ICED

Societies get the crime they deserve.
—Ancient criminological proverb

ICED

THE STORY OF ORGANIZED CRIME IN CANADA

STEPHEN SCHNEIDER

John Wiley & Sons Canada, Ltd.

Library and Archives Canada Cataloguing
in Publication

Schneider, Stephen, 1963–
Iced: the story of organized crime in Canada / Stephen
Schneider.

Includes index.
ISBN 978-0-470-83500-5

1. Organized crime—Canada—History. 2. Pirates—
Canada—History. 3. Outlaws—Canada—History.
4. Criminals—Canada—History. 5. Crime—Canada—
History. I. Title.
HV6453.C3S35 2009   364.1'060971   C2008-
905702-3

Production Credits
Cover & Interior Design: Michael Chan
Printer: Friesens

Editorial Credits
Editor: Don Loney
Project Coordinator: Pauline Ricablanca

John Wiley & Sons Canada, Ltd.
6045 Freemont Blvd.
Mississauga, Ontario
L5R 4J3

Printed in Canada

1 2 3 4 5 FP 13 12 11 10 09

TABLE OF CONTENTS

For footnotes and bibliography go to: www.storyoforganizedcrime.ca
www.wiley.com/go/iced

ACKNOWLEDGMENTS

This book would not have come to fruition without the help and support of a number of people.

I would first like to thank Saint Mary's University students and others for their help in researching the book and transcribing my notes. This list includes Jenna Theberge, Marina Colleen McKay, Harmony Kook, Danielle Masse, Amanda Gauvin, Natasha Hawley, Shauna Kennedy, and Kimberlea Clarke.

I am very much beholden to the writers and journalists who blazed a trail in the Canadian organized crime non-fiction genre and am especially indebted to James Dubro, Lee Lamothe, and Antonio Nicaso for their help and guidance with the book.

I received tremendous support from friends and contacts with Canada's policing community, including Ben Soave, Steve Martin, Glenn Hanna, Don Panchuk, Jym Grimshaw, Marc Fleming, Ben Eng, and Chris Perkins.

My many thanks to those at John Wiley and Sons who supported my vision for this book, did not complain when the finished product was twice as many pages as originally proposed, placated me through all my creative demands, and arduously toiled to ensure this book saw the light of day. In particular, I would like to thank Mike Chan, Pauline Ricablanca, and Jennifer Smith. Most importantly I am greatly indebted to the book's senior editor and my good friend Don Loney (make sure to check out Don's cameo in Chapter Ten). I am also indebted to Andrew Borkowski for his diligent copy editing and helpful suggestions.

The book has greatly benefited from the creativity of two fabulous artists: Ben Frisch, who is responsible for many of the illustrated portraits scattered throughout the book, and Adam Hilborn of Parishil Studios in Toronto, the illustrator behind Chapter Eleven's Manga-style comic strip.

Finally, my ever-lasting thanks to Meg for her love, support, and patience throughout this long process.

SRS
Halifax
February 2009

PART I
ANTECEDENTS
1596–1907

CHAPTER ONE

SHIVER ME NORTHERN TIMBERS
Pirates and Privateers of Atlantic Canada

BLACK BART

Without are dogs and murderers.
—Book of Revelation

The starless night was as dark as a black dog. The small fishing village of Trepassey, located on the southern tip of New-found-land's Avalon Peninsula, was tranquil in the pre-dawn hours, on the twenty-first day of June, in the yeare of grace one thousand seven hundred and twenty.

But amidst this early morning solitude, a dark cloud of treachery hung over the town and a foreboding wind of menace blustered into the harbour, fiercely pitching the sloops, schooners, and brigs out of their slumber. Before the sunne had broken over the horizon, the calm of the somnolent village was shattered by the hellish uproar of a grande ship coursing through the long slender reach of the harbour "with Drums beating, Trumpets sounding, and other instruments of Musick, English Colours flying." It was the sloop *Royal Rover*. And as she brazenly sailed into the dusk-veiled harbour, much unease and terror was stirred amongst the newly awoken townspeople who realized immediately what violent squall had broken their calm midst.

Pyrates!

Standing on the quarter deck of the marauding vessel, below death's flagg flying at the topmasthead, was a tall, nut-brown figure attired in the most resplendent of finery — a rich crimson waistcoat and petticoat breeches, with gold braid, a red feather in a broad-brimmed hat that sat aloft his tarry locks, and a gold chaine wrapped ten times around his neck, with a diamond-encrusted cross, once destined for the King of Portugal, dangling in the middle. He laid bare a cutlash in the hollow of one hand, and at the end of a silk bandolier flung over his shoulders he carried two pistols. The sea-roving Turk at the helm of the infectious ship was none other than Black Bart, renowned navigator and true sea dog who went into the cannon's mouth willingly, not for want of riches, but from a yearning for roving and adventure; for the wayward Captain was apt to say, "A merry life and a short one, shall be my motto!" And that destiny would grant him!

He was borne John Roberts in 1682 in the wee village of Castle Newydd Bach, a dreary blemish to be found on the southern slopes of the Preseli Hills in Wales. He would later change his name to Bartholomew, but, to his victims and enemies alike, he was known as Black Bart. Despite his errant ways later in life, he was not delivered into the vagabond class, but was sired from respectable, land-owning parents. "On the cusp of his teenage years, he was, when the young, curly sable haired, John Robert, with sable eyes, went to sea as a cabin boy." He returned to the land, but conditions were poor, and "this olive-skinned broad-shouldered young man, who be fortunate enough to stand more than two yards tall, possessing good natural parts and personall bravery, returned to the sea," whereby during the time of the Spanish Succession, betwixt the yeares one thousand seven hundred and two and thirteen, he served in the Royal Navy. His battle-hardened maritime expeditions granted John the skills of a highly proficient seaman, navigator, and natural leader of men. Nevertheless, at the end of the war, John Roberts, now 31, found himself without a vocation.

Dreaded flag of the pyrate ship *Royal Rover*

Roberts' days as a sea raider began in the yeare of our lord one thousand seven hundred and nineteen, whilst serving as third mate on a slave ship captured by the tallowy pyrate Howell Davis. In the force of the moment, and with little recourse, Roberts and other crew members were press-ganged into service aboard the wicked pyrate ship. When Davis was killed whilst attacking the town of Principe off the Guinea coast, Roberts was elected captain of the buccaneer vessel, "as he had none of the appearance of a man who sailed before the mast; but seemed like a mate of skipper, accustomed to be obeyed or to strike." For reality and in truth he loathed this wretched calling, but the extremity of want that whet his appetite for

escapades and exploits overcame his trepidations, and thusly accepted the honour— evidently concluding, "since he had dipp'd his hand in muddy Water, and must be a Pyrate, it was better being a Commander than a common Man." His life was now forever cast in the free trading commerce of the sea, without the folly swaddles, just as the Angel of Death created it. His first order as captain was to raze a select few homes of Principe as an act of revenge for the killing of Howell Davis.

Unlike the typical swashbuckling corsair, Roberts hisself was a prudish, fastidious, and pious man by disposition and custom. He dressed like a proper gentleman at all times, even in battle. Ne'er a vice ever threatened the sanctions of his piety; instead of playing cards, rolling bones, or cavorting around the barrel getting bowsy from drinking sittyated grog, he was wont to sit in his cabin alone, sipping tea and reading his Bible. Intoxicating liquor never touched his lips. He also expected the same of his crew, whom he loomed over as strict disciplinarian, not simply to impose order on the ship, but in his preferment that they be warded from the tempests of sin and idleness. Those roundhands not on duty were made to retire at nine bells every night. Women were never permitted to board his ships and the penalty for blowing off the groundsails with the gentler sex was death by dancing the hempen jig. His collection of cloyers were strictly forbidden from gambling aboard his vessels, and a man could be flogged for uttering a swear word or a blasphemy. In religious matters, all hands were expected to gather on deck every night to say prayers and Roberts ensured the Sabbath was strictly observed as a daye of reste. Any crew member who nicked from the company would hath his nose and ears split and thenceforth would be marooned. He tolerated no fighting on board; any quarrels were to be settled ashore by duelling with drawn pistols or through the brandishing of cutlashes. Roberts personally issued a standing invitation to any disgruntled swaddler to settle their mutual disagreement in a duel. No man ever took him up on this challenge; for despite his modest countenance, the Black Pyrate was one "of the most wickedness men that God ever allowed on the sea." He ordered his pyrate knots to treat their victims equally roughly "in order to make them discover their Money, threatening them every Moment with Death, if they did not resign every Thing up to them." Black Bart was indeed "the mildest manner'd man that ever scuttled a ship or cut a throat."

The two and twenty merchant vessels in Trepassey's harbour were easy prey for the Devious Captain's calculating mind, his troupe of terrifying troubadours and the thirty-two cannons and twenty-seven swivel guns of the *Royal Rover*. As the Black Vessel flew into the harbour, it met with little resistance from the blubbering lubbers aboard the ships anchored in the harbour who, for want of courage, "all quitted upon Sight of the Pyrate." One by one, Bart and his crew of forty-five swaggering skulks boarded the victim vessels. With a swarm at every turn, the cast of clapperdogeon cutthroats looted each one bare, and afterwards, the saucy sea robbers set the ships ablaze in a fire so spectacular,

some say it outshone the aurora borealis. With musketry in hand, and without feare of resistance or molestation, the maritime raiders then went ashore to gull and gut the homes and plantations of Trepassey "like madmen, who cast firebrands, arrows and death," forcing the poor villagers to deliver up their meagre possessions.

Throughout the day, the seafaring whip jacks remained in the harbour, raiding, stumping, and burning all manner of vessels that had the misfortune to sail in. By the time the sunne had descended from the cobalt sky, the scarlet scoundrels had plundered and burned to the cinder more than thirty ships great and small. "It is impossible particularly to recount the Destruction and Havock they made here," Daniel Defoe wrote in the yeare one thousand seven hundred and twenty-four, "burning and sinking all the Shipping, except a galley from Bristol, and destroying the Fisheries, and Stages

Captain Bartho. Roberts with two pyrate ships, *viz.* the *Royal Fortune*, in the foreground, and the *Ranger* to the left, with captured prizes off the coast of Guiney, 1721.

of the poor Planters, without Remorse or Compunction; for nothing is so deplorable as Power in mean and ignorant Hands, it makes Men wanton and giddy, unconcerned at the misfortunes they are imposing on their Fellow Creatures, and keeps them smiling at the Mischiefs, that bring themselves no Advantage."

Ever solicitous to find a superior vessel, and never one to disregard his good fortune, Black Bart seized and refitted the reprieved Bristol galley, after being greatly impressed by the cut of her jib, her statuesque masts a pleasure to the eye, and her canvas sails both hearty and supple; she was enough to retract the breath of any seaman worthy of his salt, and that being enough for the now-smitten and coquettish Captain, he proceeded to mount her helm. He affixed twenty-eight new guns to his newest conquest, stocked her hold with provisions looted from his Trepassey adventure, coated her bottom below the waterline with a mix of tallow, red lead, and sulphur to allow her to slip through the waters well, and topped all this off by christening her the *Royal Fortune*. After making himself master of the harbour at Trepassey for a fortnight, and having now plundered near one hundred and fifty boats and twenty-six ships at Trepassey and St. Mary's, and being fully satisfied with the execution of his old bold stratagem at New-found-land, Bart ordered his ships to beat out and stand to Ile Royale (known to later generations as Cape Breton Island), whence many French fishing boats rendezvoused, and where he was already renowned as *le jolie rouge* (the "pretty man in red").

Thereupon and thenceforthe, he swept the coast like a hungry hawk, flying a "bewildering variety of flags" as he once scribed, "to confuse our adversary as to our intent" and then, at the last moment, unveiling the black Jolly Roger to the horror of his confused quarry. With much helter skelter, he took six more sails, one being even more spectacular than the *Bristol Galley* and this twenty-six-gun ship would become the next *Royal Fortune*. With a ballast full of bustle on deck, armaments, supplies, and Bart's personal furnishings were transferred to his newest flagship. The leader of the sea gypsies also press ganged frightened fishermen into his family of freebooters, thereby and forthwith providing more complement to his strength. Those who resisted the entreaties to sign aboard were slaughtered with an unremorseful veracity so that they would never be tempted to tell tales. Reports were hastily made to His Majesty in Britain that some of the Frenchmen "were whipped nigh unto death." Other poor swabs were hood-wink'd, shackled, and heaved overboard; had their ears docked; or were encased in fetters and hung aloft from a yardarm by the hands or feet and used for target practice. As he left this scene of devastation and death, the Captain of Darkness now had as many as four hundred sea dogs under his command, a band of barnacled badgers large enough for three ships. To accommodate them all, he captured and fitted two more prizes for his piratical depredations, the *Great Ranger* and the *Little Ranger*.

The Arch Rouge steered a course due south and tooke more English prizes off the New England coast, the most lucrative being the *Samuel*, bound to Boston, about eleven weeks from London and ten from land's end, which he fell in with on the thirteenth of July one thousand seven hundred and twenty in the Latitude of Forty-four, Thirty or Forty Leagues to the eastward of the banks of New-found-land. The *Samuel* was filled with merchants and nobility, all of whom were ripe for the smouching and they submitted to their captors without hesitation. The *Boston News-Letter* of the twenty-second day of August one thousand seven hundred and twenty recounted the gloomy story "whereof the sloop being accosted and taken by two pyrate vessels, *viz.*, a ship of twenty-six guns, and a sloop of ten, both commanded by Captain Roberts, having on board about a hundred Men, all English." Foregoing the pretence of any proper formality or negotiations of terms, the bastard brigands boarded their victim vessel and their first act of debauchery was "to strip both Passengers and Seamen of all their Money and Cloths which they had on board, with a loaded Pistol held to everyone's breast ready to shoot him down, who did not immediately give an account of both, and resign them up." Next, the salty swig-men clambered below deck where they "tore up the Hatches and entered the Hold like a Parcel of Furies, and with Axes and Cutlashes, cut and broke open all the bales, Cases, and Boxes, they could lay their hands on." Chests full of baubles and trinkets would be undubbed "by shooting a brace of Bullets with a Pistol into the Key-hole" and then turned out alow and aloft. Any wares that were brought on deck, but not favoured as booty by the scurrilous scallywags, were not returned to their rightful place in the hold, but were jettisoned. If any attempts were made to overpower the sea robbers, the merciless captain threatened to fire his pistol into the ship's magazine so they would all goe "merrily to Hell together." The oceanic miscreants were now flush in the pocket having fork'd the *Samuel*'s culls to the tune of eight or nine thousand Pounds Sterling worth of the choicest goods and, still insatiated, they stripped the *Samuel* of every article of value to the profligate pyrate ships: sails, cordage, guns, ground tackle, compasses, binnacle, and hogsheads full of gunpowder.

Whilst the sea glaziers debated the virtues of scuttling the *Samuel*, they spied a sail in the distance and so left their ravaged victim afloat and shab'd off in pursuit of their new prey, which they halted by pouring a well-placed broadside into her, and she proved to be the *Snow* from Bristol, bound to Boston. The scurrilous scabbies boarded and grappled the victim ship and "because he was an Englishman, they used the master in a cruel and barbarous manner." Two days later, the dastardly dells swagged the *Little York* of Virginia, and the *Love of Liverpool.* "In three days they captured three other vessels, removing the goods out of them, sinking one, and sending off the other two."

Roberts and his ravenous rogues then made haste for the West Indies, wantonly cloying and destroying ships encountered along their path. When landfall was made at Martinique in January, one thousand seven hundred and twenty-one, the evil plotter hatched a diabolical scheme. A Jack was hoisted atop the main mast, the traditional signal of a vessel desirous to trade, and how the sea swine did fob the many merchants and traders, who sailed up to the disguised pyrate ship to barter, and in doing so were surprised with much malice and forcibly deprived of their cargo and supplies. Whilst in the West Indies, Roberts also over-mastered a French

man-of-war, carrying fifty-two guns, which he commandeered and renamed the *Royal Fortune*. Aboard the ship, the Lord of the Cannons discovered, with much glee, the Governor of Martinique, who was taken prisoner and then hanged by the neck until he was as dead as old Oliver Cromwell. The sadistic sea trotter thence displayed his distaste for the people of the West Indies by designing a jaunty new flag that showed a figure of hisself brandishing a cutlash in his right hand with each foot standing atop a skull. One skull had written beneath it the initials "ABH" (A Barbadian's Head). The other had "AMH" (A Martiniquain's Head).

Black Bart's tribute to the people of the West Indies

In June of one thousand seven hundred and twenty-one, with great aplomb and abandon, the sea-roving riff-raff arrived off the coast of Africa, whence they went hard with their watery prey and tooke four more sails, keeping one and renaming her the *Ranger*. On the coast of Liberia, the Pyrate Commander took the *Onslow,* with a cargo worth nine thousand Pounds Sterling. Having again put out from land, he sailed his private navy to the Ivory Coast and took at least six more prizes and then raided eleven slave ships, which he ransomed for eight pounds of gold dust each. One captain refused to submit to this extortion; in retaliation, Bart ordered the ship to be burned to the cinder. Eighty slaves were on board at the time.

The rampaging ruffian was now such as a threat to British trade that he was zealously pursued by the

Royal Navy and pyrate bounty hunters. The most dogged and determined of his dispatched shadows was Challoner Ogle, the commander of the British man-of-war *Swallow*. On the fifth of February in the year one thousand seven hundred and twenty-two, the *Swallow* caught up with the pyrates near Cape Lopez in Gabon. Ogle took a trick from the pyrate captain's own book and disguised his ship as a Portuguese trader. Bart took the bait and gave chase. The *Swallow* pretended to flee, but once out of sight, she slowed to a crawl to allow the pyrate ship to draw near. "Upon her coming up to the *Swallow*, the pyrate hoisted the black flag, and fired upon her; but how greatly were her crew astonished, when they saw that they had to contend with a man-of-war."

Bart was never one to swallow the anchor. Thusly, he put on "the most expensive garments in his wardrobe, made of magnificent red damask, he hung several fine pistols, handsomely carved, from his shoulders, and placed around his neck a costly solid gold chain, from which a cross of diamonds was suspended. As a finishing touch he donned his gala hat with a red peacock feather." He forthwith ordered his mongrel crew to break out the cutlashes and pistols, prime the cannons, batten down the hatches, and grope up the dingle. The fighting commenced and the "cannonading was terrific, with neither side gaining the advantage. Scuppers ran red with blood. Hoarse cries mingled with the thunder of artillery and small arms. Powder and smoke drifted over the heaving vessels. It was a desperate and bloody engagement." As the barrage reached a fevered intensity, a cry of anguish and pain was heard from the brigand captain. "He had now, perhaps, finished the fight very desperately, if death, who took a swift passage in a grape shot, had not interposed, and struck him directly on the throat. He settled himself on the tackles of a gun" and, within a moment's breath, was no more. It was on this, the tenth day of February in the year of grace one thousand seven hundred and twenty-two that the life of Black Bart — notorious pyrate, scourge of the seven seas, brother of the blade, the buccaneer with whom "the devil himself would have been afeared to go to sea with" — was ended.

When the pyrate crew realized the conclusion of their leader had come to pass they jettisoned his expired body, "scarlet damask, white plumes, and all" to be forever entombed in Davy Jones' Locker. This was in accordance with a standing command made by Captain Roberts that his body never be allowed into the hands of his enemies, dead or alive, lest he were forced to be "hanged in chains from a gibbet on shore." Deprived of their captain, the crew of the pyrate vessel surrendered to Captain Ogle, upon which a celebratory chorus of huzzahs was sung by his victorious soldiers with much gaiety. The captured turks were shopt in irons and prosecuted in a special Assize, the likes of which had hitherto never been seen in the annals of pyrate history: one hundred and sixty-nine men were charged, forty-five of them free negroes. In excess of fifty men were condemned to the gallows, from whence they all swung to the Paddington frisk. The death of Black Bart — the most successful pyrate of all time who, betwixt one thousand seven hundred and eighteen and twenty-two, sniped and stripped more than four hundred prizes, surpassing any and all others of his yoke — was a symbolic end to what many have deemed the Golden Age of Pyracy.

THE BROTHERHOOD OF THE DEEP

It can be said that the first criminal organizations in North America were pirates operating off the eastern seaboard. To be able to hunt down and pillage their victims, pirate ships required many of the essential trappings that would come to define organized crime: a reliance on violence, a nose for profitable opportunities, a code of secrecy among the conspirators, access to black markets to sell their stolen wares, and connections with the political elite to protect and even sanction their predatory activities. Most importantly, a pirate ship demanded a large crew. Pirates captured and plundered their prizes by outnumbering and overpowering the victims, so ships that could carry large crews were preferred. Other pirate captains operated a fleet of smaller sloops or brigs, which were favoured because of their speed and stealth. Regardless of the size of their vessels, pirate captains had to constantly enlist crew members, often at sea. Most of these recruits joined willingly. Others were forced into their new occupation at the point of a cutlass or a pistol.

Large crews were necessary because pirate ships relied on intimidation to frighten their quarry into compliance. And while the sight of a fully manned deck and a well-armed hull of a pirate ship was often enough to quell any foolhardy resistance by victims, the most potent purveyor of terror was the pirate flag. Whenever a pirate ship was ready to attack, the Jolly Roger would be hoisted at the top of the mainsail to signal the pirates' intentions and to scare victims into submission. Hundreds of years later, similar tactics would be adopted by the Hells Angels and other motorcycle gangs, by donning their menacing "colours" to intimidate "citizens." The Hells Angels trademark winged-head death skull insignia is nothing more than a latter-day version of the pirates' skull and crossbones.

The master pirate had to be a ruthless warrior, a competent sailor, and an astute navigator and tactician in order to locate and track down lucrative prey, as well as a disciplinarian who could keep order among a rough, unruly, and potentially mutinous crew. To help ensure order while at sea, pirates were among the first organized criminals to implement rules, regulations, and a code of conduct, a practice that would be emulated by such 20th-century criminal descendants as the Italian mafia, the Chinese triads, and outlaw motorcycle gangs. Before departing shore, a pirate captain and his crew often drew up the articles of a ship that had to be obeyed by all on board. Contravention of these rules could mean confinement in the ship's stockade, banishment on a desert island, a taste of the cat-o'-nine-tails, other forms of gruesome torture, or even death. Some common articles of one rule-bound pirate ship commandeered by John Phillips in the 1720s included the following:

1. Every man shall obey Civil Command. The captain shall have one full share and a half of all prizes.
2. If any man shall offer to run away, or keep any secret from the Company, he shall be maroon'd with one Bottle of Powder, one Bottle of Water, one small Arm and shot.
3. If any man shall steal any Thing in the Company, or gain, to the value of a Piece of Eight, he shall be maroon'd or shot.
4. That Man who shall strike another whilst these Articles are in force shall receive Moses Law (that is 40 stripes lacking 1 on the bare Back.).
5. That Man that shall snap his Arms or smoak Tobacco in the Hold without a Lanthorn, shall suffer the same Punishment as in the former article.
6. That Man that shall not keep his Arms clean, fit for an Engagement, or neglect his Business, shall be cut off from his Share and suffer such other Punishment as the Captain and the Company shall think fit.
7. If any Man shall lose a Joint in time of an Engagement he shall have 400 Pieces of Eight: if a limb, 800.
8. If at any time you meet a prudent Woman that Man that offers to meddle with her without her consent shall suffer present death.

Crews of pirate ships often had to undergo a hazing ritual that, like the military, was used to forge a cohesive squadron of mercenary combatants that was necessary if a pirate ship was to overtake a prize or to survive a sea battle. For pirates, the traditional "crossing the line ceremony" — the point at sea where a vessel intersects the Tropic of Cancer, just south of Florida — marked the beginning of ceremonies that would allow a crewman the privilege of becoming a member of the brotherhood of the deep. This spot in the hemisphere was not just a symbol; it was also the point of entry into the most profitable fishing ground for the pirate ship: the treasure-laden waters off the coast of South America and the Caribbean. Captain Woodes Rogers, the commander of an English pirate ship in the early 18th century, used a common initiation ritual called "ducking at the yard arm," which was both simple and symbolic: "Hoiste 'em halfway up to the yard and let 'em fall at once into the water."

Like their modern-day criminal counterparts, pirates were wholly concerned with financial gain. Piracy held out the promise of an income that far exceeded the meagre wage of the merchant seaman or fisherman. A few of the most successful pirate captains were able to live a life of luxury, and even buy their way into nobility with the riches they harvested from their unlawful ventures. Available to the pirate was a number of revenue-generating opportunities; the most common, of course, was to rob ships of their cargo. Port towns were also targeted, not only for their valuables, but to refit ships, re-stock supplies, and to recruit crew members. Pirates were also known to use extortion, such as blockading harbours and trade routes and then charging a fee for any merchant vessel that wished to pass.

The great age of piracy coincided with the colonization of the New World between the 15th and the 18th centuries. Not long after the Spanish and the Portuguese began to explore and lay claim to South America, pirates were attacking and looting their vessels, which were filled with gold, silver, and other precious metals. Most of these pirate ships sailed from English and Caribbean ports, often with the blessing of the British monarchy. While a ship carrying gold or silver was the pirate's greatest prize, other commodities were highly sought after, including liquor from the old country, fur from New France, cured fish from Newfoundland, and spices, sugar, fruits, tobacco, and molasses from the West Indies. In addition to their cargo, ships that fell victim to pirates were often stripped bare of their sails, navigational equipment, weapons, and anything else of value.

In order to dispose of their seized bounty, some pirates were part of a network of black marketers. These mercantilist "fences" included prominent merchants and traders, including some from nobility, who sold or bartered stolen goods and captured ships. As Michael Woodiwiss writes in his book on organized crime, piracy was an occupation that was "well protected" by the economic and political powers of France, England, and other European countries. "Pirates could not have carried on their trade without the support of merchants, gentlemen and officials, especially admiralty officials, and measures taken against such abettors of piracy were for the most part ineffective, since all too frequently those responsible for executing the law were themselves notorious offenders."

The aristocratic patron of many English pirates during the latter half of the 16th century was the English robber baron family the Killigrews. Sir John Killigrew was the vice admiral of Cornwall and the royal governor of Pendennis Castle, also located in Cornwall. In the years between 1560 and 1582, his wife, Mary Killigrew, was a Lady under Queen Elizabeth I. Together, the Killigrews were the secret financiers and brokers for syndicates of pirates that sailed the coast of Great Britain. They regarded these pirates as their agents-at-sea and even provided them with a safe haven in the waters that lay inland from their castle. The larcenous activities of the Killigrew family were not conducted entirely behind the scenes; they also had a reputation for plundering ships that had the bad luck of sailing too close to their Cornwall fortress.

In addition to their links with leading merchants, many pirates operated with the sanctioning of the sovereign of their native lands. During the reign of Elizabeth I (1558–1603), hundreds of privately held ships were commissioned by Her Majesty. In fact, many of the English pirates that plied their trade during the 1600s began as "privateers" with licences issued by the Queen empowering them to seek out and rob merchant ships belonging to enemy countries, most notably Spain. Privateering was a form of commercial warfare that was directed, not toward an enemy's military, government, or territory, but against their trade. Through hit-and-run tactics that would become the hallmark of guerrilla warfare centuries later, privateers became a potent weapon in a kingdom's arsenal during wartime. While violence and intimidation would still be key tactics in privateering, as historian Carol MacLeod writes, "perhaps the one thing that could be said for privateers was they attempted to keep bloodshed to a minimum. They were more interested in plunder than murder."

Commissioned by the Crown through "letters of marque," these mercenary commerce-raiders sailed on armed, privately owned ships that acted either as a substitute for, or an adjunct to, a state navy and attacked the ships of enemy nations at virtually no cost to the sovereign. Under British law, any prize captured by a privateer had to be taken to the Court of Admiralty, which had jurisdiction over civil matters arising from actions committed on the high seas. If the Court declared a prize to be a legitimate catch — called a "condemnation" — it was auctioned off to the highest bidder and the proceeds divided between the Crown, the lawyers and magistrates involved in the condemnation trial, and the owner of the privateer vessel. The captain and officers of the privateer ship would share in the owner's cut and anything left over went to the crew (all of whom joined under the assumption of "no prey, no pay"). Because the remuneration and functions of a privateer captain and crew were closer to that of a pirate ship than a naval vessel, the distinction between pirates and privateers was imperceptibly blurred and many consider privateering as nothing more than legalized piracy. The semantic difference between the two was that a privateer sailed with the official blessing of his government to capture and loot merchant ships, while the pirate ship plundered independent of any government.

Many privateers readily became pirates during peace time when their private warships no longer had legal standing, or when it simply suited their interest. Because of her indiscriminate issuing of letters of marque, Queen Elizabeth was responsible for a deluge of English privateers and pirates at the end of her reign. Sir Francis Drake, the first Englishman to circumnavigate the globe, is perhaps the most famous of all the privateer-cum-pirates. Although letters of marque forbade privateers from attacking towns, Drake captured a fortune through his many larcenous raids on gold- and silver-laden Spanish settlements in South America. In 1572, Drake raided the town of Nombre de Dios on the island of Dominica, stealing silver bars from the governor's mansion. A few months later, he paid an unwelcome visit to Cartagena in Panama, where his ships sailed away with as much as 30 tons of gold and silver and an untold sum of money paid as ransom by the town to avoid being razed by the invaders. Drake epitomized the government-commissioned mariners who operated in that grey area between privateer and pirate, explorer and vanquisher; he was revered in his home country as a daring naval hero, a brilliant navigator, and a visionary explorer, but was vilified by his Spanish enemies as *El Draque* (the Dragon).

THE PIRATES OF AVALON

The first pirates to come into contact with Canada sailed off the coast of Newfoundland during the early part of the 16th century. Like other seafaring pioneers, what initially drew pirates to Newfoundland was the fish. It wasn't long after John Cabot's 1497 discovery of the great cod stocks off the Grand Banks that

opportunistic thieves began preying upon the cargos of fish that were now being regularly harvested, salted, and shipped back to Europe. The earliest record of a pirate ship off the Grand Banks was in 1517. The *Mary Barking* and the *Barbara*, two British ships that had been outfitted for the Newfoundland fishery, reportedly turned to piracy as soon as they arrived in the New World. Perhaps the most famous of the 16th-century pirates operating in Newfoundland waters was Jean Ango, a French shipowner, merchant, and adventurer who became notorious for attacking English and Portuguese ships off the coast between 1516 and 1520. Sailing as an explorer and privateer under a letter of marque issued by French king Francis I, Ango was said to have amassed a private fleet of seventy ships, which he used for exploration and to harass ships that flew the English, Spanish, or Portuguese flag. He sailed to Newfoundland sometime in 1516 and upon arrival he built the port of *Havre de grace,* the chief harbour in Newfoundland for the French and Ango's main base of operations for the next five years. His private squadron of armed vessels provided protection to French ships fishing off the coast, which included attacking, pillaging, and sinking non-French vessels operating in the area. With Ango's help, France was able to establish its early dominance in the New World.

The next recorded instance of piracy off the Newfoundland coast occurred in 1523, when an English captain named Cook robbed several French ships loaded with fish. In 1546, Jean Francis, the master of a French fishing ship, reported that an English pirate had stolen a load of cod that had been freshly caught off the Grand Banks. In 1582, two English gentlemen, Sir Henry Oughtred and Sir John Perrot, raided Spanish and Portuguese boats fishing off the coast of the Avalon Peninsula. A year later, Sir Humphrey Gilbert, the English explorer who set in motion the hunt for the Northwest Passage and the settling of America, travelled to Newfoundland for the purpose of annexation on behalf of Queen Elizabeth. Many of the crew members Gilbert hired had a nefarious past and volunteered for the trip to escape prison terms or even execution. While many were experienced sailors, their employment turned out to be ill advised as the crews of at least two ships mutinied and plundered a number of French and Spanish fishing vessels in Bay Bull harbour in Newfoundland before returning to England. Richard Clarke, the captain of a fishing vessel based at St. John's, complained how the French commodore, Michel de Sance, had sailed into the harbour in 1596 with three ships and began robbing Clarke's vessels, taking the captain and his crew prisoner for nine days. In 1597, Captain Charles Leigh visited St. Mary's Harbour where he found three Basque and two French fishing ships. After a bitter fight, he captured one French vessel loaded with fish.

By the early 1600s, Newfoundland was home to numerous coastal villages and played host to hundreds of migratory fishing boats. The profitable fishing industry, a growing reservoir of manpower, an evolving infrastructure to service and supply seagoing vessels, and a strategic location astride the navigation route between Europe and the New World, combined to establish St. John's and other harbours along the Avalon Peninsula as major outposts for ships from all over Europe. This bustling maritime activity also made the coast of Newfoundland a prime hunting ground for pirates, who found easy pickings among the merchant ships that came to trade or to be refitted before setting out on the long journey across the Atlantic. Pirate ships also came to Newfoundland to rest, repair, pick up supplies, and conscript seamen.

Soon, the main draw of Newfoundland for pirates lay, not in the plundering of ships or the tiny villages that dotted the coast, but as a staging area for excursions into the more profitable waters of the Caribbean and South America. Because Spanish ships generally followed the Gulf Stream when sailing from South America to the old country, they often came within only a few hundred miles of the Newfoundland coast. Thus, it was in early 17th century Newfoundland, according to Harold Horwood and Ed Butts, that the "pirate captains set up forts, careenages, docks; recruited shipwrights, sail-makers, iron-workers, deckhands by the thousands; then sailed south, well equipped to deal with the merchant ships of all nations, including their own." As the authors note, there were three classes of English pirates during this period: those who attacked only the ships of their enemies, those who attacked ships of any foreign power, and those who attacked anything, including the ships of England.

Pirates also found Newfoundland to be a safe haven in that there was little fear of being captured since there was no government, no constabulary, no courts, no military, nor even a militia at this time. The myriad inlets and fishing villages, the erratic coastline, and the many coves also provided numerous hiding places for pirate ships, not to mention temporary storehouses for their ill-gotten booty (which has given rise to many a tale of treasure still buried along Newfoundland's craggy shores).

THE PIRATE ADMIRALS

Following the end of England's war with Spain in 1603, many British naval officers and privateers found themselves unemployed. As a result, some turned to piracy. One of those was Peter Easton, who would go on to become the most successful and feared of the 17th-century pirates. The piratical pursuits of Captain Easton took him from the English Channel to the French Riviera, Africa, the Spanish Main, the Caribbean, and Newfoundland. Easton raided both English and foreign vessels with a fleet of armed ships that at one time was said to be forty strong. His cunning was so remarkable that despite the efforts of the British Admiralty, he was never captured. Although no portrait survives of the man referred to as the "Pirate Admiral," he has been described "as a dark man of authentic build and medium stature."

Easton hailed from a fabled English family whose ancestors fought in the Crusades. He visited Newfoundland as early as 1602, when England was still at war with Spain, under a commission issued by Queen Elizabeth to take three British warships to protect the Newfoundland fishing fleet from Spanish attacks. Bestowing responsibility over British navy vessels to a private sea captain was an early indication of Easton's naval prowess. When James I succeeded Elizabeth in 1603 as King of England, he promptly ended the war with Spain, decreased the size of the Royal Navy, and revoked letters of marque given to English privateers. Stranded in Newfoundland with no source of income, Easton turned to piracy.

By 1610, the next time information on Easton is available, he was being described by his contemporary, Captain Henry Mainwaring, as a "notorious pyrate." With his private army of sailors, including some recruited from Newfoundland docks, Easton sailed back to England, where he stationed his fleet at the mouth of the Avon River. From there he extorted ships moving into and out of the Bristol Channel by demanding a fee for their safe passage. Easton's services had been secured by the Killigrew family, who financed his trip back to England and took a cut of the money Easton was able to wring from merchant vessels. After a while, Bristol merchants petitioned the Earl of Nottingham, the Lord Admiral of King James' navy, for help and he responded by commissioning Captain Henry Mainwaring to capture Easton.

Like his nemesis, Mainwaring was a brilliant seaman. Born in Shropshire, England, in 1587, he was the second of four sons and two daughters of Sir George Mainwaring of Cheshire. Henry attended Oxford and upon graduation at the age of fifteen, he worked as a trial lawyer. But the call of the sea was too strong for young Henry and, after a short stint as a sailor, he applied to the King for a letter of marque to prey upon Spanish ships. Although England was at peace with Spain at the time, his commission was approved, with the stipulation that he confine his raids to the New World. At the helm of the *Resistance*, a small but fast and well-armed ship of 160 tons, Mainwaring set sail for the West Indies. As he neared Gibraltar off the coast of Spain, the captain ignored his king's directive and began to attack any and all Spanish ships he could find. He had now crossed that fine line that separated the privateer from the pirate. His skills as a navigational tactician, his tenacity in pursuing his prey, and his violent broadside bombardments of enemy ships made him infamous among Spanish merchant vessels. Despite his impertinence towards the King's orders, his aptitude on the sea could not be ignored by the British Admiralty and, in June 1611, at the age of only twenty-four, he was deemed worthy for the post of Captain of St. Andrew's Castle, a fortress located near Southampton. That same year, he received a commission from the Lord Admiral to proceed against pirates infesting the Bristol Channel.

While Mainwaring was scouring the Channel for pirates, Easton had already set sail for the Coast of Guinea in Africa where he robbed Spanish and English ships of ivory and gold. From there he sailed to Newfoundland, arriving in 1611 with captured prize ships in tow. Easton established a fortress at Harbour Grace — the port founded by Jean Ango — and from there he began attacking ships and harbours along the coast from Trinity Bay to Ferryland. While Easton remained in Newfoundland until 1614, his main interests lay to the south. As he was stealing cargoes of salted fish and red wine from French and Portuguese vessels off the Newfoundland coast, Easton was also capturing ships, conscripting sailors, stockpiling arms and ammunition, and refitting his vessels in anticipation of setting sail to the Caribbean where he could prey on Spanish treasure.

Once in the Caribbean, Easton successfully attacked Moro Castle on the Spanish colonial island of Puerto Rico. While the capture of this supposedly impenetrable fort (which had previously withstood a siege by Sir Francis Drake) contributed to Easton's budding reputation for invincibility, the daring raid was not conducted for glory, but for profit. At that time, Puerto Rico was a vast source of gold, which was Easton's real object of desire. Among the ships accompanying Easton on his triumphant return to port in Newfoundland was the Spanish galleon the *San Sebastian*, which was said to have held the greatest treasure ever to have been captured from the Caribbean.

When Easton landed back in Newfoundland, he found Harbour Grace in the hands of a squadron of five French Basque warships, which had captured his fort during his absence. The enemy fleet, led by the largest ship, the *St. Malo*, engaged Easton, who was aboard the *San Sabastian*. With military precision, Easton captured or sank each of his adversaries, including the *St. Malo*, which sunk after being forced onto a small islet near the entrance to Harbour Grace. The Pirate Admiral then landed and recaptured his fort. Legend has it that the forty-seven men Easton lost in the battle are buried in unmarked graves at Bear Cove, just north of Harbour Grace, in a site appropriately named "The Pirates' Graveyard."

In June 1612, John Guy arrived in Newfoundland to take up his post as the first governor of the English colony, which he established at Cupid's Cove. A letter from Guy to John Slany dated July 29, 1612, reported on Easton's activities at Harbour Grace, a scant 15 miles by sea from the new colonial settlement:

Because the proceedings of one Captain Peter Easton, a pirate, and his company since, are most fit to be known, before I touch our plantation business, you shall understand what they have been unto this time. Until the seventeenth of this present, the said Captain Easton remained in Harbor Grace, there trimming and repairing his shipping and commanding not only the carpenters of each ship to do his business; but hath taken victuals, munition, and necessaries from every ship, together with about one hundred men out of the Bay, to man his ships, being now in number six.

As Guy noted, Easton remained in Harbour Grace until July 17, preparing his ships, reinforcing his fort, and recruiting men. That summer he invaded harbours along the Newfoundland coast with a fleet that was described by Sir Richard Whitbourne in his 1622 book as "ten sayle of good ships well furnished and very rich." Easton plundered thirty English vessels in St. John's Harbour and robbed French, Portuguese, and Flemish fishing vessels at Ferryland. The total damage inflicted by Easton on the fishing fleets was estimated at £20,400. As part of these latest raids, Easton recruited or forced into his service some five hundred men.

During the same raids, Easton captured Sir Richard Whitbourne, who had been sent by the King to help colonize the New World and who would later be appointed governor of a colony in Newfoundland. Because of the heavy losses being suffered by merchants and fishermen from piracy, Whitbourne was also instructed to establish a court under the British Admiralty to prosecute captured pirates. This would be the first English court of law established in the New World. By Sir Richard's own account, he was held hostage by Easton for eleven weeks "and had from him many golden promises, and much wealth offered to be put into my hands as is well known." Easton tried to persuade his prisoner to join him as his first lieutenant, but Whitbourne refused and admonished his captor "on the wickedness of piracy." This lecture seems to have borne fruit, as the Pirate Admiral made an entreaty to Whitbourne to arrange a

royal pardon for him. Easton instructed Whitbourne to tell the King that, if pardoned, he would return to England peacefully and abandon his life of piracy. If no pardon were forthcoming, he would continue to sail the high seas on his own terms.

While Whitbourne was in England advocating on behalf of the man he called "that famous Arch-Pirate," Easton was moving his headquarters from Harbour Grace to Ferryland. Located on one of the eastern-most points in North America, Ferryland boasted a harbour that was closer to shipping lanes and also provided greater security should the King or other forces decide to send a fleet against him. Easton built a fortified palace on Fox Hill, which overlooked the harbour and had a panoramic view of the ocean in every direction. He also kept his fleet of ships nearby in case of attack.

When Whitbourne arrived in England to inquire about Easton's pardon, he found that one had already been granted to the pirate in February 1612 by the King, who had scented the possibility of sharing in some of Easton's riches. By 1614, Easton still had not received his clemency, which only re-affirmed his commitment to piracy. In March of that year, Easton did hear from one of his scouts in the Caribbean that Spanish treasure ships were preparing to sail for Spain by way of the Azores, a set of islands located in the middle of the Atlantic Ocean, about 1,500 kilometres from the Portuguese mainland. Easton quickly prepared to set sail so he could lie in wait at the Azores. He knew that the Spaniards could take any one of a dozen routes through the Azores, so upon arrival he shrewdly deployed his fleet of fourteen ships in a wide arc to the west and south of the islands, covering the different possible paths that could be taken by the Spanish convoy. His strategy met with great success; the Spanish fleet sailed directly into his dragnet and, before long, Easton was cruising towards the Barbary Coast with four treasure ships as prizes.

In 1614, when word got back to England that Easton was now operating out of Newfoundland, Captain Mainwaring was commissioned five ships to hunt him down. By the time he arrived in Conception Bay on June 4 of that year he had eight ships under his command (the additional three were either captured en route to Newfoundland or belonged to independent captains who fell in with Mainwaring). After docking in Harbour Grace, Mainwaring found that the King's most famous fugitive had eluded him once again. After taking possession of Easton's old fort at Harbour Grace he refitted his eight ships and recruited more crew members. (In a letter to the King written some years later, Mainwaring lauded Newfoundland as the world's best station for refitting ships.) While still commissioned to capture Easton, Mainwaring's revamping of his fleet appears to have less to do with his original mandate and more to do with his own personal enrichment, as he began raiding vessels along the Grand Banks, stealing wine from Portuguese ships, and snatching fish from the French. On September 14, 1614, Mainwaring and his private army of four hundred mariners departed Newfoundland for Europe, having with them stolen goods valued at approximately £5,400. In his letter to the King, Mainwaring tacitly acknowledged his piratical ways, but assured His Sovereign that he only attacked vessels belonging to His Majesty's enemies. He also pronounced that into the trade of piracy "he fell not purposely but by mischance," and once in the trade, his goal was to serve his King and country.

Mainwaring was welcomed back to England and even offered a pardon by King James I — if he agreed to give up piracy. Mainwaring consented, and to show appreciation for his own clemency, he wrote one of the first discourses on pirates entitled *Of the Beginnings, Practices, and Suppression of Pirates,* which he presented to the King in 1617. Now a respectable citizen, the corsair–turned–king's courtier sailed for Dover where he rescued a Newfoundland trading fleet captured by pirates near Gibraltar. In 1618, he was knighted and, three years later, he was elected to Parliament as a member for Dover. Ending his career as a vice-admiral in 1639, Mainwaring fought for King Charles I in the English civil wars, spending whatever fortune remained to him from his days as a pirate in the losing battle against Oliver Cromwell. Because of his loyalty to the deposed King, Mainwaring was removed from Parliament in 1646. He accompanied Charles into exile in Jersey where he lived the short remainder of his life in poverty. He died less than two years later and was buried in an unmarked grave in St. Giles' Church in Camberwell.

Peter Easton fared considerably better in his retirement from piracy. After he divided the Spanish treasure among his crew, he disbanded his fleet, renounced his life of crime, and sailed off with a personal fortune estimated at an astounding £2 million. His destination was Villefranche in Savoy, near the present Principality of Monaco, which was then a French free port for pirates. Because of his considerable wealth, Easton was cordially received by the Duke of Savoy, who invited him to settle there. Easton accepted the offer, purchased a palace, and acquired the distinguished title of Marquis of Savoy. Upon learning that the Duke of Savoy actively courted the riches of Easton, Sir Richard Whitbourne wrote, "Thus in that somewhat free and easy time a pirate owning ten good ships rich with gold, and full of fighting men, was evidently a personage who sovereign princes were by no means to snub." Whitbourne also describes how Easton "covered himself with glory" while serving as an officer under the Duke of Savoy during his raids on the Duchy of Mantua. Among Easton's many accomplishments was his skill in "laying guns," which was such, "that a few shots by him produce more effect than most gunners produce with many." Easton added to his affluence by marrying into a wealthy French family and sired children of his own, and their descendants live on the French Riviera to this day. Easton remained with the Duke of Savoy until 1620, after which history fails to record any further details of his life.

THE ENEMY PLUNDERED, RUINED, AND FIRED

Although not as famous or successful as Peter Easton or Bartholomew Roberts, numerous other pirates plied the seas off the Newfoundland coast during the 17th and 18th centuries. After serving as a gunner on an English naval ship, John Nutt, who settled in Torbay, Newfoundland, with his family in 1620, was another ex-navy sailor-turned-pirate. In the summer of 1621, Nutt and several others seized a French fishing boat, fit her out as a pirate ship and, over the next two years, raided fishing and trading boats along the coast. Nutt and his crew then sailed back to England and fenced much of their bounty through the Killigrews. Before he left for England in 1623, he wrote a letter to John Eliot, the vice admiral of Devon, who had been ordered to arrest him. Nutt offered to pay Eliot £300 for a pardon, and although Eliot agreed to petition the King on his behalf, he secretly harboured plans to capture Nutt.

Eliot accepted the pirate's invitation to his ship to discuss the pardon, and according to Eliot's 19th-century biographer, Sir John Forster, "The first thing he saw, on reaching the pirate's deck, was that Nutt, even while the negotiations for his submission were in progress, had made prize of an English merchantman, a Colchester ship with a cargo of sugar and timber." When Nutt was separated from his crew, Eliot seized the opportunity and had him arrested and imprisoned. Nutt was tried as a pirate and sentenced to be hanged, but was spared the gallows by the intervention of England's secretary of state, George Calvert. As the first Lord Baltimore, Calvert was responsible for establishing a colony in Newfoundland for King James I, who had awarded him the Province of Avalon in 1621. In a clemency letter written on behalf of Nutt in 1623, Calvert acknowledges the help he received from the condemned man in protecting his plantation from pirates, "Wherein I have no other end but to be grateful to a poor man that hath been ready to do me & my associates courtesies in a plantation which we have begun in Newfoundland, by defending us from others which perhaps in the infancy of that work might have done us wrong." Calvert's letter of support may have also been prompted by his fears that the reciprocal arrangement — whereby Lord Baltimore tolerated Nutt's pirate activities in return for a cut of his ill-gotten gains — would be exposed. Thanks in part to Calvert's intervention, Nutt did obtain his pardon in 1623. After he was released from prison, he returned to the sea to loot and pillage, this time under a letter of marque issued by the king to attack French merchant ships.

Meanwhile, back in Newfoundland, Lord Baltimore was experiencing troubles with French pirates. In 1628, the Marquis de la Rade, commanding three ships and four hundred men, raided St. John's and other English settlements along the Avalon Peninsula. In retaliation, Calvert seized several French vessels that were berthed in Trepassey. In 1629, when a French pirate captured a number of ships during a raid on the fishing community of Cape Broyle, Calvert ordered one of his armed ships to give chase. The French pirates were captured and brought back to Ferryland to face justice. Lord Baltimore left Ferryland soon thereafter.

In 1637, Sir David Kirke was appointed governor of Newfoundland and, in 1639, he settled in Ferryland. Kirke was an English privateer who, in 1628, had captured Nova Scotia and Quebec from French forces in the name of King Charles I. On his way home, he looted a French fleet of eighteen ships in the Gulf of the St. Lawrence carrying supplies to New France. For his heroics, Kirke was awarded with a royal charter giving him absolute control over Newfoundland, which he abused by instituting new taxes and levying tolls on all fishing boats, the proceeds of which went into his own pocket. "Becoming governor of Ferryland meant only one thing to Sir David Kirke," Frank Galgay and Michael McCarthy wrote in their book *Buried Treasures of Newfoundland and Labrador*. "He could now legally rob every settler and summer fisherman who came to the Southern Shore area. His taxes were high and he collected without mercy." As a result, he amassed a personal fortune and, in 1639, moved in the manor that Lord Baltimore had built for him and his family. Kirke was dismissed from his post in 1651 for violating his charter by keeping the tax revenue he collected. He returned to England where he was found not guilty of the charges, but was imprisoned after successfully being sued by Lord Baltimore's heir for illegally seizing his estate in Newfoundland. Kirke died in prison in 1654, but his wife and family were allowed to return to Ferryland, and were still living there in 1673 when Captain Jacob Everson of the Netherlands captured and sacked the settlement.

By the halfway point of the 17th century, Dutch pirates had become the new scourge of Newfoundland's colonies. Between 1652 and 1674, England and Holland went to war twice and the conflicts inevitably spilled over to the protectorates of both nations. In June 1665, a year after the Dutch colony of New Amsterdam (present-day New York City) surrendered to the English, Holland's Admiral De Ruyter raided St. John's and other ports, looting and burning ships and stealing shore equipment. In 1673, the year the Dutch recaptured New Amsterdam, Captain Jacob Everson and his fleet of four ships and 152 guns returned to

Newfoundland. On September 4 of that year, he laid siege to settlements along the Avalon Peninsula. English captain Dudley Lovelace, who was a prisoner aboard one of the Dutch ships when the harbour of Ferryland was attacked, wrote, "the enemy plundered, ruined, fired, and destroyed the commodities, cattle, household goods, and other stores" belonging to the inhabitants. "They also took away 4 great guns, the fort being out of repair, and no commander upon the place." The next day, thirty fishing ships "were burned in the harbour, and as much fish as the ships could carry away, taken. They also forced the inhabitants to send 6 hogs, and one bullock, to each ship." On September 9, "the Dutch went unto William Pollard's house, 3 miles distant and plundered him of 400 quintals of fish, provisions and household stuff amounting to £400 sterling. They likewise burned at that place 40 Fishing boats, the house, warehouses, etc. belonging to the fishery in that harbour, besides several English prizes."

The Dutch continued towards St. John's, but it was saved from capture by forces organized under the command of Christopher Martin, who had spent seventeen years as vice admiral of St. John's. Despite a militia of less than thirty men, Martin was able to maintain a defensive battery at the entrance to the harbour by extracting six cannon from his vessel, the *Elias Andrews*, and constructing an earthen breastwork at the entrance of the narrows leading into the harbour. Martin and his followers also stretched a heavy iron chain from south to north through the harbour. After trapping the Dutch ships in the narrows of the harbour, several were burned to a cinder by shallops and dories that were filled with combustibles, set on fire, and steered towards the Dutch invaders.

Despite the relative calm that followed their successful defence against the Dutch, the British colonies in Newfoundland were subject to numerous attacks from French troops and privateers before the end of the century. In 1689, England and France were again at war. The French authorities, who had established a fortified beachhead in Newfoundland at their main fishing port in Placentia Bay thirty years earlier, sent out small bands of soldiers and privateers to loot and destroy English settlements. In 1690, an English privateer ship commanded by Herman Williamson

plundered Placentia. The French retaliated by their own assault on Ferryland and the Bay of Bulls. In 1692, the English Navy attacked Placentia Bay.

The battle over Newfoundland took a decisive turn towards the French around 1696 when Pierre Le Moyne d'Iberville, a soldier, ship's captain, explorer, trader, colonizer, and privateer was asked to lead a charge against St. John's and other British settlements along the Avalon coast. D'Iberville was born in Ville-Marie (present-day Montreal) and baptized there in 1661. He was the son of Charles Le Moyne de Longueuil who had come to New France in 1641 and settled at Ville-Marie where he worked as an emissary to the aboriginals on behalf of the French government. Charles was also active in the fur trade, which made him one of Montreal's wealthiest citizens when he died in 1682. Like most of his eleven brothers, Pierre took part in numerous incursions against English posts in North America, and it was because of his many military successes that he was tapped to lead French forces in their attempt to capture Avalon from the British. According to historian and biographer Bernard Pothier, this command coincided with d'Iberville's own ambitions, which were becoming increasingly commercial in nature. During his patrols of the North Atlantic as a sea captain in the early 1690s, d'Iberville was well aware of the lucrative fishing opportunities that could be realized by controlling the Avalon coastline. As a privateer, he was also promised a share of the profits of any cargo captured and "even before leaving France d'Iberville had hoped to market 200,000 quintals of cod."

D'Iberville's novel offensive strategy against St. John's was to shun the traditional sea attack, where he would face formidable cannon batteries, and approach the town from its unfortified landward flanks. Meeting some 50 miles south of St John's, d'Iberville's troops, along with another French detachment, marched north to the English capital, and captured it on November 30, 1696. After setting fire to St John's and demolishing the English fisheries along the eastern shores, d'Iberville's soldiers successfully laid siege to the rest of the coastline. Over the next four months, the French divisions destroyed thirty-six settlements, killed two hundred people, and took another seven hundred prisoner. By the end of March 1697, almost all of Avalon was in French hands. Because of his impressive victory, d'Iberville was able to satisfy his mercantilist ambitions and, as Pothier writes, spent at least "two months in Placentia marketing the cod and other booty he had amassed, and supervising the fishery he had organized on his own account, using not only his own men but prisoners from the English fishing settlements as well." Profiteering always appeared to be d'Iberville's overriding ambition, which left one French governor convinced that he "has his interests and his trade much more in view than the king's service."

Pierre Le Moyne d'Iberville

Between 1696 and 1705, the French and English continued their assaults upon one another in Newfoundland and many of these battles were between private navies. The British Navy's postponement of an attack on the French stronghold at Placentia left it up to English privateers, who boldly descended on the bay and captured a third of the French fishing fleet. As a result, France surrendered and England took control over Newfoundland for good. French authorities commissioned d'Iberville to take the fight against the English elsewhere in the New World and, in early 1706, he was commanding a squadron of twelve warships

and two thousand soldiers and privateers. His most decisive victory took place on the Caribbean island of Guadeloupe, which fell into his hands after only a day's battle. As his biographer recounts, "Once again, as in so many of d'Iberville's previous campaigns, there was much bad faith and ruthless looting; by the time the French departed on 22 April, Nevis, the garden of the Caribbean, had been completely desolated." D'Iberville did not enjoy the fruits of his Caribbean conquest, as he died shortly after his victory. Accusations that d'Iberville used his military position for personal profit culminated with a French military commission that convicted him posthumously for theft and embezzlement and even demanded his widow make restitution for her husband's ransacking of Guadeloupe.

DEAD CATS DON'T MEOW

Between 1702 and 1713, the European powers continued their running battles, this time over the succession to the Spanish throne. In the New World, the fighting not only pitted the British against the French in the north, but also the British against the Spanish in the south. As part of Britain's war effort, Queen Anne commissioned approximately one hundred privateer ships, which reportedly captured two thousand French and Spanish vessels. As a result of the 1713 Treaty of Utrecht that ended the war, the British were given full possession of Newfoundland, as well as Acadia (later renamed Nova Scotia), and the fur-trading posts in Hudson Bay. The end of the war had another consequence: it unleashed into the waters of the New World a legion of unemployed privateers, naval officers, and regular seamen. The result was a titanic outburst of piracy that would terrorize parts of the western hemisphere for the next forty years.

Unlike previous British "gentlemen" pirates, such as Easton, Mainwaring, or Drake who had military backgrounds and came from patrician families, many of the privateers commissioned by Queen Anne were men of lesser birth and distinction. Devoid of any military education or discipline, and conditioned by the predatory profiteering that came with the privateer vocation, the pirates that emerged following the war were far more ruthless, indiscriminate, and violent. Their prey was any merchant ship that sailed the bustling trading routes between European countries and their outposts in the New World. The pirate ships also benefited from a well-established privateering infrastructure in North America, which included shipbuilders and outfitters, armament suppliers, black-market buyers for the proffered booty, and sailors well schooled in high-seas thievery. As Philip Gosse wrote in his 1932 book, *The History of Piracy*, "Willing volunteers were to be found at most of these ports, the favourite recruiting ground, as before, being Newfoundland." Bartholomew Roberts was perhaps the most famous of these postwar pirates, although he had numerous contemporaries and competitors, including Henry Morgan, Anne Bonny, Blackbeard, and Captain William Kidd.

One pirate based out of Newfoundland during these postwar years was Alphonsus Kelly. Described as a "red-bearded giant of a man," the Irish-born Kelly operated out of Conception Bay, although he reportedly robbed ships as far south as the Caribbean. Kelly was conscripted into the British Navy as a young man but deserted for a life of piracy. Before long, he was the captain of his own pirate ship with a reputation as a merciless thief who punished hapless victims by lifting them over his head, cracking their spine across his knee, and throwing their broken bodies overboard. Legend holds that Kelly buried his treasure on a small island in Conception Bay, in a spot that can be found at the tip of a large boulder's shadow that is cast only during a short period of time in the late-afternoon sunshine. Kelly was eventually tracked down and either captured or killed by the Royal Navy before he could enjoy his gold. The small parcel of land is today known as Kellys Island because of the legend that Alphonsus Kelly's ghost still haunts anyone brave enough to venture near the spot where the treasure is buried.

Another exemplar of the new breed of pirate was Eric Cobham, whose viciousness was rivalled only by that of his wife, Maria Lindsay. Both shared a sadistic streak that prompted such villainous acts as tying the captain and crew of one prize to the windlass and then using them for target practice. Born in the English Channel port of Poole, Cobham was practically raised on the sea and turned to crime at a young age. By his late teens, he was part of a group that smuggled brandy from France to England, which ended with his capture, flogging, and a two-year prison term. After

his release, he began working at an inn, but quickly reverted to his old ways, robbing a wealthy guest of his gold coins. After fleeing with the loot, and leaving an innocent innkeeper to hang for the theft, he made his way to Plymouth where he bought a small ship. Cobham then recruited a crew from the local port and set sail to begin his new career as a pirate.

His first victim was an aboriginal merchant ship sailing in the English Channel and carrying an estimated £40,000 worth of gold and other cargo. Reluctant to share his new-found wealth, Cobham revealed a side that epitomized his career as a pirate. He scuttled his ship, drowned the crew, and then somehow made it to the French Mediterranean where he sold the stolen cargo on the black market. Afterwards, he returned to Plymouth, bought a new ship, and assembled another unsuspecting squadron of seamen. It was also here that he met Maria, who agreed to accompany him to North America. Together they sailed to Newfoundland and established a base on the western coast of St. George Bay. From this secretive and strategic location, they had easy access to the fur-trading ships in the Gulf of St. Lawrence, which they attacked with abandon. It was also a mere two days' sail to the coast of Cape Breton and Nova Scotia, prime hunting grounds for pirates in search of trading ships.

For at least the next ten years, Cobham was able to evade capture, in part because of his policy of sinking his victims' ships and leaving no survivors. Cobham's creed as a pirate was captured in a catchphrase he supposedly liked to repeat: "Dead cats don't meow." His strategy appeared to have paid off as he never was caught and accumulated enough riches to retire to an estate in France. Cobham was even appointed as a French magistrate, a position he held for twelve years. But even amongst the landed gentry, Cobham could not resist the lure of an easy prize when it sailed in his direction. While aboard his ship off the French coast, Cobham encountered an unarmed vessel bound from the West Indies to England. With his servants pressed into pirate duty, Cobham captured the ship and murdered the officers and crew. He then sailed the ship back to Bordeaux where she was auctioned off along with her cargo.

He and Maria gradually became estranged, in part because of her bouts with depression and alcoholism.

One day her body was found in the shallow waters at the bottom of a cliff near the couple's seaside estate in France. Suicide was suspected as her body contained a fatal dose of laudanum, a popular painkiller cocktail made up of sherry wine, herbs, and opium. The leap over the cliff may have been added for good measure. Cobham died a natural death a few years later. On his deathbed he made a lengthy confession to his priest, insisting that his story be published. His wishes were carried out, but Cobham's respectable and law-abiding heirs effectively suppressed the revelations about their disreputable heritage by purchasing and burning all copies of the book.

Another pirate active in Newfoundland waters in the first part of the 18th century was John Phillips. Born into a family of English shipwrights, and later working as a carpenter himself, Phillips immigrated to Newfoundland in 1721 to work in the island's thriving shipbuilding industry. Before his ship touched shore, however, it was captured near the Grand Banks by the pirate Anstis. Carpenters were always in high demand among sea-going vessels so Phillips' life was spared on the condition that he sign on as part of the crew. Without much in the way of options, he agreed. Soon after Phillips came on board, Anstis and his crew applied for amnesty, which was granted by the King and all returned to England. Still yearning to travel to the New World, Phillips boarded another ship bound for Newfoundland and arrived at Placentia in the spring of 1723. He began work as a fish splitter on a shore crew, but it wasn't long before he became bored with the stationary life. Along with fifteen others, Phillips conspired to steal a ship and then set sail under a pirate's flag.

The night of August 29, 1723, was chosen for the heist, but when Phillips arrived at the pre-arranged meeting place, he discovered that only four of the other conspirators had shown up. Despite the short crew, the five decided to carry out their plans and made off with a merchant schooner. After renaming her the *Revenge,* and voting to have Phillips serve as captain, the newly anointed pirates began raiding fishing fleets up and down the coasts of Newfoundland. In less than a year, the *Revenge* had captured dozens of English and French vessels, some of them heavily armed. With new recruits from the captured prizes, the pirate ships then sailed to the West Indies, where they cruised throughout the winter and added to their bounty. In early 1724, while still in the West Indies, one of Phillips' original co-conspirators, named Thomas Fern, and a small crew absconded with a recently captured prize. Furious, Phillips relentlessly chased them down. Fern and his crew were captured and prosecuted aboard the *Revenge*. In keeping with the articles to which he swore an oath, Fern paid the maximum penalty; when the *Revenge* next touched ground, Fern was taken ashore, tied to a tree, and shot.

In the spring of 1724, Phillips began to make his way back to Newfoundland to repair his vessel and take on a new crew. Before he reached shore, the pirate captain was betrayed by some new members of his existing crew, who launched a violent mutiny. Those on board who refused to take part in the uprising were killed along with Captain Phillips, who fell victim to a blow to the head from a broadaxe. The seditious crew members then decapitated their former captain and attached his head to the main mast. The remainder of his headless body was thrown to the sharks. After taking control of the ship, the pirates changed course for Boston and, upon arrival, turned themselves in to the authorities.

PULCHRUM SCELUS: PRIVATEERING AND NOVA SCOTIA

By the mid part of the 18th century, Nova Scotia would surpass Newfoundland as British North America's centre for seafaring thieves and, for the next seventy years, it would be both a victim of and a staging ground for pirates and privateers during times of war. Between 1750 and 1815, Nova Scotia was at the front and rear of naval battles staged off the Atlantic coast during a succession of wars involving her colonial master. The Seven Years War (1756–1763), the American Revolution (1775–1783), the Napoleonic Wars (1793–1811) and the War of 1812 (1812–1814) all touched the shores and people of the colony. In turn, these wars spurred the greatest mobilization of private navies in Canadian history. Hundreds of thousands of dollars in private capital was raised, hundreds of privateering ships were launched, and thousands of seamen were recruited as part of Nova Scotia's contribution to the British war-making machine in the New World.

Privately owned vessels sailing out of Halifax, Liverpool, Shelburne, and Annapolis Royal roamed the North Atlantic, and even ventured as far south as the Spanish Main in search of French, Spanish, and American merchant ships. "Privateering was an essential element to marine warfare," Maritime historian Dan Conlin wrote, "especially in colonial theatres like Nova Scotia, where it was seamlessly integrated with normal commerce and complemented state navies such as the Royal Navy." A privateering cruise from Nova Scotia began when merchants, risking their own capital, petitioned the colonial governor for permission to launch a ship in search of prizes. Private ships of war sailing out of Nova Scotian harbours and other British colonies operated under strict regulations established by the Crown. No vessel could officially go prize hunting without first obtaining a letter of marque from the governor. Before a letter could be issued, a surety had to be posted by the ship's owners. The amount would be based on the number of men the ship carried, and was usually between £1,500 and £3,000. A regular account of captures and proceedings had to be kept in a logbook and any valuable information obtained by the privateer about the enemy had to be recorded and reported to the Vice Admiralty Court. All prisoners were also to be turned over to the court. Privateers were forbidden to kill in cold blood, torture, maim, inhumanely treat, or ransom any prisoner.

Privateering ships from Nova Scotia were usually converted from merchant or fishing vessels, although in some cases ships were specially built for the unique demands of piracy. Most of the private warships were small schooners, which were valued for their speed and resemblance to enemy merchant ships. Because of their small size, however, they could only accommodate a limited number of men and armaments. This meant that privateers had to rely on cunning, stealth, duplicity, quickness, and the element of surprise to be successful. A few privateering ships relied on size and brute force and some weighed as much as four hundred tons, carried upwards of one hundred and sixty men, and were armed with as many as twenty carriage guns that shot variously sized cannonballs weighing between 4 and 12 pounds. Some ships also carried "swivels," movable cannons mounted on rails that fired buckshot at close quarters to repel boarders

or to cover the rush of their own attack. Other common armaments and supplies on board a privateering ship included: bullets, grapeshot and gunpowder; cannon charges (flannel bags stuffed with gunpowder); paper, wax, and sheet lead for making gun cartridges (each of which was handmade by rolling a lead ball and a charge of powder in paper that was sealed with wax at both ends); pistols and muskets; sweet oil and blacklead for gun lubricants; matchrope and priming wires for the cannon and muskets; grappling hooks, grapnel chains, and boarding pikes for seizing a vessel after running alongside her; cutlasses, lances, and hatchets, for hand-to-hand fighting; and handcuffs for captured prisoners.

The owners and captains of privateering ships actively recruited crewmen through newspaper advertisements, by glad-handing in the local taverns, and by "crying the town," which consisted of parading up and down the main street with bells ringing, drums beating, horns sounding, and flags flying. One typical ad for the schooner *Revenge*, which solicited volunteers for privateering expeditions against Yankee merchant ships and their French allies during the American Revolution, appeared in the *Nova Scotia Gazette* on January 12, 1779:

"THE REVENGE."

Captain James Gandy, who has been on several cruises and has met with great success.

All gentlemen volunteers:

Seamen and able-bodied landsmen who wish to acquire riches and honour are invited to repair on board the Revenge, private ship of war, now lying in Halifax Harbor, mounting 30 carriage guns, with cohorns, swivels, etc., bound for a cruise to the southward for four months, vs. the French and all H. M. enemies, and then to return to this Harbor.

All Volunteers will be received on board the said ship, or by Captain James Gandy, at his rendezvous at Mr. Pround's Tavern near the Market House, where they will meet with all due encouragement, and the best treatment.

Proper advance will be given.

God Save the King.

Crews of Nova Scotian privateer ships averaged between forty and fifty men (as compared to naval crews of several hundred or more) and most were manned by locals, including experienced fishermen. Among the most important of the crew members were the prize masters, who were responsible for sailing captured enemy vessels back to port, while the mother ship continued her search for more victims.

Privateering in Nova Scotia began in earnest around 1756 with British excursions against the French during the Seven Years War. In the summer of that year, Britain declared war on France, a formal declaration that allowed British colonial governors to issue privateering licences. In the fall, instructions from the King were received by colonial officials in Halifax that authorized letters of marque be issued. For British military strategists, the best way to strike at France was not in Europe, but at sea and in her colonies abroad. The strategic location of Halifax meant that for the first time, the small maritime city would be thrust in the middle of a large-scale international war.

During the course of this embroilment, fifteen privateer ships were armed and fitted out at the Halifax port, most of which sailed against French merchant ships in southern waters. The most famous of these was the *Musketo,* which was owned by Halifax merchant traders Joshua Mauger and John Hale. Commanded personally by Captain Mauger (who had been variously engaged as a fisherman, merchant, distiller, slave trader, smuggler, and Halifax's largest shipowner), and with eighty crew members aboard, the 120-ton schooner sailed on her first cruise in November 1756. The destination of the *Musketo* was the richest hunting ground in the hemisphere, the West Indies. Once it entered the region, the *Musketo* wasted little time in capturing a prize. Flying a French flag as camouflage, she overtook a large merchant ship, which she halted with cannon fire. The ship, however, was not French, but the *Patience* of Amsterdam, which was carrying sugar, coffee, coca, and other articles from the Dutch island of St. Eustatia. Despite its Dutch registry, Captain Mauger did not free the ship. He suspected that the cargo of the *Patience* was French property and, if this could be proved in the Vice Admiralty Court, she could be claimed as a legitimate prize. His suspicions were bolstered after seeing a crew member of the captured vessel hurl a bag overboard, which Mauger assumed was filled with invoices and other papers indicating that the *Patience* was carrying French goods.

In order to secure a confession, the privateersmen ignored their commission, which forbade any form of inhumane treatment, and applied thumbscrews on various upper and lower appendages of six of the Dutch crewmen to persuade them to talk. Despite receiving no confessions of the kind, Mauger commandeered the ship and had it sailed home in the hope it would be condemned as a French prize. Back in Halifax, the court ruled that a portion of the cargo was French property and could be confiscated and sold at auction. However, the vessel and the rest of the cargo were deemed to belong to the Dutch and were released. The court also convicted Second Officer John Crowley and the shipmaster, Matthew Pennell, of torturing members of the *Patience*'s crew. Both were ordered to pay a fine and the court costs of the tortured sailors.

The next great surge of privateering activity on the eastern seaboard began with the outbreak of the American Revolution in 1775. The upper hand in the war was quickly gained by the rebel colonies, for the Continental Congress and individual American colonies began commissioning privateers as soon as the fighting began. As the Loyalist sympathizer George E. Nichols wrote in 1908, "Our opponents had not been inactive, for in the state department of the United States are 1,624 privateer bonds issued at that time, 548 of which are credited to the State of Massachusetts, and 571 to the State of Pennsylvania." Before the end of 1776 alone, nearly 350 prizes had been taken by American privateers, causing English insurance rates for merchant ships to increase by 25 percent. By the end of the War of Independence, the impressive armada of American privateers captured more than three thousand British merchant ships.

Large and well-armed American privateering ships cruised as far south as the Caribbean, while smaller schooners harassed enemy fishing and merchant fleets off the coasts of Newfoundland and Nova Scotia. As early as April 1775, rebel whaleboats captured a British schooner off Martha's Vineyard. On September 13, 1775, Simeon Perkins, who resided in Liverpool, Nova Scotia, wrote in his diary, "Capt. Snow's fishing schooner comes in, and report that there was a small schooner alongside them last night and told them my brother, Capt. Mason and Mr. Gideon White are all taken by American Privateers. That there is a great number upon the shore, and that they have taken near 20 sail about the Head of Cape." At Cape Forchu, in Yarmouth County, the crews of two armed Yankee vessels took townspeople prisoner and captured four vessels as prizes. At Cornwallis, located on the shores of the Bay of Fundy, some thirty armed men travelled up the river in whaleboats and robbed the house of Stephen Best, stealing everything of value, including £1,000 in cash.

In the autumn of 1775, the Continental Army received information that two English brigs were sailing from the British Isles to Nova Scotia with a cargo of arms and ammunition. General Washington ordered two armed privateer schooners from Beverly, Massachusetts — the *Hancock*, commanded by Captain Nicholas Broughton, and the *Franklin*, commanded by Captain John Selman — to intercept the British ships. The two American schooners headed to the Strait of Canso, but missed the ammunition brigs. Refusing to return empty handed, the American privateers attacked and robbed local fishing boats and then sailed to Saint John's Island (now Prince Edward Island). When they arrived at Charlottetown's defenceless harbour on November 17, a raiding party threatened to set fire to the town. The colony's attorney general, Phillips Callbeck, met the intruders at the town wharf in the hope of appealing to their better judgement. "Not having heard that the rebellious Colony had fitted out Privateers," he later wrote, "I judged them to be Pirates; by their Conduct, they were actually such." Captain Selman ordered Callbeck on board his ship where he was held hostage, while other American crewman began breaking into houses and stores and stealing their contents. Among the victims was Callbeck, whose home was deprived of its furnishings, liquor, food, clothing, and his pregnant wife's jewellery. In a letter written

January 5, 1776, the attorney general expressed his outrage over the anguish suffered by his wife: "These brutal violators of domestic felicity have left her without a Single Glass of wine, without a Candle to burn, or a Sufficiency of Provisions of the bread-kind; most of the furniture of her house taken away, & for what I know all of her Cloaths." Even more frightening, as the attorney general put it, the "blood-thirsty" rebels then "sought Mrs. Callbeck for the purpose of cutting her throat" because she was the daughter of a well-known Boston Loyalist. Fortunately, they failed to find her, and instead turned their attention to the colonial governor's mansion. After two days of ransacking Charlottetown, the American privateers departed with Callbeck and Thomas Wright, the surveyor for the colony, as hostages.

Halifax was also a favourite target of the revolutionary forces due to its vibrant trading ports, well-established shipping routes to New England, and the easy access that Yankee ships had to the province's coastal communities. Many of the American privateers easily pounced on unsuspecting merchant ships while eluding capture by hiding in the many nearby coves or concealing themselves in the dense white fog that often hung along the coastline. "The Coasts hereabouts swarm with little privateers from New England," fumed one outraged Halifax native in 1776, "which getting into creeks and shoal water where men of war cannot follow them, do a great deal of mischief." The September 30, 1776, edition of the *Boston Gazette* reported on the mouthwatering inventory of one British merchant ship captured while en route to Halifax: "200 tierces of pork, 231 barrels of beef, 270 firkins of butter, 169 barrels of oatmeal, 11 tierces of beef, 1 crock of butter, 25 sacks split peas, 25 boxes candles, 30 boxes of soap, 20 barrels pork." Less than a month later, two American privateers, the *Montgomery* and the *Eagle,* intercepted another British merchant ship, the *Property*, which was bound from Haiti to Halifax. She also proved to be a valuable prize, "yielding 9,000 gallons of rum, 6,000 weight of sugar and supplies of cotton, wool, flour and coffee."

Liverpool, located near the southeastern tip of Nova Scotia, was also besieged by American privateers as it served as a stopping place for fishing vessels proceeding to Newfoundland's Grand Banks and fur traders heading into and out of the Gulf of St. Lawrence.

Simeon Perkins noted in his diary entry for September 13, 1776, that Captain Snow, another Liverpool resident, told him his fishing boat was trailed by a small American schooner and that other local ships were taken by American privateers. On October 11 of that year, Perkins noted that American privateers had "taken away 5 sail of ships, brigs, etc. Burnt; sunk and destroyed 5 or 6 more, and taken some things out of stores." Five days later, Perkins lamented the ongoing losses suffered at the hands of the American ships: "This is the fourth loss I have met with by my countrymen, and are altogether so heavy upon me I do not know how to go on with much more business, especially as every kind of property is so uncertain, and no protection afforded as yet, from Government." On October 23, he documented in his diary the "fifth loss I have met by the privateers." At the end of November, Perkins wrote that in his coastal town, the New Englanders "are much engaged in privateering, and very successful."

To make matters worse, with the British navy preoccupied with fighting the Continental Forces, Nova Scotia had little protection. According to John Dewar Faibisy, who studied the impact of American raids on Nova Scotia during the American Revolution, this left much of the province dangerously open to American pirates, who "lacked legal authority and indulged in wanton plunder" and "constantly violated their instructions by committing illegal acts in Nova Scotian waters." The result was "a tidal wave of Yankee raiders" along the shores of Nova Scotia. "With no adequate defences to halt them, myriads of Yankees descended upon the shore towns of Nova Scotia. Canso on the Eastern Shore, Maugerville on the Saint John River, Liverpool on the South Shore — numerous settlements received nocturnal visits from the heartless New Englanders. They entered harbours, rivers and coves, committing various depredations on land, burning vessels in port and at sea seizing valuable prizes." The infestation of American privateers was so bad that, on December 5, 1775, Nova Scotia's lieutenant-governor Arbuthnot proclaimed martial law throughout the colony.

Although paling in comparison to the number of American privateers, colonial authorities in Nova Scotia granted at least seventy-five privateering licences to Loyalists, who ended up capturing more than eighty American vessels during the revolutionary period. One of the first privateer ships launched from Nova Scotia during this time was the *Enterprise*, a schooner financed by Liverpool businessmen. The largest shareholder was Simeon Perkins who invested £147, a contribution motivated in part by revenge for the loss of his vessel, the *Bouncing Polly*, to an American privateer. Born in Connecticut on February 24, 1735, Perkins moved to Liverpool where he would eventually become one of town's leading citizens. In 1772, he received a commission as lieutenant colonel in the militia and would later become a justice of the peace and a member of the Legislative Assembly of Nova Scotia. The *Enterprise* — which was commanded by another Yankee-turned-Loyalist, Captain Joseph Barss, who came to Liverpool from New England in 1761 as a boy of eleven — enjoyed immediate success, capturing twelve prizes in her first cruise.

Simeon Perkins

Following in the wake of the *Enterprise* were other Nova Scotian privateering ships with such expressive names as the *Insulter* and the *Revenge*. In early

February 1777, the *Revenge* set sail with the *Halifax Bob* and, by May of that year, the pair had captured at least ten prizes. In March of that year, after learning American privateers had taken a Liverpool schooner with "two great guns," Simeon Perkins commissioned Joseph Freeman "to muster under arms 15 of the militia, or more if need be" to catch the culprits. At the time, Freeman was a sergeant in the local militia, and "a strict seaman who mustered his crew aft every Sunday morning and read aloud a selection from the Bible and certain rules of the British Navy." Freeman was successful in recapturing the schooner, but this small victory did little to deter American sea raiders. On May 20, 1778, Perkins wrote in his diary, "a number of the Privateers' men came on shore, and ravaged and pillaged a number of the houses and stores. Broken open my store, and robbed me a number of things, which I represented to the Captain, but had no redress, or scarcely an answer."

Privateers were now on the front line in the navy battle between the King and the rebel colonies. On July 10, 1780, just outside Halifax harbour, the colonial privateer brig *Resolution* was engaged by an American counterpart called the *Viper*, which carried twenty-two guns and 130 men. Both vessels suffered great damage and loss of life; eight men aboard the *Resolution* were killed while her adversary lost thirty-three men. In the early-morning hours of September 13, 1780, Simeon Perkins was awoken with news that two American privateering schooners, with between forty and fifty men, had landed in Liverpool Bay and captured the small fort at the mouth of the harbour, taking the officers, soldiers, and other occupants prisoner. Perkins, his son, and three members of the local militia took up a position on a road they knew the privateers would have to travel on their way to town, which was their ultimate destination. The mini militia ambushed the American privateers, and after the two sides traded gunfire, the rebels retreated to the fort. But Perkins and his men were able to capture their commander, Benjamin Cole. With the full militia now assembling to attack the fort, Perkins offered Cole a deal: His life would be spared if the American invaders relinquished the fort and quit the harbour within twenty-four hours. Cole agreed and after being released, assembled his men from the fort, boarded their ships, and sailed away. Upon their departure,

the American privateers spied a small private ship of war from Halifax and began firing, killing one man and wounding two others.

Despite the increased security provided by Nova Scotian privateers, local militias, and the Royal Navy, American rebels continued to plunder various townships throughout the colony. In June 1781, rebels from five Yankee schooners ransacked Lunenburg and then extorted £1,000 from local citizens on the threat of burning the town to the ground. On July 22 of that year, Simeon Perkins was informed that forty gunships had been amassing off Cape Sable during the past few days. The same day he wrote in his diary that two privateer shallops had landed in Liverpool where they invaded the home of one resident, killing "his Oxen, 4 hogs, 12 Sheep, & 9 Lambs" and stealing "Sundry Goods out of his House, Molasses, Butter, Cheese, Pots, Kittles &c. besides the Cable & Anchor to his Shallop, all her Rigging, & Some Sails &c." In August 1781, two rebel privateer ships, with a contingent of eighty men, sacked Annapolis Royal, capturing the town's blockhouse, looting homes and businesses, and holding townspeople prisoner in the ditch surrounding the local fort. Upon departing, the rebels carried away John Ritchie, the solicitor general. American privateers also ransomed colonial prisoners and prizes they captured. On November 8, 1781, Snow Parker was taken by an American privateer who, according to Simeon Perkins, "ransomed his shallop & Cargo for £40. Mr. Samuel Mack Some Days ago also ransomed his Cargo of Lumber on board Lowdowick Smith for 30 or £35. This Custom of Ransoming Shallops I fear will be a great Disadvantage, as the Privateers will now Insist upon either a ransom or that they will Distroy them, as they find the People are Able to ransom."

As with pirates of centuries past, the coastal waters off Newfoundland were also a cruising ground for American privateers and other British enemies. In 1779, the brig *Triton* was taken by an American privateer while fishing on the Grand Banks. On October 3 of that year, another British merchant ship sailing along the Grand Banks was taken by a Spanish privateer. In 1782, word reached the people of St. Mary's that an American privateer was cruising in the bay and had captured a ship that had just recently departed from the town. The privateer ship was the *Hazzard,* with a crew of twenty-four. Upon hearing the news, twenty-two men from the town armed a local fishing sloop with six carriage guns collected from the other ships in the harbour and set out to engage the enemy. They came upon the privateer after she had just sunk three fishing vessels. Following a brief engagement, the American privateer surrendered and was sailed back to St. Mary's as a prize. The governor of the colony was so impressed with the bravery of the local men that they were given the proceeds of the sale of the captured ship to divide amongst themselves.

THE LIVERPOOL PRIVATEERS

By 1784, the hostilities between America and Britain had subsided and, for the next ten years or so, relative calm prevailed over what was left of the British colonies in North America. In 1793, the calm was broken as Napoleon began his charge across Europe and declared war on Great Britain, plunging the colonies back into war mode. Before long French privateers and frigates were cruising along the coast of Nova Scotia. On April 16, 1793, a proclamation issued by Nova Scotia's governor, John Wentworth, appeared in Halifax's *Royal Gazette* extolling His Majesty's loyal subjects to apply for letters of marque to "prevent any mischief which otherwise they might suffer from the French" while doing "their utmost in their several stations to distress and annoy them by making capture of their ships, and by destroying their Commerce." In return, the "owners of all armed ships may rest assured, that His Majesty will consider them as having a just claim to the King's share of all French Ships and Property which they may make prize of."

It wasn't until 1796 that the first Nova Scotian privateer ship was commissioned, but the *Royal Edward* quickly proved her worth that year by capturing a lucrative prize in Jamaica. The ship, a Spanish schooner named *Nostra Signora, del Carminio,* was fair game as Spain had entered the war as an ally of France. On November 13, 1796, Captain John Berlinder of the *Royal Edward* wrote to the ship's owner from Kingston, Jamaica:

On the 8th inst. off Jamaica, according to your instructions, and the authority given to me by his Excellency Sir John Wentworth, I brought too and captured the Spanish schooner *Nostra Signora, del Carminio,* valued at about 18,000 dollars; and brought her in with me to this Port; which appears to me to have given the inhabitants much uneasiness, there having been no accounts of a Spanish war arrived at this place. However, I have detained the vessel, not having any doubts on my mind of the propriety of my conduct.

Between the years 1797 and 1803, Nova Scotia's lieutenant-governor issued privateering licences to more than two dozen vessels, including the *Adamant, America, Asia, Caroline, Charles Mary Wentworth, Commerce, Duke of Kent, Eagle, Earl of Dublin, Eliza, Flora, Fly, Frances Mary, General Bowyer, Hunter, Jane, Jason, Lord Nelson, Lord Spencer, Nelson, Nymph, Phoenix, Princess Amelia, Rover, Sisters, Sir William Parker, Swallow,* and *Tartar.* The period starting with the Napoleonic War and ending with the War of 1812 would become Nova Scotia's golden age of privateering.

For much of this time, Nova Scotia's privateering activity was based in Liverpool. Located on the estuary of the Mersey River, Liverpool was founded in 1760 as a fishing village, but soon became better known as a logging town. Milling the spruce and the pine trees from the surrounding virgin forests also helped transform Liverpool into a major shipbuilding centre. The harbour would also become one of Eastern Canada's most important shipping ports. Yet, the lumber, shipbuilding, and shipping industries would soon be surpassed in importance and notoriety by another trade that would truly distinguish the small town. For Liverpool would become the launching pad for many of the province's most legendary privateers. There would be so many privateer captains in town, Francis Freeman Tupper noted, that "on a propitious day the chambermaid who emptied the slops out the upstairs window might flush a convoy of them at any time. With any luck she might be able to get three and even five captains at one shot."

When the captains were not dodging the effuse of sharpshooting chambermaids, they were piloting such storied privateering vessels as the *Lord Nelson, Lord Spencer, Duke of Kent, Charles May Wentworth, Rover,* and *Liverpool Packet,* all of which sailed from

Liverpool. As historian Janet Mullins notes, "the Liverpool privateersmen were of excellent stock, all leading citizens of their community, well and favourably known to British naval officers of the time. When the wars were over, many filled positions of honour as members of parliament, judges, ship-owners, and merchants." The most famous of the local privateersmen was Enos Collins. Born in Liverpool in 1774, Collins received little of a formal education. Instead, he was reared on the sea. At the age of eleven he was a cabin boy on one of his father's fishing boats and was master of his own trading ship before he was nineteen. He served as first mate on the *Charles Mary Wentworth* in her first privateering cruise launched at the end of the century, and as the leader of numerous long-boat excursions against enemy vessels, he seldom returned empty handed. Later in his life, when he was asked to reminisce about his adventures as a privateer, he coyly replied, "You will observe, sir, that there were many things happened we don't care to talk about." His influence as a privateersman, and the considerable wealth he accumulated from this profession, was made not while a sailor, however, but as an investor. His knack for seizing profitable opportunities during wartime first became apparent during the Peninsular War (1808 – 1814), which was fought on the Iberian Peninsula with the Spanish, Portuguese, and the British forces on one side and the Napoleonic French on the other. When Collins learned that the British army was desperate for provisions during a battle near the Spanish city of Cadiz, he dispatched three ships, loaded with food and other supplies, across the ocean. The ships made it through to the British troops and the cargo was sold at a substantial profit.

Collins later became a leading Liverpool merchant and shipping magnate and was a major shareholder in what is considered the greatest Nova Scotian privateering ship of all time, the *Liverpool Packet*. Collins eventually moved to Halifax, where he consolidated his fortune through a number of investments and by founding what would eventually become the Canadian Imperial Bank of Commerce. He would also become controversial in his later years, in part because he used his considerable influence to overrule elected officials who voted on policies that went against his business interests and because he opposed democratic reforms

Enos Collins

in the colonies as well as the creation of the Dominion of Canada. Leaving an estate estimated as much as $9 million, Collins was reputed to be the richest man in British North America when he died in 1871 at the age of ninety-seven.

The first major venture of the Liverpool privateers began on December 18, 1798, when a letter of marque was granted to the *Indefatigable*, which set out in pursuit of the French privateer ship *La Minerer*, with sixteen guns and 125 men. After an engagement of an hour and a half, in which the French vessel was "much shattered," according to a 1799 newspaper account of the battle, the *Indefatigable* emerged as the victor. Her prize was $60,000 in coffee and sugar, which the French ship had just seized from an English merchant vessel. Another privateer ship to sail from Nova Scotia during the Napoleonic War was the *Charles Mary Wentworth*. Built in Liverpool in 1798 by local investors, the 130-ton brig was named after the son of Nova Scotia's governor. With sixteen cannons and a capacity for more than eighty crewmen, she became one of the most fearsome warships ever to sail from colonial Nova Scotia. On

August 15, 1798, the *Charles Mary Wentworth* began her first cruise under the reliable command of Captain Joseph Freeman. Along with his officers that included Thomas Parker, Joseph Barss, Jr., and Enos Collins, Freeman commanded a crew of sixty-seven men and four boys, far more than needed to handle a ship this size, but necessary to overpower victims and steer prizes back to port. Cruising the West Indies, the *Wentworth* spent the days in pursuit of Spanish and French vessels. On this her first voyage, she took two prizes. One of these, the Spanish brigantine *Santisima del Carmen,* bound from Havana loaded with cocoa, cotton, and sugar, was captured on September 4 and arrived at Liverpool on September 11. The cargo was auctioned off for £7,460, while the vessel itself fetched £871.10. The other prize was the American brig *Morning Star,* which had been captured by French forces.

On her second cruise to the West Indies, which began February 3, 1799, the *Wentworth* was accompanied by two schooners, the *Fly* and the *Victory.* On March 24, the Spanish brig *Nostra Seignora del Carmen* was steered into Liverpool harbour by prize master Lodowick Harrington and his crew after capturing her off the island of Tortuga, just north of St. Kitts. Filled with wine, brandy, dry goods, and other articles valued at more than £10,000, the cargo was so plentiful it took three days to auction. In May, the *Wentworth* made port with four Spanish prizes in tow. As reported by the *Royal Gazette* on May 21, 1799, these prizes included a "brig of 14 guns, and 140 tons burthen, laden with Wine, Brandy and Flour; a coppered bottomed schooner of 140 tons burthen, mounting 6 guns, laden with Cocoa; a schooner of 60 tons, and another of 40 tons, coasters, laden with dry goods and sundry other valuable articles." The cargo of the four ships grossed £16,000 at the subsequent auction and "warehouses along the Liverpool waterfront and that of Halifax where much of it was eventually sold were full of cocoa, oil, wine, brandy, dry goods, molasses, sugar and all the other commodities common in the West Indies trade."

No sooner had the *Wentworth* returned to Liverpool than her owners began to think about her next cruise. They also decided to fit out the captured *Nostra Seignora del Carmen* as a colonial privateer ship. Every bit the equal to the *Wentworth,* the newly christened *Duke of Kent* was 194 tons with three masts. After refitting, she boasted twenty carriage guns, including ten 9-pounders, thirty small arms, twenty barrels of powder, thirty-eight rounds of grapeshot, one hundred cutlasses and a crew of ninety-six men and boys. At sunrise on June 19, 1799, the *Charles Mary Wentworth* was put out to sea and headed south. Ten days later, the *Duke of Kent* followed, striking what Simeon Perkins called "a "Very Warlike appearance." At the helm of the *Duke of Kent* was Captain Thomas Parker. By July 8, the pair had captured a French schooner called the *Josephina,* carrying die wood and tobacco. On the night of July 17, under cover of darkness, Lieutenant Joseph Barss, Jr. and eighteen men sailed aboard a cutter to a small, fortified island controlled by the Spanish off the coast of Venezuela. They were successful in destroying the gun battery, but in the attack, Lieutenant Nathaniel Freeman was killed by a musket ball. Upon learning the news, Simeon Perkins reflected in his diary, "It was the only Gun fired, and they could not tell whether it was the Enimy or their own people. It is heavey News to his poor wife. She is much distressed & almost beside herself." On July 24, the Nova Scotian privateers captured a Spanish schooner, the *Nostra Senora del Carmen,* with a cargo of indigo and cotton.

In a letter dated August 12 to his Nova Scotian investors, Simon Perkins, Joseph Barss, Sr., and Snow Parker, the commander of the *Duke of Kent,* Captain Thomas Parker, made the following report while at sea:

> I am happy to embrace So good an opputunity to give you short detail of my proceedings Since I left Liverpool, after a passage of 19 days I arrived Safe of the Island of St. Christophers. the Reason of my falling so much to the Eastward, was mainly owing to the Constant Westwardly winds being in [illegible]. I maid the Island of St. Barthalomies. I then thought proper to Replenish our Water, and accordingly bore away for St. Kits. At 12, Came too in old Roads. I had the Rigin Sett up, and Water filld. mean time I went to Basseterra, and Veary luckily got a Linguist, a young man that understands the French, and Spanish tonges, veary well, who, I find, to be of great

Service to us. Having filld our water and being all Ready, at 11 P.M. 21ˢᵗ, I got under way, and steerd for Moona Pasage. A Runing down the Island of Portorico the 23ʳᵈ, at 4 A.M. fell in with and captured a Small Sloop, said to be from St. Croix, but on Strict examiniation the Capt., and Supercargo Confest that it was Spanish property, and delivered it up to me as Such. his boat being a shore, and not Sufficient ballast on board the Sloop, I thought it prudence not to Send her to Nova Scotia.

[. . .] from thence I proceeded to the passage, where I Saw Several Sails, but none of them a prize, but one Small Spanish boat. She being of no Consequence, I let them have her again. I Stretched on to the Southward, and on the 27ᵗʰ, A.M., discovered a Sail. Gave Chase, at 3 P.M., Came Nigh enough to give him a Shott, but unfortunately we Carried a way out four top mast, which oblidged us to give up the Chase. Afterwards I learnt that She was a French privateer from Curacao, bound to Gardalope. I then proceed to the Southward, brought too on the 31ˢᵗ, a small Spanish Sloop. She being emty, I dismiss him. The 2ⁿᵈ day of August I made the Main, discovered the Town or Lequirs 5 leagues distance. lay off, and on, on the 4ᵗʰ at 6 A.M., Discovered a Sail. Gave Chase at 5 P.M. was obliged to give up the Chase, She being under Cover of the Bataries in Liquira. At 3 P.M., the 8ᵗʰ, Discovered a Sail a Running down. I amediately gave Chase, and gave him a gun. I found him to be an armed Brig. It Came on dark. We lost Sight of him. at 9 P.M., being Clost in with the land, Discovered at Sail, and, Supposing it to be the Brig, Gave Chase, and prepaired for action. at 10 Came within hail. She not Giving a direct answer, I gave her a shot, She Steering for the Land, and it being Veary dark, and within half a mile of the Land, I Sheared Clost A long Side of him, and ordered him to ware amidiately, or else I would Give him an other Shot, and Sink him. he then Wore Round and Stood from the Land. I Sent my boat on board,

took Charte of him, and brought the Capt. On board. he said that he was a dian [Dane?], but with the help of my Linguist, found him to be a French man. I Kept him on board all night, and after Strict examiniation, I could not Know him from any Place but Barsalona, bound to Leguira. His Seacond (as he Called him), was a french man and all the Rest of the Crew, with Some Passengers, were Spaniards. He still persisted to be Veary bold, and dareing in Respect of Claiming the Vessel, and Cargo. But his Seacond informed me that he had distroyed Some papers, and when he Saw that we were a gowing to land him according to his own Request to the leeward, He offered the Prize master, Mr. Thos. Burnaby, 6000 Dollars if I would Release the Vessel. I then Went on board, in order to Land the Prisoners. Mr. Burnaby informed me of the Capt's offer. he then Came to me, and in presents of Mr. Burnaby, W.C. Maning, and Mr. McLeod, offered to me the Same Sum, as a Ransom, and to pay the money by 10 of the Clock, the Next morning if I would land him, which I Refused, Knoing all these Circumstances to be in my favour. I insisted on his going to Halifax, with the Vessel, but he Refused, thinking to make an afidavid man of his Seacond. he accordingly authorized him as his atorney to act for him, and took his leave when the boat Returned. he expressed himself in these words. I Know the vessel will be Condemned, and I will be left destitute, and beged me to land him, and gave me a Certificate that It was his particular Request. Which I granted. Sent the Boat on Shore, with him, with a mesage to the Capt. To Come off, but he did not Come. Knowing the evidence on board, which I send you, to be Sufficient, I maid Sail to the Northward, in Company with the Prize. at 3 P.M., the 10ᵗʰ, Discovered two Sails Coming up a Stearn in Chace. I lay under easy Sail, ordered the Prize to Range a head, and Prepared for the action. at 4 P.M. the head Vessel, being a Brig, Came up with Pistol Shott. I up Courses. She, Seeing that, wore Round. I amediately did the Same, and gave here Seaveral Shot. he hoisted an English Ensign, and Pennant. But halld them down the third Shot that I gave him, and Still Kept Runing from us. we gained on him Veary fast, but taking a Squall, our Ship water logged, which oblidged me to take in Sail for a Short time, which gave him the advantage of Rainging a head for us. at 5 P.M., he tacked Ship to the Nortward, at which time the other Vessel made all Sail, and Stood to the Southward. he being a grate Sailor, and making Short tacks, obliged me to quit the Chace for the Preservation of our Prize. by what information I Can get, She was a Brig belonging to Curacoa, 14 guns, and 150 men, and the other I Supposed to be his Prize, as I heard Guns, the day before. at 10 A.M., the 11th discovered the Island of Neavs, Continuing our Course to the Northward. I am veary Sorry to enform you that we have lost 2 french privateers, mainly owing to our Ships being Crank, not having Sufficient balast, and that of the Right Kind, which Shelfurne will Real the Benefit off, but in every other Respect She answers my expectations, and I am in hopes that you Shall hear from me again Shortly. I have Infumation of Seaveral Spanish Vessels, which I hope to fall in with.

I have had no information of the Wentworth at yeat, but hope to fall in with her dayly. having notheing more to add in particular, after my best Respects to all my owners, I Subscribe myself, Gentlemen, yours,

Simeon Perkins, Esq.)
Joseph Barss, Esq.)   Thos. Parker
Capt. Snow Parker, Esq.)

The *Duke of Kent, Charles Mary Wentworth,* and *Earl Spencer,* from a modern drawing by C.H.J. Snider

P.S., —I have wrote these few lines in hast for fear of being oblidged to part Company with the Prize Schooner, Lady Hamond, who, I have not the least doubt, but She will be a good, and Lawfull Prize. I was informed by the mate that She has more property on board than the invoice Specifies. that She has to the amount of 22000 on board.

The *Duke of Kent* did meet up with the *Wentworth* on August 16 in Mona Passage, a shipping lane running between Puerto Rico and the Dominican Republic. The two returned to Nova Scotia together with three captured French schooners. They also brought with them the *Lady Hammond*, the "Prize Schooner," which Parker mentioned at the end of his letter, a Danish ship carrying cargo worth an estimated £22,000. In October of that year, Perkins and his partners outfitted the *Lady Hammond* and re-named her the *Lord Spencer*, after the First Lord of the Admiralty. A month later, with Joseph Barss, Jr. commanding, the *Lord Spencer* was sent her out on a voyage to the West Indies and the Spanish Main with the *Charles Mary Wentworth* and *Duke of Kent*, with Thomas Parker and Joseph Freeman commanding each ship, respectively. On December 17, the *Wentworth* took her first sail on this cruise. In a letter dated December 24 1799 and postmarked St. Kitts, Captain Parker informed his Nova Scotian agents, "Nothing Remarkable Occurd on our Passage till the 17th Inst. In the Morning Discovered a Topsail schooner Under Our Lee. Imediately gave Chase, and at 1 P.M., had the pleasing Satisfaction of comeing up with, and Recapturing, the Schooner Betsey, Ownd at New Providence, from Charles Town, S.C., bound to Martinique." On board the *Betsey* were fifty-one hogsheads of tobacco, 58,000 cypress shingles, and four African slaves. Parker also reported that the privateer *Lord Nelson* "fell in with a Privateer Schooner of Sixteen Guns & 140 Men, about 2 Degrees to the Windward or Antigua, who Engaged five Glasses, had 2 men killed, & 5 wounded, his sparrs, and Riggen veary much shattered." On December 29, the *Lord Spencer* had a brush with a French privateer and three of her men were wounded in the exchange of broadsides and musketry fire. During the same voyage, the *Lord Spencer* captured two prizes, but then

Captain Thomas Parker

struck a reef, forcing her crew to be rescued by her privateering cohorts.

By the time she was sold in 1800, the *Charles Mary Wentworth* had captured eleven enemy vessels as well as a Spanish island and fort off the coast of Venezuela. Nova Scotian historian Dan Conlin believes she may have been "the first warship ever built, crewed and commanded by Canadians" and more than covered her costs through the prizes she brought back to auction. Years spent in southern infested waters made the *Wentworth* leaky and slow, however, and she was able to make only one capture on her fourth cruise. The next time the *Wentworth* was put to sea it would be as an ordinary merchant ship. During a violent storm in 1802 she capsized and sank, although no lives were lost.

Joseph Freeman would continue his privateering ways in the War of 1812, commanding the *Sir John Sherbrooke*, the largest private commerce raider ever to sail from a Nova Scotia port. His son John would also enter his father's profession during the same war as the first commander of the *Liverpool Packet*. Joseph Barss, Sr. would establish himself as a leading figure in Liverpool commerce and also became a representative in the colony's House of Assembly. After suffering the ignominy of steering the *Lord Spencer* into a reef, Joseph Barss, Jr. would redeem himself during the War or 1812 by becoming the most successful Canadian privateer of all time. Following the Napoleonic War, Thomas Parker continued seafaring, mostly by piloting merchant ships to and from Liverpool. On October 27, 1805, Parker piloted the ship *Lylly* into the Liverpool docks. Waiting for him there was Simeon Perkins, who described his friend as "very much ellivated with the prospect of gitting home and particularly as it was his Birthday." Unhappily, "the Scene was Soon changed!" A violent wind confronted the brig as it was docking and "She was under a whole foretopsail fore Sail & Mainsail one or two Staysails which appeared to me too much Sail. When they were nearly up to the Fort Capt. Parker fell overboard and was drowned." In his diary entry for that day, Perkins solemnly reflected, "how uncertain is Life. Such providences are Loud Calls and teach us the great Necessity of being prepared to meet our God."

THE BATTLE OF THE *ROVER*

*The strange privateer clearly meant business —
fighting business.*
—Thomas Raddall, *The Rover*, 1958

At the southern tip of Nova Scotia, at the mouth of the Mersey River, where they feared God and beseeched the protection of King George, there lies a small port, which by some is called Liverpool, but is more aptly known by the designation "Privateering Capital of British North America." It was in this small town, we are told, that the *Rover* was being built as a private ship of war during the winter of 1799 and spring of 1800. The financial sponsors of her creation were the Liverpool merchants Simeon Perkins, esq., Snow Parker, esq., and William Lawson, esq.

On 2 June 1800, the one-hundred-ton brig sailed on her first cruise with Captain Alexander Godfrey at the helm, a crew of fifty-five at his side, and fourteen 4-pounder guns at the ready. Seven of these guns were placed at each side of the ship's waist and positioned through ports in her bulwark. Each bulwark also had many row-ports for the 25-foot oaken oars used to propel the *Rover* on those days devoid of wind or when she was in a tight spot. The *Rover* returned to port a little more than a month later with three prizes. All were American ships captured previously by the French. On her second voyage, the *Rover* left with forty-five men and boys. Little did the crew know that their brig would become engaged in one of the most storied battles ever to involve a Canadian sea hawk. On this battle, I have endeavoured to provide all the information of this fine excitement that can be gathered from the official records, and from the personal, albeit modest, account by Captain Godfrey himself.

While cruising near Cape Blanco on the Spanish Main, 10 September 1800, the *Rover* gave chase to a Spanish merchant ship, and was able to drive her to the nearest shore. Knowing the Spaniards were trapped, the crew of the *Rover* prepared to board. But Captain Godfrey quickly realized the tables had been turned; for closing in on the *Rover* was a Spanish squadron of four warships, assembled by the Spanish governor at Puerto Rico. The squadron was well prepared for armed conflict; the lead ship *Santa Rita* mounted ten 6-pounder cannons, two 12-pounder carronades, a timber beak at the bow for ramming enemy vessels and a crew of one hundred seamen and twenty-five marines. Each of the three armed gunboats that accompanied her carried at least twenty marines as well as slaves, who manned the long oars.

The commander of the *Santa Rita* had sent out a small merchant ship as bait and after the *Rover* bit, the warships positioned themselves between their quarry and the open sea. The *Rover* was now trapped, and her imperilment became more grievous when the wind died to a weary draught, eliminating any hope that the *Rover* could out sprint her opponents. The Spaniards closed in on the Liverpool brig like sharks coming in for the kill.

Godfrey knew he was in for the fight of his life. He barked orders to his crew to prepare for battle. The gunners took their position alongside the cannons, four men to each gun. Each seaman was issued a cutlass, a pistol, or both. The young powder monkeys carried canisters of gunpowder, grapeshot, and fuses for the cannons; the master-at-arms and his corporals loaded and primed their muskets; pikes were placed along the ship's edge to slow the enemy's boarding party.

The Spanish fleet moved ever closer to the *Rover* under the cover of cannon fire from their bow guns. Godfrey ordered that fire be returned from the two guns at the stern of the brig. But he ordered his larger cannons to remain silent. By biding his time and holding back his full arsenal, he was gambling that the Spaniards would think that the *Rover* had little firepower.

"Look, cap'n," said Lodowick Harrington the master gunner urgently, "there's a mob o' men on that schooner's deck, and a squad o' soldados in each of those galleys, not countin' the black men at the oars. You let 'em get much closer and they'll try to board us."

"That's what I want," Godfrey replied. "Better than a gun fight at this range."

"You're goin' to let 'em board us?" Harrington cried.

"I'm going to let 'em think they can," replied the captain.

Outnumbered and outgunned, Godfrey's plan was to outmanoeuvre the Spanish war vessels as they neared by swiftly swinging his ship around to the starboard of the *Santa Rita* through the force of his twenty-four oars. He would then order a volley of cannon fire to be unleashed at close range. Nine-pound cannonballs would be aimed at the sails of the *Santa Rita* to immobilize her and to allow the *Rover*'s men to jump aboard the Spanish vessel from the rear. This strategy was a colossal gamble as it gave the *Santa Rita* the opportunity to drew near to and lay low the *Rover* through her own overwhelming firepower.

"Remember this," Godfrey yelled to his crew as the Spanish enemy ships drew near, "if they get aboard of us you'll have to fight like wildcats if ye hope to see Nova Scotia again. There's no hope for any man taken prisoner — nothing but hard usage and a mean death at the last. Now get to your stations and keep low. If it comes to a gun fight, the

The *Rover*

Senor will try to cripple us afore the wind comes on again — he'll shoot high for our spars and sails. But don't count on that. Keep down, shoot cool, and reload fast — you've got to move like tallowed lightning."

From the helm, Godfrey waited patiently as the *Santa Rita* inched closer and closer. Then, when he believed the time was right, the captain ordered his men to engage the enemy with muskets and pistols, while directing his oarsmen to position the ship so her stern directly faced the oncoming vessels. The cannons, well loaded with great and small shot, remained silent, but ready.

The enemy ships were now so close that Godfrey could hear the commander of the *Santa Rita* order the crew of two of the gunboats to board the *Rover*. The Spanish marines leaped into action. One boat attacked on the brig's larboard bow and the other on her larboard waist. Godfrey ordered his own men to continue firing with small arms and the stern guns.

With the gunboats less than 15 yards away, Godfrey made his move.

"Now, lads," he shouted to his first lieutenant who relied it to the lead oarsmen, "out with your sweeps to larboard — out with 'em! Lively! Lively does it! Now heave! Heave her round to starboard, fast as you can. Heave, I tell you. Put your backs into it! Pull — pull your shoulders off — this is no time for lagging. Come! Round with her. Make that sea boil. Make it boil if ye want to see home again. Ah! Now she moves—she moves! Swing, my beauty!"

With three men at each oar on the larboard side, the *Rover*'s human pistons began their giant sweeps and in unison, the mighty oaken appendages pulled the *Rover* around so as to bring her starboard in a position where she could broadside the bow of the *Santa Rita* with her full artillery.

Godfrey's strategy was working; the Spanish navy men could not see the oars because of the thick smoke from the cannons. They did not anticipate that their prey could turn so quickly, nor did they expect the heavy arms that had up to this point been cleverly concealed.

With the *Santa Rita*'s bow and foresail badly exposed, the *Rover*'s master-at-arms ordered his men to let loose a broadside of cannon fire. The gunners raked the crowed deck of the *Santa Rita* fore and aft from the starboard, while attacking two of the Spanish gunships with her portside cannons. Before long, a loud crack was heard from the *Santa Rita;* a 9-pounder from the *Rover* had struck the foretopmast of the lead Spanish ship, causing her sails and rigging to fall in a heap across her bow.

Godfrey next ordered his oarsmen to shift the *Rover* and, in doing so, began a broadside against the gunboats, doing great damage and killing and wounding many on board. Godfrey noticed that the cannon fire from the *Santa Rita* had slackened, and began close action with the schooner. He took advantage of a puff of wind to back the *Rover*'s head sails and ordered the ship to be steered so that her stern was on board the *Santa Rita*. Using this as a bridge, Godfrey ordered a boarding charge.

With cannons continuing to fire, the privateersmen leaped onto the main deck of the Spanish

With the *Santa Rita*'s bow and foresail badly exposed, the *Rover*'s master-at-arms ordered his men to let loose a broadside of cannon fire.

vessel with a flourish of muskets, pistols, pikes, dirks, and cutlasses, some jumping from the stern, others from the bow, still others swinging across on ropes attached to the main mast. A furious battle ensued as cannonballs, grapeshot, and bundle shot blasted from the two combatants; muskets were fired and the sound of steel upon steel was heard as cutlasses brandished by marines and privateersmen ferociously clashed.

Despite the thick plume of smoke, Godfrey could see the *Santa Rita* was immobile. He also saw the badly mauled Spanish gunboats limp back to the mainland. Victory was his! After a battle that lasted three turns of the hourglass, fifty-three Spanish sailors had been killed and another seventy were taken prisoner. In his own recitation of the battle, Godfrey claimed that not one of his men were killed or even hurt during the conflict.

On 16 October 1800, the *Rover* sailed victoriously into Liverpool harbour with the disabled *Santa Rita* behind her. Upon hearing the news of the *Rover*'s victory against all odds, Simeon Perkins wrote, "We Must Esteem it a Wonderful Interposion of Divine providence. O! that men would praise the Lord for his Goodness and for his wonderfull works to the Children of men."

As a reward for his gallant leadership in this battle, Captain Godfrey was offered a commission in the Royal Navy, but he declined. In 1803, this "Stirring Capable man," as Simeon Perkins described him, died of yellow fever while on a trading mission to the West Indies. He was buried near Kingston, Jamaica.

The *Rover* continued to sail on privateering missions until 1804, but these cruises garnered few prizes. Succeeding Godfrey as commander was Joseph Barss, Jr., who was at the helm until 1803. The final commander of the privateer vessel was Benjamin Collins, but he was forced to relinquish his commission when he was accused of abrogating his letters of marque by making several illegal captures. Following these allegations, the *Rover* was disarmed and for the remainder of her days she was put to work carrying fish and lumber.

A SAUCY WILD PACKET

The next great spate of privateering activity in North America began when U.S. president James Madison declared war against Great Britain on June 18, 1812. Within weeks of the declaration, investors across America's eastern seaboard rushed to commission virtually anything that could float. The first American privateer, the 30-ton *Fame*, was licensed on July 1 and during the course of the war, more than five hundred American privateering licences were issued in her wake. Some of these ships were built expressly to harass British merchant vessels, emphasizing speed, power, and range. While most of the American privateer vessels were large sloops and schooners capable of transatlantic cruises, others were little more than open fishing or pleasure boats. When a tiny 10-ton privateer put into Salem, Massachusetts, with three English prizes in tow, the September 26, 1812, edition of the *Niles Weekly Register* proclaimed, "It will not much amaze us, bye and bye, if these people go out to fight the enemy in washing tubs."

As in the Revolutionary War, American naval forces quickly overwhelmed the British colonies and less than a month after war was declared, newspapers were already reporting heavy losses. The Massachusetts-based *Newburyport Herald* contained the following colonial dispatch from Halifax, dated July 20, 1812:

> American privateers are swarming on our coast and in the Bay of Fundy. Hardly a day passes but we hear of captures made by them. A schooner hence to Liverpool, N.S. was taken last Friday near Port Medway. A schooner hence with arms and ammunition for Country Harbour was taken into that harbour on Wednesday last, also a Liverpool Schooner returning from Labrador. Two schooners from Lunnenburg were captured last week and considerable sums of money taken out of them, but the vessels were released. Indeed, so numerous are the privateers around the coast, that we consider it very improvident for any vessels to sail from this port unless under convoy.

There were also many American privateers raiding fishing boats along the coast of Newfoundland. The August 19, 1813, edition of the *Royal Gazette and Newfoundland Advertiser* filed reports on the American privateer *Frolic,* which was active around the Grand Banks:

SCHOONER CAPTURED: Tuesday morning returning to this Port, the Schooner "Hunter," Captain FERRIS, belonging to Messrs. J & R. BRINE. She sailed the 7th inst. for Sydney and was captured on the 14th off Scatari Island by the American Privateer Schooner "Frolic" and sent in as a cartel. The "Frolic" had taken seven other vessels which she destroyed, among them was the "Jane Gordon" of this Port. She fought the Privateer for two hours and finding all resistance in vain, the Captain and Mate leaped overboard and swan to shore. The Privateer's men landed twenty-four of the prisoners at Sydney and twenty others were put on board the cartel.

American privateers once again contravened their letters of marque repeatedly by raiding and ransacking towns and kidnapping local residents for ransom. But despite the yarns circulated by Newfoundlanders of Yankee pirates making cannonballs out of their victims' heads, for the most part the captives were treated amicably. In an 1836 book by the archdeacon Edward Wix, he describes the kidnapping of one Newfoundland woman at the hands of American privateers:

Saturday, 6.— Walked to the First Barrisway, where three families live, and the widow, Anne Huelen, a native, the mother of the settlements. The recollection of this cheerful old lady is unimpaired, and carries her back to the history of the island for the greater part of a century, and this a most interesting portion of the history of Newfoundland,-as it takes in the troubled periods in which the French and American privateers inflicted such incalculable hard-ships on the simple inhabitants of this coast. In 1814, soon after the loss of her husband, she was proceeding with one of her daughters, and her catch of cured salmon, to St. John's, for the arrangement of her affairs, when she was captured by an American privateer, and carried to New York. Her cargo was sold there by a writ of "venditioni exponas." She showed me her pass-papers, which were signed by James Monroe, then secretary to the President of the United States. She speaks with lively gratitude of the very humane attentions which were uniformly paid her while she was detained in New York, especially by a Mrs. Sophia Doty, after whom and Mr. Doty, she had two of her grandchildren, Sophia and Elihu, named after her return to Newfoundland. She was allowed, too, very kindly, to buy in her own schooner at the nominal price of one dollar, which a benevolent American put into the poor creature's hand at the moment, for the purpose of effecting the formal purchase.

While not as quick off the mark as the Americans, the Loyalists launched forty privateering ships before the war ended, although few of these ships were specifically built for this purpose. Instead, captured American vessels, some already refitted for privateering, were purchased at auctions by investors. The American-built ships were not only fast, but their familiar shape and rig design could be used to deceive enemy merchant ships in Cape Cod and Martha's Vineyard, the favourite cruising grounds for the Nova Scotian privateers.

One of the most unlikely privateer ships launched from Nova Scotia during the War of 1812 was the *Liverpool Packet.* A mere 53 feet in length and weighing only 67 tons, the schooner was a runt compared to most of her counterparts. "A lean-lined thing she was," wrote C.H.J. Snider in his 1928 book on Nova Scotian privateers, "straight as a gunbarrel, with bold bows, undercut stem and raking keel, and two taunt spars, longer than she was, slanting back so sharply they seemed to be falling over her narrow stern." The schooner spent the years before the war as a contraband slave ship, trying to evade the Royal Navy after the trade in humans was outlawed in the British Commonwealth in 1807. Upon capture, she wound up on a Halifax auction block in

November 1811. Would-be purchasers scoffed at the puny Baltimore clipper, ridiculing "her small carriage, unorthodox rigging, and the rank smell emanating from her bowels," the product of the "illicit human cargo that had been so recently stacked like cordwood in her belly." She was too narrow to accommodate enough cargo to make her profitable, and it was doubtful she could be converted to a fishing boat. For much of the auction, the ex-slaver, "all chewed up like a dog from a street-fight," solicited little interest. Most referred to her derisively as the "Black Joke."

Yet, one of the bidders at the auction must have seen something in her that no one else did. Enos Collins, who had recently moved to Halifax from Liverpool, purchased the much-maligned schooner for the sum of £440 on behalf of himself and his partners, Benjamin Knaut and Joseph Barss, Sr. After having her fumigated with vinegar, tar, and brimstone, she was taken to Liverpool and re-christened the *Liverpool Packet*. She began her new life carrying passengers, mail, and other small freight between Halifax and her new home port, with Captain John Freeman at the helm. Being a man of shrewd reputation, financial means, and with an uncanny knack for turning improbabilities into profitable ventures, some speculated that Collins had other plans for this ship. Whether he anticipated the upcoming war will probably never be known. What is apparent is that once colonial authorities began to issue letters of marque in 1812, Collins had in his possession a schooner that he believed was ideally suited for a new career as a private warship. With the conflict already raging, the *Packet* sailed to the Halifax dockyard where she was outfitted with five carriage guns. On the last day of August, the *Packet* hoisted the Red Jack and with a crew of forty-five, provisions for sixty days, and armaments that included two hundred rounds of canister, three hundred of roundshot, four hundred pounds of gunpowder, twenty-five muskets, and forty cutlasses, Captain John Freeman set a course for American waters.

The *Packet* snared her first victim on September 7, 1812. According to C.H.J. Snider, she laid in wait on Georges Bank, 120 kilometres off the coast of New England, with every sail "tightly furled, so that only the slender spars and low, straight body etched a faint blur against the horizon. All unsuspecting, the 325-ton American ship *Middlesex*, of six times

the *Packet's* size, sailed right towards her, on her way to New York." After the *Middlesex* and her cargo of coal, salt, and earthenware was captured, she was sailed back to Halifax and brought before the Court of Vice Admiralty for condemnation. The *Middlesex* was freed, however, when her master was able to prove the authenticity of the British licence he was carrying. On the same voyage, the *Packet* fell in with the 291-ton *Factor,* bound from Portugal to Norfolk, Virginia, with a cargo of wine. After firing a cannonball across her bow, Freeman's crew boarded the victim ship, only to discover that she had already been cleaned out by British privateers sailing on the *Hero.* A supply of wine was found on board, but when the *Factor* reached Halifax, the thirsty prize crew had "left little but the bungholes." The *Packet* finished her cruise along the New England coast around mid-October, capturing the schooner *Polly* heading from Charleston to Boston with a load of rice and cotton, the schooner *Four Brothers*, also on her way to Boston with lumber in her hold, the schooner *Union*, travelling from Philadelphia to Bath with flour and corn, and the sloop *Ambition* from Boston to New York. At the end of her first cruise, Captain Freeman parted company with the *Liverpool Packet,* no doubt satisfied with his take of nine prizes in less than two months.

The *Packet* left on her second cruise sometime in late October or early November, this time under the command of Joseph Barss, Jr. Like his predecessor, Barss headed straight for New England waters and, by November 22, a Salem newspaper reported that she had already captured at least eleven American prizes. New Englanders seethed over the success of the impertinent Nova Scotian schooner, especially given her temerity in prowling the New England shore and carrying off prizes right from under the noses of American armed forces.

It was around this time that the Americans launched their first determined effort to rid themselves of this irritant. Captain John Upjohn declared at a town meeting in Salem that since all the local privateers were at sea, he himself would lead an attack on the *Packet*, if someone could supply a vessel. He estimated that seventy men were needed for the mission, a high compliment to the *Packet*. The schooner *Helen* was made available and, after being fitted with armaments and supplied with provisions and a crew, Upjohn set sail. Several days later, he returned empty handed after acting upon erroneous information that the *Packet* had sailed for Saint John, New Brunswick. "There were dark suggestions of treachery, and hints that some informer's whaleboat must have carried the warning from the shore to the lurking privateer," C.H.J Snider wrote in 1928. "But the St. John story was just one of the amusing tales Joseph Barss was continually trying on his involuntary guests. The *Liverpool Packet* never went there in her life. If the *Helen* had persisted she would have found the scourge of Salem sooner or later about three leagues off Cape Cod Light." During the month of December, as the *Packet* resumed another tour of duty, the Boston newspapers once again decried her success, which entailed twenty-nine captures on this cruise. It was said that halfway through her current mission, the *Packet* was forced to return to Halifax for fresh hands because almost all of her crew were sailing prizes back to port.

A large part of the *Packet*'s success may have been the result of her design. As a Baltimore cutter, she had a trim physique, a sharply raked stem and sternpost, and a deep draught, which allowed her to sail close to the wind. Combined with her light weight, she was as fast as any boat on the water, an essential prerequisite for chasing down merchant ships or fleeing enemy war vessels. Her sleek design also ensured great stealth; her topsail measured a mere 16 metres in length, with a hold only 2 metres in height. Her simple rigging also meant that sails could be handled from the deck and hoisted quickly the moment a potential victim appeared. Her design was not particularly suited for long voyages at sea, but she was perfectly matched for cruising coastal waters, which provided her with a rich crop of American merchant vessels that clung to the eastern seaboard. Moreover, her American design enabled her to sail into New England waters like a wolf in sheep's clothing. One mate of a prize captured in Cape Cod took the *Liverpool Packet* for an American privateer at first, "for she looked exactly like their Virginia pilot boat, except her having waistcloths" (to conceal her midship guns).

The *Packet*'s success was also due to her master, Joseph Barss, Jr. Born in Liverpool on February 21,

The *Liverpool Packet*

1776, he was the second of Elizabeth Crowell and Joseph Barss' fourteen children. Like his father and brothers, Joseph, Jr. spent much of his life at sea, beginning in his early teens. At the age of twenty-one he was already master on one of his father's vessels and a year later he was second lieutenant aboard the *Charles Mary Wentworth*. In 1799, Joseph, who now cut a dashing figure with his fashionably long hair, thick sideburns, and boyish good looks, was given command of the *Lord Spencer*. In 1801, he succeeded Captain Godfrey as master of the *Rover*. For the next ten years, he commanded merchant vessels in the Maritimes, New England, and the West Indies.

Joseph Barss, Jr.

When the *Liverpool Packet* first set sail in 1812, Joseph, Jr. was second-in-command and a year later he became her master. His appointment was a nod to his leadership abilities, his navigational skills, and his uncanny ability to anticipate potential prey and enemy captors. "Some of the *Liverpool Packet*'s feats of changing position were marvellous," C.H.J. Snider wrote. "She must have sailed like a witch. No spot was too perilous for Joseph Barss to reach if there was a prize to be made." In one 24-hour period, he logged 250 miles between one capture at Halfway Rock off Portland, Maine, and another off Point Judith in Martha's Vineyard, all the while being pursued by American warships. Barss forged a naval intelligence system by enlisting the help of other friendly ship captains to alert him to potential prizes or to American warships sent to capture him. Barss' record as commander of the *Packet* was unequalled among privateers, and his skills as a seaman were duly recognized in November 1812, when he was promoted from master to captain. With his new commission, Barss enjoyed a resplendent Christmas with his family in Liverpool; he had captured twenty-one ships, netting his investors approximately $100,000.

On February 10, 1813, Barss received another letter of marque and, by March, the *Packet* was back prowling her favourite hunting grounds off the coast of New England. Once again, she did not disappoint her investors; between March 5 and 14, she captured at least ten American prizes, sending seven back to Halifax. While sailing towards the waters off the coast of Maine, the *Packet* fell in with the *Defiance*, robbing the large American sloop of her cargo of flour and lumber shingles, as well as her 14-foot ash oars, which Barss kept for the *Packet*. He also used the captive *Defiance* as a decoy to help capture the *John* of New York, a 130-ton brig carrying a cargo worth $20,000. Along with the *Sir John Sherbrooke* and the *Retaliation*, the three Liverpool privateer vessels were causing so much disruption to American shipping that marine insurance rates were hiked for American vessels sailing out of Boston and other New England ports.

By April, Boston newspapers were reporting that the *Liverpool Packet* had captured seven ships that month. In its May 1813 edition, the *American Shipping Intelligence* paid its grudging respect to the colonial privateer:

> The evil genius of our coasting trade has of late changed her cruising ground from Cape Cod to our north shore. About five o'clock on Saturday afternoon she took, near the outer harbour of Gloucester, the schooner *Fanny*, bound from Boston to the east-ward, having on board a cargo of corn, tar, cordage, etc. On

Saturday morning she took a sloop with wood, and sent her into Gloucester with prisoners. The privateer continued off the harbour until Sunday afternoon, when the inhabitants, provoked at seeing their port thus blockaded, sent out the brig *New Orleans*, manned with smart and experienced men, in pursuit of her, on which the privateer made off. But the brig chased until she got within a mile and a half of her, when it fell calm, and the privateer, by the sweeps (from the *Defiance*'s cargo!) and night coming on, escaped. The brig returned next morning, with no further success than having driven her from the mouth of the harbour. The armed boat *Jefferson* and privateer *Frolic* also sailed from the port in quest of the *Liverpool Packet* but returned, equally unsuccessful.

On May 23, 1813, the *Packet* returned to Halifax with the *Defiance*, the thirty-third prize she had delivered for condemnation. On June 8, she left on what would prove to be her final trip under the command of Joseph Barss, Jr. Three days into the excursion, a sail was spotted in the distance and Barss ordered his crew to give chase. Soon after the pursuit began, the *Packet*'s prey abruptly reversed course and headed in the direction of the hunter. The intended quarry was not a merchant ship at all, but the American privateer *Thomas*, commanded by Captain Shaw. The *Thomas* was at least double the size of the *Liverpool Packet* and heavily armed, with five big guns on each side and four more swivel guns on rails. Clearly outgunned, and with a third of the *Packet*'s crew away in captured prizes, Barss decided to retreat. But the *Packet* was no match for the speed of the Yankee schooner, as a stiff wind filled the large square topsails of the pursuer and cut the distance between the two. As the gap closed, the *Thomas* began to unload her cannons. Barss returned fire and in a last-ditch effort to accelerate, he ordered the heavy cannons to be thrown overboard. The *Thomas* continued to gain on the *Packet*, however, and soon was close enough that Barss was forced to surrender. A first-hand account of the battle and subsequent capture of the *Packet*, from the perspective of a crew member of the *Thomas*, was printed in the *Acadian Recorder* on June 26, 1813:

… at 9 gave chase to a sail, which proved to be a sch. under a press of sail … at half past two [the *Thomas*] commenced firing her stern chasers - at 3 she rounded too and struck her colours - ran along side and ordered her under our lee - in the act of veering she fell on board of us, her men ran forward to bear off — our men thought them going to board us, jumped on board of her at the same time the marines fired a volley of musketry, which killed 2 of our own men on her deck, viz. William Thomas and Patrick Train - and Lewis Peliham on our own deck, The schr. proved to be the *Liverpool Packet*, of 5 guns and 35 men. Capt. Barss, 3 days from Halifax on a cruise.

That same day, the *Thomas* sailed into Portsmouth, New Hampshire, triumphantly towing the enemy schooner behind her. Guarded by New Hampshire militiamen, the manacled prisoners were marched to the local jail, amidst a chorus of jeers and taunts from the assembled crowd of townspeople. As chronicled in one Nova Scotia newspaper, the crew was "treated with great severity by their captors, some of whom were heard to express regret that they had not been put to death at once." Captain Barss was subjected to particularly harsh treatment, "for he was locked in fetters, and fed on a diet of water and hard tack." Barss spent several months shackled in a Portsmouth jail, even after his crew members were freed. It was only through the personal intercession of the governor of Nova Scotia, Sir John Sherbrooke, that a prisoner exchange was made. The conditions under which Barss was released required that he never again become involved in privateering against the United States of America.

Upon his release, Barss returned to Liverpool where be began a new career as a merchant trader. In 1814, he took the *Wolverine* (ironically, the former *Thomas*, which was captured by the British in 1813) to the West Indies with an armed ship. According to a Boston newspaper dated October 28, Barss had been recaptured by the Americans, having "broke his parole" and was apparently imprisoned again. Whether this was true or not, the next record of Barss was his return to Liverpool in March 1815. By that time, his seafaring life was at an end, due to ill health. In 1817, he moved to Kentville, in Nova Scotia's Annapolis Valley, with his wife, Olivia, where they bought a farm and raised a family of nine until his death on August 3, 1824, just four years after the passing of his father.

Despite Barss' capture and subsequent retirement, the lieutenant-governor of Nova Scotia was now handing out letters of marque at a fevered pace, and, by the end of 1813, commissions were issued to twenty-one different privateers from across Nova Scotia. In March, Enos Collins launched two new ships, the *Sir John Sherbrooke,* formerly the American brig *Rattlesnake,* which had been captured by the Royal Navy, and the *Retaliation.* One of largest privateers ever to sail out of Nova Scotia, the *Sir John Sherbrooke* carried a crew of 150 men, including "many foreigners — Hamburghers, Portuguese, Swedes and other neutrals whom, the fortunes of war had stranded in Nova Scotia." She was also the most heavily armed of the Nova Scotia raiders according to C.H.J. Snider: "Eighteen long nine-pounders grinned from her gunports, nine on each side; and she had bridle ports cut in the bows, where two chase guns could be shifted, for firing straight ahead. Eighty cutlasses and boarding pikes hung in racks around her masts. Fifty muskets filled her arms chest." For a 60-day cruise, the *Sherbrooke* "put a ton of gunpowder into her magazine, and sixteen hundred rounds of grape, canister, chain, bar, and round shot." While other privateers went to sea with one anchor attached to a frayed cable, the *Sherbrooke* had a total of three anchors and four cables.

American privateers were also escalating their raids along Nova Scotia's shores. The most notable was the *Young Teazer,* a 124-ton schooner that sailed out of Portland, Massachusetts, which excelled in stealing back American prizes originally taken by colonial privateers. On June 27, after being chased by the *Sir John Sherbrooke* and the HMS *La Hogue,* the *Young Teazer* was cornered in Nova Scotia's Mahone Bay. Just when the British began to board the trapped ship, she exploded into thousands of pieces, killing as many as thirty-two crew members. Reports of the cause of the blast varied, although there is general agreement that it was deliberate. One version is that an unstable British deserter aboard the *Young Teazer,* realizing that if captured by British officers he would be hanged, threw a lit torch into the ship's magazine.

After her capture by the *Thomas,* the *Liverpool Packet* was refitted as an American privateer and fittingly rechristened *Young Teazer's Ghost.* Following little success during her initial voyages, she was sold and again rechristened as the *Portsmouth Packet.* But after only a few months under this new name, she was captured off the coast of Maine by the Royal Navy following a 14-hour chase. Now back in British hands, the vessel returned to Halifax, where she was reunited with an old friend. For a second time, Enos Collins and his partners put their faith in the small schooner, purchasing her for the same price they paid two years earlier. On November 25, 1813, another letter of marque was granted to the rechristened *Liverpool Packet,* which was now under the command of Caleb Seely. Although not as prolific as Barss, Seely was able to bring some fourteen American prizes before the Court of Vice Admiralty for condemnation by the time he retired his commission on October 14, 1814. Lewis Knaut, a prize master who sailed under Seely, was at the helm for the *Liverpool Packet*'s last voyage, receiving his letter of marque on November 11. By the first week of December, the *Packet* had sent home three ships before returning to port for the final time as a privateer vessel. During her short life as a commerce raider, from September 1812 to December 1814, that ship C.H.J. Snider called the "saucy wild packet" captured at least sixty vessels — with some estimates as high as two hundred. Thirty to fifty of these prizes were condemned by the Court of Vice Admiralty, bringing in around a quarter of a million dollars after auction. It has been said that her constant raids along the New England seaboard helped revolutionize shipping in the area by prompting the construction of the Cape Cod Canal, so that American merchant ships could avoid future privateers and pirates.

The signing of the Treaty of Ghent in December 1814 ended the last war ever fought between Great Britain and the United States. One of the final Canadian privateering ships actually set sail a month after the treaty was signed, but before the news had reached Nova Scotia. The 132-ton schooner *Rolla,* which left Liverpool in January of 1815, had her "pick of the privateering profession," Liverpool historian Janet Mullins wrote. "Fifteen of her crew of forty-five were masters of vessels." Many would never return home.

On the night of January 13, the ship sank off Martha's Vineyard during a powerful storm. In the end, "twenty-two wives were made widows and nearly a hundred children were left without a father."

Although the war accomplished little for either Britain or America, the people of Atlantic Canada realized significant economic benefits from the conflict, more than making up for the disruptions to trade that usually accompanies war. Between 1812 and early 1815, hundreds of prizes where sent home by Nova Scotian privateers. As Faye Kert states in her book *Prize and Prejudice: Privateering and Naval Prize in Atlantic Canada in the War of 1812,* privateering became "a major component of the Atlantic coastal economy. Entrepreneurs and merchant shipowners found an outlet for investment capital that would otherwise have laid idle, experienced seamen found employment, shore-based industries such as shipbuilding, ropemaking, and chandlery prospered, and the courts and auctions provided work for an array of clerks, prize agents, lawyers, and notaries." Privateering also contributed heavily to government coffers. "Buoyed by wartime speculation, military contracts, a steady supply of prize cargoes, and a populace willing to engage in trade under licence or under cover, the provinces of New Brunswick and Nova Scotia prospered."

Within the context of Canada's historical and military development, privateering was more than an economic activity; it provided a locally managed defence and offence, especially given the Royal Navy's neglect of the Canadian colonies during periods of war. As maritime writer Thomas Raddall observed, "The privateers of Nova Scotia were the first warships to be built, owned, manned and commanded on the high seas entirely by Canadians. In them the Royal Canadian Navy had its humble beginning." For historians Harold Horwood and Ed Butts, "the War of 1812 was Canada's war of independence when native Canadians, led by small groups of British regulars, fought off the one major attempt to take their country by force of arms." And it was the privateers, mainly those sailing out of Nova Scotia, who were "the principal line of defence that prevented Upper and Lower Canada, New Brunswick, and Nova Scotia from becoming American territories and eventually American states." Outcapturing their American counterparts by a four-to-one ratio, Canadian privateers "won the war at sea."

The War of 1812 was the last international conflict in history where private navies played a significant role. By the mid part of the century, most nations agreed to abolish privateering. As naval enforcement increased throughout the 19th century, the pirate ship also became a relic of the past. The last hanging in Canada for piracy took place in Halifax in 1809. A few pirates did manage to linger in North American waters, however. On April 3, 1825, while on board the English sloop *Eliza Ann,* bound from St. John's to Antigua, Lucretia Parker wrote a letter to her brother in New York that contained the following passage:

> We set sail with a favourable wind and with every appearance of a short and pleasant voyage, and not with an incident to destroy or diminish those flattering prospects, until about noon of the 11th day from that of our departure, where a small schooner was discovered standing toward us, with her deck full of men, and as she approached us from her suspicious appearance there was no doubt in the minds of any on board that she was a Pirate; — when within a full yard of us, they gave a shot and our decks were instantly evaded with the motley crew of desperados, armed with weapons of every description that can be mentioned, and with which they then commenced their barbarous work, unmercifully beating and maiming all on board except myself.

Even before piracy and privateering ended, seagoing vessels operating on the fringe of legitimacy were involved in a more lucrative and less dangerous trade: smuggling. Indeed, the international trade in contraband goods would become a mainstay of organized criminal conspiracies throughout Canada. Smuggling would also foreshadow the future of organized crime in Canada and abroad — a reliance on profit-oriented illegal activities that did not prey on people, but was consensual in nature, supplying goods and services demanded by the public. Despite this tactical shift, future organized criminals would have an ample amount of pirate in them.

CHAPTER TWO

OUTLAWS ON THE CANADIAN PLAINS

Bank Robbers, Horse Thieves, Cattle Rustlers, Smugglers,
Swindlers, Whiskey Traders, and Other Varmints

OUTLAWS OF THE BIG MUDDY BADLANDS

They terrorized towns and ranches on both sides of the Saskatchewan–Montana boundary leaving behind a trail of death-destined lead, writhing gunsmoke, and empty corrals. Who could stop this violent gang of cattle rustlers and horse thieves known as the Big Muddy Mob?

There was a time when Wood Mountain was real peaceful-like. That was before Red Nelson showed up. I reckon aint nothin' gonna be the same round here agin.

I first saw his large stoop-shouldered, bandy-legged hide propped against the side of the Shamrock Belle Saloon over yonder in Glasgow, Montana. He was lurkin' behind the corner, starin' direct at the jailhouse just 'cross the street. I figgered he was up to no good.

Nelson's bushy-browed eyes darted toward the local jail and watched real intense-like as the sheriff walked out the front and 'cross the street to bend an elbow at the saloon. After the tin horn had pushed himself past the swingin' doors, Nelson done leaped onto his horse and rode up to the hoosegow, with two more horses right behind him. He dismounted, began a-yellin', kicked the door of the calaboose open, and then strode inside like he was Buffalo Bill at one of his Wild West shows. Waitin' fer him inside the jail

cell, downright excited, were his pardners, who went and unlocked the cell door with a key made from a tin can. With his desperadoes behind him, old Red glided right past the sheriff's wife real casual-like and even done tipped his hat to her.

After Nelson sprung his gun cusses from their iron quarters the three of them jumped on the waitin' horses and hightailed it out of town. When Sheriff Willis was told about the jailbreak, he done near fell off his bar stool. He ran from the saloon and hopped onto his own horse and with a loud grunt he galloped away, hot on the heels of them escapin' varmints. But before the sheriff could get too far, slugs began explodin' into the ground right in front of his horse. She got spooked and began a-kickin', a-plungin', and a-rearin'. Willis was catapulted clear out of his saddle. After the sheriff picked himself up, dusted himself off, and soothed his bruised ego, he went off and done formed himself a posse. But as he was fixin' to do so, he found out that the town's menfolk were about as scarce as a hen's front tooth. It turned out that a right many of the menfolk, horses, and guns were on the road with Deputy Sheriff Hoke Smith. Some thought this to be right queer. Some say that Hoke was workin' fer Nelson. The deputy sheriff later had to quit when Sheriff Willis found out that he and old Red had bin writin' letters to each other. In one of his letters, Red even asked Hoke fer a loan of money!

News of the daylight jailbreak spread clean through the town and countyside. It was on this hot day in June 1895, that Sam Kelley (a.k.a. Charles "Red" Nelson) become real infamous-like.

Kelley was the leader of a ragtag, on-agin off-agin assortment of outlaws, crooks, bandits, rustlers, and desperadoes that terrorized towns and ranches on both sides of the Saskatchewan-Montana boundary. The main varmints in the Big Muddy Mob were Kelley, Dutch Henry, and Frank Jones. Kelley was knowed as "one of the wiliest, most dangerous and most wanted outlaws of the Big Muddy." He could slap leather faster than any gunslinger and was knowed as one of the quickest draws this side of Homer Watson. He could unshuck a pistol so quick-like that it seemed they leaped right from their holsters into his waitin' hands. Some folk claim he could use his .30-30 rifle to de-horn a steer at one hundert yards. This here Kelley was "a heavy set, incredibly dirty hulk of a man, who ambled, rather than walked." His face was more scarred than a brave after a Blackfoot Injun war dance and his nose looked like it had bin "sidetracked by an ungracious fist some time in the past." He could be spotted a mile away because of his wild shock of red hair, red whiskers, and red bushy eyebrows that looked like caterpillars. He was from way back yonder east, Nova Scotia to be exact. But he was no high-falutin flannel-mouth dude. He went west to work as a cowpoke in Montana and after a spell punchin' cattle, shore enough he done seen dang fit, fixin', and all-fire aimin' to git plumb clean into the life of crime not a downright smart while after arrivin' yonder there in Montana.

One of Kelley's pardners in the Big Muddy Mob was that ornery critter Frank Jones, a psychotic mudsill of a killer who was more tightly wound than a corset around the belly of Jolly Irene. He had black hair, a dark moustache that sat over a permanent sneer, and a real mean look in his eyes. By the time he hooked up with Kelley around 1899, he was already thievin' cattle. He was a real hard case and blowed plenty about all them notches on the handle of his pistol. In 1898, Kelley and a hot spur named Frank Webber, stole twenty-one head of unbranded cattle from a ranch near Estevan, Saskatchewan. A group of bounty-huntin' possemen caught up with Webber

and threw him into the old Stony Mountain Pen fer five years. But Jones got clean away.

Other members of the Big Muddy Mob were the Pigeon-Toed Kid, a half-breed named Bloody Knife, James McNabb, Edward Shufelt, Frank Carlyle and four other cowboys that folks only knowed as Parent, Wollett, Duffy, and Birch. Another gunpoke in cahoots with Dutch Henry and Frank Jones was Harry Alonzo Longabaugh. Some folk say that the three of them ran stolen horses from Montana clear across the border into Saskatchewan. Longabaugh also holed up in the Big Beaver district of Saskatchewan a spell after hightailin' it from a hot-eyed American posse that was chasin' him cause he done robbed a Great Northern Railway train in Montana on November 29, 1892. He also worked as a cow puncher at the Bar U Ranch near Calgary in 1890. He began bunkin' there after holdin' up the San Miguel Valley Bank in Telluride, Colorado, on June 24, 1889. Longabaugh even became a part owner of Calgary's high-falooten Grand Central Hotel. But he left the business around 1893. Longabaugh aimed to liquidate the pardnership and git his fair share of the profits. After reckonin' he did not git all the money he had comin' to him, Longabaugh got plenty mad at his former pardner and cussed his dirty double-crossin' mangy hide. He paid the scoundrel a final visit and this time he used his Smith & Wesson in the negotiations. His former pardner got the message and gave Longabaugh the rest of his share straightaway. Longabaugh then left Calgary fer good. Real soon after that he saw fit to hook up with another outlaw feller who was named George Parker, but who liked to call himself Butch. Along with a gang of saddle tramps, the two life pardners robbed banks and trains from Washington State all the way to Bolivia. The lawmen named this group of outlaws the "Wild Bunch." Around these parts, most folks just knowed 'em as Butch Cassidy and the Sundance Kid.

The Big Muddy Mob didn't rob trains or banks. They rustled horses and cattle. They thieved 'em from ranches on either side of the boundary line and then moved 'em real quick-like to the Big Muddy badlands where they would hole up fer a right long time, if need be. The badlands is a rocky valley located just there north of the boundary that separates the south-central part of Saskatchewan from the northeastern part of Montana. From Willow Bunch, Saskatchewan, to the mouth of the Missouri River in Montana, the Big Muddy is plumb full of desolate canyons, rugged buttes, slopin' ravines, naked cliffs, cavernous craters, and hairpin hogbacks. In some places, the valley is as much as 500 feet deep. Underneath that there rock is layer after layer of geological history that goes back a right smart while; sixty-five million years just about.

The Big Muddy is the most northern station on th' legendary Outlaw Trail, what gets started in Canada and goes all the way yonder south to Old Mexico. The trail joins together a right many escape routes, hidin' places, rest spots, and supply stations fer fleein' bandits that could go this-a-way or that-a-way dependin' on their fancy. From the Big Muddy in Saskatchewan, the route snakes southward to Miles City in Montana. Then it winds to Deadwood, South Dakota, through the Black Hills country to Hole in the Wall, Wyoming, and then onto Brown's Park, which squats along the Colorado and Wyoming border crossin'. The trail then done cuts over Diamond Mountain and through an Injun reservation to Robbers' Roost in Utah. After passin' through Arizona, the next stop is the Wilson ranch in New Mexico, and from there the outlaw gringos cross the border to safety in Ciudad Juarez in Old Mexico. After a train, bank or stage coach robbery, the thievin' long riders would high tail it hell-fer-leather direct to the trail. Most folk think it was Butch Cassidy that organized the trail and made sure it ran clear along a route taken by the Pony Express. That way, it was real close to towns, banks, railroad lines, not to mention the stagecoach routes. He made plum sure there were a station every 10 or 12 miles or so along the trail. At each of them stations, dragged-out horses could be replaced with fresh ones and supplies could gotten from ranchers. Sometimes there was no call to go all the way yonder past the Mexico border. They would just hole up and hide out with ranchers along the trail who were either in cahoots with the bandits or promised to hush up while starin' down the barrel of a Winchester. The gun slickers don't always make

a clean gitaway along the trail. But more often than not, Cassidy and his Wild Bunch left them lawmen chokin' on their dust.

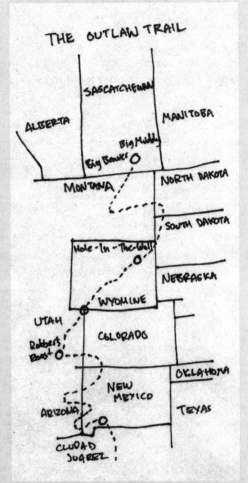

The legendary Outlaw Trail starts in Canada and goes all the way yonder south to Old Mexico.

Not far from the Big Muddy, on this here northern side of the border, was Wood Mountain. It became real famous-like when around five hundert braves, one thousand squaws, fourteen hundert Injun younguns, and more than three thousand horses from the Sioux Nation travelled to Canada in 1876 and camped there. They were scoutin' fer Sittin' Bull and his tribe, who were retreatin' from the American cavalry. The troops were real bent on capturin' 'em after Sittin' Bull wiped out General

Custer's Seventh Cavalry at the Battle of Little Big Horn in June. Word spread that there was a haven fer the Sioux in the land they called the "Great White Mother" to the north. Major Walsh of the Mounted Police was real accommodatin'-like. He offered Sittin' Bull a laurel and hardy handshake and told him that his people could stay in Wood Mountain as long as they obeyed Canadian law. The Mounties had set up an outpost at Wood Mountain, but the Big Muddy and Wood Mountain area was too dang large to be patrolled by them there horsemen and it would be a pieceways afore the men in the bright scarlet uniforms and pillbox hats could git control of the region. In the meanwhile, justice was doled out by a six-shooter and the verdict was more often than not death by hot lead.

The Big Muddy was a right fine hidin' place fer land pirates who had the law hot on their heels. It had plenty of canyons, caves, and gulches that gave cover and a mess of vantage points to spot oncomin' posses. The right small number of folk livin' in Wood Mountain meant that the outlaws didn't have to worry about no tenderfoot, greenhorn, white-collared, yellow-bellied, lily-livered, gol-danged, bush-whackin' city slicker–turned–homesteadin' settler with gumption stickin' his nose in a place where it don't belong. The Big Muddy was on the Canadian side of the line, so it was beyond the arm of the American lawmen. It was also a right far way from the Mounties' post at Wood Mountain. Varmints of all kind — cattle rustlers, horse thieves, bank robbers, smugglers, gun slick crews, and whiskey traders — holed up in the Big Muddy Badlands.

In 1874, while pretendin' to be U.S. marshals, the outlaw Charles Hart and eight of his thievin' cow punks hid out in the Big Muddy after they robbed three Manitobans plumb out of seven hundert buffalo robes. And the longhorn traders were right fired up about bein' thieved cause they had just traded fer them furs with some local Injuns! In June 1884, a lone Mountie ran into a group of desperadoes drivin' a band of stolen horses just south of Wood Mountain. When the gun-jumpy saddle bums saw the scarlet uniform, they dismounted and signalled him to pass. As the Mountie rode near the group of the men, each one dropped to a knee and covered him with a rifle. Shore enough, the redcoat just kept on ridin'.

The Big Muddy was a right fine hidin' place fer land pirates who had the law hot on their heels.

The favourite target of the Big Muddy outlaws was the Montana ranchers because them thievin' critters could cross the line into Canada with the stolen ponies and hole up in the Big Muddy afore they tried to sell their stolen heads to Canadian homesteaders. Sometimes, them dang-blasted outlaw roughriders would steal the horses from the Canadian ranchers they done sold 'em to, take 'em back to Montana and then sell 'em to the folks they originally stole 'em from! One cold day in December 1899, around noon, a few of the cowpokes on the Diamond "C" ranch in Montana were gittin' ready to chow down. They got their vittles and squatted by the campfire. But then real sudden-like with a whoopin' and a hollerin', two riders swooped down on the camp and don' captured the mess-wagon. The cowpunchers were right scared and leaped onto their own horses and hightailed in out of there with dust and stray bullets flyin' every which way but loose. One of them cowboys' horses was shot right out from under him. The cowpokes done knew the shootin' bandits were Kelley and Jones and knowin' their reputation they done kept goin' until they reached Culbertson some 25 miles away.

Sam Kelley knew the caves, grottoes, and gullies of the Big Muddy like a tomcat knows a back alley and he made a hideaway fer himself in two caves that used to be wolf dens. One cave was where the rustlin' crews bunked down and the other was a stable to hide stolen horses. Kelley was right fond of this spot because it looked out over miles of the valley and the trails used by the Mounties. If the red coats were spotted nearby, the thievin' bushwhackers had plenty of time to vamoose across to the American side where the Canadian lawmen could not touch 'em.

Around 1901 or so, the gang was joined by Frank Carlyle. A year afore, the 22-year-old had just moved out of his ma's house in Toronto to join the Mounted Police. All growed-up now, Carlyle was a right fine candidate fer the life of a Mountie. He stood five feet and eleven inches and weighed 175 pounds. He was built like all them boys of the Mounted Police are built — fer action! He worked as a fireman in Toronto fer six years and then left with a letter from his boss sayin' he was powerful honest and trustworthy. But he was about as honest and trustworthy as a bunko artist sellin' snake oil to old widows. Not long after he joined up with them Mounties, the durn fool was forced to resign because of his constant boozin' and fer becomin' a saddle buddy to horse thieves.

One of his thievin' pardners was that son-of-a-skunk Dutch Henry. Carlyle met Dutch when he moved to Saskatchewan's Willow Bunch District as a Mountie. Carlyle had already heard about Dutch, and his excitin' life was real appealin' to him. Carlyle was introduced to Dutch, and they were right proud to know one another. Folk around Wood Mountain were plumb shocked about how the two took such a right fine fancy to each other. The two began smugglin' horses across the Canadian line together and when Carlyle's bosses became suspicious-like, he quit the Mounties. Carlyle brought Dutch into the Big Muddy gang and then Dutch fetched his long-time gun-ugly pardner Edward Shufelt to join up.

Henry Jeouch came to America direct from Germany around the 1860s. Nobody knows who Henry Jeouch is. But say the name "Dutch Henry" and every manfolk, womanfolk, and chillenfolk in these parts will say, "Oh, the horse thief." Henry never lost that thick Bavarian accent, which is why most folk just knowed him as Dutch (in these here parts folks weren't learned too much about European geography). He first settled in Texas where he fought Injuns beside Wyatt Earp and Bat Masterson at the Battle of Adobe Walls. Dutch was real stocky with a head shaped like a cannonball, blond hair, blue eyes, a crooked nose, and gold fillins on his teeth. He was real funny-like and more popular than a whorehouse on nickel night. He carried a pistol specially made for him that he ordered from Minnesota. It was a .45-calibre Bisley with a 4¾-inch barrel and ivory grips that had a steer's head carved into one side.

In 1888, Dutch moved to Montana to work as a cowpoke. He was plenty known fer his love of the ponies and he once owned a horse named Dude and even decorated his mane with coloured ribbons. One time, Dutch dressed Dude in a white collar and tie, and then got made up in his own best parade chaps and peacocked around Regina playin' to the gallery! Dutch loved the attention. Besides dressin' up horses real purdy-like, Dutch was also a plenty good wrangler and some said he could lasso a horsefly at a hundert paces. When he worked as a cowpoke he cared for them there cattle real good; he kept the coyotes away and when he worked the night shift dang burnit if he weren't heard singin' them cattle to sleep.

It was not a right smart while after he arrived in Montana that Dutch began thievin' horses and cattle. In December 1893, he stole some head from a Montana rancher named Conrad Kohrs. Then he sold them head to Andrew Sherry, who done changed the brands and burned in his own mark. In 1898, a sheriff asked Sherry about some of the cattle on his ranch. Sherry told him he bought un-branded cattle from Dutch fair and square and then swore that the brands on the cattle were all his own makin'. The sheriff reckoned that Sherry was a lyin'-snake-in-the-grass and called his bluff. He fetched his rifle, shot one of the cattle plumb dead, and then skinned it near the brand. The inside of the calf's skin showed the original brand. Sherry's brand was burned direct over it. Sherry plum got hisself arrested and a price got put on Dutch Henry's head. A short while after, Dutch done got captured at Culbertson, Montana, and was locked up in the nearby stockade. But Dutch escaped after sweet-talkin' the deputy sheriff to let him go to the local saloon to borrow money from a friend. While the deputy was waitin' fer him to come back, Dutch leaped onto a horse and rode straight away without a how-dee-do. While he was on the lam, Dutch crossed into Canada with horses he stoled in Montana and hid out fer a spell in the Big Muddy. The Mounties picked up his trail and closed in on him there, but they were turned back by rifle fire. The men in scarlet then surrounded him and played the waitin' game. After a week, the Mounties sent in a Sioux Injun who caught Dutch fast asleep in a ravine and took his guns away. When he woked up, Dutch was wrassled to

Dutch was also a plenty good wrangler and some said he could lasso a horsefly at a hundert paces.

the ground like a steer and was arrested. But he was right soon out of the sheriff's hotel after his $500 bail was posted by some of his pardners. When Dutch was brought to trial on the cattle thievin' charges, he packed the courtroom with his renegade horse-stealin', cattle-rustlin', tobacco-chewin' outlaw pals. Turned out, there was no witnesses to testify agin him. Shore enough, the judge reckoned he had to throw the case out.

After he got free, Dutch took a job workin' as a cow thumper fer J. W. (Dad) Williams, one of the men who posted his bail. Pappy Williams was an old-time Montana stockman who had a real big ranch on Shotgun Crik just outside of Culbertson. Dutch was fixin' to stay a spell at the ranch, but his onery side plum got the best of him. Y'see, Dutch had a bad habit of thievin' from folks he knowed, if that don't beat all. Some said that he liked to make friends, 'cause it was easier to thieve 'em than folks he don't know. In May 1899, Dutch began stealin' horses from his boss. He would separate a band of horses while herdin' and take 'em into Canada to sell. On one drive he stole upwards of four hundert head o' horses, took 'em across to Canada, sold 'em, stole 'em back, and brought 'em back to to the U. S. of A. to sell 'em agin'!

Around 1900 or so, Dutch Henry and Frank Carlyle teamed up with Frank Jones. Shortly after that, a local sheriff from Montana named Griffith received a telegram that a hundert head o' horses had been rustled near Culbertson. Sheriff Griffith took the train to North Dakota aimin' to catch them there thieving scoundrels when they tried to unload them critters. He didn't find 'em, but he did spot several head with brands what had been worked over. Sheriff Griffith's posse then galloped to Wood Mountain where they found sixty head of branded American horses. Some half-breeds in the district also claimed they had been held up by Frank Jones and other gun slickers. The half-breeds were tough, but they were downright ascared of Jones. A $1,000 price was put on Jones' head. His desperado pardners got bounties between $300 and $500.

While on the loose, the gang began extortin' "insurance" money from ranchers so their cattle didn't git stolen. It's what some big city folk might call a "protection racket." One rancher named Cachot McGillis was brave enough to stand up to them varmints and was fixin' to go to the Mounties. When Frank Jones found out, he done decided to learn McGillis a lesson. He done rode onto his spread, done looted his house, and done drove off his horses. McGillis got all-fired angry and bellyached to the Mounted Police. When Jones found out about this, he laid in wait fer McGillis at his house "with two guns thronged to his thighs and a bloodlust brew in his brains." When McGillis returned from the Mountie detachment, he was dry gulched, hogtied, blindfolded, and taken back to the bandits' hideout, a-kickin' and a-cussin'. McGillis was forced to work as their personal slave fer a spell. He even had to look after the herd stolen from his own ranch! One mornin', Jones told McGillis that he had worked off his debt and could return home.

By now, lawmen on both sides of the line were hot after that gang of rustlers and kidnappers. A rancher near the Big Muddy named Frank King had some dry goods thieved from his home. He followed some hoofprints that led from his shack to a cabin and found what was stolen from him. He went to the Mounties, who told King that he better be plum careful about shootin' off his mouth 'cause word gets around real quick-like in these here parts and those who did the thievin' may not take very kindly to folks goin' to the law. The Mounted Police offered to give him protection when he rode home, but that durn fool said he had enough protection on account of his six-shooter. What King didn't know was that it was the Big Muddy outlaws who had done the robbin'.

Shore enough, Jones and Kelley found out King ratted on them and one day they ambushed him. After they whupped him and cleaned his plow, they hogtied and blindfolded him and took him to their hideout in the Big Muddy where they stripped him naked. Them there outlaws even held a mock trial and shore enough found him guilty and condemned him to death. King may have been blindfolded but knowed full well the sounds of cartridges bein' pumped into a Winchester when he heard 'em. He also knowed the sounds of a gun bein' cocked and reckoned his time was up. Jones had put his rifle muzzle straight in front of King's blindfolded eyes.

King was not only sightless he was also mighty deafened, what with all the cockin' and the pumpin', leather a-slappin', gun-hung cowboys a-gruntin', horses a-rearin' and sheep a-shriekin'. In spite of all the commotion he did hear a voice with a real thick accent and guessed it was that hornswaggerin' Hun Dutch Henry that he had heard so much about. King listened real intense-like as Dutch told Jones to put his dang-blasted rifle down and leave King because they were only foolin' the prisoner about killin' him. He didn't knowed that at the time how close he was to buyin' that big ranch in the sky. But fer the next thirteen days or so, King was the prisoner of the outlaws who amused themselves by trussin' him up like a Christmas turkey, tyin' him to a post and seein' how close they could shoot at him without actually hittin' him. They even made King build them a corral so they could store their stolen critters. At the end of about two weeks they let him go, without his horse, and practically naked. A vengeful Jones went alookin' fer him aimin' to drill the released prisoner, but King was able to escape back to his ranch without no more harm comin' to him.

Sam Kelley was now startin' to git plumb tired of life on the run and in 1904 he turned himself in to the sheriff at Glasgow, Montana, who threw his sorry cowhide behind bars. The next mornin' a group of his old cowpoke pals paid the jailbird's $4,000 bond. When his case came to trial there suddenly weren't enough evidence to convict Kelley of a single crime. That's the way things went around these parts. Witnesses got real scared-like or they disappeared fer a good long while. Or maybe they just got real forgetful-like. Whatever the reason, Kelley used the opportunity to quit the outlaw trade fer good.

With Sam Kelley pullin' in the horn, Dutch Henry on the run, and Ed Shufelt in the hoosegow for horse thievin', Frank Jones, Frank Carlyle, and the other remainin' pardners planned one last harebrained, half-cocked scheme — a train robbery. The plan was for Carlyle to blow up the railway bridge just west of Plentywood, Montana, and then the rest of the gang would rob the train. But the sheepfer-brains Carlyle got real locoed drunk and plum disappeared right before the heist. The bridge didn't get blowed up good and no train got thieved. He done put a big spoke in the wheel and Jones was fit to be tied. When Carlyle sobered up, he blazed a trail to the Big Muddy where he aimed to hide out fer a spell until his rabid pardner cooled down. But Jones never cooled down. On Christmas Day, two horsemen rode into the ranch where that noaccount Carlyle was holed up. He didn't knowed it at the time, but he was in a heap of trouble. Late that night he was awoken by the sounds of hoof beats. He sprung from the ground and automatically slapped leather, but before he could draw his six-shooter, the sharp crack of a rifle rang out and Carlyle was cut down like the mangy dog he was. Folks now know the place where the slug-infested, whiskey-soaked body was left to rot as Carlyle Coulee.

Nothin' much was heard of the Big Muddy Mob after that there messed-up train robbery. Edward Shufelt died afore finishin' his five years in the hoosegow. Frank Jones was tracked down by a posse after he had robbed a local constable in Montana in 1904. He was captured, and after tryin' to escape, was shot as dead as the president. The Pigeon-Toed Kid was filled with lead by a posse. Bloody Knife got drunk one night and began to shoot up the town of Ambrose, North Dakota. Townsfolk answered by shootin' him clean through. Duffy and Birch got prison sentences in Canada. Wollett and Parent were arrested and stood trial down yonder in America.

Dutch Henry also knowed it was time to go straight and got a new job roundin' up cattle in Montana. One day in early 1906, he told his ranch boss that he was gonna leave Montana fer good. Dutch handed over $100 to his boss to hold fer him until he sent fer it. He also gave his bone-handled gun to his boss' youngun and told him if he didn't come back he could keep it. On April 24, 1906, some cowboys stumbled across a body over yonder in a field in Roseau, Minnesota. It was part buried in the dirt and had a gunny sack over its head. It was pretty clear that, there body was real deadlike. Part of the face had been shot clear off, so it was hard to know who he was. Some folks around these parts were right sure it was Dutch Henry. But others in Montana, Saskatchewan, and even as far up as Winnipeg said they had seen Dutch alive and he was still stealin' horses. On January 21, 1910, a newspaper in Montana said Dutch had been killed by the Mounties 60 miles southwest of Moose Jaw, Saskatchewan. But the red coats were all-fired sure that there was no truth to that report. In February of 1910, a liveryman from Harlowton, Montana, said he knowed three men who'd swear on a bible that Dutch Henry was alive and kickin' in South America. Whatever you reckon the truth may be, Dutch Henry was never heard from agin.

Sam Kelley kept a right low profile fer the rest of his life. Some say he continued to bunk out in the Big Muddy caves up until 1909. A year later, he was an honest rancher. But he left the Big Muddy in 1913 to homestead about 40 miles northwest of Prince Albert. Kelley took with him some horses and three cowpokes from Montana. They each built a cabin around the shores of a small lake that folks would later call "Kelley's Lake." With the exception of a little rustlin' now and agin, the men were right well mannered and lived there as happy as pistol-packin' cowboys on Brokeback Mountain. T'aint much known about Kelley agin, that was 'til a hot July day in 1937 when the Mounties found a grizzled old codger at a bus stop in Smeaton, Saskatchewan. He was cold, hungry, and real confused-like. It turned out to be Sam Kelley. He was sent to the North Battleford mental hospital and passed away there in October at the age of seventy-eight. He was buried in a bone orchard not too far away.

THE NOCTURNAL DEPREDATIONS OF THESE BANDITS

Perhaps the most enduring and endearing of all Canadian folklore is that the historical development of this country was relatively free of crime and lawlessness. The origins of this myth may be traced to the mid-19th century. In the aftermath of a local burglary, an 1844 editorial in the *Toronto Star Transcript and General Advertiser* newspaper commented on the rarity of such crimes in the region, "which too frequently disturb the old country." This may not have been the first instance of this country's proclivity for benign blindness when it comes to crime. But at the very least it could be evoked as a prototype for Canadian's self-nurtured image as an immaculately well-behaved, lawful people, deferential to authority, and incrementally striving towards the characteristically unassuming goals of peace, order, and good government.

Perceptions of the abounding lawfulness of Canadians spring from a number of sources: the absence of a violent revolution; an abiding respect for good government, democracy, and the decorum of the parliamentary system; and a deference to the rule of law that apparently even surpassed that of the "old country." Numerous other factors have been cited. From its very beginning, the most populous portions of Upper and Lower Canada were amply garrisoned with British troops and local militias. Even Canada's bleak climate, which one pioneer famously described as "six months of winter and six months of poor sledding," has been viewed as an inhibitor against year-round criminal marauding. As the country expanded westward during the latter part of the 19th century, accounts of Canada's lawfulness became even more ingrained in the country's collective psyche, especially in light of the bloodshed that accompanied the settling of the American West. The most celebrated symbol of Canada's peaceful and law-abiding nature is the venerated Mountie. For unlike the U.S., the large-scale settlement of the vast western region of Canada was preceded by a paramilitary, law enforcement presence — the legendary North West Mounted Police — which, for the most part, carried out its responsibilities with great competence, doggedness, impartiality, and integrity.

Despite the idyllic picture painted by some revisionist historians and nationalists, 19th-century Canada was not immune to crime, including the organized variety. Smuggling began to escalate dramatically around the start of the century as Great Britain levied more and more taxes and customs duties on her colonies. In addition, Canada's inland economy was rife with larceny, corruption, and violence. The fur trade "exercised a profound influence in the sculpt-ing of the Canadian soul," Peter C. Newman wrote, and "more than virtually any other single experience, is the primary matrix out of which modern Canada emerged." If this is true, one must also accept that the early fur trade "became a focal point for widespread law-breaking," according to Canadian crime historian D. Owen Carrigan. Fur traders "cheated, stole, mur-dered and debauched the Indians," plying them with toxic liquor and turning their women into prostitutes. The traders realized that natives had little tolerance for alcohol and traded cheap (and often poisonous) "elixirs" for expensive pelts. Violence also characterized the fur trade. Some traders found it easier to steal the pelts rather than buy them and, in the process, com-mitted murder, genocide, and other atrocities.

In 1668, the Hudson's Bay Company was formed and, during its early history, a voracious appetite for profits and a monopoly over the fur trade meant that at times it could be extremely unscrupulous in its pursuits. The Company was the first to supply native hunters with cheap liquor in return for expensive pelts. It readily turned to violence when faced with competi-tion, especially from the North West Company, which was founded in 1783. As Carrigan stated, "Murder, theft, destruction of property, arson intimidation, and assault marked the commercial rivalry. Raids on each other's posts were common." The enmity between the two reached a bloody peak in 1816 at the junction of the Red and Assiniboine rivers. The Hudson's Bay Company seized Fort Gibraltar, built by the North West Company in 1809, and attempted to intercept its supply of pemmican (dried buffalo meat). In retaliation, a group of trappers aligned with the North West Company attacked the Hudson's Bay Red River colony killing twenty people, including the colony's governor.

By the mid part of the 19th century, the frontier outlaw carried on the organized criminal tradition of the sea pirate. The most fabled of these desper-ado groups were the Youngers, the Daltons, the Wild Bunch, the Hole in the Wall Gang, and the James Broth-ers in the United States, and, in Canada, the Markham Gang, the Campbell brothers, the Big Muddy Mob, and the McLean brothers. Like pirates, these bands of highwaymen were predatory in nature, robbing

trains, stagecoaches, banks, hotels, cattle ranches, and homes. Theft, assault, and murder were not uncommon occurrences in the settling of Canada and at various times, whole towns and regions lived in fear of vio-lent gangs. The "spread of crime in the rural districts of this province, is daily more alarming," warned a February 6, 1846, article in the Toronto edition of the usually staid British Colonist. "We hear of gangs of horse thieves, and of burglars of every description, prowling about the country in organized gangs, and the peaceable inhabitants have to guard themselves and their properties against the nocturnal depreda-tions of these bandits."

By the 1860s, Western Canada was inundated with whiskey traders. Like the fur traders in New France two centuries before, this parasitic profession was forged on the drunken and dead bodies of aborig-inal people who were given cheap liquor in return for valuable buffalo pelts. During the 1880s, construction crews building the Canadian Pacific Railroad produced another ready-made market for illegal whiskey mer-chants, not to mention prostitutes, con artists, and crooked gamblers, "all bent upon fleecing the poor railway man of his hard earned gains." The railway system was also a mecca for dishonest businessmen who manipulated stock prices, swindled settlers out of their land, and offered bribes for government contracts. On the receiving end of the bribes were politicians, some of whom were in a gross conflict of interest as they sat on parliamentary committees that awarded contracts to firms in which they had a financial interest. The various gold rushes during the latter half of the century in British Columbia and the Yukon fuelled a cornucopia of outlawed consensual vices. In 1861, a correspondent for a British Columbia newspaper reporting from the gold-rich Cariboo admonished government authorities for turning a blind eye to the well-organized and omnipresent games of chance:

> The openness and extent to which gambling
> is carried on in the Cariboo is a matter of
> general remark and surprise. Right under the
> very nose of the officers of the law, without the
> slightest show of concealment, are gambling
> tables daily opened, — covered with gold
> and surrounded with professionals and their

unsuspecting dupes. In almost every public house licensed for the sale of liquors these tables are to be seen, and are seen, by those whose business it is to suppress such vices; and the very openness with which the profession is pursued is the best evidence that it is winked at by authority...

The inability or lack of political will to enforce vice laws in and around the railway work camps or gold mines was indicative of the immense challenges facing law enforcement in Canada throughout the latter half of the 19th century. While renowned for always getting its man, the NWMP was woefully understaffed in its efforts to police an area the size of Western Europe.

By the end of the century, Canada played host to a vast array of organized criminal activities that included bank and train robberies, cattle and horse rustling, bootlegging, gambling, bookmaking, prostitution, fraud, copyright piracy, stock market manipulation, currency counterfeiting, human trafficking, government corruption, and an unstoppable trade in an assortment of smuggled and contraband goods. The introduction of opium into Canada in the last quarter of the century would also provide a glimpse into the future of organized criminality in this country.

NO REMORSE FOR DISREGARDING TRADE REGULATIONS

Smuggling is the most historically rooted, persistent, and widespread form of organized non-compliance perpetrated by Canadians. While smuggling is often carried out on a small scale by individuals for personal consumption, it has also been one of the most organized forms of illegal behaviour affecting this country. The smuggling of contraband into British North America began shortly after legitimate commerce was initiated in the new colonies and was spurred by the restrictive mercantile policies of the British and French governments. For the most part, the colonies were forced to trade only with their mother countries, which meant that the amount paid for merchandise produced in New France and British North America was low while the price of consumer goods imported into the colonies was artificially high. The early fur

traders were among the first smugglers on the continent when they began surreptitiously transporting pelts back to Europe and selling them on the black market without the knowledge of their charter company. Edicts from French authorities did little to stop fur smuggling from New France, including that perpetrated by government officials. When a French delegation was sent to the British colonies to negotiate trade matters with the English in 1682, a delegate by the name of Sieur Salvaye took the opportunity to smuggle eight hundred beaver skins from New France. French officials at Versailles considered smuggling of fur pelts so endemic that they increased the penalty for such infractions from being chained to an oar in the galley of a ship to death.

Smuggling was also rampant in the early British colonies along the Atlantic coast of North America. In a letter dated November 14, 1706, Newfoundland merchants complained about the smuggling of whale bones and fins, which was undercutting their retail trade: "The importers and traders in Whale Finns, doe find a great Decay in their trade in that commodity; which they apprehend to be chiefly occasioned by the Smuggling Trade, which is a great discouragement to the honest fair dealer, who pays the full Duty." Illegal imports into Britain's North American colonies soared between the mid part of the 18th century to around 1815. It was during this time that duties on imported goods began to rise precipitously due to Britain's insatiable appetite for revenue to finance her endless succession of wars. The stifling impositions would become an economic noose around commerce in the British colonies and, as a result, according to criminologist William Chambliss, "smuggling activities promoted an institutionalization of crime in the colonies in order to ensure their commercial survival." While the American colonies ultimately responded to Britain's heavy-handed mercantilist policies by dumping cases of British tea into Boston harbour and then rebelling against the unjustness of taxation without representation, the expression of defiance by the mother country's subjects north of the 49th parallel was more subdued — they simply evaded the taxes by bringing in shiploads of contraband tea. Dave McIntosh goes so far as to say, "the only reason Canada and the Maritime colonies did not join the revolution was that they were expert smugglers and consequently were not as enraged by customs duties as were the Americans." The contraband market flourished as "Canadians showed no remorse for disregarding trade regulations imposed by a faraway imperial authority without their consent."

Smuggling only increased after the United States became an independent country. After travelling through the northern U.S. and Upper Canada during the 1790s, François de la Rochefoucauld alluded to the repercussions of British mercantilist policies on her Canadian colonies following the founding of America, "The high duty laid by England upon all the commodities exported from her islands proves a powerful encouragement to a contraband trade with the United States, where, in many articles, the difference of price amounts to two-thirds." In a letter to the British Secretary of State dated August 14, 1788, H. Townshend, Collector of Customs on the Island of St. John (the future Prince Edward Island), reported on his efforts to suppress the flow of contraband from New York to the island. To his surprise, the smuggling was coordinated by the first governor of the island colony, Walter Patterson (who was dead by the time the letter was written), and his brother, John:

> On the 19th June last, I seized as forfeited, a Schooner of British-Plantation-Built, owned and navigated according to Law, the causes of seizure were, first; that her cargo was Imported directly from New York into this Island contrary to the provisions of a late Act of Parliament and secondly, that bulk was broke before entry; the goods were landed in the night-season at the Farm of the late Lieutenant Governor near the entrance of this Harbour, and distant about three miles from Town.
>
> Having received very correct and satisfactory Information of an Extensive Smuggling Trade intended to be carried on between the late Lieutenant Governor his brother John Patterson, and a wealthy inhabitant of the State of New York to whose daughter Mr. John Patterson is married, and being well apprized that this small vessel was to be followed by a larger ship named the Kitty in the same disgrace-

ful employ, I formed a resolution to seize this property, and by that means stop the encrease of so ruinous a Traffick.

> Accordingly in the night following I obtained a Party of soldiers from the Commanding Officer here, went to the Farm, and in company with the Comtroller made a seizure of part of the smuggled Effects, but, before we could get them to the Boats prepared for the purpose, the Servants of the late Lieutenant Governor aided by eight or nine other persons who had been sent over the water by him from Town to their assistance, (being in all about twenty-five persons armed with various offensive weapons) wrested the property out of our hands.

Townshend and the soldiers accompanying him were detained for several hours while the smugglers spirited the goods away. After he was released, Townshend heard of another shipment of contraband landing on the farm. He immediately mobilized a larger contingent of armed soldiers and "went to the farm in company with the Comtroller and seized the goods in a very artful place of concealment, and conveyed them to Town, and have since labelled them and the schooner in the Court of Vice Admiralty as forfeited."

At the end of the 18th century, the contraband market in the Maritimes was so large that illegal imports now surpassed legal landings. In their 1908 book *The King's Custom*, H. Atton and H.H. Holland estimated that contraband consumed in the Maritimes during this time made up "nearly all the tea; three-quarters of the wine; nine-tenths of the spirits; seven-eighths of the soap and candles; most of the indigo, starch, mustard, tobacco and cottons; and all the nankeens, sailcloth, cordage and anchors." In an 1811 letter to the Nova Scotia legislature, William Goodall advocated on behalf of local merchants when he wrote, "great quantities of teas and all sorts of India goods" as well as "gin, American rum and many other articles, are daily & illicitly brought into this province by the Americans as well as by British subjects residing in this country." Nova Scotia merchants who legally purchased their goods from British companies complained, "unless some steps are taken to prevent the smuggling trade from the American states, we shall soon be without a customer for the principal part of the articles that we deal in."

In his analysis of the contraband trade between the Maritime colonies and the United States in the late 18th century, W. Stewart MacNutt alludes to the factors that drove the northward smuggling of American goods: flour sold at $3.00 on the American side compared to $12.00 in New Brunswick and payment for the services of a man and a boat willing to smuggle the goods was as high as $47 a day, a princely wage for those times. So much of the contraband now entering the Canadian colonies was from the United States, it could be said that British policies prompted the first instance of free trade between America and Canada. Maritime historian Faye Kert believes that smuggling helped cement a strong trading partnership between the two countries, "The close commercial relationships between New Brunswick and Nova Scotia entrepreneurs and their American neighbours in Vermont, New York, and Massachusetts (now Maine) had evolved through years of conspiring to evade British duties."

The War of 1812 only broadened the underground commerce between the United States and British North America. Not even a wartime trade embargo was going to interfere with a commercial association that was already well entrenched between the northeastern states and the Maritime colonies. A common ruse employed by American merchants to get their goods to market in the colonies during the war was to arrange for the capture of their trading ships by Canadian privateers. Once the American prize was escorted into port at Halifax or Saint John and its goods auctioned off, the owner of the privateering ship would split the proceeds with the American merchant. Although illegal, such collusion was apparently so commonplace in the waters between the Maine–New Brunswick border that some of the so-called captures were actually pre-arranged shipments to the Maritimes.

The contraband trade was so extensive that it became a subject of inquiry by the legislative assemblies of both Upper and Lower Canada. In 1825, a committee of the Legislature of Upper Canada placed the blame squarely on the shoulders of British trade policy, concluding, "the inequality of price holds out a temptation to smuggling which is found to be irresistible." As part of his testimony in 1828 before a British committee investigating smuggling between the U.S. and British North America, a member of the Lower Canada Assembly, named John Neilson, summed up the enforcement challenges facing the Crown, "Anything that can give any profit by smuggling will come in; all the custom-house officers in the world could not prevent people, living as neighbours and friends, relations, brothers and sisters, people who visit one another almost every evening, from bringing in anything that will enable them to make a profit, or exchanging articles for mutual convenience."

Tea was, without a doubt, the most popular of the contraband smuggled into the colonies during the 17th and 18th centuries and, once again, it was Britain's mercantilist policies that encouraged the underground trade. The policy that most outraged the colonies was the monopoly given to the British-controlled East India Company over the sale of tea throughout the empire. In January of 1829, the House of Assembly for Upper Canada passed a strongly worded resolution protesting the monopoly over the supply of the "indispensable article of tea" to the colony "at prices so exorbitant, that the excess, over and above what would be deemed a fair mercantile profit under free competition, amounts to an oppressive and insupportable tax." By the 1830s, the price of tea supplied by the East India Company was more than fifty times that which was available through American wholesalers who traded directly with suppliers in China. To ensure the British monopoly, duties were slapped on all teas imported into the colonies from the United States. As Gordon Blake notes in his book on the history of customs administration in Canada, "Tea was truly Britain's gift to the smuggler. Its bulk and weight were small in proportion to its value; it had a relatively inelastic demand; and, since it cheered but did not inebriate, its prohibition tended to alienate an important and influential female public opinion in Canada."

The total amount of tea legitimately sold in Upper and Lower Canada was estimated at one-tenth of what was actually being consumed. Customs reports, court cases, and newspaper accounts from this period testify to the vast trade in contraband tea and other heavily taxed goods in British North America. In 1833, the New York *Journal of Commerce* reported that smuggling was increasing at an alarming rate along America's northern border. On the Canadian side there was "a remarkable abundance and cheapness of teas and silks," and on the American side, there was "an equal abundance and cheapness of loaf sugar and broad cloths." A November 28, 1839, article in Ontario's *Western Herald* newspaper concluded, "A vast amount is smuggled into the province. From facts that have come to our knowledge we are convinced that smuggling is carried on to an extent that but few could believe. One of the first acts of the Imperial Parliament should be to relax their prohibitions and heavy duties on imports from the States to Canada." In the 1843 case of *The Queen v. Miller*, the schooner *Dolphin* from Prince Edward Island was forfeited to the Crown following the discovery of "forty chests of tea of the value of four hundred pounds of lawful money of Canada." The illicit tea was seized on November 10, 1843, at the Port of Belleville in Ontario. On April 21, 1860, customs officials in Quebec seized a typical contraband cache of heavily taxed consumer goods, including tea, sugar, tobacco, shoe leather, and candles.

Determined efforts were made by the British government to stop the untaxed movement of goods from America into the colonies. The number of customs officers along the border was increased, penalties were stiffened, and the military was employed to prowl popular smuggling routes. The *Montreal Gazette* reported on February 17, 1817, that "smuggling has arrived at such a height that parties of the 19th Light Dragoons have been stationed between Lapriarie and St. John's to prevent it." But even these enhanced measures had little impact, due in part to the sheer determination, adaptability, and ingenuity of smugglers. Various strategies were used by Maritime smugglers to evade restrictive trading policies or customs enforcement. Cargoes were transferred from American to colonial ships in secluded coves around Nova Scotia or were landed on islands off the New Brunswick coast to be picked up by fishermen hired by colonial merchants. On land, buildings were erected that straddled the boundary; at night, goods went through the door on the American side, while in the morning they would emerge from the door on the Canadian side. Another reason the smuggling

trade could not be stopped was that the contraband market was so enthusiastically supported by suppliers, traders, transporters, merchants, and consumers on both sides of the border.

Canadian merchants were some of the most flagrant participants in the contraband traffic. In 1865, a *Globe* article stated "as fact" that "a large number of Canadian merchants are engaged in swindling the Government by means of false invoices, thereby fraudulently withholding from the Government in considerable amount of tax due under the general laws." On October 19, 1848, customs officials at the Port of Toronto seized 100 boxes of American soap worth £75 from John Ray, an employee of A.V. Brown and Company. The soap was seized at the border after the sales invoices presented by Ray, which greatly undervalued the goods, were judged to be forged. A customs official became suspicious that the invoice was not in fact prepared by the real New York wholesaler because it too closely matched the handwriting of an employee of A.V. Brown and Company.

As the clandestine trade became increasingly necessary for the economic survival of the colonies, some within the colonial governments conspired with smugglers, or at least looked the other way. Even some British military personnel stationed in Canada turned a blind eye to the smuggling trade. To get their goods to the New Brunswick ports, according to historian W. Stewart MacNutt, American smugglers had to evade their country's warships that hovered off the coast, "but having succeeded in doing so, they came under the protection of friendly British cruisers that escorted them into Saint John." In his 1833 book, *Sketches of Canada and the United States*, William Lyon Mackenzie King documented his own eyewitness account of a tea-smuggling operation from Youngstown, New York, to Fort George, Ontario, which occurred under the watchful eyes of British soldiers who made no effort to intervene. The inference he drew was that smuggling across the border "must have been nearly universal."

The lucrative profits of the contraband trade quickly expanded the ranks of the professional smuggler and, as Dave McIntosh wrote, "armed gangs of smugglers were not uncommon on the Eastern Townships border of Lower Canada and on the St. Lawrence and Niagara frontiers of Upper Canada." A letter dated

July 23, 1842, from a customs official in Ontario accuses one W. Burnham of being a serial smuggler who has "carried on for years, successfully to himself and injurious to the fair traders." Although he was known to have been engaged in smuggling for at least a decade before this letter was written, he was not caught until October 1, 1840, when, at Port Hope, officials seized eighteen chests of tea and two kegs of tobacco valued at approximately £212. Violence was also an inevitable by-product of the smuggling trade. An 1865 *Globe* newspaper article describes correspondence sent by customs officers stationed along the St. Lawrence that documented the "many instances" in which "officers have been personally assaulted by bands of smugglers while in the performance of their duties." The writer recommended, "the posting of United States troops along the river to aid in the detection and arrest of these contraband traders." Some customs officials were more aggressive in their enforcement. In 1852, the *Globe* reported that Henry Smith was "shot by an officer of the customs and his posse, while defending some smuggled goods which were about to be seized."

THE GANGS OF UPPER CANADA

In addition to consensual crimes like smuggling, 19th-century versions of organized crime were also predatory in nature. While stories of outlaw gangs are etched into the popular folklore of the American West, less is known about the equally larcenous and violent groups of villains that terrorized communities in Ontario around the middle of the century. D. Owen Carrigan describes how some of these gangs were led by men engaged in legitimate commerce, but who effortlessly resorted to violence to maintain their monopoly. In the pursuit of these ambitions, "they gathered about them groups of ruffians they used to intimidate and beat into submission those who stood in the way of their ambition. Such men were to be found competing with each other for hegemony in the lumber trade in the Ottawa Valley in the 1830s and none was more ruthless in the pursuit of power than Peter Aylen."

Peter Aylen became known as the "King of the Shiners" and, as his title implies, he aspired to great heights and resorted to any means necessary to get there. As a timber baron who sought to monopolize the lumber industry in the Ottawa Valley, Aylen capitalized on the large pool of disenfranchised Irish labourers by securing them jobs in the French-Canadian–dominated lumber camps. He set himself up as a tireless campaigner for the Irish workers, but Aylen was less concerned about their well-being, and more interested in using them as his own personal army to help satisfy his economic and political ambitions. His two hundred or so Irish-Protestant followers, who called themselves "Shiners," were already well known for their indiscriminate use of violence in the Ottawa Valley, which at the time was little more than the backwoods of a developing British colony. Aylen simply made this violence more discriminate and strategic. By sending his troops into work camps, political meetings, commercial establishments, and homes to intimidate, fight, destroy property, and even murder his opponents, Aylen was responsible for some of the most violent years in the history of Ontario.

Not much is known about the early years of Peter Aylen. Born an Irish Protestant sometime in the 1790s, he arrived in Quebec in 1815 as a seaman, jumped ship, and then made his way to Eastern Ontario where he began work in the lumber trade. By the 1830s, he controlled a number of large timber operations, owned several properties, and was a member of the "Gatineau Privilege," a group of local lumber barons intent on obtaining a monopoly in the Ottawa Valley. Despite his growing wealth, his thirst for power remained unrequited and he began to organize and manipulate Irish immigrants as part of his efforts to seize control of, not only the local timber industry, but also Bytown (which would later expand to become Ottawa). Aylen offered his Irish constituents employment and, with their help, according to Michael Cross, he promised them "a complete victory over the French Canadians who competed with the Irish for jobs in the timber camps, and who had superior skills and a better reputation for reliability." Aylen also garnered their loyalty by offering them prostitutes, some of whom were imported from Montreal. As Cross wrote, "The orgies at the 'King's' home were extended, exuberant affairs, which often combined the dual pleasures of debauchery and insult to the respectable community. For instance, after sexual appetites were satisfied, the Shiners were known to fill their women with liquor until they collapsed insensible. Then the girls were stripped naked and arranged on the public sidewalk — well illuminated with candles so they might be seen by the shocked townspeople."

Before Aylen came along, the Shiners were a loosely knit, unorganized group of Irish immigrants who helped build the Rideau Canal and, when that was completed, worked in the lumber industry. The origin of their name is obscure, and has been variously attributed to the bastardization of the French word *cheneur* (a cutter of oak), the ubiquitous shiny silk hats worn by wealthy English immigrants, or a self-designation, meaning they "shined" above all others. Besides their common occupation, the Shiners all shared the Protestant religion, an intense dislike for the English and the French, and a proclivity for violence. For the longest time, they were an "ungovernable rabble," wrote a correspondent for the *Globe* newspaper in 1856. "At first, these ruffians acted independently of one another, and without concert jeering and insulting the defenceless and unprotected, and occasionally 'pounding an enemy.'" Soon thereafter, "they moved about in couples or small gangs, like wild beasts, seeking whom they might destroy." Their reputation for group violence was cemented in 1828 when a St. Patrick's Day brawl in Bytown culminated in the death of an Englishman.

For the most part, the violence perpetrated by the Shiners, like the group itself, was without any real purpose. This changed around 1835 when Peter Aylen recognized that the violent, but leaderless, mass of Irish fury could be organized to serve his ambitions. It was then that he sought to establish himself as the leader of the Irish workers, convincing them that the French aspired to drive them from their jobs. He assured them that they had a dedicated leader and a common cause: to force the French Canadians out of the timber camps along the Rideau River. The result was the "Shiners' War," a period of organized violence in the Ottawa Valley orchestrated by Peter Aylen that peaked from 1835 to 1837.

The wave of violence began on January 5, 1835, in Bytown with the daylight murder of Charles McStravick at the hands of Shiner James Curry. In the spring of 1835, Aylen's men attacked French logging camps and boarded their rafts, beating the men senseless and destroying the tools upon which their livelihoods depended. The French Canadians fought back by ambushing rafts manned by the Shiners, but they were no match for their Irish adversaries, who took control of the Union Bridge over the Ottawa River and began demanding payment for anyone who wished to pass over it. "Although the government owned the bridge, no one dared intervene to stop the outrages," Michael Cross wrote. "All too frequently bodies were found below the bridge, victims of the playful celebrations of the Shiners above." In the summer of 1835, the Shiners terrorized the owner of a Bytown inn popular among French Canadians and ultimately set it ablaze, forcing the innkeeper and his family to flee the town in fright. When a local constable attempted to arrest an Irish raftsman on a charge of rape, the part-time police officer was beaten by three other Shiners in full view of a large crowd. After Aylen was arrested for assaulting a lawyer from Perth, his men went on a rampage. Assuming their leader was to be transported to Perth via the Rideau Canal, his supporters swarmed a steamer anchored at Bytown and, as a June 25, 1835, edition of the *Bathurst Courier* recounts, when they could not find Aylen, they "commenced an assault on the crew of one of the steamboats, and disabled the engineer and several others."

The Shiners were able to act with impunity because of the absence of a full-time constabulary and a local population that had been frightened into submission. But the causes of the violence were much deeper. In his detailed examination of the Shiners' War, Michael Cross believed the "Irish in the Valley were more than ready for a leader and for violence." They were conditioned to be more tolerant of violence as it was an everyday fact of life in their homeland. Poverty, famine, disease, foreign rule, civil war, and political and religious oppression "combined to produce a society teetering on the edge of anarchy." These traditions were simply brought over from Ireland to the Ottawa frontier. Existing animosities toward the English, combined with the reality of their own poverty, were exacerbated when they viewed the opulent conditions enjoyed by the local English gentry. Politically and economically, the Irish immigrants were made to feel like second-class citizens as the English and Scots assumed most positions of power. The completion of the Rideau Canal in 1832 created a glut of unskilled labour in the Ottawa

Valley and the Irish found it difficult to get work in the timber camps where the more experienced French Canadians were favoured by employers. The lumber barons also exploited the excess labour by driving down wages and pitting worker against worker. No moderating force within the Irish community arose to restrain these violent impulses and the Ottawa Valley at the time had few strong institutions to quell or even mediate the ongoing violence. In an article dated December 25, 1856, the *Globe* newspaper offered a more succinct, albeit crude, interpretation of the violence meted out by the Irish workers against their French counterparts in the Ottawa Valley, "'Paddy' at home is a slave; abroad, a task master; in fact he must be groaning under a load of chains, real or imaginary, it little matters which, or else he must have a 'Niggar' to wallop. The poor quiet Franco-Canadian, for the time, was Paddy's 'Niggar' here."

By the summer of 1835, Aylen was using the Shiners to help him fulfill his political aspirations. He began by forcing a coup of the powerful Bathurst District Agricultural Society, which was holding its annual meeting in Bytown in August of that year. According to Michael Cross, he arrived at the meeting with—

> a large body of raftsmen, each equipped with the dollar fee necessary for membership. Never had the friendly little aristocrats' club witnessed such a scene. Sprawling on the benches, swigging poteen from their bottles, roaring over coarse jokes, the Shiners turned the austere meeting room into a fair facsimile of a Lower Town tavern. Then came the moment Aylen had been awaiting — the election of officers. Vastly outnumbering the legitimate members, the Shiners voted out of office the entire executive and replaced them with timberers.

Elected as the president of the society, of course, was Peter Aylen.

At a meeting of the Nepean Township Council on January 2, 1837, Aylen and his hooligans tried to intimidate councillors into electing candidates who were sympathetic to the Irish migrants. When they balked at his demands, Aylen's men started to riot. In the process, two members of the council were severely beaten. By this time, Aylen's power was at its zenith. "Armed to the teeth," wrote the *Globe*'s correspondent in 1856, the King of the Shiners "would parade himself on the highways, and in the 'groggeries,' with the air of a despot, — a bold, wild, reckless outlaw, for whom nothing was too hot or too heavy, who lived without the pale of society, and who neither feared God nor honoured the kind." His continued reliance on violence, however, would prove to be his downfall, and the events of February 4, 1837, were the beginning of the end for Aylen. That afternoon, the wife and daughters of a farmer named Hobbs, who had previously run afoul of some Shiners, were returning home in their horse-drawn sleigh after a trip into town. Unbeknownst to them, members of the Shiners were lying in wait. All at once, the Irishmen leaped from the hiding spot and viciously attacked the sleigh, beating not just Hobbs, but his pregnant wife and daughters as well.

Horrified by the vicious, premeditated assault, townspeople appealed to the local magistrate for action. However, attempts at apprehending the men behind the assault proved futile. A week after the attack, a mob of angry farmers arrived in town, armed with pitchforks, clubs, and guns and announced to the magistrate that they had come to aid in the capturing of those behind the ambush. After convincing the farmers to return home, the magistrate was able to arrange for the arrest of the Shiner who'd led the attack. But this provoked even more rioting by other gang members, which peaked in March 1837. By that time, local citizens formed armed patrols and were sworn in as special constables by the magistrates. With determined community action, the Shiners were brought under control and in the spring and summer of 1837, many were sentenced to prison terms. Despite this enforcement success, Peter Aylen was never brought to justice. Well aware that the tide had turned against him, he sold his property in Bytown and fled to Aylmer, Quebec. Other than an instance in 1843 when he was accused of illegally cutting timber on Crown lands, he assumed the role of law-abiding citizen and community leader. By 1846, he became a member of the Hull Township Council and two years later he was appointed justice of the peace.

On June 13, 1845, the *Toronto British Colonist* shone a light on another violent gang operating in Upper Canada. "There has been for a considerable time past," the article explains, "a gang of Robbers in Markham and the surrounding townships, whose depredations have been carried on an extensive scale." For the next year, newspapers would be filled with stories on the Markham Gang, an "extensive and organized gang of rogues" responsible for "a great many daring burglaries and other crimes" in and around the township of Markham. A July 29, 1846, edition of the *Toronto Examiner* reported that, within the previous three years, the gang had committed various robberies in several townships. "A number of thefts, in one case of a few yards of cloth, in another of a pair of breeches, another of a few tin pans, and one of seventy or eighty dollars accompanied by brutal violence, have been perpetrated upon the farmers by persons who must have acted in concert. Great terror pervaded the minds of the timid and those living in isolated and remote places, on account of the frequency of these depredations and the apparent impossibility of detecting the offenders."

Between 1844 and 1846, the so-called Markham Gang carried out a series of crimes in and around Markham Township, close to present-day Toronto. While their offences included horse theft, pickpocketing, and counterfeiting, their speciality was residential burglaries. Membership in the gang at any one time was as many as nineteen men, although six were considered the group's leaders or more active offenders: Robert Burr, the brothers Hiram and James Stoutenborough, Nathan Case, James Green, and Henry Johnson. While little is known about the ringleaders, one outraged newspaper of the day revealed that most were from reputable and wealthy landowning families:

It was a remarkable fact that several of those charged were the sons of respectable farmers, while others were men with wives and children, cultivating farms of their own, with plenty and comfort around them! What could induce such men to commit such crimes? That a man living with his family, and owning 200 acres of land, worth 3,000 or 4,000 dollars, should join himself to a gang of ruffians, and go prowling about the country, at one time stealing from his neighbour a gun, at another three or four tin pans, and the miserable booty among half a dozen companions, with certainty of detection, sooner or later, is, we should hope, a rare occurrence.

The *British Colonist* provided some observations on the gang's rudimentary hierarchy:

From what we have learned of the gang, we should be disposed to divide them into two classes: the cavalry! And the infantry! The former, who are generally mounted on the best horses in the country, figure only in the higher branches of roguery; such as burglary, horse stealing, and in the wholesale dissemination of "Boodle!" Boodle being the flash term of the gang for counterfeit money! To the infantry is delegated the lower or democratic order of thievery! Such as pilfering from hen roosts; stealing harness, buffalo skins, blankets, &c., from stables sheds; wheat and other grain from barns and graineries; clothing, guns and other articles …

One of the distinguishing characteristics of the Markham Gang was the systematic planning that went into the execution of many of their crimes. "From the nature of the robberies committed by them, the parties were evidently quite familiar with the habits and mode of living of those they have robbed," according to the June 13, 1845, edition of the *British Colonist*. "They always watched the most favourable opportunity to enter the houses, so as to escape detection and save their booty." Most of the robberies they carried out was preceded by careful reconnaissance. Potential victims were identified and gang members were dispatched to observe them in their daily routine. Some even were able to gain entrance into the homes or businesses of prospective victims under false pretences. The gang relied on a network of informants and spies who roamed the countryside and townships gathering information on potential victims. Some of the gang's operatives were travelling salesmen or tradesmen who scouted on a part-time basis. Gang members also adopted the cloak of these professions to gather information. Either way, the "avant couriers" had to be respectable in appearance, a pretence that increased the chance that intended victims would take the advance men into their homes, allowing them to determine the location of valuables. One even gained entrance into a home on the pretext of being a roaming Methodist minister. He read psalms and prayed with the family in exchange for food and lodging, all the while trying to determine the location of their valuables.

The well-organized and disciplined nature of the criminal group was reinforced by a strict code of secrecy and loyalty. Each member pledged "to adhere to their rules and never to betray their secrets on the pain of certain death," the *British Colonist* stated in 1846. Gang members also had to follow strict rules to avoid incrimination. They were never to take stolen items to their own homes or to try to fence the goods in their own community and, if captured, they would not reveal the identity of their co-conspirators. All communication between gang members had to be oral and special horseback messengers were employed to communicate over long distances. Violence and intimidation was also used to deter anyone from "taking proceedings against the robbers, from the fear that the greater evils of fire and murder would be inflicted upon them by this desperate gang." Even judges, police constables, and jurors were not immune to these intimidation tactics; some magistrates were accused of refusing to sign arrest warrants against gang members for fear of reprisals.

One of the first public glimpses of the gang was provided in October 1845 when newspapers reported a vicious burglary committed at the home of John Morrow and his family, who lived in the Reach Township, northeast of present-day Toronto. One night, while John was upstairs in bed, his wife, Mary, heard the heavy pounding of several footsteps on the front porch. Before she could waken her husband, four men barged through the door. One intruder lunged towards Mary and with a closed fist struck her across the face, sending her to the ground. Another of the intruders bounded to the second-floor bedroom where he savagely beat her husband with a large club while demanding he hand over his cash and other valuables. A third man charged into the bedroom of twelve-year-

old Margaret and began rifling through a chest. The Morrows testified in a subsequent court case that the man who directed the robbery and doled out most of the beatings was a neighbour, Nathan Case. In his book on the Markham Gang, Paul Arculus describes the suffering the Morrow family endured at the hands of Case and his accomplices:

> Case ordered the children to stay in their bed. He returned to the kitchen where he began searching through its meagre contents. Case put a gun to Mary's ear and pointed another at her husband and demanded that they hand over the money that they had gained at the Uxbridge fair. John Morrow, now dazed, told Mary to hand them the money. She went to her purse, hidden under her pillow, and handed it to the third man. He snatched the purse and ripped it open, taking out a roll of notes while the coins fell to the floor. The second man struck John on the head again. By this time he was almost senseless. Mary dragged herself after him to the doorway. To her horror she saw that there were more men, at least ten of them, all now walking away. They were in three groups, each heading in a different direction. Several hours later John regained consciousness. John was sure that three of the men who had carried out this sadistic beating were neighbours, Nathan Case, Hiram Stoutenborough and his brother James Stoutenborough.

Warrants were issued for the three men and two others — Robert Burr and Henry Johnson — who were positively identified by the Morrows. Almost all involved in the robbery went on the lam, but not without continuing their crime spree. According to one newspaper, authorities received information that Burr and Johnson "were lurking in the neighbourhood of the village of Ingersoll in the Brock District, where a number of robberies had recently been perpetrated." A constable was dispatched with warrants for their arrest and upon his arrival, "he found the two parties lodged in the gaol at Woodstock, on a charge of an extensive robbery committed near Embro in which they had been detected, and were subsequently apprehended, through the vigilant exertions of Captain Graham, an active and efficient magistrate in the Brock District." When the men were brought to trial, details came forth suggesting the attackers knew the Morrows had received a sum of money from a local fair that day, that Mary was in charge of the family savings, and that she had even more money hidden in the house.

The attack on the Morrows was just one in a series of brazen crimes the gang committed at a relentless pace between 1844 to 1846. No robbery was too large or too small for these thieves as they strategically rambled across the countryside in their pursuit of victims. In July 1844, John Fleming and Robert Hubbard stole 110 bushels of wheat and oats from a farmer's barn. One night in August 1845, Henry Johnson entered Thomas Scripture's home while he was in bed. After being woken by a sound, Scripture went downstairs and noticed he had been robbed of a sizable amount of cash he had received in a transaction only that evening. When he later testified against Johnson in court, Scripture did not know if he had been visited by one of the gang's spies, but he did acknowledge that the thief must have known he had a quantity of money in his home that night. The way Johnson broke into the house, and his quick entry and exit, indicated that he had intimate details of the layout of the dwelling and where the cash was hidden. With equal precision and even greater stealth, gang members broke into the home of John Smith, made their way to his bedroom while he slept, fished the keys from his trousers that he customarily left on a chair by his bed before retiring for the night, unlocked a desk located off the bedroom, and stole $500 in cash. Throughout it all, Smith never awoke. While a neighbour of Smith's was attending the services at the local Methodist church, burglars broke into his house, smashed open a dresser, and removed $300 in cash (although in their haste they missed $700 that was hidden elsewhere in the dresser).

On February 12, 1846, Samson Roberts and his wife, Mary, who supplemented their income by renting out rooms in their large home located eight miles north of Oshawa, took in two strangers who were seeking shelter on that cold and snowy night. Despite the late hour, Mary served them refreshments while they sat by the fire to get warm. A few hours after going back to bed, she awoke to find one of the men standing at the foot of the stairs with a saddle over one shoulder, a candle in one hand, and a meat cleaver in the other. Threatening her into silence, the intruder entered her bedroom, opened the bureau drawers and pocketed their contents. After a few minutes, the man made his way to the front door and left. The Robertses later discovered that the burglars had rifled through almost every occupied room in the house and had stolen a variety of items, including a watch, candlesticks, several coats as well as a money box given to Mary for safekeeping by one guest. Her husband hastily assembled a posse and began tracking four sets of footprints freshly made in the snow. Along the way, they discovered a carpet bag partially buried under the snow and, later that day, found more bags full of items stolen from the house. The details of the burglary were reported to the local magistrate and David Sawyer was later charged.

The members of the Markham Gang also dabbled in forgery and counterfeiting, mostly to facilitate the disposal of the goods they stole. In particular, gang members were often paid for their stolen property in counterfeit money. As the *Toronto British Colonist* recounted in 1846, they were instructed to take stolen articles "of considerable value and easily removable" such as watches, banknotes, or horses "to Lower Canada, to the townships of Shefford and Durham, where there is a wholesale establishment for issuing counterfeit money of all sorts, and for receiving stolen goods and where the stolen articles are disposed of in exchange for 'boodle,' at the rate of $100 worth of boodle for ten dollars worth of valuable property, or for five dollars worth of bankable paper." The "boodle" would then be brought to the "small fry" of the gang, whose job it was to put the counterfeit cash into circulation.

Local law enforcement began to realize some success in breaking up the band of thieves by capturing individual members and pressuring them to inform on others. The first to be arrested in January 1846 was twenty-three-year-old Daniel Spencer, who was charged with larceny. The same month, Matthew Udell was arrested for passing a forged note, while Thomas Alsop was brought before the police court at the end of the month on a horse-stealing charge. In April, at least five other gang members were charged with larceny. By the Spring Assizes of 1846, many of those picked up were tried and most were convicted.

Robert White was found guilty of stealing a horse and sentenced to three years. Henry Johnson was tried on numerous burglary, horse-stealing, and assault charges and, after an initial acquittal, was retried, convicted, and sentenced to four years. Robert Burr, Nathan Case, and Hiram and James Stoutenborough were condemned to death, but their verdicts were changed to prison terms, including life imprisonment for Burr. The guilty verdicts and sentences that were obtained, especially for the gang's leaders, effectively put an end to one of Upper Canada's most infamous and well-organized criminal groups.

Although not as large or well organized as the Markham Gang, other criminal groups gained a certain level of infamy in Ontario during the mid 19th century. Among these were the Campbell brothers, who were at the core of a network of outlaws that flourished in the 1850s along the border between Grey and Bruce counties, about 30 miles east of Lake Huron. John and Colin Campbell operated a tavern that became a notorious meeting place for drunkards, drifters, bootleggers, and freelance criminals, some of whom congregated there to plan their robberies. By providing a meeting place and the occasional start-up capital to thieves, the Campbell brothers received a cut from robberies or would fence the stolen goods. After helping Andrew MacFarlane illegally retrieve horses that had been seized from him by the county bailiff in early 1859, warrants were issued for the arrest of MacFarlane and the Campbell brothers. When Constables George Simpson and Caleb Huyck tried to serve a warrant on the two brothers, they were confronted by a band of armed men, led by Colin Campbell. After firing his gun into the air, Campbell demanded that Huyck eat the warrants. Fearing for his life, Huyck meekly complied. Campbell then gave the two constables the option of leaving or dying. Huyck and his partner chose the former. But the two returned with a posse, and after surrounding the Campbells' tavern, they exchanged gunfire with the men holed up in the heavy log building. After several attempts, the posse set the cabin ablaze and smoked the men out. While fleeing the burning building, the fugitives adeptly used the fire's thick smoke as a cover to escape, although Colin Campbell was hit in the back by a bullet from the posse. While his wounds were not immediately

fatal, the pain forced him to seek treatment from a doctor in the town of Hanover. A local constable was apprised of his presence and Colin Campbell was arrested. Along with three others, Campbell was charged with horse stealing and assaulting a police officer. The men went to trial on September 30, 1859, where they were found guilty. Campbell went to prison, although his co-defendants were merely fined.

Another gang that gained notoriety in Ontario around the same time worked the streets of Toronto. The Brooks Bush gang — so named because of the seedy part of the city that was their base — were engaged in petty theft, robberies, and break-ins. But they are most remembered for one of the most high-profile murders to take place in Toronto during the 19th century. The slaying occurred on the Don Bridge on December 1, 1859. That night, John Sheridan Hogan, a Member of Parliament, was crossing the bridge on his way home when he was attacked by what the April 6, 1861, edition of the *New York Times* called "ten or twelve loose characters, of both sexes, known as the 'Brooks Bush Gang'." The group of ruffians robbed Hogan, beat him to death, and then threw his body into the Don River. When Hogan failed to return home that night, a search party was organized, but proved futile as his murderers made sure his body would sink to the bottom of the river by attaching heavy stones to it. On the afternoon of March 30, 1861, Hogan's body was found floating at the mouth of the river by two men out duck hunting. Despite being badly decomposed (having spent more than sixteen months in the water) the body was positively identified as Hogan. Following the confession of Ellen McGillich, a part-time prostitute who was present at the time of Hogan's death, James Browne and Jane Ward were arrested, tried, and convicted of murder. Ward was accused of delivering the fatal blow, with a stone tied in a handkerchief, while the evidence indicated that Browne threw the body over the bridge. Although the fate of Ward is not known, James Browne was executed on March 10, 1862, before a crowd estimated at five thousand people. To the very end, Browne maintained his innocence, even as the condemned man sat in his jail cell a day before the execution, listening to the construction of the scaffold, from which his own lifeless body would soon dangle.

VILE SPIRITS

Another form of organized criminality during the 19th century combined the worst of the consensual contraband trade and the violent predatory gangs of Upper Canada. The illegal liquor trade would also be one of the most socially destructive criminal activities undertaken in Canada during this century. The Canadian whiskey traffic can be traced to the earliest days of the French and English fur traders who bartered rum, brandy, and whiskey in exchange for pelts provided by native hunters and trappers. While European settlers were also a market for illicit liquor, the most organized and despicable of the distillers, smugglers, and peddlers amassed their revenues through the pernicious exploitation of aboriginal peoples. As surrogate hunters for the white man, native people exchanged their furs and pelts for a wide range of goods, including blankets, cheap jewellery, food, tobacco, clothing, shoes, metal goods, rifles and ammunition. But it was whiskey that would become the currency of choice for the European traders.

The Hudson's Bay Company was one of the original rivulets through which native people in British North America got their first taste of liquor. Historical records show that as early as the 1680s, the Company had shipped hundreds of gallons of brandy from Europe to its overseas posts to trade with aboriginal hunters. When their supply of brandy became scarce, due to England's intermittent conflicts with France, the Company began to distill its own liquor. According to Peter C. Newman, this mixture was called "English Brandy" and consisted of "cheap (almost raw) London gin to which were added drops of any of several tinctures (usually iodine) to duplicate the rich auburn colour of the real brandy." This innovation would set the die for future commercial relations between white traders and native hunters; instead of purchasing commercially produced liquor, white traders would now "distill" their own product, which greatly minimized their expenses. One whiskey trader operating from an encampment in Alberta during the early 1870s boasted how he obtained two hundred buffalo pelts, worth nearly $1,000, in exchange for $50 of homemade liquor.

The ingredients of the brutal and sometimes lethal concoctions made by subsequent traders expanded upon the original Hudson's Bay recipe. The base generally consisted of a gallon of diluted raw alcohol with three gallons of water. To this was added a variety of other ingredients, such as molasses, tea, Jamaican ginger, chewing tobacco, soap, the painkiller laudanum, and a dash of lye or red peppers to give it a bite. Red ink or even paint was added for colour. The mixture was then brought to boil to blend the ingredients and to give it an extra kick.

A review of court files in Upper Canada in the early part of the century reveals numerous cases involving the illegal distilling and distribution of liquor. Two moonshiners who appeared regularly before the courts in the Township of Bertie were Mathias Hawn and Edmund Raymond. Information for a court case prepared in 1803 alleged that the two men "carried on the trade of making and distilling spirituous liquors for sale." The court documents indicated that the men operated four stills, each of which was capable of holding 120 gallons. While it was not illegal to privately distill liquor, the two were prosecuted for failing to pay any taxes on the sale of their homemade booze.

The whites referred to their toxic mixtures by various names — "bug juice," "benzene," "Injun juice," "Injun coffin varnish," and "hoochinoo." Aboriginal people called it "firey water" and its impact on First Nations was devastating. Whiskey — and the whiskey trade — eroded their culture, destroyed their self-sufficiency, fuelled violence, and robbed proud hunters and warriors of reason, dignity, and the ability to provide for their family and their community. In 1804, Alexander Henry, a trader for the North West Company, wrote in his journal, "Indians having asked for liquor and promised to decamp and hunt well all summer, I gave them some. Grand Gueule stabbed Capot Rouge, Le Boeuf stabbed his young wife in the arm, Little Shell almost beat his old mother's brains out with a club, and there was terrible fighting amongst them. I sowed garden seeds." Reverend John McDougall, a missionary who spread the Gospel in the Canadian West during the 1870s, and whose reports on the whiskey trade helped convince the Canadian government to form the North West Mounted Police, had this to say about the impact of the whiskey trade on aboriginal people: "Mothers lost their children. These were either frozen to death or devoured by the myriad dogs of the camp.

The birth-rate decreased and the poor red man was in a fair way towards extinction, just because some men, coming out of Christian countries, and themselves the evolution of Christian civilization, were now ruled by lust and greed."

The whiskey traders were little concerned about the effect that the liquor had on aboriginal people, nor did they care about the long-term viability of the fur trade. Their goal was to obtain as many pelts as possible in the shortest period of time. As far back as the early 1700s, Hudson's Bay officials began sending communiqués to its traders cautioning them against trading brandy with their native suppliers, not out of concern for their welfare, but because they realized that drunken aboriginals made poor hunters. The profits made by bartering cheap homemade whiskey for valuable pelts, however, meant that the tradition continued for at least another 150 years. A letter written by an American politician in 1849 accused the Company of continuing to provide "immense amounts of spirituous liquor which is imported by the Hudson's Bay Company annually, not only for their trade in the British possessions, but which is furnished to the Indians who reside and hunt within the limits of the United States." Beginning in the 1860s, the Hudson's Bay Company prohibited its traders from using liquor to barter with native hunters. The void left by the Company was quickly filled by others, who were now delivering and trading liquor by the wagon- and boatload. In 1831, whiskey trader James Kipp, who built Fort Peigan at the mouth of the Marias River in northern Montana, played host to hundreds of Blackfoot Indians who unexpectedly showed up one day declaring their intention to trade. Kipp had a single 35-gallon barrel of whiskey left. Frantically improvising, he diluted it with copious amounts of water, added boiled red peppers and blackstrap tobacco, and then strengthened the mix with all the patent medicine he had on hand. By the time he was finished, he had produced 350 gallons of "whiskey," which he then traded for 2,500 prime beaver furs worth around $46,000.

In the early 1860s, whiskey traders began to cruise along the western shores of the Colony of British Columbia searching for markets among the coast-dwelling native communities. One letter dated 1866 from colonial officials to the Hudson's Bay House in London alerted them to "a considerable number of traders" who have "introduced spirituous liquors" to aboriginals in B.C. Appeals were also made to London by those fur traders who refrained from bartering liquor for pelts and, as a consequence, were at a disadvantage to the whiskey traders. One such letter from a Hudson's Bay official to his superiors in London included an urgent plea for help against competitors trading in "large quantities of liquor and goods" that had been smuggled into the colony. "And the answer from the Administrator of the Government to our repeated representation on the subject is that he has no means at his disposal to prevent it. You will thus perceive that as legitimate Indian Traders on the Coast, we have little chance of competing successfully with a fleet of smugglers." Some vessels were floating distilleries, producing liquor in stills set up in their hulls and then sold on deck to natives who would paddle to the ships in their canoes. A letter from a Hudson's Bay Company official in B.C. to the acting Colonial Secretary of New Westminster dated October 20, 1866, read, "since the beginning of July several Schooners, some with large quantities of liquor on board have cleared for the North West Coast." Among those vessels identified in the letter were the *Langley,* containing 292 gallons of rum, two cases of porter and four cases of brandy, and the *Native,* carrying 313 gallons of rum. One of the most active of the liquor-trading schooners during this time was the *Nanpareil,* which, according to the same letter, was "commanded by the notorious Whiskey seller W. J Stephens." The captain of the *Nanpareil* had already been convicted on at least one occasion "for infringement of the Indian liquor law of British Columbia and who, very soon after he was unlocked for early liberation, was, while himself trading at Nass River, selling liquor by orders on his Agents at Portland Canal, an inlet a few miles north of the line but chiefly frequented by British Indians by the Nass and Chimsyan tribes."

There were so many liquor-laden schooners sailing up and down the British Columbia coast in search of native traders that colonial officials petitioned Britain to send naval warships. On November 21, 1870, Anthony Musgrave, the governor for B.C., wrote to London pleading that a "Gunboat should be employed to watch the Coast." Despite this plea, in the same letter he acknowledges, "one Gunboat will be inadequate to exercise the necessary surveillance over several hundred miles of Coast; and I hear that without the constant employment of one or more vessels as Cruisers for this purpose it will always remain difficult to prevent the traffic." British customs vessels were already patrolling coastal waters, but they were greatly outnumbered and outmatched by the wily liquor traders. Colonial officials were told of one customs vessel that "set out on a futile chase after these smuggling Schooners — at one time eleven in number — on a coast so abounding in channels, inlets, sheltered bays, and caves as is that of British Columbia, and whence to escape is so very easy into Russian waters, beyond British jurisdiction." In 1863, several whiskey schooners escaped capture by the British warship H.M.S. *Devastation* and then sailed near enough along the coast to "barter their liquor with the natives of British Columbia." Under Commander John W. Pike, the H.M.S. *Devastation* was given the task of checking the liquor traffic along the east coast of Vancouver Island in 1862. Pike was relentless in his duties, detaining and inspecting vessels, scrutinizing paperwork, interrogating traders, seizing contraband liquor, and impounding ships. Notable casualties of Pike's interdictions were the *Hamley*, which had a cargo of 300 gallons of "vile spirits," and the *Langley*, which was impounded indefinitely for repeated liquor violations.

The whiskey ships responded to the heightened enforcement by moving their trading centres to more clandestine locations along the coast, in coves or on uncharted islands, while aboriginal middlemen picked up caches of liquor that had been submerged in designated spots. Governor Musgrave wrote that liquor-trading schooners also avoided scrutiny by clearing the ports at Victoria or New Westminster empty, and then taking liquor on board outside the harbour:

> It is true that the liquor is not on board when these Coastline traders leave Victoria; but it is not in fact known where or when they take on board the liquor which it is believed that they trade to Indians in exchange for furs. The Gulf of Georgia abounds in Islands. Bays, and Inlets affording numerous places where it is easy

to have the liquor left to be taken, or put on board by concert with other persons for such a purpose; and moreover, as the American Ports on Puget Sound are at no great distance from Victoria it is quite possible for their supplies to be obtained from thence.

WHOOP-UP

By the late 1860s, whiskey trading had also become widespread in the Northwest Territories (what is now Saskatchewan and Alberta). A number of factors conspired to cause an increase in the whiskey traffic in the territories after 1860. Principal among these was a trading post called Fort Benton. Located in Montana on the Upper Missouri River, about 160 kilometres south of what is now the Alberta–Montana border, Fort Benton has been described as "a collection of log stores, cut-throat saloons and wicked hurdy-gurdy houses." The trading fort was established by the American Fur Company, which was founded by John Jacob Astor who amassed a fortune through the monopoly he held over the fur trade in the central and western United States during the first thirty years of the 19th century. Astor became a multi-millionaire by trading aboriginal hunters cheap rotgut whiskey for expensive pelts, using his heavily armed agents to violently crush his competitors and by routinely bribing politicians. His American Fur Company also operated a profitable loansharking operation, providing credit to native customers on such items as rifles, gunpowder, flints, knives, and tools at a rate of up to 400 percent. When the native people complained about the unjust trade, Astor either had them murdered by his agents or he would send urgent cables alerting his friends in the White House and Congress about the rebellious state of the local natives, and federal troops would be dispatched immediately. He died in 1848 as America's richest man.

By 1864, Fort Benton was being managed by Isaac Gilbert Baker, who was born in 1819 in New Haven, Connecticut, and entered the fur business at eighteen years of age. The death of Pierre Chouteau, head of the American Fur Company, in 1865, and the effects of the civil war resulted in the closing of all its trading posts. As a result Baker and his brother George founded a company of their own, and in 1866 opened their first store in Fort Benton under the name of

I. G. Baker and Brother. Under Baker's management, Fort Benton became the great shantytown of Montana — the "Sagebrush Sodom," as one historian called it — playing host to a transient population of traders, hunters, prospectors, cowboys, soldiers, aboriginal, gamblers, and prostitutes. It was also the chief source of whiskey used to barter with aboriginal hunters.

Despite the importance of Fort Benton in the whiskey and fur trade, by the late 1860s the real money was to be made north of the Montana border. The demand for buffalo hides was rapidly increasing as manufacturers discovered they could be tanned into a durable leather suitable for industrial machinery belts. Along the American plains, much of the buffalo herds had already been wiped out, but north of the border, a huge buffalo population had thus far been untouched by the white man. Equally attractive to the would-be traders were the numerous aboriginal nations just north of the border — the Cree Blackfoot, Blood, and Assiniboine, to name just a few — all of which boasted seasoned buffalo hunters. It was also during the late 1860s that the U.S. Cavalry and local sheriffs in Montana began to more aggressively enforce liquor laws that prohibited the sale of alcohol to aboriginals. There were no such restrictions on whiskey trading in the Canadian Northwest, nor was there any law enforcement or any kind of government presence. All of these factors culminated in a mass northward exodus of American whiskey traders from Fort Benton. Some of these so-called "free traders" were fugitives from the law, most were men of questionable character, and almost all were lured by the profits that could be made by trading liquor with Indians in return for buffalo hides. As Duncan McNab McEachran wrote in a 1881 *Montreal Gazette* article, "This class of men have been a curse to the Indians and this whole Northwest territory. They are usually outcasts from society, who fear neither God nor man, and whose object is to destroy the senses of the poor Indians that they may rob them of whatever they may possess."

It was from Fort Benton that much of the whiskey pestilence spread north. Traders picked up their liquor and other supplies and from there wagons pulled by horses or oxen transported the traders and their whiskey north of the border. On their return trip back to Fort Benton, the wagons would be full of buffalo hides. At first, the traders travelled directly to native encampments. Before long, temporary trading posts were being set up, most of which were simply wagon camps, and native hunters were now expected to travel to these posts to trade. These centralized, stationary posts were preferred by the traders as it reduced their travel time, expenses, and the risks of entering hostile native territory. By the early 1870s, there were dozens of trading posts in Southern Alberta and Saskatchewan, all strategically located to be accessible to aboriginal populations. In 1876, one former trader reminisced about "a half-breed camp on a river called Frenchmen's river" where there were "thirteen whiskey traders within three miles."

These temporary trading camps were soon replaced by semi-permanent forts. As business picked up and the traders learned of the hazards of dealing with intoxicated customers and unfriendly native bands, the original ramshackle structures were replaced with sturdy forts, built with heavy timber and fortified with rifle ports and small cannons. Many of the forts were built at the junction of two rivers or streams so they could be better protected from attack by the water barrier. Among the forts operating during the early 1870s were Robber's Roost, located at the junction of the Belly and the Oldman rivers, and Fort Standoff, which stood where the Waterton and Belly rivers joined and which was named for the time a party of American whiskey smugglers "stood off" a U.S. marshal. Fort Slideout received its name after the occupants "slid out" one night to escape a war party of Blood Indians. Fort Spitzee, located near the High River in present-day Alberta, took its moniker from a corruption of the Blackfoot word *ipitsi,* meaning high.

Of all the whiskey-trading posts in the territories, none experienced more success and gained more infamy than Fort Whoop-Up. Standing on the high plains where the St. Mary and Oldman rivers meet, just a few miles from what is now Lethbridge, Alberta, Fort Whoop-Up was less than 100 kilometres from the American border and only a seven-day trip from Fort Benton. One RCMP historian wrote, Fort Whoop-Up "stands for everything that was wrong in the west — lawless American desperadoes dealing noxious 'whiskey' to an Indian population unaccustomed to alcohol; buffalo hides by the hundreds of thousands

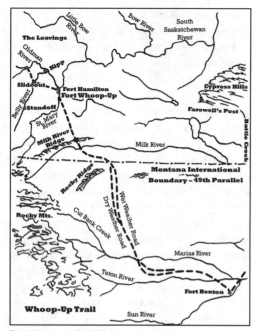

The Whoop-up Trail, Fort Benton, and Northwest Territories whiskey forts

being shipped out, leaving nothing but rotting carcasses and starving Natives; and a general atmosphere of anarchy with no accountability."

Fort Whoop-Up was the brainchild of three men: John Jerome Healy and Alfred B. Hamilton, two American traders based out of Fort Benton, and their financial backer, Isaac Gilbert Baker. The driving force behind the fort was Healy, a stout, barrel-chested Irish adventurer who sported a Buffalo Bill goatee through much of his adult years. Vain and arrogant, he loved to brag about his exploits and boasted that he was ready to fight anything from a circular saw to a grizzly bear. He was born in Ireland in 1840 and moved to New York with his family at the age of twelve. In 1858, he enlisted in the U.S. Army's Second Dragoons and served for two years before taking his discharge. He then joined a wagon train bound for Oregon but left it to prospect for gold in Montana. He later became the sheriff of Choteau County in Montana and, following his brief career as a whiskey trader, went on to such professions as newspaper publisher, ferryman, Yukon trading post operator, and promoter of Alaskan industries. Healy always talked about a new, get-rich-quick scheme and while not all of his business ventures were successful,

Fort Whoop-Up did make him wealthy. The efforts of other whiskey traders would pale in comparison with those of the daring, showy, quick-witted, and wholly ruthless Healy, who was able to wrestle the fur trade away from the Hudson's Bay Company in its own backyard, and who is considered the kingpin of the whiskey trade in the Canadian Prairies during the early 1870s.

Healy had spotted the opportunity to make money in the Canadian Northwest after a stint as a prospector around Fort Edmonton during the summer of 1863. In the late 1860s, he approached Baker about bankrolling a trading excursion north of the border. Deciding the gamble was worth the risk, Baker agreed to outfit Healy and Hamilton with a few wagons loaded with supplies. In 1869, the two men made the trip north on wagons loaded with thousands of dollars' worth of spirits, a few cases of lever-action Henry repeating rifles, and other merchandise that Baker hoped to trade with native bands for buffalo pelts. Healy and Hamilton set up a crude trading post, made up of log huts linked in a circle by a picket fence, at the confluence of the St. Mary's and Oldman rivers, which they named after Hamilton. While Fort Hamilton may not have been much to look at, it was immediately successful. When they returned to Fort Benton in the spring of 1870 their wagons were piled high with $50,000 worth of buffalo pelts.

Now fully aware of the immense profitability of the whiskey trade north of the border, Baker equipped Healy and Hamilton for another trip and even provided them with $25,000 to construct a larger, more permanent trading post. While a ragtag assortment of traders had been operating in the Northwest Territories for some years, no one had ever operated on the scale that the three entrepreneurs were envisioning. The investment was a huge sum of money at the time, but Baker was confident that a large fort could generate more business than all the other trading posts combined. Healy and Hamilton chose a spot close to the original Fort Hamilton, which had burned down, and began construction on their new trading post. The fort was built in two years by thirty-two labourers, under the supervision of William Gladstone, a former Hudson's Bay Company master carpenter. When completed, it was the largest and most secure of its kind. It was constructed of heavy, squared timbers in the form of a hollow square with a sturdy palisade loopholed for rifles and a bastion at the northwest and southeast corners. One bastion was mounted with a two-inch muzzle-loading brass cannon, while the other contained an alarm bell and a howitzer. Three wickets were carved out of the walls to facilitate trade, and a large gate made of oak was built to admit wagonloads of supplies. The exterior walls were 14 feet high and topped with sharpened stakes. The doors, windows, and even the chimneys were barred with iron to discourage trespassers. Heavy log roofs were laid across the partitions and covered with earth to protect the buildings from flaming arrows. A well was dug within the enclosure, and a short distance from the southwest corner a corral was erected for horses and cattle. Flapping from a flagpole attached to one of the bastions was Healy's personal blue-and-red flag, which resembled the Stars and Stripes. Inside, the fort contained a cookhouse, a blacksmith shop, stables, a fur-storage room, a storeroom for supplies, a stockade, and living quarters with stone fireplaces.

John Jerome Healy

Fort Whoop-Up was open for business in the fall of 1870 and quickly became the central trading post for all of northern Montana and the Canadian territories. Free traders bearing such colourful names as J.B. (Waxy) Weatherwax, Spring Heel Jack, Slippery Dick, John (Liver Eating) Johnson, and Toe String Joe flocked there to buy supplies and whiskey, while natives came to trade their buffalo pelts for whiskey and other supplies. The aboriginal traders were rarely permitted inside the palisade — the only natives allowed through the front gates were women whose sexual services were traded for liquor — instead, they had to push their buffalo hides through a small wicket near the main gate. In exchange, the aboriginal traders could receive blankets, guns, pots, axes, ammunition, and other supplies. But the item that was in most demand was whiskey, which was produced inside the fort and called "Whoop-Up wallop." An employee of the fort would stand at the trading window, with a tub of whiskey at his side, and dole out tin cups of the noxious brew. One buffalo pelt fetched two cups of whiskey. By the spring of 1871, wagonloads of buffalo pelts and other proceeds of the season's trades were transported back to Fort Benton along a soon-to-be well-worn route

that became appropriately known as the Whoop-Up Trail. The fort was tremendously successful, collecting upwards of nine thousand buffalo hides in less than a year. At the peak of the whiskey boom in the early 1870s, the trading post pulled in an annual revenue that has been estimated as high as $500,000.

There are various accounts of how Fort Whoop-Up received its name, one of which was because the aboriginal traders always "whooped it up" after getting drunk on the fort's main trading currency. After a while, white suppliers or merchants trying to gain entrance into the fort would yell "Whoop up" when asking for the main gate to be opened. While the name stuck for the white traders, the Blackfoot tellingly called the area around Fort Whoop-Up "Many Ghosts" or "Many Died." It is estimated that more than 140 native people died in the vicinity of the fort in 1871 and 1872 alone, mostly killed during drunken brawls or freezing to death in a stupor. The fort's manager, Donald W. Davis, employed enforcers called "mad dogs" whose job was to patrol the fort with guns and clubs and ward off as many drunken and aggressive Indians as possible.

Rival traders took notice of Fort Whoop-Up's success and the number of whiskey forts throughout southern Alberta and Saskatchewan swelled. Their proliferation and infamy was also attracting the attention of Dominion officials in Ottawa. In an 1872 report, Colonel Patrick Robertson-Ross, an adjutant-general of the Canadian militia on a reconnaissance mission in the Northwest, wrote that the trading posts were in "direct opposition to the laws both of the United States and the Dominion of Canada." He also documented the impact the whiskey traffic was having on native peoples and rued the lack of a government presence that allowed the traders to operate unfettered:

> The demoralisation of the Indians, the danger to the white inhabitants, and injury resulting to the country from this traffic are very great. It is stated upon good authority that during the year 1871 eighty-eight of the Blackfeet Indians were murdered in drunken brawls among themselves, produced by whisky and other spirits supplied to them by those traders. At Fort Edmonton during the past summer whisky was openly sold to the Blackfeet and other Indians trading at the Fort by some smugglers from the United States who derive large profits there from, and on these traders being remonstrated with by the gentlemen in charge of the Hudson's Bay Post, they coolly replied that they knew very well that what they were doing was contrary to the laws of both countries, but as there was no force there to prevent them, they would do just as they pleased.

The trading posts had now become a serious political issue for the new Dominion Government in Ottawa, especially since most of the forts were being operated by Americans on land the Canadian government had recently acquired from the Hudson's Bay Company. It was also an issue for American officials who were concerned that the widespread lawlessness would spread south of the border. The threat of American intervention in the form of the cavalry policing this no man's land worried the Dominion Government even more, as it would greatly compromise its new-found sovereignty in an area that it deemed its "manifest destiny." Robertson-Ross recommended that a chain of military posts with a force of 550 soldiers

be established for the territories. Ottawa decided on sending a paramilitary police force, which would accomplish the dual objectives of bringing law and order to the territories while establishing the Dominion Government's sovereignty over the land. On May 3, 1873, Prime Minister John A. MacDonald introduced a bill into Parliament that led to the creation of the North West Mounted Police.

While the new police force was being assembled, an unspeakable tragedy occurred in the territories that added to the urgency of establishing a law enforcement presence there. The authors of this tragedy were not the whiskey traders, but another group of unscrupulous white interlopers who had descended upon the plains and who were known simply as "wolfers." Along with the buffalo, wolf pelts were a valued commodity and the wolfers were notorious for using a method of killing their prey that was easy and inexpensive, but which was derided by the native peoples. They would shoot a buffalo and then poison the carcass with strychnine. The poisoned bait would guarantee a pack of dead wolves in no time. Aboriginals hated the wolfers, not

Exterior of Fort Whoop-Up, with Blood Indians

only because they respected the wolf, but because their own dogs were killed by the poisoned buffalo meat. The wolfers and aboriginals were constantly at war with one another, resulting in numerous deaths on either side. The Waterloo of this ongoing conflict took place in an area of southern Saskatchewan called Cypress Hills.

Straddling the border and rich in buffalo, wolves, bear, deer, and other wildlife, Cypress Hills had long been a favourite hunting ground for aboriginal bands. White hunters and traders were equally attracted to the area. Among them were Abel Farwell and Moses Solomon who built whiskey forts there. In May 1873, a man named Hammond, who was staying at one of these forts, discovered that his horse had gone missing. He suspected a band of Assiniboines camped near the fort and vowed to take two of their horses in retaliation. Along with a group of wolfers who had been drinking at the post, Hammond headed for the Assiniboine camp fully armed and fully intoxicated. By the time the men arrived at the native encampment, many of the braves were also drunk. Any hope of restraint or a peaceful settlement now flowed away in a river of whiskey. Who fired the first shot is uncertain. Regardless, according to Harold Horwood and Ed Butts, "the high-powered repeating rifles of the wolfers were too much for the northern Indians who were armed with ancient muzzle-loaders and some with only bows and arrows." The wolfers fired randomly into the aboriginal camp. They murdered Chief Little Soldier and mounted his decapitated head on a pole. Four women, including the chief's wife, were carried away to a nearby trading post and raped. By the time the smoke cleared, one wolfer named Ed Grace had died. By best estimates, thirty Assiniboines, including women and children, had been murdered. Upon departing, the wolfers tore down the aboriginal camp, buried Ed Grace, and rode on. In Ottawa, the Cypress Hills massacre was viewed as a crime of unspeakable proportion perpetrated by American desperadoes who were now taking over the Canadian West. The calamity only hastened the Dominion Government's resolve to ensure the new police force could assume its duties as quickly as possible.

When the Mounties left Fort Dufferin in Manitoba on July 6, 1873, they had no idea what they were up against. In October 1874, after a long and arduous journey, a detachment of the NWMP under Assistant Commissioner James Macleod arrived at Fort Whoop-Up. Anticipating a prolonged battle, he ordered his men to deploy the cannons while others took up positions well beyond the range of the fort's rifles and cannons. Still on horseback, Macleod rode straight ahead, towards the entrance of the fort, his men expecting rifles to blast from the loopholed palisade of the eerily silent enclosure any second. In a moment as anticlimatic as any in Canadian history, Macleod halted his horse, dismounted, and strode calmly through a wide-open gate. Once inside, he knocked on the door of the nearest building. A bearded, grey-haired man named Dave Akers opened the door and invited his guest to come right in. As the only white man at the post, Akers was running a small legitimate trade with local aboriginals, when he was not tending to the vegetable garden he had planted inside the fort. Long before the Mounted Police had drawn near, word had reached the whiskey traders that a large number of horsemen wearing red coats and drawing cannons were approaching from the east and they quickly packed up and quit the territories, many heading back to Montana. As the Mounties rode to the other trading posts, they found them equally deserted.

Despite the presence of the NWMP, there were still plenty of liquor smugglers and traders operating in the area. Among them was William Bond, who had his caravan full of whiskey casks, rows of rifles and revolvers, and piles of buffalo robes confiscated by the Mounties. Bond was fined $200 and sentenced to a short term in a makeshift log-cabin jail. The arrest of Bond, and four of his men, led to the discovery of one of the largest whiskey suppliers in the territory, John (Waxy) Weatherwax, a crafty and defiant Montana native who swore he would never be routed from the area. All five men arrested had been working for Weatherwax, who paid their fines, except that levied against Bond. Weatherwax continued to sell whiskey and even frequented Fort MacLeod, the newly built headquarters of the NWMP, to socialize and play cards. On February 17, 1875, Waxy's welcome ran out. He was rounded up by a patrol of Mounted policemen who surprised the trader and two other men with a large stock of liquor and hundreds of furs and robes.

Waxy was handed a six-month prison term and fined $300. He also had his horses, whiskey, robes and other possessions impounded. The following year, after he had been released from jail, Waxy's body was found a few miles from Fort McLeod with a bullet lodged in his back.

The storied Fort Whoop-Up didn't survive much longer either. Akers continued his legitimate trading business while growing prizewinning cabbages in the compound. But, in 1888, fire destroyed much of the fort and six years later Akers was shot dead by a former business partner. John Healy remained in Montana until 1882 where he farmed and worked as a district chairman of the Democratic Party. In 1877, he was appointed sheriff of Choteau County and, in 1878, he became co-owner and editor of the *Fort Benton Record,* which regularly published anti-British and anti-NWMP editorials. In one that appeared in an 1875 edition, Healy called the NWMP "mounted grabbers of the spoil." In 1885, he moved to Alaska where he went back into trading and operated a coastal schooner until around 1907. In 1908, while visiting his daughter in California, he became ill and died on September 16 of cirrhosis of the liver complicated by a bad heart.

LAWS WELL CALCULATED TO SUPPRESS CRIME

Unlike the swift end to the whiskey forts, the Mounties were less effective in enforcing the recently imposed prohibition laws in the territories and the new province of British Columbia. By the early 1880s, thousands of men were now employed on the construction of the Canadian Pacific Railway. The large number of transient labourers, the harsh and isolated conditions under which they worked, and the ban on the sale and possession of liquor within a 10-mile radius of the railway created a golden opportunity for bootleggers. Fuelled by the vast profits that could be made — a gallon of whiskey bought in the East for one dollar would be diluted and then sold in the West for as much as $50 — an underground trade in liquor west of Manitoba began to flourish once again.

At first, there was great optimism that the NWMP could curtail the supply of illegal booze along the railroad lines based on their past success with the whiskey forts. This confidence was reflected in the 1882 annual report of the force's commissioner:

> Our police work during the last year was very great. This has been largely caused by the

"Caught with the goods." Unsigned, undated drawing of whiskey-smuggling enforcement by the North West Mounted Police

construction of the Canadian Pacific Railway, which employed upwards of 4,000 men during the whole summer, some of them exceptionally bad characters. I am, however, happy to report that, owing to there being no liquor obtainable, very little trouble was given us by them. The difficulty of preventing whisky being supplied them by disreputable characters entailed a great deal of extra duty on the force. Where large amounts of money are being expended among such men as railway navies it was to be expected that many attempts would be made to supply them with liquor. Had this not been effectually stopped, I fear I should have had to report a large number of depredations as having been committed. I venture to state that it is unparalleled in the history of railway building in a western country that not a single serious crime has been committed along the line of work; and I would also add that it is a matter of the utmost congratulation to the Government, inasmuch as it must reflect great credit in the enactment and carrying out of laws well calculated to suppress crime.

It wasn't long before the optimistic spirit of the commissioner was dashed as bootleg whiskey began to flow freely into the work camps. The task set out for the Mounted Police was made all the more difficult because their jurisdiction was limited to a 10-mile stretch on each side of the railway route. Outside this limit, bootleggers, shanty bars, and saloons proliferated. Inside the dry zone, the sale and the consumption of liquor was omnipresent. Even a staunch advocate of the law like the legendary Superintendent Sam Steele — who commanded a NWMP detachment responsible for enforcement along the railway lines being constructed through the Rocky Mountains and into British Columbia — was well aware of the uphill battle that faced his small contingent of men in halting the liquor trade. He also acknowledged the frustrating irony of policing society's morals, especially when these edicts went against the will of the majority: "We soon learned that compulsion will not make people sober," he wrote. "The prohibitory law made more drunkards than if there had been an open bar and free drinks at every street corner."

The Mounties were increasingly obstructed in their efforts to obtain the co-operation of the railway workers and settlers in combatting the illicit liquor trade. In complete contrast to his cheery account written just two years earlier, the NWMP commissioner penned a more dour assessment in his 1884 report:

> The suppression of this traffic is the most disagreeable duty which the police are called upon to perform. On the one hand, they are condemned for omission or neglect of duty, and on the other for interested and undue severity. Under no circumstances, except in the case of a trader quarrelling with his associates, can information be obtained as to the possession or traffic of liquor. Settlers will not incur the odium of becoming informers, however much they may deprecate the existence of liquor manufacturers or traffic in their midst, and when I say they will not become informers, I mean that they will not give even secret information which will tend to the conviction of the law breakers. The information obtainable from the latter is meagre enough, for the profits of the traffic far exceed an occasional half fine paid to an informer, as may be supposed when a single five gallon keg of spirit easily changed hands at Standoff, the other day, at the admittedly low price of $60.

The challenges facing the NWMP in their prohibition enforcement duties continued even after the last spike had been driven into the ground in 1885. "The traffic in illicit liquor cannot, I regret to say, be said to be on the decline," the commissioner wrote in his annual report for that year. "I may safely say that the majority of the people living in the North-West do not respect and do not hesitate to break the prohibitory liquor law." By 1887, the frustration of the commissioner was equally palpable when he wrote, "The enforcement of the North West prohibitory law is more difficult than ever. The sympathy of many of the settlers being generally against us in this matter."

In addition to the unsympathetic settler, the Mounties and other law enforcement agencies had to contend with the rise of well-organized bootlegging gangs, some of which became quite powerful and violent. In Michipicoten Bay, a small town located along the northern shore of Lake Superior near present-day Wawa, Ontario, the head constable, Charles Wallace, used his position to become the town's leading bootlegger, in part by arresting all his competitors. After his own digressions cost him his job as the town's top law enforcer, he began to devote all his time to dispensing liquor. He assembled a gang of some of the toughest desperadoes in the county and, by October 1884, Wallace and his gang were selling liquor to all comers. In his quest to dominate the local trade he intimidated or beat up his rivals and bribed local law enforcement and railway company officials.

Two local lawmen who did make a determined effort to arrest Wallace and his gang — Canadian Pacific Railway agent Alexander Macdonald and Ontario magistrate Captain Burden — had their lives threatened and then, on October 9, 1884, were the target of an assassination attempt. The following day, notices were found posted around the railway office threatening death to Macdonald and all others who dared to enforce the liquor laws. The notice was signed "By Order of the Vigilance Committee." Macdonald and Burden were not easily intimidated and continued their investigation into the liquor traffic. That night, a local office of the Canadian Pacific Railway, which at the time was the temporary home of Macdonald and Burden, was besieged by more than thirty masked men who riddled the building with gunfire. The assailants then stormed the local jail. Neither of their intended victims were injured, but by the next day the town was in the grips of Wallace and his men. Three newly appointed constables were fired upon (wounding two) while more notices from the Vigilance Committee promising death to CPR officials, magistrates, constables, and informers were posted around town.

An appeal was sent to the Crown Attorney in Sault Ste. Marie, who responded by ordering police from Toronto to restore order in Michipicoten Bay. Wallace's gang bunkered down for a protracted battle, but they were no match for the armed police who were successful in seizing banned liquor and driving Wallace and many of his gang members out of town. Confident that the whiskey ring had been broken, the imported police contingent left town on October 30,

having arrested only one gang member, Harry Cleveland, an American fugitive who had escaped from the Michigan State Penitentiary. Soon after the Toronto police left, Wallace and his gang re-emerged and even paraded down the street in a heavily armed show of force. Wallace himself was carrying four revolvers, a Winchester rifle, and a Bowie knife.

Despite the show of bravado, the real reason that Wallace and his men had returned to town was to hop on the next steamer before any more police showed up. After boarding the ferry, Wallace forced the captain to cruise to a port in Michigan, where they disembarked unarmed. This proved to be a costly mistake. A sheriff and his deputies from Ontario tracked Wallace and his men and captured them in Michigan without a fight. After being transported back to Canada, Wallace and several of his cohorts stood trial in Sault Ste. Marie in November 1884. All were acquitted, however, most likely because their arrest on the American side of the border by a Canadian law enforcement official was deemed illegal. Before long, Wallace was once again selling liquor near railway work camps. This time, with his gang greatly reduced in number, local police were able to capture Wallace, but not before he had shot a constable. The fugitive was escorted to Toronto by the very police officer he had wounded and, after standing trial, was sentenced to a prison term on February 21, 1885. He was released from jail within weeks after his conviction was quashed for reasons unknown to this day. After that, Wallace disappeared from public view.

Wallace and his gang were just one of many organized groups trafficking liquor on a scale that eclipsed that of the old whiskey forts. The steady rise in the number and size of liquor seizures documented in the annual reports of the NWMP attest to the growing scope of the contraband liquor trade. During the early part of the 1880s, the average seizure from a bootlegger was between 5 and 10 gallons. By 1886, the NWMP was routinely making seizures that averaged 50 gallons. Some were as much as 600 gallons. In 1882, the minister of customs fined Hartlaub, Smith & Company $600 for illegally importing spirits into Canada under the guise of vinegar. The value of the liquor seized amounted to $10,000. Law enforcement officials were also faced with what the NWMP commissioner called a growing "ingenuity which is devoted to encompass the transgression of the prohibitory law." Liquor was now being smuggled into the country and work camps through a variety of methods, including books ("that is, zinc cases made up in the shape of books"), tins of sardines and oysters, loads of coal, oil cans and barrels, steamer trunks, imitation Bibles, eggs, tins of fruit and produce, salt and sugar barrels, false-bottomed buckets, the hollow soles of boots, and, on one occasion, a coffin carried past the lowered heads of a respectful police patrol. The Mounties also intercepted a consignment of liquor labelled as canned apples addressed to a justice of the peace and opened two barrels of oatmeal destined for the Reverend Leo Gaetz only to find that each contained 10 gallons of whiskey. Smuggling was also greatly facilitated by women's fashion of the time; one newspaper correspondent reported that liquor was being surreptitiously transported into the country by women who secreted the bottles under their expansive dresses.

While the CPR was vigorously imposing and enforcing prohibition laws, its own trains were being used to transport liquor, often with the help of those working for the railway company. As the NWMP commissioner wrote in his 1885 annual report, "there is no doubt that there has been collusion on the part of railway employees, or else this system of smuggling liquor could not be carried on. A baggageman here was tried, convicted and dismissed by the railway company for having connection with this traffic." In this competitive and lucrative market, hijackings and thefts were also common. In one instance, a railway car full of alcohol, which had been left overnight on a Calgary railway siding, was found empty when it reached its destination. Holes had been drilled through the bottom of the railway car penetrating the base of the full barrels sitting on its floor.

Organized bootlegging and liquor smuggling continued unabated for the rest of the 19th century and expanded eastward. A June 17, 1892, article in the *New York Times* declared, "the traffic in contraband whisky in Lower Canada has long been carried on by smugglers, who own a fleet of crafts to carry on the trade, and have so far, with few important exceptions, successfully evaded the vigilance of the customs officers, who, however, have hitherto been inadequately equipped to put down the traffic. Immense quantities of alcohol over-proof are sent from Boston and other points in the States up the Gulf of St. Lawrence and sold there without payment of duty." The article goes on to report that "three thousand gallons have been seized in Quebec District alone within a short time." Liquor smuggling was deemed so widespread in the Gulf of St. Lawrence that armed customs cutters were commissioned "under orders from the Dominion Government to begin a crusade against those who seek to evade the tariff laws by bringing in whisky from Boston and other ports in the States by vessels by way of the Gulf."

AN ESTABLISHED INDUSTRY

The brisk cross-border traffic in booze invigorated a smuggling trade between Canada and the United States that was already pulsating due to the high tariffs imposed on goods imported into both countries. Smuggling was also bolstered by the completion of the Grand Trunk Railway, which, starting in 1860, was running between various American and Canadian cities. The railway provided a fast and efficient means to transport contraband, while also allowing for far greater quantities to be hauled. In one operation detected in 1877, Grand Trunk rail cars would be loaded in the eastern U.S. with merchandise cleared by customs for delivery to the West and bonded through Canada. Once in Quebec, the seal of the bonded cars was broken and their contents removed (and later sold on the Canadian black market). If that was not enough, goods to be smuggled into the U.S. from Canada would be placed in the now-empty rail cars. The cars were then bonded with counterfeit American and Canadian customs seals and the contraband was transported back into the United States.

By the final years of the 19th century, a wide variety of undeclared goods was flooding into Canada from the U.S. Even when tariffs on many goods were reduced in the late 1880s, it had little impact because, as the *New York Times* observed in 1888, smuggling had "taken root as an established industry" in Canada. The list of merchandise being smuggled into the country resembled the inventory of a dry-goods store and more: cotton, clothes, shoes, boots, silks, textiles, coal, and even oil and kerosene "are the staple articles conveyed across." One efficient method of smuggling American kerosene across the border was discovered by Canadian authorities in 1883. While the temptation to avoid paying the $3.50-a-barrel duty on American oil was great, the logistical difficulties of transporting a large enough quantity to make it profitable appeared to be a significant deterrent. One enterprising group in Michigan developed a technique that overcame this obstacle to profitability. They simply placed the barrels in the Detroit River on the American side, joined twelve of them together like a log boom, and then towed the floating freight across the river to the Canadian side.

The size, organization, and sophistication of smuggling operations was now unprecedented. "It is not to be supposed that these smugglers are a 'fly-by-night' people," an 1892 edition of the *New York Times* reads, "as their operations have been reduced to a system that has baffled for a long time and still does baffle the efforts of the officers to whose ears rumours of the illegal sets come. Years of practice have enabled them to carry on their working in a workmanlike manner." In 1877, federal officials in the U.S. identified a Montreal-based smuggling operation coordinated by a D. McClannaghan, which he began while employed as an express messenger on the Grand Trunk Railway between Portland, Maine, and Montreal. He was discharged after his extracurricular activities were detected in 1865 by company officials, but his smuggling operations only expanded after that. In co-operation with an American Customs inspector, railway baggage handlers, and telegraph operators in Montreal, he devised a system of secreting goods into the United States duty free. He would obtain from the baggage masters duplicates of claim checks, which were then provided to the corrupt U.S. Customs inspector who would stamp the tickets duty paid. One claim check would be sent to a customer in the United States receiving the goods, while the other would be attached to the package to be delivered. McClannaghan then used the services of the telegraph operator to send a coded message to the customer, such as: "Pay note 7,086 S," which indicated he had shipped goods with the claim check number 7,086 by way of Springfield. In this case, the buyer would present the duplicate baggage check at the railway station in Springfield

and receive his goods without question or payment of duties. As the *New York Times* reported, "McClannaghan shipped anything that was called for — silks, laces, cloth, perfumery, &c — and he was so sure of the perfection of his arrangements that he always insured delivery. No money was asked until after the receipt of the goods. Then he required payment directly to a bank in Montreal. So successful has he been that he owns the Express Hotel and an entire block of ground in Montreal and is estimated to be worth $250,000, all of which he has made out of the commissions on his smuggling ventures."

Despite the sheer variety of goods smuggled between the two countries, by the end of the century, tobacco products had become the most popular contraband in Canada, due to the imposition of an import duty to protect Canadian cigarette manufacturers. The duty raised the cost of a small package of cigarettes imported into Canada to ten cents while in the U.S. they could be purchased at half that price. The result, according to a 1895 *Toronto Star* article entitled "Smuggle the vile cigarette," was that tobacco smugglers were now "doing business on a tremendously large scale, bringing the goods both to Toronto and to Montreal." In 1898, Dominion officials broke up one of the biggest tobacco smuggling operations to date, involving the illegal transport of thousands of cigars from Puerto Rico into Canada, via Halifax. The contraband cigars were delivered to a Halifax grocery store and from there distributed throughout Nova Scotia. The cigars were also shipped to New Brunswick, Quebec, and Ontario. "So well and systematically was the enterprise organized," the *Toronto Star* wrote, "that the goods were distributed by express and freight over the Intercolonial and other railways, and the payments collected by draft through the banks." Canada Revenue officers were dispatched to search tobacconists, grocers, and the barrooms of hotels throughout the Maritimes, Ontario, and Quebec for the contraband cigars. The result was "the biggest seizures of smuggled tobacco ever brought into Canada."

Canada was also used as a conduit to smuggle goods from other countries into the United States. In 1894, authorities in Toronto unearthed an extensive scheme that stretched from Syria and Turkey to Canada and the United States. Arrests were made in all of these countries, including the ringleaders who, according to the *Toronto Star* "are natives of Syria with unpronounceable names." As the *Star* reported, the illegal imports were—

> the very finest products of Syria and Turkey, consisting of spreads, tapestries, shawls, coverlets, and other fancy articles hand embroidered in gold, and the duty on this class of goods is 60 per cent. The modus oprandi of the smugglers was to have the goods shipped from Constantinople to Montreal, Hamilton, and Toronto, where they were unpacked and sent forward in small packages to Windsor, where the smugglers concealed them on their persons and crossed over to Detroit. The rest was then easy. Express parcels to New York and other Eastern points speedily carried the contraband articles to the best markets, where they were disposed of to large dealers in Oriental goods.

Canada's role as an international smuggling conduit into America prompted the U.S. Secret Service to station one of its agents in Toronto in 1893. His mission, according to the *New York Times,* was to "locate a well-organized gang of smugglers, who for at least a year, have been evading the United States customs officials, sending in large quantities of opium and jewerly." The head of the smuggling group, who resided in Honolulu, "was shipping largely quantities of opium, pearls, moonstones, and other precious stones to Vancouver, whence duty having been paid on parts of the shipments to the Canadian Government, the goods were shipped to points along the Canadian border and afterward smuggled across the line."

By the start of the new century, it seemed like every conceivable consumer product was being illegally transported into and out of Canada through any available mode of transportation and facilitated by an imaginative range of concealment and camouflage. In a 1904 article entitled, "The modern art of smuggling," the *Globe* newspaper summarized the breadth and versatility of this underground industry. A favourite means of smuggling diamonds into the U.S. was to "ship them from Paris or London to Montréal, charging no duty on them, and then to take them secretly across the border into the United States." The smuggled diamonds would be "hidden in the heels of shoes, in cakes of soap, in the hollow legs of dolls, in false calves, in corks of perfumery bottles, and even in cheeses." Female smugglers wrapped the diamonds "in tissue paper just the colour of their hair, in which they were well concealed." One elderly man "is said to have employed with great success a hollow cane, with which he made twelve trips across the Atlantic, on occasions carrying as much as $50,000 worth of stones in this way. He was afraid to try the thirteenth, and so bought a new cane." In addition to diamonds, "silks, laces, and shawls have been brought over in bales of hops. Iron tubing has been employed to conceal valuable goods; likewise loaves of bread, cork legs, the handles of shaving brushes, and concertinas." One "reverend-looking gentleman with white whiskers" was found to be carrying a Bible that was hollowed out and filled with watches. "Oil cans have been made with compartments to contain fine French brandy, and one dog has been known to wear the skin of a slightly bigger dog, with laces hidden between his own and the borrowed integument." Customs officers found "imitation lumps of coal filled with cigars" while "opium has been hidden in organs, and in bananas still hanging on the stalk, as well as in sausages and in the hump of a supposed hunchback." Mattresses have been stuffed "full of silks, and twenty yards of point lace were discovered on one occasion beneath a porous plaster on a man's back." In addition to the railway, smuggling was greatly facilitated by transatlantic passenger steamships and even navy vessels. The crews were the most frequent transgressors and took advantage of the many potential hiding places on board. "Officers of the United States navy are chronic smugglers, taking advantage of a certain amount of latitude which is allowed to them in fetching from foreign lands goods which are supposed to be for their own personal use. Under this disguise they are accustomed to fill many commissions for their friends in the way of purchasing rugs, silks, wines and cigars." Finally, according to the *Globe,* "one of the strangest forms of smuggling is that of illegally importing Chinamen." In one case "a dozen

Celestials were found hidden under the boilers of a steamer bound from Vancouver to San Francisco. They were literally roasted and their cries attracted the inspector's attention, who came on board at Port Townsend. Some of them died afterward."

A DESPERADO OF THE WORST DESCRIPTION

Along with smuggling, the theft of horses and cattle was a chronic problem during the waning years of the 19th century. With the opening of the Canadian West for settlement, farming, and railway construction, the demand for and value of horses and cattle rose greatly, which increased their attractiveness to thieves. The new pioneer settlements also had to contend with horse thieves from local natives, who adapted their expertise garnered after years of reciprocating horse theft that occurred between rival aboriginal bands. In his annual report for 1883, the NWMP commissioner described how Cypress Hills "was infested by horse thieves" most of whom he identified as "American Indians from the Peigan Reservation, 90 miles west of Fort Shaw, Montana." A large number of horses were stolen "from the Indians and white men in our country," he wrote and "in some cases, the thefts committed were daring," including one from a stable at the NWMP Fort Walsh settlement. Judging by the commissioner's report for 1884, the problem of horse theft appeared to be increasing in the territories:

> Further west, in the vicinity of Wood Mountain, I was informed on reliable authority that a great many horses had been stolen. Settlers there are now bringing their horses north, as they find they cannot hold them, horse stealing never having been carried on so boldly as it has been this season. On arrival at Moosomin I found the inhabitants in a state of terror, owing to the presence of strangers in the village who were looked upon as desperadoes. With reference to the remarks that horse stealing has never been so prevalent before, it is clear that the effect is explainable by the cause. As the country becomes more and more settled, so many more temptations will be presented to the marauding desparadoes, who have not to face, on this side of the line, the contingency by bullet or rope which attends their exercise of their calling on the other.

The theft of livestock necessitated a certain level of organization, regardless of how many heads were being stolen. Planning was necessary to identify a ranch from which the horses or cattle would be stolen. The theft had to be timed when ranch hands were not around; alternatively, the hands were recruited by the rustlers as co-conspirators. There also had to be a sufficient number of men to herd the livestock. A well-planned escape route, which included hiding places big enough to conceal the stolen animals overnight, was obligatory. Cattle and horses stolen in southern Canada would often be smuggled across the U.S. border, which required further stealth and organization. A market was required for the stolen stock and, in order to cover their larcenous tracks, the rustlers had to re-brand the animals. Once stolen horses were herded, the NWMP commissioner wrote in 1884, they would be driven away at the "utmost speed, the thieves riding and relieving each horse in turn, until the American frontier is crossed. Any horses that drop out from exhaustion are abandoned. With pre-arranged plans a thorough knowledge of the country, and accurate information as to the whereabouts of the police, the thieves make straight for their objective point and trust to their own determination to tide them over any unforeseen difficulties." Crossing the border also meant that the rustlers were out of the grasp of Canadian law enforcement. But this strategy was not without risk. Once on U.S. soil they were now susceptible to the vigilante justice doled out by American ranchers. One NWMP inspector reported to the commissioner that he had reports of fifteen or twenty horse thieves being "linched in the Missouri River and Musselshell regions." Although these numbers were dismissed as exaggerated, the inspector insisted, "there is no doubt that some were hanged, and others shot, but not in sufficient numbers to break up the organized gang of horse thieves."

Compared to horses, the theft of cows and steers required even greater organization and covertness because the rustlers could not rely on the element of speed when escaping (although stolen cattle was more difficult to detect than stolen horses because the cows could be butchered and their hides destroyed relatively quickly). The so-called Cuntingham, Grady and Foster Gang, was one of the more notorious bands of cattle rustlers operating in northern Wyoming and Montana as well as southern Saskatchewan and Alberta during the late 1800s. Once a part of the Hole in the Wall Gang, Cuntingham was arrested and put on trial when he was caught red-handed illegally branding eighty head of stolen cattle.

In addition to stolen livestock, horses and cattle legitimately purchased in Canada or the United States would be smuggled across the border to avoid duties. In a typical case reported by the NWMP in 1886, a herd of twenty horses and mares belonging to a Canadian settler was seized "for evading payment of Customs." The horses were purchased at Sun River in Montana, "and driven into the country by an unfrequented trail, crossing the Canadian Pacific Railway west of Swift Current, and then following down the north of the boundary." The routes used for smuggling liquor or other goods were often used by horse thieves and cattle rustlers. In a letter dated August 25, 1883, a NWMP superintendent stationed in Maple Creek, Alberta, wrote, "there is more horse stealing going on now more than I have ever known before, and horses are stolen from this vicinity nearly every night." In addition, "a great deal of whiskey" was smuggled from Montana to Medicine Hat and the same trail "evidently used by whiskey smugglers and horse thieves."

One of the largest bands of cattle rustlers and smugglers in the Canadian West was headed by brothers Samuel and John Spencer, who one U.S. Treasury official characterized as "wealthy and unscrupulous men." Working under the auspices of a cattle company called Spencer Brothers & Co. Ltd., the two operated a ranch at Milk River in southern Alberta that was strategically located close to the American border. From this ranch, according to a NWMP superintendent in Lethbridge, the brothers and their hired help "inaugurated a systematic course of smuggling cattle (A) From Canada into United States, and (B) From the United States into Canada." In a February 4, 1902, letter to the Minister of the Interior of the Dominion Government, the comptroller of the NWMP wrote, "we have had very strong suspicion for some time past that the Messrs Spencer Bros., who have a ranching lease in the Milk River country close to the boundary, have been systematically playing fast and loose with the Customs Regulations of the United States and Canada, to enable them to take advantage of the Chicago or Canadian markets, whichever at the moment happens to be paying the higher price for stock."

In April 1900, cowboys working for the Spencer brothers stole about four hundred head of cattle from Montana ranches, which they then smuggled into Alberta. In October of that year, another seven hundred were stolen and transported across the border. In February 1901, some American ranchers complained to the NWMP after Spencer and Company ranch hands gathered up some two thousand head of stray cattle in Montana and drove them across Milk River at a time when the ice was perilously thin. When confronted by an American rancher, one of the Spencers' lead hands told him that he was going to drive them across the river even at the risk of drowning them all. As it turned out, this was no idle threat. Almost half of the cattle fell through the ice on the drive. The following spring, when the dead cows thawed out, it took months to fish the bloated and foul-smelling carcasses from the river.

Despite numerous complaints and sufficient evidence as to their smuggling activity, the harshest punishment inflicted on the brothers were fines. Although they could easily pay them, they regularly turned to their stable of high-priced lawyers to fight the levies in court. "We'll law 'em," was Sam Spencer's usual retort when faced with a fine. In 1902, Canadian customs officials seized 587 head of mixed cattle from the Spencer brothers. Their cash value at the time was upwards of $20,000 and government authorities demanded a bond of $10,000 to release the cattle. The amount was paid by the Spencers, but after they undertook legal action, $4,000 of the bond was returned to the brothers, who then launched another suit for the remaining $6,000. In commenting on recent charges being laid against the Spencer brothers, the NWMP commanding officer at "E" Division in Calgary wrote that he was "certain from the outset that that Firm would contest every step." As part of their numerous criminal and civil trials, the wealthy brothers were also accused of "buying up testimony if given the opportunity."

A FISTFUL OF TERROR

You see, in this world there's two kinds of people, my friend. Those with loaded guns and those who dig. You dig.
—The Man With No Name in Sergio Leone's 1967 film, *The Good, the Bad, and the Ugly*

At the foot of Long Lake, a few miles from the town of Kamloops, British Columbia, four young men camped on a bitterly cold day, a few weeks before Christmas in 1879. The oldest, a tall, strapping man of twenty-five with a black beard, heavy brows, and dark complexion was Allen McLean. Also at the camp were his two younger brothers, Charlie, a dusky seventeen-year-old with coal-coloured hair that sat atop a squat face highlighted by high cheek bones and the beginnings of a post-pubescent moustache, and Archie, the impish, baby-faced fifteen-year-old, whose fair complexion and sandy hair belied any relation to his two older siblings. The fourth member of the group was Alex Hare, the childhood pal and inseparable companion of the three brothers who seemed to wear "a look of ineffable sadness."

They had barely started their campfire when the sound of hoof beats sheared the silence of the backwoods. Atop the approaching horse was L. William Palmer, a Stump Lake rancher who had recently lost a black stallion and rode into the camp after seeing one tied to a nearby tree. But as Palmer stared down the barrels of two cocked shotguns, he chose not to press the matter directly with the group and galloped away. Instead, he travelled a short distance into Kamloops where he laid a complaint with the justice of the peace, John Edwards. Palmer's accusations were entirely justified and in addition to his own horse, the four were also in possession of another stolen horse, which they had liberated from Palmer's neighbour. In addition, the young men were well stocked with saddles, bridles, guns, ammunition, food, and

Allen McLean

Charlie McLean

cooking utensils. All of it had been stolen from homes and stores in the sparsely settled country between Cache Creek, Kamloops and the Upper Nicola Valley.

Palmer's discovery of the encampment signalled the beginning of the end for the young thieves, who had victimized the people of the Kamloops region for close to two years and who would go on to be remembered as one of British Columbia's most villainous outlaw gangs.

If ever there were three boys who had a hole pre-dug for them, it was the McLean brothers. Their childhood was filled with poverty, segregation, neglect, and violence. Their father, Donald McLean, came to Canada from Ireland and worked as a trader with the Hudson's Bay Company. He was an arrogant and abrasive man who seemed to clash with everyone he met. He married two successive native wives, although he despised aboriginals. His first wife gave birth to six children. But he abandoned her and, in 1854, took up with another woman.

Archie McLean

She brought five more little ones into a soon-to-be fatherless world. In 1864, Donald McLean was shot and killed while he and a posse of other vigilantes were hunting down a Chilcotin Indian suspected of murdering a Hudson's Bay employee.

When their father died, Allen, Charlie, and Archie were all under the age of ten. Archie was just a baby. The boys grew up as neglected itinerants: alone, estranged from their mother, and with no land, no money, and no education. Only Archie had learned to write his name. Because they were half-breeds they did not fit into either white or aboriginal society. They were rootless with no city or town, no street, no walls, no square foot of earth to call their home. They drifted from ranch to ranch working sporadically as cowboys and shepherds, but could not find steady work. The boys did gain plenty of skills while living on the wild frontier that would later prove to be of immense value to them; they were experts when it came to horses, having practically grown up in the saddle, and because they had to hunt to eat, they were all excellent shots.

Like their father, the boys drank heavily, were quarrelsome, and made enemies easier than friends. The outcasts cursed the seemingly "pure" societies of the white towns and aboriginal reserves for their inability to understand the depths of their exclusion. These "sons of a thousand fathers" became social castaways who could rely only on one another. Not only could they see no path ahead of them, they seemed to have sensed there was none. "Having settled into a drifting existence, the McLeans slowly entered into a collision course with the ranchers and townspeople around them." When they could not find legitimate work, they turned to stealing. "They made off with anything that could be used or sold — money, livestock, food, clothing, firearms. They sometimes beat the victims of their robberies. They were tough, feared nothing, and had no sense of pity or compassion; they were as merciless with the world as the world had been with them."

In 1877, fifteen-year-old Charlie was arrested after biting off the end of the nose of a man with whom he was fighting and was sent to the Kamloops jail for three months. But he was able to escape and once reunited with his two brothers and Alex Hare, the four began a larcenous rampage across the Koot-nays, robbing farms, ranches, and even pedestrians. From G. Wilson, they stole a saddle and provisions. Four racehorses and several saddles were pilfered from John Wilson's Savona ranch. A horse and a saddle disappeared from the Kamloops aboriginal reserve. A shepherd named James Kelly was robbed of a bottle of brandy and a loaf of freshly baked bread. The storeroom at Savona's Ferry was broken into and its provisions were taken. Blankets and armaments were removed from the ranch of Thadeus Harper. James Cavanaugh of Cache Creek lost several items of clothing while George Caughill and Tom Cavanagh were deprived of their saddles. The four desperadoes even crossed the American border where they stole cattle and shaved off the hair of a native woman, a sign of contempt. One night, the boys came across a Chinese man on a lonely road and beat him so savagely he nearly died. They took from him what cash he did have, plus a bottle of whiskey.

With little law enforcement in the region and with nothing to lose, the McLean gang wreaked havoc throughout the years 1878 and 1879. They were unleashed onto society like a pack of wild dogs and were as difficult to catch as a stampeding herd of mustangs. They robbed at gunpoint and left nothing but fear and destitution in their wake. They swore to kill anyone who tried to stop them and constantly threatened to ride into Kamloops and burn it to the ground. They even tried unsuccessfully to incite an uprising among the local aboriginal bands. "Many Interior residents would as soon hear that the Four Horsemen of the Apocalypse were coming as learn that the McLean gang was near." A Victoria *Daily Colonist* reporter lamented, "This is a fine state of things, to be terrorized over by four brats, who have threatened to burn the jail in order to destroy the records of their deeds. If these vagabonds are not either arrested or driven to American territory, it may become pretty hot for us. This is a nice state of things for us, and a nice Government to allow it. At present nothing is being done and everybody scarcely likes to leave his house for fear of being robbed."

Arrest warrants were issued in 1878, first in the light in August and a second in the dark of November.

But neither brought any immediate justice. The state of law enforcement in the district was simply too weak. Kamloops and the surrounding area had only one part-time constable, John Tannatt Ussher, the son of a Montreal Episcopalian minister who came west to join the Yukon gold rush and then settled down as a rancher on the North Thompson River. Despite his slender and frail appearance, Ussher was a determined man and took his job very seriously. He eventually was able to round up Allan, Charlie, and Archie and charged them with horse stealing and larceny. While waiting in the local jail for their trial, the boys escaped by climbing over the prison wall with a rope thrown from the other side by Alex Hare.

Ussher formed a posse to find the escapees. Among the members of the party were local ranchers John McLeod and William Palmer. On December 8, 1879, after tracking hoofprints in the newly fallen snow, the posse saw four horses tied to a tree. They also spied a rifle barrel sticking out from another tree. At the end of the rifle was Charlie McLean. A sharp whistle was heard and a single gunshot rang out in the stillness of the forest. The bullet cut past Palmer and hit McLeod in the cheek, knocking him from his horse. After the first shot, a barrage of bullets exploded from behind the trees. Palmer, who was armed with a shotgun, began to fire back at Allen McLean, who crouched behind one tree as he reloaded his gun. Bullets from Ussher's shotgun pierced the tree like nails through a cross. Confident he could reason with the boys, Ussher walked un-armed towards Alex Hare. This would be a misjudge-ment with tragic consequences. After discharging his pistol in the direction of Palmer and McLeod, Alex came out to confront Ussher. He had a pistol in one hand and a Bowie knife in the other. He lunged at the constable. The two grappled. Ussher quickly gained the upper hand. That was until Archie McLean snuck up from behind and, at short range, fired his revolver at the constable's head. At almost the same moment, Hare plunged his knife into the lawman's cheek and continued slashing at Ussher's face until he was unrecognizable.

Although in pain from his own facial wounds, John McLeod continued to unload his shotgun in the direction of the young outlaws. But he suffered a second gunshot wound, this one in the leg. After close to thirty shots were exchanged, the posse retreated to Kamloops for more help, leaving the body of Ussher in the snow. Once back in town, twenty additional armed horsemen were recruited and soon they were galloping out of town to deal with the outlaws once and for all.

When the reinforced posse arrived at the camp just after dark, they found the fire still burning. Not too far away lay Ussher's frozen body, his perforated head surrounded by tufts of maroon-coloured snow. The outlaws had stripped him of his coat, boots, and gloves. The hunters made another grisly discovery not too far away: the body of the shepherd James Kelly. He had been killed in cold blood. After surrounding a cabin where the boys had taken refuge, the posse was able to capture the four by smoking them out. They were arrested, charged, and escorted to New Westminster. After a short trial, they were found guilty of the murder of John Ussher. All four were decreed to die.

"The sentence of this Court is that you be taken to the place from whence you came, and from thence to the place of execution, and be there hanged by the neck until you are dead," the judge proclaimed to a hushed courtroom. "Sentence to be carried out within a period of not less than two months' time. May God have mercy upon your souls."

"It's a well-deserved sentence, Your Lordship," Alex Hare was heard to say.

On January 31, 1881, the four young men were executed in a group hanging. As customary, photos of each of the condemned were taken just before. While still wearing their leg irons, each gazed into the camera with a calm, rapt expression like a monk in a monastery. At the time, Allan was twenty-four and Charlie and Alex were seventeen. At fifteen years of age, Archie was the youngest person ever to hang in British Columbia. Never, in the short history of the province, were such young men "wasted so bad."

HIGH NOON AT NEW HAZELTON

The commandments say "Thou shalt not kill," but we hire men to go out and do it for us. The right and the wrong seem pretty clear here. But if you're asking me to tell my people to go out and kill and maybe get themselves killed, I'm sorry. I don't know what to say. I'm sorry.
—The Minister Dr. Mahin in Fred Zinnemann's 1952 film, *High Noon*

To the townspeople he was known simply as "Doc." Despite carrying a muscular physique on his ample six-foot frame, the Reverend Donald Redmond (Doc) McLean was a soft-spoken, unassuming man. His dark hair, brushed straight back, parted in the middle and flattened to the scalp, clung to a smooth, broad forehead. His deep blue eyes were set in a long hard face with heavy bones underlined by an uncompromising chin with a cleft so cavernous it could hide a .45-calibre bullet and a jaw so square it seemed to transcend geometrical perfection. He was as out of place in the small British Columbian town as an ageless Grecian statue.

He was born in Nova Scotia and graduated from Knox College at Dalhousie University. But to the people of New Hazelton, British Columbia, his adopted home, he was the preacher who taught the Gospel to the Presbyterians every Sunday, and the horse doctor who worked for the railway contractors the rest of the week. He had a profound love for animals, which he consummated when he graduated from the Ontario Veterinary College, and put on display every time he tended to one of God's sick or injured four-legged creatures. When he wasn't caring for animals, he was killing them; he loved to fish and hunt and was known to survive in the wild for days with nothing but a piece of twine, a Bowie knife, and his British army–issued Lee-Enfield .303 rifle.

New Hazelton is a small town in northwest British Columbia, where nothing really important happens. Nestled in the bosom of the snow-capped Coastal Mountain range, the town was built on the precipice of the new railway and surrounded by picturesque natural beauty, with the 3,000-foot walls of the rugged Rocher de Boule mountains, the meandering salmon-filled Bulkley River, and the wind-swept Hagwilget canyon, named after the Gitksan word for "peaceful, deliberate people."

On one sunny April morning, Doc was walking peacefully up New Hazelton's main road, bucket in hand, heading towards the community's water pump. The drowsy smell of the hazelnut trees the town was named after hung in a misty morning air that was occasionally stirred by a chilly wind off the mountaintops. "As he strolled along the dusty street he little realized that he was about to exchange the water bucket for his rifle, a weapon he handled as skilfully as the bible."

Around the same time, Mr. Al Gaslin, a manager of a local contracting firm working on the railway, had just entered the local branch of the Union Bank of Canada. The bank had just opened for business and Mr. Gaslin was chatting casually with Mr. Bishop, one of the tellers standing behind the counter.

The bank was as unpretentious as the town and its people. It was a small, low-slung log building with bars at the windows and a wooden-plank sidewalk that ran along its perimeter and out onto Pugsley Street. The bank branch stood on the edge of town, away from most of the other buildings, but it did a flourishing business, especially during the construction of the Grand Trunk Pacific Railway.

Soon after the bank's doors opened that morning, two men walked up the main road heading straight towards the log building. Two others appeared from the edge of the lush, well-watered forest that sat between the rear of the bank and two ranges of rugged hills. Two more men came from the east side of the building. All six men, "hard-eyed and unshaven," could have easily passed for one of the many railway workers or miners who regularly attended the bank to deposit their paycheque. However, "they weren't depositors, these six. They were bent

on withdrawing. In addition, a rifle, carelessly cradled under one man's arm, and revolvers in the hands of his five companions suggested they were going to dispense with the usual bookkeeping formalities."

Inside the bank, Mr. Gaslin had $50 in cash, a few cheques, and his deposit slip in hand. Before Mr. Bishop, the teller, could take the money from his customer, two of the armed men crashed through the bank's front doors. Four others appeared almost instantaneously and took up positions at various points inside. The final gang member stood watch outside on the wooden sidewalk.

In a slurred, guttural attempt at English, one of the armed intruders shouted, "Hanz up!" Mr. Bishop and his fellow bank employee, Mr. Ray Fenton, raised their hands in shock.

The man yelling out the commands thrust one arm towards Mr. Gaslin, and greedily snatched his deposits from him. In some foreign language, he barked orders to his accomplices. Two of the men replied by leaping behind the teller's counter. Without hesitation, they pushed Mr. Bishop out of their way, sending him reeling to the floor. They then ripped open the cash drawers and seized the cash inside.

The leader of the bandits then ordered Mr. Bishop to open the safe. The frightened teller tried to explain to the threatening, gun-waving bank raider that a brand-new steel safe had been installed following a previous holdup, and as a safety precaution he had been given only half of the combination. The other half was known only to the bank's manager, Mr. E.B. Tatchell.

Despite the ruckus inside the bank, all was quiet in the surrounding town. "So far no one in the town suspected anything amiss at the bank. The unshaven lookout man in his work clothes resembled any other construction laborer waiting for a friend in the bank." The only difference was that this man was holding a Winchester under his mackinaw.

Inside, an exasperated Mr. Bishop was trying to explain to the gunmen that he could not open the safe. Suddenly, without warning, one of the bandits aimed his gun at the teller's feet and began shooting.

Outside the bank, the manager, Mr. Tatchell, was nearing when he heard the loud noises coming from inside.

"Sounded like shots," he said, turning to Doc McLean who just a moment earlier had stopped to chat with the new bank manager. Doc's perceptive eyes then glimpsed the idle figure fidgeting nervously on the wooden planks just outside the bank's front doors. In a blink of an eye, the man slipped a long gun from underneath his soiled jacket.

"It's a holdup, Doc," said Mr. Tatchell. "Over at the bank!"

Mr. Tatchell ran to take cover, while Doc quickly turned, threw aside his bucket, and sprinted towards his ministry, a small modest room above the dry-goods store. He was not running to take cover or to say a prayer. It was there that he kept his rifle.

Doc did not ponder his obligations. He did not shirk from his duty, nor would he waiver in the face of danger or doubt his cause. Some men may have waited for the lawmen to arrive. Some may have hesitated under such circumstances or questioned the very futility of intervening. Some may be apt to say cynically, "You risk your skin catching killers and the juries turn them loose so they can come back and shoot at you again. If you're honest you're poor your whole life and in the end you wind up dying all alone on some dirty street. For what? For nothing."

But unlike Cain, Doc would not forsake his loved ones. Nor would they forsake him. The people of New Hazelton did not have to be talked into upholding law and order. They knew it was their right and their responsibility.

With the courage of a true frontier settler, Mrs. McLean handed her husband his rifle almost as soon as he entered the door of his small chapel. She was a small-boned woman with short wheat-blond hair that was pulled straight back into a large chignon that did not quite cover the back of her head. A yellow ribbon looped around her hair twice. She was wearing her favourite cinnamon-coloured crinoline day dress trimmed with silver buttons. Her high cheekbones, fair complexion, and ocean-blue eyes were suggestively Scandinavian and she carried herself with a self-assuredness that would have been cockiness in one less graceful or humble.

As Doc hurried out of the room, Mrs. McLean stoically grasped the lapels of her husband's vest and looked deep into his eyes. She pressed her face to his. Her long eyelashes gently caressed his cheeks like the wings of a small butterfly. As she pulled her face away, they spoke not a word as they lovingly stared at one another. They didn't have to speak. She could read everything about her husband in his eyes, which simply said, "I've got to, that's the whole thing."

The only law enforcement official for the district was miles away. But the brave townspeople from the heartland of British Columbia — already victims of a bank robbery just six months earlier in which the young teller, Mr. Jock McQueen, nearly died from a shot to the head — were not waiting for the police to arrive. "This time it was going to be different. The robbers would not be the only ones shooting."

As the word of the robbery spread, the townspeople emerged from every business, home, and livery, with rifle or pistol in hand. They took up positions in every shielded spot that surrounded the besieged bank. Women showed their mettle by passing along ammunition to their menfolk. "Open season on bank robbers!" Mr. Harry Summer yelled. One barbershop customer receiving a morning shave threw his cover aside, leaped out of his reclined chair, grabbed his gun, and took position behind a door post "one side of his face still lathered, a rifle butt pressing the other." As Doc raced back along Pugsley Street, restaurant owner Mr. Harry Lewis ran across his path before disappearing into his diner. Seconds later he reappeared, gun in hand.

Realizing the bank was surrounded by the well-armed and implacable townspeople, the panicked lookout man sprinted from his sentry post outside and hurried into the bank to warn his partners. "He was barely through the door when the first barrage smashed into the building. Fenton and Bishop threw themselves to the floor while the robbers began returning the fire." The gunfight was on!

As returned gunfire streamed out of the bank onto the street, Doc, with his rifle in one hand and a fistful of shells in the other, weaved and dodged his way through the street and threw his lanky body behind a pile of solid galena ore that was sitting in front of the office of Silver Standard Mine. The local mining broker had just hauled the deposit from the Silver Cup Mine to advertise its rich claim. The mound of minerals was large enough to hide Doc in his entirety, solid enough to deflect any bullets, and was a mere 180 feet from the bank, well within the range of his high-powered rifle. After pushing his back up against the ore, he caught his breath, and poked his head above the pile, just in time to see the bank doors explode open and six armed men burst out.

With their guns blazing, the desperate bandits made a break for the nearby bush. One of their bullets ricocheted off the pile of ore and whizzed close enough to sheer the bristle tops of Doc's whiskers. Without fear for his own safety, Doc loaded and then pumped the bolt of his lever-action rifle. With studied care, he trained his sights on one of the thieves. In a heartbeat, he released a single 215-grain bullet through the 25-inch barrel that tore through one of the fleeing villain's shoulders, sending him crashing to the ground in screams of anguish.

The remaining bank robbers continued to retreat to the dense woods, with gun muzzles flashing. But they were now dodging bullets from all directions as more townsfolk joined in on the shootout. Bullets careened off buildings, smashed through windowpanes, splintered the wooden sidewalks, "and thudded into the stout logs of the bank."

Slugs whined past Doc's head as if destiny had marked each one for him alone. Doc knew exactly what he had gotten himself into and "was too much of a gambler not to accept fate. With him was at best an uncertain game and he recognized the usual percentage in favour of the dealer." With one probing eye affixed to his rifle's scope, he continued to coolly pinch off one shot after another, helping to fell two more of the robbers onto the wooden sidewalk outside the bank.

When the shooting finally stopped and the curtain of acrid smoke-tainted air cleared, six of the bandits could be seen "strewn along the road or the sidewalk. Two of them hadn't moved since they were hit. Three moved spasmodically and one crawled slowly to seek sanctuary under the flap of an unoccupied tent pitched opposite the bank." The throng of armed citizens slowly emerged from

Two of the New Hazelton bank robbers, lying dead, 50 feet from the Union Bank of Canada

their places of concealment and drew near to the bank. Most were out of ammunition. From inside the bank, Mr. Fenton, Mr. Bishop, and Mr. Gaslin emerged shaken but unharmed. Mr. Fenton was the only one of the townspeople who had been hurt when he suffered a scalp wound from a splinter shot out of his solid oaken desktop.

After the lawmen arrived on the scene, they had little to do but cart off the bodies of the dead would-be bandits and arrest the three wounded survivors. The sixth man escaped into the woods with $1,100 in cash. A posse followed his blood-stained trail, but failed to find him.

The unfruitful search for the missing outlaw was an anticlimax to one of the most spectacular shootouts in the history of the Canadian West. Some two hundred bullets zinged through the air during the exchange.

A month after the botched robbery, three of the captured bandits came before the local magistrate. Each received twenty years in jail. In the intervening month, as the wounded bank robbers made a steady recovery and confessed to provincial police, a wild and dramatic story of the gang's background emerged.

All were Russians, mostly from Siberia. A local newspaper reported they were members of "a lawless sect feared even in that wilderness of swamp and frozen tundra." Mr. Dzachot Bekuzaroff, the leader of the bank raid and the only one to escape, "had been a sort of outlaw chief in eastern Russia until action by the Czar's government sentenced him and his band to different forms of penal servitude." They were banished to the rock quarries of Sakhalin Island north of Japan, but when part of the islands were ceded by Russia to Japan at the end of their war, the Russian prisoners were freed. Then along came an American schooner recruiting labourers for railroad construction in Mexico. From Mexico, Mr. Bekuzaroff worked his way up to San Francisco and later to Vancouver. It was there that the bank robbery was planned with other Russians recruited from railway construction crews.

"Anyone who has been labouring under the delusion that this gang of robbers were a bunch of poor shots have another thing coming," the *Omineca Herald* cautioned not long after the story of the bank robbers was revealed. The newspaper reported further:

> They are all ex-members of the Cossacks and have had a thorough military training with all the sharp shooting and plundering frills thrown in. Anyone who had seen the man at the bank door with the rifle would never think that he was a poor shot. ... That they had planned well to "get" anyone who attempted to interfere with them is evidenced by the condition of the bullets found on some of the men. They were not only sharpened, but were split and notched. They were out to rob and kill if necessary. It was only the sharp rifle shooting of the citizens which prevented a successful robbery and a slaughter of the citizens.

The convictions were the finale to one of British Columbia's most famous bank robberies and shootouts. Two men were dead, three were in jail, and one Cossack remained on the loose. The gunfight showcased the bravery and heroics of a small northern railway-and-mining town, where nothing that happens is really important. Suffice to say, there have not been any more bank robberies in New Hazelton.

Doc felt more at home than ever in the small frontier town. He never doubted the courage of his steely spirited neighbours and he never questioned whether a man of the cloth should so readily pick up arms. He would have been lying if he said his calling did not make him hesitate for at least a fleeting second. But as long as that pile of iron ore remained on the street in front of the mining company's office, Doc couldn't help but look to the sky and smile knowingly every time he walked past it.

And if anyone should ask, the events described above took place between 10 a.m. and 12 p.m. — high noon.

EVERY CONCEIVABLE TRICK

In addition to those outlaws who robbed banks, trains, stagecoaches, and ranches at gunpoint, 19th-century Canada was also populated by those who stole through the gift of gab. In his 1920 memoir, Toronto police magistrate George Denison recalled one case of a "shrewd looking gentleman who called himself Robert Vincent and gave his address as the Prince George Hotel." One day, Vincent contacted a Toronto lumber dealer named Daniel Madden and "placed before him a very tempting proposition to make some easy money by purchasing a block of stock in the Wheloe Reinforced Cork Boat Company, which he had been fortunate enough to get hold of through a sick farmer he had met, who had no idea of its value." Vincent said the stock could be purchased for about $5.00 a share and then immediately sold for $8.50 a share to a broker in Philadelphia who was buying all he could get hold of. Vincent even introduced Madden to the "sick farmer," who confirmed he had invested in the company. Madden became suspicious and filed a report with the Toronto police, who upon investigation discovered that Vincent and his partner (the sick farmer) were con men trying to sell Madden $20,000 worth of stock in a business that had never existed. "Both men were locked up on charges of vagrancy," Dennison wrote, "and subsequently a charge of attempting to obtain money by false pretences was laid. At the time of their arrest they had more than $4,000 in their possession, which they would have cheerfully parted from in exchange for their freedom if the police had been purchasable."

Upon further investigation, Toronto police discovered that Vincent's real name was Charles Gondorf and the man who played the sick farmer turned out to be Samuel Gerne. American police had been searching for Gerne for more than two years on a charge of obtaining $40,000 by similar scams. Gondorf had been arrested in New York City on this same charge and was out on a $25,000 bond when he was picked up in Toronto. The two men had fleeced hundreds of thousands of dollars from unsuspecting victims by selling them fictitious stock and had been arrested on several occasions in the United States. In carrying out their swindles they went so far as to set up a fake brokerage office in Philadelphia, which was staffed by another accomplice. The intended victim was told to cable the Philadelphia broker and find out what he was paying for the fabricated stock. Not surprisingly, the broker always offered a very attractive price.

Despite the longevity of their fraud operations, and their numerous arrests, the two grifters had never been convicted or spent more than a few hours in jail. They were well connected to men in positions of power and the methods that had kept them out of jail in the United States were also employed in Canada. When his case came before the courts in Toronto, Gondorf was represented by a lawyer (who also happened to be a Member of Parliament) from Welland, Ontario, as well as a lawyer from New York City and one from Chicago. The men also knew an influential New York politician and a prominent bail bondsman who were prepared to put up as much as $20,000 bail for the two. In Toronto, the fraudsters were released on a bail bond of only $5,000, but once freed, Gerne was re-arrested and taken back to New York for a trial on previous charges. Upon hearing this news, Gondorf left Canada as fast as he could. The law eventually caught up with Gondorf, who also stood trial in New York. Both were convicted and sent to Sing Sing, Gondorf for five to ten years and Gerne for one to three years.

In addition to stock market scams, many other types of fraud were being perpetrated on Canadians during the last quarter of the 19th century. As D. Owen Carrigan observed, many were carried out by legitimate companies:

> Businesses across the country resorted to every conceivable trick to increase their profits. In some cases, they devised elaborate schemes to cheat the public or the government. Even gold-mining companies, which literally mined wealth, engaged in stock manipulation, the avoidance of royalty payments, and smuggling. One enterprising company in Nova Scotia, at the turn of the century, worked out a scheme to avoid royalty payments by forging duplicate gold bricks. One would be deposited in the local bank as the official product for royalty purposes and the other would be smuggled out of the country. ... In 1883, price-fixing agreements involving fire insurance companies,

cotton manufacturers, and wholesale grocers were uncovered. The corporate conspiracies against the public interest became so flagrant that the federal government was finally forced to appoint a Select Committee of the House of Commons to examine the situation.

The 1888 report of the committee revealed that price fixing was rampant in a number of industries, including "wholesaler jewelers, biscuit and confectionary manufacturers, coal sellers, oatmeal millers, cordage and barbed wire manufacturers, undertakers, stove manufacturers, and even egg buyers."

Construction around the new transcontinental railway also became a focal point for fraud and corruption. When stock for the Grand Trunk Railway was issued, bankers and contractors held back a large portion, hoping to drive up the price. "The entire venture was characterized by graft, fraudulent bookkeeping, and shoddy construction," Carrigan wrote. "Although the railroad was in debt, accounts were kept to show an operating profit, thus enabling the shareholders to be paid a dividend. The money, of course, was coming from the public purse and being voted on by the very people who stood to collect a large share of the so-called profits." The land boom that coincided with the building of the Canadian Pacific Railway also provoked a flurry of speculation that was ripe for real estate swindles. "Homesteaders were cheated out of their properties or intimidated into selling by crooked lawyers and agents, who then flipped the holdings for much higher prices." Because of the immense sums of public and private money invested into railroad construction, railroad ventures were a magnet for unscrupulous contractors who cheated the federal treasury by artificially inflating their expenses and devious promoters who manipulated stock prices.

Allegations of corruption and fraud tainted the Canadian Pacific Railway even before construction began and even ensnarled the prime minister himself. Opposition politicians and newspapers uncovered evidence that Sir Hugh Allan, a prominent railway baron and shipping magnate, had channelled $350,000 to Canada's first prime minister, John A. Macdonald, and to his Conservative Party right before the 1872 election. In return, Allan's consortium was promised the contract to build the railway. Few believed the prime minister's protestations that the political donations and the awarding of the contract were unrelated, especially when a damning telegraph was published in the press. Six days before the election, Macdonald had wired Allan, telling him, "I must have another $10,000. Will be the last time of calling. Do not fail me. Answer today." Macdonald continued to assert his innocence even after the cable was made public. "These hands are clean," he would say. But his hands weren't clean. MacDonald was censured by a parliamentary commission, his government fell the next month, and his Conservative Party was trounced in the election.

Corporate Canada's dalliance with fraud and corruption reaches all the way back to the very first public corporation formed in this country. Around 1690, directors and majority shareholders with the Hudson's Bay Company were accused of "stock-jobbing," which consisted of paying out inordinately large dividends to shareholders as a way to attract more investors and increase the share price. When the price of the stock reached a certain level, the original shareholders would unload, making a very nice profit for themselves. In his book on Canada's fur trade, Peter C. Newman wrote that in the fourteen years after it received its original charter, the Company paid no dividends. But in 1688, despite a cumulative loss of £118,014 over the preceding six years, "a fat 50 percent payout was distributed to its tight circle of eight dominant shareholders, including the Duke of Marlborough." This payout was "followed by another 25 percent declaration and, in 1690, by the largest bonus in the Company's history: a 74 percent dividend, together with a stock bonus of 200 percent in the form of a convertible dividend scrip. Vague explanations were floated that this would bring the HBC's capitalization more into line with the committeemen's estimates of what the stock was really worth, yet such a forecast of the Company's potential earnings was so far removed from the facts (in the next five years, further losses of £97,500 would be recorded)." Over the next two years, six of eight Hudson's Bay Company officials who voted themselves the bloated dividends had resigned from the company and sold their shares. In addition, the stock was continuously split, which raised the value of the company's capitalization from £10,500 to £31,500. This increased the value of Marlborough's shares by 400 percent. Buoyed by the expectation that they would cash in on another 150 percent dividend, investors snatched up the company's stock. Instead, twenty-eight years of no dividend payments followed as the company fell deeper and deeper into debt.

Of all the commercial crime perpetrated in Canada during the 19th century, perhaps none has been more widespread or better organized than counterfeiting. Based on police and media reports, currency counterfeiting in this country appears to have begun in earnest in the 1850s and for many years following, Canada would be a significant source of U.S. counterfeit cash or "green goods." In 1853, the *New York Times* reported that two investigators working for a Boston association mandated to detect bogus American banknotes were dispatched to Montreal "to purchase of a gang known to exist there, some counterfeit bills, for the purpose, if possible, of obtaining legal proof sufficient to convict the counterfeiters." Unfortunately, the investigators fell into a trap of their own making. While posing as buyers interested in purchasing the phony script, they were able to make contact with the counterfeiting gang and even obtained some fake bills. The head of the counterfeiting group "smelt a rat, however, and by a most shrewd operation, gave such information that one of the officers suddenly found himself incarcerated for having counterfeit money in his possession." After a short imprisonment, the American investigator was able to verify his credentials and was set free.

On August 1, 1854, two groups of counterfeiters were arrested in Sherbrooke, Quebec. There was some speculation that they were part of the same counterfeiting conspiracy, since their operations were located in remote homes only 5 miles from each other. When government authorities searched one of the premises they found a printing press, twenty-six platters for paper money, an 800-pound machine for stamping gold and silver coins, various engravers' tools, twenty-four moulds for running hard-money dies, ink, paper, and thousands of dollars in fake money. The *New York Times* proclaimed, "this is probably the most important arrest of the kind ever made on this continent." American government officials were particularly interested

in this case as most of the fake currency discovered was U.S. script. Two months earlier, $16,000 in counterfeit "ones, threes, and twenties" that had been "executed with singular skill" were discovered in New York State. Large amounts of gold and silver coins were also found. "The band was completely organized and had their engraver, who could make all their plates, and their printers, and their signers of the bills — all of whom are now safely lodged in the Montreal jail."

Court documents showed that four years later, in the county of Middlesex, Ontario, Hirman Biggs Smith was found in the possession of one machine and several moulds "constructed, devised, adapted, and designed for the purpose of counterfeiting and imitating certain foreign silver coins, to wit, the silver coin of the United States of America." On July 9, 1858, Smith was found with "four hundred pieces of forged false and counterfeit coins each piece thereof resembling, and apparently intended to resemble and pass for a piece of foreign silver coin to wit, the silver [dollar] coin of the United States of America. Smith was convicted of counterfeiting offences.

Advances in photography and other technology meant that the quality of counterfeit currency steadily improved over the years. In the spring of 1880, highly convincing counterfeit bills began appearing throughout the country. There were estimates that more than one million dollars in fake American and Canadian currency was being circulated. Among the phony script were copies of an American five-dollar bill of government issue, a one- and five-dollar bill issued by the Bank of Commerce, a five-dollar bill from the Bank of British North America, a four-dollar bill from the Dominion Bank, and a one-dollar bill issued by the Dominion of Canada. According to John Wilson Murray, the famed Canadian detective hired to track down the perpetrators, the counterfeiters were "so bold and so daring" that $200,000 in the bogus currency was used to pay for a large shipment of fur. "Even the banks whose bills were counterfeited accepted the counterfeits over their own counters. They denied that they ever paid any of them out again. The bills were afloat in all sections of the country and there was a great stir."

After fruitless trips to Washington, New York, and Philadelphia, Murray pursued a tip from an informant, and turned his investigation toward one well-regarded British counterfeiter named Edwin Johnson, who was known to have operated in Canada and the United States. "I remembered the tales I had heard of him," Murray wrote. "He was an Englishman by birth, who was an educated man, and had married an educated Englishwoman. He learned the trade of an engraver and the young couple moved to America, and he was supposed to be honest, and worked at his trade until, when the civil war came on, some one made a fortune out of $100, $50, and $20 counterfeit banknotes, and Johnson had been mixed up in it, and later was reported to have returned to England." Currency experts told Murray "the bills were beauties created by a master. They were the best ever seen."

Murray began his search for Johnson by travelling to Chicago to speak with a well-informed ex-counterfeiter he knew. From him, Murray learned that Johnson's last-known whereabouts was Indianapolis. After obtaining a picture of Edwin Johnson and his family, but having no luck in finding him in Indianapolis, Murray took the train back to Canada. When he arrived in Toronto, Murray visited a nearby saloon "to get a welcome-home nip." To his great surprise, at the end of the bar was Edwin's son, Johnnie. "If he had dropped from the clouds I could not have been more astonished, and if he had been the Recording Angel come to write my title clear, I could not have been more delighted. Johnnie was full. He stood alone at one end of the bar drinking." When Johnson left the bar, Murray shadowed him to a comfortable brick house on Hazelton Avenue. For five days, Murray kept the home under surveillance, but "no one passed in or out, except the butcher and the baker and the milkman." After several more days, the front door opened, "and old man Johnson himself, Edwin Johnson, the king of counterfeiters, appeared on the doorstep and walked jauntily down the street." Murray then began to trail Johnson:

He stopped in almost every saloon on his way down town, but he paid for his drinks in genuine money. He got boozy, and finally he went to the railroad-station and bought a ticket for Markham. I sat six seats behind him on the train. We both got off at Markham. He went into a saloon, and bought a drink. When he came out, I went in. There was a young bartender — a saucy, smart aleck; but I had him call the proprietor, and through him I got the $1 bill that Johnson had given in pay for the drink. I paid silver for it, and had the proprietor initial it. I eyed it eagerly when I got it. It was a new Dominion $1 bill. I had my man at last. Johnson went into place after place, buying a drink or cigar, and paying in bad bills. I followed him from place to place, buying the bills as he passed them.

After gathering his evidence, Murray confronted the elder Johnson, who confessed that he was still active in the counterfeiting business. He even agreed to show Murray his equipment. Once back at his studio, Johnson removed a tarp from a large table revealing the plates he used for the forgeries. "Johnson lifted them out as tenderly as a mother could raise her sick babe from a cradle," Murry wrote. "They were wrapped in oiled cloth, and were encased in solid coverings of beeswax." Johnson said the plates cost more than $40,000 to make, a considerable investment that was partially financed by another unnamed "party" in Canada. Murray examined the plates and "saw they were the finest in the land."

I marvelled at the firmness and precision of the strokes, the authority of the signatures, the beauty of the vignettes and medallions, the accuracy of following all the little whimsies of the engravers of the original, genuine plates. For each bill there were three copper plates — one for the front, one for the back, and one for the wedge. Each plate was about one quarter of an inch in thickness. I scored them criss-cross, and locked them up. Not only were the six Canada counterfeits in the lot, but the plates for the counterfeit States $5 bill was there. There were twenty-one separate copper pieces or plates, three each for the Bank of Commerce $10, the Bank of Commerce $5, the Bank of British North America $5, the Ontario Bank $10, the Dominion Bank $4, the Government issue $1, and the United States $5.

Johnson told Murray that he made the plates while living in the U.S. Tales of his counterfeiting operation also revealed a true family business, complete with a division of labour among his children, which included daughters Jessie and Annie — "both clever, accomplished girls" — and his five boys, Tom, Charlie, Johnnie, Elijah, and David Henry. As Murray remembered, "his daughters forged the signatures. They had been trained in forging or duplicating signatures since childhood. They would spend hours a day duplicating a single signature, and would work at the one name for months, writing it countless thousands of times. Jessie was better on larger handwriting, and Annie was better on smaller handwriting." While the daughters specialized in calligraphy, the Johnson boys "were learning to be engravers, and one or two of them were so proficient that the old man spoke of them with pride." Johnson confessed that they printed a large quantity of bills once a year, most of which was turned over to a wholesale dealer who in turn sold it to retail dealers, who then placed the bills with "shovers." After each printing, "the plates were encased in beeswax and oilcloth and buried, and the other paraphernalia was destroyed."

Edwin Johnson was placed on trial at the Fall Assizes in Toronto in 1880 and pleaded guilty to every charge. His son Tom, "the lame one" who operated a tobacco store on King Street in Toronto, was arrested in Erie, Pennsylvania, after police discovered hundreds of dollars' of bogus bills stuffed in his hollowed cane. Johnnie Johnson was arrested in Buffalo, but was able to avoid conviction in the U.S. When he returned to Toronto, he was picked up after trying to pass a counterfeit $10 Bank of Commerce note and received a 10-year jail sentence. Charlie was arrested at Sarnia, Ontario, in possession of counterfeit money and was also sent to jail. After Charlie was released, he went to Detroit, and on August 12, 1898, he and Elijah were arrested. By this time, the old man was dead and the mother and sisters were living in Detroit. David Henry, who was suspected of pushing fake bills for the family, was also living there. Acting on a tip, federal Secret Service agents searched his house and found a hollow place in the baseboard that opened with a secret

spring. Inside, the agents found close to $10,000 in counterfeit American banknotes.

Two other skilled and prolific Canadian counterfeiting groups operating during the same period were also family affairs. In 1878, the superintendent of the Dominion Police was hot on the trail of Rowland and Henry Jackson, a father-and-son duo who worked in the Stratford, Ontario, area producing and distributing counterfeit silver coins in half-dollar and twenty-five-cent pieces. A Department of Justice court brief stated that "on or about February 27, 1878, a local constable attempted to make an arrest but was fired upon and the two escaped. The two then traveled to the village of Williamsville, outside of Kingston County where they again fired upon police and escaped. The duo was ultimately captured and sentenced after another member of the gang, who had been arrested in possession of the counterfeit coins, agreed to become a Crown witness."

In May 1899, banks throughout the country complained to police about a deluge of counterfeit $1 Dominion bills. In February 1900, U.S. Secret Service agents arrested one Anthony Deckers in Maryland after he was found in possession of a plate for "one side of a $5 Molsons bank bill and cuts for other portions," according to the *Manitoba Free Press*. A search of the room he rented in Baltimore unearthed the plates and other equipment used to produce both the Molsons and the Dominion bills. At his home in Hamilton, Ontario, where his wife was arrested, police found more engraved plates. The Deckers' son was also apprehended in Woodstock, Ontario, with counterfeit bills in his possession. The conspiracy was apparently hatched in Montreal, but "when the place became too hot for the conspirators they moved west, or at least some of them did." The father was for years employed at a lithograph company in Montreal "and being a most expert engraver, one of the best in America he drew a princely salary." A year before he was arrested, he left the firm and it was around this time that the imitation $1 Dominion bills began to appear. Police suspected the forgery ring was about to produce "no less than a quarter of a million dollars in fake $5 bank notes" before it was disrupted. For the *Manitoba Free Press*, the arrests concluded one of the "most sensational schemes of the decade."

Canadian counterfeiters did not restrict their fraudulent infringements to currency. In the late 1890s, members of the American Music Publishers' Association blamed "Canadian pirates" for producing "spurious editions of the latest copyrighted popular songs." As the *New York Times* reported in 1897, the association's investigation "revealed that all of the most popular pieces have been counterfeited, despite the fact that they are copyrighted, and by unknown publishers are sold at from 2 cents to 5 cents per copy, though the original compositions sell at from twenty to forty cents per copy." Those behind the music piracy operation took out advertisements in Canadian and American newspapers "which publish lists of music to be sold at, say, 10 cents a copy. The Post Office box given belongs to the newspaper, and it takes half of all the money sent as pay for the advertising, and the other half goes to the 'pirate,' who sends the music by mail." The association estimated that in the month of May 1897 alone, five million pirated copies of sheet music were printed and sold. The result was that "the legitimate music publishing business of the United States has fallen off 50 percent in the past twelve months." Canada was accused of being a hub for music piracy due to weak copyright laws.

THE YELLOW PERIL

By the last quarter of the 19th century, a new form of organized criminality began to rear its head in North America: opium smuggling. While opium's medicinal use as an anaesthetic and all-round elixir was legal and well established among the white population, it wasn't until the arrival of the Chinese immigrant that the recreational smoking of opium was introduced in Canada and the United States. But whether the opium was being ingested by white upper-middle-class housewives or Chinese migrant labourers, it was still legal in both countries. What drove the opium trade underground was new government customs duties. At the same time, lawmakers, social reformers, newspaper publishers, and myriad other xenophobes in North America were trumpeting the arrival of an associated threat to the white, god-fearing population: "John Chinaman."

This new phase in the history of organized crime can be traced to China in the early 1850s, when word began to spread that a wondrous new land was opening up opportunities for anyone willing to work, regardless of race, creed, or colour. Gold was discovered along the Sacramento River in 1848, and thousands of Chinese fortune seekers crossed the Pacific Ocean to join in the quest for instant riches. Once the California gold mines were exhausted, many of the Chinese migrants began to work as labourers along the thousands of miles of railroad track being laid in the American West. Others turned to mining and some became merchants, many of whom set up shop in San Francisco, where the continent's first Chinatown took root.

By the late 1850s, another "gold mountain" was discovered along the west coast, this time in the Fraser River Valley of British Columbia. Chinese prospectors making their way north from California were joined by others immigrating to the province directly from China. All were looking to pan for gold in the Cariboo gold fields during the 1860s or to help construct the Canadian Pacific Railway lines starting in the early 1880s. The 1885 Royal Commission on Chinese Immigration estimated that 15,701 Chinese nationals entered Canada from 1861 to 1884. By the early 1870s, at least a third of all Chinese residents in B.C. were living in Victoria, and the city's growing Chinatown district was a beehive of economic and cultural activity. Dry-goods stores, restaurants, shoemakers, tailors, and launderers were opening on and around Johnson Street while Chinese business, fraternal, and cultural organizations were being formed. Gambling halls, houses of prostitution, and opium dens also became fixtures in Victoria's Chinatown. Forced to return from their low-paying jobs to crowded, dismal, unsanitary rooming houses, many lonely and despondent Chinese bachelors turned to gambling, prostitutes, and opium smoking. Since the Chinese residents could not patronize the white man's "houses of ill-fame," a handful of Chinese merchants in Victoria and Vancouver began to cater to this demand.

"From the days of the gold rush in 1858," Anthony Chan wrote, "gambling had been an important part of Chinatown life. Leisure moments away from the sandbars and, later, the railroads, were spent at games of chance." At first, most of the early professional Chinese gambling operations were transient in nature, catering to the scattered migrant labourers by moving from one work camp to another. As the Chinese population became more sedentary and urban, so did the gambling parlours. After the completion of the Canadian Pacific Railway in 1884, Victoria's "Fantan Alley" — which stretched one city block and was named after the popular Chinese game of chance — boasted around twelve separate gaming establishments. "Most of the gambling dens were small and could accommodate a few dozen gamblers at most," according to Chan, while "some of the larger establishments could hold up to one hundred bettors." As early as 1860, Victoria newspapers began to report on gambling houses catering to the local Chinese population. An editorial in the *Victoria Daily Colonist* on January 10, 1860, entitled "Chinese gambling," lamented a decision by the police magistrate to acquit several Chinese residents of charges stemming from their participation in a game of fantan. In 1861, the *Daily Colonist* ran a story about a police raid on a Chinese gambling house in which dozens of "Chinamen" were "rushing, shouting and tearing about the premises." Despite these media reports,

Harry Con and colleagues assert in their book on the Chinese in Canada that "between 1879 and 1894, only twelve Chinese were ever brought before the court in Victoria for infractions of the gaming laws, ten in 1879 for playing fantan, which was prohibited, and two the following year for possession of an illegal game."

Another service that could be found in Victoria's Chinatown was prostitution, which flourished due to the disproportionate number of Chinese males immigrating to Canada. The 1871 national census counted fifty-three women, less than 1 percent of the total Chinese population of 1,548. The numbers did not change much in subsequent years; in 1902, when the Chinese population in Victoria totalled 3,283 people, the number of women did not exceed one hundred. Chinese entrepreneurs were quick to realize the profits that could be made from satisfying the sexual needs of the lonely Chinese male. The first prostitutes brought to Victoria came via San Francisco, which had become the centre for the international trade in Chinese women. The "yellow slave trade" was escalating so rapidly in North

Chinese gamblers at a CPR work camp, Kamloops, B.C., 1886

America, that procurers scoured the impoverished villages of rural China for families willing to sell their young daughters. The women and girls were either taken to an underground auction block in San Francisco or sold directly to a Chinese merchant or group of merchants in Canada or the United States. They would be herded into show markets hidden in buildings in San Francisco's Chinatown or on the waterfront where they would be stripped and then paraded onto a platform so prospective buyers could inspect them and make a bid. Prices for the women ranged from $500 to $1,000. After more restrictive immigration laws were imposed in the U.S., the price of a Chinese woman rose to as high as $2,500.

As the century drew to a close, the Chinese sex trade was becoming more organized in British Columbia, although no one individual or group gained any sort of monopoly. Testimony before the 1885 Royal Commission on Chinese Immigration estimated there were "150 Chinese women prostitutes" in British Columbia around this time. Most of these, according to one of the commissioners "were living as concubines with their own countrymen, this relationship being deemed among them no offence and no discredit." Women and girls from the provinces of Guangdong, Jiangsi, and Zhejiang were now bypassing San Francisco and arriving in Victoria and Vancouver. Lee Mon-kow, a Chinese interpreter at the Customs house in Victoria, testified to the 1902 Royal Commission on Chinese and Japanese Immigration that a contract would be drawn up between a Chinese woman and a Chinese merchant or brothel operator who agreed to pay the woman's head tax, passage fees, and other expenses. Lee even cited a bill of sale for one woman that cost a merchant $302 plus $7 for clothing and $4 for her leather trunk. In return, he "had the right to her body service." As part of the contract, the woman agreed "to pay a certain sum at a certain time, to repay the passage money and the head tax and seven percent interest." When this amount was paid off through revenue generated by the sexual services provided by the woman, she would be "freed" from her indentured existence.

Once in North America, the young women would be placed in one of two types of Chinese brothels that were distinguished by the colour and class of the clientele. The "parlours" were the more opulent establishments that catered to Chinese merchants and white customers, and the women working there were generally more beautiful and better paid. The "cribs," according to Cassandra Kobayashi's 1978 essay on the history of sexual slavery in Canada, primarily served Chinese labourers and "were back alley operations where up to six women worked in slatted crates about 12'x 14', furnished with a curtain, a pallet, washbasin, a couple of chairs and a mirror. A woman who 'pledged' her body to a crib operation had a life expectancy of six to eight years after she started. After six to eight years of sexual slavery she was debilitated by disease, beatings, and starvation and allowed to 'escape' to die at the Salvation Army, or at a hospital."

In addition to gambling and prostitution, another vice closely associated with the "Chinaman" and Chinatown was opium smoking. The Chinese were central to the transport, sale, manufacture, and consumption of raw and smokable opium in North America and Chinatown was a centre of opium trafficking and smoking dens. Anthony Chan estimates that from the initial days of the gold rush in California and British Columbia, until well after the railways were finished in the 1880s, 40 to 50 percent of Chinese males in North America were addicted to opium. While this may be true, the stereotypical addicted Chinese opium smoker of the day shared company with thousands of Caucasian opiate addicts. During the American civil war, morphine was the main anaesthetic used to treat wounded soldiers and so many became possessed by the drug, that opiate addiction became known as the "soldier's disease." In the latter half of the century, opium was an ingredient in countless prescriptions and over-the-counter remedies for the treatment of a wide range of ailments, including arthritis, asthma, bowel disorders, bronchitis, cholera, colds, consumption, coughs, diarrhea, diabetes, dropsy, dysentery, erysipelas, "female irregularities," fever, fits, flatulence, gout, indigestion, inflammation, insomnia, jaundice, liver ailments, lumbago, malaria, nausea, piles, rheumatism, scrofula (the King's Evil!), tumours, ulcers, venereal disease, worms, as well as pain of any kind. By the end of the century, cocaine was also an active ingredient in many oral anaesthetics and other patent medicinal products, not to mention an original ingredient in a new soft drink, first concocted by a pharmacist in 1886, called Coca-Cola.

Opium was legally imported into Canada from the British colony of Hong Kong and the United States. Because the importation, distribution, and ingestion of opium in Canada were entirely legal during the 19th century, newspapers were filled with advertisements for raw and processed versions of the narcotic. In the early 1860s, the Toronto-based *Globe* newspaper ran an ad for bulk purchases of Turkish opium in 200-pound lots at wholesale prices. In January 1863, ads in the *Victoria Daily Colonist* promoted the impending arrival of cases of "Chinese Produce" in Victoria. G. Vigrolo and Company of Wharf Street imported opium prepared in Fooklong, China. During the 1860s, San Francisco was the primary supplier of smokable opium to B.C. and shipments ranging from small, letter-sized envelopes to large chests arrived on Victoria's and Vancouver's docks almost daily. The last six months of 1860 alone saw a total of 1,110 cases of opium imported into Victoria. Most of this came from San Francisco, although opium shipments direct from Hong Kong were increasing. In 1862 the total value of opium shipped to Canada was $810. In 1863, the value jumped to $6,640 and climbed steadily for years after that.

British Columbia also became a centre for producing the black tar opium that was used for smoking. Between 1870 and 1908, Chinese merchants opened a number of factories in Victoria and B.C.'s Lower Mainland to convert raw gum opium into the smokable form. While much of the processed opium stayed in B.C., some was shipped east to Winnipeg, Toronto, and Montreal and south to Seattle, California, and even Hawaii. While the opium factories were legal entities, they had to apply for a government licence to operate. In a letter dated January 17, 1880, to the federal minister of justice, Goon Gan of Victoria asks for information on how to obtain such a licence. Goon identified himself as an agent for "A Chinese House in Hong Kong" that is "desirous of establishing in this city a manufacturory of opium for smoking purposes, provided an exclusive right in British Columbia can be leagally obtained." By the 1880s, British Columbia was now the main North American importer, producer, and exporter of opium. Between 1881 and 1886, opium factories in Victoria increased from one to thirteen. Between 1882 and 1888, the importation

of crude opium into B.C. for refining purposes grew from 17,000 to 105,000 pounds. An1894 article in the *Manitoba Free Press* estimated there are "600 Chinamen" in British Columbia "engaged in the manufacture of opium, and 160,000 pounds of crude opium comes into the province every year." While opium production was a competitive business, a few Chinese merchants began to control the industry in B.C. By 1901, three Victoria firms with eighteen partners had established a virtual control over the manufacture of opium in the province.

The Chinese were also the first to open commercial opium dens in Canadian cities. Like taverns and saloons, they were legal, accessible to adult males, and stocked with an assortment of brands and smoking paraphernalia. The opium dens were the principal clients of the opium factories, although Caucasian-operated pharmacies were quickly becoming lucrative customers as many were now selling smokable opium to white and Chinese smokers alike. The colonial, provincial, and Dominion governments also benefited from the early opium trade in Canada. They received licensing fees from manufacturers and taxes were imposed on the retail sale of opium, although the real government money was made from tariffs imposed on opium imports. In February 1865, a 50 percent tariff on opium imported into the colony of B.C. was imposed, far exceeding the usual 12.5 percent applied to most other imports. The substantial tariff prompted the widespread smuggling of opium into Canada, helping the legal substance take its first baby steps into the nether region of the criminal underworld.

Less than a few months after the tariffs were imposed, colonial customs officials in B.C. began making seizures of contraband opium, most of which was being smuggled aboard steamer ships from Hong Kong or San Francisco. Captain Wylde, the customs officer in Victoria, made the first seizure under the new tariff laws on April 24, 1865. "Observing a Chinaman who came up by the *Enterprise* making some rather suspicious movements," the *British Columbian* reported the next day, "Mr. Wylde seized his carpet-sack, in which was found about 23 lbs of opium. A derringer was also found in his possession. 'John' was marched off to jail and his goods taken charge of by the revenue officer." Numerous other seizures would soon follow, including 18 pounds of opium discovered just days later. Because the offences were simply infractions against British customs laws, the penalties were usually small fines. The seized contraband would later be sold at government auctions. While some criticized the tariff as an unnecessary provocation of smuggling, others, such as the racist *British Columbian* newspaper, called for stringent enforcement, especially against Chinese immigrants, "as there can be little doubt that many of them will attempt to bring in a supply of their favourite narcotic about their persons. Indeed it would seem almost necessary that every Chinamen should be thoroughly searched on arriving in the colony, as we understand they have already had recourse to the artifice of secreting opium beneath the lining of their jackets." Enhanced enforcement will, no doubt, "teach these rascals a salutary lesson."

British Columbia's role as a manufacturer and exporter of processed opium increased substantially in 1890 when the United States Congress imposed its own prohibitive tariffs on opium and morphine imports. The result was that even larger amounts of raw opium were being brought into Canada (legally and covertly), processed through B.C.-based opium factories, and then smuggled into the United States to avoid the tariffs. Following the enactment of the American tariffs, opium was imported from India or China, processed into smokable form in Hong Kong, British Columbia or Mexico, and then smuggled into the United States.

Newspapers were now brimming with stories that chronicled cases of opium smuggling from B.C. into the U.S. The *Globe* reported one such case in its November 17, 1886 edition:

> Advices from British Columbia state that the United States Customs officials are finding it almost impossible to put down opium smuggling from Victoria to Portland, Or. Capt. Gardner, of the United States Customs, has been investigating the several methods employed to defraud the revenue in opium smuggling with good results. At his instigation a Chinese interpreter named Huestis has been arrested, and the authorities have discovered several of his pals, whose arrest will shortly

follow. This gang would send demijohns having false bottoms fitted with opium from Victoria to Seattle, and from there to Portland filled up with spirits over the opium. This little game has been going on for some time right under the nose of the revenue officers. The large number of demijohns going through empty to Seattle when they were filled with spirits and shipped attracted the attention of the officers which led to the discovery of the game that was being carried out.

In another case that occurred in the early 1890s, an unnamed ship jettisoned watertight barrels packed with opium into the Columbia River where a waiting fishing boat retrieved them in its nets. Raw opium would be smuggled into Victoria in this fashion and the same technique would be used to transport the processed opium into American ports. Dominion customs officials quoted in the media believed one captured vessel "has for some time been engaged in smuggling opium from Victoria, where, it is said, there is a large establishment devoted to the preparation of the drug for the American market."

An 1888 edition of the *Globe* reported that "representatives from British Columbia say the smuggling of contraband opium between that Province and the United States has grown to an enormous extent." The paper estimated that one of Victoria's thirteen opium factories would be more than sufficient to supply local demand. As such, it was clear that the "surplus is shipped to the United States." While opium continued to enter Canada primarily through B.C. ports, it was being smuggled into the U.S. at numerous spots across the border stretching as far as east as Quebec. On February 8, 1888, federal officials in the U.S. captured $25,000 worth of opium at Redwood in upstate New York. According to a *New York Times* article, the opium was brought from China via Vancouver and transported by train to Brockville, Ontario. It was then transferred across the St. Lawrence River "by ferries in summer and sleighs in winter which were met by wagons or sleighs on the American side and then shipped to New York as butter, eggs, etc." In 1891, 141 pounds of opium was confiscated in Swift Current, Saskatchewan, and a saloon in Sweet Grass, Montana, was shut down when the Mounties told their American counterparts that it was a transfer point for opium entering the United States. In an 1895 dispatch from Montana, American customs officials there alleged that "large quantities of opium" are smuggled from the Manitoba side of the border "in the stomachs of live cattle, and that a great many of cattle are also smuggled." In his 1898 book on New York's Chinatown, Louis Beck argued that opium is "smuggled into the United States by French women, who are employed for the purpose by the Chinese. The manufacturer in Victoria, B.C., makes a shipment to Montreal and then the women take the stuff and carry it over the border to some city or town, such as Burlington, where they leave it" until sufficient quantities were amassed to ship to New York City.

While the Chinese usually got most of the press when it came to opium smuggling, it wasn't long before Anglo-Saxon names connected with the trade began appearing in the newspapers. One of these was Donald McLean (a.k.a. "Little Dan" a.k.a "Opium Dan") who smuggled and sold opium while working on a passenger steamer ship. In December of 1888, James Carran was charged with smuggling opium from Canada into the United States and later confessed to shipping more than 4,000 pounds to Denver. Canadian Harry H. Hutchinson was arrested in Chicago in 1891 on a charge of smuggling opium after federal officers found 110 half-pound packages of the drug in the bottom of his steamer trunk. One of the most "notorious opium smugglers in the country," proclaimed the *Manitoba Free Press* in 1894, was arrested in Detroit by U.S. officials. Charles Kennedy was described as being "engaged in the business of smuggling opium across the border for nearly ten years and during that time has managed to elude the vigilance of the brightest men in the secret service." Along with partners, George Henderson and Edward Patterson, the arrests broke up "one of the boldest bands of opium smugglers in the country. They are believed to be three of the cleverest smugglers that operated between the Canadian frontier and the American border." Law enforcement authorities in Detroit learned that the three were arranging to transport a "heavy consignment to this city and would, in all probability, be sent to the Chinese supply depot in North Division

street." As a result of this information, according to the *Manitoba Free Press*:

> Two deputies stationed themselves outside the store and awaited the arrival of the smugglers. They waited until midnight, when they saw three white men enter the yard on the side of the store and drop several suspicious looking packages down into the cellar. The deputies swooped down on the smugglers at about 1 o'clock and took them to the station house. Over 400 pounds of opium was found on the premises. All of it was wrapped in newspapers printed in Vancouver, BC. The opium was estimated to be worth $4,000. The duty on it would be $12 a pound. The Chinamen who run the place are named Wing, Wong and Lee. It is believed the three prisoners have been in the employ of the Chinamen for over a year.

In 1894, Frank L. Gilchrest of Toronto was arrested in Detroit and charged with smuggling opium. When captured on his way to Chicago, he had in his possession 116 pounds of the drug. Canadians George Green and Stephen Wright were arrested the same year at St. Clair, Michigan, after smuggling 250 pounds of the contraband across the border.

HANDSOME PROFITS FOR THEIR OWNERS

Along with opium, Chinese nationals were also being smuggled into the United States from Canada, due in part to ever-tightening restrictions on Asian immigration to that country. This earliest form of human smuggling into North America was coordinated primarily by whites, many of whom were long-time smugglers using well-worn, covert routes between the two countries. One of these professional smugglers was Gus Brede, who began running whiskey from Montana's Fort Benton to the Peigan and Blood bands in Southern Alberta around 1880. In his book, *Sheriffs and Outlaws of Western Canada*, Frank Anderson wrote that Brede, "ran his excursions like a battle tactician" and spurned the idea of "dead heading" (returning from Canada with an empty wagon). So after he delivered his cargo in Alberta, he would smuggle Chinese nationals into the U.S. for $50 a head. "Within a few years he had established an underground railway for Orientals seeking to enter the promised land." The end came for Gus Brede with a shocking abruptness. On an August night in 1891, during a violent storm, Gus was steering one of his wagons, when out of the turbulent skies a bolt of lightning struck him on the head. He died instantly, although, miraculously, neither of the Chinese passengers sitting on either side of him were injured.

In 1884, law enforcement authorities in B.C. captured fourteen fishing ships engaged in human smuggling, each one realizing "handsome profits for their owners," as the *New York Times* put it. "As high as $80 per head for women and $80 for Chinese men are now paid to Captains of boats for running them across the boundary line." Over an eight-week period, more than "1,000 Chinamen have crossed over voluntarily. British Columbians who are protesting against Chinese immigration are facilitating their getting out of the country into the United States as much as possible." With more than a hint of exaggeration, the *Times* reported, "advices received from British Columbia state that unless some immediate steps are taken to prevent the smuggling of Chinamen into the United States from the Province before Spring, nearly the whole Chinese population of British Columbia will be transferred over to Oregon and Washington Territory." Another *New York Times* article from 1896 described one Canadian-based illegal immigration ring that was orchestrated by a "half dozen white men who are regularly engaged in the smuggling business."

> In engaging to smuggle Chinamen a guarantee is usually given and required, to the effect that the smuggled person will be taken to some safe place in the United States, but in this case it seems they were intrusted to a man who has already lost a great deal of the confidence of the Chinese merchants by leaving his charges to their own devices in exposed places. ... This regular system of smuggling is at present considered a little out of date and antiquated, and consequently the old method of using false merchants' certificates is largely being resorted to, and, in addition, a system of "fathers" is used with such success that as a fact from

twenty to thirty Chinese are allowed to get across by this means every week.

In March of 1890, the *Manitoba Free Press* reported that at Port Huron in Michigan, an investigator with the U.S. Treasury Department stopped a laundry wagon with "four 'raw' or smuggled Chinamen." Each man had cards with directions on where they were to go upon arrival in the U.S. "They also had a complete opium outfit." On one of the arrested "was found papers showing plainly he is an agent of a gang of smugglers who make a business of running Chinamen across the Canadian border." Federal agents found twenty-six letters addressed to co-conspirators located in Hong Kong, Victoria, Ottawa, Toronto, Hamilton, London, Sarnia, and numerous American cities. Information obtained revealed that $20 a head was charged for the trip across the border. The gang engaged in this "Chinese importation" was allegedly connected with or part of an opium smuggling gang.

In 1891, police traced a smuggling ring that used the Grand Trunk Railway to illegally transport Chinese citizens from "a junk shop in Toronto." With the final destination being New York City, "the Mongolians enter Canada via Vancouver and go to Toronto, where they are ticketed over the Grand Trunk and Erie to New York. Sleeping car berths are bought, and the Chinamen are asleep in their berths when they pass Suspension Bridge" which spans Ontario and New York State. "The special inspectors do not go through the sleepers, and thus they escape detection." American soldiers with the Eleventh Infantry at Fort Niagara were even accused of ferrying the "Celestials from Niagara-on-the-lake." They are picked up on the Canadian side at the mouth of the Niagara River, just across from the fort, and are paid as much as "$50 apiece for safely landing the Chinamen on this side."

Human smuggling became increasingly organized as the numbers of Chinese aliens illegally spirited into the U.S. grew. In June 1893, customs officials in Portland, Oregon, congratulated themselves after defeating what one newspaper called "the greatest attempt at wholesale smuggling ever made on the Pacific coast." Thirty-two Chinese men had been brought to Seattle "on a smuggling vessel from British Columbia." There, they were transferred to "a Northern Pacific box car, which was supposed to have contained merchandise for Portland, Ore." After receiving a tip, customs officials broke open the car and discovered the illegal human cargo. Customs officials were also investigating cases where Chinese illegals entered Canada using fraudulent immigration certificates. In one case, government officials traced forged American citizenship certificates to Montreal, although according to the *New York Times* the "heads of the conspiracy still remain in Boston." The documents certified that the signatory was a merchant who lives in the United States. The certificate was signed and sealed by the U.S. Immigration Commissioner, but upon close inspection it became clear that this signature was forged. The bogus certificates were sold for prices ranging from $25 to $100. Evidence surfaced that members of the smuggling group were trying to have a stamp produced in Montreal "which would imitate a United States Commissioner's seal, but that they were unsuccessful, and that dies for such a seal were finally sent from Boston here, where they were fitted to a stamp."

PART II

GENESIS

1908–1933

CHAPTER THREE

THE BLACK HAND OF DEATH

Extortion and Violence in Canada's Early Italian Communities

When discussing Italian organized crime in North America, most people think of the so-called Sicilian Mafia. However, there is also the 'Ndrangheta, which was founded in the southern Italian province of Calabria. In fact, the 'Ndrangheta had the greatest influence on ethnic Italian crime groups in Canada because, since the turn of the century, most of the founders, leaders, and members of these groups were Calabrian by birth or heritage.

The word "mafia" is generally used to refer to a secret, ritualistic criminal organization that began in Italy and was replicated in America, Canada, and other parts of the world. Yet, as Henner Hess notes, the word describes a phenomenon far more complex "than the headlines about a vaunted, secret criminal association suggest." It refers to a philosophy, a behaviour, and, indeed, a way of life that emerged from historically rooted subcultures in Sicily and Calabria. As a philosophy it is meant to dictate how powerful men are to conduct themselves and the role they are to play in society, or at least in their own sub-terrain of society. For criminologist James Inciardi, the word "mafia" is Sicilian-Arabic in its origins and is derived from terms meaning "to protect and to act as guardian; a friend or companion; to defend and preserve; power,

integrity, strength." Various definitions of the word that began surfacing in 19th-century Italy included superlatives that reflected the traditional ideals of manhood and manliness: power, superiority, bravery, boldness, self-confidence, revenge, respect, honour, and vainglory. Embodying these common ideals was the mafioso who is known and admired for his ability to protect and provide essential services to his kin, his friends and his associates because he is a "man of honour." Becoming a man of honour is all based on *rispetto* (respect). Every mafioso demands respect; it is the core of his power and his very being. Respect and honour for the mafioso are garnered by winning a reputation for toughness, courage, the ability to get things done, a defiance of government authority, and the use of violence against his enemies or those of his friends and associates.

As Peter Edwards and Antonio Nicaso observe, "central to a study of the mafia is its twisted concept of honour." As a man of honour, the mafioso "cannot stand the slightest offence and reacts violently when a *sgarro* (insult) is done to him. A man of honour knows he is capable of exercising violence in such a way that he frightens others into giving him deferential treatment." In other words, it does not matter to the mafioso how he obtains honour or respect; they could be forcibly extracted through threats, intimidation, extortion, revenge, or violence. Intimidation and violence, in fact, serve a number of purposes for the mafioso: to protect his kin and territory, to sustain his criminal activities, to ensure secrecy and obedience, and as a means to gain and reinforce respect, honour, and power. "The instant a mafioso cannot protect those around him with violence, his respect evaporates and he becomes a target himself. Murder is considered an honourable means of gaining and guarding power, respect and territory." In this regard, habitual criminals like the mafioso "feel the need to call themselves 'Men of Honour,' much the way those with the worst body odour in Elizabethan times often wore the most perfume."

A man also gains honour and respect by being able to keep a secret. "An *uomo di panza* is literally a man of guts, someone who can keep his secrets deep in his body," according to Edwards and Nicaso. Exemplifying this credo is the code of *omerta*, a sacrosanct canon of the mafioso that transcends secrecy; it is a term that embodies the virtues of manliness, honour and respect, self-control in the face of adversity, and non-co-operation with the government. By remaining silent, especially in the face of government interdiction, one's prestige and honour rise immeasurably. In short, "the Mafia has codes, a structure and, of equal importance, a spirit that distinguishes it from common organized crime." Power, violence, and *omerta* are intertwined and mutually reinforcing as the foundation for traditional mafia groups. "Power is seized with violence and maintained through silence."

As a powerful man, the mafioso commands a network of relationships or *partito* and, as the centre of this network, he views himself as a *padrone* (patron) to his "clients." In this role he is a provider of services, especially for those who can't or won't turn to the government — from the peasantry in Sicily or Calabria where a government presence was sparse, to the Italian immigrant unfamiliar with or suspicious of the government in a new land, all the way to the thief or murderer, who cannot go to the government for help. For Howard Abadinsky, the mafioso is "a provider of protection broadly defined. For legitimate entrepreneurs, he provides insurance against otherwise untrustworthy suppliers and/or customers and will limit competition by restricting market entry. He acts as a guarantor so that persons who do not trust one another can transact business with a significant degree of confidence; this refers to legitimate entrepreneurs and, most particularly, the illegitimate, who cannot turn to the police or courts to remedy their grievances." A related role performed by the mafioso is that of an intermediary, whether it is a commercial agent who brings legitimate businessmen or criminals together to make a deal, a political power broker who helps friends get elected to public office, or a mediator who arbitrates a conflict between two parties. To this extent, the terms "mafia" and "'ndrangheta" denote an unofficial, unrecognized, and even secret system of government headed by unelected yet influential men who seek to control a particular community. And like the government, the mafioso charges a fee for his services or expects a cut from any profitable transaction he brokers or is carried out in his jurisdiction.

As an organization, the Sicilian Mafia appears to have begun as an underground sect that emerged to fight foreign invaders and rulers. The most common explanation of the origins of the mafia — as both a moniker and a secret society — is traced to 1282 when the French invaded Sicily. To defend their island, Sicilians rallied under the anti-French battle cry *Morte alla Francia Italia anela!* (M.A.F.I.A.). Italian folklore also holds that the term was applied by the Sicilian resistance movement after hearing a mother scream out, *Ma fia, ma fia!* (My daughter, my daughter!), upon discovering she was being raped by a French soldier. Regardless of its exact origin, the mafia became a nationalistic symbol to the repressed and conquered Sicilian people. Resistance fighters were made to swear an oath under the penalty of death that they would never reveal their underground movement to outsiders and the official ruling elite, which helped lay the foundation for the sacred code of *omerta*.

As the influence of foreign forces waned in Sicily, the mafia was gradually transformed from a clandestine resistance force to a powerful political, economic, and criminal institution on the island. The abolishment of feudalism in rural Sicily during the early 19th century contributed to the emergence of the mafioso by giving rise to a new profession, the *gabellotti*, who managed rural estates for landowners. In this capacity, the *gabellotti* played the role of the *padrone* to the local peasantry, subletting farmland to them, controlling local resources, mediating disputes, and protecting them from the ruling gentry or bandits. The *gabellotti* ruled over his estate with brute force, backed up by the *compagnie d'armi*, family members or friends who were recruited because they were men of respect, meaning that they were tough, quick to use violence, and feared. By the end of the 19th century, these local *gabellotti* had become the ruling class in rural Sicily.

The origins of the social grouping that would serve as a basis for the mafia as a criminal organization emerged alongside the mafioso's rise to power. Most of the early mafia clans were formed around kinship because it was only blood relatives — *sangu de me sangu* ("blood of my blood") — where true loyalty could be found. When an exclusive reliance on kinship proved to be too restrictive, the *famiglia* began to be augmented through the custom of *comparatico* or *comparragio* ("god parenthood"), in which outsiders became members to help increase the clan's strength and power. Over time, standardized rituals were adopted to induct new members into the family, and all inductees had to swear allegiance to their *famiglia* and pledge their commitment to the principle of *omerta*. At the same time, the heads of each family (*capo di famiglia*) began networking with one another and, in some parts of Sicily, came together to form a *cosca*, a small, localized clique whereby member-families supported one another to pursue mutual objectives, divide up territories, and arbitrate disputes amongst themselves. The *cosca* was devoid of any rigid organization and was simply referred to as *amici degli amici* ("friends of friends"), the members of which were known as *aregli uomini qualificati* ("qualified men" or "men of honour"). A *zio* ("uncle") or *capo* ("head") was recognized as the leader of these informal, secretive networks and whoever rose to this esteemed position truly personified the attributes of the mafioso. Another level of organization was the *consorteria*, an alliance made up of two or more *coscas*. One *cosca* was recognized as supreme within the *consorteria* and its head was anointed as the *Capo di tutti Capi* ("the boss of bosses"). An informal network of local *coscas* emerged in various parts of Sicily, which

helped the mafiosi consolidate their power on the island (although no unified, monolithic mafia group ever became of this loosely aligned confederation). These evolving subcultures were known by various names throughout Sicily, but ironically, never by the term "mafia." In Monreale, it was referred to as the *Stuppaghieri*; in Bagheria, it was called the *Fratuzzi*, while in other towns it was known as *Cudi Chiatti* ("Flat Tails"), the *Mano Fraterna* ("the Brotherly Hand"), and the *Birritti* ("the Caps").

By the end of the 19th century, mafia dons were all-powerful in Sicily; they held sway over a large portion of the rural population, had influence over local government, and controlled a number of vital industries on the island. The mafioso was also being transformed from a protector of the Sicilian people to their subjugator, extorting money from the peasantry and merchants under the pretence of tribute or a "protection fee." These mafia groups were now incorporating criminal activities into their traditional role, which contributed to the forging of a complex and paradoxical social, political, economic, and criminal force in Sicily. As Peter Robb noted in his 1996 book, *Midnight in Sicily*, "The mafia was outlawed, but tolerated, secret, but recognizable, criminal but upholding of order. It protected and ripped off the owners of the great estates, protected and ripped off the sharecroppers who worked the estates, and ripped off the peasants who slaved on them."

In addition to the Sicilian Mafia, a subculture with similar structures, rituals, and norms was forming and evolving into violent criminal fraternities in Calabria. According to the FBI, the 'Ndrangheta originated in the 1860s, formed by Sicilians who were banished by the Italian government from their native island, an explanation that suggests the Calabrian Mafia grew out from the rib of the Sicilian Mafia. Lee Lamothe and Antonio Nicaso believe the origins of the 'Ndrangheta were indigenous to Calabria; it began as a defence mechanism for impoverished rural peasants against their aristocratic landlords. Regardless of its origins, as in Sicily, weak local governing institutions and the remoteness of Calabria from Rome helped pave the way for the emergence of power-hungry men bent on unofficially controlling all facets of local life, while financially whetting their beaks. For Lamothe and

Nicaso, "Some leaders were beneficent; others were tyrannical. But all were violent, having to first prove their manliness through homicide, preferably in public, and preferably being acquitted of the ensuing charges." Like "mafia," the term "'ndrangheta" — which was derived from the Greek word *andragathía*, meaning heroism, cunning, virtue, and manliness — is embedded with deeper meanings as to how powerful men should conduct themselves.

Traditional 'Ndrangheta groups are also based on family relationships, either through blood, marriage, or the custom of *comparatico*. All members must go through an initiation ceremony, which consists of a series of vague questions and answers, obscure symbolic gestures, the invocation of mythical knights, and references to violence and the supremacy of the 'Ndrangheta clan to which the inductee is expected to make a lifelong commitment. In 1985, police video cameras captured an undercover RCMP officer as he was inducted into a 'Ndrangheta cell during a ceremony held in a Greater Toronto apartment. After gathering the inductee and six "made" members into a circle, the leader of the cell welcomed the new member into "the Honoured Society of Calabria" and "the Family." The ceremony was described by long-time RCMP officer and organized crime expert Reginald King:

> An 'Ndrangheta group voted three times to accept the initiate into the organization. "I swear on the tip of this knife to forget father, mother, all the family, at whatever call, to answer to 'Corp of the Society', " the inductee was instructed to repeat. "There is a dark tomb wide and deep under the depth of the sea. Whoever uncovers it shall die with four knifings to the breast," the vow continued. Later, the leader explained some of the rules, the "codes of the court," as he called them. Cooperation, communication, dividing of profits, and punishment are crucial elements. "If we make a penny, a penny ... is what is divided amongst us. If (one of us) is in trouble, we are all in trouble. These are not things that are discussed with anyone," the leader said. "You are older than my brother, but because he entered (the

Society) before you ... you have to respect him. I will tell you something. When one does a swearing in, they have to do a swearing in that will last. It is not a swearing in that you can say you want to leave ... If he does (a profitable activity) and I don't know but if I find out, if he does something light, small, there are other methods in which he can pay. And you don't pay with words ... You know how it is paid? With death, that's how it is paid." And finally, catchall words of wisdom: "If you are respectful, you are respected by all. When one has respect, the other things will come." The leader did not speak of punishment without pointing out benefits, including the connections that came with being a made member.

Variously referred to as "the Honoured Society," "the Calabrian Mafia," *Fibbia*, or *N'drina*, signs of this secret society began to emerge in Calabria by the end of the 19th century. In 1888, the prefect of the city of Reggio, Calabria, received an anonymous letter alerting him to the existence of "a sect that fears nothing." Four years later, more than 250 men from several villages throughout Calabria and southern Italy were investigated for mafia-like activities.

The period in which the Calabrian and Sicilian mafiosi were consolidating their power in Italy coincided with the great Italian diaspora to North America. Beginning in the early 1870s, successive waves of Italian immigrants, most from the southern parts of the country, began arriving on the shores of the United States and Canada. By the end of the century, stories about the existence of secret societies, extortion activities, and vendetta-based violence began to emerge from the expatriate Italian communities. Secret societies were being formed by Italian immigrants who had already been inducted as members of the 'Ndrangheta or mafia clan in their native country. Other aspiring mafiosi in North America had no such past, but were endeavouring to create their own nascent organizations. Still others did not bother with such formalities, and simply bastardized the traditional "protection" services of the mafia or 'Ndrangheta by carrying out rudimentary extortion rackets that preyed upon their fellow Italian immigrants.

While the traditions and norms of these secret Italian societies were carried over from the old country, there is little evidence to suggest that entire criminal groups were transported from Italy to North America. Instead, the humble beginnings of Italian organized crime in the U.S. and Canada were the result of a potent mix of customs and traditions associated with the 'Ndrangheta and mafia, men who aspired to positions of power, respect, and honour, and the acculturation of Italian immigrants in an urban environment characterized by poverty, discrimination, marginalization, lawlessness, ambition, and corruption.

THE SOCIETY

The earliest versions of secret Italian societies in Canada were loosely structured groups, influenced by the Sicilian Mafia and the Calabrian 'Ndrangheta. "The Society," as they were simply called within the Italian communities, were "much whispered about" before they came to the attention of the media or law enforcement, Lee Lamothe and Antonio Nicaso wrote, although "even then it was made out to be more sinister than it actually was." Some of these societies followed the original philosophical credo of the mafioso and provided a range of services to Italian immigrants, such as helping to bring over family members, locating accommodations, finding jobs, providing money, and fostering social relationships. This was all conducted within the context of the traditional *partito*, where the *padrone* served as an intermediary, a broker, and a provider of services to his Italian clients in the new country. Most of these societies required regular donations from those who joined up. This money was then used to help society members who were in trouble with the law or who could not support their families. Many of the *padrones* who founded these societies, however, regularly abused their positions of power and trust and devolved into criminal piranhas who used the payment of society dues as an excuse to forcibly extract money from Italian immigrants.

Events leading to the first public discovery of a "Society" in Canada began on December 7, 1908. It was on this day that Louis Belluz, a baker in Fort Francis, Ontario, received a letter written in red ink. The letter demanded $100 and, according to a police summery of a statement made by Belluz, if payment was not forthcoming, "his buildings were to be burned and himself burned to death." After Belluz reported the extortion attempt, police traced the letter to Nicholas Bessanti and Joe Ross. Bessanti told police that he wrote the letter on behalf of a secret society he was forced to join in Fort Francis. He estimated total membership in this group at fifteen or sixteen people. His fee to join was $25, but Bessanti disclosed that he only paid $10. He spoke of an initiation ceremony where a closed circle of men crouched over a large stiletto knife and chanted oaths that consisted of arcane Italian poetry and at the end they hugged and kissed one another. "In joining the Society," Bessanti told police, "we took a solemn oath that we would obey our leader's orders: would rob, burn or kill as he directed; that we would protect one another from the hands of the law; to disobey these orders we would expect to be punished by death or otherwise as decide upon by the Society." Bessanti explained that the group "met every Saturday night in the west end of freight shed and there they decided what to do to raise money."

Bessanti also informed police that he attended a meeting where it was decided "the Baker Louis Belluz must pay over some money to them. Carmine Domic was chosen to write the letter and I was chosen to carry it to Belluz. It was also decide that an older member of the Society was to go along with me to see that I delivered the letter as instructed. Domic was instructed to write in the letter that if he, the Baker, did not put up at least $50, they would burn his house up and him in it." Bessanti was warned by leaders of the society that he would suffer the same fate as the baker if the letter was not delivered. Among those present in the freight shed while he wrote the letter was Frank Dusanti, Francesco Tino, Frank Muro, Salvador Tino, and Carmine Domic. The letter Bessanti wrote was dictated to him by the society's founder, Francesco Tino. Little is known about Tino, except that after arriving in Canada from Italy around 1907, he spent a few months in Montreal and then turned up in the Ontario town of Sault Ste. Marie. Shortly thereafter, he went to Fort William, where he reportedly killed an Italian migrant worker. From there, he fled to Fort Francis. By the time police had begun to close in on Tino, he and Frank Muro, who helped organize the Fort Francis society, had crossed the border into the United States. After warrants were issued by Canadian authorities, American police arrested the two men in the town of Hibbing, located in northern Minnesota. Tino and Muro were brought back to Canada and following a trial were convicted along with Bessanti of theft and other charges. Tino received the harshest sentence of five years.

THE BLACK HAND

Despite the existence of ritualistic Italian secret societies in North America, the most prevalent and fearsome type of criminal conspiracy operating within the early Italian expatriate communities was not carried out by cohesive organizations. The "Black Hand" was a label applied to a common form of extortion perpetrated against Italian immigrants in Canada and the United States that predominated during the first quarter of the 20th century. While these extortion schemes were no doubt influenced by the 'Ndrangheta and the Sicilian Mafia, most Black Handers eschewed a formal organizational structure, codes of conduct, or ceremonial rituals.

A Black Hand extortion attempt invariably began with a letter addressed to an intended victim. According to Jay Robert Nash, these extortion schemes were not just prosaic, but highly intimidating and potentially lethal:

> An anonymous Black Hander would threaten various types of violence to extort money from one, usually well-to-do, victim. These threats most often involved kidnapping a family member, threatening to blow up a business or shop, or to attack, injure, or kill a family member or the recipient of the Black Hand note. These notes were crudely written in broken English … and boldly demanded a certain amount of money, with specific instructions as to how the cash was to be delivered. The note would usually be decorated with a number of horrific symbols and images — daggers dripping blood, a bomb exploding, a gun smoking at the barrel, a skull and crossbones, a body dangling from a rope tied about the neck. The signature of the sender was invariably a hand imprinted in heavy black ink, thus the sobriquet, *La Mano Nera* (The Black Hand).

In 1903, New York City newspapers began reporting on the activities of Ignazio Saietta, nicknamed Lupo ("Wolf"). Saietta arrived in New York from his native Sicily in 1899 and, over the next few years, he used intimidation and violence to extort money from Italians living in Harlem's Little Italy. Either on his own, or as an enforcer for other Black Handers, he was reputed to have killed at least thirty people. According to Nash, "He simply strangled them in their homes, dragged their corpses outside to his waiting cart, and drove to a livery stable he owned. He then hacked up the bodies, burned parts of them, and buried what would not burn in his backyard." Saietta later allied himself with the Morello crime family, one of the earliest Sicilian criminal organizations in New York City. In tandem with Saietta, the Morellos were the leading suspects in the "barrel murders," a name used by the media to describe victims of the Saietta-Morello union who were stuffed inside a barrel after being beaten, strangled, stabbed, or shot to death. Saietta also branched out into currency counterfeiting

New York City Black Hander, Ignazio Saietta

along with Don Vito Cascio Ferro, a Sicilian mafioso who immigrated to the United States in 1901 and who was also a leading Black Hander in New York. Saietta's reign of terror continued until 1909, at which point he was arrested and imprisoned along with Ferro and a dozen others for counterfeiting offences.

One of the first reports of the Black Hand in Canada came out of Montreal in 1904. That year, Antonio Cordasco, a high-profile Italian immigrant who became known as *Re de la lavoratori* ("King of the Workers") while serving as the Canadian Pacific Railway's chief recruiter of Italian labour, received a menacing letter demanding money. According to Peter Edwards and Michel Auger, the letter included a "drawing of a black hand, pointing to the letters M and A" as well as a "crude sketch of a coffin, two skulls-and-crossbones, and what appeared to be a snake under the hot sun." Little is known about what transpired following receipt of this letter, but at the time, Cordasco himself was embroiled in controversy, having been accused of capitalizing on the stranglehold he had over Italian workers by defrauding them at every step of their journey from the Italian countryside to Canadian work camps. As labour historian Gunther Peck described:

> In addition to exacting between five and seven dollars for each Atlantic crossing, Cordasco charged each compatriot three dollars to get a job and another two dollars to get to the work site. Once on the job, Italian workers continued paying Cordasco tribute by purchasing their food from his traveling commissary service. Charges for all supplies consumed by these mobile men were immediately deducted from their wages and paid to Cordasco at the end of the work season. The more his compatriots traveled along Canadian Pacific Railway lines, the more goods they consumed, and the more Cordasco profited.

A July 23, 1904, letter from a fired CPR employee to a judge presiding over an inquiry into Cordasco's labour practices also accused him of bribing company officials to ensure that only Italians received jobs on the railway and that the Italian labourers would receive free passage to labour camps on CPR trains. "There

was an unwritten law in the CPR Labor Bureau at Winnipeg that no white men need apply, as it was easier and safer to extort fees from those who could speak no English." Many of the labourers who paid Cordasco did not obtain employment, and when they demanded their money back, some claimed they were threatened with violence. In this respect, Cordasco, like other Society men, turned a paternalistic *padrone* relationship into a corrupt method of extortion that victimized destitute and trusting Italian immigrants. Cordasco would later be implicated in a conspiracy to smuggle Italian nationals into the United States from Canada in partnership with the Fort Francis extortionist Francesco Tino and Vito Adamo, a Black Hander, bootlegger, and mob boss from Detroit.

In Toronto, rumours began circulating in 1904 that a Black Hand organizer was in town, although this story actually begins in New York City. In the summer of that year, Salvatore Bossito, an eighteen-year-old music student who worked in his father's restaurant on Park Avenue in Manhattan, went to the police to report a conversation he had overhead among twelve Sicilian men who were living in apartments above the restaurant. He said that the men had planned to cheat a number of Italian miners travelling through New York using a crooked game of chance. Acting upon the complaint, police arrested the plotters. The men found out it was Salvatore who had gone to police and when they were released from custody they began hatching a plot to kill him as revenge. On August 23, Salvatore's father, Francisco, allegedly found scrawled on the door of his restaurant a cabalistic Sicilian symbol that was said to be a sign of death. The elder Bossito, a Calabrian, laughed it off as a joke. Two days later, while Salvatore was working in the kitchen of the restaurant, he heard his father loudly arguing in Italian with another man. The young Bossito came out to see what the fuss was about, and upon spotting him, the stranger drew a pistol from his pocket and fired at the youth. The bullet struck Salvatore between the eyes, killing him instantly. After knocking down the father, the man escaped into the street, but was caught by police and held at the Elizabeth Police Station while a mob estimated at one thousand people gathered outside calling for his blood.

During his interrogation, the shooter confessed to police that his name was Carlo Rossati. He insisted that he killed Salvatore accidentally, claiming he had shot the young boy with a bullet meant for another man with whom he was quarrelling over the finger-guessing game *passatella*. To some, Rossati's confession was an attempt to downplay evidence that he had been summoned to New York expressly to kill Salvatore. Some pointed to the fact that the thirty-five-year-old Sicilian arrived in New York on August 23 and went straight to the restaurant. Witnesses also told police that after the shooting they had seen Rossati with some of the Sicilian men who were reported to police by Bossito. The shooting was not simply a function of revenge, the *New York Times* asserted at the time, but the result of "unfriendly relations" between Calabrians and Sicilians, who have a habit of settling "their quarrels without calling in the legally constituted authorities." Bossito was targeted, in part, because "invoking the aid of the police for any purpose" is contrary "to the Sicilian and Calabrian canon."

About three or four weeks before the shooting, Rossati landed in Toronto, telling people he had just come from Baltimore. He was described by the Toronto media as a tall, well-dressed, and stout man who "had the appearance of someone who did little hard work and his hands showed little evidence of any severe toil." While in the city, Rossati presented himself as a reformer, announcing to whoever would listen that Italians in Canada were mistreated, that they should mobilize for their rights, and that he was the one to organize them. Rossati apparently held a number of meetings in Toronto that were well attended by local Italians. Prompted by recent media reports of Bossito's murder and the activities of the Black Hand in New York City, some suspected that Rossati was in Toronto to organize a local extortion ring. An August 24 edition of the *Toronto Daily Star* recounted the story of the "murder in New York by an agent of the Black Hand who had been brought from Toronto for the purpose." The newspaper then posed the question "Has the society of the Black Hand a branch in Toronto?" Toronto city police claimed they knew nothing of the society or the man who was said to have committed the murder. A "prominent Italian" interviewed by the *Star* said that the mafia has several members in this city, but is not believed to have any regular organization. Under the headline "Black Hand in Toronto," an article in the *Globe* read, "There is very little doubt existing in the minds of members of the Italian colony in this city that Carlo Rossati, who is charged with killing young Bossito in New York on Wednesday, was successful in forming a branch of the Black Hand Society in Toronto."

The true nature of Rossati's intentions in Toronto remains a mystery. A New York City police captain denied reports that the mafia or Black Hand was a factor in the killing of Salvatore Bossito and said no death mark had been chalked on the door of the restaurant. However, the assassination of Bossito — one of the earliest murders in New York attributed to Black Handers — began a wave of media-inspired hysteria that attributed any act of crime or violence within the Italian community to this sinister society. Stories appeared in New York City newspapers on a regular basis about extortion attempts, not to mention the various bombings, stabbings, shootings, and kidnappings allegedly perpetrated by the Black Hand. Over the next five years, the hysteria spread to newspapers in New Jersey, Pennsylvania, and Ontario, which were full of sensational stories, many of them baseless, accusing the shadowy Black Hand of numerous crimes and depredations. The hysterics turned into a full-fledged panic in New York's Little Italy on October 7, 1904, when frantic parents besieged an elementary school after a local Italian newspaper published reports that the Black Hand planned to dynamite two Harlem pubic schools attended primarily by children of Italian families. The police found no evidence of such a plot.

Despite the manufactured frenzy surrounding the Black Hand, there was evidence of a number of extortion rings in New York, New Jersey, Pennsylvania, Ontario, Manitoba, and British Columbia during the early 1900s, some of which culminated in violent deaths. In February 1904, a Newark, New Jersey, man named Michael Rossati received a letter threatening to kill him and his wife if he did not pay $400. The signature was a black-ink imprint of a hand. On December 4, 1904, a New Yorker named Joseph Pagano received a letter demanding $100 or his life. The letter, written in Italian, bore a skull and crossbones. In May 1905, the fruit store and home of an Italian immigrant in Monessen, Pennsylvania, was dynamited after he allegedly refused to pay $5,000 demanded in two previous extortion letters. Numerous other bombings of Italian shopkeepers would follow in Pennsylvania and New York City. Later that year, an Italian butcher was murdered by four men in his Brooklyn store. Police explained that he had been killed, not because he had refused to accede to extortion threats, but because he had opposed a dominant political faction allied with the mafia in his native Sicily. According to press reports, his murder was carried out by "agents of the Black Hand society" in America. Hundreds of other murders would be attributed to the Black Hand or the Italian mafia over the next few years, most of them never solved. This included the death of five people on November 12, 1905, and eight people (including five children) on April 30, 1908, in New York City. In both instances, fires were deliberately set in Italian tenement buildings, and the families who died had both recently received extortion letters. As early as 1905, Detective Sergeant Joseph Petrosino of the New York City police — a legendary figure in organized crime enforcement who would go on to make hundreds of arrests of individuals supposedly associated with the Black Hand and the mafia — declared "there are thousands of Black Hand robbers and assassins in New York and Brooklyn" who are the descendants of generations of brigands from Reggio Calabria and the Palermo province of Sicily. Petrosino himself received numerous death threats warning him to cease his pursuit of Italian criminals. As part of his wide-reaching investigations, Petrosino travelled to Palermo where he was murdered by assassins on March 12, 1909.

In rural parts of the United States and Canada, Italian extortionists turned up at work and camp sites of Italian labourers toiling on construction projects. Some were so brazen that they stood at the paymasters' wickets to collect their cut of the cash wages paid to their victims. In 1905, the media reported that Italian men working on the dams in New York's Winchester County were threatened with violence if they did not pay a membership fee to the local society. "Every pay day at the different dams agents of the Black Hand band demand all the way from $1 to $5 from each man, and if refused a note threatening him with death is left at his home the next day." In Welland, Ontario, where many Italians were involved in the construction of the canal, police came into the possession of several extor-

tion letters that were sent to Italian business owners. In one letter sent to a Fred Guido, the extortionists asked for a payment of $5,000 to be delivered "at 3 a.m. in the Catholic cemetery." The letter concluded by saying, "We know you're a person who can afford to pay, if you don't you will have problems."

Numerous other extortion attempts were reported in Ontario between 1905 and 1910. In 1906, Italian workers arriving in Toronto from Port Colborne, located in the southern portion of the Niagara Peninsula, told stories about one countryman who had been terrorized into paying $30, and another who disappeared after persuading a friend to guarantee the payment of a similar amount. After asking, "Are there Black Hand Italians at Port Colborne?" the *Toronto Daily Star* wrote, "It is said that a number of the thriftier Italians have been threatened with dire penalties should they fail to pay the specified amounts. Letters have been written, but frequently the prospective victims are seen in person and significant threats used. Thoroughly frightened, four or five have returned to Italy. These men argued that it would be about as economical to buy a passage back to their native land as to respond to blackmail, and safer." In North Bay, where a large Italian community supplied labour for railroad, dam, and sewer construction, the Black Hand was considered so active that "there has been a spirit of unrest manifest in the Italian colony," resulting in "a revolt among the victims." In 1907, a North Bay merchant named Frank Dececco received "the fatal missive so dreaded by the sons of sunny Italy, informing him that he would choose quickly between death and donating one thousand to the society of assassins designated by the Black Hand symbol." Dececco was so frightened that he made out his will, bade farewell to his wife and children, and then departed for Italy before he could be "laid low by the assassin band." The same year, a number of armed robberies against members of the Italian community in North Bay were blamed on the local "Black Hand Gang." One alleged member of the gang who threatened to go to police was stabbed to death. Relying on the revelations of a self-confessed member of the Society, the *Toronto Daily Star* reported that when "the society decrees the death of a man, lots are drawn and when the assassin completes his deed of honour, a scapegoat is ready and provided with $100 and a ticket to a distant point with instructions to efface himself from the sight of the law. Then the crime is sworn on the absent man, who is generally a late-comer to the colony and little known. The scapegoat soon loses his identity among his compatriots at a distance, and the law is baffled."

In 1907, a letter written in English was passed along to police from the wealthy Toronto woman who received it. The letter demanded $500 "to be paid to the Brotherhood of the Black Hand" and warned, "If you let the letter be made public, show it to the police, or have police on the spot which we appoint to have the money paid up, both you and your husband will be murdered and your house blown up." At the bottom of the letter "Black Hand" was printed in large letters and was accompanied by the initials of no less than twenty people. In 1908, in the township of Louth, near St. Catharine's, an Italian fruit grower was sent a letter addressed to him signed "Black Hand." The letter ordered the recipient to place $500 at the end of a recently erected row of houses. The man was threatened with the torching of his residence and barns if he did not comply. While $500 was demanded, the letter curiously proposed a compromise: if $100 was provided, the writer would see to it that no harm came to the man or his family. But if no money was produced, the letter stated, the man and his family would be murdered.

One of Ontario's most sensational Black Hand episodes took place in Hamilton. In September 1909, John Taglierino, Samuel Wolfe, Carmelo Columbo, and Ernesto Speranza were arrested and charged with theft and extortion. The circumstances leading up to their arrest began in 1906 when fruit dealer Salvatore Sanzone received a letter demanding $1,000. Written in Italian, the letter commanded Sanzone to take the money to a spot on Dundas Road and pay it "over or pain of losing his life, having his family exterminated and his shop blown up." Sanzone reported the threat to police and a sting operation was set in motion. The police asked Sanzone to follow the letter's instructions, which he did. Upon arriving at the predetermined location, and under the watchful eye of carefully hidden police officers, the intended victim encountered Wolfe, Columbo, and Speranza. The men

demanded that Sanzone hand over the cash and when he complied, police jumped into action and arrested the three men.

A confession by the three Black Handers led police to Taglierino, a storekeeper who was the driving force behind the extortion attempt. Police already suspected Taglierino of engineering a number of other extortion plots within the local Italian population, but could not charge him due to the reluctance of witnesses to come forward. In September 1909, Taglierino was arrested on an assault charge unrelated to the Sanzone case, and later that year was charged with extortion. Even after his arrests, Taglierino continued to send extortion letters, which included another to Sanzone that threatened him with "painful death" if he did not produce $1,000. This letter, which Sanzone also forwarded to police, was signed by "Revolver" and was accompanied by a crude sketch of a handgun. Joseph Courto, a Taglierino minion who became a Crown witness, testified in court that Ernesto Sperzano wrote the first letter to Sanzone under orders from Taglierino. Ralph Rufus, another Taglierino underling who became a Crown witness, admitted he wrote the second letter under the "Revolver" pseudonym, but claimed to have done so after being threatened by Taglierino. Rufus was already known to police, having been charged with keeping a house of prostitution. On October 26, 1909, Speranza, Colombo, and Wolfe were found guilty and sentenced to ten years in Kingston Penitentiary. At the conclusion of the trial, the judge stated that those convicted "had been found guilty of one of the most diabolical crimes in the criminal calendar. It was more serious than highway robbery, for they not only threatened to kill the man himself, but his family as well." Taglierino would be found guilty at a later trial.

Around the same time, the town of Fernie, located in the Kootney region of British Columbia, was reeling under allegations that Black Handers were extorting the local Italian population, most of whom had immigrated to the area from southern Italy in the late 1890s in search of work in the mines or in railway construction. In 1908, a petition signed by dozens of Fernie citizens and sent to the provincial government requested that action be taken against the "Black Hand Society" which has "for its object, extortion of money; the wounding of persons who do not yield to its requests, and in many cases, it commits murder." Following a police investigation, twelve men were arrested in early July and charged with conspiracy to obtain money by threats. Police had obtained statements from at least five of the arrested men — Frank Marasco, Nicolo Cardamone, Joe Quartiere, Antonio Lento, and Louis Carosello — that they were compelled to become members of the Society and forced to pay an initiation fee. Based on their evidence, police identified the two ringleaders as Stephen Bruno and Frank Albernesse, who had come to Fernie from Spokane, Washington, expressly to organize a "Society."

While being held in advance of their upcoming trial, five of the suspects, including Bruno and Albernesse, escaped from the local jail by prying open a bolted coal-chute door. The five fugitives made their way to the dry-goods store of another suspect named G.S. Bartolo, who had been allowed out of jail to tend to his business. Upon arriving at the store, the men discovered that Bartolo was released only on the condition that he be accompanied at all times by a police escort. Another escaped prisoner ventured to the Australian Hotel, where he bought four bottles of beer. He was recognized, but got away. All the men eventually fled into the bush, where they spent the night, but turned themselves in to police the next morning. One of the escapees, a shoemaker named Jasper Jacimo, claimed the others forced him to flee the jail at razor point.

By August 1, while still waiting for their trial, a small brushfire quickly spread into town, and in less than ninety minutes, the majority of Fernie had been destroyed. Rumours began to circulate that the fire "was started by members of the Black Hand society in an effort to release their imprisoned brothers," as the August 6, 1908, edition of the *Cranbrook Herald* reported. These rumours were quashed by local fire officials who had been fighting the brushfires for days. The mayor of Fernie also denounced the story. He even went so far as to praise the prisoners, who had been released on their own recognizance when it became clear that the jail was in jeopardy of burning to the ground, and who had all voluntarily delivered themselves back into custody soon after the fire was extinguished. He also publicly stated that the prison-

ers, with the exception of five suspected leaders of the Society, had proven to be "the most efficient workers in clearing up the wrecked town."

By September, ten of the twelve accused men were committed to trial on the charge that they "did unlawfully conspire, combine, confederate, and agree together to form in the said city of Fernie a Society to be known as 'Black Hand Society', having for one of its objects the unlawful intimidation of other persons and the extorting of money from them by threats of using violence and personal injury." The trial concluded on September 19, with all the accused being convicted and sentenced. The five reputed ringleaders — Domenic Marzini, Stephen Bruno, Frank Albernesse, Joseph Ferraro, and Frank Rocco — received between six and seven years, while the other convicted conspirators — Annunziato Santori, Joseph Ferraro, G.S. Bartolo, Jasper Jacino, and Antonio Vitali, received sentences ranging from six months to two years.

Despite these convictions, complaints about extortion attempts continued to be forwarded to police in Fernie. Acting on these reports, a man named Ranier was arrested. His detention stemmed from threats made to Louis Carosella, who had provided testimony in the previous Black Hand case. Carosella was set to testify against Ranier, when he received a letter advising him to renounce his statements to police or he would be killed. Shortly before the letter was sent, Ranier escaped from the Fernie lockup, although he was soon recaptured. During the time he was on the lam, a shot was fired through Carosella's bedroom window when he was at home. He exchanged several shots with his assailant who fled after wounding Carosella in the knee. Although police never did determine the identity of the shooter, Rainer was convicted of extortion and sentenced to fourteen years.

There is some indication that the successful prosecution of the Black Handers in Fernie drove any remaining conspirators out of the province. In January 1910, a meeting of six Italian men in Winnipeg was broken up after "a well-directed fusillade of revolver shots poured into the room." The *Toronto Daily Star* reported that all the men had recently arrived in Winnipeg "from Fernie, and are known to have been connected with the 'Black Hand' there, against which there has been vigorous crusade." The men attending the meeting were all purportedly friends of Antonio Bruno, who in 1898 was shot to death in the Kootney town of Moyie by an alleged Black Hander after he refused to join the local Society. Speculation increased that the men were part of a Black Hand conspiracy when none of those attending the sit-down would disclose to police the subject of their meeting or why anyone would want to kill them.

The presence of Black Handers in Manitoba was confirmed in August of that year when a trial of six Society men began in Lac du Bonnet. In the crowded defendants' box sat Antonio Bordegoni, Frank Filletto, Frank Rolla, Petro Muto, Guiseppi Andre, and Paulo Fillippo, all of whom were accused of operating a "Black Hand Society." The case followed allegations by Pasquale Devonna that the accused had "invited" him to join the Society and was told that as a member, he might be called on to steal or kill on behalf of the Society. The fee for joining, he said, was $10. Devonna paid the fee and attended one meeting of the Society in Winnipeg where further demands for money were made from him and other new inductees. Devonna told the court that after refusing to pay, he was threatened with death, which prompted his report to police. Written statements made to police by Rolla and Muto indicated that a society did exist. However, as one police officer wrote, they refused to say anything more, "lest they would be locked up like the 'wolf,'" a reference to Ignazio Saietta who had just received a lengthy prison sentence in New York.

Pasquale Devonna

EXPOSE METHODS OF PICCIOTTERIA

Murder followed Black Hand outrage

GRIRO SAYS HE WAS VICTIM OF BLACK HAND

Victim Was Feared and Hated By His Assailant

Murder Took Place on Sunday Afternoon at Church and Front Streets, Where the Victim Was Shot Down—Prisoner Said Crime Was Outcome of Money Matter

Toronto, Sept. 19, 1911— "I am the man who shot Francesco Sciarrone and am prepared to accept the consequences. What do you want to do with me?"

Voluntarily offering the foregoing confession, Frank Griro, who fled from Toronto on July 30 last, after shooting Sciarrone, a fellow countryman at Church and Front streets, and with the Sword of Damocles precariously hanging over Griro's Mediterranean head, the fugitive, who, according to accounts, "appeared cool and collected evincing no sign of the seriousness of his actions," surrendered himself at the Agnes Street Police Station on a charge of murder.

The shocking revelations of the now-contrite Italian are concerned with the July 29 murder of Frank Sciorrone, a murder that turbulently plunged the local Italian colony into a dystopia of unrest.

Having paid close attention to the case and the proceedings of the police, upon examinations of the prisoners and his subsequent trial and accusations towards other criminal rogues; and having received much additional information on the subject from informants and witnesses, as well as the magistrate so experienced in bringing the criminal variety to justice, we are enabled to present our readers with some account and exegesis of this wicked story of blackmail, duplicity, and murder, all centering upon a pestiferous secret society that has become an excrescence of Toronto's own Italian colony.

Two days following the murder of Sciarrone, a warrant was issued for the arrest of Frank Griro, aged 25, who, it was said, both hated and feared the victim of this calamitous shooting. Police were convinced that the escapee, Griro, was the slayer, as he answered the description of the killer provided by erudite eye witnesses.

Griro, a barber by profession, is a handsome, yet jowly man, with abbreviated eyebrows that cling to the middle of his face and scars on his left jaw and right chin. He appears neatly dressed and shows signs of having been careful of his personal grooming. His speech betrays that he is a foreigner.

After leaving his flat in a rooming house at 165 York Street the afternoon of the shooting, he met Sciarrone — described as "in his mid-thirties, of medium height with a surly look and a nasty attitude" — at an Italian restaurant at 160 York Street. Witnesses told police they saw the two men walking along the street, apparently in a peaceable manner, when at the corner of Front and Church streets, Griro suddenly whirled upon the other and fired four shots in rapid succession. Griro then threw down the gun and with great velocity escaped the scene; but the wounded man picked up the weapon, moved a few steps towards the retreating

shooter, and then sank to his knees, his rapidly ebbing strength prohibiting him from pulling the trigger.

In announcing the warrant for Griro, Inspector Duncan of the Toronto police speculated that the man may be the number one member of the Black Hand society in Toronto. The Italian interpreter working for the police bolstered this supposition when he said that the killing of Sciarrone was probably over money, as it was believed the dead man was in debt to Griro. (Initial rumours that the carnage was the result of a duel fought over a woman were rapidly dispelled.) Police did link Sciarrone to Griro, not as a victim, but as a partner in the carrying-out of the sedulous extortion activities by the malevolent Black Hand Society.

Both men lived on the ill-gotten gains extorted from members of their own Italian colonies in Toronto, Chicago, and Montreal. The many Italian labourers known to the men, "were kept in constant terror, and they feared to inform police lest they draw on their heads the vengeance of the Black Hand." The unfortunate victims told stories of being forced to hand over to the coffers of the Society the entire proceeds of their labour. One prominent Italian said "all these secret societies are organized by unscrupulous men, who by much high-flown talk work on the sympathies of their more ignorant compatriots, and fill their own pockets." Members of the Italian colony "believe that once marked by the Black Hand, death sooner or later is certain, that the Society first squeezes the victim's money out of him, and finally when he has nothing left, his life goes to swell the assassination roll of the mysterious and villainous society."

Following a meticulous search of 165 York Street, Toronto police officers discovered letters and other documents "showing the extensive nature of the operations of the Black Hand Society. These communications were mostly between friends and several contained threats of inflicting punishment on certain persons with whom the writers were at outs." One epistle told of the wanderings of a member of the gang from Buffalo to Cleveland and other cities and complained that business was not as profitable as it might have been, as the writer "had to

MURDERER WANTED

WANTED ON A CHARGE OF MURDER

FRANK GRIRO alias ROSSARO

Age 27; 5 ft. 9 in.; about 140 lbs.; black hair; dark complexion; brown eyes; clean shaven; has two upper teeth gold capped; rather low, wide forehead; slightly Roman nose; two vaccin marks on left forearm; small circular scar on right forearm; one inch scar on left wrist; scar on left jaw; scar on centre of chin; wearing a blue serge suit; black Christy hat; low tan shoes; always dresses well; is a barber by occupation, but has recently kept a restaurant; is suspected of being connected with the White Slave Traffic, and is usually found around large factories where young girls are employed.

This man is an Italian, but speaks English fluently; might be taken for a Frenchman and associates with French prostitutes.

A warrant has been issued for his arrest on the charge of shooting Frank Tarra, an Italian, here yesterday. If apprehended, his extradition will be demanded.

We are most anxious to secure his arrest and any assistance rendered will be very much appreciated by this Department.

H. J. GRASETT,

Chief Constable.

Police Headquarters,
TORONTO, Canada,
July 31st, 1911.

Wanted poster issued by Toronto police for the arrest of Frank Griro

keep constant watch for the police, whose vigilance interfered somewhat with his activities."

On the body of the dead man, Sciarrone, detectives found extortion letters and fake marriage licences, which they believe were to be shown to immigration officials to allow women to enter the country who were coming to be married; in fact, police believe the forged documents were to be used to enable Sciarrone to import into the country women of questionable repute as part of the white slave trade that now engulfs the province and threatens the morals and sanctity of all good Protestant women in the city. After two weeks on the run in Detroit, St. Louis, and Chicago, the fugitive Griro gave himself up to Toronto police after succumbing "to the twittings of his own conscience." As police interrogated the suspect, "the discredited society of the 'Black Handers' so often and so indefinitely connected with Italian tragedies again leaped into prominence."

While confessing that he killed Sciarrone, Griro surprised police by claiming he was the victim in the affair and that the shooting was the result of the unrelenting terror inflicted upon him by this violent and vengeful Italian brotherhood, through the persistent demands being made upon him for sums of five and ten dollars by Sciarrone, and it was his only rebellion against the persecution that drew Griro into this fatal form of retaliation against the man for whom he had nothing but excoriating contempt.

Upon meeting with Sciarrone on that day of destiny, Griro claimed to have immediately suspected his compatriot to be the assassin appointed to kill him if he did not accede to their extortion demands. "And sooner than let them do that," stated Griro, "I decided that I would rather be hanged than shot to pieces."

A transcript of Frank Griro's statement to Toronto police detectives, taken August 10, documents one of the first personal testimonies to verify the greatly rumoured presence and demands of this secret society in Toronto:

Q: The dead man came to you and said that you had to give him $5 a week to stay there and help you in your business?

Griro: No, he wanted $5 for Society, or something.

Q: He wanted a contribution of $5 a week from you, did he?

Griro: Yes, he a Camorrist.

Q: He said he was a Camorrist?

Griro: He says he is a Camorrist.

Q: That is the dead man?

Griro: Yes.

Q: He said that he was a Camorrist and that he wanted you to pay him $5 every week.

Griro: Yes, I give him two or three weeks after I leave business, I was afraid.

In confessing his crime, and with a perspicacity that belied his Italian heritage, Griro told police of the great animus he held toward his tormentors, "I am tired of these Black Handers trailing me and persistently demanding money. They hounded me to death and when they demanded money I frequently handed it over. Besides having to face a serious charge, I am going to tell the police how this Black Hand organization, composed of a certain element of the Italian colony, has been operating in Toronto. They have been hounding the poor Italians and keeping them in a state of terror. I am one of those victims."

Griro declared that the fuglemen of the parasitic Black Hand Society in Toronto directed their attention almost exclusively to poorer classes in the Italian colony, when they made a demand for money. He said they were characters who did not treasure life, and would not hesitate to shoot men down like hunted animals and the pitiable victims of these maledictions were deterred from pursuing judicial action against their assailants for fear that a vendetta of the most excessive sort would be inflicted upon them and their family.

To Inspector Duncan, Griro disclosed other valuable information, and gave a list of the names of those prominently connected with the dreaded organization. This information was most fortuitous for it is well known that Italian crimes are most difficult for Canadian detectives to solve and, as the *New York Times* reliably opined, the "men who come here from the south of Italy and from Sicily have less control over themselves and their weapons than any other class of immigrants."

Resulting from this fortuitous information, Sergeant of Detectives Alex Mackie and his entire staff of sleuths paid unsolicited visits to three restaurants frequented by Italians on York Street, and placed under arrest, with various charges of vagrancy, possession of unlicensed and illegal weapons, and extortion being laid against seven people: James Rapola, Joe Musolino, Jim Vicceray, Mike Polesini, Salvatori Sciarrone (the brother of the deceased), Sam Carolla, Joseph Dolzini, and Mrs. Mary Clarke.

With the arrests, police believe they have broken up the Black Hand Society, which for several months past has been a miasma emanating from the Italian colony.

The effusive confessions of Griro did not simply expose the practices of a local Italian extortion ring; it brought to prominence the existence of a furtive society originating in otherwise sunny Italy and hereto unknown in Canada: the *Picciotteria*.

This clandestine opprobrium of criminals, which began in the southern province of Italy called Calabria, is committed to the most avaricious of evil activities — blackmail, extortion, kidnapping, and murder — and is made up of shooters and stabbers of the most reprehensible sort. The organization is said to have a pyramidal structure with two distinct levels: the *camorrista* and *picciotti*. Both levels are dominated by a *saccio capo* or *capo bastone*, devious organizers who coordinate robberies and extortions. To enter the society, a potential *picciotto* must be introduced by a member of the *camorrista*, and then pay a fee.

Upon joining, leading experts on the Italian secret societies tell us the member must swear "to be faithful to everyone connected to the Society of the *Picciotteria*, to help them unto his last drop of blood, to assist the other members in robberies, to present exactly all stolen goods to be divided equally with all other members cent for cent; to slash or to murder, when it is necessary, or because the boss tells him to, and spies on all people who try to get in the way of the society, including the police.

"The early *picciotti* were village toughs who made a lifestyle out of being outlaws. Their sideburns were long and wide, cutting deeply into their cheeks. They strutted about with rolling gaits, proud that they had little to do because others tended to their needs. On their necks were scarves, or *camuffi*, with ornate edges bearing peculiar and complicated fringes, always in very bright colours. These were purchased from the travelling vendors who arrived on village streets with their wagons overloaded with goods. Rounding out the distinctive look of those in the Picciotteria was their hairstyles, described often in archives as 'like a butterfly.'"

At the head of the Toronto branch of this surreptitious organization is Giuseppe (Joe) Musolino, who owns the restaurant at 165 York Street, which served as the unofficial headquarters for this mysterious association; that the place kept by Musolino was used almost exclusively for those connected with the feared society as a meeting place the police feel certain.

Italian sources inform this reporter that Musolino was initiated into the *Picciotteria* in November 1896 in Santo Stefano d'Aspromonte in the picturesque province of Calabria. Following police raids on his operations in 1901, Musolino incontinently fled to the state of New York, where he opened a restaurant in Niagara Falls, and soon after Musolino arrived in Niagara Falls, a rash of extortion letters was received by Italian immigrants living in the surrounding area. He was subsequently ordered by police to close the restaurant and vacate the city.

Upon his forced departure, the malapert Musolino moved to Toronto and settled in the Italian district in the centre of the city, where he opened his current restaurant.

Acting on Griro's information, police searched Musolino's place of business, where they found three stilettos, three boxes of gun cartridges, three boxes of revolver cartridges, a dirk, and a large amount of correspondence in Italian, addressed to different individuals who frequented the place.

Police found other incriminating evidence that connected Musolino to secret Italian societies. A few days preceding Griro's confession there arrived in Toronto a Secret Service detective from Naples in the old country who figured prominently in the famous Camorra trial that recently took place there. Remarkably, whilst walking along a Toronto street, the detective recognized two alleged Camorrists, who'd escaped from Naples following the commencement of the trial. As soon as they got a glimpse of his familiar face, the two malefactors disgorged themselves from his view with great alacrity and felicitously boarded a streetcar and escaped. Their timorous departure satisfied the detective that these Italian interlopers were here for odious purposes and their physical description was immediately given to local authorities.

When police entered Musolino's place, they discovered sitting in one of the rear rooms, seven accused Camorrists who had fled Italy after being accused of murder; one was reading from a newspaper the account of Griro's return to Toronto, and when they spotted the police, all seven of the reprobates, who were very excited, attempted to escape through the back door, but when they found the alley was blocked, they turned and ran back straight into the arms of the waiting police officers.

At the time of his arrest, Musolino was already known to police who believed he had under his thumb many of the Italian labourers who worked on Toronto's waterfront, and was arrested a few months earlier on charges of threatening, which stemmed from his Black Hand conspiracies. Police also received several anonymous telephone calls that connected him to the unsolved murders of many from the Italian satellite in Toronto, including one Italian man recently found dead at 160 York Street.

When Musolino was re-acquainted with the seven escaped Camorrists at police headquarters, detectives became certain he was the boss to all those present; the sycophantic outlaws in attendance cravenly looked at him when asked questions by police, and Musolino, with little compunction in his demeanour, directed the conversation of his pusillanimous underlings in their native language when any of the arrested was asked a question through the Italian interpreter present.

Musolino mendaciously insisted he could not speak English, despite being in North America for eight years; but when direct inquiries were made of him by police, he absent-mindedly lapsed into perfect English. Upon realizing his mistake, he would revert to Italian and profess ignorance of what he claimed were abstruse questions being asked of him.

When his murder case came to trial, Griro pertinaciously described how he was pressured with choleric belligerence into joining the abominable society by Frank Sciarrone (a.k.a. Frank Tarro), who one day dropped by Griro's workplace with another man. According to Griro, Sciarrone said, "You are a good man and a good fellow. Wouldn't you like to join the same society as I?"

Griro told the court, "I was afraid and said that I would let him know in a couple of days.

The rapacious Sciarrone then said to Griro, "You had better join, it costs only $50 to join."

The most compelling testimony of the case came when Griro was questioned by his own attorney:

Q: Did you ever give him any money?

Griro: Yes, I gave him $5 once, $4.50 another time, and $5 once more.

Q: When did you next see Tarro?

Griro: He came to where I was living at 176 Jarvis Street. We went to 169 York Street, where they were playing cards and I went in. Somebody inside told me to go to the corner of University Avenue and Queen Street, and there I met a man named Amara. He took me by the arm and we walked up University Avenue to Agnes Street. Then he said, "If I tell you something, will you tell nobody?" I said, "No." He then said, "Frank, you have money and there are some fellows that want to take it from you." I asked, "Where?" And he answered, "160 York Street." You go there and you will lose your life and money."

Q: Then what happened?

Griro: I said, "You are fooling me." He answered, "No, I am not. You leave the city, for if you go to York Street, Tarro and Musolino will take your money and put you in a cellar and perhaps kill you." I would not believe him, and he said, "You must believe me as they are in the united society."

Q: Did they tell you what the name of the society was?

Griro: Yes, it was the mafia.

Q: What is this society Tarro wanted you to join?

Griro: The Mala Vita or evil life.

Q: Is it the same as the Black Hand?

Griro: I think so. They are all the same, the Black Hand, the Mala Vita, the Mafia and the Camorra.

Q: Did you think Musolino belonged to the Mala Vita?

Griro: Yes

The prisoner then described how he had handed over sums of money to Sciarrone, but when on the day of the killing, Sciarrone sclerotically demanded all Griro had with him, all of $120, Griro steadfastly refused and said he would tell the police. Sciarrone replied he would kill him before he had a chance to do that. It was then that the shooting began.

With the trial wrapping up on November 1911, the jury sided with Griro, believing his remonstrations that he killed his tormentor in self-defence due to the ongoing villainous ways of the society that hounded the poor man's every step, and with his brave testimony and verisimilitude, Griro lifted the veil of opacity necessary to expose and effect the perdition of this Italian secret society.

"No person could find fault with your verdict," Mr. Justice Ridell told the jury. "You believed his story and you have the right to believe it." Turning to Griro, the judge dismissed him, saying, "Now you go and behave yourself, and see if you can become a good Canadian citizen." Shortly thereafter, Frank

Joe Musolino, sporting the butterfly hairstyle popular among Calabrian criminals

Griro, the Italian man of the hour, walked out of the courtroom a free man of the hour.

Musolino was convicted of illegal possession of a firearm and following another conviction for grievous bodily assault upon that of fellow colony member Michael Silvestro, Musolino was deported from the Dominion of Canada, all the while maintaining that he never belonged to, let alone, headed a secret Italian criminal society called the Camorra, Mafia, Black Hand, Picciotteria or otherwise.

"I NEVER TALKED — DONE NOTHING"

Considerably less was heard of Black Hand extortions or secret Italian societies in Canada between 1910 and 1920. That all changed in the early 1920s when Black Handers resurfaced in Hamilton with a vengeance. The first sign of their coming-out party occurred on May 24, 1921. At about one o'clock that Tuesday morning, dynamite exploded at a home on Sheaffe Street. The front windows were completely shattered, but luckily no one was injured. A police investigation revealed that two and a half months before the bombing, the owner of the home, Mr. Monaco Natale, received a letter, illustrated with a cross and a black hand, demanding

payment of $1,000. The letter instructed Natale to deliver the money to the Grand Trunk Railway Bridge on John Street. There, he would be met by someone who would take the money. The letter warned him that failure to make the cash delivery would result in the death of his entire family. Despite the threat, Natale did not comply with the letter's demands.

On September 17, 1922, a home at 32 Simcoe Street West was severely damaged by what police called "a heavily charged time-bomb." The homeowner, Vincenzo Napoli, his wife, and two boarders were in the house asleep when the bomb was detonated at 2:30 a.m., but again all escaped injury. The explosion did inflict considerable damage to Napoli's home, as well as to his neighbours', and police suspected Black Hand extortionists. Upon questioning by police, however, Mr. Napoli stated that he had never received any extortion letter prior to the bombing.

Then, on October 4, 1922, the home of Mrs. Pauline Lombardo of 36 Simcoe Street West, just two doors down from Mr. Napoli, was racked by yet another bombing. The explosion, which occurred at 12:30 a.m., was caused by a charge of dynamite that had been inserted in a hole made between the brickwork and the windowsill. Not only was the entire lower front of the house destroyed, but windows in nearly twenty houses in the immediate neighbourhood were blown out. Once again, miraculously, no one was injured. Mrs. Lombardo, an elderly Sicilian widow who lived in the house with her four children, said she knew of no reason why she was targeted, as she has never received any threatening letters, nor did she believe she was marked by the Black Hand.

The two explosions on Simcoe Street used similar types of dynamite, which led police to believe the same people were behind both. But police were baffled by the motive behind the bombings, since the occupants of the two houses claimed to have never received any threats. While no arrests were made and police had few leads to follow, there was speculation that the owner of 38 Simcoe Street had been receiving extortion letters and that the wrong houses were targeted. These suspicions were heightened at one o'clock in the morning on March 27, 1923, when the home at 38 Simcoe Street was levelled by an explosion from dynamite placed on the ledge of the front window, almost exactly where the explosives were positioned in the previous two bombings on the street. Despite demolishing the living room, the family of twelve that was fast asleep upstairs was unhurt. When asked by the *Hamilton Herald* if he knew of anything that might have prompted the bombing, homeowner Sebastino Notto would neither confirm nor deny that he was a target of the Black Hand. Nonetheless, his explanation in broken English, captured phonetically by the newspaper, was revealing, "Mebbe think me know something, but I never talked — done nothing."

The city was now in a state of fear over the well-publicized terror campaign. Unlike the previous two bombings, Hamilton police did arrest four suspects — Joseph Restivo, Charles Bardinaro, and William Pasquale of Hamilton and Joseph Scibetta of Buffalo — they believed were behind the explosion at Notto's home. They were charged with vagrancy and were also held on a warrant that implicated them in the bombing of Vincenzo Napoli's house at 32 Simcoe Street. Following their arraignment on the vagrancy charges, each was released on bail, although Hamilton police indicated that the four would face more serious charges stemming from the bombings. These charges were dropped, however, after a principal witness disappeared.

The bombings on Simcoe Street did end after the four men were arrested, although Black Hand extortion letters continued to be received by some in Hamilton's Italian community. In May 1924, a number of Italian produce dealers on King Street East received letters bearing the imprint of a large black hand. The letters demanded that the recipient deliver cash ranging from $100 to $1,000 to a designated spot in a secluded part of town. As far as Hamilton police were aware, none of the recipients of the letters heeded the threats and all filed complaints with the police. The Black Hand gained prominence again in July 1924 when Hamilton resident John Borsellino received a letter threatening his life unless $3,000 was paid. The extortion letter, which was not the first one received by Borsellino, was crudely written in Italian and signed with a cross. The letter instructed him to stuff his coat pockets with the cash, and carry on his normal daily routines, always with the money in his pockets. "When it suited their plans," the *Hamilton Spectator* reported, "a member of the gang would walk toward Borsellino and, raising his right hand in a salute with two fingers upraised, he would utter the word 'Torrino.'" Upon hearing this, Mr. Borsellino was expected to hand the money to the passerby and walk away without looking back. If he failed to follow these instructions, the letter threatened him with death.

In August of the same year, the bombings returned to Hamilton. This time the target was the home of Sam Gualliano at 23 Murray Street. Neighbours told the *Hamilton Herald* that they saw a "high-powered limousine" drive up to the curb directly opposite the doomed home between eleven and eleven-thirty that night. According to the *Herald*, "two men, who they could not recognize, alighted and crossed the road to the Gualliano home, where they disappeared in the shadow of the porch. A few minutes later, they returned to the car and drove off. Twenty minutes later, a terrific explosion was heard." Flames engulfed the home and the next day all that remained was a cavity where the cellar was located. Police investigators learned of several Black Hand letters received by friends and relatives of Gualliano during the preceding three months. The previous week, a Bay Street North building, owned by Gualliano's brother-in-law, was set on fire. At the time, police believed that the bombing, following so soon on the heels of the fire, was most likely the work of the same gang. After inspecting the remains of Gualliano's home, police found within the cellar, under charred debris that was once a house, large kegs filled with wine. The liquid stash was most likely illegal contraband, which led some to believe that the bombing was motivated by a rival bootlegging gang. (It is not known whether Gualliano was ever charged with provincial *Temperance Act* offences, although police guarding the home did have their hands full trying to restrain spectators from hauling off the undamaged kegs.)

The bombings and Black Hand extortions that gripped Hamilton during the early 1920s took place during a period where inter-gang violence was raging in and around the Hamilton and Niagara regions, due in part to the highly competitive trade in illicit booze, as well as vendettas and other clashes between competing Italian groups. Between 1914 and 1924 there were at least twenty murders affecting the Italian community in the Hamilton and Niagara regions. The decade of violence began with the 1914 murder of Peter Basile, one of the leading figures in the Basile bootlegging family, whose bullet-riddled body was found in Lockport, New York. His sister Consima Bane and her husband, Patsy, were the next victims. Both were shot to death in 1918. Following the 1922 bombing of Vincenzo Napoli's home on Simcoe Street, police theorized that the culprits were after another Italian who lived on the same block and who "some time ago figured in a stabbing affray in which he came out second best."

Jim Leala, the man who stabbed the Simcoe Street resident, was found brutally murdered in the Beverley swamp near Dundas Street. The police believe that Leala's associates may have planted the bomb to seek their revenge for his death, although if this was true, they targeted the wrong house. Leala was already well known to Toronto police as a violent bootlegger. In June 1922, Tony Leala, the brother of Jim, was found mortally wounded while crawling in a ditch on a side road near Oakville. Tony Leala was also known to police as a bootlegger and there were rumours that he was targeted by rival gangs who believed he was passing along information to police.

In 1923, Jon Sciabone, a Hamilton resident, was shot and killed in Buffalo and, shortly thereafter, his wife was threatened with a similar fate. In May 1924, Joseph Basile was murdered on the same Buffalo street as Sciabone. On November 11, 1924, local Boy Scouts, helping in the search for missing jitney driver Frederick Genesse, found the decomposed remains of Joseph Baytoizae, whose head had been completely severed from his body. Four days later, police located Fred Genesse's corpse; a sash cord was tightly wrapped around his neck five times, his left eye was gouged out, and a deep indentation marked his forehead. Both Baytoizae and Genesse were known to have provided information to police on local bootleggers. Two days following the discovery of Fred Genesse's body, the *Toronto Daily Star* waxed poetic on the series of gruesome murders that were plaguing nearby Hamilton:

> Hamilton Mountain has become a place of skulls, a mountain of human sacrifice. It is like one of the stone pyramids on which the bloodthirsty Aztec priests cut the throats of innumerable victims. Canada needs Edgar Allen Poe to write the murders of the Rue St. James and to solve the mystery of Hamilton's many Marie Rogets.... So far the Hamilton police force has produced no Poe or Sherlock Holmes. Again and again they have been baffled by the inscrutable mountains which frowns above them like an inscrutable enigma.

Despite the lack of convictions or even arrests, police in western New York believed that at least some of the murders were the work of the "Good Killers," the enforcement arm of a Buffalo crime syndicate that was attempting to eliminate all bootlegging competition on both sides of the border.

THE PRESIDENT OF VENDETTA

The era of the Black Hand in Canada came to an end in 1928 with a highly publicized case that was played out in a courtroom in Welland, Ontario. On February 21, 1928, Giuseppe (Joe) Italiano was found guilty on eight counts of extortion and related charges. He was sentenced to nine years' imprisonment, eighteen strokes of the lash, and deportation at the expiration of his prison term. Italiano was arrested and charged with threatening Frank Mango, the owner of a shoe shop in Niagara Falls.

(Translation)

"Dear Sir:- (foul language)
I have to give you reason for all you've done your not worth anything. You are no better than a jackass. You know all you've done, you shouldn't have done that you do dirty business. Now you watch yourself think it over, surely your life is short, now think over all the best you can do, watch yourself and save your life, and all your family, you needn't think we care about you and your family, we sure going to clean you out, even the cats, your house. Your house is going to be blown up in the air like a balloon. Your time is short, one week or 15 days at least if you like to save yourself and family try in some way possible

(3)

find somewhere to do what we want you know what you did, you better (swear word) You should write and pay sum of $4000.00 in this time no longer. Be sure not to open your mouth. I think you know what we are talking about. If you don't do that, we blow your building up over the river and all you have in Canada.
I sign, The President of Vendetta, we will destroy you".

Your Grave

You die the Knife go through your heart and mouth. Better for you to keep your mouth shut"

Translated extortion letter sent to Frank Mango

In November 1927, Mango received an extortion letter postmarked in Buffalo, and written in Italian, complete with a death threat and numerous expletives, demanding $4,000. The letter, which was translated into English for the trial, promised, "We sure going to clean you out, even the cats, your house. Your house is going to be blown up like a balloon. Your time is short, one week or 15 days at least if you like to save yourself and family." The letter cautioned Mango to "Be sure not to open your mouth. I think you know what we are talking about. If you don't do that, we blow your building up all over the river and all you have in Canada." The letter was signed, "The President of Vendetta, we will destroy you." At the bottom of the letter was a crudely drawn picture of a grave (with "Your Grave" written underneath) as well as two daggers pointing at a heart (subtitled with "You die the Knife go through your heart and mouth. Better for you to keep your mouth shut.").

Mango received a second letter, this time written in English, which simply read, "We have warned you. unless you pay us what you promised you will loose all you have and we will get you some where soon so look out. You can't put it over us no more. We intend

to have our rights. What comes are you ready." The letter was signed "I,h,S,B,h."

On November 7, Mango's house was rocked by an explosion, which police determined was caused by dynamite that had been placed on his front porch. Ten days later, Mango received a visit from Italiano, who told him, "The Brotherhood wants the money." Mango replied that he didn't have $4,000 but agreed to pay $400 in four instalments. Joe Italiano accepted the offer, but unbeknownst to the Black Hander, Mango had previously been in contact with police, who had his house under surveillance. When Italiano left Mango's home, with $400 in his hand and threatening letters in his pocket, he was arrested, charged, and later convicted.

THE END OF THE BEGINNING

Although it was not known at the time, the Italiano case represented the end of the Black Hand in Canada. It was a fitting end, given that the case typified the elementary and brutish tactics of early Italian organized crime in Canada and the United States. The case of Giuseppe (Joe) Italiano also seems to support the conventional wisdom that extortionists affixed with the Black Hand

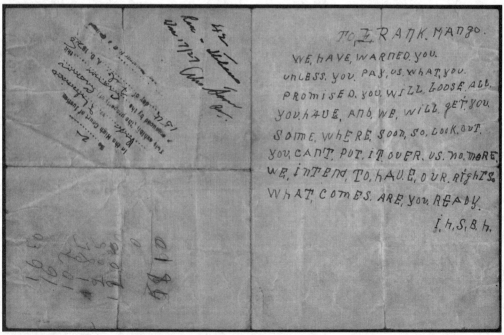

Actual extortion letter sent to Frank Mango

label were mostly independent operators. Yet, evidence continues to mount that some of the Black Handers in places like North Bay, Hamilton, Toronto, Winnipeg, and Fernie were connected to secret societies, complete with ceremonies, rituals, and a rudimentary organizational hierarchy, that were influenced by the Sicilian Mafia and Calabrian 'Ndrangheta. As further information on the Black Hand cases comes to light there are also indications that during this period there was a greater level of organization, coordination, and even international networking among Italian criminals than was previously thought. While Ignazio Saietta operated as an independent Black Hander, he also carried out his extortions and other criminal rackets with an established Sicilian organization, the Morello Family. The theory that Carlo Rossati travelled from Cleveland — which police at the time believed was a central location for the manufacture of explosives used by some Black Handers — to Toronto to "organize" local Italians and then on to to New York to murder Salvatore Bossito at the behest of a group of Sicilian criminals in that city, suggests some form of international network was in place. Evidence unveiled as part of the Griro case also shows that some "Camorrists" traveled from Naples to Toronto to be hidden by Joe Musolino and were subordinate to him upon arriving in Canada.

While the era of the Black Hand may have ended, extortion would continue to be a stock-in-trade for Italian crime groups in Canada for at least the next five decades. The Black Hand label, and the term "extortion," would now be replaced with a new and grossly misleading designation: "protection." Under the protection racket, Italian businessmen were permitted to operate in a territory under the control of a local mafioso, as long as they paid a regular fee. In return for these payments (or "tribute") the payee received protection against violence, arson, robbery, union troubles, or the non-delivery of essential supplies. The mafioso rationalized this extortion by stressing that it was part of the paternalistic duty of the *padrone* in protecting his flock. The reality was that most of the threatened calamities likely to befall the recalcitrant client would be carried out by the mafioso himself.

The protection racket, and extortion in general, is heavily reliant upon, and intertwined with, two fundamental imperatives of organized crime: intimidation and violence. While extortion can be carried out by individuals working alone, it is most credible when carried out by a group, particularly a group that has a reputation for using violence. Extortion is favoured by criminal groups that prey upon their own ethnic communities because it serves a dual purpose: it generates revenue for the perpetrators while also keeping the community in a state of fear and silence. Each successful extortion boosts the reputation, stature, and influence of the criminal group within the community it victimizes, which it then uses as a foundation to augment the grip it has over the community while expanding into other criminal endeavours.

Extortion fulfilled all of these objectives for the 'Ndrangheta, a criminal fraternity that, not only influenced the Black Handers, but also future generations of Italian criminal groups in Canada. Indeed, Italians of Calabrian descent would assume a formidable place in the annals of the Canadian underworld. While extortion and other predatory crimes would continue to be used by Italian criminal groups, the tactics of the Black Hand became increasingly outdated and those who relied exclusively on these predatory money-making ventures lost ground to the more modern criminal entrepreneur. By the 1920s, the highly profitable trade in liquor, drugs, gambling, and prostitution revealed that the greatest source of illicit money was to be made in satisfying the vices of receptive consumers. This would be the future of organized crime in Canada.

CHAPTER FOUR

CANADIAN VICE
Dope Peddlers, White Slavers, and Fantan Operators

Of Prohibition, root of all our woes.
—Milton, *Paradise Lost*, IX, 645

With the exception of the contraband smuggling trade, organized criminality in Canada before the 20th century was predatory in nature; most criminals robbed, cheated, or extorted people out of their money. These uncongenial revenue-generating enterprises would continue as a staple for organized offenders for years to come. However, by the start of the new century it was becoming clear that the greatest source of illicit revenue was to be accumulated, not by depriving people, but by providing them with the goods and services they demanded, but which were outlawed by the government. Gambling, drugs, liquor, and prostitution would increasingly be driven into the receptive environs of the criminal underworld by powerful reformist movements, panicked over the growth in society's vices, the breakdown of Victorian moral values, and the threat posed to the racial and religious purity of white, Protestant society by the flood of new immigrants. Only too happy to oblige the powerful Prohibition lobby were politicians who enacted laws regulating and criminalizing the supply and consumption of society's most popular turpitudes. The consequence of these actions would be the creation of immensely profitable underground markets, widespread law breaking, and the launching of organized crime to a new level of wealth, sophistication, violence, and power.

THE WHITE SLAVE TRADE

Prostitution is not only the world's oldest profession, it can also be one of the most financially lucrative, especially when well organized. While there continued to be plenty of freelance prostitutes during the first quarter of the 20th century, it was also during this period that the sex trade became much more organized in North America. Like most other vices, the organization of harlotry was precipitated by a heightened demand for sexual services, which itself was the result of large-scale immigration of unattached males to Canada and the United States. The wave of immigrants who came to Canada during the late 19th and early 20th centuries differed from the migrants of the past, who were primarily farm families that headed straight to rural areas. This new spate of immigrants was disproportionately made up of men, either bachelors or husbands who had left their wives and families at home until they could get established in the new country. Many of these newcomers headed to urban centres in search of work.

Among the different sectors of urban commerce that benefited the most from the overabundance of males was the sex trade. While many women came to the trade of their own volition, the heightened demand for prostitutes also resulted in the aggressive recruitment and procurement of eligible women who were forced into sexual servitude. The organization of the prostitution trade and the forced conscription of women into the profession prompted a deliberately frightening new term in the public's lexicon — the "white slave trade." The term was first popularized in England in the 1830s by Dr. Michael Ryan, a British reformer who actively campaigned against vice. Like many of the moral crusaders who followed him, Ryan's goal in his use of this phrase was to arouse moral indignation among the public while exhorting the government to intensify its efforts to combat prostitution. One of Ryan's tactics was to capitalize on the fervent anti-Semitism of the day by blaming Jews for the organized sex industry (a tactic that had long been used to demonize the loansharking industry). In reference to the white slave trade in London, Ryan wrote, "It has been proved in several cases that have come before our public magistrates, especially at the eastern end of town, that the infernal traffic in question is still carried on to a great extent, principally by Jews."

Subsequent generations of anti-prostitution crusaders in Canada and the United States overtly or subliminally identified Jews, the Chinese, blacks, and other "foreigners" as the culprits responsible for the trafficking of young women. Books, brochures, church sermons, radio broadcasts, and laughingly gullible and sensationalized newspaper articles propagated lurid tales of alien pimps, madams, and their agents forcing young Christian white women into prostitution through kidnapping, cross-border smuggling, forcible confinement, and drug addiction. The term "white slave trade" is itself a misnomer; by no means was the sex trade populated solely by the white race during this period. Women of all colours were attracted to or forced into the business. However, calculating moral crusaders knew that an exclusive inference to white women would resonate among the Anglo-Saxon population. While the extent of the white slave trade was exaggerated by social reformers, the hyperbole did make the anti-prostitution campaigns of the early 20th century enormously successful, at least as measured by the moral panic created, the number of media articles on the subject, the new legislative and enforcement initiatives undertaken, as well as the numerous international conventions adopted by the fledgling League of Nations.

Despite the exaggerated claims of the moral reformers, it would be sheer folly to deny that prostitution was becoming better organized or that women were being coerced or forced against their will into the sex trade. In America, the most infamous of the early white slavers was Mary Hastings, a Chicago madam during the 1890s who prowled the Midwest seeking trusting teenage girls. By promising them a job in Chicago, she convinced some to return with her. Once inside her three-storey brothel, the girls were supposedly stripped naked, locked in a room, "broken in" by well-endowed "professional rapists," and then forced to pleasure male callers. Hastings was also known to sell her girls to other brothel keepers at prices ranging from $50 to $300, depending on their age, looks, and health. Legend has it that one victim of Hastings managed to scrawl on a scrap of paper, "I'm being held as a slave," which was then tossed out the window of her room. The note was found by a passerby and taken to the police, who raided the brothel and rescued the prisoner. Following in the footsteps of Hastings was perhaps the most successful of the organized white slavers in North America, Giacomo (Big Jim) Colosimo. By the early 1900s, Big Jim was said to have controlled more than a hundred whorehouses in Chicago's Levee district. Known as the "King of the Pimps," Colosimo organized a regional prostitution ring in which young girls would be lured to Chicago with promises of good jobs, and then imprisoned and forced to turn tricks in one of Big Jim's many establishments.

Mary Hastings and Big Jim would help cement Chicago's prodigious reputation as the vice capital of America. In a 1909 book entitled *White Slavery*, Edwin W. Sims, the U.S. attorney for Chicago, was quoted as saying: "The recent examination of more than two hundred 'white slaves' by the office of the United States district attorney at Chicago has brought to light the fact that literally thousands of innocent girls from the country's districts are every year entrapped into a life of hopeless slavery and degradation because parents in the country do not understand conditions as they exist and how to protect their daughters from the 'white slave' traders who have reduced the art of ruining young girls to a national and international system." Like many others, Sims believed the white slave trade to be a monolithic conspiracy, "The legal evidence thus far collected establishes with complete moral certainty these awful facts: that the white slave traffic is a system operated by a syndicate which has its ramifications from the Atlantic seaboard to the Pacific ocean, with 'clearing houses' or 'distribution centers' in nearly all of the larger cities; that in this ghastly traffic the buying price of a young girl is from $15 up and that the selling price is from $200 to $600." He went on to characterize this international syndicate as "a definite organization sending its hunters regularly to scour France, Germany, Italy and Canada for victims." As part of his ongoing crime commissions in Chicago, John Landesco contended in his 1929 report that since the early part of the century, there was an elaborate system for procuring and transporting women between New York, Milwaukee, St. Louis, and Chicago.

Some of the earliest stories of organized prostitution in Canada came out of Hamilton. In 1910, officials with the YWCA told the *Hamilton Spectator*, "There is more white slave trafficking in Hamilton than in any other city of its size — in the whole of America — not Canada, but America." One YWCA official described the case of "a foreign girl" who landed at the Stuart Street Railway Station in Hamilton with no one to meet her:

> She was a pretty girl, 17 years of age, and came here in reply to an advertisement, but was not met at the station. She had only recently arrived from a European country and could not speak a word of English. On arrival at the station, she was met by a well-dressed woman, who had every appearance of being a friend. She took the girl by the hand, spoke kindly to her, and on seeing that she was a foreigner, told her to wait until she went to the telephone. Some minutes later a man who could speak the girl's language arrived at the station, with the result that she was taken to a disreputable house.

In 1911, the *Hamilton Times* reported on a new enforcement campaign that successfully rounded up a "large number of street walkers and supposed members of a gang of colored alley workers, which

the Provincial police department and the police of the largest cities in all the province had been trying for two years to break up." In 1912, under the headline "Hamilton a center of white slave traffic," the *Hamilton Herald* reported that "many young girls are enticed into lives of shame and that the white slave traffic is carried out here to a very large extent." The *Herald* reporter was told by YWCA officials "of case after case where young girls had gone wrong through being enticed to houses of ill fame by people who posed as friends." Young women arriving in the city for the first time by train are "often approached by men and women of disreputable character who in the most smooth manner endeavor to get them to go to their houses, promising the most attractive things in the way of money and comforts." One YWCA worker claimed to have evidence on "an organized gang in the white slaves traffic," in Hamilton including "a Chinaman, a colored woman, and a white man who approached young girls." According to Reverend Dr. Lyle, president of the Anti-White Slave Association, "Hamilton had the worst reputation in Canada as a city where the white slave traffic was carried on."

The Hamilton white slavers used all conceivable methods to attract young women, according to the moral crusaders and the media. "They dress sometimes like widows, or pose as very pure and humble people, and talk religion in an effort to get the young girls interested, according to a 1912 edition of the *Hamilton Herald*. "Once interested the girls are gone unless someone interferes in their behalf." Other techniques used by the "Mashers" included posing as theatrical agents searching for pretty faces or giving young girls "doctored candies and automobile and buggy rides." Reverend C.E. Burrell told the media "he had heard a woman was forcibly picked up" on a Hamilton street "and but for strong friends would have been carried off for an improper purpose." In 1913, the *Herald* ran a story about Canadian immigration authorities who blocked what they believed to be "one of the most brazen attempts at white slavery ever brought to the attention of the officials of the city." The scheme, worked by two men, was to advertise for stenographers and other female help. The man went so far as to rent an office to conduct their job interviews. After one applicant took her suspicions to police, an inspector conducted surveillance within the building where he heard propositions being made to other young women to go to Buffalo or Toronto where they would be provided with jobs as secretaries.

On June 20, 1917, the *Globe* reported that "the first case of alleged white slavery to be found in Toronto in many years was unearthed yesterday afternoon by police of No. 2 Division." Toronto police discovered that, for three weeks, eighteen-year-old Paulina Theoult was "held captive in a house at 153 Victoria Street, and by means of frequent drugging has been forced into abominable practices." Having escaped her captor and "with her right eye blackened and her face bruised and cut," Miss Theoult rushed to a local police station and told her sordid story. Her injuries, she said, were at the hands of her pimp, Rinaldo Centino, who "proved to be a dangerous character" when two police officers cornered him in his home. "Plainclothesman Scott met him at the door just as he was leaving, and in spite of Centino's objections shoved him back inside the house. Once inside the front room, which was used as a bedroom, Centino swiftly drew a razor from his hip pocket and attempted to slash the officer with it, but Scott was too quick for him, knocked him over the bed and took the razor from him. Upon searching Centino's clothing the police found that in every suit he secreted a razor in preparation for emergency."

By the early 1920s, RCMP annual reports began including brief accounts of the white slave trade in Canada. Most of the information was supplied by Reverend John Chisholm, who worked in co-operation with the Mounted Police, primarily by meeting ocean liners arriving at Montreal and caring for "unaccompanied female immigrants." Although the RCMP does not appear to have investigated many white slave cases, their annual reports did print Chisholm's accusations that "many attempts were made by infamous creatures to corrupt and entice away young women." In a 1923 report, under the heading "Protection Against Commercialized Vice," the RCMP lauded Chisholm for his work, which has "cast a vivid and unpleasant light upon the dangers which threaten the unescorted girl who travels, and upon the number of human beasts of prey who strive to trap her; some of the plots, which Mr. Chisholm and his helpers frustrated can only be described as diabolical, and the organization has saved many women from ruin and misery." Despite its apparent support for the work of Reverend Chisholm, in its annual report for 1923, the RCMP dismissed Canada's role in the international sex trade, writing, "Mexico, not Canada is the principal avenue whereby women are conveyed from Europe to the United States for improper purposes." The RCMP did acknowledge, "attempts continually are being made, however, to inveigle unsuspecting girls from Canada to questionable places in the United States, and a number of these plots have been frustrated."

In a submission prepared for the RCMP dated January 20, 1925, Reverend Chisholm cited research presented at the International Conference for the Suppression of White Slavery and Commercialized Vice, held in Geneva in 1912, which accuses Montreal of being a major source of women for the international sex trade. This study, which examined the registers used by hospitals and other medical facilities to record the names, birth places, and physical conditions of female brothel "inmates" in North and South America, found that with the exception of New York and Chicago, Montreal contributed more victims to the white slave traffic than any city in the western hemisphere. Based upon his own interviews with prostitutes who suffered from advanced cases of venereal disease, Reverend Chisholm wrote:

> On their deathbeds they confessed with sobs and tears, the awful tragedy of their brief career of sexual degradation. From their dying lips, I learned that the women in charge of the Montreal Bureaux of Employment, under false pretenses, gave them to procurers from the U.S.A., who at that time could without any barriers, take domestic servants to their country from Canada. They told me, how, after they became diseased, they were cast out of the houses into which they were forced. After they were rejected, they were arrested, examined, and deported via Canada.

That Montreal was a major source of prostitutes and sexual slaves should provoke little surprise given the renowned scope of the city's red-light district.

In his autobiography, former Montreal vice cop and RCMP commissioner Clifford Harvison reminisces about the city's brothels in the early 1920s, which "operated openly in a red-light district that covered more than a dozen blocks." These bordellos ranged from "luxurious houses where dalliance was expensive and the girls young and pretty, on down to the cheap tawdry places where intercourse was handled on a production line basis whereby girls carried tally cards punched by the matron each time a prostitute headed for the bedroom with a new customer, where it was not unusual to find twenty or thirty punch marks on the card. In one case a tally of forty-two marked a girl's effort for a fourteen hour day."

Relying on police information, the "Committee of Sixteen," a self-appointed group of private citizens who conducted their own investigation into Montreal's vice conditions in 1918, estimated the number of "houses of commercialized prostitution" at between "250 and 300, including 6 or 8 hotels operated almost exclusively as 'houses of assignment'." The group also commented on the organized nature of prostitution in Montreal, "Vice in Montreal is thoroughly systematized for the exploitation of girls and young women for the profit of third parties. Girl after girl has recounted as a warning for us to give to other girls that there is nothing in the 'life' for the girl, the madam and the pimp getting all the profit." In its report, the committee tells the story of one wayward girl who fell into the clutches of what appears to be a well-organized syndicate of white slavers:

Take the case of Mary B., 15 years old who made the acquaintance of Fred, a famous procurer, at an apartment on St. Denis Street. Mary met him through Ethel G., a thoroughly depraved girl of 17, who had already led another one of our girls astray. Mary had become delinquent and occasionally immoral before this time and it was easy for this unscrupulous man to persuade her to go with him to Madam Z. on Lagauchetiere Street. One of his infamous co-workers had already recruited another of Ethel's associates, feeble-minded Maud T., who later came to our attention and who in turn pointed out Mary to a worker of this Committee. Mary, on reaching Madame's house, saw $50.00 given to Fred by Madame Z., and she was not allowed to leave until this had been paid off by her earnings. Mary paid $12.00 a week for board and $2.00 protection money, which may or may not have been used by Madame for this purpose. Moreover, Mary was forced to buy at exorbitant prices clothes to wear in the house and later, when she was allowed one afternoon a week to go out, her street clothes. Clothing dealers had a monopoly of this business in the houses drove the bargain and divided the profits with Madame. Those clothing dealers have also been pointed out by other cases as being on hand at court to pay fines after raids, after which the girls return to work off the fines, more enslaved than ever. Mary found herself in a cheap house, in the blunt parlance of the district, a 'dollar' house. Each visitor netted her personally 50 cents, Madame getting the other half. From six to twelve visitors were received every night, and Mary was obliged to take anyone who came, Negroes and Chinamen as well. Practically no precautions were taken against disease and Mary became ill with syphilis. She still worked on, receiving her round of six to twelve visitors.

A judicial inquiry into vice and its enforcement in Montreal conducted by Justice Louis Coderre in 1924 and 1925 also documented the dozens of "houses of ill repute" operating in the city's red-light district. In his final report, Justice Coderre described the proliferation and aggressive nature of Montreal's white slavers. The agents of the city's whorehouses could be found in billiards halls, hotel rotundas, restaurants, dance halls, taverns, railway stations, harbours, and even at church doors pursuing "clients by discreet invitations." Meanwhile, "prostitution runs rampant in the streets with its addicts and its protectors who have always in their hands a card with the name and address of a public woman." The judge also decried the organized nature of the city's sex trade: "Prostitution itself, commerce in human flesh, in its most shameful form, and most degrading effect, operates and flourishes in Montreal like a perfectly organized commercial enterprise; I would dare say that few industrial or commercial establishments have as perfect an organization, as powerful methods of action, a personnel as well-groomed and as rigorous an internal discipline; I do not know of any which have in such a short time enriched so great a number of proprietors." By way of conclusion he argues, "proof made at the inquiry reveals an astonishing state of affairs and, I might say, an alarming one. Vice shows itself in our city with such a hideousness and insolence that are born of the certitude that it will go unpunished; like a giant octopus it stretches its tentacles in every direction and threatens to strangle a population which is three-quarters healthy and moral."

While appearing before the Coderre inquiry, Dr. Alfred K. Haywood — Superintendent of the Montreal General Hospital, which treated a number of the red-light district's prostitutes — provided extensive testimony that alluded to the organized nature of Montreal's sex trade. This included declarations on the efforts by pimps to procure new prostitutes, the use of drug addiction to ensnarl and imprison women, the slave-like conditions under which the women were forced to work, and the network of accomplices, such as bail bondsmen whose job it was to extricate the women after they have been charged, doctors and nurses who performed abortions on the prostitutes, and corrupt police and government officials who turned a blind eye to the city's vice industry. The doctor was personally told by "several" prostitutes who attended his hospital that they were forced into the sex trade after being "picked up in the street" and "drugged." Many of the addicted women had little other means than prostitution to support their habit. "A woman very seldom has the courage to steal," Dr. Haywood testified, "and dozens yes, hundreds of them have told me personally that they entered into houses of prostitution, where their entry had been made very easy, for the purpose of making enough money to purchase drugs."

Dr. Haywood described to the inquiry how he had hired a detective to find a missing woman he suspected was working the red-light district. In the course of his work, the detective found her in a brothel on City Hall Avenue, "in bed with a coloured man and he found in practically every room in that house coloured men

in bed with white women. He found the house full of drugs . . ." The detective brought the woman to the hospital where she told Dr. Haywood that "she was put into this house by a drug peddler" who is now in jail. "The condition I found her in was almost too pitable to explain," the doctor told the inquiry. "Her normal weight should have been a hundred and forty five pounds and at that time we weighed her and she weighed one hundred pounds." He kept her at the hospital for nearly a month and "thought we had cured her of the drug habit." She was twenty-three years old at the time, a widow of a man who died during the influenza epidemic. To deal with her grief she began "taking ten grains of morphine a day and as much as four grains at a time. She started taking the morphine five years ago and after her husband died found it necessary to get into a life of prostitution in order that she might secure money for drugs." The young woman also admitted that she "had been pregnant several times, but have been able to get rid of her baby by visiting a certain doctor who is now in jail for life for this practice." Dr. Haywood confirmed that medical professionals had been hired to perform these illegal procedures. He also noted that a pathologist working at Montreal General was approached by a brothel operator to see "if some arrangements could not be made whereby her girls could come to the hospital and be examined regularly and be given a certificate of good health." The pathologist was told he would be paid "a liberal sum for that work."

Vancouver's red-light district also thrived during the first quarter of the century, due in part to a steady migratory flow of merchant seamen, loggers, fishermen, and other seasonal labourers. The bawdy houses were tolerated, British Columbia historian Daniel Francis contends, as long as they "did not advertise themselves too blatantly, conformed to liquor regulations, and the women did not solicit too aggressively." But even in Vancouver's laissez-faire atmosphere, reformers pressured police and politicians to launch periodic crackdowns, which accomplished little except the creation of a highly transient population of pimps and prostitutes. According to Francis:

During 1907, responding to a public outcry, authorities closed the Dupont Street bawdy houses and arrested many of the prostitutes. But the brothels simply relocated around the corner in Canton Alley and Shanghai Alley, then the centre of Chinatown, and later a couple of blocks south to Shore Street, a short lane of ramshackle buildings running off Main Street. In 1910, a resident of Shore Street reported that "there are seven houses of prostitution all showing red lights" and "every night hundreds of men may be seen going to and from these houses."

At a 1928 judicial inquiry into vice and police corruption in Vancouver, one police official stated the "conditions are practically wide open so far as gambling and prostitutes are concerned," while the chief constable presented statistics showing that 489 "bawdy house keepers" had been charged between 1925 and 1927 alone. The most well known of these was Joe Celona, a politically astute über-pimp who was known as the "King of the Bawdy Houses," the "vice czar," and the "the mayor of East Hastings." Born in Italy in 1898, Celona immigrated to Vancouver shortly after the First World War and soon became well known as one of the city's most disreputable citizens. Celona owned several other well-attended brothels in the city. He was colour blind when it came to both the prostitutes and their clientele, provided cab drivers a cash payment for every referral, paid off police officers to look the other way, was rumoured to have had one Vancouver mayor in his pocket, fortified his bordellos by installing iron doors, and vigorously fought every charge laid against him. After being convicted on one occasion, Celona registered the houses he owned in the name of his wife or his brother, who were also responsible for managing some of his brothels. The people of Vancouver were aghast when they learned from the testimony of one police officer that a whorehouse Celona operated at 210 Keefer Street, in the heart of Chinatown, was "a resort that Chinamen were going to and that there were several young white girls in the resort and Chinamen stated that they went there to have intercourse with these girls."

One of Celona's associates was Frank Casisa, who was first arrested for operating a disorderly house at

Joe Celona

240 Georgia Street. According to one police officer who testified at the 1928 inquiry: "It was an old house and there was one big room in the bottom and a curtain between. There were no lights on the house, and a man would go in and he would go in with the girl at the back of the curtain, and Casisa would watch out in front for an officer and as soon as he saw any officer going to raid the house he would tip off the girl and she would go through a small cut into the house next door and get away. And I arrested him at that time and we could not get the girl. In fact I heard it was his own wife."

The inquiry heard several accounts of the brutal methods personally employed by Frank Casisa to keep his prostitutes in line. Among those testifying was Jean Smith, a sometimes housekeeper and prostitute who worked in Casisa's bawdy houses:

Smith: Well, I told [Vancouver police detective] McLaughlin that I was in the hospital with a premature birth in February; it was St. Valentine's Day when I went there. I told him how sick I was; I nearly died and Dr. Brewster was my doctor and he can tell you the condition I was in and when I came out he met me.

Q: Did you tell McLaughlin anything about the cause of the premature birth?

Smith: Yes, that he had beat me so that he had brought on premature birth.

Q: Who had beaten you?

Smith: Casisa, Frank Casisa.

Q: How did he beat you?

Smith: He threw me downstairs once. He beat me with his feet and his hands and up against the wall.

Q: When was the time that you had this trouble with Casisa when he did this?

Smith: You mean when he beat me?

Q: Yes, and caused the premature birth?

Smith: Well, he used to beat me often.

Q: When was the premature birth?

Smith: In February, in here, in this hospital.

Q: How did he beat you?

Smith: With his fists.

Q: Why did he do that?

Smith: He was just cranky because business was not good and he thought it was my fault because the business was not good. I told him he should not talk like that, but he just took his spite out on me. For no cause at all he hit me.

Q: After the premature birth you came out of the hospital?

Smith: Yes.

Q: And you went back to live with Casisa again?

Smith: Yes, I had to go back again.

Q: And it was then that you became Casisa's housekeeper, was it not?

Smith: Oh, I was the housekeeper before that.

Q: You were the housekeeper before that?

Smith: Yes, about two months before.

Q: Let us go back. Did you tell McLaughlin all about this when you went to the Police Station, that Casisa had run this house and received part of the money?

Smith: Yes.

Q: You told him that, too. Did you tell McLaughlin anything else?

Smith: Yes, I told him after I came out of the hospital that I was in the family way again; I was four and a half months and he [Casisa] tipped me to Nurse Jessop for an illegal operation; he gave

me $46 to go to her for an illegal operation. She performed it, but did not do it right and I had to go to the hospital two days later. They took me from the Balmoral Hotel in the ambulance to the General hospital here.

Q: What happened at the Balmoral Hotel?

Smith: Five days after I came out of the hospital he beat me up terribly.

Q: Casisa?

Smith: Yes.

Q: What did he do to you?

Smith: He blacked my eye and all his finger marks were on my throat and both sides of my face were black and blue and my chest here and the backs of my hand where he grabbed me like that with his fingers.

Q: Your mouth was cut?

Smith: My mouth was all cut and swollen and my nose had a great big mark upon it here and my head up here had a great big lump on and a little vein was sticking out and the proprietor of the hotel came and threw Frank out.

Q: That was the Balmoral Hotel?

Smith: Yes.

Q: In what room?

Smith: This beating was done in 614, 614, but I was in 707 when they took me to the hospital.

Q: They took you to a hospital in an ambulance that time?

Smith: Yes.

Q: As the result of the beating?

Smith: That was when the illegal operation was, when I was sick.

Q: That was five days after the illegal operation?

Smith: Yes, this beating I am just telling you was about five days after.

Q: That is in your chest?

Smith: Yes, and oh, I was terribly sick, but anyhow…

Q: What did he say about that?

Smith: He never done anything. He never even got a doctor, never got any medicine, and when I got a little better he made me work again, but I can only whisper and so after I left why

I had to go to a doctor. I was awfully sick and blood came, came up like when I was at 511 Main Street and I went to the doctor and he x-rayed my lungs in the hospital and he said it was T.B.

Q: Was there anything else?

Smith: Yes.

Q: You had a blood disease?

Smith: I had four plus Wasserman.*

Q: You contracted that?

Smith: Yes, I found out later that Frank Casisa had the same thing and I must have got it from him.

Q: Did you tell McLaughlin about that?

Smith: Yes, I told McLaughlin, but I did not know at the time it was from him [Casisa], so I told McLaughlin I did not know, but later I found out from several people.

Q: Just a minute, now. Did you sleep with Frank Casisa?

Smith: Yes, Frank Casisa came around to my window the night before last night.

Q: The night before last night?

Smith: Yes.

Q: At the hospital here?

Smith: Yes.

Q: How long did you work after the operation?

Smith: Oh, I just worked a week or so.

Q: After the operation?

Smith: Yes.

Q: You think that your physical condition — do you think you could work after a serious operation?

Smith: Well, I never worked in the house very much, just once in a way when the girls would not be on duty, while I would be there in the morning.

Q: What do you mean by "working"? Were you prostituting yourself after the illegal operation?

Smith: Oh, just twice, I guess.

Q: A week afterwards?

Smith: Yes.

Q: One week after the operation?

Smith: Yes.

Q: You were able to prostitute yourself as soon as that?

Smith: I was not able to, but had to.

THE UNIVERSITY OF GAMBLERS

Long before governments in Canada began legalizing gambling, anyone wishing to partake in a professionally run game of chance had to visit an underground gambling den, while those who preferred to bet on the horses or a hockey game had to consult with their local bookmaker. During the 1890s, the *Toronto Daily Star* ran a number of stories on the illegal gambling parlours in the city. In a May 1894 article entitled "On the throw of dice," the newspaper described the "gambling halls in full operation where many men lose most of their earnings and where a few make very comfortable livings without working." The most popular destinations for gamblers in Toronto during this time were the "poker joints," which are "frequent at the present time and have been for many years." The newspaper noted that while rooms in private houses and public buildings are devoted to friendly games where a few meet to play for sport "others are devoted to games where sharks meet unsuspecting victims and fleece them to the limit of their possessions." The paper also describes a new innovation in the gambling world that had become all the rage: craps. In October 1894, the *Star* ran stories on a "cook shop," which played host to 24-hour crap games and the numerous hotels where gambling was carried out. Six years later, the *Star* reported on a police raid at a gambling operation "for the working class" run by Frank Duffy and located in a barn at the corner of Queen and Leslie streets:

> On Saturday night Frank Duffy was chief Pooh-Bah in a gambling den; now he is a broom-maker in the Central Prison. When the police raided Duffy's place they did not find the bones rolling on green baize tables, and the players resting their weary feet on Brussels carpet. The banker did not wear a diamond pin and keep his silver in a tray. Works of art were conspicuous by their absence from the wall,

---

* The "Wasserman" is a blood test used to detect syphilis. "Four plus" indicates the presence of syphilis.

and the flickering oil lights revealed chinks in the walls and a straw-littered floor. The bones rolled on a canvas-covered table in one corner. In another greasy cards were slapped down upon another table, where a poker game, with a cent ante and a nickel limit, was in progress.

The gamblers arrested by police during the raid were described by the newspaper as "rough-clothed workingmen" and once they were all assembled at the police station, "the roster of drunks and disorderlies read like an enunciation of an Irish Colony."

By 1901, professional gambling operations in Toronto were perceived to be so widespread and the police response to them so lax, the city's Board of Police Commissioners was compelled to hold a public inquiry. In his testimony before the inquiry, the chief constable of the Toronto police, Lieutenant Colonel Grasett, blamed the low rate of police arrests on the highly mobile nature of the games: "You are probably aware that gambling is conducted now in a different way from what it used to be; at one time there were cumberous appliances necessary for the games which were very difficult to get rid of hastily; and when the police visited gambling rooms and found those implements there they had prima facie evidence of what went on; now those appliances are either too slow or else too self-evident so the gamblers resort to crap-playing, which is a game played with dice, easily disposed of — they can be thrown out of the window in an instant or concealed about the person — and to card-playing." A staff inspector added that some of the gambling operations had lookouts so that once police entered a gambling hall, it was inevitably empty.

In addition to gambling dens, bookmaking was becoming a growing source of revenue for underground entrepreneurs in Toronto. Local "horse-books" became widespread with the opening of the Woodbine Racetrack in 1874 and its decision to license individuals to take bets on site. It was not long after that hordes of unlicensed bookmakers began showing up at the track, offering better odds than their legitimate counterparts. By the turn of the century, the legion of bookmakers who stationed themselves at the track had become so plentiful that some were calling Woodbine the "University of Gamblers." Off-track betting operations or "bucket shops" were also popping up throughout the city to accommodate those who were unable to attend Woodbine or other racetracks in person. Testimony at the 1901 police commission by a self-confessed bookie named Alexander Smiley suggests that bookmaking operations in Toronto had already become well organized. In his testimony, Smiley also indicated that some bookies in Toronto were part of a larger gambling syndicate based in Buffalo. This relationship allowed residents of upstate New York to place bets on horse races at Woodbine, while Toronto residents could bet on races at various tracks in New York State through their local bookie.

This long-distance relationship among bettors and bookies was greatly facilitated by the telegraph system, which could quickly relay up-to-the-minute information on races and other sporting events between cities. The wire service became so vital to off-track betting that any self-respecting bookmaking operation had to have a "wire room," complete with a large blackboard where the odds and results from racetracks all over North America were tallied. The wire service also bolstered the cross-border network of bookmakers by facilitating the transfer of money, whether it was to place a bet, for a payout, or to settle an account. Testimony at the 1901 inquiry revealed that the telegraph was used to remit funds from Toronto to Buffalo, where central accounts were maintained. The following exchange between Smiley and the inquiry commissioners provides a glimpse into the connections among bookmakers in the two cities, the organized nature of the betting industry, and the anonymity that was maintained among participants as a protective measure:

Q: Have you got agents that can do it with more than one [race]track?

Smiley: The one house will do business on every track.

Q: The one house in Buffalo?

Smiley: Yes

Q: And you are authorized to send telegrams to them "Collect"?

Smiley: He says he does that through an agent here in town.

Q: Don't you send them yourself?

Smiley: No sir.

Q: Don't you go to the Telegraph office with them?

Smiley: No sir.

Q: You always take them to this friend; who is he?

Smiley: Have I got to answer?

Q: Yes.

Smiley: Mr. Samuel Clapp is the gentleman's name.

Q: What is his address?

Smiley: He lives on Yonge St, somewheres; I don't know exactly his number.

Q: About where ...

Smiley: Up around the Avenue, pretty near opposite Yonge St. Avenue, or College St; somewheres around there.

Q: Does he keep a store?

Smiley: He keeps a bicycle store.

Q: But he would never know who these people were on whose behalf you had sent this money?

Smiley: No sir.

Q: Do you hand him a slip showing who the money is for?

Smiley: No; I just tell him to put so much money on for me.

Q: And if it is won you distribute it later after you know the result?

Smiley: Yes.

Q: And if it is lost you pay it to Mr. Clapp.

Smiley: Yes.

Q: At once?

Smiley: No; it may be a week or two weeks.

Q: As I understand it as far as this man Clapp and the Buffalo men are concerned, the whole matter is impersonal and the only person that is accounted to is yourself, you having placed the order?

Smiley: That is all.

Q: And Clapp does not know who the individuals are that made the arrangements with you?

Smiley: No.

The front pages of the *Toronto Daily Star* were a microcosm of the contradictions that inevitably accompanied legalized horse racing. At the top of the page, on a daily basis during racing season, the results of the previous day's runnings at Woodbine would be printed. On the same page, the reader could often find a story on the latest arrest of an unlicensed horse bookie. The arrests escalated as police, posing as bettors, began regular sting operations. Even if arrested and convicted, however, the penalties for bookmaking were minimal and hardly served as a deterrent. In one 1906 case, four associated Woodbine bookmakers caught in a police sting were each fined $50 and costs, despite the fact that the court heard evidence that their daily revenue was ten times that amount. (When one of the undercover officers took the stand he told the court how he placed bets with the accused for the purpose of securing evidence and described the betting board, sheets, and tickets provided by the bookies. In detailing his undercover operation, the constable described how he wagered $2 on a horse named Judge White to place first, second, or third. "Did you bid on him because he was a judge?" the magistrate asked whimsically. "No, Your Worship," the police officer dutifully responded.)

By the end of 1906, new laws, regulations, and court decisions resulted in a bizarre legal situation where unlicensed bookmakers at Woodbine could avoid any criminal penalty for keeping a "betting place" as long as they did not operate from an enclosed or designated space. The result was an even larger contingent of bookies at the track, some of whom took bets while riding atop bicycles to ensure compliance with the court ruling. In 1907, after thirty-nine bookies were charged at Woodbine, an even bigger scandal erupted when it was revealed that the Jockey Club was selling to bookies advance information — which included the names of jockeys, the weight of horses, and their trial times — before the information was printed in the official programs. On May 31, John G. Cavanagh and Mortimer Mahoney were charged with "keeping a disorderly house" at Woodbine, where they sold information to bookies for $10 a race. Not content with simply selling information, the two were also supplying their bookmaking customers all the associated paraphernalia, including a slate listing the names of the horses, a bag with the bookie's name on it, and betting tickets.

Police were also busy raiding off-track betting parlours. In August 1909, in what the *Daily Star* called "one of the most successful raids ever carried out by the detective force of Toronto," thirty-one men were arrested on charges of being either keepers or frequenters of betting houses. "The raid took the police to all sorts of business places — a tailor shop, a barber shop, a real estate office, a pool room, a food store, etc." After police entered his real estate office, one bookie tore the telephone off the wall, while another "reached for a knife on his desk, and with one slash cut the telephone wire, in order to block the officer from getting evidence in that way."

While the earliest of the illegal horse books in Toronto were run independently by small-time operators, they were increasingly pushed out or absorbed by organized gambling syndicates based in Buffalo. Indeed, bookmaking in the U.S. and Canada was becoming increasingly organized and centralized, a development some blame on the moral crusaders. In 1905, anti-gambling coalitions in the United States pressured Western Union to abandon its $2-million-a-year horse-racing wire service. This opened up the door for underworld figures to take over the business. As a result, according to Stephen Fox in his book on the history of organized crime in America, "Western Union wires still might carry racing information, but the underworld collected it, received it, and gathered most of the profits. Reformers had once again outlawed something into the hands of gangsters." As gambling operations became better organized, a division of labour began to emerge, which included such positions as runners, collectors, enforcers, controllers (mid-level managers who hire and supervise the bookies), bankers (who control the money, pay winners, and bribe police), technicians to install the wire service, and operators to decode the information. By the 1920s, large-scale bookmaking consortiums were now operating in Canada's major cities, most of which had ties to American gambling syndicates. In December 1923, under the headline "Toronto is biggest betting place in North America," *Daily Star* correspondent Ernest Hemingway wrote that bettors could place a wager in Toronto for horse racing or sports events in cities across Canada and the United States. He estimated there were ten thousand bettors in Toronto generating profits for gambling organizations that was as much as $100,000 a day. "It has been estimated that more men are employed in illegal betting in North America than work in the steel business," Hemingway wrote. "And it all goes on under the surface."

In his inquiry into vice conditions in Montreal, Justice Coderre also discussed the increased organization of illegal betting houses in that city, which were —

> ordinarily hidden behind barber shops and tobacco stores. Their doors are open to all, which shows how safely they can be operated. They are affiliated with a central bureau which, for a certain sum, paid weekly, bring to the small places quotations and results. The probe revealed that these operations have been allowed to go on for months and years past and this without the police succeeding in catching those at the head of these activities. People holding these places are sometimes raided but as soon as their fine is paid, start again without being molested.

In Vancouver, several social clubs came under investigation in 1904 by the provincial attorney general for gambling infractions. Among these was the Playgoers' Club, which was incorporated in 1903 under the Benevolent Societies Act to foster "social intercourse, mutual helpfulness, mental and moral improvement, and rational recreation." Complaints were received by the police that gambling was taking place at this club and, in April 1904, its manager was convicted of keeping a common gaming house and was ordered to pay a fine of $97.50 plus court costs. The club folded operations after this conviction. On June 13, 1905, thirteen men were convicted of gambling at the Vancouver Chess Club. In a letter to the provincial secretary, the attorney general wrote that the informant who blew the whistle on the club "states that games, such as poker and black jack, were generally played, and that, although he frequently visited the place, he never saw a chess board there." During two separate raids of the Elks Club (not to be confused with the Fraternal Society of Elks) police found draw poker and roulette games in progress. Police also found a ledger maintained by the proprietor, Mr. J. J. Bottger, which kept track of each $1 chip that the house took as a rake-off. The Eureka Club, another of Bottger's operations, was located upstairs behind the Eureka Cigar Shop. In reference to this well-hidden gambling operation, the attorney general wrote:

> Access to it may be gained through the shop or from the lane on the north side of the building. To reach the gaming room, it is necessary to go upstairs, pass through a small room, and from that into another room; then, passing through the second room and on turning to your right, you reach the Club room. In one of the doors, through which it is necessary to go, there is a little slide — a peep-hole, the witnesses call it — which enabled the person inside who guarded the door to scan any visitor before he was admitted. The police stated that they always found this door guarded and never could reach the gaming room without considerable delay outside the peep-hole door. The gaming room is furnished with four tables, three of them, at least, being round card tables, and a number of chairs. A witness, who had played in the Club, stated that it was frequented by white men, Japanese, and, occasionally, by Chinamen. The game played was draw poker.

Despite repeated police raids, by 1910 the acting solicitor of Vancouver had declared in a letter to the mayor that the keepers of gambling dens in the city "have unlimited financial resources to contest the efforts of the police to drive them out of business."

Vancouver's Chinatown was also a hot spot for gamblers of all races and ethnicities, and during the 1920s it came under the microscope of police and the city's judicial inquiry into vice. In 1918, the *Globe* newspaper estimated, "there are over forty gambling dens in Chinatown today, and that many of these have advertisements in their windows for 'fantan' as above stated." One police official provided the inquiry with a list of thirty addresses in Chinatown that he said were operating as gambling dens between 1921 and 1928. Among the biggest gambling house operators in Chinatown were Chow Wong Lun (a.k.a. Georgie Chow) — who ran one so large that it was described

by a police officer as "an enormous barn of a gambling place" — and Joe Won Lum, who admitted to being the "bossman" of a Chinese lottery at 846 Main Street and a gambling hall outside of Chinatown on Davie Street. The inquiry was told that Lum was "dealing with pretty well high up English people who have got most of the money" and in order to better serve his white clientele, Lum sent out runners with lottery tickets that his customers could mark at their leisure. This innovative service saved the affluent Caucasian gamblers the indignity of frequenting a Chinese establishment, helped to modernize the numbers racket in the city, and made Lum a tidy profit. According to ledgers seized by police, Joe Won Lum's "small place" at 615 Davie Street was able to take in as much as $1,440 a month, while only paying out winnings of $34. Lum also confessed that he was a partner with Georgie Chow in other gambling operations.

One man more than any other stood out under the glaring spotlight of the Vancouver judicial inquiry: Shue Moy, the self-proclaimed Potato King — an appellation derived from his ownership of the largest potato ranch in Canada — but who was best known as Vancouver's "King of the Gamblers." Moy, who had come to British Columbia from China in 1899, had an eclectic career after arriving in the province. In addition to farming potatoes, he owned a grocery store, sold lumber in Victoria, and served as the postmaster in a small interior town. Although he was never convicted of a criminal offence, Moy was accused of operating several gambling houses, running a brothel, trafficking opium, overseeing protection rackets, and providing generous bribes to city officials, including the chief of police and the mayor of Vancouver. In his testimony to the 1928 judicial inquiry, one police officer named Harold Duggan, who confessed to having known Shue Moy "intimately for three years," stated that Moy had told him he had an interest in two gambling dens. Detective Ricci, of the Vice Squad, testified that Moy did not outright own any gambling halls, but had an interest in four of them located in and around Chinatown. In the following exchange between inquiry commissioners and Ricci, the police detective explains that gambling operations in Chinatown are rarely owned solely by one person, but controlled by groups of investors, through companies, benevolent societies, or other types of association:

Q: You said yesterday that he [Moy] was interested in four places; that is #54 Cordova Street East and West, 91 Pender and 119 Pender. Now, you do not know the extent of his interest in the places on Cordova Street, 54 east and west?

Ricci: I know it is a company.

Q: You did tell us there was no such thing practically as one Chinaman having a gambling house. It was always companies?

Ricci: Companies.

Q: Syndicates?

Ricci: Always depending on what district they come from in China. And these certain people come from China from a certain district; they get together; they are like a bunch of brothers. They call themselves cousins and brothers and they get a little money and chip in and start a gambling house.

In his testimony before the commission, Joe Won Lum confirmed that most Chinese gambling halls were run as partnerships. He asserted that joint ventures were essential to ensuring the solvency of the gambling houses and explained to the commission the system by which large bets were handled. Amounts too big for the smaller operations were turned over to a "clearing house" that was itself a partnership among Chinatown merchants. Detective Ricci concurred with this assessment, stating that the amount of capital required for some of the larger gambling halls to cover potential losses was greater than any one man could invest: "There is no gambling joint existing in Chinatown unless there is 10,000, 20,000 or 30,000 dollars in the back and there are very few lottery joints that start with less than $10,000. I know this myself for facts, especially in Chinatown, because they may go broke with one night, may lose $10,000 which I know somebody wins several times $10,000 and go back the next night and lose it all and be drunk for a week."

When put on the stand, Moy tried to characterize himself as nothing more than a patron of Chinatown's gambling operations, but quickly confessed to having an interest in several gambling joints in the city:

Q: Since you came to Vancouver, what have you been doing?

Moy: Oh, I am just gambling a little myself.

Q: You are a gambler?

Moy: Yes.

Q: By a gambler, what do you mean, a man who runs gaming houses or gambling houses?

Moy: No, I play most, I have a little interest in 54 Cordova East.

Q: I will come to that later, but you make your living, you say, by gambling?

Moy: Yes.

Q: Actually gambling?

Moy: Yes.

Q: You have been referred to throughout this enquiry as the King of the Gamblers. What do they call you on Water Street?

Moy: The Potato King.

Q: Why do they call you the Potato King?

Moy: I don't know, I guess I have too much potatoes to sell.

Q: It is true that you had the biggest potato ranch in Canada up at Lillooet?

Moy: Yes.

Q: And they called you the Potato King?

Moy: Yes.

Q: You are King twice in your own right. Listen, have you any convictions against you?

Moy: Never.

Q: You had an interest, he did not know much, in 54 Cordova West and 54 Cordova East. Is that right?

Moy: Yes, I have one ninth.

Q: One ninth interest in those two places?

Moy: Yes.

Q: You are, I understand, a member of the club at 91 Pender Street?

Moy: Yes.

Q: And also 119 Pender Street?

Moy: Yes.

Q: Those are clubs composed of a large number of Chinese?

Moy: 91 has 120 members, and I have one share. 119 has 160 members, and I have one share.

Q: You have one share in each of those places?

Moy: Yes.

THE GRAFT-RIDDEN CITY

To understand why organized prostitution and gambling seemed so impenetrable to government enforcement efforts, one must appreciate the extent to which vice operators were protected, or at least tacitly ignored, by police agencies and politicians, sometimes in return for generous compensation. Prostitution and gambling were often viewed as harmless vices by police and politicians and, as such, they chose to focus on more serious crimes or could rationalize taking a bribe. The result was that the underground vice industry spawned corruption in police forces and other government agencies in major Canadian cities. During the first thirty years of the 20th century, each of Canada's three largest cities had at least one judicial inquiry into government corruption resulting from organized criminal activities, and gambling in particular. Toronto's inquiry was held in 1901 (there would be more municipal and provincial corruption investigations in the years to come), Montreal's began in 1924, and in British Columbia a provincial inquiry was held in 1923 and another was convened by the city of Vancouver in 1928.

Toronto's first judicial inquiry into underground gambling and corruption was prompted by a series of articles in Toronto's *Evening News* in November of 1901. These stories charged the police department with failing to suppress professional gambling and accused some police officials of being in collusion with gambling operators and bookmakers. While the commission exonerated most senior police officials, the inquiry did find that a number of police officers were placing bets with local bookmakers.

Former RCMP commissioner Clifford Harvison referred to Montreal as "a graft-ridden city in the early twenties" where "the rot of bribery and corruption had crept into branches at all levels of Government and had spread to undermine law enforcement and to tilt, if not upset, the city's scales of justice." Harvison backed up his allegations with descriptions of mutually convenient arrangements between the local government and the city's brothels:

> While not licensed, the houses paid taxes under an indirect and smoothly organized system. By arrangement, raids were carried out during which it was required that a "madam" and a specified number of girls and "found-ins" would be available for arrest. The frequency and timing for the raids and the number of arrests required worked out in accordance with the size, location, class, and business potential for each establishment. Regular patrons, having been warned, stayed away during these brief interruptions, while the madam and her girls went visiting for an hour or so before resuming business as usual. Their places were taken by "stand-ins," derelicts recruited from the flophouses and hang-outs of the area for a set fee of two dollars. Each plea of guilty brought fines that followed a fixed scale. The fines were paid forthwith by representatives of the organization that controlled the brothels.

Similar accusations were made by a group of private citizens investigating vice conditions in Montreal. They wrote in their 1918 report that "houses of commercialized prostitution and gambling dens are tolerated and exist openly in large numbers" and fines collected from convictions of brothel operators were simply an indirect form of licensing by the city for "revenue purposes." The committee documented in its report that between May 27 and November 17, 1917, "fines collected from raids at disorderly houses amounted to $41,604.75. In practically none of these cases, according to police, do these fines result in cessation of the activities of those fined."

In his testimony to the Coderre Inquiry in 1924, Dr. Alfred Haywood of the Montreal General Hospital simply stated, "I don't think that the Red Light District could exist without the leniency being shown by somebody, whether it is police or Court officials or whoever it might be. It would be utterly impossible for a Red Light District such as ours to exist without leniency being shown." Justice Coderre did not find systemic corruption within the Montreal police. But he did conclude that senior police officials wilfully turned a blind eye to vice in the red-light district and, because of incompetent leadership or lax discipline, allowed pockets of corruption to form within the police department whereby some gambling houses were being tipped off about looming raids. In his final report, Justice Coderre summarized the evidence provided by Monsieur Dore, the proprietor of one gambling house:

One of the employees in this shop, E. Provost, remarked that at each raid by the police — about once a year — the gambling room was emptied as if automatically, a few minutes before the arrival of the constables, so that when the latter arrived, they had nothing to do but to collect the telephones, the bookmaker and two or three bettors, just as much as was necessary, in order to make a case to be put to the credit of Sgt. Archambault, specially entrusted with this service. The conclusion is inevitable: the keeper having been notified, passed the word to his clients who, ten minutes before the police came, deserted the room and took refuge on all the available seats in the barber shop. The straw-men employed by Dore and his Greek associate, docilely followed the policeman, came to court to plead guilty, received his sentence and paid his fine on the spot; the following morning business started again and went on as prosperously as ever until the next raid, about a year later.

One focus of the Coderre Inquiry was the alleged relationship between the city's chief of police and Tony Frank, a habitual offender who robbed banks and armoured cars, worked as a pimp, operated gambling halls, and ran a protection racket. While Frank was involved in multiple enterprises, much of his wealth came from the influence and power he held over other gambling house operators in the city, many of whom paid Frank a percentage of their profits, supposedly for protection from police, but more likely for protection from Frank's gang of thugs. Evidence was provided at the Coderre Inquiry by Abraham Mouckley, who testified that despite protection money paid to Frank, his gambling house was still raided by police:

Q: Did Tony Frank go and see you after you had pleaded with [Police Chief] Sauve to be lenient? Did Tony Frank say anything to you?

Mouckley: Well, Tony Frank didn't come and see me at all.

Q: What happened?

Mouckley: I got a phone call.

Q: From whom?

Mouckley: From a party. I don't know who it was from.

Q: And then what?

Mouckley: Told me to go to Tony Frank's place of business and see me.

Q: What about?

Mouckley: Yes, I went there and when I went there, he told me he never knew I was operating a gambling house, it was too bad, he heard I got raided last week, and asked me what I had decided to do, whether I should remain there or to close. I told him, I said, "If I cannot go on, I might as well close." Whether he obtained money from me for police protection — I don't think it was police protection, because I did not get any — it might have been protection from hold-ups; that is all I ever got but he got money from me.

Q: Did you pay any money to Tony Frank, and if so how many times and how much.

Mouckley: I gave him four hundred dollars.

Mouckley later conceded that the money paid to Frank was most likely to protect his gambling operations from Frank's gang. "No police protection was mentioned," Mouckley meekly confessed. "The only thing [Frank] said was — 'I will see that there will be no harm; no harm will come to you or your players.'"

Even before the Coderre Inquiry began, allegations were made at a robbery trial that Montreal city police had been tipped off about the planned holdup of an armoured car, but did nothing. The robbery, which took place on April 1, 1924, by a crew assembled by Tony Frank, was successful, but, in the process, bank employee Henri Cleroux was shot and killed. Police arrested two of the holdup men and, facing the prospect of the death penalty, they implicated Tony Frank. Coderre interviewed most of the accused, including Giuseppe Serafini who claimed that an understanding was in place between the thieves, the receivers of the stolen goods, and the police, whereby all profits from the sale of the goods would be split with certain police officers. Allegations that the gang had connections with Montreal police continued to mount when one of the robbers turned out to be a former police officer. Some speculated that one of the corrupt officers still serving on the police force was the chief himself, as it was well known that he had an ongoing relationship with Frank. However, there was insufficient evidence to pursue these charges and Frank took any corroborating evidence he may have had to the gallows. On June 24, 1924, Tony Frank, ex-detective Louis Morel, Giuseppe Serafini, Frank Gambino, Mike Valentino, and Leo Davis were all found guilty in the murder of Henri Cleroux and were sentenced to death. All were hanged on October 24, 1924.

In 1928, Vancouver City Council established a special commission to look into accusations that members of the police force were receiving bribes from professional criminals. In establishing the articles of the commission, the provincial attorney general wrote that since at least 1910, allegations had been circulating that police officers were accepting cash payments "from the professional gamblers, both Chinese and white, and from the keepers of houses of prostitution, in return for protection from prosecution." T.W. Fletcher, an alderman and member of the commission, even charged that criminal influence reached as high as the mayor. From April 30 to July 6, 1928, Justice R.S. Lennie heard 180 hours of testimony from ninety-eight witnesses, including the mayor, various police officers, other civic officials, as well as a host of alleged gamblers, gambling hall operators, bookmakers, prostitutes, and pimps. The public inquiry was headline news for weeks, with sensational evidence suggesting that gambling dens and prostitution houses were operating with immunity from the law, while top police officials and the mayor's office had conspired against any police crackdowns. In his final report, Justice Lennie wrote, "Some of these police officers both uniformed men and detectives gave evidence of instances where they were unable to secure support from their superiors and indicated that gambling and disorderly houses were carried on to such an extent and under such circumstances that they were unable to suppress the conduct of certain individuals and their positions as policemen were flouted by Chinese gamblers and the keepers of disorderly houses, as they contend because of the lack of co-operation

and interference by their superiors and the Mayor of the City." A former Liberal member of the provincial legislature, Gerry McGeer demanded that Mayor L.D. Taylor be removed from office, proclaiming, "Organized lawlessness has taken charge of the town."

Police representatives were the most forthcoming about the open nature of the gambling and prostitution houses in Vancouver and the almost complete lack of heed that their owners, employees, and patrons had for police enforcement. In his report, Justice Lennie reflected on the appearance of Vancouver police constable Angus Murdock Stewart, who was "almost ashamed to work on his beat with the number of gambling houses that were running wide open and he was particularly impressed with the disregard they had for policemen entering their places. They quite openly came out of their places counting the spots on their lottery tickets and made no effort to hide or conceal their gambling when he went in there."

The proprietors of some prostitution and gambling houses testified that they made payments to the police, which ranged from $5 to $50 a month. Most notable of these was Georgie Chow, who stated that in 1926 and 1927 he was paying $50 a month to Sergeant George McLaughlin and Inspector John Jackson to protect his gambling operation from police raids. Chow told the inquiry a detailed story concerning his alleged gift of a $360 diamond ring to Sergeant McLaughlin in early 1926, while Commissioner Lennie described a bribe reportedly given to Inspector Jackson by one "Chinaman" who "left a note naming the addresses of three gambling houses on a slip of paper enclosed in an envelope with four twenty-dollar bills. The Chinaman who delivered it was well-known to Inspector John Jackson on whose desk it was left." Lennie concluded the note "was accepted to protect those places from being further raided." While Chow's partner, Joe Won Lum, flatly denied ever paying protection money to police, one of his employees, Joe Yem, contradicted his boss when questioned by the inquiry:

Q: Did you ever know beforehand when a raid was coming?

Yem: In most of the cases.

Q: In most of the cases you knew beforehand that the raid was coming?

Yem: Sometimes I know beforehand and sometimes we don't know.

Q: When you knew beforehand what happened?

Yem: The boss man told us and led them one or two men up to the jail.

Q: I see the boss man told you, who was that— Joe Won Lum?

Yem: Yes.

Q: Where did he get his information from, do you know?

Yem: I don't know where he get his information, but he told me he pay $50 for police protection.

Asked point-blank by commission lawyers why he was providing evidence against the police since he was also paying protection money to them, Georgie Chow declared that police were not giving him the same privileges that Shue Moy was receiving. He objected to his gambling operation at 60 Cordova West being closed down by police while those of his competitors were allowed to stay open. Chow said he had gone to Inspector Jackson to complain that Shue Moy was running wide open at 54 Cordova Street West, but when Chow opened up next door at 60 Cordova Street West, police officers came and "raised hell." According to Chow, Inspector Jackson once told him, Shue Moy "is a good friend to the mayor. He can do anything he wants." In his testimony, Inspector John Jackson also alluded to the preferential treatment that Moy appeared to be receiving from the mayor's office and senior police officials:

Jackson: I say the Chief of Police and the Mayor both discussed the thing with me, that they did not want us to bother with these fellows at all, but to go down and get after these holdups and so forth. That is as far as I know.

Q: Then as a matter of fact it was due to the instructions that you received from the Mayor and the Chief of Police that these places were allowed to run under your inspectorate?

Jackson: I suppose.

Q: Eh?

Jackson: I suppose that is about it.

Q: Now, can you tell me why Georgie Chow was put out of business?

Jackson: There were several of them put out of business as we went along.

Q: For instance, take this famous place 54 Cordova Street West and I point out to you there were four raids on that place?

Jackson: Yes.

Q: And at this little place 1263 Seymour Street of Georgie Chow's there were fifteen raids in the same period of time? Was that all at Georgie Chow's at that time?

Jackson: Well, Georgie Chow and his partner, he had several other places I understand, four or five places, but this particular one at 1263 Seymour Street, it was raided fifty times; Cordova Street was raided four times and Joe Won Lum's famous 17 Crounce Alley was only raided seven.

Q: Can you give me any explanation why you were not going after 54 Cordova Street East and 54 Cordova Street West?

Jackson: No.

Q: I am going to suggest the reason was it was because you knew the Mayor wanted those places of Shue Moy's to operate?

Jackson: The Mayor did not want us to bother about it. I have told you that before and that is as far as I can go.

Jackson: And further than that Shue Moy's places in Chinatown were never raided either?

Jackson: Yes.

Q: Eh?

Jackson: Yes.

Q: In the year 1927 tell me of one single place of Shue Moy's in Chinatown that was raided in 1927? Can you do that?

Jackson: Offhand I cannot tell you, no.

In fact, much of the inquiry centred on Moy's reputed cozy relationship with the mayor of Vancouver, Louis D. Taylor. Evidence presented before the commission, including testimony by Moy himself, showed that he visited the mayor's home on several occasions and had also made a number of financial contributions to his political campaigns. Other witnesses provided more damning evidence. Ah Kim, a partner with Moy in one gambling house, testified that he paid $300 a month to the mayor so that Moy could keep his main gambling house at 54 Cordova West open. Although Moy denied he ever paid protection money to the mayor or police, he did admit it was "a Chinese custom" to give "gifts" to officials. Even more damning, the chief of police described a conversation he had with the mayor who requested "that two specific lottery joints be allowed to run as there were two Chinamen who had assisted him in his election who wished to open these places."

Also implicated in the corruption scandal was the reigning King of the Whorehouses, Joe Celona, who also was alleged to have ties to the mayor. Numerous police officers provided testimony that they were reprimanded for aggressive enforcement actions against Celona's properties. In his sworn statement to the commission, Constable William George Thompson described one encounter with Joe Celona outside a brothel he operated:

> I questioned Chinamen going in and out and searched them for narcotic drugs and gave them all the trouble I could and this caused a falling off in the business and one night Joe Celona, he said that he was Joe Celona, wanted to know why I was riding his joint all the time. I told him that it was about time that he was moving on, that I did not want to have anything to do with him, that I would take him in and charge him with vagrancy. He made a bet with me that I would be fired off the beat the next night. I asked him who was going to do all this, that he could not do it and he said "His good friends." I said "Who is your good friend?" He said "The big boss at the city hall." I said "Who is the big boss at the city hall?" He said "That is all right, you will find out." I did find out the next night. I came to work at eleven o'clock and I was told that the deputy chief wanted to see me in the chief's office. I went there and Deputy Chief Leatherdale was there himself and he said that he had a complaint that the officer on the beat, number 184, had been riding 210 Keefer Street, had been camping on the doorstep too much. He said that the man, in person, he did not know

the name of the man, had gone to Mr. Taylor, and complained, and that Mayor Taylor came to Chief Long and that Chief Long had told him to see me about it that Mayor Taylor was complaining. I said "What am I to do? Are you giving orders to lay off the place and leave it alone?" He said, "No, don't do that, use your own discretion. Don't make yourself too noticeable." I kept on myself the same as ever and gave them all the trouble I could for the rest of the month. I was only on the beat another week.

As a result of the Lennie Commission, Chief Long and Detective Sergeant McLaughlin were fired from the Vancouver City police force. Shue Moy emerged unscathed and continued to be a force in Vancouver's criminal underworld until at least the mid-1930s. The commission was a political disaster for Mayor L.D. Taylor, despite Justice Lennie's conclusion that there was insufficient evidence that he ever accepted a bribe or directly interfered with a police investigation. As Taylor's biographer notes, the mayor was not corrupt, but simply a realist who recognized that "a certain amount of gambling and prostitution was going to occur. He was not as concerned about it as he was about 'major crimes'; that is, murder and property crimes. His approach, which he stated openly, was to regulate vice crimes while at the same time committing the city's limited police resources to protecting citizens from violent crimes and tracking down serious criminals." Regardless, because of the highly publicized allegations of the inquiry, Taylor lost the mayoral race in October 1928 (topping off a horrific year for the mayor that included emergency surgery after being struck by an airplane propeller and losing his first wife to an automobile accident). But L.D., as he was affectionately called, bounced back. In 1930, he was re-elected to the first of two consecutive two-year terms as mayor, losing to Gerry McGeer in 1934. Among the many issues in that year's election was Joe Celona, who had recently been arrested for keeping a Chinese bawdy house on the top floor of the Maple Hotel on East Hastings Street and for procuring two young girls to work there. The thirty-eight-year-old Celona was convicted the following spring and sentenced to eleven years, but was released on parole less than six years later. Following a public outcry over this leniency, he was sent back to the B.C. penitentiary to serve out the remainder of his jail term.

CHINATOWN

I visited Chinatown in Vancouver, that queer district where men seem to glide from nowhere to nothing.
—Emily F. Murphy, *The Black Candle*, 1922

It is with the utmost of urgency that we alert you, our gentle reader, to one of the greatest threats facing the white inhabitants of our fine Christian Dominion. This most pernicious malediction emanates from what the *Victoria Times* calls "a vast alien colony," unassimilated, uncultured and "bound together in a secret and defensive organization with fewer wants and a lower standard of living than their neighbours, maintaining intact their peculiar customs and characteristics, morals, and ideals of home and family life" and which, by the pressure of their very numbers, can only serve to undermine "the very foundations of the white man's well being." Of course, we are referring to John Chinaman and his brethren. With the dangerous combination of "occidental ingenuity and oriental craftiness," the yellow race represents the most significant peril to the security, sanctity, and purity of British culture and civilization in North America since the Queen's Archies were defeated at Bunker Hill by the Union Army during the American Revolution of 1812.

We can only wholeheartedly endorse the resolution on the "Chinese Question" from the British Columbia Legislature of 1885 that urges the Dominion Government to curtail immigration and crack down without sympathy on the current blight of Asiatic foreigners invading our soil. "The Chinese are alien in sentiment and habits" and "do not become settlers in any sense of that word. They have no intention of permanently settling in the country, but come for the purpose of trading and labouring, in order to return to their native country with the means to make the remainder of their days in ease." The Chinese population in our fair land "chiefly consists of male adults, and thus — without responsibility of providing for a family — they come in unfair competition with white labour." These migrant labourers are nothing more than "the slaves or coolies of the Chinese race, accustomed to live on the poorest fare, and in the meanest manner, and hence their presence tends to the degradation of the white labouring classes."

We do concede they provided important labour for the building of the railway. Yet when those honest wages were not enough, they departed for greener pastures — or, more accurately, golden pastures — the abundant gold mines of British Columbia and the Yukon. Despite the economic opportunities so graciously provided to them by their host country, one cannot deny that the "Chinamen, as a class, are the smallest consumers, the least producers, and the most unprofitable of all who resort to these shores," as the *British Columbian* newspaper wrote. "Economical in their diet and nomadic in their habits, all we have in return for the really large quantities of gold they carry away is the paltry revenue derived from the Chinamen's opium and 'licee.'" Yes, the C.P.R. would never have been built without them and our laundry has never been cleaner and whiter. "But with their frugal ways, they put little back into the economy." When one thinks of John Chinaman, "it is usually as the genius of the washtub." With that said, as the *Toronto Star* points out, he also "causes much disturbance to the larger laundries by competing with their costly machinery by the dint of his two hands and the housewife's tools."

We are asked to extend our sympathy to this most baneful class of foreign scroungers, men "who follow on the heels of the hardy pioneer," yet never become colonists, let alone Christians. The "jackal-like" Chinese retain their ancestor worship in their adopted countries, "but outside of that they appear to have little interest in the religions of their native land." As our first prime minister, Sir John A. Macdonald, eloquently warned the House of Commons on May 4, 1885:

The Chinese are foreigners. If they come to this country, after three years' residence, they may, if they choose, be naturalised. But still we know that when the Chinaman comes here he intends to return to his own country; he does not bring his family with him; he is a stranger, a sojourner in a strange land, for his own purposes for a while; he has no common interest with us, and while he gives us his labour and is paid for it, and is valuable, the same as a threshing machine or any other agricultural implement which we may borrow from the United States on hire and return it to the owner on the south side of the line; a Chinaman gives us his labour and gets money, but that money does not fructify in Canada; he does not invest it here, but takes it with him and returns to China; and if he cannot, his executors or his friends send his body back to the flowery land. But he has no British instincts or British feelings or aspirations, and therefore ought not to have a vote.

It is irrefutable that immigrants from the yellow race have "prevented white men with families from coming to British Columbia" which would have "made the province a flourishing place, with happy, contented people." Equally alarming, the Occidentals "are driving the white people out of British Columbia, and if they are not stopped will soon drive them out of Alberta, Saskatchewan and Manitoba," the Dominion's precious breadbasket, first settled by white men and women who want nothing more than "to preserve the British type in our population." That this transient and congenitally procreative population scorches through their temporary country like an incendiary wildfire is vividly discernible in our Dominion. Already they have made their way as far east as Hamilton, Toronto, and Montreal. "Like most of the large cities on the continent, Toronto has quite a cosmopolitan population, and one of the most largely represented of the strange peoples is the Chinese," the *Star* newspaper reports. There among the good people of Toronto are "between four and five hundred of these Celestial visitors, and they live in all parts of the city. Consequently, there is no Chinatown with its picturesqueness but also with its enmity to sanitation."

Indeed, the Chinaman's lack of hygiene and loathsome tolerance to disease imperils his white neighbours, especially given his preference to habitat in cramped, isolated slum-like conditions. "That their custom of living in quarters of their own — 'Chinatowns' — is attended with evils, such as depreciation of property, and owing to their habits of lodging in crowded quarters and accumulating filth is offensive if not likely to breed disease. But these evils might be dealt with by police supervision." A case in point, dear reader: Toronto's housing inspector recently found dozens of cases of infraction of the city's lodging-house bylaw. The regulations call for 364 cubic feet of air space for every man, woman, and child who breathes. Yet, in nearly every Chinese domicile, "this limit was exceeded. Ten and twelve persons were sandwiched away in bunks, tiered one above all other, where only half that number should live. In one house, supposed to be a store, not a lodging house at all, thirty-seven Chinamen were found lying around the floor in a stifling, disease-breeding atmosphere." In another cellar, "a dark kind of dungeon where even sacks of rice become moldy and the atmosphere has a sodden chill," twenty-nine Chinese made their home.

The greatest cause for concern emanating from the alien Celestials and their Celestialtowns is their rampant vices and depraved immorality ubiquitously reflected in such omnipresent problems as prostitution, opium addiction, and gambling; vices that were virtually unheard of throughout much of the Dominion before the Orientals arrived. This horrible state of affairs is exemplified in Victoria's Chinatown, which is nothing more than a "nest of gambling" and where young girls are sold body and soul. Chinatown is "infected with moral and physical leprosy, and upon Britain's free soil — the helpless are shackled." The fact remains "that in Christian Canada's banner city of Vancouver there are women of the worst kind and in a state of moral degradation alongside which the history of Babylon appears like a saintly record." But to clean up such a moral and physical stain is difficult.

"The Heathen Chinee in British Columbia." From the *Canadian Illustrated News*, April 26, 1879.

"The Chinese gamblers and women proprietors are past-masters in the art of duplicity and of cheating the devil. They can lie without a smile on their faces, and swear to it without winking."

The congenital deceit of the yellow race extends to their secret gambling dens, the front of which often appear as "a shallow innocent little candy shop having a stock of candies, nuts, raisins, etc.," as the mayor of Vancouver wrote to the Dominion's minister of justice in 1910. To the trusting eye of the white man, the rear of this shop is merely a blank wall; but it is in fact a reinforced bolted door, with a small peephole, seven or eight feet up from the floor. Behind the wall is the real gambling den. And out on the street, according to his Worship the Mayor —

is a Chinaman soliciting and loading his white victims to this bolted door. He gives the high sign and the door is opened from within. Behind the gambling table within sits another Chinaman superintending the game or assisting in it or sometimes taking a hand in the play. When the police make a raid they are met in the front shop by a grinning Chinaman who "no saveys." If they undertake to force their way through the door in the back partition usually they have to exert a force with a jack-screw equal to raising about four tons in weight. When they have broken down this barrier they usually find a number of misguided white men sitting around the "chuck-a-luck" or "Fantan" tables, but the Celestials have disappeared through their underground retreats connecting "a la Frisko" the underground world of Chinatown.

> *Chinese to the right of 'em,*
> *Chinese to the left of 'em,*
> *bruised up, but bravely they leapt to their feet.*
> *Bare batons in the air*
> *they grabbed, by arm or hair,*
> *half of Hamilton's Chinese elite.*

> *Handcuffs on wrists were placed,*
> *then, sad and sorry-faced,*
> *twenty-four Chinese were led to the street.*
> *But to have seen the smile on Sergeant Walsh while,*
> *lo! it was almost angelically sweet.*

> *Back in the room were found two dollars flying round,*
> *mostly in coppers and nickels and dimes*
> *(of course there was Chinese stuff,*
> *but, you know well enough,*
> *Chinese spondulaks don't sound well in rhymes).*

> *Two tables there were seen covered with baize to green,*
> *whereon 'twas thought that the playing was done.*
> *One that was almost round*
> *Sergeant Walsh placed on th' ground*
> *and wheeled to the station, it must have been fun!*

> *They took two dozen men away*
> *and they were charged in court today*
> *with gambling on the Sabbath night*
> *which everybody knows ain't right.*
> *Those twenty-four big Chinamen,*
> *packed tight together, filled the pen.*
> *"Who's who" the sergeant couldn't tell,*
> *so all were locked up in a cell.*

Hamilton Herald, February 2, 1914, "Police raided Chinese place."

That the gambling industry is controlled by John Chinamen is evidenced by our courtrooms, which as of late are filled with "shaven heads and pigtails." Some are clad in the "latest Occidental style, with their queues carefully coiled on top of their heads. While others wore the felt soiled shoes, loose trousers, and smocks of their fatherland." The air becomes "full of the Chinese monosyllables," and the Crown Attorney's table is piled high with the paraphernalia of the various games of chance favoured by compulsively gambling Chinamen: dice, dominoes, chips, cards, lottery boards, counting machines, as well as the account books of the various games. And on those occasions that the Chinese criminal can outwit our men in blue, should it please his fancy, he might laugh into his westernized sleeve and say, "Gee whizza! Police big chumpee. Me Number 1 boy, all right."

Most threatening of all the Chinamen's vices is the smoking of opium, which is extending throughout the country "to the demoralization of the native races," a calculated strategy by the Chinese to "encourage the use of this drug amongst others of our own raising population." Police searches of Chinatown inevitably uncover a concentration of opium joints; but these are not the luxurious opium dens of the movies, "wherein smokers sprawl in comfort on plush divan while scantily clad maidens flit across deep oriental rugs to serve their every want." These gee yen dens of reality are made up of rows of dirty, smelly cubicles. "Quite often the male smokers would be accompanied by a female companion — not scantily clad oriental maidens, but unclad prostitutes employed to loll about in the nude. Apparently the presence of naked women helped to form and lend some reality to the hallucinations of the smoker." The Chinese opium smokers are, almost invariably, peaceful, docile, and sanguine. Many of them are older citizens, who have "had the habit for years and could not quite understand why, suddenly, a fuss was being made." As an intrepid scribe with the *Vancouver Daily Evening Post* perceptively observed, it is through the hopped-up Chinaman who sits precariously on the end of a flimsy straw-filled cot "in a half trance, though he smokes vigorously, and in his cadaverous face, painfully hollow cheeks, deeply sunken eyes, open vacuous mouth, and teeth discolored, decayed, and, as it seems, loose as castanets, that you read the penalties of opium smoking." While we would be grateful for the drug-induced extermination of the Chinamen, we are now well aware that opium is a disease no longer restricted to the Oriental people; it has now insidiously spread to the white race.

The non-Oriental addicts are marginalized riff-raff of no consequence to society: drifters, the unemployed, debtors, jazz musicians, Negroes, merchant seamen, university professors, and other social derelicts. The majority of these slack-twisted persons are confirmed addicts and "although only white people of low standards would smoke opium, nevertheless, they are demeaning themselves and the white race by 'stooping' to such a despised Chinese practice."

As has been said in our own House of Commons, John Chinaman is not content with simply smoking opium; he is also the exclusive purveyor of this narcotic. The trafficker, generally an Oriental, a cool, calculating scoundrel, does not take the drug himself because he knows its terrible effects on those who become its slaves. It is also well known that the "Chinese have amongst them a greater number of criminals than white people, in proportion" due to a moral character that is as weak as their tea. "Opium is the Chinese evil" and this drug is used in every Oriental house, with scarcely an exception. "The evil is growing with whites" and we have been told "on good authority that white girls of respectable parents use it." Make no mistake, the Chinaman "has taught white men and women, and boys and girls, to smoke opium." It is only natural "that the Chinaman should prefer teaching the art of 'hitting the pipe' to white 'devils,' like you and me who probably have no souls anyway, and certainly no ancestors." As magistrate Emily Murphy elucidates in her 1922 book *The Black Candle*, the peddling of opium beyond their own race, is part of a "well-defined propaganda among the aliens of color to bring about the degeneration of the white race":

It is hardly credible that the average Chinese pedlar has any definite idea in his mind of

bringing about the downfall of the white race, his swaying motive being probably that of greed, but in the hands of his superiors, he may become a powerful instrument to this very end. In discussing this subject, Major Crehan of British Columbia has pointed out that whatever their motive, the traffic always comes with the Oriental, and that one would, therefore be justified in assuming that it was their desire to injure the bright-browed races of the world. Naturally, the aliens are silent on the subject, but an addict who died this year in British Columbia told how he was frequently jeered at as "a white man accounted for." This man belonged to a prominent family and, in 1917, was drawing a salary of six thousand dollars a year. He fell victim to a drug "booster" till, ultimately, he became a ragged wreck living in the noisome alleys of Chinatown, "lost to use, and name and fame." This man used to relate how the Chinese pedlars taunted him with their superiority at being able to sell the dope without using it, and by telling him how the yellow race would rule the world. They were too wise, they urged, to attempt to win in battle but would win by wits; would strike at the white race through "dope" and when the time was ripe would command the world. "It may sound like a fantastic dream," writes the reporter, "but this was the story he told in one of the brief periods when he was free from the drug curse and he told it in all sincerity." Some of the Negroes coming into Canada — and they are no fiddle-faddle fellows either — have similar ideas, and one of their greatest writers has boasted how ultimately they will control the white men.

We have already witnessed the Chinamen's first step toward domination of the white race with the 1842 defeat of the British army at the hands of the Manchurians during the Opium War, which irrevocably weakened the vigorous and heroic effort of the Commonwealth to curtail the worldwide trade in the devil's nectar.

The chief target of the yellow dope-pushing villains are younger Christian men and women whose natural rebelliousness and naivety make them more inclined to be drawn to "banging the gong" and "taking it on the hip." In his 1908 report on the opium trade in British Columbia, W.L. MacKenzie King observed that use of the drug was spreading to young boys and girls and "to be indifferent to the growth of such an evil in Canada would be inconsistent with those principles of morality which ought to govern the conduct of a Christian nation."

As the future prime minister dutifully documented in his report, the Celestial opium trafficker is particularly interested in the white woman, who, when she becomes an addict inevitably "seeks the company of those who use the drug and avoids those of her own social status. This explains the amazing phenomenon of an educated gentlewoman, reared in a refined atmosphere, consorting with the lowest classes of yellow and black men." Their senses dulled, decent white women and girls are subjected to the influence of the Chinese dope pedlar whose ambition is to degrade, demoralize, abuse, and lure them into their brothels through opium addiction. White or aboriginal women and girls are forbidden by law to work in Chinese places where, in the opinion of society, it is dangerous to their morals to do so. Thusly, the Chinaman finds other ways to corrupt them; Celestials of great wealth and living in expensive, luxurious quarters, give snow parties "at which white women, whom they employ, act as hostesses. Young girls are invited from about the city to take part in these so-called social functions — perhaps a dance, perhaps a card party; something of that kind. Interspersed among these young people are two or three addicts who are trained and whose business it is to inveigle other people into the use of narcotics."

During a raid of one such party, Toronto police found on one of those arrested, Wah Lee, who gave 196 York Street as his address, a letter addressed to a white girl. Another of the Chinamen, "Ling Hen, who also resides, he says, at 196 York Street, had a white girl's photo in his possession." One of Toronto's most habitual Chinese dope wholesalers is Lee Jim, who between May 11, 1911 and December 9, 1913, was arrested on nine separate occasions for various offences relating to the manufacture, storage, and sale of opium. He was also known to have sold opium directly to white women. One of these arrests ensued after police found $10,000 worth of opium at 25 Chestnut Street. According to one Crown report on this case, "the ease with which the women obtained the drug indicated that white women are not infrequently seen at the Chestnut Street warehouse."

In conclusion, faithful reader, it is this inferior Oriental race, with its penchant for opium smoking and dope peddling and its desire to sexually ensnare good Protestant white women that threatens to overturn the safety, sanctity, and racial purity of this great land. It threatens our very origins, which can be traced to 1776 when the great English explorer Marco Polo discovered America, landing in the shadow of Lady Liberty at New York's harbour after circumcising the Pacific Ocean with his three ships, the *Santo*, the *Pinto*, and the *Enrico Caruso*. As the Secretary of the Asiatic Exclusion League stated in reference to the impact of the opium trade and its chief sponsor: "Here we have a disease, one of many directly traceable to the Asiatic. Do away with the Asiatic and you have more than saved the souls and bodies of thousands of young men and women who are yearly being sent to a living hell and to the grave through their presence in Canada."

A BONDAGE WORSE THAN SLAVERY

The reality of the early Chinese experience in North America, of course, was quite the opposite of the laughingly stereotypical and racist portrayals put forth by newspaper editorials, politicians, and "Anti-Asiatic" groups of the late 19th and early 20th centuries. Like many ethnic ghettos, the various Chinatowns of Canada and the United States have wrongly been held out as symbols of the insular and clannish Chinese community. Instead, they were formed as the first and subsequent waves of Chinese settlers banded together for protection in the face of racial hatred,

ethnicity-based herding, violence, and legislative dis-
enfranchisement. Some cities went so far as to adopt
restrictive bylaws to prevent the Chinese from buying
property beyond the boundaries of the Chinatown
enclave. Chinese labourers were excluded from unions,
paid lower wages than their white counterparts, driven
out of small towns and work camps, denied licences
in certain professions, such as medicine, law, and
teaching, and in some provinces, forbidden to work
on government-funded construction projects. Fears
that the Chinese male was out to anaesthetize, seduce,
and corrupt white women prompted laws in numerous
jurisdictions prohibiting the latter from working in
Chinese businesses. Chinese Canadians were denied
the federal vote until 1947 and the provincial vote in
B.C. until 1949. Of all the "ethnic" immigrant groups
arriving in Canada, only the Chinese had to pay a fee
to settle here, the infamous "head tax" that was initially
set at $50 in 1885, and then rose to $100 in 1902 and
$500 in 1903. In 1923, the *Chinese Immigration Act*
(which has been more accurately referred to as the
Exclusion Act) prohibited Chinese immigrants from
entering Canada with a few exceptions. Anyone of
Chinese descent already living in the country, including those who were born here, had to register with the
Dominion Government.

In British Columbia, anti-Chinese organizations, such as the Asiatic Exclusion League and the
Vigilance Committee, held periodic meetings, lobbied politicians, and posted notices in Victoria and
Vancouver all in the effort to force the eviction of
Chinese immigrants and citizens from the province
and the country. The outcome of these overzealous
anti-Chinese sentiments in B.C. was violence and
even mass rioting. On the night of February 24, 1887,
several hundred members of the Anti-Chinese League
held a meeting at Vancouver's city hall. The gathering
began with calls to protest the hiring of cheap Chinese
labour and ended in violence. A mob of more than
three hundred people stormed out of the meeting and
descended upon Vancouver's embryonic Chinatown
district, breaking windows, ransacking stores, and
setting fires. The mob then attacked a Chinese work
camp on the periphery of the city. They razed the
shantytown, tearing down the shacks that were the
homes of the transient workers, starting bonfires into

which their scant possessions were thrown, and forcibly loading anyone who looked even vaguely Asian
onto wagons and then driving them miles outside the
city. The violence continued to the next day and even
expanded into New Westminster.

Anti-Asian hostility erupted into violence again
in Vancouver on September 7, 1907. Following a hate-
filled meeting organized by the Asiatic Exclusion
League, a crowd of close to one thousand people
surged into the nearby streets of Chinatown where
they attacked, destroyed, and looted Chinese businesses and homes. A few blocks away, Japanese shops
and businesses were also attacked. The riot lasted five
hours and property damage was estimated at between
$50,000 and $100,000. As the *Toronto Star* reported
two days later, "Monday morning the wrecked quarters of the Orientals presented a dreary aspect. The
interior of the shops were littered with costly china,
silks, teas, and spices, worth thousands of dollars."
When Chinese merchants complained to the federal
government, R.G. MacPherson, Vancouver's Member
of Parliament, placed the blame on the victims, saying
it was an outcome of their unfettered immigration
into the province. "B.C. is white man's country," he
declared. Future prime minister Robert Borden echoed
his sentiments, saying B.C. had to be kept "a British
and Canadian province, inhabited and dominated
by men in whose veins runs the blood of those great
pioneering races which built up and developed not only
Western but Eastern Canada." Despite the callous and
racist responses from some politicians, the Dominion
Government in Ottawa did take the complaints seriously and launched an inquiry. What followed was an
unforeseen turn of events that would constitute one
of the most significant precursors to the development
of modern organized crime in Canada.

William Lyon Mackenzie King, at the time deputy
minister of labour in the Dominion Government, was
dispatched to Vancouver to assess the losses incurred by
Chinese and Japanese businessmen and to determine
what compensation, if any, should be forthcoming.
Among those making claims for compensation were
the Chinese owners of two opium-processing plants
that had been vandalized in the riots. Through these
claimants, King was shocked to learn that there was
a perfectly legal opium-processing and wholesaling

industry in British Columbia. He subsequently toured the two factories that turned gum opium into the smokable variety and later learned that there were at least seven plants in the province. He also discovered the lucrative nature of this industry; the combined gross receipts for the factories for 1907 alone were between $600,000 and $650,000. "The factories are owned and the entire work of manufacturers is carried on by Chinese, between 70 and 100 persons being employed," he wrote in a subsequent report. "One or two of the factories have been in existence for over twenty years, but the majority have been recently established." King even went so far as to buy a few grains of opium to prove how easy it was to obtain on Vancouver's streets.

King had inadvertently stumbled upon British Columbia's well-established and profitable opium industry and, although it had little to do with his original mandate, the politically aspiring King decided to make the issue his cause célèbre. "I will look into this drug business," he said to the *Vancouver Province*. "It is very important if Chinese merchants are going to carry on such a business, they should do so in a strictly legal way." But Mackenzie King had no intention of condoning or regulating a legal trade in opium. Shrewdly capitalizing on the race-based fears of the domestic opium trade, King wrote in his 1908 report entitled *The Need for the Suppression of the Opium Trade in Canada*, "The habit of opium smoking was making headway, not only among white men and boys, but also among women and girls." King was now determined to use his influence to prohibit the manufacture and consumption of opium in Canada.

He submitted his report to the Dominion Government and, that same year, Parliament passed the *Opium Act* of 1908, which criminalized the import, manufacture, and sale of opiates, except for medical use. For the first time in Canadian history, a narcotic substance was now regulated by the *Criminal Code*. Having acquired the reputation of an expert in opium and its trafficking, King was appointed to a British delegation attending the Shanghai Opium Commission in 1909. With the realities of opiate abuse and addiction now being recognized internationally, King vowed that Canada "will not only effect one of the most necessary

moral reforms so far as the Dominion is concerned, but will assist in a world movement which has at its object the freeing of people from a bondage which is worse than slavery."

By 1911, King, now a member of Wilfrid Laurier's Liberal government, introduced a more stringent *Opium and Drug Act*, which required legal drug distributors to keep records of their transactions, made opium smoking and possession a criminal offence, and expanded the list of prohibited drugs. By 1921, amendments to the *Opium and Drug Act* included a maximum seven-year penalty for the importation, manufacture, and sale of opium or any other narcotic drug mentioned in the act. In 1922, King convinced Parliament to add cocaine to the schedule of prohibited drugs. The same year, flogging and deportation were added as penalties to the narcotics legislation. In 1923, marijuana was added to the schedule of prohibited drugs. In 1929, this whirlwind of legislative action culminated in the *Opium and Narcotic Drug Act*, one of the country's most punitive pieces of criminal legislation, which increased jail sentences for trafficking and possession, broadened police search-and-seizure powers, and increased the scope of possession charges. The legislation would be in force until the 1960s.

Mackenzie King had made his mark and used this notoriety as a springboard to become Canada's longest-serving prime minister. As Neil Boyd observes in his book *High Times*, King adroitly positioned himself at the leading edge of a new "moral entrepreneurship" in Canada and abroad that "successfully marketed a new morality with respect to drug use."

THE CALAMITOUS NATURE OF THIS TRAFFIC

While the legal opium manufacturers were put out of business, the original 1908 legislation was a boon to the patent-medicine industry and to the pharmacists who legally dispensed opium and opiate-based elixirs. After opium was outlawed in 1908, pharmacists became some of the biggest dispensers of opiates in the country. Police, court, and College of Pharmacy records from Ontario show that a large number of police investigations and prosecutions were directed at pharmacists based on allegations that they were dispensing an inordinate amount of raw and processed opium. In a letter dated November 17, 1909, to the deputy attorney general of Ontario, the Crown attorney for the County of Middlesex wrote:

> [a] complaint was made to the Police Authorities here, that a firm of druggists was furnishing large quantities of opium to Chinese residents of the City. A Policeman was sent in plain clothes to purchase some. He asked for gum opium and was shown a very large quantity, probably several hundred dollars worth, and asked if that was the kind he wanted. He replied that it was and then bought a quarter of a pound, for which he paid $2.00. ... The purchaser of the opium did not produce any medical prescription or certificate, nor did he indicate in any way that he required the opium for medical purposes.

A 1913 report of an Ontario Provincial Police constable assigned to investigate illegal narcotic sales by pharmacists describes how his Chinese agent, Lee Chun, helped gather evidence. In one particular sting operation against a pharmacist named J. Urquhart, who had been suspected of selling large quantities of opium to Chinese customers, the constable made the following report:

> I shadowed Lee Chun till he entered the back door of J. Urquhart's drug store. Lee Chun came out in about 10 minutes and gave me the sign that he had bought some opium; I then entered the drug store and made search for opium. I first secured the marked bills which I had given to Lee Chun to buy the opium with, and which Mr. Urquhart had in his right hand pants pocket. I next secured some opium which he had behind the counter and which he appeared to be trying to hide, also secured a basket of opium which Urquhart said was no good and which he was going to return to the wholesaler, in all I secured ten or twelve pounds ...

Urquhart, who told the constable he had purchased the opium from a legitimate pharmaceutical wholesaler, was arrested and fined $400.

Following the new federal drug laws, some pharmacists began purchasing inordinately large amounts of opium and other narcotics from wholesalers. In a 1917 memo, an official with the Ontario College of Pharmacy in Woodstock wrote, "Quite of lot of opium has been coming in here lately from Toronto, Montreal, and London. One druggist had 50 pounds in a month as you can easily find by looking up the wholesale of record." The memo also describes a druggist in Woodstock "who professes to furnish the Chinese with laundry sundries and going around amongst them in this way he also deals opium." As part of a widespread investigation into drug retailers and wholesalers, the Ontario Provincial Police discovered a surreptitious system by which retail druggists ordered their excessive amounts of opiates from wholesalers. Attached to official orders would be handwritten notes, such as one accompanying an order from a Toronto druggist that read, "if you can spare 20 or 25 lbs Persian Gum just so you may send it along with these goods." The handwritten notes were expected to be destroyed by the wholesaler after the order was filled. Evidence showed that drug wholesalers regularly filled the large orders. Dominion Government records reveal that between January 1915 and November 1916, the Vancouver-based National Drug and Chemical Company sold 523 ounces of morphine, 59 ounces of powdered opium, 366 pounds of gum opium, and 454 ounces of cocaine. During the same period, another Vancouver wholesale druggist, J.A. Topoorten Limited, sold 37 ounces of heroin, 67 ounces of powdered opium, 4,981 ounces of morphine, 1,140 pounds of gum opium, and 4,216 ounces of cocaine. Among the customers of these wholesalers were a handful of retail druggists. One of these was O.C. Rutledge, who, during this period, purchased 1¼ ounces of powdered opium, 23 ounces of heroin, 1,518 ounces of morphine, 146 pounds of gum opium, and 1,277 ounces of cocaine. Another reliable customer of the wholesalers was S. Edgar Kee, who purchased 8¾ ounces of heroin, 3,179 ounces of morphine, 988 pounds of gum opium and 2,807 ounces of cocaine. In responding to these sizable orders, a federal official advised, "a retail druggist enjoying a lucrative trade in any large city in Canada does not legitimately use more than from five to ten ounces of cocaine in a year and that he does not so use more than 20 or 25 ounces of morphine in twelve months, such a druggist would not in the same time legitimately use more than one ounce of heroin…"

Doctors also became drug traffickers of sorts, catering to an exclusive clientele, according to David T. Courtwright in his book on the history of opiate addictions in America. "The upper-class background of many addicts is certainly consistent with the allegation that some doctors courted the wealthy client with a little morphine," he wrote. "Even worse, it was common practice for 'quack cure joints' to offer 10 to 20 percent kickbacks for referring addicted patients. The utterly unscrupulous practitioner could realize a handsome profit by addicting patients and then having them trek from one asylum to another — asylums with which he had an arrangement." Between April 1921 and March 1922, the Dominion Government prosecuted under the provisions of the *Opium and Drug Act*, twenty-three doctors, eleven druggists, and four veterinary surgeons. In its annual report for 1925, the RCMP reported that the Quebec City detachment "made a very good clean up of the drug situation" in the city, "apprehending a number of doctors and druggists." In its report for the following year, the RCMP commissioner extolled the Mounties' ongoing "purification of the medical profession by exposure and conviction of a number of it's members — few in proportion, I should add — who have sunk into the practice of dispensing these drugs illegally."

As the 1920s wore on, pharmacies and druggists were less and less a source of legal or illegal opiates, due to increased regulatory control over pharmaceutical drugs and the refusal of the retailers to stock opiates because of moral objections or the increased risk of hold-ups and break-ins by addicts. The retreat of retail druggists from opium distribution, in conjunction with the ongoing criminalization of narcotics, pushed the drug trade further underground. The expansion of the black market in opium and morphine was also quickened by a substantial growth in the supply and demand for these illegal drugs in the postwar years. During World War I, government controls severely limited the international distribution and availability of narcotic drugs. When the war ended, supply — both legal and illegal — escalated, in part to meet the heightened demands of the many morphine-addicted soldiers whose return from the battlefields in Europe or whose release from domestic hospitals swelled the addict population in major Canadian cities. In 1922, the RCMP was calling attention to "the alarming increase in the use of narcotic drugs in Canada and the growing traffic in the same." A review of year-end reports by the Mounted Police during the 1920s shows that drug trafficking had become a significant law enforcement problem in many of Canada's larger cities. As the commissioner wrote in the annual report for 1922:

> An important and arduous task is the support of the Department of Public Health in enforcing the Opium and Narcotic Drugs Act. Reference was made in the last annual report to the calamitous nature of this traffic; I regret to be obliged to state that the evil persists, and I fear has grown in some parts of the country. To check it will require the united efforts of this force and the provincial and municipal priorities, and also drastic punishment of the agents, such as the peddlers who desperately create addicts. … the figures already given show that we have been active, having arrested over one thousand persons and having secured 800 convictions…

THE MOST POWERFUL AND WEALTHY CRIMINAL ORGANIZATION

Despite the spike in demand for opium and morphine, the illegal drug trade was still a fairly primitive business in the first quarter of the 20th century; most illegal shipments into Canada were measured in ounces and most of the smugglers operated independently. For much of the 1920s, the majority of the illegal opium smuggled into the country arrived aboard passenger steamer ships from Europe or Asia. As stated in the 1922 annual report for the Opium and Narcotic Drug Branch of the Federal Department of Health, "Most of these illicit shipments are smuggled in by the crews on the incoming steamships, the drugs being carefully concealed below decks, either among the cargo or in the coal bunkers, etc. Quite a large proportion of such shipments are brought into the country by freight or cargo vessels, and particularly tramp steamers calling at Canadian ports for wheat cargoes, etc."

The opium trade became better organized as smuggling and trafficking networks began to coalesce and grow in size. While still dealing at the ounce level — or, at the most, one or two pounds at a time — opium wholesalers were becoming much more plentiful as the demand grew for middlemen who could connect overseas suppliers with street-level peddlers in Canada. Many Canadian wholesalers also doubled as retailers, often personally handling the drugs themselves. At the street level, drugs were sold in "decks," a folded piece of paper the size of a postage stamp containing between one and fifteen "grains" of opium, morphine or cocaine. These decks sold anywhere from 25 cents to $5 apiece, depending on the quantity, scarcity, or region of the country. In Vancouver in 1922, an opium addict had the choice of purchasing a twenty-five-cent deck (½ grain — about 1/50th of an ounce), a fifty-cent deck (1 grain), a one-dollar deck (3 grains), or a four-dollar deck (15 grains). Once the opium made it to Canada it was adulterated and diluted, which contributed to the profitability of the trade for the wholesaler and the street-level retailer. Given an average wholesale price of $5 for an ounce of opium, a retailer could potentially make a profit as high as $200 an ounce.

In 1922, the federal Opium and Narcotic Drug Branch declared that the illegal opium traffic "is controlled almost altogether by large drug rings, which employ numerous agents to distribute the drug. Some of these agents simply act as a medium of distribution, between a dealer with a large stock and the small peddler, and work on a commission basis." The January 14, 1992, edition of the *Vancouver World* had this to say about a particular drug ring operating in that city: "Investigations made by the authorities have led them to the conclusions that the most powerful and wealthy criminal organization on the American continent has its headquarters here. Its object is the handling of drugs. Its ramifications extend as far east as Montreal and Chicago. It will undertake to sell $100,000 worth of 'dope,' or it will sell it by the 'deck,' the small package sold by the street vendor for from one to five dollars."

In reality, most of the drug trafficking groups in Canada had little in the way of a national presence, although drug connections were being forged between groups and individuals in Montreal, Toronto,

Winnipeg, and Vancouver. As importantly, smuggling and trafficking linkages began to emerge between Canadian and American cities, the most notable being between Montreal between and New York. It was during the 1920s that Montreal became positioned as a central conduit through which opium and morphine from Europe or Southwestern Asia would be transported into New York. Vancouver was also becoming established as a major port of entry for opium from Southeastern Asia and a major trans-shipment point for other markets in the Pacific Northwest of the U.S. and as far east as Toronto. As Montreal and Vancouver increased their stature as international drug channels for the rest of North America, the quantity of opium and cocaine smuggled through these port cities began to spiral. According to one confidential RCMP report dated May 20, 1922, of the 14,000 tins of opium (114,000 ounces) that are estimated to have been smuggled through Vancouver's ports, some 9,000 tins (72,000 ounces) are sent to the United States and the balance is consumed locally, in the interior of B.C. and in Alberta. Between October 1920 and September 1921, the RCMP in B.C. investigated 477 *Opium and Drug Act* cases, from which they secured 292 convictions. One of those convicted was Nip Gar, who the media referred to as the "Queenpin" who "controlled the drug trade in Chinatown." Gar was sentenced to seven years after police made nine undercover buys from her. Other notable seizures during this one-year period included opium worth $50,000 found in the store of a Chinese merchant, concealed in a "cleverly-constructed pocket in the seat of a chair" and behind a false baseboard located behind the store's counter.

In one report from 1922, the RCMP estimated that the Canadian Pacific's *Empress* passenger ships carried "some 800 lbs of narcotics" into Vancouver during the previous year with another "1200 lbs of narcotics distributed over the other four lines from the Orient." It was the crew of these ships who were the smuggling workhorses, some working independently, some conspiring with other crew members and officers, while still others were recruited by drug trafficking rings or Chinese merchants. As the *Vancouver Daily World* reported in 1922, the smugglers capitalized on the array of potential hiding spots aboard the large ships:

Innocent passengers may be sleeping on it on the way across for a wily Oriental has a knack of hiding it in staterooms under the berths. It has even been stitched into the mattresses. Planks have been pried from the walls and thousands of dollars of cocaine and morphine concealed in cunningly contrived cavities. It has been concealed among the stores on the life-boats; in the engine room store; in the crews quarters; down in ventilators. It is anywhere and everywhere. Cunningly built up lumps of coal, seemingly innocent enough from the outside, have been broken open and reveal a few thousands dollars worth of dope securely done up in watertight packets. Solid looking blocks of wood have on very close investigation revealed themselves as hollowed out hiding places, the joints so well made and blending with the grain of the wood that only an expert could detect them.

Once the ships docked, the drugs were surreptitiously carried onshore through body packs, in passenger trunks, or in cargo. Alternatively, watertight packages would be thrown overboard to be picked up by waiting boats before the ship docked.

In March 1921, RCMP Special Agent Number 23, Constable Frank Eccles, who worked undercover at Vancouver's marine ports, wrote a confidential memo entitled "Opium & Drug Traffic, City of Vancouver and 'Empress of Russia'" in which he describes how he was told by a Chinese steward on the *Empress of Russia* that "a large quantity of Opium, Morphine and Cocaine had been taken off the boat" by three Chinese crew members and delivered to a group of Chinese drug wholesalers in New Westminster. The informant estimated that on each trip the three were smuggling "$10,000 to $30,000 worth of drugs." The RCMP constable was also told that the smugglers "employ a number of China boys to arrange for these drugs to be taken ashore in order that the Customs Department will not know who brings the drugs over, and if any of these boys are caught, their fines are paid, and they receive one dollar per tin for all opium they carry off the ship" (a tin contained around seven ounces of

smoking opium). The smuggled opium eluded customs inspections because one of the crew members "is in charge of all 2nd class cabins and after the passengers leave the ship, these drugs are stored in these vacated cabins and the doors locked, this is 'C' Deck, cabins from 300 up; also toilets and bath-rooms. During the search, they keep moving the drugs from one place to another." Once delivered, the opium was divided among the Chinese traffickers for sale locally and for disbursement to the Prairies, which was shipped through a mail order business operated by one of the conspirators. Eccles was informed that this trafficking ring has "a cache somewhere East — about two days run on the train, and drugs are distributed from there, as needed, to different points." The investigation stemming from this report led to the arrest and conviction of J.J. Wing, who the Crown alleged "to be one of the ringleaders in the narcotics trade of the city." Other confidential RCMP documents from 1923 indicated that Wing had been "carrying on a very large and presumably well protected system of import and distribution, both by a system of runners and also by the use of the mails." The RCMP estimated that Wing had "30 or 40 Runners" working for him in Vancouver.

Another RCMP report, dated April 7, 1921, contains evidence of drug smuggling and internal conspiracies among customs officers, railway police, and dockworkers. Based on evidence provided by Frank Yip, who worked on passenger ships docking in Vancouver, an RCMP inspector wrote:

Opium, Morphine and Cocaine is brought in on every vessel coming from the Orient. It is brought across by the Chinese and Japanese sailors aboard, and taken off by Chinamen, wearing vests specially made, containing thirty pockets, each for a tin of Opium. Also local Chinese visit the boats on a pretext of seeing their friends, and carry the dope off in a similar way. Yip claims that the Chinese pay $3.00 per tin for every tin taken off, to the Customs and Railway Officials. The guard on the gang-plank "Splits" with these officials, and is responsible for these people going on and off the ships at will. In wet weather when the longshoremen are wearing heavy coats, they pack it off also. Yip says that all the officials who have the handling of the ships cargoes are implicated. If the Chinese think they are being watched, they get the Railway Police to carry the stuff off.

In a memo dated July 31, 1921, Constable Eccles wrote of being informed that two hundred tins of opium and five tins of cocaine had "found its way into Vancouver last week from Victoria, B.C., to a Company here whom I know quite well, and the five lbs. of Cocaine has been shipped to Seattle already." Less than a month later, "one of the largest drug dealers in town" told him that he had just "purchased 200 tins of Opium and some Cocaine" while another "Chinaman named Yee Lun, of Yee Lun & Co, 534 Fisgaurd Street, Victoria" purchased twenty pounds of cocaine and three hundred tins of opium from Sim Yin, "the No.1 Fireman on the Empress of Asia." According to Eccles, "Yee Lun Co. is the largest dealer over there and some days ago was trying to sell to my informant 500 tins of Opium in Vancouver, but the deal fell through."

Asian crew members were not the only ones accused of opium smuggling. In an RCMP report dated October 18, 1921, confidential sources accused Captain Hopcraft, of the *Empress of Japan*, as heading "a gang of Drug Smugglers" that also involved the ship's master of arms, a baggage master, and a purser. The information received by the RCMP indicated that "four different Chinamen" regularly visited the captain's home in Shaughnessy Heights and hauled away large quantities of opium and other narcotics. "The Captain also has two China boys visiting his home daily when the ship is in port, supposed to be servants. They carry things off the ship without being searched, and they may be packing these drugs as they are interested in same. The Gangway Customs officer is well supplied with cigars and whisky for letting them off without being bothered."

Among the dockworkers accused of conspiring to smuggle opium ashore was the secretary of the longshoreman's union in Victoria. According to one RCMP memo, "it was common talk" on Victoria's waterfront that this man "had frequently brought drugs from the boats ashore." Customs officials would

also be accused of collusion with smugglers. One of those making such charges was Frank Eccles, and between 1921 and 1923, at least six customs officials were dismissed or quit due to these allegations (although there is no indication that criminal charges were ever laid against them).

In August of 1923, the accuser became the accused when Constable Eccles, along with Constable William (Doc) Smith, a fellow drug squad member, Sergeant Robert Mundy, who was in charge of the RCMP's undercover operations, and Frank Fernandez, a police informant, were arrested at Victoria and charged with illegal possession of opium. That year, a classified RCMP report disclosed that "No. 23, Special-Agent Eccles, had purchased a fast green-coloured boat in which he and an ex-Customs Officer, named James Sperring, were getting drugs from the Empress Boats." Dominion customs investigators, who were already suspicious of Eccles, followed the green boat during one of its pickups from an *Empress* ship and caught Eccles red handed with 50 tins of opium. In November of that year, Eccles, Smith, and Fernandez were convicted under the *Opium and Drug Act*. Eccles and Fernandez were sentenced to eighteen months and fined $1,000 each, while Smith was sentenced to nine months. For the attorney general of B.C., the convictions only hinted at the widespread involvement of these dishonoured police officers in the drug trade. The scandal prompted him to appoint lawyer J.P. Smith to lead a provincial inquiry to investigate accusations that Eccles and his convicted colleagues had been responsible for "framing certain drug addicts and others in order to cover the traces of their alleged graft, traffic in the business they were supposed to suppress."

Among those testifying at the inquiry was Mrs. Annie Jones who stated under oath that Eccles had used her as a drug courier and described how on one occasion she was sent to the *Empress of Russia* to pick up morphine and raw opium. Eccles, she alleged, accompanied her onto the ship and from there into a room "where a Chinese came in carrying a bundle that looked like laundry." The Chinese man gave her eleven packages, which she stowed in a skirt specially made to conceal the drugs. She told the inquiry that the packages were so heavy she did not think she would have the strength to board the streetcar to get home.

She did in fact make it home, where the merchandise was later picked up by another Chinese man who gave her $10 a package. Jones' husband also testified that two years earlier, Eccles and Fernandez went to one of the *Empress* ships and took "two sacks full of drugs" to Fernandez's home, which was then picked up by the same Chinese man. Mr. Jones testified that he was paid $1,000 by Eccles a few days later.

J.J. Wing, the convicted opium trafficker who at the time of the inquiry was serving seven years on drug charges, was also called to testify. In a startling revelation, he told the commissioners that he had bought twenty pounds of opium from two Mounted Police officers for $2,000. While being questioned by inquiry lawyers, he acknowledged that the two policemen were sitting in the room, but stubbornly refused to identify them. Wing also alleged paying Eccles $300 to take care of a police witness testifying in the drug case against him. Sergeant Mundy confirmed this testimony by admitting he had sent the material witness, a fellow Mountie, out of town on another drug investigation. (The diversionary tactic was not successful; the constable made it back in time for Wing's court case and provided evidence that helped convict him in 1921.) Wing also claimed that Constable Smith had come into his store with Eccles and two seventeen-year-old girls, whereupon he pulled out of his shoes "125 grains of cocaine" and proceeded to sniff it in the presence of Wing and the girls. He then passed the cocaine along to Eccles and to the two teenage girls. One of the girls vomited after inhaling too much. Both of the girls testified before the commission of inquiry that they had been supplied with cocaine by members of the Mounted Police drug squad.

Incredibly, when presenting his findings on February 11, 1923, Commissioner J.P. Smith exonerated the RCMP members against charges of drug trafficking, despite overwhelming evidence to the contrary. This absolution was not unexpected by the provincial attorney general who had already withdrawn his support for the inquiry because the commissioner refused to enter into the record such pertinent information as the criminal convictions of the men as well as the damning testimony provided by J.J. Wing (testimony that was made public by the attorney general in December 1923, a few weeks after he stopped co-operating with the inquiry).

Despite the unflattering light the inquiry shone on the RCMP drug unit in B.C., the Mounties continued to take the lead in drug enforcement in the country and were generally successful in tracking down some major traffickers during the 1920s. In 1921, they began investigating Lee Kim, who was described in a classified RCMP memo as "one of the largest drug dealers in the City of Victoria" and "the sole supplier of opium to small dealers and consumers in that city." Kim was also suspected of being an agent for other wholesalers and "keeps a stock in one of the numerous truck farms outside the City of Victoria, orders being fulfilled as required." Despite making Kim a priority, the Mounted Police were unable to accumulate enough evidence to charge him, primarily because he was "too smart to handle the goods himself," according to the memo. By 1927, the RCMP were able to close in on Kim, and more importantly, his boss, Lim Gim (a.k.a. Lim Jim), who was considered one of the largest opium wholesalers in all of Canada.

The investigation began early that year in Windsor, Ontario, where the RCMP made a number of arrests following a series of undercover purchases in that city. The Mounties determined that the opium was coming from Vancouver and, more specifically, Lim Gim, who at the time was the president of a large import company and one of the wealthiest and most prominent men in Vancouver's Chinese community. Lim Gim, who had come to Canada at the turn of the century, was making an estimated $900,000 a year through his various businesses, although opium trafficking was the greatest source of his fortune. "This man is wealthy," the 1928 annual report of the RCMP stated, "controlling several firms; he long has been regarded as the centre of the opium smuggling traffic in British Columbia, but hitherto no case could be made against him."

An undercover RCMP agent, posing as a New York City drug wholesaler in search of a new supply, was introduced to Lim to negotiate a large opium purchase. When the agent tried to buy $10,000 worth of opium, Gim told him that he didn't have that just much at the time, but could obtain it from a ship that just arrived in Seattle or from other ships coming to the United States. Within weeks, the undercover operative received a letter from Gim postmarked in Seattle that read, "Mr. A.B. Smith is now in town. He will be ready to do business at any time. Let me know as Mr. Smith is going away shortly." The name "Mr. Smith" was one of the many codes used by Lim, in this case an indication that two hundred cans of opium were ready for pickup. Coded telegrams were sent back to Gim confirming the date and time of the delivery. In conjunction with American narcotics agents, an undercover police officer visited Gim in his store in Vancouver in July 1927 where be obtained and paid for the opium. Gim was promptly arrested. At the conclusion of his trial, he received four years, but upon appeal by the Crown, the sentence was increased to seven years.

Despite Gim's 1927 conviction, his smuggling and trafficking network persisted unabated. A new RCMP informant, who had recently been arrested after hauling opium from an *Empress* ship, reported that Chan Sun Sing (a.k.a. Henry Chan) had asked him to offload a future shipment from the *Empress of France*. Chan was employed by the Victoria Baggage Company and had already used the informant to unload and transport a number of opium loads from *Empress* ships, including the one that got him arrested. In his latest request, Chan told the informant he was picking up the opium for Lee Kim and was to deliver it to a pre-arranged site. The RCMP learned that Lee Kim had travelled to China at the end of 1928 and returned to Victoria on the *Empress of Russia* on January 25, 1929. Accompanying Lee Kim on his cruise were three hundred tins of opium that were earmarked for at least six Chinese wholesalers in British Columbia and Washington State. The man responsible for ensuring that the shipment made it safely to Victoria and onto a ship destined for Seattle was Henry Chan. During a conversation with the RCMP informant, Chan remarked that in June 1928, customs agents in Victoria seized 350 tins of opium from the *Empress of Asia* that he was supposed to have picked up.

On August 27, 1929, the informant reported to his police handlers that Henry Chan had told him arrangements were being made for him to unload the opium from the *Empress of France* that night. Around midnight, the informant and an undercover customs officer approached the *Empress of France* in a small boat. They were told to look for a porthole that was covered in a red cloth. After spotting the cloth, the informant attached to the end of a string hanging from the porthole a half piece of paper that had been given to him by Henry Chan. The paper was hauled up into the porthole where it perfectly matched its other half. Within minutes, forty-four tins of opium wrapped in burlap were lowered to the men in the boat. The two then took the opium to the Vancouver Hotel where Lee Kim was waiting to take delivery. After Kim praised the informant for eluding customs, one of his lieutenants, named Charlie Sam, arrived to pick up the drugs. After counting the tins, Sam carried them to another room in the hotel where he was staying. Once he stepped into the hallway, the RCMP sprang into action and arrested him. When police knocked on Sam's hotel room door, it was opened by none other than Lee Kim and Henry Chan, who were also arrested. After searching both hotel rooms, the RCMP found numerous coded documents that, when translated, contained detailed information on this and other opium smuggling conspiracies. Police also found a map showing the location of certain landmarks at the southern end of Vancouver Island that were designated as drop-off and pickup points for opium taken from ships docked at Victoria. Lee Kim, along with Charlie Sam, Mah Poy, and Henry Chan were all eventually convicted under the new federal drug statute.

Now focussing primarily on major smuggling and trafficking conspiracies, the RCMP and the Dominion Customs Service continued to make a number of significant drug seizures and arrests during the late 1920s and early 1930s. On July 14, 1927, Lore Yip, who the RCMP described as the third most important narcotics dealer in Vancouver, was arrested after police found 43 pounds of opium, morphine, and cocaine concealed in the panelling between two walls of his apartment at the Sherman Hotel in Chinatown. At the time, it was the single-largest drug seizure in B.C. history. In 1931, the RCMP announced the arrest and conviction of Winnipeg-based Arthur Toole, who they touted as "undoubtedly the largest dealer in heroin in the entire West." According to the RCMP, Toole's arrest "created consternation among the drug-peddling element of Winnipeg and the West, and practically cut off the illicit supply of the drug mentioned."

THE FRENCH CONNECTION, PART I

Like Vancouver, Montreal was a major entry point into North America for opium, morphine, and heroin. In addition to its marine ports, Montreal was a popular conduit for drug smuggling because it was a terminus for nearly all Canadian and United States railways, was located close to the American border, and was connected to New York and other major American cities along the eastern seaboard through brand-new asphalt highways. Montreal's vibrant red-light district and large addict population also helped to ensure a substantial domestic market.

Quantities of opium were being seized in Montreal that was unheard of in Vancouver. In June 1918, a police raid on an old farmhouse on the outskirts of the city turned up approximately seventy pounds of raw and processed opium. Along with 240 copper boxes containing varying amounts of the drug, police also found a small manufacturing plant to turn the gum opium into the smokable variety. As the *Montreal Gazette* reported, "The boilers, machinery and raw material found in another of the rooms constituted the biggest drug plant that the police have yet raided. The quantity of opium found in the house is claimed to be the largest ever seized in Montreal." The house was also equipped to manufacture opium pipes, a number of which were seized by police. Two Chinese men were arrested at the scene and it was clear they had prepared for a long stay; there was enough food and liquor in the house to meet the needs of the occupants for over a year, police told the media. "Several revolvers and many boxes of cartridges were also found, the men evidently being prepared for any raid which might occur." Less than a year later, this record seizure would be eclipsed when police discovered 180 pounds of opium in the home of Lee Jee, a Chinese merchant with a store on La Gauchetière Street. Eighteen packages, each one containing ten pounds of opium, were seized. The packages had been shipped East from B.C. via parcel post.

Between October 1920 and September 1921, the number of drug cases investigated by the RCMP in Quebec was 167. During the following fiscal year, the number had jumped to 531 and, for the rest of the decade, the RCMP investigated an average of 250 cases annually in the province. High-profile cases also kept the narcotics trade on the front pages of Montreal newspapers. In 1924, a shipment of cocoa, phennacotin, and other goods was sent from a firm in Switzerland to a variety of companies in Montreal. All of these companies had the same address on St. Peter Street, which aroused the suspicion of customs agents. With the assistance of the RCMP, more than three thousand pounds of morphine, heroin, and cocaine were seized en route to the Canadian consignees. The wholesale value at the time was estimated at $200,000. This would be one of the largest drug seizures ever made in Canada.

In 1925, Inspector J.W. Phillips of the RCMP's Quebec Division wrote about the ever-increasing organization and sophistication of the underground drug trade in Montreal. "Slightly better progress has been made against offenders under the *Opium and Narcotic Drug Act*, but as time goes on our work becomes more and more difficult," he wrote. "The traffic in drugs in Montreal has now reached such a science and has been driven so far underground that it is only with the greatest difficulty we can obtain any good results." In its 1932 annual report, the RCMP identified Goon Lin (a.k.a. Goon Dep Bon, a.k.a. Goon Kwong Lin, a.k.a. Goon Sham) as the head of the largest opium ring "in the Chinese district of Montreal." While he first came to the attention of the RCMP in 1928, "so cunning was he and so careful with his method of delivery that it was not until February 5, 1932, that it was possible to arrest him." The RCMP described his sales routine as follows: "The usual procedure was for the customer to come in a motor car, stop before his house and send some passing Chinaman in for him; he then would emerge, identify his customer, and tell him where the delivery would take place. The customer would drive to the spot mentioned and Goon Lin procured the drug from its hiding place in one of several houses which he was in the habit of using, proceed to the spot and hand it to him." After being put under surveillance, Lin was seen making a delivery to a customer, which prompted RCMP detective sergeant W.H. Styran to arrest Lin. In Goon Lin's tightly clutched hands was a deck of opium, and in the ensuring struggle, the paper burst and both became covered with the drug. Upon searching his home, the RCMP discovered what it called a "considerable quantity of drugs." Lin pleaded guilty and was sentenced to eighteen months and a

$200 fine. Evidence presented at his trial showed that Lin was also a major wholesaler to other street-level dealers in the city.

A French-Canadian man named A. Frenette, reputed by the RCMP to "be one of the most important dealers in narcotics in Montreal," was arrested on February 13, 1932, following a high-speed chase that began after police observed Frenette making a drug delivery. He was forced to cut his getaway short as he had secreted much of the opium in the tires of his car. According to a RCMP report, the inner tubes of the car's tires were perforated "and a certain amount of drug inserted therein. The inner tube is then placed into the tire on the wheel of the car, which is inflated with sufficient air to give it the appearance of an ordinary tire. Of course the car may not be driven at a high rate of speed." Frenette was arrested, but acquitted at his trial when the Crown could not prove that the opium found in his car was his property. The same year, Hector Valade, a member of the Montreal city police, was arrested after an RCMP investigation showed he "was using his position of trust to deal in Narcotic drugs." Valade was charged, found guilty on two counts of drug trafficking, and sentenced to eight years.

Most of the illegal and legal opiates entering Montreal originated from Germany, France, or Switzerland. During the 1920s, pharmaceutical companies in these countries were the world's largest manufacturers and suppliers of legal morphine and heroin and imported huge quantities of gum opium from China and Turkey. The finished product would then be shipped throughout the world. The importation of raw opium, as well as the manufacture and export of its derivatives, were controlled by government agencies in these countries, with strict limits on quantities to be imported, produced, and exported. However, some of the companies illegally dealt in much larger quantities, most of which was diverted to international black markets.

One Montreal-based trafficker who attempted to tap into this illicit surplus was Max Faber. In 1924, a classified RCMP report acknowledged that Faber (a.k.a Max Farber, a.k.a Maxie Faber) was well known to police in Quebec "as an International Drug Trafficker, and as a man who was running a Wholesale and Retail Narcotic Peddling Joint in the Benoit Street District in partnership with one known as 'Red' Miller. This Joint was run in a very business like manner, neither of these times men peddled themselves, always employing men to do this work for them. They also ran, for a short time an Opium smoking Joint, somewhere in the 'Red Light District.'" Faber, who was born July 10, 1892, in Russian Poland, was described by the London Metropolitan Police as the "head of Maxie's Gang in Montreal" and a man who "usually dresses rather poorly" and "bears all the appearance of a Jew." The Scotland Yard report goes on to characterize Faber as "an exceptionally cunning scoundrel. In the drug traffic his part usually has been the handling of the money, leaving the passing of the poison to be performed by others." Similarly, the aforementioned RCMP report acknowledges, "attempts have been made to catch him with the goods, but with no success. He has always employed someone else to do the dirty work for him and this other person was always sufficiently well paid to ensure silence in the event of an arrest."

According to the RCMP, after closing down his "peddling joint" on Benoit Street sometime in 1922, Faber concentrated on importing opium into Montreal. Between 1922 and 1924, he made three trips to Hamburg, Germany, accompanied by his two Alsatian wolfhounds. On his first trip, he met "Lambert alias Elias, a man known locally as 'The English Jew.'" After stealing "a quantity of opium and drugs" from the Hamburg warehouse of a German drug firm, Maxie, the "English Jew," and other accomplices were arrested and convicted. When Faber and Elias were released following a short stint in prison, they "made a deal or two and collected quite a supply in Hamburg ready for shipment to either America or England." While in Hamburg, Faber arranged with the officers of passenger ships sailing for North America to transport the opium. When Faber returned to Montreal, he bribed a customs officer to clear the boxes of soap which hid the opium.

In 1924, Miquel de Maluquer, the consul for Spain in Montreal, and Ramon Tey de Torrents, an importer of Spanish goods, were convicted of conspiring to smuggle drugs from Spain into Canada through Montreal and were sentenced to six months each. It was the first time that an accredited representative of a foreign power had been arrested in Canada for a criminal offence. Maluquer was working in tandem with an international network that bought opium and morphine in Barcelona, shipped the drugs to Liverpool, repacked them in trunks, and then sent them off to Montreal. There, a corrupt customs official intercepted the trunks and delivered them to the traffickers for an honorarium of $1,000 per trunk.

Based on evidence initially provided by an informant who admitted to being involved in the smuggling trade for the past twenty years, the Mounties also began investigating a Quebec-based drug smuggling ring that was tapping into this Spanish-English pipeline. According to a 1923 RCMP report, the informant identified Mr. E. McLaughlin, a senior customs official at the Port of Montreal, as "the man who passes these drugs through at Montreal" and who received "$2,000 for every trunk he puts through." Another conspirator was "Mr. Henry Blachford, connected with the Northern Woodlands Limited, having offices at 180 St. James Street Montreal" who "acts as agent for Mr. McLaughlin; he is the man who makes all appointments and acts as middle-man." Leon Piard, the manager of a dining room on Notre Dame Street West was described as "the man who negotiates for the drugs and talks business with Mr. Blachford." When a shipment of drugs was en route to Montreal, McLaughlin, who has already received notice of the name of the ship before it has left port in Europe, proceeded to a point along the river east of the city where he could board the ship and accompany the goods to Montreal. He then relied on his accomplices in the customs service to ensure the trunks were passed through without inspection.

When an undercover RCMP officer, posing as a prospective opium pusher, had dinner with a drunk and talkative Piard, he was told if he could come up with $2,000 he could "go to Germany and make $15,000 easily." According to a report by the undercover officer, a Canadian customs official "would fix me up with three trunks and letters to certain parties in Germany and I would cross and the return trip would cost about $250 each way, buy 1500 ounces of cocaine at $1.00 an ounce, pack 500 ounces in each of the trunks, and ship it as passenger's baggage on the boat or even as freight." Before leaving Germany, the undercover smuggler was to tell the customs official on what boat the drugs would be secreted "and he would guarantee me $25.00 an ounce here, leaving a profit of about $36,000." This profit would be divided as follows; $15,000 for the buyer, $11,000 for the customs officials "and $10,000 for the Royal Mounted." Piard informed the RCMP officer that to facilitate the unloading of the drug-laden trunks, the corrupt customs agents had "three trunks exactly similar to the ones containing the junk; when the boat unloads, the trunks containing the junk are at once taken off the dock and the other three are placed in their place to comply with the manifest; these are examined and passed and shipped to any address in Montreal as given by the handler in Germany, the carrier brings them back, as the consignee is unknown at the address given and they are eventually sold as unclaimed goods."

The RCMP officer's report noted that customers of this smuggling ring included two wholesale drug firms: "Messrs. Gasgrain & Charbonneau, Wholesale Druggists, 28-30 St. Paul Street East, Montreal and Messrs. McEwen, Cameron Limited, Wholesale Druggists, 132 St. Paul Street West, Montreal." The report also states, "Two Jews, I. Lande and his brother-in-law, a man named Gordon are also interested parties and supply some of the money." An RCMP informant reported that Mr. Cameron of McEwen, Cameron, Ltd. had been until recently connected with another drug wholesaler by the name of Lyman. According to the informant, a Member of Parliament, by the name of Gault, who was on record as strenuously opposing the lash and other corporal punishment penalties under federal narcotics legislation, was a shareholder of Lyman's Ltd. The report also described him as "one of the biggest men in the drug game, he sends stuff to New York and deals locally through a man named 'Harry' from whom the informer has purchased drugs frequently but does not know his full name."*

The "Harry" referred to above may very well be

---

* The RCMP report is vague as to the identity of the Member of Parliament named Gault. It may be a reference to Andrew Hamilton Gault, who was born in England in 1882 and died in Montreal in 1958. He attended McGill University, became a millionaire through his family's businesses, was commissioned in the Second Canadian Mounted Rifles, served in the Boer War in South Africa, and used $100,000 of his own money to found the Princess Patricia's Canadian Light Infantry in 1914, which he led into battle in the First World War. On retirement from the military in 1920, he moved to England where he was elected Conservative MP for Taunton in 1924, and became well known for his progressive views. The "Lyman" in question may be Walter Lyman who owned a number of pharmaceutical firms in Montreal during the 1920s.

Harry Davis, who the RCMP identified as a client of this smuggling group while heading one of Montreal's biggest trafficking rings during the 1920s and 1930s. Davis, a Romanian by birth who had become a British subject, arrived in Canada in 1907. By the early 1920s, he had his hand in a number of criminal enterprises, including bank robbery, prostitution, gambling, bookmaking, fencing stolen goods, and drug trafficking. As part of his drug trafficking ventures, Davis was well connected with suppliers in Europe and had influential partners in New York City's underworld. In Montreal, he worked on and off with a number of other drug traffickers, including Abraham Mouckley (a.k.a. Abie Mockley), Eddie Schreider (a.k.a. Dave Schrieder, a.k.a. Eddie Davis, a.k.a. Little Eddie), Eddie Baker (a.k.a. Kid Baker), Michael Sagor (a.k.a. Mike Sagor, a.k.a. Mick Sagor), Lazarus Goldberg (a.k.a. Lazarus Oblay, a.k.a. Kid Oblay), and Charlie Schwartz (a.k.a. Fatty). Davis' principal partner in Montreal was Eddie Baker, who was born in Russia in 1898 and came to Canada at the age of two. Even as an adult, Baker was diminutive in stature, standing around five foot eight and weighing 140 pounds. He picked up his nickname "Kid" as an amateur boxer in Montreal and would later describe his occupation to police as a manager of prizefighters. By the early 1920s, he already had a criminal record, having been arrested several times under different names for being found in gambling houses. As a drug dealer, according to a 1923 RCMP report, Baker "carries on a fairly active business around St. Lawrence Main Street" and "has working for him a man named 'Jockie Fleming,' another man 'Gussie' and a third named 'Smithy.'" The report also noted that the four are "particularly prone to taking 'Gayety Girls' out to 'slumming' parties which involved sitting in front seats at the Gayety Theatre on Sunday night, picking out the girls they desired, meeting them after the show, and then visiting Chinatown where they would smoke opium." Baker also operated a mail order business through which he sent opium and morphine to other parts of the country. In a 1923 letter to the Opium and Drug Branch in Ottawa, the chief of the Winnipeg Police Force wrote that Jennie Labansky, "an old time dope" in Winnipeg, was found in the possession of a package with "four packets of morphine cubes, and another large envelope with what proved

to be morphine." The woman confessed to Winnipeg police that "one Ed. Baker living at either 226 or 266 St. Urbain St., Montreal, is where her source of supply comes from."

By 1923, Davis, Baker, and their drug dealing cohorts were well known to the RCMP in Montreal and all were subject to constant police surveillance and undercover sting operations. One surveillance report from August of that year describes the retail drug operations of Davis and Baker:

A buyer enters Davis' shop at No. 266 St. Urbain Street, he states his requirements to Davis, who tells him the price by ounce and takes his money then. Whether Davis himself or "Kid" Baker is to supervise the delivery of the drug, the buyer is usually required to wait for, say half an hour at 266 St. Urbain Street. The time is sometimes less, sometimes longer, but the procedure usually follows as detailed. Everytime "Kid" Baker takes the buyer to the place of delivery he follows this plan — the buyer is taken in Davis' car along this route, North on St. Urbain Street to St. Catherines, West on St. Catherine to Benoit, South on Benoit to Dorchester, West to St. George, North on St. George crossing St. Catherine Street, North on Jeanne Mance Street and the drug is delivered by a small Jew at the corner of Jeanne Mance and Ontario Street. Should Davis himself take the buyer to his drugs, this plan is followed: The buyer enters Davis' car and is taken North on St. Urbain, West on St. Catherines, across Bleury and then either North or South on St. Alexander Street where the car is met by the same small Jew and delivery effected. The plan of actual delivery is this: Davis or Baker on arrival at the points detailed stops his car, having the engine running, the buyers usually more than one, are in the car. The runner, the small Jew, who always carries his coat on his arm, having the bottle of drugs in the coat, appears walking, Davis or Baker starts the car and the runner jumps in. Delivery is effected to the buyers who in turn jump out of the car while the car is in motion. Davis always uses the same runner, whether he delivered at or near his place at 266 St. Urbain Street or by car.

The same report documents the work of RCMP undercover agent No.717 who, after gaining the confidence of Davis, told him he had an associate who might want to buy a large quantity of drugs. "Previously, Davis has said that he could supply any quantity up to 200 ounces without delay." On August 13, Agent 717 visited Davis at his shop on St. Urbain Street and placed an order for an ounce of opium to test for purity. Davis instructed his new customer to get into the car where Kid Baker would take care of him. With two other buyers already in the back seat, and Kid Baker at the wheel, the car followed Baker's usual route. The car stopped for a short wait on Mayor Street, about a half block west of Bleury. Baker then turned the car around and retraced his course as far as the corner of St. Catherine and Bleury where he turned north. Proceeding north on Bleury, the "small Jew" runner — who police later determined was Jockie Fleming — was seen standing near the corner of Mayor and Bleury. Baker stopped the car on Mayor Street and Fleming jumped into the back seat, promptly producing five ounces of opium. Between July 4 and October 28 of 1923, RCMP undercover agents made ten separate one-ounce purchases from Davis. While they were never able to locate the cache from which their supply of opium and morphine was retrieved, more than enough evidence was accumulated to arrest and convict Davis, Baker, and their cronies.

Even after charges were laid, Davis and Baker continued their trafficking activities. In May 1925, Kid Baker along with Kid Oblay and Fatty Schwartz, were charged again for drug sales they made almost immediately after they were released from their prior arrest. One loyal customer of Kid Oblay filed the following deposition as part of Crown's evidence for the new charges:

During the Great War, I served in the 3rd Canadian Battery Garrison Artillery. In the year 1917 I was wounded and sent to hospital, as a result of the treatment I received, I became addicted to narcotics, and have since then,

more or less, been forced to use drugs, but I am now trying to take the cure. On my return to Canada I had to find some source from which I could obtain my supplies of narcotics. I bought from a number of people, until one day, about three years ago, certainly not less, I met one known locally as Kid Oblay, a narcotics trafficker. I have bought my narcotics drugs from this man since that day, except on occasions as I have been out of town. Kid Oblay, about two years ago, used to sell two dollar decks. He was famous at that time for the purity of the drug in his two dollar decks, and he consequently had considerable success. Recently he has gone in for what might be called the wholesale traffic, selling on a larger scale. He sells from a quarter of an ounce of any drug upwards in quantity.

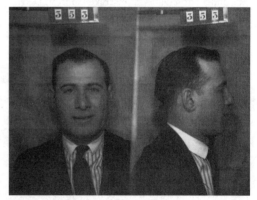
RCMP mug shot of Lazurus (Kid) Oblay

In June 1925, an undercover officer posing as an out-of-town buyer was introduced to Oblay through an informant. According to a report filed by the officer, Oblay told him "his partners were Kid Baker and Schwartz and that he resided at No. 72 Sherbrooke Street East. He also told me that they had been in the business for the past six years, they were backed up by well to do Jewish people in the City and that their methods for getting drugs into this country was an International affair and that all of their drugs went through Customs." According to the RCMP officer, Oblay told him "he could get as much as 600 and 700 ounces at the one time of 'C,' 'H,' and M.' He said that they had never been caught except for a charge now pending against them which was made by some stool pigeons, but that it was not strong enough to send them down. He also said that he knew everyone of the police and that one of them would not be able to talk to him for two minutes before he would know him." Following this show of bravado, Oblay sold the undercover officer $35 worth of opium and also told his buyer, "If I did not care to come to Montreal to get the goods myself, all I had to do was to send a money-order payable to one Fred Harris and to address it to Kid Oblay, 73 Sherbrooke Street East." During the course of another drug deal between the two men on July 3, Oblay told the undercover officer that he was "not a big man in the game," only dealing in one- and two-dollar decks, and occasionally in ten-dollar decks and ounces, and that he was supplied by a bigger source, "his boss," who dictated prices to Oblay. Around this time, Oblay's boss, Kid Baker, was under surveillance as he travelled from Detroit with a "load of drugs probably concealed on his wife's person," according to an RCMP report.

By the end of the summer of 1925, the RCMP realized they could lay even more charges against members of what they called the "Kid Baker Gang," if they could only get a corroborating witness. Fortunately for the Mounties, Naiten Erlich was arrested at a most opportune moment. Erlich was only twenty-one years old when he was picked up by the Mounties for drug trafficking, but had been working as a street dealer since he was fifteen. At the time of his arrest, he confessed to working as a runner for Baker and, as reported by a RCMP memo, was "an intimate acquaintance of traffickers he mentions and a very highly trusted man by them." Erlich agreed to become a Crown witness and began unravelling a story that substantiated much of the evidence already collected by the RCMP drug squad. Erlich confessed to being a drug addict and stated that Baker used Kid Oblay and Abie Mockley to get young kids hooked on drugs, and then employ them as their street-level peddlers. These dealers were expected to take the fall for their bosses if they were ever caught.

Unbeknownst to the young drug addict or his police handlers, Erlich was shadowed to the RCMP barracks by members of the Baker gang the evening he was arrested. When Erlich was released, Oblay and Abie Mockley confronted him and gave him the choice of either being killed or getting out of town. Erlich chose the latter. Oblay purchased a one-way ticket for Windsor and made sure Erlich was on the train that night. But the RCMP caught up with the fugitive and recorded the following statement from Erlich after he was brought back to Montreal:

Erlich: They pushed me in the corner — Oblay and Mockley did — and then Mockley started to talk fast with his hand to his pocket all the time.

Q: With his hand to his pocket — what was the idea behind that?

Erlich: He said, "I will cut your face for you if you don't get out of town." I said, "Why?" He said, "You got arrested yesterday," and they told me I was met going up to headquarters." He said, "You are not going to turn 'red.'"

Q: What did he mean by saying "You are not going to turn 'Red'?"

Erlich: Stool-pigeon.

With Erlich's most recent statement, the RCMP now had witness-tampering charges to add to the multiple counts of drug offences they had accumulated on the gang. Baker, Oblay, Mockley, and Eddie Schreider were arrested and, on November 24, 1925, they were found guilty of drug trafficking, conspiracy, and witness tampering. As the *Montreal Gazette* reported, "When the indictments were read to the accused in the afternoon the four answered guilty in their turn. Baker was called upon to make a response three times. Mouckley and Oblay twice, while 'Little Eddie' Schreider replied only in the charge of conspiracy to traffic in drugs." Baker, Oblay, and Mockley each received a three-year prison term and when they were released, none of them would ever be a force in Montreal's drug trafficking scene again. Davis was later convicted in a 1928 trial, but received only a six-month sentence. Before the end of the decade he would be back on the street and would continue on as the biggest drug trafficker in Montreal.

CHARLIE SPURTZED

That was until Fat Charlie came along. It was Charlie who would be the downfall of Harry Davis and it was Charlie who would beat his gums and begin the unravelling of one of the world's largest dope smuggling rings.

It was a hot June day in Montreal, nineteen hundred and thirty one — the kind of day where you could fry a gefilte fish on the sidewalk — that Charlie became a stoolie. Short, fat, shifty-eyed, double-chinned, swarty-faced Charlie Feigenbaum. He had a mug that looked like a tuckas, but he was a gantser k'nacker in Montreal's underworld. He had so many slots in the resort shtetls scattered throughout the Laurentians that he was called "The King of the North." He also tried his hand at bookmaking and at one time had a share in the White House Inn, the largest and most popular gambling hall in Montreal. Another major shareholder in this dice emporium was Harry Davis, the slender, impeccably dressed, aristocratic-looking clipster, with the inscrutable poker face, slicked-back dark hair, and piercing eyes the color of a burnt loaf of sour rye.

Despite his shlumperdik appearance, Charlie actually began in the schmada business. He parlayed that into dealing contraband silk, a racket bigger than a chazzer noshing at a free kosher buffet thanks to the heavy import taxes imposed by the Canadian feds. Most of the silk was brought in from New York by bronfen shmuglens returning to Canada after they had schlepped their prohibited schnapps south of the border. It was through his sneaky silk sales that Charlie first met Pincus Brecher.

Pinky was just five foot seven, and looked even shorter because he was always stooping. He had wavy black-grey hair that looked like worn steel wool, pale gaunt skin, grey and sombre eyes partly covered by drooping lids, a nose with a tip as flat as the blunt end of a hammer, no jawline to speak of, and a scar that ran from the outer corner of his left eye toward his left nostril. He had a battered face that "was as threadbare as a bookkeeper's tweed office coat after if it had been hit by everything but the bucket of a dragline. It was scarred, flattened, thickened, checkered and welted." Pinky had come

to America from Romania around the turn of the century when he was a little north of twenty years old. He moved to New York where be became a big-shot silk soykher in the Bronx.

Pinky was also in the dope trade and his chief partner was one of the most legendary k'nackers in the American mob, Louis (Lepke) Buchalter. During the 1920s and 1930s, this "diminutive hawk-nosed creature of the Manhattan streets" had plenty of shutfims in New York's mafia families. He had his meathooks in every illegal racket imaginable, which some say netted him a cool $50 mil in scratch every year. His hatchet men eighty-sixed dozens of rivals through Murder Inc., the syndicate's bloodthirsty enforcement arm. Lepke was ruthless, moraless, murderous, and remorseless. He gave even the most blood-thirsty rod merchant the hewbie jewbies. He was the kind of guy that would kill both his parents and then throw himself on the mercy of the court because he was an orphan.

Lepke was one of the biggest gownicks in the world during the last roar of the Roaring Twenties and the first dirt of the Dirty Thirties. He bought most of his hop from Paris-based Jacob Pollakowitz. The transatlantic shvindel used by Buchalter, Pollakowitz, and Brecher was pretty straightforward: the gow would be hidden in steamer trunks and then schlepped stateside by mob gees to New York or Montreal on passenger ocean liners. The palms of ships crews and customs' combers would be well oiled so they would take care of the hype-filled luggage. Most of the easing powder that landed in Montreal would end up on the streets of New York.

When Brecher met Fat Charlie he knew he could be plenty helpful in smuggling the white cross into and out of Montreal. Charlie was a natural gonif and his record as a border-tripper was unblemished. He had customs dicks in his pocket like so many pennies and nickels, and was a big-time macher in Montreal who had plenty of pull with the coppers and croppers alike.

In summer of 1930, Brecher and Buchalter were in Montreal to break unleavened bread with Feigenbaum and Davis, who was back cooling his heels on the street after his short stint in the big house. Charlie was getting a piece of the smuggling action, but he was not told he would be schlepping the foolish powder. They told him the merchandise would be Swiss watches and he would get a cut of the take if he could get the timepieces into the country. This was old schmeer for Charlie the contrabandit. He began by providing the oil of angels to his bent customs bulls so the trunks could slip through the port without being sniffed. Charlie also got his hands on shvindeled passports for some of Brecher's key loogans, including Jacob Pollakowitz.

On August 15, 1930, the first shipment of "timepieces" arrived in Montreal on board the S.S. *Montclair*. But there was a problem. The on-duty customs dick refused to allow the trunks in without snooping through them first. Feigenbaum had an ace up his sleeve just in case a raw deal like this happened. He contacted his number-one bent customs snark, Joe Lapalme, who signed the paperwork and made sure the trunks passed like a hot knife through schmaltz. For his services, Lapalme was dropped six grand. Not bad for a couple hours of work. The trunks were released to Charlie's brother, Max, and taken to his house in Montreal. Harry Davis stopped by the house a little later and emptied the trunks of their illegal medicine. To Davis, Feigenbaum was a kishef macher and any doubt about his value to the organization had been laid to rest.

Davis and Buchalter asked Feigenbaum to become a partner in their bindle business and offered him a cut of future deals. Feigenbaum's shadowy g'virs also asked him to travel to Paris to serve as a mekler with Pollakowitz and prepare the next few shipments for Montreal. While in France, Feigenbaum and Pollakowitz hacked out a system to mark the trunks filled with the joy flakes so Fat Charlie's well-oiled border schlumps would know which ones to let through. After a few empty trunks were sent across the pond to test the system, the race began for real. By November 11, 1930, four trunks full of the "O" and the "M" had been shipped from France and shtuped straight into Montreal. The trunks contained more than three hundred kilos of dope.

Charlie was now riding higher than the Star of David. He was kvelling over his partnership with some of the biggest gonifs on the eastern seaboard and was making more gelt than a public shmeckle on the take. But god forbid he should get to enjoy his success. His undoing began with a routine bust involving a couple of bindle-dealing deucers in Montreal. On October 11, 1930, Saltorio (Sam) Arcadi and Harry Tucker were pinched after they sold a kilo of morph to an undercover RCMP dick, who was posing as an American aeroplane pilot who promised to smuggle the dope into the U.S. through the air. Arcadi had already been busted for trafficking junk. A 1932 Mountie report said he had connections in the United States, and "usually dealt in a rather large way." Arcadi and Tucker were convicted and sent up to the state bucket. Tucker received a three-spot while Arcadi got a nickel's worth, plenty of time to think about his sins and to call his mother. After the two pugs were clocked, Harry Davis told Feigenbaum that he had sold them the hype.

Feigenbaum knew John Law would have a hard time connecting him to Arcadi, Tucker or the dope, so he wasn't too verklempt. But in December 1930, his shagetz customs flunky, Joe Lapalme, got all guilty and spilled his guts to his bosses, the yutz. Long story short, along with four others, including his brother Max and the French babbling brook Lapalme, Charlie was handed a stretch for smuggling silks into Canada. He ended up at the St. Vincent De Paul big top looking at five and a half years' slammer time. Once inside, he stewed over how Brecher and Davis came up with bubkis when he needed bail or a mouthpiece for court. Charlie was sore. Plenty sore. So in June 1931 he spilled the beans to the heat. He never thought he would do it, but Charlie became a spikotz.

Feigenbaum klipped and kvetched to the Mounties about those shmendriks Davis, Brecher, and Buchalter. He told them all about the dope shipments and their sources in Europe. He told them about the shady customs bulls and conspiring crews on the passenger ships. Charlie even told them about Davis selling Arcadi the junk. We should all be so lucky that we get a gift so generous that Charlie gave to those Mounted policemen! Through their own spade work, the Mounties corroborated Charlie's statements and linked Davis to 852 kilos of dope pushed on the streets of Montreal and New York between January 1 and December 31, 1930.

The bar mitzvah was over for Davis. On April 9, 1932, the harness bulls plastered him with nine counts of dope boosting and grafting public officials. Enough gow had been pulled from France "to put the whole of New York City to sleep," trumpeted Crown Lips Gustov Monnette. Bail for Davis was set at 100,000 bills. Not even the biggest shylocking schnorrer bailsman in Montreal could come up with that much shtrudel for Davis. And without so much as a mazel tov, the judge sent him off for a whiff in the joint. Jack Pollakowitz was also eyeballed as a co-conspirator and Pincus Brecher was fingered for pushing the smeck in the Big Apple. Both were indicted in the Empire City a few weeks later.

Harry's legal circus began on October 1, 1933, in the Court of King's Bench in Montreal. The Crown's court jester called more than fifty witnesses and the first to take the stand – you guessed it, Fat Charlie (Don't get me started on that shlemiel). He yipped about how he shmuglened the angel's dust for Davis and Brecher. Sam Arcadi also made the show as a Crown blabber. Dressed in snazzy blue standard-issue duds and iron bracelets courtesy of the St. Vincent de Paul pen, Sammy-the-Wop tipped out that Davis had furnished him with the illicit linctus he was shoving. The earful given by the two blobbers was so damning that the Crown glove puppet did not even bother to put any of his remaining eyes on the stand. The judicial circus took all but five days and at the end the jury slapped Harry Davis with a guilty verdict after less than an hour of lip smacking. Dressed in a brown suit, a dull white shirt, and a light brown tie that "had been tied with a pair of plyers in a knot the size of a pea," Harry sat in the prisoners' holding pad as steady as a moyel's hand at a bris, while Chief Justice Greenshields threw the Talmud at him. The judged handicapped Harry to fourteen years in the can, ten strokes of the lash, and a $3,000 fine. "I know nothing good of you," His Lordship said. "You apparently have earned the unenviable reputation of being the 'master mind' in this illicit traffic in deadly drugs." The court umpire also recommended the Crown lips start extradition proceedings against Pincus

Brecher, who had been let go by a New York judge because any criminal capers he allegedly perped were in Canada, not the States.

In December 1933, less than two months after Davis was sent packing to the joint, Feigenbaum hit the street. Fat Charlie knew that he was a marked man on the outside. He shed the protection of the Mounted Horsies because he was trying to mount a comeback in the Montreal underworld. But Charlie was no mashugga; he hired his own shtarkers, and by the spring of 1934 he was operating a sporting house at 56 Mount Royal Avenue East, providing the best odds this side of Monte Carlo. Rumours were also flying around town that he was trying to muscle in on the slot machine action in Montreal.

Charlie Feigenbaum

Charlie was back on top of the world. He was a free man, making plenty of gelt, and was his own boss. But his shtik naches would soon turn into a tsuris as big as an elephant's heine. On August 21, 1934, Fat Charlie arrived at the home of his shvegerin to take her to the family cottage in the country. With the help of his eighteen-year-old kaddishel Jackie,

Charlie was waddling back and forth between the house and the curb loading packages into the trunk of his heap. Before he was finished, he was startled by two men who had just catfooted across the street from their parked Hudson rattletrap. Each casually pulled a rod from underneath their jackets. Before the horrified peepers of the young Feigenbaum, his tatteh was mowed down in a hail of .45-calibre iron pills. Six slugs were pumped into the forty-eight-year-old schlimazel, to be exact. One drove into his leg, two drilled the abdomen, two grazed the back of his skull and the top of his head, and one burrowed into his heart like a gopher into the ground. Feigenbaum was plugged. He was plugged good. As his lead-filled body collapsed into the gutter at 5:45 p.m. that summer evening, the two paid wipers casually strolled back to their Detroit iron and sped away. After spying his blood-mottled suit, they knew right away that Fat Charlie was as dead as a wholesale discount outlet on the Jewish Sabbath.

One eyewitness wrote down the licence plate of the fleeing bucket and immediately called the public dicks. The jalopy was found abandoned on a nearby street just ten minutes later, but there was no sign of the trigger men. Six hoods, five of them American, were later held by the dime-a-pops for questioning. When the suspects were scooped up in the rented room of their flophouse, the soft shoes also found several ounces of hop and four hop sticks. But they could find no evidence linking the loogans to Fat Charlie's icing and they were released from the copper factory. Any leads on Fat Charlie's murder quickly became as cold as a bowl of shav. Charlie's dousing would remain forever unsolved.

The bulls knew that Charlie's lead poisoning was not just revenge for his backstabbing Harry Davis. He was also slated to be the star snitch at the Montreal trial of Pincus Brecher, who had just been sent gift wrapped from the American feds on Canadian dope charges. But Charlie's unscheduled absence did not help the New Yorker's case. On September 28, 1934, the fifty-seven-year-old Brecher was convicted on all counts. Brecher boasted to the courtroom that he was an odds-on favourite to win on appeal. Perhaps his outward chutzpah belied his own inner fachadick and fahklumpt state. Later that evening, Brecher broke free from the two screws who were escorting him to his room in the state hotel and hurled himself over the second-floor guardrail, landing with a klop on the concrete floor, yarmelkeh first. He was as flat as a matzoh, an instant nifter. Like the *Daily Star* reported the next day, "When the name of Pincus Brecher, New York millionaire drug trafficker, is called in Court of King's Bench for sentence on narcotic drug charges, there will be no response for the mortal remains of Pincus Breacher today lie in a morgue of Montreal Jail." Above the picture of Brecher in the *Star* it read "To a higher court."

Pincus Brecher

The stretches in the joint handed to Davis and Pollakowitz, and the croaking of Brecher and Feigenbaum, marked the beginning of the end of the gownicks' lock over the dope trade in North America. Louis Buchalter, the shtocker behind it all, was now enemy number one for American G-men.

In 1939, he was convicted on dope charges and sentenced to fourteen singles in Sing Sing. But he wouldn't have to finish his sentence. In 1944, after being convicted of murder, Buchalter was baked like a knish in the prison's barbecue stool.

Harry Davis was released from the big house in 1945 and resumed his place as one of Montreal's leading clip joint operators and edge men. One day, he was sitting in his office located in the back of his Stanley Street bookie joint. A large steel safe took up more than half the room. In one corner was a heavy, old mahogany desk covered in betting slips, receipts, an overflowing ashtray, old racing forms, and a cold cup of joe that was ground during the Meighan administration. A hat rack stood lonely in another corner with a cashmere coat carefully hung on a wooden hanger. The parquet floor was scratched and well worn with little of its original gloss finish surviving over the cheap varnish haphazardly laid over generations of dirt and the occasional cigarette butt. A window that opened onto a back alley let in the air from the garbage cans mingled unpleasantly with the musty odour of the office.

Out of nowhere a two-bit nishtikeit named Louis Bercowitz strolled into the office like he owned the joint and demanded that Davis give him his blessings to open his own gambling hall. Davis didn't much like that idea so he refused the little pisher and told him to scram. Bercowitz stormed out of the office and vowed revenge. Big talker, that Bercowitz. But Davis wasn't worried. In his business, gun punks were a dime a dozen and would-be tough guys came a nickel a gross.

But Bercowitz returned to Davis' office plenty mad on the night of July 25, 1946. He was a tough little ape who now planned on cutting a bigger one down to size. Hate filled his eyes and steamed his ears red. He was ready to jump all the way out of his brogans and trudge up and down the length of Davis like a welcome mat. Bercowitz parked his boiler at the curb outside the lane that led to the back door of Davis' office. His right hand checked the snub-nosed, spring-holstered roscoe beneath his left arm. He sat there for just a moment, eyeballing the joint. With boiled-up rage and killer courage glinting from his slitted eyes, Bercowitz plotzed into the office, pulled his rod from his trousers, and sprayed bullets at Davis, splattering the yiddisher kop of Montreal's legendary mob boss all over the walls.

After Bercowitz was nabbed by the eagle eyes he squibbed off that he snuffed Davis in self-defence; he had heard rumours that Davis was planning to bump him off. He yipped that when he confronted Davis, Montreal's big bookie told him he could "be taken care of just as easy as Feigenbaum." The jury at Bercowitz's trial thought his alibi was kosher enough and saved him from the big sleep by handing him a fifteen-year term in the barred hotel for manslaughter.

STRIVING TO WALK ON AIR

In contrast to Quebec and British Columbia, Ontario appears to have had less of a drug trafficking problem during the first quarter of the century. Periodic busts did occur in the province, such as the forty tins of unadulterated smoking opium police found hidden in a box of alarm clocks that had entered Canada through Vancouver and ended up at the Kuorg High Chong Company at 179 Queen Street East in Toronto. As in the rest of the country, the addict population in Toronto began to grow following the Great War. Harry Wodson, a long-serving magistrate in the city, also blamed a growth in demand for opium and morphine on the imposition of strict liquor laws in Ontario:

"Hundreds of cocaine and morphine victims filter through the court each year," he wrote in 1917, "but since the Ontario Temperance Act came into operation the number of young men adopting the drug habit has been steadily on the increase."

A moral panic over drug use began to take root in the puritanical province of Ontario as robberies, shootings, and other violent deeds were now being blamed on "the rapidly growing use of drugs." A February 1921 edition of the *Hamilton Spectator* quoted an unnamed police investigator who confidently stated, "We know positively that some of the worst crimes of the past few months have been 'pulled off' by dope fiends." The culprits were mostly "young chaps" under the age of twenty who were responsible for a rash of armed robberies at drug stores and other retail outlets in Hamilton while "filled with 'hop.'" Reporters wrote about "dope fiends" sitting in local restaurants and bars "lit up to the eyes" and making no effort to conceal their drug use. "One man was observed to help himself to his bit of 'snuff' in full view of many customers in the place" while another who was "delightfully 'lit up' persisted in jumping up and down striving to walk on air." Organized bands of dope peddlers were now dominating the street trade, according to the *Spectator*. "Men who are known not to have had a cent to their names have been made suddenly and mysteriously rich, through trafficking in drugs, the leader of the supposed ring according to the stories circulated making enough to buy himself a fine automobile. Others are known to have acquired fat bank accounts through the business of dope selling." To guard against police sting operations, "the sellers of drugs will not part with their wares without elaborate inquiries and introductions to make sure that their customer is 'on the level.'"

One of the largest drug importation rings in Ontario during the 1920s was headed by Rocco Perri, although many believe it was his common-law wife, Bessie Starkman, who was the driving force. "Bessie was the person who made most of the deals, corrupted many of the public officials on the Perri organization payroll, collected most of the money coming in to the Perri mob and met with many of their gangster allies in the States and ran her criminal empire with an iron fist," James Dubro and Robin Rowland wrote in their book on Frank Zaneth, the legendary RCMP undercover officer who penetrated the Perri-Starkman organization. Rocco and Bessie made most of their money by overseeing a multimillion-dollar liquor smuggling operation during the 1920s, but police in Canada and the U.S. gathered considerable intelligence connecting them to the drug trade. As early as 1922, RCMP reports were chronicling the "suspected dealing in narcotics on a large scale" by an Italian immigrant in Canada named Rocco Perri. In a March 12, 1926, letter, a U.S. Narcotics Bureau agent accused "Rocco Perry" of supplying an "Italian dope peddling" ring in Pennsylvania.

Rocco and Bessie's network of associates were strategically placed in various locations in Southern Ontario, mostly along the American border. Some were running booze into the U.S. and returning with loads of raw opium to be processed into smoking opium or morphine. One RCMP informant alleged that drugs were also brought into Ontario by seaplane, which landed on Lake Ontario near Burlington, or by dropping packages by silk parachutes onto old flying fields near Hamilton. "There is no doubt this is the cleverest gang of drug runners in the country," an undercover Mountie wrote of the Perri-Starkman gang in a 1929 memo. "The ring leaders are very shrewd and have deliberately withheld introducing a new customer until they knew more about him." If there were suspicions that police were on to them, they would "rather close down temporarily rather than take any unnecessary risks." The memo also acknowledges that Bessie "is the brains of the whole gang and nothing is being done without her consent."

By the late 1920s, as it became clear that Prohibition was coming to an end, Bessie and Rocco diversified their criminal activities by expanding their drug operations. It was during this time that the RCMP noted a substantial increase in the availability of opium, morphine, and heroin in Southern Ontario. As a result, the RCMP stepped up its surveillance of suspected members of the drug trafficking network. In 1929, under the guise of a Quebec drug dealer looking for a source in Toronto, Frank Zaneth was introduced to two of Perri's bootlegging and drug dealing cronies, Tony Defalco and Antonio Brassi. Zaneth successfully negotiated the purchase of $40 worth of morphine, which was delivered on May 8 by another Perri lieutenant, Tony Roma, who handed over to Zaneth a hundred white cubes, each weighing between 2 and 2.5 grams. By June of that year, Zaneth had purchased cocaine and morphine from Roma and Brassi on three occasions and noticed that in each buy, the drugs were wrapped in pages from Hamilton newspapers. This led him to believe that the source was located in Hamilton, a suspicion that was corroborated by an informant who identified Hamilton-based Francesco Rossi (a.k.a. Frank Ross), one of Perri's most trusted lieutenants, as his main distributor of cocaine and morphine. Through his investigation, Zaneth also discovered that the drugs sold through Perri's group were kept at the

Hamilton home of yet another underling, Nazzareno (Ned) Italiano.

Beginning on June 20, 1929, the RCMP raided Tony Roma's gambling hall in Toronto where they found drugs, money, guns, and ammunition. Roma was arrested along with Zaneth, who was still playing his drug dealing character. Italiano's Dundas Street home in Hamilton was raided at the same time and police found a supply of morphine and some of the marked money used by Zaneth in his undercover buys. Italiano and three other men were arrested. Much to the RCMP's surprise, as they were winding down the bust at Italiano's home Bessie Starkman arrived. When questioned, the startled drug doyen replied that she was just making a social call on her husband's old friend. When police searched her purse they discovered rolls of bills that added up to hundreds of dollars. Upon close inspection, they determined that none of the cash was the marked money used for the undercover drug buys. As a result, Starkman was released without any charges laid against her.

On September 23, 1929, Italiano, Defalco, and Brassi were put on trial for drug trafficking and four days later the three were convicted. Italiano and Defalco were sentenced to six months while Brassi received three years in the Kingston Penitentiary. Police testimony during the trial revealed that Rocco and Bessie had visited Italiano's house while it was under police surveillance at least three times. However, there was still insufficient evidence to link either to drug trafficking and they were never charged. Tony Roma, meanwhile, had jumped bail before the trial began and a bench warrant was issued for his arrest. Suspecting he had skipped the country, Roma became the subject of a continent-wide manhunt. It wasn't until July 27, 1936 that Roma would be captured by the FBI near the small town of Fowler, California. After being extradited back to Canada, where he stood trial on outstanding drug charges, the fifty-two-year-old Italian native was convicted on December 21, 1936, and sentenced to two years in the Kingston pen. Following his release, Roma tried to re-enter the United States, but was deported to Italy.

CHAPTER FIVE

SPEAKEASY OR DIE

Organized Crime in the Era of Prohibition

THE KING OF THE BOOTLEGGERS

It was just past midnight, October 6, 1923. Sidney Gogo was quickly offloading his cabin boat, the *Hattie C.* She was docked on the shore of Lake Ontario, at the foot of Leslie Street, in the City of Toronto. There was a moon somewhere in the autumn sky, behind the dark clouds, but only a sliver of light sliced across the surface of the bay. It was a cool night, but not too cold. A few tentative raindrops splashed into the water and sent ripples the size of Canadian dimes, then nickels, then quarters, then half dollars.

The cargo being hauled to shore was 106 bags of high-grade Canadian hooch; more than 2,400 quart bottles of Corby's special whiskey. This was Prohibition-era Ontario, and the illegal cache of liquid damnation had a street value of over twenty thousand clams. Helping Gogo with the squirrel dew was his brother James and son John. On the receiving end of the juniper juice was a group of rum-running pugs led by Francisco (Frank) Di Petro and Rocco Perri.

Before the rye sap could be completely unloaded into the waiting motor cars and lorries, the hoods were startled by the sudden appearance of Toronto's finest. Knowing they were in a jam deeper than J.M. Smucker, the Gogos leaped into the idling boat and started to scram. The lead copper spied the schooner making a break for it and barked, "Stop the engine. Come in, we've got you cornered."

The *Hattie C* did not stop. As she slowly disappeared into the dark shadow of the moonless night, the two bulls unholstered their bean shooters. The lead copper roared again, "Stop your engines or I'll sink your boat."

No good. With engines puttering, the *Hattie C* continued to ankle from the shore.

The lead bull turned to his men. "Sink it!"

In a flash, John Law's iron rods clapped thunder. Warning shots were pumped over the bow of the fleeing boat. The hot lead then found its mark in the hull. The boat sputtered to a stop. As the public dicks boarded the hobbled vessel, they made a grim discovery. James Gogo was lying in a pool of his own blood. He was drilled in the jaw by the fusillade of lead. His twenty-four-year-old nephew was lying still in his father's arms. Crimson blossoms stained his shirt. He'd been taken a .32-calibre slug to the chest. Fifteen minutes later, he was as dead as a pickled walnut.

News of the pinching and fatal metal squirting spread quickly. The front page of the *Toronto Star* howled, "Today's tragic raid was the first time the police have come in close grips with the rum runners who have been stealing into Toronto under the blanket of night and discharging their illegal cargoes of whiskey into the eager hands of bootleggers." The story would be news for weeks to come.

All eight roustabouts found at the water's edge were arrested and charged with the illegal transport of stagger juice. Three days after the early morning ambush by the state beaks, Ontario's top Crown mouthpiece ordered a probe into the gunplay and the bootlegging racket of the punks nabbed that night. The hammer and saws made a point of fingering Rocco Perri as the big cheese behind the operation and vowed to do everything in their power to send him up the river.

The trial for the men nabbed that night took place in November. By the end, Sidney Gogo and Frank Di Petro were slapped with a sentence of thirty days in the joint or a fine of a thousand singles. Di Petro was forced to pay because he was the owner of the Model 34 Marmon heap that had most of the offloaded squirl. He paid his tab, while Gogo chose to serve thirty days in the cooler.

The coppers were certain that Rocco was the real buyer of that boatload of gay and frisky. But Rocco was singing another tune, and it was not music to the elephant ears. Rocco's reason why he was at the foot of Leslie Street that night, "I run into Frank Di Petro on York Street about eleven o'clock," he said. "And Frank ask me how to get to Leslie Street, so I show him." The flatfoots pounded the pavement and were able to prove that Rocco owned the three jalopies seized at the bay. The button men thought they had caught Rocco red-handed this time for sure. But there still was not enough proof to sock him away and he was allowed to walk. Maybe he was just giving directions that night. Maybe not. It was a dark night. This wouldn't be the first time Rocco avoided the big party on the hill. All through his career as a boozeheister, Rocco would be more slippery than a Seymour River salmon spawning upstream. It was one of the reasons why he was called the "King of the Bootleggers."

Rocco Perri was small but stocky. He stood five feet four and weighed around 160 pounds. He had a swarthy complexion, a round face, a cleft chin, and a small boil scar on his left cheek. His straight black hair was fronted by a receding hairline and accentuated by a small bald spot on top. He was renowned for his loud ties, slick ace-deuce suits, and straw boater hats. Expensive Cuban stogies that looked like they were rolled by Manuel Lopez and licked shut by Mae West were often seen dangling from a crooked mouth that one typewriter jockey described as "grinning an Italian grin." To some, he was plenty confident, cocky, and well connected, with a swell eye for the rackets. Others saw him as timid and dim-witted; a two-bit hoodlum who kowtowed to his wife, Bessie, the real brains behind their wet-mule racket. It didn't much matter. The Rocco Perri gang became one of Canada's big-shot mobs during Prohibition. Rocco would also become a humdinger scofflaw in the annals of Canadian underworld history.

Rocco and Bessie

Rocco was born in Reggio, Calabria, in 1890. He came to Canada when he was thirteen, joining thousands of Italian immigrants in Ontario. In 1912, he moved to Toronto where he fell for a dame. Her name was Bessie Starkman, the Polish immigrant wife of his landlord. Bessie was of medium build, with straight shoulders and narrow hips. Her large face and wide cheekbones accommodated an oversized mouth and a pug nose. Her puss was topped by neatly plaited hair and underscored by a witchly pointed chin. This dame was no looker, but her confident mug and cocky countenance loudly proclaimed she was no kept floozy or anybody's chiselly-wink.

Rocco snatched Bessie from her husband and, in 1915, the two moved to Hamilton where Rocco began working in a macaroni factory. The next year, they opened a small grocery store hawking noodles, olive oil, tomatoes and other necessities of life for the local Italians. The store was also where their bootlegging empire was distilled. In 1916, the *Ontario Temperance Act* was now law, outlawing the sale of panther sweat in the province. Prohibition in Ontario had begun.

The banning of tonsil paint was a present to the underworld and this present came gift wrapped in C-notes. Bootleggers were now as common as a run in a dollar pair of stockings. Prohibition turned petty thugs and small-time crooks like Rocco into boozeheisters, rumrunners, gin joggers, and whiskey walkers; distillers, brewers, alky-cookers, and booze foundry founders; mobsters, gangsters, grafters, and grifters; blind pig proprietors, speakeasy supervisors, gin mill managers, moonlight innkeepers, creep joint operators, and whoopee parlour property owners; not to mention, button men, hit men, hatchet men, and trigger men; croppers, droppers, and wipers; gun punks, gun pokes, hoods, apes, loogans, and stooges; mugs, pugs and thugs.

Rocco and Bessie quickly took advantage of the demand for giggle water. They began by hawking blotto juice from the back of his grocery store; fifty cents for three fingers of nose paint. Their first run-in with the law was on January 4, 1919, when the store was raided and Rocco was cuffed with *OTA* charges. The *Hamilton Herald* reported on his January 6 appearance at the Hall of Justice:

> Rocci Perri Sussino, grocer, 105 North Hess Street must have bathed in booze, washed his teeth with it, used it for shaving, gargled his throat with it, shampooed his raven locks with and utilized it as a massage. The OTA tax on toilet water Sergeant May and Constables Coburn and Goddard found on Rocco's premises Saturday night amounted to $1,000. There were eighteen quarts of

"ski" under a bed in the living apartments above the store, a gallon can of alcohol in an upstairs kitchen, a partly filled bottle and glass in the downstairs kitchen, two dozen "dead soldiers" in the bathroom, a hundred gallons of wine in the cellar and a bunch of whiskey labels and the seal of a Canadian distillery.

In addition to having his liquid lightning confiscated, Rocco was fined 1,000 clams.

But that did not stop Rocco. He was soon blipping around the province taking orders for the red eye from an ever-expanding clientele. His cover was a travelling salesman for the Superior Macaroni Company. Rocco took advantage of all the gaping loopholes in the prohibition laws. You couldn't buy the tanglefoot in Ontario, but you could drink it in the comfort of your own home if you brought it in from Quebec or another province. It was still legal to produce it, if you had a federal licence, and Ontario boasted plenty of distilleries and breweries. This perplexing patchwork of provincial and parliamentary Prohibition prelates portended a promising platform to please the peccadillo of the parched punter. As Will Rogers quipped, "Prohibition is better than no whiskey at all."

Rocco was plenty well positioned to help fill this demand and was a regular customer at Ontario's biggest booze producers: Gooderham and Worts, Seagram and Sons, and Hiram Walker. By 1920, he was the biggest pour-out man in Hamilton. But the pint-sized Canadian market for contraband hooch was now dwarfed by the Texas mickey-sized thirst south of the border. Prohibition had just whipped into America like sand in an Arabian windstorm. The liquid Eldorado for Rocco and other snakehead salesmen had arrived. For the next dozen years, Canadian rumrunners would no longer be dumping their load of contraband liquor cargo exclusively on their own soil. They would now shoot their load into America.

Rocco moved swiftly into the business of exporting the insanity water to America and built a network of bootleggers that stretched across Southern Ontario and northern New York. By the mid-

1920s, he had a fleet of forty souped-up cars and trucks. Many were modified to carry loads of up to three hundred gallons at a time. He also launched an armada of fifty fishing boats that smuggled thousands of gallons of the devil's diet across Lake Erie to the American side. He was buying cases of 60-proof shoe polish in Toronto for as little as $18 a case and selling them across the border for as much as $120 each. During a ballyhooed interview with the *Toronto Daily Star*, Rocco beaked off that he sometimes sold as many as one thousand cases of whiskey a day. Bessie also made with the words in the same interview, saying they never dealt in less than one-hundred case lots.

Before long, Rocco and Bessie were richer than a Lindy's cheesecake. They lived in an opulent igloo at 166 Bay Street in one of Hamilton's toniest neighbourhoods. It was a nineteen-room, three-chimneyed Victorian beauty that was more pleasant to look at than the Queen, but a little smaller than Buckingham Palace. It was in the expansive living room of their classy wigwam that Rocco and Bessie threw lavish parties where politicians, judges, and other big shots rubbed shoulders with Canadian and American mobsters while sipping absinthe out of bone-china teacups strained through lumps of laced sugar. Rocco and Bessie owned a battalion of motor cars, trucks, boats, hotels, and speakeasies, where mutton-faced blonds bellowed gummy mammy songs. They were often seen driving around town in a chauffeured limo, and Bessie was always dolled up in public, wearing dresses that looked like they were cut by Michelangelo and pricey fur glad rags thicker and softer than a newly washed kitten fresh out of a newfangled electric dryer machine. Strands of expensive ice dangled from her plump neck. They were free spenders and they stepped around town high, wide, and handsome.

Because of Prohibition, their bank accounts were multiplying faster than the Dionne family. Intrepid spadework by government bean counters unearthed seven accounts opened by Bessie under various *nom de plumes*. The feds found more than 841,000 cranberries on deposit. A 1927 audit commissioned by the feds' accountants found one account at the James Street branch of the Standard Bank of Canada in Hamilton. "It is interesting to note that after 1920 the account is headed 'Mrs. Bessie Perry, In Trust,' and the deposit slips are also made out in this way," one forensic number cruncher wrote. "The deposits in this account all appear to have been made by Mrs. Perry herself." The total amount deposited into the account in a four-year period was a cool five hundred grand.

Rocco was often lurking in the shadows of a liquor pick-up or delivery. But he always kept several layers between him and his rackets. One former copper reminisced that he had personally stopped Rocco many times but never actually caught him with any illegal mouthwash. "He may have been the King of the Bootleggers but he never drove a car full of booze in his life." He didn't have to. At the pinnacle of his reign, Rocco was reputed to have an army of more than two hundred scuffers on either side of the border. His soldiers came from all different ethnic backgrounds, but his gang was mostly made up of fellow Calabrians who pledged an oath of *omerta* to Rocco. "There is not an Italian in Hamilton who would give this man away," a Mountie scribbled in a 1926 memo. "Perry is a clever and dangerous crook exercising an extraordinary influence over the men in his employ, and any who are not in his employ are afraid of him. He is the 'King-pin' directing all operations but the members of his gang, when caught, shoulder the responsibility and pay the penalty." Rocco made plenty sure that cars, boats, and other property were registered in the name of Bessie or his stooges. In a 1920 raid on their stately Hamilton manor, the law found fifteen cases of high-grade hooch in the garage. Rocco claimed the garage was leased to Tony Morano, who was rapped, convicted, and fined half a G-note. Rocco's rackets were also well protected through his religious use of state lubricant. His payroll extended to top coppers, Prohibition enforcement bulls, and customs flunkies on both sides of the border.

Rocco's rise was also due to his muscle. His climb to the top of bottle hill was scattered with stiffs who were once his rivals. He also hijacked the loads of his competitors. "Over the telephones, he received information concerning the movements of shipments by rival gangs, and over the wires he sent forth his commands to intercept the shipments," one reporter reported in 1923. Rocco was also the lead suspect in the deep-sixing of the heads of rival gangs. On September 5, 1922, Joseph Scaroni of the rival Scaroni family was found in the Welland Canal near Thorold wearing lead buttons on his suit. Near the body, police came across a shallow, freshly dug grave. The public deeks thought Scaroni was rubbed out in another part of the province and then tooled to Thorland by motor car. The "murderers probably intended to bury their victim, but were frightened away, and so threw it into the Canal in their flight," a 1922 edition of the *Globe* reasoned. Four months earlier, on May 10, Joseph's brother, Dominic Scaroni, was sent to dreamland somewhere around Lewiston, New York. He was plugged four times at close range after being taken for a ride and his bullet-riddled body tossed from a speeding car. On June 4, Tony Leala, a relative who worked for the Scaroni family under the alias of Frank Cici, was found stone cold near Oakville.

In 1926, a Red Coat wrote in a secret report, "In Hamilton during the last few years there have been several bombing outrages and murders among the Italians, and it is freely stated that these have all been in connection with the members of Perry's gang of smugglers, who are desperate men and will stop at nothing. Again the directing hand is stated to be Perry." Rocco would never be nabbed for any of the icings. He did pay his last respects at Dominic Scaroni's cold-meat party, however, and was even a pallbearer, helping to carry Dominic's Chicago overcoat down the church steps. After the Scaroni brothers were eliminated, Rocco took over their bootlegging racket. This was just another ritual in his coronation as the king of the alki racketeers and the *capo crimini* of Ontario's Italian colonies.

All through the Roaring Twenties, the state nabbers tightened the dragnet around the Calabrian Liquor King, but with only a shot glass full of success. In the early 1920s, John Cruickshank, a senior snooper at the East Hamilton police clubhouse, led a raid on Rocco's home and seized raw alcohol and several boxes of fake labels of well-known booze brands. Rocco was convicted under the *OTA* and dinged a thousand Canadians. He paid his fine in cash.

When forty-five people in the Niagara Peninsula became inanimate stiffs after drinking a batch of toxic moonshine, a warrant was issued on July 31, 1926, by a U.S. D.A. for the arrest of Rocco. The warrant was part of a case where more than ninety indictments were handed down by the State Shyster in Buffalo. The Ontario A.G. laid manslaughter charges against all the Canucks listed in the American indictment, including Rocco. But the American and Canadian charges against the King were thrown out because of a lack of evidence that tied him to the lethal embalming fluid.

On November 18, 1927, eight counts of perjury were laid against Rocco and Bessie after they spinned a load of lies to a federal commission investigating the smuggling trade. Early the following year, the pair came to trial to face the charges. Bessie won an acquittal, but Rocco was slapped with six months under state care. It would be the longest time he would ever take a load off in the slammer.

When he emerged from the can, Rocco wasted no time in throwing himself back into the illegal sour-mash racket. But he soon discovered that the King had been dethroned. The distilleries were now bypassing Canadian outfit boys like Rocco and selling direct to American syndicates. To make matters worse, by the late 1920s temperance laws were falling throughout Canada like born-again converts at a Southern Baptist religious revival. To make up for lost profits, Rocco and Bessie ramped up their dope peddling. Rocco also opened a gambling joint with Black Hander, John Taglierino.

The violent rackets in which they ensconced themselves would soon strike Rocco and Bessie like a pouncing cobra. When they returned home from a party on the night of August 13, 1930, two gun punks jumped out from the bushes and with grind organs rat-a-tat-tatting they filled Bessie's body full of daylight. She kicked off instantly. Rocco was untouched, mostly because he flew away like an uncaged canary in a room full of felines. Wrath suffused Rocco's swart face as he swore revenge-prodded bloodshed. But the trigger men were never found. The rats and mice on the street were laying even scratch that Bessie was sent on a deep-six holiday because she refused to pay the prime and the juice after going into dutch on a dope deal. She gambled, but in her final deal, there was no shuffle, no cut, and on top of the deck was her final card. The death card.

The gangland slaying of Bessie Starkman — the Queen of the Bootleggers, the moll with moxie, the original doyenne of the Canadian syndicates — added more fuel to rumours that she was the real brains behind the Rocco Perri criminal empire. In 1930, an undercover Mountie scribbled that a stalwart stoolie sang about three hatchet men from Buffalo "who did it, as he was well acquainted with the three men that called on him the previous night, and it is stated that it was the same men that killed her." The stoolie told the mounted policeman, "Rocco Perri does not dare report these men to the police as he fears that harm or possible death may come to him."

Years later, Rocco was targeted for the eternal checkout. In March of 1938, the veranda of his Bay Street shack was blown to bits by a stick of dynamite with an explosive temper. In November,

he cranked the key of his jalopy and the ignition spark set loose an eruption that ripped it apart, catapulting his engine hood across the street, and carving a three-foot-deep crater in the concrete. Two men standing nearby were injured. Rocco emerged with only minor scrapes.

For the next few years, Rocco kept a low profile. For most of the war, he was locked up by Canadian G-men as an enemy alien. On April 23, 1944, while visiting a cousin in Hamilton, he stepped outside for some air. From that day forward, Rocci Perri — Canada's answer to Al Capone, the Canadian Little Caesar, the self-proclaimed King of the Bootleggers — was never seen again. Most pundits thought that he ended up wearing a concrete leisure suit at the bottom of Hamilton Bay. But his body would never be found. A letter dated June 19, 1949, was discovered years later in the hands of a relative in his native Italy. It read simply, "Dear Cousin, With this letter, I will tell you I am in good health. Let them know I'm fine if you've heard the news." The letter was signed "Rocco Perri."

ON THE DEATH OF JOHN BARLEYCORN AND THE BIRTH OF ORGANIZED CRIME

For organized crime in North America, Prohibition changed everything. In Canada, provincial temperance laws dating back to the early 1900s kick-started the illegal liquor trade in this country. The domestic trade in unlawful booze, however, would be a drop in a cask compared to the tidal wave of Canadian contraband liquor that would wash across America following the First World War. For, in 1920, the Eighteenth Amendment to the Constitution of the United States came into effect, opening up history's single-largest illegal market. Prohibition helped create organized crime as we know it today, launching it into an unprecedented epoch of growth, sophistication, power, profitability, corruption, and violence. The ramifications of Prohibition for the organization of crime were recognized in a 1929 article in *Canadian Forum* magazine:

What has actually happened is that prohibition has given a new rallying point and a new coherence to the criminal element. There is a

demand to be satisfied, and the legal sources of supply have been stopped. The result is an illicit trade that has reached the basis of an established industry. But those engaged in it have to face competition, often accompanied by violent methods, and they cannot appeal to the protection of the law. So the trade has built up its own protective system and in many cases its own legal system as well. It has its acknowledged district heads, it has its own courts, attorneys, judges, it has its own armed forces; and the code of gangland is more binding on its members, and its breach is more severely avenged, than the laws of civil society in which the gang exists.

Before Prohibition, most criminals did not accumulate a great deal of money, power, or influence. "Criminals had always belonged to the flotsam and jetsam of society, not to the economic elite," C.W. Hunt wrote in his book *Booze, Boats and Billions*. "Now, prohibition and the enormous illegal profits it made possible was changing this perception and leading to the emergence of a new phenomenon in Canadian society — the millionaire criminal." Prohibition also taught gangsters an invaluable lesson: there was far more money to be made in satisfying the vices of a receptive public than cheating, glomming, grifting, shysting, or extorting the tenderloin citizen. Moreover, bootlegging and other consensual crimes were preferred by gangsters because it meant there were no victims to complain to police. In years to come, criminal syndicates and underground entrepreneurs would follow the precedent set by the bootlegger and focus on filling the insatiable demand for outlawed goods and services.

Prohibition in America would have enormous implications for the organization of crime in Canada, which was the main source of illegal liquor south of the border. Bootlegging became a nationwide industry, employing tens of thousands of people. Smuggling organizations were formed and quickly multiplied. Export companies conveniently sprang up just north of the U.S. border. On a daily basis, fleets of ships would set sail from Canadian ports to the shores of America, while caravans of motor vehicles crossed over the border, all carrying liquid gold. To help ensure safe delivery, the palms of government officials would be liberally greased, leading to an epidemic of corruption that to this day is unparalleled in Canadian history. Prohibition drew Canada further into the web of the American underworld and, for decades to come, the most notorious Canadian criminal groups would become branch plants of American organized crime.

Canadian distilleries and breweries regularly dealt with some of the most infamous gangsters in America and were behind the largest smuggling operations ever carried out across the 49th parallel. These companies relied on graft, duplicity, and forgery to get their product to the underground market and, in the process, they evaded tens of millions of dollars in taxes. Prohibition laws helped make Canadian distilleries and breweries some of the largest and most profitable liquor producers in the world. Encouraged by a Canadian government that was indifferent to provincial and U.S. temperance laws, these same companies were instrumental in undermining the Noble Experiment. By supplying the bulk of the liquor sold by American and Canadian bootleggers, they

contributed to the expansion and modernization of organized crime, while providing the economic power base for the rise of Italian-American organized crime, La Cosa Nostra.

The following is the story of Prohibition and the role it played in forever changing the organization of crime in North America.

"THERE'S NOUGHT, NO DOUBT, SO MUCH THE SPIRIT CALMS AS RUM AND TRUE RELIGION"

The temperance movement in British North America can be traced as far back as the early 19th century. Prohibition advocates became one of the most visible crests of a broader social and moral crusade spearheaded by well-organized, well-funded, and politically connected church congregations who blamed the demon rum for many of society's ills. After decades of pressure, the Dominion Government partially relented to their demands and passed the *Canada Temperance Act* in 1878. This legislation did not prohibit the sale of ardent spirits in Canada. Instead, it provided the provinces with the power to regulate the sale and consumption of alcohol, while its manufacture, interprovincial trade, import, and export remained in federal hands. In 1901, Prince Edward Island became the first province to prohibit the sale and consumption of alcohol and over the next fifteen years, practically every province in the country enacted some form of temperance legislation.

It was only during the last years of the war that Canada would be subject to a national ban on booze. In 1918, the federal Cabinet passed an order-in-council barring the production of liquor for personal consumption, while also prohibiting liquor imports. Most provincial governments also passed wartime prohibition legislation or reinforced temperance laws already in effect. By the end of the Great War, however, temperance laws began to fall throughout the Dominion. Quebec revoked its ban as early as 1919 and, in 1920, British Columbia followed suit. The single-greatest setback for the temperance movement in Canada occurred on January 1, 1920, when Cabinet lifted its wartime Prohibition policy. From this day forward, there would be few meaningful restrictions on the manufacture of liquor in this country. Beginning the same year, the Eighteenth Amendment to the American Constitution came into effect completely banning the manufacture, sale, importation, and transportation of alcoholic beverages in the U.S. Together, the two diametrically opposed national policies fermented an underground economy, a smuggling maelstrom, an organized criminality, and a spirit of lawlessness that was never before seen on the continent. The Canadian government's stubborn maintenance of its wet policy made a mockery of, and completely undermined, temperance laws throughout North America. It can also be cited as one of the most significant catalysts in the repeal of America's Prohibition laws in 1933.

The shared jurisdiction over liquor by the federal and provincial governments meant that, while it was perfectly legal to produce and even import booze, in many provinces it was illegal to consume it. Bewildering provincial Prohibition laws added to this incongruity. From 1916 to 1927, it was against the law to buy most spirits in Ontario, but thanks in part to the powerful grape growers lobby in Ontario, wine could still be freely purchased in the province in strengths up to 28 percent. Moreover, it was legal to order liquor into Ontario from outside the province. You weren't allowed to buy it locally, but you were allowed to consume it locally (as long as you did so in your home). As a result, Ontario residents flocked to Quebec by foot, horse, car, train, and boat to buy their booze or had it shipped to their local post office through a burgeoning interprovincial mail order business.

Ironically, Ontario's prodigious liquor industry actually came of age while that province's temperance laws were in effect. By the mid-1920s, there were breweries in Belleville, Kingston, Toronto, and Hamilton. There was also the Wiser's distillery in Prescott, the Gooderham and Worts distillery in Toronto, the huge Corby distillery in Belleville, and the Hiram Walker distillery just outside of Windsor. Unable to sell booze legally in the province, these companies shipped their cargo off to Quebec, which was then sold to customers in Ontario through the mail. In 1921, both the Ontario and Dominion governments clamped down on this booming mail order business, but the effect of the toughened enforcement was simply a harbinger of things to come.

After being cut off from legal suppliers in both Ontario and Quebec, residents of Canada's largest provinces turned en masse to bootleggers. Booze was now more widely and conveniently available in Ontario than ever before. Hotels and restaurants, the backs of stores, taxis, private residences, barns, the trunks of cars, and the suitcases of travelling salesmen all became common, albeit unofficial, sources of the drink. Underground gin mills, booze cans, grogshops, speakeasies, and blind pigs multiplied. Another popular outlet for booze in Ontario was the medical doctor or the pharmacy. Under the province's temperance law, doctors were allowed to prescribe alcohol to any patient who needed it for medicinal reasons. In 1920 and 1921, 588,000 prescriptions for medicinal liquor were issued in Ontario alone. By 1923 and 1924, the total number had risen to 810,000. One Toronto doctor dispensed 2,005 prescriptions in a single month (only to be surpassed by a medical practitioner in Vancouver who sold 4,100 liquor prescriptions in a month, an average of 136 a day). Many drugstores — now part apothecary, part speakeasy — did not even bother to keep up a pharmaceutical pretence. As B.J. Grant writes in his book *When Rum was King,* "This was the era of what was called the 'talcum powder drug-store,' the shop that carried on its shelves a few bottles of iodine, Minard's Liniment, Scott's Emulsion, cough syrups (that were highly alcoholic), a lot of talcum powder, and almost as much booze as a fair-sized liquor store." Stephen Leacock observed that in order to obtain a bottle of liquor in Ontario, one simply had to go to a local drugstore, lean up against the counter "and make a gurgling sigh like apoplexy. One often sees these apoplexy cases lined up four deep."

The underground liquor supply was no less scarce in other dry provinces. In Woodstock, New Brunswick, one newspaper editorial mused, "there are three licensed vendors in town and 1,219 bootleggers and there is a growing impression that the proportion is out of all reason." In 1921, one New Brunswick man told the media he "knew of thirty-four places or persons in West St. John where liquor can be bought. Before prohibition, he said it was difficult to buy liquor in West St. John." In Vancouver, an investigator with the Provincial Liquor Control Board estimated that in 1929 there were 7,000 known bootleggers working in the city. Prohibition also prompted the greatest proliferation of home-based micro distilleries in the history of the country. In an editorial dated April 6, 1923, the *Regina Leader* newspaper claimed Saskatchewan to be the Canadian capital for illegal stills:

> The discovery that there are more illicit stills in Saskatchewan, with a population of less than 760,000, than there is in the rest of Canada, with a population of 8,000,000, will come as an unpleasant surprise to the people of the Province. ... Out of a total of 1,606 investigations of infractions of the Inland Revenue Act carried out by the Mounted Police during the year ended September 30 1922, 962 were in this province. Of a total of 1,420 investigations of breaches of Federal Statutes in Saskatchewan during the year under report approximately 68 per cent were illicit still cases. Assuming that the estimate made by certain Inland Revenue officers is correct, where one illicit still is discovered nineteen others are operating undisturbed by the officers of the law. ... The illicit distilling industry is almost solely, as far as Saskatchewan is concerned, an adjunct of the farming industry. The fact that 962 cases of illicit distillery were investigated by the Mounted Police last year indicated that there are operating in the Province today perhaps 20,000 illicit stills, or one for every fifteen farms in Saskatchewan.

In the early 1920s, the attorney general of Alberta estimated the number of stills operating in his province at 1,140. Like Saskatchewan, moonshine operations proliferated throughout this largely rural province, prompting a 1923 edition of *Canadian Forum* magazine to suggest, "in some districts every farm-house is a potential and often an operating distillery. Many a mortgage has been washed away by moonshine."

Bootleggers and rumrunners also took advantage of the legal liquor export trade to circumvent provincial Prohibition statutes through "short circuiting," a practice where liquor exports found their way back onto Canadian shores. Vessels leaving from Vancouver with a load of whiskey consigned to be delivered

Illegal stills seized in Vancouver, circa 1917

to Mexico would sail to some unfrequented part of the B.C. coast, where they would unload their cargo and then, to avoid suspicion, return to home port only after sufficient time had elapsed to make the voyage to Mexico. In the Maritimes, cargo that was to be exported to foreign shores was unloaded on the coast of New Brunswick, Nova Scotia, or Prince Edward Island just hours after it left port. Some east coast rumrunners did not even bother to keep up the pretence of a foreign journey. In a speech to the House of Commons in 1926, one Member of Parliament cited the case of the schooner *Morso*, "which left Halifax for St. Pierre, Miquelon on August 13 with 2,632 cases and 185 kegs of liquor. In two days, she cleared Halifax again; she must have made the round trip of 1,000 miles in 48 hours, allowing no time for unloading and loading." In response to this unlawful repatriation of exported liquor, the Dominion Government forced exporters to post a bond that would require them to forfeit twice the value of their cargo if it did not reach its stated foreign destination. The surety would be returned to the exporter on presentation of a receipt from the foreign entry of port. These legal requirements were easily circumvented either by bribing customs and excise officials or by forging foreign landing certificates.

In addition to short-circuiting, booze was smuggled into dry provinces from abroad. One cartel based in Nova Scotia had freighters make several trips a year to the West Indies where they purchased Caribbean rum in bulk. Once back in Atlantic Canada, the "mother ships" would offload the kegs to small motor boats, which would scurry back to the shores of New Brunswick for offloading and distribution. To keep police off their scent, gang members phoned in anonymous reports of fictional bootleg liquor sightings in locations far from the real offload site. Police in New Brunswick received so many false reports that after a while they stopped responding to all tips provided by the public. This smuggling group also operated their own counter-espionage system using a network of rural telephone operators who were on their payroll. Not only would these internal conspirators tap into police communication networks, but the telephone lines could also be thrown out of whack during the times that police dispatchers were trying to communicate information about a smuggler's whereabouts. The immense challenges facing law enforcement in the Maritimes was recounted in a desperate telegraph dated September 11, 1926, sent from an RCMP detachment in Amherst, Nova Scotia, to its headquarters in Ottawa: "Smuggled liquor pouring into this country in enormous quantities stop unless ten men from Mounted Police Force sent here tomorrow country will be swamped with smuggled liquor stop Department advised of this situation before by me before stop please notify Halifax to send ten men not later than tomorrow stop."

THE FOUR-THOUSAND-MILE ANDORRA

Following its enactment of national Prohibition laws in 1920, America would be supplied with illegal booze from a diverse number of countries. Canada was by far the greatest source, however, outstripping all other countries combined. Estimates of Canada's share of America's contraband liquor market ranged from 60 to 90 percent. As historian Ralph Allen wrote, "To anyone interested in assuaging the sudden thirst of a hundred million Americans, Canada was the promised land, a smuggler's paradise — an Andorra with a border four thousand miles long, and an undefended border at that. At each end lay enough open water to float a thousand Mojacas." In their 1931 report, a U.S. federal commission examining enforcement of Prohibition laws in that country wrote, "Importation is chiefly from Canada, both directly and indirectly, since Canada is a large producer and is exceptionally convenient, by proximity and by geographical conditions and conditions of transportation, as a base for smuggling operations."

It was not simply geographical fate that solidified Canada's role as the chief supplier of illegal booze to the United States. While American lawmakers were closing their own spirituous beverage floodgate, the Canadian government was opening theirs by lifting the nationwide wartime prohibition on liquor production. Safe, name-brand, high-quality booze was now available from Canada, in sharp contrast to the often hazardous and unsanitary rotgut that was secretly being produced in American stills and bathtubs. To make American enforcement matters worse, the Canadian government made only token efforts to restrict the tsunami of Canadian booze that was crashing down on American shores. In fact, Ottawa bent over backwards to facilitate the manufacture and export of Canadian liquor. The Dominion Government allowed any exporter with even the most suspect of credentials and the least seaworthy of boats to purchase from a Canadian distillery, as long as they promised to ship to an offshore location. Cuba and the West Indies were the most frequently listed destinations for Canadian liquor, but of course, the booze was being sent short distances to U.S. ports. The situation became so ludicrous and so infused with government corruption that one boat was recorded as leaving the same Canadian port for Cuba four times each day. While American officials pleaded with the Canadian government to clamp down on its illegal exports, Ottawa did just the opposite: it allowed exporters to clear shipments directly to the

Political cartoon from the October 30, 1920, edition of the *Literary Digest*, lampooning how Canada was major source of contraband liquor for America.

United States. In the end, an unspoken, yet mutually beneficial partnership emerged between the Dominion Government, liquor producers, and rumrunners. Together, this tacit triumvirate would pose a major challenge to America's Prohibition laws.

At first, Canadian rumrunners imported liquor from other countries for re-export to the United States. During the first full year of American Prohibition, the import of scotch whiskey into Canada increased from an annual value of $5.5 million to $23 million. The Dominion Bureau of Statistics shows that, between 1925 and 1929, the value of all liquor imports into Canada increased from $19,123,627 to $48,844,111. Canadians soon realized that greater profits could be made by producing liquor domestically and then exporting it to the American market, so breweries and distilleries quickly popped up throughout the country. By 1927, there were eighty-three breweries and twenty-three distilleries, all federally licensed, in Canada. In Ontario, sixteen distilleries and twenty-nine breweries were legally established in 1920 alone. In one Atlantic Canadian town with a population of just over 25,000 there were no fewer than twelve bottling plants, all of which manufactured beer and ale. In 1924, almost 4.5 million gallons of spirits were produced in Canada. By 1929, this had jumped to more than 11.5 million gallons. A U.S. Coast Guard intelligence report from the late 1920s estimated that only 20 percent of the liquor produced in Canada was consumed domestically. The other 80 percent found its way into the United States.

The earliest attempts to smuggle liquor across the border were often for personal consumption or small, local sales. And while these smuggling efforts were often quite amateurish, they were not without imagination or ingenuity. Suits with secret pockets were filled with flasks. The legs of rubber boots were stuffed with pint bottles. Deep-pocketed carpenters' aprons were worn under baggy suits. Rubber inner tubes and garden hoses carrying booze would be tightly wound around bodies. Hot-water bags dangled from necks. Small bottles were tucked inside oversized shoes. Suitcases and steamer trunks with false bottoms were lugged across the border. Women concealed liquor in their bloomers, their corsets, and even in false rubber breasts. Bottles were wrapped in baby blankets and coddled by innocent-looking women crossing the border. Infants would also be perched atop liquor bottles in baby carriages. Hollowed-out baseball bats, wooden carvings, potatoes, and baked bread filled with booze were found by U.S. Customs agents. One man reportedly hurried across the International Bridge at Buffalo carefully carrying two dozen eggs, each of which had been emptied and refilled with whiskey. Gas tanks, tool chests, jerry cans, and maple syrup tins would be filled to the brim. A double-amputee war veteran boasted that he could carry 36 pints at any one time in his hoallowed-out artificial arm and leg. On a larger scale, horses pulled sleds carrying logs that had been hollowed out and filled with hundreds of bottles.

The money that could be made from running rum attracted the involvement of otherwise law-abiding citizens, and those smuggling for personal consumption evolved into or were quickly joined by the professional rumrunner. Immediately following the enactment of Prohibition in the United States, small independent groups dominated the early liquor smuggling traffic. Residents living along the Ontario side of the Detroit River ordered liquor from Quebec and then sold it for big profits to Canadian and American smugglers. During the first seven months of 1920 alone, 900,000 cases of whiskey were shipped to the Windsor area from Quebec for "personal consumption" (increasing the per capita consumption from a prewar total of nine gallons to 102 gallons). Some Canadian rumrunners moved from supplying domestic markets to smuggling across the U.S. border. Others were truck drivers or fishermen, lured by the considerable financial rewards their skills now offered. Known as the "little fellow," the independent rumrunner often worked alone, travelling by car across the many back roads that hugged the U.S. border or navigating the numerous waterways into United States via rowboat, canoe, fishing boat, or pleasure craft. As Vernon McKenzie wrote in a 1926 edition of *Maclean's* magazine, "A new 'profession' has developed during the past years — that of professional smuggler. Previous to the enactment of Prohibition in the United States smugglers were, comparatively, isolated outlaws. A competent authority estimates today on this continent there are 100,000 men whose sole business is that of smuggling."

"THEY CALL ME A SMUGGLER. THAT IS WRONG. I AM A RUM-RUNNER."

One of these men was Ben Kerr of Hamilton. He was a plumber and boatbuilder by trade but turned to smuggling the lip trop after the war-to-end-all-wars ended. He was a lean man who carried a self-satisfied look. His mouth was narrow, his grin was taut, and he liked to crack wise. At his peak, he employed between eight and twenty pullers at any one time. His office was Lake Ontario. His desk was a motorboat. His paycheque was a wad of dead presidents. He was one of the biggest and the best of the early independent shine movers.

Orders were arranged between Kerr and the Corby's distillery. The load of eel juice would be rattled by rail from the Belleville plant to Whitby, Ontario, where it was picked up by Kerr and his jobbers and loaded onto one of his boats. The stated destination on export documents was either Cuba or Mexico, but the load was always dumped at a pre-determined spot on the shore of Lake Ontario, near Rochester, New York. The American palookas got their booze, Kerr got his commission, and everyone was happy. Kerr made even more mazuma by smuggling raw Yankee alcohol back into Canada on his return trips.

Kerr was a savvy sailor who knew Lake Ontario like Mary Pickford knew the Turkish baths. He owned three boats to transport his loads of lubrication to the American shores: the *Martimas,* the *Lark,* and the *Voyageur.* The *Martimas* was the slowest of the three, but she could haul the most — as many as 1,200 cases at a time. She was forty-two feet long and perfectly suited "to the early days of rum running when reliability and carrying capacity, rather than speed, were the most important qualities of a black ship." Kerr travelled under the cover of the night's darkness and even refused to make deliveries when a full moon was out. He didn't use his lights to avoid being spied by the seafaring bulls and moved as quiet as a shadow on water. Kerr was also one of the first hooch racketeers on Lake Ontario to make use of a swell new technology called radio. By 1925, he was making eighteen jaunts a day across the lake and was grossing between 2,400 and 3,600

clams on each trip. He had more dough than an army baker and built up a bank account that at one time had a balance of 45,000 big ones. He owned a large home in one of Hamilton's most well-heeled neighbourhoods, as well as a marina with thirty houseboats that provided plenty of rental cabbage. His friends and associates were among the highest of Hamilton's highbrows.

Kerr wasn't too keen on greasing the palms of John Law and that was part of the problem; he wouldn't play the game. He spouted off that he could outwit any state hammer at any time. Most of the time he could. He was nicknamed the "phantom bootlegger" because he was one of the most elusive smugglers operating on the Great Lakes. The Prohibition coppers had been trying to catch him for years, but Kerr always appeared where he was least expected. On the evening of May 26, 1925, Ben Kerr's luck began to run out.

Kerr and his beerocrats were busy unloading crates of suds from the *Maritimas* into a dory that was attached to the shore by a cable. U.S. coastal Prohibition-men glommed the activity and a cordon of thirteen keystones closed in. Kerr tried a clean sneak by cutting the cable and racing his boat to open lake. The Customs cruisers gave chase and, as they closed in, Kerr ordered his boys to toss the rest of the barleybroth overboard. The coppers' .30-calibre Lewis machine guns belched. Two rounds of lead were fired across the bow of the *Martimas.* Kerr kept catfooting away. The coasties then gave him the works and raked the hull of the boat. Eight slugs found the mark.

The P-men boarded the *Martimas,* but found only eight cases of Dow ale. They did find another sixty cases in the dory and six hundred cases on shore. They also discovered that Kerr and his dousers had more arms than a Hindu elephant god. Three repeating shotguns, one double-barrelled shotgun, three rifles, and two automatic revolvers were confiscated. All were fully loaded. To dissuade pirates from hijacking his hooch, Kerr and his loogans always strapped on the iron.

The capture of the "King of Lake Ontario Rum Runners" and eleven of his plumbers was hailed as a great victory for the Prohibition agents. Despite being pinched by the P-men, Captain Ben was supremely confident he could beat the rap and blew his horn more than Louis Armstrong. He wouldn't pipe down and boasted to the American newsies, "the rest of the rumrunners are too yellow to come over here very often." Bail was set for most of the prisoners at the sky-high rate of $60,000. The largest bail — $100,000 — was set for Kerr.

He was tried in Rochester in September 1925 and was ready to cop a guilty plea when he caught wind that he was also to be tried for manslaughter. This charge arose from a tragic tryst with two sport fishermen who were out on the lake during a night as dark as a black boot. Their boat accidentally rammed into Kerr's reinforced hull and broke apart as easy as a wet snickerdoodle. Both men went to the big fishing pond in the sky. Kerr was operating his boat at night without lights, so he was criminally negligent in the two fishermen's long goodbye. Kerr had crapped out and was now hotter than a two-dollar pistol. After reading about his indictment in the Rochester newspapers, Kerr got wise, dummied up, and skipped town. The local D.A. responded by putting a bounty on Kerr's noodle.

It would only get hotter for Kerr. In 1926,

he was named as one of the culprits behind the liquor-poisoning deaths of forty-five stiffs and was arrested in Hamilton on a warrant charging him with manslaughter. But the government's case collapsed when it could not produce evidence to tie Kerr to the toxic booze. Charges against Kerr, Rocco Perri, and dozens of others were dropped. The discharges meant that the hard work of the P-men once again went straight into the toilet.

Kerr returned to rumrunning and even had a new boat custom built for him. The *Pollywog* was powered by two six-cylinder 180-horsepower engines and was capable of skirting across the sea at thirty-five miles an hour while carrying a hundred cases of neck oil. On a stormy night, in February 1929, Kerr and a jobber named Alf Wheat were crossing Lake Ontario in the *Pollywog*. The ship was partially disabled after recently been given the hot-lead treatment from yet another run-in with a U.S. Customs picket boat. Three weeks after he left on that routine trip across the lake, Kerr's bloated and frozen carcass washed ashore. He was identified from a cluster of maple leafs tattooed on his arm and one remaining sock that had been knitted by his mother.

HATCH'S NAVY

As the demand for Canadian liquor steadily grew south of the border, the small shipments of the lone smuggler were no longer sufficient. The independent little fellow was being pushed out by larger and better-organized smuggling groups. Professional criminals were now flocking to the highly profitable trade like lions to a feeding. In a 1923 article, journalist William McNulty wrote that the first shipment of smuggled liquor from Canada into the U.S. was made in 1917, the year the *American War Time Prohibition Act* was passed by Congress. "At first only Canadians were involved in the traffic, but in 1919 American smugglers began to run liquor over the international border. In 1921, the American-Canadian whiskey manufacturing and smuggling gangs made their debut. The individual smuggler who did not expand beyond his modest beginnings was squeezed out by their new competitors, or else they joined the gangs." The *Detroit News*

reported in 1920 that the business of transporting contraband liquor into the U.S. from Canada had already become "intricately organized" by bands of astute operators.

The independent who owned his own truck or boat was actively recruited by smuggling groups or Canadian liquor producers and would be paid by the hour or by the number of cases they could deliver. If caught, some of the syndicates that underwrote the shipments would pay the legal fees of their contracted rumrunners. Other smuggling groups owned their own fleet of cars, trucks, or boats, employed sales agents to take orders from American customers, and then arranged for pickup or delivery. One American group operating along the Detroit River had one of its crews purchase the liquor at the export docks in Windsor, another transported the liquor across to a designated location on the U.S. side, a third team picked up the cases and transported them to nearby warehouses, while yet another team trucked the booze to its customers in Detroit.

It was not long before the underground liquor trade in Canada was dominated by a few well-organized bootlegging syndicates, such as those headed up by Rocco Perri, Max Worztman, Roy Olmstead, or Albenie Violette. Some of the Canadian bootleggers hid behind legitimate fronts. Federal investigators determined that between June 1924 and June 1926, the Regina Vinegar Company illegally removed some "four thousand gallons of alcohol from the company's bond," according to a 1928 report of the Royal Commission on Customs and Excise, which investigated the contraband liquor trade and accompanying corruption. However, the alcohol "did not go into the vinegar mix, but was taken from the company's premises and used elsewhere, apparently in the bootlegging business." These suspicions were confirmed when investigators discovered that the owners and managers of the Regina Vinegar Company were Z. Natanson and S. Diamond, "two well-known bootleggers." Notwithstanding these sorts of corporate fronts, at the pinnacle of the contraband liquor trade in terms of size, organization, sophistication, and veiled legitimacy, were legitimate Canadian distilleries and breweries that amassed substantial profits by selling to Canadian and American bootleggers and by coordinating the export and transport of huge quantities of booze to the United States.

The rumrunning trade also benefited from advancements made in the horsepower and reliability of motor vehicles. The introduction of the six-cylinder engine allowed many a rumrunner to escape capture at the hands of law enforcement. Six-cylinder cars were so popular with liquor smugglers, they became known as "Whiskey Sixes." Rear seats were removed from Packards, Hudsons, Buicks, and Studebakers to make room for extra cases of liquor. Gas tanks were divided so that one part carried a little gas while the other stored bottles. The fabric tops of cars would be separated and between the two layers a storage space four inches deep was constructed that could carry 180 pint bottles. Cars were rebuilt with false floors and storage areas running the length of the drive shaft that could conceal 480 quarts at a time. The suspension of liquor-smuggling cars would be reinforced to support the heavy load. Some rumrunning vehicles dragged dust-inducing chains to obstruct the vision of pursuing law enforcement officers. For wintertime operations, oversized skis would be attached to the front axle of cars and trucks, which were then driven across the frozen rivers and lakes separating Canada from the United States. The doors would be swung open or completely removed in case the car broke through the ice or encountered a fishing hole and the driver had to bail out quickly. Propelled by strong gusts of wind, iceboats were also used to transport booze on frozen lakes and rivers and were often preferred over cars as they were lighter, faster, and safer.

Soon, caravans of cars and trucks were transporting large quantities of liquor. Heavily armed enforcers would sit alongside the drivers to protect shipment from hijackings, while lookouts would travel miles ahead to scout out police roadblocks or spots vulnerable to ambushes by rival bootlegging gangs. In two confidential reports written in 1926, the RCMP in New Brunswick detailed the system used by one rumrunning group headed by Thomas Nowlan, "Usually the routes are governed by a block system, that is, a decoy car travels ahead; this has no liquor as a rule, if stopped the driver phones to certain places where it is understood the autos carrying liquor must not pass unless the road is clear; if the decoy car is stopped, then the loaded cars take another route, or hides until the word comes that all is clear." One of the reports also observed, "there are as many as 12 autos used, three taking one route and three taking another and so on. The idea being that if three are caught the other nine get away." The RCMP officer who wrote the reports conceded that very few of the liquor caravans are caught, for the simple reason that "they are well organized and have every Customs Officer spotted through their spy system."

Boats also became a staple of the rumrunner and had several advantages over motor vehicles. They could accommodate larger payloads, sail in international waters where they could not be touched by American law enforcement, and could navigate directly to the ports of major cities, such as New York, Boston, Detroit, and Seattle, or land along the thousands of miles of unguarded American coastline. A 1920 article in a London, Ontario, newspaper reported that Canadian rumrunners, with secret caches of liquor, waited in hiding at night among the trees and tall grass on the Canadian side of the Detroit River. Pocket torches would be waved using a primitive system of signals for "yes" and "no" or "stop" and "go" while their American customers coasted up and down the river with empty rowboats looking for the signal to come ashore. Then the bargaining would begin. Once the deal was closed, the liquor changed hands and was transported across the river.

Rowboats soon gave way to outboard motorized vessels, which in turn were replaced by fishing boats. As the U.S. Coast Guard commissioned faster enforcement vessels, open fishing boats were replaced by high-powered speedboats, custom built for rumrunning. It wasn't before long that the large smuggling groups were using fleets of boats. The biggest Canadian flotilla ever assembled for rumrunning purposes was put together by Herb and Harry Hatch, two brothers who began their careers bartending at hotels and saloons around Belleville, Ontario, and who would go on to make millions from a liquor empire built by supplying the underground American market. At the centre of their empire was Gooderham and Worts Ltd., the distilling giant that would become a major supplier to some of North America's biggest bootleggers. These included Rocco Perri who, under the alias of J. Penna, was on the phone almost daily placing large orders. (He later began using the alias J. Johnson because, as he admitted in court, too many orders were going to J. Penna.) In 1911, Harry Hatch opened a retail liquor store in Whitby, Ontario, where he catered to the residents of Oshawa, which was dry at the time. When all of Ontario went dry in 1916, Harry began a mail order business in Montreal. In 1921, he was hired as the sales manager for the Canadian Industrial Alcohol Company, which owned and operated both the Corby and Wiser distilleries in Ontario. Within two years, Harry's cunning as well as his natural marketing skills helped increase sales for the Corbyville distilling operation from 500 to 50,000 gallons a month, primary by selling to customers south of the border. Before the end of the decade, the Corbyville distillery was one of the largest liquor producers in the world.

Most of Corby's products were transported across the Great Lakes as part of one of the largest ongoing liquor smuggling conspiracies that ever took place in North America. In 1927, a federally appointed auditor estimated that liquor diverted from the warehouse of the Walkerville distillery to the United States, using bogus bills of lading from other countries, totalled more than $2 million. Due to a lack of records maintained by the distillery, the auditor acknowledged that this value was only the tip of a multi-million-dollar smuggling iceberg overseen by the Hatch brothers. Herb Hatch assembled his armada by purchasing defaulted mortgages on boats from indebted fishermen, who were then recruited to run the booze across Lake Ontario to the U.S. side in a flotilla of fishing boats. "Hatch's Navy" would become so successful that Rocco Perri put his fifty fishing boats operating on Lake Eire under the control of Herb Hatch.

To increase their payload capacity, the Hatch brothers slung large fishing nets on each side of their boats, running from bow to stern. The nets would then be loaded with booze. Once on the other side of the lake, the cargo would be deposited on the sandbars for retrieval by American buyers. An added benefit of this system was that if U.S. Coast Guard boats were seen approaching, the nets could be cut in a matter of seconds, allowing their contents to quickly sink to the bottom. To salvage their sunken booty once the coast was clear, all of the nets were marked with a buoy and a large piece of salt. When the salt melted, the buoy would float to the top — signalling the location of the submerged liquid treasure. To ensure the liquor would actually sink, wooden cases were replaced with cardboard and pockmarked with holes. To help them sink even faster, the bottles were wrapped in lead. While this cargo-jettisoning system worked most of the time, it was not foolproof. Bootleggers once tried this manoeuvre in shallow Lake Erie waters near Munroe, Michigan, but before the cases could be reclaimed by the smugglers, the tide had receded. Lakeshore residents who woke up the next morning could hardly believe their eyes: bags containing bottles of beer, whiskey and wine were scattered along the beach. One local fisherman was quoted in the media as saying he had "his best catch in forty years."

Numerous modifications were also made to boats to accommodate the needs of rumrunners. The Hatch brothers had twin Packard engines installed in many of the fishing vessels used on the Great Lakes, and legend has it that some of the larger ships were fitted with as many as four airplane motors. Entire boats were painted grey or black to make them less visible at night and cabins were lopped off and pilothouses lowered to reduce their profile on the water. Some boats carried multiple nameplates, so they could clear Canadian Customs under one name and then arrive in American waters with a completely different name. Exhaust pipes would be extended underwater to muffle the loud roar of their powerful engines and some boats were outfitted with armour plates on their pilothouses for protection in the case of a shootout with the U.S. Coast Guard. Still other boats were equipped with devices that belched out a billow of low-hanging black, choking smoke if a pursuing coast guard cutter got too close.

Canada's east coast shipbuilding industry was one beneficiary of the demand for custom-built boats. New boat registrations in the Maritimes increased steadily throughout Prohibition. In the peak years of 1928 to 1930, ninety-two boats were built, the majority for rumrunning. In fact, the Nova Scotia shipyards began to specialize in designing and building vessels expressly for the liquor smuggling trade. To accommodate greater payloads, boats built at the Metechan shipyard in Nova Scotia increased in length and weight from 70 feet and 40 tons in 1926 to over 100 feet in length and 118 tons in 1930. The cargo capacity was also increased to hold up to 1,600 cases of liquor. For the power needed to outrun enforcement vessels, many were installed with two or more V-8 car engines. Despite these substantial augmentations, the boats were designed with a low profile that was flatter, sleeker, and stealthier.

Communication also became more advanced. Morse code replaced the flashlight as the preferred system of communication for the seafaring rumrunner. Among the thousands of different codes used was one discovered in the home of a member of one of the largest liquor smuggling operations run out of the Maritimes:

KDP   Position
KDU   Proceed to position
KDC   Our scout boat is patrolling around
KON   Come close but keep outside limits
KTW   Unable to work tonight as the shore is
      red hot.

Morse code was eventually replaced in some ships by new radio technology, including radio wave direction finders that enabled rumrunners to locate Coast Guard surveillance technology.

Not only was booze smuggled above the water, it was also transported below the surface. Stories circulated about pipelines being constructed through which bulk liquor would be pumped directly from shore to waiting tankers. Police discovered that sleds filled with cases of liquor were being dragged across the bottom of the Detroit River with the aid of steel cables and automobile engine–powered pulleys attached to concrete anchors along the opposite shorelines. The *New York Times* reported in 1920 that "electronically operated torpedoes loaded with whiskey are being sent across the Detroit River from the Canadian to the American shore." Citing a government informant, the newspaper wrote that three torpedoes 10-, 15-, and 25-gallon capacities were being used (while one with a 50-gallon capacity was currently under construction). Each one was fitted with a copper casing, and "a propeller at the nose actuated by electric storage batteries." The torpedoes would submerge to 100 feet and required about five minutes to cross the river. A red flag on one side of the river and a white one on the other side "comprise the targets at which the operators direct their torpedoes." After they make their journey to the Detroit side, the liquor-filled torpedoes were emptied and then "ballasted with water and sent back."

When the traditional methods of land and sea transport faced heightened threats of hijacking or detection by law enforcement, the railway system was increasingly used. Cases would be stacked into freight cars, or bulk liquor would be pumped into empty oil tanks. Shipping booze by rail was done mostly by liquor producers or large syndicates with enough money to pay for the several boxcar loads and to withstand the occasional loss of one to police. In collusion with corrupt railroad employees, the waybills for the freight were described as anything but booze. Railroad cars full of liquor originating in Canada would be labelled and routed to Mexico by way of the U.S. While in the United States, however, a mysterious problem often inflicted the loaded railcars, requiring them to be taken off the train and then switched to a convenient siding. It was there that the whiskey was unloaded and distributed to local bootleggers. In a memo dated October 23, 1926, a RCMP corporal describes how the rails were used by Consolidated Exporters Corporation Ltd. to smuggle liquor from Vancouver to Seattle:

> I have the honour to report that on the 21st, inst, at 6.00, pm, I received information from an Informant, (who wishes his name not to be divulged) to the effect that 300 cases of Whiskey had been loaded sometime the last few days into an empty oil tank of a freight train around the G.W. Rly Freight Yards, Vancouver, B.C. The 300 cases of Whiskey would eventually land into the U.S.A. on the other hand, it is possible, that it might be switched back into Canada. The informant went on to say, that the freight train would pull out of the G.H. Rly Freight Yards, Vancouver on the night of the 21st inst, for Seattle, Wash, U.S.A. the freight train with oil tank would then be broken, and this particular freight car with oil tank would be switched on to some convenient siding near Blaine, or Bellingham, where the 300 cases of whiskey would be unloaded.

Some smugglers aspired to even higher ambitions, literally. In October 1921, the first airplane loaded with liquor was reported to have left Winnipeg for the United States. Ten years later, in April 1930, sixty-two planes loaded with Canadian liquor allegedly cleared from Ontario airfields for points in Ohio, Michigan, Indiana, and Wisconsin. The planes generally flew at night, and landed on crudely made runways in unpopulated areas. The runways would be illuminated by the headlights of the cars and trucks waiting for the payload.

A NATION OF BOOTLEGGERS

By the mid-1920s, bootlegging had become a national industry in Canada. From British Columbia, liquor was routinely smuggled into Washington State and as far south as California. Most liquor-laden ships consigned for delivery in Mexico rarely sailed past Washington's Puget Sound. The Manitoba Refineries, a liquor export company based in British Columbia, was regarded by the Royal Commission on Customs and Excise as "a typical illustration of what is and has been the practice at the ports of Vancouver and Victoria in connection with all so-called shipments of liquor in transit." The ship *Chris Moeller* cleared the Port of Vancouver with a cargo of 17,779 cases of liquor owned by the Manitoba Refineries. Her official destination was San Blas, Mexico. Shortly after disembarking from Vancouver, she called at the port of Victoria to take on an additional 3,700 cases. Customs officers became suspicious of the large cargo and refused a clearance from Victoria pending an investigation. Two pieces of evidence suggested to customs investigators that this cargo was not in fact destined for Mexico. First, the liquor was originally imported from Great Britain and was shipped to Vancouver by way of the Panama Canal, which would have brought it past its Mexican destination. Second, investigators deduced that San Blas was a small village located far inland with no port or harbour. Customs officials concluded, "the alleged consignee is fictitious and that it is not intended that the liquors should be delivered at San Blas, the port of destination, but rather that the same should be made available elsewhere to rumrunners or bootleggers for consumption in the Western states."

One of the most prolific west coast smugglers was Stuart Stone, who was active from 1920 to the end of Prohibition in 1933. By the mid-1920s, he was commanding mother ships like the five-masted schooner *Malahat*, which could carry a cargo of 100,000 cases — 60,000 in the hold and 40,000 on deck. Captain Stone would moor the floating warehouse off the west coast of the United States, but in international waters, and supply a steady stream of customers in speedboats, pleasure crafts, and fishing boats who would purchase the liquor and transport it back to the mainland. Charles Hudson captained another west coast mother ship called the *Coal Harbour*, a three-masted schooner that could carry 10,000 cases of liquor. Peter C. Newman tells the story of one trip where the ship was captured by the U.S. Coast Guard off the California coast while safely outside the

12-mile limit that constituted American jurisdiction. "Hudson learned that rival rumrunners had given the Coast Guard skipper $25,000 to testify that the *Coal Harbour* had been inside the limit, but the skipper backed Hudson's story after receiving $25,000 from lawyers for the Vancouver liquor exporters. The *Coal Harbour* was released, her cargo intact."

In 1922, a number of brewery and distilling companies from B.C. and back East formed the Consolidated Exporters Corporation Ltd. and set up a large warehouse in downtown Vancouver, close to the rail yards and port facilities, to supply smugglers. Many west coast rumrunners were also supplied by Henry Reifel, one of the largest distillers and bootleggers in B.C. during Prohibition. Reifel, a German immigrant who settled in British Columbia in the late 1880s, had learned to brew lager beer at the Chicago Brewing Company before making his way to Nanaimo where he began an apprenticeship at a large bottling company. In 1890, the Nanaimo Brewing Company was launched and after two highly profitable years, and a few company mergers later, the ambitious Reifel became the brewmaster and a minority shareholder in the Union Brewing Company of Nanaimo. By the early 1900s, the new company was one of the most profitable breweries on the west coast, thanks to Reifel's skill as a brewmaster and his shrewd business sense. By 1908, along with his brothers and sons, he built the Canadian Brewing and Malting Company in Vancouver, which later amalgamated with other companies to form Vancouver Breweries Ltd. in 1919. With his brothers, he established British Columbia Breweries and, with his sons, he founded the British Columbia Distillery Company Ltd. In 1926, the family formed Brewers and Distillers of Vancouver Ltd. as a holding company for their two distilleries and four breweries. The Reifels also operated their own export companies, which supplied west coast bootleggers with liquor from their distilleries and breweries to smuggle to the U.S. According to an RCMP report from 1940, Frank Eccles, the former RCMP undercover agent who was convicted of opium possession during the 1920s, was at the same time "actively associated with the Reifel Interests, and was, what might be termed, 'Shore Skipper' for their smuggling activities."

In 1925, members of the British Columbia legislature's Public Accounts Committee accused Henry Reifel and his companies of smuggling liquor to the United States through his export companies. It was also rumoured that, from his posh oceanfront mansion on Vancouver's Marine Drive, Reifel directly piped liquor to waiting ships. When Henry and his son George crossed into the United States in July 1934, smuggling charges were laid against the two based on evidence that the products of Brewers and Distillers Ltd. "found their way into the commerce of the United States during the period of prohibition." The pair could only leave the country after paying $200,000 in bail. In 1934, as a result of the charges, Henry and his two sons were forced to resign as directors of Brewers and Distillers Ltd. The case did not go to trial as the Reifels agreed to pay U.S. authorities $500,000 in back taxes and fines, plus the $200,000 in bonds already forfeited when the two never showed up in Seattle for their arraignment.

Henry Reifel, circa 1929

In Saskatchewan, farmland located right on the American border was used as a staging ground to sneak booze onto the U.S. side. Farmers were recruited to help smugglers by allowing the illicit inventories to be stashed in their barns and lending out tractors and other farming implements to transport the liquor across the border. The prairie province was also home to no less than sixty-nine liquor-export houses, and, by the end of 1920, they were already selling 28,000 cases a month, 95 percent going to the United States. Many of the export houses were controlled by Meyer Chechik and Harry Rabinovitch through the Prairie Drug Company and the Regina Wine and Spirit Company. According to a 1928 report by the Royal Commission on Customs and Excise, the latter company broke numerous laws during its short existence:

> The Regina Wine and Spirit Company conducted an export liquor business at Regina and certain border towns in Saskatchewan. They compounded, labelled and sold liquors on a wholesale scale with a licence and contrary to sections 187 and 196 (inclusive) of the Excise Act; and in violation of the provisions of the Food and Drug Acts 10–11 George V, chapter 27, and the regulations made thereunder. They applied false trade marks and false descriptions to such goods, contrary to the provisions of section 488 of the Criminal Code; they used United States Revenue strip stamps and Scotch liquor labels on goods bottled by them contrary to law. These companies kept a double set of books and false accounts for the purpose of deceiving the Government as to the extent of their operations and their income. Their cash receipts for sales from July, 1920 to December 21, 1921 exceeded $2,200,000 and the returns made by them do not show all the profits.

In one interim report, the Royal Commission could not mask its incredulity when discussing the lack of government scrutiny over the ownership and operations of Saskatchewan-based companies, which hid behind the veil of legitimacy to cloak their bootlegging operations:

> We refer to the Canada Drug Company, the Yorkton Distributors, the Prairie Drug Company, the Regina Wine and Spirits, Dominion Distributors and the Regina Vinegar Com-

pany. All of these companies appear to have conducted their business in persistent and open contravention of the laws and regulations governing excise, and even the most casual observer could not have failed to detect their irregularities. These companies were owned and controlled by the Bronfmans, the Chechiks, the Natansons, the Diamonds and Rabinovitch, and yet they were seriously expected to carry on a bona fide "drug" and "vinegar" business. That such a condition of affairs could have existed at all, let alone have continued for several years, shows not only a lack of intelligent and efficient supervision on the part of the collector of the port but serves to demonstrate a breakdown in proper and efficient supervision on the part of the Department [of Customs and Excise] as a whole.

From Southern Ontario, booze-filled boats sailed across the Great Lakes to the small seaside towns of upstate New York and Michigan, with deliveries extending to larger cities such as Duluth, Toledo, and Cleveland. From the Niagara region, they crossed into Buffalo. Through Lake Champlain, they travelled to Plattsburg, New York, and Burlington, Vermont. Despite the multitude of smuggling routes, there was probably no spot across the U.S.-Canada border that was as porous as the Detroit River. Seventy miles long, but less than a mile across in some places, smugglers could cross from one shore to the other in just a matter of minutes. Along a 15-mile stretch of the northern side of the Detroit River, there were at least two dozen government-licensed export docks that served as the launching pad for Canadian liquor. A 1929 article in the *New York World* estimated that 75 percent of the liquor exported to the United States came from the Windsor district via Detroit. Dominion records appear to back up this assessment; statistics from the Department of National Revenue for 1927 show that of the 4,252,583 gallons of beer, ale, and porter exports from Canada, 2,993,547 gallons were shipped from Windsor. "There before our astounded eyes were the boats, on runners, loaded down to the gunwales with kegs and cartons of beer," journalist Roy Greenaway wrote as he witnessed the flurry of export activity on the Windsor docks one winter's day. "They were spaced out at approximately hundred-yard intervals. We soon counted twelve, and more were shooting out from the shelter of the canals on the Canadian side. The men who were dragging and shoving them across the ice looked like pirates in their toques and high rubber boots." In the first months of 1920, one estimate placed nearly 24 percent of the population of Ontario living within a few miles of the Detroit River as connected with the illegal liquor business in some way or another.

In the Maritimes, "rum running, smuggling, and bootlegging was a way of life," J. W. Calder observed in his book on Canada's east coast during the Prohibition era. William McNulty estimated that in 1922, "no fewer than 500 vessels of all sorts and descriptions were engaged in smuggling whiskey from the maritime provinces of Canada to the New England seaboard." The coastal stretch from Boston to Atlantic City was so populated with booze-laden ships that it became popularly known as "Rum Row." Mother ships would anchor in international waters and then unload their cargo onto speedboats. In 1931, the National Commission on Prohibition Enforcement in the U.S. reported on the scope, sophistication, profitability, and adaptability of liquor smuggling along the eastern seaboard:

> This form of transportation has been elaborately organized, often with special craft, with radio stations, and with efficient service for soliciting business, directing the movements of boats, ascertaining the movements of enforcement agents, and giving warning of their activities. It has developed all manner of ingenious apparatus, using the newest methods of engineering and of science. The organizations can operate profitably if they can land one boat load of five. The margin of profit is more than enough to take care of all ordinary activities of enforcement agencies. When an organization of this sort is broken up, it is quickly set up again by reorganization of experienced violators knowing exactly what to do and how to do it.

Many of the mother ships anchored off Rum Row operated under the British flag, but were registered in Canada and belonged to Canadian owners, many of them working for American syndicates. A letter dated April 3, 1930, from a Canadian diplomat in Washington noted that during the first few months of 1930, the U.S. Coast Guard at New York "has reported the names of thirty different vessels of British registry as having been observed while laden with liquor off the entrance to the New York Harbour. Three of these vessels were registered in Newfoundland, twenty-three were certainly registered in Canada, and the remaining four are probably Canadian, although I have no definitive information on this point."

Vessels that frequented Rum Row were often crewed by fishermen and other experienced sailors from Nova Scotia, New Brunswick, and Newfoundland. In 1925, *Maritime Merchant* magazine reported that about half of the hundred vessels that made up the Lunenburg fishing fleet in Nova Scotia were engaged in the rum trade, some being leased to American bootleggers for as much as $4,000 a month. In his autobiography, *I Was a Rum Runner*, Nova Scotia's Don Miller estimated that "ninety percent of Lunenburg's fleet were involved at one time or another." So many fishermen had forsaken their original profession that the *Lunenburg Progressive Enterprise* newspaper reported in 1924 that a local fish plant was forced to close. Some contended that rumrunning was one of the few reliable sources of income during the recession that gripped the Maritimes during the 1920s. By renting out their boat or captaining a vessel full of booze, fishermen could make more in a week than they did all year catching fish. Others believed it was a U.S. tariff on Canadian-captured fish that forced many Maritimers to the smuggling trade. An editorial in a 1923 edition of the *Globe* newspaper describes the conditions and enticements that stirred Maritime fishermen to enter the rumrunning trade, as well as the typical smuggling methods of the Nova Scotia rum ships:

> Canadian fishermen have been shut out of the United States market by the tariff and are tempted by American agents with plenty of money to employ their idle ships and crews in carrying liquor cargoes. The tempter lays down

the cash, insures the vessel against any calamity, and charters it as a coasting freighter. The ship clears from Yarmouth in the ballast for St. Pierre, where she takes on a cargo, clearing for Nassau, in the British Bahamas. But before she reaches her destination she has discharged her cargo along the Atlantic coast. She loads at Nassau with clearance papers for St. Pierre, and again her cargo disappears before she completes her northern voyage.

The role of the Canadian Maritimes in supplying bootleg liquor to America was heightened when the U.S. Coast Guard began commissioning destroyers, minesweepers, and cabin cruisers and hundreds of smaller vessels along Rum Row. The result was that many rumrunners were driven away from the U.S. seaboard towards the safety of what would become "Rum Row North" — the coastal waters that ran off the Maritime provinces to the northeast as far as New-foundland. The creation of Rum Row North also situated the French Islands of St Pierre and Miquelon at the forefront of the Atlantic coast's underground liquor trade. "Now if you are never in St Pierre," advised Jack O'Hearts, a bootlegging character in a Damon Runyon story, "I wish to say you miss nothing much, because what it is but a little squirt of a burg sort of huddled up alongside some big rocks off Newfoundland, and very hard to get to, any way you go. Mostly you go there from Halifax by boat, though personally I go there in 1924 in John the Boss's schooner by the name of the *Maude*, in which we load a thousand cases of very nice merchandise for the Christmas trade. The first time I see St. Pierre I will not give you eight cents for the whole layout, although of course it is very useful to parties in our line of business."

Located some 20 miles off the coast of Newfoundland, the French colonial outposts were free from any restraints on the sale or consumption of liquor and boasted deep-water ports and docks that were open year-round. When the SS *Sable Island* docked at St. Pierre on July 1, 1922, with a cargo of 12,000 cases of Canadian Club whiskey, "it marked the beginning of the most frantic period of activity the colony had ever seen," according to Jean-Pierre Andrieux's book *Prohibition and St. Pierre*. Soon, the island became

"flooded with booze to the point where at times when the fog rolled up the streets of the small island with the nightly tides they would carry a distinct Scotch flavour." The two islands became an oceanic mecca for bootleggers and a logistical haven for Canadian distilleries, which set up transhipment facilities for liquor bound for the American coast. Andrieux estimates that 95 percent of all import activities on St. Pierre were controlled by the Canadian distilleries. The same distillers had a fleet of eighty or more vessels available on call to deliver whiskey from St. Pierre to points in the United States and Canada. Canadian government export figures also revealed the value of the French islands to liquor producers in Canada; for the nine-month period ending in December 1929, Canada exported 747,944 gallons of rye whiskey to St. Pierre and Miquelon. After Rum Row was cordoned off by an enlarged American enforcement presence, St. Pierre received 1,624,956 gallons for the same period ending 1930. Over the course of the following year, Canadian rye whiskey exports to St. Pierre jumped to 2,042,692 gallons. A branch of the Canadian Imperial Bank of Commerce was even established on the island to facilitate commercial transactions. When American Prohibition ended, the CIBC promptly closed the branch.

Joining the rum rows off the Atlantic coast were the rum trails that ran from New Brunswick into Maine. In 1921, journalist William McNulty estimated that "one hundred booze-filled vehicles passed daily over the border, including those operated by "at least three dozen Maine syndicates." One of the suppliers to these syndicates was Albenie Violette, perhaps the largest and most successful bootlegger in New Brunswick during the 1920s. "Joe Walnut," as he was nicknamed, was described by Canadian customs agent W.G. Carr as "a typical French Canadian of the woodsman breed. Tall and slim, agile as a cat, dark featured, with thin cruel lips. His eyes were black as coal, yet slightly protruding, the white bloodshot from constant drinking. He was reported to have a fiendish temper, and few scruples." Violette purchased large quantities of both raw alcohol and distilled spirits from suppliers all over the world, which he then wholesaled in Canada or the U.S. He also produced his own liquor. A booze foundry with a capacity of 50 gallons was built under the floor of his barn in St. Leonard to distil imported denatured alcohol that was then poured into bottles with fake labels of popular brands. Up until his death in 1929, Joe Walnut was probably one of New Brunswick's biggest private importers of raw alcohol.

Violette's bootlegging activities made him a wealthy man. He owned a stable of cars and boats, an automotive dealership, several bottling plants, and hotels in New Brunswick and Maine. He also owned local politicians, judges, liquor inspectors, and even had his nephew made the chief of police of his hometown. These connections would come in handy for Violette. After the Canadian National Railway police secretly seized a boxcar of raw alcohol, valued at $80,000, they waited for Violette to show up to collect his goods. Even after receiving a tip that a trap had been laid for him, Joe insisted on reclaiming his merchandise and went down to the rail station where he offered a bribe to a CNR officer. The bribe was refused and Violette was arrested and charged with trespassing on railway property and attempted theft. He was turned over to his nephew, the chief of police, and released on his own recognizance. When he appeared in court, the more serious charges against Violette were dropped. In the end, he was fined $100 for trespassing.

Violette enjoyed matching wits with law enforcement authorities and regularly taunted customs officials by using fictitious names on his declaration forms, like Albert Soucy or B. Temperance. On one occasion, local police seized and then quarantined eight barrels of Violette's homemade booze in a hotel cellar behind locked door and police guard. Undaunted, Violette had his son enter the cellar through a secret entrance and replace all barrels with eight replicas full of water. When the case went to trial, he was acquitted and the barrels were returned to him. Without skipping a beat, Violette accused the government of tampering with his ardent spirits and then had his lawyer file a civil suit against the New Brunswick Board of Liquor Commissioners. He won the case and was awarded $8,954 in damages. In another show of impertinence, Violette let it be known where he would be one night while running a load over the Maine–New Brunswick border. American Prohibition officials responded by setting up a roadblock at that very spot. As Violette's car sped closer to the roadblock, the U.S. federal agents frantic-ally signalled for it to pull over. Violette did not stop. Instead, he crashed through the blockade, smashing into the Prohibition officers' car, and overturning his vehicle. After searching his car, but finding no liquor, the two hapless federal agents found themselves on the receiving end of a barrage of accusations and expletives from Violette who accused them of damaging his car and endangering his life. The customs agents knew little about the wily French Canadian and his thespian skills. For his tirade was all an act. While the Americans were trying to calm Violette down, a heavy truck barrelled down the road heading toward the U.S. border. The truck slipped past the gap made in the blockade by Violette and sped into Maine carrying a large cache of his liquor. Even this was not enough for Violette. He later instructed his lawyers to sue the Prohibition officials for trespassing, alleged negligence, recklessness, and a violation of the highway laws. Both federal agents were arrested by Maine police and damages were paid to Violette by U.S. authorities to keep the matter out of the courts.

A TIDY BIT TOWARDS CANADA'S FAVOURABLE BALANCE OF TRADE

The underground liquor trade was driven by the most basic of economic laws: that of supply and demand. Outlawing liquor did little to squelch demand. It did, however, provide enormous revenues for distillers, brewers, bootleggers, and criminal syndicates. The money that could be made from skirting Prohibition laws proved to be irresistible to thousands of people and more than offset the risks of capture. In 1929, the average wholesale price of Canadian-made spirits, including excise and sales tax, was $16.20 an imperial gallon. The bootlegger's price in the U.S. averaged $55 an imperial gallon. As early as 1920, the *Detroit News* figured that the smuggling organizations who "keep the alcohol deluge flowing across the Canadian line" were sharing in net profits that totalled $100 million. And that was only for Detroit.

Prohibition made many Canadians rich and turned a sizable number into millionaires. An investigation into the finances of New Brunswick rumrunner Thomas Nowlan revealed that between 1923 and 1927 he had deposits of more than $830,000 at a branch of the Canadian Imperial Bank of Commerce. In 1926, the revenue produced from the smuggling operations of Ontario-based Max Wortzman was estimated to be worth $1.4 million. These fortunes were being amassed during a time when the average annual income in Canada was $3,000, a nickel would buy a malted milk or man's linen shirt collar; twenty-five cents would buy a package of MacDonald's CutBrier cigarettes or a meal at the Woolworth's lunch counter; $2 would rent a modest hotel room for one night; $4.50 would buy a Black Siberian Wolf Muff; $10 would cover the price of a men's gabardine suit or two women's wash dresses; $1,000 would buy a Ford coupe motor car; and $7,000 would finance a detached, solid-brick, eight-room home with hardwood floors and electric fixtures on Spadina Avenue in Toronto.

Prohibition in America also proved to be a financial windfall for Canada's economy and spurred an air of entrepreneurship that had rarely been seen in the young Dominion. Thousands of Canadians and Canadian companies made money directly or indirectly from supplying booze to the United States. Canadian distilleries and breweries grew to be some of the largest and most profitable producers of spirits in the world. Numerous other industries benefited, including export-related firms, transport companies, hotels, restaurants, and boat building. American currency sprayed into the country like an out-of-control fire hose. In addition to revenue brought into the country from the sale of liquor, tourism flourished as thirsty Americans streamed into the wet provinces. American Prohibition, the *Financial Post* observed, "has provided a tidy bit towards Canada's favorable balance of trade."

The Canadian and provincial governments also profited handsomely from Prohibition in the United States. Provincial governments made millions from their monopoly over liquor sales, provincial taxes, as well as licensing fees for export warehouses. According to the Dominion Bureau of Statistics, from 1920 to 1928, annual provincial liquor revenues increased from $3,837,000 to $22,755,000. The financial windfalls accruing to the governments of wet provinces did not go unnoticed by the dry ones. By 1927, almost every province had repealed its temperance laws and began cashing in on the huge demand for liquor. Municipal governments were reported to be milking Prohibition

through the collection of fines. From January to August of 1920, the city of Windsor collected $259,500 in fines from those illegally in possession of liquor. It was the federal government, however, that profited the most from Prohibition. The Bureau of Statistics estimated that the Dominion Government's annual liquor-related revenue increased from $8.5 million in 1919 to $49.8 million in 1928. By the fiscal year ending March 31, 1928, approximately one-eighth of all Dominion Government revenue was derived from the trade in alcoholic beverages. All told, according to a 1932 article in *Maclean's* magazine, the estimated revenue accruing to the provincial governments from liquor sales and taxes between 1922 and 1932 was $152 million. For the same period, the Dominion Government reaped $399 million from the liquor trade.

The Canadian millionaires that most profited from the evasion of Canadian and American liquor laws did not organize crime gangs. They formed companies. These businessmen were the owners and operators of some of Canada's largest and best-known distilleries and breweries, like Joseph E. Seagram's and Sons, Consolidated Distilleries, the Wiser Distillery Company, Gooderham and Worts, Hiram Walker and Sons, John Labatt, O'Keefe's Beverages, B.C. Brewery Limited, and the Carling Export Brewing and Malting Company. These companies, and the men who ran them, were the consummate and matchless Prohibition profiteers. The Canadian conglomerates that grew fat off Prohibition were some of the first corporations to be vertically integrated, handling all aspects of their trade including production, distribution, sales, export, financing, and marketing. They were also the most corrupt, unethical, and duplicitous corporations ever to operate in this country. Canadian liquor producers aggressively pursued distributors and consumers in dry jurisdictions and did not shy away from selling to dangerous criminal syndicates. Export houses were set up within walking distance of the U.S. border and sales agents were sent to America to drum up business. Canadian distilleries and breweries directly organized massive smuggling operations that transported millions of gallons to the United States or into dry provinces. They forged export documents, fraudulently listed the consigned destination of exported liquor as anywhere but the U.S., used counterfeit landing certificates from foreign ports, set up shell front companies, misrepresented the contents of their products, forged liquor labels, and bribed customs officials.

While investigating the Saskatchewan-based Franco-Canadian Import Company, federal investigators found in the desk drawer of its manager, Harry Rabinovitch, 50,000 forged U.S. Customs duty paid excise strip stamps. Harry Low, the managing director of Carling Export Brewing and Malting Company, used stolen Canadian and U.S. customs seals and shipping documents to divert railway cars of beer to the U.S. camouflaged as other commodities. Hiram Walker and Sons used fictitious consignees and false landing certificates for alleged shipments to Central America and Cuba. "The traffic had been carried on by means of fictitious consignees, clearances of false declarations as to destination, false return clearances and false landing certificates," a 1928 Department of Customs and Excise report investigating liquor exports from Canadian distillers stated. "In a large number of the cases, the goods so shipped were allowed to remain in sufferance warehouses for an extended period in order that shippers or consignees might find purchasers for the same in the United States."

Not content with their millions in profits, these companies also went to great lengths to avoid paying sales and excise taxes. Consolidated Distilleries was repeatedly accused of fudging its books to underestimate their profits and tax liabilities. Gooderham & Worts of Toronto listed all orders for liquor, no matter what their origin, as foreign destinations to capitalize on tax-exempt exports. Joseph E. Seagram's and Sons evaded income tax by distributing profits to its three principal shareholders in the guise of loans. When these companies were subjected to government audits, stalling tactics were used to keep investigators away from their accounting records. It was also common for company books to mysteriously go missing. The Royal Commission on Customs and Excise reported on one attempt by government-appointed accountants to audit the books of the O'Keefe Beverage Company:

> On the 26th of October, 1926, the accountants, P.S. Ross & Sons, under instructions from the Department of Customs and Excise, presented themselves at the office of the above named company to make an examination of their books. Access to the books was refused to them. On the 10th of December, 1926, another attempt was made by one of the representatives of the accounting firm with no more success. On the 26th of December, 1926, the representative of the same accounting firm, accompanied by one of the customs officials of the Customs Department, came to the office of the brewery and then were admitted to make the examination of the books, but they soon discovered that all the books, vouchers, invoices that could give any information of the dealings of the company previous to September, 1926 were missing.

The commissioners concluded that the books of the O'Keefe Beverage Company "are concealed purposely, and their whereabouts are known to the officials of the company and can be produced by them if they are so minded." An alternative theory is that rather than turn their books over to the Royal Commission, managers at the O'Keefe Brewery had them burned.

When the records of the liquor producers were discovered, auditors uncovered a cornucopia of irregular and illegal accounting practices. In the case of one liquor exporting company, the Royal Commission found $990,000 of unvouchered expenditures, and "it was impossible to find any official of the company who could or would give a satisfactory explanation of these items." Investigators also discovered dual sets of books maintained by these companies that existed solely "for the purpose of deceiving the Government as to the extent of their operations and their income." More than fifty breweries and twelve distilleries in Canada became the subject of tax investigations and audits by the Royal Commission. Based on these forensic audits, the commission calculated the following taxes and duties owed by just a few of these liquor producers: Consolidated Distilleries Limited ($973,667), Gooderham and Worts ($488,223.34), O'Keefe's Beverages Limited ($320,000), B.C. Brewery Limited ($114,428.21), Joseph E. Seagram's and Sons ($156,601.17), Carling Export Brewing and Malting Company ($129,416.11), Wiser Distillery Company Ltd. ($86,078.04), and Dominion Distillers ($20,580.30). These penalties represented only a fraction of the taxes evaded by

Canadian liquor producers. In 1935, the U.S. Treasury Department threatened to go after Canadian liquor producers for approximately $60 million it claimed was owed to the American government from evaded excise and customs tariffs.

Despite the many accusations, no executive of any major liquor producer in Canada during the Prohibition years was ever convicted of a criminal offence. On November 2, 1928, an indictment was returned in the U.S. District Court in Buffalo against some thirty defendants, including Gooderham and Worts and its chief officer, Harry Hatch, charging them with offences against the *National Prohibition Act*. In 1930, Hatch travelled to Buffalo and pleaded not guilty to the charges. With the case still pending in 1932, Hatch wrote to no less than the Right Honourable R.B. Bennett, prime minister of Canada, exhorting him to "authorize Major Herridge [Bennett's minister in Washington and brother-in-law] to discuss this matter informally with the United States authorities at Washington with a view to having this indictment discharged insofar as I am concerned." All charges against Hatch were eventually dropped.

While directly controlling the flow of illicit booze to the United States, the Canadian liquor executives were well insulated from the rumrunners and kept many layers between their legitimate corporate facade and the illegal markets. The Canadian liquor producers endowed the underground liquor market with a scope, sophistication, efficiency, and organization that was unparalleled in the history of the contraband trade. Their organizational structure and business practices were even emulated by America's biggest criminal syndicates. By supplying organized smuggling syndicates, Canadian liquor companies were partially responsible for the rise of some of the most powerful and most violent criminal enterprises in the U.S., including the Italian-American mafia (hereafter "American mafia"). These Canadian companies and their principals would be as culpable as any gangster in undermining and contributing to the repeal of Prohibition in the United States. In turn, American Prohibition and U.S. criminal syndicates helped Canadian distilleries become some of the largest, most profitable liquor producers in the world, while producing some of Canada's richest and most fabled family dynasties.

THE WHISKEYMAN

The most famous of the Canadian family dynasties to make its fortune from Prohibition was that of the Bronfmans. By the time he died in 1971, family patriarch Samuel Bronfman was a billionaire who had built one of the world's largest liquor empires. At their height in the mid-1960s, Bronfman-controlled companies claimed more than one-fifth of the U.S. liquor market.

Sam was one of eight children of Yechiel Bronfman who emigrated from the Bessarabian region of Russia to Saskatchewan in 1889. After trying their luck in farming, wood fuel delivery, and even horse trading, the family entered the hotel business, buying the Anglo-American Hotel in Emerson, Manitoba. The lore surrounding a teenage Samuel Bronfman is that after watching his father complete a horse sale with a ritual drink at a bar in the Langham Hotel in Brandon, he urged him to abandon the horse trade for the more profitable hotel business. By 1912, the Bronfman family owned four hotels in Manitoba, and in just a few years, the family was buying and selling hotels in Manitoba, Saskatchewan, and Ontario. Even in their early years, the Bronfmans were dogged by accusations of harbouring illegal activities. In 1908, when the family was renewing the liquor licence for their Balmoral Hotel in Yorkton, Saskatchewan, they were accused by local townspeople of previous liquor violations and condoning illegal gambling in their inns (an accusation perhaps fuelled by anti-Semitism, given that such charges could have been levelled at many hotels during this period). In his biography of the Bronfman family, Peter C. Newman also notes that some of the Bronfman hotels were accused of being nothing more than glorified brothels ("If they were," Sam would say later, "then they were the best in the West!"). Despite the isolated gambling and prostitution accusations, the prodigiously entrepreneurial Sam realized that the true money-making potential of hotels during this period was in the sale of booze. From these humble beginnings, Sam and his brothers found their true calling.

The family's road to its global liquor empire, however, appeared to be blocked early on. Prohibition was taking hold throughout Canada, and, in 1916, both Manitoba and Ontario had adopted temperance laws, dealing a severe blow to the family's hotel businesses. Undaunted, the brothers embarked on what at the time could be seen as an inauspicious and ill-timed business move: they entered the whiskey trade. Yet this decision was simply an early indication of the cunning and opportunistic business sense of Sam and his older brothers, Harry and Abe. They recognized that while the temperance laws in Manitoba and Ontario prohibited the local sale of liquor, both provinces allowed booze to be imported from outside provincial boundaries. With this in mind, Abe Bronfman, the oldest of the four brothers, moved to Ontario where he set up a liquor mail order house that catered to the Winnipeg market. He later moved to Montreal, where he set up another mail order company to supply liquor to eastern Ontario. In 1916, Sam purchased the Bonaventure Liquor Store Company in downtown Montreal where he filled mail orders sent in from throughout the country. By capitalizing on Canada's porous temperance laws, the brothers not only made their first fortune, they also established a pattern of wily decisions that would characterize their Prohibition-era liquor operations. As Peter C. Newman aptly put it, the Bronfman's expertise in manipulating the system and avoiding the full force of the law was so adept that the federal and provincial liquor laws seemed to be drafted in such a way as to maximize the Bronfman brothers' bootlegging profits.

The enactment of national Prohibition in Canada in 1918 virtually wiped out the Bronfmans' mail order liquor business, but true to form, Sam and Harry took advantage of another loophole in provincial Prohibition legislation. They realized that Saskatchewan still allowed the sale of liquor for medicinal purposes. With this in mind, Harry obtained a licence to establish a wholesale drug company and, in 1919, with the newly acquired provincial licence in hand, he founded the Canada Pure Drug Company in Yorkton, Saskatchewan, which Bronfman biographer Michael Marrus called "a thinly disguised liquor outlet that soon pumped more whiskey into retail drugstores than any other wholesaler in Saskatchewan." This new business venture was another crucial turning point for the career of the Bronfman brothers. No longer were they simply taking advantage of legal loopholes. They were now breaking the law. In addition to importing

and legally supplying medicinal alcohol to doctors and pharmacies in that province, the same liquor would be flavoured, bottled, and then labelled for the underground market in Canada and the U.S. In their investigation of the Bronfmans, one of the Royal Commission's conclusions was that the Canada Pure Drug Company "was never engaged in the drug business, but confined its activities to the sale of alcohol in the western provinces and to purchasers from the United States." The commission documented evidence "that the company imported from the United States about 300,000 gallons of alcohol, brought it to Yorkton, and had it compounded and bottled." The company then "labelled the compound as Scotch whiskey."

Years before the Royal Commission would level such accusations, Harry continued to work around, underneath, and above the law. His next move was to use the family's wholesale drug firm to obtain a bonded warehouse licence from the federal government. With both licences, he could now import and export liquor to and from Canada. With this in mind, Harry embarked on yet another gamble: he bet the Canadian government would continue to allow liquor to be imported and exported regardless of the wartime ban on production. He was right again. Finally, he gambled that national Prohibition would soon be a reality in the United States, shutting down distilleries in that country and opening up a huge export market for Canadian liquor. Once again, he was correct. Relying on highly placed contacts in the Unionist federal government, the Canada Pure Drug Company was granted bonded warehouse status and, almost immediately, the Bronfmans began importing massive amounts of liquor into Canada. "They filled one warehouse until the floors creaked, then another, then another," James Gray wrote. "Then, with all the facilities overflowing, another twenty-seven cars of whiskey arrived on the siding. The liquor would then be reshipped to the export houses that were springing up all over Western Canada, including those which they were establishing in Alberta, British Columbia, and Ontario."

Events continued to turn in the Bronfmans' favour. In 1920, national Prohibition was repealed in Canada, which allowed them to resurrect their mail order liquor business on a national scale while establishing warehouses across the country. By 1921, Sam's mail order business had spawned at least sixteen companies across Canada, most of which he did not even bother to incorporate. When Prohibition in the United States began, the Bronfman family could not have been in a better position. They had warehouses filled to capacity with imported liquor, had a well-oiled mail order business in place, export companies were established coast to coast, sales agents were hired in the United States, and a string of "boozoriums" were set up along the Saskatchewan–North Dakota border from which American customers could conveniently purchase their liquor.

Despite the vast profits already rolling in for the family, they set their sights even higher. The brothers realized that even more money could be made in liquor production. The Bronfman family was now in the distilling business. In the early 1920s, Harry set up the Yorkton Distributing Company and purchased ten 1,000-gallon redwood vats and a machine that could fill and label a thousand bottles an hour. The liquor all came from the same vat, but were poured into bottles with different brand names (many of which resembled existing high-quality brands of competitors). Once Harry got the Yorkton plant running smoothly, it was processing an average of 20,000 gallons a month, which produced gross monthly revenues of $500,000 and an annual profit of over $4.5 million. While Harry kept turning out more booze, Sam travelled about the country, establishing a network of connections with Canadian and American bootleggers and smugglers.

Now fully immersed in the underground liquor trade, the Bronfmans became increasingly vulnerable to government enforcement as well as the violence of the bootlegging trade. The year 1922 would not be a good one for the Bronfman family on both accounts. They became the subject of a tax audit by the Department of National Revenue, which discovered that the wealthy family had failed to file any income tax returns between 1917 and 1922. As a result, they were forced to pay $200,000 in back taxes and fines. Worse still, on October 4, 1922, Paul Matoff, a brother-in-law of the Bronfmans' who also operated the family's boozorium in Bienfait, Saskatchewan, was murdered by a shotgun blast while unloading a shipment of liquor at the lo-cal railway station. The killer, who was a mere 10 feet from Matoff when the 12-gauge shotgun unloaded, also made off with $6,000 in cash from Matoff as well as the diamond ring on his finger. Speculation about the motives included Harry's contention that it was a simple case of a robbery gone wrong. Others claimed the murder was a blunt warning to the Bronfmans from their American customers that they shouldn't water their whiskey so much. Another theory is that the assassination was a reprisal for Matoff's role in the arrest of members of Minnesota's notorious Kid Cann gang, which had previously hijacked a Bronfman car loaded with booze. Two American bootleggers who had been customers of Matoff were formally charged with the murder, but were later acquitted. Despite numerous leads, his murder would remain unsolved.

Matoff's death occurred in the midst of a spate of robberies and violence at Saskatchewan's liquor warehouses and export houses. Local newspapers, politicians, and townspeople were aghast and linked the violence and local crime sprees to the bootlegging trade and the Bronfman brothers in particular. Because of the public outcry, the Saskatchewan and Dominion governments moved to outlaw the export business in the province. By the end of 1922, the province of Saskatchewan — the birthplace of the Bronfman family fortune — had effectively expelled their most famous citizens. Like other events in the lives of the determined Bronfmans, the brothers turned what seemed to be a setback to their advantage. Sam packed up and moved to the friendlier climes of Montreal, where he established the headquarters of his ever-expanding empire. In 1924, he founded Distillers Corporation Limited and built what would become one of the world's largest distilleries. In the same year, the family consolidated its fortunes under the privately held Brintcan Investments Ltd., which at the time was worth around $3.5 million. In 1926, the Bronfmans' corporate interest would go public to finance their expansion in the booming liquor export market. In 1928, Sam purchased Joseph E. Seagram's and Sons Ltd. and its historic Waterloo, Ontario, distillery. After merging numerous corporate entities, Seagram's became the world's largest producer of spirits.

By the mid-1920s, the Bronfmans controlled all aspects of their liquor business from distilling

Sam Bronfman, circa 1936

Companies and warehouses were also established in the West Indies and Mexico, which meant that the Bronfmans' international transhipment points now encircled their main market, the United States. Their liquor shipments to the United States were facilitated by Canadian and foreign customs agents who were on the Bronfmans' payroll and who stamped the bills of lading with their country seals for shipments they never saw. The Bronfmans also forged landing certificates from foreign ports so they could be reimbursed by the Canadian government for the bond required for liquor exports. A hierarchy of real and shell companies, nominee owners, fictitious names, domestic and foreign bank accounts, and elaborate money laundering operations were all used to conceal their illegal exports and their enormous profits. These crews and other rumrunning employees were well protected by the Bronfmans as the bail and legal expenses of various individuals charged with Prohibition-related offences were put up by the family's many subsidiaries. By the end of the 1920s, the Bronfman companies were generating annual revenue in the tens of millions of dollars. In 1930 alone, the Atlas Shipping Company had deposited $3,794,907.99 into the account of the Distillers Corporation Ltd. A federal investigation revealed that a shell company set up by the Bronfmans to facilitate the bootlegging end of their distilling operation was the recipient of more than $8 million.

to distribution and export. They expanded to the east coast, where they acquired bonded warehouses in Saint John and Halifax. They owned some of the largest distilling plants in the world, but were also importing British liquor, which was then exported to the United States by a fleet of schooners via Rum Row. The Bronfmans set up a new firm to act as an intermediary between Seagram's and American bootleggers, called the Atlas Shipping Company, which bought whiskey from Seagram's or imported it from abroad and then resold it to bootleggers. At first, the company shipped much of its liquor to Windsor. When the federal government began closing down export docks on the Windsor side, Sam established warehouses in St. John's, Newfoundland, and stepped up his liquor deliveries along Rum Row. Around 1930, when the Canadian government began banning liquor shipments to the United States, the Bronfmans set up shop on St. Pierre. The Northern Export Company was established on the island as a Seagram's distribution facility and catered almost exclusively to American bootleggers. It wasn't long before the company became the island's largest trader.

In accumulating these revenues, the Bronfmans and their agents dealt with some of North America's most notorious rumrunners, bootleggers, and gangsters, including Ontario's Rocco Perri; Meyer Chechik and Harry Rabinovitch of Saskatchewan; Frank Costello and Meyer Lansky of New York; Cleveland's Moe Dalitz; the Purple Gang from Detroit; the Reinfeld Syndicate of New Jersey; and Charlie Solomen, a major player in the Boston underworld. Even competitors such as Lewis Rosenstiel, who later ran the giant Schenley Distillers Company in the U.S., got his start during Prohibition by purchasing booze from the Bronfmans during his trips to Montreal. Some have alleged that Sam Bronfman flew to New York to solicit business from U.S. bootleggers and personally wooed Meyer Lansky over fancy dinners. In turn, Lansky reportedly arranged for Bronfman to attend a Jack Dempsey fight in New York in 1923. Whether Bronfman and Lansky ever met is uncertain, but in his old age, Lansky, a principal architect of modern organized crime in America, would bitterly ask, "Why is Lansky a 'gangster' and not the Bronfman and Rosenstiel families? I was involved with all of them in the 1920s, although they do not like to talk about it and change the subject when my name is mentioned."

During a special U.S. Senate Committee hearing into organized crime held in 1951, Frank Costello — a New York mobster so powerful and influential that he was referred to as the "Prime Minister of the Underworld" — was confronted over his reputed ties to Sam Bronfman. Although he first denied ever "personally" buying liquor from the Bronfmans, after repeated questioning Costello nervously provided this rambling and confused admission, "… what I meant is if I bought liquor from him, that means I met him in the United States and brought it from him in the United States … I come to the conclusion that I never bought it from him in Canada … I bought it in New York … either from Bronfman or independent people … I want to make it specifically on the record that I bought it in New York, whether it was Bronfman or anyone else, and if Bronfman shipped it to anyone else, I bought it from someone else." Through its own investigative work, the committee may very well have unearthed the identity of that "someone else." Committee members confronted Costello with testimony he made before the New York State Liquor Authority in 1947 "in which he stated that one Harry Sausser was the person through whom he arranged the importation of liquor from Canada."

Another regular Bronfman customer was Joseph Reinfeld, a naturalized American citizen from Poland who presided over a massive New Jersey–based bootlegging organization, which, according to the U.S. Senate investigation, "imported nearly 40 percent of all the illicit alcohol consumed in the United States during prohibition." U.S. Treasury investigators stated before the committee that they had uncovered bank deposits made by the syndicate of "around $25,000,000" and estimated that the "Reinfeld Syndicate collected approximately $60,000,000 from their illegal liquor distributorships." An October 21, 1929, letter marked secret from the Canadian Legation in Washington to the secretary of state for external affairs in Ottawa described the Reinfeld syndicate as "a

highly organized smuggling ring, operating on a very large scale, maintaining its own fleet of ocean-going vessels, fast motor boats, as contact ships, a radio station to direct operations and houses along the coast which the newspapers call well supplied armouries." Based largely on the testimony of retired U.S. Treasury agents, the Senate committee accused the Bronfman family of being the primary source of liquor for the Reinfeld syndicate, going so far as to declare that during Prohibition this group of "notorious bootleggers" were "partners in some of Bronfman's operations." The committee also alleged that the Reinfeld syndicate was laundering its profits through Canada:

> This syndicate, dealing largely with the Bronfman interests which owned the Bronfman Distillery of Canada, carried on what they described as the "high seas operation." The system under which they operated consisted of bringing liquor from Canada, France, England, Scotland, and Germany to the little St. Lawrence River island of St. Pierre et Miquelon and there transhipping it to "rum runway" 12 miles off Sandy Hook. At that point the syndicate's customers took over and ran the liquor into the United States. Much of the money received would be sent in the $100,000 and $500,000 lots, frequently in gold to Canada so that in case this country got too hot for them, they would have something if they had to flee.

At the height of its operations, the Reinfeld syndicate was reportedly purchasing 22,000 cases a month from Bronfman companies. Historian Stephen Fox also contends that tanker ships owned or leased by Reinfeld would travel to a Bronfman dockside warehouse in Montreal or St. Pierre where the booze was pumped directly into large copper-lined tanks in the ship's hull. It would then set sail to the New Jersey coast where it would anchor a hundred yards offshore. A small boat would bring out a hose lined with linen and "twenty-five thousand gallons of Canadian whiskey would be pumped into oaken tanks on shore."

The business relationship between Bronfman and Reinfeld was significant for a number of reasons. Not only was Reinfeld one of the first American customers of the Bronfmans (he was selling their whiskey in his Newark saloon-turned-speakeasy as early as the summer of 1920), but as Reinfeld's primary supplier, the Bronfmans helped to nurture the largest American bootlegging operation during Prohibition. Reinfeld also helped to revolutionize bootlegging, first by operating on such a grand scale, and second by cutting out the middleman and purchasing and shipping whiskey directly from Canadian distilleries to American shores. When the Canadian and American government began to clamp down on Canadian liquor exports to the U.S., it was Reinfeld who allegedly advised Sam Bronfman to ship his American-bound whiskey from St. Pierre.

Sam's dealings with Reinfeld also exposed him to other American mobsters. This included Abner (Longy) Zwillman, one of America's most influential gangsters who helped start the infamous Murder Incorporated, and who sat on the so-called Mafia Ruling Commission in the 1950s. Longy made his first of many millions by running Canadian liquor, using surplus World War I armoured trucks to offload booze-filled ships from Canada. In 1923, at the age of nineteen, he muscled his way into acquiring a 50 percent partnership in Reinfeld's smuggling syndicate, and, according to Zwillman's biographer, Joe Reinfeld had Longy negotiate directly with Sam Bronfman in Montreal. Recognizing Zwillman's ambitious nature, Reinfeld reportedly admitted, "My biggest mistake was sending him to Montreal to meet Sam Bronfman. Now he's got the connection too." After America's Prohibition laws were repealed, Reinfeld, Zwillman, and James (Nuggy) Rutkin, created a new liquor importing corporation called Browne-Vintners. "To avoid public disclosure of the investors," the special U.S. Senate Committee reported in 1951, "all the stock of this corporation was held by a nominee." Stephen Fox alleges this nominee was an employee of Seagram's in Montreal, who "laundered" the initial $250,000 investment provided by the former American bootleggers. In 1940, Browne-Vintners was sold to the Bronfman-owned Seagram's Distilleries for $7.5 million.

As the 1920s drew to a close, their many years of covert activities began to catch up with the Bronfmans. The Royal Commission investigating smuggling and corruption with the Customs and Excise Department had placed the Bronfmans' family businesses under a very unflattering light and recommended that bribery charges be laid against Harry, based on the testimony of customs officer Cyril Knowles. Because of the attention paid to the Bronfmans by the Royal Commission, they became the centre of a political storm in Saskatchewan. Before gaining power in the province in 1929, the Conservative Party had repeatedly called for the prosecution of the Bronfmans. Once the party achieved power, it wasted little time in going after Harry. On November 29, 1929, he was arrested on the instructions of Saskatchewan's attorney general and charged with attempted bribery and witness tampering. The bribery charged stemmed from his alleged offer of graft money to Knowles eight years earlier. The second charge stemmed from an incident wherein Harry attempted to extricate his brother-in-law, David Gellerman, from a charge of selling whiskey to William Denton, an undercover provincial liquor commission agent. Denton told the court that in 1922, Bronfman gave $1,200 to the two witnesses to leave the province, which they did. When the case was dismissed, due to the absence of the material witnesses, Denton claimed that Harry offered him $2,250 as a reward for shepherding the two out of Saskatchewan. Predictably, on September 13, 1930, Harry was acquitted of the tampering charges. After the trial, he invited the jury to a party in his suite at the Hotel Saskatchewan where he reportedly filled a bathtub full of whiskey to celebrate.

By the time American Prohibition ended in 1933, Seagram's was poised to capture the market once again, this time legally. It had amassed vast inventories of aged and blended whiskies, and had an extensive distribution network already in place. Americans had developed a taste for Seagram's Seven Crown American Whiskey and V.O. Canadian Whiskey and they became some of the best-selling brands in the post-Prohibition era. The Bronfmans purchased distilleries in the U.S. and Sam moved Seagram's main office to New York City.

Despite the end of American Prohibition, Canadian and U.S. authorities were not through with the Bronfmans. In 1934, the Canadian government, now under the control of the Conservative Party of R. B. Bennett, launched a nationwide investigation into the liquor smuggling industry. Prime Minister Bennett was highly critical of his predecessor, Mackenzie King, for failing to combat liquor smuggling and, more specifically, for not prosecuting the Bronfmans. Near the end of this sweeping investigation, an RCMP memo reported, "in five provinces of the Dominion and in the United States the RCMP were last night trailing sixty-one Canadians against whom stands a blanket warrant charging them with conspiracy to evade payment of more than $5 million in customs on smuggled liquor." It was the biggest investigation in the history of the force, stretching from Prince Edward Island to British Columbia. As part of its prosecution, the Crown alleged that conspirators collectively handled approximately $50 million worth of contraband liquor.

Among the sixty-one defendants were all four Bronfman brothers. Late in 1934, the Crown charged the four with conspiracy to evade payments of duty on liquor shipped to St. Pierre (which the government claimed was short-circuited back onto Canadian shores, thereby evading federal excise tax) and "conspiring to violate the statutes of a friendly country" (i.e., the United States). The bail for each was set at $100,000. As part of the investigation into the Bronfmans, thousands of documents from their companies were seized. The Crown's case was fatally weakened, however, when the RCMP could not gather sufficient evidence from Seagram's headquarters. Accusations quickly surfaced that Sam Bronfman ordered the destruction of thousands of incriminating papers, "almost certainly with a view to shielding their early operations from inquisitorial eyes," according to a 1935 article in the *Globe*. Other Bronfman companies used for smuggling purposes conveniently went out of business, and their assets were transferred offshore. On June 15, 1935, the Bronfmans were acquitted of all charges. As a reward for his diligent defence, their lead lawyer was awarded one thousand free shares of Seagram's stock. While once again escaping criminal charges in Canada, the U.S. Treasury Department demanded millions of dollars in excise and customs tariffs it accused the Bronfmans of evading. After negotiations with the Treasury Department, the Bronfmans' bill came to a mere $3 million.

With the last of their Prohibition-era legal wranglings behind them, the Bronfman empire expanded at a dizzying pace. Under Sam's leadership, Seagram's sales topped the $1 billion mark in 1965. Sam himself would often feign innocence when confronted with his nefarious past. In an interview with *Fortune* magazine in 1966, Sam rationalized his export-driven business during Prohibition without a hint of moral compunction: "We loaded a carload of goods, got our cash, and shipped it. We shipped a lot of goods. Of course, we knew where it went, but we had no legal proof. And I never went on the other side of the border to count the empty Seagram bottles." On November 12, 1963, Harry Bronfman passed away. Eight years later, on July 10, 1971, Sam died of cancer, leaving the empire in the hands of his family. Following the death of the two brothers, the Bronfman family would assiduously endeavour to yarn a mythology of the origins of the family fortune. Regardless, in both their legal and illegal operations, the Bronfman family became the most successful of all Canadian liquor producers and suppliers. This is appropriate enough, given the Yiddish translation for the name Bronfman is "whiskeyman."

MY AMERICAN GANGSTER

The Bronfmans were only one of many Canadian liquor suppliers that worked with the American criminal syndicates that increasingly monopolized the underground liquor trade. Most of America's infamous Prohibition-era gangsters were supplied with booze from Canada and many dealt directly with Canadian distilleries and their export subsidiaries. Some even set up accounts and lines of credit with their Canadian suppliers. This mutually profitable partnership catapulted the Canadian liquor industry to new heights and also helped transform the organization of crime in the United States. By supplying American bootleggers, Canadian liquor producers contributed to the modernization, consolidation, and expansion of organized crime throughout North America. If Prohibition provided the jump-start to American organized crime, then Canadian distillers were the jumper cables. As Stephen Fox writes, "organized crime in America was permanently transformed by thirteen years of Prohibition." Gangs moved beyond their own neighbourhoods and an "informal cooperation among bootleggers in different states was increasingly systematized." By the late 1920s, the major bootleggers of the Northeast and Midwest had organized themselves into the "Big Seven." This group included some of the most influential and dominant names in American organized crime — Johnny Torrio, Charles Luciano, Frank Costello, Meyer Lansky, Charlie Solomon, Waxey Gordon, Longy Zwillman, Benjamin Siegel, Al Capone, and Moe Dalitz — all of whom bootlegged Canadian liquor. At a 1929 meeting in Atlantic City, the biggest names in American gangsterdom met to divide up the rackets and to ensure peace among the competing groups. As part of the meeting, Cleveland's Moe Dalitz "took the floor and told the bosses that there should be an end to the cutthroat underbidding on liquor from Canada and Europe," according to John William Tuohy. "If that happened, he said, prices would drop and they would all make more money. All the bosses agreed." For the first time, the U.S. underworld was united "under one thought, one direction."

Johnny Torrio, the man who initiated the Big Seven, the Atlantic City conference, and the idea of a national commission of criminals, was one of the first Chicago gangsters to make direct contact with Canadian distilleries and breweries. Forever trying to apply business principles to his rackets, Torrio recognized that he could maximize his profits by directly smuggling whiskey from Canada, rather than purchasing it from middlemen. Al Capone, a Torrio disciple, was also a major importer of Canadian liquor. Through a network of alliances with other bootleggers in Detroit, St. Louis, and Philadelphia, Capone obtained huge quantities of liquor from Canada, Cuba, and the Bahamas. Rumours persist to this day that Capone personally travelled to Saskatchewan in June 1926 to strengthen his ties with his Canadian sources. This included stops in Moose Jaw, which was directly linked by rail to Chicago, where he reputedly hid from police in the tunnels under the town, and in Bienfait, where he met with Sam and Harry Bronfman. One of Capone's alleged suppliers was Rocco Perri. When questioned about a possible acquaintance with his Canadian counterpart, Capone spat out what would become one of his most famous quotes: "Do I do business with Canadian racketeers? I don't even know what street Canada is on." A Chicago syndicate headed by Al's brother Ralph

supposedly owned twenty airplanes that regularly flew into Canada to pick up liquor.

Stefano Magaddino, who was once described as "the grand old man of the Cosa Nostra" made millions by moving bootleg whiskey from Canada's Niagara region into Buffalo's underworld (which he would dominate for many years to come). Francesco Castiglia (a.k.a. Frank Costello) purchased liquor directly from Sam Bronfman's St. Pierre operations, most of which was then transported to New York City where it would be sold to the highest bidder. Costello's former lawyer and biographer contended that the "boss of all Bosses of the Mafia" also worked directly with Nova Scotia shipbuilders to manufacture "rummies of a new character." It was through his involvement in bootlegging that Costello forged a historic partnership with Charles (Lucky) Luciano and Meyer Lansky, both of whom also purchased liquor from Canadian distilleries and bootleggers. By helping to establish the five New York mafia families, the three men could rightly be considered the fathers of modern-day organized crime in America.

Cleveland's Moe Dalitz, who is considered to be second only to Meyer Lansky as America's most influential Jewish gangster, was a loyal customer of the Bronfmans and other Ontario-based liquor producers. He used barges to float empty trucks across Lake Erie to the Canadian side where they would disembark and drive to distilleries or export warehouses. The barges would then be sailed back and the booze distributed throughout Ohio, Pennsylvania, and New York. Dalitz and his partners in Cleveland's Mayfield Road Gang moved so much Canadian whiskey across Lake Erie that it became known as "the Jewish Lake." William (Big Bill) Dwyer, one of New York City's most prolific bootleggers and a former employer of Frank Costello, also brought liquor across the Great Lakes in armoured speedboats. (In 1925, Dwyer used $75,000 from his bootlegging profits to purchase the Hamilton Tigers hockey team, which was then moved from Ontario to his hometown and renamed the New York Americans.)

The Purple Gang, a loose confederation of Jewish gangsters from Detroit's east side, was once the city's biggest and most violent criminal syndicate. In addition to shoplifting, extortion, gambling, insurance fraud, kidnappings, and contract murders, they were heavily involved in distilling, brewing and hijacking contraband liquor. They later began importing Canadian whiskey from Windsor, which was then diluted at one of the gang's many "cutting plants." One faction of the Purple Gang was the so-called "Little Jewish Navy," a group of smugglers who brought liquor across the Detroit River via motorboats. When Chicago's Al Capone decided to set up a base of operation in Detroit, he was told in no uncertain terms by the Purple Gang that he was not welcome and that the "river belongs to us." Ever the incisive businessman, Capone avoided a war with the Purples by hiring them as his agents in Detroit. From that time on, the Purple Gang affixed Old Log Cabin labels to bottles of Canadian Club whiskey, which were then sold to Capone for distribution in Chicago. It was the hijacking of a shipment of Old Log Cabin whiskey by Capone's archrival Bugs Moran that led to the massacre of seven of Moran's men on Valentine's Day in 1929.

Joseph P. Kennedy, the son of a Boston liquor dealer and the father of a future American president, is also reported to have made millions from smuggling booze into America. In one book documenting the many transgressions of the Kennedy generations, Seymour Hersh quotes a former employee of the elder Kennedy who said he "heard anecdotes, rumours, and stories of bringing Haig & Haig scotch from Canada to Cape Cod and to Carson's Beach in South Boston." Another of Kennedy's biographers asserts that he arranged for the transport of liquor from Canada and England to Rum Row where "organized crime syndicates" including those run by Frank Costello "picked up the liquor on the shore." In a 1973 interview conducted just ten days before his death, Costello told journalist Peter Maas that he had been contacted by Kennedy who wanted help bringing liquor into the country and that the two became "partners" in the liquor industry. Joseph Bonanno, who headed one of New York City's mafia families, also alleged that he worked with Kennedy smuggling liquor from Canada. In his 2003 biography, Ted Schwarz claims that Joe Kennedy even brought his eldest son and namesake into the liquor importing business. "And in Boston, Joe Kennedy and his father understood the new opportunity for making money. They had established sources for liquor coming from

Canada and other parts of the world." Schwarz claims that Joe Jr. obtained Canadian whiskey through his father for the tenth reunion of his Harvard graduating class. Kennedy was also linked to Samuel Bronfman and his steady customer Joe Reinfeld by Diamond Joe Esposito, Chicago's powerful underworld boss during the 1920s, who allegedly supplied Cuban sugar to all three men. Through his political connections, Esposito boasted that he met with U.S. president Calvin Coolidge where he asked that the three men "receive special protection and all rights to bootlegging."

The most concrete evidence of Kennedy's involvement in bootlegging Canadian liquor comes from the Royal Commission on Customs and Excise, which linked Kennedy and British Columbia brewmaster Henry Reifel. Along with their breweries, the Reifel family ran Joseph Kennedy Ltd., a holding company that operated several bonded export houses in British Columbia. With sons George and Harry presiding as president and general manager, respectively, the company was headquartered at 1206 Homer Street in downtown Vancouver. According to a 1928 report of the Royal Commission, the sole business of this company was "the export of liquor to the United States." In addition to smuggling booze, the commission also documented "a great many irregularities, some of a very serious nature, in connection with this company." This included attaching "forged United States revenue stamps to bottles containing liquor bottled by this company." Another associated company accused of being used by the Reifel family for smuggling purposes was the Kennedy Silk Hat Cocktail Co., which shared its offices with Joseph Kennedy Ltd. on Homer Street in Vancouver.

In a letter to the RCMP's director of Criminal Investigations from the Customs Department dated October 9, 1926, an undercover agent accuses the Kennedy Silk Hat Company, Henry Reifel, and other west coast exporters of short-circuiting liquor consigned to foreign ports:

> Large shipments of liquor in transit between
> Europe and central American ports are landed
> at Vancouver and held in Sufference sheds
> until convenient to tranship to certain boats
> engaged in rum running. ... Among water

front employees, such as Stevadores, Checkers, and Police, with whom I conversed, It is the opinion that a large quantity of the tran-shipped liquor never reaches the foreign Ports to which it is consigned, but is landed in Canadian waters, and ultimately returns to Vancouver for distribution among local bootleggers by such firms as Consolidated Exporters Ltd., Manitoba Refineries Ltd., Kennedy Silk Hat Cocktail Co. &c. Henry Reifel, R.T. Morgan, and other prominent men connected with distilleries and Breweries in B.C. are freely spoken of as being the leading men in these activities.

The agent also notes in his letter that Captain Aubrey T. Gowe, president of the B.C. Grain Stowing Contracting Co. claimed he had personally dealt with Reifel and Kennedy, although no details are provided

on the nature of these meetings. Following the end of Prohibition, Kennedy entered the legitimate world of liquor importing, and in a few years established himself as the largest distributor of scotch in the United States. In 1946, Joe Reinfeld and Longy Zwillman bought Kennedy's Somerset Importers.

Dwarfing all other west coast bootleggers on either side of the border was Roy Olmstead, a former lieutenant in the Seattle police force who ran "one of the most gigantic rum-running conspiracies in the country," according to the *New York Times*. Dubbed by the Seattle press as "King of the Puget Sound Bootleggers," Olmstead purchased the majority of his booze in British Columbia. As Puget Sound historian Daryl C. McClary writes, "Olmstead reasoned that an unlimited source of good liquor in British Columbia, Canada, plus an untapped market for booze in Seattle, equalled the perfect combination for a very profitable business opportunity. Bootlegging just needed someone to

The "Gray Block" located at 1206 Homer Street, Vancouver, home of Joseph Kennedy Ltd., liquor exporter, circa 1925

organize and run it like a business; Roy Olmstead was just the man for the job." Olmstead's ships loaded two to four thousand cases at a time at Vancouver's and Victoria's ports. He took advantage of the Canadian government's tax-free exemption for liquor destined to non-American foreign ports by listing his ships' destination as Mexico. After leaving port, however, the ships' cargo would be unloaded on small islands in the Haro Strait northeast of Victoria, where it was stored until picked up by speedboats that took the cases to designated spots along the coast of Washington State and Oregon. With the combination of his tax-free liquor and the discounts he received on his bulk purchases from Canadian suppliers, Olmstead was able to undersell his competitors in Seattle by as much as 30 percent. At his peak, Olmstead's organization was delivering two hundred cases of Canadian liquor to the Seattle area on a daily basis, grossing between $200,000 and $250,000 a month. Olmstead went so far as to purchase a radio station that law enforcement officials believed was being used to send coded messages to his Pacific fleet, providing information on where the cases were to be unloaded and warning them where Coast Guard vessels were patrolling.

In addition to his many rumrunners and bootleggers in Washington State and Oregon, Olmstead also had a number of operatives in British Columbia. In one of the largest liquor smuggling cases prosecuted in the U.S., Olmstead was indicted along with ninety-one other people. Of these, according to a former assistant attorney general in charge of Prohibition, "many lived in Canada." Among those Canadians indicted was Russell Whitehead, president of National Canners Ltd. of Vancouver, lawyer F.R. Anderson of Victoria, twenty-seven directors of the Consolidated Exporters Corporation, and the entire crew of the steamship *Quadra*, which was owned by Consolidated Exporters and was captured with a load of liquor by a U.S. Coast Guard cutter off the coast of San Francisco.

The American investigation began in October 1924, when Canadian customs officials seized the *Eva B*, one of Olmstead's rumrunning boats, arresting three men and confiscating 784 cases of liquor. Olmstead was eventually arrested, and while out on bail, he continued to smuggle booze from B.C. In 1927, the U.S. assistant district attorney for Oregon,

Roy Olmstead

George Heuner, learned from an informant who had loaded ships for Olmstead in Vancouver, that the Seattle-based bootlegger was now transporting enormous amounts of Canadian liquor to the Oregon coast. As part of his investigation into Olmstead, Heuner directed Federal Prohibition Bureau agents to investigate Sterling Traders Ltd., a British Columbia company that Olmstead relied upon for his liquor supplies. In a December 3, 1927, letter, one of these federal agents, R.E. Herrick, reported that an informant had observed the loading of "a shipment of whiskey which was shipped from Vancouver, B.C. in a box car load of wheat screenings to Portland, Oregon in June 1927." The letter also relayed a startling discovery made by the informant: that American "Federal Prohibition Agent Alfred Hubbard loaded this shipment of whiskey into the box car at Vancouver, B.C." In another communiqué written three days later, a senior Prohibition Bureau official acknowledges that Herrick has "reasonable grounds for believing that the Sterling Traders Ltd. of Vancouver, B.C., is concerned with the sale of the smuggled liquor and the shipment of it by sea to points off the Oregon Coast, and that the liquor itself is probably being purchased by Roy Olmstead,

Arthur Boyd, Ed Morris, all of Seattle, Washington, and suspended Prohibition Agent Alfred Hubbard." The letter concludes, "The United States Attorney for the district of Oregon considers this the largest and most important smuggling case that has come up in his district during his term of office."

"STEP ON HER, KID. MAKE IT QUICK."

For every year that Prohibition was in effect, the competition between rival bootlegging groups became more fierce and more violent. Rumrunning cars and boats were routinely ambushed and hijacked by heavily armed assailants. A 1923 article by William McNulty conveyed the Darwinian laws of the bootlegging industry that inevitably paved the way for an unprecedented level of violence on both sides of the border:

> "Might is right" was the motto adopted by the gangs. In the wake of the whiskey shipments of 1922 came a veritable stream of blood, an orgy of violence and theft. The gangs began to attempt the annihilation of the weak in order to limit competition. On the sea schooners loaded with whiskey were stolen; motorboats filled to the gunwale with the forbidden liquid were seized; and even steamers fell into the hands of "hijackers," as the whiskey pirates were known.

In one of the single-largest cases of hijacking during this period, the steamer ship *Lutzen*, which departed from Montreal with 4,300 case of scotch whiskey officially consigned for Bermuda, was overtaken by a "modern Captain Kidd" thirty-six hours out of port and out of signalling range from other ships. As the *Globe* newspaper reported on February 12, 1924, "When the buccaneers bore down on the *Lutzen* out of the blue the Captain and the crew of the latter were too astonished to put up a fight. Besides, they said, they were armed." The hijackers boarded the ship, bulldozed the crew into obedience, shackled the liquor agents in irons, and then took command of the vessel, "while the pirate captain set the *Lutzen*'s bow dead for Rum Row, off the Long Island coast." Upon arrival at their destination, "the captured vessel competed with other rum ships, selling the scotch at $30 a case, it was said,

till the last of 4,300 cases had gone over the side." A New Jersey aviator reported that he had sighted the commandeered vessel, although the name "Lutzen" had been painted out and substituted with "Lion." Before they could be captured, "the buccaneers sent signals to the Long Island coast, and a steam tug came chugging out before daybreak that morning and took all the marauders on board." The thieves "escaped with about $129,000 in their pockets. This was the last heard of them."

Another bloody example of the risks assumed by seafaring rumrunners occurred on September 24, 1924. The *Beryl G*, a fishing boat sailing off the coast of British Columbia with 350 cases of liquor, was hijacked by three men, one of whom was wearing a police uniform. In addition to the liquor, the hijackers made off with $3,000 in cash. In the course of the robbery, the lone men aboard the fishing boat, William Gillis and his teenage son Bill, were shot to death and their bodies thrown overboard, but not before they were handcuffed together, tied to an anchor, and slashed with a knife so that they would sink faster. The brutal murders set off lengthy investigations on both sides of the border. After a year's search, Owen Baker and Harry Sowash were captured in the U.S. and extradited for trial in British Columbia. On January 14, 1926, the pair was executed at the Oakalla Penitentiary in Burnaby. It was to the hangman that Baker purportedly muttered his final words, "Step on her, kid. Make it quick."

Because ambushes and hijacking became such an accepted part of the underground liquor trade, most caravans of cars and trucks were heavily armed. As the *New York World* described in a 1929 article, "The rum runners sleep atop their loads with drawn weapons until a convoy can be made up. These convoys are preceded by a 'fix' car, a light automobile containing no liquor. This is manned by men who make a 'fix' if they can. If they can't other methods are adopted, usually accompanied by copious gunnery." One such battle occurred in June 1920 when a party of hijackers attempted to entrap a group of rumrunners near the Amherstburg Distillery in Ontario, at a spot known as the Indian Burial Ground. The town of Amherstburg, located not far from Windsor, had become the "headquarters for one of the most rapid and reckless bands of hijackers operating on the Detroit River," a 1929 *Maclean's* magazine article warned. "With the true delicacy which marks the modest tribe, these young gentlemen elected to entitle themselves the 'Blood and Guts' gang":

> Word came to their ears of a considerable cargo of liquor stored in a barn near the river-front town of Sandwich. It was the intention of the original owners to load this valuable consignment on a scow and jerry it across the river under the cover of darkness. The hour of departure had been set for one in the morning and the business of loading was to start around midnight. The playful little lads of the Blood and Guts gang planned to ambush the loading party at the moment the scow was ready for clearance, take them by surprise and rush the cargo. Afterward they would ferry it over themselves and dispose of it in their own market. It looked simple, but in some mysterious manner — there was almost as many spies on the waterfront as there were bootleggers — word of the projected raid was carried to the owners of the shipment. Therefore, when the merry marauders from Amherstburg arrived on the scene of their proposed operations, they were considerably annoyed to be greeted by a welcoming committee which poured a fusillade of revolver fire into their ranks. ... To their credit it must be set-down that the bold buccaneers did not in this emergency disgrace their gory title.

The battle between the two sides raged for three hours before the would-be hijackers fled. During the gunfight, it was estimated that some three hundred bullets had been fired.

Violence among rum-running gangs was particularly fierce in Southern Ontario. The Windsor-Detroit border was the site of ongoing bloodshed and lawlessness unmatched in any other part of Canada. However, it was the Niagara bootleg war of 1920–22 that has become a symbol of the violent nature of the bootlegging trade in Canada. This particular spate of carnage was blamed on competition and vendettas between the Scaroni and Perri gangs. Some of the victims whose murders have been attributed to the region's bootleg traffic during this violent period include:

- Thomas Mathews, who was found stabbed to death near his Stoney creek property;
- Ralph Mandrolo of Niagara Falls, who had his head blown off by a shotgun blast;
- Fred Tedesca, who was shot in Guelph supposedly on the direct orders of Dominic Scaroni;
- Angelo Fuca, who was plugged on a Hamilton street;
- Frank Pizzuto of New York City, whose body was hacked beyond recognition;
- James Saunders (whose real name may have been Nunzio Corazzo), who was stabbed to death "by a man strong enough to drive the knife or stiletto through him in a single blow";
- George (Toni) Timpani, who had four bullets fired into his head as he climbed Clifton Hill in Niagara Falls;
- Vincenzo Castiglione, whose bullet-riddled body was soaked in oil and then set ablaze in Hamilton;
- Mike Lobosco, who was shot outside his barbershop; and
- Maurrizzio Bocchimuzzo, whose body was found by hunters on the outskirts of Niagara Falls, New York with a handwritten sign nearby reading "Death! Here! Look!"

The bloodletting ended around the summer of 1922 with the elimination of Joseph and Dominic Scaroni and the consolidation of their bootlegging racket by the Rocco Perri organization.

While the carnage was concentrated among members of rival bootlegging gangs, law enforcement officials were not immune to threats and acts of violence. Between 1920 and 1932, one estimate of the death toll associated with the underground liquor trade in the United States was five hundred Prohibition agents and two thousand civilians, most of them rumrunners and allied gangsters. Enforcement officers in Canada were also the victims of bootlegging-related violence. In Edmundston, New Brunswick, two charges of dynamite exploded within three minutes of each other at the homes of local police constables. Both policemen, according to the *Daily Gleaner* newspaper, had been "very active in this district against rumrunners, bootleggers, etc." and both had turned down large bribes to look the other way. Three men, two from Maine and one from New Brunswick, were arrested and charged with attempted murder. The men were hired by Archie Dube, who confessed to police that he was contracted by "high-ups," in the New Brunswick illicit liquor traffic, and who were connected with a powerful syndicate made up of New York, Quebec, and New Brunswick bootleggers. One of the bombers confessed that he had been provided $25 for the job.

Violence also extended to those working jobs within the distilling and brewing industries. In September 1927, Sam Low, a wealthy liquor exporter and younger brother of Harry Low, the vice-president of Carling Breweries, was kidnapped and held for a $35,000 ransom. His kidnappers were alleged to be from Detroit. John Allen Kennedy, a mid-level bookkeeper for Carling, whose initials and signatures were on suspect cheques under investigation by the Royal Commission, was murdered just before he was to appear as a witness for hearings concerning federal tax evasion by Canadian breweries. He had been shot through the head at short range.

EMPEROR PIC

Emilio Picariello, a.k.a. Emil Picarello, Emperor Pic, Pick, the Bottle King, family man, entrepreneur, the Godfather of working-class Italian immigrants, an Italian Robin Hood, a murderer—just who was the man?

Pic was already a legendary brewheister in the Great Canadian West. His real name was Emilio Picariello. He was born in Sicily in 1875 and moved to Fernie, British Columbia, with his family in 1911. He stopped growing at five feet eight inches tall, but was built like the front of a draught horse. He had shoulders the size of the Rockies, a meaty neck, a broad Cro-Magnon jaw, a thick-lipped blubbery mouth, a handlebar moustache that could steer a Schwinn, a rounded bulldog nose, and brows as expansive and as lush as a British Columbia redwood forest.

By December 1914, Pic was hawking vino as the local rep for the Pollock Wine Company. Four years later he set up shop in Blairmore, Alberta, and became the sole agent for a Lethbridge brewery. When Prohibition drained Alberta on April 1, 1918, Pic began running bingo from its wet neighbour to the west. At the start of American Prohibition, he expanded his B&A racket south of the border.

The dope on Emperer Pic was that he was making dough hand over fist. The big dog had a big brass collar. He owned six touring rattletraps, each one capable of holding dozens of cases of illicit hooch. He relied on various pilot men to deliver the scrog and even employed a full-time mechanic.

By the early 1920s, Pic had already had plenty of run-ins with the bulls. His hotel was raided and his car was frequently stopped and searched. To cope with John Law's roadblocks, he equipped his whiskey sixes with bumpers made from piping filled with concrete. Pic's Italian-made *testicolis* must have also been filled with concrete. One night, after his whiskey-filled heap became stuck in the mud during a rainstorm, he asked a couple of provincial coppers for help. After a few minutes of pushing by the two public dicks, Pic was dislodged and drove away with his load of illegal hooch. On another occasion, as Pic was returning from a trip into Montana, an American P-man jumped on the running board of his Buick just inside the American border. With one wing on the steering wheel, Pic catapulted the other out the driver's-side window, fastened a viselike grip around the man's neck, and held him until his crate had safely crossed into Canadian territory. Once on the other side, the American lawman was helpless to do anything to Pic. That was just fine with the audacious Pic. "He thought of it as a sport. A game. A run. A vocation. A skill. But never murder."

The Pic also had a gentle side. He was always the first to help someone in need. He handed out toys to kids at Christmas and delivered grub to hungry families. He lent money out at no interest. When the coppers opened his safe after he died, it was filled with promissory notes. Many were from police. Pic was a big dog with a big heart.

On September 21, 1922, provincial lawmen were in Blairmore on the blink for Pic after receiving a tip

Portrait of Emilio Picariello and family, 1915

that he had a load of 40-rod red eye. Around four bells, First Class Constable Steve Lawson and the town's chief flattie, Jonathan Hougton, eyed a small caravan of Detroit boilers heading into town. The first was driven by J.J. McAlpine, Pic's mechanic. The second was handled by Pic's nineteen-year-old son, Stephen. The third was piloted by the Pic himself.

When the caravan of roadsters snorted past the lead coppers, they reported the arrival of His Majesty the Emperor to the provincial P-agents, who then paid a visit to him at his castle, the Alberta Hotel. It was a rough-edged building with small dried-out planter boxes on the window ledges. The late-afternoon breeze made the ends of the headless plants tap-tap against one cracked window. A wedge of sunlight sliced through the dirt street and fell noiselessly on the front entrance of the hotel. Pic purchased the hotel in 1918, and it became a front for his ski business. Beneath the flophouse, he excavated a small room where he stashed his outlawed hooch. Leading to the cave was a tunnel large enough to drive one of his Special Six McLaughlin Buick touring hippos.

After being served with a warrant to search his jalopy, Pic hopped into his chariot and sounded his horn as a signal. The P-men rushed to the rear of the building in time to see Pic's son blip out to his own bucket and light a shuck for high ground in a thundering hurray. The provincial black and whites then snorted off to their own prowl cars and made a beeline in the same direction. The elder Pic followed suit and was soon in the thick of the chase.

After spotting the cars speeding his way, Constable Lawson stepped in the middle of the street and flapped his wings like a hen laying a square egg. But Pic Junior twisted his tiller and scooted around the stationary copper. Lawson pulled out his roscoe, drew a bead on the car, and sprayed metal. Stephen drew two pieces of lead into his left mitt. Lawson commandeered the car of a local resident and gave chase. The law-hounded son of the bottle king flew across the winding dirt roads like a crow searching for field mice in a prairie autumn. His large Buick rear fishtailed along tight hairpin turns. Its large tires kicked gravel and stone into the afternoon air. In hot pursuit, Lawson squeezed off a third pellet before

he was forced to pull over with a flat tire. With the law choking on his dust, Stephen Picariello safely crossed the provincial line to freedom.

Later that day, Lawson confronted Emilio, exclaiming, "You might as well bring the boy back, for if you don't, I will." Pic ventured out in search of his son, but he failed to find him and returned to Blairmore. In the evening, he learned Stephen had been nabbed and sent to the University of Young Delinquents. In the dark of the night, Emilio set out to retrieve him.

Florence Lassandro, the twenty-two-year-old housekeeper and nanny to Pic's children, insisted on coming along. This was not the first time she accompanied Pic. Emilio often urged Florence to ride along with him on some of his bootlegging trips. He believed the P-men would be less suspicious if a young woman was inside his car. She was born Philomena Costanzo in 1901 in Calabria, Italy, and immigrated with her family to Fernie. As a teenager, Florence married Charles Lassandro, who became one of Pic's delivery boys. Her semi-masculine features were set off by a Romanesque nose, lids that drooped over her brown eyes, a protruding chin, and large brows that expanded along their outer corners. In her mug shot, Florence displays an eerily calm countenance, set off by a Mona Lisa smile.

The judge who presided over Florence's trial said that her "relations towards the boy, Steve, who was shot, were something more than friendly." When she inquired about Steve's condition with a local police officer, "she said that she thought a great deal about him but that it was not necessary to tell her husband."

While the two searched for Stephen, Pic suddenly stopped the car, pulled a heater from under his coat, loaded it, and placed it on his lap. After a short distance, he stopped the car again, drew another gun from under the seat, and thrust it into Florence's narrow lap. "For protection," he growled like a rabid dog. "They used guns this afternoon, we meet them on their own terms!"

As Pic continued his revengeful journey into B.C., he stopped to talk to some men gathered at the CPR station at Crow's Nest. The men would later tell the court that Pic waved his automatic cannon and threatened that if his boy had been harmed, he would kill Lawson that night.

Pic returned to Alberta and confronted Lawson at his home. With a pent-up fury, Pic accused him of plugging his son and demanded that the harness bull produce his boy. Lawson swore he did not know his whereabouts. Pic's eyes had a murderous glassiness to them. His breath came in short gasps and he said, through tight lips, and pointing at the gun clenched in his lap, "If you don't cut out this shooting, I can shoot too!"

Lawson spied the gun and lunged for it. A struggle ensued. There was a deafening roar. The smell of gat powder filled the air. A lead lug whizzed past Florence's feet. Other shots rang out wildly. One hit the speedometer. Another smashed through the windshield. Glass rained down over the inside of the car. The smell of gunpowder filled the air. Lawson loosened his grip on Pic and ran to the safety of his barracks. Pic's piece blasted away at the unarmed provincial flat foot. A pile driver knifed through Lawson's shoulder at the back. His torso jerked with the impact of the .38-calibre slug. He stumbled backwards and fell to the ground with a thud. Within a few minutes, he was ripe for the lilies. Watching the forty-one-year-old constable expire were his wife and one of his five children.

Coldly and snollygosteringly, Pic turned to Florence and demanded she take the rap for the shooting. "You shot … yes, by accident … them then you shot … when you saw his gun … someone shot at you and you shot back in self defence… A woman can, you know. To protect herself … a woman can. They no touch a woman … Listen! You say you did it. I go free and with money I get the best lawyers. Then you go free too." As he barked out the orders, Florence went wooden on him.

Pic was elbowed by the choirboys the following morning. Florence faced the show that afternoon. As instructed by Pic, she dutifully confessed to popping Lawson, but she would not be the only one stuck with a first-degree-murder charge.

It was a short trial that ended with a conviction for both, followed by appeals all the way to the Supreme Court of Canada, a stay of execution, and a clemency plea to the prime minister. But there was no leniency for the pair. Emilio and his nanny were hung at the Fort Saskatchewan Pen on May 3, 1923.

In a letter to his family the day before he mounted the thirteen steps to swing on the gallows pole, Emilio Picariello penned the following:

> My dear wife and children. I expect this
> will be the last letter I will be abel to write

Police mug shot of Florence Lassandro

to you and the children. I go to the scaffold tomorrow as an innocent man, and I am prepared to meet my maker. I hope that you and the children will lead good and happy lives together and that we will all meet again. according to the will you already have from me you are the sole executor until Steve our son becomes of age and then you will both become trustees and I wish that they all get an equal share. I want you to know that I do not owe any body. I want you to know that Mr. E. Gillis has already had $4500.00 from me and I consider I have over paid him for work he had never done. all other lawyers are paid in full. ... I want you to remember all the people I have helped at different times they have forgotten me know and don't come to help or cheer me. I will say good bye with love to you all children till we meet again and may god bless and keep you all safe kis all the children for me.

Your loving Husband and Father
Emilio Picariello

The final official statement made by Philomena Costanzo was transcribed into a letter to the minister of justice in Ottawa by her priest. She pleaded for mercy and for the truth. "Lawson was shot by a thirty eight revolver but I don't know how it happened. I am positive that I never had a gun in my hands." Florence would be the first and the last woman ever to be executed in Alberta.

ASSURANCE AND PROTECTION

A New York police reporter wrote once that when you pass in beyond the green lights of a precinct station you pass clear out of this world, into a place beyond the law.
—Raymond Chandler, *The High Window*, 1942

Like violence, corruption was an unavoidable consequence of Prohibition. It is doubtful that Canada or the United States ever experienced the level of government corruption that emerged during this period. Thousands of police officers, customs officials, liquor inspectors, Prohibition officers, politicians, and judges on both sides of the border were convicted of graft connected to the contraband-liquor trade. Thousands more were never exposed. The temptation to look the other way was often too great to pass up; a single bribe to a police officer could exceed his annual salary. Customs officials were enticed to look the other way or to call in sick on days when trucks full of Canadian liquor would rumble across the U.S. border. Other law enforcement personnel were on the payroll of criminal syndicates and received a regular payment or a pre-determined cut from a successful delivery. Some government agents provided armed protection to bootlegging caravans and even trafficked in the very product they confiscated (which led to the accusation that a Prohibition agent's zeal in enforcing the law was often in direct proportion to the payload of the rumrunner). In 1929, the entire crew of the U.S. Coast Guard's Cutter 219 was apprehended and then convicted after they had seized a boatload of contraband Canadian whiskey and transferred it to another rumrunning vessel. In what was called the worst scandal in the history of the Detroit Police Department, the commander of the Harbor Patrol was forced to retire after it was discovered that he used police boats to convoy liquor from Canada to the American shore and even ordered patrolmen under his command to help unload the liquor. (As payment for their help, the commander shared the bootleg liquor with his men.)

Between 1920 and 1926, 750 U.S. Coast Guard employees were dismissed due to "misconduct and delinquency," according to a June 1929 edition of the *Congressional Record*. Over the next two years, an additional 550 were charged with "extortion, bribery, solicitation of money, illegal disposition of liquor and making false reports of theft. In the same period, the federal Prohibition Bureau fired 1,600 agents with cause. "The grounds for these dismissals," a 1931 U.S. government commission summarized, included "bribery, extortion, theft, violation of the *National Prohibition Act*, falsification of records, conspiracy, forgery, perjury and other causes which constitute a stigma upon the record of the employee." Of this total, 257 were criminally prosecuted. While he was a member of the New York State House of Representatives, Fiorello La Guardia sarcastically surmised that it would take 250,000 police officers to enforce Prohibition laws in New York, and another 250,000 to police the police.

In 1921, Cecil Smith, a Windsor taxi driver–turned–bootlegger, was sentenced to five years after he admitted in court that he offered $2,000 to an Ontario Liquor Licence officer to walk away from twelve cars being filled with cases of liquor at the Windsor depot of the Canadian Pacific Railway. In court, he confessed that he had also provided a case of liquor to "express company agents" to release the booze shipment before government inspectors arrived. Smith admitted that over the course of one year, he had paid more than $90,000 in bribes to government officials.

Canadian liquor producers were also directly involved in graft. In a document prepared for the Royal Commission on Customs and Excise entitled "Private notes for counsel re: John Labatt Ltd.," a commission staffer summarized evidence provided by Mr. Burke, a Labatt's manager in charge of exports. Under the heading of "Special Payments," the staffer wrote that Labatt's paid "sums of money to various persons in order to carry on their export business, and for this purpose the company had a secret fund which was known as the 'Snake Fund.' We gathered that unless gratuities were given their business would be hampered in every possible way. Mr. Burke stated that while a portion of that money was paid to Customs officers, it was only for clerical services in making entries and not by way of corruption."

Maxwell Henderson, who worked as an accountant for Seagram's and who would later become the auditor general of Canada, claimed that both the Liberal and Conservative parties expected large financial contributions from liquor companies. While testifying before the Royal Commission, Henry Reifel admitted to providing nearly $100,000 to provincial political campaigns in 1925 and 1926. A Liberal Party "bag man" in Vancouver named William McArthur admitted to receiving four cheques between January and June 1926 totalling $40,000. Reifel told the commission that he did not receive any "promises" in return for the donations, although he acknowledged he recorded these payments in his company's financial ledger as "assurance and protection." Reifel recommended to the Royal Commission that a law be made prohibiting campaign contributions because "you never get any return on the money."

Clement King, a director of the Hiram and Walker Distillery in Windsor admitted that his company had paid out over $250,000 to politicians in a three-year period. Emilio Picariello would routinely deliver his political payments to a go-between, who forwarded it to elected officials. The Alberta bootlegger supposedly tailed the intermediary one day to an office and discreetly waited outside until he was sure the money had changed hands. He then walked into the office and introduced himself as "the man who is paying you the money." As he turned to leave, Pic explained to the startled official, "I just wanted to see where my money was going."

Unsurprisingly, customs officials on both sides of the border were the rumrunner's most sought-after government ally. A hundred-dollar bribe to an American customs officer could open up the border for hours, allowing tens of thousands of dollars' of contraband to be safely delivered. Canadian Customs and Excise officials were paid to sign export documents for foreign ports knowing the cargo was destined for the United States. Some customs officials were gracious enough to sign a number of blank liquor export permits, leaving the rumrunner to fill in such required information as destinations, cargo size, and departure date. One customs report on corruption at Canadian ports noted that liquor imported from Europe landed in Vancouver and was "held in Sufferance sheds until convenient to tranship to certain boats engaged in rum-running." Some of the imported liquor would be consumed while in the Port of Vancouver, "with the knowledge of the Customs Officer on duty, who is invited into the different rooms to partake in the hospitality of those in possession of liquor." The Royal Commission into Customs and Excise uncovered the existence of a "snake fund" out of which customs officials in Windsor "were subsidized for passing American rum-running cars without inspection on their homeward journey to Detroit, and for 'tipping off' the drivers if they were likely to be searched on the American side." Several customs agents admitted to receiving "payments of $10 per car for those so passed."

The immense scope and blatant nature of the graft shocked the minister of national revenue, William D. Euler, when he visited Windsor in 1928 to personally observe rumrunning operations. "I could see the United States Customs office in the other shore," Euler recollected in a media interview. "And I could also see that it was not difficult to detect any boats that left the Canadian shore to go to the American side." The minister asked a Detroit bootlegger where customs officers happened to be when all the illegal liquor streaming uninterrupted across the river. "It just happens that they are not there when we go across," the man replied.

The single-most infamous episode of corruption in Canada during these years involved Joseph Alfred Bisaillon. As the chief preventative officer for the Department of Customs and Excise in Montreal, Bisaillon became what historian Ralph Allen called "one of the most incredible sitting ducks in the annals of public malfeasance." During his tenure with the Dominion Government, and despite a modest paycheque, Bisaillon owned houses on both sides of the Quebec–Vermont border. One home was located in a well-known smugglers' den known as Rock Island. In addition to smuggling liquor into the U.S., he was also accused of selling stolen cars that had been illegally transported into Canada from America, and was also hauled before the courts for conspiring to help smuggle $35,000 worth of opium into Canada (a lack of evidence allowed him to walk free from the drug charges). In 1924, Bisaillon pulled rank on two Quebec Liquor Commission officers who had just seized 16,000 gallons of contraband alcohol. He dismissed the two officers from the scene and then permitted the two American smugglers to escape. While he impounded the illicit cargo, he was still charged by the Crown with conspiracy. These charges were also dismissed for lack of evidence. In the incident that eventually led to his downfall, Bisaillon was found to have deposited $69,000 into his personal bank account, despite the fact that his annual salary was only around $2,500. While this revelation may appear to

have been just one of many examples of government corruption brought about by liquor smuggling, it in fact initiated a series of events that would expose the colossal scope of the contraband trade affecting Canada and the culpability of the Dominion Government in encouraging (or at least ignoring) smuggling into and out of the country. The incident also precipitated the most significant constitutional crisis ever faced by the young country.

On February 3, 1926, H.H. Stevens, a Conservative M.P. from British Columbia, rose in Parliament and linked Bisaillon to widespread sleaze within the Liberal government. "I find running through all of this thing like a slimy, evil influence, the name of Bissaillon," he discharged in a multi-hour rant in the House of Commons. He referred to Bisaillon as "the worst of crooks, he is the intimate of ministers, the petted favourite of this government. The recipient of a moderate salary, he rolls in wealth and opulence, a typical debauched and debauching public official." After talking until four in the morning, Stevens was able to convince the House that corruption within the Department of Customs and Excise was endemic. The result was the formation of a special Commons Committee to investigate the administration of the department. Through hearings held between February and June of 1926, the committee documented extensive corruption, stretching from port inspectors all the way to the highest levels of the department. At the centre of the committee's investigation was Bisaillon, who stood accused of buying, transporting and selling contraband liquor and was estimated to have "had a turnover in the last two years of $1,500,000." The lead investigator of the inquiry concluded, "To my mind, only one inference can be drawn: that Bisaillon was doing business with the knowledge of his superior officers." The committee went so far as to implicate the minister of customs and excise himself. Evidence was presented showing the minister, Jacques Bureau, along with his deputy minister had "a large quantity" of seized liquor transported from Canada Customs warehouses in Montreal to their Ottawa homes. Even before the hearings wrapped up, an article in *Maclean's* magazine labelled the Department of Customs and Excise as "corrupt and debauched" and damned the entire Dominion Government for an unprecedented level of neglect, incompetence, and corruption. "Politicians and procurers, servants of the Government and prostitutes, graft in public places high and low, inefficiency almost unparalleled, are intermixed in a nauseous mess, comparable in gravity to nothing else previously been placed before a nose-holding and well-nigh despairing citizenry."

The committee's report landed like a political bombshell in the House of Commons on June 29, 1926. Many personally blamed prime minister W.L. Mackenzie King for allowing liquor smuggling and corruption to career out of control. The House of Commons went so far as to adopt a motion that it had lost confidence in the minority Liberal government. With few options, the prime minister visited the governor general and asked that Parliament be dissolved. In a surprise and unparalleled move, the governor general, Lord Byng, refused the Prime Minister's request and instead handed power to the Conservative Party, sparking a major constitutional crisis. The new government fell just three days later, however, and a general election was called.

Before Parliament was disbanded for the election, the House of Commons resolved that "since the Parliamentary inquiry indicates that the smuggling evils are so extensive and their ramifications so far reaching that only a portion of the illegal practices have been brought to light, the House recommends the appointment of a Judicial Commission with full powers to continue and complete investigating the administration of the Department of Customs and Excise and to prosecute all offenders." With little delay, the Royal Commission on the Department of Customs and Excise was created. From November 1926 to September 1927, the commission travelled the country hearing more than 15 million words of testimony. Although the inquiry was only incidentally mandated to examine the liquor smuggling problem, bootlegging inevitably became its principal focus. With the power to subpoena, the commission wasted little time going after some of the biggest fish in the bootlegging sea, including Rocco Perri, Bessie Starkman, Ben Kerr, Thomas Nowlan, Herb and Harry Hatch, Sam and Harry Bronfman, and the employees, officers, and directors of every major distillery, brewery, and export company in the country.

The commission's report was presented to the House of Commons on January 27, 1928, and expanded upon the parliamentary committee's revelations of widespread corruption at all levels of government. The findings of the commission forced the Dominion Government to take more seriously the smuggling of Canadian liquor to the United States. The re-elected Liberal government clamped down on liquor exports and numerous criminal investigations were launched. The department of customs and excise was re restructured to minimize future corruption, and greater customs enforcement powers were handed over to the RCMP. Some Canadian distilleries and breweries had their licences revoked while others faced tax investigations.

HOW POWERLESS WE ARE

Despite increased enforcement, from the outset of the Noble Experiment, the enforcement of Prohibition laws in Canada and the United States. was a grand exercise in futility. As historian Andrew Sinclair points out, those circumventing the laws were more organized and better funded, and often, received greater support from the public than those enforcing the laws. As a result, "the inadequate were forced by their country to pursue the prepared." On the American side, Congress initially entrusted enforcement to a new bureau within the Treasury Department. However, only 1,500 positions were created for the country as a whole. To make matters worse, according to a 1933 U.S. commission that studied Prohibition enforcement, political connections seemed to be more important than skills or experience in getting hired, and training was almost nonexistent. Federal Prohibition agents were, in the words of one U.S. Treasury official, "a most extraordinary collection of political hacks, hangers on, and passing highwaymen." To frustrate enforcement efforts even further, the courts did not seem to take bootlegging offences very seriously. During 1928, 6,200 violations of the Prohibition law occurred in the two federal districts of northern New York. Only 1,200 cases came to trial, while a mere 120 convictions were secured. "I arrested a prisoner last summer with a load of ale," one commander of a New York Coast Guard station wrote in a letter to his bosses. "He was fined $1.00 in court and as his carfare was $1.15 home, a collection was made in the court room and carfare paid to him."

U.S. Customs was handed the impossible job of trying to defend thousands of miles of border from liquor smugglers. As one bootlegger declared, "There are at least fifty roads from Canada leading into the United States through Plattsburg [New York], and there are only about fifteen United States customs officials to guard these fifty or more bootlegging trails." Gradually, more funds were dedicated by Congress to combat the problem, more personnel and equipment were added, and there was better coordination between local, state, and federal agencies. The U.S. Coast Guard was provided with faster and better-armed ships designed expressly to catch the high-powered rumrunning vessels. The increased American enforcement effort met with some initial success. In the Detroit region, during a two-year period in the latter half of the 1920s, 634 boats, 964 liquor-toting automobiles, 46,594 cases of beer, 6,644 barrels of beer, and 16,560 cases of whiskey were confiscated. Despite this success, U.S. Customs continued to be hampered by high levels of corruption, incompetence, bureaucracy, a rapid personnel turnover, and a lack of resources. A popular analogy that depicted the helplessness of the Coast Guard concerned a recently commissioned speedboat; while on routine patrol, it ran out of fuel and had to be towed to dock by a rumrunner.

A serious effort by the Dominion Government to combat the smuggling problem was conspicuously lacking throughout much of the Prohibition era. U.S. officials implicitly blamed the smuggling problem on a Canadian government that legally allowed and financially benefited from the production and export of liquor. "The rum runners are obeying every Canadian law," a Detroit Prohibition chief began, "and violating every law of the United States." Washington repeatedly appealed to Ottawa to stop the export of Canadian liquor to the United States, but for much of the 1920s the Canadian government declined to undertake any such measures. In a speech to Parliament, the minister of national revenue in the Liberal government defended the Canadian practice of clearing liquor cargoes that eventually ended up in the United States, saying that securing America's borders was an American, not a Canadian, problem. Upon advice from the Canadian Department of Justice, the minister even declared that no law existed in Canada to prohibit the shipment of liquor to the United States.

At times, federal authorities in Canada seemed to bend over backwards to accommodate the contraband liquor trade. With jurisdiction over the production and export of liquor, the Dominion Government approved liquor production and liquor export facilities in all of the provinces, regardless of whether they were wet or dry. And like the bootleggers, the Canadian government knew exactly where to go for the big action. A 1929 Customs and Excise Department memo entitled *Departmental Regulations Regarding Exportation of Duty Paid Intoxicating Liquors* designated seventeen docks in the Windsor area alone "for the acceptance of entry and clearance of such goods for export." Chester Walters, chief of the Hamilton Dominion Tax Office, ruled that bootleggers and rumrunners who filed federal income tax returns were entitled to deduct the amount of their *Ontario Temperance Act* fines as legitimate expenses incurred in the course of their business. However, those who had their liquor seized by government authorities were not entitled to any reduction, as that was counted as a capital loss.

Eventually, the Mackenzie King government grudgingly made a few modest efforts to address the tidal wave of Canadian liquor flooding the United States. In 1924, Canada and the United States signed the *Convention to Suppress Smuggling*. While American officials pushed the Canadians for a complete embargo on all liquor exports to the United States, the prime minister refused, fearing that Canadian voters would see him as toadying to the Americans. Instead, among other provisions, Canada agreed to provide the U.S. with information on vessels cleared to the United States. In effect, Canada Customs agents would telephone their American counterparts whenever a boat loaded with liquor was officially cleared for the United States. In 1928, this practice was discontinued at the request of U.S. authorities, perhaps due to the overwhelming frequency of the calls, perhaps due to the rampant corruption in customs agencies on both sides of the border, or perhaps due to the ease with which bootleggers circumvented the reporting requirements. Rumrunners found that providing false destinations or false names of boats to Canadian customs officials was sufficient to throw a wrench in U.S. Customs' interdiction efforts. One Canadian member of parliament estimated that there were five thousand instances in which Canadian customs agents communicated the wrong name of a boat or captain to their U.S. counterparts. "An unbelievable number of the boats were called *Daisy* and their skippers Bill Smith," he remarked. After 1928, lists of liquor clearances for the U.S. were mailed on a weekly basis to local U.S. Customs offices, a trifle late to catch rumrunners who were departing Windsor for a scant five-minute trip across the river to Detroit.

It was only after the Royal Commission issued its final report that the Dominion Government made any serious attempts to combat liquor smuggling. In 1929, Ottawa closed down a number of export docks throughout the country, including almost all along the Detroit River. Customs officials also began to prohibit small, rickety crafts from taking on loads to foreign destinations they could not possibly reach. On June 1, 1930, legislation prohibiting the export of Canadian liquor destined for delivery in a country that outlaws its importation came into force. Immediately, seizures were made by Dominion authorities and, less than two weeks later, liquor prices in Detroit increased by 50 percent. The move also signalled to some liquor producers that their export-fuelled prosperity was no longer guaranteed. In 1930, the *Financial Post* advised its readers not to buy shares in Carling Brewery because in the future it will "have to rely on [the] domestic market."

The augmented enforcement measures on both sides of the border, however, proved too little, too late. By 1930, it had become clear that there was no stopping the underground trade in Canadian liquor. For every new enforcement initiative introduced on either side of the border, the resourceful and resilient smuggler simply modified his *modus operandi*. Increased enforcement also served to weed out the smaller, independent smugglers, leaving the trade to the larger, better-organized, and more violent criminal syndicates. American officials acknowledged that even with the increase in seizures, they were confiscating no more than 5 to 10 percent of the total amount of booze coming from Canada. In a 1926 letter to the director of customs investigations, one RCMP member admitted, "how powerless we are to cope with the situation successfully. We may get an occasional haul but this only means a drop in the bucket as the saying goes." The *Philadelphia Evening Bulletin* argued that Prohibition "can not be enforced in its entirety, even if the military power of the Federal Government were to be put behind it, as long as there shall exist the present division of popular sentiment throughout the country." The *New York World* editorialized that "State and federal officials brandish the feeble mop of a badly organized prohibition enforcement system at this gigantic and cunningly controlled flood tide."

THIS SINISTER SLOTH

The hopelessness of curtailing liquor smuggling — combined with the ever-growing organization and sophistication of the bootleg liquor trade, the accompanying problems of violence and corruption, the unpopularity of Prohibition, and widespread lawlessness — led to the gradual repeal of temperance laws throughout Canada and the United States. By 1927, most Canadian provinces had annulled their laws. In 1933, the Twenty-first Amendment to the Constitution of the United States officially killed Prohibition in that country.

Ironically, the Canadian liquor industry, which for over a decade had flouted American law, was given privileged access to the U.S. market soon after Prohibition was repealed in that country. It would take some time for America's brewers and distillers to meet the pent-up demand and Canadian booze was safe, reliable, and of high quality. The flood of orders from the United States helped the shares of Canadian distillers shoot through the roof, contrary to the predictions of the *Financial Post*. Hiram Walker's common stock rose from $5 to $35. Consolidated Distilleries went from fifty cents to $9. Distillers Corporation stock catapulted from $5 to $20 a share.

Besides the vast benefits Prohibition provided the Canadian liquor industry, the repercussions of the great social experiment were lasting and profound. With its paternalistic overtones, Prohibition foreshadowed the rise of the welfare state and its ideological penchant for intervening in the lives of its citizens for their own good, whether such intercessions were welcome or not. Prohibition also kick-started a development that coincided with the rise of the welfare state: the expansion of the criminal justice system, which was now the government's main tool to control other personal vices, such as drugs and gambling (despite the precedent-setting failure in controlling the public's thirst for the demon rum).

Prohibition also had implications for the maturation of Canada as a country that increasingly yearned for its own identity and independence. Prohibition immediately followed the First World War where, for the first time, divisions of Canadian troops fought as national units instead of being parcelled out to support and reinforce British regiments. American Prohibition continued Canada's evolution toward independence from Britain. The 1924 *Convention to Suppress Smuggling* signed with the United States was the first international treaty Canada negotiated without Britain's involvement and signalled the start of made-in-Canada foreign policies. The Bisaillon scandal and its political aftermath was a major impetus for the *Statute of Westminster*, passed by the British Parliament in 1931, which granted legislative and political independence to Canada and other Commonwealth countries. Prohibition also helped to strengthen a Canadian nationalism that would steadily be built upon a defiance of America and its new-found continental and international power. Indeed, the uniquely (English) Canadian process of nationalistic self-identification would largely be forged by efforts to differentiate the country from the overshadowing American behemoth. The defiance exhibited by the Liberal government towards America's Prohibition laws, and its insolent role in undermining these laws, was driven in part by this emerging sense of Canadian identity. At the centre of this defiant nationalism was the Liberal Party of Canada and its politically astute and populist prime minister, William Lyon Mackenzie King, who led the patriotic cheerleading in the Dominion by obdurately refusing to bow to American pressure. In his repudiation of the United States, King showed he was more concerned with popular nationalistic sentiments, economic interests, and re-election, than kowtowing to the American government.

Unfortunately, the indifferent and often obstructionist position taken by the Dominion Government towards American and provincial temperance laws also fermented extensive lawlessness, organized criminality, violence, and corruption within Canada. As Ralph Allen wrote, "It took half a dozen years or more before Canada fully comprehended the impossibility of providing both an operating base and the raw materials for a multi-billion-dollar criminal industry while itself remaining untouched by the crimes involved." Under the banner "Why this Sinister Sloth?" the *Globe* editorialized in 1928 that, "not only does the Department of National Revenue continue to make possible large scale criminal operations against a friendly neighbour by its unrestricted issuance of liquor export clearances. It does so with a cynical disregard of the nullifying of such operations on the laws both of the Dominion of Canada and the various provinces." Through the charity extended to liquor smugglers, the Canadian government was instrumental in creating an environment that tolerated and even celebrated law-breaking. Paradoxically, the lawlessness that emerged in many parts of Canada belied the country's most defining characteristic — that of a law-abiding, peaceful, deferential people. Thus, in promoting a Canadian nationalism, a cherished symbol of the Canadian identity may have been further diluted.

It took a high-profile corruption scandal, a parliamentary inquiry, a Royal Commission, and the fall of the Liberal government to force federal politicians to realize the repercussions of their inactions. By the end of the 1920s, the Dominion Government was, according to Allan Everest, "waking up to the disagreeable fact that smuggling *into* Canada was on the increase, with a consequent breakdown in Canadian law enforcement and the loss of considerable revenue. American bootleggers, who were already breaking the laws of one country, saw no reason to observe those of Canada. Where once they went back to Canada with empty cars and boats, they now found double profits from smuggling in both directions." The minister of customs himself stated in 1925 that at least $50 million worth of smuggled goods entered Canada in the course of a year. As a 1926 article in *Maclean's* magazine reported, "Truck-loads of liquor are running to the United States, and truck-loads of silks, denims, radio supplies — even jewellery — are run into Canada, on the return trips. Smugglers soon learned that primary principle of economics of transportation, that it does not pay to return empty." The contraband goods being smuggling into Canada cost the Dominion Government millions of dollars in lost duty. Because these goods were sold on the black market at heavily discounted prices, Canadian businesses also suffered. The tardy enlargement of the Canadian government's enforcement efforts had less to do with American pressure, and more to do with a realization of the damage being inflicted on Canada by smuggling.

Among other things, Prohibition will be remembered for producing the greatest mass participation of the North American public in unlawful activity. It should have come as no surprise that even the most well-intentioned Prohibition laws would have little impact on consumption. Since Neolithic tribes discovered the fermentation process and began consuming berry wine around 6400 B.C., liquor has been the drug of choice. Government edicts were not going to change this. Temperance laws lacked the necessary acceptance by the majority. A small minority of moral reformers, social do-gooders, and political opportunists foisted a social and personal morality upon a recalcitrant population. Prohibition blurred the distinction between ordinary people and criminals. Because of Prohibition, otherwise law-abiding citizens were now breaking the law on a regular basis, without any significant repercussions or social stigmas. Many people were on the side of the bootleggers and in some places, according to Art Montague, smuggling was "so ingrained as a way of life that rumrunning was more acceptable social behaviour than trying to stop it." While many rumrunners and bootleggers may have been viewed innocently as outlaw heroes of the day, a more dangerous symbiotic relationship was being forged between organized crime and mainstream North American society.

Prohibition illuminates the monumental challenges societies face in their attempt to regulate vices. It also shows how outlawing such vices helps create and nurture organized crime. Prohibition demonstrated that no matter how illegal a product may be, or how much its supply is restricted, demand will persist. And if the price is right, there will always be someone to fill that demand. Because of the huge demand for booze, the criminal element in North America became larger, better organized, wealthier, and more powerful than ever before. Prohibition required a level of organization and sophistication that was not necessarily required for such pre-existing rackets as gambling, extortion, kidnapping, prostitution, or even drug smuggling. The contraband liquor industry flourished via a network of distillers, exporters, financiers, bootleggers, shippers, importers, retailers, transportation companies, banks, insurers, enforcers, and corrupt government officials.

Prohibition forged a more elaborate form of logistical organization for criminal entrepreneurs and, following repeal, this new organizational structure was carried over to other forms of criminal conspiracies, in particular drug trafficking. Ambitious efforts to coordinate the activities of different criminal organizations and to settle disputes, such as the Atlantic City Summit and the National Mafia Commission in the United States, would never have been needed or been possible, without Prohibition. The underground liquor trade also became international in scope, and this experience proved to be invaluable for future transnational criminal activities, such as the smuggling of narcotics, cigarettes, and people. Prohibition turned neighbourhood gangs into criminal empires. In short, Prohibition brought organized crime into the modern age, cementing it onto the North American landscape.

While Prohibition was responsible for launching many criminal organizations in Canada, the most notable of these did not evolve into the type of continuing and diversified criminal conspiracies witnessed in the U.S. following the repeal of temperance laws. Instead, most of the Canadian criminal syndicates dissolved, with their ringleaders and subordinates either retiring with their profits or returning to previous law-abiding occupations. Others moved on to fill the demand for other outlawed goods and services, such as drugs and gambling. For the next few decades, the Canadian criminal element would not be beholden to the large distillers and brewers. They would, instead, become subservient to the American mafia. As Canada was gradually pulled into the economic web of America, a similar process was occuring in the North American underworld.

PART III

ASCENDANCY

1933–1984

CHAPTER SIX

LA COSA NOSTRA COMES TO CANADA

The Ascendancy of the Italian Mafia in North America

By 1934, the dawn of a radically different criminal underworld had arrived in North America. Organized crime was now more widespread, more sophisticated, more entrepreneurial, more consensual, more transnational, and more Italian. Indeed, for the next fifty years, the so-called Italian mafia would become the single-most dominant organized criminal force in Canada and the United States. The mafia would become synonymous with organized crime and for good reason — it set the standard for all other crime groups that followed. The scope and influence of the mafia in North America was deemed so great during the postwar years, that some believed it constituted a single monolithic organization whose threat to the legal, economic, and moral values of democratic societies was second only to that of Communism. To investigate and counter this threat, there were at least five presidential or congressional commissions formed in the U.S. and at least six provincial or federal commissions in Canada between the end of the war and the early 1980s. To differentiate the American variety of Italian organized crime from its Sicilian foils, a distinctive new moniker — La Cosa Nostra — was applied by U.S. law enforcement in the early 1960s. Roughly translated from Italian as "this thing of ours" or "our

thing" (the abstract way mafia members referred to their secret criminal society), this sinister-sounding designation was created to help scare the public into supporting the war against organized crime waged by the Kennedy administration and led by Attorney General Robert Kennedy.

In Canada, most government officials were less alarmed by the threat posed by the Italian mafia. In fact, for many years the attitude of Canadian politicians and some senior police officers was to deny that an ongoing criminal conspiracy based on the principles of the Sicilian Mafia even existed in this country. Technically, they were correct. Unlike the United States, where the Cosa Nostra was primarily made up of Sicilians, most mafiosi in Canada were from Calabria, or at least could trace their roots to the Italian province. As such, the secret Italian criminal societies that arose in Canada beginning in the 1930s were mostly influenced by the traditions of the 'Ndgrangheta (although for the most part there is little difference between the customs and traits of the Sicilian and Calabrian Mafia).

There are many reasons why the Italian mafia reigned so supreme in the American and Canadian criminal underworlds in the decades that followed Prohibition. Their organizational structure incorporated a rational hierarchy, complete with a capable, ambitious, and visionary leadership, and a business-like approach that stressed entrepreneurship and the timely exploitation of any illegal or legal business opportunity that had the potential to make money. As Robert Stewart writes, the Cosa Nostra fashioned their money-making ventures "in a systematic, expansive, protracted, diversified and synergistic manner," which means that "the gambling operation feeds the loansharking operation, which in turn generates the debtor businessperson, who then forfeits his business, or the debtor warehouse worker who pinpoints a valuable item in storage to be stolen, or the debtor police officer who can be compromised and corrupted, etc., etc." This rational commercial infrastructure was complemented by emotionally grounded contrivances — in particular, membership in an exclusive secret society, and the use of the "family" as the core of each Italian crime group — which promoted shared bonds, values, and goals within each crime family and across different families that were a part of "this thing of ours." The Cosa Nostra also benefited greatly from the partnerships they formed with other like-minded criminals, regardless of their race, religion, ethnicity, nationality, or location. American and Canadian mafia groups effectively incorporated the essential tactics of organized crime, in particular the use of violence and corruption, while the code of *omerta* ensured other crucial tenets of a criminal organization — loyalty, discipline, and silence — were maintained to protect the mafia members from arrest and prosecution.

The steady stream of Italian immigrants into Canada and the United States also meant there was an abundance of prospects from which to recruit members. Most of these immigrants came from the mafia strongholds of Sicily and Calabria and, although only a small fraction were made members of the mafia or 'Ndrangheta, an intensive police crackdown on organized crime in Italy during the postwar years did result in an exodus of experienced mafiosi who would be influential in establishing the traditions of the secret societies in their adopted countries.

The Italian mobsters also learned the lessons of Prohibition better than anyone else: the biggest criminal profits were to be made by satisfying society's vices and, more specifically, by controlling the manufacture or wholesaling of illicit goods, while working towards a monopoly over a particular market or territory. Italian criminal groups emerged from Prohibition with a substantial financial war chest that was re-invested into a number of illegal and heavily regulated goods and services that were in high demand. As Richard Hammer writes, for criminal entrepreneurs the Great Depression of the 1930s was in some ways superior to the heady days of the 1920s in that the "racketeers were the dispensers of dreams and escape — in the form of alcohol, gambling, money, drugs and sex — and by the early thirties they had enormous wealth and clout."

The end of Prohibition had little effect on the emerging on the emerging mafia groups in Canada; they quickly capitalized on the increased costs of booze by providing a cheaper tax-free product that was produced in massive underground distilleries or was shipped in from abroad. It was illegal gambling and bookmaking, however, that became the single-reatest source of income for organized crime in the years immediately following Prohibition. Like booze, gambling enjoyed a popularity that cut across social classes and ethnic groups. The demand for commercial gambling outlets fuelled a dramatic increase in underground casinos, floating card games, illegal lotteries, and bookmaking operations. In 1938, the *Toronto Daily Star* ran a series entitled "Canada in the bookies' web," which investigated the "vast octopus of bookmaking" that spread from Montreal to Vancouver. Up until the end of the Second World War, the illegal gaming industry in Canada was characterized by pure competition; no one individual or group dominated. This changed at the end of the war as Italian-Canadian crime groups, backed by the money, organization, and muscle of the American mafia, began their hostile takeover of the independent professional gamblers and bookmakers. The takeover of illegal gaming in Canada by the Cosa Nostra was part of a larger plan: to gain control of ethnic Italian criminal organizations in the country, which could then be used as ground troops to monopolize the country's most profitable criminal rackets.

If any one individual can take credit for the Cosa Nostra's invasion of Canada, it was Charles Luciano, the far-sighted and highly ambitious American mobster who has been widely cited as the father of modern organized crime. Inspired by the Roman Empire, Lucky Luciano sought a comparable criminal dynasty and in 1933 even created a governing Mafia Commission in the U.S. Made up of the heads of the major mafia families in New York and other American cities, the Commission acted as a sort of board of directors for the Cosa Nostra and, although it had little formal powers, it was respected enough to mete out binding decisions in disputes that arose between different families. Luciano's grand vision also resulted in the partitioning of the United States and Canada into twenty-four separate regions, each of which would be under the jurisdiction of a particular mafia family. The implication for Canada was that it would be treated as a protectorate of the Cosa Nostra. As a result, the Montreal mafia became a wing of New York's Bonanno Family, southwestern Ontario fell under the influence of the Detroit mob, while the rest of Ontario's underworld became the fiefdom of Buffalo's mafia boss Stefano Magaddino.

The servitude of Italian-Canadian crime groups to their American counterparts escalated in the early 1950s when a crackdown on organized crime in the U.S. prompted mafia leaders in that country to relocate many of their illegal gaming operations to Quebec and Ontario. Independent professional gamblers and bookmakers in Canada were put out of business, or at the very least were forced to pay a percentage of their revenues to the Cosa Nostra. Canada was also established as a major "lay-off" centre for the American mafia's bookmaking operations (a "lay-off man" takes bets from other bookmakers who are trying to insure against heavy losses, if one horse or sports team receives heavy betting, by placing bets on the favourite with the layoff man). Through their expansion into Canada and Cuba, their move into Las Vegas, as well as shrewd investments in national and international wire services (which instantaneously transmitted information on sporting events), the Cosa Nostra created an international gambling and bookmaking network the likes of which had never been seen. As Alan Phillips wrote in a 1964 *Maclean's* article, "this underworld federation is first and foremost a gambling cartel, a monopoly so well-concealed that some policemen refuse it credence. Gamblers call it 'The Combination.' Through a network of affiliates, a small bettor

Charles "Lucky" Luciano

in Saskatchewan can bet on a fight in Sweden, a dog race in Florida, or a horse running on any track in America."

The American mafia also began taking over other criminal rackets in Canada. As RCMP commissioner Clifford Harvison stated in a well-publicized address to the Canadian Club in Toronto on November 6, 1961: "the American syndicates are showing an increased interest in Canada and they are moving to take over direct control of some existing criminal organizations and to expand their criminal activities. They are already active in the field of gambling, narcotics trafficking, counterfeiting, and in the protection rackets. There are some indications and there is some evidence that the syndicates have already started to treat Canada as an area for expansion of their activities." Commissioner Harvison's comments prompted President John F. Kennedy to remark in 1962 that his administration's war against organized crime must be succeeding if so many gangsters were fleeing to Canada.

THE CANADIAN CONNECTION

In addition to incorporating Canada into its gambling network, the Cosa Nostra was establishing its northern neighbour as a part of its international pipeline for drugs smuggled into the United States. Throughout the 1930s, Canada's coastlines and official maritime ports were well-travelled entry points for opium exported from Asia and morphine and heroin processed in Europe. The illegal drug supply dwindled precipitously during the war years, but by its end, the amount of opium, morphine, and heroin smuggled into Canada escalated to unprecedented levels. By 1947, the number of RCMP investigations under the *Opium and Narcotic Drug Act* had jumped by 40 percent over the previous year and in 1949 they increased by another 28 percent. The spike in supply was due to a heightened demand, which stemmed from the return of thousands of morphine-addicted war veterans and a rise in drug-friendly counterculture movements such as the beatniks. Supply also increased as the end of the war meant fewer obstacles to production in Southeast and Southwest Asia as well as the escalation of merchant shipping. The sheer profitability of the heroin trade also contributed to an abundance in supply; wholesalers paying US$3,500 for a kilo of heroin in Europe were generating revenues as high as $40,000 a kilo once it was diluted and sold on Canadian streets. A final reason the heroin supply increased in the postwar years was that production, smuggling, and wholesale distribution became concentrated in the hands of a confederation of drug trafficking syndicates — the French *L'Union Corse*, the Sicilian Mafia, the American Cosa Nostra and the Canadian 'Ndrangheta — that together constituted one of the longest ongoing heroin trafficking conspiracies of all time.

At the start of the 1940s, Italian mafia families in the U.S. and Canada began supplanting Jewish groups as the largest illegal dispensers of opiates and, for the next forty years, they held an almost complete monopoly over the wholesale distribution of Turkish heroin in both countries. Their main suppliers were French Corsicans, who had become the world's biggest heroin producers. The criminal syndicate behind what would be called the French Connection was *L'Union Corse*, so named because most of its leaders and members hailed from Corsica, an island located southeast of France in the Mediterranean Sea. *L'Union Corse* rivalled the Sicilian mafia in terms of the scope of its criminal operation and, according to a 1972 edition of *Time* magazine, it "is more tightly knit and more secretive than its Sicilian

counterpart." Following the end of the Second World War, *L'Union Corse* was making millions from its various illegal ventures, which included theft, extortion, counterfeiting, gambling, prostitution, immigrant smuggling, and its most profitable enterprise, heroin trafficking. The group was able to operate unfettered for years due to its infiltration of local, regional, and national government agencies in France.

Until the mid-1970s, the world capital for heroin production and distribution was the French port city of Marseilles. Located less than an hour's plane ride from Corsica and with direct maritime connections to opium sources in Southwest Asia and to heroin markets in North America, Marseilles became the hub for the conversion of Turkish opium and Lebanese morphine into heroin. Those who took a leading role in the *L'Union Corse*, such as François Spirito, Paul Carbone, Joseph Orsini, Paul Mondolini, Antoine d'Agostino, and Jean Jehan, were responsible for supplying thousands of kilos of heroin during the height of the French Connection in the 1950s and 1960s. Carbone and Spirito were the original forces behind *L'Union Corse* and its foray into heroin production and smuggling. During the 1920s, they began importing opium from Turkey and morphine from Lebanon or Germany, which was converted into heroin in labs in Paris. Following a temporary interruption in the heroin trade because of the war (during which time Carbone was killed by the French Resistance after it was discovered that he and Spirito was collaborating with the Nazis), Spirito and his lieutenant Joseph Orsini organized the many independent opium smugglers and heroin processors into a centralized syndicate and set up processing plants in Marseilles. They also entered into a partnership with Corsican crime lord Joseph Renucci, who had connections with opium and morphine suppliers in Turkey and Lebanon as well as a powerful friend in Charles Luciano, who was now setting up his own drug smuggling networks. By the end of the 1940s, a seamless international narcotics cartel was in place whereby brokers working on behalf of the Corsicans purchased opium in Turkey, which would be smuggled into Syria or Lebanon to be processed into morphine, and then shipped to one of the many clandestine laboratories in Marseilles, where it would be processed into heroin and then smuggled to the U.S. and Canada.

Quebec's cultural, commercial, and linguistic ties to France, the subservience of the mafia in the province to the American Cosa Nostra, as well as Montreal's inviting seaports and close proximity to New York, made the city a major entry point for heroin being shipped into North America. According to a 1963 U.S. Senate Committee on organized crime, "in the early 1950's, the clandestine processing of heroin from morphine base had shifted to the hands of the French Corsican traffickers, along with a substantial share of the import trade into the United States. The advent of the Corsicans as major traffickers brought changes in the smuggling operations; for years, the main port of entry had been New York but now the French Corsicans supplied the drugs to their French-speaking Canadian confederates for smuggling into the United States." One of the first French-Canadian customers of the Corsicans was Lucien Rivard, who in turn was supplying two of Canada's biggest heroin dealers in the immediate postwar years: the Mallock brothers.

George Mallock

John and George Mallock originally hailed from Winnipeg where they were well known to local police as small-time criminals. Around 1947, John began dealing small amounts of heroin in Winnipeg while his brother was serving time for assault. Business prospered and as the revenues accumulated, he built his own drug-dealing organization, forcing out competition in Manitoba and then moving into Saskatchewan and Alberta. When George Mallock was released from jail in 1949, John was already one of the biggest heroin traffickers in the prairie provinces. The two brothers then struck out on an even more ambitious quest: to take over the lucrative heroin traffic in British Columbia. According to a 1950 RCMP report, during the summer of that year, the Mallock brothers "took up residence in Vancouver and set out to take control of the distribution of illicit narcotics in that city with the intention of eventually extending their operations into the Western United States." While John was organizing new deliveries through Lucien Rivard, George and another member of his trafficking network, named William Carter, were supplying street-level dealers in Vancouver and Seattle. By July, the Seattle office of the U.S. Bureau of Narcotics was alerted to their presence in the city and one of their agents, Henry L. Giordano (who would later head the bureau), was dispatched to Vancouver as part of an undercover operation. Through a police agent, Giordano was introduced to Carter and, in September of that year, he purchased an ounce of heroin from him. This led to the arrest of Carter and then the Mallock brothers after police discovered in George Mallock's possession $500 in the marked money that was used to buy the drugs. Police also seized heroin with an estimated street value of $20,000 from George's common-law wife.

A judge set the Mallock brothers' bail at $20,000 each, but they easily raised the funds, while leaving behind their destitute partner, William Carter. When their trial began on January 30, 1951, John and George were nowhere to be seen and bench warrants were issued for their arrests. While the two were on the run, Carter was convicted and sentenced to seven years. By the end of November 1951, the RCMP had learned that the brothers had managed to sneak into the United States, with the help of Lucien Rivard, although it wasn't until late 1953 that George was captured. Even while on the lam, they were working on drug deals; George visited Rivard in Montreal in September 1953 where he purchased a kilo that was sent to Winnipeg, while John had travelled to Mexico to purchase heroin there. While in Montreal, George Mallock was also buying directly from Corsican Antoine d'Agostino, who was emerging as a major heroin supplier to Canadian dealers. In 1953, George was arrested in New York City along with d'Agostino's chief courier, and was extradited to Vancouver where he was sentenced to twenty-one years in March 1954. His brother's trail was picked up in Mexico, but before he could be arrested, he died just a month after George's conviction. Some believe the highly suspicious car accident that took John Mallock's life was orchestrated by d'Agostino, who exacted revenge when he was never fully paid by John for five kilos of heroin he purchased from d'Agostino.

John Mallock

In addition to the Mallock brothers, Rivard was supplying members of the Montreal mafia. Throughout the 1950s, the Cosa Nostra and its Canadian branches were the biggest patrons of the heroin trafficking arm

of *L'Union Corse* and their relationship was highly flexible. On some occasions, the Corsicans arranged to smuggle the drugs out of Europe to New York or Montreal, where it would be wholesaled to mafia groups. On other occasions, individual members of American and Canadian mafia groups coordinated the smuggling, which sometimes entailed working through a Sicilian intermediary. Regardless, by the end of the 1950s, the mafia had a stranglehold on the wholesale distribution of Corsican-processed heroin in the United States and Canada.

In addition to the Corsicans, Charlie Luciano was also behind the massive postwar heroin trade. Despite his varied career as a mobster, he actually began as a drug trafficker and was first convicted in 1915, at the age of eighteen, for selling morphine and heroin. By the mid-1920s, he and another prolific mafia narcotics dealer named Vito Genovese were financing heroin shipments to America. When Prohibition ended, Luciano ramped up his drug trafficking activities, negotiating deals with Corsican suppliers Spirito and Carbone, diverting legally produced heroin from Italian pharmaceutical firms (a 1950 investigation by the Bureau of Narcotics alleged that over a four-year period at least 700 kilos of heroin had been supplied to Luciano from the Schiaparelli drug company), and working with his Cosa Nostra colleagues to set up distribution networks in the U.S. When Luciano was deported to Italy in January of 1946, he began working with mafia families in Sicily to import opium from Turkey and the Far East, as well as morphine from Lebanon. Freighters would offload the opium or morphine to fishing boats waiting off the coast of Sicily, and once on shore, the drugs would be transported to heroin processing labs, like the one in Palermo that was disguised as a candy factory. Luciano was also organizing what was called the "American Colony," a network of other deported Italian-Americans who he posted throughout Italian and French ports to coordinate drug shipments back to the U.S. in tandem with New York's Lucchese, Genovese, and Gambino families.

A major turning point in the development of the international heroin trade, and Canada's role in the trade, purportedly occurred over a four-day period in October 1957 when Luciano hosted meetings in

Palermo at the Grand Hôtel des Palmes. Attending the meeting were a delegation of American mafia leaders, most notably Joe Bonanno and his underboss Carmine Galante, as well as Sicilian mafiosi Gaetano Badalamenti and Tommasso Buscetta. Among the outcomes of the meeting was the establishment of a transatlantic heroin trafficking accord between Sicilian and North American mafia families to smuggle heroin from Marseilles to Sicily and then to the United States and Canada. The FBI believed it was at this meeting that Joseph Bonanno was convinced to participate in the Cosa Nostra's international heroin trafficking network. Whether this claim is true, there is no doubt that starting in the late 1950s, members of the Bonanno Family in New York and Montreal became much more active in organizing the importation and distribution of heroin, which significantly increased Montreal's role as a North American access point for European-processed heroin.

As Lee Lamothe and Adrian Humphreys write, Gaetano Badalamenti was highly receptive to the partnership, recognizing the American market for heroin would generate untold profits for the Sicilian families. However, the greedy Badalamenti made a decision behind the back of his American mafia partners that escalated the role of Canada in the new global heroin trafficking hierarchy even further. He directed his underling Tommasso Buscetta to travel to North America, but "rather than deal strictly through the Bonanno Family receivers, Buscetta was instructed to create a parallel pipeline from Sicily to Montreal, Windsor, Toronto and, from there, into the United States. Both networks would pass through Canada en route to America." The result of this historic meeting, according to the 1963 Senate committee, was the establishment of a well-coordinated and highly flexible international trafficking conspiracy whereby heroin manufactured in Marseilles would take what the committed described as "one of several routes toward its eventual destination in the United States. A large part of the heroin is sold by the Corsican racketeers to their close associates, the mafia traffickers in mainland Italy or in Sicily. From any of a number of Italian seaports — Naples, Milan, Genoa, Palermo, Rome — shipments are routed to this country by way of certain ports of entry — notably New York and other Atlantic seaboard ports, Montreal or Toronto in Canada, or Mexico City. The French traffickers also deal directly with heroin buyers in the United States, Canada, and Mexico."

The Palermo meeting was followed a month later by a summit of Cosa Nostra leaders from every corner of America and Canada. Held at mafia associate Joseph Barbara's country estate in the town of Apalachin in upstate New York, it has been asserted that one of the purposes of the meeting was to hammer out the details for the distribution of the heroin in America and Canada by the different mafia families. Some believe that the decisions made at this meeting reaffirmed the use of Ontario and Quebec as landing and distribution points for heroin destined to the United States. Facilitating the importation of the heroin into Canada were the branch plants of the American Cosa Nostra — the Cotroni group in Montreal, which reported to the Bonanno Family, and in Ontario, Anthony Sylvestro, the Agueci brothers and John Papalia, who reported to Stefano Magaddino in Buffalo, but who also worked with New York City's Genovese Family.

The U.S. Bureau of Narcotics estimated that between the end of the Second World War and 1963, the Cosa Nostra was responsible for 95 percent of all the heroin smuggled into the United States. While this estimate may be a slight exaggeration, what cannot be denied is that during roughly the same period, police in United States and Canada investigated dozens of major importation conspiracies that brought in thousands of kilos of almost pure heroin and which led to the conviction of more than three hundred people in the two countries. Many of these were "made" members of mafia families. As illegal drug use skyrocketed throughout the 1960s and 1970s, Montreal and Toronto continued to serve as conduits for European heroin imported into North America. The only difference was that the mode of transportation had shifted from the sea to the air, which meant that airports in both cities became the sites for some of the biggest heroin busts in the country.

In 1971, the Nixon administration persuaded Turkey to ban the cultivation of opium in exchange for subsidization of alternative crops. That same year, an official agreement was reached with French authorities to crack down on the extensive heroin processing and trafficking network based in Marseilles. The result of these measures was a major reorganization of heroin trafficking: Turkey was replaced as the chief supplier of heroin by the "golden triangle" of Thailand, Burma, and Laos and the "golden crescent" of Pakistan, Iran, and Afghanistan. The breakup of *L'Union Corse* provided the Sicilian and American mafia families with an even greater monopoly over the Southwest Asian heroin traffic and Sicily resumed its role as a major heroin processor in the mid-1970s. By the late 1970s, Sicilian Mafia families in partnership with their American colleagues, and the Bonanno Family in particular, established another massive heroin importation conspiracy, which came to be known as the Pizza Connection because much of the heroin that made it into America was sold through mafia-connected pizza parlours.

The disruption of the Pizza Connection by American and Italian law enforcement signalled the end of the mafia's dominance in the global heroin trade. But the international heroin partnership forged between the French Corsicans, the Sicilian Mafia, the Cosa Nostra and its Canadian subsidiaries in the postwar period remains one of the biggest ongoing drug trafficking conspiracies in the 20th century. It not only transformed Italian organized crime and modernized the international narcotics trade, but it gave Canada and Canadian mobsters a pivotal role in the global heroin traffic, while further pulling the country's criminal underworld into the orbit of the Cosa Nostra.

CHAPTER SEVEN
ÂLLO POLICE
The Montreal Mafia and Other Crime Organisé in Quebec

RUM ON THE ST. LAWRENCE

Despite the end of Prohibition, contraband liquor continued to be one of most profitable sources of illegal revenue for criminal groups in Quebec. While the American market dried up for Canadian bootleggers, a steady increase in liquor taxes at home reinvigorated a domestic contraband market. And in what can be considered a case of Canadian karma, the increased liquor taxes spurred the smuggling of low-cost booze from St. Pierre and Miquelon, the United States, and the West Indies into Canada. With a vast smuggling infrastructure already in place, and the opening of the St. Lawrence Seaway as a shipping route in 1937, Montreal was the destination of choice for fleets of motorboats that transported thousands of cases of booze into the city on a monthly basis. In its annual report for 1938, the RCMP acknowledged there was "considerable" liquor smuggling activity in the Lower St. Lawrence River "most of which was brought over by larger vessels from St. Pierre and Miquelon. No fewer than sixteen contact boats were seized in the Lower St. Lawrence, twelve of which were forfeited for having smuggled liquor on board, and destroyed."

During the 1930s, the biggest illegal-liquor dealer in Montreal was Joe Normandin, who, according to the same RCMP report, "had been engaged in the traffic for a number of years and had built up a complicated system which made it extremely difficult to secure information regarding his activities." After several truckloads of liquor were seized by the Mounties in 1936, Normandin was arrested, convicted, and sentenced to four months in jail and fined $2,000. In 1937, he was freed after his lawyers successfully appealed the conviction and, upon release, he immediately returned to peddling illegal liquor. His network of bootleggers was now under intense law enforcement scrutiny, however, which resulted in more liquor seizures and arrests. On August 24, 1937, a truck carrying 97 gallons of alcohol was stopped by police and one of Normandin's drivers was charged and sentenced to twelve months. On November 12, 1937, the RCMP discovered 3,034 gallons of illegally imported American and European spirits in the basement of a west end Montreal home. The ensuing investigation linked the cache to Normandin, who was again arrested and charged. A month later, police stopped another one of his trucks with more than 321 gallons of illicit liquor and Normandin on board. He tried to escape but was captured and once again placed under arrest. This time, he was sentenced to twelve months in jail, which was to run concurrent with his previous sentences.

Large quantities of smuggled liquor destined for Quebec were also being landed in the Maritimes. In its 1938 annual report, the RCMP wrote, "liquor vessels were quite active throughout the entire navigation season off the coasts of the three Maritime Provinces. The bulk of the shipments apparently originated at Mt. Martin's French West Indies, which has become the chief point of trans-shipment for rum intended for the Canadian trade." Mother ships hovered in international waters, while under the cover of darkness "cargoes of alcohol and mixed liquors are illegally loaded on schooners and motor boats." These cargoes were then landed on the shores of Cape Breton, the northern coast of New Brunswick and Quebec, and in the Bay of Fundy.

A 1936 report by the Canadian Department of Transport described how the S.S. *Reidun*, flying the Norwegian flag, unloaded a cargo of more than 30,000 cases of liquor in international waters off the coast of Nova Scotia between November 10 and 13, 1935. Over the course of those four days, five Canadian-registered speedboats made several trips to relieve the freighter of its cargo. The *Reidun* had been charted by the Shaw Steamship Line of Nova Scotia, and an employee of the company was reported to have boarded the vessel 100 miles off St. Pierre to oversee the offloading onto the smaller boats. The Department of Transport had evidence that Shaw Steamship Line had chartered at least two other freighters for similar purposes, including the *Trajan* (which offloaded 14,838 cases of spirits) and the *Anders* (5,085 cases). All of the cargo was ultimately delivered to Montreal. In 1939, the RCMP initiated an extensive investigation targeting what they considered to be the single-largest liquor smuggling organization operating off Canada's east coast. By the end of the year, charges were laid against forty-eight people, of whom forty-two were convicted. Thousands of gallons of liquor were confiscated, as were numerous ships, most of which were forfeited to the Crown. The organization's smuggling activities were so widespread that as part of the investigation the RCMP examined approximately 75,000 postal money orders, 50,000 railway express delivery receipts, 50,000 express waybills, and 15,000 postal money orders.

Those who preferred to avoid the risk of smuggling liquor into the country set up illegal distilleries. On the afternoon of September 16, 1937, Quebec Liquor Commission officers seized a large commercial still in the Rosemount district of Montreal and arrested Romeo Berube of Montreal, Max Bittman of Cleveland, and Robert McCullen of New York. A fourth man, who had the misfortune of arriving with a truckload of sugar, molasses, and yeast just after the provincial officials showed up, was also arrested. The still was located at the rear of a bankrupt bakery called Mother's Tasty Pies. The bakery had been purchased by the bootleggers and its former owner was paid to reopen it as a cover for their illegal liquor production. After being handed two-year terms, Bittman and McCullen sought to reduce their sentences by providing information on a province-wide network of stills of which they were only a small part. An investigation was launched that led to the arrest of six more men on conspiracy charges. Among them were Sam Chernoff and Robert Pageau. Chernoff was already well known to Quebec police, having been arrested in 1934 on charges of conspiring to defraud the government of $250,000 by illegally importing 15,000 gallons of alcohol from the United States. After a long court case, all were convicted; Chernoff was sentenced to three years and Pageau to two. Other investigations that spun off from this case resulted in the arrest of another forty-five people who were tied to the province-wide network. Police marvelled at the scope and sophistication of the operation; experienced American engineers were brought in to build commercial-capacity stills; numerous bankrupt businesses were purchased as fronts; elaborate distribution schemes that transported the liquor across the province were set up; and an insurance policy of weekly payments of $25 were made to the families of any of the conspirators arrested and jailed.

By the start of the Second World War, the majority of the contraband liquor available in Canada was smuggled into the country, due to the domestic rationing of ingredients necessary for homemade distilling, such as sugar or molasses. In addition to liquor, numerous other products were being smuggled into the country because of shortages of goods or outright bans that were in place due to wartime conditions.

Among the contraband most frequently seized by border officials were tobacco products, tea, coffee, silks and other textiles, cars and car parts, and household electrical appliances. In addition to goods that were being smuggled in, Canada was also a source of contraband for black markets in wartorn Great Britain and Europe. An April 5, 1943 memo from the Paymaster Captain of the Canadian Navy read, "large scale smuggling of tea, tobacco and cigarettes has recently been discovered in N. Ireland" and the "Canadian corvettes are alleged to be the worst offenders." The majority of contraband cigarettes found in the U.K. "are American or Canadian and one 25 lb. case of tea is addressed to N.S.O., Halifax, and is still wire bound." The memo ends with a request from the British Admiralty that steps be taken to warn "the Masters and crews of H.M. Canadian ships of the serious consequences which may follow detection of such trafficking."

In the postwar period, cigarettes became the commodity of choice for most smugglers, once again owing to Canadian tax hikes that increased the cost of a pack to an all-time high. The enormous volume of cigarettes illegally crossing the border pushed seizures under the *Customs and Excise Act* to their highest level since statistics were maintained. In 1945, more than 3,223 seizure reports were made by federal agencies, an increase of 722 cases over the previous year. This escalation, according to a RCMP report, is largely "accounted for by the increased number of seizures made of non-duty paid cigarettes entering from the U.S.A." While a large proportion of these seizures were from individuals bringing tobacco products across the border for personal use, the RCMP also investigated a number of well-organized cigarette smuggling operations. In 1950, more than 450,000 cigarettes were seized from one smuggling group alone. During the late 1940s and early 1950s, the RCMP was also busy investigating groups that were smuggling new cars, stolen in the United States, into Canada.

In 1954, concurrent investigations in Quebec and New York uncovered what police called a $3-million black market in babies in which more than one thousand were smuggled out of Montreal and then sold in the U.S. over a ten-year period. According to a Canadian Press report that year, information obtained by police indicated that most of the babies were sold in the United States to Jewish couples "who were led to believe the French-Canadian and other Christian infants were born of parents of the Jewish faith." The American buyers reportedly paid from $3,000 to $10,000 for each baby. Most of the infants were said to have come from unwed mothers in Quebec who were "given amounts up to $50 and their living-in expenses paid," the Canadian Press article stated. "Others had their babies snatched away virtually without the mothers' consent." The infant racketeering schemes included the falsification of birth records and involved lawyers, doctors, nurses, and nursing-home operators. "The rings are said to have thrived because official child-placement agencies in the United States have long waiting lists, particularly of Jewish couples."

THE VICE CAPITAL OF CANADA

Contraband liquor, untaxed cigarettes, and black market babies were not the only revenue generators for organized criminals in Quebec following the end of Prohibition. Throughout the Great Depression, the Second World War, and the postwar years, Montreal's vice economy continued to thrive. Despite judicial inquiries, new laws, and intensified police enforcement, the city's reputation as a "wide-open town," the "vice capital of Canada," and the "Paris of North America" remained intact. As Alan Phillips wrote in his 1963 exposé on organized crime in Canada, the city's "two hundred night clubs offered entertainment second only to New York. Its bordellos were famous. Its wide-open dice games drew an international clientele. You could bet any sum on a game or a horse through fifty-some wire-serviced bookmakers." Montreal's reputation as a sink of iniquity was bolstered during the postwar years with the invasion of American mobsters, who brought with them scores of bookmakers, crooked stockbrokers, strong-arm crews, and heroin importers. At the vanguard of the American interlopers were senior members of the Cosa Nostra, who carried across the border ambitions to take over and consolidate Montreal's rackets. Responsibility for overseeing the Quebec interests of the American mafia was eventually delegated to a man who went on to become perhaps the most successful and powerful mafioso in Canadian history: Vincenzo Cotroni. As the head of the Canadian wing of New York City's Bonanno Family,

Cotroni ruled over a criminal empire that lasted more than forty years.

The foundation for Vic Cotroni's ascension as Canada's leading mafia don was Montreal's gambling and bookmaking industry, which expanded dramatically throughout the 1940s and 1950s due to a number of reasons. This included the large number of troops transiting through the city on their way to and from Europe, the introduction of long-distance telephone and the wire service, a crackdown on illegal gambling in the United States, and the consolidation of Quebec's betting operations by well-oiled American syndicates. By the mid-1940s, a gambler could lay a bet in one of over two hundred establishments in greater Montreal that collectively generated $100 million a year in revenue. A 1946 *Time* magazine article describes how gambling at the luxurious Mount Royal Bridge Club, located in a small municipality just beyond the westernmost limits of the city, often took in as much as $100,000 on weekends through its crap games and roulette wheels. A series of *Montreal Gazette* articles published in the summer of 1945 reported that during their peak periods between 9 p.m. and 4 a.m., the city's barbotte houses — so named after a dice game similar to craps — employed close to four hundred people who collected $75,000 in bets every hour. One of the largest barbotte houses, the University Bridge Club, located at 1222 University Street, "is always open and you can walk in as easily as in any local store," a *Gazette* reporter observed. "After climbing a flight of stairs, you are welcomed by the checkroom attendant, who directs you politely to the first smoke filled room where the 'big' table is." With single bets as high as $1,000 and an average of about $4,700 on the table for each roll of the dice, clients who placed less than $25 on the table were generally frowned upon. To accommodate players, most of the barbotte houses had their own restaurant with waitresses who brought sandwiches and soft drinks to the players so that they would not lose their seats at the table. In addition to gambling, the *Gazette* reported, barbotte houses also sold many other "commodities rarely seen in law-abiding places."

In addition to these clubs, there were the floating barbotte games that were ferried from one location to another by taxis and moving companies in only a matter of minutes. For those who preferred to play the lottery, Montreal's Chinatown was the place to be. Lottery tickets were available from numerous Chinese merchants, with draws occurring at 2:30 p.m., 8:30 p.m., and 11:30 p.m. For those too impatient to wait, "quick draws" were offered. Gamblers in Montreal also had the luxury of betting on horse races from all across North America through local bookmakers equipped with long-distance telephone and telegraph connections, including one who had been lodged for years in a building at the corner of Ontario and St. Lawrence and who shared office space with a printer that supplied racing sheets.

Between July 5 and July 18, 1945, police raided forty-two gambling houses in Montreal, arresting 515 people. Since most of the charges were not for criminal infractions, the majority of those taken into custody were released after pleading guilty and paying a $100 fine (for the operators) or a $25 fine (for the "found-ins"). The *Gazette* estimated that during the mid-1940s, the city of Montreal took in approximately $300,000 annually in fines against those "found guilty of offences against morality — that is gambling and prostitution." As in years past, police and other city officials were accused of lacking a serious commitment to shutting down the underground gambling halls, which was evidenced by the small fines, the absence of jail time, and the fact that most operations were up-and-running twenty-four hours (or sooner) after they had been raided by police. One press report described how, following a police raid at 9:30 p.m. on a Wednesday night in July 1945, the University Bridge Club was "going 'wide open' again" by midnight with more than one hundred clients "crowding around the same four tables that have been there for some months." It continued its operations as usual on Thursday "while its alleged operator and 37 found-ins were being arraigned in Recorder's Court." On September 28, 1945, the morality squad padlocked thirty-one barbotte houses in raids that lasted from the early afternoon to midnight. By October 2, the *Gazette* noted that twenty-one of the games that had supposedly been shut down were "still going openly at the same locations as before while two others [had] moved to a nearby address after leaving a man to give the new location to all comers. Three establishments are really closed while one of the civic addresses given by police as having been padlocked does not exist." After its original location was padlocked by police, the University Bridge Club moved to a nearby street. Reporters visiting the old address found a man casually sitting at a small table providing the new address to anyone unaware of the move.

The lax enforcement of the law on gambling operations was epitomized by a commonly used law that mockingly became known as the "comedy of padlocks." Municipal statutes stipulated that police must padlock establishments that provided illegal gambling or prostitution if two offences had been committed in the span of twelve months. However, these ordinances were easily circumvented by crafty operators working in tandem with corrupt government officials. Padlocks were fastened to dummy doors, brick walls, kitchen cupboards, and, in one case, a tool shed located behind a building. In some establishments, gamblers were inconvenienced when the only room available to padlock was the coatroom, or worse, the bathroom. A screwdriver was always handy in one apartment building that housed numerous barbotte games to quickly remove the numbers from the apartment doors to be padlocked so they could be fastened to others that were empty. Before long, the barbotte operator found this too inconvenient and simply had all the apartment door numbers written in chalk. Two newspaper reporters who visited six establishments that were supposed to have been padlocked a day earlier found five of them still open while the sixth had moved to another location. As they walked up the stairs of one barbotte house, the reporters spotted a set of double doors. On one of the doors was a padlock and a court-ordered seal marked "closed by police." As they went in through the adjoining unlocked door, they realized that it opened onto the same room as the sealed door. Once inside they found the room filled with dice-throwing players crowded around four tables.

Allegations of lackadaisical enforcement, protection of gambling operations, and corruption within the Montreal police force resulted in yet another public inquiry — the Commission of Inquiry into Gambling and Commercialized Vice in Montreal — this one held between 1950 and 1953 under Justice François Caron. One long-time manager of a gambling house testified before the inquiry that the officer in charge of a police raiding party was normally "given a $20 or a $50 bill as a tip from the management of the house." The witness made it clear that this was not a bribe to the police officers, however. "It was just for being gentlemen and carrying out their duties."

The morality squad of the Montreal police was also accused of receiving bribes from Chinese lottery houses, each of which was charged a monthly $100 levy by leading Chinatown merchants who then passed the graft money to police officials. Deals were purportedly arranged between some gaming operators and city police whereby the former would be allowed to operate unfettered, as long as the latter were given the opportunity to conduct "show raids" every so often. During these raids, the management of a gambling house would offer up "stooges" or "straws" who would be arrested. Because police also had to show they were seizing prohibited gaming equipment, the gambling house operators offered up old decks of cards, dice, chips, roulette wheels, folding tables, and even "dummy tables" that were prepared by carpenters who were kept on staff for such purposes. A member of the police morality squad told the commission that when raiding a brothel, they ordinarily arrested the woman who opened the door. One forty-seven-year-old housekeeper who worked in many of the twenty-four brothels operated by Montreal's most enterprising madam, Anna Beauchamp, admitted that she had been arrested on eighty-five separate occasions. Mme Beauchamp was a familiar figure at the courthouse. The flamboyant brothel operator would arrive in her chauffeur-driven Cadillac and then stride down the corridors in her mink coat, swinging a large red handbag. Before she paid the fine for her "straw women," she would chat with the other madams and police officers to whom she would provide advice on which brothels should be raided in the upcoming month.

Barney Shulkin, who had worked for fifteen years as a slip writer at one of Montreal's largest bookmaking operations at 286 St. Catherine Street West, was informed by the commission that, before 1947, he had been convicted 102 times as a keeper of a betting house. He told the inquiry that this number sounded about right to him, but he assured the commissioners he never spent any time in jail, except on those occasions when he had to wait in the holding cell before his boss, Louis Klitzner, came to pay his bail or fine. When questioned, Shulkin told the inquiry he made $30 a week, but denied it was part of his job to be arrested:

Q: How can you explain that you were arrested so many times as keeper of the "book?"

Shulkin: I don't know. I think it's because the informer always picked on me.

Q: What happened when the police raided the place?

Shulkin: Well, they rushed in, and everybody was scared.

Q: Were you scared, too?

Shulkin: Sure, I was scared. You see them come in like that. Some of the people tried to run away, others wanted to jump out the window.

Q: But you weren't sufficiently scared to quit?

Shulkin: Well, it's a living. I have to work.

Q: What did the police do when they raided the place?

Shulkin: They rushed for the counter and took the money on the counter, and then they lined up everybody and the fellow in charge of morality took the names.

Q: After the police raid what happened?

Shulkin: All the people went out and we were left alone.

Q: Who was left alone?

Shulkin: The keeper and employees. Naturally, half an hour later they came back.

Q: Who came back?

Shulkin: Why, the people who were betting.

Q: Did the police come back?

Shulkin: Oh, no. But maybe they went to visit some other place.

"THE HORSES FORGOT TO WIN"

Before the takeover of Montreal's vice rackets by the American mafia, many of the city's gambling and bookmaking operations were run by Jewish syndicates. Upon his release from prison in the mid-1940s, Harry Davis resumed his position as Montreal's most powerful gambling czar. Not only did he run his own gaming houses, but he had a say in who else could operate in the city's red-light district and received an estimated 20 percent of the net returns from other gambling operators. Davis was also an investor in the largest gambling house in all of Greater Montreal, the Mount Royal Bridge Club. The sprawling edifice, which was built on rural property in the Montreal suburb of Côte Saint-Luc at an estimated cost of $100,000, was located directly across the road from the home of the town's police chief and lone constable. A 1945 *Montreal Gazette* article describes how taxi drivers were paid double their fare to transport customers to the club, which included "hundreds of prominent citizens." Opened in the summer of 1944 by "a powerful syndicate headed by a local sports promoter and a Toronto operator," the building was subdivided into several rooms, had a capacity of close to 150 people, and featured craps, roulette wheels, *chemin de fer,* and barbotte. The death of Harry Davis in 1946 sparked an even greater proliferation of gambling venues in Montreal, as the profit potential increased due to the elimination of Davis' automatic cut. Eddie Baker, who ran a bookmaking operation at 362 Notre Dame Street West, attempted to fill the void left by the death of his old drug trafficking colleague by demanding protection money from barbotte operators. But Baker was outmanoeuvred by a rival named Harry Ship, who would go on to become the new "King of the Montreal Gamblers." It was also Ship who would inadvertently provide the beachhead that allowed for the takeover of Montreal's underworld by the Cosa Nostra.

Born in 1915, Harry Ship was a mathematics student at Queen's University before dropping out and beginning a career as a bookmaker's clerk. Although little is known about Ship, he possessed a number of attributes that propelled him to prominence among professional gamblers in Montreal: he had a great mind for business, was well respected among his peers, was highly innovative when it came to using new technology, and was a brilliant mathematician. In 1940, he began Montreal's largest bookmaking enterprise at the time when he converted several apartments in a St. Catherine Street residential building. Ship equipped each apartment with five telephone lines and several blackboards. Adapting the headsets worn by Bell telephone operators with long extension cords, each bookie was now free to take calls and write bets on blackboards simultaneously — an innovation that allowed Ship to cut personnel costs by combining two jobs into one. Business became so brisk that Ship used partitions to subdivide apartments into halves and then quarters. Each cubicle housed a slip writer, five telephones, and one or more blackboards, and the partitioned apartments became so stuffy that the bookies were often found working in their underwear. Ship had Barney Shulkin's brother Joe supply racing forms from his nearby printing office and, by 1943, he was contracting with the telegram service of the Canadian National Railway to receive the results of horse races and sports scores. He also had a sports ticker service installed in the hall of the building and, in 1946, this was hooked up to a Trans-Lux projector, which illuminated onto a large screen the racing information coming in over the ticker service.

Harry Ship's bookmakers took bets on races and sporting events from across North America. His long-distance bills (all addressed to and personally paid by Harry Ship) were so large that the Bell Telephone Company required him to make a monthly deposit of $500 (which was raised to $1,000 as the number of telephones multiplied). His bookmaking operations covered so many events and his slip writers took so many wagers that blackboards had to be replaced on a monthly basis. When he appeared before the Caron Commission in 1952, Ship admitted that between 1940 and 1946 he grossed more than $1 million annually from his bookmaking business, most of which was deposited into a bank account registered in the name of the Victory Cigar Store. During the same period, Ship's St. Catherine Street operations was raided thirty-four times by police, leading to thirty-seven convictions against his bookies, the padlocking of various apartments in the building, and thousands of dollars in fines. "The fines we paid took care of the

One of Harry Ship's slip writers working in a partitioned cubicle

police department's salaries, or a large part of them, and the city coffers were getting fat," he said. "I think that's why we were tolerated."

Despite his substantial revenue, Ship cried poverty when he was arrested on gambling charges in 1946. "The horses forgot to win," he laconically explained to Justice Caron. On January 8, 1948, the thiry-three-year-old was convicted on three counts of operating an illegal gaming house and was sentenced to six months in prison. Ship's assertion that he was broke may very well have been true. He was an inveterate gambler who had no qualms about betting thousands of dollars on a single horse race or sporting event. Because of his chronic gambling, Ship became indebted to Frank Erikson, one of the biggest and wealthiest bookmakers on the American eastern seaboard. By taking lay-off bets from other bookies across the United States and Canada, Erickson reportedly made bank deposits that totalled more than $6 million over a period of just four years. Erikson had numerous silent partners in his

gambling and bookmaking operations. Among these were some of America's most powerful mobsters — Meyer Lansky, Lucky Luciano, and Frank Costello. Whether or not he knew it at the time, Harry Ship was now indebted to the Cosa Nostra.

Enter Luigi (Louis) Greco and Frank Petrula, two Montreal-based criminals with ties to Costello and Luciano, who became aware of Ship's indebtedness and saw this as a golden opportunity to take over his rackets. Greco and Petrula both got their start in Montreal's gangland as bodyguards for Harry Davis. Greco was a short, squat man, with matching dark brown hair and eyes and a face that bore a passing resemblance to that of Babe Ruth. Born on September 19, 1913, Greco emigrated from Sicily to Montreal as a child with his family and was only a teenager when he received his first conviction for assault. After he began working for Davis as a bodyguard, Greco quickly moved up the ranks due to his ready use of violence and the cash he generated for Davis by robbing gambling

Harry Ship (centre) in a Montreal courtroom during his 1946 trial

operations that refused to pay protection money. In 1936, Greco was convicted of armed robbery and sentenced to eleven years in prison. Frank Petrula was the son of Ukrainian immigrants and specialized in car theft, bank robberies, and drug trafficking. He was described in a 1963 article on Quebec organized crime as the embodiment of the quintessential Hollywood movie gangster: "He was darkly good-looking, thin and high-strung, and dressed like a clothing ad."

Petrula and Greco took over many of Davis' rackets when he was killed in 1946 and viewed Ship's operations as another stepping stone to controlling professional gambling in Montreal. With the backing of Frank Costello and Charles Luciano, Greco and Petrula had Erikson pressure Ship to take the two men on as partners in his Montreal bookmaking operations. Erickson, Costello, and Luciano probably did not need much convincing; not only would they receive a cut of the profits, but all three were well aware of the opportunities that stemmed from establishing

a presence in Quebec. Erikson and Costello were interested in moving some of their American bookmaking and gambling operations to Canada because of the government crackdowns in the United States, while Luciano recognized Montreal as a key entry point for heroin imported into North America from Europe. Ship had little choice but to take Petrula and Greco on as partners.

Before long, Costello and other American crime bosses began instructing their bookies and other hired help to pack up and relocate to Montreal, with assurances from Greco and Petrula that they would be provided protection from the municipal and provincial police. By the spring of 1953, the groundwork had been laid for a radical re-alignment of the city's criminal world. This included the arrival of some of the largest criminal combines from the United States, the establishment of Montreal as one of the biggest bookmaking centres on the continent, the eventual consolidation of local rackets under New York's mafia

Frank Petrula

Luigi Greco (centre) in court, circa 1955

families, and the transformation of organized crime in Quebec into a branch of the Cosa Nostra.

As RCMP commissioner C.W. Harvison put it in 1962, a number of well-known bookmakers "made their permanent residence in Montreal, operating there behind the facade of commercial establishments, conducting their operations by batteries of telephones, and connected to other bookmakers in Vancouver, Calgary, Edmonton, Saskatoon, Winnipeg, Toronto, Windsor, Hamilton, Ottawa, Quebec City and the Maritimes, as well as all major cities in the U.S.A." Leo Schaffer transferred his massive bookmaking network from Chicago to Montreal. Gil Beckley, Cincinnati's leading bookie, drove straight to the city in his Cadillac. Morris Schmeizer (a.k.a. Max Courtney) and his partner, Frank Ritter (a.k.a. Frank Reed), who had set up gambling operations in the Bahamas with money from Meyer Lansky, began a giant lay-off business between New York, Miami, and Montreal, piling up telephone bills that ran as high as $15,000 a month. Gordon Collins arrived via New York and set up his bookies in two Montreal apartments that were linked together by a phone extension so bets taken by phone in one apartment were recorded in another. Lookout men stood at the front of the building with buzzers to announce the arrival of police, and lit cigars were always at the ready to incinerate the chemically treated flash paper that was used to record bets. Almost all of the newly arrived bookmaking operations were connected to wire services, including the storefront located at Ontario and St. Lawrence streets, where a master control fed race information into a battery of phones that supplied almost fifty bookie joints. Bets that totalled millions of dollars monthly flowed in from every part of North America. One journalist estimated Gordon Collins' revenues to be $3 million a year, while Charlie Gordon, who hailed from Shreveport, Louisiana, and leased a suite in Montreal's Crydon Hotel, claimed that the profit for one season of football bets alone was $2 million. Overseeing each of Montreal's newest professional gamblers was a personal attaché to the heads of the New York families who ensured their bosses received an appropriate cut.

The favourable climate Montreal offered to American bookmakers, combined with the substantial revenue now being generated, meant that the appearance of high-ranking New York criminal overlords in the city was inevitable. Of all the American gangsters who arrived in Montreal during the postwar years, none was more powerful, more ruthless, more closely connected to the heads of the New York families, and more influential in the Cosa Nostra's takeover of organized crime in Montreal, than the man called "Mr. Lillo." In 1953, Carmine Galante, an underboss with the Bonanno Family, relocated from Brooklyn to Montreal to run the New York families' bookmaking and gambling operations in the city. But this was not enough to satiate his Machiavellian ambitions; he wanted a cut of all criminal rackets and any business operating on the fringe in Montreal. As Lee Lamothe and Adrian Humphreys write in their history of the Montreal mafia, "Mature as the city's underworld was by Canadian standards, it was a shadow of what Galante envisioned it could be: nightclubs and restaurants were not being shaken down thoroughly enough, pimps and madams operating brothels were paying a mere pittance and back alley abortionists had somehow escaped altogether the underworld imperative of paying kickbacks to the mob to be allowed to work in peace." Galante also recognized the pivotal part Montreal played as a gateway for European heroin entering North America and was determined to expand that role, while enriching himself in the process.

Galante was in his early forties when he arrived in Montreal. He was a short, bald, paunchy, bespectacled man who always seemed to be chomping on a cigar. Yet, his unobtrusive exterior hid an unremorseful hit man with dozens of murders under his belt and a lust for power that drove his long-time quest to become New York's *capo di tutti capi*. Galante was born on February 10, 1910, the son of a fisherman who had immigrated to America from Castellammare de Golfo in Sicily. His criminal career began as early as the age of eleven when be formed a street gang made up of other youth from New York's Lower East Side. He entered mafia circles while still a teenager and, by 1930, was arrested and put in jail after hijacking a truck and shooting a police officer during the getaway. When he was released from prison in 1939, he began working as a hit man for Vito Genovese, one of New York's most powerful mafia dons at the time. Sometime during the 1940s, he defected to the Bonanno Family and quickly rose to the level of underboss.

Carmine (Mr. Lillo) Galante

Galante was the most senior American mafioso to be stationed in Montreal, and it was not long after his arrival that he began organizing the city's underworld on behalf of the New York families. Assisting him was Luigi Greco, Frank Petrula, Harry Ship, and a promising young gangster named Vic Cotroni. Galante began by demanding protection money from the city's gambling dens, bookmakers, drug traffickers, brothels, nightclubs, thieves, and shady stockbrokers — as much as $300 a week from each plus 25 percent of their revenue. Those who refused to pay were faced with violent attacks, arson, or police raids. By 1954, Galante was extending his influence to Montreal's legitimate businesses by investing in nightclubs, bars, and restaurants. He also brought in from New York City an ex-burglar named Earl Carluzzi to set up Local 382 of the Hotel, Restaurant and Club Employees' Union, which allowed Galante to control the hirings and firings of all staff in these service industries, while raiding union funds. During his time in Montreal, Galante also established a local *decina* (cell) of the Bonanno Family, swearing in fellow Italians as members, establishing himself as the boss, and anointing fellow Sicilian Luigi Greco as his underboss.

One of those Galante swore in as a member of the Bonanno Family was Vincenzo (Vic) Cotroni.

Although he was not a Sicilian, Cotroni quickly impressed Galante and the two became friends and later godfathers to each other's children. Cotroni's standing in the Montreal *decina* would soon surpass that of Greco and in a few years he would take over from Galante, paving the way for his long career as one of Canada's most powerful criminals.

"IF HE WERE OF NO FURTHER USE, HE WOULD BE DEAD"

Vincenzo Cotroni was born in 1911 in the small Calabrian village of Mammola. In 1924, he, along with his parents, two sisters, and younger brother, Giuseppe, immigrated to Canada and settled in Montreal. Rather than attend school, Vic, as he was often called, worked briefly as a carpenter's apprentice and then as a wrestler under the name "Vic Vincent." He became a student of Armand Courville, a well-known local wrestler and coach who gave lessons to aspiring young pugilists and who had financial interests in bars, speakeasies, and gambling houses. It was Courville who introduced Vic to Montreal's seamier side and, before long, his student was involved in bootlegging, petty theft, cheque kiting, passing counterfeit money, and working as a political goon that stuffed ballot boxes and terrorized voters on election day. The two became good friends, business partners, and criminal associates for the next fifty years. By his early twenties, Vic had already accumulated a criminal record, although he never spent more than six months in jail. One of the charges laid against him was for rape, but it would later be dropped when the victim agreed to become his bride. His reputation for violence appeared to be a contradiction for the young man who was shy, reserved, and unemotional, and whose drooping lips, thick nose, and oval face made him appear slow and dim-witted.

In 1942, Armand and Vic bought the Café Royale, a popular nightclub located in the heart of the red-light district and frequented by many of Montreal's criminal elite. In 1944, Cotroni, Courville, and two drug-dealing brothers from Marseilles, named Edmond and Marius Martin, opened a bar called Faisan Doré, which became popular among politicians, lawyers, and judges. Cotroni, Courville, and other investors also became partners in a number of

A young Vic Cotroni

would not allow Galante's prostitutes to work there. Cotroni was charged with wilful damage, but his only penalty was a $200 fine after Silver was pressured to revise the damages to his club to a paltry $1,000. As Vic rose through the ranks of the Montreal mafia, he now had a number of soldiers reporting to him. He also proved to be as strict a disciplinarian as Galante. One night, while Harry Ship was dining in a Montreal restaurant, he was confronted by a man with his topcoat pulled over his head, who fired two bullets into each of his legs. Ship was attacked because of persistent rumours he wanted out from his role as lay-off man for Galante's bookmaking operations. As Alan Phillips wrote in 1963, "This was simply a warning — to him and others — to stay in line. If Ship were not serving the syndicate still, if he were of no further use, he would be dead."

Vic Cotroni's influence in the Bonanno Family's Montreal wing grew exponentially when Galante was deported from Canada in 1954. After a succession of lieutenants sent from New York to manage Bonanno Family affairs in Montreal were deported back to the U.S., Vic and Luigi Greco were appointed as joint heads of the Montreal arm. However, Vic would quickly outmanoevure Greco for sole possession of the *capo decina* position in Montreal. By the end of the 1950s, the emerging don had grown quite wealthy from his interests in a wide variety of profitable enterprises, including extortion, gambling, bookmaking, labour racketeering, prostitution, and loansharking. Also joining him in his criminal endeavours were his two younger brothers, Giuseppe (Pep) and Francesco (Frank). Neither would ever rise to the heights of their older brother, although both would become key players in the American mafia's international heroin trafficking network.

gambling operations, which they ran out of apartment buildings. In tandem with Courville, Vic re-entered the corrupt world of Quebec politics and, in 1947, he was charged with and later acquitted of voter impersonation. While Courville can be credited with Vic's criminal apprenticeship and his growing influence in Montreal's underworld, it was Vic's relationship with Carmine Galante in the early 1950s that sent his career as a mobster spiralling. He began as one of Galante's strong-arm men and reportedly caused $30,000 damage to the Chez Paris nightclub, because its owner, Solomon Schapps (a.k.a. Solly Silver),

JUNK DEALER

I have seen the exact manner in which the junk virus operates through fifteen years of addiction. The pyramid of junk, one level eating the level below (it is no accident that the junk higher-ups are always fat and the addict in the street is always thin) right up to the top of tops since there are many junk pyramids feeding on peoples of the world and all are built on basic principles of monopoly: (1) Never give anything away for nothing. (2) Never give more than you have to give (always catch the buyer hungry and always make him wait). (3) Always take everything back if you possibly can. The pusher always gets it all back. The addict needs more and more junk to maintain human form ... buy off the monkey.
—William Burroughs, *The Naked Lunch*, 1959

Bonanno, Galante, Greco, the Cotroni Brothers, Petrula — junk dealers…underworld entrepreneurs, phantom purveyors of misanthropic misery; like vampire bats, giving off a "narcotic effluvium, a dank green mist" that anaesthetizes their victims and renders them helpless in their enveloping presence. All vital cogs in boosting Montreal's mantel as North America's premiere junk funnel; a large inviting marine port spread open like a seasoned whore … invisible hierarchy of captains; panhandlers of political power … Montreal is not a young land: it is old and dysfunctional and corrupt. Shoot the junk through the watery mainline, son. You can smell it coming in and feel the cool hard cash coming out; a rush of pleasure, overflowing bank accounts, gleeful accountants prostrated across black-inked ledgers. This is the yen of the gangster; a need without conscience or moral direction, rancid ectoplasm shot out by unrelenting yobs coughing up money like phlegm.

And always the junk pushers. Practiced, smooth, unapologetic. Bonanno: cool, calculating New York mafioso, all sharped up, with greedy insect eyes, controlling la belle ville in la belle province through the Cotroni clan… French-speaking mobsters communicating with Corsicans, the wily refiners transforming hop into junk …

American and Canadian narcs think Frank Petrula is working with Joseph Bari of New York's 107th Street mob. Bari is a main pusher of Mexican brown heroin … adobe junk … the country's biggest export next to migrant labourers. Petrula is suspected of being his largest customer. A 1945 secret Mountie report reads, "…opium comes from Mexico into California and it is placed in cans there and shipped in large quantities direct to New York City." In through the out door: a vast network of ecto-connections; in lead zeppelins hovering over humanity; sopping up what the city oozes. Petrula travels to NYC to purchase the junk for transport back to Canada. The "107th St. mob will only sell into Canada in a twenty-to-twenty-five-thousand dollar lot." Traffickers in the white meat, flesh of the white centipede "found in a land of black rocks and iridescent, brown lagoons, exhibit paralyzed crustaceans in camouflaged pockets of the Plaza visible only to the Meat Eaters."

Petrula and Greco fly to Italy in 1954 on the orders of their boss Carmine Galante and meet with Charles Luciano to import Sicilian-processed junk into Montreal. Petrula and Greco return to Montreal with a suitcase that had more in it than silk suits and toiletries. The Mounties catch a whiff and raid Petrula's home. No drugs are found, but they discover something of even more value. Their law enforcement smile ignores the misadventure of a balloonist or a circus animal run amuck. In a wall safe hidden behind tiles in the upstairs bathroom police find $18,000 in cash and detailed notes. Figures … numbers … names … the Galante-Cotroni four-flushing, political-buggering, street-hustling gang shelled out $94,000 to at least six newspapermen (rag men) and one radio reporter (Can you say Canadian payola?) to denounce and discredit the reform-minded Civic Action League and its mayoralty candidate, Jean Drapeau during a recent municipal election; that top cat has been a thorn in the side of Montreal's mobsters for the past four years as one of the legal beagles on the Caron Commission, Drapeau ran on a platform to clean the city of vice and gangsters. Pop! Bang! Shoot! Fix! The mayor is a junkie, but can't take it direct because of his office … so he has his own circle of power dealers … from time to time he makes contact with them and gets recharged … his face a flash of intensity slipping faute de mieux into the inexplicable cleavage of corrupt Quebec governments.

Petrula's papers also show money paid to goons who trash Civic Action League committee rooms, who stuff ballot boxes and terrorize voters at polling stations. Ever pop C-note into the mainline? It comes back to hit you like a speedball … pure pleasure … electricity through the circuits … "a need without body and feeling"… The C-note-charged brain is a "berserk pinball machine, flashing blue and pink lights in electric orgasm." C-note pleasure cannot be felt by a thinking being, "but the first stirrings of insect life." A veritable phone book of key Galante-Cotroni men — Carmine, Vic, Luigi, Harry, Vincenzo, others … Squatting on a three-ring binder of information, a panorama of naked fools in black and white, drunk on money, stretched across Montreal. The notes blacken Petrula's eye and his underworld mugwumps are furious. A crackle of short sharp shocks and the smell of singed flesh, identities revealed hang in the air like soiled laundry on a clothesline. Drapeau is still elected as mayor and mounts a campaign to force the American mugwumps out of Montreal. Petrula is a spent force in the Montreal mafia and is targeted for removal. In 1956, the feds accuse him of tax fraud to the tune of $220,000. In June 1958, Petrula vanishes and is never seen again; his algae-covered body languishes somewhere at the bottom of the Saint Lawrence Seaway. "The gangster in concrete rolls down the river channel … They cowboyed him in the steam room … Is this Cherry Ass Gio the Towel Boy or Mother Gillig, Old Auntie of Westminster Place?? Only dead fingers talk in Braille …"

The American mugwumps scamper back home leaving a trail of ectoplasm slime as their trail, pieces of turf hanging from their black souless shoes. 1955. Galante is deported back to the U.S. and is replaced in Montreal by brother-in-law Tony Marulli. But Marulli is forced to leave the country and in 1956 Salvatore (Little Sal) Giglio, a Galante underboss in the Bonanno Family, is sent to Montreal. More religious devotees of superseded, unconscionable, deals, doodling in Etruscan, addicts of junk not yet invented, black marketers of the soul, exorcists of telepathic sensitivity, gynaecologists of the spirit, investigators of violations censured by insipid paranoid checker players, undoers of disconnected warrants taken down in the hebephrenic shorthand costing unmentionable mutilations of the soul, unofficial of uncontested police states, brokers of nightmares and nostalgias resting on sanitized cells of junk sickness and bartered for the last remaining raw materials of the will. With the help of Vic Cotroni, Giglio takes up where Galante leaves off, exacting protection from the remaining bookies and expanding Galante's heroin trafficking network. One more shot … tomorrow the payday. The way there is short. Come-ons and bring-downs are the different side of the same coin. The junk dealer has to see the vein … blood blossoms like a bubbling cauldron … currents of movement from the two

criminals dancing with their captors; delayed justice, proceeding through unknown portals.

1957. Lucky … Carmine … Bonanno … Corsican processors … Sicilian suppliers expand the world's junk traffic; the boys are like enigmatic old men again in the high cool quarters of their own vacuous visions of mortality … hoisting the sails of society's junk-fuelled morbidity … Turkish junk is sent to Marseilles, converted to heroin, and smuggled into Montreal and then America. The disease ignores borders and travels through the international mainline like junk through a vein … half of the continent's junk is entering through Montreal … Montreal's A-1 gig as a major junk mainline for North America goes aces up … controlled by the Bonanno-Galante-Greco-Giglio-Cotroni consortium; money sealed in translucent ambers of success that could never by equalled by their traditional rackets. The commandant murmurs orders through clogged telephone lines as signal flares of junk orgasm burst all over the skies of North America. Galante's face brightens with flashbulb intensity threatening any moment to explode, and entrusts the Montreal end to Giglio and the Cotroni brothers. Pep Cotroni … becomes the Montreal mafia's lead man in trafficking junk … fluent in French, he forms an alliance with Corsican junk wholesalers in Marseilles. (All standing there, syringes in one hand, holding their pants up with the other, abdicated flesh burning in the cold white halo of Times Square; sick, sweating, single cell organisms running cold and desperate for another fix. Shoot it through the mainline, son.)

Pep falls into the world on February 22, 1920, and slovenly follows in his brother's criminal footsteps … Vic's subservient mugwump … Pep makes a name for himself through armed robbery and by fencing stolen bonds. He is "a free-wheeling, free-spending, tough, pushy, ex-con, head of a band of bank robbers whose million-dollar break-ins have made them the most successful of all time." He enters the banks like ghosts with ghost fingers … moving through mirrored alleys of time and space where no life can survive as usual … only the pallid have no sense or smell of death and cower in the corner like a captured fly caught in a cobweb. He is affable enough, brown eyes, two small scars on his eyebrows and forehead, a wart above his right buttock (so says a 1959 FBI memo) and a rapidly receding hairline that makes his head look like a Penny Ford gumball machine covered by a thin layer of translucent olive-oil skin. 1937 and Pep has already been charged eight times for various offences; in 1949 he is convicted of receiving stolen bonds and spends four years in the St. Vincent de Paul iron bungalow. The years are hard on Pep. The sailor spots his serpent. Disintoxicafied observations. Paranoia of social withdrawal. Sheepish adherence to mafia protocol while his free brother dines on caviar on the outside; dead electoprotoplasm of illicit wealth … Flesh dead, tender, toneless … Pep's bloodshot yellow animal eyes gone out, "dying inside, hopeless fear reflecting the face of death."

Pep deals junk as an effluvium of crusty skin flakes off his suit, with a mildewed stench like an old discarded syringe. He works Corsican junk wholesalers and visits Paris several times a year (his is arrested once by French police and cannot explain the torn American dollar in his pocket);

his couriers run fifty kilos a month from Montreal to New York using Cadillacs with secret back-seat compartments (occluded from space-time by a welders torch wielded by a laughing hyena locked out from the zoo). The junk is delivered to Galante and Big John Ormento in NYC who cut it and dispose of it to the street pushers. Pep and Vic are suspected of being behind thirty-one pounds of pure heroin seized from the French freighter, the SS *Saint Malo* in 1955. Canadian brass supplying the junk throws up groaning into the volcanoes of America leaving eyes bloodshot in their sullen faces; passing out incomprehensible dialects, with burned cigarette holes in their pale skin. Shoot it up the main street, son. Pep Cotroni is now A1 in the international junk market. (Power calls forth a prostitution of the mind, a cerebellum stimulation similar to schizoid substance [note similarity between the exercise of power and a C-soaked brain]. Eventual result of power — especially true of the weak-minded rich and privileged where large doses dulls the monotony of money — is enduring despair

Giuseppe (Pep) Cotroni's 1949 mug shot

St-Vincent-de-Paul
6984

and a state of terminal vegetative schizophrenia: total lack of concern, autism, nearly deficient of cerebral occasions.)

Fast-forward to 1959. Time jumps like a broken typewriter … Edward L. Smith, a Canadian drug courier and former Montreal chauffeur for Carmine Galante is copped by U.S. narcs at the American border with a stash of junk in his car travelling from Montreal to New York. Sniggering customs agents copulate to the anguish of a trapped rodent. Lonely librarians unite. Rats take heed. Smith becomes a double agent and promises to introduce an undercover narc to Cotroni and his suppliers. A thirty-year-old U.S. Narc Bureau agent named Patrick Biase poses as a New York junkie named Dave Costa who wants to get into the business of pushing. The square wants to come on hip. April 1959. He is introduced to Pep Cotroni by Smith, who whispers in a forged, eviscerated junkie voice. Cotroni cannot deny his protoplasmatic core and accepts Costa's offer of $14,000 for two kilos of junk, $4,000 more than he could get in New York. The dream police disintegrate into globs of joy hot on a doughy, balding junk dealer, coughing and spitting up a trail leading to the mafia. June 1959. Their faces melt from the heat. Cops, dogs, & secretaries snarl at their approach. The providential capitalist god has fallen to unassailable despicability. Junk pushers don't break. They bend; elastic, expandable, resilient, flexible — endless putty stretched into perpetuity, blazing a trail to the Cosmos.

The undercover narc returns to Montreal (schlup, schlup, schlup) and purchases the junk from Cotroni. Rene Robert makes the delivery: 98.2 percent pure junk. June 18. Costa buys another two kilos. A double this time waiter, the singles keep leaking. It is again delivered by the Frenchman Robert. It tests 100 percent pure junk. Shoot it up straight to the police station boys. Cotroni supplies the narc another two kilos on credit. Biase is smooth … nameless grey and ethereal … and can make any junk dealing rube (Note: Make in the sense of "dig" or "size up"). June 24. Cotroni and Robert arrived in New York to negotiate a third purchase. There is the man on roller skates throwing money to the bums, a corpulent drag queen walking his pet rabbit through the East Forties, cab drivers of Absolute Reality gazing into rearview mirrors that are their lives, an old junkie squatting on brittle bones in a pile of excrement pissing down a rusty subway staircase, a businessman in a red-hot blaze of fire, burning flesh, stretches (and stenches) to the darkened horizon, wearing three-piece, white-collared costumes hiding their crimes, bankers, wholesalers, industrialists, opium farmers of Wall Street … The world is full of junk dealers, turning on a spit over a fire of burning swastikas. (Note: New York and Montreal have more junk dealers per capita than anywhere else in the world.) July 8. Biase-cum-Costa meet with Cotroni and Robert in Montreal under to purchase more junk. When an agreement cannot be reached, Cotroni and Robert are arrested by the Mounties. November 9, 1959. Pep Cotroni, thirty-nine years old, is awarded ten years in jail and an $88,000 fine. Robert receives an eight-year sprint on the same charge. Hesitant half-parodies that dissolve in shadows … pockets of mouldy ectoplasm swept away by a junk dealer coughing and spitting and retching in the sick shadow of justice. Pep is offered a plea bargain if he implicates his brother and Carmine Galante in the transactions. Pep refuses and takes the fall for his brother. Sibling Mafia Hierarchy. One top copper belches, "I'm sure [Vic] used Pep as protection against being out front. Vic was the boss so his brothers were expected to be the guys out front, protecting the eldest from any direct involvement in anything." Pep goes where his brother never does … a place "specially designed for the containment of ghosts: precise, prosaic impact of objects … washstand … door … toilet … bars … there they are … this is it … all lines cut … nothing beyond … Dead End … And the Dead End in every face …"

The six kilos of junk used to charge and convict Cotroni and Robert is taken to New York and used as evidence in a junk conspiracy case against almost forty defendants. The city swarms with every conceivable junk dealer — Slav, Chinese, Italian, Jew, Gentile, Scot, Aryan.

Police conclude the junk smuggling operations are part of a huge conspiracy (to fill conspicuous consumption followed by junk-sick mornings) that smuggled hundreds of kilos of French junk into the United States through Canada. May 1960. Store shutters slam like a sharp new guillotine blade on a cold winter day. Riot noises in the background, a panic suctions the city, cold turkey — a thousand hysterical junkie bettors with money to burn. A federal grand jury in New York cops Carmine Galante, John Ormento, Vito Genovese, and future Bonanno capo Natale Evole; spectral vendor of the junk, spirits as grey as ashes, sweeping out the junkies' souls like a vengeful ecclesiastical choirboy. They are blind from money, their bodies "a mass of scar tissue hard and dry as wood." They are accused of peddling more than 600 kilos of junk (worth a cool $600 million on the streets) since 1954.

The trial of Galante, Ormento, and nineteen others begins on November 14, 1960. The Corrupt versus the Corrupt. Two years later, fourteen are convicted and sentenced to refrigerate from nine and a half to forty years. Carmine Galante receives twenty years and a $20,000 fine. Big John Ormento receives forty years. Others like Salvatore Giglio and Angelo Tuminaro (wait for it) skip bail. The slow, anguished, irregular beating rhythm of a dying cardiac, the clang, clang, clang of the jail cell convulsing on a criminal career; the sycophantic sinner is no more as the Alabama lie detector crashes down on his head … like an old brown photo that is exposed in the sunlight.

Lucien Rivard blows into the scene and fills the hole left by the arrest of so many big-shot junk pushers. Short, paunchy, black eyed, "the conscious ego that looked out of the glazed, alert-calm hoodlum eyes — would have nothing to do with this suffering of his rejected other self, a suffering of the nervous system, of flesh, and viscera and cells." Shoot it in the French mainline, son. Rivard is already a major player in the junk trade (a former partner of Pep); wholesaler, retailer, financier, smuggler, they are all his bag. Rivard leaves Cuba — where he runs a casino and organizes international junk and gun smuggling junkets until he and his mugwump criminal comrades are kicked out by Castro (future betrayer of revolutionary proletariat power) — and balls the jack to Montreal in 1959 shortly before the arrest and conviction of Pep. Timing is everything. This

Lucien Rivard, circa 1952

is the yen of the pocketbook alone; a want without emotion and without body, earthbound needs, rancid ectoplasm swept away by junk dealers, coughing and spitting out junk and inhaling money. Rivard has connections with Corsican pushers like D'Agostino and the two work together "to make Montreal the wholesale depot for the U.S." The long streets look like an endless parade of pathetic priests and rabbis and mullahs pining for blood transfusions from pagans and atheists while coveting undocumented sexual trysts with lonely domesticated Eisenhower-era, amphetamine-popping suburban housewives. Shoot her in the mainline father.

1960. The RCMP is told that Rivard is in Acapulco at the same time four international junk dealers, boots laced up tight, are blowing up a storm in Mexico. "Something falls off you when you cross the border into Mexico, and suddenly the landscape hits you straight with nothing between you and it, desert and mountains and vultures; little wheeling specks and others so close you can hear wings cut the air (a dry husking sound), and when they spot something they pour out of the blue sky, that shattering bloody blue sky of Mexico, down in a black funnel..." Donkeys ... palms ... dusty weed-filled streets ... merchandise carts ... pushed by young brown lions ... no rigour mortis here ... Fellow Corsican and former Saigon police chief, Paul Mondolini, the balding, scowling heavy-browed thief whose armed robbery of the Aga Khan in 1949 made him 200 million francs richer and one of the world's most wanted criminals. He is there. The city is visited by an epidemic of junk dealers ... Junk dealers tend to merge together into a unified, but rotting body ... frantic skeleton smirk of unceasing junkies glazed over with white sunshine ... the unintended dead are left for the "H" vultures. The blind junkie shields his bloodshot eyes in the afternoon sun.

October 10, 1963. Joseph Michel Caron and his wife are nabbed at the U.S.-Mexican border crossing into the U.S. at Laredo, Texas. Dust filled, government sanatorium of invisible boundaries, spectral corridors of smugglers and illegals pouring like effluence into a giant desert toilet. A border narc checks the padding of the car seats and is suspicious of their hardness. He rips the seats open and finds 35 kilos of junk (second-biggest catch to date in U.S. history). Caron spills: he is delivering the junk to Lucien Rivard and blows the works on Mondolini and some Mexicans as suppliers. Joselito ... Paco ... Pepe ... Enrique ... Boys look up from street ball games, bull rings, and bicycle races as sirens whistle by and fade away. An indictment is handed down by a grand jury in Texas and leads to warrants for Rivard. June 19, 1964. Rivard is arrested in Montreal on a charge of smuggling junk into the U.S. He sits in the Bordeaux Prison and awaits his extradition hearing. A follower of rebellious unthinkable trades, addicts, not yet digested, reduced to an unmitigated habit of longevity ... power; philistine bureaucrats of the junk state ... overseers of constitutional carnage ... brokers of junk welfare ... doling out instantaneous lobotomies, dismantling the wings of Icarus ... The 6-foot centipede gnaws at the iron door.

1964. The summer screams in a false falsetto. Rivard's lawyers fight his extradition. Pierre Lamontagne is the Canadian lawyer hired by the Amer-

ican government to seek Rivard's exile to America. A seemingly silky spread of dollars, he is offered a $20,000 bribe to stop objecting to Rivard's release on bail because he is telling the judge that if the prisoner is released he would most certainly fly. The court agrees and refuses Rivard bail. The man who offers the bribe to Lamontagne is Raymond Denis, executive mugwump assistant to the immigration minister, René Tremblay, of Lester Pearson's Liberal government (he sits in the office catching insects with his long tongue). Lamontagne is also pressed by another Liberal Party mugwamp: Guy Rouleau, M.P., Prime Minister Pearson's parliamentary secretary. The mugwump men with their shiny red empty faces come with alabaster briefcases full of multicoloured graft to smooth out the politicos saying Rivard is a good friend of the party and it would be good for the party if Rivard is released. Guy Masson, a Montreal Liberal organizing mugwamp, carries a briefcase full of tainted promises, dreams of power and a $60,000 donation to the Liberal Party by Rivard's wife if her husband is freed (hold her, she is desperate) ... everyone looks like a junkie ... The Liberal Party is a power junkie ... continual dreams of command (those addicted to power have done far more damage than those addicted to junk) ... And every decade there is one mugwump who shoots it straight into the party's mainline; clean and cold hard cash; the C-note connection; you can feel it going in, a rush of orgasmic political power right through your electoral war chest. "Your head shatters in white explosions. Ten minutes later you want another shot...you will walk across town for another shot."

Lamontagne gets the morals and does not accept the bribe; he passes information about the bribe to justice minister Guy Favreau, who refuses to press charges. (In his previous life as immigration minister he also does not deport gangsters when found in the country — story to be continued!) Favreau does a striptease at his government desk as the disease of power permeates his brain like frenzied rock and roll fans storming the stage, throwing acid into the faces of their heroes, open bathroom stall doors, burning in effigy bankers and accountants. August 10, 1964. Lamontagne takes the allegations to the Mounted Police. They investigate, but conclude there is insufficient evidence to lay charges. Orders from faraway headquarters; distant rumblings of charades by politico-plasmid police throwing great creamy power eunuchs off Parliament Hill. They put on their electric smiles. Junk dealers and politicians have no shame … they are impervious to the repugnance of others … It is doubtful that shame can exist in the absence of caring … a soiled paper rose twisted on a wire hanger in the filthy Passaic, leaped on the waters, crying, crying. They stand on the edge of the abyss with "dead cold, undersea eyes, eyes without a trace of warmth or lust or hate or any feeling no … at once cold and intense, impersonal and predatory."

The affair hits the newspapers in November 1964 when opposition parties begin a relentless campaign against Favreau. Mr. Attorney General chews his cud, sprawled out in his office, surrounded by simpering dark-eyed political sycophants. The story is headline news for months. It causes such a ballyhoo that the feds are forced to form a commission of inquiry headed by Frederic Dorian, chief judge of the Quebec Superior Court. Squads of lawyers and judges with thin lips and large egos moving with the syncopated rhythms of their own power and self-worth. Gabfests are held from December 15, 1964, to April 9, 1965. And as it is about to come to a close … Another twist. March 2, 1965. Fade-in to the Bordeaux Prison. Rivard and a collegial fellow monkey inmate named Durocher ask to hose down the outdoor rink; guards say yes (despite a balmy four degrees Celsius); the two blow the prison scene using a gun carved out of wood and blackened with shoe polish. The most famous manhunt in Canadian history begins. By car, boat, plane, horse, and skateboard, but it isn't until July that Rivard is recaptured, unarmed and in his bathing trunks, his shiny red face, sunburned and wet from frolicking in the water while at his cottage in the Laurentians, a place given over to free love, hideaways, chestnuts, and continual bathing.

So leave us to return to the stricken capital. June 1965. The air is cloyed with a sweet evil smell of middle-class hypocrisy as husbands and fathers slip out to play craps while wives and mothers sit around and sip pousse-cafés through chilled straws and watch the pool boy. Dorian submits his report and confirms that Rivard's friends tried to parlay their connections with Liberal Party mugwumps and offered bribes to secure his release. Guy Rouleau offers his resignation as parliamentary secretary. The scandal also forces justice minister Favreau's resignation. It forces him to eat and digest the scales of justice like a trapped boa constrictor, and he is finally convicted in the court of public opinion only after burning his party with a flame thrower – the court of inquiry ruling that such means were not justified and after losing humanity's passport was, in consequence, a creature without species, country, political party, or riding. Rivard is shipped to the U.S. In September 1965, a Texas judge sentences him to twenty years.

For the 1965 election, Prime Minister Pearson recruits a number of new Liberal candidates from Quebec in an attempt to put a new face on his party government. Among the new recruits is Pierre Elliot Trudeau. An enlightened Canadian romantic or just a plain polemist? (Rhetorical question.) On November 8, 1965, Canadians blast the joint with another Liberal minority government. Trudeau becomes justice minister. On December 14, 1967, at the Liberal Party convention — where political junkies stand and cheer passionately and real citizens wig with their new unrestrained addiction, drinking the tea of the disposed, and the last nothing but a hopeful little bit of hallucination; instead, the concrete void of insulin — Pearson announces his retirement from politics. Pierre Trudeau sits like Buddha in a lotus position as he is chosen the new leader of the Liberal Party of Canada (By God I don't have to take this! I will metabolize my own junk!). He combs his hair like a Canadian Caesar and pirouettes his way to the ultimate power-junkie position in Canada. The commandant of cool is a sharp dresser and wears a cape to a football game. Nembies, bennies, junkies, dollars, junk dealers, Big "C," goofballs, politicos, amp heads, yellow jackets, power, businessmen, yen pox, graft, hotshots, tea. "A rabid dog cannot choose but to bite. Assuming a self-righteous position is nothing to the purpose unless your purpose be to keep the junk virus in operation. And junk is a big industry." Shoot it in the mainline, son.

THE GODFATHER OF MONTREAL

By the early 1960s, with Carmine Galante and Pep Cotroni in jail, Salvatore Giglio on the run, and Luigi Greco relegated to a subordinate role, Vic Cotroni tightened his control over the Montreal arm of the Bonanno Family. His stature as mafioso was also evident; while his brother and other members of the Montreal and New York mafia groups were being convicted on drug trafficking charges, all strictly adhered to the code of *omerta* and shielded their don from prosecution. Throughout the 1960s, the soft-spoken and taciturn man, who never learned to read or write, reigned as the most powerful criminal in Quebec. He was also one of the wealthiest and was not shy about enjoying and even displaying the spoils of his profession, whether it was his ubiquitous bodyguards, the chauffer-driven limousines, his luxurious duplex in Montreal's exclusive Rosemount District, or his palatial summer estate in Lavaltrie on the St. Lawrence River, which housed a six-car garage, a vineyard, a greenhouse (complete with a full-time gardener), a boathouse, and a sunken swimming pool.

While he preferred to remain in the background, Vic's prominence in Montreal's criminal underworld could not be veiled and he was increasingly exposed to the glare of the media and the government spotlight in both Canada and the United States. In 1962, the name "Vincent Cotroni" was placed on the U.S. attorney general's list of persons engaged in organized crime activity, while Quebec police were monitoring his whereabouts, activities, and conversations. He took on an unlikely foe by suing *Maclean's* magazine for $1.25 million in damages after a 1963 article referred to him as the "godfather" of the Montreal mafia. The trial judge concluded that Cotroni's reputation was indeed "tainted" by the article, but ruled that the defendant was entitled to an award of only two dollars, one dollar for the English version of the magazine and another for the French version. Vic's imprudent strategy had backfired on him; not only did the lawsuit thrust him even more into the public eye, but the ruling was an implicit recognition of his criminal stature. Even worse, the two dollars in damages awarded to him was an embarrassing blow to the prestige and honour of the mafioso.

Cotroni's ties to the Bonanno Family were also displayed for the world to see in the summer of 1964, when Joseph Bonanno flew to Montreal and declared to Immigration Canada that he wished to make an investment in Quebec and perhaps even become a Canadian citizen. "At the immigration office, I repeated my intentions of investing in a Canadian business for the purpose of expanding a cheese plant and hiring more people," he wrote in his 1983 autobiography. "I was helping Canada reduce its unemployment." But Bonanno's attempted emigration north of the border had less to do with his altruistic interest in the Canadian labour market, and more to do with his desire to escape an escalating conflict that was engulfing his family in New York, a conflict he created and would perpetuate for years to come.

Joseph Bonnano

Joseph Bonanno was born on January 18, 1905, in Castellammare del Golfo, Sicily. He came to America with his family in 1908, but returned shortly thereafter to his hometown. As a youth growing up in Sicily he learned the way of the mafioso and, like many of his ilk, he was also an anti-Fascist who became involved in the underground movement to depose Mussolini. Whether it was because of his opposition to the Italian dictator or his involvement with local mafia groups (or both), Bonanno was forced to flee Sicily and returned to America in 1924. He settled in Brooklyn and before long was working for a local mafioso as a bootlegger and an illegal lottery operator. Even as a young man, Bonanno's brains, superior organizational skills, and opportunistic instincts set him apart from his more thuggish associates. When violence broke out between two rival Italian criminal factions in New York during the late 1920s, Bonanno aligned himself with the winning side and was rewarded with his own family and a position on the newly created Mafia Commission. Bonanno was only twenty-six years old at the time, the youngest of all the heads of the five New York families. Under his leadership the family prospered and he was soon a millionaire. Gambling, loansharking, prostitution, labour racketeering, and drugs would be the family's primary money-making ventures, but over the years he also invested heavily in legitimate businesses, including clothing factories, cheese producers, moving and storage companies, pizza parlours, cafés, and funeral homes.

Bonanno's arrival in Canada in 1964 sparked a flurry of press coverage, not to mention great consternation within the Canadian government, which came under tremendous pressure by American government officials to deport him to the United States. Canadian officials found a legal reason to do so when they discovered on Bonanno's immigration documents the declaration that he had never been convicted of a criminal offence. As his son Salvatore (Bill) Bonanno defiantly describes in his own autobiography:

> … the Canadians said he had lied on an entry visa form where he had been asked to state if he had ever been convicted of a crime. He had answered — truthfully — in the negative. The Canadians pointed to a violation of wages and hours statute that had been filed against him in 1941 by the federal government when he was a partner in a garment factory in Brooklyn. But the charge had been against my father's company, not against him personally. His company paid a four-hundred-dollar fine at the time. The U.S. Justice Department, through the Canadians, were grasping at straws.

Joseph Bonanno refused to accept extradition, knowing that if he was deported the FBI would have just cause to arrest him upon his arrival on American soil. During his legal wrangling in Canada, Bonanno would spend close to ninety days in Quebec's Bordeaux Prison, where he was treated like royalty by the other inmates. In the end, his lawyers and Canadian officials worked out a face-saving deal for both sides: Bonanno would not be officially deported from Canada, but instead would be released from jail a free man as long as he agreed to return to the U.S. voluntarily.

Bonanno's arrival back in America did little to quell the growing storm that was brewing within mafia circles over his trip to Montreal. When Stefano Magaddino found out about his cousin's northward expedition, he was livid and allegedly proclaimed, "he's planting flags all over the world." Magaddino suspected that Bonanno was trying to muscle in on his rackets in Ontario and that his trip to Canada was a ploy to that end. Characteristically, Bonanno rejected the allegations that he had gone to Canada to expand his interests. Instead, he had travelled there to escape the conflict engulfing him in New York: "What bothered Stefano about my Canadian trip was not that I went to Montreal but that I might use Montreal as a jumping-off point to encroach on his cherished Toronto," he wrote in his autobiography. "There was no truth to this. I was looking to extricate myself from my world, not to entangle myself in territorial disputes."

The disputes were largely of Bonanno's own making and confirmed Magaddino's suspicions of his aspirations beyond New York. In addition to Canada, Bonanno had established gambling and prostitution interests in California, bought a home in Arizona, and claimed a large part of the American Southwest as his territory. Bonanno's aggressive attempts at expansion and his not-so-subtle desire to become the *capo di tutti capi* of the Cosa Nostra were of great concern to the heads of the other New York families. They were justifiably even more outraged when they learned that Bonanno had placed contracts on the heads of mafia leaders Carlo Gambino and Thomas Lucchese of New York, Sam Giancana of Chicago, Frank DeSimone of Los Angeles, and Magaddino in Buffalo. Responsibility for the assassinations was given to Bonanno's top enforcer, Joseph Magliocco, who in turn delegated the responsibility to Joseph Colombo. Instead of carrying out the murders, Colombo reported the plot to the Mafia Commission.

Bonanno was ordered to appear before the Commission to explain the allegations, but he steadfastly refused. The Commission mulled over several forms of punishment for Bonanno and did not rule out killing him and dispersing his family's interests, which would have resulted in handing control of Montreal to Magaddino. Their final decision was surprisingly lenient: Bonanno would be stripped of his authority as head of his family and replaced by his lieutenant, Gaspar DiGregorio. But true to form, Bonanno refused to accept the decision of the Commission. The result was a civil war within the Bonanno Family pitting the DiGregorio faction against those still loyal to the old boss and who fought under the leadership of his son Bill. Dubbed the Banana War, the conflict was blamed for a number of deaths in New York as well as Montreal. The senior Bonanno would also become a casualty of the war. On October 21, 1964, the eve of his scheduled appearance before a U.S. grand jury, Joseph Bonanno was kidnapped at gunpoint on Park Avenue before the astonished eyes of his lawyer. For the next nineteen months, he was held hostage by Stefano, who was backing the DiGregorio bloc. Bonanno eventually agreed to step down as the head of the family and accept the Commission's decision on a successor. As a result, he was set free from captivity. Once freed, however, Bonanno reneged on his offer and threw himself into the war to regain control of his family.

Throughout the conflict, Vic Cotroni was careful not to take sides. As Peter Edwards writes in his biography of the Montreal godfather, Vic was placed in a highly untenable position, "He couldn't have wanted to defy the Commission," writes Edwards. "But he also couldn't afford to offend Bonanno, who represented his link to the riches of the American market and who was, in effect, his boss. Lives would be lost, as well as money, if Joe Bonanno's bitter personal rivalries were allowed to divert energies from money-making to in-fighting. At the very least, Joe Bonanno's arrival [in Quebec] disrupted Vic Cotroni's seclusion." Vic's preferred isolation was interrupted again in 1966 when Bonanno sent a delegation to Montreal to ensure that control over his Canadian interests were maintained during the conflict. Among the delegates sent north was his son Bill, who met with Vic Cotroni and his lieutenants in November of that year. Following one of the meetings, Montreal police arrested Bill Bonanno and his men when three loaded handguns were discovered in their car. Among those nabbed were Louis Greco and Peter Magaddino, brother of Buffalo mob boss Stefano. On December 2, 1966, thirty-four-year-old Bill Bonanno and his American entourage were deported from Canada. For the next two years, a battle of attrition was fought over control of the New York family. In 1968, just when Bonanno appeared to be winning, he suffered a debilitating heart attack. While he was recuperating, Bonanno finally agreed to a compromise with the Commission: he would be banished to Arizona where he could retain control over his rackets in the Southwest, but had to relinquish control over his family's operations in New York and Montreal.

In retrospect, Vic Cotroni actually benefited from the conflict in that he emerged with greater autonomy from the Bonanno Family. Nonetheless, for years to come, he would continue paying his respects to his American superiors by sending millions of dollars to New York, generated from his highly profitable criminal activities. By the mid-1960s, his gambling interests alone were multifaceted: Montreal continued to be a major bookmaking centre for North America, he oversaw numerous gambling operations in the city while expanding into the Ottawa-Hull region, tribute continued to be extracted from independent professional gamblers and bookmakers, and family members and associates were arranging junkets from Montreal to mob-controlled Las Vegas. In addition, money continued to pour in from extortion and protection rackets, drug smuggling, loansharking, and labour racketeering.

Vic Cotroni also controlled a number of legally incorporated businesses in Montreal, including construction companies, food importing firms, ice cream manufacturing and distribution operations, as well as hotels, restaurants, and bars. The businesses thrived, in part because they had an edge over legitimate competitors by circumventing labour laws and health codes, while using intimidation and violence to bankrupt rival companies. One Cotroni-controlled business was Montreal's biggest meat wholesaler, while another had an almost total monopoly over the sale of Italian ice cream in the city. Vic Cotroni's investments in the hospitality sector were bolstered by his influence over the Hotel and Restaurant Employees International Union. Officials with the union could be relied upon to keep labour peace within the family's hotel and restaurant businesses and to stir up union troubles among the competition. (In the early 1980s, Montreal's Local 31 of the Hotel and Restaurant Employees International became the only union ever to be barred from the Quebec Federation of Labour due to unethical conduct, which included police allegations that it had ties to Vic's younger brother, Frank.)

To carry out his numerous criminal and semi-legitimate business ventures, Vic built a productive and sturdy mafia unit. At the core of the organization was some twenty made members who, in the words of crime historian D. Owen Carrigan, were "cemented together by family ties, friendship, common ethnic origins, and a strict code of loyalty and silence." Vic based the structure of his *decina* on that of the New York families, with the core membership made up only of Italian "men of honour." While full-fledged membership in the Montreal mafia was available only to those of Italian descent, there was no discrimination based on what part of Italy a made member hailed from. Testifying before the Quebec Organized Crime Commission in 1975, Dr. Alberto Sabatino, a senior official with the Italian national police, stated that the Montreal mafia was an "exceptional" mixture of Calabrian and Sicilian gangsters and that it was "unusual" to see the two regional groups working as one mafia organization. "Such a mixture of Calabrian and Sicilian gangsters does not occur in Italy," Dr. Sabatino said. What Sabatino did not know at the time was that cleavages did exist between the Sicilian and Calabrian factions, which would soon result in a wholesale transformation of the organization's leadership and hierarchy.

Most of the made members of the Cotroni *decina* did not specialize in any one particular criminal endeavour, but were in charge of or worked in a particular geographic district in Montreal. With such names as St-Laurent Gang or the Sorrento Gang, each cell was headed by a high-ranking member and made up of several *picciottis* (soldiers) who, in turn, had a number of people under their command. During the 1960s and early 1970s, Vic's most senior lieutenants were Luigi Greco, Nicola Di Iorio, Frank Cotroni, and Paolo Violi.

From his pizzeria, Luigi Greco ran the group's gambling, loansharking, and extortion interests on the west side of the city. Unlike his ostentatious Calabrian boss, Greco was an unassuming Sicilian Mafia traditionalist who lived in a modest middle-class home and performed many of the menial functions at his small restaurant, such as baking pizzas and cleaning the floors.

Nicola (Cola) Di Iorio was considered Vic Cotroni's most brilliant deputy. Born in Montreal in 1922, he learned the ropes from family soldiers Jimmy Soccio and Diodato Mastracchio and then rose through the ranks until he began reporting directly to Cotroni. Intelligent, well connected, and politically astute, Di Iorio had Vic's utmost respect and served as his most trusted adviser. He also became the organization's chief political corrupter. Di Iorio was particularly successful in building strong ties with the Quebec Liberal Party during the late 1960s and early 1970s. Along with Frank D'Asti, his second-in-command, the two made financial donations to Liberal politician Pierre Laporte in his failed bid for the leadership of the provincial Liberals in 1969, and when he ran in the provincial election in 1970. Jean-Jacques Coté and René Gagnon, Liberal Party organizers and Laporte's principal campaign aides, later admitted that they met with Di Iorio and D'Asti in 1969 to obtain contributions for Laporte's leadership campaign, and again in April 1970, just two weeks before the provincial election. There has been much speculation that the second meeting was personally attended by Laporte and another Liberal Party candidate, Jerome Choquette. Following the election, police secretly recorded D'Asti and Di Iorio discussing how they could wring favours from Laporte if he was appointed attorney general. In particular, they wanted to end the constant provincial police raids on their nightclubs and gambling dens. While the two later expressed disappointment when Laporte was instead named minister of labour, police did overhear them talking about assurances they supposedly received from Coté, who promised them the same level of support from the new justice minister, Jerome Choquette. Police also received information that Vic Cotroni was planning to expose the alleged underworld links of Pierre Laporte to pressure the Quebec cabinet to halt an ongoing provincial inquiry into organized crime. The plot thickened when members of the extremist Quebec separatist group Front de Libération du Québec kidnapped and murdered Pierre Laporte in October 1970. Just days before the kidnapping, the FLQ Manifesto, which was read on the CBC French-language network, included the allegation that the Liberal Party's recent provincial election win "was nothing but the victory of the election riggers, Simard-Cotroni." The reference was to the perceived influence of the Cotroni clan and the wealthy Simard shipbuilding family in the provincial Liberal Party.

Heading the so-called St-Laurent Gang was Francesco (Frank) Cotroni, the fifth of six Cotroni children. Frank was born in Montreal in 1931 and, by the late 1950s, he was a senior member of the *decina*. Fluent in Italian, French, and English, his nickname was the same in all three languages: "Il Cice," "Le Gros," "The Big Guy." Unlike his older brother, Frank never shrank from public attention, nor was he content to operate in the background; he became directly involved in a cornucopia of criminal activities, from gambling and loansharking, to extortion, counterfeiting, bank robbery, pornography, murder-for-hire, smuggling, and drug trafficking. Frank threw himself with reckless abandon into his illegal endeavours and, as a consequence, was arrested more times than his brothers Vic and Pep combined.

Frank was first arrested in September 1960 for possession of a deadly weapon (he was carrying a gun that fired armour-piercing bullets). Along with seven others, he was charged with conspiring to rob the Decarie Boulevard City and District Savings Bank in 1967 after police found a 53-foot tunnel leading directly to the bank's vault from a nearby home. There had been a spate of bank robberies in the Montreal area in recent years, most of them the work of the local mafia, according to the Montreal police. Despite his arrest and police pronouncements, however, Frank was acquitted on all charges after his co-conspirators, several of whom were convicted, protected their boss by refusing to rat him out. On February 18, 1971, Frank Cotroni took the unusual step of holding a press conference to clear his name after being arrested and jailed by Mexican authorities in Acapulco. A month earlier he was charged for being in possession of stolen jewellery (it was a case of mistaken identity and he was not charged) and then being accused by American Express of using a stolen credit card (which forced the hand of Mexican authorities who decided to expel him from the country). Montreal police conceded this was the first time they had ever heard of an alleged mafia leader staging a press conference, and in inimitable Frank Cotroni style, he even made sure there were drinks and hors d'oeuvres on hand. "He wore a conservative black suit, black patent leather shoes, a wide racy tie striped with maroon and a very expensive nouveau-gauche-style ribbed white shirt," according to the *Toronto Star*. "His kinky black hair had been newly styled, and his stubby fingers were freshly manicured." Frank Cotroni's press conference was not only a first for a Canadian gangster, it also reflected his audacious personality; one of the reasons he was in Mexico was to work out a deal to export cocaine and heroin to New York City.

Vic Cotroni's fourth lieutenant, and the man he would one day share power with, was an Italian immigrant known in Montreal as "The Godfather of St. Leonard." His name was Paolo Violi and he would be responsible for ushering in a new era for the Montreal mafia, not once, but twice. Paolo Violi was born into the mafia subculture on February 6, 1931, in Sinopoli, a rural village on the Calabrian peninsula. Italian police accused his father, Domenico, a shepherd by trade, of being the boss of the 'Ndrangheta in Sinopoli and was once even exiled from the village under that country's anti-mafia laws. The elder Violi was also deported from Canada after a report from Italian police provided to Canadian immigration authorities described him as a retired mafia chief. Paolo himself was in trouble with the law from a young age. A 1947 Italian police report described the sixteen-year-old as "a dangerous person with an impulsive nature and a violent disposition, capable of anything."

Paolo immigrated to Canada in 1951 and began his new life in Southern Ontario. His first brush with the law in his adopted country occurred in Toronto in 1955 when he was charged with involuntary manslaughter in the death of Natale Brigante, another recent Italian immigrant. Brigante's death apparently resulted from a quarrel between the two men over a woman, an argument that dated back to the old country. One version of the murder is that Brigante was lured to a parking lot in Toronto by a phone call and found Violi waiting for him. After a brief joust, Violi pulled a .32-calibre pistol and shot Brigante twice. He died on the spot, but not before stabbing Violi under the heart. Police picked Violi up in Welland and charged him with manslaughter, but he was acquitted in court. According to one account, he successfully claimed self-defence, using his stab wounds as proof.

Violi gained his Canadian citizenship in 1956 and by the early 1960s he was running bootleg liquor into Toronto from Quebec, where dozens of clandestine stills operated by the mafia were each turning out hundreds of gallons of 165-proof liquor on a daily basis. In 1961, Violi was convicted of possessing illegally manufactured liquor (and was rumoured to have used his trips to the Toronto courthouse to run booze into Ontario). Around this time Paolo was also ingratiating himself with Giacomo Luppino, the leader of the 'Ndrangheta in Hamilton who reported to Buffalo mob boss Stefano Magaddino. Because Paolo was the son of his old friend Domenico, Luppino took him under his wing and even allowed him to court his daughter Grazia. Whatever Paolo's intentions may have been toward Luppino's daughter, it was an astute move by a young man desperate to join the ranks of the mafia.

In 1963, Paolo left Ontario for Montreal, supposedly on the orders of Luppino so he would not clash with another ambitious Hamilton mobster named John Papalia. Accounts differ on whether Magaddino approved of Violi coming within the orbit of the Montreal mafia and, by extension, the Bonanno Family. While it is possible that Magaddino may have felt betrayed by the move — and was reportedly persuaded to spare Paolo's life by Luppino — some also believe that he backed the decision to send Violi to Quebec and may even have instigated it to provide him with a toehold in the province. When he arrived in Montreal, Paolo opened Violi Pizzeria in the city's north end, which he used as his base to extort members of the Italian community of St. Leonard. He also became involved in currency counterfeiting, while continuing to run bootleg liquor to Ontario. Before long, he had befriended Frank and Vic Cotroni and used the association as a stepping stone to become a part of the Cotroni organization, to which he was already paying tribute. At the same time, he maintained close ties with the Luppino family and, in 1965, took Grazia Luppino as his bride. Violi now had the best of both worlds: he was part of Ontario 'Ndrangheta royalty while expanding his influence with Quebec's leading mafia clan.

Violi became an important bridge between the Hamilton and Montreal mafia *decinas*, while also playing an emissary role with other families within and outside of Canada. Police observed Vic Cotroni and Paolo meeting with known mafia members from Italy and, in March 1963, police learned that Violi was one of the participants at a Montreal meeting with American Cosa Nostra members to discuss the distribution of counterfeit money printed in the U.S. On November 28, 1966, Paolo Violi, Vic Cotroni, Giacomo Luppino, and Luigi Greco met with Bill Bonanno and other members of the Bonanno Family in Montreal. While Paolo would pay his respects to both Cotroni and Luppino, as well as Bonanno and Magaddino, he was playing a dangerous game. According to Peter Edwards, "Paolo Violi clearly had his own ideas. He privately told Luppino that the Cotroni family should strike out on its own and should be subordinate to neither the Magaddino nor the Bonanno family. Violi displayed dangerous signs of hubris as he belittled the abilities and judgment of Vic Cotroni and his close associate Louis Greco."

By the late 1960s, Violi was making his move to take over the Cotroni *decina* and by the end of the decade he was second only to Vic, having surpassed Luigi Greco, Frank Cotroni, and Nicola Di Iorio in the hierarchy. By the early 1970s, Violi's stock had risen so high that police began referring to the Montreal mafia as the "Cotroni-Violi Family" (although technically it was not its own "family," but a wing of the Bonanno Family). Violi was also forging strong links with other Canadian, American, and Italian mafia groups. Police wiretaps revealed frequent contact between Violi and such men as John Papalia, who was the godfather of Violi's second son, and Joe Gentile, the leading mafioso in Vancouver, who was godfather to one of Violi's daughters. Police wiretaps also picked up numerous conversations between Violi and members of mafia groups from Italy or America, concerning the settling of disputes and accepting new members from Sicily into the Montreal organization. Between 1972 and 1975, a number of long-distance phone calls and face-to-face meetings took place between Paolo Violi, Vic Cotroni, and high-ranking mafiosi from Italy, such as Settecasi, head of the mafia in the Sicilian province of Agrigento, Leonardo Caruana, a member of the Settecasi family, as well as Pietro Sciarra, Camelo Salemi, and Giuseppe Cuffaro, another senior Sicilian mafiosi. On April 22, 1974, for example, Sciarra, Salemi and Cuffaro discussed with Violi recent changes that had taken place in the Sicilian Mafia, among them the election of Leonardo Caruana as a *capo de madamento* (district boss). While he was a Calabrian, Violi showed great respect for his Sicilian associates and frequently turned to them for advice. For Violi, his connection to these men of honour represented a link to the historical traditions and sacrosanct principles of the mafia. According to the Quebec Police Commission, it was clear that regardless of whether a made mafia member was located in Italy or Montreal, they were all considered "friends," meaning they are all part of the same honoured society. Violi referred to this in a May 10, 1974 conversation with Camelo Salemi, "Some people who come from Italy have the same privileges when we know they're 'residents' from over there. They come here … they're recognized by everybody." Salemi agreed, responding, "In our mob, it's a friend and we gotta recognize a friend and that's that."

Paolo Violi

While membership in the Montreal *decina* was restricted to Italians, like other mafia groups in North America, this core membership served as the infrastructure for a larger criminal network, which over time included hundreds of associates from all types of ethnic, racial and religious backgrounds — French, English, Irish, Slavic, and Jewish, among others. Certain non-Italian associates were deemed so important they reported directly to Vic Cotroni or Paolo Violi and were even assigned soldiers to work under their supervision. Despite their power, however, these associates could never become made members. Paolo Violi confirmed as much on May 10, 1974, when he spoke of one French Canadian who worked as an enforcer for him: "Yeah, but you gotta know that the guy who was with us, he's a good *picciotto*, a French *picciotto*. He's good … Yeah, but he's not one of ours …" Armand Courville, according to the 1977 Quebec Police Commission report on organized crime, was "without any doubt one of the most influential and respected non-Italian partners of the Cotroni-Violi family." Courville — who was described in one 1975 newspaper article as standing "about five feet high" and measuring "about the same in circumference" with "cauliflower ears and slicked-back greying hair" — continued to be Vic Cotroni's closest partner in a number of illegal and legal enterprises, ranging from gambling houses, nightclubs and restaurants to real estate firms, and meat processing plants. Courville even told the Commission that he was the official business agent of "his friend." Cotroni was also godfather to Courville's son, Vincent.

THE APPRENTICESHIP OF WILLIE OBRONT

"There's more to you than mere money-lust, Duddy, but I'm afraid for you. You're two people, that's why. The scheming little bastard I saw so easily and the fine, intelligent boy underneath that your grandfather, bless him, saw. But you're coming of age soon and you'll have to choose. A boy can be two, three, four potential people, but a man is only one. He murders the others."
—Uncle Benjy in *The Apprenticeship of Duddy Kravitz* by Mordecai Richler, 1969

What with all the money rolling into the Cotroni-Violi coffers, it was inevitable they would need a little help on the financial end. The Cosa Nostra had Meyer Lansky. The Montreal mafia had William Obront. *"The Boy Wonder was just another bum at the time. Funny isn't it? I mean his phone bills alone last year must have come to twenty G's (he's got lines open to all the tracks and ball parks all day long, you know), but only ten years ago he would have had to sweat blood before he coulda raised a lousy fin."*

The Quebec Police Commission, a pretty good authority on Montreal mobsters from St. Urbain Street and beyond, once wrote that William Obront "appears to have been the individual charged with accomplishing various tasks for the Cotroni-Violi group, particularly in the corporate and financial spheres. He met regularly with individuals identified as being members of the Cotroni-Violi group and was asked to undertake responsibilities ranging from a menial to an extremely important nature." *"Anyway, he's broke like I said. So he walks up to the corner of Park and St. Joseph and hangs around the streetcar stop for a couple of hours and do you know what? ... He's pulled for milking pay phones. Or stealing milk bottles, maybe."*

William Obront — "Willy" or "Obie" to most — was born in Montreal on March 27, 1924. Even as a young boy, he looked middle aged; with lazy black eyes, a sullen face, a drooping neck, and a receding hairline. His most notable feature was his youthful lips, which contrasted with the remainder of his ripened face, abbreviated stature, and unremarkable personality. But that scheming little bastard was a shrewd financial and corporate wizard and used these skills to become a powerful racketeer. *"All that time…he's collecting streetcar transfers off the street and selling them, see. Nerve? Nerve. At three cents apiece he's up a quarter in two hours, and then what? He walks right in that door, MacDonald, right past where you're standing, and into the back room. There, with only a quarter in his pocket, he sits in on the rummy game. Win? He's worked his stake up to ten bucks in no time. And you know what he does next?"*

Obie first came to the attention of the police as a shareholder in the Hi-Ho Café and the Bal Tabarin Nightclub. Both were well known as hangouts for members of the Montreal underworld. Beginning in 1950, he was part owner of the Beret Bleu nightclub along with Peter Adamo and Frank D'Asti, but sold his interest to Vincenzo Soccio in 1958. *"Around the corner he goes to Moe's barbershop and plunk goes the whole ten spot on a filly named Miss Sparks running in the fifth at Belmont. On the nose. You guessed it, MacDonald, Miss Sparks comes in and pays eleven to one. The Boy Wonder picks up his loot and goes to find himself a barbotte game. Now you and me, MacDonald, we'd take that hundred and ten fish and buy ourselves a hat, or a present for the wife maybe, and consider ourselves lucky. We mere mortals we'd right away put some of it in the bank. Right? Right. But not the Boy Wonder. No Sir."*

He ran a thriving loan-shark business that generated millions of dollars in profit, and set up companies like Trans-world Investments Ltd. (incorporated October 12, 1961) which provided financing to legal and illegal business ventures. One loyal and highly leveraged client of Obie's was

Willie (Obie) Obront

Mitchell Bronfman. The nephew of Sam Bronfman first turned to Obie in the early 1960s when he began an executive airline service and could not get at his share of the family fortune because it was tied up in trust. Between 1962 and 1974, his Execaire Aviation Limited, located at Dorval Airport, rarely showed a profit, so Bronfman was borrowing larger and larger sums from Obie. During those years, Bronfman sent 1,199 personal cheques to Obie amounting to $2,473,316. Between 1967 and 1974 alone, Bronfman borrowed $1,417,250 from Obie and ended up accumulating interest totalling $1,037,031. By 1974, Bronfman still owed Obie around $200,000, but this money was seized from him in 1975 by the Quebec Department of Revenue as part of the $1,058,000 that Obie owed in back taxes. *"How that goniff manages to keep out of jail beats me."*

Obie also made millions from playing and manipulating the stock market and maintained trading accounts with at least seven brokerage firms in Montreal. In addition to helping finance high-pressure boiler-room operations, Obie was manipulating share prices through heavy trading with associates and company insiders. He was eventually charged with more than four hundred counts of fraudulently manipulating stock market shares over a fifteen-year period.

Obie's dexterous financial and criminal mind and his tight relationship with Vic Cotroni and Paolo Violi made him a top associate in the Cotroni clan during the 1960s and 1970s. In 1973, Obie played a key role in helping the Cotroni group take control of bookmaking in the Ottawa-Hull area. Larry Tucker, Obie's long-time employee, was appointed to oversee the extensive bookmaking operation with enforcement assistance from former Luigi Greco bodyguard Leslie Coleman. His job was to ensure that local bookmakers came under Tucker's control. Posing as the local salesman for Obront's meat business, Tucker was soon supervising a network of bookmakers in the Ottawa-Hull region that handled around $50,000 in bets a day, with 25 percent of the volume going to Paolo Violi. *"Picture him, MacDonald, a twenty-nine-year-old boy from St. Urbain Street and he's not even made his name yet. All night he spends with those low-lifes, men who would slit their mother's throat for a lousy nickel. Gangsters, Graduates of Saint Vincent de Paul. Anti-semites, the lot. If he loses, O.K., but if he wins — If he wins ... MacDonald."*

Obie himself was a degenerate gambler and confessed to the Quebec Police Commission that he sometimes bet as much as $50,000 a weekend using bookies on both sides of the border. When Obie appeared before thecommission, he was asked how he could bet in one day more money than he claimed to have earned in a year. "I don't generally lose," he replied. *"Imagine him, MacDonald. It's morning. Dawn, I mean, like at the end of the film. The city is awakening. Little tots in their little beds are dreaming pretty little dreams. Men are getting out of bed and catching shit from their wives. The exercise boys are taking the horses out. Somewhere, in the Jewish General Hospital, let's say a baby is born, and in the Catholic hospital — no offence, MacDonald — some poor misguided nun has just died of abortion. Morning, MacDonald, another day. And the Boy Wonder, his eyes ringed with black circles steps out into God's sunlight — that was before his personal troubles, you know — and in his pocket is almost one thousand de-isollers — and I should drop dead if a word if this isn't true."*

A key role played by Obie in the Cotroni *decina* was to serve as the organization's chief banker and financial adviser, which meant he was responsible for laundering millions of dollars in illicit revenue. As part of his money laundering operations, he opened numerous bank accounts and incorporated myriad fake and legitimate companies to hide, legitimize, and invest vast amounts of dirty money. The Quebec Police Commission estimated that over the course of 1974 and 1975 alone, Obie handled more than $84 million for the Montreal mafia and its associates. Obie was well at ease in the business world and, between 1950 and 1975, he was involved in thirty-eight companies, as owner, shareholder, or director. Despite his pretence of corporate legitimacy, rarely did Obie ever play by the rules, as the Quebec Police Commission observed in their 1977 report *Organized Crime and the World of Business*:

> One of the characteristics common to all the companies incorporated in Quebec in which William Obront was known to have had interests, openly or through a front-man, is the fact that they almost never complied with the laws concerning the information required annually from companies in Quebec ... People who hide behind many real or fictitious corporations are also trying to cover their tracks and mislead the police, the income tax authorities and the public. Tycoons are very adept at using this technique. William Obront did not invent or create this method, but he made use of it on a grand scale for a long time.

As the Cotroni clan's money man, Obie was called forth to assist in financial matters both large and small. He was asked to come up with financing for drug deals that required millions of dollars in cash, but was also tapped for a thousand or even a few hundred dollars. In 1974, a shepherd who was already paying tribute to Paolo Violi approached his don to help finance the transportation of a load of lambs and goats from Texas to Quebec. Violi responded that he did not have the $5,000 on him and then called Obie and told him that a friend who deals with goats and lambs needed a cheque for $5,000. Obie asked Violi to send the shepherd

over and he would provide it to him immediately. In May 1972, professional gambler Sol Teblum met with Paolo Violi for permission and money to run gambling junkets from Montreal to Las Vegas. After first consulting with Obie, Violi gave Teblum his blessing, but laid down two conditions. First, Teblum had to share 25 percent of his profits with him. Second, he was to go through Obie for the initial financing. *"That morning he takes the train to Baltimore, see, and that's a tough horse town, you know, and they never heard of the Boy Wonder yet. He's only a St. Urbain Street boy, you know. I mean he wasn't even born very far from where I live. Anyway, for six weeks there is no word. Rien."*

During the early to mid-1970s, Obie maintained at least nine personal accounts at four banks and from 1974 to 1975, at least forty-six people and fourteen companies made deposits — ranging from $2,500 to $1.7 million — into these accounts. During this two-year period, the deposits, which were made up of Obie's own revenue plus that being laundered for other members and associates of the Cotroni *decina*, totalled over $18 million. Obie's annual declared income during this time was around $38,000. When his taxable income for the years 1965 to 1973 was re-assessed, the government figured he had undeclared income of $2,197,801, which meant he had an unpaid tax bill of $1,058,102.79 (plus fines and interest). After the assessment, Quebec's Department of Revenue seized Obie's assets and charged him with tax fraud to the tune of $469,238.59. He was also sentenced to twenty months in jail in 1979 and was ordered to pay $683,046 in back taxes and fines or face another twenty months. *"Then one day, MacDonald, one fine day, back into town he comes, only not by foot and not by train and not by plane. He's driving a car a block long ..."*

Obie was also the public face behind the Cotroni group's infiltration of Montreal's Expo 67. In the spring of 1967, Liberal politician and former Quebec justice minister Claude Wagner announced that four companies controlled by the Montreal mafia and its associates were supplying the meat and vending machine concessionaires at the world's fair. Joe Frankel, who Wagner called "a chief of Montreal bookies," owned a company called Fleur de Lys Vending Machines that had a contract to supply Expo 67. Frankel in fact was working for Obie who at the time operated Obie's Meat Market (officially owned by his uncle Ben Obront), which also had obtained a contract to provide meat to the Expo 67 concessions. Wagner even produced a map of the Expo warehouse area that showed a space was reserved for Obie "which allows him to do business in meat at Expo." Obie was not only the biggest supplier of meat to the fair, but he was also the only one who had cold-storage lockers on site. "*... and do you know what, MacDonald? He parks that bus right outside here and steps inside to have a smoked meat with the boys.*"

Almost ten years following the world's fair, the Quebec Police Commission made a stomach-turning discovery: most of the wieners and burgers sold by Obie's Meat Market to Expo 67 — 400,000 pounds to be exact — was unfit for human consumption. "Meat from animals that die of disease or natural causes is being sold on a large scale," one commission official said in 1975. "It's supposed to be used only for dog food." Gilbert Massey, who worked at the Cotroni-controlled Reggio Foods Inc. from 1967 to 1972, testified to the commission that at least two tons of sausages made from unfit meat was processed by the company. A butcher who worked at Reggio Foods provided the commission with his recipe for a batch of hamburger patties supplied to Expo 67: twenty pounds of turkey giblets, forty pounds of beef, sixty pounds of horsemeat, and seven or eight pounds of protein. After Reggio Foods supplied the Quebec Summer Games in Rouyn-Noranda in 1973, more than forty athletes became so sick that events had to be cancelled. Acting on a tip, government authorities seized over 20,000 pounds of horsemeat from the freezers of the school where the athletes were housed. The meat was found in boxes that had originally carried a horsemeat label, but all the labels had been removed. "*By this time he owns his own stable already. So help me, MacDonald, in Baltimore he has eight horses running. O.K.; today it would be peanuts for an operator his size, but at the time, MacDonald, at the time. And from what? Streetcar transfers at three cents apiece. Streetcar transfers, that's all. I mean can you believe that?*"*

*All italicized text from Mordecai Richler. 1969. *The Apprenticeship of Duddy Kravitz*. Toronto: McClelland and Stewart, pp. 24–26.

THE FRENCH CONNECTION, PART II

During the late 1960s and early 1970s, mafia groups in Italy, Canada, and the United States continued to be responsible for much of the heroin sold in North America. Montreal would also carry on as a major gateway for European-processed heroin entering the continent during this period. The only real difference from years past was that the transportation of choice was no longer ocean liners, but airplanes. A 1970 Quebec judicial inquiry into crime stated, "the Montreal International Airport plays an important part in the transporting of large quantities of narcotics." Further, since 1967, there had been "an appreciable increase" in the number of couriers arrested stepping off planes from Europe. In 1967 alone, twenty-one drug couriers were arrested at the airport, most of who were arriving from France or Italy. On May 28, 1967, Josephine Noelle Kontoudenas and Marius Frontieri were found with 16 kilos of heroin wrapped around their waists. On October 26, a search of Michael Bernard and his wife, Yvonne Marie Louise, uncovered another 16 kilos of heroin hidden in the false bottoms of their two suitcases. On December 12 and 13, six Italian citizens with Argentinean passports were arrested with 36 kilos after arriving on separate flights from France. On September 5, 1968, Paul Antonorsi was caught with six kilos of pure heroin after getting off his flight in Montreal. The Quebec crime probe concluded "these importations were not isolated but were in fact connected with each other and that several of the suspects had successfully eluded customs officials on previous occasions."

After being arrested in New York on October 27, 1971, French citizen Michel Mastantuono confessed to helping smuggle 419 pounds (190 kilos) of heroin from Paris to New York via Montreal from 1969 to 1971. Mastantuono, who oversaw the Montreal end of the operation while he worked as a bartender at the Chez Clairette nightclub, recruited a number of French and French-Canadian entertainers who wittingly and unwittingly smuggled the heroin from Europe hidden in amplifiers and automobiles. One of the entertainers he used was his lover, Danielle Ouimet, a beautiful B-movie actress from Quebec. In the summer of 1970, Mastantuono travelled to France with Ouimet and purchased a Citroën DS21 automobile, which was then filled with 40 kilos of heroin and shipped to Montreal and then New York. The organizers behind the massive smuggling operation were members of New York's Gambino Family, Joseph and Anthony Stassi. Based largely on the court testimony of Mastantuono, the two brothers were convicted and sentenced to twenty-five and thirty years, respectively, for conspiring to smuggle a total of 528 pounds of heroin into the United States. In return for his assistance, Mastantuono received a new identity through the federal witness protection program while Danielle Ouimet was sentenced in March 1976 to five years' probation.

Among those illegally importing drugs into Montreal was Frank Cotroni, who dealt in both heroin and cocaine. Police first linked Cotroni to heroin smuggling when he was spotted in the company of Sicilian mafioso Tommasso Buscetta, who was under surveillance while he intermittently lived in Montreal in 1969 and 1970. Buscetta, who attended the landmark 1957 meeting in Sicily that mapped out future heroin trafficking by the mafia, became a key player in its international smuggling efforts. While on the lam after being convicted in *absentia* by an Italian court for his part in the murder of seven police officers in a 1963 shootout, Buscetta relocated to Brazil where he helped run the Sicilian Mafia's South American narcotics operations.

Cotroni met frequently with Buscetta in Montreal, not only to coordinate the smuggling of heroin into North America, but also to expedite the illegal immigration of Sicilians into Canada and ultimately the United States. A Canadian Immigration Department intelligence report from 1969 alleged that mafia groups in Italy, Canada, and America were working together to sneak Sicilian migrants into America where they were used in such low-level criminal activities as drug smuggling and muscle-for-hire or employed in mafia-run businesses as dishwashers, trash collectors or construction labourers. Most of the smuggling routes ran through Quebec and were coordinated by the "Cotroni-Violi family" in conjunction with the New York crime families, according to the report. Another immigration document from 1972 accuses the "Cotroni brothers" of smuggling more than 1,000 Sicilians into the United States in recent years. "A handful has been deported; the rest work as 'slaves' in mob-run restaurants, bakeries and construction companies, or as hoodlums."

The usual procedure was for the Italian migrants to come to Canada on official visitor permits, receive forged government documents, such as passports or social security cards, and then enter the U.S. In a 1971 *Toronto Star* article, the attorney general of Ontario spoke of whole Sicilian villages being funneled into America through Canada. On December 9, 1969, American customs officers at the Champlain, N.Y., border crossing arrested Buscetta and two New York mafia members as they tried to slip into the U.S. Buscetta, who was caught with four Canadian passports, managed to escape back into Canada. He did eventually make it into the U.S. and was arrested in New York City in August 1970 for being in the country illegally. At the time of his arrest he was using a forged Mexican passport and travelling under the name Manual Lopez. Buscetta was deported to Italy and, in 1984, became the single-most important turncoat in mafia history when he provided Italian authorities with information that led to more than 350 arrest warrants.

In addition to helping transport illegal immigrants into the U.S., Frank Cotroni was also moving cocaine into the country. On November 9, 1973, Cotroni, along with Frank D'Asti, fellow Montrealer Guido Orsini (who also worked with Cotroni and Buscetta in smuggling immigrants), Paul Oddo of New York, as well as Claudio Martinez and Jorge Asafy Bala of Mexico, were indicted by a federal grand jury in Brooklyn for conspiring to import and distribute nine kilos of cocaine in New York in 1971. The state's main witness was Giuseppe Catania, a long-time drug dealing associate of Tommasso Buscetta, who had been

Frank D'Asti

indicted in August 1973 for his involvement in smuggling more than 300 kilos of heroin into the U.S and Canada. Catania told police that Buscetta introduced him to Frank Cotroni, who purchased nine kilos of cocaine from him. Catania had obtained the coke from Jorge Asafy Bala, a major Mexican heroin and cocaine wholesaler. The drugs were then smuggled from Mexico by Claudio Martinez who delivered it to Paul Oddo in New York on January 8, 1971. After being arrested on an international warrant by the RCMP in Montreal, Frank Cotroni battled extradition all the way to the Supreme Court of Canada. But the court refused to block his deportation and, on March 24, 1974, Cotroni was sentenced to fifteen years and a fine of $20,000 in a New York City courtroom. He would join fifty-nine-year-old Frank D'Asti, who just three weeks before his own arrest on the cocaine trafficking charges had been sentenced in a New Jersey courtroom to twenty years for heroin smuggling. D'Asti was arrested in the lobby at New York's Plaza Hotel in December 1973 and charged with conspiring

to smuggle ten kilos of heroin from Canada to the United States the previous year.

A THOUSAND MEN

The convictions of Frank Cotroni and Frank D'Asti were not the only setbacks that plagued the Cotroni *decina* during the early 1970s. Around this time, Willie Obront was awaiting trial on various fraud, tax evasion, and forgery charges. Among his other problems, Frank Cotroni was arrested in Montreal in 1972 after trying to extort $250 a week from a Greek restaurant owner. That same year Luigi Greco lost a $200,000 investment when British customs officials seized 3,395 pounds of hashish at an English port. In December, he lost his life after being fatally burned at his pizzeria when the solvent he was using to clean the floor caught on fire. In 1973, Antonio (Tony) Mucci, a Cotroni soldier, was arrested after shooting newspaper reporter Jean-Pierre Charbonneau while Conrad Bouchard, a key associate of the Cotroni clan, was implicated in a scheme to smuggle 100 kilos of heroin into America with the alleged backing of high-profile American financier Robert Vesco. The Quebec Police Commission began hearings on organized crime in 1973 and almost immediately focussed its attention on Vic Cotroni. In a widely publicized statement by police officials who appeared before the commission in November of that year, Vic was described as the "godfather" of the Montreal mafia. In the summer of 1974, he was subpoenaed to testify before the commission.

Throughout this turmoil, Paolo Violi was tightening his grip over the Montreal *decina*. With Frank Cotroni in prison and Luigi Greco dead, two potential obstacles to his leadership ambitions had been removed. Violi was also given control over Greco's and Cotroni's soldiers and territories, which only added to his power and authority. Violi's leadership ambitions were given a boost on October 20, 1973, when he met with Gambino *capo* John De Matteo in New York City. The Gambino Family had taken control of the Bonanno Family following Joseph Bonanno's forced retirement and De Matteo was inviting Violi to represent the Cotroni wing at an upcoming meeting in New York to elect a new leader for the family. The position was to be voted upon by all of the Bonanno Family captains and, much to Violi's delight, his vote was being courted by one of the candidates, Philip Rastelli. On February 25, 1974, Violi left Montreal for New York City and, at the meeting held at the Americana Hotel, helped elect Rastelli as the new head of the family. Rastelli had already been installed as the acting boss by the Mafia Commission and knew Violi while serving as the family's liaison to their Montreal arm. In exchange for his vote, Violi petitioned Rastelli for more men, a request that was motivated by his desire for soldiers who would be personally loyal to him. Rastelli apparently agreed to Violi's request, but would not commit to any timetable.

Violi exhibited great deference to Rastelli and actively lobbied the new Bonanno *capo* to install him as interim leader of the family's Montreal branch. This request was prompted by the September 1974 jailing of Vic Cotroni, who had been cited for contempt by the Quebec Organized Crime Commission, which described his testimony to the inquiry as "voluntarily incomprehensible, disconnected, vague, hazy and equivalent to a refusal to testify." While Vic had already delegated responsibility to Violi for much of the day-to-day operations of the Montreal *decina*, Paolo wanted to ensure his leadership was formalized. On January 9, 1975, Violi asked one of his most trusted advisers, Pietro Sciarra, to go to New York to plead his case before Rastelli. Violi told Sciarra, "You're gonna talk. The best thing is to explain your case before. You're gonna say to him: Paolo sent me here, actually, and seeing as Vincent's inside, all that time … things there, everybody, somebody's gotta take responsibility now. So then Vincent, when he was sent down, he didn't see none of us to hand things over to somebody." A few weeks later, Violi told Joe Di Maulo, a fellow member of the Cotroni group who travelled with Violi to New York, that he'd obtained what he wanted: Rastelli had made him the acting *capo* for the Montreal wing, at least until Vic was out of jail. "He said to me: when Vincent gets out, have him call me, and if a change has to be made then, I'll talk to Vincent. But for the time being, you take over." While Vic's lawyer won a reversal before his year-long sentence was up, Violi's strong ties with Rastelli and his ongoing consolidation of power now placed him on almost equal footing with the aging Cotroni.

Like other mafia traditionalists, Paolo Violi stayed true to many of the prevailing customs and beliefs

that underpinned his calling. Police wiretap recordings revealed a man obsessed with ensuring he was accorded the respect he felt was due him. In 1972, Violi expressed his indignation to Vic Cotroni about one Louis Stoll, whom Violi felt was insolent while he was arbitrating a dispute between Stoll and Abe Isalf. He took particular exception to Stoll's outbursts toward Isalf, an associate of Violi and Willie Obront, "But this guy lost his temper and honour toward me and I was only there to discuss business. So I will tell Obie that the fucker does not know who the people are and I am surprised of you because you had to prepare him of my visit. Now for this respect which he didn't have toward me … I don't want to do a grave thing but I have to show him something and for this he will have to pay me $50,000. So he will learn for the next time." As the Quebec Police Commission noted, Violi was "quite upset by Stoll's attitude since he expected that Obront would have explained to Stoll how influential a person he, Violi, was and that Stoll would consequently have acted with the proper 'respect.'" Instead of physically harming Stoll, Violi decided to impose a fine, "once again illustrating the analogy of the parallel system of government" that the mafia represented to men like Violi.

In addition to respect, Violi also viewed loyalty and the code of *omerta* as supremely important. During one discussion with Giuseppe Cuffaro on May 10, 1974, Violi made it clear that the affairs of the Montreal *decina* were not to be discussed with any outsiders, including members of other mafia families. When Cuffaro asked whether as an associate of the Montreal group he could work with "friends" from outside the *decina*, Violi answered, "You can, but you can't talk to them about affairs of the family..." Loyalty and secrecy was also intermeshed with the mafia hierarchy, and the lowly soldier was expected to unquestioningly obey every order from his superiors and, if necessary, take the fall for them. This was never more apparent than in 1973 when two of Violi's *picciotti*, Moreno Gallo and Tony Vanelli, obediently bowed to his orders that they plead guilty to the murder of rival drug trafficker Angelo Facchino, whom they killed at the behest of Violi.

Paolo Violi also revelled in the mafiosi's time-honoured role as arbitrator. In one conversation with

Pietro Sciarra on April 22, 1974, he outlined what was expected of the mafioso: "Uncle Petrino, we're here to do the thinking, to arrange things for this one and that one. … and our job, all the time, is to straighten things out." One of the many mediation "clients" served by Violi was Réal Pelletier, who was in a financial dispute with a contractor who built his home. After receiving a number of anonymous telephone calls threatening his wife and children, Pelletier's brother-in-law Ralph Di Zazzo set up a meeting with Violi, who promised Pelletier the problem could be settled if he agreed to pay $5,000 to the contractor. After Pelletier balked at this amount, Violi persuaded him to pay $2,500 to settle the affair. In his testimony before the Quebec Police Commission, Harry Ship commented on the mediation services that Violi provided in a dispute between himself and Willie Obront. When Ship was asked how it was that Violi had been accorded power to provide binding arbitration decisions, he had this to say:

Ship: Well, my view about Violi is that he is highly respected by certain people for some reason or other.

Q: Well, which kind of people?

Ship: Let's say people that are on the fringe of legitimacy and he is called in arbitration and he makes decisions.

Q: In the same respect when you attend these types of meetings where Paolo Violi acts as "arbitrator" to what extent would you question his decision?

Ship: I would accept his arbitration as a rule

Q: In this case it seems that Obront also accepted it?

Ship: No question about it.

Violi often charged a fee for his arbitration services, whether his clients wanted the services or not. Lino and Quintino Simaglia learned this lesson the hard way. In 1971, Violi told the two brothers, who ran a small business, that he could settle a problem they had with a Toronto-based company. A few months later, Violi demanded they make a $1,000 payment every Christmas for the services he rendered. Testifying before the provincial crime commission, Lino said that

they did not dare refuse this command and, as a result, were unable to afford gifts for their children during the holiday season because they had to give Violi his $1,000 "Christmas present" every year.

For Violi, his role as a mediator stemmed from his larger function as a *padrone* to those within and outside mafia circles, which involved using his influence and contacts to provide opportunities and expedite transactions for his "clients." Paolo once told a *picciotto* named Antonio (Tony) Teoli to go through him when fencing stolen goods, "But I told you before, when you have something … tell me, because I know my way around better than you do … do it this way because I know people who get a few more dollars." Teoli told the provincial crime commission that during 1973, "I made lots of deals, including heroin, and I talked them over with Paolo." Teoli was referring to a taped conversation with Violi who instructed him to go see Guido Orsini who could provide heroin at a price that was far less than Teoli's current suppliers.

Like other mafiosi, Violi's self-appointed role as a *padrone* was simply another way to exercise his power, while whetting his beak financially. Police recorded one exchange on March 27, 1974, where a twenty-three-year-old *picciotto* named Massimo Di Rodolfo incurred Violi's wrath because he had fenced stolen jewels without consulting him first. Violi caught wind of the $4,000 transaction and summoned Di Rodolfo to his Reggio Bar where he unleashed a verbal tirade, assessed a $600 fine, and warned him in the future that any stolen merchandise must be brought to him. Before being dismissed, the young thief apologized profusely while professing his respect for Violi, "Paolo, I've always respected you, I've never done anything … Whenever I do anything, I'll always come to you. I made a mistake … You're the boss, Paolo." In her 1979 biography of Violi, Ann Charney wrote that his "insistence on respect and how it ought to be expressed drove him to exercise absolute control, and to demand a cut from every transaction, even when it involved a ridiculously small sum of money." In one instance, Violi insisted on an offering of sheep as tribute. No crime was too petty for Violi and he rarely displayed any discrimination in his choice of victims. In August 1973, he chastised two of his men, who specialized in stealing presents from wedding receptions, for bringing him "nothing but cheap stuff." Violi then referred the two *picciottis* to "a good place that would bring in a lot of money." The target turned out to be Violi's own neighbour, whom he knew went away every weekend. Violi even suggested the two thieves follow him home that night so they could case his neighbour's house.

As part of his self-anointed role as *padrone*, Violi, like Cotroni before him, demanded tribute from those doing business in the neighbourhoods he considered his territory. Violi's insistence on payments extended to both illegal and legal commerce, and at the height of his power, he was collecting protection money from every Italian shopkeeper in the St. Leonard district. One day, Giuseppe Petrozza, manager and owner of the Tricolori Pizzeria, was paid a visit by two of Paolo's soldiers, Massimo Di Rodolfo and Tony Mucci, who demanded $5,000 from him. Wiretaps and Mucci's own testimony before the provincial crime commission reveal that it was Violi who had "suggested" they extort the money and even provided instructions on how to do so. He told Mucci to first pass by the store to make sure there were no police around. He then instructed him to tell Petrozza "they want $5,000," and if the owner resisted, to "give him a few slaps in the face." Another Italian immigrant who ran a small window-washing business testified to the commission that he received a phone call asking him to draw up a bid for a contract to clean the windows at Violi's Reggio Bar. When he arrived with his bid, two of Violi's soldiers forced him down to the basement and, with a gun pointed at his head, was ordered to make out three cheques, each for $500. Later on, Paolo came down to the basement to close the deal and when the man begged Violi to intercede on his behalf, he was released but not before having to write two cheques. After the man bravely refused to take on Violi as his partner, he soon began losing most of his customers, which forced him out of business.

When he wasn't demanding tribute from local Italian businesses, Violi was methodically trying to corner certain local industries. He gained a monopoly over the sale of Italian ice cream in the north end of the city through force and intimidation. One witness before the crime commission testified there were only two firms making Italian ice cream in the Montreal area, "and the second wasn't allowed to sell it because Violi didn't want it to." In 1969, a newly arrived Ital-

ian immigrant named Mauro Marchettini opened a pool hall on the same block as the Reggio Bar. Before long, suppliers refused to make deliveries to the new business and after failing to heed a warning to close down, Violi unleashed his merciless brother Francesco, who beat Marchettini with a wooden paddle he used to make ice cream.

Despite his petty and brutish nature, Violi was also known to have a more genteel side. "As a mobster, he played his role with a warm smile and a friendly handshake," a *Toronto Star* reporter once wrote. "He drove around Montreal in a white Cadillac and frequently offered rides to those he knew." Anne Charney tells the story of Bob Beale, president of the St. Leonard Home and School Association in the mid-1960s, who vigorously opposed the removal of English language instruction at local schools, and as a result found himself harassed by nationalist extremists. Violi despised the Quebec sovereignists and offered Beale moral support. "If he saw me passing by he would call me over, invite me in for a coffee and tell me what a great job I was doing," Beale was quoted in Charney's 1979 article. "'My Boy' he would say — he always called me that — 'we admire you and we appreciate this.'" Violi even went so far as to station some of his men around Beale's house for protection. Violi's hatred of the sovereignists was surpassed only by his antipathy towards competing French-Canadian mobsters. Police intercepted one conversation between Violi and Vic Cotroni where Paolo brags about his attempted hit on Pierre Lacerte, who had threatened to murder him:

Violi: Last night I went to do the guy, but you didn't see it in the papers.

Cotroni: No ... he's dead?

Violi: No, he's ... the asshole didn't die!

Cotroni: You shot him?

Violi: Yes, three good ones in the head.

Cotroni: They know you did it?

Violi: No, no, no, no, no, no. But I'm telling you I did it, with another *picciotti* who, we went there. He was asleep. Bang, bang, bang. I fired three shots.

Cotroni: Did he recognize you?

Violi: No, no. He was asleep in the house, it was in the house.

Cotroni: You hit him with a couple. How many? And he got away?

Violi: Yes. But they don't have a name, but even if he lives, I don't think he'll be like before. That's if he doesn't die.

Cotroni: You'll shoot him again ...

Violi: Ha, ha, ha, ha ...

Violi was most likely lying to Vic about the attempted hit in order to impress him, although he was involved in ordering some of the various murders in the Montreal area that police blamed on inter-gang rivalries during the 1960s and 1970s. Between 1963 and 1969, 110 slayings were attributed to organized crime, seventy of which occurred in 1968 and 1969. A 1969 provincial inquiry into crime in Quebec blamed a number of the deaths on battles between the Magaddino and Bonanno families for control over Montreal's rackets. In fact, the violence was the result of ongoing conflicts between numerous criminal factions in the city, including the Italianmafia, French-Canadian mobsters, Irish criminal groups, and outlaw motorcycle gangs. The violence peaked in 1975, when there were more than two hundred murders in the province, including seventy-three that police categorized as gangland executions.

On the front lines for the Cotroni *decina* in their battles against rival French-Canadian mobsters was Joe Di Maulo and his brother Vincenzo. On May 4, 1968, Gilles Bienvenue and Albert Ouimet, two men associated with a French-Canadian gang led by Richard Blass, were shot to death by masked gunmen. Three days later, Roger Larue, a member of the Blass gang who had vowed revenge, was seen in a heated argument with Joe and Vincenzo. Larue was murdered hours later. In October 1968, Joe Di Maulo opened fire on Richard Blass, who was wounded in the head and back but survived. On May 6, 1969, Vincenzo Di Maulo and two other Cotroni soldiers pumped a dozen bullets into another French-Canadian gang member. A number of bystanders witnessed the killing, which helped lead to murder convictions against the three men. On March 12, 1971, Joe Di Maulo and three others were found guilty of first-degree murder in the slaying of three French-Canadian gangsters, but had their convictions overturned on

appeal. On July 10, 1973, two Cotroni soldiers were slain after they were accused of selling poor-quality heroin to drug dealer Angelo Facchino. Paolo Violi was outraged and blamed it on members of a French-Canadian motorcycle gang who worked with Facchino. "They shot up some Italian *picciotti* and that's no good for any of us," Violi told Vic. "They've got to be dealt with."

Paolo's call to arms resulted in a meeting among the *decina*'s ranking members. Their goal, in Violi's own words, was to "figure out what the hell we're going to do with these Frenchmen." During another meeting between Violi and Frank Cotroni on July 31, 1973, Frank tells Paolo that he knows the French-Canadian men involved in the murder, saying they were "crazy, crazy, crazy ... They've killed something like 10 guys already!" Frank agreed to take care of these men, while Violi said he would handle Facchino. He gave the job to Tony Vanelli and Moreno Gallo and on September 2, 1973, Facchino was murdered. A few weeks later, police wiretaps recorded Violi fuming over the death of another of his *picciotti* named Tony Di Genova, who was killed in retaliation just twelve days after Facchino was assassinated. Violi told two unidentified men that the Di Genova murder "never should have happened" and the only reason it did was because Frank Cotroni wasted too much time in taking care of the "Frenchmen" who ended up assassinating Di Genova. "I told Frankie to leave the Italian [Facchino] to me and to hit the Frenchmen first ... He should have gone into the club, clients or no clients, lined everybody up against the wall and rat-a-tat-tat." At a meeting held at the end of September attended by Vic and Frank Cotroni, Paolo Violi, Nicholas Di Iorio, and Tony Mucci, the decision was made that there would be no reprisals for the Di Genova hit, at least for the time being.

THE BROTHERS DUBOIS

Paolo Violi's contempt for French-Canadian criminals was returned with equal vehemence by Claude Dubois, the leader of Montreal's only other crime group that could seriously rival the strength and scope of the Cotroni clan during the 1960s and 1970s. "They put Violi as a big king," Dubois once remarked in an interview. "To me, Violi's a punk. He tried to go and collect a guy for $100 a week with a punch in the nose. You don't call that a king. For me, he's a punk, no?"

Claude Dubois knew plenty about punks and gangsters. At its height, the Dubois network of criminals comprised about two hundred men loosely organized into independent gangs of several dozen members. At the centre of this criminal constellation were nine Dubois brothers: Raymond, Jean-Guy, Normand, Claude, Rene, Roland, Jean-Paul, and twins Maurice and Adrien. The Quebec Police Commission paid the Dubois brothers the ultimate compliment when it wrote in its 1977 report, "Some maintain that the ruthless methods of the Dubois, the large number of toughs gravitating about each of the nine brothers, as well as the widely dreaded cruelty of their hirelings, make them the most influential criminal group at the present time on the Island of Montreal."

The brothers grew up in a poor family in the working-class district of Saint Henri in southwest Montreal and began cultivating a reputation for toughness and criminal behaviour during their teenage years. The older brothers — Jean-Guy, Raymond, Normand, and Claude — "were physically sturdy, aggressive, given to brawling and closely united as a group, having quickly learned the truth of the saying that in unity there is strength," the commission wrote. "Together they constituted from the very beginning a gang that was perfectly cohesive, with which few in that part of town could compete." The cornerstone of their criminal fortunes was intimidation and violence and they reigned like feudal lords over legitimate and illegitimate businesses alike in the territories they controlled. They terrorized the owners of bars and nightclubs, forced them to pay protection money, and then took over their businesses. They used similar tactics to organize a network of pimps, prostitutes, drug dealers, loan sharks, strippers, thieves, and fences. When the Cotroni *decina* began to show signs of weakness during the early 1970s, the Dubois brothers expanded into their territory in both the east and west ends of the city. They virtually wiped out a rival Irish gang and took over lucrative drug markets in Montreal's downtown by outmuscling motorcycle gangs.

Their criminal careers began with a series of burglaries and armed robberies during the early 1950s.

Claude Dubois

By the end of the decade, five of the brothers were charged with, but later acquitted of, murdering a waiter who was shot in a bar after a quarrel. By the 1960s, the brothers began specializing in extortion, targeting the owners and employees of nightclubs, bars, and taverns in the eastern part of the city. If an owner refused their demands, the brothers and their associates would make nightly visits to the establishment where they would threaten the staff and patrons, pick fights, vandalize the premises, and attack the proprietor until he finally gave in. Charles Houle, the owner of a bar on Notre-Dame Street West, told the police commission how Raymond Dubois paid a visit shortly after the bar opened in 1965 and demanded that he be paid $100 a week. When Houle testified before the commission in 1975, he was still paying protection money, which he estimated had totalled more than $50,000. Once a Dubois brother gained a foothold in a particular business, he would force the owner to hire gang associates as managers and staff. The newly hired personnel would then collect protection money, control the hiring of personnel, and oversee criminal activities on the premises, including drug trafficking, loan sharking, gambling, and fencing stolen goods.

Those who refused a Dubois brother or associate paid the ultimate price, as was the case of Louis Fournier, owner of the Jean Lou Cabaret, who was murdered on June 20, 1971. After rebuffing the brothers, Laurier Gatien, the owner of the nearby Tavern Montréal, endured several attempts on his life that involved shootings, knifings, and attacks with billiard cues and balls. Despite police protection, and the conviction of Dubois-hired assassins, Gatien finally relented to the pressure and sold his tavern in October 1973.

Claude Dubois extended this protection racket to pimps and prostitutes who were forced to purchase a "work permit" for $35 if they wished to ply a street or an establishment controlled by a Dubois family member. He also extracted a percentage of their revenue. When one prostitute refused to pay her fee, acid was thrown into her face. The Dubois brothers also muscled their way into a booking agency for strippers, the Paul Calce Agency. Claude Dubois collected $250 a week from the agency, which in return received a monopoly over booking dancers at Montreal's strip joints. By the 1970s, the Dubois gang had become the foremost loan sharks in the west end, using the bars they took over as their offices. To obtain a loan, a borrower had to visit one of the Dubois-controlled bars and if the loan was approved, the money was either given directly to the borrower or delivered by a courier. Cash repayments were expected to be made at the same establishment. The interest on most loans ran about 30 percent a month.

The Dubois brothers prospered throughout the 1970s as they continued to expand their territory and criminal activities. A 1977 Quebec Police Commission report described most of the gang as living in "opulence if we can judge by the external manifestations of wealth, such as town houses, country houses, expensive cars and an ostentatious life style." The brothers' success as a criminal organization can be attributed to their family bond, which gave the gang "a kind of loyalty and cohesion that protect against internal dangers such as defection, stool pigeons, or power struggles," according to the commission, which also observed that "nine brothers and their friends, in a cohesive nucleus, can put up a firm resistance against attacks from outside and make convincing use of threats of reprisal." There was never any formal hierarchy to their organization;

each brother, either individually or in tandem with another, controlled a particular territory or criminal activity and had his own small army of soldiers, which was often shared among the brothers.

In addition to their intermittent battles with the Montreal mafia, in 1973 the Dubois brothers began an open war with the McSween gang, a smaller group of Irish-Canadian mobsters who had controlled territory adjacent to that of the Dubois brothers for a number of years. Pierre McSween and his brothers Jacques and Andre began working with the Dubois brothers in the mid-1950s to help support their fatherless family. They committed thefts, burglaries, and truck hijackings for their criminal contractors, who in turn supplied the McSweens with weapons, getaway cars, and hired hands for a cut of between 10 and 20 percent of the loot. In the early 1970s, the McSweens began operating more independently and, by 1973, they controlled a number of rackets in a portion of downtown Montreal just east of Dubois territory. Among the most profitable of the McSweens' criminal activities was a loan-shark business that brought in $7,000 to $8,000 a week. They also scored big on a crooked bookmaking operation that took bets on the time the Montreal Canadiens scored their last goal in their home games. There were very few payoffs, however, as Jacques McSween had an arrangement with the official timekeeper at the Montreal Forum to ensure that the time of the goal reported in the newspapers was altered. The rigged lottery brought in between $15,000 and $18,000 a week for the McSweens.

The Dubois brothers were intent on driving the McSweens from their territory and launched what would be called the "war over the west end." More than a dozen lives were lost on both sides, but the French-Canadian gangsters emerged victorious, enabling them to extend their territory. When the smoke finally cleared in June 1975, nine men linked to the McSween gang were dead. In the Montreal version of the St. Valentine's Day Massacre, four men were killed on February 13, 1975 when Dubois hit men opened fire in the bar of the South Shore Lapiniere Hotel, a McSween hangout. Three of those killed had no association with the gang. "They weren't cool killers," Pierre McSween told the police commission. "They stood too far back and sprayed the place ... Cool guys would have walked up to the table and put a bullet in the target's head, that way nobody else gets hit."

Among the war dead was Jacques McSween, who was killed on October 5, 1974, after being ambushed at his home by Jean-Guy, Adrien, and Claude Dubois. All three men were charged with the murder based on evidence provided by Donald Lavoie, who was at the scene of the crime but insisted his role was confined to driving the getaway van. Despite his remonstrations, Lavoie was the Dubois brothers' most prolific killer. He confessed to single-handedly murdering fifteen people, participating in thirty-four others, and possessing evidence on seventy-six killings in total. In 1980, Lavoie began working as an informer for the Montreal police and in exchange, he entered the witness protection program and was able to escape charges in all of the murders to which he confessed.

The war was instigated when Real Lepine, a friend and drug trafficking associate of the McSweens, was killed in a bar on Notre Dame Street West after refusing to deal drugs sold by Adrien Dubois. The Dubois brothers — especially Adrien, Claude, and Roland — had logically branched off into drug trafficking and by the mid-1970s, they controlled the sale of marijuana, hashish, LSD, amphetamines, and cocaine in the west end and centre of the city. The drugs were distributed through a web of dealers working in the licensed establishments under control of the brothers. In late 1973 and early 1974, Montreal police seized nearly two million tenuate pills, a prescription-based amphetamine being distributed by Adrien Dubois.

Claude Dubois gained control over the drug trade in parts of the downtown area by scaring away one of Montreal's most vicious motorcycle gangs. As the Quebec Police Commission wrote, "The Claude Dubois gang is so strong that it was able to take over this important territory, almost without striking a blow, from a greatly feared motorcycle gang, the 'Devil's Disciples,' noted for their violence and for the bloody battles they had with rival factions." The Disciples had carved out a profitable drug trafficking enclave in Saint-Louis Square in downtown Montreal around 1972, which quickly became the city's largest open-air drug market. Viewing this as an intrusion into his territory, Claude Dubois dispatched a group of hired muscle to expel the bikers and between August

1974 and January 1976, fifteen members of the Devil's Disciples were killed.

In a telephone conversation that took place on July 12, 1975, Jean-Guy Giguere, who had just met with Claude Dubois, informed Claude Ellefesen, the leader of the drug dealing wing of the Disciples operating in Saint-Louis Square, that Dubois had put a contract on Giguere's head and that of his associate Pierre McDuff (who was murdered in his car just a few days following the conversation). By the end of the phone call Ellefesen made it clear that he had no intention of crossing the "big one," Claude Dubois:

Ellefesen: Another thing ... Dubois, the big one ...
Giguere: Hm ... hm ...
Ellefesen: He knows I was makin' money out of "dope" you know ...
Giguere: Oh! Yeah.
Ellefesen: Like, he wanted to take over my business.
Giguere: Oh! Maybe.
Ellefesen: Like, you know, I didn't bug him, man, I just got the hell out.
Giguere: Yeah.
Ellefesen: I started business somewhere else.

On November 17, 1975, the Quebec Police Commission began hearings that focussed on the Dubois brothers and, on December 8, a special police task force was established to dismantle their gang. By the fall of 1976, the constant police attention began to take its toll on the brothers; their network of criminals began to unravel, their drug markets withered through police undercover operations, and their foothold in Montreal's bars and other businesses was slipping away. Many of the gang's most notorious and loyal associates had either met violent deaths, become police informants, or had fled Montreal. By 1977, Claude and Adrien were charged with perjury for providing false testimony to the commission, and Roland and Normand faced assault charges. Earlier that year, Jean-Paul received a year's sentence for possessing the proceeds of a $100,000 jewellery theft and was also charged with contempt and perjury by the commission. On April 27, 1977, Jean Guy Dubois was found guilty of second-degree murder in the death of Jean-Guy Fournier. On November 12, 1982,

Claude Dubois, the driving force behind his family's sprawling criminal empire, was convicted of ordering the 1973 murder of Frank Cotroni's brother-in-law, Richard Desormiers, at the Mons Pays bar and was sentenced to life imprisonment without parole for at least twenty-five years.

INSTANTLY OBSOLETE

The government and police cordon that closed in on the Dubois brothers was no less yielding for Paolo Violi and the criminal organization he was now leading. In May 1975, the Quebec Police Commission began hearings into the tainted-meat scandal, which resulted in a scathing report, descriptively entitled *The Fraudulent Marketing of Meat Unfit for Consumption and Fraud in Connection with Horse Meat*. The hearings also led to fifty-five police raids in Quebec that resulted in the seizure of more than 500,000 pounds of meat and a city of Montreal injunction shutting down Reggio Foods, which was enforced through a twenty-four-hour police presence at the company's plant.

Willie Obront had fled Canada in August 1974 so he would not have to appear before the commission and relocated to Miami. His presence in the U.S. had become an embarrassment to the American government, however, especially when it was learned that the Canadian mobster was able to bypass the usual five-year waiting period for naturalization. When extradition proceedings were undertaken by the Canadian government in May 1976, he fled again, this time to Costa Rica, but was expelled the same month. Under RCMP escort, he was brought back to Canada where he was sentenced to a one-year prison term for his refusal to testify to the commission. Around the same time he was convicted of tax evasion and fraud, including a charge of fleecing creditors of Obie's Meat Market out of $515,991, and was sentenced to four years in prison. The Quebec Police Commission also forced Armand Courville into retirement after his controlling interest in Reggio Foods was exposed and many of his other businesses were forced into bankruptcy following revelations at the hearings.

In November 1975, Paolo Violi was sentenced to a year in prison and a $25,000 fine for conspiring to manipulate Buffalo Gas and Oil shares on the Montreal Stock Exchange. That same month, Violi, Vic

Vic Cotroni in 1975

Cotroni, and Hamilton-based mobster John Papalia were arrested for conspiring to extort $300,000 from a Toronto stock promoter. To make matters worse, the Quebec Police Commission began new hearings the same month, focussing again on the Montreal mafia. By early December, evidence presented before the public hearing confirmed that Paolo Violi and Vincenzo Cotroni were "co-directors" of the Canadian division of a powerful New York crime family. On December 1, Violi was subpoenaed to testify before the commission. He was handed his notice to appear upon arriving at Dorval Airport in Montreal after being whisked from Toronto by police where he was being held on the aforementioned extortion charges. Just before he was transported back to Montreal, Violi was arrested by the Ontario Provincial Police, acting on a Canada-wide warrant charging Violi with conspiracy to commit grievous assault.

This charge stemmed from a 1972 attack on Pasquale Tullio by two of Violi's soldiers. Paolo had ordered the assault on behalf of Michael Cutoni who had paid Violi $375 to avenge his honour after Tullio had struck Cutoni during an argument over money.

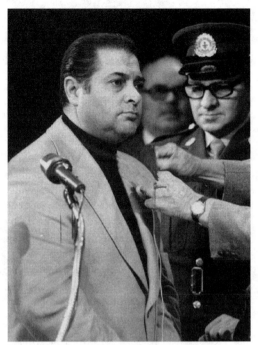

Paolo Violi appearing before the Quebec Police Commission

At Violi's preliminary hearing the judge acquitted him of the assault charge because neither Cutoni nor Tullio would testify that Violi was involved in the attack. Despite this victory, Violi was sentenced to one year in Bordeaux Prison on December 2, 1975, for refusing to answer questions before the provincial crime probe. His stay in prison was short; just before Christmas he was released on bail by the Quebec Court of Appeals after his lawyers successfully petitioned the Supreme Court of Canada to scrutinize the constitutionality of the Quebec Police Commission. Violi now appeared to be untouchable. That was until the commission introduced stunning evidence that would prove to be fatal to Violi's honour and power.

In December 1970, Bob Menard, an undercover police officer posing as an electrician, began renting a flat above Violi's Reggio Bar, located on Jean-Talon Street in the St. Leonard district of Montreal. This allowed police to plant electronic listening devices throughout the bar and Violi's adjoining offices. Along with the telephone bugs already in place, police now had almost unlimited access to conversations Violi and his colleagues held in his de facto headquarters. In a

media interview following the end of his undercover duties, Menard described his unease as he walked into the bar, along with an undercover policewoman posing as his girlfriend, and encountered Violi face-to-face for the first time, "He was sitting way at the other end of the room with half a dozen flunkies around him. When he looked up to examine us I remember being struck by his eyes. They were the most piercing eyes I'd ever seen. They seemed to look right through you, and I'll tell you, they shook me up a lot more than the questions." After interviewing Menard, Violi informed him that he could rent the flat. It would be the single-worst decision Violi ever made in his life. In his quest to generate a little more revenue for himself, Violi provided a crucial opening for "Project Benoit," the most revealing surveillance operation ever launched against the Montreal mob. Beginning in October 1975, the provincial crime commission began to release selective transcripts of the recordings. The result, according to journalist Anne Charney, was that "Violi's private conversations, revealed for all the world to hear, made him vulnerable not only to public authority but also the authority of the mafia. In a world where silence, *omerta*, is a first commandment, the daily serialization of Violi's rule rendered him instantly obsolete."

The most serious threat to Paolo Violi came not from the government, however, but from within his own crime group. The cleavages that were festering between the Sicilian and Calabrian members were now coming to a head. The result would be a power struggle that lingered until 1981, resulting in more than twenty casualties in Montreal and Italy. The main instigator of the internal strife was the *decina*'s most errant and rebellious member, Nicolò (Nick) Rizzuto. Born on February 18, 1924, Rizzuto grew up in the small Sicilian town of Cattolica Eraclea, located in the province of Agrigento, a mafia stronghold. After marrying Libertina Manno, their first child, Vito, was born on February 21, 1946. Their daughter, Maria, would arrive soon after. Rizzuto had married into the local mafia family, which was led by his new father-in-law, Antonio Manno. When he immigrated to Canada with his wife and children in 1954, Rizzuto renewed contact with his mafia family members and other Sicilian mafiosi who had already relocated to Montreal. Most likely recruited by Luigi Greco, he

Nicolò (Nick) Rizzuto

became a member of the Cotroni *decina* sometime in the late 1950s or early 1960s. While working under the Calabrian leadership of Vic Cotroni and Paolo Violi, Rizzuto steadily built his own crew of expatriate Sicilians drawing from a well-established network of mafia members and prospects that had immigrated to Canada from the province of Agrigento.

Among his most faithful allies in Montreal were the Caruana and Cuntrera families. The patriarchs of the two clans, Pasquale Cuntrera and bothers Leonardo and Liborio Caruana, were born in Siculiana, a small village on the southern shores of Agrigento. Joined by blood and intermarriage, the two families formed a criminal clique that ruled their village. In the early 1950s, Pasquale Cuntrera and Leonardo Caruana were arraigned on homicide charges and fled Sicily for Canada. For the next twenty years, family members from three generations began to emigrate to various parts of the world — Canada, England, Venezuela, Switzerland — where they forged what would eventually become one of the world's largest drug trafficking conspiracies. The Cuntreras settled briefly in Montreal before moving to Venezuela, headquarters for their

international drug network, while the Caruanas moved to England and then Venezuela before finally settling in Canada. Wherever they were located, the families were unwavering partners of Nicolò Rizzuto.

While Rizzuto made a significant contribution to the financial coffers of the Montreal *decina*, he grew increasingly frustrated with the Calabrian leadership. As Peter Edwards and Antonio Nicaso write, instead of following the orders of Violi and Cotroni, "Rizzuto glibly ignored them, doing whatever he pleased, whenever he pleased. Worse yet, newly arrived Sicilian mobsters in Montreal gravitated toward him, while ignoring old Calabrian leadership." Rizzuto's rebellious behaviour was an extension and perhaps even a deliberate provocation of the chasm that was fermenting between the Sicilian and Calabrian factions of the Montreal mafia. In a 1967 article entitled "Mafia families active in Canada," the *New York Times* reported, "the Canadian police have seen indications of disharmony between Greco and the Cotroni brothers." This was due in part to the elevation of the Calabrian Vic Cotroni to the highest post in the Bonanno Family's Montreal wing, relegating the Sicilian Greco to a subordinate role. As one senior Canadian police officer told the newspaper, "Greco is only a door opener for Vic Controni." Greco had good reason to be insulted. Not only did he share Sicilian roots with the Bonanno Family leadership, he also had seniority over Cotroni in the family hierarchy. If Greco was resentful, it rarely showed; by all accounts he faithfully served his don until his death in 1972. The difference between Luigi Greco and Nicolò Rizzuto was that Greco appeared willing to accept a subservient role for himself and his fellow Sicilians in the Cotroni *decina*.

Rizzuto's frustration peaked when Cotroni's protégé and fellow Calabrian Paolo Violi was appointed interim leader in 1974, prompting him to operate even more independently. Rizzuto's wayward behaviour infuriated Violi, who constantly complained about his lack of respect for the leadership of the *decina*. In one conversation taped by police, Violi grumbled that Rizzuto "goes from one thing to the other, here and there, and says nothing to nobody, he does things and nobody knows nothing." As the Quebec Police Commission wrote in their 1977 report, Paolo and Vic's main grievances against Rizzuto "were that he was a lone wolf, that he stayed away from occasions where members of the family could meet and discuss together, that he showed respect neither to his superiors nor to those placed under his charge, that he lied about his real intentions, that he by passed the line of command and acted on his own initiative in important matters, and finally that he would come and go without letting anyone know what he was doing."

The mutual antipathy between Rizzuto and Violi only grew as Paolo did everything in his power to contain the growth and influence of the Sicilians within the Montreal mafia. In a number of conversations taped by police, Violi made it clear that any new Sicilian recruit would have to serve a five-year probation period before they could become a made member (in contrast, Carmine Galante, who was now heading the Bonanno Family after being released from prison in 1974, was initiating recent Sicilian arrivals into the New York family with little or no waiting period). On April 22, 1974, Paolo explained his rules to Pino Cuffaro, "No 'cause you see, Pino, things here, I know all about how it is in America. Someone who comes here from Italy, it's orders and you better believe it, he has to stay here for five years under us … After the five years are up, then everyone can see what he's like …" On May 10, 1974, Violi said in reference to one Sicilian prospect, "We're keeping him near us. When the right time comes, we'll have him sent here, but today there's no chance, 'cause the positions are all taken for now." For Peter Edwards and Antonio Nicaso, Violi's membership rules were a means to establish some independence from both Sicily and America; he "was giving a Declaration of Independence of sorts, saying that the colonies had grown up and expected some respect. Especially the Calabrians in the colonies like him." But given his oft-repeated request for more soldiers, Violi's insistence on the five-year probationary period should more rightly be seen as a strategic ploy to ensure that the Sicilian bloc did not grow so strong as to outweigh the dominant Calabrian faction.

Vic Cotroni and Paolo Violi felt so betrayed by Rizzuto's contemptuous and provocative actions that they moved to have him formally expelled from the Montreal *decina* and even considered seeking permission from New York to have him killed. But Violi was smart enough to know that New York would never sanction such an extreme move, especially given the drug trafficking revenues that Rizzuto was generating. Vic Cotroni also preferred a mediated settlement and, in conjunction with Violi, sought advice and arbitration from numerous senior mafiosi in New York and Sicily, some of whom travelled to Montreal to adjudicate the dispute. Violi went so far as to travel to New York at the beginning of 1972 to discuss the Rizzuto problem with Natale (Joe Diamond) Evola, the new boss of the Bonanno Family. Evola promised Violi that as soon as he had put his own family affairs in order, he would send an envoy to Montreal to settle this quarrel. In September of that year, two ranking members of the Bonanno Family arrived in Montreal and, after sitting down with each side, decided that Rizzuto should stay in the Montreal *decina*. This decision infuriated Cotroni who, in one police recording, fumed that he had the power to kick Rizzuto out, "Me, I'm *capo decina*. I got the right to expel."

But Vic and Paolo were not about to challenge the authority of New York and, while both lost face as a result of the decision, they exacted some revenge when Paolo was named interim head of the family in 1974. This appointment was the final affront for Rizzuto, who fled to Venezuela the same year to join the Cuntrera family in Caracas. With their growing narco-wealth, the influence of the Cuntreras and Rizzuto grew among their mafia colleagues in North America. Despite his distance from Quebec, Rizzuto had no intention of forsaking his membership in the Bonanno Family or its Montreal wing. While Nick and the Cuntreras were establishing their international base in Caracas, Vito Rizzuto and the Caruana brothers remained in Montreal to help coordinate the importation of heroin and cocaine and to maintain a foothold in the city and in the Cotroni-Violi organization until such time as the opportunity presented itself to launch a coup.

That moment came in 1976 as Violi's power and stature within the Bonanno Family was decimated by the public release of the police wiretap transcripts. While Violi's selection as interim head of the Montreal *decina* had the blessing of New York, he would never be forgiven for allowing himself to become enmeshed in the police dragnet. Violi made matters worse by telling Carmine Galante that the Sicilian faction of the Montreal mafia continued to ignore his author-ity. It was no coincidence that around this time Nick Rizzuto was spending much more time in Montreal. He also travelled to New York City where he met with Galante, in part to seek permission to remove Violi, who, he argued, had become a liability and an embarrassment to the family. The events that followed over the next few years are proof that Rizzuto received the permission he sought from New York to eliminate Violi and his supporters. Pietro Sciarra, Paolo's most trusted adviser who backed him in his battle against Rizzuto despite the fact that he was Sicilian, was the first to go. On February 14, 1976, as he was leaving a Cotroni-owned movie theatre with his wife, Sciarra was shot dead (ironically the couple had just watched the Italian-language version of *The Godfather, Part II)*. Francesco Violi, the tall and physically imposing younger brother by nine years, was next on the list. If Sciarra was targeted because he was Paolo's *consigliere*, Francesco was second on the list because he was Paolo's most loyal enforcer. On February 8, 1977, while Paolo Violi languished in jail on extortion charges, Francesco was ambushed at his family's import business by two gunmen who barged into his office, forced him against the wall, and shot him execution style.

In May 1977, Violi was freed from a Toronto jail after the Ontario Court of Appeal reduced a six-year sentence handed to him and Vic Cotroni on extor-tion charges. While Violi must have suspected that he would be the next target, he carried on with his life and attended his regular hangouts. On January 22, 1978, he received a phone call inviting him to play cards at the Reggio Bar, which he had sold some months earlier to brothers Giuseppe and Vincenzo Randisi. Paolo promised his wife that he would be home in time for dinner. After arriving at the bar, he settled into a chair at a table behind a partition at the back of the room and began playing cards with three others. Around 7:30 p.m., two masked men entered through the back door and walked straight toward the table. Approaching Violi from behind, one of the hired killers pointed a 12-gauge Italian Lupara shotgun — a traditional mafia execution weapon — at the back of his head and pulled the trigger. A second superfluous but symbolic bullet was also fired into the top of his skull. One of the men playing cards with Paolo was said to

have kissed him on the cheek — the traditional *bacio della morte* (kiss of death) — right before the fatal shot was fired. Paolo Violi was forty-six years old.

The media reported that Violi knew for months that a contract worth as much as $50,000 had been placed on his life. But, as Peter Edwards and Antonio Nicaso write in their book on Canadian mafia mur-ders, "Paolo Violi had had no plan to fight back. He had willingly gone to his old café — the centre of the fiefdom he had once controlled — to die." He had betrayed the code of *omerta* and now, as a man of honour, was willing to accept the consequences. Other organized crime experts dispute that he went to the bar knowing he would be killed. For Lee Lamothe and Humphreys, Violi — whom they characterized as "a relatively unintelligent thug and provincial thinker who had an inflated view of his own power" — was completely unaware "he was being drawn into a trap by the Rizzuto Family the day he died. He believed a meeting was being arranged for the following week that would accommodate the use of Montreal as a heroin pipeline into the United States; the arrange-ment, he was told, would leave him in control of the day-to-day organized crime activities of the Quebec underworld."

Whether Paolo had accepted his fate or not, there was little uncertainty about who was behind the hit. Police were well aware of the feud between the Calabrian and Sicilian factions and also had numerous clues to work with in uncovering Violi's assassins. Several weeks before the murder, Montreal police began following a white van loaded with guns, ammunition, and ski masks. They felt certain they were on the trail of hired killers, but did not know the identity of the intended victim.

Police crime scene photo of Paolo Violi

Frank Cotroni arriving at Montreal's Dorval Airport in 1979 after being released from U.S. custody

Due to a lack of resources, police had to call off their surveillance just a month after it began and only a day before Violi's murder. On the basis of the information already gathered from the aborted surveillance, police were able to quickly identify five suspects in Violi's death and arrested three of them. All had connections to the Rizzuto and Cuntrera families: Domenico Manno was Nick Rizzuto's brother-in-law, Agostino Cuntrera was a member of the Cuntrera family, and Giovanni DiMora had married into the Cuntrera clan. Despite the evidence against them, the three were able to get away with pleading guilty to murder conspiracy charges and received minimum sentences ranging from five to seven years. Police were unable to wrest any confessions on who ordered the hit.

Nick Rizzuto returned to Montreal shortly after Violi's murder and, along with his son, assumed control of the *decina*. While the elimination of Violi removed the last obstacle to Sicilian control of the mafia in Quebec, Nick and Vito did build a working relationship with members of the Calabrian faction. However, it was their Sicilian network, in particular the Caruanas and Cuntreras, that would form the nucleus of this new chapter in the Montreal mafia's history. Due to the shared origins and close relations between these three families, Italian authorities began referring to them collectively as the Siciliana Family, a title that refers to the region of Sicily from which all three families originated. With much of his ambitions realized, Nick Rizzuto passed the reins of power to his capable son, Vito, and returned to Venezuela to rejoin the Caruanas and Cuntreras. The Siciliana Family was to ensure Montreal continued as a gateway for drugs imported into North America, whether it was heroin now being processed in Sicily, cocaine from South America, or hashish from Pakistan and Lebanon. Rizzuto's rise to power was paved through drug trafficking and when he took power he steered the Montreal mafia away from localized criminal ventures, such as extortion and theft, towards the much more lucrative trade in narcotics. As Peter Edwards writes, the Montreal mafia was being transformed from a neighbourhood-based group that "mediated community disputes while parading as living embodiment of manly honour" to a multi-national drug trafficking conglomerate. And it was Rizzuto's partners, the Cuntrera-Caruana group that

"represented the new spirit in the Mafia. They took as their role-model the daring venture capitalists."

The Sicilians' consolidation of their power over the Montreal mafia was heightened as the remainder of the old guard began to die off or join forces with the new leadership. Police considered Paolo's brother Rocco to be only a minor participant in the Calabrian faction. Nonetheless, he was seen by the Sicilians as a threat and in order to eliminate the possibility of reprisals, Rocco had to go. On October 17, 1980, he was killed with a single shot to the heart while he sat at his kitchen table with his sons. A year earlier, Pep Cotroni died (of natural causes) after eight years of freedom from prison and his own successful return to narcotics trafficking. The remaining members of the Montreal mafia now pledged their fidelity to Nick and Vito Rizzuto. Among those who accepted the changing of the guard was Frank Cotroni, who was released from a U.S. prison into a vastly changed Montreal underworld on April 25, 1979. He was welcomed into the Rizzuto-led mafia, or at least tolerated, because of his drug trafficking experience.

On July 12, 1979, Carmine Galante was shot dead as part of the New York mafia's ongoing power struggles and as a direct result of his own unrelenting ambition to become the don of all dons. Galante's death was symbolic for organized crime in Montreal, for it was he more than anyone else that made the mafia in that city a branch plant of the New York families. And like that of Paolo Violi, his murder also marked a turning point for the Montreal mafia insomuch as the Rizzutos began to slowly seek greater independence from New York. While the Rizzutos did not immediately cut ties with the Bonanno Family, over the years they gained considerable autonomy to the point where they were no longer considered simply a *decina,* but an autonomous "family" in their own right.

As for Vic Cotroni, his life was spared because of the status he enjoyed in Montreal's gangland, but also because it was only a matter of time before his cancer-riddled body would cease to function. On September 16, 1984, Vincenzo Cotroni, the mafia don who built Canada's most powerful criminal organization, died of cancer at the age of seventy-four. His funeral featured a twenty-three-car procession, massive floral arrangements, and a seventeen-piece brass band. The passing of Vic Cotroni was equally symbolic for the consolidation of the Rizzutos' power. Over the next two decades, Vito Rizzuto would entrench his position as the most powerful mafia don, and perhaps the most powerful criminal in all of Canada, while increasingly asserting his independence from the Cosa Nostra, thereby establishing one of Canada's first truly independent mafia families.

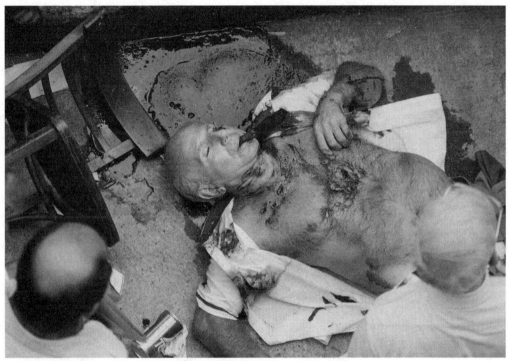

The body of Carmine Galante immediately following his 1979 assassination, cigar still firmly clenched in his teeth

THE UNDERTAKER, THE THREE DONS, THE ENFORCER, AND OTHER TALES OF THE MAFIOSI IN ONTARIO

'NDRANGHETA HOWL

I saw the best criminal minds in Ontario destroyed by sloth, carelessness, and greed

Rocco Perri, the once tip-top daddy of the bootleggers,
       now under cement bedsheets, upping some real crazy watery riffs?
But beat me daddy, eight to the bar
       'cause the three dons straight from Calabria are re-animating the 'Ndrangheta in Ontario, a
       sweet swinging sphere for The Society

At the top of the pops sat Don Stefano
       portly, balding Undertaker; one bad boss reigning from his Buffalo pad
       with Ontario under his thumb while he dines on Italian flesh, long gone
To solitude! Waving! Don Stafano! I'm with you in Ontario, where you mine the anti-Victorian under-
       ground and plot the next criminal revolution

The Sylvestro and Cipolla families putting it down into illegal jazz water, craps, and hops
       Jive, jump, kicksville;
       Making the scene
       Laying it on Ontario
A new generation of junk dealers, and if that don't turn you on brother
       you ain't got no stitches

Dan Gasbarrini
       a solid wig, totally uncubistic hep cat,
       a member of the Magaddino clan

Carrying the hop out west
    high, fly and too wet to dry
The void is no longer in Ontario

Johnny Pops in Hamilton, pressed stud
    stay cool, hang loose, and don't admit nothing
My solid pigeon, that roscoe is a killer-diller
    an e-flat dillinger, hell-bent on taking over Toronto the Good.
They stone his soul to its body again
    from its pilgrimage to a cross in the darkness under the loveless!
Corrupt Moloch! The heavy judger of men!
Moloch whose eyes are a thousand black jacks, billy-bats, and knuckle-dusters!
Gangster in Moloch!

Vincent Feeley and Joseph McDermott,
    hip to the hipsters of gamblers, all rejoicing in Toronto's secreted soul
    that shivered the city down to the last honest copper
    with the echoes of shuffling cards and rolling dice and counted dollars
    the mad hatters of Toronto who bang the same bebop rackets
I'm with you in Toronto where you will split the subterranean heavens
    and resurrect your living human soul from the dustbin of irrelevancy

His friends called him "Maxie", the sabbath-observing gambling boss who blew
    and then was dragged off to the Town Tavern to bop with the Enforcer
Never to be the same again
    hincty, hung up, a link in a chain that leads to insanity
    one crazy cat, frantic threads, while continuing alone, his back lifts to Heaven!
Heaven which exists and is everywhere about us! Visions!
Omens! Hallucinations! Lunacies! Crazy man.

The Agueci brothers, Vito and Alberto
    their evenings in Sicilian rose gardens
    knee high in white butu powder brought over to satiate America.
The one-eyed shrew that does nothing but ingest and vomit and ingest again
Angel-headed hipsters burning for the ancient heavenly connection to the visible mad man
    and to be a victim
tramped down the stroll, burned flesh, tapsville, eclipse of the doom
    bought, sold, and done for

Big Boss Giacomo Luppino
    falling in and digging the happenings in Steel town suburbs
    Calabrian, Mafiosi, Magaddino capo, head of La Camera di Controllo
Ontario mobsters of Steel town I'm with you, says Magaddino the master
    righteous, putting it down, way down
    besides the flapping laundry of suburbia

Michele Racco, undisputed Siderno daddy
    copasetic, cool, a real gone, ding-dong daddy
Mooch the system
    but he don't go for that magoo
    he gets the signal, cool and clear
Moloch the incomprehensible prison!
Moloch the soulless jailhouse and Parliament of sorrows!

Vople using his Big Apple connections,
    to become a member of the Magaddino Family.
Volpe in Toronto where you tear it down, just to build it up again
    suave hep cat, the cat's pyjamas, a solid wig
    busting his four-flushing conk, putting the bite on everyone
    only to be dragged off to the airport! To solitude!
I'm with you in Toronto where you laugh at this invisible hypocrisy
I'm with you in Toronto where you scream in a straightjacket
    that you're innocent and the immortal should never die
But you are not the living end
You are the end

A history of 'Ndrangheta
    manifested in the Commisso brothers,
    big barracudas, bottom dealers, midnight ramblers
    vipes, but too many vops
    boots laced up too tight. flipped out violence
    blowing in off Lake Ontario only to be done in by a chop-beating wired biker

Extortion is the Musitanos' bag
    and they go crazy on their own reign of terror
Squall, ball and climb the wall
Putting it down with dynamite, blasting others wacky
    peeling the ears, loose as a goose, and getting in with the Devil's Disciples
Only to be abandoned and turned in
    after clipping cokehead Domenic, the glorified drugstore cowboy
Canceling his Christmas. Scratching him from the big race.
The Eternal Checkout. The Big Chill.
And if I'm lying, I'm flying
Daddy-O

THE UNDERTAKER AND THE THREE DONS

Rocco Perri set the stage for the rebirth of Italian secret societies in post-Prohibition Ontario. While Bessie may have been the brains behind the couple's extensive bootlegging and drug trafficking business, it was Rocco's network of Calabrian-born compatriots that carried out the dirty work. This Calabrian connection would also foreshadow organized crime in Ontario for many years to come. By the 1940s, however, Perri was already considered part of the old guard of racketeers. This sentiment was particularly strong among some of the up-and-coming mafiosi on both sides of the Canada-U.S. border who were intent on taking over the rackets once dominated by the Perri-Starkman gang. Following two attempts on his life in the late 1930s, Perri disappeared for good in 1944. Although there has been some speculation that he escaped Ontario alive, others believe his destiny was not unlike that of his criminal associates. One ill-fated crony was John Deluca who, in 1945, was murdered and then disembowelled, a symbolic gesture of contempt inflicted upon the enemies of the mafia. Another was Louis Wernick, whose body was found in a snowbank in Islington, Ontario, early the same year. The January 29, 1945, edition of the *Globe and Mail* reported that the forty-two-year-old bootlegger and drug dealer was "taken for a ride" and then beaten and shot to death sometime around the middle of the month. An investigation into his death reached over the border and, although his killers were never caught, newspapers speculated that Wernick was most likely murdered by a "Buffalo dope syndicate." A secret U.S. Bureau of Narcotics report from 1944 provided evidence that Wernick was buying heroin from Frank Lojacono of Buffalo, who represented the same group that supplied Rocco and Bessie. Other Perri associates, such as Paul Doneff and Giovanni (John) Durso, also vanished around the same time.

Rocco Perri's disappearance signalled the end of an era for Ontario's criminal underworld. The independent mobster who achieved power during Prohibition was now being replaced by a tightly knit group of men, many of whom also hailed from Calabria and whose criminal roots were much more firmly planted in the traditions of the 'Ndrangheta. They also had less autonomy in that they were answerable to mafia families in the United States. Most notable among the new Calabrian crime bosses in Ontario were Anthony (Tony) Sylvestro, Calogero Bordonaro (a.k.a. Charles Bardinaro), and Santo Scibetta. The so-called "three dons" were instrumental in re-animating the 'Ndrangheta in Ontario. Their rise to power, which began almost immediately after the repeal of Prohibition in the U.S., was bolstered by their close association with the Magaddino crime family in Buffalo. At the top of the family hierarchy sat Stefano Magaddino, the portly, balding don who not only resembled Nikita Khrushchev, but wielded power like a Soviet dictator. He was known as the "Undertaker" because of his funeral business and has been given credit for the quaint mafia

custom of the double-decker coffin in which the body of a gangland victim would be quietly disposed of by placing it under that of the funeral parlour's legitimate client. He would later be called "the grand old man of La Cosa Nostra," a testament to his influential role and longevity in the American mafia. A cousin of Joe Bonanno, Magaddino was born in Castellamare del Golfo in Sicily in 1891. He became involved in mafia activities at a young age but was forced to leave the island following the murder of his brother at the hands of the rival Buccellato Family. He immigrated to the U.S. and settled in Brooklyn, where his credentials as a mafioso helped establish him as a leader among a group of Castellamare criminals. Sometime during the 1920s, Magaddino relocated to Buffalo to escape the inter-family warfare that had been exported to Brooklyn and which led police to suspect his involvement in the murder of several Buccellato Family members. Once in Buffalo, he became the largest bootlegger in western New York, importing most of his liquor from Ontario. He consolidated his power on both sides of the border through his unflinching use of violence. Some believe he was behind what the newspapers of the day called the "Good Killers," a group of enforcers and hit men who systematically eliminated competitors in western New York, Southern Ontario, northern Pennsylvania, and eastern Ohio. Following the repeal of Prohibition, he put together his own mafia family and moved into loansharking, extortion, labour racketeering, fraud, theft, gambling, and drug trafficking. Illiterate, but with a strategic mind and a ruthless demeanour, Magaddino's wealth and power were recognized when he was awarded a seat on the mafia's ruling commission. As part of the partitioning of North America by the commission, Magaddino was granted jurisdiction over much of Ontario, which he jealously guarded until his death in 1974.

The alliance the three dons forged with Magaddino provided them with their own heightened level of power and prestige in Ontario's underworld, which was instrumental in fuelling the re-emergence of the 'Ndrangheta in the province and its growing dominance in gambling, bookmaking, illegal liquor production, and drug trafficking. Santo Scibetta is believed to have already been a made member of the Magaddino Family when he arrived in Hamilton via

Buffalo following his deportation from the U.S. Little public information is available on Scibetta, in part because he was able to avoid police scrutiny for much of his life. This in itself is a remarkable testament to a man who could rightly be considered one of Ontario's most powerful and respected mafia figures until his death in 1985. As Hamilton mob authority Adrian Humphreys noted in 1999, "As an old man, after seven decades of Mafia activity, Scibetta became a sort of universal *consigliere* for Ontario's mafia groups, and would slowly wander from his modest Hamilton home on Dundurn Street South near Aberdeen Avenue to all manner of offices, restaurants, and parking lots, listening to proposals by young mobsters, giving his nod of approval for the plans and reaping a cut of the profits." When Santo Scibetta moved to Hamilton he joined his older brother, Joseph, who had been an active Black Hander and, along with Calogero Bordonaro, was behind a number of extortion-related bombings in the city during the early 1920s. When he was not extorting the local Italian population, Bordonaro was bootlegging liquor for Rocco Perri. By transferring his allegiance to Magaddino, Bordonaro emerged from the Prohibition era as a powerful member of the Buffalo family until his death in the 1960s. He also sired the first lawyer ever to be a made member of an American mafia family — his son, Ignazio (Harold) Bordonaro — who, like his father, would enjoy a long tenure with the Ontario wing of the Magaddino Family.

Tony Sylvestro also worked for Rocco Perri as a bootlegger and a drug trafficker, as did his brother Frank. Tony took up residence in Guelph and branched off into "highgrading," a popular racket among Canadian mafiosi that involved purchasing stolen gold from corrupt miners and then re-selling the gold on the black market. In addition, he became one of Stefano Magaddino's biggest Canadian heroin wholesalers during the 1940s and 1950s. Tony Sylvestro died in 1962, but not before he ushered his sons into their own criminal careers. His eldest boy, Sam, would be convicted of bookmaking offences in Guelph in the 1950s and 1960s, while younger brother, Frank, was arrested on loansharking, bookmaking, and extortion charges.

Another criminal clan in Guelph that worked closely with the Sylvestros was the Cipolla family.

Stefano Magadinno

"There are two Italian families in this city that bring discredit to these citizens," Justice Bruce Macdonald wrote in his 1964 report on organized crime in Ontario. "These are the Cipolla and Sylvestro alias Sylvester families. Through these two families, criminals congregate at Guelph and the city is used as a meeting place to plan many major crimes." The Cipolla family, which had been in Guelph since the 1920s, operated a fruit market and a restaurant that was used as a front for bootlegging, gambling, currency counterfeiting, and drug trafficking. In December 1927, the patriarch of the family, Matteo (Big Joe) Cipolla was sentenced to a five-year term in Kingston Penitentiary for drug offences. On August 9, 1933, he was arrested again, along with Alexander Duarte, of Niagara Falls, New York, Giuseppe Coddaro of Welland, Ontario, and Mike Trotta, of Niagara Falls, Ontario, and charged with selling ten ounces of cocaine and 2 pounds of gum opium. The arrests followed an undercover operation in which an RCMP officer posed as a physician from Detroit looking to purchase large quantities of narcotics. He was able to negotiate a drug buy in the U.S. from Duarte, who was supplied by Cipolla. Matteo's sons, Charles and Frank, followed in their father's footsteps and amassed criminal records that included possession of an illegal weapon, possession of counterfeit currency, and drug trafficking. In 1931, police arrested Charles Cipolla for his part in a conspiracy that was about to ship $20,000 in counterfeit American cash from Toronto to Winnipeg. Police reported that the bogus bills were the same type seized by U.S. Treasury agents when they raided a printing plant in the basement of a suburban Buffalo bungalow. Charles was convicted and sentenced to Kingston Penitentiary where he joined his brother Frank who had already been convicted after being found in possession of $40,000 in counterfeit bills the previous year.

The Sylvestro and Cipolla families were also behind the operation of illegal stills in Ontario. The size of these secret distilleries dwarfed anything that was known to be operating in Canada during Prohibition, thanks in part to the guiding hand of Magaddino who provided start-up capital and sent experienced engineers, distillers, and construction crews from south of the border. In its 1937 annual report, the RCMP alluded to the illegal stills when it described how "several large plants were seized during the past year" which are "of similar construction and capacity and the same gang of bootleggers are suspected of being responsible for the majority of the plants, although they are refrained from actually operating the still, relying on their employees to take the rap when they have the misfortune to run afoul of the provisions of the *Excise Act*." One police bust carried out on a 200-acre estate near Woodbridge in York County uncovered a distillery capable of producing two hundred gallons of 63 percent-proof liquor a day. The still was so large it occupied two stories of the house, extending from the ground-level bathroom into the second-floor bedroom through a hole cut in the floor. Five people were arrested, including Cipolla, who police observed tending to the still and stirring large vats of mash.

The Sylvestro family was behind the province's largest-known bootleg distillery, which was discovered by the RCMP on February 19, 1937, in a Toronto factory that was being rented from the Liquid Carbonic Corporation Ltd. To camouflage their illegal operation, a sign was erected on the front of the building that read, "Dominion Oil Reclaiming Company." The lessees even

went so far as to scatter a few empty oil drums around the yard to add an air of legitimacy. Below the main floor of the factory, a tunnel led to a huge still as well as several hundred five-gallon cans filled with alcohol. In a garage attached to the building, police found a five-ton truck, loaded with 1,200 gallons of distilled liquor ready for delivery. Under the garage was a 5,000-gallon mixing tank fitted with a revolving agitator, driven by a large electric motor, and a conveyor belt that fed sugar into the mix tank. Nearby were two 1,000-gallon tanks filled with alcohol and connected to a four-spout filter that filled the five-gallon cans. In another part of the building was a 4,400-gallon hot-water tank and three 10,000-gallon steel tanks, each containing mash in various states of fermentation. By the end of the raid, the RCMP had seized 22,700 pounds of sugar, 6,020 gallons of alcohol, 34,160 gallons of mash, 539 gallons of molasses, and eighteen electric motors ranging from one-quarter to 10 horsepower. At the time of the raid, six men — Morris Joseph, Hyman Topp, Abe Moore, Sam Pizzolo, George Rogers, and Patrick O'Brien — were arrested and later convicted and fined. Sam Pizzolo, a close associate of the Sylvestro family, was in charge of the operation.

Starting around the mid-1930s, Ontario's Calabrian Mafia families, and Tony Sylvestro in particular, helped fuel the expansion of the opium and heroin trade in the province. "For a considerable period prior to June, 1936," the RCMP wrote in its 1938 annual report, "there appeared to be very little heroin available in Toronto, but, during the latter part of that year, it became apparent large quantities of heroin were being brought into Toronto for illegal distribution." RCMP investigators traced the source of the Turkish heroin to "two gangs, the heads of which were found to be Italians." The first was controlled by Carman Chiovitti and Louis Spadacini, while the second, and the larger one, was headed by James Pugliese. What the RCMP did know at the time was that both were being supplied by Tony Sylvestro. At the end of June 1937, James Pugliese, Sam Pugliese, Margaret Pugliese, Charles Mulligan, and John Murphy were arrested by the RCMP in Toronto and charged under the *Opium and Narcotic Drug Act*. The amount of narcotics seized was small, but there was sufficient evidence to show that James Pugliese had been one of the chief sources of heroin in Toronto. Following a brief trial, he was sentenced to three years in the Kingston Penitentiary. In 1937, Chiovitti and Spadacini were also arrested following a high-speed chase through Toronto. While they were being pursued by police, a small package was thrown from their car, which turned out to contain several capsules of heroin. After being convicted of illegal possession of drugs, Chiovetti was sentenced to three years while Spadacini was sent away for nine months.

Further evidence of Magaddino's involvement in Ontario's heroin trade began to emerge in 1938 with the arrest of Luigi and Dante (Dan) Gasbarrini in Toronto on drug trafficking charges. That year, information was obtained by the RCMP drug squad that heroin being sold on Toronto streets was coming from a source in Hamilton. On November 3, 1938, members of the RCMP followed a street-level trafficker from Toronto to a house on Sheaffe Street in Hamilton. When he left the house, the man was stopped by the Mounties and relieved of five capsules of heroin. The RCMP then raided the house where they discovered Luigi Gasbarrini, his wife, and their daughter. Twenty minutes later, their son, Dan, arrived. After searching the home, police found 162 capsules of heroin, each around 2.5 grams in quantity. The father and son were placed under arrest and, following their trial, Luigi received a six-month sentence, while Dan was acquitted. Dan Gasbarrini, who would go on to become a member of the Magaddino crime family, had come to Hamilton from Italy with his parents in 1926 at the age of six. By thirteen, he had dropped out of school and, following some odd jobs, he embarked on a career as a teenage bookie. During the Second World War, he was stealing and fencing war bonds. When he was hauled before the courts on theft charges, the main witness for the Crown failed to appear (and was never heard of again) and the charges were dropped. Gasbarrini became firmly entrenched in Ontario's Calabrian Mafia when he married the daughter of Tony Sylvestro. The marriage also pulled Gasbarrini deeper into Sylvestro's and Magaddino's heroin trafficking universe. By the 1940s, classified reports from the U.S. Bureau of Narcotics and the RCMP documented the flow of Mexican brown heroin from Buffalo to Hamilton and then on to Toronto and Vancouver, as well as Turkish heroin that was moving from Ontario to Buffalo and then to the eastern seaboard. In May 1949, two of Sylvestro's main distributors, Carmen Chiovitti and Dan Gasbarrini, were arrested on drug charges in a Vancouver hotel after the RCMP obtained an adjoining room to conduct surveillance. The two were supplying heroin to the Vancouver market and, before the bust, police traced a large amount of funds that were being wired from B.C. to Dan Gasbarrini in Hamilton. On October 11 of that year, ten men were put on trial in Vancouver on drug charges and, before the end of the month, five of the conspirators, including Chiovitti and Gasbarrini, were found guilty. After appeals by the two men were dismissed by a higher court, each was sentenced to seven years.

While Magaddino controlled much of Southern Ontario, Windsor was considered the jurisdiction of Detroit's mafia families. When he appeared before a U.S. Senate hearing into organized crime in 1963, former Detroit police commissioner George Edwards stated that Southwestern Ontario is treated as a "suburb" by the Motor City mafia. Among the Detroit mafiosi most active in the Windsor area during the 1950s and 1960s was Pietro (Peter) Corrado, who owned a 100-acre farm just outside Windsor. Corrado died in 1957, but at the time Detroit police believed he had actually gone into hiding as the farm continued to be registered in his name for years to come. As in the days of Prohibition, southwestern Ontario was of great strategic benefit for the Detroit mob, especially when it came to smuggling. In the 1950s, Windsor and the surrounding area became a launching pad for heroin imported into Detroit. The region would also serve as a staging ground for the smuggling of illegal Italian immigrants into the U.S.

Beginning in the 1950s, Pietro Corrado and his son Domenic helped ensure the Detroit families were well supplied with manpower by sneaking Italian nationals across the border to work in mafia-owned businesses in Detroit (but not before they were put to work on Corrado's Windsor-area farm). "At first they worked for starvation wages — because their bosses used the threat of deportation to hold them in virtual slavery," the *Toronto Telegram* reported in 1961. "Later, those with the proper strong arm qualifications were given jobs in the Mafia's real business — crime.

Because these men were pawns in the hands of the syndicate, they made ideal henchmen." The illegal immigration schemes continued until the 1970s under the supervision of other Detroit mafia members living or working out of Windsor, most notably Nicholas Cicchini, Onofrio (Mono) Minaudo, and Giuseppe (Cockeyed Joe) Catalanotte.

Onofrio Minaudo was the most senior member of the Detroit mafia on the Canadian side during the late 1950s and early 1960s. Born in Sicily sometime in the early 1900s, he entered the U.S. illegally around 1924. After he left Italy, Minaudo was convicted *in absentia* by an Italian court of a double murder as well as other offences and was sentenced to life imprisonment. While on the lam, he settled in Detroit and soon was running a mob-controlled bar and bowling alley. After working with the Purple Gang during Prohibition, he became a made member of the Detroit mafia where he specialized in labour racketeering and was a principal suspect in a number of unsolved murders in the city. He was deported from the U.S. in 1953 and wound up in Cuba, where he became involved in mafia-run casinos and drug smuggling. He first came to Canada on a tourist visa in 1956, moving to the Windsor suburb of Riverside. Undercover as a bakery owner who conveniently made daily bread deliveries to Detroit, Minaudo operated as a Canadian underboss for the Detroit mafia. Police Commissioner Edwards testified to the 1963 Senate hearings on organized crime that three Windsor bakers — Minaudo, Cicchini, and Catalanotte — were linked to the mob in Detroit and coordinated the smuggling of heroin, hidden in loaves of bread, across the river. Although no heroin-filled bread was ever seized, police on both sides of the border did arrest a number of drug couriers linked to Cicchini during the 1950s. This included the February 1956 arrest of Giuseppe Indelicato who was nabbed in New York City after travelling from Italy with three pounds of heroin.

THE ENFORCER

In the fall of 1957, two men entered the Bay Street office of Toronto stock promoter Philip Owen and beat him so viciously they knocked a tooth through his cheek. Owen laid charges against the men, but this only prompted numerous threatening phone calls as well as another attempt to attack him while he sat in his car at a red light. He eventually withdrew the charges and then collapsed into a nervous breakdown that required a six-week stay in the hospital. Following Owen's harassment, stories began to circulate around Toronto's financial district that other stockbrokers and businessmen were assaulted and extorted by mysterious figures. The pattern for each was painfully similar. In one encounter described by *Toronto Star* columnist Pierre Berton, a man of medium build entered the office of a brokerage firm and walked straight into the office of a broker. Once inside, he gave the man his name and then asked, "Does that mean anything to you?"

"No," the broker replied.

The stranger responded, "Well, it's going to. I'm your new partner." The broker immediately rejected the outrageous offer.

"Don't you know who I represent?" the stranger demanded. "I represent people from the other side." The broker began to grow angry.

"Now look," the stranger said, "I don't want any trouble with you."

"What do you want?" asked the broker.

"A thousand dollars a week—for protection."

"What kind of protection?"

"Protection against everything." The broker told him to leave or he'd call the police.

"Call the police eh?" replied the man. "We'll have to learn you the ABC's. We'll have to give you a few lessons."

A few minutes after the threatening stranger left, two other men walked into the broker's office. One was swinging a blackjack. They paid no attention to his fellow employees and beat the broker unconscious before leaving. Numerous other stockbrokers were known to have been threatened and attacked. One victim paid $12,500 after he was warned, "You're going to come home one day and find your wife and kids in the garbage can." To some of the intended victims, the man who usually initiated the threats referred to himself as Johnny. To others, he was known by another nickname: "The Enforcer."

John (Johnny Pops) Papalia was the son of Rosie Italiano (the cousin of Rocco Perri's drug dealing minion Ned Italiano) and Anthony Papalia, who had immigrated to Canada from Calabria around the beginning of the century and settled in Hamilton. Johnny was one of seven children — six boys and one girl — who were raised on Railway Street in Hamilton's lower-class Italian neighbourhood. Sometime in the 1920s, Anthony Papalia began bootlegging liquor and would continue to do so for years following the repeal of Prohibition laws. (When he was interned as an enemy alien during the Second World War, his occupation was listed simply as "Bootlegger.") His first employer was fellow Calabrian Rocco Perri but, in later years, Anthony worked for Tony Sylvestro and become active in the various criminal rackets carried out by Ontario's Calabrian Mafia families. Papalia's ties to Sylvestro, and ultimately Magaddino, were exposed when he was interrogated by police for his possible role in the murder of Bessie Starkman.

Born on March 18, 1924, John Papalia grew to be a skinny, often sickly-looking kid, but had a tough reputation, even at a young age. He went to school with Dan Gasbarrini, marking the beginning of a partnership that would last for decades. Like his future partner-in-crime, he dropped out of school around the age of thirteen. It was as a young teenager that Papalia embarked on a criminal career, first becoming involved in theft and bootlegging before moving on to more violent crimes, such as extortion and muscle-for-hire. By 1943, Papalia had relocated to Toronto where he began running with a gang of other young toughs. While in Toronto, he received a four-month sentence for a residential break-in, the first of many convictions that would see him in and out of jail for the rest of his life. Before the end of the decade, he was pushing heroin for one of Toronto's biggest traffickers, Harvey Chernick, who was supplied by Anthony Sylvestro. In 1949, at the age of twenty-five, Papalia was arrested near Union Station after being caught with fifty capsules of the white powder. He was sentenced to two years less a day.

After his release from jail in 1951, Papalia headed to Montreal where he used his connections to land a job as an enforcer for Carmine Galante, working under the command of Luigi Greco. It was in Montreal that Papalia cemented his credentials with important mafia figures and picked up invaluable career experience through his merciless extortion of professional gamblers and shady stockbrokers. Ac-

cording to writer Adrian Humphreys, sometime in the mid-1950s, Papalia was called back to Ontario by Stefano Magaddino and inducted into his family. By this time, Galante had firmly incorporated Montreal into Joseph Bonanno's orbit and Magaddino was building up his own Canadian base in Southern Ontario. While the Buffalo boss already had the three dons and other mafiosi running rackets for him in Ontario, Magaddino required "a young, firm, hands-on boss to move the organization into rich, new areas of growth." John Papalia would be one of his top selections. "Johnny was not to supersede the older dons of Ontario who already answered to Magaddino," writes Humphreys, "but rather work with them, taking on the role of hands-on boss, with the old dons remaining almost as *consigliere*, advisors, and arbitrators; spiritual leaders who were paid tribute through both respect and cash payments. Although insolent with anyone from outside his criminal fraternity, Johnny remained acutely respectful of his *Mafiosi* elders, allowing these old dons to maintain influence over him."

John Papalia, circa 1950s

When he returned to Hamilton around 1954, Papalia was thirty years old and a made guy. Alan Phillips depicted Papalia in his 1963 *Maclean's* magazine article on the Ontario mafia as follows, "His taste in clothes and girls was costly and he had the hoodlum's habit of always carrying a thousand dollars. He was not a big man, about five-foot-eight and slight, with a scarred right cheek, hooknosed and black haired, soft-spoken and well mannered — except when slugging someone with a blackjack." As soon as he arrived back home, Johnny Pops began assembling his own criminal crew. Among his closest recruits were enforcer Fred (Gabe) Gabourie, a former Hollywood stuntman named Jack Weaver, professional gambler Donald (Red) LeBarre, enforcers Art Tartaglia and Frank Marchildon, his brothers Domenic, Frank, and Rocco, and brother-in-law Tony Pugliese. By putting together a gang that included non-Italians, Papalia broke with 'Ndrangheta tradition in Ontario, but the men he hand selected were fiercely loyal to their boss and most would maintain lifelong relationships with him.

Back in Hamilton, Papalia began to branch out into gambling, loansharking, extortion, and peddling stolen stock certificates. He also set up legal companies, partly as a cover for his illegal enterprises. One early indication of the overlap between his commercial and criminal interests was the 1954 gangland-style murder of Tony Coposodi, a driver working for the Crown Taxi Company, which Papalia started with his brother Domenic. In 1958, John Papalia began the Monarch Vending Machines Company with Art Tartaglia and, in Toronto, he founded the Star Vending Machine Company in partnership with Alberto Agueci, another member of the Magaddino Family. Papalia's companies enjoyed a distinctive edge over their competitors. Business owners who had gambling debts owing to Papalia had no choice but to accept his companies' vending machines on their premises. Bribery was also used to place machines into other businesses and, if that didn't work, Papalia could always rely on intimidation and violence as a marketing tactic. Another competitive edge was that much of the merchandise sold through the vending machines was stolen. Not long after Papalia's companies were established, railway cars, transport trucks, and warehouses filled with cigarettes were hijacked in the Hamilton-Niagara region.

"At first it was mostly break-ins," an Ontario provincial police officer was quoted as saying in a 1963 interview with *Maclean's* magazine. "They'd hit the warehouse. Then they started hitting the railways. Now it's the transports. It's spread across the province and into the States and Quebec. We believe it's the same Toronto gang; their MO is the same. One stole forty thousand cartons in eight months in 1962–63. In one month this group ran up a gasoline bill of five hundred dollars following cigarette trucks, charting their routes and stops." The same method was used with cargo-filled railway cars. "They get the number. They know where it stops. They don't hit till they're sure it's safe, about once every month or six weeks. Then they back up a one-and-a-half-ton truck and load up about ninety cases, worth eighty to a hundred and twenty dollars a case on the black market."

By the late 1950s, many of Papalia's criminal ambitions had been satisfied. He was a made member of the Magaddino Family, he worked closely with the senior dons in Ontario, and he maintained strong connections with mafia figures in Montreal and New York. Magaddino also tapped Johnny to take the lead in his most ambitious plans in Ontario to date: to take over illegal gambling in Toronto.

WHAT'S THE ODDS?

Like most other big cities in North America, gambling and bookmaking became the most profitable of all organized criminal activities in post-Prohibition Toronto. According to a former RCMP commissioner, for every dollar bet legally at the racetrack, three to five dollars was bet illegally off track. Hockey was also a favourite among Toronto gamblers and it was no coincidence that many of the city's illegal betting parlours encircled the famed Maple Leaf Gardens, which was built in 1931. A 1938 *Toronto Daily Star* article touted its hometown as one of the biggest illicit betting centres on the continent, boasting a citywide network of bookmakers "located in small stores, running elevators, driving taxis, in factories and office buildings, poolrooms and hotels." Toronto police estimated that in 1936 the largest bookie in town had annual revenues of approximately $500,000. Beginning in the 1930s, Toronto bookies relied heavily on the Canadian Racing and Financial News company, which not only distributed the *Daily Racing Form* (a legal publication), but occupied a downtown office with a wire service that immediately reported the results of horse races from around North America and Cuba (an illegal practice in Canada at the time because it facilitated off-track betting). When Toronto police raided the office in 1936, they found eighteen women working a bank of telephones and recording the results of various races. The operation was owned by Moe Annenberg, the American millionaire publisher of the *Philadelphia Inquirer,* who also owned a chain of racing papers and the Nation Wide News Service, which wired racing results across the continent.

Toronto also had more than its fair share of underground gambling dens. During the 1930s, the largest and most prosperous was the Brown Derby, a luxurious restaurant-club located on the Lakeshore Highway in the suburb of Etobicoke. On June 16, 1938, eleven police officers equipped with sledgehammers smashed their way through a thick, heavily barred door that served as the club's entrance. Inside, they arrested thirty-nine people and seized gambling equipment, including several tables used for blackjack, stud, and draw poker. At one end of the room hung a huge tapestry that hid a cashier's cage. On the north side of the building was a mezzanine with a catwalk

and a long chalkboard that listed the horses, jockeys, and odds at local and American tracks and recorded race results once they were received by long-distance telephone. Among the raiding party was the chief of the York police, who answered one ringing phone and was promptly informed of the results of a horse race just held in Santa Anita, California. Beneath the mezzanine on the ground floor were wickets where patrons placed bets and received their payouts. The building also incorporated a number of elaborate precautions against police raids or robbery attempts. Police had to break down five doors to get to the main betting parlour and, once inside, they found a bouncer armed with a sawed-off shotgun who sat in a cubicle lined with a quarter-inch of steel guarding the cashier's room, which itself was hidden behind a mahogany panel. A 100-foot underground tunnel led from the basement to beyond the large fence that ran along the perimeter of the club's backyard and, on the night of the raid, police officers arrested the shift manager who was attempting to flee through the tunnel with $2,000 in cash.

The same night, Manny Feder was arrested in his suite at the Royal York Hotel and charged with operating the Brown Derby as a common gaming house. This was at least the second time in three years

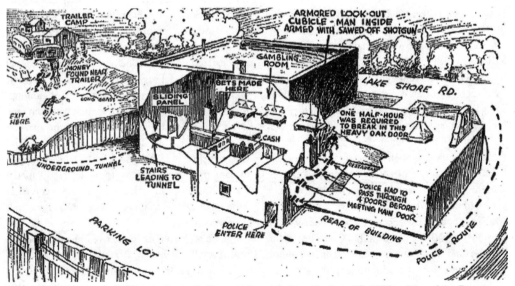

Sketch of the elaborate and secure Brown Derby gambling club, from the June 16, 1938, edition of the *Toronto Daily Star*

the Derby had been raided and Feder charged. When he was arrested the second time, police confiscated a key to a safety deposit box in the hotel, which they opened to find $6,850 in cash and two dozen loaded dice. (They were loaded with weights so when rolled as a pair, the combination would not add up to seven or eleven, a winning combination in craps. This was just one of many tricks used by crooked gamblers, which also included rounding or cutting edges of die so they would roll to certain numbers, or altering the backs, fronts, or sides of playing cards for the benefit of crooked dealers and players.) The Brown Derby was shut down, but Murray Feder and his financial backers simply moved their gambling and bookmaking operation to another spacious location in Etobicoke, which they re-opened as the Combine Club. A few months later, police raided the nearby Brockwood Country Club. As part of the raid, police found dice, card tables, and a roulette wheel that one newspaper called "the best ever seized in Toronto." Police believed that Feder also had a controlling interest in this club.

Beginning in the early 1940s, "there was an alarming upsurge in organized gambling in this province, particularly in gaming," Justice Wilfred Roach wrote in his 1962 report on organized gambling in Ontario. This increase in "gaming" (a legal term that differentiates games of chance from other types of gambling, such as sports betting) was fuelled, in part, by a provision in the *Criminal Code of Canada* that allowed bona fide social clubs to provide certain games of chance, although it prohibited any rake-off by the club. Professional gamblers took refuge behind incorporated social clubs to operate elaborate underground casinos, using letters patent from the Department of the Provincial Secretary. Charters for social clubs were rarely cancelled, and if a gambling den was shut down, the charter was used to open a "social club" at another location. In 1950, the chief of the Toronto police wrote, "One of our big problems in dealing with the common gaming house particularly, is the Chartered Club, which can operate under certain provisions set out in Section 226(b)(ii) of the Criminal Code, but in our opinion (and we say this after careful consideration), many of these clubs operating under provincial charter are nothing but 'fronts' for professional gambling activities. The most unfortunate feature is that these

charters are issued by the Provincial Government for a specified organization, but only in a few cases are they issued for a specified street address or city or 'town location,' with the result that the charters seem to 'float' from one location to another, further complicating the situation for the Police." Professional gamblers bought out existing social clubs or obtained control of dormant charters and reactivated them by filing annual returns. In his 1962 report on organized gambling, Justice Roach described one club on Yonge Street in Toronto that was able to obtain a number of charters over a nineteen-year period (one was purchased for a mere $1,700). He described the club as "a den occupied in succession by one family of wolves after another, each wrapped in the sheep's clothing of a social club charter."

Along with his partner, Dan Gasbarrini, John Papalia set up a lucrative gambling hall in Hamilton in 1955 under the auspices of the Porcupine Miners Social Club charter, which they put into good standing by having front men pay the government fees that had fallen into arrears. The charter, which was originally issued in the late 1920s to set up a club for miners working in the Northern Ontario town of Timmins, was secured by Tony Sylvestro (one of the club's silent partners) from a shady mining official he knew from his highgrading days. After three years at its new location in Hamilton — 740 kilometres from Timmins, but only a block away from police headquarters — the club's charter was revoked when police determined it was being used for professional gambling. Years later, Gasbarrini told the press, "For two years the police never bothered with us although they knew it was going on. But we never paid anyone off. It was just that we ran an honest game and had some of the best people in town coming to it." The club was closed down, he said, when police "stopped looking the other way." Not to be deterred Papalia, Gasbarrini, and their associates became involved in various other underground gambling clubs throughout Southern Ontario.

One police report from 1950 indicated that Toronto's small Chinatown, located along two blocks of Elizabeth Street in the downtown core, had "no less than 8 Clubs operating under Provincial charter" that were "being used in many instances to cover up professional gambling operations." These gambling halls were operated by "syndicates" that rigged many of their games. Another report noted that between July 15, 1946, and May 15, 1947, "a store at 76 Elizabeth Street was raided on at least nine separate occasions and its proprietors charged with keeping a common gambling house." In each raid, a different proprietor was charged, suggesting to police that managers were being rotated through by whoever controlled the gambling club. Less than a block away, at 92 Elizabeth Street, police were equally busy; between October 26, 1946, and May 15, 1947, the small store was raided by police at least eight times, with a different manager being charged with keeping a common gaming house each time.

As illegal gaming and bookmaking increased in Toronto, so did the level of violence. Gambling joints were particularly susceptible to armed robberies, not only because of the large amounts of cash on hand, but because the victims could be expected not to file a police report. In December 1936, Toronto police were in the midst of investigating at least four robberies of illegal gambling operations, only one of which was reported. The violence was also a product of the many crooked games of chance that were being run. In one such operation on Jarvis Street, men leaving taverns were met by attractive women who enticed them to nearby apartments where they lost their money on games with stacked cards, loaded dice, and fictitious horse races. Police learned that one victim who protested his losses was beaten and then dumped in a back alley. Besides "clipping" their victims in card and dice games, the gang behind this racket was also known to make money by extorting other bookmakers and gambling dens. Police identified the leaders of this gang as John (The Bug) Brown, Michael (Mickey) Macdonald, and Joseph Constantineo. In January 1939, the three were found guilty of assaulting and robbing bootlegger James Elder in his Church Street apartment. Brown also faced charges of armed robbery, arising from the holdup of a secret gambling den. Macdonald was later arrested and tried for the murder of Jimmie Windsor, who was killed in his home, in front of his family, on the night of January 7, 1939. "The leader of the murder squad shot Windsor down in cold blood and as he lay dying with a bullet through his abdomen, kicked him in the head," a *Toronto Star* article reported.

"Windsor might have talked, even with a bullet in his stomach, but repeated kicks stunned him so that there was no need to fire another shot to silence him for good." Police were told that Windsor refused to pay a weekly $25 protection fee for his Yonge Street barbecue and dance hall. Macdonald was convicted of the murder and sentenced to hang, but four days before his execution he was given a reprieve by a court of appeal, which called into question much of the evidence provided by Crown witnesses. At the end of his second trial — and despite his confession that "I'm as good as on that rope right now!" — Macdonald was found not guilty. Nonetheless, he was transferred to Kingston Penitentiary to serve the remaining fifteen months of a two-year term for the robbery of James Elder. Around the same time, his brother Alex was sentenced to ten years for the armed robbery of a Port Credit bank in which a teller was shot.

Michael (Mickey) Macdonald

Another by-product of Toronto's underground gaming industry was a thriving loan-shark business. In 1961, the *Toronto Telegram* told the story of one group of loan sharks who stationed themselves right outside of gambling houses. One heavily indebted hotel owner had borrowed $5,000 and was required to pay $6,000 two weeks later. After a few months of avoiding his creditors, the man wound up owing more than $10,000. As the threats against him and his family escalated, he was forced to sell his home to settle the loan. In another case reported by the newspaper, "a Toronto playboy" who was delinquent on a $1,000 loan was confronted "by two strong arm men" in a Bay Street bar and forced to sign over the ownership of a new convertible car. A Toronto lawyer whose gambling losses amounted to more than $100,000 and who fell behind in his loan payments to the gang was forced to provide them with legal services, which included establishing dummy corporations that were used as fronts for loans and loan payments.

During the 1940s and 1950s, the biggest and best-known professional gamblers in Toronto were Joseph McDermott and Vincent Feeley. The man considered the brains behind their operation was Joe McDermott, who was described in a 1963 *Maclean's* article as "an exuberant crafty man" who "respected knowledge." He enjoyed legal texts, especially those dealing with betting and gaming, and even attended a Supreme Court session that was hearing a gambling case involving sections of the *Criminal Code*. "If anyone in Canada knew how to run a gaming house it would be Joseph McDermott," Toronto lawyer David Humphrey told a 1962 provincial commission on organized crime. McDermott had a violent side as well. He kept a baseball bat behind a door at one of his clubs and when one patron was caught cheating at cards, it was forcefully deployed to break the man's arm before he even had a chance to collect his winnings. Vincent Feeley, a high-school dropout who forged his own discharge papers to avoid service in the Second World War, was largely responsible for the bookmaking end of the operation. He once admitted that he rented safety deposit boxes under fictitious names — and put nothing in most of them — so he could use the bank cubicles and phones to call his customers and associates and to calculate his bookmaking sheets. Feeley also appeared to prefer footwear to bank accounts; police once found $10,000 hidden in one of his shoes.

In the 1950s, police investigations revealed that McDermott and Feeley had an interest in a number of gambling clubs in Ontario, including the Centre Road Veterans' Club in Cooksville, the Jordan Club and Riverdale Club in downtown Toronto, the Roseland Club in Windsor, and the Frontier Club in Fort Erie. The average daily value of bets recorded at the Jordan Club alone was $30,000. Their largest and most profitable venture, however, was the Centre Road Veterans Association, which was granted a provincial charter as a social club in 1957. Other gambling halls they controlled operated under federal charters obtained from army, navy, air force, and merchant marine veterans groups. The membership lists for these "social clubs" numbered in the thousands, and McDermott became a master at manipulating provincial and federal laws by obtaining licences in the names of nominees or transferring licences between different clubs. To travel to their gambling operations scattered across the province, McDermott and Feeley had a private airplane at their disposal and both were licensed pilots. McDermott also reportedly bought a helicopter for $44,000 in cash produced from a suitcase.

James McDermott

McDermott and Feeley had another ace up their sleeves in the person of Sergeant John F. Cronin, second-in-command of the anti-gambling squad of the Ontario Provincial Police, who protected their operations while raiding competitors. They lost the services of Cronin who retired in 1954, but their relationship with the anti-gambling squad continued under Constable Robert Wright. In 1961, the twenty-seven-year-old police officer was committed to stand trial on charges of bribing OPP undercover agent Constable George Scott and obstructing justice. Wright's co-defendants were forty-year-old Joseph McDermott and thirty-six-year-old Vincent Feeley, who were charged with obtaining information illegally from a police officer, obstructing justice, and keeping a common gaming house. During the trial, Scott testified that he received $1,000 in bribes from Wright for tipping him off on impending OPP raids. He also alleged that Wright had given him McDermott's unlisted telephone number and was to call him with any information on any planned police visits to his "social clubs." In a secret diary discovered when he was arrested on May 28, 1960, Wright had written that he was attempting to trap Constable Scott who he suspected of being in league with the two gamblers. Feeley and McDermott's lawyers admitted both men were professional gamblers and that McDermott had readily taken the tipoffs that flowed to him. But he stressed the Crown had failed to show any evidence that either McDermott or Feeley passed even a dollar to Wright or Scott. Following a nine-day trial the three defendants were found not guilty of conspiring to bribe a policeman. (As McDermott returned to the prisoner's box before the jury's verdict, he leaned over to the press table and was heard to ask, "What's the odds?")

Despite their acquittal, the three still faced other bribery and corruption-related charges, while McDermott and Feeley faced illegal gambling charges. Their ongoing trials were highly publicized affairs, not only because of the salacious details that came out on Toronto's underground gambling scene, but because frequent references were made to senior police officials and provincial government officials who were accused of being on the take. Among those mentioned in the first trial were provincial attorney general Kelso Roberts, past and present senior officers with the OPP, and several Toronto lawyers. The man who was second-in-command of the OPP's anti-gambling squad was made deputy chief of the Peterborough Police Force because gamblers bribed the selection committee, according to George Scott, who told the court he heard this information from Robert Wright.

The negative publicity generated from the trial also prompted greater government action against professional gambling operations. This only stoked the media frenzy due to revelations of the lucrative nature of these operations and the large amounts of bets being placed or laid off in Ontario. On February 1, 1960, Norman Joseph, an American connected to Buffalo gambling syndicates, and Michael Genovese, a front man for Papalia's Porcupine Club and a wholesaler in Tony Sylvestros' drug trafficking network, were convicted of keeping a common betting house at the Alexander Motel on Highway 20 outside of Hamilton. Betting sheets seized by police showed an average daily take of $22,900. On September 13, 1960, police raided one Toronto home and confiscated betting slips showing that $65,000 had been wagered on various sports and horse races over the last four days. A week later, police tracked down another Toronto bookie who took an average of $37,000 a day in bets. Most satisfying to police was the closure of the legendary gambling clubs operated by McDermott and Feeley, including the Centre Road Veterans' Club in Cooksville, the Jordan and Lakeview clubs in Toronto, and the Roseland Club in Windsor. Police raids had become so frequent at the Centre Road Veterans' Club that a local plumber was on call to drain the septic tank because so many die were being flushed down the toilets in moments of panic.

The increased police activity did little to satisfy members of the province's political opposition parties, who were out for government blood. On May 2, 1961, one member of the Co-operative Commonwealth Federation demanded that Ontario premier John Robarts act against criminals in "high places," contending that he was shielding government officials who were co-operating with organized crime figures. At the end of November 1961, John Wintermeyer, the Leader of the Opposition in the Ontario legislature, made similar accusations against the government. He claimed that certain gambling operations posing as social clubs were somehow immune to police interdiction. "Between 1957 and the middle of this year," he said in the legislature, "thirty-one so-called social clubs lost their charters as a result of illegal gambling in Metropolitan Toronto. Yet at the end of this period there were still twenty-four clubs in the Metro area suspected of illegal gambling by the police."

The onslaught of illegal gambling and corruption allegations led to the creation of a provincial Royal Commission, headed by Justice Wilfred D. Roach. The inquiry, which began public hearings on March 20, 1962, and concluded with the commissioner's report dated March 15, 1963, heard accusations that prominent politicians intervened to secure charters for social clubs despite police reports showing the clubs were being used for professional gaming. One witness from the provincial government estimated that in the previous eleven years, five provincial secretaries issued a total of twenty-seven charters (overriding the objections of police). In the end, Justice Roach cleared most government officials, including Kelso Roberts, of any wrongdoing. Unfounded rumours of high-level corruption in the Ontario government were largely the work of Joseph McDermott, who Justice Roach called "an audacious liar who will stop at nothing to advance his own cause." However, Roach did recommend that OPP deputy commissioner James Bartlett and District Inspector J. Allan Stringer be removed from the provincial police force because of evidence "pointing to an association between Stringer and Feeley." Both men resigned in disgrace.

Singled out in the final Royal Commission report were McDermott and Feeley. Following the release of the report, McDermott offered to surrender two club charters he controlled, an offer that was made from Burwash Reformatory where he was serving eighteen months after finally being convicted for conspiring to corrupt a police officer. The report also documented the growing presence of American gambling syndicates in Ontario. When the report was issued, mafia families from various parts of the U.S. were in the midst of a two-decade-long campaign to cash in on and consolidate gaming and bookmaking operations in the province. In 1948, Detroit police commissioner Harry Toy stated publicly that Windsor was a "central wire service" that supplied all the bookie establishments in Detroit. In 1951, while testifying before Senator Kefauver's organized crime committee in

Washington, D.C., the new commissioner of the Detroit police repeated the claim that Windsor was the source of illegal racetrack wire information for Detroit and other American cities. He said an investigation into one bookmaking operation in Detroit uncovered an "intricate network" of racing information, which originated in Toledo, Ohio, then went to Windsor, and from there to Detroit. According to FBI reports, Frank Costello, the powerful New York mob boss who had poured much of his Prohibition-era profits into illegal gambling, had controlled Windsor's bookmaking syndicates since the mid-1940s. By overseeing Windsor's bookmaking operations, the FBI concluded, Costello was able to control bookmaking in Detroit and parts of Ohio.

A 1950 *Toronto Daily Star* article claimed that, in 1945, Costello sold his Detroit bookmaking interests to Howard Kerr of Windsor, who was once described as the "best handicapper" in the horse-race business in America. By 1949, Kerr was muscled out of the Detroit-Windsor bookmaking market by Peter Liccavoli, the long-time Detroit mafia boss, who around the same time employed a Hamilton woman to oversee a "travelling prostitution system, whereby women are interchanged among large cities, from Boston and Montreal to Chicago and Detroit," according to the *Star*. The 1964 government inquiry into organized crime in Ontario also established that Vito Giacalone, a kingpin in the Detroit gambling scene, had a financial interest in McDermott and Feeley's Roseland Veterans' Club in Windsor area, and was even arrested there as a found-in during an OPP raid. In 1958, a police intelligence report alleged that McDermott and Feeley went on a hunting party in Moosonee, Ontario, with Detroit mobsters Domenic Corrado, Vincent Meli, and Anthony Tocco. McDermott covered the party's expenses, a bill of around $2,000.

Outside of Windsor, the Magaddino Family was behind La Cosa Nostra's takeover of gambling in Southern Ontario. He no doubt received a cut from John Papalia's clubs in Hamilton and also backed the Sylvestro and Cipolla families in establishing Guelph as an important link in a multimillion-dollar cross-border bookmaking network. Guelph police estimated that $15,000 to $30,000 a day in illegal bets were handled through bookies in the city. One of the first signs of

Magaddino's foray into Toronto's underground gambling industry was revealed on March 26, 1947, when police raided an illegal betting place located in the rear of a fruit store on Dundas Street. Arrested and charged with keeping a common betting house was Carmen Chiovitti, the Magaddino Family member who had just been released from a 1937 drug trafficking sentence. Also arrested were his brother Samuel and their mother, who had a purse in her apron pocket containing more than $2,000 in cash. (She later used the money to provide bail for herself, her sons, and those arrested as found-ins.) Samuel took the rap by pleading guilty, allowing his brother and mother to escape conviction, although the sentencing judge did mention Carmen's considerable criminal history, which included charges on ten separate occasions related to illegal gambling, drugs, contraband liquor, and assaulting a police officer.

There were other indications that the Magaddino Family and other upstate New York gambling syndicates were extending their reach into Ontario. Sam Rich, a Buffalo bookmaker, had moved into a Toronto hotel and was taking bets from all over the U.S. On March 28, 1961, Toronto police raided the premises at 353 Betty Ann Drive in Toronto, where they charged Reuben Stein and Sam Band for keeping a common betting house. While the police were on the premises they intercepted incoming telephone calls in which large bets were being placed or laid off from numerous American and Canadian cities, including Queenston and Buffalo, New York, Chicago, Cleveland, Miami, Hamilton, Guelph, and Montreal. That same year, the New York State Commission of Investigation released a report called *Syndicated Gambling in New York State*, which provided evidence that Toronto, Guelph, Hamilton, Niagara Falls, and Montreal were part of a bookmaking network that fanned out across upstate New York. "Layoff centers are maintained in several cities in Canada," the report stated. "There is an extremely close relationship between major bookmakers in Canada and those in the Buffalo, Niagara Falls, Rochester, Syracuse and Albany areas. Many of these bookmakers in Canada are transplants from New York city who periodically shift their operations from the one site to the other." The close relationship between bookies in upstate New York and Southern Ontario is a function of geography, according to the

report, as "bookmakers tend to operate on a regional basis. Thus, the small bookmakers in the central New York area lay off primarily with contacts in their own immediate geographical section." The report described one Toronto-based betting operation that netted nearly $500,000 during two months of the baseball season by taking layoffs from bookies in upstate New York.

By the late 1950s, Stefano Magaddino had firmly incorporated many of Ontario's bookmaking operations into his fold, turning numerous cities into important layoff centres, while taking an interest in numerous underground casinos throughout Southern Ontario. Yet, despite the encroachment of the mafia on Southern Ontario, some large-scale gambling operations in Toronto continued to be run by independents. At the behest of Magaddino, John Papalia was determined to change that once and for all.

THE MOST REMARKABLE CASE OF MASS BLINDNESS IN SCIENTIFIC HISTORY

Papalia's efforts to consolidate the mafia's hold over underground gambling operations in Toronto began around the late 1950s. By the early 1960s, almost every major illegal gaming and bookmaking enterprise in Toronto (outside of Chinatown) was either in partnership with, paying protection to, under the control of, or being shut down by Magaddino through John Papalia and his crew. An April 1961 article in the *Toronto Telegram* described the plight of one bookmaker operating in the downtown core who told the newspaper that three tough-looking men paid him a recent visit and ordered him to close shop. "When he objected he was told it would be better for his health if he complied, and he did." This story was repeated by at least five other bookies in the city. "Those in the know say the mobsters want to wipe out the small bookies so all the money will filter through big-time outlets, which they hope to control." The takeovers continued throughout the first half of the 1960s, as Allan Phillips summarized in his 1964 *Maclean's* article:

> The syndicate has been tightening its control in Toronto. Its former employees appear in other combines, no doubt as watchdogs. Some of the best-known bookmakers of the Fifties are being squeezed out. One of the biggest —

Maxie Bluestein

he netted a quarter of a million dollars a couple of years ago on sports bets — has been reduced to taking bets on the street. Another has quit and is in the scrap-metal business. A third is in the stock market. A fourth, once big, applied for a gun permit and has opened up retail stores in Sudbury and North Bay, the only two northern Ontario cities east of the Lakehead with bookmakers. When one would-be free-enterpriser said that he wanted to get in the business, a friend, a bookie, asked, "Have you got permission?"

Not even the most powerful professional gamblers in Toronto could escape the mafia's reach. Joseph McDermott and Vincent Feeley were providing a cut from their Veterans' Club revenue to the Detroit families before it was shut down by police. By 1958, the Ramsey Club in Niagara Falls, which the two also controlled, was being run by Benny Nicoletti on behalf of Stefano Magaddino. In 1960, McDermott and Feeley reportedly received a visit from Peter Magaddino, Stefano's brother, who sought to tap into their connections with the Anti-Gambling Branch of the Ontario

Provincial Police. With Ontario's biggest gambling operators under the thumb of the American mafia, Johnny Pops now turned his attention to the last of the big independents in Toronto: Maxwell Bluestein.

His friends called him "Max" or "Maxie" and he was described by one journalist as "a tough man with deep blue eyes and very dark hair, which only accentuated the pallid flesh of his harshly featured face. Although a man of very few words — he hardly spoke at all, in fact — he was bold, cocky, and clever, and was into gambling's biggest bucks." Bluestein had long been involved in Toronto's criminal world and recorded his first conviction in 1934. In 1946, he was one of three men charged with assaulting Ernest Steinberg, who was most likely attacked because he had given police information that led to a raid on a local gambling joint. A classified RCMP report from 1945 accused Maxie Baker (his real name) and associates of being "the main heroin distributors in Toronto" and "definitely connected with the peddling of illicit narcotics in this City."

By the 1950s, Bluestein had become wealthy enough to live in the fashionable Forest Hill district of Toronto. He had an interest in several popular gambling clubs, including the Cooksville Veteran's Club, but his jewel in the crown was the Lakeview Club at Eglinton and Bathurst, which he ran with Joseph Zeldin and Samuel Binder. Incorporated as a social club, it operated for more than three decades and, by the 1950s, had become Toronto's pre-eminent gambling establishment. If this were not enough, Maxie always had several crap games floating around town. Notwithstanding these profitable businesses, most of his money came from sports books and he was known to have employed at least two hundred runners in Toronto to take wagers. Betting slips seized by police following a raid on the Lakeview Club in 1960 showed a daily average of $37,700 over a nine-day period. In his testimony before the Roach Commission, Bluestein argued that this estimate was excessive, but he did admit that his daily intake was more than $10,000. In addition to his gambling operations, he was known to have investments in a finance company, hotels, and apartment buildings.

In 1958, John Papalia asked Bluestein to meet with him at the Westbury Hotel in Toronto. When he arrived, Maxie found he would be sharing company with representatives of mafia families from Montreal, New York, Buffalo, and Detroit. Pops told Bluestein in no uncertain terms that he was to merge his operation with the mafia's gambling interests in the city and, in return, would receive a percentage of the take. Maxie refused and for the next three years, Papalia and his men placed intense pressure on him to capitulate, which included recurring threats as well as tips to police that resulted in raids on his Lakeview Club. Fiercely independent, Maxie began to fight back. He started by feeding information to the police on Papalia's gambling's outlets. He applied for a gun licence, but was turned down following a criminal background check. He then arranged for goons to come in from Detroit to rough up Papalia, hoping that it would scare him off. It didn't work. When the Detroit enforcers discovered Papalia's mafia connections they immediately backed off and even lent their support to his move against Bluestein.

In July 1960, the Lakeview Club was raided by police and Bluestein and his partners were convicted of keeping a common betting house. The stingy Bluestein chose four months in jail over the $15,000 fine, but this would prove to be a grave tactical error on his part. After finding out that Papalia was ratcheting up his efforts to take over Bluestein's gambling operations, Maxie promptly paid his fine and was released from jail. Before long, Bluestein was called to another meeting with Papalia, which was to take place on March 21, 1961, at the Town Tavern, a popular Toronto lounge and restaurant. Papalia had arranged for the restaurant to be packed with his friends, associates, and other professional gamblers and bookmakers so they could watch Bluestein surrender, or, if he continued to refuse Papalia's entreaties, to observe the consequences. Bluestein arrived at the restaurant, settled into a table with some friends, and then sealed his fate by rejecting a drink ordered for him by Papalia. Maxie was well aware of the significance of this seemingly charitable offer; if he accepted the drink it would signal his intentions to give in to Papalia's demands. At about one o'clock in the morning, as Bluestein was picking up his things at the hat-check counter, Papalia asked him to step into the lounge, which by this time was dark and deserted. At the same time, Papalia's henchmen, Freddie Gabourie, Jack Weaver,

and Frank Marchildon, had sidled up towards the counter. The men now had Bluestein surrounded and moved in for the kill. Instinctually, Maxie pulled a pocket knife and was able to stab Marchildon several times. But he was outnumbered. In his *Toronto Star* column that appeared a couple of weeks later, Pierre Berton describes the rest:

> A moment later, in full view of 100 persons, including the personnel of the Town Tavern and the steady customers, they administered as terrible a beating as it is possible to give to a man without killing him. Iron bars, with ropes tied to them for better leverage, rained down on Bluestein's head and across his forehead, eyes and cheekbones. His scalp was split seven or eight times. Knuckle dusters smashed into his eyes and a broken bottle was ground into his mouth. When Bluestein dropped to the floor be was kicked in the face. His overcoat, torn and slashed, was literally drenched in his own blood. His scalp later required 20 stitches.

With the help of Berton's column, Bluestein's thrashing would be front-page news for weeks to come. The publicity not only provided Papalia with a new notoriety, but it confirmed to many the existence of the mafia in Ontario. Four days after the beating, metro police announced that the attack was the work of a secret organization that was attempting to take over the city's gambling operations. The April 8, 1961, edition of the *Toronto Telegram* howled that the beating was conducted by "three of the most notorious racketeers in Ontario," members of the Italian mafia that were muscling in on Toronto's gambling rackets. Metropolitan Toronto chairman Fred Gardiner charged that the planned attack was "evidence of the introduction of gangsterism into Toronto" and promised that the police commission would look into the incident.

Despite the widespread publicity, police were severely hampered in their ability to lay charges. Topcoats belonging to two of Bluestein's attackers were left in the Town Tavern, but, as the *Telegram* reported, "both bore the trademarks of the professional gangster — frayed patches where labels had been removed earlier to prevent identification." Bluestein was not co-operating with police and threats against the lives of witnesses meant that few came forward. As Pierre Berton wrote on April 7, customers at the Town Tavern that night had been stricken by "perhaps the most remarkable case of mass blindness in scientific history." Police eventually did convince witnesses to come forward and two months after the beating occurred, Freddy Gabourie, Jack Weaver, and Frank Marchildon surrendered to police. Papalia was also charged but had disappeared from sight. A massive manhunt was undertaken, while surveillance was conducted on Papalia's known associates. One man being tailed by police in the hopes he would lead them to Papalia unexpectedly pulled a baseball bat from his car and swung wildly at his two police shadows. At the same time, he appeared to be throwing a packet into the gutter. The man was overpowered by the two officers, who also retrieved the small package. Inside, they found two capsules of heroin. As a result, Alberto Agueci was charged with illegal possession of narcotics and possession of a dangerous weapon.

Papalia did eventually surrender to police, with some speculating that he was forced to by his mafia superiors in order to take some of the heat off the syndicate. On May 11, 1961, dressed in a tailored suit, wearing dark glasses, and with a white handkerchief shielding his face from the media's cameras, John Papalia gave himself up to Hamilton police. He was quickly hustled off to Toronto and after appearing before a magistrate, he was released on bail. On his way out the door, he stomped on the foot of a television cameraman and spat at a newspaper photographer. A month later, three men were convicted and sentenced to jail for the beating. John Papalia was given eighteen months, Frank Marchildon was sentenced to nine months, and Fred Gabourie received four months.

That night at the Town Tavern was seen by many as a seminal event in the history of organized crime in Ontario. It confirmed the presence of the mafia in the province, exposed their efforts to take over Toronto's underground gambling industry, and helped trigger the creation of a Royal Commission into gambling and organized crime. As organized crime writer James Dubro explains, it was also significant in that the attack backfired on Stefano Magaddino and John Papalia in their quest to establish a mafia monopoly over Toronto's criminal rackets:

Since the Mafia's lifeline is in its ability to instill fear, Johnny "Pops" and the Mafia, in the end, lost the fight to Maxie Bluestein. Not only did Maxie stand up and fight, he inflicted his own share of damage. And he showed everyone that all one had to do to overcome the Mafia was to fight back, even if it meant risking your own life. Many on the street argue that Maxie was never the same after the terrible beating he received from "Pops" and the boys. But Bluestein did hold on to his gambling in Toronto and "Pops" did go to jail for the beating after many of the reluctant witnesses were shamed by Pierre Berton and others into coming forward. Papalia didn't take over Bluestein's operations or Mafia operations in Toronto. In fact, he has never been able to take over mob operations in his hometown of Hamilton. After the Bluestein beating, Papalia was never as big as he once appeared to be. He had lost a lot of respect, a vital and all-too-fragile commodity for a Mafia boss.

While Bluestein held his own against Papalia, he was never the same following the beating. He was suspicious of everyone and rarely left his swank Forest Hill home. In 1973, he discovered four sticks of undetonated dynamite under his car, which only contributed to his well-founded sense of paranoia. The same year, he shot and killed a close friend, David Stillman. He was found not guilty by reason of insanity — he denied the killing and even refused to accept that Stillman was dead — and was committed to a mental institution. In time he was released and, on October 30, 1984, he died at his home following a heart attack.

THERE IS SO MUCH JUNK IN CANADA IT'S LYING AROUND IN BAGS

While the American mafia and its Ontario branches were busy trying to corner the illegal gambling markets, they also had their sights set on incorporating the province into an international heroin network. The province would not only be a destination for the drug, but, more important, it would serve as a gateway to the United States. Ontario had already been used on a limited basis by mafia families to smuggle heroin into North America, but it was during the late 1950s and early 1960s that it began to flow into Ontario in record quantities. American mafia leaders attending the October 1957 meeting at the Grand Hôtel des Palmes in Palermo and the Apalachin conference in upstate New York a month later reportedly decided that Ontario would be one of the continent's main conduits in their expanding heroin importation plans. During the latter half of the 1950s, Settimo (Big Sam) Accardi was coordinating the smuggling of heroin, hidden in suitcases and cans of anchovies, from Sicily and Marseilles into Canada and the United States while he lived in Toronto. The 6-foot, 215-pound member of New York's Genovese crime family took up residence in Toronto after he skipped bail pending a trial on heroin trafficking charges in New York City.

Another major figure responsible for establishing the Ontario connection was Alberto Agueci, the Magaddino Family member who also lived in Toronto and who maintained strong contacts with heroin wholesalers in his native Sicily. Agueci was born in Salemi, Sicily, in 1922, two years after his brother, Vito, another Magaddino Family mafioso. As the brothers grew older, both became involved in mafia activities in Sicily and, in 1950, Alberto was refused entry into the U.S. due to Italian police reports that documented his criminal ties. But he was accepted into Canada, first settling in Windsor and then Toronto. When he entered the country, he carried with him a letter of introduction from Rosario Mancino, a Sicilian Mafia boss who was one of the biggest international heroin traffickers at the time. Vito followed his brother to Canada and the two opened a bakery in Toronto, while specializing in heroin importation and trafficking in Ontario and western New York on behalf of the Magaddino Family. In his testimony to the 1963 Senate Committee on Organized Crime, Joseph Valachi, a low-level soldier with the Genovese Family, made this brief, but significant, reference to Vito:

Valachi: … Vito Agueci himself is a member from Canada.

Q: From Canada?

Valachi: Yes.

Q: He is a member of another family though?

Valachi: In Canada.

Alberto Agueci

Q: The Buffalo family?

Valachi: Buffalo and Canada is all one. When I say Canada, I mean Toronto.

Q: He was not a member of the Genovese Family?

Valachi: He was a member of another family in Buffalo, Stephen Magaddino.

Through his contacts in Sicily, Alberto Agueci began bringing over small quantities of heroin into Canada, often sending his brother to make the purchases. Alberto's Sicilian suppliers assured him they could get their hands on an endless supply of almost pure heroin from Corsican gangsters. Now all he needed was a larger market. The opportunity to supply the biggest heroin market in North America presented itself when Alberto was introduced to Vincent Mauro and his two lieutenants, Frank (Frankie the Bug) Caruso and Salvatore Rinaldo. All three men were made members of the Genovese Family, New York City's most prolific heroin retailers at the time. Rinaldo, who would later turn state's evidence and testify against his Canadian drug dealing colleagues, was working as a small-scale heroin distributor for Mauro in New York, but his suppliers were inconsistent and rarely had the large quantities he desired. The man who would bring Alberto Agueci and Vincent

Mauro together and cement the relationship between supplier and distributor was none other than John Papalia. As two of the most prominent members of the Magaddino Family's Canadian wing, Agueci and Papalia were close associates, having worked together on a number of scams in Ontario. One of their swindles was rigged bingo games where tiny printing presses that manufactured winning cards were smuggled into bingo halls. They also became partners in illegal gambling operations and liquor smuggling, and the two co-owned the highly profitable Star Vending Machine Company. Papalia was also close to Vincent Mauro (a.k.a. Vinnie Bruno), the heavy-set native of Greenwich Village who reported to Anthony Strollo, the Genovese underboss who oversaw the family's heroin trafficking in New York.

In October 1958, Papalia introduced Alberto Agueci to Mauro, who then put Agueci in contact with Caruso and Rinaldo to work out the details of their fledgling heroin smuggling partnership. "I was told we were going to work together," Rinaldo later told a New York City courtroom. "Agueci and Papalia would take care of their end in Canada and bring the stuff from Europe and we would take care of our end here." Rinaldo told the court that the joint venture was hatched in March 1960, after fellow Genovese solider Joseph Valachi returned from Canada and proclaimed there was "so much junk in Canada it was laying around in bags." The date provided by Rinaldo was perhaps a deliberate lie, although Valachi did spend a few days in Toronto under the care of Alberto Agueci and John Papalia in January 1960, while he was on the lam after being charged with drug trafficking in New York (while at Alberto Agueci's Toronto home he received a phone call from Anthony Strollo ordering him back to New York to give himself up to police). Regardless of how and when the partnership started, it was a perfect fit for both sides: Alberto Agueci had access to substantial quantities of heroin in Sicily, but he lacked a distribution system in a large North American market. The Genovese Family had a large market and a distribution network, but did not have a reliable supplier. Agueci informed Magaddino of their plans and was guaranteed a healthy percentage of the drug profits. In return, he pledged legal help and bail money if his men ran into trouble. Magad-

dino's influence over heroin trafficking now stretched from Southern Ontario through to western New York and the Ohio Valley all the way to New York City. In the early 1960s, police intelligence indicated that his organization included two Ontario residents who worked as drug wholesalers (Alberto Agueci and John Papalia), six who operated as local suppliers in Southern Ontario and the Buffalo-Niagara Falls region of New York, and two Buffalo residents who smuggled the heroin across the U.S.-Canada border.

Before being imported into North America, the heroin was first transported from laboratories in France to Agueci's Sicilian hometown of Salemi where it would be sewn into quilts or secreted in false-bottomed suitcases. From there it would be carried to New York City by unwitting Italians travelling via passenger ships. Helping out with the Italian end of the operation was Salvatore Valenti, a mafia-connected travel agent in Sicily whose job was to arrange for the voyage of the Italian nationals and to ensure the drug-laden luggage found its way into their hands. When the ocean liners arrived in New York, the Italian passengers would be met by Matteo Palermi, a Sicilian immigrant living in New York who would pick up the suitcases and deliver them to the Brooklyn bakery where he worked. Once the suitcases were safely in his possession, Palermi would contact Agueci or Rinaldo and tell them how many "boys" (code word for the number of kilos in each suitcase) had arrived. The luggage was then picked up from Palermi and the heroin removed, diluted, and sold to wholesale and retail customers throughout New York City, including other Genovese soldiers like Joseph Valachi and Salvatore Maneri. Rinaldo would turn over the funds generated from the sales to Vincent Mauro or Frank Caruso who would then provide a cut, in the form of $5,000 bank drafts, to John Papalia. In addition to the unsuspecting Italian tourist couriers, Alberto Agueci and Papalia also had Scopelliti, an Ontario-based mafia prospect in his early twenties, make at least one trip to Italy to smuggle heroin to New York. Smaller quantities of heroin were also brought into Canada via Toronto, where it would be repackaged and spirited across the border to be distributed in western New York by Magaddino Family members or in Detroit where it was wholesaled by Nicholas Cicchini.

By the end of the 1950s, dozens of kilos of heroin were being shipped to New York without a hitch. Things were going so well that steamer trunks were now being used to accommodate larger quantities and plans were afoot to make a one-time purchase of 300 kilos. By the summer of 1960, however, the well-laid plans of Agueci et al. began to go astray. One steamer trunk arriving in New York had the wrong address and was almost intercepted by U.S. Customs at the harbour. But what ultimately exposed the drug ring was the arrest of a low-level trafficker working for Joseph Valachi named Ralph Wagner, who squealed on his supplier. This not only led police to lay heroin trafficking charges against Valachi in late 1959, but it also prompted around-the-clock surveillance of other Genovese Family members. The police attention bore fruit on October 21, 1960, when Matteo Palermi and Salvatore Rinaldo were arrested in New York in possession of a trunk containing 10 kilos of heroin that had just been unloaded from a passenger ship. Under intense interrogation, the two men provided information that allowed police to piece together the French, Italian, American, and Canadian cells that made up the international heroin smuggling network. In January 1961, a multi-force investigation was launched comprising the U.S. Bureau of Narcotics, the RCMP, and Italian and French law enforcement agencies. In Toronto, police turned up one frantic telegram from Alberto Agueci inquiring about the mislabelled steamer trunk and also learned that numerous Italians living in Canada had made return trips to their homeland at his expense. At the same time, federal and municipal police were zeroing in on the main Genovese Family members behind the operation, Italian police were investigating the Sicilian suppliers, and French authorities were positioning themselves to shut down the Corsican heroin processing plants.

The day of reckoning arrived on May 22, 1961, when a New York grand jury indicted twenty-four people alleged to be part of the international drug ring, including Vincent Mauro, Frank Caruso, Salvatore Rinaldo, Salvatore Maneri, Matteo Palermi, Joseph Valachi, John Papalia, Alberto Agueci, Vito Agueci, and Rocco Scopelliti. In announcing the indictments, U.S. district attorney Robert Morgenthau estimated that, since 1958, the conspirators had smuggled more

than 110 pounds of pure heroin, worth around $7 million, into New York City. The district attorney's office later announced that in the previous ten years, mafia groups based in Sicily, America, and Canada had been working together to smuggle heroin with a street value of more than $150 million into the U.S.

Two days after the indictments, police in New York launched a series of pre-dawn raids arresting twelve of the accused. A few days later, the Agueci brothers and twenty-one-year-old Rocco Scopelliti were picked up in Toronto. John Papalia was out on bail after his arrest for the Bluestein beating and once again had disappeared. Following a telephone tip, Toronto police tracked him down and arrested him on Toronto's Yonge Street the morning of June 13, a few hours after the RCMP had moved his name to the top of their Most Wanted list. Almost immediately, U.S. authorities began extradition hearings against the Canadian suspects. The Agueci brothers and Scopelliti were ordered to be extradited around the middle of June after an Ontario magistrate permitted the withdrawal of their Canadian charges. On July 7, 1961, Papalia was ordered extradited to the U.S. Four days later he would be convicted of assaulting Bluestein, a conviction he welcomed, thinking it would prevent him from being sent to the U.S. Canadian justice officials would not be so accommodating and pushed for his extradition, a process that would drag through the courts for almost a full year.

Of the twenty-four people indicted, eleven were put on trial in a New York courtroom in November 1961. Absent from this initial trial were the four men most responsible for the drug conspiracy: Alberto Agueci, John Papalia, Vincent Mauro, and Frank Caruso. Most of those charged had been released on bail, including Mauro, Caruso, and Salvatore Maneri who took the opportunity to flee the country. Vito Agueci and Rocco Scopelliti were unable to come up with bail money and languished in a New York jail while Alberto Agueci had to sell his home in order to post his $20,000 bail. Although Magaddino had agreed to provide bail money for his Canadian dope peddlers, the Agueci brothers and Scopelliti soon discovered he was not a man of his word. Furious over this betrayal, Alberto stormed his way to Buffalo to confront Magaddino sometime in the summer of 1961. Some say he threatened to reveal the don's involvement in the heroin smuggling conspiracy if he did not come up with the bail money. Other reports suggest he threatened Magaddino with death. Either way, Magaddino never relented and Agueci would pay the ultimate price for his insolence.

On October 8, 1961, Alberto bid his wife farewell as he left Toronto to travel to New York for his preliminary hearing. He would never make it. When Agueci failed to show up for his trial, it was assumed that he had jumped bail. However, on November 23, 1961, about halfway through the initial trial, two hunters stumbled across the charred, mutilated remains of his body in a field near a Rochester interchange of the New York State Freeway. Agueci was not only murdered, he had first been tortured. A blowtorch had been applied to his face, blinding him. His ankles and wrists were bound with nylon cord and he had been tied to a tree with barbed wire. The blowtorch was also applied to his genitals, which were then cut off and shoved into his mouth. Eight teeth had been knocked out and three ribs were split. About 30 pounds of flesh had been filleted off his body while he was still alive. What was left of his remains was doused in gasoline and set aflame. Police believe his torment may have lasted for several days before he was finally put out of his misery. His ghastly torture and murder was meant to be a signal to anyone else who entertained ideas of threatening Don Magaddino.

Despite the absence of the main conspirators, the trial went ahead as scheduled and continued until the end of December. Prosecutors argued that John Papalia and Alberto Agueci purchased around 100 kilos of heroin in Italy and arranged for its transport to Canada and the United States. Among the evidence presented in court was ten plastic bags filled with 10 kilos of pure heroin discovered in the false bottom of a trunk seized from Salvatore Rinaldo, who told the court that Agueci and Papalia were his suppliers. Matteo Palermi testified that he was first approached in October 1958 by Alberto Agueci who told him he would be smuggling diamonds, not heroin. Palermi informed the court that it was Agueci who often picked up the drug-filled luggage from him and confessed to taking a suitcase with 10 kilos of heroin from Rocco Scopelliti at Pier 84 on the Hudson River on August 10, 1960. Palermi said he had been paid $300 for his work and when he

demanded more money, Agueci told him they could not afford it, as they needed every cent for a deposit on 300 kilos of heroin. When the jury delivered their verdict, all eleven of the defendants were found guilty. Joseph Valachi received twenty years, Vito Agueci was sentenced to fifteen, and Rocco Scopelliti was given ten years. When the sentences were handed out in January 1962, U.S. Attorney General Robert Kennedy called the investigation and subsequent convictions, "the deepest penetration the federal government has ever made in the illegal international traffic of drugs."

The unravelling of the international heroin ring did not end with these convictions. In February 1962, sixty-seven-year-old Nicholas Cicchini of Windsor was convicted of conspiring to traffic in heroin and possession of counterfeit money. Cicchini was snared in April 1961 after a drug dealing associate named John Simon sold heroin to an undercover agent working for the U.S. Bureau of Narcotics in Windsor. On May 1, the agent was referred to Cicchini by Simon, who boasted to the agent that he could obtain large quantities of heroin and counterfeit money. The 100 percent pure heroin could be purchased for $11,000 a kilo, while fake American cash could be bought at the price of $35 for $100 bills and $15 and $50 bills. On May 8, Simon met the agent at a tavern near Windsor and handed him a cigarette box containing a small amount of heroin. The agent then drove to the parking lot of a nightclub where he was introduced to Cicchini. After some negotiating, Cicchini agreed to sell half a kilo for $5,500 and promised his customer he would introduce him to his source from whom he could obtain larger quantities. On May 11, 1961, Cicchini met the agent again in the same parking lot, and was paid $5,500 in marked money in return for a brown paper package containing half a kilo of heroin that later tested to be 99.2 percent pure. On May 24, the agent once again met with Cicchini, who advised him that due to the arrest of his suppliers in Toronto he could not come up with a previously promised delivery of four kilos for at least a month. He did, however, offer to sell the agent another kilogram for $10,500 as well as $1 million worth of counterfeit U.S. dollars. The agent asked Cicchini if he could arrange a meeting with his suppliers, but was told "You'll never meet them." On July 9, another rendezvous was held, at which time Cicchini advised the agent that because of the recent arrests, he could no longer supply him with heroin. Realizing that Cicchini was not bluffing, police moved in and arrested him. Along with Simon, Cicchini was charged with various narcotics and counterfeiting offences. At the conclusion of their trial in January 1962, the two defendants were convicted and sentenced. Cicchini received twelve years while Simon was handed six years.

Around the time that Cicchini and Simon were being prosecuted, Vincent Mauro, Frank Caruso, and Salvatore Maneri were being tracked down in Spain following an international manhunt. When the fugitives were arrested in Barcelona they were all carrying false Canadian passports in the names of three Hamilton, Ontario, residents (most likely supplied by Canadian lawyer and Magadinno Family member Harold Bordonaro). The three men were deported to the United States to stand trial on the drug charges, along with thirty-seven-year-old John Papalia, who was finally extradited to the U.S. in March 1962. A year later, on March 4, 1963, the long-awaited trial of John Papalia, Frank Caruso, Vincent Mauro, and Salvatore Maneri came to an abrupt end, a mere two hours after jury selection was completed. The four defendants decided to change their pleas to guilty. As a result, Papalia received a ten-year sentence, while the three New York men received fifteen-year terms. Anthony Strollo was able to escape any charges that arose from the drug busts, although a month following the convictions he disappeared from his New Jersey home and was never seen again. It is widely believed that he was murdered on the orders of Vito Genovese, who held his underboss responsible for the mistakes that led to the dismantling of the drug ring.

In April 1963, Settimo Accardi, who had been on the lam since 1955, was arrested in Italy and flown back to New York to answer federal narcotics charges. This time, the judge set Accardi's bail at a record-setting $500,000, an amount that assured the prisoner would not have the opportunity to escape justice again. On August 25, 1964, the sixty-year-old was sentenced to a fifteen-year term and a $16,000 fine. After being imprisoned in Atlanta, Accardi told fellow inmate Vito Agueci that in September 1960 Stefano Magaddino had refused to pay for $20,000 worth of heroin that Accardi had sold him as punishment for smuggling drugs while living in Toronto without his consent. Accardi told Agueci that he had not responded to an invitation to meet with Magaddino because, as the *New York Times* reported, "he knew his days would have been numbered."

The arrests of the mafia-connected heroin traffickers continued in the summer of 1963 when the RCMP broke up a ring headed by Charles Cipolla, which was supplying Toronto and Hamilton. The five-month undercover investigation resulted in the confiscation of heroin worth around $120,000 on the streets and the arrest of twelve people, although only five were charged. Fifty-year-old Charles Cipolla, described by one newspaper as the "short, swarthy owner of a Guelph fruit store and restaurant," was sentenced to twenty years' imprisonment, the stiffest sentence for a drug offence handed down in Ontario to date.

"COMPARATIVELY FREE OF ORGANIZED GANGSTERISM"

The years 1963 and 1964 continued to be high-profile ones for organized crime in Ontario. In 1963, the U.S. Senate Committee on Organized Crime heard mafia turncoat Joseph Valachi proclaim that the Cosa Nostra stretched into Ontario. At the same hearings, senior officers with the Buffalo Police Department testified that in Toronto, Hamilton, Guelph, and Niagara Falls, Ontario, there were at least twenty members of a crime syndicate headed by the "irrefutable lord paramount" Stefano Magaddino. The presentation was accompanied by an organizational chart entitled "The Magaddino Empire of Organized Crime." On the right hand of the chart, in a square marked "Canada," were the names of the Vito and Alberto Agueci, Charles and Frank Cipolla, Dan Gasbarrini, John Papalia and his two brothers, as well as Paul and Albert Volpe.

In March 1963, Mr. Justice Roach presented his report on organized gambling in Ontario to the provincial government. He acknowledged that it had reached a "staggering" volume, but concluded that little evidence existed suggesting "there was organized crime in the province in any alarming extent except in the field of organized gambling." He also denied the existence of the mafia in Canada, writing, "There is no evidence before me that it does subsist in organized crime or that any of the activities of those engaged in organized crime were in any way associated with the Mafia." The findings certainly contradicted recent events, and some observers later accused Roach of whitewashing the commission's findings in order to take the pressure off the provincial attorney general and the Conservative government, which had been accused of corruption and the failure to take sufficient action against organized crime in the province. Yet, Justice Roach was not the only one in denial over the existence of the mafia in Ontario. Two years before he appointed the respected jurist to head the commission, Ontario Attorney General Kelso Roberts declared that Canada was "comparatively free of organized gangsterism." When Detroit police commissioner Harry Toy stated publicly in 1948 that Windsor was now part of Detroit's network of bookies, the chairman of the Windsor Police Commission snorted, "It is difficult to believe that a responsible public official of Detroit would make such scurrilous statements about a 'friendly' neighbour, its police force and its citizens generally." In the early 1960s, Toronto's chief of police disputed a report that a local "numbers racket" was flourishing and didn't believe the mafia was active in the city. In his statements before the Roach Commission, Hamilton's chief constable Leonard G. Lawrence did not believe that organized crime had a hand in narcotics trafficking or gambling operations in the city, nor did Hamilton play host to any sort of mafia organization.

One high-ranking law enforcement official whose take on the existence of the mafia in Ontario was not so blinkered was RCMP commissioner C.W. Harvison. In a press conference at the Canadian National Exhibition in Toronto on August 16, 1963, the head Mountie appeared to disagree with his colleagues and the Roach Commission report released just a few months earlier. He suggested that mafia crime syndicates from America were making incursions into Canada, and were involved in drug trafficking, counterfeiting, bootlegging, and stock market manipulation. The controversy provoked by his comments, combined with the discovery of corruption within the OPP's anti-gambling squad, led to yet another provincial commission in Ontario, this one headed by Judge Bruce Macdonald, who delivered his report on January 31, 1964. In startling contrast to the conclusions of the Roach Commission, Justice Macdonald asserted, "Organized crime has existed in

Ontario and in some cases still does, in varying degrees from time to time as conditions change." He also stated there was solid evidence that American criminal syndicates had infiltrated Ontario. Although no one group had a monopoly over a particular region or criminal activity, he did confirm that "certain persons to wit: Alberto and Vito Agueci, John Papalia and possibly Rocco Scopelliti and in all likelihood several others having known contacts and associations with them and others in Canada and in the United States, were members of the so-called mafia or Cosa Nostra and made unsuccessful efforts to obtain control of certain organized criminal operations in Ontario."

The political storm that was brewing over whether the mafia existed in Canada escalated even further in December 1964 when Justice Macdonald revealed that the Windsor-based mobster Onofrio Minaudo was provided a visa to enter Canada in 1960, despite being deported just two years earlier. After his presence in the country was discovered in 1961, Minaudo was ordered to be immediately deported, but for some reason was allowed to stay until 1964, even though he had been convicted of drug trafficking and other offences in 1962. Macdonald told the press that his commission never received a reply from the federal minister of immigration Guy Favreau when he tried to find out why Minaudo was allowed to remain in Canada. A day after Macdonald's public comments, two members of the federal New Democratic Party filed a series of written questions asking the Liberal government in Ottawa for information about the deportation of Minaudo. They also inquired about Giuseppe Catalanotte, who was deported from Canada on November 5, 1964, more than a year after the order was actually made.

A native of Arcano, Italy, Catalanotte was one of the Detroit mob's most vicious enforcers and was suspected of numerous murders during the 1930s. Like Minaudo, he settled in Windsor after entering Canada on a short-term visitor's visa in 1957. He obtained the visa from the Canadian embassy in Cuba, where he ended up after being deported from the United States for convictions ranging from drug trafficking to extortion. The scandal was heightened when External Affairs Minister Paul Martin admitted that, as a private lawyer, he had received a "normal legal fee" from Minaudo in 1960 after making representations to the

Immigration Appeal Board that his deportation order be squashed. The petition was somewhat successful in that Minaudo was allowed another six months in the country. Martin and the appeal board were cleared of any wrongdoing or corruption, but the affair tainted both considerably (some say it put an end to Martin's aspirations to be leader of the federal Liberal Party). After finally being deported from Canada, Minaudo settled in the Sicilian village of Custonaci. In May 1965, his sixty-year-old, bullet-riddled body was found by Italian police, who suspected he may have been killed in revenge for murders he committed in that country forty years earlier. "The people in that area of Sicily never forget," a Canadian embassy official in Rome told the media. "There, vendettas run for generations." The FBI had another theory: they believed that senior members of the Detroit mafia had ordered the hit after finding out that Minaudo, whom they no longer welcomed in their territory, intended to sneak back into Canada. Giuseppe Catalanotte, who relocated to the same Sicilian province as Minaudo, disappeared in 1966, despite being under police surveillance.

Throughout all of this, Canadian immigration officials were busy deporting other Detroit gangsters. In September 1965, fifty-eight-year-old Sam Finazzo, a ranking member with the Detroit mob, was arrested while entertaining friends at his cottage in Kingsville, Ontario. He was expelled soon after due to his criminal record. In July 1966, the heirs to Detroit's mafia leadership, Anthony (Big Tony) Giacalone and Domenic (Fats) Corrado, were arrested in Montreal after they stepped off a plane from Windsor. Following an immigration hearing, the pair, who said they were travelling to the religious shrine at Ste. Anne de Beaupré in Quebec, were deported back to the U.S.

MR. LUPPINO

Q: How long have you known Natale Luppino?
A: I have known his brother between fifteen and twenty years.
Q: That is Jim Luppino?
A: Yes.
Q: Is his name Vincenzo and he is called Jim?
A: I never called him Vincenzo. It is Jimmy, I know him as.
Q: Do you know Giacomo Luppino?

A: Who's Giacomo?
Q: Is that his father?
A: I know his father but I didn't realize his name was Giacomo.
Q: What did you understand his father's name to be?
A: Mr. Luppino.

—Testimony by Paul Volpe before a 1974 Royal Commission investigating violence and corruption within Ontario's construction industry

During the mid-1950s, John Papalia would be joined in Hamilton by another powerful mafioso and future Magaddino Family member named Giacomo Luppino. Born in 1900 in the village of Oppido in Calabria, Luppino came to Canada in 1955, already a member of an 'Ndrangheta clan in Italy. Settling in Hamilton, he would go on to be Magaddino's most trusted and reliable Ontario lieutenant and one of the most respected mafia dons in Canada. While little is known about Luppino's initial years in Canada, it was around the late 1950s or early 1960s that he and Santo Scibetta were chosen by Magaddino to oversee his Ontario interests. Influenced by his Calabrian roots, the organization Luppino set up in Ontario reflected the structure, rules, and codes of the 'Ndrangheta. He was the *capo decina* of the Hamilton wing of the Magaddino Family, but was also in charge of *decinas* in other regions of Ontario. In keeping with 'Ndrangheta organizational tradition, different areas of the province were broken into *aubbocatos*, distinct territories that separated different families or wings of a family. Luppino became the *capo di tutti capi* over all of Magaddino's branches in Ontario, putting him in charge of *decinas* operating in such *aubbocatos* as Hamilton, Guelph, Oakville, and Toronto. In one revealing police recording, Luppino used a business analogy to describe the organization of the 'Ndrangheta in Ontario and the different branches he oversaw in the province, "It is the same as saying there is a company at Hamilton, at Toronto and there is a head of each. Toronto represents the centre and Hamilton represents the commanding point. In Oakville, there are two, but all these *aubbocatos* are represented by one. In other words, we have to play the way I say."

Following the lead of the mafia's ruling commission in the U.S., Luppino also established *La Camera di Controllo*. Made up of the heads of the various *decinas* in Ontario, the goal of this "board of control" was to ensure co-operation, to avoid territorial infringement, and to resolve any problems that may arise. The board, which answered to Magaddino, was reflective of Luppino's great reverence towards his boss, his respect for the American mafia Commission (which he once called "eight of the best") and his adherence to the traditional role of the mafioso as a mediator and arbitrator. Luppino has been described as "a master strategist" who built bridges and brokered deals between different mafia leaders. He was frequently consulted by mob figures from throughout North America and intervened to settle numerous disputes that arose over the years. By setting up the *Camera,* he forged strong relationships with other 'Ndrangheta leaders in Ontario and also maintained ties with the Montreal mafia through a cordial relationship with Vic Cotroni and later, with his future son-in-law, Paolo Violi.

Notwithstanding the respect and influence Luppino garnered from other mafia leaders, there was no doubt that the source of his power emanated from his close association with Magaddino. He was extremely deferential to his don and also delighted in any opportunity he had to meet with him. Police once recorded a fawning Luppino gush about the highlight of a Buffalo wedding he attended — that Magaddino had talked to him at the reception for a whole twenty minutes! Magaddino also respected and often heeded Luppino's advice, which was most apparent in 1966 after Luppino talked him out of any reprisals against Vic Cotroni, who had met with the son of rival Joseph Bonanno.

Luppino was largely illiterate and spoke little English (although he once confessed to his wife that he wished he could speak the language because "people here are much easier to cheat than in Italy"). He was a mafioso in the classical sense in that he lived a modest life, believing that it was not wealth but respect and honour that defined the worth of any man. At one point, police wiretaps caught Luppino lamenting that his sons did not come to seek his counsel, which to him was a sign of disrespect. One Hamilton police investigator, who for several years secretly monitored the movements of Luppino, recounted the time that "old man Luppino" arrived for a meeting and "everyone went around kissing his ring like he was the Pope and showed him a tremendous amount of respect." Luppino revelled in such displays and, according to the police officer, "he'd rather have someone call him Mr. Luppino than give him $10,000." In one conversation with his like-minded son-in-law Paolo, both complained about how the American mafia, with its emphasis on making money, had lost the "old country ways of operation" and conflicted with the traditional ways of the mafioso.

Like other mafia traditionalists, Luppino shunned material wealth. He lived in a humble bungalow in a quiet Hamilton neighbourhood, where he grew tomatoes and often strolled down the street greeting his neighbours. Upon his death in 1987, he was described by some who lived on the block as a quiet, kind man who sat on his veranda and passed out candy to children. But Luppino's home was also his control centre and the site for numerous visits from other mafiosi who came to pay tribute, seek his counsel, broker a deal, or settle a dispute. As one newspaper obituary said of him, "He wielded authority from the back yard of his modest home in Hamilton, where visitors from as far away as Italy came to talk about murder and extortion next to a clothesline of flapping laundry." Neighbours acknowledged that he constantly had people visiting his home, but he would make sure their cars never blocked the driveways of other houses on the street.

Beginning in 1967, police began a five-year surveillance operation on Luppino, which included wiretapping his Hamilton home. Information gleaned from "Operation Orbit" provided great insight into the life of the mafia don and the existence and structure of his 'Ndrangheta organization. In one recording, Luppino and a visitor laughed out loud about the way the mafia was portrayed in a television crime show and spoke about how there were no initiation rites or ceremonies. However, it became clear that Luppino did follow some time-honoured 'Ndrangheta customs. Made members had to pay dues and pass along a percentage of all profits from criminal or legal activities to him. He was also recorded discussing how one obligation of an 'Ndrangheta group was to make financial contributions to a "welfare assistance program" to help its members through difficult times. At one point, Luppino told a young mafioso in Toronto to take a collection across Southern Ontario to care for the widow of an associate and her six children. Despite his paternalistic nature, Luppino was still the head of a criminal group that made money from extortion, loansharking, fraud, counterfeiting, migrant smuggling, drug trafficking, and murder. Remarkably, although his reign lasted for more than thirty years, Luppino was never charged with any criminal offence in Canada.

"YOU KNOW, UH, 'NDRINA"

While Mr. Luppino ruled his criminal fiefdom with the backing of Stefano Magaddino, Toronto was home to other 'Ndrangheta clans that were connected to Antonio Marci, the *capo crimini* (boss of all bosses) in Calabria. During the 1950s and 1960s, Marci forged a loose network of 'Ndrangheta cells in the United States, Canada, Germany, Switzerland, South America, and Australia, in part to facilitate his international heroin smuggling operation. Each cell was based on 'Ndrangheta tradition: a small family of blood relatives formed the nucleus while other members and associates were related through marriage or god parenthood. While each cell generally followed this template, and worked with one another, for the most part they operated autonomously from Marci. Some of the original members of the Toronto cell, which was founded in the late 1950s, had already been inducted into the Honoured Society in Italy, while their sons and other younger recruits took the ritual oath in Toronto. Because most of the Society men that were transplanted in Toronto hailed from a small port on the eastern coast of Reggio di Calabria called Siderno Marina, police began to refer to the Toronto cell as the Siderno Group.

The undisputed head of the Siderno Group up until his death in 1980 was Michele (Mike) Racco. Born on December 12, 1913, in Siderno Marina, Racco was already a member of the 'Ndrangheta before he immigrated to Canada in the early 1950s. Short, with bulging eyes, heavy lids, and thick eyebrows that made his face look almost reptilian, Racco established an 'Ndrina cell in Toronto that grew steadily as he recruited men of Calabrian descent locally and from Italy. By the early 1960s, Racco established a local commission (a *crimini*) which settled disputes and maintained discipline among the city's 'Ndrina members. As the head of this ruling board, Racco became the *capo crimini* for Toronto.

From his small bakery on St. Clair Avenue in the city's Italian district, Racco oversaw a secret criminal society that at any one time included between fifty and one hundred members and which was involved in bootlegging, counterfeiting, extortion, immigrant smuggling, and drug trafficking. The bakery was also a popular meeting place for members of the Honoured Society and, like Luppino, Racco played the role of the traditional mafia don. He rarely became directly involved in criminal activities; instead, his job was to help create opportunities for other Siderno Group members. He valued respect and honour over money and saw himself as a *padrone* to his constituents, providing jobs and loans to community members and safe passage to Canada for Italian immigrants. Racco was much sought after for advice or to solve disputes and maintained strong ties with like-minded criminals, among them Giacomo Luppino in Hamilton, Vic Cotroni in Montreal, Paul Volpe in Toronto, as well

Michele (Mike) Racco

as members of other 'Ndrangheta cells in the United States and abroad. Police intercepted one telephone call from the U.S. in which the man on the other end solicited Racco's advice on how to resolve a territorial dispute between two 'Ndrina clans in New York. At one point during the conversation the man on the other end of the line appeared to have difficulty understanding Racco, who responded in frustration, "Jesus Christ, I can't really go into details here. You know, uh, 'Ndrina." Although Racco preferred mediation to violence, he is suspected of sanctioning the death of two Toronto 'Ndrangheta members in the late 1960s.

Among those who sat on the original *crimini* with Racco was Rocco Zito. Born in Fiumara, Calabria, in 1928, his father, Domenic, was a member of the Vincenzo Crupi group, which was involved in petty smuggling, rustling, and extortion in the 1930s. Italian authorities considered the group to be an 'Ndrangheta clan, a designation that would later be used by Canadian authorities to deny his father landed immigrant status. Zito was believed to have become a member of the 'Ndrangheta before he tried to sneak into North America in 1949, first as a stowaway on a New York–bound ship and again after trying to cross into Texas from Mexico. Both times he was captured and deported. In 1952, a murder charge levelled against him was dismissed by Italian courts and three years later he legally entered Canada via Montreal where he began working for the mafia transporting bootlegged liquor to Toronto. By the late 1950s, Zito had relocated to Toronto where he became an enforcer for Alberto Agueci. When Paolo Violi was arrested on liquor offences in 1960, police found Zito's telephone number in his pocket. Zito was granted Canadian citizenship in 1961, the same year police found an illegal still in his home, which cost him a criminal conviction and a $100 fine. The following year, he was observed attending a meeting in Hamilton at the home of Giacomo Luppino along with other known mafiosi from Quebec, Ontario, and Buffalo. The purpose of the meeting, according to police, was to plan a network of stills across Ontario and Quebec. The following year Zito became a member of the Toronto *crimini*.

Zito also firmly adhered to the traditions expected of the mafioso. He kept a low profile and lived with his wife and five daughters in a small bungalow in Toronto. He maintained a wide circle of contacts and was always available to dispense advice, make a deal, or loan money. Like Luppino and Racco, he was continuously meeting and working with fellow gangsters from Ontario, Quebec, the U.S., and Italy. When Tommasso Buscetta was in Toronto in the late 1960s, he met frequently with Zito. In 1970, Zito was observed by police with Paolo Gambino, the brother of Carlo, New York City's most powerful crime boss at the time. After meeting with Vic Cotroni and Paolo Violi in Montreal, Gambino travelled to Toronto to work with Zito in establishing a heroin pipeline through Toronto (Zito later told police that Gambino was a neighbour of his cousin in New York who had come to seek advice on a personal matter). Zito was also observed having lunch in Toronto with Frank Cotroni in the early 1980s. According to one police report, during a private party held in 1985 at a Toronto restaurant, Don Zito's hand was kissed by at least twenty-five men. Following the death of Mike Racco in 1980, Zito was elevated to the head of the *crimini* in Toronto, but he was forced to vacate the post in 1986 when he was convicted of killing Rosario Sciarrino, a freelance photographer who had borrowed $20,000 from Zito in 1981. After falling behind on his payments, and allegedly insulting Zito when the two men met on January 13, 1986, Sciarrino was shot and killed. An autopsy revealed that Sciarrino had also been beaten with a heavy object, resulting in more than a dozen fractures to his face and head. Zito surrendered to police four days later and was charged with second-degree murder. He was convicted of manslaughter and sentenced to four and a half years in jail.

It wasn't until the late 1960s that a spate of violent events provided police with their first glimpse into the existence of the Honoured Society in Toronto. On January 6, 1967, thirty-four-year-old Salvatore Triumbari, the president of Cynar Dry Ltd., was shot and killed outside his Toronto home. Shortly after his death, the Cynar bottling plant was set ablaze causing $100,000 in damages. On June 29, 1969, forty-three-year-old Filippo Vendemini was killed in the parking lot behind his Bloor Street shoe store. The next day, the *Toronto Star* reported that he had been killed "in the traditional, make-sure Mafia way: he was shot once in the chest as he left his car, then dispatched with two more bullets in the head as he lay on the ground." Powder burns were found on his head wounds, indicating the killer stood over him and fired the shots from no more than a foot away. Vendemini was a former employee of Cynar Dry Ltd. before opening his shoe store in October 1968.

Toronto police suspected that the mafia was behind the two murders, but only had circumstantial evidence. Both men had immigrated to Canada in the early 1950s from Siderno Marina and, by the early 1970s, information had surfaced that they were members of the mafia in Canada. As journalist Peter Moon describes in a 1971 article on the 'Ndrangheta in Ontario, Vendemini's final hours strongly suggest that his murder was gang related, "The first phone call made by the Vendemini family after he was shot was to a family friend named Rocco Zito. The last man to see Vendemini alive, apart from his killer, was a member of the Montreal mafia. Vendemini drove the man to Hamilton where they met a member of the Hamilton mafia. Vendemini then drove the Montreal man to the Toronto airport and returned home to where his killer waited. When the police searched Vendemini's body they found $600 in cash in his pants' pockets and the telephone number of two Montreal mafia members." A few years later, police reported that Triumbari had held an initiation meeting for the Honoured Society in the basement of his house the night before he was murdered. Police initially suspected both men were killed over control of illicit liquor sold in Ontario as Vendemini was known to have taken part in the bootlegging operations set up in the 1950s by mafia groups. The commonly accepted theory, however, is that Michele Racco, at the behest of senior 'Ndrangheta leaders in Calabria, ordered the deaths of the two because of their involvement in the ritual disfigurement of an 'Ndrina member in Italy.

Around the time of the murders, Italian shopkeepers in Toronto were experiencing a rash of violent attacks; store owners and employees were beaten or shot at and their stores were bombed or set on fire. A classified Toronto police memo from 1971 stated, "a closer check of the many fires in the Toronto area has disclosed a number of incendiary fires in the Italian Community. There were thirty-two fires in the Toronto area in 1970 that were connected with the Italian

problem." Cosimo Racco and Ernest Commisso, who together operated several bakeries in Toronto and who had no involvement in the Honoured Society, were the targets of a number of attacks. On July 17, 1968, two shotgun blasts were fired from a passing car at Cosimo Racco and his wife. On March 28, 1969, the home of Ernest Commisso was broken into by thieves who stole jewellery, liquor, cheques, and cash. In the early morning of March 31, 1969, a bomb shattered the storefront windows at the Commisso Brothers and Racco Italian Bakery on Kingcourt Street in the suburb of York. On June 2, 1969, Ernest's brother Anthony was shot three times in the legs. A bakery opened by former employees of Commisso and Racco was decimated by dynamite on June 16, 1970, and, less than ten days later, a nearby bakery was also destroyed by dynamite. On December 20, 1972, dynamite tore a hole in the roof of the Commisso Brothers and Racco Bakery. This was the second bombing of the bakery and the fourteenth reported bomb blast in 1972 targeting Italian businesses.

Despite the ongoing violence, police had little success in gaining the co-operation of the victims or other informants. One Italian merchant complained to police that he was threatened if he did not pay $2,000 to an Italian man who police already suspected of shaking down other shop owners. Police arrested the extortionist, but when his case came to trial, the merchant changed his story, testifying it was all a misunderstanding and that the man was simply asking for a loan. As a result, the charges were dropped. Even without the co-operation of victims, police were becoming certain that the violence was part of an extortion racket carried out by a secret 'Ndrangheta society that was now publicly being called the "Siderno Group." A July 7, 1972, article in the *Toronto Star* was one of the first to link the violence and extortion attempts to this newly discovered criminal syndicate:

> The Siderno Group, some of whose members belonged to the Mafia in Calabria, have brought an extortion technique with them that is peculiar to Calabria, according to Italian police. Victims receive anonymous letters which order them to carry a stated sum of money with them while they drive or walk along a

route outlined in the letters. The letter tells the victim that somewhere along the route he will encounter a sign giving him further directions or he will meet "our representative." Invariably the terrified victim follows the instructions only to find there is no sign and no "representative." All this increases his fear.

The *Star* reported that "a full family" of the Honoured Society had established itself in Toronto. "While the group's members are for the most part unostentatious in the way they live — many operate small businesses or work in factories — they have grown powerful enough to earn the respect and co-operation of other organized criminal groups."

Michele Racco used his power to bring an end to the extortion-related violence, but by that time a police task force had already accumulated a wealth of information on the Siderno Group. On March 20, 1971, police wiretaps picked up a phone conversation between two men who discussed an upcoming meeting where "youth of honours" were "brought forward" for initiation into the Society. Two of the six new recruits were the sons of senior Siderno Group leaders, Vincenzo (Jimmy) Deleo and Michele Racco. Based on the recordings, police scrambled to set up a surveillance team around the Ossington Avenue home where the meeting was to take place. When some of the twenty men attending the meeting began to leave around 9:35 p.m. police raided the house. At 10:30 p.m. Jimmy Deleo phoned Mike Racco and told him police had "blocked all the lanes over there, they've surrounded the place."

On April 14, police intercepted a phone call from Mike Racco to another Society member named Santo Femia in which they discussed the possibility of having a meeting at either Femia's house or that of fellow member Frank Caccamo. Racco cautioned that only a small number of people should attend to avoid suspicion, "If we are going to get together at Caccamo's home fifteen or twenty people at most. Then we do it during the daytime. But if we say were going to be too many, it's not right. But if we decide that all of us should get together, then we squeeze ourselves and make it Friday night."

"*Compare* Mike," Femia replied, "some of the older fellows you could tell not to come because they already know what's going on. But to the young guys, the new ones that came in, you know they don't know each other. They don't know how things are. They don't know this one or that one. But to satisfy them also, we all are going to meet."

The meeting they discussed was held on April 30, 1971, at the home of another Society member named Cosimo Stalteri, and police counted at least twenty-three men in attendance. While police were collecting information from their surveillance, they still did not have enough to lay charges or to prove the existence of a criminal organization. The evidence they so desired would be provided to them courtesy of Mike Racco's firebrand son, Domenic, whose actions over the next year would trigger a cycle of events that would irreversibly confirm the existence of the 'Ndrangheta in Toronto. Born and raised in Toronto, Domenic surrounded himself with the sons of other Siderno Group members. With his Mediterranean good looks, he could be as charming as his father. But unlike his restrained *padre*, Domenic Racco was impulsive, erratic and ill tempered — characteristics that would emerge with dire consequences on July 19, 1971. That evening, the nineteen-year-old was out with his friends and fellow "youths of honour," eighteen-year-old Frank Commisso and nineteen-year-old Joseph Deleo. After getting into a shouting match with another group of young men outside a bowling alley on Yonge Street, an infuriated Domenic rushed home where he retrieved a gun. Intent on avenging his honour, he returned to the scene and fired six shots at the men who had hurled anti-Italian insults his way. Although five of the bullets found their mark, all three of the victims survived the shooting.

On July 30, police arrested and charged Commisso and Deleo with attempted murder. Police also announced a search was under way for Domenic Racco, who had disappeared. After corroborating the mob connections of the three boys, police used the shooting to snare other suspected members of the Siderno Group. They raided homes and businesses of the young men's relatives, where they found weapons, explosives, and counterfeit money. At least seven other people were arrested, including Joseph Deleo's fifty-year-old father, Vincenzo, who was charged with being an accessory after the fact to the shooting and possession of a prohibited weapon (a switchblade). In other raids, police arrested Giuseppe Fragomeni, Francesco (Frank) Caccamo, and Antonio Stalteri. Michele Racco was also arrested and charged after a gun was found in his bakery (he was later acquitted of the charge). On August 25, Domenic, who had fled to Albany, New York, where he hid out in the home of an 'Ndrina member, returned to Toronto via a chartered plane and surrendered to police. At the conclusion of his trial on January 26, 1972, he was found guilty of three counts of attempted murder and a week later he was sentenced to ten years.

Although none of those arrested provided any revealing information on the 'Ndrangheta in Toronto, police did make one discovery that would prove to be a significant breakthrough in their efforts to prove the existence of the secret society in North America. When searching the home of thirty-three-year-old Francesco Caccamo, police found a twenty-seven-page document, handwritten in an antiquated Italian script, in his kitchen cupboards. Experts from Canada and Italy would later conclude that the papers outlined the rites and structure of the *Honorata Società*. It was the first time such an authentic document had fallen into the hands of police in North America. The heading on the first page was *Come Formare una Società* ("How to Form a Society") and the preamble partially read: "My stomach is a tomb, my mouth a bleated work of humility." Another section dictates the initiation rites of an inductee who symbolically vows to take "a bloody dagger in my hand and a serpent in my mouth" should he betray the Honoured Society. A 1972 *Globe and Mail* article described the remainder of the document as a "a tangle of centuries old archaic Italian, the phrases laced with flowery, mystic imagery dealing with such matters as collecting opinions from society members, punishing members who don't surrender their guns at meetings, catechism-like initiation rituals and the proper words to be used when separating a member from the group."

Dr. Alberto Sabatino, the head of a special mafia investigative unit in Italy, testified at Caccamo's trial on weapons and currency counterfeiting charges that the papers were "for a certainty" one of the *condici* (sets of rules and ritual) of the *Honorata Società* and that, in the thousands of raids conducted by Italian police in the past ten years only two similar documents had been found. Sabatino said the papers outlined the basic structure of a 'Ndrina cell, which includes three levels or ranks — *camorrista*, the highest rank; *picciotto*, a middle rank; and "youths of honour," the lowest rank. There were also references to the pledges and obligations of members, the most important being a vow of silence. Sabatino pointed out that the Italian word *d'umilta* appears throughout the document and should be interpreted the same as the word *omerta*, the Sicilian Mafia's oath of secrecy. The document also refers to the term *mastro di sgarru*, another important obligation of members that has to do with vendettas against enemies of the Society. Another term was *baciletta*, which Sabatino defined as "extorted money" collected by Society members that should be "given to the ones who need it, the ones who have been arrested, for the defence lawyers, to help the people the police are looking for."

Sabatino and other experts told the court that whoever was in possession of the papers held a high rank in the Society. This testimony prompted the Crown to paint Frank Caccamo, a construction foreman who arrived to Canada in 1959, as the *maestro di giornato* of the 'Ndrangheta in Toronto. "He was always there for meetings," one Crown attorney argued. "They had to have him there to ensure compliance with the rules." At the conclusion of his trial in August 1972, Caccamo was found guilty on all charges. More significantly, in his summation the trial judge stated that the document found in Caccamo's home was an authentic set of rules and rituals for a secret criminal society and, because it was in his possession, Caccamo was associated with this Society. On that basis, the loaded gun found in Caccamo's home must be for a purpose dangerous to the public peace. This decision and the authenticity of the document were upheld by an Ontario appeals court and the Supreme Court of Canada. This meant that Ontario became the first jurisdiction in North America, and the first outside of Italy, to recognize the existence of the Honoured Society as a secret criminal organization. The sentencing judge accused Caccamo of leading a "Jekyll and Hyde existence" and imprisoned him for one and a half years. He also recommended that he be deported to Italy upon release. In 1976, the

Immigration Department began deportation hearings against Caccamo on the grounds that he belonged to a subversive organization.

That same year, Domenic Racco would once again give in to his impulsive, violent, honour-obsessed temperament. While behind bars, he paid his twenty-two-year-old cousin and American 'Ndrina clan member Frank Archino, Jr. to travel to Toronto from his home in upstate New York to lay a "real good beating" on his brother-in-law Antonio Commisso. Racco had learned that Commisso refused to repay a debt and therefore had dishonoured the family. The scheme to injure Commisso became known to police when a Toronto constable pulled over a car carrying Archino and his twenty-year-old accomplice, George Mickley, for a routine traffic check. Their suspicious behaviour led to a more thorough search of the car, which turned up a .38-calibre pistol hidden in the spare tire along with directions to Commisso's home. Police were also given a mislabelled and unsigned letter at a Canada Post depot that was traced to Domenic Racco. The letter included two $100 bills and maps to Commisso's home and place of work. The letter, in Racco's handwriting, made it clear that Commisso was to be beaten, and if necessary, shot, but not killed: "If Possible — Just a Real Good Beating. Without Doing Anything Else. If not Possible — Then Just GO Ahead As Originally Planned. Blast The Legs. But Remember NO HIGHER Than The LEGS. IMPORTANT — NO DEATH." The letter innocently concluded, "Once you've received this, send me a card saying Hi just to let me know you got it." When Archino was arrested by police in Toronto, he was promised a reduced sentence if he would become a Crown witness and testify against his cousin. Archino agreed and told police how he and Mickley stole the .38-calibre revolver in New York and then visited Racco in jail.

Based on Archino's confessions, Domenic Racco, Archino, and Mickley were charged in November 1976 with conspiring to wound Commisso. When the case came to court in March 1977, however, Racco was able to intimidate his cousin to such an extent that Archino changed his testimony halfway through the preliminary hearing. From the prisoner's dock in the courtroom, Domenic reportedly made a number of hand motions and other gestures that warned Archino of the penalty of testifying against a fellow 'Ndrina member. If his threatening pantomimes were not enough, there were also reports that enforcers from the Siderno Group were occupying the front rows of the courtroom's public seating area. When Archino was put on the stand he declared that police forced him to sign a statement saying that Racco had asked him to shoot Commisso, an about-face that prompted Racco to burst out laughing. The judge had no option but to acquit Domenic of the charges. While Racco avoided another criminal sentence, further damage had already been done to the 'Ndrangheta. Before recanting his confession in court, Archino had given police extensive information on the Honoured Society in Toronto and New York. When asked why he would follow Racco's orders, Archino told police, "For the honour of the family." When asked what he meant by "family" Archino replied, "Italian, the organization." Archino admitted to being an 'Ndrangheta member, having gone through an initiation ceremony in Toronto, and also identified Domenic Racco and his father as members. After serving his sentence for conspiring to wound Commisso, as well as additional counts of perjury and contempt of court, Archino moved back to New York where he later became the business agent for Local 452 of the International Laborers Union in Troy. Archino disappeared in September 1993 after embezzling $570,000 from the union.

"I KNOW HOW THIS GUY PERFORMS"

When Mike Racco was searching for a good lawyer to defend his son on his attempted murder charges, he turned to Paul Volpe. Not only did Volpe refer his own lawyer, David Humphrey, but he also arranged for Humphrey to escort Domenic back to Toronto to face arrest. A classified 1977 RCMP intelligence report on Volpe described him as a "central figure in a large criminal organization of well known criminals involved in various known and unknown criminal activities." Police investigations also revealed "that Paul Volpe was extremely well established with other major Canadian organized criminals," although law enforcement agencies have "achieved little success in gathering evidence against Volpe. This is due entirely to the fact that Paul Volpe, consistent with classical organized crime behaviour, has remained both insulated and isolated from direct criminal activity." Notwithstanding the assistance Volpe provided to Mike Racco or his connections with other mob figures, Volpe had more than his fair share of rivals and enemies. Although he was one of the initial Canadian members of the Magaddino Family, he was disliked and distrusted by many of his mafia contemporaries because of his stubborn independence, his duplicitous demeanour, his high-profile stature, and his constant intrusions into the territories of other mafia groups. He had fallen in such disfavour with Stefano Magaddino that it was rumoured he came close to putting a contract on Volpe's life in 1968, but was dissuaded from doing so by Giacomo Luppino. Volpe's list of enemies grew to be so long, that police had no shortage of suspects in his untimely death.

Appropriately enough, Volpe means "fox" in Italian and, as Peter Edwards and Antonio Nicaso make clear, "like his vulpine name-sake, Paul Volpe was clever and a loner by nature." He was regarded by many of his peers as—

A young Paul Volpe

> troublesome and distant, a man who jealously guarded his secrets and the fortune he had gained through loan-sharking, gambling and labour racketeering. They would also suspiciously eye him as a bit of a moralist, someone who looked upon lucrative businesses like pornography, prostitution and narcotics trafficking as dirty and beneath his dignity. As a statement of the distance Volpe maintained from traditional mob figures, he settled outside Toronto's mob enclaves in Woodbridge, St. Clair West and College Street, preferring instead to live apart in Schomberg, northwest of Toronto, in a flood-lit Tudor mansion with a turret that he had bought from a county court judge. A large Canadian flag flew outside the manor, which, fittingly, was called Fox Hill.

Paul Volpe was born in Toronto on January 29, 1927, to Elizabeth and Vito Volpe. Not long after Paul's birth, his father — a tailor with no criminal background, but little ambition or reliability — abandoned his wife, who was left to bring up six children: Frank, Eugene, Albert, Joseph, Paul, and Laura. Beginning in the late 1940s, Paul was delivering bootlegged liquor for his older brother, Albert, and by the 1950s he was helping to organize underground poker games along with Albert and Eugene. His experience with these seemingly innocent, yet profitable, criminal activities, his observations of the other street-level criminals and vice rackets that abounded around his home on Walton Street in downtown Toronto, and a growing friendship with Vincenzo (Jimmy) Luppino all helped to whet young Paul Volpe's criminal appetite. He was now determined to enter the big time of crime: membership in a mafia family.

Around 1957, after visiting New York City on several occasions to establish a connection with one of the major crime families there, he was able to meet and begin working for Vito de Filippo, a member of the Bonanno organization (who, nine years later, would be arrested in Montreal along with Bill Bonanno after meeting with Vic Cotroni and Paolo Violi). De Filippo was impressed with Volpe's money-making abilities, while his physically imposing stature, complete with broad shoulders and thick neck, also conveyed the impression that he was ready-made for the life of a gangster. Volpe also clearly benefited from the relationship, according to his biographer James Dubro:

Volpe realized that working for Vito gave him invaluable entrée into the secret world of the traditional Sicilian Mafia, a connection that could help establish him in his home base in Toronto. As a native-born Canadian, Paul Volpe didn't naturally possess the old-world, secret-society traditions. He didn't even speak Italian, let alone understand the intricacies of the Mafia societies, and he had been born and bred and was now based in the more cosmopolitan, sophisticated world of Toronto, rather than the tightly-knit Hamilton Italian community. Through Vito de Filippo, Volpe found out that successes in the criminal underworld depended a lot on building up a larger-than-life image and becoming a "name" to be reckoned with. This required connections to top criminals, establishing "respect" through both contacts and intimidation, and an ability to put together a well-oiled criminal machine. The Mafia was to be his ticket to success.

Sometime during the late 1950s and early 1960s, Volpe was able to use his New York mafia connections, as well as his friendship with Jimmy Luppino, to become a member of the Magaddino Family. Sponsored by Jimmy and Harold Bordonaro, and initiated in Hamilton, Volpe became one of Magaddino's Toronto representatives during the 1960s, which helped to fill the void left by John Papalia's imprisonment in 1962. While he had already made an enemy of Papalia by operating in Hamilton, Volpe wisely ingratiated himself with Luppino and the Bordonaro families. His mafia links first came to public attention in 1963 when Buffalo police named him and his brother Albert as two of the twenty Canadian members of the Magaddino crime syndicate. By this time, Paul was active in loansharking, gambling, and fraud in Toronto but, due to his new-found public infamy and the resulting police attention, he and Vito de Filippo fled North America and began running a casino in Port-au-Prince, Haiti. With investments from mafia families in Buffalo, New York, and Montreal, the two were able to turn the casino into a moderate success. Homesick for Toronto, however, Volpe returned to Canada in 1965 and, three years later, he had completely divested himself of his Haitian adventure.

Volpe made news again in 1965, when he and his brothers Albert and Eugene embarked on a fraud-and-extortion scheme that targeted Toronto stock promoter Richard Angle. After going to police, Angle was fitted with a miniature radio microphone and transmitter to gather evidence at future meetings with Volpe and his associates. At one meeting held in a Toronto hotel room in March 1965, Angle was pressured by Volpe to cough up $17,500. Also attending the meeting was a man from Buffalo who called himself "Mr. Palmer." The mysterious Mr. Palmer was in fact Pasquale Natarelli (a.k.a. Pat Titters), a top lieutenant in the Magaddino Family. The police recorder captured efforts by Natarelli to convince Angle that by agreeing to their demands he would be protected by powerful forces:

> "Look, I mean, I don't know how else to convince you, Dick. Look, look. With us, with us, its like having City Hall behind you. You can't make a mistake. ... I don't care, I don't care who you. ... what you do, how you do it, who you hurt. You know Dick, with us you're always right. ... From this moment on, you go home and sleep like a baby, with peace of mind, all right? Untroubled, believe me, because if you get in trouble you'll know that our word is bigger than a police .45 or all the money in the world. ... Nobody at any time will ever bother you. If they bother you, you get in touch with me and we'll take anybody that's on your back right off."

In blunter terms, Natarelli told Angle that he better come up with the money "or blood will run in the streets of Toronto." These threats were backed up by the presence of another Buffalo mafia enforcer, a 285-pound behemoth that Palmer called "Cicci" and who made menacing motions with a fork as he sat in the corner of the hotel room. In a subsequent conversation with Volpe, Angle inquired about the man with the fork. "You're lucky he didn't have an ice pick in his hand," Volpe replied. "I know how this guy performs." Police believed the recordings proved that Angle was being defrauded and extorted and on March 17, 1965, Paul, his brothers, and Natarelli were arrested and charged.

Their trial began in September 1965, but was aborted when a juror complained he couldn't understand English. An appeal was launched by the Crown, but the judge in the second trial also ended it without a verdict when the jury reported itself deadlocked. In the third trial, Paul Volpe had one of his enforcers, David McGoran, offer a bribe to a juror, who contacted police. McGoran was arrested and later convicted of jury tampering, but his interference forced Judge Harry Waisberg to declare a third mistrial in November 1965. In the fourth trial, the defendants were acquitted, but the Crown appealed this verdict, charging that the judge had misdirected the jury. The Supreme Court of Canada agreed and ordered a fifth trial, which was unprecedented in Ontario legal history. As this trial drew near, Paul and Eugene Volpe agreed to a bargain that would see them plead guilty to a lesser charge. On June 21, 1968, Paul Volpe was sentenced to two years, just three days after he was married to an ex-model from Denmark. His brother Eugene was sentenced to three months, while Alberto avoided the trial by skipping the country. Pasquale Natarelli was also unavailable for the Canadian trial, having already been sentenced to twenty-six years in an American penitentiary for conspiring to rob a Brink's armoured truck and to steal $500,000 in jewels from a Beverly Hills hotel. Richard Angle continued to work as a stock promoter, although following the trial Revenue Canada seized $120,000 he had transferred to Bermuda, on the grounds of tax evasion. Angle contended the transfer was simply to put the funds out of reach of Paul Volpe.

After being released from prison in 1969, Volpe enjoyed boom times for the next ten years. His success was based on a potent mix of ambition, brains, charisma, charm, greed, treachery, intimidation, leadership skills, business acumen, connections, and the ability to surround himself with capable associates and subordinates. Terms used by friend and foe to describe Volpe ranged from the very negative ("egocentric," "materialistic," "unscrupulous," "a human parasite"), to the very positive ("engaging," "very likeable," "essentially decent," a "fascinating, intelligent, interesting guy"). Volpe always looked the part of the gangster, wearing the latest in loud Italian fashions, driving expensive cars, carrying around large wads of cash — all the trappings that projected the image of a powerful, wealthy made guy who deserved respect. But he also deviated from the mobster stereotype; he rarely swore, didn't drink, didn't smoke, and doted on his Danish wife, who was a vice-president of a high-end women's fashion store in Toronto. He loved to garden and watch movies, although his greatest sense of satisfaction seemed to be derived from scamming people. He was a great judge of the wants and vulnerabilities of others and once he got his hooks into a victim, he wouldn't let go until he had shaken every last penny loose. He could be very loyal to his closest associates, but he had little compunction about betraying anyone if it meant another buck for him.

Volpe's success was also due to a partnership with another habitual Toronto criminal named Nathan Klegerman, an abstemious, gregarious, part-time University of Toronto philosophy student who specialized in fencing stolen diamonds and who has been described as possessing "a canny deviousness, intelligence, tremendous efficiency, and great organizational skills." Klegerman was initially drawn to Volpe in order to cash in on the latter's notoriety and began using him as hired muscle. When Klegerman was charged with possession of $80,000 in stolen gems in 1964, he claimed that he did not know the jewels were stolen when he offered them as collateral for $1 million in loans. Klegerman was convicted of possession of stolen goods and was sentenced to prison.

During the 1970s, the two enjoyed a mutually beneficial partnership. Volpe provided Klegerman with clout and protection within the criminal world and Klegerman introduced Volpe to new ways of making money, such as jewellery theft and stock market frauds. He also helped Volpe run his criminal rackets as a more cost-effective, businesslike enterprise and oversaw the pair's most profitable joint venture: loansharking. "Klegerman's ingenuity and organizational ability and Volpe's charisma and 'respect' on the street made for a formidable criminal combination," James Dubro noted. Klegerman's contacts in the crime world also proved to be of great benefit to Volpe who, like John Papalia, eschewed the traditional tight-knit Italian mafia family for a multicultural network of criminal specialists. Together, they established a highly profitable and versatile criminal organization. "Volpe had natural management skills and was a born talent-spotter. Working in a Canadian context, he naturally went for the best people, regardless of their backgrounds, when structuring his crime family. Creatively, Volpe brought together under his leadership an ethnic mix of people with diverse talents and skills." Among the specialized talent that Volpe and Klegerman recruited was Chuck Yanover, an enforcer and weapons expert, the loan shark Murray Feldberg, Ron Mooney, who specialized in burglaries and crooked card games, Sam Shirose, a card shark who organized poker games on behalf of Volpe, and enforcers David McGoran, Ian Rosenberg, and Fred Wang.

Volpe also continued to work with other mafia colleagues, and by the early 1970s, he and Natale Luppino, whose son was Volpe's godchild, had their eye on Toronto's construction industry. Much of the construction in Toronto's postwar housing and commercial building boom was carried out by firms owned by Italian-Canadians, with the labour being chiefly provided by Italian immigrants. For opportunistic ethnic Italian criminals like Volpe and Luppino, this presented an opening to extort unions and construction firms while hiding behind contractors, supervisors, and immigrant labourers frightened into silence. The result, according to a 1974 report by Justice Harold Waisberg who was appointed to head a Royal Commission that investigated violence and corruption in Ontario's construction sector, was that between 1968 and 1974, "a sinister array of characters was introduced to this industry."

The events that paved the way for Volpe and Luppino to infiltrate the construction industry began with a meeting at a Toronto restaurant in the spring of 1971. It was here that Cesido Romanelli, the owner of several Toronto-area construction, drywall, and lathing firms, agreed to hire Natale Luppino as an "escort" for $150 a week. Romanelli would later employ Joseph Domenic Zappia of Ottawa as another escort for eastern Ontario. When he was officially hired by Romanelli Construction in May 1971, Luppino had little experience in the industry, although his previous convictions for fraud and assault made him an ideal candidate for the tasks he was hired to carry out. Luppino was used by Romanelli to intimidate unions representing the tradesmen working for him, not only to ensure union peace, but to help him gain control

over the unions themselves. Around the same time, Volpe began working for A. Gus Simone, business manager of Local 562 of the Lathers International Union. Simone was allied with the Toronto Building and Construction Trades Council, which at the time was backing a drive by five affiliated unions to organize concrete workers. Volpe and Luppino were brought in by Simone to "convince" the heads of other rival unions to join Simone's cause, while Romanelli served as the "bag man" for a group of contractors who made payoffs to the corrupt Simone in return for a steady supply of quality workers and to ensure labour peace.

One of the most prominent targets of Romanelli's hired goons was Jean-Guy Denis, business manager of Local 124 of the Plasterers Union. Denis was pushing for an agreement with Romanelli, but the contractor's response was to try to persuade Denis to allow his company to use piece workers on his Ottawa jobs. Romanelli was involved in several large construction projects in Ottawa at the time and either wanted the unions in his pocket or the jobs to be performed by non-union workers. The two could not reach a compromise, and when their talks broke down, Luppino and Zappia paid Denis a visit and demanded he set up a separate union and provide membership to people of Romanelli's and Luppino's choosing. Denis rejected their offer. At another meeting, Luppino offered Denis a bribe of five cents an hour for every hour worked by his seven hundred to eight hundred men if he would stay off the job and let someone else take over as head of the local. Again Denis turned Luppino down. Denis would testify before the Royal Commission that on the evening of January 8, 1973, two men forced their way into his house. He was not home at the time but his sixteen-year-old son was. The men beat the teenager so savagely that he had to spend a week in hospital with a concussion and internal injuries that required surgery. Jean-Guy, who fought in the Second World War, still would not give in and as a result his own life would be threatened several times.

Luppino and Volpe also terrorized independent contractors and union leaders to force them to join with Romanelli and Simone. According to Toronto police records, between 1968 and 1972 there were 234 acts of wilful damage, twenty-three acts of arson, fifteen assaults, and five explosions, as well as numerous thefts and break-ins at Ontario construction sites. Among the many acts of violence was the bombing of two lathing companies in 1972 and the shooting of Bruno Zanini, a union organizer and former labour reporter for the *Toronto Telegram* who was conducting a freelance investigation into labour racketeering. He told police that a man wearing a stocking over his head shone a light in his eyes in the parking garage of his apartment building and then fired two shots, one of which struck him in the leg. Acme Lathing Ltd. was twice bombed with dynamite and, on July 3, 1972, its office was strafed with automatic gunfire. Another company, Gemini Lathing Ltd., was also bombed. At the time, the two companies were engaged in merger talks, which led police to believe that Cesido Romanelli, who also owned a lathing company, was trying to prevent the creation of a powerful competitor. Although neither the police nor the Royal Commission could prove it, Paul Volpe was hired to assure such a merger did not happen.

Toronto police received a break in their investigation into the attacks when a woman called to complain that she had found dynamite in her fridge. This tipped off investigators to Thomas Kiroff, a former member of the Vagabonds Motorcycle Club, and Volpe enforcer Charles Yanover (a.k.a. Chuck the Bike). Yanover was later photographed on a custom-made motorcycle that matched the description of the one seen in front of Acme the night of the shooting. Witnesses testifying before the Royal Commission stated that around the time of the bombings, Kiroff had given about fifteen sticks of dynamite with fuse and blasting caps, similar to those used in the bombings, to several people for safekeeping. When searching an apartment used as a safe house by Yanover, police found rifle barrels used in the strafing of the Acme Lathing building. Justice Waisberg contended that a number of cheques made out by Romanelli to Zappia, but cashed by Natale Luppino, were payments for the shooting and bombings of Acme and Gemini companies.

On December 19, 1974, Judge Waisberg produced his two-volume report, which acknowledged that organized crime had infiltrated Toronto's construction industry. He concluded that Volpe, Luppino, Zappia, Yanover, and Kiroff were most likely responsible for the violence that plagued the industry and had been hired and paid by Romanelli. His report asserted that union boss Gus Simone was conspiring with contractors such as Romanelli and had received "numerous gifts of labour and material from contractors who were in contractual relations with his union." The report also expressed surprise that Simone could afford a home worth $100,000, which he built in 1972, on a declared annual salary of $17,000.

The Waisberg report exploded onto the headlines when it was tabled in the provincial legislature in 1974. The *Globe and Mail* gave it front-page coverage and Paul Volpe, Natale Luppino, and Chuck Yanover figured prominently in the articles. Following the release of the report, police continued their investigations into the many allegations made during the inquiry. Cesido Romanelli, Natale Luppino, and Joseph Zappia were charged with perjuring themselves at the commission and while Zappia and Luppino were convicted, Romanelli was found not guilty. In 1976, Gus Simone was fined $20,000 after he pleaded guilty in tax court for failing to report $43,210 in income, much of it under-the-table payments from contractors. Despite this conviction, he went on to become the business manager for Local 675 of the United Brotherhood of Carpenters and Joiners.

Paul Volpe's top enforcer, Chuck Yanover, emerged from the Royal Commission and subsequent police investigations relatively unscathed and would go on to have a varied and eccentric criminal career. A gun-loving, motorcycle-riding, criminal mercenary at heart, Yanover was described by fellow biker and mob hit man Cecil Kirby as standing about 5-feet-9-inches tall, with "thick glasses that hide ferret-like eyes" and "heavy lips and a long nose" that fill out "a Weasel-like face." In 1976, the thirty-one-year-old Yanover was arrested as part of an extortion plot and, when police raided his home, they seized a folding rifle that could hold up to twenty-five rounds of ammunition. In April 1977, he was arrested again on weapons charges when police found two loaded rifles and a large quantity of ammunition in his home. In 1979, Yanover was convicted on his 1976 extortion and weapons charges and sentenced to eighteen months. Three years later, in perhaps one of the most outlandish cases to be heard in a Toronto court, Yanover was one of two defendants who admitted to plotting the assassination of the South Korean president and then defrauding the North Korean men who allegedly sponsored the planned hit. In 1981, Yanover and Alexander Gerol were promised between $200,000 and $400,000 by the North Korean men to kill President Chun Doo Hwan. The assassination was to take place while Chun golfed with Philippine president Ferdinand Marcos at a resort on the island, in what one bemused attorney referred to as "the annual dictator's golf tournament." Yanover pledged to his North Korean clients that he would "muster the Sixth Fleet for a three-pronged amphibious landing in the Philippines with helicopters and armies," according to his defence lawyer. Yanover and Gerol were charged with attempted murder and conspiracy to commit fraud. On February 17, 1984, Yanover was sentenced to two years, but only on the offence of defrauding the North Koreans after the judge accepted Yanover's argument that he was only interested in the money and never intended to carry out the assassination. At the time of the sentencing, he was already serving nine years for bombing a Toronto disco on January 9, 1980, as well as for his role in an unsuccessful plan to overthrow the government of Dominica.

Paul Volpe also emerged unscathed from the inquiry. When he was forced to testify before the commission, Volpe, who called himself an independent "labour consultant," gave very little away, although he raised a few eyebrows when he presented a net worth statement indicating his most significant asset was $55,500 in cash (technically, this was true as most of his assets were registered in his wife's name). Neither Judge Waisberg nor the police could directly implicate Volpe in any of the violence and he escaped criminal charges. In subsequent years, Volpe continued to have influence with at least one trade union leader. In the late 1970s, Volpe referred two men to Gus Simone who appointed them international representatives of Local 1190 of the Carpenters Union, which at the time was involved in a bitter dispute with another union over residential housing construction. The dispute became the subject of a police investigation when a series of fires caused about $3 million in damages to houses under construction. The two men appointed representatives were Cesido Romanelli, who held the job for three weeks before his death from natural

causes on January 17, 1983, and Peter Scarcella, a Volpe lieutenant. At the time of his appointment, Scarcella was on probation after pleading guilty in January 1982 to three counts of offering secret commissions in connection with a scandal involving Metro Toronto municipal garbage dumps.

The publicity surrounding the Royal Commission actually bolstered Volpe's gangland reputation. But it also raised his profile among police and for the next ten years he would be in and out of court on a number of charges. In September 1977, Volpe and others were arrested for conspiring to keep a common betting house. The charges were laid following several joint federal, provincial, and municipal police investigations that began in 1975 and focussed on his gambling and loansharking operations. As part of one investigation, police raided Volpe's Toronto Bridge Club on Bathurst Street, which offered numerous games of chance and also housed a bookmaking operation with direct connections to American-based gambling syndicates that supplied daily betting lines. Targeted in another investigation dubbed "Project Oblong" was Flite Investments, a lending company Volpe operated with Klegerman and fronted by associate Murray Feldberg. Flite Investments was essentially a loansharking operation that Volpe and Klegerman used to provide operating capital to other criminals at usurious rates. A police report that summarized the surveillance conducted as part of Project Oblong conceded that the "entire investigation was confused by the endless parade of unidentified individuals" who were approaching Volpe for money to finance a legal or illegal scheme. "Paul often entered into these schemes, but regardless of the outcome he was 'guaranteed' his money — a solid investment. It became obvious that Paul Volpe would become involved in almost any scheme or 'scam' which suggested a large profit. Due to Paul's position and authority, as well as the respect and fear he commanded from the criminal element, Paul's money would be returned even when it was a losing scheme." Volpe and Klegerman were also putting tens of thousands of dollars on the streets by blackmailing a manager at a Bank of Montreal branch. They had filmed him while engaged in a homosexual act, and used this to force him to provide more than $300,000 in loans to Volpe associates and clients, none of whom had any intention of paying the loans back. When police decided to wrap up their surveillance in 1978, dozens of people were arrested and convicted of various offences relating to loansharking, gambling, infiltration of legitimate businesses, bank fraud, corruption, extortion, theft, hijacking, fencing of stolen goods, stock fraud, money laundering, and tax fraud.

Between 1976 and 1981, Volpe, his brothers, Nathan Klegerman, and others were charged with even more offences that resulted from various police investigations. In 1976, they were accused of conspiring to smuggle $1.6 million in diamonds into Canada. In 1978, they were in court after being connected to a fraud scheme dating back to 1972 in which they purchased diamonds and other gems from merchants with bad cheques, worthless stocks, and unpaid promissory notes. In total, the scam netted gems with a retail value of $2.5 million. One victim, the Zahler Diamond Company, sold them $450,000 worth of diamonds between 1972 and 1975. On February 4, 1980, Volpe was sentenced to eight months for the illegal possession of electronic wiretap equipment, which was found in his home by police in 1977. At his trial Volpe said he purchased the devices as part of his hobby of collecting electronic gadgets. After an appeal, his sentence was reduced to sixty days. Also in 1980, he pleaded guilty to running an illegal gambling operation out of the Toronto Bridge Club and was fined $8,000. In 1981, he and three other men were charged with conspiracy to commit fraud and criminal breach of trust over a proposed $4.5 million sale of the Citytv building on Queen Street in November 1980. (Police said a deposit was placed on the building by one potential buyer, but it was subsequently sold to another buyer. While Volpe was charged, he was unwittingly roped into the fraud by a corrupt lawyer.) In September 1981, the Volpe brothers and Nathan Klegerman pleaded not guilty to charges arising from their fraud against the Zahler Diamond Co. After a mistrial due to the illness of one juror, the accused were acquitted of all charges.

In 1977, Volpe began investing in real estate in Atlantic City, like so many others who were trying to capitalize on the 1976 law that legalized gambling in the coastal resort town. In 1980, New Jersey law

enforcement authorities, who were monitoring Volpe's investments, stated that all his transactions up to this point were legal. Yet, true to form, Volpe was not content to make money simply by flipping real estate. He also began defrauding others who invested with him. When any property was sold at a profit, the money was reinvested immediately so when his partners wanted to cash in, they were told the money was tied up. And Volpe "just kept on doing that," one New Jersey police official told the media in 1983, "pyramiding the property, utilizing the investors' money." When investors pushed Volpe to get their money back he used "strong-arm tactics to keep control of that money." If the investors insisted, Volpe would only provide them with their original investment and no more. "Then, eventually, the organized crime people control the property, and although they're not turning it over, they can see that in a couple of years they can probably turn it over at a profit. Then, so they won't have to meet mortgage payments, they may put that property in receivership or bankruptcy to tie everything up for a period of time. Then they start a new company which ultimately takes control of the property." Among those Volpe cheated was John Cocomile, a Toronto lawyer who had invested more than $200,000 and was told he could expect a profit of at least $1 million within two or three years. Volpe had secretly sold the property, however, and refused to share the profits. Volpe did eventually agree to pay Cocomile $12,000, but his payment was accompanied by the following terms: "if you cash the cheque I'll break your fucking neck."

Volpe's Atlantic City venture was yet another example of his talent for making money, his inveterate dishonesty, and his refusal to limit his operations to his home base of Toronto. Atlantic City was outside the Magaddino Family territory, but Volpe was able to secure the backing of Angelo Bruno, the head of the Philadelphia mob. Part of the conditions was that Volpe would provide a cut to Bruno and would also have to work with Nicodemo (Little Nicky) Scarfo, Bruno's hotheaded and homicidal representative in Atlantic City. Around the time Volpe was making his move into New Jersey, Scarfo was positioning himself to take over the Bruno family, which resulted in at least a dozen deaths, including the March 1980 murder of

Angelo Bruno. When Scarfo became the new head of the family, he was far more aggressive than his predecessor in ensuring Volpe cut him in on his real estate action in Atlantic City. This included sending three of his men to Volpe's Toronto home to request a "donation" to the "Philadelphia Church."

"I KNOW YOU'LL KILL ME, VIC"

When Paul Volpe was released from jail on his extortion charges in the late 1960s, he was joined on the street by John Papalia, who in January 1968 was paroled from his U.S. narcotics conviction on humanitarian grounds because he was suffering from tuberculosis. When Papalia returned to Hamilton his health miraculously recovered and he immediately began to re-establish his presence in Southern Ontario's underworld. But he now faced competition from other mobsters, including those in the Luppino family, the Siderno Group, and Paul Volpe, not to mention other emerging crime groups, like the outlaw motorcycle gangs. Ontario's gangland became even more factionalized when Stefano Magaddino died of natural causes on July 19, 1974. His death caused a split in the family as two of his lieutenants, Joe Todaro and Salvatore (Sam) Pieri, jockeyed for power. Magaddino's passing and the resulting interregnum was the beginning of the end for his family's sway over its members in Southern Ontario, who were increasingly exercising their independence. This was most apparent with Paul Volpe, who persisted in solidifying his reputation as a lone wolf. The family squabbles also put Volpe, who pledged whatever loyalty he could muster to Sam Pieri, on a collision course with John Papalia, who aligned himself with the Todaro faction of the family.

Once back in Hamilton, Papalia was reunited with his long-time criminal acquaintances. Using a popular Hamilton nightspot called Diamond Jim's as his headquarters, he threw himself back into gambling, loansharking, extortion, drug trafficking, and money laundering. One frequenter of Diamond Jim's described how Papalia audaciously coordinated his rackets from his new command post:

> It was just like in the movies. "The man" always had a table reserved for him up front centre. He'd arrive in his big car and first his boys would go in and check out the place. Then Papalia would come in, dressed in a flashy suit, sunglasses, his hat pulled down. He'd sit down at his table with his boys around him, and he'd deal right there. He was that brazen about it. You'd see the guys come up to him — mainly young guys dealing in street drugs. He'd talk to them, money would change hands, they'd go away and someone else would come. That was Papalia's style, never gave a damn about anybody.

Papalia also began investing in real estate and legitimate businesses in Hamilton, including bars, restaurants, autobody repair shops, and construction firms. In addition to funds generated by his criminal activities, the investments were also being made with money sent from American crime syndicates as part of an international money laundering operation put together by mafia financier extraordinaire Meyer Lansky. Arrangements to launder U.S. mob money through Canada were allegedly made at February 24, 1970, meeting in Acapulco, which was attended by Lansky, John Papalia, Vic Cotroni, and Paolo Violi, among others. The idea was to send criminally generated cash from the U.S. to Canada where it would be laundered and the funds reinvested in U.S. enterprises in order to return the money south of the border. Other Canadians, in particular John Pullman of Toronto, were identified as key Lansky associates, and facilitated his money laundering interests in Canada primarily through real estate investments. In 1974, an article appeared in the *Toronto Star* based on an interview with Inspector Thomas Venner of the RCMP's intelligence unit in Toronto. The article asserted that "laundered crime money is invested in every kind of business" in Metro Toronto, which included "investments in hotels, restaurants, small shopping plazas, and increasingly, in recent months, real estate." A 1975 police report from British Columbia estimated that, in the previous two years, more than $6 million from "two major crime families based in New York and New Jersey" was invested "in vice establishments on Yonge Street in Toronto." According to a 1970 edition of the *Hamilton Spectator*, that city "also became one of the major centres for the investment of money gained through organized crime across North America, and the Hamilton Mafia became important in the laundering of money gained by illegal means."

Papalia's brash return to Hamilton did not go unnoticed by the police or the media. On August 31, 1971, he was remanded to appear in court to face an assault charge after throwing a court clerk off the veranda of his Railway Street home while being served with a summons. Papalia apologized in court and the clerk withdrew the charges. In 1974, he and five others were arrested following raids on the Monarch Vending Company and two Papalia associates, Michael Dipaulo and Tom Campisi, were charged with illegal betting and bookmaking offences. John and his brothers Frank and Rocco were also charged with assaulting and obstructing a police officer, while his close associate Donald LeBarre was arrested after police found marijuana in his home. Papalia's name was also splashed over the newspapers when allegations became public that Clinton Duke, a businessman with a criminal past and ties to Papalia and Stefano Magaddino, was on friendly terms with senior Ontario Provincial Police officials (a subsequent provincial inquiry found no improper conduct on the part of the police officers).

Police were also becoming aware of the cooperation between mafiosi from Hamilton and Montreal. On October 16, 1968, Paolo Violi travelled from Montreal and met with Dan Gasbarrini at Giacomo Luppino's home. On June 22, 1972, a veritable who's who of the Canadian mafia turned out for the wedding between Domenic Luppino and the daughter of Siderno Group member Remo Commisso. Among those attending the wedding were John Papalia, Paul Volpe, Paolo Violi, Vic Cotroni, Pietro Sciarra, Frank Sylvestro, Rocco Scopelliti, and the entire Luppino and Commisso clans. Also in attendance was Giuseppe Settecasi, the mafia family head for the Sicilian province of Agrigento who was passing through Ontario after his unsuccessful attempt to reconcile the disputes between the Calabrian and Sicilian factions of the Montreal mafia. On February 19, 1974, John Papalia travelled to Montreal where he met with Violi and Cotroni for three days. The purpose of this meeting, as well as subsequent ones held with Vancouver mob boss Joe Gentile, was to hatch a scheme spearheaded by Violi in which shell companies would be set up to launder money.

John Papalia, circa 1970s

A year later, Papalia, Cotroni, and Violi were charged with conspiracy to commit extortion. The con, dreamed up by Sheldon (Sonny) Swartz, a semi-legitimate businessman with loose ties to Papalia, involved defrauding Stanley Bader, a Toronto stock promoter who had partnered with Swartz in a money-lending/loan-shark business. In 1973, Swartz and Papalia conspired to trick Bader out of $200,000 by telling him that a recent scam he pulled in Montreal had victimized Vic Cotroni, who they claimed was going to kill Bader unless the money was returned. To add credibility to the swindle, Papalia made a cameo appearance before Bader as the Cotroni enforcer. Bader was told that of the $300,000 he had originally defrauded in Montreal, Swartz had already provided "The Enforcer" with $100,000, but Bader would have to produce the other $200,000. The story was completely fictitious (and was being perpetrated without the knowledge of Cotroni), but a gullible and terrified Bader was convinced and gave Swartz a suitcase with the full amount in hundred-dollar bills. Celebrations over the financial windfall were short-lived for Swartz and Papalia, however. Bader grew suspicious and in early 1974 he started making discreet inquiries in Montreal mob circles. Vic Cotroni and Paolo Violi soon heard about the threats they supposedly made and became furious, not because the family's name had been used without their knowledge or consent, but because they did not receive a cut of the money. Papalia was confronted by Cotroni and Violi who demanded $150,000 from him. This order was recorded by a police wiretap, which exposed the original scam. In the most business-like terms, Violi told Papalia, "You, Johnny, know these things, that [we] have to work all together but instead you did it alone. You used our names. Don't you want us to be friends? Bring $150,000 and no one will know anything. ... Be aware that we don't like crooked things ... and we respect each other but with us you have to come straight." Cotroni was less diplomatic, warning Pops that if he did not cough up the money, "we'll kill you." Papalia acknowledged Cotroni's power and sincerity by simply replying, "I know you'll kill me, Vic."

Based on the wiretap evidence, co-operation from Bader, and a follow-up investigation, Papalia, Cotroni, Violi, and Swartz were arrested in November 1975. The following year, the four were convicted of extortion in a Toronto courtroom and sentenced to six years. Violi and Cotroni appealed their sentence, arguing that since their involvement was secondary to the original offence, they deserved a lesser sentence than Swartz and Bader. An Ontario Court of Appeal agreed and reduced their sentence to six months. The fifty-three-year-old Papalia had no such luck and was kept out of circulation until 1982. That same year, Stanley Bader was greeted at the front door of his Miami home with a hail of bullets. It had been almost a month since the last threatening call warned him, "Look over your shoulder — you won't live out the week." Another phone call to Bader told him, "This is in revenge for five years ago."

VIOLENT, LEAN, CUTTHROAT, AND VINDICTIVE

Two years before John Papalia was released from jail, Michele Racco, the respected head of Toronto's Siderno Group, died of cancer at the age of sixty-six. Attend-ance at his funeral, held on a cold day in January 1980, was a testament to his influential status in the criminal world. His pallbearers included other members of the Toronto *crimini,* while cars bearing licence plates from New York, New Jersey, Ohio, Connecticut, and Quebec lined the two-mile-long procession. It was one of the biggest funerals ever held in Toronto. With Racco gone, the Siderno Group was now without its founder, its leader, and its moderating influence. His son Domenic, who by this time had been released from prison on his 1972 attempted-murder charge, was now trying to replace his father. But it was Rocco Zito who assumed the post of *capo crimini* due to his seniority and because most of the other senior Sidernese mafiosi in Toronto were wary of Domenic's ongoing erratic and violent nature (which was made even more acute by his cocaine addiction). Domenic's leadership aspirations were also being challenged by another powerful faction of the Siderno Group: the Commisso brothers.

It was in 1961 that sixteen-year-old Cosimo Commisso and his fourteen- and thirteen-year-old brothers, Rocco and Michele, immigrated to Canada along with their widowed mother. Despite their youth, all arrived with a family history of 'Ndrangheta involvement. The father of the three boys, Girolomo Commisso, was a member of an 'Ndrina clan in the Siderno area of Italy until he was gunned down in a feud in 1948. When they arrived in Toronto, the fatherless boys were taken under the wing of Michele Racco. By the 1970s, Rocco (or Remo, as he was usually called) began assembling his own 'Ndrina clan, anointing himself *capo bastone* (head of the family), with his older brother, Cosimo, assuming the position of *sotto capo* (underboss). By the middle part of the decade, Remo had been given a seat on the governing *crimini* in Toronto (around the same time his cousin, Cosimo Commisso, was taking over as the *capofamiglia* of the Calabrian Mafia in Italy after his predecessor, Antonio Macri, was murdered by rivals). As James Dubro relates in his 1985 book, *Mob Rule,* "the most serious, structured, and respected group within the Siderno mafia in Toronto was to be that run by Remo Commisso. The fashionable Remo, who was often seen wearing silk scarves around his neck, established his pre-eminent position through a combination of ruthlessness and 'connections' — in the United States, Hamilton, Montreal, Toronto, and, most significantly, in the old country itself." By the end of the 1970s, Remo and his brothers had put together a criminal enterprise that "rivalled the best of the Sicilian Mafia structures existing in the United States and which was, in terms of pure muscle and audacity, one of the most powerful mafia groups in Canada." Together, Remo and Cosimo "controlled a criminal organization that imported and distributed heroin with the Vancouver mob and the Calabrian Mafia in Italy, fenced stolen goods across North America, printed and distributed counterfeit money throughout Canada and the United States, ran a vast extortion network in Ontario, arranged insurance and land frauds in the Toronto area, and engaged in contract killings and contract-enforcement work across Canada and the United States — the whole gamut of violent criminal activities one usually associates with the Mafia."

Their first notable run-in with the law occurred in August 1976 when Cosimo and Remo were flown to Vancouver from Toronto with a police escort to face charges of counterfeiting currency, which stemmed from a raid on a Vancouver warehouse that uncovered $1.3 million in near-perfect American tens, twenties, and fifties. Among the others arrested was Vancouver mobster Camelo Gallo, who pleaded guilty to conspiracy charges. The brothers also generated considerable revenue through their infiltration of Toronto's construction industry. As Cecil Kirby states in his biography, when he began working for the Commissos as an enforcer in 1976, "I learned quickly that their big thing for making money was the construction industry. They probably made more from extortions in the construction industry than they did from trafficking in heroin — and it was a helluva lot safer." They had positioned themselves as a collection agency for contractors trying to settle outstanding debts. "The Commissos would collect money owed to a contractor and take a percentage of it. They didn't let legal technicalities or stalling tactics get in the way." The brothers also used trade unions to shake down companies and individuals who owed money to their contractor clients. For a fee or a percentage of what was owed a contractor, the Commissos would send "union goons" to visit construction company managers and extract payments by way of beatings, shootings, bomb-

Rocco (Remo) Commisso

ings or wildcat strikes. When they were not extorting contractors, they were rigging bids on government construction contracts by intimidating companies that competed against their clients. "Once their man got the bid, they became his partners," according to Kirby, "and their people — plasterers, electricians, plumbers, cement suppliers — would be used on the job. They'd inflate the cost of the job, pocket the profits, and run like thieves while the public or business paid the price."

Like other organized criminals, the Commissos relied heavily on intimidation and violence. Not only was the threat of violence used as a basis for their extortion-fused activities, but the brothers were personally involved in carrying out vendettas against their enemies. As children and teenagers, Remo and Cosimo were raised on violence 'Ndrangheta style and they were taught that no act of aggression against the family should be forgotten or go unpunished. Remo travelled to Italy at least twice during the 1970s for the purpose of murdering enemies, carrying out vendettas, and recapturing the family's honour. When assassins injured their uncle Vincenzo Commisso as part of the successful attack on his boss, Antonio Macri, in January 1975, the Commisso nephews exacted revenge the same year by slaughtering members of their rival family in their home in Italy. In 1982, Remo avenged the murder of his father committed more than thirty years prior after travelling to a small Calabrian town and slaughtering the sons of his father's suspected killers. As James Dubro puts it, "Remo Commisso has always believed in the old country and the old values, the Mafia the way it used to be: violent, lean, cutthroat, and vindictive." His brother was no less vicious, according to Cecil Kirby, "Cosimo wasn't tough — he was homicidal. He'd kill you as soon as look at you if he thought you were crossing him, if he thought it was good for business, or if he thought you had insulted him or his family. The lives of other people meant nothing to him."

In carrying out their reign of violence in North America, the Commisso brothers relied on paid enforcers and none was used more or became as infamous as Cecil Kirby, an outlaw biker-turned-freelance-hit-man. Kirby's biographer, Thomas Renner, describes him as small framed, but solidly built with sky-blue eyes, curly, reddish-blond hair and an "impish, almost boyish face that often breaks into an infectious smile." An RCMP officer assigned to handle Kirby after he became an informant characterized him as "schizophrenic." He had a "dual personality" that "ranges from a very kind person to a vicious, hot-tempered, violent individual who is quite capable of killing."

Kirby came to the Commisso brothers in the spring of 1976, when he was just twenty years old. He had just left the Satan's Choice Motorcycle Club, which he had joined in 1969. On orders from the Commissos, he carried out a spree of violence, using a specialty of many biker enforcers — explosives. When Kirby became a police informant in 1980, he told his handlers that he could provide evidence on at least eighteen bombings, several extortions, and three arsons that he carried out for the Commissos.

One of Kirby's first assignments in the fall of 1976 was to blow up a car belonging to Antonio Burgas Pinheiro, a Brampton-based salesman for Appia Beverages Ltd., which competed against another beverage company controlled by Siderno Group members. On November 11, 1976, Kirby left a stick of dynamite in the mailbox of the owner of Pozzebona Construction to persuade him to pay a plastering bill to a Commisso client more promptly. In December 1976, Kirby was promised $10,000 to kill one Dennis Mason who was to testify against a Commisso ally in an upcoming trial. Kirby was given five sticks of dynamite by Cosimo, which he attached to Mason's car, but the dynamite failed to explode and even if it did, he had targeted the wrong Dennis Mason. On May 3, 1977, he dynamited the Wah Kew Chop Suey House on Elizabeth Street in Toronto after the Commissos had been contracted by the Kung Lok, a local Chinese criminal group. According to Kirby, the restaurant was targeted because it was running a gambling operation without the permission of the Kung Lok leaders, who couldn't do the job themselves because they were under intense scrutiny by Toronto police. One restaurant employee was killed in the explosion.

In 1978, Kirby received $2,000 after he placed a bomb at the doorstep of Ben Freedman, a construction contractor who was in debt to subcontractors and who had hired the Commissos as their collection agency. In March and April 1978, Kirby set off bombs at two Mississauga apartment buildings owned by brothers Jerry and Roman Humeniuk, who owed money to some electrical contractors. Kirby also detonated an explosive at the home of Dr. Roman Humeniuk. In May 1978, Kirby was instructed to extort money from Max Zentner of Montreal, a developer who was in debt to a Commisso associate. Kirby was to target Zentner's partner, John Ryan of Hamilton and, on August 1, 1978, Kirby blew up Ryan's car in his driveway and received $3,000 in return. During the summer of 1978, Kirby was busy setting fires at a tavern and a home in Toronto as well as a hotel in Acton, Ontario. In July 1980, he was instructed by Cosimo to bomb the home of Maury Kalen on behalf of Willie Obront over a $100,000 debt that Kalen allegedly owed to him. Kirby detonated a stick of dynamite at Kalen's Toronto home, but discovered later that the intended victim no longer lived at that address.

Between June and August 1978, Kirby travelled to Montreal on several occasions to murder Irving Kott, an occasional associate of Willie Obront and Vic Cotroni, who made millions from manipulating the stock market. The Commissos told Kirby they were acting on behalf of one of Kott's business partners who would benefit financially from his death, but Kirby believed it was Vic Cotroni who wanted him dead because he thought

Kott had cheated him in one of his stock market scams. After an aborted attempt to shoot him, Kirby planted an explosive in Kott's car, but when it was detonated the intended victim was nowhere near. Instead, two innocent passersby were injured. In the fall of 1980, Remo directed Kirby to break the arms or the legs of Alphonso Gallucci who owed $54,000 to a Commisso associate. At first Kirby agreed, but then changed his mind because of the lack of advance money.

By this time, Kirby was growing weary of the Commisso brothers' demands, especially given their growing stinginess in providing advances and final payments and the consistently incorrect information on targets they were providing him. He also feared that sooner or later he would become one of their victims, given all he knew about their criminal affairs. So, in November 1980, Cecil Kirby contacted the RCMP and volunteered his services as an informant, an almost unheard-of offer for someone in Kirby's position. His contract with the Mounties, which was negotiated (and revised) in 1981, promised him immunity from prosecution for his past crimes, police protection for him and his family, and an expense allowance of $1,950 a month. In return, Kirby agreed to provide everything he knew about the Commissos and even became an undercover agent to collect more damning evidence that could be used against the brothers, who still looked upon Kirby as their number-one enforcer.

In February 1981, Kirby informed his RCMP handler, Constable Mark Murphy, that Cosimo Commisso had told him he was to meet with someone from New York who wanted Kirby to travel to Connecticut to kill "some broad that was causing a problem." The unnamed New Yorker turned out to be Vincenzo (Vincent) Melia, a Canadian citizen who led an 'Ndrina group in Connecticut. Melia suspected his brother's girlfriend, Helen Nafplotis, was a police informant and he had contacted Cosimo to arrange for a hired killer as part of what James Dubro called a "hit-man exchange program" between Canadian and American 'Ndrangheta groups. Melia met Kirby on February 22, 1981, at a motel in Stamford, Connecticut, and supplied him with a .38-calibre revolver, the keys to the home of Nafplotis, her picture, a car, and $5,000 in cash. Kirby was promised another $5,000 when there was proof of the murder. After working with

the FBI in Connecticut, who placed the woman in a protection program, Kirby returned to Canada and met with Cosimo to inform him that the job had been carried out. At one point Cosimo asked Kirby, who had been fitted with a police recording device, "But you did it? When you did it, Tuesday?" The RCMP now had Cosimo Commisso for conspiracy to commit murder.

If this was not enough evidence for the police, the Commisso brothers tasked Kirby with his most important assignment to date: the assassination of Paul Volpe. Cosimo had already asked Kirby to kill Volpe lieutenant Peter Scarcella, who was also working with the Commissos and who Cosimo suspected was providing Volpe with information on their operations. Cosimo called off the hit, however, most likely because he could not receive permission from his superiors, either in Toronto or the U.S. The reasons are still unclear as to why the Commissos asked Kirby to eliminate Volpe. No doubt, they saw him as a competitor and also had a personal dislike for the man, having been cheated by Volpe in a real estate deal. There were also suspicions that Vic Cotroni had ordered the hit or at least had relayed orders from New York to the Commissos, perhaps as retribution for Volpe's intrusion on American territory through his New Jersey excursions. Volpe was also becoming an embarrassment to the mob due to his high-profile nature, which included naively agreeing to an extensive media interview that became a prominent part of two groundbreaking documentaries on organized crime in Canada aired on the CBC in 1977 and 1979. Whatever the reason, a police recording of a discussion between Cecil Kirby and Cosimo Commisso on March 31, 1981, reveals that the decision to kill Volpe was conditional on approval from a higher authority:

C.K.: What about Volpe?

C.C.: I'm waiting for an answer, O.K.?

C.K.: Alright.

C.C.: And maybe we know next week. You see what I mean?

C.K.: O.K.

C.C.: See what I mean. It's not us.

C.K.: Someone else.

C.C.: Right. O.K., you see what I mean?

An older Paul Volpe

Whoever the higher authority may have been, Cosimo did receive the go-ahead. On April 23, 1981, he told Kirby that Scarcella was no longer a target, while hinting that Remo had a more important one in mind:

C.C.: We gonna put you on the payroll and when things are done you gonna get a bonus for it. Ah, Scarcella, forget about it for now. Just don't worry about it for now.

C.K.: For how long?

C.C.: A month, two months, we don't know yet. There's another guy.

C.K.: What the fuck's going on?

C.C.: There's another guy that I want you to take care of instead of him. He [Remo] wants to do another guy.

C.K.: You don't want to do him, you want to do another guy?

C.C.: Yes, not him for now, O.K.?

C.K.: Well, who the fuck is this other guy?

C.C.: Ah, I'll show you, next week you'll see.

C.K.: Another guy?

C.C.: Yeah.

C.K.: Holy fuck. Make up your minds. What, a close friend of Scarcella's?

C.C.: Yes.

C.K.: Not Volpe?

C.C.: I'll show him. Maybe you know the guy a little bit. But don't worry about his name, you see him, O.K.?

Cosimo later told Kirby that Volpe was in fact the target and offered him $20,000 for the hit. When Kirby informed his shocked police handlers, a plan was put in place to carry out a mock assassination in an attempt to entrap Remo Commisso. As James Dubro points out, "the police had more than enough evidence against Cosimo Commisso, but lacked hard evidence against Remo Commisso, for whom his older brother was acting as a kind of insulation. It was decided that Kirby's final sting would be to obtain admissible evidence on the murder contracts against Remo Commisso, who, as we have seen, was considered to be the real leader of the Commisso family." Police already had Kirby's agreement to double-cross the Commissos; now all they needed was the support of the intended victim. Constable Murphy along with Sergeant Al Cooke of the Toronto police visited Volpe at his home and, after telling him a contract had been taken out on his life, persuaded him to go along with a plan to convince Remo Commisso that Kirby had actually carried out their orders. Not only did Volpe agree to help out, but he also consented to hand over his wallet to police, which would then be taken by Kirby to Remo as proof that he had fulfilled the contract. The two police officers also convinced Volpe that he and his wife should spend the day at the RCMP's Toronto headquarters for safekeeping.

Despite his unpredictable nature, Volpe's agreement with all of these requests must have been a great surprise to police. As Dubro observes, "This ready cooperation with the police, as well as his willingness to strike back through official channels instead of using his own muscle and power to retaliate against the Commissos for their lack of respect, was a major breach of mob etiquette, and it was to cost Volpe dearly when the extent of his co-operation became generally known on the street."

On the morning of May 16, 1981, while Volpe and his wife were enjoying some Mountie hospitality, Cecil Kirby met with Constable Murphy and was given Volpe's wallet. By 11:15 a.m., Kirby, who was body-packed with listening devices, arrived at Remo Commisso's home. After greeting Kirby at the front door, Remo escorted his visitor to the bathroom and turned on the faucet in the sink. Despite the attempt to muffle their conversation police did pick up sufficient incriminating evidence against Remo Commisso:

C.K.: Volpe he's dead.

R.C.: How come?

C.K.: I just killed him an hour ago ... Cosimo told me you and he wanted it.

R.C.: ...you should never come here.

C.K.: I need some money okay, okay ... I need some money and I want to get ... out of the country.

R.C.: Tell me how I'm going to get it to you?

C.K.: Well a thousand or something just to get me out of here ... [pulling Volpe's wallet out] I took this right out of his back pocket.

R.C.: You should have thrown [it] away ... All right, don't worry; we'll take care of you. You know we respect you like a brother. Don't worry.

Police now had enough evidence on the Commisso brothers. In May 1981, thirty-six-year-old Cosimo, thirty-four-year-old Remo, and thirty-three-year-old Michele were arrested in Toronto and charged with three counts of attempted murder and counselling to commit assault causing bodily harm. At the same time, the FBI arrested fifty-two-year-old Vincenzo Melia and twenty-four-year-old Jerry Russo in Connecticut and charged them with conspiracy to commit murder. In July of that year, both men were ordered by a U.S. district court judge to be extradited to Canada. Vincenzo Melia was later convicted in a Canadian court and received nine years for his role in plotting the murder of Helen Nafplotis. In August, the three Commisso bothers pleaded guilty to conspiring to commit murder. Remo and Cosimo were sentenced to eight years in jail, while Michele received a two-and-a-half-year sentence. Two years later, based on

evidence provided by Cecil Kirby, Cosimo and Remo were slapped with an additional thirty-nine charges resulting from offences that took place between 1976 and 1980. Following another trial, Cosimo was sentenced to an additional eight years while Remo received another six. In total, Cosimo received more than twenty-one years, while Remo was given fourteen and a half years for conspiracy to commit murder, counselling to commit murder, possession of property obtained by crime, conspiracy to commit extortion, counselling another person to commit an indictable offence, causing bodily harm, and conspiracy to defraud. Not long after the Commissos were convicted of these offences, Paul Volpe contacted the RCMP to tell them a $100,000 contract had been put out on Cecil Kirby, who was now in a witness protection program. This was his way of saying thank-you to the Mounties and to Kirby.

MEETING WITH PEOPLE "FROM OVER THERE"

Paul Volpe was lucky enough to escape one attempt on his life. But circumstances were conspiring to remove any remaining hopes that he could escape the contract that was still hanging over his head. In 1981, Sam Pieri, one of Paul Volpe's last remaining supporters in the Magaddino Family, died. Volpe was now even more isolated and dangerously unprotected from his enemies while his standing within the family was rapidly deteriorating. For a number of years he refused to pay tribute, and his foray into Atlantic City only confirmed his maverick status. Joe Todaro, who was now in control of the Buffalo family, wanted nothing to do with Volpe. Other American mafiosi, especially Nicky Scarfo, began treating Volpe as a pariah. Todaro's ascension to the leadership of the Buffalo mob also bolstered his biggest Canadian supporter, John Papalia, who never hid his desire to get rid of his rival. Volpe was also losing many of his key associates and enforcers. Nate Klegerman had fled Canada to escape a number of criminal charges, Chuck Yanover was in and out of jail, and Fred Wang was dead of a drug overdose. On April 22, 1977, the bodies of Volpe enforcer Ian Rosenberg and his girlfriend, Julie Lipson, were found by their five-year-old child. Both had been shot in the head while sleeping. The hit was most likely ordered by Volpe because Rosenberg had become extremely erratic and unreliable and Volpe worried that he was co-operating with police after being charged with extortion.

On Sunday, November 13, 1983, Paul Volpe, dressed in a white turtleneck sweater and green corduroy trousers, informed his wife that he would be having lunch with Pietro Scarcella and then had to go to the airport where he would be meeting with people "from over there." This was most likely a reference to American mobsters, either from the Magaddino or Scarfo family. He said that he should be home by early evening. When he failed to show up that night, Volpe's wife became frantic. On Monday morning, she nervously called their lawyer, David Humphrey, who contacted the Toronto police. After he informed them of Volpe's planned meeting at the airport, police searched the airport parking lots for the leased BMW he was driving. They eventually found the car on the second level of the Terminal Two garage. After spotting blood on the tailgate, they opened the trunk and discovered Volpe's lifeless fifty-five-year-old body, curled up in a foetal position and lying in a pool of his own blood. There was so much blood that police thought his throat had been slashed. Upon closer inspection it was discovered that Volpe's killers had shot him in the back of the head.

Scarcella confirmed with police that he had lunched with Volpe that day, but his boss had driven away on his own. Investigators determined that Volpe had been killed almost immediately after he left Scarcella as the time recorded on the airport parking lot stub was a little less than half an hour after he drove away from the restaurant. Police reasoned that he was most likely shot at one of the numerous construction sites near the airport, which would have been abandoned on a Sunday. His body was then stuffed into the trunk of his car and driven to the airport parking lot by one of the killers. Volpe's murder would never be solved, in part because there was no shortage of potential suspects or motives. He already had enemies in Ontario — such as John Papalia and the Commisso brothers — who would have dearly liked him out of the way. He had alienated himself from the Magaddino Family, had stepped on the toes of the vicious Nicky Scarfo, and had defrauded dozens, if not hundreds,

of people, including fellow mobsters. His high-profile TV and court appearances were also a great cause of concern to his mafia colleagues who desired anonymity, plus there was lingering embarrassment that Volpe was still around a full two years after he was originally slated to die. If that were not enough, his co-operation with the police over the planned hit by the Commisso brothers was an inexcusable sin in mafia circles. As Chuck Yanover wrote in a letter from jail, "Paul got what he deserved, nice guy or not, since he did what he did when he broke the code of ethics."

The most plausible theory is that Volpe's meeting that Sunday was with members of the Todaro-led Magaddino Family. The murder was performed in clear mafia fashion, according to Peter Edwards and Antonio Nicaso: "Mob protocol dictated that the killer must be from Volpe's own crime family, the Buffalo mob. He was their responsibility and his death would ensure greater harmony, both inside their ranks and with the Philadelphia mob." The shot from behind also suggests that Volpe trusted his killer enough to turn his back on him. Another theory behind the murder was that it was ordered by Frank Cotroni who was making a move into Toronto and wanted Volpe out of the way. Regardless of who ordered the assassination or actually pulled the trigger, it would have to have been sanctioned by the Magaddino Family and perhaps even New York's Mafia Commission.

THEY WERE INTERESTED IN COLLECTING THE MONEY

When plans were afoot to stage the first assassination attempt on Paul Volpe, Cecil Kirby's RCMP handler Mark Murphy told him that Volpe's good friend Jimmy Luppino used to visit him every day in Toronto until it became known that a contract was taken out on his life. If this was true, it speaks volumes about the tenuous nature of friendships and loyalties among those who belong to the Honoured Society. The anecdote may also reflect personally on Jimmy Luppino, another typical brutish thug raised within the 'Ndrangheta tradition. Like his father, Jimmy relied heavily on the most tried-and-true of his profession's criminal calling — extortion, backed up by violence and intimidation. His reputation became so notorious in Hamilton that he admitted to "renting" out his name for $1,000 to other criminals to be used during their own extortion bids. His brother Natale was equally violent and, by the mid-1970s, had been convicted of assault, possession of a deadly weapon, and extortion. Of the ten children sired by the fertile Giacomo Luppino, his five sons, Jimmy, Natale, Rocco, Antonio, and John would become the public face of the family's criminal province. And like loyal sons and devotees to the time-honoured custom of *omerta*, they protected their father at all costs.

The extortion plots hatched by the brothers and their associates mostly victimized businesses, often to gain a monopoly in a particular industry. In September 1978, forty-one-year-old Rocco Luppino, along with Domenic Musitano, the owner and operator of a Hamilton haulage company, and Angelo Natale, president of the Ontario Haulers Association, were charged with conspiracy to commit extortion after police discovered a protection racket operating within Ontario's independent trucking industry. Freelance truck drivers were threatened with violence, damage to their trucks, and a loss of business if they refused to join the Haulers Association. Police officials stated that if the conspiracy had succeeded, the association could eventually have gained a monopoly over the trucking industry in Ontario. The extortion ring was also trying to influence the issuing of public commercial vehicle licences in order to control the dump truck industry in Southern Ontario. All three were convicted of extortion-related offences in 1979.

In 1981, forty-nine-year-old Antonio (Tony) Luppino, his thirty-four-year-old brother, Johnny, and twenty-nine-year-old Geraldo (Gerry) Fumo were all convicted in connection with the fraudulent takeover of Tops Continental Meats of Hamilton. As part of his testimony in court, Domenic Returra, the owner of the meat-packing and pasta plant, said the accused began by offering their services in collecting delinquent accounts and eventually ended up controlling 60 percent of the business. Returra's troubles began when he mentioned to a salesman that he was having problems collecting money from his customers. Before long he was paid a visit by the three men. Returra offered them ten cents on each dollar collected, but the men had grander ideas. Demanding to see his books, they told Returra that they were interested in buying the company and wanted a

glimpse into its financial state. Afterwards, they forced him to sign a contract that handed over shares in the company. Among the tactics used to persuade Returra to sign was a visit by Luppino brother-in-law Paulo Violi. At the end of the six-month trial, Tony Luppino received fifteen months in jail while John was handed twelve months, and Gerry Fumo, eighteen months. The trial received extensive publicity in the local and national media, not only because of the high-profile nature of the defendants, but because of the precedent set in the case of *Regina vs. Fumo and Luppino and Luppino*, whereby county court Judge McWilliams recognized the existence of a secret criminal organization known as "'Ndrina."

Among the close associates of the Luppino family were brothers Domenic and Anthony Musitano. Born in 1937 and 1947, respectively, they ran a real estate business, a bakery, a haulage company, and a scrapyard in Hamilton, when they were not tending to their criminal enterprises. Domenic — whose physical appearance has been described as a stuffed olive ("short, rotund, and with grey-green pop eyes") and a cross between actor Danny DeVito and a bowling ball — had a legendary temper; in his younger days he was sentenced to seven years after shooting and seriously wounding a fellow motorist who honked at him one too many times. Domenic's violent ways were passed down to him from his uncle Angelo Musitano, who had served seven years in a Calabrian jail for the mentally disturbed after shooting another man during a fight at the age of twenty. Shortly after he was released in 1937, the "Beast of Delianova," as he was so appropriately nicknamed, shot and killed his widowed sister for becoming pregnant out of wedlock. After murdering the brother of the man who impregnated her, as well as another local farmer who owed him money, Musitano went to France where he boarded a ship bound for Canada. Not long after, an Italian court found him guilty of murder and sentenced him *in absentia* to thirty years. By that time Musitano had arrived safely in Canada and took up residence in Hamilton. For the next twenty-five years he lived under the alias Jim D'Augustino, bleach salesman. On May 8, 1963, Hamilton police received a letter from Interpol requesting assistance in locating "one Angelo Musitano, killer" who was believed to be living in

Domenic Musitano

the city. Almost two years later, on March 3, 1965, he was captured in the kitchen of his brother Pasquale's home and deported to Italy where he began serving his thirty-year sentence.

Like the Luppinos, Domenic and Anthony Musitano's bread and butter was extortion and they embarked on their own reign of terror in Hamilton during the late 1970s. Between December 1978 and June 1980, at least six explosions ripped through Italian businesses in the city. The first occurred on December 29, 1978, at the Genuine Bakery owned by Gino Meranageli, causing more than $10,000 damage. On May 3, 1979, La Favorita Bakery had its windows blown out by a large blast, causing more than $15,000 in damages. Police determined that the explosion was caused by the ignition of gasoline that had been poured into the store through a hole drilled in the roof. This would not be the last time the bakery was targeted. On June 3, 1980, several sticks of dynamite stuffed into a cardboard tube were discovered undetonated in the doorway of the store. Other local businesses owned by Italian-Canadians were also preyed upon. On November 10, 1979, Grand Prix Motors, owned by Gino Bartolozzi, was rocked by an explosion that destroyed part of the car dealership. Bertulia D'Agostino, who at the time was operating Alba Collision, told

the *Hamilton Spectator* that many Italian business owners had been approached about paying protection money. She recounted how she was visited by two men shortly after her body shop was opened in 1978 and advised that it would be in her best interest to sign over 50 percent of the business to them. The visit was preceded by a flower delivery from the two men offering congratulations and good luck in her new venture. After she repeatedly turned down the partnership offer, the body shop became the victim of arson in September 1980. In April 1981, D'Agostino's home was also set ablaze. Rope that had been soaked in gasoline was placed inside the house and shredded newspaper was used to ignite the fire. Damage to the home was estimated at $65,000.

As the bombings and arsons continued, police were able to close in on the perpetrators. Their first big lead was the discovery of the unexploded dynamite at La Favorita Bakery. After identifying the source the explosives, police began an intensive investigation that involved thousands of hours of physical surveillance, informant work, and wiretaps. In October 1980, police arrested four suspects: Anthony Musitano, Douglas Cummings, Elizabeth Wala, and Leslie Russell Lethbridge. Cummings, who was nicknamed "Fingers" because he lost two of his appendages in an industrial accident, was a former member of the Wild Ones Motorcycle Club. He admitted to being hired by Anthony Musitano to coordinate the bombings after meeting him at a cockfight arranged by the Wild Ones at Cummings' farm. Cummings and Lethbridge were also responsible for assembling the bombs and obtained their dynamite through biker contacts working at a quarry. When Cummings became the chief suspect in the bombings, police began around-the-clock surveillance on him. Bugs were planted in his car and the home he shared with Elizabeth Wala, and police recorded one conversation in which Wala expressed concern over whether they would be paid for their botched attempt to dynamite La Favorita Bakery. She then provided police with their most solid lead as to who was ultimately behind the bombings:

> He won't be happy with that bakery. Because remember, we phoned him to get paid the next day ... We've been working for the ... Mafia ...

Everything that's been done is got to do with them … Those gang fights with the Mafia, all those places that have been blown up and all that, all it is is just the Mafia dispute, eh, and all they're doing is blowing each other up. They [police] finally got rid of the fucking bikers. Now they got to worry about the Mafia. Don't get no rest in this city … Everybody's running around with bombs, it's true … You know this is bomb city, right? This place has more bombings than any other city in the whole of Canada for the size of it, I'd say.

In January 1983, Anthony Musitano, Douglas Cummings, Elizabeth Wala, and Leslie Lethbridge were found guilty on explosive conspiracy charges. Musitano and Cummings were sentenced to life imprisonment, while Lethbridge was handed an eighteen-year term. Wala was given fifteen years. Two years later, the Ontario

Court of Appeal reduced Musitano's and Cumming's sentences to fifteen years, Lethbridge had his reduced by five years and Wala's sentence was cut to seven years.

The investigation led police and the media to examine more closely the relationship between the local mafia and outlaw bikers. In October of 1980, the *Hamilton Spectator* reported that a "group headed by Giaccomo Luppino of Ottawa Street South, the closest thing Canada has to a Hollywood-style 'Godfather,' has established a pipeline with the bikers for contract work." The newspaper goes on to say, "the bikers are being played for suckers in the incidents, taking all of the heat and very little of the profit. Paid by the mob anywhere from $400 to $1,000 an assignment, the bikers have placed bombs or incendiary devices at extortion targets. The extortionists, meanwhile, reap greater rewards, from $25,000 cash to complete takeovers of businesses worth more than $100,000."

BLOOD ON THE TRACKS

This is the city. Hamilton, Ontario. I work here. I carry a badge. My name's Thursday. The story you are about to read is true; the names have not been changed to expose the guilty.

October 22, 1978. 8: 35 a.m. We were on a stakeout at the Tim Hortons on King Street West when I heard the news from headquarters: Domenic Racco was granted a conditional release. He was twenty-nine years old. Parole officials deem him no threat to society. I begged to differ. I'm a cop. I work bunko.

As soon as Domenic was back on the street, he began trafficking in narcotics. Cocaine to be precise. Domenic saw narcotics as the surefire way to get ahead in the mob and get rich at the same time. He believed he has the divine right to "inherit his father's mantle of power and respect" and to be anointed the all-powerful leader of the 'Ndrangheta in Toronto. But it's got to be a fixed race to let a wild horse like Racco win. You see Domenic was not just selling cocaine. He was abusing it. And if reefer is the flame, and heroin the fuse, then cocaine is the bomb. With cocaine,

Domenic Racco

the idea is to get so high that you don't know who or what you are. There is no such thing as a quickie or one to be sociable. In coke-snorting circles if you're not flying you're a square. And "flying" means you don't know who you are or what you're doing. No matter how you slice it, that's dangerous. I know. I'm a cop.

February 1982. Domenic Racco is arrested following a narcotics investigation. Cocaine with a street value of $200,000 is seized. We suspect his wholesaler is Domenic Musitano. He had strong ties to Domenic's father, Michele, before he died. We believe Musitano fronts Racco the cocaine to sell in Toronto. He is paid back with a cut from the Raccos' narcotics revenue. But we can't prove it.

Racco makes two crucial mistakes in his dope-peddling business with Musitano. First, too much of the cocaine fronted to him never makes it to the streets. Instead, it goes up his nose. Second, he begins to move into Hamilton's cocaine market. But that market is under the control of the Musitano family. Perhaps he has snorted most of the cocaine provided to him by the Musitanos. Perhaps the Musitanos demand that Racco pay him for the narcotics seized in 1982. Perhaps it is both. Whatever the reason, Domenic Racco owes Musitano a large amount of narcotics money. Possibly as much as $500,000. Despite their attempts to collect the money owed to them, Racco cannot or will not pay.

Tuesday, March 1, 1983. Domenic's brother Tony is handed a life sentence in the Millhaven maximum security prison near Kingston, Ontario. His sentence is the result of his conviction under *Canadian Criminal Code* Section 81(1), conspiracy to possess explosive substances with intent to cause explosions. But Tony continues to offer advice to family members who visit him regularly in jail. It is at Millhaven that the conspiracy to murder Domenic Racco is hatched. Domenic and Tony Musitano's patience with Racco had run out. They seek permission from the leaders of the Siderno group. With Racco's father now out of the picture, the plan to murder him is set in motion.

We secretly record the Musitanos' conversations at their home, at their scrapyard, over the telephone, and at Millhaven. Our wiretaps pick up conversations about killing "the one from Toronto." But at the time we still don't know who it is they are going to hit.

Monday, November 21, 1983. We were responding to a call for service at the Dunkin' Donuts on John Street when we get a dispatch from headquarters that Giuseppe Avignone is visiting his uncle Tony Musitano at Millhaven. He is accompanied by a family associate named Giuseppe Chiarelli. Our wiretaps pick up their discussion about the planned hit:

Chiarelli: …who's gonna do it?
Avignone: … it's up to you.
Musitano: What's the name … Mike?
Chiarelli: He can't do it no more Tony.
Musitano: His brother?
Avignone: No. Rosario is too scared.

Tony Musitano suggests a bunkmate from the Millhaven maximum-security prison. His name is William Rankin. He is due to be released soon and may be interested in the job. Rankin is a degenerate alcoholic and narcotics abuser who has been in and out of prison since he was seventeen. He has been charged more times than a dying automobile battery. Rankin takes the job and Musitano tells him to get hold of Avignone as soon as he is released from jail:

Avignone: Um, tell this guy when he comes down to kill him, he owes me nothing.
Musitano: He can look after that when he comes out. That's no problem …
Avignone: Tell him… tell him we gotta that … you guys want December 7th?
Musitano: Yeah.
Avignone: Tell him to get a hold of me as soon as he comes out. The next night after that, he's happy.

Wednesday, December 7, 1983. Rankin is released from prison and is picked up by Peter Majeste. Majeste is a criminal associate of Rankin's. Avignone meets with Rankin, who is promised $20,000 for the murder. Rankin recruits a couple of other two-bit punks from Hamilton to help carry out the contract, thirty-six-year-old Graham Court, and thirty-three-year-old Peter Denis Monaghan.

Thursday, December 8, 1983. We record another conversation at Millhaven maximum security prison. This time it is between Tony Musitano, Giuseppe Avignone, Joe Spanno, Vince Nicoletti, and Joe Chiarelli. The men discuss the hit and their plans for paying Rankin:

Avignone: Tonight we are busy, eh? Don't you two disappear.
Musitano: What's on tonight?
Avignone: Going for a ride. Just in case, you know, just in case we forget to … So you are sure this guy knows what he has gotta do? That bastard's not going to get all cash after he does it.
Musitano: Yeah, well, I hope so, you know.
Avignone: Well, when you told him half up front.
Musitano: Well, you can work that out with him Thursday?
Avignone: He's gonna come around and …
Musitano: I know. He knows that. He knows nothin's for free.

Friday, December 9, 1983. 9:30 a.m. Racco is busier than a one-legged tap dancer. He visits his lawyer Meyer Feldman who hands him a cheque for $21,506.83. The money is from the sale of real estate property Racco and his mother owned. Racco immediately goes to his bank and deposits the cheque. He then asks to withdraw more than $20,000 in cash. The teller tells him the bank does not have that much cash on hand. So she gives him a certified cheque for $8,000 and $12,500 in large bills.

Friday, December 9, 1983. 8:48 p.m. Racco signs in at the RCMP headquarters as part of his bail conditions for his narcotics trafficking charges.

Friday, December 9, 1983. 9:00 p.m. Racco heads to Oakville where he meets with Domenic Musitano. At the meeting Racco endorses the $8,000 cheque over to Musitano. Racco is still unaware of his fate. Racco is so thick he couldn't smell a rat in a room full of cheese.

Saturday, December 10, 1983. 1:30 a.m. Racco returns to his apartment at 1333 Bloor Street West in Mississauga, Ontario. He is grievously assaulted by two men and then forced into a brown Pontiac station wagon and driven to a field outside of Hamilton, in a town called Milton.

Saturday, December 10, 1983. 9:22 a.m. Rankin calls Giuseppe Avignone and tells him he needs to see him in person. The two meet at a Tim Hortons at the corner of King and Caroline. Coincidentally, two police surveillance teams are already at the scene. Rankin is overhead demanding the $20,000 owed to him. Musitano tells Rankin that his payment will not all be in cash and it will not all be delivered at once.

Saturday, December 10, 1983. 10:15 a.m. We get a call that the body of Domenic Racco has been discovered sprawled across an abandoned railway spur approximately 150 feet off Derry Road in Milton. So I ask the girl to make my coffee and cruller to go and we head out to Milton. Once at the scene, we find three sets of footprints in the snow leading to his body. Only two sets leave the scene. Racco had been shot three times in the head and twice in the chest with a .38-calibre revolver. He was as cold as a three-day-old cup of coffee in a Regina snowbank.

Sunday, December 11, 1983, 9:00 a.m. My partner, Bill Cannon, and I meet with our boss, Captain Stubing, to discuss the Racco hit. We were too late to help Domenic. But at least we can bring his killers to justice. That's my job. I am a cop. The Musitanos are now our number one suspects in the murder.

Thursday: Captain.
Stubing: Joe.
Cannon: Captain.
Stubing: Bill.
Thursday: Racco.
Stubing: Check.
Thursday: Musitanos.
Stubing: Hmm.
Thursday: Rankin.
Stubing: Check.

Thursday: We think we heard what we need to know.

Stubing: Where?

Thursday: Tim Hortons.

Cannon: On King Street.

Thursday: Check.

Stubing: At the corner of James?

Cannon: No, the other one.

Stubing: The one across from the park?

Thursday: No, a block from there.

Stubing: On the corner of Queen Street?

Thursday: No sorry. Another block over.

Cannon: You know the one at King and Caroline?

Stubing: Yes.

Cannon: Right across the street from that one.

Stubing: Check.

Cannon: Check.

Thursday: We have surveillance teams at every Tims in the city.

Stubing: Check

Cannon: In case Musitano and Rankin meet again.

Stubing: Uh-huh.

Thursday: Bill and I are off to stake out D & M Scrapyard.

Stubing: Check.

Cannon: It's owned by Domenic Musitano.

Stubing: Check.

Thursday: Check.

Stubing: Joe?

Thursday: Yes, Captain?

Stubing: Are you stopping by the Tim Hortons on your way?

Thursday: Uh-huh.

Stubing: Can you pick me up a medium double-double and a honey dip?

Thursday: Check.

Stubing: Check.

Cannon: Check.

Monday, December 12, 1983. Racco's murder is all over the news. Even with all the heat, Domenic Musitano still tries to cash Racco's certified cheque for $8,000. He sends Avignone to give it to Edward Greenspan. He was once Racco's lawyer. Greenspan's secretary tells him that Racco had just been murdered. They will not accept the cheque. Avignone becomes so distressed the secretary has to help him from the office.

Meanwhile, William Rankin is becoming more and more of a problem for the Musitanos. He is getting drunk and bragging about his "connections" with the mob.

Thursday, December 22, 1983. Rankin is in a serious automobile accident. He is driving a brown Dodge that Avignone gave him as partial payment for carrying out the murder. He runs from the scene faster than a junkie hepped up on goofballs. We find out the plates are stolen. Then we strike gold. The car's ownership is traced to D & M Scrapyard. Bingo. We are now trailing Domenic Musitano twenty-four hours a day. Sooner or later he will slip up. They always do. They get nervous or sloppy. That's when we catch them. That's my job. I'm a cop.

Sunday, February 5, 1984. A family conference is held at Millhaven maximum security prison. Domenic Musitano consults with his brother Tony about what to do with "Billy" Rankin, who has been shooting his mouth off around town:

Tony: Yeah, been busy.

Domenic: Ah everything's quiet. A bit of heat.

Tony: Yeah, I've been reading the paper with that guy here

Domenic: Ah [expletive], he's crazy

Tony: Huh?

Domenic: That guy you sent down, the [expletive] apple. What's his name?

Tony: I dunno.

Domenic: Billy-y-y.

Tony: Yeah, yeah, yeah.

Domenic: He's going around Hamilton braggin' that he worked for them [the Commissos].

Tony: Oh yeah?

Domenic: I ain't, if they connect him with me it will come down on your [expletive] head ... I'm tired of giving him the money.

Tony: Twenty thou... [Tony then asks about the "screws" — the police.]

Domenic: Screws asking about ... this Billy guy ...

But I heard this before that he [Rankin] goes out in Hamilton braggin' in the [expletive] joints, you know, bars that he is working for the Commissos so ah … ah …

Tony: 'Cuz he was in with Michael [Michele Commisso].

Domenic: I don't know who he was in with. I'm just telling you, tell those guys [the Commissos] if the guy goes near them he's no [expletive] good. He's N.G. … Drunk. Drunk every day. Smashed my car. Everything else … I got cops, one street, the other street, the other corner, behind me … I can't even go to the toilet I'm telling you.

With each passing day, evidence of the Musitanos' role in Racco's death becomes clearer. Our next big break is when William Rankin's friend Peter Majeste is arrested for driving without a licence. He is the other half of a half-wit. He is pulled over in the same brown Pontiac station wagon that witnesses spotted in front of Racco's apartment the night he was abducted. The car is seized because of an overdue rental payment. Our forensic department inspects the car and takes wool and animal fibres from the seats. They match the clothes Racco was wearing at the time of his death. Polyester fibres from the car seat upholstery are also found on the overcoat worn by Racco.

Friday, March 8, 1984. Rankin drinks himself into a stupor, gets into his car and hits a lamp standard. The responding police officers find a photograph on the back seat. It is a picture of Rankin and Anthony Musitano taken at the Millhaven maximum security prison. Written on the back is the following: "Domenic: As you can see your brother sends his respect with me to you. Yes, he's the person I listen to and respect. His words and mine concur. No other person, family or otherwise. You were told to help me so please do not ever attempt to project the illusion that I am responsible to you. Talk to Tony. Capice! Bill." The photo is Rankin's one-way ticket back to jail. His alibis are thinner than the gold on a Las Vegas wedding ring. We take

him in for questioning and he spills his guts like an alcoholic after a three-day bender.

Tuesday, March 20, 1984. Arrest warrants are issued for Anthony Musitano, Domenic Musitano, Giuseppe Avignone, and William Rankin. The charge: *Canadian Criminal Code* Section 465(1), conspiracy to commit murder. A search of 48 Colbourne Street in Hamilton locates two loaded handguns under the basement staircase. Both are .38 calibre. One is a Smith & Wesson. Ballistics proves that it is the same weapon that killed Domenic Racco.

Monday, February 18, 1985. In the Ontario Supreme Court in the jurisdiction of the Township of Milton, thirty-eight-year-old Anthony Musitano, twenty-three-year-old Giuseppe Avignone, and thirty-three-year-old William Rankin plead guilty to conspiring to murder Domenic Racco. All three are sentenced to prison terms of between five and twelve years. Anthony Musitano receives twelve years to be served concurrent with the life term he began in 1983. "If Anthony Musitano is not the worst offender in the worst offence he comes microscopically close to it," Judge Osborne tells the courtroom.

Thursday, January 11, 1990. Graham Court and Peter Monaghan are in custody awaiting trial for the 1984 slaying of Hamilton grocery store owner William Rutledge when they are charged with the murder of Domenic Racco. The investigation into the Racco murder is re-opened after Graham Court makes incriminating statements to a police informant about the murder while in a police holding cell after being charged with the Rutledge murder. He tells the informant how he and Monaghan grabbed Racco at his apartment, knocked him unconscious with a billy bat and then took him to the train tracks where he was shot five times. He tells the informant they were paid $4,700 and a small quantity of cocaine for the job. The informant reports the information to us. He talks to us for hours. We ask him for just the facts. Court and Monaghan are tried and found guilty in 1991. But the sentences are overturned by an Ontario appeals judge. He cites allegations of systematic abuses by police and prosecutors. The audio tape recording made of the confession to the informant mysteriously disappeared while the Crown counsel did not disclose contradictory evidence to the defence counsel.

Justice sometimes comes late. Sometimes it never comes at all. But it has no expiry date. Sure, we can't take every punk mobster off the street. We can't change the world. Just our little corner of it. I know that upholding justice may seem "square" to some people. And being a police officer may seem like an endless, thankless job. We also make mistakes. We are only human. But it's a job that still has to be done. And I am damn glad to do it.

OPEN CITIES

For some provincial politicians the high-profile, back-to-back murders of Paul Volpe and Domenic Racco was proof positive that organized crime in Ontario was out of control. In January 1984, a member of the provincial Liberal Party demanded a Quebec-style public inquiry, arguing, it "appears to be a completely runaway situation in organized crime." The reality was that the two murders were symptomatic of Ontario's fractured and factionalized criminal underworld. In reference to the mafia's attempts to dominate Toronto, James Dubro wrote in 1985 that the city "was always considered too large, disparate, and broken up to be handled by one family, and hence it became a more opportune ground for independents and new mafia groupings; and Italians then, as now, were not the only ones interested in or organized enough to run effective organized crime operations." In short, Toronto and, to a lesser extent, Hamilton were "open cities"; that is, they were "open to many different mob groups operating simultaneously in different areas."

Stefano Magaddino considered most of Ontario his turf, but was thwarted in his attempts to monopolize the province's most profitable criminal rackets. While the mafia families in Hamilton were firmly united under Giacomo Luppino, Toronto's largest mob operations were divided between Paul Volpe's organization, which had become virtually independent of Buffalo, and the Siderno group. The growing tension between these two factions were fuelled by a combination of Volpe's arrogance, the passing of Michelle Racco, the brutal ambitions of the Commisso brothers, as well as the American mafia's last-ditch effort to display its muscle in the city.

Whatever power or dominance the Italian mafia did have within Ontario's criminal world ended in the 1980s. The deaths of Paul Volpe, Michelle Racco and Domenic Racco, the jailing of Rocco Zito, the Commisso brothers, and the Musitanos, and the infighting within the Magaddino Family created a power vacuum that could not be filled by the mafia or the 'Ndrangheta. The symbolic end came with the 1987 death of Giacomo Luppino, whose last fifteen years were not kind to him. His power and influence was already waning following the death of Stefano Magaddino. He was under constant police surveillance, his sons were in and out of jail, and criminal trials were exposing the existence of the 'Ndrangheta in Hamilton. His son-in-law Paolo was murdered in 1978, while his loving wife died in February 1982. The onset of senility in the early 1980s relegated him to St. Joseph's Hospital and it was there that he died on March 19, 1987, at the age of eighty-eight. The 150-car procession at his funeral was the last great mafia burial to be held in Canada, yet few mob leaders attended. His sons tried to take the place of their father, but simply did not have the clout or the connections he enjoyed. Johnny Papalia was spending so much time in jail that he was unable to wield any real power and had already lost a significant amount of credibility after failing to co-opt Max Bluestein in the early 1960s.

The power vacuum created in the late 1980s opened the door for an even greater fractionalization of Ontario's organized crime scene as a diverse range of professional criminals, including the Chinese triads, outlaw motorcycle gangs, Russian criminal groups, the Colombian "cocaine cowboys," as well as mafia groups imported from Quebec and Sicily, crowded into the province. The future of organized crime in Canada would be a continuation of the past and current trends. Like Quebec, Ontario would continue to be a branch plant for a number of foreign criminal organizations representing a diverse range of nationalities and ethnicities. By the time Giacomo Luppino had passed away, a new chapter in the history of organized crime in Ontario and Canada was already under way.

PART IV

PROLIFERATION

1985 – 2006

CHAPTER NINE

CHALLENGING THE MAFIA HEGEMONY

The Expansion, Proliferation, and Internationalization of Organized Crime

By the mid-1980s, a number of significant trends in the world of organized crime were becoming apparent. One of the most discernible was the proliferation of criminal groups, which began in the early 1970s and gathered speed during the 1980s and 1990s. While the Italian mafia was dominant in much of the North American underworld during the postwar years, by the start of the new millennium, a plethora of powerful organized crime groups and networks representing a diverse range of ethnicities and nationalities were active. As D. Owen Carrigan writes in his 1991 book on the history of Canadian crime, "the Mafia hegemony was challenged from at least the early seventies by a number of local gangs, then by the motorcycle clubs, and finally by a number of ethnic organizations. Today, many elements of organized crime co-exist, share the market for their illegal activities, compete against, and assault and murder each other." Foremost among these new organized crime "genres" in Canada were the English- and French-Canadian motorcycle gangs, the Chinese triads, the Colombian cocaine cartels, and Eastern European crime groups. Although not as widespread or dominant, a myriad of other crime groups and networks emerged within the Vietnamese, Iranian, Indo–Canadian, Jamaican, Irish, Sri Lankan,

Nigerian, Lebanese, Saudi, and aboriginal communities. Soon to be ingrained in the annals of Canadian criminal history were groups sporting such names as the Hells Angels, the Outlaws, the Rock Machine, the West End Gang, the Kung Lok Triad, the Big Circle Boys, the Medellin Cartel, the Cali Cartel, the Solntsevskaya Organization, the Spangler Posse, and the Mohawk Warrior Society.

As the number of crime groups multiplied, so did the range of organized criminal activities carried out. Crimes that catered to demand from the public — in particular, drug trafficking, cigarette and liquor smuggling, migrant smuggling, gambling, loansharking, and prostitution — were the biggest money-makers, although predatory offences were also reappearing in the repertoire of many existing and budding crime groups. While extortion, fraud, counterfeiting, and theft have long been a staple of criminal groups, by the start of Prohibition they took a back seat to the so-called consensual crimes. During the 1990s, however, there was considerable growth in the scope, variety, and regularity of fraud and counterfeiting crimes being carried out on a continuing and conspiratorial basis. Traditional street-level crimes, such as automobile theft, credit card theft, pickpocketing, and hijackings also became better organized. The sexual slave trade that was such a cause of concern in the early part of the century re-emerged with a vengeance in the 1990s, as prostitution, migrant smuggling, and human trafficking coalesced to form a transnational and highly profitable trade in women. Even the environment could not escape victimization as crime groups became involved in the illegal dumping of (hazardous) waste and the trafficking of endangered wildlife.

Another characteristic that came to define organized crime beginning in the 1980s was its transnational nature. For much of the century, most criminal groups were confined to or controlled a well-defined local or regional territory or market. Any large-scale international movement of drugs or contraband was often conducted by two or more different groups, each of which was located in a different country (as personified by the French Connection). In the last few decades, the world's major organized crime genres — the Italian mafia, the Chinese triads, outlaw motorcycle gangs, the Colombian cartels, and Eastern European criminal groups — have become truly multinational in scope, with cells located in various countries. The transnational nature of modern organized crime is also characterized by an enormous increase in the quantity of illegal drugs and contraband being moved across borders.

Canada has not been immune from the globalization of crime and plays a number of roles in the worldwide organized crime theatre. Most notably, it continues to serve as a branch plant for transnational criminal organizations and a transit point for the international movement of illegal goods. According to the U.S. State Department's 2002 *International Narcotics Control Strategy Report*, "heroin, cocaine, and MDMA (ecstasy) are trafficked through Canada, as international drug traffickers take advantage of Canada's proximity to the United States, less stringent criminal penalties as compared to the U.S., and the constant flow of goods across the U.S.-Canada border." Canada has also stepped up its role as a conduit for undocumented immigrants, primarily from Asia, who are illegally entering the U.S.

In addition, there is evidence that Canada has become a centre of operations for some transnational crime groups. Since the return of Hong Kong to China in 1997, ethnic Chinese crime groups have shifted resources, people, and certain criminal activities to Toronto and Vancouver. Canada also has the highest concentration of Hells Angels chapters in the world. The country supplies an embarrassingly rich assortment of illegal and contraband goods, a tradition that began when British Columbia became a major producer of smokable opium in the early part of the century. This tradition continued through Prohibition, when Canada was America's main source of illegal liquor, and found new life in the 1970s, when the country surfaced as a major producer of synthetic drugs. By the end of the 1990s, Canada had established itself as the continent's preeminent supplier of high-grade marijuana, methamphetamines, and ecstasy. It has also become an international centre for telemarketing fraud and the counterfeiting of currency, bankcards, and digital entertainment products. All of these developments led the *Wall Street Journal* to assert in 1998 that Canada has become "one of the most important bases for the globalization of organized crime."

Another significant trend in the world of organized crime has been an increase in the co-operation and networking between different criminal groups. Modern organized crime in Canada and abroad can best be characterized as a fluid network of many autonomous buyers, brokers, financiers, middlemen, and distributors from different groups, ethnicities, nationalities, and countries that come together to make deals by capitalizing on each other's specialties and strengths. In a 2005 article, criminologist James Finckenauer of Rutgers University writes that most contemporary organized crime conspiracies are "loosely affiliated networks of criminals who coalesce around certain criminal opportunities. The structure of these groups is much more amorphous, free floating and flatter, and thus lacking in a rigid hierarchy." In a Statistics Canada survey of police agencies exploring organized crime, the respondents indicated that 93 percent of the criminal organizations they investigated in this country had links with other crime groups. The purposes of these linkages were to combine expertise, share personnel, facilities, or smuggling routes, exchange goods and services, or to expand into new markets. In its 2006 annual report, the CISC elaborated on these relationships:

… law enforcement is identifying crime groups that are based on temporary alliances of individual criminals who merge their particular skills to better achieve success in specific criminal enterprises. Once a specific criminal venture is completed, these individuals may continue to collaborate on further criminal activities, or the group may dissolve. Although the individuals may go their separate ways, they sometimes reform into new groups based upon the skill requirements of new criminal opportunities. The nature and success of such networks are largely determined by individual characteristics and skills among those who act as their component parts.

Drug trafficking epitomizes the new networked structure of organized crime in that few criminal groups independently carry out all the essential functions of the drug trade, from production to street-level distribution. Instead, drug trafficking conspiracies, both domestically and internationally, are generally made up of a network of individuals and groups, each of which specializes in one or more aspects of the trade, such as supplying the raw material or processed product; arranging financing; brokering the purchase, transportation, or distribution; physically transporting the goods; or storing, wholesaling, and retailing the product.

THE WEST END GANG

One Canadian crime group that has come to personify the underworld's emerging spirit of co-operation is Montreal's West End Gang, a moniker applied by police to a network of professional criminals, mostly of Irish descent, who grew up in the slums of Montreal's West End. Despite its changing leadership and a varying cast of characters over its forty-year existence, the West End Gang went on to become one of the biggest importers of hashish and cocaine in the country, working closely with other criminal entrepreneurs from drug suppliers in the U.S., Colombia, Pakistan, and the Middle East to wholesalers and retailers in Canada, including outlaw motorcycle gangs and the Italian mafia.

The origins of the West End Gang can be traced to the early 1970s, when a veteran thief named Francis Peter (Dunie) Ryan began assembling a network of like-minded associates. Born in Montreal on June 10, 1942, Frank Ryan was the product of a poor Irish family headed by an itinerant and absentee father. He began his life of crime by stealing racks of fur coats and other garments from delivery trucks. By the 1960s, he had a string of convictions for armed robbery, possession of a false driver's licence, possession of stolen goods and, in 1965, criminal negligence causing death after he accidentally killed a pedestrian while driving his Pontiac Bonneville convertible. This conviction was overturned, but instead of viewing this acquittal as an opportunity for redemption, his resentment over being charged in the first place only fuelled his descent into the criminal world. As Dan Burke explains in his 1987 biography of Ryan, following the acquittal he began frequenting the Country Palace, a club on Montreal's Sherbrooke Street that would spawn a new phase in his criminal career. "Hoods from all over the city, but especially the Irish Catholic ghettos, gathered at the Country Palace. Primarily strong arms and bank robbers, the Irish Canadians were an important element of the Montreal underworld, and the nightclub was a mine of contacts for Ryan. There, through the Irish-Canadian links with the Boston underworld, he found the bridge to bigger opportunities and his first costly setback."

The setback was a botched armed robbery that occurred one summer day in 1966 when Ryan and three other men he had befriended in Montreal held up the Essex County Bank and Trust in Lynn, Massachusetts. All four were caught by police and convicted for armed robbery. Ryan received fifteen years for his part, but only had to serve six. After his release from prison in 1972, he returned to Montreal where he went on a binge of jewellery-store heists. By 1973, he had set his sights on banks and armoured cars and began assembling a crew made up of career criminals with expertise in deactivating security systems, picking locks, and cracking safes. Among those joining his new gang in the 1970s were "Porky" McGurnaghan, Paul April, Kenny McPolland, Peter White, Allan Ross, and the Mattick brothers.

While enjoying some limited success with his band of thieves, by the mid-1970s Ryan realized that the real money to be made was in drugs. Through his contacts in Montreal's Irish criminal community, and using his robbery proceeds as financing, he began to purchase and sell small quantities of hashish, the city's most popular illegal drug. By the end of the decade, he had made enough money to import hash shipments and, before long, he was one of the biggest distributors in the city. Under Ryan's leadership, hash arrived at the Port of Montreal by the ton and was then distributed through a network of wholesalers that extended west into Ontario and east into the Maritimes. Dan Burke describes how, on one occasion, "Ryan watched from the window of a Spanish restaurant as $250,000 worth of hash was transferred to his runners in a Park Avenue parking lot. He had lookouts posted on every corner and — one witness swears — a helicopter hovering overhead." In the late 1970s, Ryan diversified into the rapidly expanding cocaine market by tapping into American sources through his cousin Peter White. By the next decade, he was Quebec's biggest cocaine trafficker, purchasing directly from South American suppliers while wholesaling to Frank Cotroni, the Hells Angels, and others. All the while, Ryan was building up a network of some two hundred criminals who were engaged in drug trafficking, bank robberies, jewellery theft, and hijackings. He was now worth an estimated $50 million and was rumoured to carry around a briefcase with $500,000 in cash, which he put back onto the streets through a profitable loan-shark business. By the time of his death, it was said that he had almost $10 million owing to him, including a $700,000 drug debt that had been accumulated by members of the Hells Angels.

Ryan was also owed $200,000 by estranged West End Gang member Paul April. Instead of paying Ryan the money owed him, however, April was planning his murder. On November 13, 1984, after luring Ryan to a motel room through the promise of a tryst with a young woman, April and accomplice Robert Lelièvre jumped Ryan and, with two guns pointed at his head, demanded to know where he kept his cash-filled briefcase. Ryan tried to make a break for it, but was cut down by a barrage of bullets from Lelièvre's shotgun. As Ryan lay dying on the ground outside the motel, he was shot a final time through the cheek with a .45-calibre pistol. When word reached senior West End Gang member Allan Ross that April was boasting about the murder

of his good friend and colleague, he approached Yves Trudeau, the Hells Angels' most prolific hit man, to do away with April. Less than two weeks after Ryan's death, April, Lelièvre and two other men were killed in an apartment by an explosive that Trudeau had rigged to a VCR. In March 1985, Eddie Phillips, who Ross suspected was responsible for renting the motel room where Ryan was killed, was shot to death by a motorcycle-driving assailant.

With the murder of April and Phillips, Allan (the Weasel) Ross established himself as the new leader of the West End Gang. Ross had also grown up in Montreal's West End tenements and began his own criminal career robbing jewellery stores and stealing cars before working for Ryan as a drug courier. Ross quickly picked up where his old boss left off and began personally arranging cocaine shipments from Florida to Montreal. He even expanded Ryan's sprawling drug empire by sidestepping his Florida middlemen and travelling to South America to do business directly with Colombian suppliers. By the end of the 1980s, he was buying hundreds of kilos of coke at a time, most of which was being shipped to Florida and then

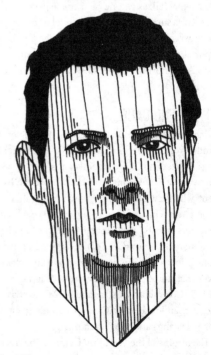

Frank Ryan

on to the Port of Montreal where it was offloaded by dockworkers he had on his payroll. He was even sending shipments of cocaine by boat to Europe. By the latter half of the 1980s, he had come under the radar of the U.S. Drug Enforcement Administration, which considered him one of the biggest drug traffickers in the world.

The Americans began by arresting Ross' suppliers, couriers, and pilots in the U.S. and through the threat of long jail sentences, were able to gather enough evidence to tie Ross to the importation of thousands of kilos of cocaine and marijuana into Florida. Despite knowing full well that he had already been indicted *in absentia* in a Florida courtroom, Ross still travelled to the Sunshine State in 1991 to take care of some business. Whether he was deluded by visions of his own invincibility or simply motivated by greed, the trip would be a career-ending mistake for Ross. After being tipped off about his presence in Florida, the U.S. Marshals Service arrested him on October 7, 1991. (Before he was even fingerprinted, Ross reportedly offered his captors $200,000 to let him go.) On August 1,

Allan (The Weasel) Ross

1992, the forty-eight-year-old Canadian was sentenced in a Tallahassee courtroom to thirty years and a $10-million fine for conspiring to import over 10,000 kilos of cocaine and 3,000 kilos of marijuana into the U.S. between 1975 and 1989.

Ross' legal troubles did not end there. In 1993, a Fort Lauderdale judge convicted him of the 1985 murder of David Singer, a small-time drug dealer from Montreal. The prosecution argued that Ross feared Singer knew too much about his part in the murder of Eddie Phillips and had hired two hit men to kill Singer while the intended victim was in Fort Lauderdale. Among those testifying against Ross in this latest trial was Yves Trudeau, who told the court that Ross hired him to avenge Frank Ryan's slaying. Ross was spared the death penalty, but did receive another thirty-year sentence after being convicted for Phillips' murder and yet another cocaine trafficking offence. In 1995, a Florida appeals court overturned these convictions, ruling the state should not have prosecuted him in the same trial on two unrelated charges. Despite this ruling, Ross would languish in a Florida jail due to his life sentence from his earlier drug conviction.

The fact that Ross was captured and prosecuted in the U.S. became a major embarrassment for police in Canada given that his massive drug trafficking empire was headquartered in Quebec. Many began to question how Ross and his coterie of traffickers were able to operate with such impunity in Canada for almost ten years. Another intriguing question arose: if American law enforcement had concrete evidence on Ross' drug trafficking, why did they not contact police in Montreal for co-operation or contact the Department of Justice to request extradition to the U.S.? The answer was that in their investigation of Ross the Americans had become aware that he had access to confidential RCMP information, although at the time they did not know the source. They suspected that Ross had an RCMP member on his payroll.

In an interview with the CBC news program *the fifth estate* in 1993, Inspector Claude Savoie, the Officer in Charge of the RCMP's drug section in Montreal for much of the 1980s, downplayed suspicions of a mole within the force, and then offered a bewildering explanation as to why Quebec's biggest drug baron was not captured in Canada, "Allan Ross, for us from '86 to '91, was not one of our problems. Allan Ross — everybody says he was the head of this. People were saying this. But I must say that in my work, I wouldn't be able to say that. And we were never sure, we never had him pinned." In a subsequent interview, Savoie acknowledged that Ross may have infiltrated the RCMP and, in an astonishing *mea culpa*, even alluded to his own complicity, "I know with Allan Ross there's no doubt there was word always out you know that he had access to somebody, and you know maybe he did, he probably did … And I gather from you wanting to talk to me that you feel maybe I was one of those people on the list and that's fair game, I guess … Sometimes people can make a mistake. What can I tell you?" Journalists at *the fifth estate* had already learned that while Ross was under indictment in Florida, Savoie had met with him in an Italian restaurant in Montreal and in the office of Ross' lawyer. When asked to explain the meetings, Savoie said he was trying to convince Ross to become an informant. He then changed his story, saying that since the Americans were after Ross, he was trying to cajole him to work out a deal with the RCMP. Savoie's weak and conflicting remonstrations were further undermined by the fact that he went to these meetings alone and did not alert his superiors, two blatant deviations from normal RCMP procedure. At one point, Savoie phoned the Drug Enforcement Agency to find out what they had on Ross, but the DEA refused to provide him with any information.

Then, on December 21, 1992, while sitting in his new office at RCMP headquarters in Ottawa (following a promotion to assistant director of criminal intelligence) and with two RCMP internal investigators waiting in another office to interview him on suspicions that he was providing information to Allan Ross, Inspector Claude Savoie took out his service revolver, placed the barrel against his temple, and put a bullet through his head. Before pulling the trigger, he wrapped the gun in the sleeve of his jacket to dampen the noise. A subsequent inquiry found that he had accepted $200,000 from Allan Ross. Savoie's wife and three children buried him on Christmas Eve that year. Attending the funeral was a number of Mountie colleagues, but none were wearing their uniforms, nor was an honour guard present.

Despite the jailing of Ross, as well as the public disclosure of Canada's biggest case of police corruption in years, the West End Gang's drug trafficking activities only grew bigger in subsequent years. When Ross was imprisoned in Florida, Gerald Matticks took over the reins and barely skipped a beat in furthering the group's standing as one of Canada's biggest drug importers. The youngest of fourteen children, Matticks was born and raised in the West End. Gerald, along with three brothers, Fred, Robert, and Richard, were dutiful contract employees for both Frank Ryan and Allan Ross. When they began working for Ryan in the 1970s, the brothers specialized in the hijacking of tractor-trailers in and around the Port of Montreal. Using information obtained from insiders working on the docks, they would whisk away tractor-trailers full of imported merchandise using heavy-duty tow trucks. In 1971, Gerry and his brother John were charged with attempting to murder a police informant who accused the brothers of trying to stop him from revealing their crimes on the waterfront. The Matticks avoided conviction when witnesses testified in court that they were drinking with them at a bar when the shootings took place. Gerry and Richard were acquitted in 1981 of a truck hijacking that occurred eight years prior, but pleaded guilty in 1992 to the 1988 theft of a tractor-trailer. They were sentenced to serve forty-five weekends in prison and fined $10,000.

By the 1990s, Gerald Matticks was a millionaire with investments in various legitimate businesses, including a transport company, a meat-wholesaling business, and a restaurant. At the height of his power, Matticks also displayed a big heart that matched his large frame. He donated food baskets to the poor, provided frozen turkeys to families and toys to children at Christmas, paid for the repair of leaky church roofs, threw out dollar bills from his float during St. Paddy's Day parades, and dished out free meals from his restaurant to people who lost their electricity during winter storms. All the while, he was a cunning and circumspect drug smuggler, importing thousands of kilos of hashish and cocaine, which he wholesaled through his own network, supplying the elite of Quebec's underworld — the Hells Angels, the Rock Machine, the Rizzuto Family, as well as Asian and Russian criminal groups. Like his predecessor Allan Ross, Matticks was able to move large quantities because of the influence he had in the Port of Montreal. He virtually controlled the hiring of "checkers," a waterfront job responsible for overseeing the movement of containers off ships and essential to ensuring the safe passage of drugs through the port. Gerald's son Donald even worked on the docks as a checker for fifteen years before being caught up in a police dragnet in 2002. He would later tell a parole board that he began working at the port at the age of twenty-four and used his position to sneak drug-filled containers past the port gates without being inspected.

The provincial drug squad finally caught up with Gerald Matticks on May 26, 1994, when he, his brother Richard, and nine others were charged by the Sûreté du Québec in connection with a 2,650-kilo shipment of hashish found in a shipping container on the Montreal waterfront earlier that month. At the time, it was one of the largest hashish seizures ever in Quebec. The SQ announced that the Matticks would also be charged in connection with another 1,000 kilos discovered in March. When the case came to court, however, allegations began to surface that the provincial police had planted incriminating evidence against the Matticks. In June of the following year, all of the charges were dismissed by a Quebec court judge who ruled that the SQ had fabricated evidence, falsified documents, and provided inconsistent testimony in court. Four police officers were charged and allegations of corruption reached the highest levels of the provincial police. The four were eventually acquitted, but the highly publicized outcome of the case precipitated the formation of a public inquiry to delve into the practices of Quebec's provincial police force. The commission's report released two years later revealed embarrassing details about the SQ, not only in relation to how they mismanaged the Matticks case, but how it had broken the law in other criminal investigations during the 1990s. The report concluded, "A crisis of values has shaken the Sûreté du Québec from the beginning of this decade."

Despite their acquittal, the Matticks brothers could not count on the incompetence of the provincial police or the luck of the Irish forever. In 1997, sixty-three-year-old Richard was sentenced to three years for cocaine trafficking after being caught in a

police sting operation. Matticks had agreed to sell a police agent eight kilos of cocaine following an introduction by Giovanni Cazzetta of the Rock Machine, who was arrested along with two other West End Gang members. The jailing of his brother did little to deter Gerald who was now ramping up his hashish and cocaine smuggling. In December 1999, Matticks and his drug-dealing partner Louis Lekkas — the former owner of a vitamin store who began working with Matticks as a chicken salesman — were behind a 2,363-kilo shipment of hash that was landed at the Montreal port. This was followed a month later by another load of over 20,000 kilos, although this was seized by police. In April 2000, they brought in 265 kilos of cocaine from Panama, some of which was sold to the Hells Angels. Later that year, Matticks and Lekkas imported 4,037 kilos of hash and sold 1,500 kilos to the Angels. Another consignment in October 2000 brought in 5,485 kilos of hash, but this was also seized by police. Their last shipment of 9,000 kilos of hash landed at the Montreal port in February

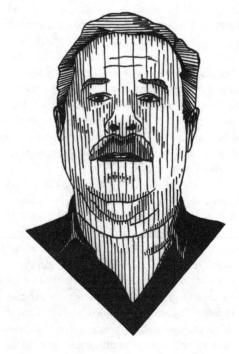

Gerald Matticks

2001. In a little over a year, Matticks and Lekkas were behind eight shipments, which brought 44,093 kilos of hashish and 265 kilos of cocaine into Montreal. Police estimated that once on the street, the drugs had a value of around $2 billion.

While police had strong suspicions that Gerald Matticks was behind the two hashish shipments seized in 2000, they had insufficient evidence to lay charges. But their fortune was about to change. During a widespread investigation of the Hells Angels cocaine trafficking activities, Matticks' name was discovered among documents seized from the Angels. According to spreadsheets the bikers used to track their own massive cocaine and hashish trafficking conspiracies, they owed Matticks almost $7 million for drugs purchased from him. Surveillance conducted as part of the investigation also captured Lekkas lugging bags full of cash from one Angels-controlled apartment in Montreal. Police were able to show that he was picking up a monthly average of $500,000, which he would take to Matticks' sprawling and heavily secured rural estate.

Police now had evidence to show Matticks was the Quebec Hells Angels main hashish supplier and, as part of a massive sweep that targeted the motorcycle gang and their associates at the end of March 2001, Matticks was charged with a number of drug trafficking and conspiracy offences. Lekkas was arrested as well and quickly turned on his former partner by becoming a Crown witness. On August 6, 2001, Matticks pleaded guilty to drug charges and received a twelve-year sentence. While in jail, he was hit with a bill for $2.1 million from the Quebec government for taxes owed on his drug sales.

Another member of the West End Gang, John McLean also became an informant after he was arrested and, in exchange for a guilty plea and a relatively light sentence of eight years, he agreed to provide evidence against Gerald's son, Donald. Based in part on McLean's information, a joint police task force began Projet Boeuf, a sly reference to the French nickname the Hells Angels had given Gerald Matticks (which may have derived from his meat business, his beefy neck, or both). In an early-morning police raid on December 4, 2002, Donald was one of fifteen men arrested for conspiring with his father to import multi-ton ship-

ments of hash and coke through the Port of Montreal between 1999 and 2001. In 2005, the forty-one-year-old Matticks pleaded guilty to fourteen charges of conspiracy and drug smuggling and was handed an eight-year sentence.

Following the conviction of Gerald Matticks, veteran crime reporter Michel Auger wrote that despite the jail term, "his people are still there." Auger was referring to the West End Gang's influence at the Port of Montreal, which was still intact despite the recent convictions. The waterfront is vital to the West End Gang's ongoing hashish smuggling, according to Inspector Serge Frenette, head of the organized crime division for the Montreal police, "because it's hard to hide 4,000 pounds of hash in the trunk of a car." Sure enough, on May 10, 2006, the RCMP seized 989 bales of hashish, weighing around 22,500 kilos, from a ship that departed from Angola in Southern Africa and which was destined for the Port of Montreal. The hash had been transported part of the way by an "undercover" ship chartered by the RCMP and crewed by police officers. Once in Montreal, a controlled delivery of the hash was made by police to a home about 50 kilometres southeast of Montreal. Three men were arrested — Peter Toman, his son Andrew, and Sidney Lallouz — all from Montreal and all affiliated with the West End Gang, according to the RCMP. All three men were convicted and sentenced to terms ranging from two years for Andrew Toman to eleven years for his father, who police called the mastermind behind the operation.

SEVERAL ESTABLISHED BOOKMAKERS

Despite the many revenue-generating ventures at the disposal of criminal groups, illegal gambling and bookmaking continued to be a mainstay of organized crime in the 1980s and beyond. In the 1970s, the underground gaming markets began to shrink in Canada with the advent of legalized gaming, including off-track betting and casinos, not to mention the many lotteries run by the provincial and federal governments. To compete, professional gamblers and bookmakers began offering their clients better odds, more convenience and selection, as well as credit and on-the-spot loans. Criminal groups also branched out into new lucrative forms of gambling that were outlawed or difficult to regulate, such as video lottery terminals and Internet-based gambling.

A 1996 classified report by the Criminal Intelligence Service Ontario stated that the many types of illegal gambling in the province were taking in an estimated $10 billion a year. Three years later, the provincial government established the Illegal Gaming Enforcement Unit and that year, 941 gambling-related charges were laid against 623 people. Because it was still prohibited in Canada, professional bookmaking emerged as the most widespread and profitable form of illegal gaming in the country, taking in more than $1 billion annually in Ontario alone. In their 1992 report on organized crime, the Canadian Association of Chiefs of Police revealed that bookmaking activity in Metropolitan Toronto "is dominated by several established bookmakers who are in the 60 to 70 year age group. These individuals are financially established and very active in sports betting action. They rely on younger individuals to generate new action and to act as a shield between themselves and law enforcement." In November 2002, an Ontario court levied fines and forfeitures totalling $300,000 against Dario Zanetti, who was in charge of a vast interprovincial bookmaking ring that police believed was being run by the Montreal mafia. "He's working for the Rizzuto crime family, and he took the rap for his bosses back in Quebec," one police officer told the press. The financial penalties were the culmination of a police operation code-named "Project Juice," in which more than three dozen people in Toronto, Montreal, and Ottawa were arrested in April 2001 following a seven-month investigation. As part of a plea bargain, charges were dropped against nine other men — Leonardo Bitondo, Francesco Cardinale, twin brothers Martino and Antonio Caputo, Domenic Defillippo, Vincenzo Loggozzo, Vincent Lopresti, Robert Marchese, and Giuseppe Renda. Police said that over a five-month period, the bookmaking ring took in more than $20 million in wagers on professional and college sports, using a web site, BlackBerry pagers, and Palm Pilots to take bets.

Video gaming machines have also become a source of illegal revenue for criminal groups in Canada. The Hells Angels, Chinese crime groups, the Italian mafia, and the Russian "mafiya" are all said to be involved in the illegal operation of video lottery terminals. In 1993, the head of the organized crime squad for the Montreal police claimed that illegal video gambling machines in the city were tightly controlled by the Rizzuto Family and were second only to drugs as a revenue generator. Francesco Cotroni, the son of long-time Montreal mobster Frank Cotroni, began working in the video poker business after he was released from prison in 1990 on charges of conspiracy to murder, while his brother Santos was charged in 2000 after about fifty video lottery terminals were seized by police. The charges were later dropped as part of a plea bargain. In 1996, the Criminal Intelligence Service Ontario estimated there were some 25,000 illegal video gambling machines in the province, "most of them distributed and controlled by a southern Ontario crime family and motorcycle gangs." The machines were estimated to generate around $500 million a year in revenue. The 2000 annual report for the Criminal Intelligence Service Canada stated that in Western Canada, "video gaming and lottery machines are the newest, and possibly the largest, illicit source of gambling income available to organized crime groups. The machines can earn up to $2000 per machine, per week, making this an extremely lucrative business. The cost of the machines ranges between $2500 and $5000 and is quickly paid off."

Illegal gaming has also been revolutionized by the Internet. In 1997, there were around fifteen web sites that offered online gambling, according to the FBI. One year later, there were at least 140 sites hosted around the world. Today, the number of web sites offering professional gaming services is in the thousands. Gambling web sites can be broken down into two categories: those that offer casino games such as blackjack, roulette, and poker and those that take bets on racing and sporting events. Internet gambling sites provide numerous features that are ideally suited for organized crime. Most are hosted outside the U.S. and Canada, which effectively puts them beyond the reach of the legal systems of both countries. In addition, the offshore location and faceless technology of web sites provides shady operators the opportunity to rig games. The Internet offers a distinct advantage over conventional gambling operations in the sheer volume of bettors and bets that can be accommodated. An investment of as little as $100,000 can purchase the hardware and software required to establish a gambling web site capable of reaching millions of prospective bettors and can take in tens of millions of dollars in wagers twenty-four hours a day.

Canadian companies and entrepreneurs have become involved in the Internet gaming industry by developing software and even starting up their own gambling web sites. In the first prosecution of a Canadian online gambling firm, Vancouver-based Starnet Communications International Inc., pleaded guilty to an illegal gambling charge in 2001. While it only paid a fine of $100,000, the court ordered the forfeiture of $6 million which it deemed to be the proceeds of crime. The company has since reinvented itself under a different name, World Gaming, and a new location, the Caribbean island of Antigua. In another case, Francesco del Balso was arrested in Quebec in March 2007 after police shut down a sports bookmaking operation that in the space of just eleven months took in almost half a billion dollars in bets and netted del Balso a profit of around $17 million. All bets were made through a web site called World Sport Centre (www.betwsc.com). Police linked del Balso and his bookmaking operation to the Montreal mafia. He was arrested as part of a sweep of the Rizzuto Family and its associates in November 2006.

While the glut of government-run lotteries and legal casinos may have taken some of the profit out of the underground gambling industry, police believe it has reinvigorated another organized criminal activity that has long been coupled with gambling — loansharking. In March 2001, three Toronto-based members of a Chinese criminal group pleaded guilty to lending money at usurious rates. Police alleged that they operated a loansharking ring in Casino Rama, located 70 miles outside of Toronto. "Most of the victims willingly went to these people just to get money to gamble," according to an official with the Casino Intelligence Unit of the Ontario Provincial Police. The loans averaged about $5,000, with 10 percent being taken off the top right away (so a borrower would only receive $4,500 cash on a $5,000 loan). The borrower then had to repay the entire $5,000 within an agreed-upon time, usually three days. If the amount was not paid within the specified period, another $500 would be tacked on to the principal. In 2003, Quebec provincial police

(Sûreté du Quebec) announced they had broken a loansharking ring that also preyed on gamblers, this time at a Montreal casino. Among the seventeen people arrested on 124 criminal charges was a casino security guard and the father and three half-brothers of the goaltender for the Montreal Canadiens at the time, José Théodore. The *Journal de Montréal* reported that police seized $85,000 in cash from a safety deposit box belonging to the senior Théodore and that the security guard arrested had ties to the father. Police alleged that seventy-one-year-old Ted Nicholas Théodore had been running a loansharking operation out of his Montreal wig shop for almost twenty years. Before his arrest, he had enlisted family members and others to provide loans and collect debts from gamblers at the Montreal casino, operating primarily in the bathrooms where there are no surveillance cameras. Many of the initial charges were dropped, but Ted Théodore did plead guilty to two charges of loansharking and possessing an unlicensed weapon.

"THERE IS NO IMPORTANT SOURCE COUNTRY, OTHER THAN CANADA ITSELF"

By the mid-1970s, the world of drug trafficking began to go through dramatic changes. While the Italian mafia — in particular the Rizzuto-Caruana-Cuntrera criminal troika — continued to supply Canada with thousands of kilos of cocaine and heroin, they now had to compete (and co-operate) with scores of other trafficking groups, most notably Chinese drug trafficking syndicates, Colombian cartels, outlaw motorcycle gangs, the West End Gang, and Persian heroin dealers, among others. The Hells Angels, the Outlaws, and other biker gangs in Canada established themselves as the biggest producers of illegal chemical drugs in North America. During the 1980s, crack cocaine began to appear in large Canadian cities, propelling the ascendancy of Jamaican crime groups in Central Canada and Hispanic traffickers on the west coast. By the late 1980s, the Italian mafia was supplanted as the world's largest heroin suppliers by Chinese drug traffickers. Around the same time, outlaw motorcycle gangs in Canada shifted their focus to cocaine, marijuana, and hashish, which meant that much of the trendy new chemical drugs of the day, in particular ecstasy, had to be imported from the Netherlands and

Israel. By the start of the new millennium, chemical drug production returned to Canada, this time under the control of Chinese crime groups.

The first seismic shift in global drug trafficking began to be felt in the early 1970s when Chinese syndicates began filling the void in the North American heroin market that was created with the downfall of French and Sicilian heroin processors. Since then, the high-quality "China White" heroin, which is produced from opium cultivated in the mountains of the "Golden Triangle" — Myanmar (formerly Burma), Thailand, and Laos — has steadily gained market share in Canada. Through the supply of heroin, Chinese criminal groups assembled some of the biggest and most sophisticated drug trafficking networks in the world and soon dominated the Canadian heroin market west of Montreal. During the 1970s, most of the Southeast Asian heroin imported into Canada entered the country through Vancouver and Toronto by couriers travelling on commercial aircraft who concealed the drugs in luggage or wrapped around their body. By the late 1980s, multi-kilo shipments of almost pure Southeast Asian heroin were being landed at Vancouver's bustling marine ports in cargo containers. According to 1985 estimates, a kilogram of pure heroin was worth about $225,000 at the wholesale level in Canada. By the time it was diluted to around a 5 percent purity level and sold by the "capsule" (for about $50) the drug had a street value of more than $10 million.

Around the same time, Iranian gangs were responsible for around 40 percent of the heroin traffic in Montreal and Toronto area, according to Montreal police. The Persian dealers, who had come to Canada and claimed refugee status along with thousands of others fleeing Iran following the Islamic revolution, were behind Quebec's glut of Southwest Asian heroin, which was produced from opium grown in the "Golden Crescent" (Afghanistan, Iran, and Pakistan). In his 1989 book, *Merchants of Misery*, Victor Malarek cites Montreal police officials who linked at least three hundred Iranian immigrants to various drug rings in the city. "The gangs are generally made up of young men from the same village, town or region in Iran, and many of them have links to Southwest Asia's infamous 'Golden Crescent' area," he writes. The Iranian dealers

were able "to avoid a deadly and costly bloodbath with the established mobs which dominated the city's heroin trade" by creating a new market, which involved selling low-priced heroin through bars in Montreal.

Malarek credits Shahrokh Amadzadegam as the man most responsible for organizing Iranian heroin smuggling and trafficking groups in Montreal. Also known as "the Shah," Amadzadegam arrived in Canada at the age of thirty-one on a student visa on April 12, 1980, and immediately asked for refugee status. He already had connections to opium, heroin, and hashish suppliers in the Golden Crescent and, by the mid-1980s, he had organized a small band of Iranian nationals who sold heroin and hashish mostly in the downtown core of Montreal. On March 24, 1984, he was arrested and charged with kidnapping, extortion, and conspiracy after he had held hostage the courier of a drug wholesaler who Amadzadegam accused of supplying substandard hash. Four months later, the Shah was sentenced to two years after being arrested in possession of 18 kilos of hashish. Upon his release from jail, the Shah began arranging for the import of large quantities of heroin into Canada, smuggled by couriers through Mirabel airport. After two couriers were arrested in 1988, they led police directly to the Shah, who was arrested and convicted on various drug charges and sentenced to twenty-five years. In 1989, another Iranian national named Mohsen Goldadanishtiani was sentenced to twelve years for importing heroin into Canada. Goldadanishtiani, who had fled Iran in 1986 and applied for refugee status in Canada upon arrival, was described by the sentencing judge as the head of an international gang of smugglers responsible for bringing in millions of dollars' worth of heroin into Canada.

Regardless of the source country or the trafficking group, a significant and deadly trend in Canada's drug markets has been the rise in heroin's purity and its drop in price, a combination that signalled its overabundance on the street. By the early 1990s, purity levels at the wholesale stage were as high as 99 percent while at the street level purities were as much as 85 percent. The result was an epidemic of overdoses among addicts who were accustomed to heroin that was only 5 to 8 percent pure. Of the fifty-three heroin-related deaths in Ontario in 1992, thirty-six involved heroin that was between 80 and 85 percent pure. The number of overdose deaths in British Columbia increased from sixty-seven in 1989, to eighty-four in 1990, one hundred and twenty-four in 1991, and one hundred and sixty in 1992 (mostly involving Southeast Asian heroin).

The second most significant change in the drug trafficking world was the meteoric rise in the demand for and supply of cocaine that began in the mid-1970s. From that time through to the mid-1990s, Colombian groups were some of the biggest cocaine wholesalers in Canada. And while both the Medellin and Cali cartels were the foremost importers and wholesalers in the country during this time, they were both competing with (and supplying) a number of large cocaine trafficking criminals in Canada, most notably, the Hells Angels, the Italian mafia, the West End Gang, Jamaican "posses," and Asian criminal groups. As the Criminal Intelligence Service Canada noted in 1985, a year in which cocaine prices were at their highest, the astronomical revenues accruing to cocaine traffickers at all levels attracted numerous criminal groups to the trade:

> Depending upon where it is distributed, a "retailer" can buy a single kilogram of pure cocaine from a "wholesaler" for between $60,000 and $95,000. Then the retailer cuts the drug to 50% purity and sells it on the street as a mixture of 50% cocaine and 50% filler. Since one gram of this mixture contains only ½ gram of cocaine and sells for $100 to $300, the actual selling price for cocaine has doubled to between $200,000 and $600,000 for a kilogram of pure cocaine.

In their drug intelligence estimates for 2001, the RCMP estimated that around 15 metric tons of cocaine enter Canada each year, although not all of that is destined for the Canadian market. Increased enforcement along the southwest American border and coastal areas has led to the use of Canada as a trans-shipment point for cocaine destined for the United States. Cocaine shipments to Canada are sent by sea or air, directly from Colombia, or are routed through other South American or Caribbean countries. The U.S. is also a cocaine intermediary country

for Canada, with much of it transported across the border by tractor-trailers or cars. As with heroin, the price of cocaine began to drop in Canada in the 1990s while purity levels steadily increased; cocaine seized in Canada during this time averaged around 75 percent purity levels, although shipments that were as high as 98 percent pure were not uncommon.

The largest cocaine seizure in Canadian history occurred on February 22, 1994, at Shelburne, Nova Scotia, a customs marine port on the southwest coast of the province, when 5.4 metric tons of cocaine with a potential street value of a $1 billion was found in the rear hold of a 13-metre wooden fishing boat, the *Lady Teri Anne*. While this may have been the largest, police and customs were regularly seizing single shipments that were in the hundreds of kilos. During the late 1980s, the Medellin cartel flew at least two planes into Quebec carrying 500 kilos of cocaine in each, while another flight with a similar amount crash-landed in New Brunswick. In November 1992, the second-largest cocaine seizure in Canada was made after air force jet fighters chased a Convair 580 until it landed at a remote airstrip in Quebec with 4,323 kilos of cocaine aboard. In July 2002, the RCMP seized close to 600 kilos from a sailboat that was cruising up the eastern seaboard of Cape Breton. In the summer of 2004, RCMP intercepted a sailboat named *Friendship* off the coast of Nova Scotia carrying more than 500 kilos of cocaine. On January 22, 2005, the Canada Border Services Agency seized 218 kilos of cocaine at Pierre Elliott Trudeau International Airport in Montreal during a routine inspection of luggage taken off an aircraft arriving from Haiti. In November 2005, the RCMP in Montreal discovered 300 kilos hidden inside three drums that were part of a shipment of 216 barrels of lubricating oil. Other sizable seizures that year included 400 kilos found in a marine container at the Halifax port, 329 kilos at Toronto's Pearson airport, and 218 kilos at Montreal's Trudeau airport. In January 2006, 126 kilos were discovered inside a propane tanker truck that had crossed into B.C. from the United States.

While Canada is an importer of heroin and cocaine, it is a source country for synthetic drugs. In its 1983 annual report, the Criminal Intelligence Service Canada predicted, "domestic clandestine laboratories will remain the principal source for chemical drugs on the Canadian market through 1985." Sure enough, subsequent RCMP drug intelligence reports documented the discovery of eight clandestine laboratories in Ontario and Quebec in 1984, nine in 1985, and seven in 1986. Each lab was manufacturing methamphetamines, amphetamines, or phencyclidine (PCP or "angel dust"). The 1983 CISC report also anticipated that outlaw motorcycle gangs were "expected to become increasingly involved in the production and distribution of chemical drugs in Canada through 1985." In fact, biker gangs began monopolizing the production and trafficking of chemical drugs in Canada and the U.S. in the early 1970s. They held on to this monopoly until the mid-1980s, when they began to abandon chemical drugs, due to the difficulty in obtaining precursor chemicals, the ongoing busts of laboratories, and their interest in the new drug of choice, cocaine.

The void in chemical drug trafficking was quickly filled by Quebec criminals, including those associated with the Montreal mafia. Beginning in the early 1980s, Willie Obront became involved in a network that produced methaqualone (commonly known as Quaaludes) as well as a fake version (using the less potent and cheaper diazepam). Most of the drugs were exported to Florida where Obront and other Quebec mobsters had relocated. In 1987, police raided two secret laboratories that were manufacturing the counterfeit pills in Quebec, resulting in the confiscation of approximately one million diazepam tablets, as well as 34 kilos of diazepam powder, which could have produced several million more tablets. The RCMP estimated that between 1981 and 1986 these two pill factories supplied the United States with approximately 13.5 million counterfeit methaqualone tablets.

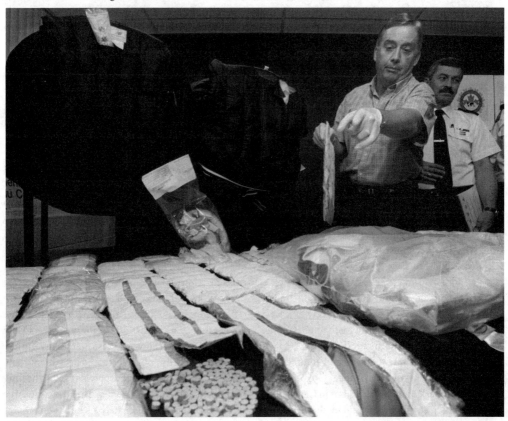

RCMP Staff Sergeant Bill Matheson and Superintendent Ben Soave display ecstasy pills and body-packs seized from two passengers arriving at Pearson airport in Toronto on May 17, 2000.

By the early 1990s, Canadian law enforcement agencies began intercepting imports of a new "designer drug" that had already gained widespread popularity in Europe. The pharmacological name of the drug is methylenedioxymethamphetamine, but it is commonly referred to by its abbreviation MDMA and is best known by its street name —"ecstasy." Ecstasy comes in a pill form and generally contains between 70 and 120 milligrams of MDMA. The profit margin for MDMA is extremely high: during the mid-1990s, one ecstasy pill that sold for $35 to $40 cost about fifty cents to $2 to produce. Throughout the decade, most of Canada's supply of MDMA was imported from the Netherlands and Belgium by couriers arriving on commercial air flights. In 1999, seven separate seizures at Pearson airport in Toronto netted 12,925 pills. In February 2000, two Hamilton teenagers arriving on an Air Canada flight from France were caught at Pearson body-packing more than 34,800 pills. Another 73,000 pills were discovered following searches of five people returning to Canada from France between January 15 and February 1, 2000. On May 4 of the same year, 144,000 ecstasy pills were discovered at Montreal's Dorval Airport stashed inside computers that had arrived on a cargo jet from Belgium. On May 17, 2000, the RCMP at Pearson airport found 170,000 tablets hidden in crude body-packs strapped to three passengers who had just flown in from Rotterdam. In December 2000, the RCMP seized another 150,000 MDMA tablets in Toronto that had been shipped via DHL from Brussels by an Israeli drug trafficking organization. The shipment was destined for the United States. In May 2001, almost 860,000 tablets were seized from an air cargo shipment to Canada declared as bedsheets.

In addition to imported ecstasy, Canadian police also had to contend with the domestic production of MDMA as well as "crystal meth," the street name for a popular new smokable version of methamphetamine. The rebirth of synthetic drug production in Canada in the late 1990s was due to intensified enforcement actions in the U.S., restrictions on the sale of precursor chemicals, the lack of such restrictions in Canada, the ease with which ecstasy and crystal meth can be produced, the high profit potential of both, the country's proximately to the large U.S. market, as well as the presence of criminal groups with plenty of experience in drug manufacturing. In June 1999, the RCMP dismantled a laboratory in Sainte-Julie, Quebec, that had sufficient chemicals to produce 750,000 MDMA tablets. In October of that year, police uncovered a laboratory in Chilliwack, B.C., with a potential to produce two million ecstasy tablets. A month later, two MDMA labs were discovered in Ontario, the first in a rural area near Hawkesbury and the second in a large apartment complex in Mississauga. Eight MDMA labs were discovered by Canadian police in 2000. Between November 2002 and July 2005, police dismantled seventeen labs in midwestern Ontario alone. In July 2003, police busted an ecstasy lab in the basement of a middle-class Scarborough home, confiscating 93,000 pills and more than 100 kilos of powder, which police believe was a combination of ecstasy and methamphetamine that could produce more than 800,000 pills. Later that summer, Canada Customs agents at the Port of Montreal found 260 kilos of MDMA powder, enough to produce 2.6 million pills. The discovery was made aboard a freighter that had originated in Belgium and was ultimately destined for B.C. A controlled delivery was made to Vancouver by rail and when it arrived on the west coast, police arrested its recipient, Chi Fai Leung, of Burnaby, who was charged with possession for the purposes of trafficking.

By 2005, illegal drug labs were being discovered across the country. "Clandestine laboratories, particularly those producing methamphetamine, continue to grow rapidly and are being reported in British Columbia, Alberta, Saskatchewan, Manitoba, Ontario, and Quebec," a September 7 RCMP press statement read. The RCMP noted that British Columbia has the highest concentration of illegal drug labs in Canada, followed by Ontario. On June 27 of that year, Vancouver police removed toxic chemicals from a methamphetamine lab located in a multi-million-dollar home in the affluent neighbourhood of West Point Grey. Inside, police found 85 litres of solvents, 40 litres of muriatic acid, 80 kilos of red phosphorous, along with heating equipment and condenser tubes. The lab was so large it could produce approximately 4.5 kilos of methamphetamine every twelve hours, according to police. Also in June, Calgary police made one of the largest ecstasy busts ever in that province, seizing 213,000 tablets worth about $4.25 million during a search of a home. The seizure was the result of an eight-month investigation that was initiated after police learned a shipment of ecstasy was coming to Calgary by land from Vancouver. The 250-milligram ecstasy tablets were laced with 20 milligrams of methamphetamine, which is supposed to increase the intensity of the high. In addition to the drugs, $25,000 cash, two stun guns, a semi-automatic rifle with a partially loaded clip, and body armour were seized from the residence. One thirty-two-year-old man, Hui Xu (a.k.a. Phillip Tu), was charged.

In its 2005 *International Narcotics Control Strategy Report*, the U.S. State Department declared that the sharp increase in the production of ecstasy north of the border had created conditions "for Canada to become a major U.S. supplier of this dangerous drug." According to the State Department, criminal groups prefer to locate their ecstasy labs in Canada because, unlike the U.S., there is no requirement to register pill presses, which are imported legally from China and the United States into Canada. Federal penalties for ecstasy offences in the U.S. are also much harsher than Canadian criminal penalties. The growing frequency of ecstasy seizures by American authorities at Canadian border crossings only corroborates the State Department's contentions.

Between January and May 2005, American customs agents along the Washington State border seized more than 500,000 doses of ecstasy that were being smuggled in from B.C. This amount was nearly double the 258,026 pills seized in 2004 and more than ten times the 2003 total of 47,686. On May 9, 2005, two Indo–Canadian men from Abbotsford were arrested after they attempted to smuggle 48,000 ecstasy pills across the border. "Most of the actual movement of the goods is done by Indo–Canadian organizations, either on their own as little freelancers or as subsidiaries to either the [Hells] Angels or some of the more structured Indo–Canadian groups," a U.S. border services official told the media. On June 12, American border agents in Washington State arrested a man and a woman and seized 167,000 ecstasy pills that were being smuggled in a pickup truck. On June 23, 2005, two Quebec men were arrested in New York State

with 350,000 ecstasy tablets and 15 kilos of cocaine. According to the Drug Enforcement Administration, the two men were part of an organization that was "providing ecstasy directly from the source and going to wholesale distributors in the New York City area." On August 1, 94,000 ecstasy tablets were discovered in a car driven by a Windsor man that was entering the U.S. through the Detroit-Windsor Tunnel. On August 12, another 204,000 pills were intercepted entering the U.S. by ferry from Walpole Island. By the end of 2005, approximately 2.4 million MDMA tablets were seized at U.S. border points in New York, Michigan, and Washington. "The continuing rise in domestic Ecstasy production has given Canada an increased role as a source country in both the domestic and international markets," the RCMP wrote in its 2005 drug intelligence report. "This was confirmed in 2005 by escalated cross-border MDMA trafficking from Canada to the United States and overseas smuggling of MDMA and methamphetamine, particularly to Japan and Australia."

Ecstasy smuggling to the U.S. did now slow in 2006. In January, American border officers charged two seventeen-year-old Canadians after 5.3 kilos of the drug was found in their vehicle as they crossed the B.C.–Washington State border. In February, a thirty-nine-year-old man from Lillooet, B.C, was arrested at the Sumas, Washington, port of entry when American officials found 51,000 ecstasy pills in the spare tire of his car. On March 16, U.S. agents at the B.C–Washington State border searched a truck with B.C. plates and discovered 671,000 tablets of ecstasy and 375 kilos of marijuana hidden inside 128 industrial drums. On May 5, three men were taken into custody at the Peace Arch crossing in Washington State, after border officials found three bags containing 75,000 multicoloured ecstasy pills hidden under the back seat of a southbound vehicle. In June, Illinois State Police charged a fifty-seven-year-old Guelph man with transporting 50,000 ecstasy pills. A state trooper discovered the drugs after stopping him for a traffic violation. According to a court affidavit, the man told authorities he was paid $20,000 to bring the drugs from Canada into the U.S.

While Canada has been a source for illegal chemical drugs since at least the early 1970s, even the recent spike in the production of ecstasy and methamphetamine cannot compare with the country's largest and most profitable illicit cash crop: marijuana. By the end of the 1990s, there were thousands of marijuana "grow operations" in the country and the number only increased in the new millennium. And these were not simply mom-and-pop gardens that contained a few plants. According to a 2002 RCMP report entitled *Marihuana Cultivation in Canada: Evolution and Current Trend*, "every year, several multi-thousand plant operations are discovered, both indoor and outdoor." Profit is the most obvious attraction. With a "comparatively small initial investment, the grower can potentially reap profits of well over $1,000,000 within the first year for an operation capable of producing a few hundred plants of high quality marijuana about every three months," the report says.

For much of the 20th century, Canada has imported most of the cannabis consumed in the country. According to RCMP estimates, of the foreign marijuana seized in or en route to Canada in 1999, at least 5,535 kilos came from Jamaica, 825 kilos came from South Africa, and 860 kilos came from Mexico. In recent years, however, Canada has not only become self-sufficient in marijuana, it has become an exporter to the United States. As a 2005 RCMP report states, "the Canadian marihuana market is supplied predominantly by domestically cultivated products. The exportation of Canadian grown marihuana is much greater than any marginal importation of foreign marihuana. As a result, there is no important source country, other than Canada itself, for marihuana found on the Canadian market." While cannabis has been cultivated in Canada for several decades, by all estimates production has exploded in recent years. RCMP figures indicate that from 1994 to 2002, the amount of domestically grown marijuana seized in Canada grew by more than 600 percent (from 6,472 to 54,372 kilos), a statistic that is reflective of both the growth in production and increased enforcement attention. In 2003, the RCMP estimated the annual production of marijuana in Canada to be at least 800 metric tons (approximately 5 million plants).

Marijuana production is now a major industry in Canada, generating billions of dollars a year in revenue and employing thousands of people. In 2001, British Columbia's Organized Crime Agency estimated the marijuana cultivation industry in that province is "a $6 billion annual cash crop." In a 2004 study entitled *Marijuana Growth in British Columbia*, Stephen Easton, a professor of economics at Simon Fraser University, wrote that there were as many as 17,500 grow operations in the province in 2000. While Canada's westernmost province has long been the epicentre of pot production in the country, cannabis cultivation has spread to other provinces. A study prepared for the Ontario Association of Chiefs of Police suggests that indoor marijuana grow operations in that province increased by more than 250 percent between 2000 and 2002. In 2002, Ontario was home to as many as 15,000 cultivation operations, producing marijuana worth up to $12.7 billion (ranking it as the third-largest agricultural crop in the province). Between September 8 and 19, 2003, a police task force in eastern Ontario seized more than 12,000 marijuana plants.

The proliferation of marijuana grow operations throughout Canada is due to a number of factors. These include the relatively low level of capital required to begin operations, an exceptionally high profit potential, a large and receptive consumer market — both domestically (Canada ranks fifth in the world in per capita marijuana consumption and first among industrialized nations, according to the 2007 United Nations *World Drug Report*) and internationally (due to its proximity to the largest drug-consuming country in the world) — the introduction of and advances in cultivation technology, the internationally recognized quality of Canadian-grown pot, and the relatively lenient penalties for marijuana offences in this country.

The entry of established organized criminal groups into the Canadian marijuana industry has also bolstered the production, distribution, and export of domestically grown pot. In the early 1970s, the Royal Commission on the Non Medical Use of Drugs concluded that the Canadian marijuana market at that time was "loosely organized" and "largely free of professional criminal involvement." Today, marijuana production in Canada has become what the RCMP calls "a staple for all crime groups." In 1996, police raided a warehouse in a suburban Montreal industrial park that housed a hydroponic facility with 11,000 plants in full bloom. This installation was traced to the

Rockers, a motorcycle gang affiliated with the Hells Angels. While there is little doubt that biker gangs are involved in this profitable enterprise, they may in fact be second to Asian crime groups in terms of the number of grow operations and quantities produced. Vietnamese groups have been particularly active in establishing grow operations in urban and suburban residences. They are highly organized and control all aspects of the business, including locating, renovating, and equipping homes for cultivation; operating hydroponic stores and nurseries to supply the necessary equipment, seeds, plant clones and fertilizers; employing crop sitters; and distributing the final product. In more recent years, Chinese criminal syndicates have been linked to some of the largest outdoor grow operations in the country and are seen as a major force behind the escalation of Canadian-grown pot being smuggled into the U.S.

Unlike most traditional cannabis-producing countries — such as Mexico, Colombia, Jamaica, Cambodia, or Vietnam, where tropical temperatures provide ideal outdoor growing conditions — the majority of Canada's marijuana crops are raised indoors. In addition to providing ideal year-round growing conditions, indoor "grow ops" also avoid the need for large plots of land, which enhances privacy. As importantly, indoor pot producers have taken advantage of specialized horticultural technology and cloning methods that have led to a rise in the potency of the drug. Canada is now internationally renowned for producing a powerful yield of marijuana popularly known as "BC Bud," "Canadian Gold," or "Canadian hydro."

While most indoor grow operations are housed in the country's urban centres, there has been an exodus to the suburbs, where growers can take advantage of large homes to accommodate bigger crops. Houses have been custom built or modified to accommodate large grow operations. A Criminal Intelligence Service Ontario report describes the housing preferences of a typical suburban marijuana producer. First, the home should be at least 2,000 square feet in size. The inside of the home should be unfinished to accommodate the rewiring that is needed to hook up the 1,000-watt lights and other electrical equipment as well as the electrical bypass system commonly used to steal the large amounts of required power. A fireplace is also preferred to vent the telltale odour from the high concentration of plants and a large, attached garage is mandatory to conceal the loading of vehicles used to tote the harvest away. Once the grow operation is set up, a "crop sitter" — often a recent immigrant who may bring along his family to avoid suspicion by neighbours — is paid a nominal wage to tend to the plants. A typical suburban grow operation produces around five hundred plants every quarter with a total retail value of close to $2 million.

As the scale of individual grow operations expanded, the trend has been to move away from residential homes to industrial spaces that can accommodate larger operations. The sheer size of marijuana grow operations has reached "unprecedented levels," the RCMP observed in 2002. The largest pot farm ever found in Canada was located in a former Molson Brewery in Ontario. On January 12, 2004, police raided this farm, seizing 30,000 marijuana plants in various stages of production. The pot factory (which one attending officer called "little Saskatchewan") operated twenty-four hours a day and was capable of producing as many as three or four crops annually that could be worth as much as $100 million. Plants covered more than 60,000 square feet of space and hundreds of thousands of dollars were spent to convert the old brewery, including the addition of dormitory-type living quarters for up to fifty workers. Many of the plants were maturing inside twenty-five beer vats that had been turned into hothouses with the installation of a thousand high-powered lights and

Indoor marijuana grow operation found by police in a former Molson Brewery in Ontario

a filtration system that pumped fresh air into the vats and then removed the unmistakable skunk-scented air, which was filtered and then sent into a separate self-contained room. A month later, police in Edmonton raided a warehouse where they found a grow operation with more than 5,600 plants. The warehouse had an electrical system that regulated 212 grow lamps, supported by two additional electrical transformers. Six people, all from British Columbia and all of Chinese descent, were arrested at the scene. At the end of the year, Winnipeg police uncovered what, at the time, was the second-largest grow op found in Canada in a warehouse only two blocks from downtown police headquarters. A predawn raid on December 2 ended with the seizure of over 10,000 plants.

By 2003, police began discovering grow operations in more remote locations. On September 19, 2003, Canadian military police showed reporters 783 mature cannabis plants they had seized from a field located midway between Montreal and Quebec City. The land is owned by the Department of National Defence and is used as an ammunition-testing ground. In November, RCMP officers seized 3,600 marijuana plants and 1.6 kilos of dried pot from an elaborate grow operation in two underground bunkers, 30 kilometres west of Dawson Creek in B.C. In October 2004, sixteen people were arrested in connection with a major grow operation in the tiny community of Seymour Arm, at the north end of Shuswap Lake in B.C. police discovered 20,000 marijuana plants located in attics, basements, and bunkers, some of which were capable of holding more than 5,000 plants at a time. "We figure that just over half of the residents were involved in this well-organized criminal enterprise," an RCMP spokesperson told the media. Sûreté du Québec officers carried out one of the largest marijuana seizures in the province's history on June 23, 2005, when they discovered 17,000 plants in a farmer's field. Two men police believe were linked to a Chinese crime group were arrested. The location of the grow op on farmland signalled a new trend in which organized criminal groups were buying big, cheap, vacant farms located in more northerly parts to be used to grow their cannabis crops. In addition to the secrecy that remote properties provide, the warm summer days and cool nights allow for excellent growing conditions. Producers have even enriched the clay soil, while new strains have been tested to determine which ones grow best in the northern climate. Outdoor crops also allow for economies of scale in that a large amount of pot can be harvested from relatively inexpensive farmland, compared to the smaller yields grown indoors in expensive urban and suburban homes.

The high potency of Canadian marijuana has inevitably led to increased demand in the United States. The result, as a 2001 American National Drug Intelligence Center report succinctly states, is that "Canada is increasingly becoming a source country for high-grade marijuana to the United States." While the quantity of Canadian pot imported into the U.S. is estimated at only one-fifth of what comes from Mexico, there has been a steady rise in exports from Canada. This is reflected in an increase in the quantity of Canadian pot seized in the U.S.: from 2,235 kilos in 2000 to 9,487 kilos in 2002. In its 2004 annual report, the White House Office of National Drug Control Policy concluded, the "marijuana Americans smoke comes from three main sources: U.S. outdoor and indoor cultivation, Mexican outdoor cultivation, and high-potency indoor cultivation from Canada." The report estimates that on an annual basis, Mexico supplies approximately 5,000 metric tons, 2,500 metric tons are grown domestically in the U.S., with roughly 1,000 tons coming from Canada.

The great demand for potent Canadian cannabis in the U.S. results in a substantial increase in its price as soon as it crosses the border. As a 2000 report by the DEA states Canadian-produced cannabis "sells for $1,500 to $2,000 per pound in Vancouver. Smuggled to Bellingham, Washington, the price increases to about $3,000; if brought to California, it can sell for as much as $6,000. In New York City, Canadian marijuana has sold for up to $8,000 per pound. DEA officials in Portland, Maine, report that high potency Canadian-grown marijuana is sold in the region at up to five times the price of domestic and Mexican marijuana." The inflated price fetched in the U.S. contributes to greater profits for producers and distributors, which in turn has led to increased production in Canada and the smuggling of larger amounts across the border. (The only comparable price markup in Canada is by the federal government. Documents released in April 2007 show that Ottawa applies a 1,500 percent premium on the medical marijuana it sells to sick patients. While the feds pay its licensed suppliers $328.75 per kilo, those with prescriptions to purchase small amounts from the government end up paying the equivalent of $5,000 per kilogram. As *Maclean's* magazine editorialized, "the government is charging criminal street rates for providing pot to the sick, and yet it continues to argue that legalizing and regulating the pot trade would be a terrible affront to the nation's morality.")

At the end of June 2006, Canadian and American police dismantled one B.C.-based smuggling network that used remote mountainous locations as staging points for helicopters and airplanes transporting thousands of kilos of B.C. marijuana to Washington State and hundreds of kilos of cocaine into Canada. Code-named "Frozen Timber," the two-year investigation ended with the seizure of 3,640 kilos of ma-

rijuana, 365 kilos of cocaine, three aircraft, and $1.5 million in American cash. Six people were arrested in Canada while forty arrests were made in the U.S. The key Canadian figure in the smuggling ring was Daryl Desjardins, who according to police, was subcontracted by several criminal groups, including the Hells Angels, the Montreal mafia, Indo–Canadian gangs, and Asian crime groups, to ferry the drugs between the two countries. Desjardins was arrested in a Bell Jet Ranger helicopter on May 10 after allegedly transporting 150 kilos of pot across the border. Desjardins was convicted of smuggling and trafficking in a B.C. courtroom and sentenced to four and a half years. In a less sophisticated smuggling operation, three men were arrested by DEA agents who had been monitoring the efforts of the trio as they toiled for eight months digging a 110-metre tunnel that ran from Aldergrove, B.C., to Lynden, Washington. The

Photograph released by the U.S. Drug Enforcement Administration showing a cart in the 110-metre tunnel built under the Lynden/Aldergrove border crossing

tunnel was constructed using shovels, a mechanical winch to raise and lower cartloads of drugs, and a sump pump to drain off water. It was wired for lighting and its walls were reinforced with concrete, steel, and about 1,000 two-by-six-inch wood supports spaced two inches apart. The cost involved in building the tunnel and acquiring the property on both sides of the border was in excess of a million dollars, which led police to believe it was funded by at least one well-heeled criminal organization. The men were arrested in Bellingham, Washington, after they had transported 42 kilos of marijuana through the tunnel. The tunnel was later filled in by government contractors.

Farther east along the border, the Buffalo Niagara region has become a major distribution point for Canadian marijuana, according to the DEA. In the first two and a half months of 2004, U.S. Border Service agencies made forty-nine seizures of Canadian pot totalling 1,930 kilos. In all of 2003, a mere 504 kilos was confiscated in ninety-nine separate seizures. One of the biggest hauls was at the Peace Bridge border crossing at Niagara Falls on February 13, when four Toronto-area men were arrested after 581 kilos were seized from a tractor-trailer. Five days later, three other men were charged with trying to smuggle 228 kilos into Buffalo sealed in vacuum-packed bags stuffed inside boxes marked as coffee.

THE "KLONDIKE OF ORGANIZED CRIME"

While Canada was quickly establishing itself as a net exporter of cannabis and synthetic drugs, it remained highly vulnerable to the illegal import of a wide range of legal goods. It was not until the late 1980s and early 1990s that the scope of contraband smuggling into and out of Canada would rival that of the cross-border liquor trade during Prohibition. By 1993, there was between ninety and one hundred million cartons of contraband cigarettes in the country, representing around 40 percent of the $12.4 billion Canadian cigarette market. Contemporary tobacco smuggling can be traced to February 1991, when the Canadian government increased the excise tax on the domestic sale of cigarettes by 140 percent. This was followed by a number of provincial tax hikes. No similar tax increases were imposed on Canadian tobacco products that were destined for export, however.

This resulted in a substantial difference between the price of exported Canadian cigarettes and those sold domestically, prompting a massive outburst in tobacco smuggling that typically began with the lawful export of tax-exempt Canadian cigarettes to the United States and the illegal repatriation of these exports into Canada. Between 1991 and 1993, cigarette exports to the United States rose 824 percent. Most of these exports were smuggled back to Canada and then distributed through networks of wholesalers, legitimate retail outlets, and street vendors, who sold them for far below their legitimate market price. In 1990, the estimated retail value of contraband tobacco products seized by law enforcement agencies in Canada was $17.2 million. By 1993, this had climbed to $53.4 million.

The evasion of duty and taxes created an irresistibly high profit margin for black market cigarettes. Research conducted in 1998 by the consulting firm KPMG stated that one case of a thousand cigarettes smuggled into Canada across the New York–Ontario border had a landed cost of $636. When transported to British Columbia, the same case could potentially sell for up to $1,750. The profit potential attracted a diverse range of individuals and groups to a smuggling trade that became increasingly organized, sophisticated, and voluminous. Like the illicit liquor traffic during Prohibition, one of the most prominent features of contemporary tobacco smuggling was the central role played by well-organized groups and networks, including outlaw motorcycle gangs, Asian crime groups, aboriginal smuggling brokers and transporters, and Eastern European organized crime.

According to an indictment filed in a New York State court, an eight-month sting operation by Canadian and American police known as "Operation Orienteer" uncovered a cigarette and liquor smuggling network that earned US$687 million between 1992 and 1996. Larry Miller, the man behind the immense smuggling operation, personally conducted $78 million in cash transactions during these five years, according to a forensic audit. He was making so much money that he purchased a Learjet for $2.5 million to commute between his homes in Las Vegas and Massena, a small town in upstate New York.

Massena is strategically located for smuggling between Canada and the U.S., due to its proximity to the border and, more important, to the Akwesasne native reserve, which had become the single-largest smuggling flashpoint along the border. In 1994, RCMP commissioner Norm Inkster said that as much as 70 percent of the contraband tobacco entering Canada was coming through Akwesasne. Populated by the Mohawk nation, the 14,000-acre reserve has the unique distinction of straddling the U.S.-Canada border, making it ideally suited for smuggling. The reserve's territory actually falls within five jurisdictions — Canada, the United States, Ontario, Quebec, and New York State— and agreements have been negotiated with federal, state, and provincial officials in both countries that uphold the right of the Mohawk people to cross the borders that cut through the reserve without being impeded by any government.

These factors, combined with a well-honed smuggling infrastructure, has meant that a variety of contraband, drugs and weapons, cross through the reserve, with resident smugglers constantly shifting products based on demand and profitability. For years, Akwesasne was a funnel for firearms illegally entering Canada from the U.S. and also served as a storage and distribution centre for weapons sold to criminal groups in Ontario and Quebec. In recent years, Akwesasne has also become what one district attorney with New York's northern office called "the most significant source of alien smuggling across the northeast border." Officials with the U.S. Border Patrol Agency estimated that in 1999, between three hundred and five hundred illegal migrants a month were being smuggled from Canada into the U.S. through the reserve. In December 1998, U.S. attorney general Janet Reno announced that Canadian and American law enforcement agencies had broken up the largest immigrant smuggling conspiracy ever uncovered on America's northern border. "Operation Over the Rainbow II" targeted a migrant smuggling scheme jointly undertaken by Chinese and Mohawk criminal groups that ferried as many as 150 people a month from Mainland China to Canada, and then through the reserve, before ending up in New York City. The price of a one-way ticket was as much as $47,000 and the smuggling enterprise raked in an estimated $170 million. The reserve has attracted the attention of numerous

smuggling groups and other criminal organizations, native and non-native alike, turning it into what a senior police official from nearby Cornwall called the "Klondike of Organized Crime." In addition to Chinese crime groups, other criminal beneficiaries of the reserve include the Montreal mafia, Vietnamese marijuana traffickers, the Russian Mafiya, Indo–Canadian gangs, and members of Hells Angels. As a Mohawk grand chief once opined, "On their maps, the gangsters put a pin at Akwesasne, and said, 'This is where it's easiest to cross.'"

At the centre of the smuggling activity on the Akwesasne reserve is the Mohawk Warrior Society, which began as a paramilitary organization and is best known for its militant actions in the name of the Mohawk people. The society gained national attention in Canada when it led a sixty-seven-day armed standoff with Canadian police and the military during the Oka Crisis of 1990, a land dispute that pitted the Mohawk nation against the town of Oka, Quebec, and which resulted in the death of a Quebec provincial police officer. The transformation of the Warrior Society from a political, paramilitary movement to a criminal organization began when some of its members started providing security for native criminal entrepreneurs who began exploiting the reserve's strategic position. The money generated from this new vocation helped the society purchase an arsenal of weapons, while convincing some members to become directly involved in smuggling themselves. The Mohawk Warriors' contention that status Indians are not subject to any form of taxation on tribal land and are entitled to unfettered access across the international border, combined with their view of tobacco as a spiritual substance, helped rationalize their entry into the cigarette smuggling trade, which began in early 1988.

The man who profited the most from Akwesasne's unique geopolitical location was Larry Miller, a thin, silver-haired, chain-smoking, American businessman from Las Vegas. Through a company called LBL Importing Ltd., which Miller incorporated with two brothers from Buffalo named Lewis and Robert Tavano, cigarettes were imported into the U.S. from Canada tax free and then smuggled back across the border through the reserve. At the height of his smuggling operation in 1995, Miller had an average of twenty-six tractor-trailers packed with contraband cigarettes crossing the border every day. Most of the smokes imported by LBL were the popular Canadian brand Export "A," which was produced by RJR-MacDonald, of Canada, a subsidiary of RJR Reynolds based in Winston-Salem, North Carolina. Police later learned that the management of the parent company and its Canadian subsidiary conspired with the Miller organization. A subsidiary of RJR-MacDonald, called Northern Brands International, was incorporated, and Leslie Thompson, a director of Canadian sales for RJR, was appointed to work with Miller to export the tax-free cigarettes to the U.S. and then smuggle them back to Canada. Northern Brands sold tax-free Export "A" to LBL and another Miller-connected company. Canadian and American customs authorities were told that the cigarettes would be stored in bonded warehouses on the American side of the Akwesasne reserve and then legally transported to Estonia and Russia. Instead, they were smuggled into Canada.

During its first year in business, Northern Brands was earning an average weekly profit of US$1.3 million, making it the single most lucrative unit of RJR Reynolds. Les Thompson later claimed in an interview on the CBS news program *60 Minutes* that more than five billion cigarettes from RJR-MacDonald and its new subsidiary went to warehouses on the Akwesasne reserve every year, and at one point, 60 percent of RJR's business in Canada was from the sale of contraband cigarettes. Thompson said executives at RJ Reynolds appointed him to oversee the smuggling scheme and were well aware of the illegal operation.

In 1995, Operation Orienteer, a joint task force of American, Canadian, and Mohawk police, had undercover police officers posing as smugglers work out a deal to transport truckloads of Miller-supplied liquor and cigarettes from the U.S. to Canada. The operation culminated in June 1997, when police in both countries laid close to five hundred charges against forty-five people. As part of its indictments, the U.S. Justice Department estimated that assets targeted for seizure in the U.S. from the Miller organization were worth US$583 million. Larry Miller was arrested in July 1997 in Syracuse on charges of conspiracy to defraud, aiding and abetting smuggling, and money laundering. At the time of his arrest, he faced another

forty charges in Canada. In the end, nearly two dozen people were convicted of smuggling, racketeering, fraud, and money laundering in American and Canadian courts. In December 1999, Miller was sentenced in a U.S. court to twelve and a half years in prison and agreed to forfeit to the government up to $160 million in personal assets, including his $1.5-million share in a Russian casino. Also sentenced that month was Leslie Thompson who received five years and was fined $20,000. Among the others convicted was Miller's thirty-three-year-old son, Nicholas, who, in an Ottawa courtroom, was handed a conditional sentence of two years less a day, and former Mohawk tribal chief L. David Jacobs, who was sentenced to twenty months in U.S. federal prison for accepting bribes and kickbacks from Miller. In December 1998, Northern Brands International Inc. pleaded guilty to conspiracy offences in the United States and was fined $15 million.

On the basis of these convictions, the government of Canada filed a US$1-billion lawsuit on December 21, 1999, against RJR-MacDonald Inc. and several related companies claiming they conspired with smugglers to defraud governments in Canada of billions of dollars in tax revenue from 1991 to 1995. The lawsuit, which alleged that company executives authorized the smuggling conspiracy, was filed in U.S. Federal Court in Syracuse under the auspices of the *Racketeer Influenced and Corrupt Organizations Act*, legislation that was created to prosecute organized crime cases. In June 2000, a district judge threw the case out, concluding that the Canadian government was using the U.S. courts to collect taxes that had been evaded. The Canadian Department of Justice appealed the decision, arguing that the defendants had broken U.S. racketeering laws. In December 2000, an appeals court in New York affirmed the lower court's dismissal of the Canadian lawsuit. In the face of these setbacks, the Canadian government shifted course, and in February 2003, the RCMP laid six counts of fraud and one count of conspiracy against JTI-MacDonald (the subsidiary of Japan Tobacco Inc. that had purchased RJR-MacDonald in 1999) and eight of its former executives. In August 2003, the federal government renewed its effort to recoup its lost cigarette taxes, this time through the Canadian court system, when it launched a $1.5-billion civil suit in Ontario Superior Court against JTI-MacDonald and more than ten other companies. By 2006, one former vice-president of sales for RJR-MacDonald from the early 1990s was convicted and sentenced to eight months of house arrest resulting from the RCMP investigation. In the summer of 2008, the tobacco companies pleaded guilty to federal charges and were forced to pay $1.5 billion in criminal fines and civil penalties.

When Canadian taxes on tobacco products were lowered in 1994 in an attempt to steer cigarette buyers away from the black market, liquor once again became the commodity of choice for contraband smugglers. Like most other goods smuggled into Canada from the U.S., the illegal liquor market was the result of a substantial difference in the price of booze between the two countries (approximately 80 percent of the price of liquor in Canada is taxes versus an average of 40 percent in the United States). During the early 1990s, the RCMP and Canada Customs were seizing tractor-trailers containing as much as 1,700 cases of liquor. Based on this volume, liquor that would cost between CDN$23,300 and $36,666 in the United States would have a street value in Canada of between $223,333 and $253,333. The Liquor Control Board of Ontario estimated that during the first half of the 1990s, one in ten bottles of booze in the province was contraband, leading to an underground liquor economy worth around $644 million annually. In Quebec, one in every three bottles of liquor sold in the province was believed to be untaxed. In addition to the U.S., the French islands of St. Pierre and Miquelon also continued to be a big supplier of illegal liquor for Quebec and the Maritime provinces. Once in the country, the booze is dispersed through a network of bootleggers who sell it to individuals and to bars and restaurants. In 1992, Ontario liquor inspectors charged 179 bars with selling illegal liquor and that number jumped to 368 in 1993.

In 1997, Gary Nicholls, the former president of a transport company, was jailed and fined $1 million for running what police called the largest liquor smuggling operation since Prohibition. Nicholls got into the trucking business in 1992 and it wasn't long before he was illegally transporting truckloads of liquor, purchased from U.S. distillers, wholesalers, and bars, into Canada. He avoided duties and taxes by claiming the imported liquor was ultimately destined for Europe. Once in Canada, thousands of cases were diverted to bonded warehouses and then sold to middlemen. The operation involved an intricate series of smuggling networks from the east to the west coasts of both the U.S. and Canada, with individual participants specializing in such areas as liquor purchases, transportation, financing, marketing, distribution, bribery, the forgery of customs stamps, and money laundering. Police discovered that between 1992 and 1994, Nicholls brought 180 truckloads of black market liquor into Canada for a profit of $6 million, while avoiding approximately $12.7 million in Canadian duties and taxes. The cocksure Nicholls — who owned a bar in his hometown of Barrie, Ontario, called Smuggler's Cove, and drove around in a luxury car with vanity plates that read "SMUGLR" — once confided to a friend that he had more than $1 million stashed in a bank account in the Cayman Islands.

One of the single-largest liquor seizures in Canadian history occurred in May 2000, when more than 40,000 cases of booze, worth an estimated $8.4 million, were confiscated in Niagara Falls. Canadian and American law enforcement agents also confiscated several modified vehicles used by the small but highly organized ring of smugglers who snuck thousands of cases of cheap American liquor into Canada at border crossings in Niagara Falls and Fort Erie. The liquor was purchased from stores in Maryland and transported to warehouses in Niagara Falls, New York. From there, the cases were smuggled into Canada in trucks with heavy-duty shock absorbers and overinflated tires to conceal from customs officers that the trailers were filled with hundreds of full 1.75-litre bottles. Police said the smuggling group made up to twelve crossings a week. The liquor was then distributed to bars and clubs in Southern Ontario.

Contributing to the large contraband market for booze are the numerous illegal stills that have been set up throughout Canada. The more sophisticated underground distilleries pass off the homemade booze as popular American and Canadian brands, complete with counterfeit labels. In January 1999, Montreal police made their largest-ever seizure of raw alcohol when they opened the back doors of two tractor-trailers at an east end warehouse and discovered 36,000 litres of 96.3-proof alcohol, packed in eighty black metal barrels. Police believed its black market value was around $3 million. A subsequent investigation showed that the raw alcohol had been transported from Europe and was part of a smuggling operation with links to Russian organized crime. Police received a tip on the shipment a month earlier and tracked it from the Maltese Islands in the Mediterranean Sea to New York. It was then transported by truck across the border to Montreal.

As in the past, the illegal entry and exit of drugs, cigarettes, booze, and other smuggled goods has in some instances been assisted by corrupt workers at Canada's official ports of entry. Nowhere is this more apparent than at the country's three largest marine ports in Montreal, Vancouver, and Halifax. Corrupt border officials and dockworkers were active at the ports during the height of opium and liquor smuggling during the 1920s and also lent a helping hand when heroin was smuggled through the ports of Montreal and Vancouver beginning in the 1940s. A 1968 probe commissioned by the Montreal Port Council surprised few when it revealed that the waterfront had been infiltrated by the local mafia clan. By 1998, the Criminal Intelligence Service Canada wrote that criminal organizations were "firmly entrenched in all major Canadian seaports and are responsible for the bulk of the contraband entering Canada through the ports":

> It is usually accomplished through the placement of criminal members, associates, relatives, and friends in legitimate employment positions at the port. This presence allows criminal organizations to acquire valuable knowledge of import and port procedures and to monitor law enforcement activity at the port. Associates in key positions facilitate the movement of contraband into the ports and ensure that it remains concealed until it can be removed and distributed on the contraband market. They also facilitate the theft and diversion of legitimate imported goods and assist

in the export of illegal goods, such as stolen vehicles, from Canada to other countries.

In its 2001 annual report, the CISC reported that "major crime groups such as outlaw motorcycle clubs, Asian crime groups, East European-based criminal organizations and Traditional organized crime have developed long-term alliances or temporary deals to jointly use their connections at any North American marine port to initially move contraband into one country and subsequently either way across the U.S.-Canada land border."

Corruption linked to organized crime has also been discovered at Canadian airports. Separate drug investigations in 1996 and 1998 at Toronto's Pearson airport resulted in the arrests of baggage handlers and a terminal supervisor who were on the payroll of Colombian cocaine traffickers. An internal review of security clearances granted to airport workers undertaken by Transport Canada in 2004 discovered seventy-three cases deemed suspicious or incomplete enough to forward to the RCMP for further investigation of possible criminal ties. The audit of the clearances granted to 131,000 "air side" employees, like baggage handlers, caterers, security guards, cleaners, and shop workers, was ordered in March of that year after the federal auditor general reported that as many as 4,500 airport employees and sixteen airport businesses may have direct or indirect ties to "biker gangs, organized crime and drug trafficking." In July 2007, eleven people were charged in connection with drug smuggling at Pearson airport. Police told the media that the group, which was smuggling cocaine, ecstasy, marijuana, and cash through the airport, had operatives working inside the airport and used their security-cleared positions to move drugs and money to and from Canada. A 2008 intelligence report by the RCMP entitled "Project Spawn" assessed the extent of criminal activity and organized crime infiltration of Canada's eight largest airports. The assessment revealed that between January 2005 and August 2008, 1,326 people had been identified as being involved in criminal activity at the airports. Of this total, 298 were airport employees. The report concludes, "organized crime is clearly present at Canada's Class 1 international airports. The facilities are susceptible to criminal exploitation and infiltration, particularly at the major international airports that receive frequent flights from either source or transit countries for various types of contraband."

THE MOTHER OF ALL SNAKEHEADS

In addition to legal and illegal merchandise, people are one of the most profitable "commodities" smuggled across national borders, making migrant smuggling one of the fastest-growing and most profitable organized criminal enterprises in the world. For years, Canada has been seen as a sanctuary for illegal immigrants, in part because most anyone who lands here can immediately claim refugee status and then access the country's social services. But while Canada may be a destination country for some immigrants entering the country illegally, it is mostly used as a transit point for those who wish to covertly enter the United States.

Beginning around 1983, immigrant and law enforcement agencies in Canada began noticing a sharp increase in organized migrant smuggling into the country. According to that year's annual report from the Criminal Intelligence Service Canada, the groups carrying out people smuggling "vary from small, informally organized networks that smuggle a few people each year, to large, well-structured organizations which operate at the international level and are involved in smuggling hundreds of people annually." By 1992, the agency reported, "organized crime groups have a wide and varied base of operations in Canada and abroad which are utilized for the smuggling of illegal immigrants. Many of these groups are international, ethnic based crime groups who use their connections in foreign countries to relocate their associates to Canada." Around this time, police and immigration officials in B.C. were investigating at least three illegal alien smuggling groups in the province, each of which catered to a different ethnic group. Among them was a smuggling ring that was responsible for the movement of between eighty and one hundred Indian and Trinidadian nationals into Canada and then the U.S. A report by the Canadian Association of Chiefs of Police stated that the illegal migrants were flown from their home countries to Toronto, where they were met by someone who arranged their airline passage to Vancouver. Once on the west coast, the illegals were met by a driver who took them, in the early hours of the morning, to unmanned sections of the Canada-U.S. border. After they crossed the border, a driver transported them to an airport in Seattle. From there, they flew to Los Angeles and eventually to Miami, Florida. The principal in this smuggling ring, a Miami travel agent, supplied his clients with counterfeit green cards for a fee of $4,500. Other investigations in 1991 revealed the existence of smuggling rings that transported Haitians, Sri Lankans, and Somalis into Canada while supplying them with fake passports and visas. Upon arrival, the immigrants claimed refugee status. Another New York–based criminal group was facilitating the smuggling of Polish nationals through New Brunswick into the U.S.

A 2005 federal study, entitled *Illegal Migrant Smuggling to Canada*, estimated that 12 percent of people who arrived in Canada without proper documents between 1997 and 2002 were directly linked to an "escort" or "facilitator" (someone who provided services including a travel document, air ticket, safe house or referral to people smuggling contacts). "Canada has emerged as a preferred destination in the human smuggling marketplace," according to the report. The study says migrant smugglers promote Canada as a preferred destination by highlighting its generous immigration regime, the ease with which refugee status can be claimed, and strong odds of refugees obtaining citizenship.

Human smuggling syndicates have been known to charge their clients anywhere from $500 to $50,000, depending on the destination, the distance, and the range of services offered. Smuggled migrants are brought to Canada aboard airliners, passenger ships, and even in cargo containers, while most of those choosing to go on to the U.S. are taken across unmanned land border crossings. The source countries for illegal migrants entering Canada are located in every corner of the world, from Asia to Eastern Europe, the West Indies, Africa, and the Middle East. However, the vast majority entering Canada come from the southern provinces of China. Since at least the early 1990s, the largest human smuggling operations affecting Canada have been carried out by organized Chinese syndicates.

One of the biggest migrant smuggling rings using Canada as a transit point to the U.S. was headed by a diminutive grandmother from the Fujian province named Cheng Chui Ping. Known as the "Mother of All Snakeheads," or more commonly as "Big Sister Ping," she reportedly turned a small migrant smuggling sideline involving a few friends and relatives into a multi-million-dollar empire. In conjunction with other smugglers, she transported thousands of people out of China to Hong Kong, Thailand, Belize, Guatemala, Mexico, Africa, Canada, and eventually to New York City from the mid-1980s to the early 1990s. Ping was one of the first Chinese "Snakeheads" — a term used to denote a migrant smuggling organizer — to transport large numbers of illegal migrants by boat. She even moved from China and set up her headquarters in Manhattan, where she began working with members of the local Fuk Ching triad. Ping also integrated extortion and human trafficking into her smuggling operations by turning the more destitute illegals into hostages, indentured slaves, and prostitutes until they could pay their transportation fees. In 2005, Ping was convicted in the U.S. on charges that included conspiracy to commit alien transportation, money laundering, and trafficking in ransom proceeds. She was sentenced to thirty-five years in jail.

Artist rendering of Cheng Chui Ping at her sentencing hearing in March 2007

With the precedent set by Ping, migrant smuggling has increasingly been tied to "human trafficking," which the United Nations defines as "the recruitment, transportation, transfer, harbouring or receipt of persons, by means of the threat or use of force or other forms of coercion, of abduction, of fraud, of deception, of the abuse of power or of a position of vulnerability

or of the giving or receiving of payments or benefits to achieve the consent of a person having control over another person, for the purpose of exploitation." Canada is both a destination and transit country for criminal groups that lure thousands of people from overseas with the promise of jobs and an escape from poverty. Once in the country, they toil in slave-like conditions, while young women may be forced to work in strip clubs or brothels. "Canada is a destination for persons trafficked into prostitution, and, to a lesser extent, forced labour, with victims coming primarily from China, Thailand, Cambodia, Philippines, Russia, Korea, and Eastern Europe," a 2003 U.S. State Department report on human trafficking concluded. "Traffickers also use Canada as a transit point for moving victims from these countries to the United States." The State Department estimates that between 1994 and 2003, at least 15,000 Chinese entered Canada illegally, "many of them paying thousands to smugglers only to end up working as indentured servants or prostitutes." Vancouver and Toronto are seen as hubs for organized crime groups that traffic in people.

As part of the many international human smuggling and trafficking operations, thousands of foreign women are recruited or forced by organized criminal groups to work as sex trade workers in Canada. In March 2000, the RCMP infiltrated a multi-million-dollar prostitution ring in Southern Ontario that, over a four-month period, smuggled as many as 280 Korean women into the U.S. where they were forced to work in massage parlours in Los Angeles and New York. The next month, following raids at Toronto-area strip clubs, police brought 650 criminal charges against more than two hundred men accused of pimping hundreds of women from Eastern Europe, Latin America, and Asia. In 2001, an undercover operation in Vancouver uncovered a prostitution ring that was importing Malaysian women into the city. Police found eleven women, ranging in age from seventeen to thirty, living and working in two apartments furnished only with mattresses in the living rooms and bedrooms, and bathrooms, containing nothing but toilet paper, mouthwash, and condoms. At least five of the women told Vancouver police that their boyfriends in Malaysia had brought them to Canada on the promise of a vacation. The boyfriends turned out to be recruiters for an international network of human traffickers. Once in the country, they had their passports taken from them and each were sold for an estimated $15,000 to a local prostitution ring. The women were then locked in primitive brothels and forced to service as many as fifteen men a day. The rise in Canada's migrant sex trade in the new millennium is partially blamed on a 1998 decision by the federal government that gave a blanket exemption to foreign exotic dancers to work in Canada. Under a "labour mobility program," temporary work permits were issued mainly to women from Eastern Europe to fill the demand for the dancers in the country. This ruling was made despite repeated concerns voiced to the federal minister of human resources that it facilitated the trafficking of women.

The coupling of migrant smuggling and human trafficking points to the broader role of organized crime in the prostitution trade. It is difficult to gauge the extent to which prostitution in Canada is organized and how much of it is freelance. Police have investigated province-wide and even national networks of pimps that ship prostitutes between different cities and provinces. A CIA report released in 2000 identified a gang in B.C. called the West Coast Players that specialized in prostituting Canadian teenagers locally and in Southern California. On May 15, 2003, police in Quebec announced the arrest of forty-four people following a widespread investigation into teenage prostitution that was allegedly controlled by a street gang called the Wolf Pack. Police said the gang had links to members of Hells Angels, who took a cut of the profits. Police arrested seventeen suspected gang members, seventeen suspected clients, and ten others. According to a Canadian Press report:

> Gang members allegedly recruited young girls at teen hangouts like video arcades, malls, and high-school dances. The girls were lavished with praise, jewellery and other gifts until they fell in love, police say. They eventually had sex — some of them for the first time — with the gang members, who then slowly lured them into sleeping with other men, police said. The teens earned up to $100,000 a year and all of it often went to their pimps, authorities allege. Once they turned 18, they were booted

out of the prostitution ring, police say. The gang was believed to have 20 girls working for them at any given time.

The Hells Angels and other motorcycle gangs have long been involved in the trafficking of women, not only as prostitutes, but also as exotic dancers, which is exercised through their control of agencies that represent strippers and through investments in hundreds of strip bars, massage parlours, and escort agencies. In Montreal alone, there are close to four hundred escort agencies advertising their services in the Yellow Pages or at the back of newspapers. As described by a 2003 *Montreal Gazette* article, the industry is made up of a close circle of operators, some of whom have ties to organized crime groups, and who employ "an ever-changing cast of characters, with the call girls themselves acting essentially as freelancers who move easily from one agency to another." A typical rate for an "escort" in Montreal is $125 to $200 an hour, with the agency collecting about from 40 to 60 percent. The ownership structure of some agencies "is a bewildering maze of shell companies, fronts of varying sophistication, and short-lived businesses." Many of the companies are registered to nominees, who are used because they have no criminal past, and addresses provided in incorporation documents are invariably fake.

"IT HAD TO BURN"

The recent rise in human trafficking and the sexual-slave trade is indicative of another trend in the world of organized crime: a renewed emphasis on criminal activities that prey on society's most vulnerable people. This trend is epitomized by the growing trade in child pornography, which has become ever more organized, widespread, and profit driven since the advent of the Internet. Frauds that target the unprotected, the trusting, the naive, and the greedy have also become much more prevalent, organized, and sophisticated. When counterfeiting is incorporated into the mix, the variety of fraud schemes perpetrated against individuals, companies, and governments is sweeping. The range of activities includes cheque kiting, bank card fraud (theft and counterfeiting of credit and debit cards), deceitful telemarketing, stock market manipulation, advance fee fraud, fake lotteries and sweepstakes, tax fraud, insurance fraud, bankruptcy fraud, marriage fraud, adoption fraud, advance fee fraud, pyramid, Ponzi and other deceptive get-rich-quick schemes, identity theft, and the counterfeiting of currency, government documents, computer software, digital entertainment, electrical appliances, clothes, batteries, toys, auto parts, and thousands of other consumer products.

Since the start of the 1990s, fraud schemes carried out by criminal groups have increased dramatically in terms of their frequency, variety, the number of victims fleeced, the amount of money scammed, as well as their economic and social impact. In November 2004, the U.S. Federal Trade Commission released the results of a survey that suggests that nearly 25 million Americans — 11.2 percent of the adult population — were victims of some type of fraud. Consumer fraud complaints made to the commission in 2003 increased by 73 percent over 2002. According to the Association of Certified Fraud Examiners, fraud and abuse cost American organizations more than US$400 billion annually. While comparable figures are not available for Canada, industry, government, and law enforcement organizations like the Canadian Bankers Association, the Competition Bureau of Canada, and PhoneBusters have all gathered statistics indicating the rise in numerous forms of fraud in this country.

One reason accounting for this increase is the more organized nature of contemporary fraud scams. Police cases have shown that well-established criminal groups carry out various types of frauds, but are particularly dominant in bank card fraud, advance fee fraud, identity theft, and counterfeiting. Not only are more Canadian citizens, companies, and governments being robbed, but Canada has gained a reputation as an enclave for organized fraud and counterfeiting schemes, leading the *Edmonton Journal* to proclaim, "international gangs and cosmopolitan criminals have turned Canada into a billion-dollar stage for sophisticated scams."

A worrisome common denominator in many modern swindles is the theft of a victim's personal information. Since the start of the 1990s, there has been a substantial escalation in the theft and unauthorized use of names, birth dates, addresses, credit card information, social insurance numbers, and other personal information. This information is then used by criminals to open credit card and bank accounts, obtain mortgages, acquire driver's licences, passports, and other government documents, redirect mail, or to rent or purchase vehicles. In other words, while the theft of personal information is a serious crime in itself, it also facilitates other profit-oriented crimes, like credit card fraud, mortgage fraud, and illegal immigration. Identify theft has become so prevalent that some insurance companies are now offering policies that will pay the costs that victims incur as they try to fix credit histories ruined by imposters.

In March 2006, more than one hundred people in the Ottawa area were victimized by an identity theft ring that used an online employment advertisement to lure people into submitting resumés. Those who responded to the ad received official-looking letters and e-mails indicating they had been selected as candidates for a $70,000-a-year job as a "programmer analyst" and that they should submit an application form with a $20 processing fee. The application forms asked for the full name, social insurance number, driver's licence number, and a mailing address. Those behind the fraud used this personal information to obtain more than sixty credit cards, driver's licences, and social insurance cards in other people's names. At least $500,000 in charges was made on the phony credit cards issued in the victims' names.

The theft of personal information is one reason why credit card fraud has skyrocketed in recent years. According to the Canadian Bankers Association, the number of Canadian credit cards used fraudulently has risen sharply since statistics were first kept in 1983. From a low of 19,200 that year to 32,851 in 1990, the total number of "fraudulently used" cards escalated to 146,310 in 2003. Financial losses to banks and credit card issuers have also risen substantially: from $17.4 million in 1983 to $201 million in losses for a 12-month period ending in June 2005. Canada has one of the highest per capita losses from credit card fraud in the world, while Toronto is considered an international epicentre for the counterfeiting of bank cards.

The rapid growth in bank card fraud began in the early 1990s, the same time that major criminal organizations began counterfeiting credit and debit cards. In its 1992 annual report of the Criminal Intelligence Service Canada wrote, "infractions against the credit card industry are increasing at an alarming rate. Major organized crime groups are largely responsible for the theft and fraudulent use of credit cards. Criminals of Asian descent, particularly from Hong Kong, account for a large percentage of crimes again the credit card industry." Sophisticated criminal groups have transformed the nature of credit card fraud, and by doing so have contributed to the rise in the number of victims and financial losses. Organized criminals do not physically steal credit cards from wallets and purses, but produce authentic knock-offs, which results in much higher dollar losses compared to thefts (primarily because consumers usually do not find out about the charges until they check their monthly statements). The most lucrative type of credit card fraud is the production of altered or newly embossed credit cards, according to the 1992 report of the Canadian Association of Chiefs of Police, "Organized crime groups involved in this activity are highly sophisticated organizations with worldwide networking in place. Credit cards produced in Toronto may be embossed with information received from one part of the world then forwarded to another part of the world for illegal purposes." Chinese criminal organizations are at "the centre of activity for most credit card related offences" and are the biggest players in producing and distributing forged and altered credit cards. In addition, fake credit cards produced abroad are taken to Toronto where they are sold in lots.

Counterfeit credit cards are usually encoded with personal and banking information from victims who have had that information stolen from them. A common method of obtaining this information is called "skimming," a term that refers to the theft of the account information from the magnetic strip on the back of a victim's credit or debit card. Skimming begins when a customer's bank card is swiped through the card reader at a retail store. The person behind the counter, who is complicit in the theft, then swipes the card again through a small computerized reader under the counter and out of the customer's view (alternatively, the point-of-sale card reader may be tampered with to record the banking information). The data is downloaded onto a laptop computer and is later retrieved and encoded on to a counterfeit credit or debit card, which is produced in the thousands by legally purchased credit card–embossing machines. In February 2002, an international credit card skimming and counterfeiting ring based in Calgary was cracked following a fifteen-month investigation by fourteen government agencies. More than 450 criminal charges were laid against sixty-three people, including members of a Chinese crime group based in Calgary. Electronic data was stolen from thousands of legitimate credit card users at more than 116 retail merchants across North America. Gang members would then emboss this information on blank cards. The fake credit cards, which were perfect in every detail, were then sold through the criminal group's extensive international network of contacts for between $500 to $1,000 each. The fraudulent cards were found in at least thirty-four countries. Police discovered eight well-equipped counterfeit credit card factories in Calgary, Edmonton, Toronto, and Greater Vancouver.

Debit cards are equally susceptible to skimming and counterfeiting. In June 2006, police in Montreal busted a debit card fraud ring that may have victimized as many as 18,000 people. More than forty stores in the Montreal area were fitted with modified Interac keypads that recorded data from debit cards and which were being run by cashiers who were members or associates of a street gang that had ties to a larger criminal organization behind the operation. Debit cards issued by one bank were targeted and police later learned that an employee working at a call centre for the bank was supplying the fraud ring with personal information on clients that had swiped their cards through the illegal keypad. Almost $2 million had been drained from the accounts of the bank's customers. That same month, police in Durham, Ontario, busted a counterfeiting operation that targeted debit card users at a local restaurant. With the assistance of a restaurant employee, a debit payment machine was rigged to steal information from bank cards while a pinhole camera was concealed in the ceiling to film victims as they entered their PIN number. Two men were arrested early one morning after police watched one of them climb a ladder and reach into the ceiling tiles to retrieve the video equipment. Later that day, Durham police executed a search warrant at a home and recovered blank debit cards as well as five pinhole cameras, instruments for reading and writing credit card data, computer hard drives, and thousands of credit and debit card numbers. They also seized cash and a fake Canadian citizenship card.

In addition to skimming cards though point-of-sale terminals, automatic teller machines are also subject to tampering to extract data from bank cards. In a typical scheme that was carried out at a bank in Halifax in 2003, a narrow electronic card reader was inserted into the ATM slot where debit cards are inserted. After a number of cards had been inserted into the ATM, the crooks retrieved the electronic skimmer, downloaded the information onto a computer and then embossed it onto fake debit cards that were used at other ATMs. The Interac Association in Canada estimated that $70.4 million had been stolen as a result of debit card skimming in 2005, up from $60 million in 2004 and $44 million in 2003. Eastern European crime groups are among the biggest perpetrators of debit card fraud in Canada.

Bank card forgery is an extension of an underground industry that has historically flourished in Canada: currency counterfeiting, which can be traced as far back as the 1840s, continued into the next century, and picked up steam in the postwar years. During the 1930s, Aldor Tardif was considered one of the biggest currency counterfeiters in Quebec and was convicted several times. In 1937, the RCMP tracked him down when they received a tip from a spiritualist, who had been consulted by a client (Tardif) wanting to know if it was safe to continue producing counterfeit money. Around the same time, the RCMP was investigating a gang in B.C. that was involved in forging postal orders. A member of the gang would purchase a post office money order in the amount of one dollar. The money order was then treated with a chemical solution to erase ink. Once the original ink was gone, the money order was rewritten for a larger amount, usually $40 to $55.

Counterfeiting became a more serious problem in the postwar years as advances in offset printing, copying, and graphic arts attracted the attention of the criminal element. In 1963, RCMP commissioner C. W. Harvison told journalist Alan Phillips that counterfeiting has increased tremendously. "Ten years ago we investigated about twenty cases a year. Today

it's about two thousand." The larger counterfeiting networks of the day employed dozens of people, each of whom specialized in a particular function, such as developing the plate, obtaining the proper paper, printing the currency, or "pushing" the fake product. Since the late 19th century, currency counterfeiting has been centred in Montreal. By the early 1960s, according to Phillips, there were three large counterfeiting groups located in the city, "one in the east end; one in the west and one downtown." The groups ran off "sample proofs for their backers, the men who finance new issues, who give them the go-ahead for the run. Paper and ink are usually bought through some other firm, or hijacked. The plate is destroyed and the counterfeit, 'the bundle,' is cached. When the backer has held it long enough to feel sure it will not be traced — and the longer the surer — the organization goes into action." Once it left the printers, the forged cash was provided to distributors who passed it along to their "pushers" or "passers" who put the bills into circulation, mostly by purchasing small-ticket items. To protect the organization, each participant was isolated from the other; the pushers did not know the printer, or vice versa, making it difficult to trace the fake currency back to its source. The pushers, Phillips wrote, "all begin at the same hour, work a weekend, perhaps only two hours, then leave town." The west end Montreal group specialized in American twenties, fifties, and hundreds, while the east end group specialized in American twenty-dollar bills and was known to send their pushers to Winnipeg and Vancouver, as well as Ohio and as far away as Switzerland. After being nabbed by Vancouver police, one of the pushers escaped, but he tried to jump a picket fence during his getaway and impaled himself. The midtown Montreal group turned out ten-dollar bills and used freelance distributors. "They flooded the west in 1960, and in 1961 they hit Vancouver, Calgary, Regina, Winnipeg, the lakehead, and points between," Phillips wrote. "Their bills turned up in Newfoundland, Maine, Jamaica, and California, and are still coming in. At the lakehead a pusher, Conrad Brunelle, was arrested. A businessman from Montreal flew out and put up his bail."

In addition to currency, during the 1960s and 1970s counterfeiters were also busy producing forged postal money orders, travellers' cheques, stock certificates, bond coupons, racetrack betting slips, company cheques, birth certificates, driver's licences, registration blanks, and licence plates. In a 1969 memo entitled "Mafia (Cosa Nostra) U.S.A.," the RCMP documented a connection between Italian crime groups "in Windsor, Detroit, Michigan, and Sicily in the transporting of counterfeit currency." Among those under investigation were Sicilian crime boss Caesar Badalamenti and New York mafioso Joseph Bonanno, as well as Pietro DiLorenzo and Vincenzo Mazzola, who were convicted in Detroit for possession of counterfeit currency. Both men were also related to Montreal businessman Giuseppe Saputo, who had sponsored the entry of Joseph Bonanno into Canada in 1964. The memo states that Italian tourists brought over to Canada were used to smuggle Canadian-produced counterfeit American currency to the U.S and Italy. DiLorenzo and Mazzola smuggled $1 million in fake U.S. bills to Sicily in May 1962 in the trunk of Mazzola's Buick.

Currency counterfeiting began to escalate further in the 1990s, due in part to the widespread availability of personal computers, desktop publishing systems, digital imaging devices, colour printers, as well as the new-found ability of more sophisticated counterfeiters to replicate security features. By 2001, a rash of counterfeit money was in circulation in Canada, prompting several large Canadian retailers to stop accepting hundred-dollar bills. The five people arrested in Windsor on counterfeiting charges in July 2001 typify the new generation of forgers; from their operation, the RCMP seized personal computers, printers, chemicals, and paints for placing the optical security devices on the bills, as well as heat-stamping machines for embossing the notes to give the impression of raised printing.

In May 2006, Peel Regional Police shut down a major counterfeiting ring that churned out more than $2.4 million in fake Canadian money. After raiding a small warehouse located inside a Mississauga industrial park, police found a 1960s-vintage German printing press, which had been adapted to place the silver foil strips down one side of the fake $20, $50, and $100 bills, and which was capable of producing thousands of pages of counterfeit banknotes a day. Police also seized five guns, including a sawed-off shotgun used to rob

a Canadian Imperial Bank of Commerce branch in 2005, ammunition, bulletproof vests, computers, inks, papers, a hot stamp press, dies, foils, thirteen point-of-sale terminals, pinhole cameras, DVD recorders, credit and debit card readers, and forged credit cards. More than 10,000 debit and credit card numbers were also found stored in seized computers. Thirty people were arrested and charged with 469 criminal counts. Among those arrested were five men and an eighteen-year-old woman police alleged were behind the CIBC robbery. Also arrested were a number of young women who were hired to push the fake money by purchasing merchandise from major retail stores, which would then be returned for a refund. A month later, police in the York Region, just outside Toronto, arrested six people who produced and circulated 70,000 bills adding up to $2 million. The raid turned up five presses used to make the bills as well as another $400,000 that had yet to be put into circulation. Investigators also found materials and equipment to make phoney debit, credit, social insurance cards, and driver's licences. All of those arrested were between the ages of twenty-two and twenty-four.

Organized crime groups are also heavily involved in product piracy — the counterfeiting of consumer goods. In a 2006 report, the International Anti-Counterfeiting Coalition wrote that the "low risk of prosecution and enormous profit potential" has attracted organized crime to the product counterfeiting industry. In addition to credit cards, Chinese criminal organizations are extensively involved in pirating computer software and digital entertainment products, plus transporting counterfeit products out of China into North America using well-established drug smuggling networks. Chinese crime groups have also flooded Canada and other countries with counterfeit cigarettes. In December 2003, police in Toronto raided a warehouse and found cheap cigarettes from China that had been placed in forged packages of popular Canadian brands. Police estimated the street value of the cigarettes at $2.6 million. Also found in the warehouse was a small amount of ecstasy and approximately five hundred pieces of counterfeit designer clothing.

The International Anti-Counterfeiting Coalition claims that the Canadian market in forged products is worth between $20 billion and $30 billion annually. They also accuse Canada of doing little to stop the illegal industry. In 2003, the United States Trade Representative put Canada on its Special 301 Watch List, which designates countries deemed by the U.S. as failing to provide adequate protection or enforcement of intellectual property rights. Another international group — the Congressional International Anti-Piracy Caucus, a bipartisan committee of U.S. legislators formed to address product counterfeiting — placed Canada on a list of nations that are the world's top sources of pirated copies of movies, CDs, and software. Other countries on the list include China, Russia, Mexico, India, and Malaysia. In its 2006 Country Watch List, the congressional committee contended, "Canada's piracy situation deteriorated in 2005 with increased unauthorized camcording and piracy by 'street vendors.' Canada has become a source of camcorder piracy, which is quickly distributed via thousands of counterfeit DVDs circulated throughout the world. Pirated entertainment software remains widely available in legitimate retail establishments, many of which also offer console circumvention devices and services. Canada's lax border measures appear to permit the importation of pirated products from East Asia, Pakistan, and Russia."

Deceitful telemarketing — a term used to describe a range of activities in which the telephone, fax machines, e-mail, and the Internet are used to fleece victims of money or property through deceit, high pressure sales tactics, and falsehoods — is another pervasive type of organized fraud in Canada. For the Competition Bureau of Canada, deceptive telemarketing is "spreading like a plague." PhoneBusters, an Ontario-based call centre for suspected telemarketing fraud, estimates that "on any given day, there are 500 to 1,000 boiler rooms operating in Canada" grossing between $1 billion to $5 billion annually. Some of the top telemarketing scams in the world, according to the National Consumers League in the United States, are phoney prizes and sweepstakes (the promise of a prize, which never materializes after a fee has been paid), advance fee fraud (a promise to transfer large amounts of nonexistent cash following the payment of an upfront fee), business opportunities (for which highly exaggerated promises of profits are made), and loans or credit cards (empty promises of personal or business loans or credit cards requiring payment of fees in advance).

Telemarketing fraud is nothing new, although up until the 1980s it was mostly restricted to pushing shares in speculative stock through high-pressure sales tactics and deceit. While most of these "boiler-room operations" were legally licensed brokerages, they clearly existed on the wrong side of the business ethics divide. In a 1937 article entitled "Swindlers on Rampage," the *Financial Post* cites examples of "some of the high-pressure selling being conducted from Toronto." In their attempt to capitalize on the mining boom at the time, the shady brokerage operations were the "most pernicious of all the factors making for an unhealthy market situation." Behind these operations are "men whose reputations are so notorious, that they dare not let their presence in Toronto be publically known." By the 1940s, Toronto had become infamous as the new North American capital for boiler-room operations. "That Ontario has become the hang-out and happy hunting ground for the stock shyster and racketeer is clearly the opinion held by many Securities Commissioners in the United States," the *Financial Post* reported in a 1944 article. "Ontario is now regarded as the main plague spot of North America so far as securities selling is concerned." The problem continued after the war, as Alan Phillips summarized in a 1963 *Maclean's* article, "Canada's post-war mining boom had spawned a species of con men who trade on U.S. interest in our new strikes. These stockateers sell shares in worthless bushland known as moose pasture by telephone campaigns so high-pressured the offices they originate in are called boiler shops." The "elite among these gentry," Phillips wrote, are "the promoters, men who put up the capital, set up the company structure, and manipulate the price of shares on the market. These are men of sharp intelligence, sound financial training, and a clear perception of human cupidity." By the early 1950s, the Ontario Securities Commission was successful in cracking down on the shady brokerage firms, but many just fled to Montreal. The result, according to Phillips, was that, by 1955, "Montreal had become a haven for sixteen boiler shops, each paying ten percent of their take to the syndicate, who had provincial authorities on their payroll."

That "syndicate" was the Cotroni mafia group, which had its hand in numerous boiler room operations in Quebec. Some were set up by Willie Obront and his partner, Harry Workman, who gained a foothold in the fly-by-night brokerage industry by taking over existing firms. They particularly targeted those that had a good reputation, but were floundering and receptive to new partners. As the Quebec Police Commission on Organized Crime wrote in 1977, "To organize a high-pressure sales operation the promoter needs to have absolute control over a brokerage firm approved by the Quebec Securities Commission. With this end in view, Harry Workman, through Ronald Golden, advanced $1,000,000 to Eddy Brown, owner of a brokerage firm which was experiencing some financial problems." This arrangement gave Workman control over Brown's privately owned Castle Securities Limited, which he turned into a high-pressure sales operation. On the front lines of Workman's boiler room were "qualifiers," men who phoned potential clients (most of whom were chosen from telephone books), promising innocuous information on the stock market. Those who agreed to receive more information were sent two or three letters that appeared to be unbiased, but actually pushed highly speculative stocks of companies that were giving kickbacks to Workman. The "qualifiers" were also responsible for collecting information about those who expressed interest, which was entered on cards that were forwarded to salesmen. The salesmen then called the potential client and tried to sell a small number of shares to get their hooks into a client. If an initial sale was made, a more experienced salesman or "loader" called the client to unload even more shares through high-pressure sales tactics. When questioned before the Quebec Police Commission, one of Workman's managers, Andre Robitalle, explained the role of the "loader":

Q:　　In plain English, a loader was another salesman, probably more skillful than experienced, who was responsible for exactly that, overloading the client?

Robitalle: That's right.

Q:　　Using high-pressure sales techniques.

Robitalle: That's it.

Q:　　To build up a head of steam, no more, no less?

Robitalle: Yes, sir.

Q:　　Hence the expression the "boiler room"?

Robitalle: That's right.

Q:　　The whole thing had to heat up?

Robitalle: It had to burn.

After reviewing the files of 177 clients of one of Workman's loaders, the commission concluded that fifty-seven had purchased 32,675 shares after refusing to buy more. Some were forced to purchase even after they made repeated requests to sell and to have their accounts closed. A letter from one angry client presented before the commission summed up the typical plight of the unsuspecting investor: "Today I received your note which says: we confirm that you have bought 2,000 shares of A.I.S. Resources Limited. I have never brought shares. I told you: I haven't any money. I authorized no one to buy any shares whatever in my name. I refuse this note because I haven't the money to make such a purchase. I return your note which was sent to me absolutely against my wishes. Signed A.H." In those rare situations where a salesman acquiesced and began selling a client's shares, only a small quantity would be sold over several weeks or months, so as not to weaken the market standing of the company.

By the end of the 1990s, Toronto police estimated there were about 150 telemarketing boiler rooms in the city. The RCMP in Montreal stated that at least fifty were located there, collectively generating around $60 million in revenue annually. In May 2001, Steven Baker, an official with the U.S. Federal Trade Commission in Chicago, told the media that Canada was the source of more than one-quarter of the telemarketing fraud in the U.S. cross-border telemarketing fraud had become so widespread that in 1997, Canadian prime minister Jean Chrétien and U.S. president Bill Clinton agreed to establish a binational working group to study the problem. The result of the study was the establishment of a multi-agency task force and the secondment of an FBI agent to the RCMP's Commercial Crime Section in Toronto. In November 2001, the task force dismantled one of the biggest fraudulent telemarketing operations in the country when twenty-five people were arrested following a raid on its operations in Laval, Quebec. The men behind the operation, Nayer Amhed, Gary Gacionis, and Vasilios Kolitsidas, were charged with fraud, conspiracy, and participating in a criminal organization. The investigation was launched after hundreds of senior citizens, mostly American, complained they were bilked of up to $50,000 each. The scam, which took in up to $1 million a week, had the suspects posing as lawyers, police officers, and customs agents to convince elderly victims, who had already lost money to fake lottery scams, that they had recovered their lost winnings. To collect the money, however, the victims were told they had to send in thousands of dollars for fees and taxes. Many of the victims' names were on a list of "repeat offenders" who routinely played bogus lotteries and were known as easy prey. During one month in 2001, the telemarketers made 1,971 calls and received or were about to receive money from 533 victims, including 117 victims who had sent in more than $1.2 million. The twenty-five people arrested either pleaded guilty or were convicted. The reputed architect behind the operation was Denis Morin-Baribeau, who was convicted in a Massachusetts courtroom in 2003 of two counts of telemarketing fraud and wire fraud and sentenced to ten years. Baribeau allegedly had ties to the Quebec Hells Angels.

On October 5, 2004, U.S. attorney general John Ashcroft announced the arrest of more than 135 people worldwide in what he called the most extensive multinational enforcement operation ever directed at deceitful and fraudulent telemarketing organizations. Dozens of separate investigations led to the discovery of around five million victims, who suffered losses totalling $1 billion. Police arrested more than one hundred people in the United States, while an additional thirty-five were arrested in other countries, including Canada. In Illinois, three Toronto residents were indicted on twenty-four counts of mail fraud, wire fraud, and conspiracy for their alleged role in a telemarketing operation based in Toronto. Known as "First Capital," they charged people with poor credit between $189 and $219 for a credit card that never arrived. Approximately 35,000 people were fleeced out of approximately $7 million. A Nigerian citizen was extradited to the United States for his alleged role in a Vancouver-based group of Nigerian nationals who operated a fraudulent lottery scheme that targeted elderly U.S. residents. Prospective victims were told they had won a Canadian lottery and were directed to send taxes and processing fees to Canada. Approximately 1,700 people lost more than $3 million.

The Vancouver-based operation was one of hundreds run by Nigerian crime groups, which generally specialize in e-mail-based telemarketing schemes. As the Internet became more widespread during the mid-1990s, the public and police began to notice unsolicited e-mails, supposedly from Nigerian government officials or businessmen, requesting help in stashing millions of dollars of stolen government or corporate money. The advance-fee fraud typically entails a mass solicitation that is sent out via e-mail to potential victims whose e-mail address has been "trolled" from the Internet. The message claims to be from an official with the government or a large private sector institution in Nigeria, such as a bank or an oil company, who is requesting an urgent and confidential business relationship. The targets are promised that a large sum of money (often in the tens of millions of dollars) will be deposited into their bank account. In return, the recipient of the e-mail is offered a percentage of the total amount that purportedly will be wired from Nigeria (or another African country). The funds that are purportedly to be deposited in a target's account are frequently described as money that must be quickly and surreptitiously transferred out of an African country due to a number of reasons, such as a civil war, bankruptcy fraud, an unclaimed bank account or inheritance, or the embezzlement of money from a government or business. Regardless of the specific claim, the source of the funds is frequently held out as illegally derived. This tactic is used to increase the credibility of the offer (capitalizing on the well-known corruption in African countries) and to deter any victims who accept the offer from going to police due to their own perceived complicity in an illegal transaction. The solicitation will ask the prospective victim to respond to the e-mail, providing his or her name, address, phone number, and banking information. Subsequent correspondence will ask for a "processing" fee from the target before the money can be transferred. This fee is often in the tens of thousands of dollars. Once the processing fee is deposited, the funds are quickly withdrawn, and the perpetrators either disappear or attempt to coax even more money from the victim. Some schemes have gone so far as to have victims fly to an African country, where even more money is extorted from them through intimidation and violence.

Criminal groups have not only brought the get-rich-quick scam to a new level, they are also turning "unorganized" crimes like auto theft, into well-organized, sophisticated, and transnational operations. Beginning in the mid-1980s, auto theft in Canada began to increase steadily, which according to a 1998 RCMP intelligence report entitled "Project Sparkplug," is "largely attributable to the fact that increasingly sophisticated organized crime groups have flooded the stolen car market." Approximately one in five cars stolen in Canada can be traced to organized groups, according to 2002 study by Statistics Canada. Criminal organizations in Canada are involved in the theft of mostly new luxury cars, which are exported to foreign markets where profits are high and the chances of being detected are low. As the RCMP note, "organized crime groups are involved in every process of auto theft for export, from placing orders for specific makes/models/years, commissioning the thefts, counterfeiting the identity of the cars and accompanying paperwork, transporting the cars out of province, as well as arranging for their illegal export out of the country." Auto theft for export includes several stages, which may occur in different parts of the country. A car stolen in Manitoba, for example, may be driven to Ontario where it will be given a counterfeit vehicle identification number, licence plates, and ownership information and then taken to a port in Montreal where it will be transported via marine containers for shipment overseas. Organized auto theft is perpetrated by outlaw motorcycle gangs and Eastern European crime groups, as well as other networks of criminals that have come together specifically to steal and export cars. This includes a network of Middle Eastern thieves operating in Quebec that police allege have funnelled their profits to terrorist groups.

Organized auto theft often works on a network basis with a specialized division of labour: established crime groups work through middlemen who delegate the theft to street gangs or criminals who specialize in auto theft. These specialists include young offenders who have been recruited expressly to protect the upper levels of the theft ring by hiding behind the more lenient youth criminal justice penalties if they are caught. The network may also include people who are responsible for dismantling the vehicle, altering the Vehicle Identification Number, or exporting the vehicle overseas. Montreal has become the auto theft capital of Canada partly because of the presence of a number of criminal groups that take advantage of the city's ports to ship stolen vehicles abroad. In 1995, police blamed Russian crime syndicates, working closely with local auto theft rings, for the theft of hundreds of luxury cars from Montreal streets. The operation was dismantled following the seizure of eleven stolen cars found in a marine container on the waterfront, just before they were to be shipped to Europe. Police also located five more marine containers full of stolen cars that had already reached Belgium. The Russian criminals would place orders with Montreal-based car thieves for up to one hundred vehicles at a time that were ultimately shipped overseas to intermediary countries like Belgium, Germany, and Finland before ending up in Russia. In 2001, two other men linked to Russian crime groups, Igor Stepanchikov and Rotislav Serniak, were charged with thirty-nine counts of theft, conspiracy, fraud, and counterfeiting related to the theft of more than 120 cars from around the Greater Toronto Area. Most of these cars were transported to marine containers, taken to various ports, including Halifax, loaded onto ships, and then delivered to Eastern Europe. As part of the investigation, police raided a storage facility in Greater Toronto where they discovered duplicated keys for stolen vehicles, blank counterfeit vehicle identification number plates, blank provincial motor vehicles permits, government-issued identification, counterfeit money and credit cards, equipment used to produce counterfeit credit cards, and more than $70,000 in Canadian and U.S. cash. Stepanchikov was charged in 1998 along with nine other people linked to Russian and Chinese crime groups after the RCMP broke up a currency and credit card counterfeiting conspiracy.

In April 2001, six Ontario and three American law enforcement agencies cracked a Lebanese auto theft ring that had stolen hundreds of cars, mostly from Toronto. Dozens of people were named in Canadian and U.S. arrest warrants, including nineteen in Ontario. In total, more than 250 criminal charges were laid in both countries. Police also recovered $7.9 million in cash and 193 stolen vehicles that were located as far away as British Columbia, Utah, and Ohio. After the cars were stolen from dealers' lots, private residences, and public parking lots, the VINs were changed and, in some cases, the autos were registered with new plates that were issued in the United States. The plates were brought to Canada where they were attached to the stolen vehicles, which were then driven to the U.S. As part of the investigation, police also confiscated more than 4,000 ecstasy tablets, along with fraudulent and stolen credit cards.

CHAPTER TEN

A STRANGE AND TERRIBLE CANADIAN SAGA

The Hells Angels and Other Outlaw Motorcycle Gangs

THE WILD ONES

The first-known motorcycle club to be formed in North America is said to be the McCook Outlaws, which was established in 1935 out of Matilda's Bar on old Route 66 just outside of Chicago. The origins of contemporary outlaw biker gangs, however, are generally traced to the period immediately following the Second World War as tens of thousands of American soldiers drifted back home. While reintegrating themselves into society, some began to reject the values of postwar America. War to them had meant exhilaration while America in the late 1940s and 1950s, had become boring, repressive, and conformist. One way to reproduce the adrenaline rush of combat was to ride a high-powered motorcycle, and soon the U.S. west coast became the mecca for ex-soldiers and other young men who roamed the highways on powerful motorcycles looking for excitement and adventure. According to Howard Abadinsky, the first postwar biker group dedicated to "mocking social values and conventional society through acts of vandalism and general lawlessness" was started by a group of army veterans from California and called the POBOB (Pissed-Off Bastards of Bloomington).

A seminal event in the early history of motorcycle gangs took place in a small town called Hollister, located outside of Oakland. On July 4, 1947, an annual motorcycle hill-climb race sponsored by the American Motorcycle Association grew violent, prompting local police to arrest a POBOB member for fighting. Hundreds of motorcyclists reportedly congregated to demand his release and when the local authorities refused, they rioted and tore up the town. The Hollister riot was later depicted in the 1953 film *The Wild One*, starring Marlon Brando, a movie of rebellion that helped fuel the outlaw biker phenomenon. Legend has it that the word "outlaw" was first applied to deviant and rowdy bikers by the sheriff of Riverside, California, which hosted a biker rally on the Labor Day weekend of 1947 that was also marred by drunken lawlessness. The AMA had become so repulsed by the black eye that gangs like the POBOBs was giving to mainstream motorcyclists that it publicly condemned them as only "one percent" of motorcycle enthusiasts. Revelling in their image as social outcasts, rebel bikers adopted the "one-percenter" moniker to distinguish themselves from the majority of motorcycle riders and, eventually, the rest of society. This label would signal the start of a concerted effort by "outlaw bikers" to cultivate a lifestyle and image that would give rise to a subculture dedicated to challenging the accepted norms and values of mainstream American society.

By the start of the 1950s, some POBOB members from San Bernardino had formed a new motorcycle club and adopted a name favoured by Second World War fighter pilots: the Hells Angels. In 1950, the first official chapter of the Hells Angels Motorcycle Club was founded up in Fontana, California, and halfway through the decade, the club had chapters and affiliate clubs in other towns and cities in the state, including Vallejo, Sacramento, Richmond, and the San Francisco Bay area. It also established a chapter in Oakland, which would later become the unofficial headquarters of the club. Around the same time, the McCook Outlaws changed its name to the Chicago Outlaws and eventually would become the Outlaws Motorcycle Nation. For years to come, the Outlaws MC was second only in size and power to the Hells Angels MC and the two would grow to become bitter enemies.

During its initial years, the Hells Angels and similar one-percenter clubs existed simply to seek adventure and to raise hell. There was no intent on becoming a criminal organization per se; the bikers just saw themselves as the last bastion of freedom within an increasingly repressive and conformist society. By the 1960s, the Angels began adorning their jackets with the club's official symbol: the grinning, winged death skull. By gilding their jackets with such defiant and repulsive patches as Nazi swastikas and others proclaiming "1%er," "FTW" (Fuck the World), "69" (as in the sexual position), and "coke" (as in the drug, not the soft drink), the outlaw bikers put their self-nurtured subculture on display to signal to the world that they had purposely cut themselves off from the majority culture. Within this subculture, there were also certain universal traits that the outlaw biker had to live up to: toughness, violence, sexual prowess, transience, and risk taking. Like the mafiosi, the one-percenters were all about bravado and portraying traditional masculine characteristics. The desired image was reflected in attire that began to emerge in the mid-1960s: the dirty and tattered leather jacket (cut off at the sleeves), grease-encrusted jeans, steel-toed boots, long, unkempt hair and beards, and skull-and-crossbones jewellery. Last, but not least, biker bravado was symbolized by the motorcycle, which had to be a big, loud, Harley-Davidson. Moreover, the motorcycle traditionally ridden by the outlaw biker could not be straight out of the factory; it had to be highly modified, a reflection of one-percenter status as well as each member's individuality and quest for nonconformity. As Hunter S. Thompson wrote in his classic 1967 book on the Hells Angels, "The outlaws tend to see their bikes as personal monuments, created in their own image, however abstract, and they develop an affection for them that is hard for outsiders to understand." In short, the modified Harley-Davidson motorcycle reflects the sacred principles of the outlaw biker: large, manly, nonconformist, individualistic, fast, adventurous, rebellious, phallic, and loud, yet staunchly patriotic (hence the American-made Harley).

The motorcycle is also a symbol of and a vehicle (literally) for a transient lifestyle that rejects the dreary stability personified by middle-class suburban existence. According to sociologist Daniel Wolf: "Outlaw bikers view themselves as nothing less than frontier heroes, living out the 'freedom ethic' that they feel the rest of society has largely abandoned. They acknowledge that they are antisocial, but only to the extent that they seek to gain their own unique experiences and express their individuality through their motorcycles. Their 'hogs' become personal charms against the regimented world of the 'citizen.' They view their club as collective leverage that they can use against an establishment that threatens to crush those who find conventional society inhibiting and destructive of individual character."

While the Italian mafia purposely disassociated itself from mainstream society by nurturing its own subculture, their self-ostracism pales in comparison to that undertaken by outlaw motorcycle gangs, whose antisocial dress and behaviour was a conscious expression of their contempt for civil society and their view that those in mainstream society are saps and suckers. This is best reflected in a comment made by Jean-Guy Bourgoin, a member of the Rockers, a motorcycle club associated with the Hells Angels in Quebec. When asked what he thought of regular "citizens," he replied, "I look at people who get up at 7, stuck in traffic for 10 bucks an hour, then come back at night ... They're the fools, we're the ones who are sensible."

The latter half of 1960s were the Hells Angels' formative years in its evolution towards a criminal organization, as it was then that they began trafficking in drugs. Club members had been introduced to marijuana, acid, and methamphetamines by America's other burgeoning anti-establishment subculture during this period, the hippies. Members of the Hells Angels began selling methamphetamine (otherwise known as "speed" or "crank") and as the profits grew with the expanding market for hallucinogenics, they began manufacturing chemical drugs. For the next twenty-five years, the Hells Angels, Outlaws and other one-percenter motorcycle gangs practically monopolized the production and trafficking of methamphetamines and phencyclidine (PCP or "angel dust"). The growing popularity of rock concerts also shaped the reputation and future criminal activities of the Angels; concerts became a prime opportunity to sell drugs while many one-percenters hired themselves out as security. They soon branched out into other illegal and semi-legitimate entrepreneurial activities, in particular trafficking in women (as strippers and prostitutes), the theft and resale of motorcycle and car parts, and muscle-for-hire.

With revenue pouring in from drug sales and their reputation and infamy spiralling due to increased publicity, America's premier biker gang spread across the U.S. By the early 1970s, there were ten Hells Angels chapters in California, eight chapters in other states, and three international chapters with approximately five hundred members worldwide (although the majority were still in California). The Outlaws MC were also expanding in an effort to challenge the Hells Angels for supremacy in the American biker fiefdom. Like their rivals, the Outlaws were transformed into a criminal organization through their involvement in the production and distribution of chemical drugs, although as noted in a 1986 report from the President's Commission on Organized Crime, they also "became involved in extortion, armed robbery, rape, mail fraud, auto theft, and witness intimidation." In addition, the Outlaws diversified into semi-legitimate businesses including "pornographic bookstores, massage parlors, marine sales and storage, and the Basic Bible Church, … an apparent money-laundering front."

From the 1970s onward, the outlaw motorcycle subculture was characterized by proliferation, expansion, consolidation, and sophistication. The number of one-percenter gangs that started up in the U.S. and Canada increased exponentially; by the end of the 1970s, there were more than one hundred outlaw biker gangs in Canada alone. Not only were new clubs founded, but the Angels and the Outlaws embarked on a strategy of expansion and consolidation by issuing new club charters, taking over or building alliances with existing motorcycle clubs, and setting up subservient puppet clubs. Through their expansion and consolidation, the Hells Angels and the Outlaws established an international network of chapters, while eliminating competitors through takeovers, intimidation, and violence. In his 1978 book, *Wayward Angel*, George Wethern, a former senior member of the Oakland chapter of the Hells Angels, noted that the club's carefully controlled expansion was highly strategic. "We didn't believe in granting charters just for the sake of growth, nor to provide us with a place to stay when we were on vacation. The additions were designed to contribute to our image and business concerns, by providing a drug route link, manufacturing a drug, supplying chemicals or distributing drugs in an untapped area." According to a 1979 report from the Criminal Intelligence Service Canada, expansion north of the border also meant "the capability of harbouring fugitives in other jurisdictions" was enhanced and when "violence from Canadian gang rivalry" erupted, "American bikers of both the Outlaws and the Hells Angels could be summoned to participate."

In 1977, the Hells Angels made their first inroads into Canada by taking over the Popeyes Motorcycle Club in Quebec and, over the next ten years, they established other chapters in Quebec, Nova Scotia, and British Columbia. Faced with the growing power of their enemy, the Outlaws quickly scrambled to catch up and that same year the club went international when it absorbed several chapters of the Satan's Choice motorcycle club in Ontario and one in Quebec. While there were an estimated nine hundred outlaw motorcycle gangs scattered throughout North America, by the late 1980s, four groups would come to dominate the one-percenter world: the Hells Angels, the Outlaws, the Pagans, and the Bandidos. The four had a combined strength of around two thousand members, although it was the Angels that were clearly on top with more than sixty chapters internationally compared to approximately thirty-five for the Outlaws, forty for the Pagans, and thirty for the Bandidos. What truly distinguished the Angels from the other clubs was that almost a third of its chapters were outside the U.S.

As the Hells Angels and other one-percenter motorcycle clubs expanded and matured, their wild and anarchistic behaviour was gradually replaced by a more businesslike approach and the adoption of a rigid set of rules, regulations, and codes. This evolution can be traced to the mid-1960s when Hells Angels legend Ralph (Sonny) Barger became president of the Oakland chapter. Influenced by his stint in the U.S. Army, he began promoting a paramilitary organizational structure and rigid internal discipline. While one-percenter clubs once offered members a hedonistic freedom from society's restraints, by the 1980s, they had become very structured, highly regimented, and thoroughly rule-bound. The larger clubs adopted a written constitution and bylaws, a chain of command, strict rules governing the behaviour of its members, mandatory meetings, and the collection of dues. In 1966, the Hells Angels even became incorporated and, in 1970, their infamous horn-winged, helmeted death's-head logo was officially registered as a protected trademark.

The organizational structure of a chapter is relatively consistent throughout most one-percenter clubs. The officers of a chapter consist of a president, vice-president, secretary treasurer, road captain, and sergeant-at-arms. The president has the final say over all the business of the chapter and may take a cut of most of the (illegal) business carried out by members. The secretary treasurer is responsible for collecting cash on behalf of the chapter, acts as bookkeeper, and keeps minutes at meetings. The sergeant-at-arms, a position usually filled by the toughest member of the chapter, serves as an enforcer, maintains order at meetings and on biker runs, and is responsible for internal discipline. The road captain organizes the logistics and security for the time-honoured biker run. Full-patch members are those who are allowed to wear the colours of the biker gang. Most MC clubs require that a chapter must have at least six members and few have more than twenty-five. Each chapter has prospective members (called "strikers" or "prospects")

who spend from one month to one year (the "striking period") on probationary status. To become a full member, a prospect must first be sponsored by an existing member, and then, during their probation period, he must prove himself worthy by following orders that may require him to commit illegal acts (a practice that helps keep law enforcement agents from posing as prospective members). Initiation rituals vary by club and by chapter. Legend has it that during the 1960s and 1970s, a Hells Angels prospect had to go through a bizarre and sometimes horrific initiation ritual that involved soiling his colours with dirt, grease and excrement to create the mangy look that set one-percenters apart from mainstream society (although Sonny Barger denies that the initiation of new members ever went to this extreme). Today, there is less emphasis on these initiation rituals, although prospects are still expected to commit one or more crimes as part of their probationary period.

The heightened organization of outlaw motorcycle gangs helped them gain a virtual monopoly over the production and distribution of chemical drugs. In 1977, the San Francisco Police Department estimated that the Hells Angels controlled 90 percent of the methamphetamine trade in northern California while, the same year, the RCMP estimated that biker gangs controlled 75 percent of the methamphetamine market in Ontario. It was around this time that the Outlaws helped turn Canada into a major source of chemical drugs. For years, the most profitable narcotic distributed by the Outlaws in the U.S. was "Canadian Blue," a sedative made up of diazepam, commonly referred to by the brand name Valium. The drug was produced by the Satan's Choice in makeshift laboratories in Ontario and Quebec and then smuggled across the border to the Outlaws' stronghold in the American Midwest. Canadian Blue was so popular in the U.S. that a pound fetched $12,000 across the border compared to only $8,000 in Canada. Satan's Choice members were producing other drugs as well, which became evident in 1975, when police raided a secret laboratory in a remote corner of Ontario and found nine pounds of PCP tablets and 236 pounds of its chemical ingredients. After several Ontario and Quebec chapters of the Satan's Choice were absorbed by the Outlaws in the late 1970s, drug production skyrocketed. In a 1986 publication, the RCMP and the DEA reported that the St. Catharine's chapter of the Outlaws was "capable of supplying kilogram quantities of cocaine and methamphetamine as well as 100,000 dosage unit consignments of counterfeit methaqualone (diazepam) on a regular basis."

In 1982, the RCMP ended a two-year undercover operation with the arrests of twenty-two people, most of whom were members of the Outlaws or the Hells Angels. Along with the arrests, police seized fifty-one pounds of phencyclidine powder, 10,787 PCP tablets, and 34,800 tabs of LSD. When a laboratory in Madoc, Ontario was busted in 1983, police found enough chemicals to make $3.6 million of methamphetamine. Members of Toronto's Satan's Choice and Para-Dice Riders were arrested in that raid. In 1984, Toronto police raided another outlaw biker lab and seized about 2.8 kilograms of methamphetamine, with a street value of $4 million, arresting a chemist and his assistant in the process. In July 1985, Quebec provincial police (Sûreté du Quebec) showed off a laboratory they claimed was responsible for producing part of the $8 million worth of synthetic drugs seized at Hells Angels hiding places across Quebec the month before. The lab, which was set up in a Montreal home, was capable of producing 15 pounds of methamphetamines a week, which could have generated an annual revenue of $25 million. Police estimated the cost of the lab equipment and chemicals needed to produce the drug was a mere $3,000. In its 1987 national drug estimates, the RCMP wrote that outlaw motorcycle gangs in Quebec are "believed to be responsible for much of Canada's PCP production, while the gangs located in Ontario are active in the production of methamphetamine."

Throughout the 1970s and 1980s, the outlaw biker subculture changed dramatically, with less emphasis on their original hell-raising adventurous, shocking, counterculture ways, and a greater preoccupation with criminal entrepreneurship and making money. By the 1980s, the Hells Angels, the Outlaws, and other major biker groups were no different than most criminal organizations in that they had become focussed almost exclusively on profit-oriented pursuits. As outlaw biker expert Yves Lavigne notes, the original bonds of the outlaw bikers soon took a back seat to making money: "Some Hells Angels made big money in the drug business, and suddenly they had something to lose, something to protect. Their bank accounts came first and the brotherhood second. When a member threatened their income, they beat or killed him. The Hells Angels Motorcycle Club was no longer an organization that sheltered social misfits. It became an enclave for some of the underworld's most cunning drug manufacturers and dealers."

For George Wethern, an outlaw biker club structure is perfectly suited for drug trafficking. Because of their reputation for violence and anti-establishment attitudes, one-percenters are ideal candidates for this line of work and each chapter can fulfill all the necessary tasks, from manufacturing, to wholesaling, street-level distribution, enforcement and transportation. While the structure of a chapter was not designed as an infrastructure for a criminal organization, Daniel Wolf argues that outlaw biker clubs are in many ways "pre-adapted as vehicles of organized crime":

> Para-military organization lies at the core of their tight knit secret society. It is a society capable of enforcing internal discipline; including an iron-clad code of silence which ensures that information about club operations never goes beyond the walls of the clubhouse. Uncompromising commitments of brotherhood generate cohesion, mutual dependence, and a sense of a shared common fate. The lengthy socialization required to become a legitimate "biker" and the two years of proving oneself as a striker in order to become a member make the infiltration of a club by the police a virtual impossibility. The political structure of the club, the anti-establishment attitudes and high-risk nature of the individuals involved, and the marginal social environment in which they operate have the potential to produce a clubhouse of crime.

Thus, while one-percenter MC clubs and individual chapters still function as a sort of social or fraternal order for its members, they have also evolved into a network of criminal conspiracies and associations that orbit around individual members of a chapter. As with other crime groups, the members of the major outlaw biker clubs have a network of associates and connections through which they carry out their own criminal rackets. As Antonio Nicaso puts it, "Belonging to the Hells Angels guarantees to each member the possibility of running an illicit activity."

By the 1980s, the Hells Angels and other biker gangs in Canada were using these networks to become involved in the importation and wholesaling of cocaine, which eventually became their largest source of revenue. According to the RCMP *National Drug Intelligence Estimate* published in 1987, "cocaine importation and trafficking are believed to account for a significant percentage of the illicit revenue generated by the four British Columbia chapters of the Hells Angels. In Alberta, the Rebels, the Grim Reapers, and the Kings Crew outlaw motorcycle gangs are all involved in cocaine trafficking. The Rebels are also believed to be responsible for supplying cocaine at the pound level in Saskatchewan. Outlaw motorcycle gangs are also largely responsible for the importation of cocaine into the province of Manitoba, where the Los Brovos gang is acting in association with the Grim Reapers and the Satan's Choice motorcycle gangs ... In the province of Quebec, the Hells Angels are also involved in cocaine importation and trafficking." Accounting records seized by police in 2001 showed that the Quebec Hells Angels were wholesaling at least 2,000 kilos of cocaine a year. A member of a B.C. chapter even relocated to Colombia to coordinate purchases and shipments, including a shipment of 205 kilos seized in Vancouver in 1995.

As outlaw motorcycle gangs evolved into organized crime groups, violence was increasingly used as a strategic tool to further their profit-driven activities. The Hells Angels in particular are notorious for trying to monopolize a particular territory or drug market, and the outlaw biker world has been characterized by unrelenting violence between competing gangs battling over territories and illegal markets. The Hells Angels and the Outlaws have been fighting intermittently since 1974, and a 1986 report from the President's Commission on Organized Crime in the U.S. points out that despite the Angels' well-founded penchant for violence, the Outlaws are no shrinking violets: "Their reputation for violence is strong. According to the Broward County Sheriff's Office in Ft. Lauderdale,

Florida, the Outlaws were responsible for as many as 77 murders between 1966 and 1979; another 15 murders in North Carolina have been attributed to the gang. Friction between the Outlaws and the Hell's Angels has resulted in massacres on both sides." The Outlaw insignia once boasted the initials "GFOD" (God forgives; Outlaws don't) and "AHAMD" (All Hell's Angels must die).

The Hells Angels have also taken on another rival biker group, the Bandidos, and the conflict between the two has been particularly ferocious in Scandinavia of all places. During the 1980s, the Angels began setting up chapters in Denmark and when they were challenged by a local biker group, they wiped them out; thirteen people were killed before the local club threw in the towel and disbanded in 1986. The remaining members joined a new club that eventually became a chapter of the Bandidos, furthering a war that would cost even more lives. In 1996, the conflict escalated when military-grade weapons were used in Denmark, Sweden, and Finland. That year, while the Copenhagen Hells Angels were hosting a party at their headquarters, an anti-tank grenade was fired into the compound from the roof of a nearby building. Two were killed and nineteen were wounded. Later that year, a jury in Denmark convicted two Danish members of the Hells Angels of murdering a Bandidos member during an ambush at the Copenhagen airport. In 1997, the Norwegian headquarters of the Bandidos was destroyed by an explosion, killing one person and injuring four others. All were innocent passersby. In an unsuccessful attempt to assassinate an imprisoned Bandidos leader, the Hells Angels launched a rocket-propelled grenade into a jail in Denmark.

From the very beginning, violence has been an integral part of the outlaw motorcycle subculture. While violence was originally used indiscriminately as an extension of the one-percenters' deviant lifestyle, it has increasingly been deployed for strategic purposes: to take over or protect drug markets or geographic territories, to ensure members are loyal and stay in line, to intimidate and terrorize victims and entire communities, and to dissuade anyone within or outside the club from becoming a state witness. Carrying out a murder or assaulting a rival is also one way a prospect could become a full member. After two men were severely beaten by low-level members of a Quebec Hells Angels chapter in 2002, a member of a puppet club later told police "the guys all want to get promoted." Violence and intimidation have even been used against police and other criminal justice officials. In the most infamous Canadian example, Maurice (Mom) Boucher, the de facto leader of the Hells Angels in Quebec during the 1990s, was convicted of ordering the assassination of two federal corrections officers. This was on top of numerous bombs that he ordered to be placed at police stations. The larger one-percenter clubs even have specialized units that are tasked with carrying out violence and other enforcement functions. Hells Angels enforcers are adorned with Nazi storm-trooper-like lightning bolts tattooed underneath the words "Filthy Few," the Outlaws have their "SS Death Squad," while the Pagans maintain the "Black T-Shirt Squad." The Rockers, a Montreal-based puppet club of the Quebec Hells Angels, had a special assassination squad called the "football team" as well a "baseball team," made up of members and associates who were responsible for carrying out beatings of rivals.

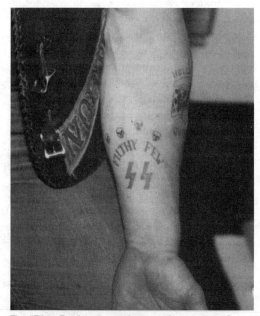

The "Filthy Few" tattoo on the arm of a member of Quebec's North Chapter, signifying that he has killed for the club. The skeleton heads above signify how many kills the member has under his belt.

As part of their strategic tool kit, the more sophisticated biker groups have also become well known for their intelligence gathering and counter-surveillance activities, which is directed against both rival gangs and law enforcement agencies. Police raids on biker clubhouses have turned up electronic surveillance equipment, confidential police radio frequency lists, and scanners. While searching a Hells Angels clubhouse in Alberta, the Edmonton Police Service discovered scanning equipment connected to personal computers that were monitoring transmissions from electronic pagers used by police. Physical surveillance of police is also frequently conducted. In one Ontario city, a motorcycle repair shop owned by members of a biker gang was set up across the street from a gas station where police cars as well as private vehicles belonging to peace officers regularly filled up. From this observation post, licence-plate numbers and descriptions of cars and their occupants were recorded. Some chapters even have a designated intelligence officer who is responsible for compiling dossiers, including photographs, physical descriptions, work and home addresses, vehicle descriptions and licence-plate numbers on rival gang members, police, journalists, and witnesses. Police searches of the clubhouses and homes of the Quebec Hells Angels and its puppet clubs have turned up photos of police officers and civilians working for a special biker task force; documents containing the names, addresses, and social insurance numbers of provincial police officers; as well as police and Crown reports on undercover officers, informants, and witnesses. According to the Union of Canadian Correctional Officers, during the 1990s members of biker gangs were actively compiling information on prison guards across the country.

Biker gangs also routinely conduct surveillance on their rivals. Stéphane Gagné, a former member of the Rockers motorcycle club, testified in court in 2002 that his boss, Maurice Boucher, ordered him to videotape attendants at the funeral of Frank Cotroni. The video, which was shot through a small camera hidden in a tissue box, was meant to keep tabs on associates of the Montreal mafioso and long-time drug trafficker. The assignment was part of a surveillance campaign against those who dared to stop the Hells Angels from taking over control of Quebec's drug trade. Gagné said similar surveillance was also done on members of rival biker gangs to assist Hells Angels hit men in identifying their targets.

Women play an important intelligence-gathering role for biker gangs and many have been planted in law enforcement agencies, courtrooms, and government licensing bureaus, where they have access to vital information. Steve Caretta, a former member of the Outlaws in Ontario, once confessed that they paid "a guy in the department of transport to run [drivers'] licences through the computer" to help ensure new prospects were not police agents. Caretta said that through this information he learned that at least two would-be members of the Outlaws were undercover officers. According to former Ontario Satan's Choice member Cecil Kirby, his club utilized the service of a woman employed in the Ontario Provincial Police who had access to classified databases:

> Club members carried her number around in their wallets. If a member was worried about the cops, all he had to do was call her number, and she'd access the police computer to see if there were any warrants on him. When we spotted a rival gang member, we'd also use her to see if there were outstanding fugitive warrants on him. If there were, we'd have someone in the club call the cops and tip them off to where that rival was and who was with him. It was a good way of avoiding trouble and getting rid of rival gang members. We could also check out anyone's criminal record through that computer. This helped us spot people trying to infiltrate us from rival gangs or from the cops.

For Kirby, the Satan's Choice had "the upper hand in Toronto because we had the best intelligence network around. We were able to move on the other gangs faster than they could move on us because we had such good sources and good information on the habits of the other gangs."

In 2002, Tony Cannavino, head of the Quebec Provincial Police Association accused the Hells Angels of recruiting civilians working in law enforcement agencies to steal information from police computers.

Cannavino said at least four people with access to police databases in Quebec were charged that year for selling information to members of the club. The Angels reportedly paid up to $10,000 to workers who helped steal data. The infiltration of police agencies by outlaw biker gangs is not limited to civilian employees. A 1988 investigation by the Ontario Provincial Police accused Niagara Regional Police members of links with members of motorcycle gangs. In January 1999, the RCMP began investigating allegations that some Edmonton police officers had been leaking information to the Hells Angels, damaging several federal investigations into the biker club.

Government agencies are not the only targets of outlaw biker infiltration and corruption. In February 2002, a Canadian Senate Committee studying Canada's security confirmed that the Hells Angels have infiltrated companies and unions that operate on Canada's marine ports to facilitate the import and export of drugs and other contraband. While other organized crime groups, such as Montreal's West End Gang, have penetrated the waterfront, on a national level, "The most significant criminal influences within the marine ports are linked to the Hells Angels," according to the 2004 annual report of the Criminal Intelligence Service Canada. In their 2003 book on the Hells Angels, Julian Sher and William Marsden allege that beginning in the 1980s, the motorcycle club created "a patchwork of full-patch members and associates to infiltrate the ports of Vancouver, Montreal and Halifax" placing them in "key positions to facilitate a 'tailgate operation,' so called because the bikers can organize the movement of drugs from a container right onto one of their waiting vehicles with exquisite precision."

Driven in part by drug sales and an unappeasable monopolistic drive, the 1990s was a period of consolidation in the biker world as the three largest clubs — the Hells Angels, the Outlaws, and the Bandidos — expanded in terms of chapters and members by swallowing up smaller clubs and setting up new chapters and puppet clubs throughout the world. By 2002, the Hells Angels had 217 chapters with approximately three thousand members in twenty-seven countries, the Outlaws had a membership of 1,200 spread over 128 chapters in ten countries, while the

Bandidos had 140 chapters and approximately 2,500 members in twelve countries. The same year, Canada was home to thirty-four Hells Angels chapters with around 450 members and another 150 prospects and "hangarounds." Biker gangs were also indefatigable in diversifying their criminal activities during the 1990s; in addition to drug trafficking they also had their hand in large-scale theft, telemarketing fraud, counterfeiting, loansharking, extortion, prostitution, and the smuggling of and trafficking in illegal weapons, stolen goods, alcohol and cigarettes. Their largest source of revenue, however, continued to be drugs and, in addition to synthetic drugs and cocaine, the Hells Angels have been cited by police as a driving force behind Canada's bourgeoning homegrown marijuana industry.

By the new millennium, the Hells Angels had evolved into one of the largest and most powerful transnational crime groups in the world. As the club evolved from a group of motorcycle-riding rowdies to sophisticated criminals, its counterculture underpinnings largely disappeared and were supplanted by efforts to promote an image of respectability; members are seen less on their motorcycles wearing their traditional colours, and more frequently driving around in luxury cars (and minivans) in everyday street clothes. When their colours are worn, they are clean and pressed, in stark contrast to their past preference for dirt and grime. Members and associates are chosen, not because of their physical proportions or anti-social predispositions, but for their intellect, cunning, criminal expertise, or connections. Outlaw bikers have also tried to downplay their violent, deviant subcultural origins by engaging in philanthropy, such as the annual Toys-for-Tots motorcycle parade or charity golf tournaments that raise money for cancer research.

FEAR AND LOATHING IN CANADA

In a closed society, where everybody's guilty, the only crime is getting caught. In a world of thieves, the only final sin is stupidity.
—Hunter S. Thompson

We were somewhere near Halifax on the edge of the ocean when the drugs began to take hold. I remember forgetting why the hell I was in Nova Scotia in the first place and was even more confused when the sky became dark with what looked like a large flock of loons. Then it was quiet again. My editor had taken off his shirt and was pouring a full can of Molson Export on his chest, supposedly to ward off the UVA rays.

A publisher had foolishly given me a contact to write a book on the history of organized crime in Canada and the manuscript was already a year overdue. For these sins, my editor was dispatched to babysit me. He is a bespectacled, squirrelly, greying bass player, who looks like he had one too many wedgies as a kid, but who, no doubt, emerged from these traumatic episodes with far more character than his latent-homosexual tormentors. My editor had a soft spot for beer and mescaline and was muttering to himself while in a narcotic-induced trance about America's bastardization of the English language.

It was almost dusk now as the smell of sea air and lobsters filled our lungs, but we were closing in on the object of our intentions: the Thirteenth Tribe of Halifax. I was researching the part of the book dealing with outlaw motorcycle gangs and my editor and I agreed that as part of this pseudo-ethnographic research it would be immensely beneficial to not only meet with the subjects, but to sample their wares; yes, the pathologically misunderstood band of motorcycle-riding Rotarians were simply filling the Canadian dream of controlling the mode of production (although they ignored the other half of the dream, which is not to annoy anyone while chasing the first half of the dream). Narco-entrepreneurs! Canadian narco-entreprenuers to boot!

In other words, we were looking to score some speed. Crank. Methaphetamines. I was a Doctor of Philosophy, after all, and was well known for my participant observation research. Besides, "there was also the socio-psychic factor. Every now and then when your life gets complicated and the weasels start closing in, the only real cure is to load up on heinous chemicals" and then drive like a bastard from Halifax to Vancouver travelling into the womb of the Canadian subcultural criminal psyche.

We thought we would start on the east coast to explore the oldest one-percenter biker gang in the Maritimes and then drive west, visiting each province along the way. We had rented a red 1968 Cadillac convertible, complete with leather seats and an all-new 472-cid V-8 engine with 375 bhp. What the actual theme of the story was, we had no idea. Was it on Canadian criminality? Canadian subculture? The Canadian dream? Canadian entrepreneurs? The latter-day versions of Horatio Alger or Conrad Black?

My deranged publisher had given me an advance of $3,000, much of which I had already spent on dangerous drugs. The trunk of the car looked like a pharmacy from Woodstock. We had four ounces of pot, seven saltshakers full of cocaine, sixty-five pellets of mescaline, five sheets of blotter acid, three baggies of psilocybin mushrooms, two bushels of khat, four bottles of Valium, nine grams of Lebanese blonde, two packs of Dramamine, a vile of methedrine, a 14-cubic-inch canister of helium, a 26-ounce bottle of tequila, a bag of limes, a two-four of Molson Export, three-quarters of a carton of Craven "A" King Size, and a bottle of water to chase down the mushrooms and pills. But what we really wanted was some speed, which worried me the most because there is nothing more pathetic than a middle-aged academic whose metabolism and heartbeat have just been cranked far past the level of physiological, cognitive, and emotional acceptability. But we knew we would get some of the wicked stuff soon because we were about to meet up with the Thirteenth Tribe.

For years, the Tribe was the dominant biker gang in Nova Scotia. It was founded in Halifax back in 1968 and was originally made up of a bunch of former navy personnel. The Tribe quickly attracted a large number of rowdy and unmanageable characters, and by 1971, the criminal element had taken over the gang and many of its members had been busted for assault, possession of a dangerous weapon, and resisting arrest. "Club members took a defiant and hostile attitude toward police and authority in general," D. Owen Carrigan wrote in the greatest understatement since President Lyndon Johnson talked about the prospect of increasing America's "police action" in Vietnam. During the early 1970s, the Thirteenth Tribe "launched a virtual reign of terror in metropolitan Halifax," Carrigan said. "They gang-raped a teenage girl, viciously beat a policeman working with the city drug squad, assaulted a Dartmouth man, and shot at another police officer patrolling a busy downtown street in his squad car." The cops quickly rounded up most of the rabble who were convicted and given sentences ranging from three to twelve years. Following the crackdown, the remnants of Tribe toned down their wanton violence and focussed on dealing speed, which they were buying from the Popeyes Motorcycle Club in Montreal or the Grim Reapers in Alberta.

After a few days on the east coast, we were ready to head west. Like the Maritimes, the speed we picked up was too weak with little staying power, and we had already collected as much information as we can use on the Tribe. Plus my editor had finished off most of the mescaline and was now jerking his head back in a succession of short violent thrusts in a valiant effort to dislodge the contents of two saltshakers full of cocaine that were fully inserted into each nostril and which caused his head to start smoking like a giant Persian hookah. He then began bouncing his smoking head into the headrest in a fit of psychotic epileptic episodes accompanied by blood-curdling screams about giant slugs crawling down his back.

"You greedy voracious whore," I shouted while simultaneously slapping him on the back of the head with a rolled-up Sunday edition of the *Chronicle-Herald*. I stepped on the gas and fired the Red Rocket back onto the Trans-Canada to take us to where I knew we could get a fresh batch of crank straight out of the pill press: Quebec!

The Satan's Choice had one chapter in Quebec. It was located in Montreal and during the first half of the 1970s, it was locked in one of the first major biker wars in Canada. Their enemy was the Popeyes, who were one of the first outlaw clubs in Quebec, with roots stretching back to the 1950s. With chapters in Montreal, Quebec City, Sherbrooke, Sorel, Trois Rivières, Gatineau, and Drummondville, the

Popeyes were famous for the prostitutes and strippers they handled, but also provided muscle to the Italian mafia and the Dubois brothers. By 1977, the Popeyes had between 250 and 350 members, which made them the largest biker gang in Quebec and the country's second largest after their archrival the Satan's Choice.

The battle between the Satan's Choice and the Popeyes was over the chemical drug market in Quebec. The Choice chapter in Montreal was smuggling drugs from Asia and Europe to peddle, but around 1974 they broke out the home chemistry sets and began setting up meth labs along with the Devil's Disciples MC. Together the Choice and the Disciples monopolized chemical drugs in Montreal, and the Popeyes wanted a piece of the action so they began a war. After the Popeyes found one of their brothers hanging in a cemetery and had to remove another one whose legs had been crushed after being pinned against a wall by the front bumper of a car, they backed down. The Choice became the dominant biker gang in the province.

The Satan's Choice and the Popeyes were the more refined and civil of the biker gangs in Quebec. A 1980 report from the Quebec Police Commission's inquiry into organized crime described how a gang called the Black Spiders terrorized a village near Quebec City, demanding townsfolk pay a toll to use local streets. In Mont-Joli, the Flambeurs biker gang, "in groups of 15 or 20, or sometimes more, spent their evening loitering, driving their motorcycles at excessive speeds by holding impromptu bike races on the streets, insulting passersby, and committing all kids of illegal acts, such as (a) taking and pushing drugs; (b) extorting $2 from passing motorists in exchange for unhindered passage; (c) damaging parked cars; (d) drinking alcohol in the street and throwing bottles at motorists; (e) vandalizing stores inside and out; (f) enticing children to take drugs; (g) urinating on the street, and blocking pedestrian's way." During a melee at an unlicensed bar called Chez Bidou in Saint Gédéon, members of the Missiles MC ransacked the place, badly injuring a bartender and a waitress. In Sherbrooke, the Gitans and the Atoms were battling it out, which resulted in six murders in 1973 and 1974. The Gitans

were already infamous for attacking and robbing homosexuals, gang raping minors, and transmitting venereal diseases. With no mincing of words, the Quebec Police Commission described one-percenter biker gangs as:

> ... idle parasites with no respect for any authority; they take drugs; they are down-and-outs; they are diseased. They have no legitimate goals, and no ambitions. They expect nothing of society, and have nothing to give. They are violent, and constitute a threat to themselves and to those around them. For that reason they are more dangerous than the mafia or other organized criminal gangs unearthed in the past who kill, traffic in drugs and offensive weapons, steal, receive stolen cars and motorcycles, and who assault, rape and intimidate.

Me and my editor didn't like Quebec too much. The violence was out of control and made it difficult to score any decent speed. We also couldn't understand a thing people were saying. Meanwhile, in between his sporadic acid rushes, my editor was raving wildly about the differences between time, space, and the proper use of semicolons and was becoming more and more erratic after he ate a handful of mescaline, which he chased down with highballs mixed with equal parts of tequila and magic mushrooms.

"You bastard son of a whoring mule train driver!" I screamed in his general direction while clobbering him in the balls with my hard-copy edition of *Moby Dick*.

My editor was now having drug-induced nightmares about being forced to eat some imaginary concoction of french fries mixed with curds of cheese and thick gravy and I was so nauseated by the thought of such a far-fetched gastronomic torture that I knew it was time to leave the province before both of us puked all over the leather upholstery of the Red Ranger. "Jesus, bad waves of paranoia, madness, fear and loathing — intolerable vibrations in this place. Get out. Flee." But do it right. Remember: Conrad Black.

We didn't bother stopping in Ottawa or any part of eastern Ontario. We knew that Toronto was the centre of the Canadian biker universe at the time. There were eighteen one-percenter gangs in Ontario by the end of the 1980s, with chapters in a dozen cities, and a membership exceeding one thousand. The biggest was the Satan's Choice, but there were also the Black Diamond Riders, the Iron Hawks, the Last Chance, the Outlaws, the Para-Dice Riders, the Vagabonds, the Wild Ones, the Red Devils, the Lobos, the Chosen Few, the Queensmen, the Henchmen, the Bad News, Crazy Horse, Crossbreeds, and the Coffin Wheelers. Unlike the Choice, most clubs just had a single chapter.

As we spied the tip of the CN Tower looming over the concrete horizon we were both shocked and delighted to see what had overtaken our car on either side: "outlaw motorcyclists wearing chains, shades and greasy Levis" storming along both sides of the Red Rover in perfect biker-run unison; members of the Satan's Choice, the largest and most powerful motorcycle gang in Canada with nine chapters in Ontario (Ottawa, Kingston, Toronto, Richmond Hill, Peterborough, Hamilton, Kitchener, St. Catharines, and Windsor) and one in Quebec. The menace is on the loose again; the "hundred-carat headline, running fast and loud on the early morning freeway, low in the saddle, nobody smiles, jamming crazy through traffic and ninety miles an hour down the centre stripe, missing by inches." They were like "Genghis Khan on an iron horse, a monster steed with a fiery anus, flat out through the eye of a beer can and up your daughter's leg with no quarter asked and none given; shoe the squares some class, give 'em a whiff of these kicks they'll never know."

We knew the Choice was really the only biker club we needed to see in Ontario. They were better organized, more powerful, more successful, and cranked out more speed than anyone else in Canada. Each chapter had ten to fifteen members, one-time member Cecil Kirby recalled in 1986, "but a lot of people in the community thought a chapter had as many as three or four hundred because they were so loud and violent and because the members of other chapters would often join one chapter on a run on a town." At its peak in the mid-1970s, the club had 220 active, full-time members. Almost all of them were in Ontario. By the early 1970s, they were smuggling and selling chemical drugs provided by the Outlaws. Then they graduated into production. They were the first biker gang in Canada to set up their own labs and employ their own chemists, but they continued to work with other American bikers to import ingredients and recipes and then to export the finished product. By the mid-1970s, the Satan's Choice was famous throughout the biker world for producing the best downers around — "Canadian Blue." In Toronto, the Choice co-operated with the Vagabonds and the Para–Dice Riders and the city was divided into three zones for drug trafficking.

The Vagabonds were a relatively small but well-respected and affluent gang that was made up of long-time, hard-core bikers. In addition to synthetic drugs, they also sold cocaine locally when its popularity began to skyrocket. In addition to the Choice, the Vagabonds scored their drugs from biker groups in the American Midwest. The Para-Dice Riders was established in 1971, "a powerful, but low-profile outlaw motorcycle gang with a strong foothold in Toronto's working class east end," according to a 1986 RCMP report.

Beginning in the mid-1970s, police began targeting the Choice and through a series of raids they severely wounded the club. On August 6, 1975, the RCMP, OPP, DEA, and several municipal police departments descended on a cabin that had been converted to a PCP laboratory. It was located on a remote island on Oba Lake, 150 miles north of Sault Ste. Marie in northwestern Ontario. They seized nine pounds of PCP and 236 pounds of ingredients that were one step away from completion. The cops arrested Alain Templain, a member of the Saint Catharines chapter of the Satan's Choice and the owner of the cabin, as well as Bernie Guindon, founder and national president of the Satan's Choice. After being convicted and sentenced to seventeen years in prison, Guindon entrusted the club's presidency to Garnet (Mother) McEwen, also from the Saint Catharines chapter, who convinced four chapters to break away and join the Outlaws. They were "tense for action, long hair in the wind, beards and bandanas flapping, earrings, armpits, chain whips, swastikas, and stripped down Harleys flashing chrome as traffic on the 101 moves over, nervous, to let the formation pass like a burst of dirty thunder." Guindon felt so betrayed by McEwen that he placed a $10,000 contract on his head. The contract was never carried out, but McEwen was not too popular with his biker brothers when he skipped town with about $30,000 from the club's treasury. He fled to Calgary, but the local bikers like the Chosen Few thought he had come west to establish a new Outlaws chapter and they persuaded him to return to Ontario in 1980. He left Alberta after being released from a Calgary hospital where he was forced to sojourn after receiving a heavy beating with his own wooden leg.

In August 1977, police in Ontario nabbed more than forty members and associates of the Satan's Choice and the Vagabonds and seized over $800,000 worth of speed, $100,000 in stolen property, as well as nine handguns and eight rifles. The cops laid 191 charges including drug trafficking, breaking and entering, possession of stolen property, possession of counterfeit money, and possession of restricted guns, knives, and swords. The arrests hit the Choice hard and they lost their supremacy in the province forever when the club split up in 1977 and half the members went over to the Outlaws. Despite its disappearing power and influence, the Choice did not take kindly to competition in its territory. William Matyiek, a former member of the Golden Hawks Motorcycle Club, had been told to shut down his club's operations by the Choice. He refused. So members of the Choice walked into a tavern, surrounded Matyiek and shot him three times in the head. The Outlaws behind the attack were tracked down by police and their trial began on September 4, 1979. Witnesses were intimidated and told not to testify; the car of one witness was shot at while parked in front of his home. Six members were sentenced to life imprisonment for the murder.

Ontario was the place to be for the best biker action but I didn't like the province any better than Quebec. The air made my eyes water and we couldn't seem to shake the huge red reptile that kept gnawing on the back of the leather seats and threatening

to tunnel his way into the trunk where he would discover our stash. So we decided to hightail it into Manitoba. Right after crossing the provincial border — which coincided with finishing off the last of the acid — we began spotting mosquitoes the size of pterodactyls!

"No I can't be seeing this," I cried out loud, while my editor, half-baked and breathing heavily, was shampooing his hair with a mix of tequila and a purely herbal mix of mushrooms and Lebanese hash.

"You vile puss-filled vesicle," I shrieked as I pistol-whipped him with the butt of my .44 Magnum handgun, one of those large-bore Colt Anacondas with the dual-use cartridge and bevelled cylinder.

We both knew we had to get out of Manitoba as fast as possible. My blood was too thick for this Idaho-wannabe province. We spent enough time there to find out that Manitoba had three outlaw motorcycle gangs during the 1970s, two of which are based in Winnipeg: the Los Brovos and the Spartans. The Spartans were history by the end of the decade, but the Brovos had to contend with a new rival, the Silent Riders, which was made up of dissident members who split from Los Brovos and formed three chapters. Both groups became big suppliers of speed, grass, and cocaine in the province. Whoever came out on top in the inevitable war, a 1986 joint RCMP and DEA report predicted, "the Hells Angels will then likely incorporate the victor into a new club chapter and proceed with plans to make Winnipeg a major distribution centre for drugs and stolen motorcycle parts."

When we arrived in Alberta we learned that the top bikers in Calgary were the Grim Reapers, which was established in 1958. In the early 1970s, they were challenged by the Outcasts, which was made up of the remnants of three clubs that the Reapers had wiped out. Apparently, they were equally intent on doing the same to the new club. One day the Reapers invited the Outcasts to a party at their clubhouse to convince them. When Ronald Hartley, the drunk and defiant president of the Outcasts, proclaimed he would not disband the club and for good measure would also wipe his ass with the Reapers, he was ceremoniously beaten to a pulp. In the best of outlaw biker tradition, Hartley got up and started partying again, but he collapsed and had to be rushed to Calgary General, where he was pronounced DOA. In another outlaw biker tradition, none of the Outcasts or Grim Reapers ratted out Hartley's attackers to police. He probably would have wanted it that way. The only problem was that police charged all thirteen Reapers at the party. They were all convicted of second-degree murder, although in April 1973, an Alberta Appeals Court reversed the murder convictions of twelve of the thirteen members. The supremacy of the Reapers didn't last long; by 1977 there were five other biker gangs in Alberta — the Chosen Few, the King's Crew, Lucifer's Union, the War Lords, and the Rebels — with a total membership of about 275 members, although only around a hundred could be considered hard-core bikers.

As we jumped into the Red Dragon to head to B.C. there were signs we might be losing control of the situation. I already felt a little uncomfortable driving around without my licence and no insurance. But I felt less uncomfortable after consuming a gram of the Lebanese blonde. An all-consuming body stone. That is the main advantage of hash:

Dr. Gonzo Schneider

pure sedated pleasure. The air is sweeter, the sky is bluer, food tastes better, music sounds more wondrous, and people are less pedantic. "You just blunder around doing anything that seems right, and it usually is."

Cannabis sativa is the perfect drug for British Columbia. A friend from Toronto once said that someone lifted Canada on its eastern side and all the nuts rolled into B.C. What kind of rat bastard would say such a thing? It turns out that most people in B.C. probably take pride in that characterization. As we rolled into Vancouver, my editor told me he felt nervous surrounded by all the coffee shops. So he finished off all the mushrooms and reverted to his normal state of psychosis.

"You malignant inoperable cancer tumour," I bellowed while he tried to lick the dead bugs off the windshield of the Red Wagon. I glared at him through insanely glazed and bloodshot eyes and, in a sudden fit of rage that must have been the result of a PCP hangover, I lopped his head off with the machete I had stored under the front seat of the car.

I was now at the end of my trip, alone, and still without any conclusion on the Canadian character that could be discerned by studying this great missing link in Canada's genealogy. What would Conrad Black do in this situation?

I think he would say, "Go west, scumbag!"

So I entered B.C. in search of the province's most powerful outlaws: the Satan's Angels MC. By the early 1980s, they had chapters in Vancouver, White Rock, Nanaimo, Powell River, and Victoria. The Satan's Angels were major players in British Columbia's synthetic drug trade and didn't tolerate competition; one of the club's bylaws is "No member will disgrace the club by being yellow." The Satan's Angels "strip colors off other bikers like scalps" and ride roughshod over the L'il Devils in Vancouver, the Devil's Escorts in Kamloops and the Gypsy Jokers in Oregon. On the wall of their clubhouse, they have a collection of stolen colors hanging right next to the coats of arms of the Vancouver City Police and the Royal Canadian Mounted Police.

Charles (Chuck the Duck) Drager tasted the vengeful wrath of the Satan's Angels when he and a bunch of other restless bikers were patched over to the Ghost Riders MC of Washington State. The Angels demanded that Drager and his biker cronies stop wearing their new colours — a wheel of a motorcycle partly cloaked by a white cloud. When they refused, Ghost Riders members were attacked. After losing a rumble in a B.C. campground, the Riders were forced out of the province and set up shop in the friendlier confines of Alberta. By the early 1980s, Drager grew tired of the biker lifestyle, partly because of the ongoing harassment of the Satan's Angels and partly because of a serious motorcycle accident that killed his girlfriend and left half his face on the pavement. After he departed from the gang, he found the head of a duck on his car. It was Halloween so he laughed it off as a harmless prank. But one morning, a Ghost Rider showed up at Drager's apartment door and fired four .22-calibre bullets into his head. The assassin then pulled out a blade and started to shear Drager's head from the rest of his body. He was interrupted when a neighbour walked by the front door and had to run off without his trophy.

By the mid-1970s, the Satan's Angels were the nucleus of an alliance of motorcycle clubs on the west coast, which also included the Gypsy Wheelers of White Rock and the 101 Road Knights of Nanaimo. But as they watched the Hells Angels and the Outlaws patch over smaller clubs and gain more power back east, the Satan's Angels realized that the best defence against their entry into B.C. was to consolidate their power by patching over smaller one-percenter clubs in the province. By 1977, the Gypsy Wheelers and the Road Knights had exchanged their colours for those of the Satan's Angels and, in 1980, the Bounty Hunters of Victoria did the same. The Satan's Angels did not stay independent for long. Another group of Angels had been eyeing them for a long time and it was only a matter of time before they would roll into B.C.

After finishing up with the Satan's Angels in B.C. I decided to ditch the Great Red Shark and stay in Vancouver. So what did this trip teach me about the Canadian condition? Can I draw an analogy between this elusive national identity and a band of violent, anarchic, drug-dealing motorcyclists? I should. I am, of course, the original Dr. Gonzo. Alas, it was too much for my feeble brain. Fuck it. The line between self-identification and masochism was already too blurred and I did not want to risk finding out that there was nothing on the other side. Besides, my credit card was confiscated by a cashier at a 7-11 in East Van. This time I had to pull back, hold out, step aside, and play for time. Freedom, independence, individuality, excitement, that all sounds pretty good. But how do you reconcile that with a satiated feeling of place; and even one's place in the universe? It is like that old joke about the biker who goes to his doctor and tells him that his old lady thinks she is a chicken. The doctor tells the biker he should bring her in to the office so he can help her. The biker said he would, but he needs the eggs. And I guess that is probably what Conrad Black would say as well.

A MORE FIERCE TYPE OF BIKER

December 5, 1977 will be remembered as a seminal day in the history of outlaw bikers and organized crime in Canada. For it was on this day that the first Canadian chapter of the Hells Angels was founded in Sorel, Quebec, when the Popeyes Motorcycle Club was "patched over" (although only a fraction of its members were considered suitable to wear the colours of the Hells Angels). One of the ex-Popeyes who would go on to play a significant role in establishing the Angels as a major criminal force in Quebec was Yves (Le Boss) Buteau. Born in 1951, Buteau was president of the Popeyes when he was personally courted by Sonny Barger to persuade his fellow members to join the Angels. Barger had such respect for Buteau that he personally awarded him his new colours, backed him as president of the new Sorel Chapter, and even anointed him as the only Canadian to wear the "Hells Angels International" rocker on the bottom of his colours. As the first Hells Angels' chapter president in Canada, the savvy, strategically minded, and business-like Buteau was responsible for carrying out Barger's vision of the "new" Hells Angels by transforming the remnants of the Popeyes into a well-oiled, disciplined, money-making machine. Buteau demanded that the newest Hells Angels keep a low profile and to refrain from violence directed at ordinary citizens. He also criss-crossed the province and the country contacting other biker gangs in an effort to establish new Hells Angels chapters while setting up connections with drug distributors. By the end of the decade, the Montreal chapter had become a major source of chemical drugs for Quebec and other provinces.

The founding of a Hells Angels chapter in Canada was partly driven by the Outlaws' takeover of three Satan's Choice chapters in Windsor, Saint Catharines, and Ottawa in March 1977. In response to the new Angels chapter in Quebec, the Outlaws established its presence in that province when it patched over the Rockers MC of Montreal in February 1978. A pact was also forged between the Outlaws and several other remaining Satan's Choice chapters in Ontario that formally recognized the members of each club as equals, assuring them of mutual hospitality on biker runs and assistance in the event of territorial intrusions and attacks by the Hells Angels. The deal cemented an informal relationship between the two clubs that already saw them co-operating on the production, smuggling and distribution of drugs and the provision of safe havens for fugitives from either country. Before the ink on the agreement was even dry, Howard (Pig Pen) Berry, an Ontario Satan's Choice member wanted for attempted murder in Peterborough, was arrested in North Carolina while in the company of the president of the Lexington Outlaws chapter. On July 26, 1976, police in Saint Catharines, Ontario, arrested James Starrett, a thirty-year-old American Outlaws member who had escaped from a Florida jail cell in 1974 after being convicted of murdering a Fort Lauderdale woman whom he had shot in the face at point-blank range when she objected to being part of a gang rape. On August 27, 1976, another Florida Outlaw, William (Gatemouth Willie) Edson, was arrested in Kitchener after being smuggled into Canada across the Detroit River by Lenny Braund, president of the Detroit Outlaws, and Stephen Dow, president of the Windsor chapter of the Satan's Choice. Edson was wanted by Fort Lauderdale police after he was accused of torturing one woman, burning her with cigarettes and heated spoons after she broke the cardinal rule of

wearing a friend's Outlaws colors. Two years earlier, Edson was involved in the kidnapping and murder of two Hells Angels and an ex-member in Florida, which helped spark the war between the two clubs. After being captured in Chicago, Edson became a state witness and helped to convict his Outlaw colleagues for the death of the three abducted men. By aligning itself with the Satan's Choice, at the time the largest federation of one-percenter chapters in Canada, the Outlaws strategically prevented the Hells Angels from gaining a foothold in Ontario while establishing its own toehold in Quebec.

Although the two gangs had been battling since 1974, the Hells Angels' ruling council "formally" declared war on the Outlaws in early 1978. And while the war may have begun in the U.S., it quickly crossed over to Canada where it was energized by the determined efforts of both clubs to expand throughout the country and gain control over the synthetic drug market. The northern front in the war opened in Montreal with the Angels drawing first blood. On February 15, 1978, Hells Angels hit man Yves (Apache) Trudeau shot Quebec Outlaws member Robert Coté as he sat in a Montreal bar drinking with a biker comrade. Both were former members of the Rockers, which had been patched over to the Outlaws earlier that month. Coté died in hospital five days later and, in a show of force intended to intimidate the Angels, some three hundred Outlaws attended Coté's funeral.

Over the next four months, gang warfare spread across the city, punctuated by car bombings, attacks on clubhouses, woundings, and more deaths. On March 21, Gilles Cadorette, the twenty-seven-year-old president of the Outlaws' Montreal chapter, was killed after a bomb planted in his car exploded. On April 26, Athanase (Tom Thumb) Markopoulos, a twenty-one-year-old member of the Outlaws, was killed after two unknown assailants pumped six bullets into his back while he waited to be let into a locked corner store just 50 feet from the Montreal clubhouse. On October 12, the Outlaws struck back when two hit men casually walked into Montreal's Le Café Tourbillon and shot to death Jean Brochu and Georges (Chico) Mousseau, two Hells Angels members, as well as Guy (Gator) Davies, a member of the Wild Ones from Hamilton who was in town to discuss the possibility of his club

Yves (le Boss) Buteau

becoming the first Hells Angels chapter in Ontario. Two other Angels attending the meeting were wounded in the gunfire. Although the assassins were never found, police strongly believed they had been dispatched by the American Outlaws' leadership to stop the Angels from setting up shop in Ontario. Retaliation by the Hells Angels came on November 10, when Outlaws member Brian Powers was murdered after answering the door at his posh Montreal home. The man standing on the other side of the door, Yves Trudeau, fired nine .45-calibre bullets into his head. Trudeau struck again on March 29, 1979, when he detonated an explosive that killed Roland Dutemple, who was targeted for removal after the Angels learned he had provided information that led to the 1978 murders at Le Café Tourbillon. In May, Outlaw Donald McLean and his girlfriend were killed when a bomb planted by Trudeau and fellow Angels Yves Buteau and Jean-Pierre Mathieu detonated as he started his Harley-Davidson. McLean had already been seriously injured as a passenger in Gilles Cadorette's car when it exploded a year earlier.

The death toll climbed south of the border as well, which included four Outlaws and a female associate who were slaughtered in their sleep at a home in Charlotte, North Carolina on July 4, 1979.

For the remainder of 1979, both the Hells Angels and the Outlaws vigorously canvassed other biker gangs in Ontario and Quebec in an attempt to set up more chapters and selectively recruit what the Criminal Intelligence Service Canada called "hard-core criminal-type members." While the Angels were winning the war in Quebec, the Outlaws were expanding in Ontario; by the end of 1979, they had chapters in Windsor, St. Catharines, Hamilton, Toronto, Kingston, and Ottawa. Unable to make any headway in Ontario, the Hells Angels focussed on fortifying their strength in Quebec and, in September of that year, a second chapter in the province was established. Based in Laval, the "North chapter" was created when the existing Montreal chapter, which was now overflowing with members, was divided into two. Among the founding members of the new Laval chapter were many of Canada's first Hells Angels: Réjean (Zig Zag) Lessard, Laurent (L'Anglais) Viau, Jean-Pierre (Matt le Crosseur) Mathieu, and Jean-Guy (Brutus) Geoffrion. Michel (Willie) Mayrand and Guy-Louis (Chop) Adam also joined the North chapter that year while a former Popeye, Gilles (Le Nez) Lachance, joined in 1981 after he was released from his six-year sentence for manslaughter.

By the end of 1980, more than twenty people belonging to or associated with the two rival gangs had been murdered in Quebec, while another thirteen had been wounded. Between 1981 and 1984, the CISC estimated that another forty-two murders in Quebec were linked to the Outlaws–Hells Angels feud as well as battles between other motorcycle clubs fighting for control over the drug trade. Among the casualties was thirty-two-year-old Yves Buteau, who was killed on September 9, 1983, by Gino Goudreau, a small-time drug trafficker who had been repeatedly warned by Buteau to stop selling in Montreal parks located within Angels territory. Goudreau, whose brother was a member of the Quebec Outlaws, shot Buteau twice in the chest outside Le Petit Bourg bar, a Hells Angels hangout in Montreal. Goudreau also shot and killed thirty-six-year-old Angel and Vietnam War veteran René Lamoureux and wounded Guy (Frenchy) Gilbert, a Satan's Choice member from Ontario who was in Quebec to discuss a patchover with Buteau. Goudreau was arrested and charged, but when his case was tried, he was acquitted after convincing the court he killed in self-defence. Once freed, Goudreau was rewarded by the Outlaws for the murders — and for halting another attempt by the Angels to gain a presence in Ontario — by granting him membership in its Quebec chapter. The day after Buteau's funeral, a young boy found an undetonated remote-control bomb, made up of dynamite and 50 pounds of nails and gravel, lying on the side of the road close to where the procession of bikers had passed the day before. In May 1984, thirty-three-year-old Outlaws Quebec chapter president Daniel Savoie and another member died after two men on motorcycles riddled their car with machine-gun fire as they were driving on an open stretch of highway in Quebec. Savoie's brother, Bernard, was killed in March of that year when his car was demolished by a remote-control explosive device while his other brother, Robert, was sent to hospital after being shot in April.

Despite the carnage in Quebec, the Angels-Outlaws rivalry had yet to seriously impact Ontario. This was due largely to the ongoing efforts of the Outlaws to thwart the prospect of the Angels' patching over existing one-percenter clubs in the province combined with the unwillingness of these clubs to get sucked into the war. Despite an intensive recruitment drive, the advances of the Angels were rebuffed by most of the province's established gangs, who vowed to remain neutral in the conflict. Meanwhile, the Outlaws continued to win over converts in Ontario, patching over London's Queensmen in 1983 and Toronto's Iron Hawgs in 1984. The takeover of the Iron Hawgs turned the weekend bikers into hard-core drug dealers, according to one Hawg-turned-Outlaw who became a Crown witness in the 1986 drug trafficking trial of his colleague, Stanley (Beamer) McConnery. Former Outlaw Maurice Couling also testified that he bought about 60,000 hits of LSD as well as cocaine from Robert (Bobby) Marsh, a former president of the Hawgs who had convinced his fellow bikers to join the Outlaws in order to expand their access to drugs. Marsh himself was persuaded to patch over after a

Hells Angels funeral procession for Yves (Le Boss) Buteau

1983 meeting with McConnery, who at the time was national president of the Outlaws and a member of the St. Catharines chapter. Marsh would go on to become a major supplier of cocaine and synthetic drugs after he became president of the Canadian Outlaws. A Crown prosecutor at the trial told the court that McConnery advised Iron Hawgs members in no uncertain terms that "if they remained 'fence sitters' in the war between the Hells Angels and the Outlaws, their [drug] supply would cease as had happened to the Para-Dice Riders Motorcycle Club." After the patchover, McConnery and Marsh began supplying speed and cocaine to their fellow bikers. Those who became members of the Outlaws were required to sell 1,000 hits of LSD in order to pay for the handgun that was necessary for membership in the club, according to one former member. Club members also contributed to a war chest to buy weapons, dynamite and grenades in anticipation of an Ontario front in the war against the Hells Angels.

Speculation that the conflict between the Angels and the Outlaws would engulf Ontario was rife in law enforcement circles. A June 1979 edition of the *Globe and Mail* reported, "Specialists in biker intelligence in several Ontario police forces say bikers are arming themselves in preparation for war this summer. They say the clubs are stockpiling not only legal rifles and shotguns but illegal weapons such as pistols, automatic weapons, and even anti-tank rocket launchers and hand grenades stolen from Canadian Armed Forces bases at Borden and Petawawa." The war between the two enemies never did fully materialize in Ontario, at least not to the extent to which it raged in Quebec. However, Ontario was not spared smaller wars between independent one-percenter clubs. From 1979 to 1984, Hamilton became a battleground for a conflict that pitted the Angels-backed Wild Ones against the Hamilton chapter of the Outlaws, which had absorbed the city's Satan's Choice chapter in 1977. The Wild Ones were also engaged in a running battle with another independent club, the Red Devils. The main casualties of the dozens of bombings set off were four members of the Wild Ones. Dennis Stewart died September 5, 1979, in Niagara Falls after a bomb wired to his car's ignition exploded. Two other members were killed earlier that year when they accidentally detonated a bomb they were constructing in their van. By the end of the year, the fifteen-member Wild Ones club began teetering on the brink of extinction when another five of its members faced a gang-rape charge. All were acquitted in early 1980, however, after the main witness refused to testify. In May 1979, Hamilton police were called to her home to dismantle a bomb made up of a gelled explosive, eight sticks of dynamite, detonators, and an alarm clock.

Violence also erupted between the Satan's Choice and the Outlaws as they both attempted to establish their pre-eminence in Ontario. The Outlaws had effectively dissuaded the remaining Satan's Choice

chapters in the province from joining forces with the Hells Angels, so the Choice initiated a coalition with the Chosen Few and the Lobos motorcycle clubs in Hamilton. In 1983, an Outlaw member named David Eugene Sequin ran amok in the Chosen Few's headquarters in Emeryville, Ontario, killing three people and seriously wounding three others. Among the dead was club president Edward Bruce Morris, a twenty-one-year-old member, and a seventeen-year-old prospect. Sequin, who was placed on Canada's Most Wanted list after escaping from police, was killed in a gunfight with police in Steger, Illinois, in July 1985. In May 1984, a member of the Red Devils was killed in their Hamilton clubhouse in a hail of gunfire that tore through the building. A few months later, a member of the Satan's Choice was killed in Kitchener while riding his motorcycle after several shots were fired at him from a passing vehicle. On September 3, 1987, forty-year-old Donald Melanson, president of the Toronto-based Vagabonds Motorcycle Club, was found dead by a chambermaid in a North York hotel room. Police ruled that he had died from a gunshot wound to the head, most likely by someone he knew. Melanson, who was nicknamed Snorkle or Snorko because of his prominent nose, had just been convicted of drug trafficking and was to appear in court in a few days for sentencing. He already had an extensive record and had served several years in jail, although he had been acquitted on charges of attempting to murder three undercover police officers in 1973. Melanson recently relinquished the presidency of the Vagabonds in anticipation of the jail term he was about to receive. Melanson was buried following a procession of 125 motorcycles and a hundred cars that included representatives of biker groups from all over North America. His killer was never found.

In addition to Ontario and Quebec, intermittent biker battles flared up in other provinces. In Manitoba, the Silent Riders and Los Brovos, which both had about one hundred members each, were locked in a five-year struggle to gain control over Winnipeg's drug and prostitution trades. In 1983 and 1984, there were four car bombings that police attributed to a settling of accounts between the two gangs and in July 1984 Silent Rider Ronald Gagnon was hit in the chest with a shotgun blast while standing on the back steps of his

Winnipeg home. Police discovered his body a day later, but, according to one newspaper account, they "had a difficult time removing it because Mr. Gagnon's two vicious guard dogs — who obviously failed to protect their master from his assailant earlier — did a stalwart job of protecting his body from police." The same year, six homes and businesses belonging to members of the two clubs were dynamited. In May 1985, Los Brovos member Stanley Potter was shot and wounded, but refused to file a complaint with police. In September of that year, Ronald Gagnon's brother David was stabbed to death in a brawl and a Los Brovos member was charged with manslaughter in his death. In March 1986, a St. Boniface house that doubled as a Silent Riders' booze can was rocked by a powerful explosion that tore off much of the front of the two-storey structure. Following a series of raids, the Winnipeg police and the RCMP seized more than two hundred legal and illegal weapons as well as drugs. In a landmark court case in 1986, a provincial judge revoked the firearms certificates of all members of both clubs. By 1990, the war had ended victoriously for the Los Brovos after several of their foes were arrested and thrown in jail.

In Alberta, the two dominant biker groups, the Grim Reapers and the King's Crew, began fighting in 1983 when five sets of King's Crew colours were stolen by members of the Grim Reapers at gunpoint. The charred remains of the colours were dropped off at the offices of the *Calgary Sun* newspaper. Over the next four years, the two clubs traded gunfire, bombings, beatings, stabbings, and kidnappings. The war's first fatality was King's Crew member Ronald (Wrong Way) Moore, who died in June 1983 when a bomb exploded under the seat of his car. Police knew retaliation was imminent when Moore's newspaper obituary contained the promise "WE WON'T FORGET." The war's next victim was another King's Crew member named Steven Joell, who was gunned down at his home on January 22, 1984. Following a three-year lull, the rivalry was renewed in 1987 when both of the gangs' Calgary clubhouses were strafed by automatic gunfire. In September, the Grim Reapers' clubhouse was completely destroyed by an explosion. This was followed in October by the disappearance of King's Crew member Louis Aaron Blatt. His body was never found, although police theorized that he was abducted

and killed by the Grim Reapers after his inscribed King's Crew ring was found in a burned-out van just east of Red Deer. In November, simultaneous police raids against the Grim Reapers and King's Crew were launched all over the province, resulting in the seizure of drugs and over 150 weapons. Along with convictions for drug and weapons offences, the Crown successfully petitioned a provincial court judge to prohibit all King's Crew and Grim Reapers' members from owning or possessing firearms or other offensive weapons for periods ranging from three to five years.

A FERTILE SPRINGBOARD

Following its conquest of Quebec, and frustrated by its inability to expand into Ontario, the Hells Angels set their sights on other provinces. At the top of their list were two provinces strategically placed for their ambitious national plans: British Columbia and Nova Scotia. Like Montreal, Vancouver and Halifax are port cities and thus fit neatly into the Hells Angels' ambitious smuggling ventures. Vancouver was also within easy reach of the Angels' California stronghold. According to a 1986 report by the RCMP and the DEA, Vancouver had become a "fertile springboard" and "an important transit point for drugs, weapons and other contraband. As a result of their meetings with Canadian motorcycle gangs, it became possible for the Hells Angels to set up a pipeline from the United States through British Columbia and across Canada to Quebec." Vancouver was also attractive because the Lower Mainland had one of the country's largest addict populations, providing a lucrative new drug market for the Angels. The Halifax port was eyed as an important entry point for cocaine from South America and Florida. A presence in both provinces also allowed the Angels to establish the outermost flanks in their planned coast-to-coast network of chapters.

On July 23, 1983, after almost a year of partying and meetings with senior officers of the Quebec Hells Angels, the Vancouver, White Rock and Nanaimo chapters of the Satan's Angels was patched over. Later that year, a fourth Hells Angels chapter, located in East Vancouver, was formed. Made up of hard-core biker criminals, the East End chapter would become the unofficial headquarters of the Hells Angels in the province. For biker expert Daniel Wolf, the instantaneous and simultaneous emergence of four B.C. chapters "was a major international coup for the Hell's Angels MC conglomerate. It virtually locked up the Canadian west coast and made the Hell's Angels' position in British Columbia unassailable. Neither of the two remaining outlaw clubs in B.C., the Tribesmen of Squamish or the Highwaymen in Cranbrook, would seriously consider forming an alternative coalition, let alone confront the Angels by merging with the Bandidos in nearby Washington or the Outlaws MC. Both of the smaller (fifteen-member) clubs decided to align themselves on an associate basis with the new Hell's Angels."

By the mid-1980s, the Hells Angels were in control of "all outlaw motorcycle gang activity in British Columbia," the joint RCMP and DEA report concluded. "The Hells Angels West Coast criminal activity includes trafficking in illicit drugs as well as business interests believed to be fronts for illegal activities. There are now more than forty registered companies in British Columbia which are controlled by or under the influence of the Hells Angels." The Nanaimo chapter also purchased a large swath of land outside the city and, at a massive party in 1986, "Angel Acres" played host to more than 2,500 people from around Canada and the world. Among those in attendance were representatives from the Para-Dice Riders, Satan's Choice and Vagabonds from Ontario, the Rebels from Alberta and Saskatchewan, the Grim Reapers from Alberta, and the Vikings from Quebec. Like most other chapters, the main revenue of the B.C. Hells Angels came from drugs, such as marijuana, methamphetamines, PCP, LSD, as well as pharmaceuticals stolen from drugstores

and warehouses. They also established a particular niche that soon became the single-largest source of revenue for Hells Angels chapters all over Canada: cocaine trafficking. Not long after the four B.C. chapters were established in 1983, hundreds of kilos of coke began to pour into the province from California, Quebec, or directly from South America for distribution in B.C., Alberta, and Saskatchewan.

On December 5, 1984, the Angels officially spread its wings to the other coast when it took over the Thirteenth Tribe of Halifax, a move made "to consolidate control of drug trafficking on Canada's East Coast," according to the RCMP and DEA. On the very same day, the Gitans motorcycle club in Sherbrooke became the third Hells Angels chapter in Quebec. By the end of the year, the Angels had chapters or affiliate clubs in nine out of ten provinces. They had four chapters and about seventy-two members in British Columbia, three chapters with sixty-nine members in Quebec, and one chapter with eight members in Halifax. They had also set up partnerships with clubs in Alberta, Saskatchewan, and Manitoba. Around this time, the Outlaws dominated Ontario with about eighty-five members in eight chapters, although their thirty-eight members in Quebec were greatly outnumbered by their foe. Despite their dominance in Quebec and across the country, as well as their growing sophistication as a criminal organization, the erratic and ultraviolent nature of the Quebec wing of the Hells Angels would come to the fore in 1985 with a cannibalistic display that accomplished in one day what the Outlaws could barely muster in one year.

EASY RIDER

While Sonny Barger is trying to transform his international band of ass-kicking, chopper-riding, beer-drinking, hell-raising social screw-ups into a well-oiled criminal machine, the coked-out North chapter is spending more time partying than taking care of business. The Quebec Angels' most senior dude, Yves (Le Boss) Buteau, convenes a meeting of both of the province's chapters in the spring of 1982. He lays down the law. He is furious. He looks like someone just fired a bazooka up his ass. He puts the burn

into the brothers and demands the North chapter quit putting so much coke up their noses and start making the chapter a little money. Buteau even bans the brothers from using cocaine. The hard-partying North chapter ignores the ban. Their lust for coke leads to the unimaginable: killing brothers from their own chapter. That year, Denis (Le Cure) Kennedy, who boasts a Filthy Few tattoo, and Charles (Charlie) Hachey, are offed and then tossed aside like a couple of burned-out whores. Hachey was heavily in debt to West End Gang leader and cocaine king Peter Frank (Dunie) Ryan. The North chapter had been working with Ryan, who was supplying them with blow and hash, sometimes in exchange for speed that the gang's chemist Jean-Guy (Brutus) Geoffrion cranks out in the club's drug lab. The North chapter also becomes Ryan's errand boys, debt collectors, and hired killers. Ryan exploits their drug-fuelled homicidal tendencies when Patrick Hugh McGurnaghan, the forty-four-year-old brother of West End Gang member Porky, rips Ryan off for drugs and cash. Ryan hires Apache, that psycho hit man. McGurnaghan is wasted on October 27, 1981, when his Mercedes explodes like a '74 Springer with open drag pipes.

By 1982, after most of the cocaine that had been fronted to them goes up their nose, Kennedy and Hachey owe Ryan more than $305,000. The two brain-dead cokeheads concoct a scheme to save their asses. To help them out, they recruit Robert (Steve) Grenier, a twenty-three-year-old striker with the North chapter, and his girlfriend, Marjolaine Poirier. They plan to kidnap one of Ryan's children. But Ryan sits atop of shitload of money, which buys a lot of ears on the streets. He gets wind of the plot and screams at his buddy Apache Trudeau like a freaked-out banshee. Apache Trudeau and five other guttersnipes from the North chapter decide to exterminate Hachey. Hachey, his girlfriend, and Kennedy go tits up in January 1982 and their bodies are thrown into the St. Lawrence River.

Things begin to spin out of control like a bald Dunlop on a rain-splattered highway and there is no one to keep things straight. The 1983 death of Le Boss Buteau, the Angels' anal-retentive leader, helps sets in motion a chain of events that take the Quebec Angels to the brink of self-destruction. The carb was opened full throttle and there was no one around to hit the brakes. The men who replace Buteau are Michel (Sky) Langlois, who becomes the Canadian president, and Réjean (Zig Zag) Lessard, who becomes president of the Montreal chapter after bolting from the North chapter like a '57 Sportster with a 1340cc V-twin engine. Lessard is born in 1946 and after dicking around for twenty years he joins the Popeyes. He becomes an Angel in 1977 when the club is patched over. He earns the name "Sky" because he has a pilot's licence and owns a

plane. Lessard grows up in the Eastern Townships and becomes a brother in the Marauders biker gang in Asbestos, Quebec. Called "Zig Zag" by his biker brothers, Lessard sells drugs, assaults citizens, and parties hard. In 1979, the Marauders split up and Lessard and some other brothers join the Angels. Zig Zag is a member of the Filthy Few. "A revolver cylinder is tattooed on his right arm. Six skulls, instead of bullets, stare out the holes. Lessard has a back pack — the Hells Angels colors tattooed on his skin — to deny rival bikers the honor of stealing his colours." Zig Zag is an epileptic so he goes cold turkey on the drugs around 1983 and begins to take care of business. He's a non-smoking, non-drinking, granola-eating health freak who is all balls and biceps. He is also a kick-ass organizer and helps mastermind the Angels' growth in Quebec by buying into King Barger's dream of turning the Angels into a criminal conglomerate. By 1985, the Angels have another chapter in Quebec. They also control the chemical drug market in Eastern Canada. North chapter brothers Zig Zag, Tiny Richard, and Sam Michaud feel their coke-crazed fellow brothers are dragging their club's colours down. In 1983, they quit the chapter and haul ass back to Sorel for good.

After Ryan is killed by Paul April on November 13, 1984, Trudeau and his equally vicious sidekick, Michel Blass, attend the funeral a few days later. The new West End Gang leader, Allan (The Weasel) Ross makes Blass and Trudeau a deal: wipe out Paul April and they can split $200,000 in cash. In addition, the $300,000 debt owed by the North chapter is wiped out, plus Ross will donate another $100,000 to the chapter. The Weasel delivers $25,000 to Apache as a down payment. Apache knows April and visits him at his apartment. Trudeau notices April doesn't have a television set, so he offers to bring him one along with a VCR. Around 4 a.m. on November 25, 1984, Trudeau drives Michael Blass to the apartment. Blass delivers the TV set and VCR, which is packed with thirty-five pounds of explosives. The timing device is wired into the VCR. Also in the VCR is a tape of the *Hell's Angels Forever*, a movie co-produced by the president of the Angels Manhattan chapter, Sandy Frazier Alexander. Three other asswipes besides April are in the apartment. Blass sets the VCR timer to five minutes and then clears out of the place, saying his car is illegally parked. Five minutes later, "an explosion flattens the walls in eight apartments, sends elevators to the basement and blows the windows out of 13 units in a building 75 feet away." The four ignorant slobs are killed instantly. Eight others in the building are totally messed up.

Zig Zag hauls ass to Manhattan and bitches to ex-marine Sandy Alexander about the cokeheads in the North chapter. Alexander tells Zig Zag to deal with the problem himself. Zig Zag hatches a plot to eliminate the entire North chapter in one wholesale purge. Few will miss them: "Most of the stringy greaseballs are candidates for deviants anonymous."

Lessard signs the death warrants of Laurent (L'Anglais) Viau, chapter president, Jean-Guy (Brutus) Geoffrion, the chemist, Guy-Louis (Chop) Adam,

chapter secretary, Michel (Jambe de Boils) Mayrand, Regis (Lucky) Asselin, and Yves (Apache) Trudeau. They are to die on Saturday, March 23, 1985. The other bros will be forced into retirement or will have to join the slimmed-down North chapter. Yvon (Le Pére) Bilodeau and Jean-Pierre (Matt le Crosseur) Mathieu will be retired. Michel (Jinx) Genest and Gilles (Le Nez) Lachance's sorry asses will be spared and they will be told to join the Montreal chapter.

All North chapter brothers are invited to a party for the four Angels chapters in Quebec and Nova Scotia on Saturday, March 23, to be held in the new Sherbrooke chapter's clubhouse in Lennoxville, 160 kilometres east of Montreal. The plan is to kill the targets on the spot. In on the plot with Zig Zag are former North chapter members Tiny Richard, Sam Michaud, Randall (Blondie) Mersereau, the vice-president and a founding member of the Halifax Angels, Georges

Scumbag members of the Quebec Hells Angels North chapter

(Bo-Boy) Beaulieu, president of the Sherbrooke Angels, prospect Gerry (Le Chat) Coulombe, Robert (Couleuvre) Tremblay, a former brother with the Gitans who became an Angel when the club was patched over in 1984, Jean-Yves (Boule) Tremblay, who just received his colours from the Montreal chapter, Patrick (Frenchy) Guernier of the Halifax chapter, as well as Quebec Angels Jacques (La Pelle) Pelletier and Gaétan (Gaet) Proulx.

Tiny orders Boy Beaulieu to pick up some sleeping bags at a sporting goods store in Sherbrooke. Boule Tremblay tells Le Chat Coulombe to rent a cube van and to make damn sure to wear gloves while inside. He is also given a box containing bottles of cleaning fluid, a jacket, and a big-ass knife. Coulombe delivers the van to Tremblay at the Sorel clubhouse. Coulombe is handed guns by Pelletier, Richard, and fellow Angel Denis Houle. He brings the guns to Lennoxville the morning of March 23.

Some of the North chapter brothers are suspicious of the church meeting that is planned. They ignore the invitation and only three shit-for-brains from the North chapter — Adam, Geoffrion, and Mayrand — show up. Lessard reschedules church for the next day and demands that ALL North chapter brothers attend. Church starts in mid-afternoon on Sunday, March 24, 1985. Close to forty Angels and prospects from Quebec and Nova Scotia make it. They are greeted at the door by Boule Tremblay. Le Chat Coulombe stands guard outside the Lennoxville bunker armed with a 12-gauge shotgun. Other prospects, like Norman (Biff) Hamel and Claude (Coco) Roy, are forced to wait outside as five brothers of the North chapter are slaughtered inside the clubhouse. (1) "Luc Michaud shoots Brutus Geoffrion in the right cheek and upper left side of the head. One bullet goes out the back of the skull. The other lodges at the base near the spine." (2) Willie Mayrand falls to the floor after being blasted. His brother, Richard (Bert) Maynard, a striker with the Angels, watches him become a cold corpse. (3) Chop Adam runs out the front door like a cat with diarrhea racing for the sandbox. Tremblay is on his heels and fires seven times at close range. Bullets shatter like bombs inside his skull and lungs. (4) Viau slumps to the ground.

Pelletier points a gun at him. Another biker stands over him and fires one deadly bullet into his head. (5) Mathieu dies unarmed with his .357 Magnum and .45-calibre revolvers at home.

Pelletier and Guernier train their guns on Le Nez Lachance who is chugging a beer at the clubhouse bar when the slaughter begins. Le Nez Lachance, Le Père Bilodeau, and Bert Maynard are ordered to stand in the corner, while the floors are washed and the five sticky corpses are dragged into the garage and thrown into a pile like a bunch of rusted Jap rice-wagon chassis. Zig Zag tells the three brothers they will not be harmed as long as they keep their mouths shut. Lachance is offered membership in the Montreal chapter and accepts.

The five dead brothers are wrapped in sleeping bags, weighted down with chains and cement blocks, and loaded into the rented van being driven by Gaétan Proulx. Le Chat Coulombe rides shotgun. From a ferry crossing at St. Ignace de Loyola, the bodies are dumped into the St. Lawrence River.

The next day, Lessard calls a meeting of all Quebec and Halifax Angels and tells everyone of the murders and explains the reasons behind them. He says the North chapter had done a burn and had to be taken care of. Lessard also sends brothers to talk to the B.C. chapters. Le Chat Coulombe and Biff Hamel are ordered to rent two large trucks and clean out the North chapter's clubhouse and their murdered brothers' apartments. Zig Zag announces the North chapter is officially disbanded and orders that the motorcycles and other shit belonging to the victims and other brothers from the chapter be given to the Halifax chapter. Zig Zag puts contracts on the heads of missing North chapter brothers Apache Trudeau and Regis Asselin. Jacques Pelletier and Denis Houle are ordered to eliminate Asselin, who finds out about the plot beforehand and makes sure to keep out of harm's way. But he can't stay in hiding forever. On May 2, 1985, he is shot in the abdomen six times as he leaves his old lady's Laurentian home, but survives after driving himself to hospital.

A few days after the slaughter, the Quebec provincial cops learn of the disappearance of Viau, Geoffrion, Mathieu, Mayrand, and Adam. They have a wiretap at the Sherbrooke clubhouse and launch operation "Chant du Coq." More than four hundred cops raid one hundred sites across Quebec and Nova Scotia. At least fifty brothers are arrested. About $8 million worth of blow, hashish, LSD and PCP, in addition to submachine guns, rifles, baseball bats, machetes, sleeping bags, and a cement block attached to chains are seized. When the cops swoop down on the Lennoxville bunker, they find sensor wires under the driveway, closed-circuit television cameras on posts, six guard dogs (which had to be tranquilized), a complex system of floodlights and burglar alarms, and bear traps in the surrounding forest. The walls of the building are reinforced with steel plates and several rifles lie under each window. Police find secret rooms that can only be entered through electronically controlled panels. Behind the panels, the cops find one John Belushi–sized shitload of cocaine. The choppers of the missing men turn up in Halifax. Another missing brother is added to the list: Claude (Coco) Roy. He was originally spared because "he was one of the few North chapter bikers to know where the group stashed its drugs and money. The murderers were hoping to get their hands on the loot." Coco was shit-kicked to death at a rural motel in early April by Michel Genest and Normand Hamel. The execution was ordered by the leaders of the Quebec Angels because they feared Coco would squeal.

Police believe the disappearance of six men is the work of the Outlaws. But there still is not enough evidence to figure out what happened to the missing scumbag bikers. That changes on June 1. Asswipe journalist Yves Lavigne describes:

The bodies rot slowly from the inside out for 69 days at the bottom of the murky St. Lawrence River. The dead Angels, like hairy, tattooed wineskins, bloat with methane gas. The swift current jostles the corpses as they lighten, then slides them along the muddy seaway bottom through clinging weeds. The 30-pound blocks they are chained to resist and the Angels tug gently at their anchors. The more they rot, the more they swell. The

bodies float suspended beneath the surface like grotesque circus balloons above a field of undulating slimy green arms. Brutus Geoffrion, the biggest of the murdered Angels, breaks surface first. A fat, soggy sleeping bag bobs in the waves near the Bertheirville ferry crossing between Sorel and Saint-Ignace Island at 1:30 Saturday afternoon on June 1. The 40-year-old mechanic's body is smothered with mushrooms and other fungi that feed on his flesh and help it decay. A padlock fastens 18 feet of chain wrapped around his body to a cement block.

Willie Mayrand's soggy ass is dredged out of the river by police divers the next day. On June 3, L'Anglais Viau is dredged from the bottom. He is in the foetal position. Later that day, the remains of Coco Roy are recovered. Two days later, another couple of hairy asses with decomposed bodies attached are found. They are the remains of Chop Adam and L'Anglais Viau.

A coroner's inquest is held. The corpses could only be the remains of Hells Angels, but the cops need more evidence before charges can be laid. The coroner concludes that the killing of six brothers was planned by Zig Zag. He acted as the "master of ceremonies."

The coroner, police, and prosecutors are helped by Angels who become rats: Trudeau, Coloumbe, and LaChance. Apache Trudeau is among those North chapter brothers who smells something fishy and skips the fatal church meeting. He books into a detox centre on March 17, 1985, and stays for a month. Three killers are sent there to plug Apache, but they can't get the job done because too many people are around. When he is released, Apache accepts a contract offered to him by Zig Zag to murder "disgraced" Angel, thirty-five-year old Jean-Marc (La grande gueule) Deniger. In return, Apache receives Deniger's Harley, which had been seized by the Angels. On May 1, 1985, Apache strangles Deniger, wraps the body in a sleeping bag, and stuffs it on the floor of Deniger's Chevrolet station wagon. Apache is anxious to claim his motorcycle and anonymously phones a reporter at the *Journal de Montréal* to tell him where he can find the body. Two months later Apache is serving a one-year stint at Bordeaux Prison for possession of an illegal weapon. He learns about the $50,000 price on his sorry ass and becomes a rat. The cops offer him immunity from past murders if he testifies against his brothers who committed the murders. Apache agrees and also provides information on ninety other murders.

Apache Trudeau "carves his way into underworld legend with bullets, bombs and a strangler's hands strengthened by a primal lust for death." His gutter-sniping soul "is a relic of pre-moral, pre-social, pre-literate man. How it gets into a 20th-century body is anyone's guess." Trudeau's entry into the world on April 2, 1946, "is nature's vicious afterthought and cruel joke." The dark-haired, lantern-jawed Apache is Canada's most prolific killer. He whacks forty-three people between September 1970 and July 7, 1985. Twenty-nine are shot, ten are blown up, three are beaten to death (including a mother defending her son), and one is strangled. "The scrawny hit man plans each killing meticulously. He often befriends targets to learn their habits and ices them when they least expect it. His cold-blooded professionalism earns him the nickname 'The Mad Bumper.'" He is also nicknamed "Apache" after he cuts off a rival gang member's ear with a hatchet. He later claims he was one of the first Hells Angels in Canada to earn the "Filthy Few" tattoo. It then becomes his job to hand out these decorations to other bloodstained brothers. He was an early president of the North chapter, and is responsible for kick-starting the Hells Angels' graveyard — a spot along the St. Lawrence River where all the gang's corpses are dumped.

Joining Apache is Le Chat Coulombe. Three months after the massacre, he is promised he will receive his colours and be initiated into the club. He calls his biker brother, Gaet Proulx, who has heard nothing about it. Coulombe begins to worry that he is next on the hit list and then goes to the cops and tells them Lessard described the mass murder plan while driving with him to a dentist's appointment just before the bloody ass-kicking. Gilles (Le Nez) Lachance fears "he may be forced to join the gang's diving club" and after he is arrested on February 21, 1986, he rolls over like an overweight Superglide on a hairpin turn. He is the only rat who actually witnessed the massacre.

Coulombe, Trudeau, and Lachance give the cops enough information to make a murder case stick. On October 2, 1985, twenty-seven Angels from Quebec and Nova Scotia are charged with first-degree murder. Among the busted are Rejean Lessard, Luc Michaud Jacques Pelletier, Robert Richard, Michel Langlois, Randall Mersereau, Robert Tremblay, Gaétan Proulx, Georges Beaulieu, and Denis Houle. On October 31, 1986, Michel Genest is found guilty of the first-degree murder of Claude Roy. Genest is sentenced to life imprisonment. On December 4, verdicts are reached in the trial of three others. Jacques Pelletier, Luc Michaud, and Rejean Lessard are found guilty of first-degree murder and sentenced to life imprisonment. In one ball-grabbing verdict Tiny Richard is found not guilty. Born in 1950, Tiny was a brother with the Popeyes when it was taken over by the Angels in 1977. He stands over six feet tall and weighs more than three hundred pounds. The dude is one big tubba shit. Two days earlier, one of the jurors in the trial is charged with obstruction of justice after he confesses he received $25,000 from his hash dealer to convince his fellow jurors not to convict the four on trial. He was promised another $75,000 if they are found not guilty. On June 17, 1987, four Halifax Hells Angels, including Randall Mersereau, are found not guilty by a Quebec jury on charges of first-degree murder. Following the trial, a black, four-door Jaguar blasts them away. Behind the wheel is Tiny. Despite the acquittals, the Halifax chapter is decimated when almost every one of its brothers are jailed for various offences. On October 31, 1999, Mersereau disappears and is presumed dead. He had parted company with the Angels and was rumoured to be forging links with archrival Bandidos. A year later, his brother Kirk and sister-in-law, Nancy, are murdered in their rural home. Kirk Mersereau had placed $50,000 bounty on the head of his brother's killer.

Robert (Snake) Tremblay goes into hiding in England, where the English Angels let him crash in a small London apartment. It takes more than a year, but his French-Canadian ass is collared by Scotland Yard. After spending six months in an English prison, he is sent back to Canada in July 1987 on murder charges. That year, Tremblay and Gaetan Proulx are convicted of premeditated murder and sentenced to life. Neither is eligible for parole for at least twenty-five years. But in 1995, Proulx is released on a technicality. Most of the other accused receive lesser sentences for accessory to murder. Georges (Bo-Boy) Beaulieu receives a nine-year sentence. Michel (Sky) Langlois, who was not directly implicated in the murders, disappears after police issue a warrant for his arrest in February 1986. He sneaks into Morocco, where he gets stoned on hash for the next two years. On April 13, 1988, Langlois and fellow Angels René Hébert and Guy Auclair turn themselves into police in Sherbrooke. Langlois receives a two-year prison sentence.

In March 1986, Apache Trudeau saunters into a courtroom and pleads guilty to manslaughter in the death of forty-three people. The plea bargain is part of a promise to help the cops solve another forty murders and fifteen attempted murders. The judge sentences him to life imprisonment and wishes him "Good luck." Trudeau will be eligible for parole in seven years and when released he will be given a new identity and relocated. In 2004, the fifty-eight-year-old degenerate is freed from jail, but is arrested on ten counts of sexual assault against a young boy and thrown out of the witness protection program.

Coulombe and Lachance rat out their brothers and are given easy time and new identities. Michel Blass also becomes a rat. Even though he pleads guilty to twelve murders, he is only charged with manslaughter.

Tiny goes on to become the national president of the Canadian Angels before dying of a heart attack at his home on February 23, 1996. The forty-six-year-old biker had slimmed down to a bonerack 230 pounds. But it is not enough to take the strain off his ticker. More than three hundred people attend Tiny's funeral.

Zig Zag Lessard converts to Buddhism while in jail and has all four of his gang tattoos removed. In February 2006, he is granted permission to take an escorted leave. He uses it to visit his aging parents. He then meditates at a Buddhist centre with his Zen master and a police escort.

ONE OF THE WEALTHIEST OUTLAW MOTORCYCLE GANGS IN THE WORLD

The bloodletting in Quebec and subsequent arrests and prosecution of Hells Angels members proved to be only a temporary setback for the rapidly expanding motorcycle club. While the Outlaws tried to capitalize on the Angels' internal problems, they had their own troubles. In January 1985, close to five hundred police officers descended on Outlaws clubhouses and other Ontario properties belonging to its members. The raids, which took place in twelve cities in the province and capped a fourteen-month undercover investigation by a special biker task force, dealt "a severe blow" to the Outlaws criminal activities, according to one police spokesperson. Approximately 125 arrests and more than six hundred charges were laid, most of them related to drugs and weapons. Police seized marijuana, cocaine, methamphetamine, a suitcase that contained a portable synthetic drug lab, rifles, shotguns, a machine gun, an automatic handgun, and more than $460,000 in cash. Among those arrested were Canadian Outlaws president Bobby Marsh and former president Stanley McConnery, who were both charged with numerous drug possession, manufacturing, and trafficking offences. The following year, both Marsh and McConnery were convicted and sentenced to five years apiece.

The Outlaws were dealt another blow in April 1989, when an eighteen-month investigation into cocaine production and trafficking led to the arrest of twenty-six members in Ontario and Quebec. Through undercover work, police were able to identify and infiltrate a faction of the club, made up primarily of senior members, who oversaw all cocaine trafficking in the two provinces and had even purportedly set up a laboratory near Kingston, Ontario, that refined cocaine paste imported from South America. (The lab was actually never found. Police believe it was shut down by its operators when it became apparent that investigators were closing in.) Among those charged was Daniel Bronson, a member of the Ottawa chapter and the man police believed had become the club's national president following the arrest of Marsh. Four months later, police struck again, raiding Outlaws clubhouses in Quebec and Ontario and arresting another thirty members and associates on cocaine manufacturing and trafficking charges.

While the police were cutting a swath through the Outlaws in Ontario, the Quebec chapters of the motorcycle gang were systematically targeted by their arch enemy, as Yves Lavigne explains in his 1999 book, *Hells Angels at War*:

> The Hells Angels tackled the Outlaws in their Joliette stronghold and whittled the chapter down one biker at a time. A confident and cocky contingent of fifty Hells Angels and supporters toured Joliette bars on August 2, 1990, in a show of force and defiance they knew the Outlaws could not match. They would not rest until all Outlaws were dead. Outlaws leader Claude Meunier, 39, parked his bike outside a motorcycle repair shop in Montreal's Cote-Saint-Paul one day during the first week of September 1990. He was riddled with bullets fired from a passing car before he could get off. Police found a semi-automatic pistol in a storm drain a few blocks away — the trademark disposal of a professional hit … By the end of 1990, there were only ten Outlaws in Quebec, and they kept to themselves in south-west Montreal, in Valleyfield, and in Chateauguay. Quebec Outlaws president Johnny (Sonny) Lacombe, 46, would not leave his Chateauguay house without bodyguards. The Hells Angels had blown up his mother's car in early November in an attempt to kill his brother, Bertrand.

By the early 1990s, the Hells Angels had mounted a remarkable comeback in Quebec. Not only was its main rival on the ropes, but it was rebuilding existing chapters and adding new ones. In 1988, they inaugurated their newest clubhouse in Saint-Nicolas, a suburb of Quebec City, when the local Vikings and the Iron Coffins motorcycle clubs were patched over. Before long, the Angels had taken over much of the cocaine market in and around Quebec City. By 1992, the province was home to four Hells Angels chapters, located in Sorel, Sherbrooke, Quebec City, and Trois-Rivières. They also exerted control over other numerous one-percenter clubs in the province. In contrast, the Outlaws still had only one chapter in Montreal with a membership of just eight and no allies among other biker gangs in the province.

The Hells Angels continued to reign supreme in British Columbia as well. They had an estimated sixty-five full-patch members in five chapters — located in Nanaimo, White Rock, East Vancouver, Coquitlam, and Haney — and could count on at least three puppet clubs in the province. They also exerted significant influence in other Western provinces through their ties with the Rebels and Grim Reapers in Alberta, the Rebels in Saskatchewan, and the Los Brovos in Manitoba. By the mid-1990s, the CISC was calling the B.C. Hells Angels "one of the wealthiest outlaw motorcycle gangs in the world."

With sixty-nine chapters spread out over thirteen countries and four continents, the Angels had clearly established themselves as the world's most powerful outlaw motorcycle group. As their illegal drug empire expanded, they were also emerging as one of the world's largest criminal networks. Yet despite their growing national and international prominence, the Angels had still not cracked the most prized jewel in the Canadian criminal crown: Ontario. By the early 1990s, there were fourteen motorcycle gangs in the province with more than 480 members. And while recent enforcement actions against them took its toll, the Outlaws were still the most powerful and influential gang in Ontario.

TOTAL WAR

It is Maurice (Mom) Boucher who, more than any other person, has been held responsible for the bloodiest gang war ever fought on Canadian streets. The eldest of eight siblings, Boucher was born on June 21, 1953 to a working-class family in Causapscal, a small town on Quebec's Gaspé Peninsula. At the age of two, his father moved the family to Montreal where he worked in construction and settled his family in

Hochelaga-Maisonneuve, one of Montreal's poorest neighbourhoods. While he was close to his mother, Maurice had a strained relationship with his father, who was an alcoholic and abusive. He quit school in grade nine and, a year later, had developed a serious drug problem. Unable to find work and needing cash to support his habit, Maurice Boucher resorted to petty crime. He served his first jail time in 1976 when he received a forty-month butcher sentence after he and an accomplice burst into a butchers shop and robbed a seventy-one-year-old butcher of $138.39 after threatening him with a sawed-off shotgun and a meat cleaver. When he was released, Boucher reverted to his old ways, committing numerous thefts, some in tandem with his brothers. Before the end of the decade, he had been charged with extortion and possession of a stolen credit card. His foray into the world of biker gangs began in 1978 when he joined the SS, a white-supremacist biker gang named after Adolf Hitler's feared secret police. The gang folded in 1984, the same year Boucher was handed a twenty-three-month sentence for sexually assaulting a sixteen-year-old girl. After being set free in 1986, Boucher had his eye on the big time of outlaw bikerdom and was rewarded with prospect status in the Montreal chapter of the Hells Angels. The Lennoxville massacre and its aftermath had made room for a new generation of bikers, and the Angels leadership prized criminal entrepreneurship above all else. The determined Boucher quickly made a name for himself as one of the gang's most productive drug dealers.

Boucher became a full-patch member on May 1, 1987, and, three days later, twenty-three-year-old Martin Huneault, president of the Laval-based Death Riders biker gang, was shot to death by a hooded gunman in Laval. The Death Riders had a large chunk of the city's drug market and had thus attracted the attention of the Hells Angels. The murder of Huneault, who opposed any alliance between the two clubs, not only cleared the way for the Death Riders to become a Hells Angels puppet club that month, it allowed the Angels to take control of drug trafficking in Laval. His death was also Boucher's first step in his mercurial rise to the top of the Hells Angels hierarchy in Quebec. No one was ever arrested for the murder of Martin Huneault, but just hours after his funeral, police spot-

ted Death Riders Mario Martin and André Richard meeting with Boucher and fellow Angel Normand Hamel. While Boucher was establishing the foundation for his future career as a feared drug baron in the late 1980s, he was still carrying out violent thefts. In 1988, he was arrested for hijacking a truck in Ontario, using nothing more than a board with a nail as his weapon. After he was released from jail in 1990, Boucher would rarely get his hands dirty through such petty crimes. With his eyes set on an executive position in the Angels, he kicked his drug habit and, by the early 1990s, his ambitious nature and natural leadership abilities earned him the presidency of the Montreal chapter.

While barely literate, Boucher was a calculating criminal who went to bed early every night and woke up around dawn every morning on the belief that it was easier to spot police surveillance during the daylight hours. He had a singular drive to monopolize Quebec's cocaine market and establish the Angels as the dominant one-percenter biker club in the province. In order to help achieve these goals, Boucher created and supervised a puppet club called the Rockers, which was founded on March 26, 1992. The Rockers were his main drug trafficking and enforcement arm and served to insulate Boucher and other Hells Angels members from police and prosecution. They were central to Boucher's plans to control the cocaine trade in downtown Montreal. Each member of the Rockers was assigned a specific area to sell coke and other drugs supplied by their Angel overlords. They were also tasked with identifying virgin territories that could be taken over by the Angels' drug trafficking machine. Boucher personally received $500 for every kilo of cocaine sold by the puppet club.

In addition to the Rockers, Mom Boucher was instrumental in creating and heading the Nomads, which would become the Hells Angels central cocaine trafficking clearing house for Quebec as well as its most powerful chapter. With Boucher taking the lead, the Quebec Nomads chapter was created with four goals in mind: to provide overarching leadership for the growing number of Hells Angels in Quebec, to coordinate drug trafficking in the province, to help promote the expansion of the biker club into Ontario and beyond, and to oversee (and escalate) the war against the Rock

Machine and other rivals. Among the other Hells Angels "elites" who became founding members of the Nomads were: Normand (Biff) Hamel, Boucher's close associate, ex-SS member and the godfather of the Death Riders; Walter (Nurget) Stadnick, the Hells Angels national president; Donald (Pup) Stockford, his close associate from Hamilton; Louis (Melou) Roy, former president of the Trois-Rivières chapter; his right-hand man, Richard Vallée; David (Wolf) Carroll, a senior member of the Halifax chapter; Denis (Not Reliable) Houle, one of the participants in the Lennoxville massacre, and Gilles (Trooper) Mathieu, who had joined the Angels in 1980 and had become one of Boucher's closest advisers. As Hells Angels tradition dictated, the Nomads chapter was not restricted to any one city. Instead, their territory was all of Quebec.

Under Boucher, the Quebec Hells Angels trafficked whatever made them money — synthetic drugs,

Maurice (Mom) Boucher flashes the peace sign to photographers outside a Montreal funeral home in April 2000.

hashish, cocaine, and even bootleg Viagra. Cocaine was the biggest money-maker, however, and Boucher was instrumental in the Hells Angels new centralized cocaine trafficking system in Quebec. The Nomads purchased the drug in massive quantities (as much as 1,000 kilos at a time) and individual chapters and puppet clubs were required to purchase their cocaine for resale from the Nomads. In a six-month period in 2000, for example, the Trois-Rivières chapter bought a total of 164 kilos of cocaine and 105 kilos of hash from the Nomads. Police observed couriers carrying bags of drug cash to nondescript apartments used by the Nomads to be counted, stored in safes, and meticulously recorded on computer spreadsheets. The day that police stopped the banking operation, they seized $5.5 million in cash. Police also confiscated the accounting spreadsheets, which indicated that the Nomads had supplied 2,000 kilos of cocaine and another 2,000 kilos of hash in one eight-month period in 2000. That year, the Quebec Hells Angels pulled in an estimated $900 million from drug sales. Despite their growing control over Quebec's drug trade, it still was not enough for Boucher, whose intolerance for any competition set the Hells Angels on a crash course with an upstart competitor in the province: the Rock Machine.

The founder of the Rock Machine was Salvatore Cazzetta. Born in 1954, he grew up in Saint-Henri, the tough working-class neighbourhood in southwest Montreal that also spawned the Dubois brothers. Cazzetta was also a former member of the SS biker gang, but unlike Boucher who gravitated toward the Hells Angels when the club dissolved in 1984, he decided to go his own way. He was repulsed by the thought of being associated with a gang that would execute its own members. Aside from these moral misgivings, his ambitious side also cautioned him against being swallowed up by a large, international organization in which he would have little clout. Instead, Cazzetta set up his own criminal group. Sometime in the mid-1980s, he convinced his twenty-seven-year-old brother, Giovanni, who at the time was a member of the Outlaws, to join him in creating a new breed of criminal organization; one that came with all the trappings of a one-percenter biker club — a formal membership based on fraternal and criminal ties,

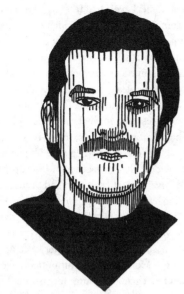

Salvatore Cazzetta

a network of semi-autonomous chapters that controlled certain jurisdictions, and involvement in the drug trade — but without the usual one-percenter accoutrements, such as the colours, the patches, and the motorcycles that attracted so much public notoriety and police attention. Rather than wear colours, Rock Machine members wore gold rings with an engraving of an eagle's head. By the early 1990s, the brothers were calling themselves the Rock Machine and had established a chapter in Montreal and another in Quebec City. Together, the two chapters had a membership of about twenty members, but could count on more than a hundred associates, most of whom were employed as drug wholesalers and retailers.

Under the leadership of the Cazzetta brothers, the Rock Machine was made up of an assortment of refugees from defunct one-percenter biker clubs, drug dealers, and shady businessmen. Among the early members of the new criminal enterprise were Renaud Jomphe, André Sauvageau, Gilles Lambert, Martin Bourget, Richard Lagacé, Nelsen Fernandez, Johnny Plescio, and Paul (Sasquatch) Porter. As Yves Lavigne emphasizes, the Rock Machine was not made up of "a bunch of punks who decided to become criminals." Instead, "they were established criminals" who had "access to lawyers, accountants, and financial

advisors." According to former member Peter Paridis, full-patch members had to pay $1,000 in dues a month. "All that money went to pay lawyers, or take care of guys behind bars." A shrewd and charismatic criminal entrepreneur himself, Salvatore Cazzetta recognized that to survive and prosper in the underworld one must forge partnerships. He also knew that his fledgling organization could not compete against the Hells Angels on its own, so he cultivated affiliations with other criminal organizations in Montreal, including the Rizzuto Family, the West End Gang, South American cocaine trafficking groups, and the remnants of the once-powerful Dubois gang. It was from these groups that the Cazzetta brothers and their associates were purchasing most of their cocaine. The Rock Machine was also running a number of semi-legitimate businesses in Montreal, including bars, tattoo parlours, and motorcycle repair shops, which they also used as fronts to sell drugs, launder money, and put together criminal deals. At the dawn of the new decade, the group held a growing portion of the city's lucrative cocaine trade and was making enough money to purchase and renovate a new Montreal clubhouse that was later valued at more than $1 million.

While the Rock Machine successfully operated for almost ten years with little attention being paid to it by the public, the media, or the police, that changed in April 1992 when Giovanni Cazzetta was charged with possession of three kilos of cocaine. He pleaded guilty to the charges in the spring of 1993. The next year, his brother was indicted in Florida as part of a sting operation in Jacksonville. In co-operation with police in Montreal, two American law enforcement agents posing as cocaine suppliers set up a deal with William (Billy) McAllister, a senior member of the West End Gang, his associate Paul Larue, and Rock Machine member Nelsen Fernandez, to purchase 10,000 kilos of cocaine, which was to be shipped to Cazzetta back in Canada. Police terminated the sting operation in March 1993 and arrested McAllister at his chalet in the Laurentians while Paul Larue was nabbed in Vermont. Larue, who pleaded guilty in 1993 and was sentenced to seventeen and a half years in prison, agreed to testify against McAllister, who was extradited to Florida where he was also convicted. Salvatore Cazzetta went on the lam and even managed to escape capture after giving false identification to a police officer who arrested him for drunk driving. He was finally captured in Fort Erie, Ontario, on May 8, 1994, but wasn't extradited to the U.S. until March 1998. Once inside a Florida courtroom, he pleaded guilty to drug charges in June 1999 and was sentenced to twelve years. After three years in an American jail, where he earned his high-school diploma, Cazzetta was transferred to a medium-security prison in Quebec in 2001. Nelson Fernandez was able to avoid extradition to the U.S. and, as a free man in Canada, rose through the ranks of the Rock Machine.

During the 1980s, the Rock Machine and the Hells Angels coexisted peacefully, due to Boucher's respect for Cazzetta who had connections to the Rizzuto Family, the only criminal organization that Bouchard dared not antagonize. When the Cazzetta brothers were in jail or on the run in the early 1990s, however, Boucher decided he could negotiate a sweet deal with a leaderless Rock Machine that would see the group and its drug business absorbed into the Hells Angels organization. He increased the pressure by sending in members of his puppet clubs, the Rockers and the Evil Ones, to wrest control from the Rock Machine's markets. When the Rock Machine failed to cave into Boucher's demands, the prospects for a peaceful coexistence between the two competitors began to disappear.

The shots that signalled the start of the war were actually fired by the Rock Machine. On July 13, 1994, two men brandishing shotguns walked into a Harley-Davidson repair shop in Montreal and killed the owner, Pierre Daoust, who was linked to the Hells Angels affiliate, the Death Riders. The next day police arrested five members of the Rock Machine — Frédéric Faucher, Martin Blouin, André Sauvageau, Normand Baker, and Guy Langlois — in a motel room in suburban Montreal while they were preparing for an attack on the Evil Ones. Police seized three radio-detonated bombs, 12 pounds of dynamite, and a silencer-equipped pistol. Three days later, Michel Boyer, a Rock Machine associate, was arrested in east Montreal as he and another man were preparing to kill Maurice Boucher. The two were caught with dynamite and a remote-control detonator capable of triggering three bombs simultaneously.

On October 19, 1994, a drug trafficker named Maurice Lavoie was murdered as he was getting out of his car at home. Lavoie had recently begun buying cocaine from the Hells Angels, which infuriated his former suppliers, the Pelletier brothers, who wholesaled cocaine to a small army of street dealers. Police viewed Lavoie's murder as a signal from the Pelletiers to their other drug dealing retailers that they should think twice before going over to the other side. A little more than a week later, in what can be considered as the shot heard around Quebec, thirty-two-year-old Sylvain Pelletier was killed when a bomb planted in his Jeep exploded. The death of a high-level drug trafficker like Sylvain Pelletier — who had been marked for execution by the Hells Angels in retaliation for the death of Lavoie and for his refusal to be absorbed by the motorcycle gang's cocaine network — served to escalate the nascent conflict to another level. As Yves Lavigne notes, Mom Boucher committed a tactical error when he began going after independent drug trafficking groups like the Pelletier brothers, which only galvanized his enemies. "The Angels got greedy, and in the heat of war decided to go after the entire drug market in Montreal instead of the portion controlled by the Rock Machine. As the Hells Angels threatened bar owners and killed gang members through their associates, they created more anger than fear in the underworld." As the territory of the independent drug dealers came under siege, they realized "they had a common enemy and the battle for drug turf turned into a fight for survival. The Rock Machine, independent drug gangs, and a group of bar owners called the Dark Circle, who allowed the sale of narcotics in their establishments, banded together to create the "Alliance" to fight off the Hells Angels and even take back from the biker gang drug territory they felt was theirs." The formation of the powerful Alliance led to a battle of attrition with the world's biggest biker gang, which explains the longevity of the war and its unprecedented death toll.

On November 4, 1994, six days following the murder of Sylvian Pelletier, twenty-nine-year-old Rock Machine member Daniel Bertrand was killed and three others were wounded by automatic gunfire at a downtown Montreal bar. On December 4, Rock Machine member Bruno Bandiera was murdered a half a kilometre from the Rockers' clubhouse in the Montreal suburb of Longueuil when the bomb he was transporting in a stolen Plymouth Voyageur minivan exploded prematurely. Police believe the van was to be parked outside of Cri-Cri restaurant, one of Mom Boucher's favourite downtown hangouts. Boucher got lucky again on December 16 when another explosive-filled van stationed outside the restaurant was towed to the city pound because it was parked illegally. In order to destroy the evidence, Rock Machine operatives detonated the explosives while it sat in the police auto lockup. A month later, Rock Machine member Daniel Senesac was killed in the Rosemont district of Montreal when the bomb he was transporting detonated. The flak jacket he was wearing did little to save him and it took forensic experts a week to identify his shredded remains.

The new year signalled a brief international expansion of the war when thirty-four-year-old Rock Machine member Normand Baker was gunned down while sitting with his girlfriend and another couple at the Hard Rock Cafe in Acapulco, Mexico. Witnesses reported that the bathing suit–clad gunman walked up to their table and yelled "Happy New Year" before shooting Baker in the head. The assailant tried to escape by jumping through the restaurant's plate-glass window, but was tackled by other diners and restaurant employees. Francois (Frank) Hinse, a prospect for the Trois-Rivières Hells Angels, who had been vacationing in Mexico with five other members of the chapter, was arrested by Mexican police. After being transported to the police station across the street from the restaurant, he was charged with murder. Baker, who reportedly had been shadowed by Hinse all morning, was targeted because the Angels had information that he was involved in the murder of Pierre Daoust. Despite the numerous eyewitnesses, a Mexican judge threw the murder case out of court citing insufficient evidence (and amidst allegations that he was bribed $700,000 to secure the Canadian's freedom).

Back in Canada, Jacques Ferland, a forty-two-year-old chemist who manufactured PCP for the Rock Machine, was shot in the head at his home in Quebec City on January 30. On February 27, Claude Cossette, who had links to the Alliance, was killed by gunfire as he sat in a van parked in front of his home. Cossette, who had been previously injured when his booby-trapped car exploded after he turned on the

ignition, was shot in the head at point-blank range. Claude (The Peak) Rivard, who dealt drugs for the Pelletier brothers, was killed the same month and in the same manner as he sat in his car at a red light in a Montreal suburb. A police cruiser happened to be passing by at the time of the shooting and a high-speed car chase ensued, but the two assassins, Serge Quesnel and Hells Angel member Richard Vallée, managed to escape on foot.

The next month, Quesnel struck again, murdering drug dealer Richard (Chico) Delcourt on March 23. Quesnel would later admit in court that he convinced Delcourt to travel to Quebec City with him, and along the way he pulled the car over along a deserted rural road and fired three shots from his .357 Magnum. He then threw the body to the side of the road and sped away. Quesnel, who was paid $10,000 to kill Delcourt and split $15,000 with Vallée for the murder of Rivard, was a hit man for the Trois-Rivières chapter of the Hells Angels. Born in 1970, Quesnel began his criminal career as a teenage shoplifter before moving on to more serious crimes, including armed robbery and drug trafficking. The darkly handsome man with a teardrop tattooed under each eye committed his first murder at twenty-three. In what Quesnel would later admit was an effort to advance his reputation in the underworld, he and Eric (Nose) Fournier killed thirty-nine-year-old drug dealer Richard Jobin on September 9, 1993.

The following month, Quesnel committed his second murder, once again with his partner, Nose. This time the victim was Martin Naud, a mechanic who had sold drugs for Quesnel and who was suspected of knowing too much about the Jobin slaying. After ambushing Naud at his home, Fournier wrapped his own shoelace around Naud's neck while Quesnel rammed a pair of scissors through one eyeball and then slit his throat. After they were certain Naud was dead, Quesnel doused the body with alcohol and set it on fire. In November 1994, Quesnel was introduced to Louis (Mélou) Roy, president of the Trois-Rivières chapter of the Hells Angels and one of the club's most powerful members in Quebec. "Melou was the richest Angel in Quebec, and I was his protégé," Quesnel wrote. "We travelled together, and I could see that he was among the most powerful members of the 'profession.' He carried a booklet with the names, addresses, licence plate numbers, and descriptions of fifty or so undesirable individuals. When I saw it, I realized that the Trois Rivières Hells Angels were very powerful." As Quesnel points out, Roy's influence extended beyond his own chapter; he controlled several biker clubs affiliated with the Hells Angels and supervised a drug trafficking network that was almost province-wide.

During their first meeting in the Trois-Rivières clubhouse, Roy offered Quesnel a job as a hired killer with a $500-a-week salary plus a commission of at least $10,000 for each murder. Quesnel enthusiastically accepted the offer and with an advance of $2,000 and the promise of $8,000 more, he was handed his first assignment: to kill Rock Machine associate Jacques Ferland. While his accomplice, Mercenaries biker club member Michel (Pit) Caron, sat in the getaway car waiting, Quesnel snuck into Fernand's home and shot him. Quesnel was then tasked with an even more important mission: to murder Gilles Lambert, one of the most senior members of the Rock Machine. "The Hells Angels had decided to strike a major blow by eliminating many of the Rock Machine's bigwigs in Montreal in one go," according to Quesnel. The price on Lambert's head was $50,000.

Serge Quesnel

Quesnel knew that if he murdered Lambert his stock with the Hells Angels would rise considerably, perhaps even resulting in membership in the club. But Quesnel's dreams came crashing around him in 1995 when Michel Caron became a police informant and fingered him in the Ferland and Delcourt murders.

Quesnel was arrested by the Quebec provincial police on April 1 and charged with the two murders. Like Caron, Quesnel also decided to co-operate with police and testify in court against his former bosses. Despite confessing to five murders, he received a sentence that made him eligible for parole after twelve years (he also received $390,000 in cash). Information provided by Quesnel and Caron led to the arrest of thirteen Hells Angels members and associates, including Louis Roy, who, along with another founding member of the Trois-Rivières chapter named Sylvain (Baptiste) Thiffault, was charged with an array of offences, including conspiring to murder Ferland, Delcourt, and Claude Rivard. The jury at their trial did not find Quesnel or Caron to be credible witnesses, however, and Roy and Thiffault were acquitted in April 1997. Quesnel was also a Crown witness in the murder trial of Richard Vallée, who was acquitted as well.

By the middle of 1995, the resolve of the Angels to wipe out its competitors deepened when Mom Boucher and his eight associates from the Montreal, Trois-Rivières, and Halifax chapters formed the No-mads. In addition to the seventy-five full-patch Hells Angels members in the province, the Nomads could count on hundreds of associates. Jean-Guy Bourgoin, a founding member of the Rockers, was once heard telling another Rocker that the financial remuneration for eliminating Rock Machine members and associates was $100,000 for a full-patch member, $50,000 for a prospect, and $25,000 for a hangaround.

The second half of 1995 would be a pivotal period in the biker war. Although it was far from over, a single violent act would spark public outrage and an unprecedented legislative response. It all began on August 9, 1995, the day the war claimed its first innocent victim. A remote-control bomb planted by the Hells Angels in a Jeep parked across from the Saint-Nom-De-Jesus School in Montreal was detonated, critically wounding eleven-year-old Daniel Desrochers. He underwent surgery at the hospital but died a few days later. As Julian Sher and William Marsden write: "More than any other single event in the biker war, the killing of Daniel Desrochers galvanized public opinion. Images of the carnage on the street and his funeral packed with tearful schoolchildren were flashed on TV screens across the country. The public outcry was aimed more at the police than at the bikers. Why couldn't the police and the government protect citizens from a gang of thugs? Suddenly it was no longer good enough for police to shrug off the latest gang killings as a 'settling of accounts.'"

Before police and politicians had a chance to respond, the war took the life of the first full-patch member of the Hells Angels. On September 15, Richard (Crow) Émond was shot six times in the parking lot of an east end Montreal shopping centre while getting out of his car with his girlfriend. He died an hour later in hospital. The thirty-nine-year-old Émond, whose vest sported the Filthy Few patch, had just recently replaced Louis Roy as president of the Trois-Rivières chapter. Later that night, three men died when a bomb they were attempting to plant outside the clubhouse of the Jokers, a biker club controlled by Émond, exploded prematurely. The victims could not be immediately identified because the explosion scattered body fragments up to 100 metres away, but police later confirmed they all had links to the Rock Machine. "We know that three persons were killed," one provincial police spokesman told the media the next morning. "There were too many body parts for only one victim." By the end of November, four more deaths were attributed to the biker war. Among those killed was Michel Boyer, the Rock Machine associate who was caught by police a year earlier with dynamite that was to be used to kill Mom Boucher.

As the bodies piled up, Quebec public security minister Serge Menard announced the creation of a special task force, "Project Carcajou" (French for wolverine), which was to be made up of close to one hundred police officers from the RCMP, the Quebec provincial police, and the Montreal police. In November 1995, the squad arrested more than forty people from both sides of the war. Among those taken into custody were six members of the Hells Angels–affiliated Evil Ones, who were arrested on drug trafficking charges, and another twenty Rock Machine members, including four from the Dark Circle who were accused of plotting to murder Nomads Denis Houle and Normand Hamel while they were incarcerated at a Laval prison. The Dark Circle, which became the de facto hit squad for the Alliance, averaged between fifteen and twenty members at any one time, most of whom

could be identified through a necklace they wore, which had a pendant engraved with a palm tree and an island. According to journalist Paul Cherry, the Dark Circle did not have a president but was run by a four-man executive committee made up of respected Montreal criminals and semi-legitimate bar owners. Like other partners in the Alliance, members of the Dark Circle were on good terms with some Hells Angels, and even purchased cocaine and other drugs from the Sherbrooke chapter. However, Boucher's unyielding monopolistic ambitions forced them to abandon their former suppliers and band together with his enemies to protect their turf. All four members of the Dark Circle implicated in the attempted assassinations pleaded guilty and were sentenced to prison terms of less than three years.

Following a relative calm in the first half of 1996, where each side traded only a single murder, by the spring the hostilities resumed, with the venue for the war shifting to Quebec City. The Rock Machine chapter in that city had joined forces with the Roberge brothers, an independent drug trafficking group, to wage what the CISC called "a ferocious struggle with the Hells Angels for control of bars and drinking establishments involved in the distribution and sale of drugs." The surge in violence in Quebec City began with the January death of Hells Angels associate Glenn Cormier. In March, a Rock Machine–affiliated drug dealer named Roland Lebrasseur was murdered by a member of the Rockers, named Dany Kane. In July, the rivals traded two more deaths of low-level drug dealers. In August, Rock Machine founder Salvatore Cazzetta, who was in the Parthenais Detention Centre in east end Montreal while awaiting an extradition order to Florida, was attacked by at least six inmates armed with homemade shivs and socks stuffed with batteries. In October, two senior members of the Montreal chapter of the Rock Machine — thirty-eight-year-old Christian Deschesnes and thirty-seven-year-old Renaud Jomphe — were gunned down in a Chinese restaurant in Verdun. Jomphe had become somewhat of a public spokesperson for the Rock Machine after vehemently denying to the media that the Rock Machine was responsible for planting the bomb that killed Daniel Desrochers. In October, a stolen Hydro-Quebec van, filled with

90 kilos of dynamite, was found unexploded near a Verdun warehouse used by the Rock Machine as a meeting place. Explosives experts later said that, if the bomb had been detonated, it could have levelled the surrounding neighbourhood. A month later, a 23-kilo explosive was found outside the Hells Angels Quebec City clubhouse but was dismantled before it was set off. In December, Bruno (Cowboy) Van Lerberghe, a member of the Quebec City Hells Angels, was murdered when a gunman walked into a restaurant and fired six shots at him in broad daylight. Before the end of the year, police attributed the murders of three more men to the biker war.

For CISC analyst Jean-Pierre Levesque, 1997 proved to be "the year outlaw bikers went from waging a turf war to a total war." At least twenty-eight more deaths were added to the body count, which meant by year's end, the war had claimed sixty-eight lives. In addition, there were "71 attempted murders, 81 bombings, and 93 cases of arson against gang-related businesses and bars, for a total of 313 violent incidents" since the war began. Among those murdered in 1997 were Robert McFarlane, a Nova Scotia businessman killed in Halifax on February 27 by Dany Kane and fellow hit man Aimé (Ace) Simard. Scott Steinert, a member of the Montreal Hells Angels chapter who lived in a seventeen-room mansion in Laval, was bludgeoned to death on November 4, just three weeks after being married. His bodyguard and Hells Angel hangaround, Donald Magnusen, was killed at the same time.

Steinert was as ambitious and psychotic as Boucher and long envisioned becoming president of his own Hells Angels chapter in Ontario. He became a full-patch member of the Montreal chapter in 1996 under the sponsorship of national president Robert (Tiny) Richard and received a Filthy Few patch not long after acquiring his colours. He had a long record of criminal convictions for assault, uttering threats, and narcotics possession and, by the time of his death, had become a central player in the biker war. He supervised a team that was responsible for manufacturing and planting bombs, participated in assassinations of rivals, and, according to one former Rocker club member, was even seeking out aerial photographs of Montreal to help plot strikes against the Angels' enemies. When he

went missing shortly after his wedding, police began to suspect he was dead. But his body would not be found until April 15, 1999, when it was recovered from the St. Lawrence River, not far from the Angels Quebec City clubhouse. Magnusen's body floated to the surface just upriver in May 1998.

While police logically deduced that Steinert and Magnusen were killed by enemies of the Hells Angels, information provided by Dany Kane indicated that both had in fact been purged by their own club. Magnussen was on the outs with other senior club members, in part because he was suspected of being a police mole. Pressure was also being placed on Boucher to remove him by the Montreal mafia, after Magnussen beat up the son of Vito Rizutto outside a bar. Kane also told police that Steinert was targeted for removal because he was responsible for planting the bomb that killed eleven-year-old Daniel Desrochers. Ultimately, it was his close relationship with Magnussen and the belief among senior Quebec Angels that Steinert was becoming too undisciplined that was behind his violent ouster from the club.

In addition to the latest Hells Angels' internal cleansing, what truly marked 1997 as the year of the "total war" was a new strategy undertaken by the megalomaniac Mom Boucher as he escalated his reign of terror. He was now plotting a campaign to destabilize the criminal justice system by intimidating and even assassinating police officers, prison guards, and high-ranking members of the provincial government. Hells Angels' informants would later reveal the existence of a hit list, created by Boucher, which included the names of Quebec public security minister Serge Ménard and Montreal police chief Jacques Duchesneau. Boucher's plan reportedly had another goal: to dissuade any Hells Angels member or associate from becoming a police informant. As Michel Auger writes, "the sentence for killing police officers and prison guards, normally twenty-five years, cannot be reduced — the criminal must serve the full term. The loyalty of any biker who committed such a crime was therefore assured: he could not hope to get a reduced sentence by informing against his associates and becoming a Crown witness."

On June 26, 1997, two members of the Rockers, Stéphane (Godasse) Gagné and André (Touts)

Tousignant, gunned down forty-two-year-old prison guard Diane Lavigne as she drove home following the end of her shift at Montreal's Bordeaux Prison. On September 8, Gagné and another Rocker named Paul (Fon-Fon) Fontaine struck again. This time the victim was Pierre Rondeau, a forty-nine-year-old guard at Rivière-des-Prairies jail in northeast Montreal who was shot while sitting behind the wheel of an empty prison transport bus. After receiving a tip from an arrested drug dealer, Gagné was picked up by police on December 5. He confessed to the murders and agreed to provide evidence implicating Boucher. Less than two weeks later, on December 18, 1997, Mom Boucher was arrested as he was leaving Montreal's Notre-Dame Hospital where he was being treated for throat cancer. After being charged with two counts of first-degree murder, he was whisked away to a high-security unit built for him at a Montreal correctional facility for women where he was held without bail. Paul Fontaine was also arrested, although police were unable to locate Tousignant.

In their attempts to contain the war, the Wolverine Squad adopted a dangerous strategy in 1997: incapacitate one side through intensive enforcement on the assumption that a war cannot be fought if one side is disabled. Understandably, police targeted the weaker side. On January 29, police arrested seven people belonging to or associated with the Rock Machine on allegations they conspired to murder Maurice Boucher by parking a van full of explosives in front of the Cri-Cri restaurant in 1994. In May 1997, more than five hundred police officers conducted sixty-six separate raids on Rock Machine clubhouses and properties in Montreal and Quebec City, arresting eighteen members and seizing drugs, weapons, and 325 kilos of explosives. Police also confiscated the group's Montreal clubhouse, homes, businesses, motorcycles, cars, boats, and jewellery as the proceeds of crime. Among those arrested were Giovanni Cazzetta and sixty-three-year-old Richard Matticks of the West End Gang. Cazzetta had been lured by an acquaintance, who had become a police agent, to introduce him to Matticks in order to purchase 15 kilos of cocaine for a fictitious Calgary-based distributor. Matticks said he could not obtain that much on such short notice, but did agree to sell him nine kilos for around $350,000.

Cazzetta, Matticks, and two other West End Gang members who delivered the coke to the police agent were arrested and charged with drug trafficking. In a surprise move, Matticks and his two henchmen pleaded guilty and were sentenced to three, four, and two years, respectively. Cazzetta, who was still on parole from his 1993 drug conviction when he was arrested again, was convicted in 1998 and drew a nine-year prison term after pleading guilty. Federal proceeds-of-crime convictions also forced Giovanni to forfeit almost $600,000 in assets, including luxury cars and his gold Rock Machine ring. Giovanni's sister Maria was sentenced to one year for possession of the proceeds of crime, while Gilles Lambert, who police described as "one of the No. 1 guys" in the Rock Machine, received three years on similar charges. A year later, Giovanni's older brother, Salvatore, pleaded guilty to drug trafficking charges in a Florida courtroom and was sentenced to twelve years.

While the Rock Machine was reeling under increased police attention, the Hells Angels continued to add to their strength in Quebec with the founding of the South chapter in March 1997. Based in Saint-Basile-le-Grand, just southeast of Montreal, the new chapter was created by long-time Hells Angel Michel (Sky) Langlois and Normand Labelle and included six other members and two prospects. All of the new members had no previous criminal convictions within the last five years, a deliberate move by the Angels to establish a chapter that could avoid being classified as a criminal organization under new federal legislation. The legislation, which was to come into force in June of that year and was enacted as a result of the biker wars in Quebec, amended the *Criminal Code* to make participation in a criminal organization an indictable offence, punishable by up to fourteen years in prison to be served consecutive to any other offence. But the re-organization of the Quebec Angels could not protect Langlois from drug trafficking charges. On October 14, 1998, he was charged with conspiring to import 178 kilos of cocaine seized in January, and the following year he was convicted and sentenced to five years in prison and a $20,000 fine.

The year that Langlois was arrested marked the fiftieth anniversary of the Hells Angels, which now stood at 125 chapters with 1,600 members in twenty-two countries. The year was also marked by more biker bloodshed in Quebec. On February 20, 1998, Rock Machine member Denis Belleau was murdered at a restaurant in Quebec City. The killing was the third gang war–related attack in the region over the past ten days. A week later, a charred, fingerless corpse was discovered in a wooded area in Quebec's Eastern Townships, but it wasn't until a month later that the deceased was identified as Nomads prospect André Tousignant. He had been killed on the orders of Boucher who was worried that he would become a Crown witness. Tousignant had been shot several times and then his fingers had been cut off and his corpse set aflame in an attempt to prevent identification. His body was still smouldering when police found it. Earlier that day, his partner, Stéphane Gagné, pleaded guilty to the first-degree murder of Diane Lavigne and the attempted murder of fellow prison guard Robert Corriveau, who was wounded when Rondeau was killed. The Crown dropped a second murder charge for Rondeau's death in return for Gagné's testimony against Boucher. Gagné was convicted of first-degree murder and sentenced to life in prison with no chance of parole for twenty-five years. He admitted to police that the assassinations were carried out so he could secure a promotion within the Hells Angels.

Over the remainder of the year, at least twenty more people were murdered as part of the war, most of whom were allied with the Rock Machine. Among those killed was Rock Machine member Richard (Bam Bam) Lagace, who was shot outside a Montreal gym on July 30. On September 8, Johnny Plescio, a thirty-four-year-old member of the club, was killed inside his home after his assailants lured him to his blank television near a window by cutting off his cable connection on the exterior of his house. On the other side of the window, standing atop a lawn chair, was a gunman who fired thirty-two shots into the house. Eleven reached their target. Before the end of October, Jean Rosa and Pierre Bastien, two Dark Circle members who had been targeted by the Angels because of their involvement in the murders of Hells Angels members, were shot point-blank in separate incidents in Laval. Both were murdered as they exited their cars at their suburban homes. Bastien was shot with his eight-year-old daughter sitting in the back seat of his car.

On November 10, Rock Machine member Stéphane Morgan and his bodyguard, Daniel Boulet, were slain together in a flurry of bullets while sitting in an idling Chevrolet Celebrity outside Morgan's home. Only minutes after a pedestrian found the dead bodies, police received calls about a burning minivan a few blocks away. By the end of 1998, the war had resulted in 103 homicides, 124 murder attempts, 9 missing persons, 84 bombings, and 130 deliberately set fires.

Amidst the ongoing bloodbath, Mom Boucher's trial for the murder of the two prison guards began on November 2, 1998. Stéphane Gagné was the main witness for the Crown; in fact, the informant was all the Crown had to link Boucher to the two murders. Gagné began his life of crime by selling drugs in school when he was only thirteen years old. A few years later, he was breaking into homes and businesses to support his own drug habit. By the mid-1990s, he was purchasing cocaine by the kilo from the Rockers and it was through the Nomads' puppet club that he first met Boucher in 1993. The two hooked up again in 1995 when both were serving short sentences at Sorel prison; Gagné was imprisoned after selling a kilo of coke to a police informant, while Boucher had been convicted of a weapons offence. When Boucher heard that Gagné had been beaten by Rock Machine members for refusing to urinate on his picture, he took him under his wing. The two were reunited on the outside and Gagné was rewarded with hangaround status with the Rockers. From there, the new recruit was given various duties, from selling drugs under the supervision of André Tousignant and Paul Fontaine, to collecting drug debts (earning him the nickname "Godasse," Quebec slang for old shoe because he was so good at putting the boot to indebted drug dealers), to blowing up a Rock Machine clubhouse and assassinating prison guards.

During Boucher's trial, Gagné testified that, on the orders of Boucher, Fontaine and Tousignant were to murder prison guards. The two men then recruited Gagné to help out and he was sent to conduct surveillance of Montreal-area prisons for potential victims. On June 26, 1997, Gagné and Tousignant followed Diane Lavigne as she drove home from work. Dressed in black jogging suits and riding a Japanese motorcycle, the two pulled up beside her van and Gagné opened fire. The next day Gagné met with Boucher, who told him that he was pleased with his work and that he shouldn't worry just because his victim "had tits." On September 8, Gagné struck again, this time with Fontaine as the two ambushed a prison transport bus driven by Pierre Rondeau. According to Gagné, it was Fontaine who killed Rondeau after jumping on the hood of the bus and firing three shots through the windshield as the bus stopped at a railway crossing. Gagné shot another guard, Robert Corriveau, but he survived. The two men fled the scene in a stolen van, which they set on fire in a parking lot, before driving away in another car. Gagné and Fontaine then went to Montreal's Saint-Luc Hospital where they stood guard for Louis Roy, who was recovering from an attempted murder after being riddled with bullets outside his father's motel in Jonquière. Despite being hit in the lungs, liver, and legs, Roy survived following emergency surgery. After pulling guard duty, Gagné was provided $5,000 to take a vacation in the Dominican Republic, partly to provide him with an alibi to explain the burn marks on his face after he got too close to their burning getaway van. When he returned to Canada, Gagné was rewarded for the murders by being made a prospect for the Rockers while Fontaine and Tousignant received similar privileges with the Nomads.

Throughout his trial, Boucher's defence team hammered away at the Crown witness to such an extent that Gagné had little credibility in the eyes of the jury. As a result, on November 27, 1998, Boucher was pronounced innocent of all charges. After the verdict was read, Boucher strode out of the courtroom to the applause of his supporters and, later than night, he and his entourage attended Montreal's Molson Centre where he watched boxer Davey Hilton defeat Stéphane Ouellet. Since he had began his life of crime, Boucher had forty-three criminal charges laid against him, yet he did not spend more than two years in jail in total. Boucher's renewed confidence in his invincibility would only fuel his violent propensities and monopolistic aspirations.

With Boucher back on the street, the war raged along at a fevered pace, with the Rock Machine bearing most of the damage. Among the murders attributed to the war in 1999 were thirty-eight-year-old Richard

Relative, the brother-in-law of Salvatore and Giovanni Cazzeta, and thirty-six-year-old Tony Plescio, another Rock Machine member who joined his brother Johnny in purgatory when he was shot six times outside a McDonald's after dropping his children off for a party. Police also added to the body count that year when forty-one-year-old Serge Boisvert, an associate of the Rock Machine, was felled by sixteen police bullets after he refused to drop the AK-47 assault rifle he was randomly firing while walking along a street in a small Quebec town. According to his brother Hector, he was "certainly" high on drugs at the time. "He knew he was going to die soon, eventually, that is certain," Hector Boisvert told the media when asked about his brother's thoughts on associating with the Rock Machine.

The biker war only became more violent in 2000. More than thirty people with suspected ties to either side were murdered. On April 17, forty-four-year-old Norman (Biff) Hamel, one of the few active Angels who participated in the Lennoxville massacre and a founding member of the Nomads, was killed by two gunshots while being chased through a parking lot in Laval. Between February and October, at least eleven members or associates of the Angels were killed, not at the hands of their rivals, however, but as a result of further purges orchestrated by Mom Boucher. Ten days following the death of Hamel, sixty-nine-year-old André Desjardins, the former director general of Local 144 of the International Association of Plumbers and Pipe Fitters and former vice-president of the Quebec Federation of Labour, was shot to death in the parking lot of a restaurant where he had lunched with Boucher just the day before. Desjardins was a central figure in Quebec government inquiries into union corruption in the 1970s and more recently was alleged to have been involved in loansharking with the Hells Angels. According to Julian Sher and William Marsden, Boucher was trying to convince Desjardins to forgive a loan made to a friend of his. Apparently, Desjardins refused the request. On June 22, former Trois-Rivières chapter president and current Nomad Louis Roy disappeared. Despite his long-standing influence within the Hells Angels in Quebec, police speculated that he was another victim of Boucher's housecleaning because of his refusal to join in with the Nomads' centralized cocaine cartel. Elias Lekkas, the former drug dealing partner of West End Gang leader Gerald Matticks, testified in court that Roy had been called to a meeting in a meat-processing plant belonging to Matticks and was ground like hamburger. His cocaine markets and personal assets were divided among his Hells Angels "brothers."

Other victims of the Angels' pogrom were police informants. Boucher was obsessed with rooting out moles in his organization and he even received some inadvertent help from police in doing so. On December 4, 1999, members of a Hells Angels affiliate gang called the Scorpions stole the laptop of an Ontario Provincial Police investigator from his Sherbrooke hotel room. The officer, who was conducting surveillance of members of the Hells Angels while they partied at the hotel, was out of the room at the time. Inside the computer were photos of Rock Machine members and associates, which the Angels used to identify targets for future assassinations. The computer also held confidential information that enabled the Angels to figure out that Claude Des Serres, a drug dealer working for Rockers member Serge (Pacha) Boutin, was a police informant. Boutin would later tell police he was ordered to drive Des Serres to a chalet in the Laurentians in February 2000. Waiting there were Nomads Normand Robitaille and René Charlebois who took Des Serres to the chalet's basement and shot him to death. Des Serres' police handlers had lost track of him and when his corpse was discovered in a snowbank outside the chalet, he was still wearing his recording device. Boutin was charged with the murder of Des Serres, which prompted him to become a Crown witness.

The purges were just another part of Mom Boucher's "total war," which also targeted journalists. On September 13, 2000, veteran crime reporter Michel Auger was ambushed in the parking lot of *Le Journal de Montréal* and shot five times in the back. Despite the multiple wounds, he remained conscious and was lucid enough to call 911 on his cell phone. Auger was rushed to the hospital and, following the surgery, pulled through. A few blocks from the crime scene police found what had become a telltale sign of a biker gang attack, a burning minivan. Like most other murders that were carried out during the war, the hit men were never found. Following the gangland shooting of Auger, organized crime and outlaw biker groups resurfaced as a topic on Parliament Hill. The Bloc Québécois introduced an emergency motion to amend the *Criminal Code* to criminalize membership in known organized crime groups and, in conjunction with Quebec's minister of public security, called on federal justice minister Anne McLellan to consider suspending the freedom-of-association provisions in the *Charter of Rights and Freedoms* for gang members. While the justice minister dismissed such proposals as draconian, she did agree to meet with provincial justice officials in Quebec City to discuss a more comprehensive anti-gang strategy.

Coincidently, the leaders of the warring factions were also discreetly meeting in Quebec City. On September 26, Maurice Boucher, along with fellow Angels Norman Robitaille, Richard Mayrand, and Alain Ruest met with Rock Machine leader Frédéric Faucher and his lieutenants, Michel Comeau, Jean Duquaire, and Nelson Fernandez. The meeting, which was arranged by lawyer Denis Bernier, who had defended Rock Machine members in the past, took place in a conference room in a Quebec City courthouse, of all places. "They wanted to be sure they were in a neutral place, without danger," Bernier told the media. While it is conceivable that the two sides were anxious to end the bloodshed — especially the Rock Machine, which was losing the battle of attrition — the leaders of the two sides were also under pressure by other influential criminal leaders who were angry that the war had brought too much attention to Montreal's gangland. Some believe it was Vito Rizzuto, the only man who Mom Boucher felt was a higher power than him, who had persuaded the Hells Angels leader to negotiate a truce. Whatever the reason, when news was leaked that the heads of Quebec's most violent criminal organizations were using a government facility, let alone a courthouse, to meet, public indignation once again reached a boiling point. Quebec premier Lucien Bouchard called the meeting "totally unacceptable" while his public security minister expressed frustration that there was little the government or police could do because the meeting was perfectly legal. The anger that was aroused by the meeting was also accompanied by some guarded optimism that it could bring about a truce in the six-year war.

This hope was further raised when a more public tête-à-tête was held between the two sides on October 8 at the Bleu Marin restaurant in downtown Montreal. It was there that Boucher and Faucher, surrounded by their subordinates, announced that a truce had been reached. A photographer from the French-language crime tabloid *Âllo Police* was even invited to record the historic moment. The next day, the public were able to see the two beaming criminal leaders shaking hands and making toasts to their new peace pact. Observers noted that the public nature of the meeting was a deliberate attempt to signal to the police, legislators, and others in the criminal world that serious efforts were being made to find a peaceful end to the war. Others believe that Boucher, whose acquittal of murder charges was being appealed by the government, was trying to soften his public image in case he had to go before another jury.

While sporadic violence continued, the worst of the war appeared to be over. In addition to the tenuous truce, other developments — some within control of the bikers, some out of their control — intervened to help put an end to the bloodshed. Most significantly, just days following the announcement of the ceasefire, the war's most belligerent general was once again taken out of commission. On October 10, a Quebec appeals court overturned Boucher's acquittal in the murder of the two prison guards, declaring that the judge presiding over the original trial gave flawed instructions to the jurors, influencing their not guilty verdict. Within hours of a new trial being ordered, Boucher was arrested on murder charges and escorted back to his special cell at Montreal's Tanguay prison for women.

Police also continued their assault on the Rock Machine. On December 6, fifteen people associated with the gang were arrested by police following thirty-four raids in the Quebec City area. Among those arrested were club president Frédéric Faucher and Marcel Demers, a founding member of the Quebec City chapter. With the arrests, police announced that twenty of the thirty-two members of the Rock Machine's Quebec City chapter were now in jail or in police custody. The raids took place around the same time a trial for eight Rock Machine members on charges of drug trafficking, murder, and participating in a criminal organization was in progress in Montreal. The Crown's main witness was Peter Paradis, a former senior Rock Machine member and self-proclaimed "chief warrior for one of Canada's most ruthless bike gangs." Paradis had escaped one attempt on his life only to be sentenced to a twelve-year prison term in March 2000 for drug trafficking and participation in a criminal organization. His testimony against his former colleagues included information on how he'd planned and sanctioned at least four murders drug dealers associated with the Hells Angels. In March 2001, four of the accused were convicted. Two months later, on May 11, 2001, Frédéric Faucher pleaded guilty to twenty-eight charges and was sentenced to twelve years in prison. As part of his plea agreement, he admitted to being involved in seven bombings that killed two rival gang members between 1996 and 1997. Demers pleaded guilty to seventeen counts of drug trafficking and was sentenced to nine years.

Frédéric Faucher is escorted by police on December 6, 2000, in Quebec City, after he was arrested.

PATCHOVER PARTIES

The jailing of Boucher and Faucher signalled the beginning of the end to Quebec's most vicious biker war, but by no means did this end the expansion plans for either group. Before Faucher was sent away, he was instrumental in reinventing the Rock Machine. On June 2, 1999, the gang negotiated hangaround status with the Bandidos Motorcycle Club and officially became its own motorcycle club, complete with red and gold Rock Machine colours and the use of "MC" at the end of their name. More surprising, the club announced it was expanding into Ontario, setting up two new chapters in Kingston and Toronto. All nine of the new Toronto chapter members were former Outlaws. The developments were particularly troubling for the Hells Angels, who still did not have a presence in Ontario and watched as their international nemesis, the Bandidos, gained a foothold in Canada. In addition to its new Ontario clubhouses, the Rock Machine also unveiled "the Palmers," a puppet club with chapters in Montreal and Quebec City, which was created to compete against the Angels-affiliated Rockers.

The Rock Machine now had two chapters in Quebec and three in Ontario with seventy-five members in total. Their rapid expansion was a great surprise, especially given that many were administering the last rites to the club in the face of the Hells Angels juggernaut. What made the rebirth of the Rock Machine even more impressive was that the man behind it all — Frédéric Faucher — was not yet thirty years old. Born in Quebec City on December 16, 1969, Faucher dropped out of high school and briefly worked installing sprinkler systems before joining the Rock Machine sometime in the 1980s. By the early 1990s, he was recognized as an intelligent up-and-coming member who had a keen business sense when it came to drug trafficking and did not hesitate to get his hands dirty by delivering and detonating explosives during the war. Faucher was also smart enough to realize that if the Rock Machine was to compete with the Hells Angels, it would have to become as large and as international as their rivals. For Faucher, 1997 was a pivotal year as he positioned the Rock Machine to compete against the Angels while trying to establish himself the leader of his club. In March of that year, Faucher proved his mettle to the gang by detonating a truck full of dynamite at the gates of the Hells Angels Quebec City clubhouse. On September 11, Claude (Ti-Loup) Vézina, the Rock Machine's president at the time, was arrested and Faucher became the gang's new leader. With Vézina, the Cazzetta brothers, and Mom Boucher behind bars, and with the war's tide turning in favour of the Hells Angels, the young leader began a succession of astute manoeuvres that would prolong the survival of the Rock Machine, at least for the short term.

The month after Faucher became the head of the Rock Machine, he invited George Wegers, vice-president of the Bandidos, to Canada to discuss the prospect of the Rock Machine being made an official chapter. Wegers was highly receptive to the invitation. Like the Hells Angels, the Bandidos were always in an expansionist mode. The timing was particularly right for the Bandidos as they were currently locked in an international war with the Hells Angels, which had become especially bloody in Scandinavia. As a 1998 report from the Quebec provincial police stated it was a match made in heaven for both organizations, "After 4½ years of fierce resistance against the Hells Angels, the Rock Machine now appears to be on its last gasp, and therefore needs now more than ever before to solidify its alliance with the Bandidos. Even if this is late in coming, recent information from the Wolverine squad leads us to believe that the [Bandidos] have not abandoned the idea of positioning themselves in Canada."

The Bandidos Motorcycle Club was formed in 1966 in the Texas county of Galveston by former marine Donald Chambers. Like their founder, most of the original members were Vietnam War veterans. The group adopted the red and gold colours of the Marine Corps and their official patch was a crudely drawn cartoon of a scowling, pot-bellied, sombrero-wearing, sword-brandishing and pistol-toting bandit. For much of the 1970s, the Bandidos were concentrated in Texas with chapters scattered throughout other southwestern states. Their principal source of revenue was cocaine and methamphetamines, which they produced in labs in Texas. Six years after founding the club, Chambers was sentenced to life for murdering two men in El Paso after discovering they had sold him baking powder instead of cocaine (he forced the two to dig their own graves at gunpoint before shooting them). Taking over as president was Ronnie Hodge, who modernized the club in an attempt to emulate the ambitions and structure of the Hells Angels. This included a national and international expansion by patching over smaller one-percenter clubs and then imposing strict rules and regulations that had to be followed. Unlike the Angels, the Bandidos developed a national organizational structure, with a "mother chapter" based in Houston comprising a president, four regional vice-presidents, plus regional and local chapter officers. Like the Hells Angels, the Bandidos also have elite Nomads chapters made up of senior members that are in charge of security, counterintelligence, internal discipline, and establishing new drug routes. By the 1980s, the Bandidos were the third-largest one-percenter motorcycle club after the Hells Angels and the Outlaws, with whom they allied themselves in the late 1970s to counter the dominance of the Angels and to maintain a steady source of cocaine. By the mid-1980s, intensive law enforcement efforts diminished the Bandidos' strength in the U.S., prompting an international expansion into Australia, Europe, and Scandinavia. According to the CISC, by 1998 the Bandidos had sixty-seven chapters and about six hundred members worldwide.

On October 28, 1997, Faucher threw a lavish dinner in George Wegers' honour at a swanky Quebec City restaurant, although the party did not end so well when police interrupted the affair by arresting Faucher and twenty-two other Rock Machine members. Wegers, who had criminal convictions in the U.S. for weapons and drug charges, was deported three days later. After serving as hangarounds with the Bandidos for a year and a half, the Rock Machine became probationary members in November 2000. In a ceremony held on December 3, 2001 in Vaughan, Ontario, five Canadian chapters of the Rock Machine (Montreal, Quebec City, Kingston, Toronto, and Niagara Falls), were patched over to the Bandidos MC Nation. About a hundred bikers and guests, including representatives from Bandidos chapters in Sweden, Denmark, and the United States, came to Canada to welcome their new full-patch brothers into the international motorcycle club.

Probationary members of the Bandidos at a January 6, 2001, ceremony in Kingston, Ontario, where new recruits received their colours

To counter the growth of the Rock Machine and the subsequent entry of the Bandidos into Canada, the Hells Angels ramped up their own expansion plans in Canada. A puppet club called the Damners had already been established in Quebec and New Brunswick. In July 2000, the Winnipeg chapter of the Los Brovos became an Angels' prospect club. Most significantly, the efforts of the Angels to expand into Ontario finally paid off. On December 29, 2000, the Hells Angels' clubhouse in Sorel, Quebec, played host to an extraordinary patchover ceremony: more than 160 members of four Ontario motorcycle gangs — the Satan's Choice, Para-Dice Riders, Last Chance and Lobos — received full-fledged membership in the Hells Angels. It was the single-largest patchover in the history of the Canadian Hells Angels and one of the largest in the club's international history. Provincial police from Ontario and Quebec watched as industrial-sized sewing machines were lugged into the Sorel clubhouse with newly crested members sauntering out afterwards.

In a move clearly motivated by the recent arrival of the Bandidos on Canadian soil, all of the Angels newest members were allowed to bypass the probationary stages and become full-patch members of the motorcycle club. According to Julian Sher and William Marsden, the "Angels came up with an offer the Ontario bikers could not refuse. The Bandidos were giving their new recruits only prospect status: trade in your patch, sign up with us for a year as a Bandido-in-waiting and then — with luck — you'll make it into the club. But the Angels proposed a straight patch-for-patch swap." The result was that "overnight, the Angels had gone from no chapters in Ontario to a dozen, more than four times the number of chapters and five times the number of members of the Bandidos. From the Satan's Choice they got entrenched chapters in Thunder Bay, Sudbury, Simcoe County, Keswick, Kitchener, Oshawa and Toronto East. The Para-Dice Riders gave them strong clubs in Toronto Central and Woodbridge. From the Lobos, they got a shabby chapter in Windsor, and the weak Last Chance delivered Toronto West."

The Hells Angels scored another coup in 2002 when a number of Rock Machine members and prospects refused to join the Bandidos and instead jumped over to their rivals. Among the newest probationary Angels were four inmates at the Rivière-des-Prairies jail. Four senior Rock Machine members outside of prison also transferred allegiances, including Salvatore Brunetti and Nelson Fernandez, who automatically received full-patch status within the Nomads. The fact that Brunetti was a former member of the Dark Circle convicted in 1996 for plotting to kill Nomads Denis Houle and Normand Labelle did not seem to prejudice his candidacy for the Hells Angels most elite unit.

The entry of the Bandidos into Canada and the expansion of the Hells Angels into Ontario naturally led to fears of yet another biker war. These fears began to be realized in 2001 with the violent deaths of three new Bandidos members. On January 18, Réal (Tintin) Dupont, who specialized in intelligence gathering for the biker gang, was shot while sitting behind the wheel of his car outside a hockey arena in Montreal. He died later in hospital. When police searched his home, they found computer files full of information on Hells Angels members. On February 14, Michel Gauthier a convicted drug trafficker who had hangaround status with the Bandidos, was found dead at the wheel of his car in a wooded area about 140 kilometres north of Montreal. He had been shot in the neck and head. Other gang-related violence included the abduction of a member of the Damers Motorcycle Club by the Bandidos in New Brunswick, as well as at least twenty fires set in Montreal bars known to be controlled by Hells Angels drug dealers. Notwithstanding these incidents, as well as future episodes of violence and murder, the war between the Hells Angels and Bandidos never did fully materialize in Canada. By 2006, an average of just six killings a year was attributed to biker gangs in Quebec compared to an annual average of thirty-five during the 1990s. Including the recent Bandidos' deaths, between July 1994 and March 2001, the biker war claimed at least 157 lives, including 17 innocent people. In addition, 167 attempted murders, 16 disappearances, 140 arson cases, and 190 bombings in Quebec were attributed to the conflict.

OPERATION SPRINGTIME

Any prospect for a continuation of the conflict between rival biker gangs were snuffed out on March 28, 2001, when more than 2,000 police officers launched raids against the Hells Angels and its affiliates in Quebec. Dubbed "Operation Springtime," it was the largest one-day police operation ever launched in Canada: 288 searches were conducted in seventy-seven locations; 130 people were arrested; twenty buildings, twenty-eight vehicles, thirteen motorcycles, seventy firearms, one stick of dynamite, 120 kilos of hashish, 10 kilos of cocaine, $12.5 million in Canadian cash, and $2.6 million in American cash were seized. The massive sweep was the culmination of three police investigations launched in Quebec in 1998 that entailed thousands of hours of police surveillance, the recruitment of bikers as police informants, and close to fifty wiretaps that intercepted more than 264,000 conversations over a period of one and a half years. In total, Operation Springtime targeted for arrest 142 outlaw bikers and their associates, including eighty of Quebec's 106 full-patch Hells Angels members, the entire Nomad chapter, as well as every member in the Rockers and Evil Ones puppet clubs. When the dust settled, forty-two members of the Hells Angels (including all the Nomads) and the Rockers were each charged with thirteen counts of first-degree murder, three counts of attempted murder, various drug trafficking offences, and the new offence of participating in a criminal organization. Of the Hells Angels and Rockers named in the arrest warrants, fourteen were already behind bars on previous convictions or awaiting trial on other charges. Boucher learned of the new charges from his jail cell, as did fellow Nomad Richard Maynard, who was serving a sentence after police arrested him earlier that year while in the possession of photos of the Bandidos' new Canadian members.

Perhaps the most fitting symbol of the war's end occurred on May 6, 2002, when Maurice Boucher was found guilty of first-degree murder in the death of two prison guards and sentenced to life imprisonment, with no chance of parole for at least twenty-five years. The main witness in this trial was once again Stéphane Gagné, who by this time was much more polished and credible when he took the stand and who was supported by other bikers who had become Crown witnesses.

By the time of Boucher's conviction and sentencing, the trial of the dozens of defendants rounded up as part of Operation Springtime had begun. A new courthouse for the trial was built close to the Bordeaux Prison, with an underground tunnel linking the two complexes to lessen possible security breaches in the daily transfer of the prisoners. The courthouse, which cost taxpayers $16.5 million, included a prisoners' dock that could accommodate several of the accused at one time. The Crown's strategy was to divide the defendants into different groups, based on the club to which they belonged and the seriousness of their offence. The result was two planned "mega-trials": one for thirteen members of the Hells Angels and Rockers who were charged with murder and attempted murder, as well as other offences, and the second for seventeen members of the Rockers charged with conspiracy to murder, drug trafficking, and participation in a criminal organization.

The first mass trial began on April 19, 2002, and was slated to hear testimony from an astonishing 750 witnesses. But no evidence was more critical to the Crown's case than that gathered by a police informant named Dany Kane. While a Hells Angel hangaround and then a member of the Rockers, Kane was working as a mole for the RCMP and later the Quebec provincial police. From 1994 — the time he began wearing a wire, meeting with police handlers, photocopying documents, and providing computer disks from Hells Angels computers — to his death in 2000, Dany Kane would become the most productive informant ever to infiltrate the Hells Angels in Canada. His job as police agent meant that Kane was living a double life. He was not only a contract killer for the Angels (participating in at least eleven murders between 1994 and 1997), but was the husband and father of four children. He was also the gay lover of fellow hit man Aimé (Ace) Simard, whom he had met through a personals ad. Born in 1968, Kane began his association with the Angels in the early 1990s as a hangaround with the Montreal chapter, serving under the command of Scott Steinert, who himself was just a prospect at the time. Kane's life as a police agent began in 1994, when he contacted the RCMP while serving a sentence for firearms violations. After carrying out various assassinations and other jobs for the Hells Angels, Kane was made a full-fledged Rocker in 1995. In this new position, he often acted as a bodyguard and driver for

A photo of Maurice (Mom) Boucher's colours, which was submitted as evidence at his 2002 trial

Nomads David Carroll and Normand Robitaille, a job that elevated Kane's status as a police agent.

In February 1997, Kane and Simard were ordered by Carroll to travel to Nova Scotia and eliminate a drug dealer named Robert MacFarlane who owed the club money. The two faithfully carried out the orders. The only problem was that Kane was a police agent at the time. After it was revealed that Kane was involved in MacFarlane's slaying, his contract with the RCMP was terminated and he was arrested and sent to Halifax where he was charged with murder. These charges were dismissed in November 1998 when the judge declared a mistrial due to the inconsistent evidence and testimony provided by police. Kane returned to the Rockers and was given a new contract by the Quebec provincial police. It was in this capacity that Kane provided information crucial to the investigations that led up to Operation Springtime. But Kane would never see the fruits of his labour. On August 7, 2000, the thirty-one-year-old was found dead by his son in his garage at home. He was asphyxiated by carbon monoxide poisoning and his death was ruled a suicide. Autopsy photos showed a body covered with tattoos, including "Support 81" (No. 8 for "H" and the No. 1 for "A"), lightning bolts, a naked Viking woman, a motorcycle and "Support Big Red." Kane left a suicide note that reflected an identity crisis of existential proportions brought about by his multiple lives. In his rambling note, he scribbled, "Who am I? Am I a biker? Am I a policeman? Am I good or evil? Am I heterosexual or gay? Am I loved or feared? Am I exploited or the exploiter?" Ace Simard would be discovered dead on July 18, 2003, in a prison cell in Saskatchewan after being stabbed more than one hundred times.

The evidence collected by Kane proved too much for six of the Rockers on trial. By November 2002, they cut a bargain with prosecutors and pleaded guilty to murder, drug trafficking and participation in a criminal organization. Among those copping guilty pleas were Mom Boucher's twenty-seven-year-old son, Francis, who received a sentence of ten years. Stéphane Faucher, another member of the Rockers and a prospect with the Nomads, also became a Crown witness. Faucher admitted to planting five bombs given to him by Mom Boucher outside Montreal police stations in April 1999 (none of which exploded due to malfunctioning detonators). He was sentenced to twelve years. Stéphane Jarry, the secretary treasurer of the Rockers, who reportedly purchased up to 10 kilos of cocaine a month for resale, was handed an eleven-year term. Kenny Bedard, who was caught by police in possession of a 9-mm Luger, a ski mask, binoculars, and photos of Rock Machine members, was sentenced to ten and a half years. Vincent Lamar, a one-time president of the Rockers and Nomads prospect was sentenced to ten and a half years, while Pierre Toupin received eleven years. Salvatore Brunetti, the former Rock Machine member, avoided a murder charge due to the short period he spent as a member of the Nomads, and was sentenced to only three years for drug trafficking and participation in a criminal gang.

Among the others on trial for murder were Nomads Denis Houle, Gilles Mathieu, Normand Robitaille, and René Charlebois, Nomad prospect Guillaume Serra, and Rockers Jean-Guy Bourgouin, Daniel Lanthier, Sylvain Laplante, and Pierre Provencher. Crown prosecutors argued that the assassinations of thirteen rival gang members showed a consistent pattern: a victim was shot with a Cobray automatic gun, usually outside his home after getting out of a vehicle, and the shooters used a stolen getaway vehicle that would later be torched to hide fingerprints or any DNA evidence. On September 11, 2003, the eleven-month trial came to an abrupt end when all nine pleaded guilty to lesser charges of conspiracy to commit murder, drug trafficking, and participation in a criminal organization. The four Nomads — Charlebois, Houle,

Mathieu, and Robitaille — received twenty years, while the other five received fifteen-year sentences.

By June 2004, the majority of the Hells Angels and Rockers charged as part of Operation Springtime were found guilty. Most were convicted of or pleaded guilty to charges of drug trafficking, conspiracy to murder, and participation in a criminal organization. In addition to the life sentence imposed on their leader, Mom Boucher, at least eight members of the Nomads ended up serving sentences of twenty years or more. In January 2004, two Nomads, Pierre Laurin and Paul Brisebois, pleaded guilty to second-degree murder in the May 1, 2000, slaying of Patrick Turcotte, a twenty-five-year-old Rock Machine drug dealer. In March, two other Nomads, Michel Rose and André Chouinard, avoided a trial for first-degree murder by pleading guilty to drug trafficking, conspiracy to commit murder, and participation in a criminal organization. The Crown argued the two imported more than 4 metric tons of cocaine from Colombia into Quebec. The bikers also tried to cheat and kill the supplier who brokered the deal, Sandra Antelo, who agreed to testify against them. Chouinard was sentenced to twenty years while Rose was handed a sixteen-year term. At the end of May, Paul Fontaine, who had disappeared in 1997 shortly after Stéphane Gagné became a government informant, was arraigned in Montreal on multiple charges of murder, including those relating to the death of prison guard Pierre Rondeau as well as two Rock Machine associates. After being acquitted in one trial, Gregory Wooley, a senior member of the Rockers who was one of the Angels' main hit men, was sentenced to thirteen years in June 2005 after pleading guilty to conspiracy to commit murder, trafficking, and belonging to a criminal gang. One of the few Hells Angels to escape justice was former Halifax chapter member and Nomad David (Wolf) Carroll who, despite rumoured sightings in the Caribbean, has yet to be found.

IN FULL CONTROL

While Operation Springtime hit the Hells Angels hard, the resilient motorcycle club quickly bounced back and even saw its membership increase. Before the raids were conducted, the gang had 106 full-patch members in Quebec. By 2002, police estimated the number had risen to 124 (although this figure includes incarcerated members). And while the Nomads chapter was wiped out, by 2002 the five remaining chapters in Quebec survived unscathed. Another chapter was added that year when the Sherbrooke Angels split in two with half its two dozen members forming the new Estrie chapter, located not too far from Sherbrooke in Quebec's Eastern Townships. In addition, the Hells Angels still controlled a number of puppet clubs, including the Evil Ones, the Jokers, the Rowdy Crew, the Damners, the Blatnois, and Satan's Gang. Their drug trafficking network also rebounded when the Trois-Rivières chapter took over the Nomads' coordinating role in the club's cocaine trafficking business.

During the time the Hells Angels were under siege in Quebec, they were increasing their strength throughout the rest of Canada. In July 1997, the Grim Reapers of Alberta patched over to join forces with the Hells Angels and, as the 1999 annual report of the Criminal Intelligence Service Canada noted, the arrival of the Angels in Alberta "brought a noticeable increase in violent crime, as they coerced independent drug dealers into their distribution network. The disbandment of the Kings Crew of Calgary placed the Hells Angels in full control of biker-related criminal activities in Alberta." By 2002, the Angels had chapters in Calgary, Edmonton, and Red Deer. In Saskatchewan, the Saskatoon-based Rebels Motorcycle Club received their red-and-white colours in September 1998. Another chapter was added in Regina at the end of 2001. In 2000, the Hells Angels established their long-coveted Winnipeg chapter when it patched over the Los Brovos and over the next seven months, ten people were shot, including members of the new Hells Angels chapter and the rival Spartans club. Twenty people linked to the two biker groups in Manitoba were arrested and charged with more than one hundred weapons offences after police seized 20 kilos of explosives, 486 rounds of ammunition, and dozens of weapons.

The British Columbia Hells Angels celebrated their fifteenth anniversary in 1998 by adding a new Nomads chapter in Burnaby. It was their seventh chapter in that province and the tenth Nomads chapter internationally. Unlike their counterparts in Quebec, the Hells Angels in B.C. were able to fly below police radar for many years and the few attempts to prosecute

members were generally unsuccessful. In the fall of 2004, the *Vancouver Sun* reported that more than thirty criminal prosecutions launched against the Hells Angels in B.C. over the past decade had failed.

The only weak point in the Hells Angels national network was on the east coast, where the Halifax chapter was wiped out after a series of arrests and convictions in 2001 and 2002 reduced the chapter to three full-patch members. To make matters worse, their clubhouse was forfeited to the government in January 2003. A judge granted the Crown's forfeiture request during the sentencing of four members on drug trafficking charges. Michael McCrea, the president of the Halifax chapter, was allegedly warned by senior Angels in Quebec to rebuild the chapter by recruiting enough people to satisfy the six-member minimum requirement. To date, however, the Hells Angels have no Canadian chapter east of Quebec.

Despite this setback, the club continued its expansion in Ontario and, by 2002, there were sixteen Hells Angels chapters in the province with more than 250 full-patch members, prospects, and hangarounds. Among the new clubhouses was one established in 2002 in Vanier, just southeast of Ottawa, home to the six-member Ontario Nomads. The chapter is primarily made up of former Rock Machine members, including its president, Paul (Sasquatch) Porter, who bolted to the Angels (after surviving two attempts on his life by Angels hit men) at the end of 2002. Porter was able to maintain a low profile throughout the biker war, despite his leadership role with the Rock Machine and the fact that his six-foot-four, 400-pound frame is hard to hide. Police believe that it was Porter who persuaded several members of the Rock Machine to jump to their rival, instead of signing up with the Bandidos, even though Porter was involved in the initial negotiations with the Bandidos. According to police intelligence reports, the Nomads control more than 80 percent of the capital's drug trade, in part because of Porter's past affiliation with the Rock Machine, which maintained safe houses in Vanier during Quebec's biker war. In 2004, Porter was arrested by Quebec provincial police for masterminding a car theft ring that stole luxury SUVs, which were then smuggled out of the country and sold around the world. The sixteenth Ontario chapter was opened in Hamilton in 2005. The Angels had long had their sights on Hamilton due to its large drug market and its junction along major smuggling routes between New York State and Toronto.

Much of the credit for the Hells Angels' growth across Canada has been given to a member of the Quebec Nomads named Wolodumyr Stadnick. Known as Walter or by his nickname "Nugget," Stadnick began his biker career as a Wild One in his hometown of Hamilton. But at the age of twenty-six, his ambitions took him to Montreal where he applied for, and was accepted into, the Montreal chapter of the Hells Angels. In 1984, only two years after becoming a member, Stadnick was seriously hurt while riding in formation with his colleagues as they travelled to pay their last respects to Yves (Le Boss) Buteau, the president of the Montreal chapter who had just been gunned down. A priest, who was rushing to see the Pope on the Quebec stop of his Canadian tour, ran a stop sign and crashed into the phalanx of bikers. One prospect, Daniel Matthieu, was killed, while Stadnick was severely burned and lost several fingers.

Despite the accident and his diminutive stature (he is only five-feet-four inches tall), Stadnick quickly rose through the Angels hierarchy. On a national level, his influence within the biker club even surpassed that of Mom Boucher. Yet the two were a powerful combination, according to Julian Sher and William Marsden. Boucher would give the Angels "the power base in the Quebec drug and sex trade that they need to expand; Stadnick would give them the vision and direction to make that expansion happen." While Boucher remained intent on conquering Quebec, Stadnick's goal was to build a Hells Angels empire in Canada that stretched from coast to coast. In 1988, he was elected national president and used the office to methodically establish chapters across the country, with particular emphasis on Manitoba and Ontario. "Stadnick realized that if the Hells Angels stood any chance of becoming a truly national empire, they had to fill the huge gap in Central Canada — and that meant Manitoba and Ontario," Sher and Marsden write. Manitoba was important "because it was the axis of distribution for any drugs moving east and west in the country," while Ontario was critical because it was "the Golden Horseshoe for drugs, prostitution and all other proceeds of crime." As Boucher was busy prosecuting

Members of the Wolverine squad talk with Paul Porter, after he was detained in a raid on the Rock Machine clubhouse in Montreal.

his war, Stadnick was travelling across Ontario and Manitoba trying to convince other biker gangs to join the Hells Angels, while establishing the infrastructure for a national drug pipeline. In January 1992, he was caught at the Winnipeg airport with $81,000 in cash and, on another occasion, Winnipeg police discovered $15,000 in $1,000 bills tucked inside his solid-gold Angels death's-head belt buckle. By 2000, Stadnick's hard work paid off when the Los Brovos in Winnipeg patched over and more than 160 bikers in Ontario became Hells Angels.

As part of Operation Springtime, Stadnick was arrested while vacationing in Montego Bay. He was extradited to Canada and, in June 2004, a Quebec superior court acquitted him of thirteen first-degree murder charges and three counts of attempted murder. But Stadnick, along with fellow Nomad and long-time associate Donald Stockford, were convicted of five charges, including conspiracy to commit murder, participation in a criminal organization, and drug trafficking. Financial records taken from the Hells Angels spreadsheets showed that between March 30, 1999, and December 19, 2000, Stadnick and Stockford spent more than $10 million to purchase 267 kilos of cocaine and 173 kilos of hashish as part of the Nomads drug consortium. The two were sentenced to twenty years, but with time already served, it worked out to only a further thirteen years behind bars. Each man was also fined $100,000 or another eighteen months in prison.

In addition to Stadnick's efforts, the Angels' takeover of Ontario was due to intensive law enforcement actions against existing biker gangs in the province, which greatly weakened two long-time provincial obstacles to the Hells Angels — the Satan's Choice and the Outlaws. "Operation Dismantle," a province wide, joint force operation that targeted the Satan's Choice, crippled their chapters in Sudbury, Thunder Bay, Hamilton, and Milton. Between 1996 and 1998, more than 1,300 charges were laid against 197 people who were members or associates of the biker gang. As part of the police raids, around $1 million in drugs and $2 million in property were seized, along with eighty-four weapons and 5,400 rounds of ammunition. Among the Choice members arrested were six accused of bombing the Sudbury police station in December 1996, including the president of the Hamilton chapter, thirty-four-year-old John Croitoru, also known by his World Wrestling Federation name "Johnny K-9." In January 2005, Croitoru was charged with two counts of first-degree murder for the 1998 deaths of Hamilton lawyer Lynn Gilbank

and her husband, who were killed in their home by a shotgun-wielding intruder. Croituru — who was also known in wrestling circles as Bruiser Bedlam, Taras Bulba, and the Terrible Turk — was convicted as part of the 1996 bombing but was not convicted of murder after the Crown prosecutor withdrew the charges. No reason was given for dropping the charges, although there were rumours that it was related to a shoddy police investigation.

Following Operation Springtime, the Bandidos attempted to grab back some of the drug trafficking territory lost by the Rock Machine in Quebec, but were quickly foiled by police. In the summer of 2001, Montreal bars used by the Hells Angels to sell drugs were plagued by twenty-seven arsons, which police intelligence suggested were set by the Bandidos to intimidate bar owners to allow their drug dealers to work the sites. The investigation into the spate of arsons contributed to the formation of "Operation Amigo" and, on June 5, 2002, charges were laid against sixty-two members or associates of the Bandidos and its puppet club, the

Walter Stadnick (facing the camera) as he leaves a Winnipeg funeral in the early 1990s

Killerbeez. As part of twenty-nine searches conducted across Quebec and Ontario, police seized 197 kilos of hashish, two hundred marijuana plants, thousands of Viagra pills, and firearms. All of the Bandido's twenty-five full-patch members in Quebec were arrested, including their national president, Alain Brunette, and two key Montreal members, Normand Whissel and Serge (Merlin) Cyr. Both men were among eleven people charged with conspiracy to murder, which dated back to their role in the Rock Machine's war with the Hells Angels. Other charges included drug trafficking and membership in a criminal organization. Salvatore Cazzetta, who had just been transferred from the U.S. to a Quebec prison to finish his twelve-year drug trafficking sentence, was charged with participating in a criminal organization, with police alleging he was giving orders to gang members over the telephone from his cell at Archambault Penitentiary. The investigation also resulted in the arrest of a contract employee with the Quebec automobile licensing bureau, who police believed was providing Rock Machine and Bandido members with information from the bureau's database, which was used to identify and locate Hells Angels and their associates for extermination. By the fall of 2004, around forty-eight members of the Bandidos had pleaded guilty. Brunette, Whissel, and Cyr were sentenced to eight, fifteen, and nine months, respectively. Cazzetta's charges were eventually dropped. Following the arrests and convictions of most of the Quebec Bandidos, police claimed their influence in the province had been severely hampered and any future war that may have been fought with the Hells Angels in the province had been pre-empted.

By 2002, the Hells Angels' other main rivals, the Outlaws, had eleven chapters in Ontario, although their membership was less than half of that of the Angels and their numbers were steadily dwindling. Some had left the club as part of the massive patchover to the Angels in 2000, while others were behind bars. As part of "Operation Charlie," an investigation targeting the St. Catharines chapter of the Outlaws, nine members and associates were arrested on numerous charges related to drugs, prostitution, and attempted murder. Chapter president Mario Parente, who had been jailed for three years in 1988 for manslaughter, was charged with fourteen counts of drug trafficking

and weapons offences. A year later, the London chapter was weakened by police raids and the murder of two prominent members. On August 12, 2002, William Hulko, the president of the Outlaws Kingston chapter, was found dead in his jail cell at the Quinte Detention Centre Ontario while awaiting trial on sex charges. Known as "Wild Bill" to his fellow bikers, the fifty-nine-year-old was found dead by guards. Corrections officials said he died of natural causes.

Two weeks later, more than five hundred police officers launched a massive sweep against Outlaws chapters across Ontario. On August 26, 2002, "Project Retire" concluded with the arrest of thirty-five Ontario Outlaws — half of its full-patch members — who faced such charges as attempted murder, drug trafficking, assault, weapons violations, and participation in a criminal organization. Mario Parente, now the Outlaws national president, was among those arrested. Simultaneous raids were conducted on their clubhouses in the U.S., resulting in the arrest of the club's international president, Frank Wheeler, in Indianapolis. Wheeler was charged with the murder of rival Hells Angels members, racketeering, and extortion. Outlaws national vice-president Dennis Pellegrini, who at the time was in charge of Ontario, was also arrested in Michigan and charged with drug offences. Following the raids in Canada, the Ontario Provincial Police announced they recovered five stolen motorcycles, one stolen pickup truck, forty-four firearms and about $1.6 million in illegal drugs. Five of the Outlaws clubhouses in Ontario were also seized by police. Most of those arrested pleaded guilty and were jailed.

With the Satan's Choice and Outlaws reduced to rubble in Ontario, only one biker gang had any chance of standing in the way of a total Hells Angels conquest of the province: the Bandidos. The prospects of becoming a major force in the province were slim, however, given it only had one twelve-member chapter in Toronto. These hopes were put to rest for good as a result of a bloody and bizarre slaughter reminiscent of the 1985 Hells Angels Lennoxville massacre. On April 8, 2006, the bodies of eight men were found dead in three cars and one tow truck parked in a farmer's field about 30 kilometres west of London, Ontario. They had all been shot at different locations before being brought

A police officer paints over the entrance gate to the Outlaws' clubhouse in St. Catharines on September 25, 2002, after it was shut down following raids a month earlier.

to the field and left in the four vehicles. The dead included six full-patch members of the Toronto chapter of the Bandidos: George Jesso, George Kiriakis, Luis Manny Raposo, Francesco Salerajno, John Muscedere, and Paul Sinopoli. The two other victims were Jamie Flanz, who police said was a prospect with the club, and Michael Trotta, who was described as an associate. Muscedere was believed to be the national president of the Canadian Bandidos. The killings were the worst mass murder in Ontario's history.

Following what a senior provincial police officer referred to as an "internal cleansing," five people were arrested and charged with first-degree murder

two days after the bodies were discovered. Four men and one woman were arrested following a lengthy police standoff outside the nearby farmhouse of one of the accused. Among those arrested and charged was fifty-six-year-old Wayne Kellestine, a full-patch member of the Bandidos, whose house was only a few kilometres from where the bodies were found and who had a history of violent and erratic behaviour as a member of other motorcycle gangs. Kellestine was charged with eight counts of first-degree murder. On June 16, police in Winnipeg charged three other men with eight counts of murder, two of them full-patch members of the Bandidos (including a former

John Muscedere, president of the Bandidos in Canada, in a photo taken on December 1, 1999, while he was a member of the Loners Motorcycle Club in Ontario

Manitoba police officer) and the other a prospect with the local chapter.

Before the killings, members of the Toronto Bandidos chapter had tried to make inroads in Alberta and Manitoba, setting up probationary chapters in Calgary and one in Winnipeg. But they had little success in either city. With the arrests and jailings in Quebec following Operation Amigo, their numbers were too low in Canada to sustain the club's presence. Speculation was rife that the murdered Bandidos members may have been contemplating a jump to the Hells Angels. Kellestine was particularly hostile to the patchover of more than 160 Ontario bikers to the Angels, which police believe led to an attempt on his life by two Hells Angels associates on October 22, 1999. When his home was searched the next day, police found a variety of firearms, including three semi-automatic weapons, three rifles, a 12-gauge shotgun, and ammunition. Kellestine, who loved weapons as much as his Nazi memorabilia, was charged with twenty-two

counts of weapons and stolen property offences and was sentenced to two years. It was following his release that he had joined the Bandidos in Ontario.

An alternative theory behind the mass murder is that it was Kellestine who wanted to leave the Bandidos for the Hells Angels and was either removing any internal obstacles or trying to curry favour with the Angels by wiping out its competitors. Either way, some believe that Kellestine may have just wanted to kill the national president, John Muscedere, but events simply spiralled out of control. Yet another theory is that the deaths were simply the result of a drug deal gone wrong (just hours before the murder Durham police were trailing three of the eight ill-fated Bandidos to Kellestine's farmhouse, although at the time the police officers did not know the men were delivering 200 kilos of cocaine).

The deaths and subsequent arrests of the Ontario Bandidos were the final nail in the coffin for the biker club in Canada. "The Bandidos no longer exist in Ontario," Detective Inspector Don Bell of the province's Biker Enforcement Unit told the media. This was confirmed by police officials in Texas, where the Bandidos have their international headquarters. The Bandidos president, Jeff Pike, had already revoked the Canadian affiliate's membership and barred its former members from wearing the Bandidos colours. The April massacre and the subsequent arrests were already a major embarrassment to the Bandidos leadership. The last straw was the revelation that a former police officer had joined their probationary Winnipeg chapter. In fact, Pike told reporters that Michael Sandham, who had worked for the local police in East St. Paul, a municipality just north of Winnipeg, went to Texas to share his "big plans" for the expansion of the Bandidos in Canada just days before he was arrested. Sandham apparently met with Bandidos leaders on June 6, but was immediately stripped of his colours after they learned about his law enforcement background. "As far as I was concerned, our conversation was over," Pike told the *Winnipeg Free Press* in a telephone interview. "That made him automatically not a member of my club." By the beginning of 2007, after being shut out of Ontario for close to thirty years, and less than seven years following their dramatic entry into the province, the Hells Angels had become the dominant force in Ontario's outlaw biker world.

WITH INTENT TO INSPIRE FEAR IN THEIR VICTIM

Now that police had virtually eliminated most of the Hells Angels' competition, they began re-training their sights on Canada's most powerful and only national outlaw biker group. Just days following Operation Springtime at the end of March 2001, more than two hundred police officers executed search warrants on twenty-seven locations in and around Calgary, including the Angels' fortified clubhouse in the city. Among the fifty-one people charged were six full-patch members, two ex-prospects, one hangaround, one ex-hangaround, and thirty-nine associates. At the time, the Calgary chapter had sixteen members. The raids also netted an Uzi machine gun, eleven rifles, thirty shotguns, along with 11 kilos of cocaine, 1.5 kilos of methamphetamine, as well as more than three thousand Valium, morphine, and

ecstasy tablets. A total of 275 drug and weapons charges were laid.

In February 2002, a twenty-two-month investigation into the Hells Angels in the Quebec City area was capped by the apprehension of twenty-nine people on drug charges. Among them were six full-patch members of the chapter and five members of their puppet club, the Downtown Damners. According to the RCMP, 'Operation 4H' was the most successful operation against the Hells Angels in Quebec City to date. Police laid a total of 1,018 charges and dismantled an important drug network that was controlled by the Hells Angels and extended from Quebec to New Brunswick."

In November of the same year, more than 350 police officers swooped down on the Trois-Rivières chapter and its affiliate club, the Jokers. Three members of the Hells Angels and the entire membership of the puppet gang were arrested. Police alleged that the Jokers were the main drug trafficking group for the parent club on Montreal's south shore. As part of the raids, police seized three kilos of cocaine, 170 marijuana plants, ecstasy, and magic mushrooms, as well as cash, fourteen vehicles, and several weapons. In all, forty people were arrested or were being sought on warrants. This included Marc-Andre Hotte, who was named in a warrant as part of Operation Springtime, and Paul Magnan. Both were members of the Trois-Rivières chapter at the time. With the latest arrests in Quebec, police announced that more than seventy known Hells Angels members in the province were behind bars or awaiting trial on criminal charges. Magnan, Hotte, as well as two senior Jokers later pleaded guilty to drug trafficking and participation in a criminal organization.

In April 2003, the Hells Angels in Greater Toronto were targeted by "Operation Shirlea," which resulted in the arrest of eighty-four people, including fourteen full-patch members from five chapters, two former members, and three members of the Red Line Crew puppet club. The Shirlea police task force, a reference to the Hells Angels chapter located on Shirlea Avenue in Keswick just north of Toronto, zeroed in on the drug trafficking activities of the Ontario Hells Angels, which police said was responsible for funnelling hundreds of kilos of cocaine through the province's streets. As one media report put it, "Within a year or two of the mass baptism in Sorel, Hells Angels or their associates were running sophisticated narcotics operations from one end of Canada's most populous province to the other: in the economic core of Toronto, but also east to Kingston and Belleville, southwest to London and north to Thunder Bay." Police alleged that the cocaine was purchased directly from Colombian traffickers, although most came from their "Quebec connection." Seized as part of the raids were 6.2 kilos of cocaine, 441 grams of hashish, about 2,400 prescription pills, ninety-three marijuana plants, and 16.7 kilograms of harvested marijuana. Police also found sixteen handguns, six sets of Kevlar body armour, and a crossbow.

In December 2003, police from the Organized Crime Agency of B.C. raided the Nanaimo clubhouse of the Hells Angels after discovering 10 kilos of cocaine from a tractor-trailer with Ontario licence plates at the Nanaimo ferry terminal. Police alleged the coke was linked to a member of the Hells Angels from the Keswick, Ontario, chapter and was part of the ongoing shipment of "multi-kilograms" from Vancouver Island to Toronto, with Hells Angels members at both ends of the operation. A fifty-three-year-old member of the Nanaimo chapter named Lea Sheppe, was charged in March 2005 with drug trafficking offences, while a member of the Keswick chapter was flown to B.C. to face similar charges.

On February 26, 2004, police staged another series of raids in Quebec targeting members of the Hells Angels, arresting forty people on charges that included drug trafficking and participation in a criminal organization. Among those arrested were twelve full-patch members of the South chapter, three members from the Montreal chapter, one from the Rockers affiliate, and four from the Evil Ones. The raids were the culmination of a thirty-month investigation that began shortly after Operation Springtime. One day before the raid, Jacques (Israel) Emond, a member of the Sherbrooke chapter, was charged along with five other people as part of what police were calling a loansharking ring that that took in more than $3 million annually by charging interest as high as 300 percent per year.

In October 2004, Winnipeg police arrested thirty-five people who were members or associates of the Zig Zag Crew, a puppet club of the Hells Angels, following a ten-month investigation called "Project Othello." During the busts, police seized 1.75 kilos of cocaine, 6.5 kilos of marijuana, 150 marijuana plants, and a small amount of methamphetamine and ecstasy. Police also confiscated $250,000 in Canadian currency and $7,000 in American cash along with a house and two vehicles. Police believe the drugs they seized were supplied by local members of the Hells Angels. The Zig Zag Crew was formed in 1998 by a member of the Los Bravos and consists of about a dozen members who, according to police, are supervised by junior members of Winnipeg's Hells Angels chapter.

In January 2005, drug trafficking and firearms charges were laid against four members of the Hells Angels' Vancouver chapter and six members of its Prince George affiliate, the Renegade motorcycle club. Among those arrested was Norman Krogstad, the fifty-seven-year-old president of the Vancouver chapter. Krogstad, who was charged with fourteen counts of drug trafficking, is the highest-ranking member of the Angels ever to face criminal charges in B.C. The charges were laid after a Renegade member became a police agent and bought more than nine kilos of cocaine from another senior East End chapter member, Cedric Smith. Police alleged the cocaine was supplied to Smith by Krogstad. Police seized 14 kilos of cocaine, 11 kilos of marijuana, more than $100,000 in cash, and three stolen John Deere Golf Course lawn tractors valued at more than $100,000. Four handguns, a sawed-off shotgun, a fully automatic AK-47 assault rifle, and ammunition were also seized.

On June 2, 2005, Shawn Boshaw, a member of the London, Ontario, chapter of the Hells Angels, who police believe was at the centre of the drug trade in Peterborough, was arrested as dozens of raids across the province also nabbed twenty-eight other people. Fourteen search warrants were executed in Peterborough where police seized cocaine, ecstasy, marijuana, Oxycodone, steroids, Percocet, and $50,000 in cash. Later that month, police arrested and charged sixteen people for their connection to drug trafficking and organized crime in the Greater Kingston Area and other locales in eastern Ontario. This included two Hells Angels members from its Nomad chapters in Ontario, Brett Simmons and James Belbeck, as well as

Richer Geneau, a ranking member of the Hells Angels in Gatineau, Quebec. A total of 102 charges were laid, ranging from drug trafficking to participating in a criminal organization. Cocaine, ecstasy, marijuana, and other drugs with a retail street value exceeding $1 million were seized from traffickers allegedly working for members of the Angels. The arrests were made as part of "Project Dante," a joint force investigation launched in September 2003 that targeted the Ontario Nomads chapter. Simmons, who was arrested while sleeping at the Nomads Ottawa-area clubhouse, was one of the Rock Machine members who defected to the Angels while in prison. Nicknamed "Lucky Luke," after surviving a bomb explosion that killed three of his Rock Machine comrades, he served eight years on attempted-murder charges. When he was released from jail, he joined the Ontario Nomads chapter, becoming a key lieutenant to president Paul (Sasquatch) Porter. Simmons' election to the Ontario Nomads gave the chapter eight members; however, his arrest along with Belbeck left the gang with only six, the bare minimum to keep their status under Hells Angels rules.

In July 2005, Madam Justice Michele Fuerst found Steven (Tiger) Lindsay and Ray Bonner, both members of the Woodbridge, Ontario, chapter of the Hells Angels, guilty of extortion and of committing that crime "in association" with a criminal organization. The ruling was viewed as a significant victory for lawmakers, as it was the first decision under the 1997 organized crime legislation that ruled the Hells Angels to be a criminal organization. On January 23, 2002, Lindsay and Bonner were both wearing their colours when they arrived at the home of a Barrie, Ontario, businessman who had sold them faulty equipment that was supposed to steal satellite television signals. By wearing the Hells Angels colours, Lindsay and Bonner "presented themselves not as individuals, but as members of a group with a reputation for violence and intimidation," Justice Fuerst wrote in her decision. Lindsay demanded that the businessman pay him $75,000 or he would "end up in hospital." The man was so terrified that he never slept in his home again. Lindsay and Bonner deliberately evoked their membership in the Hells Angels "with intent to inspire fear in their victim," according to Justice Fuerst.

Also in July 2005, police raided the Vancouver clubhouse of the East End chapter of the Hells Angels, while a simultaneous raid was conducted at a clubhouse of a satellite chapter in Kelowna. Police arrested six full-patch members and laid a variety of drug, extortion, weapons and participation in a criminal organization charges. As part of a twenty-three-month investigation dubbed "Project E-Pandora," police seized more than 20 kilos of methylamine, 20 kilos of methamphetamine, 20 kilos of cocaine and 70 kilos of marijuana. A month earlier, the RCMP in Kelowna had already seized more than 1,000 marijuana "clones" (stems from potent "mother plants" that are clipped to produce other pot plants) from the home of Joseph Bruce Skreptak, a member of the East End chapter. Police also turned up $200,000 in cash, as well as handguns, fully automatic weapons, silencers, eleven sticks of dynamite, and four grenades. Later that year, police and prosecutors in British Columbia continued to score victories in their battle against the Hells Angels when Edward Krogstad and two other members of the B.C. Hells Angels pleaded guilty to drug trafficking charges laid in January. Along with fellow East End chapter member Cedric Baxter Smith, Krogstad pleaded guilty to eleven counts of cocaine trafficking, and the two were sentenced to four years in jail. By the end of 2005, seventeen of the approximately one hundred full-patch Hells Angels in B.C. had been charged with or convicted of various offences.

On January 18, 2006, officers from the joint forces investigation "Project Husky" charged twenty-seven people in Northern Ontario, Quebec, and Alberta for their connection to a major drug trafficking ring. Project Husky, a two-year, covert operation focussing on Hells Angels members and associates, began in January 2004. During the investigation, a number of drug seizures, including cocaine, marijuana, ecstasy, Percocet, and OxyContin, with a street value of $2.3 million were made. The investigation found strong ties to the Quebec Hells Angels, and the drugs were being distributed there, according to police. Those charged include five members of the Thunder Bay chapter, as well as Andre Watteel, a former Satan's Choice member who was patched over in 2000 and then went on to become the president of the Kitchener Hells Angels. The drug network was brought down after the successful infiltration of the Thunder Bay chapter by a police agent who spent nearly two years undercover. The agent was so convincing that a police-owned tractor-trailer he made available to his Hells Angels associates was painted in Angels' red and white and published on the back page of the Ontario Angels' 2006 calendar.

In February 2006, three full-patch members of the Manitoba Hells Angels, including chapter president Ernest (Ernie) Dew, his wife, and ten other associates were arrested and charged with drug offences. The investigation resulted in the seizure of around 7 kilos of cocaine and three kilos of methamphetamine. Dew, a former member of the Los Bravos, was personally courted by Walter Stadnick in his efforts to patch over the club to the Hells Angels. All of the accused faced charges ranging from drug trafficking and extortion to participation in a criminal organization. At the time of the arrests, five members of the Manitoba Angels were already in prison or facing charges on unrelated offences.

At the end of September 2006, police in Ontario launched early-morning raids that resulted in the arrest of thirty people. Among those were fifteen Hells Angels members. The sweep was part of an eighteen-month undercover operation and resulted in the seizure of 50,000 hits of ecstasy, 13 kilos of cocaine and two kilos of crystal meth. Cash totalling $470,000 was also confiscated. At the centre of the raids was the Hells Angels' Oshawa chapter, where police uncovered a plot to kill a "recruiter" who was trying to rebuild the Bandidos bike club. Police confirmed that they acted on information provided by a senior member of the Oshawa chapter who had become a police inform-ant. His identity was not revealed, but the *Toronto Star* reported that he was a former Satan's Choice member who was part of the massive patchover to the Angels. The informant's revelations led to charges of conspiracy to commit murder, drug trafficking, and participation in a criminal organization against five of his cohorts from the Oshawa chapter as well as a member of the Nomads.

On April 4, 2007, police in three provinces fanned out in early-morning raids on Hells Angels clubhouses and other properties, arresting members and associ-ates in Southern Ontario, British Columbia, and New Brunswick. The crowning jewel of the raids was the seizure of the Angels Toronto Hells clubhouse at 498 Eastern Avenue, which was meticulously choreo-graphed for the media. Members of the provincial Biker Enforcement Unit and Toronto police smashed through the two-storey cinder-block building and a few hours later, with television cameras rolling, police removed the gang insignia from the exterior wall and unfurled their own banner announcing that the property had been seized by police. That raid, which resulted in 31 arrests and 169 charges, followed an investigation that began with information provided by an informant. Police seized nearly 500 litres of the date-rape drug GHB, nine kilos of cocaine, more than eighty weapons, and $500,000 in cash.

"OUR CLUB IS NO LONGER REALLY A REAL BIKER GANG"

Allen McMillan, a professor at Central Washington University, once wrote that most of the major outlaw motorcycle groups move through four stages of de-velopment: (1) the club shows rebellious and antisocial activity that is random and non-utilitarian; (2) a police response causes less committed members to drop out while members of weaker clubs either disperse or join stronger clubs; (3) the remaining clubs are better able to exercise discipline and control over their membership, particularly control over violence, which now changes from random and non-utilitarian to instrumental; and (4) the leadership uses organizational skills and intimi-dation in utilitarian criminal pursuits and the group becomes a fully committed criminal organization.

This theoretical framework is somewhat appli-cable to Canada, except for the fact that it was not a police response that contributed to the reduction of the number of biker gangs in the country. It was the voracious appetite of the one-percenter clubs themselves, and of the Hells Angels in particular, which came out on top in the Darwinian world of outlaw motorcycle gangs. As Hells Angel David (Wolf) Carroll once said to his biker protégé Dany Kane, "The Nomads judge you by the size of your portfolio. If you don't have money, you're no good. Our club is no longer really a real biker gang. There are some members who have told me they don't even like biking."

Police remove the Hells Angels sign from their clubhouse on Eastern Avenue Toronto.

The Hells Angels are unprecedented in the annals of Canadian organized crime in that they are the first truly national criminal organization, with cells and/or associates in every province and territory. Canada has become somewhat of an international stronghold for the motorcycle club; there are more Hells Angels members per capita in Canada than any other country in the world. Moreover, although Canada has about one-tenth the population of the U.S., the Angels have 450 full-patch members in this country, compared to about 700 south of the border. With some 2,000 members and prospects in twenty-two countries, this means that almost one in four Hells Angels worldwide resides in Canada. With between 180 and 190 of these Canadian members belonging to fourteen Ontario chapters, Canada's largest province can also boast one of the highest concentrations of Hells Angels in the world, establishing a power base, not just for Canada, but internationally. At one point, the Greater Toronto Area alone was home to ten Hells Angels chapters, with approximately one hundred members.

Experts on outlaw motorcycle gangs have argued that the growth of the Canadian Hells Angels in numbers, power, and criminal stature is not simply due to the dog-eat-dog world of organized crime, but is also a result of the lack of attention, various miscues, and even a systemic ineptitude by Canada's criminal justice system and its law enforcement branches in particular. Biker expert Yves Lavigne does not attempt to hide his contempt for the bureaucratic inefficiencies, lack of interagency co-operation, and incompetence that has plagued law enforcement's response to outlaw motorcycle gangs. Police have "failed to predict the movements of the Hells Angels for twenty years" or to "halt or even slow their growth," he writes. "The police allowed biker gangs to take the country and gave us a play-by-play description as each province fell." Julian Sher and William Marsden agree, criticizing police agencies and government policy makers for allowing the Hells Angels to expand almost unfettered across the country. They accuse Canadian police of "ignoring the bikers for too long" and allege that police were so "plagued by rivalries, incompetence and a general underestimation of the threat posed by the bikers" that they "did little to take on the Hells Angels until their power made them virtually impregnable."

Ostensibly, it is not the police or the government who should take the blame for the birth of outlaw biker gangs in Canada and the spectacular rise of the Hells Angels as a powerful criminal organization. Nor should the blame be placed on America, the international birthplace of the one-percenters. Outlaw motorcycle gangs emerged, proliferated, and grew wealthy and powerful in Canada because Canadian society provided all the necessary preconditions. Indeed, the Hells Angels and other motorcycle gangs truly are a strange and terrible Canadian saga.

THE SWORD OF THE TRIAD

illustrated by Adam Hilborn

SOMEWHERE IN THE BOWELS OF TORONTO'S CHINATOWN, MEMBERS OF THE KUNG LOK, THE CITY'S MOST FEARED CHINESE CRIMINAL SOCIETY, ARE INDUCTING A NEW RECRUIT INTO ITS RANKS...

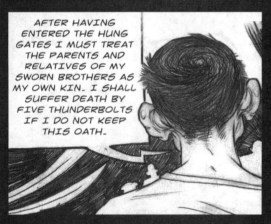

AFTER HAVING ENTERED THE HUNG GATES I MUST TREAT THE PARENTS AND RELATIVES OF MY SWORN BROTHERS AS MY OWN KIN. I SHALL SUFFER DEATH BY FIVE THUNDERBOLTS IF I DO NOT KEEP THIS OATH.

BEFORE THE GATE OF LOYALTY AND RIGHTEOUSNESS ALL MEN ARE EQUAL.

WHEN HONG BROTHERS VISIT MY HOUSE, I SHALL PROVIDE THEM WITH BOARD AND LODGING. I SHALL BE KILLED BY MYRIADS OF KNIVES IF I TREAT THEM AS STRANGERS.

I SHALL NOT DISCLOSE THE SECRETS OF THE HONG FAMILY, NOT EVEN TO MY PARENTS, BROTHERS, OR WIFE. I SHALL NEVER DISCLOSE THE SECRETS FOR MONEY. I WILL BE KILLED BY MYRIADS OF SWORDS IF I DO SO.

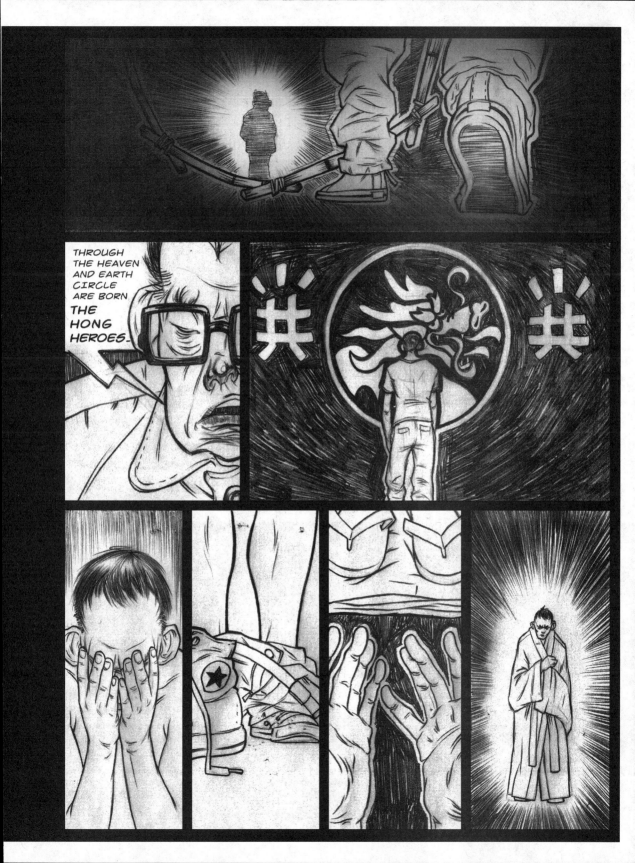

THROUGH THE HEAVEN AND EARTH CIRCLE ARE BORN **THE HONG HEROES...**

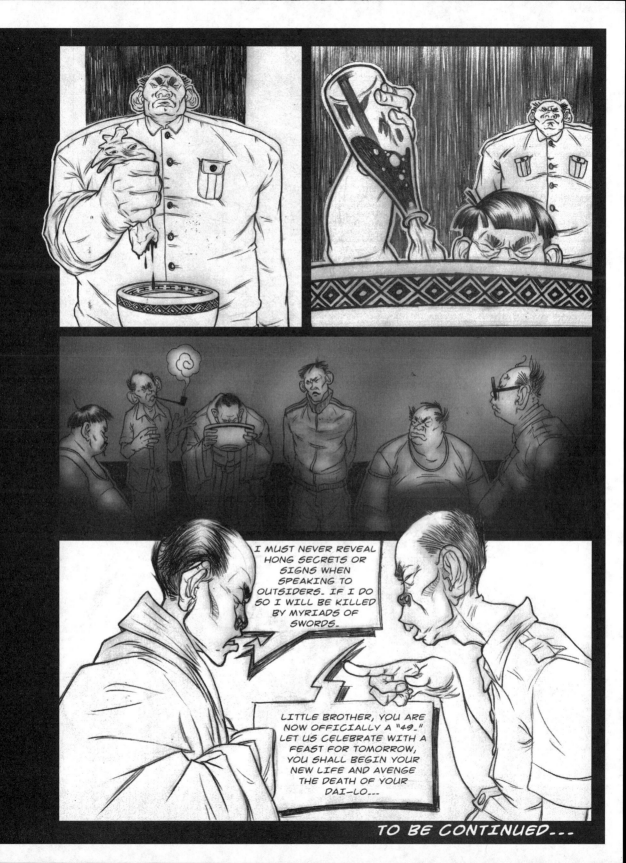

CHAPTER 11

IT'S RAINING CORPSES IN CHINATOWN!

Asian Organized Crime in Canada

Asian organized crime is not new to Canada. Chinese merchants in Vancouver were behind some of the largest opium smuggling and trafficking rings in the country during the first half of the 20th century. Canada's first Chinatown in Victoria was home to illegal gambling halls, brothels, and opium dens, most of which were controlled by leading Chinese merchants. Some Chinese associations in Vancouver, Toronto, and Montreal were used by powerful members for such illegal endeavours as extortion, prostitution, gambling, opium trafficking, and people smuggling. Beginning in the 1970s, Southeast Asian heroin began to supplant the Turkish variety in North America and, before long, Chinese drug trafficking syndicates had surpassed the French Corsicans and the Italian mafia as the world's biggest heroin suppliers. By the mid-1970s, a rash of extortions within Toronto's Chinese community exposed the presence of Canada's first modern triad. Around the same time, Chinese street gangs emerged in Vancouver. A few years later, aggressive Vietnamese gangs began to challenge the Chinese triads for supremacy in the Asian underworld in both cities. At the end of the 1980s, a network of professional criminals, originally made up of ex-military from Mainland China that had been labelled the Big Circle Boys, were being blamed for a series of violent robberies, home invasions, and pickpocketing in Vancouver and Toronto. Within ten years, this loose network would evolve into one of the largest and most sophisticated criminal conspiracies in the country. By the start of the next decade, intelligence information fuelled fears that a number of leading Hong Kong triad members were applying for Canadian citizenship in anticipation of the colony's return to Chinese control in 1997. In the years that followed, the scope of Asian organized crime groups and their illegal activities in Canada escalated dramatically. These domestic developments are reflected in the ever-growing scale of Chinese organized crime on the world stage; today Chinese criminal groups and networks constitute one of the biggest transnational organized crime threats in the world.

黑社会

Contemporary Asian organized crime in Canada can be broken down into six overlapping categories: (1) local street gangs made up of both youth and adults; (2) Chinese triads, which evolved from gangs that relied primarily on extortion in Toronto's Chinatown into sophisticated transnational criminal syndicates with links to Hong Kong, Taiwan, and Mainland China; (3) non-triad Chinese criminal networks that tend to specialize in one particular criminal activity, such as drug trafficking or migrant smuggling; (4) a loose network of criminals from Mainland China who commit a wide variety of crimes including sophisticated frauds, counterfeiting, drug trafficking, and people smuggling (the Big Circle Boys); (5) Vietnamese crime groups, which include violent street gangs in Toronto and Vancouver and later some of the biggest marijuana producers and traffickers in Canada; and (6) Indo–Canadian crime groups that are largely confined to British Columbia and are involved in cocaine, marijuana, and synthetic drug trafficking and smuggling.

The so-called triads are the oldest and most structured of the Asian criminal organizations. While their origins can be traced back centuries to revolutionary movements and mutual aid societies, their evolution into modern criminal entities began in earnest in Hong Kong and Mainland China during the early part of the 20th century. Their criminal empires expanded following the rise to power of Mao Tse Tung and the Communists in the late 1940s, when many triad members fled to the more favourable climes of Hong Kong and Taiwan. At the same time, leaders of the nationalist forces who fought the Communists relocated in Burma (now Myanmar) where they established Southeastern Asia as one of the biggest sources of heroin in the world. The criminal networks associated with the Hong Kong–based triads expanded internationally in the 1960s, exploiting the growth of expatriate Chinese communities as well as the rapidly expanding heroin markets in North America. Today, powerful Chinese criminals use triad societies to further their vast international conspiracies through what the U.S. National Security Council calls "traditional Chinese practices of networking."

There is probably no organized crime genre whose origin is more shrouded by myth and obfuscation than the Chinese triads. Some have traced their beginnings back to the White Lotus Society, which was founded by monks in the 12th century who then revolted against the Mongol occupation of China during the 13th and 14th centuries. Others place the triads' beginnings in 17th-century China, where covert

societies tried to overthrow the Manchu (or Quing) dynasty (which ruled from 1644 to 1911) in order to return the country to the Ming dynasty (in power from 1368 to 1644), which represented the majority ethnic Han Chinese. By the early 19th century, numerous rebel groups were operating in Mainland China, such as the Tian Di Hui (Heaven and Earth Society), San Tian Hui (Triple Dot Society), and the San He Hui (Triple Unit Society). Collectively, these secret societies were referred to as the Hong Men (Hong refers to "Hongwu," the reign designation of the first Ming emperor, Zhu Yuanzhang). The avowed revolutionary aims of these societies made them outlaw organizations in the eyes of the Quing rulers and any known member was subject to death.

Like the terms "mafia" or "Cosa Nostra," the "triad" appellation is a Western concoction. It was reportedly coined in the 1820s by Dr. William Milne, a British educator working in Asia who, in his writings about the secret societies, recognized the importance of the number three in their names. The number three symbolizes how the founders of the early triads viewed the metaphysical philosophy underlying their movements — united by and living in harmony with the three primary forces of the universe: heaven, earth, and man. For years, the number three (in all its mathematical permutations) saturated the many ritual aspects, organizational structure, member initiation, and criminal operations of the historical secret societies and their future criminal reincarnations, including those operating in Canada.

While the intentions of the original triads were political in nature, others were formed by clans or tradesmen as mutual aid societies (the revolutionary groups also incorporated benevolent services into their mandate to varying degrees). As with the Italian mafia, some of these groups began to incorporate criminal activities, such as extortion, kidnapping, and piracy, to help fund their operations (and which originally targeted the wealthy landowners and merchants who supported the reviled Manchu Quing dynasty). By the mid 19th century, the secret societies had spread throughout Southeastern Asia, including Hong Kong, which was formally ceded to Britain by the Treaty of Nanking in 1842. Colonial records from this time suggest that the secret societies continued as both a political and criminal force under British rule. As one colonial official wrote in 1845, "Hong Kong has been infested by members of the Triad Society, the members of which operate under the shelter of a political maxim … perpetrate the grossest of enormities." Like the Quing rulers in China, the British colonial government avowed to crush what many Chinese were now calling the "Black Societies." The English and Chinese administrators in Hong Kong did not distinguish between those triads that functioned as revolutionary, criminal, or benevolent groups and, in 1845, an ordinance for the "Suppression of the Triad and Other Secret Societies" was adopted. But the outlawing of the societies simply drove them further underground, while causing them to infiltrate legitimate workers guilds and merchant associations, and they increasingly operated behind these facades.

By the start of the 20th century, the Hong Men societies threw their support behind the revolutionary leader Dr. Sun Yat-sen, who himself was a member of the Tian Di Hui triad, one of the major financiers of his Republican movement (some have argued he became a triad member to take advantage of the vast membership and resources of this and other secret societies for his revolutionary goals). In 1911, the Republicans, with strong support of the triad societies, staged a revolt in Canton, which spread rapidly throughout Southern China and on January 1, 1912, the Republic of China was born. The overthrow of the Quing dynasty signalled the birth of the new modern criminal triad as the revolutionary cause of some societies was replaced with criminal endeavours that included extortion, protection rackets, illegal gambling, and drug trafficking. The influence of triads in Republican China became all-pervasive and many triad society members went on to be powerful members and financiers of the Chinese National Party or "Kuomintang," a political group founded in 1912 from a collection of revolutionary groups that had overthrown the Qing dynasty. In order to rise in the party, civil service, or armed forces, it was essential to be a triad "brother." Merchants, bankers, and businessmen also discovered that triad membership oiled the machinery of commerce. Triad societies also allied themselves with the various warlords who controlled much of the nation and had great influence in the weak Chinese military

under the command of another triad member, General Chiang Kai-shek.

During the Second World War, many of the criminal triad societies worked for Japanese occupying forces, running gambling houses, brothels, and opium dens. They also served in an espionage capacity by helping police suppress any anti-Japanese activity. The 1949 takeover of Mainland China by the Communists, who shared with the Quing and British rulers the same antipathy towards the triads, sparked an exodus of society members to Hong Kong, helping to cement the colony as triad central. At one point, more than three hundred triad societies existed in Hong Kong, according to James Main, a former superintendent of the Royal Hong Kong Police. Taiwan also emerged as a hotbed for the secret societies, when members of the triad-infested Kuomintang fled to the island. Other remnants of the Kuomintang-Nationalist army took refuge in Burma's northern hills and became active in the opium and heroin trade (with support from the CIA, which for years worked with opium growers and heroin traffickers in the Golden Triangle to help finance their joint efforts with Chiang Kai-shek to destabilize Communist China).

Government authorities in Hong Kong blamed the triad societies for a 1956 riot in the city, in which a mob of nationalist sympathizers looted shops and attacked property belonging to those with ties to the Communist Party. As a result, an aggressive clampdown was launched against the secret societies, resulting in the arrest and/or deportation of thousands of triad members. The triads were not completely wiped out, however, and made a comeback in the 1960s, thanks in part to their infiltration of the Royal Hong Kong police. Not only were numerous police officers accepting bribes to protect the triads and their criminal operations, some were members of the secret societies. The level of corruption in the Hong Kong police was deemed so endemic that, in 1974, the Independent Commission Against Corruption was established. The commission identified a number of triad-connected police officers, which prompted some to flee to other countries, including Canada.

By the 1980s, there were around fifty triads in Hong Kong, although not all were involved in criminal activities. Among the largest and most criminally active were the Sun Yee On, the Wo Shing Wo, the 14K, the Wo On Lok, and the Wo Hop To. Founded in the early 1950s, the Sun Yee On (meaning New Righteousness and Peace) is considered the largest of the Hong Kong triads, with approximately nine hundred members by the late 1980s. Some estimates have placed its worldwide membership as high as 25,000, although this is a highly inflated number that includes non-active members and those who were extorted into paying a membership fee. Even if membership in a triad were this high, only a small fraction would be involved in criminal activities. With that said, members and associates of the Sun Yee On carry out a wide range of crimes and use its infrastructure to work with other criminal triads. This work includes gambling and heroin trafficking, and what the Sun Yee On is perhaps best known for: its infiltration of Hong Kong's entertainment industry and the extortion of entertainers, promoters, and production company executives. The 14K grew out of the Hong Fat Shan Society, which was founded in Guangzhou in the late 1940s by Nationalist army lieutenant-general Kot Siu-wong, supposedly on the orders of his superior, General Chiang Kai-shek. Originally made up of former Chinese nationalists, Hong Fat Shan was created as an alliance of existing triad societies to fight Communist forces. It later became known as the 14K in reference to the street address of the original headquarters of the alliance at 14 Po Wah Road in Canton. When the Communists took over in 1949, many of its members fled to Hong Kong. Today, its worldwide membership is said to total 20,000, although its structure can best be described as a loose-knit network that is made up of at least thirty subgroups that share approximately 1,000 criminally active members. Collectively, the 14K is heavily involved in heroin trafficking and migrant smuggling. Taiwan's largest triad is the United Bamboo, which was formed by a mix of native Taiwanese and triad members who fled Communist China in the mid-1950s. They operate internationally with cells located in the United States, Canada, and throughout Asia, and are involved in drug trafficking, extortion, bank fraud, illegal gambling, prostitution, migrant smuggling, and gun running.

Historically, most triad societies share a similar hierarchical structure with specific responsibilities assigned to each position. This hierarchy has also been adopted by criminal triad groups in the past. The Dragon Head (Shan Chu or Chu Chi) is the leader or head of the society. Also called the Mountain Lord or the First Route Marshal, this position, which may be elected, reigns supreme over the triad society. Below him are three positions of equal rank. The first is the deputy leader (the Fu Chan Chu), also known as the Second Route Marshall or the Assistant Mountain Lord, who serves as a key adviser to the Dragon Head and may make decisions in his absence. Next are the Incense Master (Heung Chu) and the Vanguard (Sing Fung), who administer the triad rituals and ceremonies and may have the power to discipline members. The White Paper Fan (Bak Tse Sin or Pak Tse Sin) acts as a general administrator and adviser and in criminal circumstances may be responsible for paying off police and gathering intelligence information. The Red Pole (Hung Kwan) is the enforcer who is responsible for carrying out internal discipline and ensuring external security. If a society operates as a criminal group, the Red Pole may be responsible for carrying out retribution against those who do not give in to the group's extortion demands. At the next level is the Straw Sandal (Cho Hai), who is responsible for internal communications and may also collect extorted money. Finally, there are the rank-and-file members, or soldiers, known as Sey Kow Jai or Sze Kau.

Besides their titles, the officers of a triad society are known by numbers divisible by the revered figure three as well as the number four (which is believed to symbolize the earth, sun, moon, and heaven, and/or may have been derived from the four gates of the sacred Temple of Heaven, which is located in present-day Beijing and was originally constructed as the Temple of Heaven and Earth between 1406 and 1420 during the Ming dynasty). These numerical titles are deeply ritualistic, and are influenced by Chinese superstitions, fables, and numerology. The higher the rank of the society's officer, the greater their assigned number. The Dragon Head is number "489" and is also referred to as "21," the sum of the three-digit title. The number "21" is also the sum of three (meaning Heaven, Earth, and Man) multiplied by the lucky number seven (meaning that the Dragon Head embodies the society). The Chinese character for "21" also resembles the Chinese character for "hong," which also means the Dragon Head represents and embodies the Hong Men Society. The Deputy Leader, the Vanguard and the Incense Master are all known as "438" or "15," the sum of three (creation) multiplied by five (longevity). Next in the numerical hierarchy is the Straw Sandal, who is "432." (Four times thirty-two equals 128, which, according to a folk tale popularized by the Chinese Republicans as part of their propaganda against the Quing dynasty, is the number of Buddhist monks who began the first clandestine Hong Men Society. Another Chinese fable tells how some of the rebelling monks escaped from the Manchu emperor's soldiers in a straw sandal that miraculously changed into a boat). The Red Pole is assigned "426" (this title is derived from four times twenty-six plus four, which equals 108, the numerical designation for Man). The lowest-ranking member of a triad group is a 49 (four times nine is thirty-six, the numerical designation for heaven and the number of oaths required from each society member).

Chinese numerology also permeates the operational aspects of the triads, with the number three once again assuming special significance. An anonymous letter sent in 1929 to a Chinese court interpreter in British Columbia forcefully urged him not to translate certain documents that police had confiscated from an arrested drug trafficker named Lee Kim. In the letter, the translator was warned to think over these threats "three times," which may have been a not-so-veiled reference to triad involvement in the drug trafficking case that was about to go before the court. The sum of money requested in a kidnapping or extortion plot may also be a specific numerological triad-inspired quantity. The Kung Lok, Toronto's first-known triad, often demanded $36.30 as part of their extortions carried out against immigrant Chinese high-school students. Others were required to pay $72 (the numerical designation for Earth), while at least one waiter in a Chinese restaurant in Toronto filed a complaint with police that he was paid a visit by two local triad members who demanded $1,080. While these monetary figures have ritualistic significance to the members of the Toronto-based triad, they were also used to intimidate victims, mostly Chinese immigrants, who would be cognizant of the secret criminal societies and the significant of its numerical sacraments.

In addition to its ritualistic use of numbers, some criminal triad societies have practised an elaborate initiation ceremony for new members, which dates to at least the late 18th century. Each prospective member must first obtain a sponsor, who receives a payment on top of an initiation fee paid to the society by the recruit. A traditional membership ceremony is overseen by the Incense Master and the Vanguard and can take up to eight hours to complete. The ceremony is held in a triad "lodge," which can be anyplace as long as it is properly decorated with the appropriate flags, banners, and name of the Dragon Head. Upon entering the designated lodge, the initiate passes through three "gates" (the various offshoots of the original secret societies were often referred to as "Hong Gates"). Before passing through the first gate (which contains a written warning that reads: "On entering the door, do not proceed further if you are not loyal"), the recruit does a ritual dance. He then passes through an archway made up of crossed swords, a process called "Passing the Mountain of Knives." The second gate is named the "Loyalty and Righteousness Hall" and a sign on the arch announces: "Before the gate of loyalty and righteousness all men are equal." After passing through this gate, the recruit pays his fee, which is handed over to the Vanguard in a red envelope (extortion victims have also been known to hand over money to triad members in red envelopes). The sign on the third arch states, "Through the Heaven and Earth Circle are Born the Hong Heroes." Beyond this arch is the third gate, the "Heaven and Earth Circle," which is often a bamboo hoop. Passing through the hoop is meant to represent the initiate's rebirth into the world of the triad society. On the other side of the Circle is the main hall. The prospective member stands before an altar at the end of the hall, and listens to triad poetry read by senior society members. When the recital is over, the recruit washes his face, removes his clothes, and is given white robes and straw sandals to wear. Again, this symbolizes that his old life has been washed away and he is now prepared for his rebirth as a triad member. He then stands in front of the altar and swears thirty-six oaths (most of which pledge loyalty to the triad and the recruit's fellow members upon threat of such lethal consequences as being struck by five thunderbolts or being killed by a myriad of swords).

All those present at the ceremony then drink a mixture of blood from the recruit and others present (pricked from their fingers) as well as blood from a dead chicken (the decapitation of a live chicken symbolizes the fate of any member who betrays the triad). A little wine is added for flavour and after the mixture has been consumed, the bowl is broken to represent the fate of those who might betray the brotherhood. The ceremony concludes with the burning of the yellow paper, which has the names of those at the ceremony written on it, along with a statement that describes the purpose of their relationship (why they have joined together as a group). This final ritual is meant to signify the bonds of brotherhood between the participants. (In some initiation ceremonies, the ashes of the burnt paper are added to the blood-and-wine mixture before it is drunk.) When the initiation is complete, the recruit is now officially a "49" and the ceremony ends with a celebratory feast.

For criminal triads, the intricate initiation ceremony is not simply an opportunity to pay homage to the history and traditions of the Hong Men society, but is meant to instill awe, respect, fear, loyalty, and discipline among new recruits. Toronto's Kung Lok, a loosely affiliated branch of Hong Kong's Leun Kung Lok, was believed to have used a variation of this traditional ceremony when it initiated many of its members during the 1970s and early 1980s. One teenage inductee of a Kung Lok initiation ceremony held in Ottawa told police it included the beheading of a live chicken and the ritual drinking of blood from each prospect. Eyewitnesses also described an extravagant altar in the makeshift lodge that was adorned with the name of the Canadian Kung Lok founder, Lau Wing Kui. These elaborate ceremonies are rarely performed by present-day triads (the AIDS scare in the 1980s put an end to the drinking of human blood).

Like an outlaw motorcycle gang chapter, a triad society does not necessarily function as the infrastructure for a criminal operation, nor is the hierarchy necessarily representative of each member's responsibilities in a criminal enterprise. While the infrastructure of a triad may not itself be used for criminal purposes, they do house members who are professional or occasional criminals. Triad membership is a valuable asset because it facilitates criminal activities in the same way that membership in a business association facilitates the activities of a legitimate businessperson. Members of the same triad will often work together in legitimate and illegitimate business undertakings, while members from different triad societies will also come together to work on a joint criminal venture. For example, a member of one triad may provide security or police protection for an underground gambling hall operated by a member of a different triad, while ambitious criminal ventures, such as international drug trafficking or migrant smuggling, may be the product of co-operation between members of different triads. As one chief inspector of the Royal Hong Kong Police put it, triad membership is a "lubricant" which "facilitates personal contacts and co-operation between different Triad groups or individuals." Adds a former member of the 14K triad who testified before a 1992 U.S. Senate subcommittee on Asian organized crime, "Triad members do favours for each other, provide introductions and assistance to each other, engage in criminal schemes with one another ..."

Within a particular triad society there may be several subgroups, each of which is led by a "Dai-Lo" (elder brother) whose role, much like the mafioso, is to help create criminal opportunities, provide advice to the lower-echelon members, facilitate criminal partnerships and networks, and mediate disputes. Triad members and subgroups usually operate with great autonomy from the senior officers of a triad society, who may not even be involved in criminal activities let alone receive any share of the profits from the crimes of its members. Like an outlaw motorcycle gang or a modern mafia family, the senior members of a criminal triad are responsible for carrying out their own business enterprises through a network of junior members and external associates. As such, the hierarchy of a triad exists primarily in the relationship between the senior members (the elder brothers) and the junior members (the "Sai-Lo," or little brothers). The elder brothers broker criminal deals and delegate responsibilities to the little brothers, while providing them with direction, resources, connections, and protection. The little brothers are also expected to take the initiative to generate criminal opportunities on their own and to pass along a cut of the revenue to their big brother.

Toronto's first-known triad, the Kung Lok, was established solely for criminal purposes and initially blended a traditional hierarchy with this syndicated approach to carrying out crimes. Under the original "Dragon Head," who founded the triad branch in 1975, were thirteen "elder brothers," many of whom he personally recruited in Toronto. Each one had his own network of criminal underlings who mostly carried out extortions against Chinese immigrants and businesses. A Toronto-based federal immigration analyst wrote in a 1980 report that one senior Kung Lok member named Danny Mo, who held the position of Red Pole, "may have as many as 50 young followers of his own. Whether these followers have been initiated into the Kung Lok or are so far simply followers of Mo is unknown."

In short, a triad strictly defined is not a criminal organization. A triad may have several hundred and even several thousand members worldwide, but only a small proportion may be involved in illegal activities (which may even be carried out only on a part-time basis, as triad members often own legitimate businesses). The criminal portion of a triad is usually made up of a few individual members who operate their own criminal enterprises, alone or along with other triad members, associates, youth gangs, or like-minded criminals. Today, most triad groups are a triad in name only; their structure is not based on the traditional hierarchy and most do not practise the elaborate initiation ceremonies. Its "members" evoke Hong Men society jargon and rituals primarily to gain respect and to instill fear in their victims and the public.

"A SYSTEM OF SECRET SOCIETIES, WHICH ENCOURAGES CRIME AMONGST THEMSELVES"

It wasn't long after Chinese immigrants arrived in British Columbia that Hong Men societies were established in the province. While the original Canadian branches of the triad societies pursued the same political objectives as their predecessors, they were also formed as a united bulwark against the discrimination and ostracism they experienced at the hands of the larger white society. As such, some of the societies became a surrogate government for Chinese expatriates, providing a quasi-legal system that dispensed justice and mediated disputes, provided social welfare services, helped protect members against white vigilante justice, and offered recreational activities for the largely male population, such as gambling, prostitutes, and opium. The first-known Chinese triad society in Canada was founded in 1863 in Barkerville, a small gold-mining town in northeastern British Columbia. Founded by Chinese miners, it was called the Hong Shan Tang and was believed to be a branch or at least an offshoot of a similarly named society in San Francisco, which itself was associated with Hong Men societies in the Guangdong province of Southern China.

The Barkerville Chee Kung Tong building, now a national historic site

In 1876, the Hong Shan Tang was renamed the Chee Kung Tong (also known or spelled as the Chi Kong Tang, Zhigongtang, the Chih-Kung T'ang, the Cheekungtong or the CKT for short) and, besides Barkerville, they established societies in other British Columbia towns, including Quesnel Forks, Cumberland, and Rossland. The goal of the CKT was to contribute to the overthrow of the Quing dynasty back in China, but it also provided protection, mediation services, social welfare assistance, and even lodging to its members in B.C. The constitution of the original CKT society — which was discovered in 1960 in the ghost town of Quesnel Forks, located about 100 kilometres from present-day Quesnel — indicates that the society was a fraternal association founded to promote harmonious relations among Chinese immigrants, while helping to promote their advancement through business and work. The preamble of the constitution reads, "The purpose in forming the Cheekungtong is to maintain a friendly relationship among our countrymen and to accumulate wealth through proper business methods for the benefit of all members. Thus, those who do mental work and those who do physical work are devoting their strength to this common goal." Anthropologist Erin Payne writes that the Chih-Kung T'ang provided "an arm of authority that could protect the Chinese man from white racism, and from windows left open in English law to permit racism. It also assisted Chinese men in realizing their financial goals" and "protected them from each other where existing laws were an inadequate reflection of Chinese values." In his book on the history of the Chinese in North America, Anthony Chan contends that the social aid programs offered by the CKT and other triad societies in B.C. were "important tools for gathering overseas recruits, spreading anti-Qing propaganda and raising money for the struggle in China."

Another CKT chapter was established in nearby Yale, B.C., in 1882, with one local newspaper reporting that a "temple" was being built by the society. By 1885, according to Payne, "there were over 40 Chih-kung T'ang chapters in the province, and that same year Barkerville, enjoying some resurgence, became the Chih-kung T'ang Headquarters for the Cariboo." One CKT chapter was founded in Victoria in 1876, although as Harry Con and colleagues wrote, "It appears that the secret society lodge in Victoria had little to do with those in the Cariboo at this time. Not until the late 1880's did a regional structure emerge linking the various branches in British Columbia, and not until 1919 was a Canada-wide convention of the Cheekungtong held."

From the very beginning, the Hong Men chapters formed in B.C. do not appear to have been shrouded in the level of secrecy that characterized their forebears in China. Some even erected lodges or "temples," with the name of the society on the exterior, which served as their lodge where members openly congregated. On October 27, 1903, the local newspaper in Rossland, B.C., reported on the dedication of the "Gee Kong Tong" building there. Among those at the dedication ceremony were the "local president," the "Kootenay master," and "the master of the Fraternity for British Columbia." But the public nature of the Canadian societies did not stop the anti-Chinese lobby from stereotyping them as secret, subversive, criminal organizations. An 1885 resolution on the "Chinese Question" tabled in the legislature of British Columbia referred to "a system of secret societies, which encourages crime amongst themselves, and which prevents the administration of justice." While some triad societies in B.C. operated secretly due to their continued opposition to the Quing ruling party in China, the media of the day characteristically failed to understand their complex nature. By the turn of the century, numerous associations were being formed throughout Canada and the U.S. as merchant guilds, labour associations, or community-wide benevolent societies. Many were formed around a shared trade or region of China; there were associations for railroad workers, laundry workers, medical practitioners, and for those who shared the same dialect or place of birth. On the surface, most of the societies were less concerned with affairs back in China, and more focussed on furthering the cause of Chinese immigrants in the new land as well as the personal or business affairs of society members. Some were loosely organized, while others had a structured hierarchy that borrowed from the triads and required members to pledge an allegiance to one another as "brothers in blood oath." Their bonds were further strengthened through mystical, religious rituals, as well as secret codes and signs.

There is no evidence to suggest that the early Chinese societies in B.C. were criminal organizations. However, because some of the societies were controlled by Chinese merchants who were the main suppliers of opium, gambling, and prostitutes, they were used to cater to the "recreational" needs of Chinese bachelors. At the same time, the Chinese societies in B.C. saw themselves as a sort of moral regulator. Rule Seven in the constitution of the CKT founded in Quesnel in 1876 lays out a code of proper behaviour that the society expected its members to follow so as not to give it a bad name. The constitution threatened "severe punishment" for those who caused trouble in brothels or gambling houses.

A CKT branch was first established in Vancouver in 1892 and, according to Terry Gould, by 1923 there were fifty-four societies in the city's Chinatown. Among these were twenty-six formed around clan ties, twelve based on one's birthplace in China, and five based on occupation. The most prominent of the B.C. societies was the Chinese Consolidated Benevolent Association, which was founded in Victoria in 1884 after thirty-one local Chinese societies came together to establish an umbrella organization that provided loans and facilitated business opportunities for budding Chinese entrepreneurs while offering social assistance to the less fortunate. The CCBA was also a political advocacy group that spearheaded opposition to the anti-Chinese movements and the racist government policies that were being introduced. In keeping with its paternalistic intentions, the association's original constitution pledged to provide financial and legal aid to any member who was beaten, robbed or owed money, or unjustly accused of criminal or bad behaviour by whites. The CCBA also advanced a moral code for its members, provided assistance to anyone in the Chinese community convicted of a criminal offence, and pledged to combat one of the most serious social problems within the overseas Chinese population: the trafficking of Chinese women. Article Twenty of the CCBA's constitution read, "If anyone informs the Association that a young girl has been kidnapped and sold in this city, the buyer will be forced to set the girl free. The Association will look after sending her to the Tung Wah Hospital in Hong Kong, which will inform the family. In case the girl has no family, the Tung Wah Hospital will arrange for her to marry a decent man."

THE FIGHTING TONGS

The stereotypical perceptions that people had of the Hong Men societies in B.C. were greatly influenced by what was known about the triads back in China. It also stemmed from the media coverage of the Chinese-American "tongs" — a word that can be roughly translated as a meeting hall or gathering place — some of which were degenerating into violent criminal organizations by the turn of the century. For Peter Nepstad, the descent into corruption was always a looming danger for the Chinese-American tongs:

> Every merchant, labourer, and wage-earner was a member of an Association, and therefore had to pay fees. In return for those fees, the association provided protection. It's not hard to imagine how quickly such a system could become corrupted. Part of the larger Chinese benevolent association's responsibilities was protection, and the groups who provided that protection became the first tongs. ... Gambling houses, opium dens, and the like were particularly in need of protection from thugs who would raid them, so tongs were created by the owners of these places to protect their interests. The business was so lucrative that tongs began fighting among themselves, competing for territory.

In New York City, the On Leong (Peaceful Dragon), a society originally formed to serve Chinese merchants, was involved in the sexual slave trade and controlled a number of gambling houses in Manhattan's Chinatown. Its competitor was the Hip Sing (Prosperous Union) society, a workingman's association active in gambling and prostitution. The year 1904 marked the beginning of a bloody "tong war" between the Hip Sing and the On Leong. According to Howard Abadinsky, many of America's "fighting tongs," which he defines as Chinese societies that now operated primarily as criminal groups, had ties to other chapters and societies in different parts of the U.S. The result was that that a purely local dispute between the On Leong and Hip Sing helped ignite battles between tongs in other cities where rivalries were already brewing over politics, regional dialectics, territory, fundraising, or criminal rackets. Violent battles between the Hip Sing, the On Leong, and other rival tongs were played out in the Chinatown districts of New York, San Francisco, Chicago, Baltimore, St. Louis, Pittsburgh, and Boston until 1927. The term "hatchet man" also entered the North

American vocabulary to describe the hired killers (based on their weapon of choice) who were dispatched to the front lines of the various conflicts. A peace accord was reached after government officials threatened to deport more than two hundred of the tong leaders if the killings continued. Despite the peace treaties, the battles did leave their mark: some 350 Chinese were left dead throughout the country and the number of tongs had been reduced by about half.

The Chinese societies in Canada were far less violent and criminal compared to their American counterparts and no tong war ever materialized in this country. However, sporadic violence did break out between some Chinese societies, which the media automatically assumed was the start or part of a tong war. The June 6, 1905, edition of the *Globe* newspaper, for example, reported the following:

> A Tong war has again broken out on Vancouver Island. The renewal of the struggle between rival Chinese societies has been signalized by the blowing up of a house at Cumberland. The bunks were crowded with Celestials when dynamite was exploded beneath the premises, but all the Orientals except two escaped without serious injury. … Scattered along the 150 miles from Victoria to Cumberland are Chinese who are taking an active part in this mysterious Tong war. The present incident is but one of a series of outrages which followed the murder of two Chinamen in a theater in Victoria. Then came the attempt to blow sky high a Celestial shack at Nanaimo. This was followed by a similar outrage at Cumberland. Next a Chinaman was mysteriously killed at French Creek; now comes more use of dynamite at Cumberland.

Police did investigate the prospect of warring factions within Vancouver Island's Chinese community, but concluded that most of the violence consisted of isolated incidents. In 1920, the *Globe* alerted readers that police would be placing a "special watch" on all Chinese residents in Windsor, Ontario, "following indications that two factions of Chinese are fighting against each other. Reports to the police today indicate that the factions are engaged in a Tong war." In May 1925, the provincial police in B.C. claimed that the murder of two prominent members of Vancouver's Chinatown was the result of an "an internal tong feud." Lum But (a.k.a. Fred Lambert) and Ng Hong were shot to death and two other men were seriously wounded. The violence was not the result of a tong war, but part of a two-year-old dispute between factions of the Vancouver-based Shon Yee Society on how to apportion $40,000 collected in Canada to finance the construction of a hospital in China. Two men, Shui Sing and Shen Say Yung, were charged with murder.

Some of the conflicts that did arise between different Canadian tongs were not fought over criminal rackets, but were tied to politics back in China. During the early part of the 20th century, the Hong Men societies in China were throwing their support behind fellow triad member and leader of the Republican forces, Dr. Sun Yat-sen. Canada's first triad society, the CKT, was also active in supporting, financing, and arming Sun Yat-sen in his effort to overthrow the Quing dynasty and establishing a new Chinese republic. But as Harry Con et al. wrote, "The fall of the Qing dynasty did not usher in a millennium of stability and modernity in China. Instead, the next several years were ones of factionalism, division, and violence, which was reflected in the life of Chinese communities in Canada." The political infighting among the Republicans in China "exacerbated existing conflicts and introduced new ones, especially in the largest Chinese communities of Victoria and Vancouver." In particular, a power struggle emerged over control of Vancouver's powerful Chinese Consolidated Benevolent Association between the CKT (which became known as the Chinese Freemasons in 1920) and the local Kuomintang association (formed in support of Sun's Chinese National League). The conflict between the two groups was exacerbated when each vied for Sun Yat-sen's favour. (Before they became the Freemasons, the CKT raised large amounts of money and ran weapons to China to support his cause, and even sponsored Sun's visit to Vancouver in 1911 while he plotted the overthrow of the Quing dynasty. Sun is believed to have joined the Honolulu branch of the Chee Kung Tong in 1906.)

While there was little if any bloodshed between the Freemasons and the Kuomintang in Vancouver, there were episodes of violence in Toronto, where both groups had chapters. According to Anthony Chan, the two tongs were also operating gambling halls in the city and, in 1929, they were "in the midst of a ferocious battle" over who controlled professional gambling in the Chinese community. As part of this battle, the Kuomintang provided information to Toronto police regarding "certain Freemason gambling houses, widely known in Chinatown as money-making operations." The police acted on this information and numerous raids were conducted in 1929 and 1930. In one month alone, police conduct ninety raids on Chinese gambling halls in Toronto.

After thirty-five-year-old Low-Hee-faye was attacked as he walked along Elizabeth Street in the heart of Toronto's small Chinese community, the March 27, 1930, edition of the *Globe* shrieked, "a Tong war is brewing again in Chinatown." Low-Hee claimed he was beaten by hatchet men who were brought in from the U.S. by criminal elements allied within the tongs to seek retribution against those who provided police information on illegal activity in Chinatown. However, the assault was an isolated incident between those in the Chinese community who supported the monarchists and those who supported the Republican parties in China (Low Hee-faye supported the latter). Toronto police dismissed rumours that the local Chinese societies had brought foreign hatchet men into the city. They did confirm that investigations into a number of Chinese gambling houses in the city were being conducted. In his book on Asian organized crime in Canada, James Dubro contends that the Republican/Nationalists in Toronto "ran a police-protected gambling house that was in fierce competition with one run by a pro-Monarchist group who opposed the Nationalists in China and were in alliance with a rival underworld group in Toronto's Chinatown."

Between December 1933 and February 1934, the media began trumpeting a one-day tong war in Montreal that appeared to be a continuation of the rivalry between the local chapters of the Chinese Freemasons and the Kuomintang, which were also accused of operating gambling halls in the city. As the *Toronto Star* reported on December 13, 1933:

Blame for the tong war which started in Montreal's Chinatown early yesterday and which ended on the first day of the campaign, with six wounded, three seriously, and 25 prisoners in the hands of the police, is laid on the depression. Control of the gambling dens, which police last night were convinced is the chief cause of the war between the two tongs, also carries with it control of the relief bureaus for unemployed Chinese, which are largely financed by levies on the gambling houses. The funds hitherto administered by the Kao Ming gang led by Jim Lee, have been the object of attention from the Chee Keong tong with headquarters at the Dart Koon club under the leadership of George Huan, superintendent of the Montreal Chinese hospital, and head of the Chinese Masons, who is accused of seeking to make himself the uncrowned king of Chinatown.

TRIAD MEN IN OUR TOP CITIES

While there is little evidence that the Chinese tongs in Canada were extensively involved in organized criminal activities, police investigations during the postwar years did reveal that Chinese merchants, working in cartel-like partnerships, were active in professional gambling, prostitution, and opium trafficking.

On the west coast, an inquiry into corruption in the Vancouver Police Force during the mid-1950s shone an unwelcome spotlight on the Chinese gambling clubs. The inquiry's final report concluded there was evidence pointing to "an increase in gambling in Chinatown" since 1949. During the first half of the 1950s, police estimated there were twelve main underground gambling clubs in Vancouver's Chinatown, although this number was disputed. While Chinese gambling halls did most certainly exist, allegations that they were controlled by local tongs were unsubstantiated. When he appeared before the corruption inquiry, the provincial attorney general testified that numerous Chinese social clubs housed professional gambling operations, but did not produce any substantial evidence to support his claims. This lack of evidence did not stop the attorney general from revoking the licences of some Chinese social clubs without requiring their successful prosecution in court, a move that was supported by Vancouver City Council.

There was no controversy surrounding Vancouver's continued role as a major port of call for opium and heroin smuggled from Southeast Asia. By the 1930s, the amounts entering the country substantially increased as production in China skyrocketed after Japanese forces invaded the country and boosted production of the profitable export. Opium was now flooding into North America, resulting in some of the largest seizures to date. One of the biggest ever made in British Colombia occurred on January 8, 1937, when the vessel *Gyokoh Maru*, dragging her anchor near the terminals at New Westminster, pulled up eleven bundles attached to a length of rope. When the packages were opened, 550 tins of opium were found. According to the RCMP's annual report for that year, "This is the first time in a number of years that the method of dropping opium overboard to be dragged for at a later date has come to our notice." Four days later, six hundred tins of opium were seized in New York, and in March another six hundred tins were found aboard a docked steamship. That same month, government agencies confiscated five hundred tins in Hong Kong and another three hundred in Shanghai.

The Second World War greatly curtailed the supply of opium to North America but, following the end of the war and the Communist takeover of China in 1949, imports of heroin processed from Southeast Asian opium began to steadily rise on the west coast of Canada and the United States. As the Nationalist Kuomintang army retreated to the opium-rich hills of Burma and Thailand, they began financing their attacks on Red China by supplying the Hong Kong triads with opium and heroin. When it became clear that their CIA-backed insurgency was failing, many former officers and soldiers turned to opium production and heroin processing full time. In their 1965 annual report, the RCMP made note of the spike in the potent "white" heroin in Canada that "has always been the choice of addicts." However, the supply and quality had been erratic. "Generally speaking, the Hong Kong sources were not well organized and seldom active for periods long enough to enable development of prosecution

evidence." This began to change in the 1950s and, from that point forward, the RCMP drug units on the west coast in particular were kept busy investigating the importation of what was coming to be known as "China White."

Following the takeover of China by the Communists, many triad members, as well as a host of Chinese gangsters on the mainland, fled to Hong Kong, establishing it as a regional criminal stronghold for Asia and a major trans-shipment point for heroin and opium. The 14K triad began its long and extensive involvement in the international heroin trade when it started shipping opium from Kuomintang suppliers in Burma to North America and Europe. The precedent for triad involvement in opium and heroin trafficking was set by Tu Yueh Sheng (a.k.a. Big-Eared Tu), the powerful leader of a triad society operating out of Shanghai from the early 1900s to the late 1940s, called the Green Gang. From his base in Shanghai, Tu dominated the heroin and opium trade. Big-Eared Tu aided Chiang Kai-shek's rise to power by supplying the Kuomintang with much-needed funds. In the late 1920s, he was also helping the Kuomintang's Nationalist cause through a vicious crackdown on Shanghai's Communist Party organizers and labour activists. His pact with Chiang Kai-shek strengthened the Green Gang's influence with the Nationalist government in China, and Tu became one of the most powerful men in the country during the 1920s and 1930s.

As triad members were fleeing China, police in Canada began to suspect that some were illegally entering the country and settling in Vancouver and Toronto. Their fears were stoked by what appeared to be an upsurge in the illegal immigration of Chinese nationals into Canada. By the end of the 1950s, the RCMP had launched a number of investigations into well-organized illegal immigration schemes. The problem had escalated to such a point that the Mounted Police set up a special unit, later known as the Passport and Visa Fraud Section. The RCMP estimated that between 1950 and 1959, upwards of 11,000 Chinese may have entered the country illegally, using false pretences and forged documents. They soon discovered that most of the illegal immigrants were being brought to Canada by a sophisticated smuggling racket operated by Hong Kong–based syndicates. The federal government was particularly worried that Communist Chinese intelligence agents were among those taking advantage of these services.

A 1959 article in the *Toronto Telegram* quoted unnamed police sources who said that between 70 and 90 percent of the Chinese entering Canada from Hong Kong in the previous ten years had done so illegally. "So widespread has been the fraud and such the implications, that RCMP headquarters in Ottawa has stationed Inspector H.F. Price and Cpl. J. Medley to this colony to co-operate with the Hong Kong police force and Canadian immigration officials. Their task will be a long one." The illegal migration scheme took advantage of a legal loophole in restrictive Canadian immigration regulations that allowed members of the immediate family of Chinese-Canadians to settle in the country. Brokers working for criminal syndicates in Hong Kong offered Chinese-Canadians a cash payment and an all-expense-paid trip to Hong Kong to fake a marriage with a prospective immigrant, who had already paid a cash fee to the broker. Once in Hong Kong, the "newlyweds" were provided with forged marriage papers. "So clever and so expert are the forgeries that Canadian immigration officers have been unable to prove the fraud even though suspected," the *Telegram* reported. "When the local screening of the applicants was complete, forms were forwarded to Ottawa where, apparently in good order, they received the formal approval of the Department of Citizenship and Immigration, and the new Chinese immigrants were as good as in."

In 1960, the RCMP located several hundred illegal Chinese immigrants in the country, who were referred to the Immigration Department for deportation. Among these were sixteen Chinese nationals whom the RCMP called the "principal agents" behind the immigration scheme and who were charged with seventy-nine criminal and immigration counts. When the news of the illegal immigrants became public in July 1960, the Canadian media began referring to the Chinese syndicates behind the migrant smuggling as "triads." Under the headline "Dreaded Chinese 'mafia' controlled migrant racket; Triad men in our top cities," the *Telegram* wrote:

> The Chinese immigration racket smashed by the Royal Canadian Mounted Police has been operated under the "protection" of the most dreaded underworld organization of the Far East official sources said here today. The immigration racketeers were controlled by Triad — Mafia-like groups which have tentacles in rackets all over the world. While Triad societies are not suspected of direct involvement in the smuggling of an estimated 11,000 Chinese into Canada in the last decade, they are believed to have taken a substantial slice off the top of payments made to the immigration racketeers.

Based on information provided by police sources, the *Telegram* dropped another bombshell:

> A high source said that Triad agents have been identified in the major Canadian Chinatowns. The name of Triad turned up in both the Canadian and Hong Kong aspects of the investigation — the first evidence that these powerful Oriental underworld societies had penetrated organized crime in Canada. ... They draw revenues believed to be fabulous mainly by selling "protection" to the whole gamut of Oriental racketeers. They thus have financial interests in smuggling, gambling, narcotics, prostitution, white slaving, murder, kidnapping and piracy.

The newspaper also reported that the RCMP seized documents from the homes and offices of the brokers implicated in the illegal immigration scheme that included copies of contracts "requiring an illegal immigrant to pay for his passage by working at an assigned job — usually in a laundry or restaurant — up to 13 hours a day for five years at a wage of $100 a month."

In a *Maclean's* magazine article published in 1962, entitled "The criminal society that dominates the Chinese in Canada," Allan Phillips wrote that Chinese immigrants were being smuggled into the country "in junks with lockers concealing up to 200." He named the Chee Kung Tong as the Canadian organizers of the illegal immigrant conspiracy and contended that triads operating in Canada were recruiting prospective members from Hong Kong, who were then smuggled into the country. Phillips labelled the CKT as "the overseas branch of the Triad society" and backed up his claim by citing an RCMP investigation "that uncovered two books explaining the secret Triad ritual, reprinted by a Chee Kung Tong official in Toronto." However, as James Dubro rightly points out in his book on Asian organized crime in Canada, while the CKT began as a triad society in British Columbia, and continued to practise some traditional rituals, by this time it could no longer be consider a triad, let alone a criminal organization. With that said, some members of Canadian tongs were involved in the smuggling of Chinese immigrants to Canada. As Phillips notes, "three days after one Hong Kong broker was arrested, his Canadian agent flew out to take charge in the Triad-controlled area. Two Canadians, Wong Lai-yap and Chen Ping-hsuin, were among those convicted in Hong Kong as agents."

In addition, Phillips reported, "Uncle Jack" Wong, the long-time president of the Chee Kung Tong in Montreal, "is also boss of the biggest Chinese gambling joint in the city, the Victoria Sporting Club. Last year three young Chinese walked into his club and smashed it up." Phillips was correct in that Wong controlled a number of illegal gambling clubs in Quebec in the 1950s and 1960s, some of which were vandalized on the orders of a rival Chinese gang leader who was attempting to extort Wong. Uncle Jack's foe was found murdered just a few weeks later. Wong continued as the "King of the Gamblers" in Montreal until the mid-1970s when police finally closed his illegal clubs.

Back in Vancouver, police raided six Chinese gambling clubs in 1979 and charged thirty-three people, who were collecting a rake-off that ranged from 2 to 5 percent. None was convicted, however. The Chinese Freemasons were also accused by law enforcement agencies of housing "active criminals," and their early history as a triad society was dredged up to help substantiate these assertions. A 1979 report from the Criminal Intelligence Service Canada stated:

> ... consistent with the past, major Chinese criminals are operating from within a local legitimate ethnic fraternal organization, "The Vancouver Chinese Freemason Society." Present total membership is approximately

453; of this number approximately 45, or 10%, have been identified as active criminals. Members of the Chinese Freemasons are also covertly identified as "Hung Mun". The "Hung Mun" is the true Triad operating in South East Asia. Because it is now outlawed, they are also referred to as, "The Black Society". Locally the "Hung Mun" adopted the title, "Vancouver Chinese Freemason Society" to gain acceptance and respectability in Canada. The fraternal nature of this society (blood oaths) leads investigators to suspect that certain "respectable" members of this society have financed some large heroin transactions and other criminal endeavours. It should be noted that not all members of the Chinese Freemasons are criminals, but it is obvious that the majority of major criminals are members of this society.

The report also alleged that "the four major Chinese social (gambling) clubs" in Vancouver's Chinatown are "primarily operated and controlled by members of the Chinese Freemasons. Many of these members have been, and in some instances still are involved in the following crime categories: 1) heroin importation and trafficking; 2) illegal gambling; 3) procuring; 4) loansharking; and 5) stolen property."

THE FIVE DRAGONS

While Chinese criminals based in Toronto, Vancouver, and Montreal were linked to gambling, prostitution, drug trafficking, and illegal immigration, there were no criminal triads in the country before 1970. Chinese-Canadian organized crime began its great leap forward in the early 1970s, due in part to the relaxation of immigration laws for ethnic Chinese during the mid-1960s. Tens of thousands of immigrants, mostly from Hong Kong, came to Canada, including a small minority of criminals who saw the country as a land of opportunity and began secret societies and gangs in major urban centres. Not only did triad leaders from Hong Kong achieve landed status under new immigrant categories (in particular, the entrepreneur category), but the influx of Chinese immigrants greatly expanded the number of potential victims for their extortion activities as well as customers for its gambling operations. A sizable majority of the new Hong Kong immigrants were young people, many of whom were sent to be educated in Canada while their parents remained in Hong Kong. This created a population that was highly vulnerable to the triads and youth gangs, either as new recruits or as victims of extortion.

Among the new immigrants to Canada in 1974 were the so-called "Five Dragons," five former staff sergeants in the Royal Hong Kong Police Force who fled to Canada the year the anti-corruption drive in the British colony began. The sergeants were among the many police officers in Hong Kong who were on the take, had ties with local triads, were involved in criminal activities, or all of the above. Each of the staff sergeants was the non-commissioned officer in charge of a particular district in Hong Kong, which put them in control of their respective police division. The five men illegally earned millions of dollars during their corrupt period of service, which was generated from graft payments and the proceeds from gambling or extortion rackets in which the sergeants had an interest. The five men — Lui Lok, Choi Bing-lung, Chen Cheung-you, Nam Kong, and Hon Kwing-shum — came to Canada under a federal immigration program intended to attract entrepreneurs to the country. All flew to Vancouver from Hong Kong sometime in 1974.

The most senior of the Five Dragons was Lui Lok. He had been awarded a number of medals by the Hong Kong police force while accumulating the largest illicit fortune of the five. To the junior police officers that worked for him, he was reverentially referred to as Tai Lo ("the Big Boss"). The Hong Kong media later dubbed him the "$600 Million Man" in reference to his reputed illicit worth. There was speculation that Lui Lok was even a senior member of the 14K or the Sun Yee On, two of Hong Kong's most criminal triads. When he applied to come to Canada, Lok stated in his immigration application he would be bringing in at least $1 million to start a business. This prospective investment, combined with his former occupation as a police officer, qualified him for landed immigrant status. After arriving in Vancouver, all five men made sizable investments in apartment and office buildings in Vancouver and Toronto. Along with other ex–Hong Kong police officers, and a prominent architect from Hong Kong named Clifford Wong, their largest outlay was the purchase of an office building and adjoining apartment complex in downtown Toronto, valued at more than $50 million.

In 1977, following a CBC television documentary that first made the story of the Five Dragons public, Immigration Minister Bud Cullen said that when they were admitted to Canada, none had been convicted of any crime in Hong Kong and officials in his department were unaware they were under investigation for corruption. (Apparently, immigration officials were also not curious how a former police officer could save $1 million. In fact, Lui Lok eventually brought far more money into the country.) Cullen added that his department found out about the allegations after they arrived in the country, but there was no evidence of wrongdoing in Canada to warrant any federal action. Following the publicity brought about by the CBC program, the immigration minister ordered an investigation into the five men and his department's handling of their immigration applications. Around the same time, Hong Kong tried to extradite Hon Kwing-shum, who had been charged with corruption, but the Federal Court of Canada dismissed the Canadian Immigration Department's deportation order. Before the federal government could take any further action against the five men, they liquidated most of their Canadian assets and left the country.

While Lui Lok had ties to triads in Hong Kong, neither he nor his four colleagues established a secret society in Canada. The honour of setting up the first-known modern triad group in Canada goes to Lau Wing Kui, who founded chapters of the Luen Kung Lok in Toronto and Ottawa during the mid-1970s. Born in Hong Kong on April 19, 1929, Lau Wing Kui became a member of Hong Kong's Tung Lok Society, a subgroup within the larger Luen Kung Lok triad. He ran a number of legitimate businesses in Hong Kong, including a legal casino, but through the Luen Kung Lok he became involved in illegal gambling, extortion, loansharking and drug trafficking. He was also known to have collected graft money for corrupt Hong Kong police officers. Lau arrived in Canada with his wife and two daughters on December 22, 1974, after being granted entrance under the entrepreneur category (thanks in part to the suppression of his voluminous police files by corrupt Hong Kong police officials). Lau was far from the stereotypical physical portrait of a gangster; at five foot two and 123 pounds he was slight, almost fragile looking. But with his tailored suits, greying temples, polite demeanour, and fluency in Cantonese, English, Portuguese, and Spanish, he carried himself with a certain air of distinction and authority. He told Canadian consular officials in Hong Kong that he wanted to open a restaurant in Toronto. His real motive was to start a criminal triad society. He no doubt recognized the city's Chinatown as virgin territory where he could make a lot of money by exploiting the traditional codes of silence and mistrust of police by the immigrant population.

Lau Wing Kui

By 1976, he had established the Kung Lok — which means "the house of mutual happiness" — in Toronto, with a subgroup in Ottawa under the leadership of Cheang Chi Wo (a.k.a. Danny Cheang). According to a 1984 report of the Criminal Intelligence Service Canada (CSIC), his Canadian chapters operated with

a certain amount of autonomy, "but ultimate control and direction came from the parent group in Hong Kong." Using his Fair Choice Restaurant in Toronto's Chinatown as a front, he actively recruited and initiated a number of young immigrant Chinese men into the triad society (which masqueraded as a kung fu club). Among the thirteen "elder brothers" recruited by Lau were Mo Shui Chuen (a.k.a Danny Mo), a martial arts expert who became the triad's fierce Red Pole enforcer; Leung Kin-hung (a.k.a. Peter Leung),who was given the position of Straw Sandal; Kwan Yee Man (a.k.a. Charlie Kwan), the group's treasurer, as well as Yue Kwok Nam (a.k.a "Big John" Yue), who operated his own youth gang before being initiated into the Kung Lok. Each of Lau's lieutenants was expected to recruit other "49" boys and operate their own criminal cells.

Before long, the Kung Lok was a criminal force in Toronto's Chinatown, running illegal gaming clubs, forcing existing clubs to pay protection, and extorting money from Chinese immigrants and businesses. While the triad was most active in Southern Ontario, it had connections in Montreal, Vancouver, and Saint John, New Brunswick. By 1980, the Kung Lok had a core membership in Toronto of about 150, but could count on another 250 associates across the city and country.

Toronto police first became aware of the Kung Lok in 1976; an intelligence report that year described how six of its "elder brothers" met regularly in a Lombard Street restaurant. Over the next two years, the Kung Lok would be joined in Toronto's Chinatown by a chapter of another Hong Kong triad, the 14K, as well as the Ghost Shadows, a non-triad Chinese gang that was first reported in New York City in the early 1970s and which shook down Chinese restaurants, merchants, and entertainers in Manhattan while protecting the gambling operations of the On Leong Tong. A July 15, 1977, article in the *Toronto Star* reported, "the Toronto–New York connection [of the Ghost Shadows] has been confirmed by police in both cities." One 1977 robbery in Toronto that was typical of the Ghost Shadows saw three Chinese youths, armed with handguns and a machete, steal nearly $2,000 from patrons of an underground Chinatown gambling hall.

By 1977, there were about four hundred Asian gang members in Toronto, most of whom ranged in age from sixteen to twenty-five. "They are recruited for the most part from high schools and universities," a 1977 Metro Toronto Police intelligence document read. "Many are on student visas and some are overstays; a sizable portion do not even attend classes or attend only enough to achieve marginal passes. A disturbing number come from well-to-do families and meet the classical definition of spoiled adolescents — these are easy pickings for gang members who take their money in return for the empty gestures of brotherhood and companionship which the gang seems to offer." Other recruits are landed immigrants, "who hold lowly jobs such as waiters and kitchen help. For them, the gang is a way to achieve 'face' within their own ethnic community in a simple straightforward way that is easily understood and never challenged."

A 1979 intelligence report prepared by the Toronto office of the federal Immigration Department described how members of the Kung Lok were trying to recruit from the city's secondary schools as well as the Erindale campus of the University of Toronto. In 1980, the analysts documented "reliable information" it had received "to the effect that the Kung Lok are considering the recruiting of Vietnamese refugees of Chinese descent into their midst." The fact that many young Vietnamese males had received some military training was considered an asset to the Kung Lok recruiters, "they are all fighters, willing to bully around and have no respect [for] authority." A month later, the Toronto office reported "information, of unknown reliability" indicating "that 10 Vietnamese youth (presumably of Chinese ethnic origin) have been inducted into the Kung Lok." While most of the recruits for the Kung Lok, 14K, and Ghost Shadows were already living in Canada, the 14K was known to have imported men who have already been initiated as triad members in Hong Kong.

Following an upsurge in robberies, extortions, assaults, and shootings in Toronto's normally quiet Chinese community, "Project Quay," a joint forces unit made up of the Metro Toronto Police, the Ontario Provincial Police, and the RCMP, was established. Between November 29, 1977 and May 1, 1978, the new unit made more than one hundred arrests on a wide range of charges, including extortion, assault, obstruction of justice, impersonation, theft, possession

of stolen goods, operating a common betting house, as well as offences against the *Immigration Act.* The enforcement actions and ongoing surveillance of the Kung Lok and the Ghost Shadows, "has sharply limited their criminal activities," the 1979 annual report of the Criminal Intelligence Service Canada read. "It has also prevented open street warfare between them. Unit vigilance has visibly upset the gangs and it is reported the Kung Lok are disorganized and breaking up. The Ghost Shadows remain strongly united but have been frustrated to a point that they admit they have to operate outside of Toronto." While police did enjoy some success against both gangs, the optimism of the CISC report was premature.

Despite the considerable intelligence information the police task force collected on Lau Wing Kui, he was not one of those arrested. But police had the last laugh on January 11, 1980, when Lau was ordered deported under Section 40 of the *Immigration Act,* which at the time allowed the federal cabinet to pass an order-in-council to expel any landed immigrant who, based solely on law enforcement intelligence information, is considered to have criminal associations or poses a danger to Canada. Lau left the country before he could be served the deportation notice and went to the Dominican Republic where he had gained citizenship in 1978. He eventually returned to Hong Kong, and later began working for millionaire gambling magnate Stanley Ho at the Hotel Lisboa on the island of Macau, located off the coast of Hong Kong. While his wife and children remained in Toronto, there were reports that some of Lau's triad followers from Toronto joined him in the Dominican Republic, while others went to New York and Boston to form new links with other Chinese criminal groups before returning to Canada.

Lau Wing Kui's abrupt departure prompted an internal power struggle among some of his triad's elder brothers. The man who quickly came out on top was Danny Mo. Described as a natural criminal leader who possessed "a skilful blend of personality and brutal force," Mo was from an affluent Hong Kong family. Before he became involved in crime, on a full-time basis, he was the part owner and maître d' of a restaurant in Toronto. When he took over the reins of the Kung Lok in Canada, he embarked on an expansion drive through

Danny Mo

the forced recruitment of Chinese visa students and by importing gang members from New York and Boston. He was also busy extending the reach and influence of the gang through his contacts with Hong Kong triad leaders as well as deals reached with other triads and Asian gangs in Montreal, Vancouver, San Francisco, Los Angeles, Boston, and New York. A federal immigration intelligence report dated November 8, 1980, states that "some form of alliance may have been established between the Kung Lok of Toronto and the On Leong of New York. It has in fact been reported that the Kung Lok is now referring to itself as the 'On Lok.'"

Under Mo, the Kung Lok's extortion racket victimized Chinese businesses and underground gambling clubs throughout Metro Toronto while wringing "membership fees" from immigrant Chinese students in Toronto, Ottawa, London, and Windsor. The victims were often asked to pay "lomo" — short for "lucky money" — or to make a "donation." Police gathered evidence indicating that one member of the Kung Lok extorted $20,000 to $30,000 from various students within a couple of months. Restaurant owners or managers were asked by gang members to "drink tea"

with them, yet another euphemism for extortion.

The Kung Lok's extortion attempts were generally successful (in that few victims went to police) in part because most victims were immigrants from Hong Kong who were already well versed in triad tactics and traditions. Members of the Kung Lok used this to their advantage and frequently demanded quantities of money that reflected the ritualistic numerical tenets of the triad societies. Demands for payments of $36.30, $72, and $1,080 were common. In 1983, the CBC news program *the fifth estate* broadcast a segment entitled "Lomo," which included an interview with a Chinese visa student attending a Toronto high school who was extorted by members of the Kung Lok:

Student: They beat me up and asked me for money — a thousand eighty dollars.

Q: A thousand and eighty.

Student: Yes.

Q: How badly did they beat you up?

Student: I got black eyes really bad, and blood from nose and mouth

Q: How many people were beating you?

Student: At the time was four people I think.

Q: Four of them beating up on you? In your apartment?

Student: In my apartment and two of them have a gun.

Q: Two had guns?

Student: Yeah.

Q: What did they say to you when they were beating you up?

Student: He asking for money and if I didn't pay the money, they cut my leg and hands.

Q: They'd cut your leg and hand off?

Student: Yes.

Q: Did you believe that kind of talk?

Student: At the time I believed it.

Q: You believed it.

Student: Yeah. I think — I heard there's one gang in Toronto is named Gum Lok.

Q: Gum Lok. So you knew when they came that that's who you were dealing with.

Student: Yeah.

On May 13, 1981, two "49" members of the

Kung Lok — thirty-year-old Chun Chung (Francis) Ching and thirty-two-year-old Tai Loong (Paul) Tang — where charged with attempted extortion and assault after trying to rob $1,080 from Charles Chan, a twenty-six-year-old waiter at a Chinese restaurant in Scarborough. Police said Chan was attacked on March 29 and then threatened with further harm unless he forked over the "lomo." Chan was one of the few victims of the Kung Lok to go to police. When Toronto police searched Tang's house, they found a hundred-year-old book on the history of Chinese secret societies. With it was a scribbler, which contained handwritten notes in Chinese describing the initiation ceremonies for the Kung Lok. A translation of the text showed that the ceremony closely followed the ancient rituals of the original Hong Men societies and included a description of how to set up the room in which the initiation was to be conducted. Tang testified in court that the book was given to him four years earlier by his friend, Danny Mo, but he could not read much of it because it was written in antiquated Chinese characters. Both defendants, who were accused in court by the Crown of belonging to a secret Chinese crime syndicate, were convicted of extortion, and sentenced to two years each.

Danny Mo also followed a popular Hong Kong triad tradition when he tried to garner a monopoly on the booking of Chinese entertainers from Hong Kong and Taiwan in Canada and the U.S. While the companies he formed with other triad leaders in Canada and the U.S., such as the Toronto-based Oriental Arts Promotion Company, were incorporated legally, Mo used intimidation and violence to force out competing promoters and wrest protection fees from Hong Kong entertainers wishing to perform in Canada. Hong Kong triads have control over large parts of the Chinese entertainment industry and Kung Lok's first leader, Lau Wing Kui, was the first to bring this practice to Canada. In 1977, the *Toronto Star* interviewed one tour promoter who admitted to paying $700 in protection money to an unnamed gang during the appearance of a Chinese opera group in Toronto the year earlier. When contacted by telephone in the U.S., the promoter said, "It wasn't as bad as in New York; we had to pay more there and we paid $1,000 each to four different gangs."

When the troupe he was promoting completed its tour in Vancouver, the presence of police at every performance prevented further extortion attempts. Asked why he didn't contact police in Toronto, the promoter replied, "We were afraid."

Despite the fear the Kung Lok had instilled in the local Chinese community, they were not immune to violence themselves. On July 12, 1981, thirty-four-year-old Richard Castro — Danny Mo's part-Chinese, part-Portuguese Kung Lok treasurer who also ran small gambling and loansharking operations — bled to death after his throat was slashed with a broken drinking glass in a parking lot in Chinatown. His attacker was thirty-year-old Wing-Chan Lo, another Chinese criminal who was in the country illegally and who had a record that included armed robbery, statutory rape, drug possession, and escape from police custody. Close to 150 people watched Castro as he lay bleeding on the ground, but, like other gang-related murders in Chinatown, no one admitted to seeing anything. Wing escaped to the U.S. by swimming across the Niagara River in July and, following an intense manhunt, he was arrested at a Buffalo bus station in March 1982. He was sent back to Canada where he was convicted of manslaughter and sent to jail for six years. An accomplice, who held Castro down while he was being gored, was sentenced to three years in jail on the same charge. The two men escaped murder charges because Lo had been beaten twice in the past by Castro and his Kung Lok associates after trying to help a friend who owed money to the gang.

"THESE GANGS KNOW LITTLE FEAR"

In addition to Chinese gangs, Toronto's Chinatown would also fall prey to a violent and implacable breed of Vietnamese criminals. The first wave of refugees from Vietnam who arrived in Canada just after the fall of Saigon in 1975 were the middle- and upper-middle-class supporters of the South Vietnamese government. Virulently anti-Communist, many were officers in the armed forces. One of the first Vietnamese criminal organizations in Canada consisted of battle-hardened South Vietnamese army veterans who formed an outfit called the "Viet Nam Hai Mgoi" (Vietnamese Military Overseas). Their ultimate goal was to overthrow the Communist regime in their homeland. With chapters in Edmonton, Calgary, and Montreal, the group was accused of raising funds for their cause by extorting money from Asian businesses. A federal intelligence document dated January 2, 1981 reported on "a group of 20 to 30 Vietnamese Chinese with former military experience and in their mid 20's have banded together in Vancouver to form a gang called the 'Sat Kong'. To date the gang appears to have concentrated its efforts toward intimidation of persons it considers to be pro Communist in outlook." After a botched invasion attempt by some of their members launched from a camp in Thailand in 1984, the Vietnamese anti-Communist movements quickly fizzled out.

A larger influx of Vietnamese refugees entered Canada in the early 1980s, directly from Vietnam or from refugee camps in Hong Kong, Thailand, and other places in Southeast Asia. The "boat people" were a mix of urban and rural residents who escaped repression under the new regime and the Vietnamese gang members who emerged in Canada in the 1980s came to the country in their twenties after growing up surrounded by the horrors of war. Following the cessation of hostilities, many were sent to brutal Communist re-education gulags and/or escaped the country only to be imprisoned in grim, overcrowded refugee camps where they were exposed to crime, drugs, gangs, weapons, violence, and numerous other adversities. Some arrived in Canada already hard-boiled criminals and members of gangs formed in the refugee camps. Most were highly susceptible to gang life in their new country: they had no grasp of English, little education, few meaningful career prospects, no family to support them, difficulty in adjusting to Canadian society, and a well-founded aversion to police and government authority.

The earliest of the Vietnamese gangs in Toronto averaged around thirty members mostly between the ages of fifteen and twenty-five. Most gangs were made up either of ethnic Vietnamese or ethnic Chinese from Vietnam. (Of the thousands of people who came to Canada from Vietnam, more than half were ethnic Chinese and spoke both Vietnamese and Cantonese. The two ethnic groups generally did not get along and this carried over to the gangland scene where there was often mutual hatred and loathing between the Hong Kong Chinese, the ethnic Chinese from Vietnam, and

ethnic Vietnamese.) Regardless of their makeup, the Vietnamese gangs had little in the way of a hierarchy and most had a transient membership.

While the Vietnamese gangs were less structured than their Chinese counterparts, they followed the precedent set by the Kung Lok and concentrated their criminal activities in Chinatown, extorting business owners and robbing Chinese-run gambling halls and Asian stores. Vietnamese gangs were behind a rash of robberies in Toronto's Chinatown that followed a similar pattern. "The perpetrators watch a targeted business and wait until the owner leaves with the receipts at the end of the day," Constable R.B. Hamilton of the RCMP described in a 1987 article on Asian gangs in Canada. "As he approaches his car they intercept and rob him. The suspects wear balaclavas. One perpetrator uses a revolver, while a second carries a large butcher knife. They terrify their victims by yelling and threatening them with death if they do not cooperate. ... These gangs know little fear."

Around 1983, the Vietnamese gangs in Toronto began to challenge the local supremacy of the Kung Lok by robbing the underground gambling dens they controlled or were supposed to be protecting. A typical robbery took place around 4 a.m. on September 15, 1983, when Vietnamese gunmen burst into a Chinese gambling club on Dundas Street West, lined up a dozen gamblers against the wall at gunpoint, and then relieved them of several thousand dollars. Police learned of the robbery after one victim went to police (there was little co-operation from any of the other victims). Two days after the heist, Sergeant Barry Hill of the Metro Toronto Police's Asian Crime Unit told the media that there had been three armed robberies of Chinese gambling houses in the past few days. "Only one was officially reported," he said, "but it appears the Vietnamese were responsible." He also noted that operators of gambling houses in Chinatown pay between $300 and $500 a week in protection money to the Kung Lok, but stepped up police enforcement "has diluted the power of the Kung Lok and that has enabled the Vietnamese to take liberties they couldn't have taken a year or two ago." He added that the Vietnamese gang members are feared more in Chinatown than the Chinese gangs due to their indiscriminate use of violence and that a showdown with the Kung Lok was inevitable.

Senior Kung Lok member Big John Yue experienced firsthand the audacious fearlessness of the Vietnamese gangs when, in September 1983, he was severely beaten by a number of youth who reported to Asau Tran, the charismatic, well-dressed leader of a thirty-member Vietnamese gang that police called "Asau's Boys." That same month, metro police issued murder warrants for two men wanted in the slaying of nineteen-year-old Hong Trieu Thai, who died after a bullet severed his spinal cord. Two other men were shot but survived. The escaped shooters, described as armed and extremely dangerous by police, were thirty-year-old Asau Tran and twenty-eight-year-old Sang-Minh Nguyen.

Tran had come to Canada as a refugee from Vietnam in 1979. He served in the South Vietnamese Army during his youth and when the war ended, he fled to Hong Kong, where he was placed in a refugee camp. It was there that Tran began his life of crime and soon he had assembled his own coterie of young criminals. Once in Toronto, he quickly made a name for himself in Chinatown's underworld and because he was an ethnic Chinese, he obtained work as an enforcer for the Kung Lok, collecting protection payments from gambling houses. He gained his first taste of notoriety when he was arrested for the murder of Hong Trieu Thai, which was part of a conflict between different Vietnamese gangsters (although by other accounts, Tran was accused of shooting Thai outside a local dance simply because he was shown up on the dance floor). Tran and his two accomplices were arrested but later acquitted because a key witness had disappeared. The acquittal contributed to Tran's reputation and, before long, he had started his own gang. Through equal measures of brutal violence, magnetism, strong leadership skills, and ties to Vietnamese gangs in Boston, New York, and California, Tran attracted a loyal following and for a time became the most powerful gang leader in Chinatown. He started his own gambling, extortion, and prostitution rackets and organized a band of armed thieves that specialized in knocking over jewellery stores. Most of the robberies were undertaken by youth under eighteen, a tactic used by Tran, who knew they would receive lenient sentences under the *Young Offenders Act* if caught.

Young Vietnamese men were also increasingly being used as enforcers for the Chinese triads in Toronto. In January 1985, the owner of a Chinatown restaurant who was also a prominent 14K member narrowly escaped being killed by one inept Vietnamese hit man, who was hired by the Kung Lok triad. As the eighteen-year-old pulled a .22-calibre handgun from the front of his pants, a thread caused the hammer to cock and the gun fired into the floor. The intended victim escaped onto the street, where the would-be killer shot him in the chin. The man was not seriously hurt, and did not intend to report the shooting, but his injury was bad enough that he had to go to the hospital, which prompted emergency room doctors to file a report with police. The gunman was later arrested and jailed for four and a half years. The 1985 shooting confirmed to police that the Kung Lok had begun accepting Vietnamese youths as members. Not only did they use them as hired muscle, but they also hoped to tap into their knowledge of the Vietnamese gangs and to act as lookouts for Kung Lok–connected gambling operations. The strategy backfired, however, as the new members tipped off other Vietnamese criminals as to where the floating games were being held and many were robbed.

By the mid-1980s, Tran and other Vietnamese gangs were as powerful, if not more powerful, than the local triad groups. They were extorting most Vietnamese merchants and restaurants and had even taken over from the Kung Lok in providing protection to the Chinese-run gambling halls. A September 6, 1986, article in the *Toronto Star* declared that the "viciousness of Vietnamese gangs in Toronto has created an unprecedented crime wave and climate of terror that are forcing businessmen to flee the downtown for the relatively safer streets of Scarborough." The article followed closely on the heels of a weekend robbery spree of Chinatown businesses. During a burglary of one restaurant, the fifteen-year-old son of the owner had a gun pointed at his head and was threatened with death if he would not open the cash register. Another restaurant owner was robbed at gunpoint while his staff was threatened with a butcher knife. In October 1986, members of a Vietnamese gang displayed a complete lack of respect for the Chinese triads when they refused to pay a $300 bill at a restaurant owned by the prominent 14K member. He did not complain to police.

Asau Tran is taken into custody by Toronto police sergeant Benny Eng.

In 1986, the Asian crime squad laid eighty-eight charges against Asau Tran and twenty-seven other gang members, following an eleven-month investigation into Vietnamese-run protection rackets, including one that extorted Chinese entertainers performing in Toronto. The investigation also uncovered a juvenile prostitution ring run by Tran and other Vietnamese gang members.

An all-out war between the Kung Lok and its Vietnamese nemeses never did occur in Toronto; the Vietnamese gangs prevailed with minimal bloodshed after taking control of most of the Asian gaming houses and pushing the Kung Lok out of Chinatown by the mid-1980s. By this time, Tran had expanded his criminal network to more than a hundred people through active recruitment and the absorption of existing gangs. In his 1987 article, R. B. Hamilton wrote that Toronto was home to two Vietnamese gangs. "One gang is estimated to have approximately 150 members, and the second, 120 members. Both have connections in Montreal, Ottawa, Kitchener, Winnipeg, Edmonton, Calgary, Vancouver, New York, Washington, San Francisco, and Los Angeles." In the article, Hamilton discussed another emerging characteristic of the Vietnamese gangs:

> These criminals are transient. Borders mean nothing. Gang members travel extensively, committing criminal acts as they go from city to city. Having committed a crime in one city, members will then go as far away geographically as possible, to another city, to avoid detection and arrest. They then continue their criminal acts in the new location. Once they believe the heat's off and that they are safe from repercussions, gang members will usually return to their original city.

The connections between Vietnamese criminal groups in different cities throughout Canada and the U.S. meant that one local gang would organize a local robbery, which would be carried out by Vietnamese gang members imported from another city. In December 1986, two Vietnamese-run jewellery stores in Toronto were robbed by seven men who were later arrested in Lowell, Massachusetts. Police gathered evidence that they were responsible for similar robberies in Montreal, Calgary, Chicago, and Seattle. In June 1987, two Vietnamese gang members from San Francisco were arrested in Toronto after robbing an illegal gaming house just five hours after their flight touched down in the city. In the years to come, the number of Vietnamese gangs operating in Toronto would multiply, leading to one of the bloodiest gang wars the city had ever seen.

LOTUS BOY

Vancouver was also home to a number of Asian gangs starting in the early 1970s. In 1974, city police broke up what they called "a major extortion ring" operating in Chinatown and arrested twenty-six-year-old Kwok Kin Wong. In court, Crown prosecutors described Wong as the leader of the "Soccer Club," a gang of Chinese youth that range in age from twelve to twenty-six. When police searched the club's headquarters at 111B East Pender in Chinatown, they seized what was described as an "accounts book." Written in Chinese characters, parts of the book documented names and protection fees paid to the club by Chinese businesses.

Another entry indicated a connection between the Soccer Club and the Wah Ching, a triad-like gang of Chinese criminals operating in San Francisco. The Crown asked the provincial court judge to impose the maximum fourteen-year prison term on Wong, who had been convicted of extortion. The conviction was the first major break for Vancouver police, which had seen extortions of businesses in Chinatown increase in recent years. Chinese community leaders had become so concerned about gang activities that in 1973 a group of them asked police if a specific Chinatown patrol unit could be formed. The police, also concerned about the rise in crime, agreed.

The euphemistically named Soccer Club was the first of many Chinese gangs operating in Vancouver that could be described as part youth gang, part triad, and part criminal organization. The origins of the gang were literally that of a soccer club made up of immigrant Chinese youth living in East Vancouver. It began in 1965 and two years later some of its members were working together committing petty crimes, such as theft and break-and-enters. "The wrong element got involved with that group and took it over," one Vancouver police official told the media in 1978. At its peak in 1973, the club had around fifty members who were involved in armed robberies, extortions, loansharking, and drug trafficking. By the mid-1970s, the Soccer Club had morphed into the Jung Ching — which can roughly be translated as "Chinese Youth" — which was a more structured gang. Their rebirth was prompted by the San Francisco–based Wah Ching, which now had a controlling influence over the Vancouver gang.

The Wah Ching emerged in San Francisco in the late 1960s as a street gang and then evolved into a criminal organization that ran protection, prostitution, gambling, loansharking, and narcotics rackets out of the city's Chinatown. By the 1970s, it had expanded to Los Angeles where it controlled most of the criminal vices in that city's Chinese community. According to the California Gang Investigator's Association, during the 1970s and 1980s, "there may have been as many as two hundred Wah Ching members and five hundred criminal associates in California. Although primarily headquartered in San Francisco, they developed strong associations with Asian crime groups and gangs in Los Angeles,

Seattle, Vancouver, Toronto, Boston, and New York. They also purportedly developed close ties to Hong Kong's Sun Yee On and the 14K Triads."

With guidance and support from the Wah Ching, Vancouver's Jung Ching grew in size and strength, although its membership never exceeded more than twenty-five to thirty active members. By the end of the 1970s, the Jung Ching disintegrated in an internecine power struggle, and factions split off to form two rival gangs: the Gum Bong ("Golden Rod," or "Invincible") and the Bak Mel (literally, the "White Eyebrow," a traditional form of kung fu fighting). The two gangs did not last long, while the weakened Jung Ching survived for only a few more years in a truncated state before it merged with the Lotus Family.

The Lotus Family was founded in 1976 by Ling Yue Jai (a.k.a. David So, a.k.a. Lotus Boy) as a splinter group from the Jung Ching. The Lotus Family was originally made up of around forty Chinese immigrant youth from Hong Kong who were recruited from high schools. The tight-knit gang was held together by its magnetic leader, David So, who had an almost cultlike following among his young recruits. In March 1977, So was handed a two-year prison term for assault and possession of a dangerous weapon following the brutal beating of two Chinese youths by seven lead-pipe-wielding Lotus Family members. "There's something about Lotus Boy — you could call it charisma, I suppose," Vancouver police constable Bob Murphie of the Chinatown detail mused in a 1978 media interview. "The members of his gang find him very attractive and they've remained loyal. Whenever a youth gang leader goes to jail, the other members of the gang usually just say the hell with him, pick a new leader and carry on. But not the Lotus Family. They're waiting for Lotus Boy to get out — they've kept the faith."

This faith was apparently not strong enough, for in 1978 Park Shing Lo took over as leader of the Lotus Family in So's absence. In his 2004 book on Vancouver's Asian gangs, Terry Gould describes Park as a "short, violent muscleman" who frequented "grungy Eastside pool halls," but was also "one of the pioneers of the modern Chinese-gang scene." He got his criminal start in the late 1960s as a member the Soccer Club and later the Jung Ching. "Back in those days Park was a graceful persuader with a subtle mind, and in 1978 he'd helped to engineer a merger between the Jung Ching and the emerging Lotus and took control of both and then of the Asian entertainment business in Vancouver." Park also continued the Jung Ching's alliance with the Wah Ching in San Francisco.

The sworn enemies of the Lotus Family were the Red Eagles. Also known as the Hung Ying, the gang began as a mixture of ethnic Chinese from Hong Kong, the Philippines, and Vietnam. The Red Eagles were based out of the east side of Vancouver and made money by extorting restaurants and Chinese students. In conjunction with the local Gum Wah ("Golden Chinese"), a gang made up of Chinese and Filipino youth, the Red Eagles also became involved in street-level heroin trafficking. Headed by a computer store owner named Wayne Shi ("Chicken Wings") Mah, the Red Eagles reportedly had ties with Hong Kong's 14K triad. There were five other Chinese youth gangs known to Vancouver police in the early 1980s: the Star Wars, the Wild Animals, the Ching Tao, the Yee Tong, and the remnants of the Jung Ching. These gangs were much smaller than the Red Eagles, the Gum Wah, or the Lotus Family, each of which had between forty and fifty hard-core members, most of whom were in their teens or twenties.

Around 1982, Vancouver's Asian gang scene was joined by the Viet Ching, which was made up mostly of ethnic Chinese from Vietnam who arrived in Vancouver in the early 1980s (the name Viet Ching was derived from slang used to refer to Vietnamese of Chinese descent). Like the existing gangs, the Viet Ching was not a triad society, but structured itself like one; it had a hierarchy and often used the same designations for members as a traditional triad. The average Viet Ching member was in his thirties and the criminal gang was extremely aggressive in their attempts to take over the traditional Chinatown rackets of extortion, burglary, gambling and loansharking, which sparked numerous battles with the Lotus and Red Eagles.

For the remainder of the 1980s, numerous clashes were reported among five of the city's largest gangs: the Red Eagles–Gum Wah, the Lotus Family, the Viet Ching, another Vietnamese gang called the Jung Chieng, and a multi-ethnic gang called the Los Diablos. Vancouver police noticed an escalation of violence around 1984, when gang fights began breaking out at high schools and outside nightclubs. Police blamed the Lotus Family for instigating the violence when it went on the offensive in a series of attacks against the Red Eagles. At first, the weapons of choice were lead pipes and baseball bats. This was followed by an increase in the use of knives and even meat cleavers and machetes. Gang members then began using guns.

For Professor Robert Gordon of Simon Fraser University, who studies Vancouver's criminal gangs, the mostly teenage gang members who were fighting amongst themselves should be viewed separate from the "gang elders." By the mid-1980s, the Lotus Family, the Red Eagles, and the Viet Ching had become less of a street-level collection of thugs and more of what Gordon calls a "criminal business organization," a gang that that exhibits a formal hierarchical structure that includes a mix of adult leaders in their twenties, thirties, and even forties and the rank-and-file members in their teens and early twenties. The younger gang members were expected to carry out lower-level "street activities," including theft, arson, auto theft, and buying and selling handguns for older gang leaders or other established crime groups in Vancouver and beyond. "We know they have ties with gangs in San Francisco, Toronto, Edmonton, Calgary, Hong Kong," Peter Ditchfield of the Vancouver police said of the gangs in a 1984 media interview. "We know they have elders in many of these cities giving them advice and using them for protection and as go-betweens." While the Red Eagles, the Lotus Family, and other gangs that emerged during the 1980s earned money from extortion, prostitution, and theft, the real money was in drugs. The "elder brothers" in a gang, often working with members of triads and other Asian crime groups in Canada, the U.S., or Hong Kong, would set up heroin deals and then have a junior member courier the drugs from Hong Kong to Canada where it would be sold by gang members or wholesaled to other drug dealers. In a rare media interview in 1986, an unnamed leader of the Lotus gang said that some Wah Ching members from San Francisco have been to Vancouver, "but just for a visit. We can go to another city if we need to lay low, and the guys take care of us."

THE MOST CRIMINALLY ACTIVE AND SUCCESSFUL TRIAD

The crime and violence that plagued Chinese communities in Toronto and Vancouver was an outgrowth of the escalation of Asian organized crime in cities throughout North America. As the Chinese and Vietnamese criminal groups proliferated and struggled for control over finite territories and criminal markets, violence between gangs was inevitable. Some of the worst carnage occurred in the U.S. On September 4, 1977, three young Chinese men entered the Golden Dragon restaurant in San Francisco and began shooting. Five people were killed and eleven were severely wounded. It was the worst mass slaying in the city's history at the time. On December 23, 1982, a thirteen-year-old boy was among three people who were shot dead in the Golden Star bar located in New York's Chinatown after three masked men burst in and began firing randomly. Eight others were wounded. Police said the targets were gang members and the killings were part of a turf war between rival Chinese tongs. On February 18, 1983, three Vietnamese men gunned down fourteen people in the Wah Mee gambling club in Seattle, making it the city's worst mass murder.

The gang violence was one of the topics on the agenda of a remarkable summit that took place at the Miramar Hotel in Hong Kong in January 1983. It was at this meeting that various leaders and representatives of triads and other Chinese criminal groups from Hong Kong, the U.S., and Canada met to discuss a possible detente. This subject was part of a broader agenda, set by the host of the meeting, Lau Wing Kui, the former leader of Toronto's Kung Lok. His goal was to formalize co-operation between the Hong Kong triads, the American tongs, and other Chinese gangs in Canada and the U.S. in order to coordinate criminal activities among the different gangs, divide up territories, and minimize gang wars. Ostensibly, triad leaders in Hong Kong wanted to gain a foothold in and exert control over the Chinese underworld in North America in anticipation of their exodus from the British colony before it was annexed by China in 1997.

Among those attending the meeting were Kis Jai (a.k.a. Peter Chin), leader of the New York Ghost Shadows; Vincent Chu (a.k.a. Vincent Jew), the head of the Wah Ching in San Francisco; Tony Young, the Wah Ching leader in Toronto; and Danny Mo, the Canadian Dragon Head for the Kung Lok. Among those invited, but could not attend, were Tin Lung (a.k.a. Stephen Tse), head of Boston's Ping On triad, and William Tse, the leader of the Wah Ching gang in Los Angeles. In his testimony before the 1984 President's Commission on Organized Crime, Sergeant Barry Hill, at the time a Chinese gang specialist with the Metro Toronto Police, stated that Lau Wing Kui delegated responsibility to Danny Mo to bring the different North American criminal factions together into one cohesive, continentwide network. Mo was apparently selected as the peace broker and deal maker, not only because he belonged to the same triad as Lau Wing Kui, but because he was already criss-crossing the country forming partnerships and pacts with other triad leaders. The meeting also resulted in a realignment of territories, which purportedly included "officially" granting San Francisco's Wah Ching jurisdiction over Vancouver, giving it the rights to control local gangs in the city. The meeting allegedly concluded with the ritual burning of the yellow paper to symbolize the participants' bonds of brotherhood at the start of their new joint venture.

Royal Hong Kong police found out about the meeting and, during an interrogation, Lau Wing Kui told them he had heard that Danny Mo was involved in an illegal immigration scheme that brought Chinese citizens into Canada and when he was in Hong Kong, he had a number of forged Canadian immigration documents with him. Whether this information was passed along to Canadian authorities is unknown, but when Danny Mo returned to Toronto, he was arrested on immigration charges. Others picked up by police included fifty-two-year-old Sean Herbert Pollock, a personnel officer with the federal Immigration Department, who was charged with conspiracy, breach of trust, and accepting secret commissions, and Oscar Wong, a Toronto lawyer who ran unsuccessfully for city council in the 1982 civic election, who was charged with conspiracy and offering a secret commission. Revelations from informants that Chinese citizens wishing to relocate to Canada were paying thousands of dollars to have their immigration status "looked after" sparked a joint investigation between the RCMP and Metro Toronto Police in 1982. The next year, the task force confiscated hundreds of counterfeit Canadian immigration forms from a printing shop located in the heart of Toronto's Chinatown.

The illegal-immigration probe was part of an all-out assault launched by police in Toronto against the Kung Lok. In 1980, one "49" boy was charged with four counts of fraud, two counts of possession of stolen credit cards, and one count of possession of counterfeit U.S. money, while another was charged with twenty-five counts of fraud. By March 1982, Toronto police reported that fifteen members of the Kung Lok were before the courts. Two faced murder charges and thirteen were charged with extortion. In 1984, Mo was charged with two counts of armed robbery, which was the most serious case that police had against him to date. The charges arose from a March 21 robbery, in which $15,000 worth of tickets for a show promoted by Wilson Tang of Vancouver were stolen at knifepoint from a Toronto ticket agent by two men wearing stocking masks. Toronto police later arrested Walter Ip and Tom Leung, two Kung Lok members, and charged them with robbery. Charges against Ip were later dropped in return for his testimony against Mo. During his trial, the Crown told the court that Mo assumed he had the exclusive rights to bring Hong Kong entertainers into Toronto, which prompted him to order the two men to steal the tickets. Ip told the court that Mo was behind the robbery, but in a second court appearance three days later, he recanted that story. The judge said he believed Ip was pressured to change his story and accepted his original testimony. Mo was convicted of the charges in June 1985 and sentenced to four and a half years. But the guilty verdict was appealed and, because of a legal technicality, it was dismissed and a brand-new trial was ordered. During his second trial, Walter Ip refused to testify again and even went so far as to leave Toronto. The charges against Mo were stayed.

Mo now seemed untouchable and his reputation in Toronto's Chinese community increased exponentially. A 1986 police intelligence report said, "all evidence indicates the Kung Lok is the principal threat to law and order in the Chinese community in Toronto." By this time, however, the Kung Lok had already reached its zenith. By 1985, police had shut down five gambling halls the triad either controlled or received money from through extortion or robberies, thereby depriving Danny Mo of a principal source of revenue. This void was filled by the Vietnamese gangs who joined police in pushing the Kung Lok out of Chinatown's most lucrative rackets, resulting in a considerable loss of face for Mo and his triad. Danny Mo's high-profile arrest and trial was also causing dissension in the ranks of the Kung Lok and an internal power struggle ensued. By the mid-1980s, a number of senior members of the Kung Lok had achieved their own level of success and fortune, erecting fronts as respectable businessmen while overseeing such traditional rackets as extortion, robbery, and gambling. Some were also branching out into more ambitious operations, like counterfeiting, heroin trafficking, and migrant smuggling. As a *Globe and Mail* reporter wrote in 1986, "the leaders of Toronto's most powerful oriental organized-crime gang, the Luen Kung Lok triad, are businessmen in their 30s and 40s who have fought their way to the top and now sit comfortably behind desks, far from the streets where their money is made, police say." In keeping with a general trend where triads were assuming a decentralized form, Mo's lieutenants began operating more independently than ever, with some even breaking away and forming their own gangs. In 1988, the Criminal Intelligence Service Canada estimated the Kung Lok membership in Toronto at four hundred although only between eighty and one hundred were active members. Two years later, the number of active members had dwindled to around fifty.

The takeover of the Chinatown rackets by the Vietnamese gangs, combined with the autonomous branches set up by senior Kung Lok members, meant that, by the start of the new decade, the illegal enterprises of the Kung Lok had "shifted from the traditional crimes of extortion, gambling and robberies, into new areas such as the manufacturing of fraudulent credit cards, alien smuggling and the illegal sale of alcohol and cigarettes," according to a 1992 report from the Canadian Association of Chiefs of Police. In addition, some cells were now trafficking in cocaine, which they reportedly obtained from Italian mafia sources. The new decade also signalled the presence of more criminal triads in Canada. The 1992 CACP report noted "an increase in the number of Triad members and criminal associates in Canada over the past several years, most noticeably in British Columbia, Alberta and Ontario." In addition to the Kung Lok and 14K, a 1993 classified federal intelligence report discussed the Canadian presence of the Sun Yee On, Wo Hop To, and Wo Shing Wo triads from Hong Kong as well as the Taiwanese United Bamboo. "Many of these triads have apparently maintained links with their parent societies in Hong Kong or Taiwan and almost all utilize Vietnamese street gangs to undertake much of their street-level drug trafficking," the report said. The members of these triads "are hardened, professional criminals who use the triad mystique to glorify themselves."

During this period, the 14K triad was considered the largest and most powerful triad in the world, although the Canadian and American chapters operated independently of Hong Kong. In the early 1980s, most of the members of the 14K in Canada were originally from Hong Kong, but as the years passed, it recruited new members from the Vietnamese community, while absorbing the remnants of the now-defunct Ghost Shadows. In 1988, the CISC estimated the number of members in Toronto's 14K chapter at 150, although only forty were criminally active, mostly in heroin trafficking, migrant smuggling, gambling, theft and extortion. Four years later, the CISC estimated its active criminal membership in Ontario at approximately fifty.

A CLOCKWORK BANANA

But brothers, this biting of their toe-nails over what is the cause of badness is what turns me into a fine laughing malchick. They don't go into the cause of goodness, so why the other shop? If lewdies are good that's because they like it and I wouldn't interfere with their pleasures, and so of the other shop. And I was patronizing the other shop. More, badness is of the self, the one, the you or me on our oddy knockies, and that self is made by old Bog or God and is his great pride and radosty. But the not-self cannot have the bad, meaning they of the government and the judges and the schools cannot allow the bad because they cannot allow the self.
—Alex in *A Clockwork Orange* by Anthony Burgess, 1962

What's it going to be then, eh?

There was the existing yiquins, that is the Red Eagles–Gum Wah, the Lotus Family, the two Vietnamese yiquins — the Viet Chin and the Jung Chieng — and a new yiquin in town — the Los Diablos, which was started by a six-foot-two-inch droog from Iran named Babbak (Bob) Moieni. The Diablos were a nasty mix of white, Hispanic, Portuguese, and East Indian qingnans that dressed themselves in the height of yiquin fashion, which in those days was a loose-fitting red-and-black puma tracksuit. The Diablos began around the middle part of the 1980s

and at its total max it had 251 nasty droogs. They were located in the southeast corner of Vancouver, along the southernmost stretch of Kingsway that cut through the jiangyu of the Red Eagles–Gum Wah. Moieni was also recruited by the Lotus Family in 1987 and before you knew it, my brothers, he was made a zhanshi, there being where he could use his martial arts and with a long hard bat collect the old lomo from Chinese fanguans and gambling parlors, and later pull the old horrorshow chiing on the enemy yiquins of the Lotus. The Lotus Family kindly invited Moieni to participate in the old ultraviolence against the Red Eagles–Gum Wah droogs.

Now, Vancouver in the 1980s was yiquin-infested and you may have forgotten, oh my brothers, what things were like then, things changing so sukky and everybody forgetting, newspapers not being read very much anymore unless there was a story about some horrorshow louguis committed by a qingnan who is wuwu from drinking too much tea-plus-hailouying at the Korova bubble bar. We, that is me, your humble narrator, and my fellow droogs, like to down the tea with knives in it, as we used to say, to sharpen us up and make us ready for a bit of the old ultraviolence and other sorts of zhanshi, zuixng, or lougui.

Between 1983 and 1984, the Vancouver city jingfang listed thirty-two zuixngs committed by the yiquins. Horrorshow zhanshi between Asian yiquins have the city's jingfang fearing the rivalries are reaching an ultranasty level. A zhanshi between yiquins at a downtown kezhan in June 1983 meant that the reliable old jingfang laid attempted qianging charges against suspected droogs of one of the yiquins. And then there was some of the nasty horrorshow zhanshi outside Churchill Secondary Hong in November 1983, where there were many droogs brandishing about their daos and then out comes the blood, my brothers, real beautiful, and this led to the arrest and conviction of Herman Lam, just twenty years old, who the jingfang described as a zuzhang of the Lotus Family and an instigator of the zhanshi. Lam was sent off to banfang for four years while two other droogs, eighteen-year old Rick Tang and nineteen-year old Edward Jung, received two years less a day in the same banfang. In April 1984, a masked paoman shejied and qianged twenty-year old Kenneth Yang in an East Hastings pool hall and with a flash flash flash escaped through a back door and shortly afterwards, a letter surfaced, signed "Chinatown Death Squad," that threatened to qiang yiquin droogs. Park Lo, the zuzhang of the Lotus Family, blurb blurb blurbed to the media that he was threatened with "execution" by the "Chinatown Death Squad."

In November 1984, two droogs with the Red Eagles were shejied and another was jued and the same month, Hy Hang, the fine young zuzhang of the Viet Ching and two of his teenage droogs chased a Jung Chieng droog out of downtown gambling kezhan into an alley where he was ordered to kneel which, my brothers, made him pant widely with a sort of wuff wuff wuff. A semi-automatic pao was pointed at his guallaver, but how lucky it was for him that the gambling kezhan was under the watchful eye of the reliable old jingfang and the three droogs were immediately daibued. After his time in court, Hy Hang was acquitted when the wuff wuff wuffing Jung Chieng droog failed to show up in court and Hang's two teenage droogs were convicted of weapons offences but were only given probation with one of the them already a suspect in the jueding of a Red Eagle droog.

But myself, I couldn't help feel a bit of disappointment at things as they were in those days.

Nothing to fight against really. Everything as easy as kiss-my-sharries. Still, the night was young.

What's it going to be then, eh? A Red Eagle droog named Daniel Da Long Chen was given four years in the banfang early in 1985 after he was yufaned for possessing a dangerous weapon (he tried to machete a bunch of meng standing outside a downtown kezhan). The year before, he was yufaned on a charge of louqianing lomo from a Chinese fanguan employee. There were also other lomo louqians of Chinese shopkeepers and the old lougui from the mansions of those rich and well-to-do Chinese families. In October 1983, Chinese engineer Johnson Ting was snatched by some yiquin droogs and was held a prisoner for six days while his wife tried to raise $300,000 in ransom beng. Ting was freed by the jingfang who raided the Kingsway motel room where he was held captive. In 1985, three droogs burst into the apartment of a Hong Kong student, ripped off her clothes and with an oh oh oh threatened to publish photos of her horrorshow nazzis in local Chinese newspapers unless she handed over $20,000. The Jingfang arrested three droogs who belonged to the Lotus yiquin after she boo hoo hooed to them and they were all sentenced to three years in jail.

The yiquins were blamed for qianging Jimmy Ming, the manager of the Yangtze Kitchen Fanguan and his wife Lily. The two were snatched on January 20, 1985 from their Chinatown home and, oh my brothers, the droogs on the old surprise visit to their HOME, entered real horrorshow with a smash smash smash through the basement window, and then picked them up by the waishen and demanded $700,000 in beng from the Ming family. Their bodies were found in March in dense brush on a steep hill below the Squamish Highway in North Vancouver. They had been strangled to death and their bodies dismembered real horrorshow like. There were lots of promises by the nasty bangfei that they would return the two unharmed if the ransom was paid but their autopsies showed that the two were qianged right after they were snatched. The jingfang believe the Mings were bangfeied by Vietnamese yiquin droogs. The Yangtze Kitchen Fanguan gave jobs to a lot of Vietnamese refugees and one ransom note sent to the Mings' family said, "You have a good business. We don't have anything." The jingfang suspected the Viet Ching because four of their droogs were busboys at the fanguan, but the jingfang could not gather enough information to charge anyone and the Ming qianging was never solved (boo hoo hoo).

In April 1985 Ricky Choi, a middle-aged manager of a Chinatown fanguan called the New Diamond, was shejied to death on the street. Turns out, my brothers, that Choi was the second in command of the Red Eagles, a real horrorshow zuzhang. Four of his yiquin droogs saw the qianging, but not one of them would co-operate with the jingfang, saying in a shouty howly sort of way, "we'll look after the situation ourselves." This qianging also remains unsolved.

The Vancouver jingfang, in a very officious and formal manner, declared Chinese and Vietnamese yiquins were "public enemy number one" and then went off and arrested a number of yiquin droogs and because of the bam bam bam on their guallavers all the yiquin droogs went home and laid real low for awhile. And things were like quiet until the summer of 1986 when the Red Eagles launched a series of horrorshow gongdas on the Lotus, Jung Ching, and Viet Ching yiquins that included chiings and shejiings. The Los Diablos, with the help of their friends the Lotus Family, were also trying to jinjin on the East Vancouver jiangyu of the Red Eagles and take over their fandu markets. On August 16, 1986, six Red Eagles gongdaed and chiinged two Lotus droogs at a dance at the Sandman Inn.

On January 23, 1987, a sixteen-year old Viet Ching yiquin droog named William Yeung followed fourteen-year-old Lotus yiquin droog Tony Hong into the crowded Golden Princess Theatre in East Vancouver and, after being handed a pao by another Viet Ching who was in for a little of the old ultraviolence, shejied Hong between the yans and after glurp glurp glurping to the old hospital, survived, but lost one yan. After walking home, because he was still just a growing droog who needed a good night's sleep for hong the next day, Yeung was picked up by the jingfang and charged with attempted qianging. A week earlier, the same theatre

was longuied of $646 by pao-toting droogs and the Jingfang believed the same three droogs louguied a Chinese fanguan of $600 and then louguied $1,600 from another man after his car was surrounded by three Asian droogs wearing hankerchiefs and masks that completely covered their guallavers. In 1988, Yeung was tried and yufaned as an adult and then sent off to the banfang for eight years for qianging Tony Hong. The sentencing judge said in adult talk that Yeung's action was an "attempted, cold-blooded public execution."

In October 1987, the zuzhang of the Red Eagles, Wayne Shi ("Chicken Wings") Mah, was standing in front of a downtown kezhan when suddenly he was shejied making him cough with a hack hack hack. But he was only wounded, my brothers.

And the new year was the same, oh my brothers. On February 28, the Viet Ching and the Red Eagles shejied it out at the Akasaka kezhan on hip Richards Street in downtown Vancouver. Leading the charge was the Viet Ching zuzhang Hy Hang, who shejied one rival droog in the shoulder. And then sixteen-year-old Bob Moieni, the Los Diablos zuzhang and Lotus Family jinjin, was qianged on September 18, 1987. Moieni came from an Iranian family and had been run run running with the yiquins only since he was kicked out from old Killarney high hong just a year earlier. A month before he was qianged he told his older sister that he was committing very nasty deeds and she thinks he was trying to get out of the Lotus, because a couple of days later he told his family that if any Lotus yiquin droogs phoned, they should say he was not around.

Then the plainclothes jingfang visited Moieni at home, talking quietly, with only a mur mur mur being heard outside his bedroom door. His mother was convinced her little boy was opening his rot about the Lotus as a way to get the jingfang to convince the hong to allow him back in. The night before he was qianged, one of the zuzhangs of the Los Diablos named Yawer Khan led about a dozen of his old droogies to the parking lot of a McDonald's for a bit of the old ultraviolence with the Red Eagles–Gum Wah who hung out there on a nightly basis. On the way, Khan phoned Bob to tell him about the old 21-on-1 and Moieni showed up at the tail end of the zhanshi to watch Yawer Khan get chiened to the ground with a pool cue and an ow ow ow coming from the middle of his huanging guallaver. Now in those days, my brothers, the teaming up was mostly twenty by thirty, and this would be real, this would be proper, this would be an all-out zhan, the huanging, the qianging, and the zhanshi. Sometimes the yiquin would make for an all-out army, but it is better to roam in small packs where you can truly perform a nasty horrorshow gonda.

The jingfang arrived and began arresting everyone, including Moieni who was let go a couple of hours later and the next morning he slept in while his mother and two sisters left home for work and hong. His sister locked the door on her way out but, oh my brothers, it wasn't locked, when his mother came home just after 4 p.m. and found her son lying all prostrated on the living room floor in a pool of his own red glorious huang, bound and gagged, a hole in the middle of his foreguallaver. Beside his body was a turnip with a shejied track through it, having already been used to keep the old pao bang bang banging as quietly as possible. Moieni's qiang meant the Vancouver jingfang now had five yiquin qiangings under investigation.

For two years after Moieni's qianging, oh my brothers, open zhanfare raged between the Lotus-Los Diablos on one side and the Gum Wah on the other (the Red Eagles had fallen to pieces by this time and its droogs were absorbed by the Gum Wah). Each side was also fighting with the Vietnamese yiquins and the ultraviolence was real horrorshow like. In the first three weeks of the 1988 hong year, the jingfang were called to various chiings, yiquin fights, juedbings, and least fifty of the old drive-by shejiings.

One of these shejiings was a horrorshow running pao gongda that happened around 1:30 a.m. on July 6, 1988, when droogs of the Gum Wah and Los Diablos yiquins fired at least sixteen shejieds at each other on an unlit, abandoned railway overpass in East Vancouver. Three droogs were sent to hospital with paoshejied wounds. Caught in the crossfire were Phu Ha, who was shejied in the chest, Wing Quon, who suffered a shejiedpao wound to the back, and Mario Flores, who was shejied in the groin. The jingfang seized a shejiedpao, a nine-millimetre handpao and a longpao near the scene of the shejiings.

At the end of 1988, my brothers, the jingfang were putting the old lid on the old yiquin baoli and even broke up some of the nasty yiquins. Five droogs of the Viet Ching and about nine droogs of the Los Diablos were put in the banfang. A special Los Diablos jingfang squad made thirty-four daibus. The Yiquin zuzhangs cancelled meetings and recruiting came to a standstill, oh my brothers, and the Viet Ching was crippled by daibus and gongdas by the other nasty yiquins. They had fallen on rough times when at least seven of its droogs, including their horrorshow zuzhang Hy Hang, who was given a year in the banfang in December 1987 after pleading guilty to using a female qingnan as a changfu. Hang was is already in the banfang after being caught for shejiing off his pao at the Akasaka kezhan in 1987.

By the winter of 1989, the Lotus yiquin was now saying Chinatown was all theirs and tried a final push, real horrowshow like, against the Gum Wah by sending its droogs to recruit in their jiangyu, with orders to qianging any Gum Wah droog who might interfere. But here was a surprise gonda by Lotus droogs and what followed, oh my brothers, was ever more of the ultraviolence with gondas and drive-by shejiings and on December 28, two droogs were shejied in the legs and another went to the old hospital in critical condition with horrorrshow injuries to the guallaver after a bit of the old ultraviolence with an iron bar.

Faizal Dean, a student at Sir Charles Tupper high hong, took over the zuzhangship of Los Diablos around 1989, and then began selling the old kekeyin. By August 1990, several senior Los Diablos droogs were sent home from prison and tried to take over the yiquin from the newer East Indian–Canadian droogs. The old ultraviolence meant the yiquin was coming to an end, especially with the arrest and conviction of Dean for the October 11, 1991 qianging of a droog named Parminder Chana. The Los Diablos buggered off around 1992 because of all the pressure from the jingfang, the nasty horrorshow qiangings of yiquin zuzhangs, and because the yiquin droogs were just getting older.

The Lotus Family became the strongest yiquin in the city with 122 droogs, including those of the Vietnamese persuasion. There was still some sporadic baoli, especially by Vietnamese yiquinsters like the two who were qianged in a downtown Vancouver fanguan on January 26, 1991, with a blurp blurp blurp after a man walked into the fanguan, had a real horrorshow row with a group at a table and then real quickly pulled out a handpao and fired. The jingfang believe the qiangings were part of a zhan between the Viet Chin and the Gum Wah. After a bit of a lull for six years, the zhan was renewed with six attempted qiangings in Greater Vancouver by Vietnamese yiquins who were gongdaing each other again. What's it gonna be then, eh?

THE BIG CIRCLE BOYS

In 1993, the Coordinated Law Enforcement Unit of British Columbia released a study that examined police and court data related to criminal gangs in Greater Vancouver. As of 1990, there were twenty-eight gangs and 976 "gang subjects" in the Lower Mainland, according to the report. Asian gangs accounted for 44.7 percent of all "gang subjects," non-Asian gangs accounted for 38.8 percent, while 16.5 percent were not associated to any particular gang (although the report acknowledged that it was difficult to determine the exact number of members in each gang as new players continually surfaced). The age of gang members ranged from thirteen to sixty-five years, with the average age being twenty-three. Fifty-two percent of gang members were born outside Canada and the majority (73.3 percent) came from Asia, in particular Vietnam, China, or Hong Kong. Twenty percent of the foreign-born gang subjects entered the country as refugees.

While most of the ethnic Chinese that were active in Canada's triads and street gangs came from Hong Kong, Taiwan, or Vietnam, a new Asian criminal force, made up of immigrants from Mainland China, was making its mark in Canada. Known in English as the Big Circle Boys, this loose association of criminal groups would be responsible for a dramatic upsurge in the scope and sophistication of organized crime in the country, which included commercial theft, heroin trafficking, marijuana production, immigrant smuggling, currency counterfeiting, as well as cheque and credit card fraud.

The original Big Circle Boys were Chinese nationals, mostly former soldiers and officers who had been purged from the People's Liberation Army and the elite Red Guards during Mao's paranoid "Great Proletarian Cultural Revolution" of the late 1960s. For years, they were confined to prison camps around the provincial capital of Guangzhou, where, along with millions of others, they were "re-educated" in a bid to rid China of its anti-revolutionary bourgeois elements. The prison camps were outlined with big red circles on Chinese government maps of the time, leading to their name "Dai Huen" or "Big Circle" (which is also Cantonese slang for the city of Canton, the former name of Guangzhou). According to Lee Lamothe and Antonio Nicaso, between 1969 and 1975, several of the imprisoned soldiers were released from the prison camps while others escaped. Most headed to Hong Kong where approximately twenty-five of them formed a loose-knit gang of criminals. "With the military training they received as Red Guards and the brutality they had suffered in the camps, the BCBs settled comfortably into a life of crime, specializing in armed raids; their trademarks were their extreme violence, their propensity for carrying and using guns, and their well-planned operations, aiming for high-dollar targets. Jewelry firms, cash-transit companies, casinos, and payroll offices were their regular targets." Intelligence information gathered by the Royal Hong Kong Police Force on those behind the rash of crimes revealed the shared origins of the perpetrators, which led them to coin the name Dai Huen Jai (Big Circle Boys).

During the early to mid-1980s, dozens of the ex-Guard officers, soldiers, as well as other hardened criminals left China and Hong Kong for Europe, mainly the Netherlands and Britain, while others went to North America, in particular Canada. Some were smuggled into the country illegally and most claimed refugee status upon arrival. By the late 1980s, they had already made their mark in Vancouver and Toronto where they became known for their violent kidnappings, armed robberies, and home invasions. While some tenets of the triad hierarchy were applied by the original Big Circle Boys to their own gangs in Canada, they are not a triad, let alone a unified criminal organization. They are devoid of the structure, initiation ceremony, formal membership, or rituals that characterize the traditional triads. Instead, from the very beginning the Big Circle Boys were made up of numerous small autonomous gangs, consisting of between ten and thirty people at any one time, that are scattered throughout Canada (and the world) but which frequently co-operate on joint criminal ventures. The organizational strength of the Big Circle Boys lies in their vast networking, which means that criminal conspiracies are planned and carried out between different BCB cells (and other willing partners) located in different cities or countries, while BCB "members" may drift in and out of one or more BCB group or specific criminal venture. For example, Toronto-based Big Circle criminals may operate an immigrant smuggling operation with BCB members in New York City while simultaneously importing heroin in partnership with a Hong Kong–based BCB faction. Big Circle Boys are also known to work with a variety of other criminal syndicates, including Chinese triads, Vietnamese gangs, Eastern European crime groups, outlaw motorcycle gangs, and aboriginal criminals.

BCB groups pursue a wide range of profit-oriented criminal activities that are both rudimentary and sophisticated, predatory and consensual, as well as local and international. While their initial crimes in Canada consisted primarily of robberies and extortions, within a few years they graduated to drug trafficking, people smuggling, organized prostitution, loansharking, credit card fraud, and the counterfeiting of currency, cigarettes, digital entertainment products, and computer software. Today, the BCB are considered the leading players in some of the most sophisticated piracy, counterfeiting, and fraud schemes in the world. In a 1998 interview, Sergeant Jim Fisher, an Asian organized crime expert with the Vancouver police, described BCB members as highly mobile, sophisticated criminals who treat their activities like a business, network incessantly, and learn from mistakes. Fisher recounts one raid where he found

a BCB gang member studying a Crown counsel report on a credit card counterfeiting case, trying to determine how the accused was caught.

Organized groups of criminals from Mainland China first came to the attention of Vancouver police in the late 1980s following a number of armed robberies committed within the city's Asian community between November 1986 and January 1987. Police gathered evidence indicating that the robberies were being committed by new Chinese immigrants with assistance from senior members of the Lotus Family, whose job was to identify potential victims and supply the firearms. The author of a 1987 Vancouver police intelligence report did not refer to this new criminal element as a gang. "They are more a loose association of people who have a number of things in common. They have committed crimes but so far they are not organized like some of the other gangs we have in the city." A 1989 report prepared by Constable Bill Chu of the Asian Organized Crime Unit in Vancouver stated there were approximately thirty members of this emerging crime network in the city, "with numbers increasing steadily." Most were identified as former Red Army soldiers who were in their twenties or thirties. Police in Vancouver also began to associate the local BCB with a new form of violent robbery in the Chinese community — home invasions. One of the first of these that police became aware of occurred in 1990, when a group of men forcibly entered the residence of a ninety-four-year-old Chinese man. He was tied up, threatened with a gun, and then robbed of hundreds of dollars in cash. The same year, Chinese social clubs were held up by masked Asian men armed with automatic revolvers who made off with jewellery and money.

Along with the influx of Hells Angels chapters, the arrival of the Big Circle Boys on the west coast constitutes the most significant development in British Columbia's modern criminal underworld. Within a few years of their initial appearance in Vancouver in the late 1980s, the local BCB group not only put an end to the fighting between rival gangs, but brought them all into the BCB network in a subordinate capacity. "What we found is that the gangs had been organized into a sort of super gang," Detective Bill Lean of the

Vancouver police major crime squad told the media in 1991. Police intelligence suggests that around this time the major gangs in the city were carrying out specific criminal tasks for BCB members. The Viet Ching conducted robberies, break-ins, extortions, and helped manufacture and circulate fake credit cards. Members of the Gum Wah helped in the importation and trafficking of heroin, while the Lotus Family recruited teenage criminals to carry out break-ins, home invasions, and other thefts while also running errands for BCB members. A lower-echelon member of the BCB — what the police call a "Street-Gang Captain" — planned specific crimes with gang leaders. He also funnelled the proceeds of their crimes to his superior and was responsible for paying the young gang members. Within the local BCB, the Street-Gang Captain reported to the "Road Boss" who was responsible for planning the criminal activities to be carried out by the subordinate gangs. The Road Boss reported to a lieutenant of the BCB group, who along with the leader of the group, identified criminal opportunities, worked with other criminal organizations, negotiated international drug deals, and along with the Road Boss "subcontracted" the dirty work to the subsidiary gangs. Evidence of this new coordinated effort came to light when police arrested eleven people following a jewellery store robbery in August 1991. In a raid on one safe house in Vancouver, police found members of the Big Circle Boys, the Lotus Family, the Gum Wah, the Viet Ching, and the Taiwanese triad, the United Bamboo.

Around 1988, some of these mainland Chinese criminals migrated to Toronto from Vancouver or arrived in the city directly from Hong Kong. They came to the attention of Toronto police later that year following a wave of pickpocketing in Chinatown stores and on subways and streetcars. Thousands of dollars in cash were stolen, along with hundreds of credit cards that were doctored and then used to buy $400,000 in luxury goods for resale. Stolen Bell Canada calling cards were also used to contact criminal triad members in Hong Kong, who were working with them to smuggle immigrants and drugs into Canada. Bell Canada estimated that they were defrauded out of long-distance charges worth $10,000 a month. The Toronto-based BCB was also behind an armed robbery in February 1990 that stole $32,000 in cash, jewellery, and fur coats from an upscale downtown Chinese beauty salon. On April 4, 1990, they were blamed for an armed robbery of a Chinese travel agency and, a day later, a Chinese electronics store was robbed by two armed men who fit the description of those who had victimized the travel agency. Earlier that year, Toronto police busted a number of BCB-linked brothels in Chinatown and Scarborough that were run out of private homes and businesses. The prostitutes were from Malaysia and had been brought into the country under the pretence of legitimate jobs as maids. Police discovered that Toronto was part of an international sexual slavery ring that moved the women between Amsterdam, Copenhagen, New York, Los Angeles, Toronto, and Vancouver. There were also at least a dozen kidnappings in Scarborough during 1990 that were attributed to the BCB. By the early 1990s, police believed there were some three hundred people connected to the Big Circle Boys in Metro Toronto.

BCB groups in Hong Kong, Toronto, and New York were also behind one of the single-biggest heroin smuggling conspiracies ever investigated by Canadian police. From 1988 to 1990, up to 545 kilos of nearly pure heroin was shipped from Thailand to Eastern Canada. From there it was taken to Toronto and Montreal, where it was broken down into smaller lots, and then smuggled to New York City. The undercover investigation began in March 1990, five months after half a kilo of 99 percent pure heroin was seized in Scarborough. The investigation, involving law enforcement in Canada, the U.S, and Hong Kong, ended in February 1991 when police arrested seven people in Toronto and six in New York City. Police seized a total of 11 kilos of heroin and $8.6 million in American cash from two homes in Brooklyn. They also found a submachine gun, several handguns, body armour, heroin presses, and cloth cylinders used to smuggle the heroin from Thailand.

By the early 1990s, there was a steady influx of criminals from Mainland China into Canada. Some snuck into the country through elaborate people smuggling operations, while others claimed they were political refugees using the crackdown on the Tiananmen Square pro-democracy protest as their cover. The BCB became active in Calgary sometime in 1990 and the next year it was blamed for a burglary at a fur store in which $500,000 in merchandise was stolen. According to a 1992 report on organized crime by the Canadian Association of Chiefs of Police, immigrant criminals from the Mainland quickly took over Chinese gambling operations in Calgary and used members of the Vietnamese gang the Young Dragons as security and to collect gambling debts. They were also involved in prostitution and cocaine trafficking in Alberta. The CACP concluded, "members of the Big Circle Boys are responsible for a tremendous increase in criminal activity committed in Asian communities throughout Canada's major urban centres."

In 1992, four Chinese men linked to the BCB were arrested in Reno, Nevada, in possession of forged credit cards, counterfeit cheques, as well as $150,000 in cash, after cashing or attempting to cash fraudulent cheques at casinos in Reno and Lake Tahoe. When they were booked by Reno police, all listed Toronto as their home address. Later that year, nearly 10 kilos of high-grade heroin was discovered at the Port of Vancouver inside a container of marble tiles shipped from Hong Kong. In January 1993, Toronto police arrested three Chinese nationals as part of a province-wide fraud scheme in which fake companies were set up as a guise to obtain the social insurance numbers of people applying for jobs. Once they had the numbers, fake drivers' licences were acquired and bank accounts opened. Bad cheques were then deposited in the accounts and money was withdrawn. A month later, twenty-five-year-old Tow Chan was arrested as part of the same investigation. He was also accused of passing more than $500,000 in counterfeit commercial cheques in greater Toronto over a two-week period. Similar cheques turned up in other Canadian cities. Police suspected that BCB criminals in Toronto were producing counterfeit corporate cheques, which were distributed across the country and cost banks an estimated $10 million. In March 1993, a shipment of 6.9 kilos of 97 percent pure heroin was discovered in a consignment of picture frames airmailed to Vancouver from Thailand. One man, who police said was linked to the BCB, was arrested and charged in Hong Kong. In August, three Chinese nationals were charged in Toronto with the kidnapping of two refugees from Mainland China.

In April 1994, a seven-month undercover investigation by police in Ontario led to the arrest of seventeen people on fraud charges over a counterfeit credit card operation. The bogus cards, embossed with valid credit card numbers, were manufactured in Scarborough and sold on the street in Toronto for $300 to $500 each. Police said those behind the fraud had the capacity to put any name on a card and could also provide phony identification, including Ontario driver's licences and social insurance cards. During the investigation police discovered that some of the men were also trying to smuggle stolen luxury cars from North America to Vietnam via Singapore. In 1995, police raided fourteen homes and four businesses in the Toronto area, arresting sixteen people and seizing thousands of dollars' worth of machines used to emboss and encode credit cards. They also found two thousand blank credit cards and counterfeiting machinery capable of forging Canadian social insurance cards and Ontario driver's licences. A few months earlier seven thousand blank cards had already been confiscated. In 1996, Toronto police received a call about a robbery-in-progress at a home in Scarborough and when they arrived, they found one man with a self-inflicted gunshot wound to the head while another was found hiding in a backyard shed with a bag of stolen property containing cash, credit cards, and jewellery. Police said the men were members of a New York City Big Circle Boys group. In October 1999, police broke up a network of criminals involved in selling drugs, weapons, and counterfeit money. The six-month undercover operation revealed co-operation between a Russian criminal group and a BCB gang. Police seized more than $1 million in drugs, $38,000 in counterfeit money, forged Canadian and Chinese passports and weapons.

By the late 1990s, it was estimated that there were between three hundred and five hundred people connected to the Big Circle Boys in the Toronto area with between 250 and four hundred in Vancouver. By the end of the decade, the BCB was made up of two generations; the remaining ex–Red Guard soldiers and criminals that came to Canada via Hong Kong in the late 1980s and early 1990s, and younger gang members, mostly immigrants from China, Hong Kong, and Taiwan. Today, the term "Big Circle Boys" has come to refer generally to ethnic Chinese gangs of criminals from Mainland China who frequently work together in a fluid network of localized groups, some of which only have a tenuous connection to the original generation of immigrant Mainland Chinese gangsters.

BORN TO KILL

Like Chinese crime groups, over time the Vietnamese gangs operating in Canadian cities expanded their territory beyond the Asian communities while branching out into a wider range of criminal activities. By the 1990s, police in Toronto, Montreal Vancouver, Calgary, Edmonton, and Ottawa were all reporting the presence of Vietnamese gangs, including the Born to Kill and the Flying Dragons, both newly arrived imports from New York City. According to a classified 1993 federal intelligence report on Asian organized crime, these two new criminal groups "have challenged the traditional gang and criminal structures in place in the major centers. This development has resulted in a dramatic increase in criminal activity with a corresponding higher rate of violence."

The Born to Kill took its name from an insignia worn by U.S. troops during the Vietnam War (some of the original gang members had the initials "BTK" tattooed in the webbing of their skin between the thumb and forefinger) and was formed in New York in 1988 when members of existing Vietnamese crime groups in the city broke away to set up their own gang. Unlike most Vietnamese gangs, the BTK was well structured from the outset with an established organizational hierarchy. The gang originally made its money by pressuring merchants in New York's Chinatown to sell BTK-manufactured counterfeit Rolex and Cartier watches. One former leader of the gang, who was later convicted of murder, said in a media interview that he made up to $13 million from the sale of fake designer watches. The gang also pursued more traditional criminal ventures such as armed robberies, extortion, drug trafficking and enforcement for established Chinese triads and tongs. The BTK gained notoriety in New York City after some of its members threw a bomb loaded with .22-calibre bullets at a police car, supposedly in retaliation for the arrest of several merchants who were selling their fake watches. Since its founding, the Born to Kill has been locked in a bloody feud with the more established Ghost Shadows, fighting for control over heroin, prostitution, and extortion in New York's Asian community. Dozens were killed as a result of the protracted conflict.

The BTK established itself in Toronto in the early 1990s and immediately embarked on a binge of armed robberies, not only in the city's Chinatown, but throughout Southern Ontario. "The victims have been jewellery store owners of Asian descent," according to a 1992 report on organized crime from the Canadian Association of Chiefs of Police, "however, this pattern is beginning to change with Caucasian jewellery store owners, in both large and small urban centres, falling victims to Vietnamese perpetrators." The BTK also carried out a series of attacks on existing Vietnamese gangs leading the CACP to exclaim, "the level of violence exercised by Vietnamese criminal groups in Metropolitan Toronto has reached epidemic proportions."

The increase in violent robberies and gang clashes in Toronto was also due to the recent arrival of another vicious Vietnamese gangster, Trung Chi Truong. An ethnic Chinese, Truong fled Vietnam in 1979 at the age of nineteen and, after a short stay in a Malaysian refugee camp, came to the U.S. By the mid-1980s, he had become an enforcer with the Ping On triad in Boston, but before long he had set up his own gang of Vietnamese refugees that specialized in armed robbery. Truong was also a trendsetter of sorts for Asian criminal groups in that his gang was highly mobile; they committed robberies up and down the eastern seaboard and even across the border into Ontario and Quebec. His presence in Toronto was felt as early as 1986 after two Chinatown jewellery stores were robbed. Police had gathered enough evidence to link Truong and seven of his gang members to the robberies, but before arrest warrants could be issued, Truong was nabbed by police in Massachusetts for a violent armed robbery there. In June 1988, he was sentenced to eighteen years in jail. After only five months, however, he escaped from a minimum-security prison and made his way to Canada where he embarked on yet another wave of violent robberies of Chinatown stores and underground gambling dens in Toronto and Montreal with a gang that was estimated at between forty and sixty young men.

Trung Chi Truong

Truong's presence in Toronto put him in direct competition with Asau Tran, who had been released from jail in 1989 following a nine-month sentence for extortion. Three violent Vietnamese gangs were now vying for supremacy in Toronto's Chinatown and the result was an open and bloody war. Between December 1990 and August 1991, eighteen people in Ontario, almost all of whom were Vietnamese, were shot in or around the Chinatown district. Ten died from their injuries. Some of the deaths occurred as a direct result of the conflict, while others were innocent people who fell victim to the homicidal tempers of gang members.

The shooting rampage began when two Vietnamese gunmen walked into the Kim Bo Restaurant on Dundas Street around noon on December 27, 1990. They hurried to a table of seven located near the back of the restaurant and began firing before running off with their lookout. Thirty-one-year, old Dan Vi (Danny) Tran was killed. Two of his dining partners were also shot, but survived. Danny Tran's murder

was a carry-over from the Vietnamese gang war that was raging between the Flying Dragons and the BTK in New York. Tran, who was a member of the Flying Dragons, was marked for death after he was identified as one of four men who wounded a dozen people in a hail of automatic gunfire at the July 29, 1990 burial of Vihn Vuu, a Born to Kill member who was the victim of an unsolved slaying in Manhattan. Tran escaped to Canada and went into hiding in Toronto. A few months after Tran's death, Son Long, a member of New York's BTK gang was arrested in Manhattan and charged with his murder. The second shooter, Thanh Tat, a Vietnamese gang member in Winnipeg who had strong ties to the BTK, was tracked down and arrested in Vancouver.

The next well-publicized murder occurred on the night of February 3, 1991, when gunmen fired eight shots into twenty-nine-year-old Vinh Duc Tat on Dundas Street, not far from the Kim Bo Restaurant. Known on the streets as Lee Mo, he had come to Toronto in 1988 from the U.S. after spending time in a refugee camp in Thailand. Tat worked for Trung Chi Truong in Toronto, but began his own small band of thugs that extorted protection money from Vietnamese-run gambling houses in Chinatown. His killer was never found, although both Asau Tran and Truong were under suspicion as neither tolerated competition. Less than two weeks later, on February 15, 1991, one of Asau's men was stabbed to death following an argument in front of a Vietnamese café on the outskirts of Chinatown. One Vietnamese man was arrested in Ottawa and charged with second-degree murder. Amidst this carnage, the single-worst atrocity occurred on the morning of Sunday, March 3, 1991, at the A Dong restaurant on College Street when four men linked to Trung Chi Truong fired upon another group of Vietnamese men, killing three and wounding the fourth. None of the victims were part of any gang; police said they were killed simply because they insulted Truong's trigger-happy gunmen inside the restaurant, causing them to lose face.

The war's highest-profile victim was Asau Tran, who was killed on August 16, 1991, after being ambushed by two assassins as he was leaving a Chinatown restaurant. They first shot at his knees with automatic handguns and, as he lay helpless on the ground, thirty more bullets were pumped into his head. A fellow gang member and a waitress also died after being caught in the barrage. Tran's murder was never solved but it was most likely the result of a contract placed on his head by Trung Chi Truong. Before fleeing, the killers left a white glove — the same type worn by police officers at funerals — and a piece of paper bearing the badge number of a Chinese police officer with the Asian Crime Unit. Police interpreted this as a sign that the killers knew that Asau had provided police with information on Truong's whereabouts, which led to his arrest on March 3 and his deportation to the U.S. a few weeks later. Truong had escaped a number of attempts on his life and may have been aware that Asau Tran had been pressured by local triad leaders to get rid of him due to the robberies his gang carried out against the triad-controlled gaming houses. Tran's execution ended the war between rival Vietnamese gangs in Toronto. Following his death, and the deportation of Truong, other gangs, such as the Born to Kill and the Flying Dragons, filled the void. This new era was not without its own bloodshed, however, as Vietnamese gangs fought for control over street-level heroin sales.

THE EAST INDIAN MAFIA

By the mid-1990s, a new spate of gang violence was engulfing another populous Asian community in Canada, this time in Vancouver. After the Hispanic leaders of the Los Diablos left the gang scene due to jailing or death, the void was filled by young Indo–Canadian men. Shedding its mixed ethnic roots, the Los Diablos morphed into what soon would be called the "East Indian Mafia." This new ethnic incarnation of street-level gangsters was primarily involved in retail cocaine sales and, later, the smuggling of marijuana and chemical drugs into the U.S. The profile of the original Indo–Canadian criminals varied. Some were from immigrant families originating in India or Fiji while others were second- or even third-generation Canadians. Some were from well-off families, while others were from the working-class neighbourhood of South Vancouver. There was little formal hierarchy in the earliest of the Indo–Canadian drug trafficking groups and, as the police and the public found out over the years, there was also little loyalty to one another; allegiances constantly shifted and friends turned against friends over drug deals gone wrong or for revenge. The one defining characteristic of the Indo–Canadian drug traffickers was their wholesale use of lethal violence.

Among the Indo–Canadian criminals that emerged out of the defunct Los Diablos was Bhupinder Singh (Bindy) Johal. During the early 1990s, he sold cocaine for a pair of brothers named Ranjit (Ron) Dosanjh and Jimscher (Jimmy) Dosanjh. But Johal branched off to work in a dial-a-dope operation with Faizal Dean, a fellow student at Sir Charles Tupper high school who was trying to resurrect the Diablos. Johal and the Dosanjh brothers were now competitors, setting in motion a wave of killings between Indo–Canadian drug dealers that would cost the three their lives while taking almost one hundred more by the end of 2006. The bloodletting began on February 25, 1994, when Jimmy Dosanjh was killed in broad daylight after being shot seven times with a Browning 9-mm semi-automatic handgun in an alley in East Vancouver. His brother was killed the morning of April 19 when the truck he was driving in East Vancouver was sprayed with bullets fired from the rear of a car that pulled alongside him. The murder of the two brothers set off a chain reaction that resulted in a series of drive-by shootings in South Vancouver and eight more murders over the next four years.

Bhupinder Singh (Bindy) Johal

Johal became the prime suspect in the Dosanjh murders and, in 1995, he and twenty-four-year-old Sun News Lal were charged with first-degree murder in Jimmy's death. The two were also charged in Ron

Dosanjh's death along with four others: Preet Sarbjit (Peter) Gill, Rajinder Kumar Benji, Ho Sik (Phil) Kim, and Michael Kim Budai. Crown prosecutors argued that Johal ordered Jimmy Dosanjh's death after hearing rumours he had taken a contract out on Johal. (Police believe that Glen Olson, a neighbour of Bindy Johal, who was shot to death on April 24, 1995 while taking his dog out for a walk, was the innocent victim of assassins originally dispatched to kill Johal by Dosanjh before his own death on April 19.) A Crown witness argued that Ron Dosanjh's murder was ordered by Johal to prevent him from avenging the death of his brother. Prosecutors claimed that Johal offered $30,000 for the hit, which was carried out by Kim. In a decision that stunned the city, the jury acquitted Johal and his co-defendants on the two counts of first-degree murder in October 1995. In a bizarre twist, it was learned that Gillian Guess, one of the jurors at the trial, was having an affair with one of the defendants, Peter Gill, while he was out on bail. Guess was charged with and later convicted of obstruction of justice and received an eighteen-month jail term.

The Crown successfully appealed the acquittal of the six men, but before a new trial could begin, twenty-seven-year-old Johal was killed by a single gunshot to the back of the head while on the dance floor of a Vancouver nightclub on December 20, 1998. Although there were some three hundred people in the bar at the time, police could not find one witness willing or able to describe Johal's shooter. At least four of Johal's associates had also been killed in a four-month period preceding his death. When he was murdered, Johal was awaiting trial on the charge of kidnapping Randy Chan after a drug deal apparently went sour. The kidnapping occurred October 25, 1996, when a Johal associate named Roman Mann went to buy two kilos of cocaine from Chan, the younger brother of Lotus gang member Raymond Chan. Mann accused Chan of selling him diluted coke and then took him hostage. At one point during the fifty-six hours Chan was held captive, he was locked in the trunk of a car being driven around the city by Johal, who was calling Raymond Chan's pager, demanding five kilos of cocaine if he wanted to see his brother alive. (Roman Mann was also charged in the kidnapping but he was murdered before going to trial. Raymond Chan died in 2003 after being severely beaten by a group of men.)

Johal had been charged with a string of other offences over his short criminal career, including aggravated assault, obstruction of justice, and possession of dangerous weapons. He was also a suspect in at least one other murder. Johal's temper was legendary; in 1989, he received a sixty-day sentence and was kicked out of school for beating up his vice-principal at Sir Charles Tupper Secondary. He was also convicted of possession of a dangerous weapon after he smashed the passenger window of a car with a baseball bat. In 1997, he was sentenced to sixteen months for viciously attacking two men in a bar with a broken beer bottle. In a 2004 interview with the *Vancouver Sun*, Bal Buttar, Johal's main lieutenant, claimed he ordered the murder of Johal because of his erratic behaviour, which included killing off a number of his own drug-dealing associates. Buttar said that Johal had formed a five-member hit squad called "The Elite," which was responsible for at least twenty-five murders. When he made these allegations, Buttar was a blind quadriplegic, the aftermath of being shot twice in the head in August 2001. Buttar turned to "The Elite" to gun down Johal at the Palladium nightclub. He told the *Sun* he also used the hit squad a few more times after he took over Johal's drug-dealing network.

The murders of the Dosanjh brothers and Bindy Johal created a vacuum at the top of the Indo–Canadian criminal underworld resulting in a deadly power struggle and a rash of revenge killings. By 2002, fifty people linked to rival Indo–Canadian drug dealers were dead. Victim number fifty was twenty-seven-year-old Gurjinder Singh (Gary) Sidhu, who was killed by multiple gunshots on April 1, 2002. Police believe Sidhu's murder was revenge for the September 2001 death of twenty-four-year-old Kam Jawanda, who was shot outside the Richmond home of Sarbjit Singh Danda, a former associate of Bindy Johal. A few months later, cocaine dealer Robbie Kandola was shot to death as he got out of a cab in front of his apartment building in downtown Vancouver. Buttar confessed he was behind this murder because he believed Kandola had ordered the assassination of his younger brother six months earlier. One of the three men behind Kandola's murder, Kamaljit Singh Sangha, turned up dead in September 2002. On November 18, Davinder Singh Gharuis was shot outside his New Westminster home. He was a

Kandola associate as well as the close friend of Jaskaran Singh Chima, who was murdered in March 2002. Buttar told the *Sun* newspaper that he dispatched "The Elite" to kill Chima because he was suspected of being another one of the shooters who executed his brother. By 2005, about a hundred men had died as a result of the running battles between Indo–Canadian drug-dealing gangs. Despite Buttar's confessions, most of the cases remain unsolved. Among the more recent victims was twenty-seven-year-old Gerpal (Paul) Dosanjh, cousin of Jimmy and Ron Dosanjh, who was shot inside an east Vancouver restaurant on March 6, 2004.

In a federal study entitled *South Asian-Based Group Crime in British Columbia: 1993-2003*, the gang-related activities, drug dealing, and out-of-control violence of young Indo–Canadian men were blamed on a combination of cultural issues and the lure of Vancouver's lucrative drug trade. Indo–Canadian men are treated like spoiled "princes" at home by parents who are too busy earning a living and trying to get ahead to spend time with their children, the report said. In turn, this has "contributed to a breakdown in family communication, especially between father and son." The study contends there is a "consistent pattern where Indo–Canadian criminals are from families who provided their sons with money, freedom, favouritism and a discipline inconsistent with their siblings (primarily female), coupled with the culture's distrust of the police and an emphasis on preserving face or honour." The study also acknowledges that the allure of Vancouver's "explosion of lucrative criminal opportunities in the illicit drug smuggling trade" compounds these underlying cultural causes.

THE ASIAN CONNECTION

The influx of Indo–Canadian men into British Columbia's drug trade was just another chapter in a story of how criminal elements within Canada's different Asian communities have become increasingly involved in the country's modern drug trade. This story can be traced to the start of the 1970s, when the Golden Triangle of Southeast Asia began displacing Turkey as Canada's biggest heroin supplier west of Montreal. Accordingly, Chinese syndicates were also surpassing the French Corsicans and the Italian mafia as the world's biggest heroin producers and suppliers.

The shift in supply also meant that Vancouver's role as a port of entry for heroin would increase considerably in subsequent years. A classified intelligence report by the American Bureau of Narcotics and Dangerous Drugs that was leaked to the *Washington Post* in 1973 stated, "concomitant with the influx of Chinese, a steady flow of Southeast Asian heroin enters the Vancouver drug trade." The report goes on to say that "after the drugs reach the Chinese community in Vancouver, they are distributed to tong or 'benevolent' associations in the Chinese Community who, in turn, wholesale the drugs to their respective Chinese families or tong affiliations in Seattle, Portland, San Francisco, Chicago and New York." While it is questionable that the Chinese benevolent associations in Vancouver were behind the importation of heroin into Canada, over the next few years there was no disputing the fact that Vancouver had become a well-travelled port of call for Chinese heroin smugglers and traffickers.

In 1974, indictments handed down in New York City detailed an intricate international trafficking network that had smuggled close to 136 kilos of pure heroin and 45 kilos of gum opium into North America between 1970 and 1972. On its own, the processed heroin had a street value of around US$200 million. The drugs were smuggled in from Bangkok, Singapore, and Hong Kong by Scandinavian merchant seamen and handed over to Chinese distributors in Canada and the United States. Along with San Francisco, Vancouver was a key destination point and nine people were arrested in the two cities. The six arrested in Vancouver were Bing Hing Low, Paul Jang, She Teen (Tony) Wong, Chee Ying (Robert) Lee, Chian (Johnny) Chow and Victor Leung. At the time, "Operation Sea Wall," which was jointly conducted by the U.S. Drug Enforcement Agency (DEA) and the RCMP, was the largest investigation of Southeast heroin trafficking for both agencies. The conspiracy was based out of Hong Kong and more than sixty people were involved, according to the DEA.

A month before Operation Sea Wall went down, British Columbia's Coordinated Law Enforcement Unit seized around four kilos of heroin in Vancouver and charged Fook Lay Tang and three others from Hong Kong. The same month, the RCMP and Canada Customs intercepted around 3.5 kilos of black market morphine and codeine that had been mailed to Vancouver from Hong Kong. The RCMP in Vancouver arrested the package's recipient, Yuen Yuk Lam. On January 9, 1975, the Co-ordinated Law Enforcement Unit seized close to four kilos of heroin in Vancouver and arrested four people from Hong Kong. According to a CLEU report from that year, "evidence suggests that the heroin was brought in for speculative purposes, and that other shipments had been imported in November and December by the same organization." On March 27, the RCMP and Canada Customs discovered another four kilos that had been shipped to Vancouver from Hong Kong and hidden inside thirty-six lantern batteries. Three months later, the Vancouver RCMP nabbed just under two kilos of heroin and charged Sin Lap Ng of Vancouver and Mai See Cheung of Hong Kong. On July 3, CLEU seized another two kilos at the Vancouver airport that had been body-packed by a passenger on a flight from Hong Kong. By the end of the year, B.C. law enforcement agencies had confiscated around nine kilos of heroin body-packed by passengers landing at Vancouver airport aboard flights from Hong Kong. The single-largest seizure occurred in October when Canada Customs found 4.5 kilos. Two couriers, Ng Kwok Kin and Tse Ring Kwan, were charged with conspiracy to import heroin.

The quantity of heroin captured in B.C. would only increase in the years to follow. This was partially the result of greater drug interdiction efforts in Vancouver. It was also due to the escalating supply of "China White," which, in turn, was the product of recent bumper crops in the Golden Triangle and a far greater level of organization and sophistication in the smuggling and distribution of Southeast Asian heroin. The former Chinese Kuomintang army officers and soldiers that controlled the opium fields in the Golden Triangle were expanding production while establishing heroin-processing labs throughout Burma and Thailand. Working closely with them were members of Hong Kong and Taiwanese triads who were ramping up the smuggling end of the partnership.

On June 27, 1976, forty-four-year-old Ng Sin Lap (a.k.a. Shian Si Wu, a.k.a. Ho Lin Ng) was arrested in Vancouver when he tried to sell two kilos of uncut heroin to undercover police officers posing as drug wholesalers. The agents offered Ng $90,000 cash for the heroin, which had been smuggled into Canada by a Hong Kong schoolteacher. Police said Ng was planning even bigger shipments — as much as 100-pound loads to the U.S. and 50-pound shipments for Canada — which were to be supplied by contacts in Hong Kong and Taiwan. Ng had immigrated to Canada from Taiwan in 1970 after working as a typesetter for a news agency in Taiwan. Before that, he served as a captain in the exiled Kuomintang army in northern Burma, Thailand, and Laos. At the time of his arrest, Ng was a director of the local Kuomintang association in Vancouver (although there was no evidence that his involvement in the drug business was known to other directors). Ng pleaded guilty in September 1976 to trafficking in heroin and was handed a twenty-year term.

In January 1977, the *Toronto Star* reported that an international investigation that began seventeen months earlier had dismantled a Hong Kong–based heroin trafficking ring that was believed to have shipped over 1,500 kilos of the drug to North America through Vancouver, Toronto, and New York. Fourteen people were arrested in six countries. Eight of those were named in a two-count conspiracy indictment sworn out in Vancouver and all but one were residents of Hong Kong. All were alleged to belong to what police described as "one of the world's most influential heroin trafficking rings."

By the end of the decade, the Criminal Intelligence Service Canada was reporting there were "six major heroin trafficking organizations in existence in the Vancouver area, all of which are involved at the 'importing' level." In 1983, the CISC predicted that heroin from Southeast Asia would "capture a greater market share in the next few years." A 1985 RCMP drug intelligence report estimated that the Golden Triangle of Thailand, Burma, and Laos was supplying 66 percent of the illicit heroin market in Canada, while Southwest Asian heroin, produced in Pakistan, Afghanistan, and Iran, made up 34 percent of the market, most of it still entering the country through Montreal. Before the mafia-run Pizza Connection was busted in 1985, Southeast Asian traffickers controlled a meagre 5 percent of the heroin market on the U.S. east coast. By 1989, they were supplying 80 percent of the market.

Following the precedent set by the French Connection, Canada became an important conduit for Southeast Asian heroin entering the United States, and New York City in particular. Heroin shipped to Vancouver via Hong Kong or Bangkok was smuggled into Washington State or transported to Toronto or Montreal where it would be driven or flown across the border. Toronto also emerged as a direct entry point for heroin imported from Southeast Asia, which was often routed through Europe first. Most of the heroin smuggled into Canada at this time was still being body-packed by airplane passengers arriving from Hong Kong. (Residents of Hong Kong were favoured as couriers because they did not need a visa to get into Canada, so they were spared stringent checks by Canadian Customs and Immigration.) Behind the shipments were Hong Kong–based criminal groups, the 14K triad and the Big Circle Boys. Once in the country, the heroin was wholesaled to associates in Chinese and Vietnamese crime groups and street gangs. By the mid-1980s, Asian heroin suppliers were shipping quantities of heroin into the United States and Canada that made the French Corsicans and Italian mafia look like street-corner pushers. In 1985, 97 kilos was seized at the Seattle International Airport from two couriers who hid the drugs in metal ice buckets. One of the couriers escaped custody and was later murdered in Thailand, while the other refused to disclose who was behind the shipment and as a result was sentenced to a long jail term. It was later learned that both couriers worked for Kon Yu-lueng (a.k.a. Johnny Kon), the head of a Big Circle Boys cell in New York City who the DEA later described as "probably one of the two or three biggest heroin dealers in the world." Kon was arrested in 1988 and charged with importing 453 kilos of heroin into the U.S. between 1984 and 1987. In 1986, 22 kilos of heroin concealed in picture frames was seized at JFK Airport, while later that year police raided a Chinese restaurant in Manhattan and seized 15 kilos of pure heroin.

While much of the Southeast Asian heroin destined for the U.S. was shipped directly to east coast seaports or east coast airports, Toronto's Pearson International Airport continued to be a prime Canadian conduit for drugs destined south of the border. In two related cases in 1986, the RCMP arrested members of New York–based Chinese gangs with connections to Hong Kong triads as they tried to pick up heroin in Toronto worth an estimated $20 million. In both instances, the drugs had been body-packed by couriers who had flown to Toronto from Hong Kong via Western Europe. Once they landed in Toronto, the couriers phoned Hong Kong and transmitted a code indicating they had passed through Canada Customs safely. They then called their New York City contacts and arranged to meet them in downtown Toronto for the pickup. In the first case, which occurred in February, the heroin was smuggled in by a teenager from Hong Kong who told police she was duped by her mother into wearing a handmade girdle containing millions of dollars' worth of pure heroin hidden in fourteen secret pouches. After being caught at the airport, the young woman co-operated with the RCMP and made a controlled delivery to a Holiday Inn in downtown Toronto that resulted in the arrest of two members of New York's Tong Lok triad. In the other case, one of the two pickup men was a member of New York's Tung On street gang, which has ties to the Sung Yee On triad in Hong Kong.

In February 1989, "Operation White Mare," a multi-agency task force involving law enforcement agencies in the U.S., Canada, Hong Kong, and Singapore, led to the arrests of more than fifty people in Toronto, Buffalo, New York, Los Angeles, San Francisco, Chicago, Vancouver, Singapore, and Hong Kong. All were implicated in one of the largest heroin smuggling operations to date. At the centre of the conspiracy were Peter Woo and David Kwong, two New York City merchants. Woo was a long-time heroin broker who brought together suppliers in Asia with buyers in New York and brokers in Canada. The heroin usually arrived in Vancouver concealed in hollowed-out rubber tires for lawn mowers and golf carts. It was then shipped to Calgary where it was stored while triad members in Toronto set up sales to American customers. Once a deal was made, the drugs were shipped to Toronto where it was carried across the American border by "mules" recruited from the city's Chinese community. In March 1988, police received information that Woo and Kwong were plotting to bring into New York, via Canada, hundreds of pounds of 90 percent pure heroin worth about $1 billion on the street. The shipment was so large that Khun Sa, Burma's biggest heroin supplier, personally assigned his close associate, Chan Hok Pang, to plot the shipment's route. Pang reportedly dealt with members of the Sun Yee On and 14K triads to arrange to ship the drugs to Canada. On March 21, Peter Woo flew from New York to Vancouver and then travelled to Calgary to meet with his Canadian liaison Cheung Wai Wong (a.k.a. Kenny "Baby Face" Wong), who lived with his mother, four brothers, and two sisters. The RCMP picked up Woo's trail in Vancouver and followed him as he travelled east. On February 21, 1989, FBI agents and New York City police raided three houses in Queens and seized more than 362 kilos of heroin. At the third location, they also found $3 million in cash. Among those arrested and charged were seventy-one-year-old Peter Woo in New York, Kenny Wong in Calgary, and Chan Hok Pang in Hong Kong.

In a spinoff from the White Mare operation, Veng-Tat Lau, a Brampton, Ontario, restaurant owner, was arrested in New York City on May 6, 1989, for his role in an international network that smuggled heroin from China into the U.S. The undercover operation began in February of that year when a DEA agent in Hong Kong disclosed a plan by Lau to import heroin from China to the U.S. via Hong Kong and Canada. With the help of the agent, who Lau was using to coordinate the shipment, a sting operation was undertaken. The drugs were transported from China to Hong Kong and then placed aboard a freighter destined for Vancouver. Once in Canada, the boxes were transported by CP Rail to Ontario and flown to New York on May 5. The next day, New York City police seized 39 kilograms of heroin that had been concealed inside five of three hundred boxes containing umbrellas.

THEY WILL FOLLOW THEIR PREY

By the early 1990s, the only international criminal trade that rivalled drug trafficking in terms of revenue was the smuggling of people from Asia to North America. With the impending handover of Hong Kong to China in 1997, the small smuggling syndicates that moved hundreds of illegal immigrants were blossoming into sophisticated multi-country operations that were now moving thousands of illegals, mostly from Mainland China. The first public glimpse of this new era of people

smuggling occurred in August 1990 when "Operation Overflight," an undercover investigation jointly conducted by the RCMP, Metro Toronto Police, Ontario Provincial Police, and federal immigration officials, busted a group that had reportedly transported more than four thousand people from Mainland China into Canada over the previous five years. Seized documents showed the smuggling organization was soliciting clients in China while offering the same service to people in Canada who wanted to bring relatives to this country. Between thirty and forty people from China were smuggled into Canada each month, and each were charged up to $15,000 a head to get into the country. They were levied an extra $4,500 if they wanted to enter the United States.

The Chinese passengers were first gathered in groups of four to six in Hong Kong. Each group was assigned an "escort," who made all the travel arrangements, acted as translator, and was responsible for accompanying their group to Canada. (An escort made a commission of $1,000 for each person.) The group was then flown to Bangkok, where they were given forged passports and other counterfeit travel documents. From there they were put on chartered planes and taken on a circuitous route — stopping in one or more countries, such as Pakistan, the Czech Republic, Finland, England, the Netherlands, Belgium, Italy, Belize, Brazil, Panama, Haiti, or the Dominican Republic — before finally arriving in Canada. Most of the illegal aliens entered the country through Toronto or Montreal and were told by their escort to claim refugee status once they landed. The escorts were supposed to destroy all false travel documentation before they arrived at their final destination. In one excursion that was typical of the smuggling operation, a chartered aircraft arrived at Mirabel airport in Montreal in April 1990 with forty-seven Chinese nationals on board. After being smuggled out of China to Hong Kong, they and their escort boarded a plane to Panama. There, they received new travel documents and were then flown to Haiti. While in Haiti, they were given Hong Kong passports and flown to Canada, via the Dominican Republic on board the chartered aircraft.

Operation Overflight led to the arrest of six people in Canada and eight in Hong Kong, as well as the seizure of forged passports and other travel documents. Among those arrested were Chiu Sing Tsang, who was described in court as the "CEO" of the smuggling network, and his wife, King Fon Yue. Tsang was based in Toronto and had entered Canada with forged immigration documents in 1988. He had escorts and other key operatives stationed in more than a dozen cities around the world and had ties with Chinese criminal groups in various cities, including the Kung Lok in Toronto, the 14K in New York and Hong Kong, as well as other Mainland Chinese gangsters in New York and China. The operation made a profit of between $8,000 and $10,000 for each person smuggled into the country. The overall profit was conservatively estimated at $10 to $15 million. All the while, King Fon Yue was collecting welfare while living in Toronto.

In 1984, the Criminal Intelligence Service Canada had predicted that migrant smuggling from Asia would "escalate at a higher rate as the end of the British lease over Hong Kong draws nearer. Several organized smuggling rings now bring people to Canada from Hong Kong. Some of these people had made their way to Hong Kong from the People's Republic of China." As inferred by the CISC, Hong Kong had already been established as a major transit point for illegal immigrants being smuggled from Communist China. In late 1991, Hong Kong police uncovered fifteen different immigrant smuggling syndicates that were moving people from Mainland China to North America. A 1993 classified Canadian intelligence report documented the heavy involvement of Chinese triads in this smuggling activity. One Sun Yee On triad enforcer was the director of a travel agency that was a "front organization for Sun Yee On," which arranged documentation and flights that moved bogus refugee claimants on board leased planes from Southern China to North America via Belize.

In December 1990, another alien-smuggling ring operated by members of the Big Circle Boys gang in Vancouver was busted. Only thirty to forty people from China were successfully smuggled into Vancouver before the operation was shut down, but most of these had "criminal histories and/or Asian gang affiliations," according to a 1992 report by the Canadian Association of Chiefs of Police. "Passports were purchased in Vancouver, photo-substituted and

sent to the P.R.C. where a fraudulent entry stamp was affixed. These passports were then given to individuals who planned to claim refugee status upon arrival in Canada." The fee for the service was between $12,000 and $20,000. Four men said to be behind the smuggling operation were arrested. Police linked these men to other offences in Canada ranging from credit card fraud to an attempted contract killing of a witness in a Toronto court case. This latest people smuggling case raised fears among Canadian law enforcement officials that dozens and perhaps even hundreds of immigrants being brought into the country illegally since the mid-1980s were hardened criminals, including members of the Big Circle Boys and Hong Kong–based triads. The larger fear was that Hong Kong's triads and the BCB were transferring their centre of operations to Canada in advance of 1997.

Intelligence assessments from the early 1990s reported that some triads had already begun expanding their networks worldwide, focussing on countries with large Chinese immigrant populations, such as the U.S., Canada, Australia, and the Netherlands. Because of Canada's liberal immigration laws, combined with the federal government's aggressive push to attract Hong Kong entrepreneurs, Canada was seen as the number one destination for most residents leaving Hong Kong before 1997. Many believed Canada was also the preferred spot for triad members and other criminals seeking to resettle themselves, given its lax immigration laws, its strong trade ties to Asian countries, the large existing Chinese communities into which they could blend, the port systems through which drugs could be smuggled, and the country's proximity to the U.S. An additional incentive, according to the Taiwanese *Chinese Times* was that "Hong Kong triads prey on businessmen. So if their targets are moving overseas, they will follow their prey, especially to Canada."

As early as 1986, Toronto police reports were suggesting that some Chinese triad leaders had already moved themselves and their money to Toronto. Three triads in particular were said to be "funnelling millions of illegally earned dollars into Toronto real estate and businesses to form a power base from which to direct their worldwide crime operations," according to a *Globe and Mail* article. In his 1992 testimony to a U.S. Senate subcommittee examining Asian organized crime, Detective Inspector Roy Teeft of the Toronto police stated that more than 140 triad members from Hong Kong had already applied to migrate to Canada. A classified federal intelligence report on Asian organized crime from 1993 summarized the concerns of Canadian officials, while citing more conservative numbers of triad members who had applied to live in Canada:

> Currently, over 30,000 Hong Kong residents per year are being issued immigrant visas by the Canadian Commission in Hong Kong. Among these are members of triads — at least 13 identified triad members have applied to immigrate to Canada — as well as members of other organized crime groups based in Hong Kong. These organized crime groups are seeking footholds in Canada by legal and illegal means, often with the intention of continuing their criminal activities in Canada. ...We believe Canada has become a significant international base for Hong Kong–based criminal organizations. The activities of these groups pose a significant risk to law and order in Canada. As 1997 approaches, and immigration from Hong Kong to Canada increases, we expect the problem to escalate.

A confidential Immigration Department report prepared by staff at the Canadian Commission in Hong Kong, dated September 21, 1993, provides specific information about "17 new triad figures" who have applied to enter Canada. Among this group was a "major player in a massive triad syndicate that smuggles aliens into Canada (including other criminals)." The report's authors also wrote that "four more triad enforcers — (senior) triad office bearers who arrange gang warfare, beatings, torture and murder — have also applied to enter Canada." The enforcer with the Sun Yee On triad who ran the travel agency in Hong Kong wanted to immigrate so he could join his daughter in British Columbia. (Some immigration officials suggested that Hong Kong gangsters had already sent family members to Canada to obtain landed immigrant status so that they could later apply under the family reunification category.) Another applicant was a former Hong Kong

policeman who became an enforcer with 14K. "He has applied as an investor in the Quebec business immigrant program, claiming to manage a restaurant and private club." Another former policeman, described as a member of Sun Yee On, who had convictions for gambling and assault, "has applied to immigrate to Southern Ontario as a restaurateur." In a 2001 report, the United States Drug Enforcement Administration stated that during the late 1990s, Vancouver "emerged as a key operational headquarters for ethnic Chinese criminal elements."

"THERE WASN'T A WEED IN THE FIELD"

Even the best law enforcement intelligence information cannot confirm whether Canada became home to large numbers of triad members and headquarters to their international operations. What is clear is that the scope and sophistication of Asian organized crime in Canada expanded dramatically throughout the 1990s and into the next millennium. Not only did Southeast Asian criminal groups elevate Canada's role as a destination and transit country for heroin and illegal immigrants, it helped establish the country as an international centre for currency counterfeiting, credit card fraud, product piracy, and the production and export of high-grade marijuana and chemical drugs. These developments paralleled the international growth of Chinese organized crime and the diversity of its illegal enterprises. Collectively, criminal syndicates with roots in Hong Kong, Mainland China, and Taiwan represent the most widespread transnational organized criminal phenomenon in the world, with a presence in dozens of countries and tentacles in every conceivable profit-oriented criminal activity.

Asian criminals continue to be the largest suppliers of heroin in Canada and have become heavily involved in the trafficking of cocaine as well as the production and distribution of marijuana and synthetic drugs. Because Canada has become such a well-established transit country for Southeast Asian heroin, as well as a source for marijuana and chemical drugs, many of the Asian drug trafficking investigations undertaken by federal and state enforcement agencies in the U.S. have a Canadian link.

In December 1998, 70 kilos of 99 percent pure heroin was seized from a storage locker in the Vancouver suburb of Richmond. The investigation focussed on major heroin importation operations by a transnational network made up of Chinese nationals from the mainland. The amount of heroin seized led the RCMP to speculate that much, if not all, was destined for the U.S. Members of this syndicate were also producing counterfeit documents and credit cards and were smuggling illegal migrants into Canada. This heroin seizure was eclipsed less than a year later when the RCMP and Canada Customs hauled in 156 kilos in the fall of 2000 in two related cases. On September 2 of that year, the RCMP's Asian Organized Crime Unit in Vancouver arrested seven men with connections to a group of ex–Mainland Chinese drug suppliers, charging them with smuggling more than 99 kilograms of nearly pure heroin, which was shipped from Guangdong province in China. The heroin intercepted in Vancouver was found compressed into fifty-five airtight plastic bricks and hidden inside the false bottom of a shipping container. Two days later, police and customs agents in Toronto intercepted another 57 kilograms of heroin, along with 17 kilos of ecstasy pills and $1.2 million in Canadian and U.S. cash. The drugs seized in Toronto had been shipped by rail after arriving in Vancouver from China concealed in 1,700 fake duck eggs, which were hidden among a larger consignment of 174,000 real duck eggs. The two shipments of heroin were estimated to have a street value of at least a quarter of a billion dollars and was almost twice the size of all Canadian heroin seizures typically made in a year. Three people were arrested in Toronto in connection with the second seizure. Among those arrested was fifty-year-old Wei Hong Sun and her son Zhi Yong (Chris) Huang, who operated the food wholesale business where the eggs were delivered. Police told the media that the mother was at the "top of the echelon" in the criminal organization and was behind the importation of both shipments. She later received a seventeen-year sentence and was forced to forfeit $2.5 million in cash and other assets.

In the early 1990s, Vietnamese crime groups began working as street-level heroin distributors for Chinese drug wholesalers in Ontario, British Columbia, and Alberta. By the end of the decade, Vietnamese criminal groups were displaying an increased level of autonomy while establishing their own niche in

Corporal Steve Wade, of the Vancouver RCMP, displays 70 kilos of 93 percent pure heroin seized from a storage locker in Richmond, B.C., on November 26, 1998.

Canada's crowded illegal drug market. Some began importing heroin on their own, using couriers to body pack up to five kilograms of heroin from China, Hong Kong, or Vietnam. The drugs were usually brought through the Vancouver International Airport for distribution in B.C., Alberta, and Washington State. Vietnamese groups also became heavily involved in street-level cocaine sales, especially in Greater Vancouver. Another criminal forte of the Vietnamese groups is marijuana production. According to the 2003 annual report of the CISC, "Vietnamese-based groups continue to be extensively involved in the large-scale cultivation and trafficking of residentially-grown marihuana. These groups are entrenched in B.C. and Southern Ontario and are expanding marihuana cultivation in Alberta and Atlantic Canada. These operations are typically highly organized with extensive interprovincial networks and drug distribution networks to the U.S." In its 1999 annual report, the CISC estimated that "Vietnamese criminals in Vancouver now are responsible for approximately 80 percent of the hydroponic marihuana grow operations that are investigated by the police."

The large profits and low risks involved in growing marijuana in Canada has also attracted Chinese criminal groups. In the summer of 2005, large marijuana farms discovered on rural properties in various provinces were linked to Hong Kong–based triads as well as to criminals with roots in Mainland China. In late July, the Ontario Provincial Police arrested and charged Zhi Ji Chu after discovering more than 21,000 plants on a farm near Iroquois Falls east of Timmins. The crop was planted in mounds to make them look like potatoes and was meticulously cared for. "There wasn't a weed in the field," a police spokesperson told reporters (apparently with no pun intended). During that summer, police raided two other large outdoor grow ops in Ontario, containing 15,000 and 7,000 plants, respectively. Both fields were being tended by Chinese immigrants. In Manitoba, the RCMP discovered five large grow operations in August and September, all located on farmland. In total, 41,700 pot plants were seized, with the largest boasting 13,200 plants. In at least three of the sites, migrant Chinese labourers were found tending to the crops. In September, police seized nine thousand marijuana plants from a farm in Nova Scotia and arrested Chi Keung Mak, who could not speak English and who was known by his new neighbours simply as "John." Also in September, police found close to 30,000 plants at a rural property in Adamsville, New Brunswick. Part of this crop included a strain of marijuana that grows less than a metre high, which supposedly is to help avoid detection by police aerial surveillance. Two Chinese males were arrested at the farm. The RCMP in New Brunswick stated that this and three other pot farms found that month in New Brunswick were the work of Chinese criminal groups that have links to Hong Kong and Mainland China. The Mounted Police speculated that Asian crime groups are relocating to provinces like New Brunswick and Nova Scotia because of an increased crackdown on marijuana grow operations in Central and Western Canada.

The quantity of the marijuana discovered on the farms, and in Canada generally, was far greater than the domestic market could absorb, which confirms that a great deal of the pot produced in Canada is shipped to the U.S. In its 2006 *National Drug Threat Assessment Report*, the U.S. Justice Department wrote, "increasing distribution of high potency marijuana by Asian criminal groups as well as expansion of domestic high potency marijuana production appears to be significantly raising the average potency of marijuana in U.S. drug markets, elevating the threat posed by the drug." The report goes on to blame the "sharp rise in marijuana smuggling from Canada via the U.S.-Canada border" on Asian criminal groups, which are "increasing their position as wholesale distributors of Canada-produced marijuana" in the United States.

Chinese crime groups in Canada have also become involved in the production and distribution of synthetic drugs. In September 2005, the RCMP raided a home in Richmond, B.C., that housed a large-scale ecstasy lab containing 200 kilos of the illicit drug worth an estimated $15 million. Police were tipped off after Transport Canada officials found a package addressed to the Richmond residence from Shanghai that contained 600 kilos of the precursor chemical sodium borohydride. In combination with other chemicals, it was enough to produce 15 million ecstasy pills with a street value of $300 million, police said. Four men of Chinese descent, including two Richmond residents and two Hong Kong residents, were arrested. A day later, the RCMP found another clandestine ecstasy lab in Richmond in a home owned by Alfred Luk, prompting the Vancouver RCMP Drug Section to conclude that the two sophisticated labs were linked to one Chinese organized crime group. Chinese criminal syndicates are also known to import large quantities of finished ecstasy into Canada, which, along with the Canadian-produced pills, are then exported to the U.S. According to the 2006 U.S. *National Drug Threat Assessment Report*, "Canada-based Asian criminal groups with access to MDMA from Canada and Europe have surpassed Russian–Israeli drug-trafficking organizations as the primary suppliers of MDMA to U.S. drug markets."

Along with drugs, immigrant smuggling continues to be a major source of revenue for Asian crime groups. Some intelligence reports even maintain that drug traffickers are leaving the heroin trade to concentrate on people smuggling full-time. The profit margins can be just as big, while the punishment, if one is apprehended, is relatively minor compared to drug trafficking offences. Most of the illegal immigrants are from Communist China and enter Canada using forged passports and other travel documents or have no paperwork and claim refugee status once in the country. The majority of those who arrive are smuggled into the U.S. One Canadian immigration official estimated that 70 percent of all refugee claimants from the Chinese province of Fujian, the biggest source of illegal immigrants to Canada, disappear once they arrive in the country and never show up for their immigration hearing.

In December 1998, two Chinese people smuggling networks were dismantled and forty-seven people were arrested by Canadian and American authorities. Over a period of at least two years, these groups reportedly brought as many as 3,600 people from the Fujian province to New York State through Vancouver and Toronto. Most had been provided with fake passports and other travel documents to get into Canada and had passed through one or more intermediary countries before arriving by plane in Vancouver or Toronto. Once in Canada, they were instructed to claim refugee status. The fee was as much as $50,000 per person and all of the passengers had to pay a deposit before leaving China. Before being snuck across the Canada-U.S. border, they were taken to Toronto and held until another portion of their passage was paid off. From Toronto, they were driven to Eastern Ontario and then smuggled into the U.S. across the St. Lawrence River through the Akwesasne reserve. Once on the other side, they were transported to New York City where many were held until they worked off their debts in restaurants, sweatshops, and brothels. Police believe that over the course of two years, the smugglers moved 100 to 150 people per month for a total estimated profit of $170 million. During one sixty-day period, the smugglers orchestrated thirty-three separate trips across the border.

In the summer and fall of 1999, Canadian authorities intercepted four ships that were being used to smuggle more than five hundred illegals from the Fujian province into British Columbia. Each ship carried no fewer than one hundred people. One ship, apprehended about fifty nautical miles west of the northern tip of Vancouver Island at the end of August, had 190 people on board. It was an old dilapidated fishing trawler that was taking on water, leaking diesel fuel and oil, had no anchor, and was rusted thin in places. It had no life jackets or life rafts. Like most illegal migrants from China, almost all aboard the four ships claimed refugee status once they were taken into custody.

As federal authorities tightened security at traditional entry points for illegal immigrants, such as airports, people smugglers began testing new entry routes into the continent. One fresh approach was to have the illegals pose as vacationing passengers on transatlantic cruise ships. At least thirty-one people from China entered or tried to enter Canada illegally after disembarking three cruise ships that docked in Halifax in the fall of 2005. Seventeen of them were carrying false South Korean passports. The Chinese passengers said they needed to get off the ship because of seasickness, then slipped past border control agents, and made their way to the Via Rail station near Halifax's cruise ship terminal. All of them jumped on a train for Toronto and have since disappeared.

In many of the people smuggling cases organized by Asian criminal syndicates, if the illegal immigrants cannot afford the thousands of dollars it costs to book passage to North America, they are forced to pay off their debts with their labour. They also may be used to smuggle drugs in return for safe passage. Asian migrant smuggling has also become critically interconnected with the sexual slave trade in Canada and the U.S. According to a 1993 federal intelligence report:

> With the growing involvement of Asian crime syndicates, the Asian sex trade has become big business. Many of the women, wanting to escape poverty or menial jobs at home, are lured to Canada with promises of waitressing or office employment. Upon arrival here, however, many are kept virtually as slaves, their passports and papers confiscated. They undertake to repay their fare from their earnings while their employers contrive that they remain in debt for as long as they continue to attract punters. The women are often sent to other syndicate-owned brothels in major

A Chinese immigrant smuggling ship is towed to Esperanza Inlet on the west coast of Vancouver Island.

urban communities and, during the transit may be used as narcotics couriers.

In September 1997, police and immigration officials in Canada and the U.S. arrested about forty people involved in a prostitution ring that smuggled women from Thailand and Malaysia into North America through Vancouver. They were then forced to work in brothels and massage parlours in Vancouver, Toronto, and Los Angeles. The women, who ranged in age from sixteen to thirty, were recruited by brokers working for Hong Kong–based syndicates. They were forced to work off debts that were as much as $40,000. The prostitution ring was estimated to have made $2 to $3 million a year.

In April 2005, Michael Ng, the forty-two-year-old owner of a small massage parlour in a Vancouver strip mall, was the first person charged with human trafficking offences under Canada's recently enacted *Immigration and Refugee Protection Act*. An eleven-month investigation found that Ng brought women into Canada under false pretences and then forced them into prostitution. He initially became the target of a police probe on May 11, 2004, when one of his female employees phoned police to report that he had assaulted her. In addition to the human trafficking offences, Ng was charged with running a common bawdy house and living off the avails of prostitution.

Despite the legalization of many forms of gambling, Asian crime groups still have a hand in illegal gaming, including professionally run underground mah-jong clubs, casinos, lotteries, and sports betting. Some of these gambling operations come with their own "credit" department, while Chinese loansharking operations have also been popping up at legal casinos that attract Asian gamblers. In 2001, the Ontario Provincial Police wrapped up a two-year investigation into Kar Kit Ng, Shui Ming Wu, and Qi Ming Chen, who had been running a loansharking operation inside Casino Rama in Orillia. The gang typically charged borrowers 10 percent interest for a three-day loan, the equivalent of 1,200 percent annually. After pleading guilty, the three received fines of $61,000, $15,000, and $16,000, respectively, and were banned from Canadian casinos for two years.

The Big Circle Boys network is considered to be the country's leaders in sophisticated "commercial crimes" that involve forgery and counterfeiting of items including bank cards, passports and government-issued identification, cigarettes, computer software, digital entertainment, and countless other consumer products. The BCB take advantage of their national and international network to produce counterfeit goods in one part of the country and then have the goods distributed by cells in other parts of the country. This network also facilitates the sharing of personnel, expertise, and resources. In 1998, BCB criminals in Toronto produced over $1 million in counterfeit currency, which was then moved to Vancouver, where a local BCB group wholesaled the notes to smaller criminal groups in the province.

Chinese crime groups are also responsible for most counterfeit credit card fraud in Canada. Their market is international in scope and estimates provided by credit card companies suggest that they manufacture and distribute 75 to 80 percent of all forged Canadian credit cards in use worldwide. The Big Circle Boys are major contributors to the global counterfeit credit card market and are continually developing new technology to defeat the security mechanisms that have been implemented. In 1998, police in Ontario dismantled a BCB counterfeit credit card operation that had resulted in a loss to Canadian banking institutions of more than $16 million.

In 2002, police cracked a number of credit card counterfeiting rings linked to the Big Circle Boys. On July 3, the Organized Crime Agency of B.C. announced they had arrested members of a Vancouver BCB group that was counterfeiting credit cards and trafficking in hundreds of kilograms of marijuana. Arrest warrants on multiple charges were issued for twelve people. The provincial agency discovered another BCB-linked credit card factory in Vancouver with equipment and materials imported from California. Information from legitimate credit cards was stolen through a process of "skimming" legitimate cards at retail stores. The stolen data was then downloaded into a laptop computer where lists of numbers would be produced for sale.

These lists would be sent by fax to Vancouver where a broker would sell them to someone with access to the counterfeit credit card factory. Earlier that year, police in Calgary laid 478 criminal charges against sixty-three people involved in a multi-million-dollar credit card fraud. Using stolen information, a duplicate card — impeccable in every detail, including built-in holograms and anti-theft security device — would be produced and then sold on the street for between $500 to $1,000.

Ontario and British Columbia continue to be the main bases of operation for Asian criminal groups, although they have established a presence in almost every province. No longer do they confine their activities to large cities, but are also moving into smaller towns and rural areas where they set up credit card or cigarette counterfeiting plants, operate marijuana farms, or sell heroin at the retail level. In British Columbia, the Big Circle Boys are the dominant Asian organized crime force in the province where they are involved in credit card fraud, heroin importation and trafficking, immigrant smuggling, synthetic drug production, organized auto theft, and the smuggling of marijuana supplied by Vietnamese crime groups into Washington State. Vietnamese crime groups in B.C., some of which have between two hundred and three hundred members, are dominant in the street-level heroin and cocaine trade in Vancouver and on the Island and are known to co-operate in the drug trade with Chinese criminal groups, the Hells Angels and Indo–Canadian gangs. The Lotus Family continues to be active in B.C. and, in 1998, the Criminal Intelligence Service Canada puts its membership at more than one hundred. Through its involvement in cocaine and heroin importation and trafficking, credit card fraud, extortion, and cellular telephone cloning, members of the Lotus gang has connections with the Big Circle Boys, the Hells Angels, and Indo–Canadian crime groups. In its 2001 annual report, the CISC charged that Asian crime groups in the Lower Mainland were targeting high schools with large English-as-a-second-language populations "as a labour pool for a variety of lower-level criminal activities, as a source of recruits and as insulation to shield senior members from the attentions of rival gangs or law enforcement."

In Alberta, Asian criminals dominate street-level cocaine trafficking in urban centres and control a significant portion of marijuana grow operations in the province. In 1998, police in Calgary arrested senior members of the Kung Lok and Wo Sing Wo triads on drug- and immigration-related charges. The Kung Lok has been in Calgary since the early 1980s and is active in the importation of heroin, prostitution and gambling, credit card frauds and illegal alien smuggling. By the early 1990s, its membership was around sixty-five people. Two years later, law enforcement estimates pegged the number of active members in the group at between ten and twenty. In Saskatchewan, Asian crime groups are primarily involved in the importation of cocained heroin from British Columbia and Alberta for distribution throughout the province. They are also involved in selling contraband liquor and cigarettes. In Regina, Chinese immigrants with links to the Big Circle Boys in Vancouver are involved in currency and credit card forgery, drug trafficking and the theft of autos. In 1998, one police operation targeted an Asian gang in Winnipeg suspected of trafficking, cocaine, which was imported from B.C. Thirty-five men and women were arrested in May 1999.

In Ontario, the Big Circle Boys have turned Toronto into the credit card counterfeiting capital of the world and use Pearson airport to smuggle heroin and illegal immigrants into the country. Chinese triads, the BCB and Asian youth gangs regularly share expertise and personnel in the pursuit of numerous other criminal enterprises in the province, including organized prostitution, auto theft, the importation and production of chemical drugs, and the importation of counterfeit cigarettes and numerous other pirated products manufactured in Asia. In Quebec, according to the 1998 annual report of the CISC:

> ... more than 350 hard core Asian-based criminals are divided among 35 loosely structured gangs, two thirds of which are national or international in scope. These gangs regularly share personnel and expertise and are involved in heroin trafficking and loansharking. They also stage home invasions, although the extent of this activity is difficult to gauge as up to

95 percent of victims do not file a complaint. Outside of these 35 known gangs, Quebec is also the base for approximately 50 Vietnamese subjects engaged in organized shoplifting throughout Ontario and Quebec. The fruits of their labours are disposed of within their own community. Police in Quebec have curtailed the activities of approximately 20 individuals of Cambodian and Laotian origin who had committed thefts from machines of the Société de loteries vidéo du Québec during the first six months of 1997.

Leaving no part of the country uncovered, the Big Circle Boys and Chinese criminals with ties to Hong Kong triads, have established a presence in the Maritime provinces. The Port of Halifax has been used as a conduit for heroin imported from Asia, while illegal Chinese immigrants are being smuggled into the country through the port and along the thousands of kilometres of unguarded shoreline. The discovery of vast marijuana farms in New Brunswick and Nova Scotia that are tended by Chinese immigrants are also signs that the BCB and triad-connected criminals have moved east.

Numerous questions still abound concerning the Chinese triads and Big Circle Boys, the two most dominant Asian organized crime genres in Canada and the world. Their exact origins, the size of their active membership, their organizational structure, and whether traditional rituals and ceremonies still apply are all subjects that continue to be shrouded in uncertainty and controversy. In 2000, the U.S. National Security Council stated there were fifty triad groups and subgroups in the world with an estimated membership of between 50,000 and 100,000. While some triads have been said to include as many as 25,000 members worldwide, this number includes individuals only loosely associated with the group, such as legitimate businesspeople, tong members, youth gang members, and other associates, not to mention those who have been subject to extortion or forced to take out a membership. The number of active criminal members in a Hong Kong–based triad, such as the 14K, are perhaps in the hundreds and given the loose structure of criminal triads today, much of its illegal activities are carried out by small cells that come together to undertake specific criminal conspiracies in conjunction with other associates and criminal groups.

Some Chinese criminals continue to use triad jargon and rank structure to exploit the mysticism associated with the once-powerful triad societies mostly to impress new recruits, enhance their credibility with business partners, or to instill fear in the public, especially among ethnic Chinese living overseas. In traditional strongholds like Hong Kong, Taiwan, Canada, and the United States, triad groups have lost much of their power and only account for a fraction of Asian organized crime in these places. The Phoenix of Asian organized crime that has arisen from the ashes of the once-powerful triads is the Big Circle Boys, a title that is now just a vague umbrella term applied to a loose network of gangs, primarily made up of Chinese nationals from the mainland. This criminal network constitutes the most widespread, diverse, and sophisticated criminal conspiracy in Canada and perhaps the world. While the Italian mafia may have set the standard for organized crime in the 12th century, the Big Circle Boys are setting the standard and raising the bar for transnational organized crime in the new millennium.

CHAPTER 12

A DIFFERENT KIND OF SNOW

The Colombian Cartels Come North

THE LAND OF TRANQUILITY

It was as if God had decided to put to the test every capacity for surprise and was keeping the inhabitants of Macondo in a permanent alternation between excitement and disappointment, doubt and revelation, to such an extreme that no one knew for certain where the limits of reality lay.

—Gabriel García Márquez, *One Hundred Years of Solitude*, 1970

On the sixty-sixth day of a heat wave, the crops were almost completely devoured by the frogs, which seemed to have been the only thing raining down from the clear skies during the stubborn drought that had plagued the poor northern New Brunswick village for more than two months. The name of the remote village was Tranquila, an English bastardization of *La Terre de la Tranquilité*, the name first given to the lush, Eden-like area by early French settlers. It was a truly happy village where there was a punctilious conformity, no one was over thirty, no one died, and even things lost eventually re-appeared. But the townspeople had killed so many frogs that the rotting carcasses

were making the children sick, while the adults were plagued with the embarrassing malady of psoriasis. So Michael had the unenviable job of collecting the remains of the celestial amphibians and with a wheelbarrow full of small brown corpses, he crossed the parched land to dump them into a large pile behind the hills. The sun-drenched village had been sad since May. The earth, sea, and sky were of a singular dirt-brown colour, and the village's crop of corn, which, in most summers stood erect, tall and green, was now decaying in the absence of any rain and the unforeseen assault of the gluttonous amphibious interlopers.

The waves of heat rising from the ground were so dense that Michael first thought that the white fuselage of the downed airplane lying in the thick brush bordering the village was a mirage. He had to go very close to see that it was in fact the battered shell of a small plane. Startled by the sight, he ran to retrieve his wife, who, along with her own aged mother, was putting a cold compress on the forehead of her child who had a high fever. He had been sick since the deluge of green frogs. He had just been cured of the vice of eating dirt and his father built him his own room with no windows or doors so the frogs could not get in. Michael took his wife to where the plane quietly rested and the two gazed upon the crashed wreck as if in a trance. It was a small plane, one that could scarcely fit more than a dozen passengers. It read "Commander 980" on one side of its white nose cone, just below a sticker of a Canadian flag that had been ripped in half horizontally, disconnecting the red maple leaf from its thin stem and revealing another yellow-blue-and red-coloured flag. A swath more than a kilometre in length had been cut through the dense bush and preceded the tail of the plane like a makeshift runway. It lay on its belly with no trace of any landing gear or ventral fins. A full-grown fir tree was lodged in the few propeller blades that remained and its wings, dirty and pockmarked, were hopelessly entangled with branches and uprooted shrubs.

After a few minutes of inspecting its exterior, Michael climbed into the plane through the cockpit, which had a gaping hole in its side. There was no sign of death, but neither was there any sign of life. Behind the cockpit there were no passenger seats. Instead, the plane was almost completely filled with burlap sacks. He opened one sack to discover inside a dozen small packages, each one the size and weight of a telephone book of a medium-sized Canadian city. All were tightly wrapped in a gold foil that had been secured by duct tape. A label was affixed to each of the packages containing large black script that read *Calidad perfecta para nuestros mejores clients.*

Michael pulled a knife out of the top pocket of his coveralls and began to cut away at the tape and the foil of one of the packages. Overestimating his own strength, the knife dug into the dense contents and when the knife was removed, Michael noticed that at its tip were the faint traces of a coarse white powder. He disregarded the inconvenience of the packaging, and with a determination his wife had rarely seen in his eyes, he greedily ripped open the package down the middle, spilling white powder over his hands, coveralls, and onto the floor of the plane. Michael was not a well-educated or well-travelled man, but he knew what he had stumbled across. About a month ago, the newspapers reported that the RCMP had arrested two Colombian

men and a Canadian at a privately owned airstrip about 250 kilometres from the village. The Mounties had also confiscated more than 500 kilograms of cocaine. The newspapers said that because of increased enforcement in America, the Medellin Cartel was now flying cocaine into remote areas of the Maritimes where it was offloaded and then smuggled by land south of the border. Michael could not determine why the plane had crash-landed just outside his village. But he supposed that it had run out of fuel before it could find the well-hidden private runway.

On the following day, Michael alerted the other villagers of his find and took them to the plane where he had them carry the many sacks into one of the communal barns that housed the chickens and cows and hay. Michael had planned on awaking early the next morning and making the two-hour drive into town to report his discovery to the RCMP. But just after sunrise when he walked into the barn to pick up one of the packages to take with him to the nearest RCMP detachment he was startled by what he saw. The once-anaemic and sickly-looking cows were bounding about and mooing at the top of their lungs. Michael looked to the corner of the barn and saw that one of the sacks he had found in the plane had been chewed open by the hungry cows and almost two whole packages had been completely devoured. At first he did not know what to make of it. When he caught sight of one cow whose udder looked like it was about to burst, he now realized the full extent of what had happened. He grabbed a bucket and began milking her and could not believe his eyes; from what was one of the sickest and driest cows in the barn came forth a thick white jet stream of milk.

After filling up five 2-gallon buckets, Michael grabbed one of the unopened packages and rushed to his house. An idea had washed over him with a divine lucidity. In the kitchen, he sliced open the package, measured out a tenth of a gram of the white powder into a baby bottle, mixed it with formula, and ran into the bedroom to his wife and crying child, whose skin was now covered by a green moss that was sticky to the touch like wet gum. Despite the opposition of his wife, he placed the bottle in his child's mouth, who began sucking with a growing strength and vitality that had would have seemed impossible just a few days earlier. In only a matter of minutes, his pain subsided, his fever was reduced, and his energy had been regained.

Michael then ran to the well in the centre of the village and began mixing the contents of the package with a bucketful of the minute amount of water that sat many metres below the surface. When he was done mixing, he took his largest watering jug and headed directly to his crops. One by one, he poured a small amount of his fertilized mixture onto the brown and dying fruits and vegetables. It took him until sunset, but he was able to moisten each and every corn stalk, tomato vine, carrot top, and apple tree. Exhausted and with a bad case of sunburn, Michael walked back home, ate a small meal his wife had prepared for him, and slipped into bed. He had conveniently forgotten about his planned trip to the RCMP detachment.

The next morning, Michael and his wife awoke at the first light of dawn to the most miraculous sight; from their bedroom window they looked upon their crops, which were now sporting a vast array of healthy colours; yellow, and green, and red and orange! Still in his pyjamas Michael bounded out of his house and began peeling back the husk of a corn cob taken from a 12-foot-high stalk, to reveal rows of sunshine-yellow kernels. He leaped over to his tomato vines to view with amazement what looked like fire-engine-red pumpkins. He bounced around his crops like a giant cricket, digging up potatoes the size of footballs, carrots that practically glowed with an orange effervescence, and green peas that were greener than an evergreen. He then ran into the barn and began milking his cows. All had their feed supplemented with the miracle additive and were now producing enough milk to quench the thirst of the entire village.

In the afternoon, he hurried from home to home, exhorting his neighbours to come and gaze upon the rejuvenated crops. After Michael let them in on his secret, he took them to the barn and revealed the hidden cache of burlaps sacks. The rest of the villagers agreed that the health of their crops, and their animals, and their children outweighed any moral and legal imperatives that accompanied their find. Only Michael's wife understood that the village's decision was not made out of calm consideration and prescience, but out of the vagaries of a new and dangerous addiction. For the remainder of the summer, the villagers augmented their meagre supply of water with the potent fertilizer, raising crops and cattle fit for a king. They threw a party so joyous that it was surpassed only by the wake held after Big Mama's funeral caravan a few years earlier.

Michael was now treated like a hero and an archangel. The village's sickest and most fragile came to him in search of reprieve from their unfortunate ailments: one who never learned to walk; another who could only sleep during a lunar eclipse, and another who woke up every morning to untie things she'd tied up just the day before. The villagers were making all sorts of conjectures about Michael's future status.

In spite of his new-found notoriety, even Michael could not have foretold the visit by men who claimed ownership over the miracle powder that had fallen from the sky. Michael was the first to encounter the armed men milling about the fringes of the village close to where the plane had crashed. Some of them were dark skinned with ruddy complexions and spoke a foreign language. Others were white skinned, spoke English, and wore ratty, matching red, black and white vests with a crest that included the word "Angels" stitched atop a picture of a winged skull. Michael knew that angels were often sent to earth to help the innocent — or to escort them to heaven — but these imposing, scruffy, foul-talking men did not look or sound like typical angels. One, who appeared to be the leader, was called Gabe or just Spider, probably because of the large spider's head that sat atop his broad shoulders. Familiar with the greed and violence that filled the hearts of some men, Michael was reminded that God often used magic tricks to confuse the immoral and unrepentant.

Michael did not doubt the purpose of these men and knew they would stop at nothing to retrieve their valuable packages. In a poor village chafing under the invasion of ravenous frogs and tax collectors that gave nothing in return, there would be no sympathy for the ambulatory acrobats of illicit aeroplanes and their nefarious fare who had disturbed the probity of the village. Michael ran back to the village to warn the others. He first stopped by his own house to grab his rifle and then ran door to door exhorting his neighbours to do the same. Before all the men from the village could be gathered in a makeshift militia, the foreign-sounding men and the winged English-speaking angels descended upon the village and, spotting the heavily armed farmers, pulled out their own arsenal and began unleashing a barrage of bullets. The villagers, who outnumbered the intruders ten to one, returned fire and, because of their years of experience as hunters in the northern bush, none missed their target.

Quickly, the villagers gathered up the bodies and in their horse-drawn carriages and wheel-barrows transported them to a heavily forested area hidden behind a small hill about a mile from the village square. The villagers were overwhelmed by the most primordial expressions and were unrepentant. A deep mass grave was prepared and the bodies were thrown into the cavernous hole — making sure the angel with the spider's head was on the bottom — and then the hole was filled.

The villagers now naively believed they would be safe from future human intruders and went about their business like priests tending to their catechism, looking after their enlarged crops, milking their bloated cows, feeding their chickens until they were the size of ostriches, and wiling away the afternoons racing horses that were faster than Apollo.

But the village was due another visit, this time from a force they knew they could not eliminate so furtively. Back in Edmundston, the Mounties had arrested two brown foreign-speaking men con-spicuously out of place among the pale Maritimers. This led to the discovery of an arsenal of weapons, passports with the pictures of the three brown men who were now buried beneath the ground, broken plates, and pictures of dark clouds in the trunk of their car. They also found maps of New Brunswick and circled in red was an area close to Tranquila. On the back of the maps, written in what appeared to be Spanish, was a detailed description of the downed plane, the pilots, and the cargo.

Expecting to encounter a heavily armed band of modern desperadoes, the local Mounties called for backup from other detachments. After almost two days of searching, the tactical force of close to thirty police officers arrived at the site of the plane and began searching the general area.

But these new intruders were also spotted by the villagers who were maintaining an around-the-clock vigilance for possible trespassers. With a hue and a cry, the alarm was sounded and a phalanx of villagers, who were all irritable because of a highly contagious case of insomnia, descended on the armed officers, whose uniformed identity was veiled by the thick bush and the hallucinogenic paranoia of the armed villagers. Without warning, Michael and his neighbours fired indiscriminately into the forest. The gunfire was returned. When the smoke cleared, six of the villagers, including Michael, and five police officers, were dead. After even more police reinforcements arrived, the whole village, including the cows and the chickens, were arrested and taken to Fredericton where they were arraigned, charged, tried, and sentenced for first-degree murder. The mass grave was excavated, but police found only the remains of the three brown men. The bodies of the Angels were nowhere to be found. A few weeks later, the frogs also disappeared for good.

THE CHESS PLAYERS

Beginning in the mid-1970s, the criminal underworld in North America began undergoing significant changes as the popularity of cocaine skyrocketed. The drug was no longer associated with deviants and desperate drug addicts, but with the affluent glitterati. Except for the spike in popularity of marijuana in the 1960s, never before had any illegal drug enjoyed such a mercurial rise in demand in such a short period as cocaine did in North America during the late 1970s and 1980s. The enormous profits that ensued from the rapidly expanding cocaine market proved highly alluring to many existing and fledgling crime groups. Yet, it was the Colombian "cartels" that exercised an almost global monopoly over the highly popular drug, fuelling their rise as the world's most profitable and sophisticated organized criminal conspiracy.

Up until the mid-1970s, the Colombians were the largest processors and suppliers of the cocaine that made its way into the U.S. and Canada. But they did not control its importation or distribution in these countries, which was under the control of Cuban nationals, the Cosa Nostra, outlaw biker groups, and a varied assortment of other criminal entrepreneurs who were able to establish connections with Colombian sources. Realizing that the most money was to be made in the wholesale distribution of the drug, some of the more ambitious Colombian suppliers embarked on a campaign to take over all aspects of the international cocaine trade. They began by building up their own capacity to ship their product from Colombia to the U.S. and Canada, systematically eliminating or joining with their competitors, pulling together a transnational distribution system, and establishing cells within the two countries to handle importation, marketing, and distribution.

In their quest to monopolize the cocaine trade, many of the independent Colombian suppliers came together as a loose business co-operative. At the forefront of this cocaine revolution was an amalgam of businessmen and criminals from Medellin, Colombia, who formed an alliance that would become one of the largest, most profitable, and most violent transnational criminal operations of its day. Among the founders of the so-called Medellin Cartel were José Gonzalo Rodriguez Gacha (a bodyguard who would go on to pioneer new land-based smuggling routes to America through Mexico), Carlos Enrique Lehder-Rivas (the American-born marijuana dealer who revolutionized cocaine exporting by pioneering the use of private airplanes for bulk shipments), the Ochoa brothers (Fabio, Jorge, and Juan David) who invested portions of their ranching-family fortune into cocaine, and a common street thief and aspiring drug mule whose bloody reign as the self-anointed leader of the cartel would make him the most public and vilified symbol of Colombian cocaine traffickers, Pablo Emilio Escobar Gaviria.

Pablo Escobar, left, is shown with his wife and son while attending a soccer match in Colombia.

Lehder is credited with bringing the men together in 1978 and suggesting they begin transporting large quantities of cocaine using his growing fleet of airplanes via Norman's Cay, an island just 200 miles from the Florida coast. The Ochoa brothers were the venture capitalists and established one of the first Colombian distribution cells in Florida. Lehder and his partner, George Jung, coordinated the airborne transport of cocaine. Gacha established Tranquilandia — a sprawling cocaine processing complex located in the Colombian jungle that included nineteen separate laboratories capable of producing 300 tons of cocaine a year, a 3,500-foot runway, and a dormitory that could house as many as eighty people — and teamed up with Mexican intermediaries to transport the finished product to America via land routes. Escobar gradually took charge of supply, production, enforcement, transportation, and government corruption. The elimination of competitors, through the formation of a cartel and the unrestrained use of violence, combined with the development of an international organizational structure, mass marketing, a fleet of airplanes, trucks, and mother ships, sophisticated processing labs, and massive payoffs to Colombian government officials allowed the Medellin Cartel to consolidate its operations and dominate the cocaine market throughout much of the 1980s. At the peak of its power in the middle of the decade, the cartel was said to have controlled roughly 80 percent of the cocaine market in the United States and was generating revenues between $40 and $60 million a month, prompting a 1989 edition of *Forbes* magazine to list Escobar as one of the ten richest men in the world.

The only other Colombian drug trafficking syndicate that rivalled the Medellin-based traffickers was the Cali Cartel, which was headed by Gilberto Rodriguez Orejuela, who was also known as "the Chess Player" for his carefully planned business moves. Assisting him was his younger brother, Miguel, a lawyer who was reputed to be such a micromanager that he personally monitored the cocaine conglomerate's electric bills and magazine subscriptions, and José Santacruz Londono, a one-time engineering student who became New York City's principal cocaine supplier during the early 1990s. The Cali Cartel was generally less reliant on the indiscriminate use of violence compared to its Medellin counterpart, preferring government corruption and a more businesslike approach. As Ron Chepesiuk writes, "at the height of its power in the early 1990s, the Cali Cartel was running its criminal empire more on the model of a multinational corporation than a criminal enterprise. It treated its members like company employees, hired the best person for the job, used business strategy to market its illegal product, and shifted operations from one locale to another as economic and political conditions necessitated." The Cali Cartel perfected the corporate approach to international illicit narcotics trafficking. Reporting to Gilberto Rodriguez Orejuela, the acknowledged CEO of the cartel, were his senior vice-presidents responsible for finance, supply, production, transportation, marketing, sales, and enforcement. Under these men was a cadre of regional directors who headed importation and distribution cells located in different jurisdictions in the United States, Canada, and Western Europe. As the U.S. Drug Enforcement Administration put it, the "Cali leaders ran an incredibly sophisticated, highly-structured drug trafficking organization that was tightly controlled by its leaders in Cali. Each day, details of loads and money shipments were electronically dictated to heads of cocaine cells operating within the United States. The Cali drug lords knew the how, when, and where of every cocaine shipment, down to the markings on the packages. The Cali bosses set production targets for the cocaine they sold and were intimately involved in every phase of the business — production, transportation, financing, and communications."

The ascendance of the Cali Cartel during the late 1980s and early 1990s was due in part to the self-destruction of the Medellin Cartel, which was brought about by the campaign of terror Pablo Escobar launched in Colombia in which hundreds of government officials, police, prosecutors, judges, journalists, and innocent bystanders were murdered. His orgiastic use of violence, which was used to eliminate competitors, silence informants, and intimidate the government into banning the extradition of Colombian nationals to the U.S., prompted an intensive government clampdown in Colombia and the U.S. against Escobar and his Medellin colleagues. Carlos Lehder was extradited to the U.S in 1987 where he was tried and sentenced to life without parole for shipping at least 16,000 kilos of cocaine into the U.S. since the late 1970s. José Rodriguez was gunned down by police in Colombia in 1989 and, following the largest manhunt in the country's history, Pablo Escobar was killed by the Colombian National Police in 1993. The Ochoa brothers turned themselves in to Colombian authorities in the early 1990s in exchange for lenient prison terms. Although behind bars, the brothers continued to organize cocaine shipments to the U.S. and in 2001, four years after the Colombian government passed a constitutional amendment allowing the extradition of its citizens, Fabio Ochoa was sent to the U.S. where he was convicted and sentenced to a thirty-year term on drug trafficking and money laundering charges for his role in shipping an estimated 30 tons of cocaine into the United States every month from 1997 to 1999.

With the implosion of the Medellin Cartel in the late 1980s, the Cali Cartel became the world's dominant cocaine marketers for much of the 1990s, supplying between 70 and 80 percent of the cocaine reaching the United States and 90 percent of the drug sold in Europe. The new-found pre-eminence of the Cali Cartel also made it the number-one target of the U.S. DEA. In 1995, fifty-nine people associated with the cartel were indicted in a Miami courtroom, among them Gilberto and Miguel Rodriguez, José Santacruz, and some of their top lieutenants. Because they could not be extradited to the U.S. under Colombian law at the time, they were sentenced by a Colombian court, with Gilberto receiving thirteen years and Miguel being handed a twenty-one-year term. Santacruz was also arrested and jailed that year, but escaped before being sentenced. A year later he was shot dead by Colombian police. When evidence came to light that the Rodriguez brothers continued to orchestrate the export of large quantities of coke into the U.S. while behind bars, the American government took advantage of extradition laws enacted in Colombia and, on September 27, 2006, Gilberto and Miguel Rodriguez Orejuela pleaded guilty in a Florida courtroom to federal cocaine trafficking offences. Each was sentenced to thirty years in prison and together they were forced to forfeit a whopping $2.1 billion in cash and assets.

The dismantling of the two major Colombian trafficking networks resulted in a rapid decentralization of the cocaine industry as hundreds of smaller operators in Colombia filled the void. Realizing that the large omnibus trafficking organization was too rigid and vulnerable to government interdiction, the new cocaine entrepreneurs formed smaller *cartelitos* that specialized in certain specific functions. For example, one would transport the coca base from the fields to the labs, another would process the paste into cocaine, while another would purchase the final product and sell it to overseas buyers, most of whom were independent from the Colombian suppliers. The Colombians were also facing stiff competition from other South American cocaine trafficking groups, including those from Bolivia, Peru, and Chile. The largest of the post-Colombian cocaine traffickers, however, were the extensive and ultraviolent Mexican syndicates, which picked up right where the Medellin and Cali cartels left off.

Despite the fragmentation of the cocaine industry and the rise of the Mexican drug conglomerates, it was the Colombian cartels that set the standard for modern international drug trafficking and the transnational criminal organization. The Colombians were able to reach the pinnacle of the global cocaine trade due to the convergence of many factors. One was simply good timing — they began to take over the trade during the

Miguel Rodriguez Orejuela, in handcuffs, is led before the press at Bogota police headquarters August 6, 1995.

mid-1970s, just as cocaine was becoming the drug of choice in North America. The Colombian traffickers also took advantage of their country's topography of jungles, mountains, and forests that allow coca fields, cocaine-processing laboratories, and airstrips to remain hidden from government forces. Colombia's proximity to the major coca producers of Peru and Bolivia helped establish the country as the single-largest processor of cocaine while nearby transshipment points in the Caribbean and Mexico greatly facilitated transportation to the U.S. The country's Atlantic and Pacific coastlines are also of immense strategic value to cocaine exporters. The history of violence, lawlessness, and government corruption within Colombia also helped produce and protect the numerous drug dealers that rose to power in the country. In short, according to Lee Lamothe and Antonio Nicaso, the "Colombian criminals found themselves in a prime location to exploit the transportation of cocaine out of South America: their country not only had easy access to plum coca growing regions, but also good weather, busy seaports, endemic corruption, and an underworld well experienced in smuggling all manner of goods."

The Colombians also rose to the forefront of the cocaine industry because they were astute, innovative, and ambitious criminal entrepreneurs. They learned the trade from their Cuban and Mexican drug trafficking predecessors with whom they worked in the 1960s and early 1970s and vastly improved upon the techniques and methods used by their teachers. Like other underworld innovators, such as Charles Luciano and Meyer Lansky, the Colombians viewed the intense and often violent competition among small groups as counterproductive. As such, they formed strategic partnerships, not only among Colombian suppliers, but with criminal groups from other locations and nationalities, including Bolivian and Peruvian coca paste suppliers, the Mexican, Dominican, and Caribbean groups that help to transport and distribute cocaine at a wholesale and retail level, as well as a broad range of traditional and emerging crime groups that became major clients in North America and Europe. They also forged partnerships with political extremist groups in Colombia that protected their jungle laboratories and airstrips.

Carlos Lehder

As businessmen, the masterminds between the Medellin and Cali cartels realized the importance of the economies of scale of a large conglomerate and expanded into more extensive distribution networks. The Colombians moved their product to overseas markets in quantities that had never been seen before in the drug trafficking world. They abandoned the inefficient system of body-packing for massive cocaine cargos shipped through the air, land, and sea. Carlos Lehder convinced his associates in the Medellin Cartel that they could fly large quantities of the processed powder in small airplanes to market, thereby avoiding the need for countless trips by drug mules. "He was to cocaine transportation as Henry Ford was to automobiles," U.S. prosecutor Robert Merkle once said of Lehder (who reportedly came up with the innovation at a February 1977 meeting with George Jung in Toronto). Not to be outdone, the Cali Cartel began flying Boeing 727 passenger airplanes filled with cocaine to Mexico, which was then smuggled into the United States by land in tractor-trailers. The cartels also took a page from the Prohibition-era liquor smugglers by using seagoing motherships for multi-ton consignments destined for the United States, Canada, and Europe. Cocaine also arrived at the ports of the United States and Canada in marine containers.

The Colombian cartels have been touted as the most innovative and sophisticated of the transnational criminal genres because of the unique way they structured their organization and illegal activities. The two cartels revolutionized international drug trafficking; first, through the vertical integration of the cocaine business (they were organized to control almost every step of the process, including coca refinement, transportation, financing, wholesale distribution, etc.) and second, through their inventive structure, which ingeniously merged the organizational traits of the criminal syndicate, the multinational corporation, and the terrorist group. Both innovations were characterized by an intricate division of labour and a compartmentalization of specialized functions that was used to maximize efficiency and productivity. Carl Florez and Bernadette Boyce contend that it was the "expertise of hundreds of specialists," similar to that employed by a multinational corporation, which kept the cartels "functioning smoothly and efficiently." Their staff included accountants, lawyers, chemists, realtors, travel agents, and graduates of some of the world's top business schools. The Medellin Cartel was the first foreign drug trafficking entity to establish distribution cells in North America. Each cell contained between five and fifty paid employees who were supervised by a *caleño,* a mid-level manager handpicked and supervised by the upper echelons of the cartel. The distribution cells were often very fluid in that one might be established solely to receive and distribute a single shipment of cocaine. Colombian nationals would be located in an area where the cocaine was to be imported and distributed, often arriving months before the shipment arrived, and then disappearing after the cocaine had been distributed and the money collected and laundered. Following the breakup of the cell, or after a police raid, the Cali Cartel leadership was known to conduct internal "audits" to improve their overseas operation or to ensure their employees or subcontractors were faithful and that the proper security precautions were followed.

Numerous other precautions were undertaken to maximize security and to guard against police interdiction. According to Lee Lamothe and Antonio Nicaso, the cell managers would "determine from local underworld players what lawyers were loyal, what accountants or banks were amenable to taking cash in large quantities, and what the opportunities were for corruption among police and the judiciary." Law enforcement agencies had few opportunities to infiltrate the overseas cells, as they were mostly made up of Colombian nationals who were related to or well known by the cartel's senior or mid-level managers. One criterion used by the Medellin Cartel for recruiting their overseas employees was that they had to have family members in Colombia who would be used as potential hostages in case their expatriate relatives were tempted to become a government informant or entertained ideas of stealing from the corporation. The *caleños* preferred to sell to people they knew, preferably other Colombians, and prospective North American customers were often rigorously screened. This could have included establishing a customer's credentials through a "franchise inspector" that was appointed by the cartel's top management. A strict code of conduct among those working in the overseas cells

was also rigidly enforced, with particular emphasis being placed on keeping a low profile. Even the *caleños* were instructed to live a modest lifestyle and to blend into their neighbourhoods. They were often required to own a legitimate business, not only to erect a guise of legitimacy, but to help launder funds. The semi-autonomous, self-contained, and often code-named cells of the cartels, whereby each one operated with minimal identifying knowledge of the others, was also used to help shield the entire infrastructure; should one of the cells be compromised, the operations of the other cells would not be endangered.

The Cali Cartel was also highly sophisticated in its use of technology, employing computers, pagers, cellular telephones, fax machines, radar, surveillance equipment, and other hardware. In his 2002 article entitled "The Technology Secrets of Cocaine Inc.," Paul Kaihla writes, "The drug lords have deployed advanced communications encryption technologies that, law enforcement officials concede, are all but unbreakable. They use the Web to camouflage the movement of dirty money. They track the radar sweeps of drug surveillance planes to map out gaps in coverage. They even use a fleet of submarines, mini-subs, and semisubmersibles to ferry drugs — sometimes, ingeniously, to larger ships hauling cargoes of hazardous waste, in which the insulated bales of cocaine are stashed." Technology was also central to the Cali Cartel's sophisticated intelligence gathering and counter-surveillance operations, which monitored the actions of its employees, competitors, potential clients, and government agencies. When Colombian authorities raided the offices of a front man for the cartel on May 18, 1994, they seized an IBM AS/400 mainframe computer worth around $1 million. The contents of the hard drive contained the work and residential telephone numbers of U.S. diplomats and enforcement agents based in Colombia, along with the entire call log for the phone company in Cali. Police later determined that the computer, which contained custom-built software that was able to cross-reference phone numbers in Cali with those of American and Colombian government officials, was being used to identify potential informants within the cartel.

While the Colombian drug traffickers modelled their vertical integration after multinational business corporations and borrowed their cellular structure from terrorist groups, they assiduously used the tactical tools of successful criminal organizations: corruption and violence. For years, the Cali Cartel leaders deployed a steady stream of narco-graft — including a $6 million contribution to the successful 1994 presidential campaign of Ernesto Samper — that helped insulate its leadership from government crackdowns. In contrast, Pablo Escobar's rise to power was very much based on his systematic use of violence, which not only targeted competitors and informants, but was used to destabilize the Colombian government and judicial system. It is estimated that the Medellin Cartel was responsible for the deaths of more than two hundred judges and a thousand policemen. In 1984, Escobar even arranged for the assassination of Colombian minister of justice Rodrigo Lara Bonilla, who crusaded against the cocaine traffickers and was responsible for one of the most successful interdictions against the cartel — the March 1984 raid on the Tranquilandia. In retaliation, on April 30, 1984, hired assassins riding on the back of two motorcycles, ambushed the justice minister's car and murdered him in broad daylight. A few months later, Pablo Escobar was indicted for Bonilla's murder. And although the Cali bosses were known more for their use of corruption, they did not shy away from violence, especially in their competition with the Medellin Cartel. This included the formation of a hit squad known as PEPES (People Persecuted by Pablo Escobar), which was behind the deaths of at least sixty of Escobar's relatives and associates. What also distinguished the Colombian cartels' use of violence was their strategy of targeting the family members of their rivals and government officials. Not only was murder frequently used, but the methods were often quite sadistic, such as the *carte de corbata,* the notorious "Colombian necktie" in which the victim's throat is cut longitudinally and the tongue is pulled through to hang like a tie.

THE COLOMBIAN COWBOYS IN CANADA

One of the most sinister and dangerous underworld groups eyeing Metro are the so-called Colombian Cowboys.
—*Toronto Star,* March 4, 1984

While cocaine had been imported into Canada in small quantities since the early part of the century, the first signs of the direct involvement of Colombian traffickers in the country became visible around the time they began to consolidate their hold over the North American cocaine market. On February 22, 1974, Rafael Orjuela Rodriguez, who hailed from Medellin and who was linked to Pablo Escobar long before he rose to the top of the drug trafficking world, was arrested and charged in Brampton, Ontario, after being caught with a few kilos of cocaine. Around the same time, he was indicted in eastern New York for similar offences. He was convicted and sentenced to seven years in Canada, but returned to the drug trade upon release. Fifteen years after his first arrest, he would be detained for outstanding warrants, at which time he was trying to arrange a shipment of 100 kilos of coke to Canada.

Cocaine smuggling into Canada in the early 1970s also bore the hallmarks of the embryonic Colombian trafficking groups, which were relying on female couriers to sneak small quantities across the border after taking a circuitous travel route. In July 1974, a Colombian woman was arrested at Toronto International Airport when customs officers found a kilo of cocaine hidden inside six hollowed-out coat hangers in her baggage. Canada Customs had been tipped off about the women by police in the U.S., who found out she was to pass along the coke to a man in Buffalo who was then to take it to New York City. The woman departed from Bogotá and then flew to Baranquilla, Colombia, then to Panama City, and then to Jamaica, before landing in Toronto. A month later three people carrying Colombian passports were arrested and charged in Vancouver after police seized two kilos of uncut cocaine, which was brought over from Colombia via New York and Seattle and then transported across the border by bus, body-packed by a female passenger. The Colombians then sold the coke to street-level distributors in Vancouver, one of whom paid in counterfeit money. When one of the Colombians purchased two $5,000 drafts at a local bank branch with cash, an astute teller discovered that ten of the $100 bills were fake and the police were called. After escorting the man back to his hotel room, police found cocaine in a suitcase bundled in cellophane and surgical tape. Almost $9,000 in cash and $35,000 in bank drafts were found in another suitcase. Police were also able to identify and arrest his two accomplices, including the female drug mule who admitted to smuggling the drugs across the border.

By the end of the decade, customs officials at Toronto's Pearson airport were making cocaine seizures on a monthly basis, which up to this point was unheard of. According to the 1979 annual report of Criminal Intelligence Service Canada, a spike in demand for cocaine in Ontario was behind the increase in cocaine smuggling: "Cocaine trafficking and its use is increasing throughout the Province at an alarming rate. Hamilton–Wentworth Regional Police report a 100-percent increase over the past two years in charges under the *Narcotic Control Act* and the *Food and Drug Act*. Metropolitan Toronto police reported seizing $180,000 worth of cocaine in March 1978. This figure represents a greater value than the total combined seizure of all other drugs for that one-month period." For the first six months of 1978, customs officials at the Toronto airport seized almost 12 kilos of cocaine, which was, on average, 97 percent pure. Two of the busts involved Peruvian women with one-kilo packages of cocaine taped to their torsos. Early that year, Canada Customs made their biggest bust yet when, acting on an anonymous tip, they nabbed Charles Lawrence Diamond. Described by the *Toronto Star* as an "elegant, expensively dressed man in his late 30s," Diamond was caught with 4.5 kilos of cocaine hidden in specially built aluminium containers that had been inserted between the lining and exterior shell of his two suitcases. The cocaine was traced to Colombia, but to cover his tracks Diamond had flown from Santa Cruz to Buenos Aires then to Lima before flying to Toronto. The court set bail for Diamond at $150,000. Three days later two men flew in from New York with a suitcase full of cash posted his bail.

By the early 1980s, the quantity of cocaine smuggled into the country began to increase dramatically. In February 1981, 72 kilos bound for Canada was seized in Caracas, Venezuela, following a nine-month investigation by the RCMP, the DEA, as well as Colombian and Venezuelan police. Police arrested eleven people who the RCMP alleged were part of a Colombian group that was capable of supplying the Canadian market with $1.3 billion in cocaine annually. The undercover operation had RCMP officers, posing as millionaire drug traffickers, travel to Miami, Buffalo, the Bahamas, Colombia, and Venezuela in order to penetrate the group. Despite the fact that the RCMP could not produce the $6 million asking price for the 72 kilos, four Venezuelan citizens and one Colombian were arrested in Caracas. In Canada, charges of conspiracy to import cocaine into the country were also laid by the RCMP against Colombians Joaquin Montanchez and Hernando García in Toronto. Warrants were also issued for the arrest of two Miami men and two other Colombians, including Alejandro Vasquez-Caicedo, who the RCMP said headed the group. In 1984, the RCMP drug squad broke up a Colombian drug trafficking cell that was attempting to establish a transportation and distribution network between Buffalo and Toronto. Nine kilos were seized from a private airplane at the Buffalo airport and a further 71 kilos that was to be flown to Buffalo was confiscated in South America. According to the RCMP, all of the coke was ultimately destined for distribution in Toronto. A large portion of a massive 2,700-kilo cocaine shipment seized in Hicksville, New York, in June 1988, was also earmarked for Toronto.

For much of the 1970s and 1980s, the majority of the cocaine entering Canada first transited through the United States, and then came across the border primarily through a land crossing or via the air. Police investigations also revealed close co-operation between Medellin cells in the two countries. When the U.S. government made Colombian drug traffickers their number-one enforcement priority in the mid-1980s, Canada's stock as an entry point for cocaine entering both the domestic and American market rose considerably. Colombian drug trafficking groups had already acquired the same affinity for the Canadian coast as other smugglers had enjoyed for centuries. In May 1979, Canadian authorities seized a shipment of 33.5 tons of Colombian marijuana off the coast of British Columbia and, in June 1980, 22 tons were seized off the coast of Nova Scotia.

Montreal also figured "prominently in the cocaine market in Canada in 1984," according to the RCMP's 1985 *National Drug Intelligence Estimate*, "serving as the leading national distribution centre while doubling as a regional distribution point serving Eastern Canada." One noteworthy seizure that exposed Montreal's role as a hub for cocaine importation and distribution occurred at the port of Miami in February 1985, when 1,100 kilos were discovered in a cargo container filled with cut flowers destined for Montreal. As the RCMP acknowledged in its report on the seizure, "intelligence indicates that the traffickers were trying to capitalize on the St. Valentine's Day market by smuggling the contraband in a legitimate cargo."

The qualities that made Montreal attractive as a conduit for cocaine smugglers were the same as those that established the city as a major entry point for heroin for so many decades; the cocaine could be landed via the city's marine ports, flown in through the Montreal airport, or driven to and from New York City by car or truck. Well-established smuggling routes and local expertise already existed and smugglers could also count on corruption and lax security at the airports, marine ports, and border crossings. The South American exporters could also count on capable and willing partners in the Montreal mafia, most notably the Caruana, Cuntrera, and Rizzuto families, who had already transferred part of their operations to South America in the 1960s as part of the global drug trafficking network they were building.

One shipment that arrived at Montreal in October 1974, most likely choreographed by the transnational Cuntrera-Caruana-Rizzuto faction of the Cotroni *decina*, consisted of 5.5 kilos of pharmaceutical cocaine that had been shipped from London, England, and disappeared from a bonded warehouse at Dorval Airport. "That's an inside job and that's organized crime," an RCMP inspector told the media at the time. In one of the decade's most high-profile busts, Alberto Sanchez Bello was arrested in Montreal in 1974 after he sold 4.5 kilos of cocaine to undercover RCMP officers. Sanchez had smuggled the cocaine through Dorval and was able to avoid customs inspection by producing a genuine Bolivian diplomatic passport that had been issued with the help of a secretary to the president of Bolivia.

The Montreal area was also the location of at least two cocaine processing laboratories operating in the mid-1980s. The discovery of the two labs in 1984 and 1985 was surprising, not only because they were the first labs of their kind discovered in Canada, but also because, up to that point, the vast majority of cocaine making its way into North America had already been processed from paste to its crystalline form in Colombia. The labs contributed to the growing evidence that Montreal had now become a nucleus for the cocaine trade on the east coast of Canada, while also revealing the mobility and adaptability of the Colombian drug traffickers, who relocated to Canada because of the growing restrictions on the chemical precursors necessary to process coca paste in Latin American countries. The first lab was discovered by the RCMP drug squad in August 1984 in the garage of a suburban Montreal home. Three kilos of processed cocaine and 500 kilos of coca paste along with chemicals and equipment were seized while a Peruvian national and a Canadian were arrested. In April 1985, a larger lab was discovered by police in Rosemere, a residential suburb about six kilometres north of Montreal. It had apparently begun operations a day earlier and was raided following a year-long police investigation. Within the garage adjoining the suburban bungalow, police found around 30 kilos of coca paste, 1,000 litres of acetone, 80 litres of pure alcohol, and 40 kilos of hydrochloric acid, all of which was required to transform coca paste to its crystalline form. Police learned that the paste had been imported into Canada from Peru in a false-sided suitcase a few days before the raid on the home. Five people were arrested and charged: Jean Renault, a partner in a Montreal law firm; his brother Guy; an Air Canada steward named Carl Veilleux; Francois Salbaing of St. Adele, Quebec; and Francisco Salazar of Lima, Peru. During their trial, the Renault brothers were identified as the main organizers behind the drug lab by Salazaar, a thirty-three-year old chemist who told the court he arrived in Montreal on April 23, 1985, from New York City to help the two set up the lab. The necessary equipment and chemicals were bought the next day and a small batch of cocaine was produced.

At the end of the trial all of the accused were convicted and sentenced: Jean Renault received fourteen and a half years, his younger brother was handed an eight-and-a-half-year sentence, Salazaar received eleven years, Carl Veilleux, whose house contained the lab, was sentenced to nine years, and Salbaing, who bought the lab chemicals, was given four years. An arrest warrant was also issued for Ernesto Barreto-Morales, the suspected Peruvian supplier of the raw cocaine, who lived in Montreal from 1980 to 1984 while working for the Medellin Cartel. Barretto-Morales was captured in the Netherlands after he was caught at Amsterdam's airport with a false passport and $60,000 in American currency. Before he could be extradited to Canada, however, he escaped from Dutch custody. While Barretto-Morales avoided capture on this occasion, he would be arrested twelve years later as part of a cocaine smuggling conspiracy along with Frank Cotroni and his son, Frank, Jr.

"THE POPE DID SO..."

By the end of the 1980s, Canada was emerging as a major entry point for cocaine entering North America. The Colombian cartels had established cells in the country to oversee the importation and domestic distribution of cocaine. These cells were also responsible for establishing Canada as a conduit for cocaine entering the U.S. "Millions of dollars a week, maybe tens of millions of dollars a week" are being earned by the Medellin Cartel in Montreal alone, a U.S. DEA official at the American embassy in Ottawa told the media in September 1989. "We are making much larger seizures than we've ever made before in Canada and we're making a lot more seizures of cocaine coming from Canada to the U.S." Two months before these statements were made, a senior RCMP officer told the media that Canada was virtually powerless to stop Colombians from using the country as an entry point for cocaine because of the insufficient resources dedicated to intercepting incoming planes and ships suspected of carrying drugs. The sobering pronouncements were made following one of the largest cocaine importation schemes to be uncovered in the country to date.

Behind the conspiracy was Alejandro Vasquez Caycedo, a senior manager in the Medellin Cartel who reported directly to Pablo Escobar. One of his tasks was to find new routes for what the *Toronto Star* called an "air force of cocaine" into North America. The man Caycedo relied on to help expedite this mission was a Canadian pilot named Doug Jaworski. It was rare for the Medellin Cartel to trust any non-Colombian with such important duties, but this rule was frequently

broken when it came to pilots, who were in high demand due to the cartel's reliance on small aircraft to smuggle their product into North America. Born to an Air Canada pilot, Jaworski had been flying planes since he was a teenager. He was even given a Cessna by his parents at the age of seventeen. After his mother and father moved to the Caribbean, Jaworski and his airplane moved to Florida.

With his falsetto voice and boyish looks, Jaworski seemed out of place in the world of cocaine smuggling. His initiation took place in the early 1980s when he discovered tens of thousands of dollars in small bills tucked inside the panelling of a plane he was hired to deliver to clients in Bolivia. After confronting the buyers, he demanded an extra $15,000 for delivery, which he received. Soon he was being offered similar cash amounts for the delivery of planes to cocaine suppliers in South America. In a few years, he was locating, selling, and delivering planes to cocaine smugglers, recruiting other pilots and drug mules, and transporting planeloads full of coke and cash in the conspiracy to smuggle thousands of kilos of cocaine into Canada.

Jaworski's move to the big time of cocaine smuggling occurred in the spring of 1988, when he travelled to Medellin to meet with Caycedo, who wanted him to broker the purchase of a Commander 980 aircraft. After Jaworski successfully delivered the plane, Caycedo entrusted the Canadian pilot to carry out another crucial assignment: to find an airstrip in Eastern Canada to which the Colombians could fly cocaine that would then be transported to Medellin cells and other Colombian wholesalers in Toronto, Montreal, New York, and Western Canada. Shortly after receiving these instructions, Jaworski turned on Caycedo. On December 16, 1988, the twenty-nine-year-old pilot walked into the RCMP detachment at Toronto's Pearson airport to offer his services as an informant. In exchange for $200,000, protection for him and his family, and an agreement that he not be charged for past crimes in the United States, Jaworski agreed to become an undercover agent. His assistance set off a domino effect of police investigations that uncovered a network of interconnected cocaine importers and wholesalers that together made up one of the biggest drug trafficking conspiracies in Canadian history.

Unbeknownst to Jaworski or the Mounties, Caycedo's planes began their first sorties into Canada in January 1989. Their destination was the St. Robert airstrip just outside Sorel, Quebec, about 80 kilometres northeast of Montreal. After sending in a test flight to gauge security in the Atlantic corridor, Caycedo was able to fly at least two other cocaine-heavy planes into Quebec undetected. The unmolested flights emboldened Caycedo, who was now anxious to fly even greater quantities into Canada. The Sorel airstrip and the ground personnel entrusted to offload the cocaine had been organized by a Medellin *caleño* known simply as Raoul, who was working with a Montreal cell with direct ties to Pablo Escobar. The cell had been transporting cocaine into the city by land from New York, but with Caycedo's help larger quantities were now being delivered by air directly from Colombia to Canada. To this end, Caycedo was also desirous of an airstrip in New Brunswick, as it was closer to Colombia than Quebec and therefore meant less fuel had to be carried and more cocaine could be packed into a plane. He envisioned small planes with enlarged fuel tanks making the thirteen-hour flight from Colombia to the Canadian east coast nonstop, each one carrying up to 600 kilos of coke.

After considering at least seven locations in New Brunswick that would suite Caycedo's plans, Jaworski and his Mountie handlers settled on the privately owned Weyman airfield, located in Burtts Corner, about 30 kilometres northwest of Fredericton. The airstrip was ideal for smuggling purposes; it was close to the Atlantic coastline, largely hidden from view by a thick forest, and close to a provincial highway. After Jaworski convinced Caycedo that the airstrip would suit his needs, Pablo Escobar was apprised of the plans and personally approved the delivery of hundreds of thousands of dollars needed to purchase the airstrip and take care of other expenses. "The Pope did so ... You know I've seen it," Diego Ganuza, a Cuban-born, Miami-based pilot with the Medellin Cartel reportedly said after Escobar ordered the release of the funds. On February 24, 1989, Jaworski met with Ganuza, who had just flown into Montreal with a vinyl gym bag containing $430,100 in cash. Jaworski took the money straight to the Mounties who marked it as evidence and then convinced the owners of the Weyman airstrip to

co-operate in an undercover sting that was planned for Caycedo's incoming flights. A few weeks later, Jaworski deceived Caycedo into believing that he had used the cash to successfully purchase the landing strip.

In the meantime, Caycedo continued to run planeloads of coke from Colombia to Sorel, Quebec. One March 12, Ganuza was at the helm of a twin-engine Rockwell Turboprop Commander 980 along with co-pilot Hector Crisostomo Cedeno, a Venezuelan-born resident of Colombia. On board the plane were 500 kilos of cocaine. But the flight did not go as smoothly as planned. U.S. Air Defense picked up the Commander over Southern Florida after it had entered American airspace illegally and two F-16 fighter jets were dispatched from Maine to track the small plane. As it became clear that it was headed to Canada, a Blackhawk helicopter carrying U.S. Customs agents took off to search for the RCMP and for permission to fly into Canadian airspace. By 11 p.m. that night, the Commander was closing in on the Sorel airfield with Blackhawk helicopters in close pursuit. Once the plane entered Canadian airspace, however, the Americans were forced to circle in the air, waiting for permission to land. Through their night-vision binoculars, they helplessly looked on as a small truck greeted the Commander on the tarmac of the deserted airstrip and duffel bags were transferred from the airplane into the back of the idling truck. The American pilots received permission to land after a ten-minute wait, but by that time the loaded truck had sped away from the airport. When they touched ground, the U.S. Customs officials were able to capture the pilots of the Commander and forced them, and the airport manager, to lie face down in the airport's parking lot while they searched the plane. No drugs were found on the aircraft, which had no serial numbers, a phony Canadian licence, a makeshift Canadian flag painted on the fuselage, no passenger seats, and extra fuel tanks.

The RCMP and local police arrived around midnight and arrested Ganuza and Cedeno, but since no drugs were found, they could only be charged with such minor infractions as illegal entry and bringing a stolen plane into the country. The pair easily came up with $23,000 in cash to pay their fines before being deported by Canadian immigration officials on March

16, 1989. Ganuza returned to the U.S. where police in Miami placed him under surveillance. The truck that sped away that night with 500 kilos of almost pure cocaine was never found by police. It would have been one of the biggest cocaine busts in Canada to date. According to the RCMP, most of the cocaine was destined for the U.S. although at least 25 kilos had been earmarked for Toronto and another 25 was slated for distribution in Montreal.

Despite this near miss, Caycedo forged ahead with his plans to fly planeloads of coke into New Brunswick, secure in his belief the Weyman airfield was now under the control of Jaworski. On April 2, 1989, Caycedo spoke with Jaworski and informed him that an airplane carrying another 500 kilos of coke would be arriving any day. Jaworski immediately passed the news along to the Mounted Police, who dispatched a team to the airport to sit and wait. Sure enough, at 8 p.m. the next day, a white twin-engine Aero Commander 1000 with no reported flight plan was spotted gliding in, barely above treetops that surrounded the airfield. According to a 1990 report by the Canadian Association of Chiefs of Police, the "airplane had been on a direct flight from Colombia and contained 500 kilograms of high quality cocaine with an estimated street level value of $250 million. The cocaine was the property of the Medellin cartel, Medellin Colombia."

As part of "Operation Overstep," the undercover task force conducted jointly with American law enforcement and police in Fredericton, Montreal, and Toronto, the RCMP planned to allow the aircraft to land unmolested. Once the cocaine was unloaded and the plane refuelled, it would be allowed to return to Colombia in anticipation of another trip that Caycedo had planned three days later. Jaworski had arranged with Caycedo to coordinate the unloading of the planes, although he failed to tell him that the ground crew would be undercover police officers. The RCMP planned to hang on to the 500 kilos until the other flight arrived so all the drugs could be seized as part of a massive controlled delivery that would also allow them to arrest the recipients of the cocaine wherever they may be. The RCMP was forced to quickly change its game plan, however. As they watched the plane approach the runway, the pilot crash-landed after a wing hit a tree. As a result, its landing gear was

damaged, leaving it unable to take off again. The two pilots panicked and ran off into the nearby woods, leaving the Mounties no choice but to track down and arrest José Ali Galindo-Escobar and Fernando Augusto Mendoza-Jaramillo. When the RCMP officers searched the plane they found five hundred individually wrapped one-kilo packets of cocaine. The drugs were removed from the aircraft, placed on a truck, and then taken to RCMP facilities in Montreal. A secondary plan was enacted whereby undercover police agents were to control deliver a 500-kilo load of sugar in individually wrapped packages to the intended recipients of the cocaine in Montreal.

On April 4, Jaworski called Caycedo and deceived him into believing that the plane had safely landed and the cocaine successfully unloaded. Caycedo then provided him with contact information for "John," the Medellin caleño in Montreal that was to take delivery of the merchandise. On April 5, around 9 p.m., RCMP undercover agents delivered the van of sugar to John at a pre-arranged downtown corner, with close to one hundred police officers providing backup. When John arrived, the "coke" was transferred to a van, which the police followed to a garage of a townhouse in the Little Burgundy district of downtown Montreal. At 11:15 p.m. that night, police raided the townhouse and arrested everyone inside. The next day, police in Montreal arrested three other Colombian nationals — Richard Delgrado-Márquez, Carlos Mario Ortega-Gonzalez and Flora Emilse Currea-Miry — who police believed to be members of Medellin cells in Montreal and New York and who were to split the cocaine.

In August of that year, the Canadian Justice Department began extradition hearings to bring Diego Ganuza to Canada from Florida to face charges. At the same time, Canadian officials asked the Colombian government to extradite Vasquez Caycedo, who had been charged in absentia in a Fredericton courthouse with conspiracy to import cocaine into Canada. Because Colombia did not extradite its citizens to other countries at this time, Caycedo never did face justice in Canada. Along with Pablo Escobar, he was intent on ensuring the two Medellin Cartel pilots incarcerated at the York County Provincial Jail in New Brunswick also escaped punishment. As Peter Edwards describes, the two men set in motion plans for a trip to Canada by armed Medellin Cartel mercenaries. "In June 1989, above a bowling alley, Caycedo and Pablo Escobar met with a career criminal connected to political terrorists in Medellin to talk about breaking the pilots out of the York County Jail. They built a small-scale mockup of the jail from photographs and mental notes drawn from visits by the pilots' families. Even if it looked simple, the cartel would leave no details to chance. At the Medellin meeting, an informer would later tell the Mounties, it was agreed that they should use 'as much force as necessary' to free the pilots." The men hired for the planned prison break were connected to armed extremist groups and were promised almost $1 million between them for the prison break. "The team that Pablo Escobar and Caycedo selected for the New Brunswick job had a long history of violent crime, especially bank robberies, stretching as far away as Sweden," according to Edwards.

In the summer of 1989, as the two pilots sat in the Fredericton jail awaiting their trial, a group of at least five Colombian and Cuban citizens slipped into New Brunswick from the U.S. Their first task was to conduct a reconnaissance mission that included surveying the prison and its security, planning their assault, and developing an escape plan. But while they were in Edmundston on September 13, a convenience store cashier grew curious over the rare presence of Hispanic men in the New Brunswick town. With the well-publicized cocaine seizure and the jailing of the foreign pilots fresh in her mind, she grew increasingly suspicious as she noticed the men transfer packages between a van and a white Buick. Thinking it may be drugs, she contacted the RCMP, who passed the tip along to the local police. The Edmundston City Police responded and, following a search of the van, they uncovered an arsenal of guns and ammunition. A second and third vehicle were also found containing weapons and other equipment. Among the cache seized by police were an Uzi submachine gun, a Soviet 762x369 assault rifle, an Israeli 565 assault rifle, six 9-mm semi-automatic pistols, tear gas, a deactivated Japanese hand grenade, more than three thousand rounds of ammunition, burglary equipment, a generator, a high-powered cutting disc, camping gear, survival equipment, and several maps of New Brunswick. Four men were arrested in Edmundston

and a fifth was captured in Saint John while carrying two .22-calibre handguns as he was returning a rental car. Police believed that two more men were still at large. The five men arrested were all carrying false Venezuelan passports in the names of William José Rodriguez, Tito Sanchez, Euovio Manzano, Osvaldo Gonzalez, and Wilmer Roman Zanabria. While police initially suspected they were in town to prepare for another shipment of cocaine, they realized the true purpose of their visit when they discovered two other Venezuelan passports, each containing a picture of one of the two pilots awaiting trial. The planned assault on the 130-year-old cinder-block provincial jail was detailed in a 1990 report on organized crime by the Canadian Association of Chiefs of Police:

> The seized vehicles included a mini-van that, on the day of the attempt, was to be backed up to the fence surrounding the York County Provincial Jail where the pilots were held. Once in place, as the exercise period began, two members of the assault team would exit the van armed with the assault rifles, while a third member at the rear of the van would operate the generator and an electric cutting disc to open the fence. The exercise area was to be entered and the pilots armed. All persons were to escape in the van and drive a short distance and switch to another vehicle also previously seized in Edmundston. All were to drive about seven kilometres to a secluded area where another vehicle change was to be made and the abandoned vehicle hidden under camouflage. The fugitives would then continue towards the New Brunswick/Maine border using back roads and woods trails. A woods trail leading to the St. Croix river near St. Stephen, a New Brunswick/Maine border town, was the last destination in the province. At this point, the group planned to cross the river in a zodiak rubber raft previously purchased in Saint John. Upon entering the United States, a recreational vehicle would transport the fugitives to Florida for passage to Panama and on to Colombia. The support team was made up of as many as 20 persons, mostly having

American citizenship, but of Colombian descent. Their job was strictly that of a support role, such as the renting of vehicles, returning of same, transportation, etc.

Court appearances by the two pilots and the five captured soldiers of fortune were made under the strictest security measures ever put in place for a trial in New Brunswick. More than two dozen specially trained RCMP and Fredericton emergency response members carrying 9-mm machine guns, sniper rifles, shotguns, and pistols were positioned around the courthouse. The two separate trials went off without a hitch and on November 14, 1989, after entering guilty pleas, José Ali Galindo-Escobar and Fernando Augusto Mendoza-Jaramillo were sentenced to twenty-two years for drug smuggling. On December 21, 1989, the five men captured in September pleaded guilty to charges of conspiracy to commit a jailbreak and were sentenced to between nine and ten years' imprisonment.

Through their busts and ongoing intelligence gathering, police were now aware of at least three Medellin cells in Montreal, one of which took possession of the cocaine from the flights into Sorel and another that was to receive the 500 kilos landed in New Brunswick and delivered to the code-named "John." According to Peter Edwards, Caycedo "also had links to Hell's Angels bikers and the well-established West End Gang. Hell's Angels had accompanied cartel members as they timed the drive from Sorel airport to the nearest police station. They were confident the twenty-two minutes the drive took was plenty of time for a getaway. The West End Gang began working under the Colombians in cocaine trafficking shortly after the South American criminals started showing up on the streets of Montreal in the early 1980s."

Despite the success of Operation Overstep, Colombia, Quebec, and the Maritime provinces would continue to be linked together by the importation of hundreds of kilos of cocaine ultimately destined for Montreal. In September 1990, police in Pennsylvania found 1,350 kilos of cocaine stashed in duffel bags aboard a circa-1940 DC-3 plane that had departed from Colombia but was forced to land at the airport in Allentown after running out of gas. The aging cargo plane had snuck into the airport by "piggy-backing"

another aircraft — an age-old military manoeuvre whereby one plane closely follows another, making the former undetectable to radar. The RCMP later reported that the plane was destined for an isolated airfield near Halifax and an offload team was to pick up the cocaine at a nearby drop point and transport it to Montreal, Toronto, and New York. In May 1991, the Quebec Provincial Police put on display 545 kilos of 94 percent pure cocaine, which was seized at Mirabel airport after arriving in April on a cargo flight direct from Medellin and hidden in thirty boxes that contained hammocks. Police replaced the cocaine with sugar and waited for someone to show up and claim the freight. When no one materialized after a couple of weeks, police assumed the distributors were tipped off about the seizure and pulled the plug on the operation.

Around the same time, police became aware of another shipment of cocaine, estimated at between 800 and 2,000 kilos, that was to be delivered to the east coast. An approximation of the size of the illegal cargo was only possible because most of the cache was sitting at the bottom of the ocean 20 kilometres off Cape Race, Newfoundland. The mother ship carrying the payload had sunk after smashing into an iceberg at the end of April and only parts of the boat and 35 kilos of the cocaine could be recovered. The Dominican crew rescued by the Coast Guard was brought to St. John's and charged while Paulin Bolduc, described as the architect behind the huge shipment, was arrested at his home in the Eastern Townships of Quebec shortly after the ship sank. Bolduc was a major Quebec drug dealer with ties to Colombian suppliers. He also had worked with Paul Larue, an associate of the West End Gang, whose own drug dealing would lead to a fourteen-and-a-half-year sentence in Florida (he later implicated a sitting Quebec Superior Court judge who would be convicted in Canada for laundering $1.7 million in drug money when he was Larue's defence lawyer). While behind bars in the U.S., Larue told police that Bolduc had informed him there were 2,000 kilos of cocaine on board the now-sunken ship. Bolduc initially escaped arrest by fleeing the country but he was eventually found, arrested, and in 1996, sentenced to twenty-one years.

In November 1992, the Canadian military and the RCMP made their largest seizure to date after air force jet fighters chased a Convair 580 through the skies of Eastern Canada until it landed at a remote airstrip in Casey, Quebec, about 300 kilometres northeast of Montreal. The twin-engine plane usually holds around forty passengers, but on this flight all the seats were removed to make way for 4,323 kilos of cocaine. The RCMP had been placed on alert after the U.S. Coast Guard informed them of a suspicious plane that was heading north to Canada from Colombia's Guajira Peninsula. When it landed, more than fifty Mounties stormed the plane and found the cocaine, some of it wrapped in gold foil labelled with the slogan "Perfect Quality for our Best Customers." The street value of the cocaine was estimated at $2.7 billion. Police arrested the four men aboard the plane — three Colombian nationals and the Canadian pilot, fourty-four-year-old Raymond Boulanger. After cordoning off the area, two other Canadians were arrested in a truck near the airfield that was carrying fuel for the plane. According to one police spokesperson, the six men were transferred to a secret location out of fear that Colombian drug lords might try to mount another "commando operation" to free them. Police also confirmed a link between the cocaine seizure and a raid undertaken the next day on a 6,000-square-foot cocaine processing laboratory in an industrial park in Laval, Quebec, which contained what one newspaper called "rows of gleaming industrial-sized equipment to refine most types of illegal drugs on the market."

Boulanger was convicted and sentenced to twenty-three years in prison for his role in the conspiracy. In 1998, he ran away from a halfway house after being granted day parole and, two years later, he was arrested in Colombia after reportedly being kidnapped by the extremist Revolutionary Armed Forces of Colombia and released after his $100,000 ransom was paid by his wife. Colombian officials stated that Boulanger had apparently argued with the insurgency group over a required payment for a cocaine shipment to Canada. Boulanger was extradited back to Canada and returned to jail, with an additional four months tacked on for his premature departure from the halfway house. In the summer of 2001, he escaped from custody again, this time when he was left at a church to cut the lawn as part of an unescorted community service program. He was arrested two months later while using a false identity to cash a cheque in Montreal.

In February 1994, the RCMP, along with Canadian military fighter jets and the navy destroyer *Terra Nova,* combined to haul in 5 metric tons of cocaine from the hold of a fishing boat named the *Lady Teri Anne* off the coast of Shelburne in southwestern Nova Scotia. It was the largest cocaine seizure ever made in Canada. Capping a three-year investigation, police and the military were waiting for the ship, although their intelligence indicated a cargo of only 1,000 kilos. Two weeks earlier, the 90 percent pure cocaine had been transported by private aircraft from Colombia to a small island in the West Indies, where it was loaded onto a freighter, the *Pacifico.* From there, the ship sailed to its final destination, just a few nautical miles off the coast of Nova Scotia, where 170 bales of cocaine were offloaded to the *Lady Teri Anne.* Several criminal groups were implicated in this drug smuggling conspiracy, among them the Cali Cartel (which supplied the cocaine), the Rizzuto Family of Montreal, a Lebanese group, and an organization from the northeast shore of New Brunswick. Nine people from Quebec, New Brunswick, and Italy were arrested. Despite the recent massive seizures, they had "relatively little long term impact," on cocaine supply in Canada, the Criminal Intelligence Service wrote in their 1996 annual report. "Supply and demand factors, coupled with the sheer numbers of criminal groups involved in the cocaine trade as a whole, ensure the continued survival of Colombian-based cocaine trafficking organizations both in Canada and abroad."

PROJECT AMIGO

Intelligence information gathered through Operation Overstep was put to good use in Ontario, where a police task force named "Project Amigo" targeted the recipients of cocaine being smuggled into Eastern Canada. According to an April 8, 1989, article in the *Globe and Mail*, the investigation had uncovered within Toronto "a well organized and insulated network for the distribution of cocaine, and the laundering of illicit profits, directed by interests in Colombia." After a year-long investigation, involving 120 municipal and provincial police officers, Project Amigo culminated with a massive sweep on May 17 that resulted in twenty-six arrests and the seizure of 60 kilos of cocaine and $135,000 in cash. In the end, forty-four people, including some closely connected to the Medellin Cartel, faced more than ninety charges. Police officials told the media that the arrests included members of an organization that was bringing up to 400 kilos of almost 100 percent pure cocaine into Toronto on a monthly basis, generating an annual revenue of roughly $40 million. Among those arrested was thirty-six-year-old Nicolas Canizares, who police described as "a prominent lawyer in the Toronto South American community." Others who faced multiple charges were Wilson Castro, Carlos Eduardo Silva, Manuel Padilla, Hernando Arias, Freddy Valencia and his brother, Gabriel Valencia-Posada. Castro and Canizares were identified as the heads of two Medellin cells in Toronto that had been active in the city for at least a decade. In November 1989, the *Toronto Star* reported that the two men "ran highly organized 'crime cells' with a distinct chain of command that included their salesmen, the warehousers who stored the narcotics and the runners who delivered the goods. Although the two cells operated independently, they supplied each other when their colleagues ran low on drugs. Each cell had about 30 people working for it." In October 1989, Nicolas Canizares was handed a twelve-and-a-half-year sentence, while Wilson Castro received thirteen and a half years. Canizares was also disbarred from the Law Society of Upper Canada.

The Amigo squad first learned about the Toronto-based Medellin cells in February 1988 when four people were arrested by city police following an undercover operation that seized three kilos of cocaine, much of it still wrapped in Colombian newspapers. The drug bust actually began as an investigation into the theft of precious metals from Inco mines in Sudbury. Stolen ore concentrates that contained gold, silver, platinum, and other precious metals worth about $16,000 were bought as part of the undercover operation, and when the February raid went down, police came across the cocaine when searching for other stolen minerals. The man at the centre of the stolen-mineral investigation was Charles (Chuck the Bike) Yanover, the former accomplice of deceased Toronto mobster Paul Volpe. In addition to theft, Yanover was charged with conspiracy to traffic in narcotics. It turned out that one of Yanover's cocaine suppliers was Nicolas Canizares. Yanover owed the lawyer $120,000 for the cocaine that

had been seized during the OPP raid and, to pay off the drug debt, he planned on purchasing even more coke to resell. Knowing that Canizares no longer trusted him, Yanover turned to Saul Spatzner to purchase the coke. Spatzner, a plumber by trade who hailed from Ecuador, had already been dealing coke to support his own $1,500-a-week habit and had become one of Canizares' most reliable customers. By the time he was working with Yanover and Canizares, Spatzner had become a police agent after being arrested on trafficking charges. As part of Project Amigo's extensive undercover work, which already involved the purchase of cocaine from Nicolas Canizares and Wilson Castro, Spatzner negotiated a May 1989 deal to buy five kilos from Canizares and his right-hand man, Manuel Padilla. He told the two suppliers the coke was for the Vagabonds Motorcycle Club. When Padilla showed up outside Spatzner's apartment with the cocaine hidden inside a bag of disposable diapers, he was arrested by a dozen undercover police officers.

Throughout the late 1980s and early 1990s, the investigative repercussions resulting from Project Amigo continued to reverberate throughout Ontario. One offshoot of Amigo was "Project Nipas," which culminated in October 1989 when police arrested twenty-five Toronto-area residents during a ten-month probe that ended in the seizure of around 12 kilos of pure cocaine, a .357 Magnum handgun, and $100,900 in Canadian and American currency. In December, a second import ring centred in the Peel Region was disrupted when twenty-five people were arrested and approximately 13 kilos of cocaine was seized. The investigation also led to the seizure of 918 kilos of 90 percent pure coke on a small Caribbean island in October, which police said was destined for Montreal and Toronto. As part of this investigation, police were able to persuade another Colombian insider, code-named Picaro, to inform on his suppliers after he was arrested on drug charges for the third time in 1988. The Colombian native became involved in drugs almost as soon as he arrived in Canada in the early 1970s. He began as a courier, smuggling cocaine on commercial flights from Colombia and gradually began his own distribution cell in Toronto, while helping a Toronto-based Medellin cell launder money. Picaro's information was crucial in leading police to the

918 kilos seized in October and identifying the intended recipients in Toronto, José Pedro Alvarez and Libardo Arango. The two Colombians were arrested and, in September 1990, pleaded guilty to conspiring to import cocaine and received twelve and fourteen and a half years, respectively.

In "Project Sombra," an eleven-month undercover operation that became public at the end of 1990, Toronto police arrested twenty-three people they alleged belonged to a cocaine smuggling and wholesaling trafficking group that was supplying at least seven other criminal groups in Canada. Police estimated that the "The Company" was responsible for about 30 percent of all the cocaine sold in Ontario and Quebec. As demand grew, the group arranged for a single shipment of 122 kilos to be transported to Toronto, with even more being smuggled from Miami by a fleet of fifteen identical Ford pickup trucks. As part of the investigation, police found a set of accounting books that detailed a sophisticated operation that was bringing thousands of kilos of cocaine into Toronto and Montreal and laundering more than $100 million in cocaine revenue over the course of three years.

During the period that Amigo and its spinoff investigations were taking place, senior Toronto police officers were telling the media that six or seven Colombian cocaine rings were operating in the city. Some were cells of the Medellin and Cali cartels, while others were doing business with the cells or dealing directly with cartel managers in Colombia or Miami. In its 1992 report on organized crime, the Canadian Association of Chiefs of Police observed, "Representatives of Colombian trafficking organizations, such as the Medellin and Cali cartels, dominate the upper echelons of the Canadian cocaine trade. These groups view Canada as a trans-shipment point for cocaine destined for the United States, as well as an expanding market in its own right." The steady increase in cocaine seizures in Ontario and the rest of Canada reflected the "overall cocaine availability in Canada. Cocaine is widely available in most parts of the country and demand for the drug escalated in many jurisdictions. While cocaine purity in both wholesale and retail quantities remained high, street cocaine prices dropped, in some cases by as much as 25%."

In keeping with its international organizational principles, the distribution networks of the Medellin Cartel in Toronto were compartmentalized into semi-autonomous cells. According to a 1989 *Toronto Star* article, at the top of each distribution cell was "the importer" who doesn't handle the cocaine or receive the money, but "simply oversee and arrange through other people." If police start to get too close to the importer, "he is transferred to other branch plant operations on the continent, a circuit that includes Montreal, Vancouver, New York, Los Angeles and San Francisco. Next are the dealers who divide the shipment into multi-kilogram packages. They in turn pass it off to an even larger group of dealers who break the contraband into kilogram amounts. From there it is onto the multi-gram distributors and then finally the gram dealers, who turn the cocaine into crack, mixing it with water and baking soda."

The cartel mangers and employees generally came to Canada on visitor's permits, usually staying for three to six months before returning home. Others stayed for longer periods, with some applying for landed immigrant status. They were instructed to blend into the community, obtain jobs or start small businesses, buy modest homes and drive compact cars. In his 1989 book, *Merchants of Misery,* Victor Malarek cites information provided by Sergeant William Blair, at the time a Metro Toronto Police drug enforcement officer (and future chief of police), that "about twenty people, all from South America, are at the top level of the Colombian drug-dealing network in Southern Ontario, with most living in the Toronto area. Because of the tight-knit structure and operating procedures of the gangs, they are considered 'untouchable' by law enforcement agencies."

The man viewed as the most powerful of all the cocaine barons in Toronto during the 1980s appeared to be a mild-mannered Colombian immigrant, with an infectious grin and a penchant for panama hats, who ran a bookstore on Bloor Street. Bernardo Arcila was also "the biggest Canadian distributor of cocaine in our history," James Leising, a Toronto-based federal Crown prosecutor told *Maclean's* magazine in 1995. "He was *the* supplier for Toronto and Montreal, and his organization reached as far as Newfoundland. He grew the Canadian market by leaps and bounds." According to Victor Malarek, Arcila was known in cocaine trafficking circles as "The General" and had close ties "to the top echelons of the Medellin cartel in Colombia" as well as direct links to other Colombian syndicates operating in Montreal, New York City, and Miami. "His five fingers are the cells or franchises operating here. Each of the organizations is not as structured as the Mafia but they are organized along family lines, and they are linked to the Medellin cartel."

Bernardo Arcila

Arcila came to Canada from his native Colombia in 1972 as a poor twenty-nine-year-old immigrant with his wife and their five-year-old son, Juan Fernando. The family settled in a small apartment near the University of Toronto and Arcila obtained a job as a truck driver for the Shopsy's delicatessen chain. Through his social ties with other Colombian expatriates, he became involved in a group of cocaine importers, the same group that employed the future Crown witness code-named Picaro. At first his role was to let the group use his apartment as a stash house. He then worked as a courier earning $1,000 each time he smuggled cocaine from Buffalo to Toronto in his Volkswagen (his family was often with him to help evade suspicion at the border crossing). By 1982, Arcila was selling at the ounce level in Toronto, and then branched off to form his own importation network, bringing in shipments from the Miami connections that were supplying his former accomplices in Toronto.

As Paul Kaihla writes in his *Maclean's* magazine exposé of Arcila, he "made one of the most insightful decisions of his criminal career" in 1983 when he went into business with Italian mafia groups in Toronto and abroad. "By going outside the Colombian underworld and tapping into a ready-made network of criminals prepared to distribute an illegal product, Arcila vastly expanded the retail market for cocaine." In particular, he forged a partnership with Diego Serrano, who had links to Calabrian Mafia families in both Canada and Italy, and who himself was desperate for revenue due to his failing door-making factory and his inability to repay a $500,000 bank loan. Arcila promised he would pay off Serrano's bank loan. All he had to do was smuggle cocaine from Miami and then use his mob contacts in Toronto to unload the merchandise. Serrano agreed to work for Arcila and was paid $30,000 for each carload he brought into Canada (Arcila was making approximately $1.4 million on each load). Arcila's other ace-in-the-hole was his direct connection to Pablo Escobar, who reportedly invited him to his estate near Medellin several times during the 1980s because he was such a lucrative customer.

By 1986, Arcila had a fleet of Japanese cars shuttling between Toronto and Miami. Each car was equipped with hidden compartments in the gas tanks, behind the seats, and in the side-door panels to accommodate up to 28 kilos of cocaine (Japanese cars were chosen because they were easier to modify than American autos). The cocaine was packed in newspaper, covered with thick plastic, smeared with grease, and then repackaged with more newsprint to throw off the detector dogs at the border. At least five cars a month were travelling to Toronto from Miami. By 1988, Arcila and dozens of his associates were under surveillance as part of Project Amigo. Police believed they had enough evidence to convict Arcila when on November 28, 1988 an undercover officer saw him hand a brick of cocaine to a courier. But senior police officials deferred any immediate action against him because it would have meant exposing the undercover operation before it had gathered sufficient evidence on all its targets. When the Amigo raids went down in May 1989, Arcila was among the dozens who had a warrant issued for his arrest. But he would never be captured. Sensing that the police were closing in,

Arcila drove with his family to Niagara Falls in April and slipped over the border using a fake name. He then fled back to Colombia.

Upon his departure, Arcila put Diego Serrano in charge of his Toronto operations, while he played the role of supplier from his native Colombia, in partnership with the Cali Cartel boss Gilberto Rodriguez Orejuela. Estimates of the amount of cocaine brought into Toronto by Arcila and Serrano over a four-year period starting in 1987 are between 5,800 and 12,000 kilos. Their partnership ended in 1991, when an eight-month investigation dubbed "Project Tome" came to a conclusion with the arrest of twenty-one people and the seizure of 58 kilos of cocaine. Among those charged with conspiracy to import and traffic in cocaine and money laundering was Diego Serrano, the man the *Toronto Star* accused of being the leader of "the country's largest cocaine smuggling ring." Another key Serrano partner charged was forty-seven-year-old lawyer Anthony Morra, who had sold undercover detectives 10 kilograms of cocaine. When he was arrested in his Mississauga office, his pockets were stuffed with $100 bills, some of the $133,000 in marked bills he had received as a first instalment from the sale. In addition to his drug dealing and money laundering duties, Morra had also been Arcila's personal lawyer. In 1993, Morra was convicted and sentenced to six years for his part in the conspiracy. Serrano was able to escape the Canadian police dragnet by fleeing to Italy. But in January 1992, the forty-four-year-old was captured by Italian police and, following an extradition hearing, was escorted back to Canada by two metro police officers in September 1993. In November 1994, Serrano received a ten-year sentence. Despite an international warrant for his arrest, Arcila has never been captured.

THE LATIN PALACE

Project Amigo and subsequent investigations provided a glimpse into the vast profits that were being made from cocaine trafficking in the 1980s, the immense wealth accumulated by the cartels' managers, and the sophisticated money laundering methods being used to clean the narco dollars. In the years before he fled Canada, Bernardo Arcila had sent tens of millions of dollars to Colombia, which were invested in thousands of acres of land in the central Magdalena Valley, where he reputedly operates several cattle ranches. Arcila also amassed an impressive real estate portfolio in Ontario, including several houses and condominiums in Toronto and five lots in Ontario's pricey cottage country near Georgian Bay. He also owned several luxury cars, such as the $58,000 Mercedes-Benz he purchased with cash, and was a partner in a number of businesses that were used in part to launder drug money. Diego Serrano not only lifted himself out of debt, but grew quite wealthy through his partnership with Arcila. He purchased a fashionable Italian restaurant on Dufferin Street in Toronto, spending $3 million in renovations, and also owned a $14-million, five-storey condominium in Italy, which housed his personal $5-million penthouse suite. Wilson Castro owned fourteen houses in Metro Toronto and paid the rent for three apartments. Many of the homes were occupied by members of the Medellin cell he managed, while the apartments were used as stash houses or as business offices. (One apartment converted to an office contained six computers that were used to keep track of the cell's drug transactions and cash disbursements.) Nicolas Canizares owned three houses, including one in Rosedale, Toronto's most upscale neighbourhood, and also maintained five bank accounts. His colleague, Manuel Padilla, owned close to twenty homes along with an interest in the Latin Palace, a two-storey building in Toronto that operated as a South American disco, which was valued at $1.1 million in 1989.

The real estate, companies, and other assets were utilized by Bernardo Arcila, Nicolas Canizares, William Castro and their ilk to hide and legitimize the vast profits from their cocaine trade, which is consistent with the reputation of Colombian drug traffickers as adept money launderers. The Colombian cartels were the first organized criminals to have personnel dedicated almost solely to money laundering. In Toronto, mid-level managers within some of the cells were appointed to oversee the movement of money. Others were used as nominee owners of property, businesses, and bank accounts or as "smurfs" (who were tasked with depositing small amounts of drug cash into numerous bank accounts spread across the city and abroad). Members of the cell Canizares managed controlled at least seven retail businesses, two investment firms, three restaurants, and a string of numbered companies, all of which were used to launder drug profits. While considerable revenue was invested locally, much of the drug money was sent out of the country through wire transfers, bank drafts, or as cash smuggled across the border.

The Medellin Cartel leadership in Colombia was also using Canada as part of its international washing machine. In her 1994 book, *Thieves' World,* Claire Sterling notes that a Geneva judge ordered the arrest of five men associated with a German fugitive, Andreas Behrens, who was wanted for laundering several million dollars through Canada on behalf of Pablo Escobar. In the early 1980s, Luis Pinto, an American described by one RCMP official as "the chief money launderer for a group of Colombian cocaine traffickers," transferred $600,000 from his Florida bank to a Montreal branch of the Royal Bank before he was convicted of drug trafficking offences in the U.S. (and in the process admitting to laundering approximately $40 million). The account was in the name of Pinto's relatives, but RCMP officials working with the FBI had evidence that at least $400,000 in the account was drug money. On May 11, 1989, just one week before Project Amigo went public, the Supreme Court of Ontario froze $13.5 million in the account of a Toronto branch of the Swiss bank of Canada. DEA officials alleged that the Panamanian bank that was the registered holder of the account arranged through its Colombian parent company, Banco de Occidente, electronic wire transfers into the Toronto account of the Swiss Bank Corporation (Canada), a foreign subsidiary of Switzerland's second-largest bank. The DEA claims the money was part of the proceeds of a $1.2-billion cocaine and marijuana trafficking conspiracy that was linked to the Medellin Cartel. In August 1989, Canada received $1 million from the U.S. government for its assistance in successfully carrying out the largest investigation into money laundering in American history.

When the RCMP Proceeds of Crime Unit established an undercover currency exchange business in downtown Montreal in September 1990, one of its most regular and profitable customers was a Brazilian representative of the Cali Cartel. Jorge Luis Cantieri, who ran a number of import-export companies that were fronts for the cartel, was introduced to the Mountie-run Centre International Monétaire de Montréal (CIMM) by Giuseppe (Joseph) Lagana, a lawyer whose principal client was mafia don Vito Rizzuto. Lagana was already a client of CIMM and, along with a couple of junior lawyers in his law firm, had delivered at least $15 million in Canadian cash to the undercover storefront operation in exchange for larger denominations of Canadian and American currency. In his 1999 book on organized crime, Jeffrey Robinson writes that Lagana was a law student in the late 1970s when he first met the Brazilian in Montreal. "Cantieri had been trafficking in Canada probably since the 1970s, had gotten caught in 1985 — he was charged with trafficking 20 kilos of cocaine and 8.2 kilos of hashish, worth $14.5 million — and was supposed to have been sent away for twelve years. When he got out on early release, he flew straight to Colombia to get connected again, set himself up, and went back into business." Shortly after being released from jail in 1991, Cantieri began using the services of CIMM "and remained one of the exchange's best and most loyal customers." He made his final $1-million deposit just one day before the RCMP shut down the undercover operation on August 30, 1994, and arrested fifty-seven people on hundreds of counts of money laundering and drug trafficking offences.

Lagana's involvement with Cantieri was to ensure that sufficient money was sent to South America for cocaine purchases at the behest of Vito Rizzuto and Frank Cotroni. The CIMM services most preferred by Cantieri were the conversion of Canadian cash (which was the proceeds of local cocaine sales) to cashier's cheques or bank drafts in U.S. funds. According to Robinson, over a four-year period $40 million in cheques and drafts were sent abroad and then deposited into Cali Cartel–controlled accounts at two hundred different banks. Cantieri was so trusting of the (undercover) staff at CIIM that he asked for their assistance in smuggling cocaine into Canada. Pierre Rodrigue and David Rouleau, two members of the Sherbrooke chapter of the Hells Angels, had placed an order with Cantieri for 1,000 kilos of cocaine to be delivered to their chapters in the U.K. Working in an undercover capacity, the RCMP chartered a freighter and, with help from U.S. Customs agents, sailed it to Colombia, picked up 558 kilos of cocaine and brought it back to Montreal, where it was seized. Among those arrested on drug trafficking and proceeds-of-crime charges that resulted from the reverse sting operation was Cantieri, who received a fifteen-year prison term, Rodrigue and Rouleau, who were sentenced to six years each, and Joseph Lagana, who was given a thirteen-year sentence.

Despite the successful prosecutions, the sting operation was not without controversy. The RCMP came under fire when the *Ottawa Citizen* published a series of articles in June 1998 that accused the covert-exchange business of assisting drug traffickers in laundering millions of dollars in drug proceeds over a four-year period. Because the RCMP's Montreal Proceeds of Crime Section was so overwhelmed with the volume of cash processed through the exchange it could only seize $16.5 million from the $141.5 million in drug money that passed through the operation. The RCMP was accused of helping to move more than $94.7 million in drug money to Colombia in 1992 and 1993.

In addition to money laundering, another tactic used by the Colombian cartels was corruption. Within Canada, police cases and intelligence revealed the complicity of a wide range of professionals in cocaine importation schemes, including lawyers, accountants, airport baggage handlers, customs officials, and police. One of the most high-profile cases of police corruption in Canada that implicated the Colombian cartels revolved around forty-one-year-old Jorge Leite, who fled to Portugal after suddenly resigning from the RCMP on May 22, 1991, amid allegations that an insider within the force was leaking information to the Cali Cartel. Suspicions that a mole was working for the RCMP began about a year earlier when confidential police information began showing up at arrest sites, including those that appeared to have been wiped clean of incriminating evidence. When the investigation into a leak started, Leite was with the RCMP's drug squad in Montreal and was assigned to protect its star witness, former Medellin Cartel pilot Doug Jaworski. After a two-year internal investigation, the Mounties accused Leite of taking more than $500,000 in payoffs from the Cali Cartel over a four-year period and, in 1993, he was charged with corruption, fraud, and breach

of trust. In a statement the RCMP said was signed by Leite while in Portugal, he admitted to receiving $45,000 in payoffs as well as a $40,000 minivan from Ines Barbosa, the reputed Montreal "godmother" of the Cali Cartel, for providing her with information on RCMP drug investigations. Search warrants filed in Canada claimed that Leite sold information to Barbosa on at least forty-nine different occasions. Leite admitted to taking the payoffs, but said he did so in order to infiltrate the drug cartel. The Mounties claim that Leite was deeply involved with Barbosa and that just days before he fled to Portugal in 1991, Leite had flown to Cartagena, Colombia, at the request of Barbosa, to arrange shipments of cocaine to Canada with leaders of the Cali Cartel. After charges were laid against Leite, the Canadian government embarked on a fruitless effort to bring the international fugitive back to Canada for trial. While Portugal steadfastly refused to extradite him, they did agree to put him on trial on the Canadian charges in 1998. But Leite never showed up for the trial, prompting Interpol to issue an international warrant for his arrest. Leite was eventually captured and, in 1999, he was convicted, although the judge levied a lenient sentence of four years' probation, saying the RCMP failed to prove its case against their former employee.

The most persistent evidence of cartel-linked corruption in Canada has been uncovered at Toronto's Pearson International Airport. Between 1997 and 2000, at least twenty people from the airport's immigration section, Canada Customs, ramp-handling crews, and private contractors were arrested on drug and corruption charges (although not all were connected to the Colombian cartels). In January 1999, two Canada Customs officials were arrested and charged after making off with a suitcase containing $1 million in U.S. cash generated from cocaine sales that they identified during the course of their inspection duties. Most of the corruption at the airport, however, was in aid of the Colombian drug dealers, not to rip them off. For much of the 1990s, the RCMP and Canada Customs tried to infiltrate a ring of corrupt baggage handlers they suspected were on the payroll of Colombian drug dealers. The airport workers secretly removed luggage and cargo filled with cocaine from newly arrived planes and then smuggled them out of the airport. It was said that the baggage handlers were paid up to $10,000 for each cocaine-filled bag removed from a flight.

On January 12, 2000, Daniele Cappa, a terminal supervisor at the airport, was one of seven men arrested on U.S. charges relating to a smuggling network that moved more than 80 kilos of cocaine into Toronto from southern Florida in 1998. Cappa and other airport employees snuck large amounts of cash, which was used to pay for the drugs, past U.S. Customs inspectors stationed at Pearson airport and onto U.S.–bound flights. All the suspects were extradited to the U.S. to stand trial and, in 2003, Cappa pleaded guilty to sneaking $180,000 in U.S. cash strapped to his body through customs and security checkpoints while working at the airport. In his confession to police he said that once he made it past the security checkpoints, he headed for a bathroom in the secure passenger waiting area, where he gave the cash to Brett Matheys, who would then fly it back to Florida. Matheys was an accomplice of Nestor Fonseca, a Cuban national living in Brampton, Ontario, who orchestrated the cash and drug smuggling operation and who sold the coke to distributors in Metro Toronto. In 2004, the RCMP investigated Steven Young, a Montreal airport worker who allegedly tried to smuggle five kilos of cocaine into Canada through Montreal's Dorval Airport by taping it to his body. Young was working for a catering firm that serviced aircrafts and had received a security clearance that allowed him to bypass customs and other security checkpoints.

KIND OF A FACILITATOR FOR THE CARTEL

By the mid-1990s, Colombian drug trafficking organizations continued "to play a dominant role in the Canadian cocaine trade," as the 1996 Criminal Intelligence Service Canada (CISC) annual report on organized crime states. "Financial records recently seized in Canada, the U.S.A. and several South American countries indicate that some of the most prominent Colombian criminal organizations are present and active in Canada." Among these was the Cali Cartel, which was responsible for a growing proportion of cocaine imported into the country following the collapse of the Medellin Cartel.

One of the most powerful Cali Cartel bosses in Canada was Ines Barbosa, a rare example of a woman who had risen to a managerial level within a criminal group. Barbosa first came to the attention of police when she was one of seven people arrested in Montreal in December 1990 after the RCMP found eight kilos of 90 percent pure cocaine hidden in bowling balls. A year later, she was convicted and sentenced to a five-year prison term for trafficking and conspiracy to import cocaine. While in jail, her name came up again as the RCMP investigated Jorge Leite, who was introduced to Barbosa sometime in 1990. Before she was sentenced in late 1991, the RCMP suspected she was behind two shipments of 1,000 kilos of cocaine sent to the Port of Montreal in April and May of that year. Both shipments were seized by the RCMP, but as police waited in the shadows, no one showed up to claim the $750 million cargo, leading police to speculate that Barbosa was tipped off by Leite that the drugs were under surveillance. In the arrest warrant the Mounties prepared after Leite escaped from the country, Barbosa was identified as "one of the leaders of a Colombian organization that imports and traffics large quantities of cocaine in Canada."

In 1994, Barbosa was implicated in a drug trafficking conspiracy in the U.S. where thousands of kilos of cocaine were delivered from California to New York and New Jersey using Winnebago motorhomes driven by Quebecers posing as tourists. The couriers, who were paid $20,000 for each shipment, would rent the recreational vehicles in Quebec, drive to California, pick up the drugs, and then drive to New York and New Jersey. Police believe that Canadian citizens (and Canadian-licence-plated vehicles) were used because they would be subject to less suspicion by police compared to Colombian or Mexican nationals. Those recruited also had to have a clean record so they did not attract suspicion by police or customs officials. It was estimated that the Quebec couriers transported one metric ton of cocaine per month over a period of a year. The investigation led to the arrests of sixteen people in February 1994, including four Quebecers who were arrested in California near the Nevada border while driving two motorhomes with a total of 685 kilos of cocaine packed into hockey bags. According to DEA officials, the markings on the cocaine indicated that it had been supplied by the Cali Cartel. Raids on homes in Montreal led to the arrest of eleven people and the seizure of three kilos of coke, $670,000 in cash, and three fully loaded 9-mm handguns. Among those arrested in Quebec were Montreal resident Jorge Berrardo, a Colombian national who worked for Ines Barbosa and who was described as the boss of the operation. She would later be charged, convicted and sentenced to the Joliette Prison for Women in Quebec, where Barbosa served time with Canada's most notorious female inmate, Karla Homolka.

In Ontario, "Operation Opbar" snared other Colombian drug traffickers with Cali connections. The arrests stemmed from undercover work that began on July 11, 1996, when an RCMP officer, posing as a cocaine trafficker, was introduced to Patricio Narvaez by a former Colombian drug trafficker-turned-police-agent. After selling 4 ounces of cocaine to the undercover officer a few weeks later, Narvaez introduced the RCMP member to his superior, Octavio Zapata, a Colombian citizen living in Mississauga. On October 22, Zapata agreed to sell the undercover officer one kilo of cocaine for $31,500. The following day, Zapata delivered the drugs to a rendezvous point in a parking lot in Mississauga. Following this meeting, Zapata, who had already been arrested in the U.S. in June after 510 kilos of cocaine was seized in New Jersey, asked his client if he would assist in smuggling cocaine into Canada. The undercover Mountie agreed and, on April 1, 1997, he met with an Ecuadorian named Edilberto Vasquez-Yepes and sixty-six-year-old Colombian José de Jésus Kratc-Usman. Introduced as the "Inspector," Kratc told the police officer he represented a "company" and was responsible for the security of any loads arriving in Canada. According to the RCMP, Kratc was the highest-known Cali Cartel executive ever identified in the Greater Toronto Area. His main role in the cartel was to assess smuggling operations and ensure that proper security was in place. He had the final say as to whether cocaine was to leave South America for ports in Canada. Satisfied with the measures that had been put in place for this shipment, Kratc gave his approval and then promptly left for Venezuela. In October, a container arrived at the Port of Halifax containing more than 300 kilos of cocaine, packaged in 50-kilo allotments within six larger boxes of suede work gloves. The drugs were then delivered to Narvaez, Zapata, and Yepes in Mississauga on October 15,

1997. At that time, the three men were arrested, but not before Narvaez told the undercover officer that the suppliers in Venezuela had an additional 2,000 kilos of cocaine en route to Canada. That shipment, if in fact it was sent, was never found by police, nor was Kratc-Usman, despite an international warrant alleging he was responsible for smuggling tons of cocaine on a weekly basis into Canada.

While the Cali Cartel had become the dominant international force in cocaine trafficking by the mid-1990s, the Canadian market was highly competitive, with a number of different players — Colombian and otherwise — involved in importing and wholesaling. In particular, the Rizzuto Family and the West End Gang, as well as the Hells Angels, were emerging as some of the biggest cocaine importers and whole-salers in the country, often negotiating directly with sources in Colombia. Police also began to notice greater co-operation between the major players. In September 1995, for example, police in British Columbia seized 305 kilos of cocaine. According to the Criminal Intelligence Service Canada, "This seizure constituted part of a much larger shipment of 700 to 1,000 kilograms that had been orchestrated by the Hells Angels and the Colombians in Vancouver." Police intelligence information suggested that this shipment, and others like it coordinated by the Cali Cartel, were being sold to members of the Hells Angels in Quebec and B.C. and to the Rizzuto Family and the West End Gang in Montreal.

Information that led to this seizure had been provided by Rodriguez Ernesto Albornoz, a forty-six-year-old Colombian who became an RCMP agent. He told the Mounties that two associates of the Rizzuto Family would be travelling from Montreal to pick up 120 kilos of cocaine in Vancouver and that he was to accompany them. True to his word, on Friday, September 24, 1995, Albornoz left Montreal for Vancouver, along with two other Colombian nationals and Sylvain Malacket, a Montreal drug dealer who was later described by one police investigator as "kind of a facilitator for the cartel." A police surveillance team watched from the shadows as the two Colombians carried large duffel bags from a house in east Vancouver to a minivan. The two men then drove off, but were tailed, pulled over by police, and arrested. Each pleaded guilty to possession for the purpose of trafficking, and was sentenced to seven and five years, respectively. An October 2, RCMP news release stated that they had raided the east end safe house and seized 150 kilos of cocaine, along with $190,000 in cash and an assault rifle. What the news release failed to mention was that no one was charged as a result of the seizure, despite the fact that four or five suspects were found in the house and taken into custody. One of those arrested and then released was Eugene Uyeyama, who, like Albornoz, was an RCMP agent.

According to a 1997 *Maclean's* magazine article, Uyeyama was "rising up the ranks of an organization controlled by a local Colombian-born drug lord," when provided evidence that led to the seizure of 400 kilos of cocaine in Vancouver on February 12, 1996. The drugs were found sealed in the false bottoms of 2,400 aluminum pots and pans that had arrived in a cargo container that had originated in Colombia. A few months earlier, Uyeyama had given the RCMP drug squad an aluminum pot that had a thin pancake of cocaine secreted in its bottom, which he had taken from a previous shipment that had arrived undetected in Vancouver. On February 21, RCMP undercover officers initiated a control delivery of the pots and pans, which was destined for a warehouse in the Toronto municipality of North York. Before the goods were delivered, RCMP in Toronto snuck into the warehouse and installed surveillance equipment. While inside, they discovered boxes filled with thousands of mops that were later traced to a shipment that left Colombia on December 5, 1995, and arrived in Toronto, via New York, on January 30, 1996. The name of the receiver on the bill of lading was Jorge Quintero, the same person who signed for the cookware shipment that was delivered to the warehouse by the RCMP undercover team on February 21. Police determined that the mops and the cookware were produced by factories in Colombia controlled by the Cali Cartel.

More information on the nationwide smuggling operation came to light when local police in Cambridge, Ontario, located around 100 kilometres west of Toronto, raided an autoglass repair garage. Inside, they found three Colombians, all wearing surgical masks, who were in the process of removing cocaine from clear plastic rings, which had come from the handles of mops, and then using a hydraulic press to turn the small amounts of coke into one-kilo bricks. In total, police recovered 10,757 empty plastic rings and 38 kilos of cocaine. Each plastic ring held more than one ounce of cocaine, which led police to estimate that the men had pressed and distributed 348 one-kilo bricks before the raid.

Because of the ongoing seizures, Cali Cartel leadership became suspicious that it had informants working in its midst and sent a team to Canada to plug any leak. By all accounts, their intelligence gathering was 100 percent accurate. On December 21, 1995, firemen discovered the charred remains of thirty-five-year-old Eugene Uyeyama and his thirty-year-old wife, Michele, in their Burnaby, B.C., home. They had been doused with gasoline and set aflame, but not before being bludgeoned and strangled to death. Assassins struck again only days after the shipment of cocaine was delivered by undercover police to the Toronto warehouse. On March 7, 1996, Ernesto Albornoz was shot in the head in his Montreal apartment. Agents with the Colombian cartel were also suspected in the massacre of five people on an Abbotsford farm in September 1996. Three of those slain had criminal records and were known to have connections to the cocaine trade in the Greater Vancouver Area, according to police.

In June 1996, RCMP units in B.C. and Ontario launched simultaneous raids against those behind the smuggling network, which was channelling the entire 84 percent pure inventory to the Toronto market. Ten people were originally arrested, most of whom were from Colombia and other South American countries. This included the three men who received the February cookware shipment in Vancouver, as well as the three Colombians arrested in Cambridge. Among those sought by police was thirty-three-year-old Jorge Enrique Quintero, who managed to elude capture despite being under RCMP surveillance, and fifty-eight-year-old Margarita Lopez (a.k.a. Graciela Botero-Gonzalez), who police believe was the Cali Cartel manager ultimately responsible for the seized cocaine shipments. Thirty-four-year-old Sylvain Malacket skipped bail after being charged, but was captured on the island of Aruba and brought back to Canada. He would also be charged with organizing the murder of

Ernesto Albornoz. (Police allege that Malacket had previously been hired by the Hells Angels to arrange the assassination of a rival drug dealer, but the man hired to do the job killed the wrong person.) Career criminal Robert Moyes was later convicted of first-degree murder in the deaths of Eugene Uyeyama and his wife as well as the five people killed in Abbotsford. He confessed that he and another man he knew only as "Black Mike" had been hired by Salvatore Ciancio, who he alleged was the head of a drug trafficking group in B.C. that was working with the Colombians. However, Ciancio was found not guilty when the judge ruled that Moyes was an unreliable witness. Mark Therrien was also found guilty of five counts of first-degree murder in the Abbotsford slayings, confessing that he had been hired by Moyes.

MOTHER ORGANIZATIONS

While the Medellin, and especially the Cali Cartel have long been held out as the epitome of the vertically integrated, multinational criminal corporation, their operations in Canada suggest a structure that is more complicated. Like most modern criminal organizations, there was a considerable amount of network building among a number of independent cocaine importers, wholesalers, and traffickers both within and outside the Colombian community. As the CISC points out in its 1996 annual report, "the conventional understanding of Colombian trafficking organizations as stratified, wholly self-contained entities is not entirely correct." Colombian drug trafficking conspiracies are "essentially decentralized organizations that are not dependent on a rigid hierarchy in order to function." As the CISC adds in its 1997 report, while many Colombian drug traffickers "are associated with specific groups in Colombia, they function with a great deal of autonomy in Canada. Alliances of convenience between groups are not uncommon, even when those groups are linked to different parent organizations back in Colombia. As well, links with non-Colombian groups, particularly Italian-based criminal organizations, are often developed." What was true in Canada, as well as anywhere that the Colombian cartels operated, was that they were among the most adaptable and sophisticated criminal groups to do business.

By the new millennium, as the Medellin and Cali cartels were being dismantled and replaced by a number of smaller Colombian and Mexican cocaine suppliers and wholesalers, Colombian traffickers had a decidedly smaller presence in Canada. Instead, they largely played the role of long-distance suppliers to the diverse number of criminal groups importing and wholesaling cocaine in Canada. The new cadre of Colombian cocaine suppliers now expect their Canadian customers to come to them and even to arrange the transport of the cocaine back to Canada themselves. Many of the dominant criminal groups active in Canada are involved in the importation and wholesaling of cocaine in Canada, including the Hells Angels, the Italian mafia, Chinese drug trafficking groups, and Eastern European organized crime organizations. These groups have nurtured strong contacts with Colombian suppliers or middlemen, have the resources to finance large shipments, use time-tested smuggling routes, and have well-established distribution networks in Canada.

Some of the largest cocaine seizures made in Canada (or of shipments heading to Canada) have occurred in recent years and have been traced to individuals and groups that are clients of Colombian suppliers. In July 2002, the RCMP seized more than 590 kilos of cocaine, with an estimated street value of $160 million, before it reached the eastern shore of Cape Breton. Four Quebec men were arrested in Cape Breton on July 4 after the RCMP intercepted a sailboat that made its way up the eastern seaboard to a remote beach of the island. In May 2003, the RCMP made a seizure in international waters, 1,100 miles southwest of Costa Rica in the Pacific Ocean, of approximately 1,360 kilos of cocaine. The captain of the boat was arrested, as were two men in Colombia. The RCMP alleged that the accused conspired to import massive amounts of cocaine into the Canadian market through Vancouver using a large yacht. On July 6, 2004, the RCMP announced they had uncovered a major drug smuggling ring when they intercepted a sailboat named *Friendship* off the coast of Nova Scotia. The 49-foot sailboat was transporting more than 500 kilos of cocaine and had departed Antigua for Nova Scotia in June. According to the RCMP, between June 16, 2003, and June 23, 2004, some Quebec residents conspired with South American suppliers to import several tons of cocaine into Canada and England. In total, nine people were arrested.

On January 22, 2005, the Canada Border Services Agency seized 218 kilos of cocaine at Pierre Elliott Trudeau International Airport in Montreal during a routine inspection. The cocaine was concealed in luggage aboard an aircraft coming from Haiti. In July of the same year, two North Vancouver men were arrested by French authorities after French police stopped their 20-metre, Canadian-registered sailboat in international waters with 1.5 metric tons of cocaine on board. The vessel had sailed from Venezuela and was destined for Spain. The seizure was precipitated by an investigation that was initiated in May when U.S. law enforcement agencies learned that a Canadian-based criminal organization was in the process of transporting 1,000 kilos of cocaine from the Caribbean to Spain. The investigation led to the arrest in Spain of four Canadians and the seizure of another ton of cocaine in October. An RCMP drug enforcement official stated that "a Canadian organization operating in Europe" organized the shipments of huge amounts of "highly pure" Colombian cocaine through the Caribbean before taking it to Spain. One of the suspects, a fifty-five-year-old man identified only by his initials, M.M., was "one of the most important drug traffickers in Canada," the Spanish Interior Ministry said in a statement.

In November 2005, the RCMP in Montreal discovered 300 kilos of cocaine hidden inside three drums that were part of a shipment of 216 barrels of lubricating oil. The investigation revealed there were four or five similar shipments of oil into the city from Venezuela during the previous year that may have also contained large amounts of Colombian cocaine. What made the intercepted shipment particularly frightening was that the cocaine was laced with heavy doses of a chemical additive used by veterinarians to kill tapeworms in domestic animals. The November shipment was destined for Olco Petroleum Group Inc., located in east end Montreal, according to the bill of lading. Olco officials have denied any knowledge of the cocaine and no arrests were made.

In September 2006, Portuguese authorities seized a yacht carrying 800 kilos of cocaine off the coast of their country and arrested four Canadians on board. It was believed that the British Virgin Islands–registered *Lady Mary* loaded the drugs about 2,400 kilometres southeast of Portugal's mid-Atlantic Azores archipelago from a mother ship that had set sail from South America.

CHAPTER 13
RETURN OF THE ITALIANS
The Canadian Connection, Redux

Beginning in the early 1980s, Italian criminal groups began to lose their dominance in North America's underworld, due to increased in fighting, intensive law enforcement efforts, defections of made men to government informant programs, successful prosecutions, and competition from other organized crime genres.

In 1986, the U.S. Department of Justice enjoyed the most significant prosecution of organized crime figures in American history. In what became known at the "Commission Case," a number of the bosses and other members of New York's mafia families were convicted of conducting the affairs of "the Commission of La Cosa Nostra" in a pattern of racketeering. These racketeering offences included the murders of Carmine Galante and two of his associates because, as prosecutors argued, their deaths furthered the Commission's effort to resolve a Bonanno Family leadership dispute. During their trial, the mafia bosses admitted the existence of the Commission, but denied its involvement in criminal activity. Their feeble pleas fell on deaf ears; all of the defendants, including the bosses of the Colombo, Genovese, and Lucchese families were found guilty and received heavy jail sentences.

John Gotti, who in 1985 had become the head of the powerful Gambino Family, earned the nickname "the Teflon Don" when he escaped prosecution in 1986 and was acquitted in two subsequent trials. By 1992, he was finally convicted on federal racketeering charges, based on incriminating wiretap evidence and the testimony of his former underboss Sammy (the Bull) Gravano. Gotti was sentenced to life without parole and died in prison in 2002. The conviction of Gotti — whose brashness, arrogance, and shameless self-promotion betrayed many of the principles of the successful gangster laid out by the likes of Arnold Rothstein, Meyer Lansky, and Charles Luciano decades ago — was a symbol of the downfall of the once-mighty mafia in America.

In Canada, the death or incarceration of powerful mafia figures like Vic Cotroni, Paolo Violi, Giacomo Luppino, Paul Volpe, Michelle Racco, and the Commisso brothers left a big gap in the leadership ranks of the Italian mafia in this country. The organized crime void in both America and Canada was filled by numerous other mobsters, including another generation of Italian immigrants from Sicily and Southern Italy.

The influx of a new cohort of gangsters from Italy actually dates back to the early 1970s, when American mafia leaders, in particular Carmine Galante of the Bonanno Family, began importing them to do their violent bidding. These foreign recruits were seen as more ruthless, more violent, and more subservient compared to the American-grown variety because of their upbringing in the old country where they were taught to respect and obey their family bosses. La Cosa Nostra was suffering from "the Americanization of the sons of Little Italy," Jean-Pierre Charbonneau wrote in his 1975 organized crime book, *The Canadian Connection*. "The children of immigrants, detached from ancestral values and direct knowledge of ghetto poverty, no longer had respect for their old chiefs or the ambition of their elders. Young second and third generation Italian-Americans weren't buying the Honored Society's ways. They were too Americanized and failed to show the respect of old 'mustached Petes' demanded." There was a particular need for soldiers who were willing to carry out the violent orders of their bosses. A similar observation was made by a 1972 *Toronto Star* article. The American mafia "is having generation-gap problems," it read. The more recent "generation of sons and godsons is happy to inherit the multibillion-dollar empire of organized crime but unwilling to do the dirty work attached to the job. Money was now more important than respect. As a result the mob has been forced to import killers from Sicily where no gangster holds himself above such work."

By the end of the 1980s, there were two significant and overlapping changes occurring within the mafia in North America: the incursion of the Sicilian recruits and the slow disintegration of La Cosa Nostra as an "honoured society" where the traditions and principles of the mafioso were now being usurped by its revenue-generating ambitions, which was driven primarily by narcotics trafficking. The fact that Sicily had now eclipsed France as Europe's biggest source of processed heroin only escalated the transformation of the mafia in Italy and North America.

Inevitably, criminal networks whose ranks were predominately made up of immigrant Sicilian drug traffickers were becoming a force in Canada, leaving a classified 1986 report of the Criminal Intelligence Service Canada to remark, "The Sicilian Mafia is the newest organization in Ontario having established itself during the mid-60s. They appear to be the minority, however they are powerful because of strong connec-

tions to known Mafia members in Sicily. Their business is the importation of heroin." A public report issued by the CISC two years earlier warned, "The Sicilian Mafia are gaining in strength [in Canada] but have not as yet established any sort of control except in the field of heroin smuggling and distribution. In this area they are definitely dominant."

LE NEVEU

A key player in helping fill the Cosa Nostra's labour pool in the late 1960s and early 1970s was Frank Cotroni, who facilitated the entry of young Italian men into Canada and then arranged for their transportation to the U.S. by supplying false papers and smuggling them across the border. His illegal labour brokerage work was interrupted by a prison term for cocaine trafficking, which he began serving in an American penitentiary in 1975.

FBI documents show that when Cotroni was convicted that year, he tried to lessen his sentence by appearing to co-operate with federal authorities. In particular, he volunteered to reveal the whereabouts of approximately $850,000 in counterfeit U.S. currency and the plates used in the production of the fake dollars. The FBI soon learned, in part through surveillance of Bonanno Family members, that this offer was in fact a scam being perpetrated by Cotroni in that he had purchased the counterfeit currency and the plates for $100,000 so he could have something to offer as part of a plea bargain. Cotroni's plan had potentially grievous consequences when Bonanno captain Alphonse (Sonny Red) Indelicato caught wind of Cotroni's offer to the feds, and, not being aware of the apparent fraud, had ordered Cotroni to be killed. During the course of a drug investigation, the FBI intercepted a phone call by Genovese Family member William Masselli, which alerted them to the contract on Cotroni's head. These intercepts also captured the efforts by Masselli to cancel the contract by explaining the fraud to Indelicato. Masselli was overhead declaring to another unknown man:

> They were gonna whack this guy out for nothing. See how you can get whacked out for nothing? ... They were almost gonna mark that guy wrong, that Cotroni, Frank Cotroni.

So Sonny Red calls me down, this week and I know him good, Sonny Red. ... That's why I'm showing you this and I want you to go, it goes no further than here because this guy happens to be with us. I wanna know what the fuckin' story is behind it, in the meantime I gotta go back down there Monday or Tuesday and tell him you're marking the guy for no fuckin' reason ...

Maselli did straighten out the confusion sometime in 1979 and the issue appears to be forgotten by the time Indelicato was murdered in May 1981.

Frank Cotroni was paroled on April 25, 1979, after serving one-third of his sentence, and when he returned to Montreal he encountered a radically different mafia. Paolo Violi was dead, his brother was in forced retirement, and the Sicilian wing was now fully in charge under the leadership of Nick Rizzuto and his son Vito. A new era had begun in which the Rizzuto Family would establish the Montreal mafia as the most influential and powerful Italian criminal organization in Quebec and, eventually, all of North America.

Frank Cotroni was tolerated by the Rizzutos because of his drug trafficking connections. Yet, it must have been a tense relationship and there have been claims that Frank was plotting a violent overthrow of the new leadership of the Montreal mafia. At the very least, he set out to show that he was still a force to be taken seriously in the criminal underworld and threw himself back into his old line of work with his usual reckless abandon. As his biographer Peter Edwards wrote, when he stepped off the plane in Montreal in 1979, the confident and charismatic Cotroni "looked more like a prince returning from the Crusades than a drug trafficker coming home from Lewisburg Prison's Mafia Row. His hair was worn in a well-groomed, cavalier style, flowing halfway over his ears. And his eyes shone even brighter than his perfect teeth as he strode through Dorval Airport in Montreal, his New York lawyer John Iannuzzi in tow." Cotroni's stay at a U.S. penitentiary helped expand his drug associations and soon after he returned to Canada he would be supported by a new underling who would help him try to recapture some of his past glory. This new

lieutenant would, however, turn out to be Frank's worst nightmare.

Cotroni first met Réal Simard in Quebec's Parenthais prison during the early 1970s while he was awaiting extradition to the U.S. on his cocaine smuggling charges. Born in 1951, Simard was the nephew of Vic Cotroni's long-time business partner Armand Courville. In his 1987 autobiography, Simard wrote about being the child of an impoverished family headed by an abusive, alcoholic father and leaving home at the age of thirteen. He was a teenager when he joined a loose-knit street gang in his east end Montreal neighbourhood. Before long he was holding up banks with his childhood friend Raymond Martel. During one bank heist, Martel was captured as Simard waited in the getaway car. Simard managed to avoid arrest, but was soon picked up by police after another of his bank-robbing cronies, Jean-Paul Saint-Armand, was arrested and became an informant. As a result of evidence provided by Saint-Armand, Simard was convicted and handed a six-year prison sentence. Cotroni had learned that Simard was Courville's nephew, and when they met in prison he agreed to take him under his wing. "When you get out, come see me," Cotroni told his future protégé. Little did Simard know that he would be used as a pawn in Cotroni's ego-driven attempts to regain power in Montreal and beyond. In his biography, Simard maintains that his new boss was intent on taking down the Sicilian wing of the Montreal mafia.

Frank Cotroni's magnetic presence in Montreal was felt immediately upon his return; he was regularly seen holding court in the city's best steakhouses, attending boxing matches and Montreal Canadiens games, dispensing advice to whomever flagged him down, and being chauffeured around in his black, four-door Lincoln Continental. By the summer of 1979, Simard was working as Cotroni's bodyguard, chauffeur, and personal assistant. Over the next few years, Cotroni would regard Simard as a nephew and, in his fluent French, even began referring to him as *le neveu.*

By 1980, Cotroni promoted his new employee to hit man, and the first contract handed to him was to assassinate nightclub owner and hashish wholesaler Michel (Fatso) Marion, who was believed to have had a hand in the death of some of Cotroni's associates in the 1970s. On January 18, 1980, Simard killed Marion while he was eating breakfast in a Montreal restaurant. After shooting two bullets into his victim's rotund body, he fired a third one right at his head, because, as his mentor Frank Cotroni once advised him, "You never leave a body without giving it a bullet in the head." Marion's slaying, according to Peter Edwards, "would serve as a calling card of sorts for Frank Cotroni, announcing graphically that he was back on the streets and in a serious mood."

On June 18, 1981, Simard murdered Giuseppe Montegano, a low-level cocaine dealer in the city's north end. Frank Cotroni suspected he was a police informant and, to make matters worse for Montegano, he had been in a dispute with Cotroni's coke-dealing sons over the quality of the cocaine he sold them. Montegano was lured to the Argigento Social Club, which was owned by Frank's oldest son, Francesco, under the pretence that Montegano was to be paid the money owned to him by Franky Junior. Simard, and accomplices Francesco Raso and Daniel Arena, lurked in the shadows inside. The three had concocted a plan to abduct Montegano when he entered the private club and then kill him at another location, so as not to get blood all over Franky Junior's clean floors. Their plans went awry when Montegano became suspicious after walking into the bar and tried to escape through a window. As Montegano was fleeing, Simard shot him twice in the head. Réal, Franky Junior, and Raso were arrested a few days later, but all were released in a matter of hours.

Cotroni's killing spree did not end with Montegano. He was worried that Michel Pozza, the Montreal mafia's university-educated accountant and money launderer, had shifted his allegiance to the new Sicilian leadership. In Frank Cotroni's eyes, Pozza could no longer be trusted and he told Réal Simard "something has to be done about him." On the morning of September 28, 1982, Simard pulled a .22-calibre pistol on Pozza and shot him several times, right in front of Pozza's home. The fifty-seven-year-old mob bookkeeper died almost immediately. Police had been conducting surveillance of Pozza, part of an investigation into labour racketeering, but it had been called off the night before he was killed because of a manpower shortage. When

police searched the dead man's body and home they found a receipt showing Pozza had sent $2.6 million to a bank account registered to Sergio and Giovanni Ciancimino. The two were sons of Vito Ciancimino, a former mayor of Palermo and a dominant figure in Sicilian politics for thirty years. Police later concluded that the money had come from Vito Rizzuto's close drug dealing associates, the Cuntrera brothers, and was a payment for heroin that was sold by Michele Greco, who operated a heroin lab in Sicily. (Two years later, the sixty-year-old Ciancimino was arrested by Italian police on charges of having links to the American mafia and illegally exporting millions of dollars to Canada on the Sicilian Mafia's behalf. Key pieces of evidence against Ciancimino were documents bearing his or his sons' names found on the body of Michael Pozza. Palermo police were working on the hypothesis that Ciancimino had smuggled millions of dollars into Canada to invest into real estate and securities. The money was believed to have come from narcotics trafficking or other criminal activities by mafia groups in Palermo for which Ciancimino was laundering money. Other evidence tied Ciancimino to the "Pizza Connection" drug trafficking operation involving Sicilian heroin producers and American mafia distributors.)

American law enforcement agencies were also monitoring Frank Cotroni's relationship with heroin dealing members of New York's Genovese Family. Classified FBI reports from the early 1980s linked Cotroni to 115.5 pounds of heroin seized by U.S. Customs on January 27, 1982, from a Brooklyn warehouse. The heroin had arrived in port on an Italian ship the day before concealed in crates containing espresso machines. An FBI report, dated May 17, 1982, stated that one member of the Genovese Family "is dealing 'junk' on a large scale with Frank Cotroni out of Canada" and "travels to Montreal on a regular basis to set up the wholesale shipment of 'junk' from the Cotroni's in Canada to the United States, and that the Cotroni's have strong connections in Sicily which give them an unlimited supply of 'junk.'" The FBI also discovered that Cotroni wired $93,000 to a bank in Italy as a partial payment for another heroin shipment that was due to arrive on July 26, 1982.

Meanwhile, the ever-ambitious Cotroni was attempting to stretch his influence beyond Quebec into

Ontario, where he wanted to establish his son Paolo as some sort of underworld colonial governor. There were also suggestions he was setting the stage for his own voluntary exile from Rizzuto-dominated Quebec. With the fractionalized nature of Ontario's underworld, Cotroni felt the timing was ripe and in the summer of 1983, he sent his trusted lieutenant Simard to scout the territory. Ever mindful of mafia protocol, Cotroni made sure he had the blessings of John Papalia, who was in charge of the province on behalf of Buffalo's Magaddino crime family. One of Simard's first orders of business in Ontario was to meet with Papalia in a bar in Hamilton. Cotroni confirmed in a phone call to Papalia that Simard was his emissary and Papalia gave him his blessings to operate in the province. What the two men did not know that day was that a police surveillance team was photographing the meeting.

After being given the green light, Simard invested money in Prestige Entertainment Inc., which booked Quebec dancers for Ontario strip joints. "The Toronto clubs were not producing much, and had not for a while," Simard wrote in his autobiography. "The head of the Commisso family had been in prison since 1981, and no one was looking after things. Ontario was 15 years behind Quebec when it came to making money from clubs." The enterprise was so successful that Simard was soon renting a suite at the swanky Sutton Place Hotel and driving around town in a Mercedes-Benz. While the booking agency was a money maker, Simard also wanted to incorporate the bars served by Prestige into a budding drug network he was putting together for Cotroni in the province. Dealers working as bouncers, bartenders, and waitresses were placed in over a dozen clubs and Richard Clément, a Cotroni associate, was brought to Toronto to watch over the operation. Cotroni himself visited Toronto on a monthly basis and while in the city, he was chauffeured around by professional boxer Eddie (The Hurricane) Melo. When Melo was checked out by police, they found his official employment included that of an organizer for Local 75 of the Hotel and Restaurant Employees International, a union deemed so corrupt that in 1981 it suffered the unceremonious distinction of becoming the only union ever expelled from the Quebec Federation of Labour, due to charges of uncomfortably close ties with hotel management and

Frank Cotroni. Based on intercepted communications, a 1982 FBI report "determined that Frank Cotroni (LCN, Montreal), has established contacts with LCN factions in Toronto" on behalf of representatives of the New York mafia families to help them "make entree into certain labor unions in Canada and Eastern U.S." Police surveillance of Cotroni revealed that he had shared drinks with union officials during one of his sourjourns in town, and when Cotroni lieutenant Claude Faber came to Toronto, Local 75 was billed for his room. Police were also interested in a lunch meeting Cotroni had in Toronto's Little Italy with Rocco Zito, the new leader of the 'Ndrangheta cell in the city that police referred to as the Siderno Group.

While Toronto police were tailing Cotroni, prosecutors in the U.S. were preparing another drug trafficking case against him. On August 30, 1983, the RCMP arrested Cotroni in Montreal at the request of the U.S. government after a federal grand jury in Connecticut indicted him for conspiring to distribute heroin in the New York area. Six other people were named in the indictment, including four men the FBI labelled as associates of the Genovese Family: Anthony (Guy, Sr.) Digirolamo of Connecticut, Joseph (Joe Crow) Delvecchio of New Jersey, as well as New Yorkers Oreste (Ernie Boy) Abbamonte and Michael Corcione, two men Cotroni met in prison. The indictment alleged that Cotroni was the intermediary between heroin suppliers in Canada and distributors in the U.S. and that between April 26 and May 28, 1982, he arranged for the delivery of heroin from Canada to his American co-defendants. During the period in question, FBI surveillance caught Cotroni receiving tens of thousands in cash from his co-defendants as payment.

After being picked up in Canada, Cotroni was granted bail of $100,000 and was told to reappear in court on October 3 for an extradition hearing. Despite the real possibility of yet another jail term in the U.S., Frank continued to instruct Simard to further cement his interests in Ontario. While in Toronto, Simard had heard that fellow Montrealers and reputed cocaine dealers Mario Héroux and Robert Hétu had come to the city with the intention of assassinating Richard Clément. The two men were supposedly hired by George Cherry, a Montreal boxing gym owner and trainer who was owed money by Clément. "We decided to kill them before they killed him," Simard would later tell a jury. Réal set up a meeting with the two men in their Toronto hotel room for 7 p.m., on November 29, 1983. Shortly after 6:30 that evening, Simard and Clément knocked on the door of the hotel room where Héroux and Hétu were waiting for what they expected would be a meeting to discuss a cocaine deal. Instead, within seconds of Hétu opening the door, Simard and Clément began firing upon the two men. Simard shot Hétu at least twice in the face while Clément fired four bullets into the neck and head of Héroux. The two gunmen then traded places: Clément fired a third bullet into Hetu's head while Simard shot Héroux in the face.

Héroux died at the scene, but Hétu never even lost consciousness and had the foresight to write down the names of his two assailants on hotel stationery. Réal Simard was arrested the next day by Toronto police, and upon hearing that he was about to be arrested as well, Clément fled to Lebanon. Simard was charged with murder and attempted murder and, in 1984, he was convicted and sentenced to life. Police had hoped to make a deal with Simard to try and implicate Cotroni in these and previous murders, but Simard did not crack and stayed true to his vow of *omerta*. "Then I read a book, *Out on a Limb*, by Shirley MacLaine," Simard later told a reporter. "That made me decide to turn, to become a police informer. The book made me realize I had a soul. Always my head and my heart could accept what I was doing, but my soul never could. I listened to my soul." Simard's new-age spiritual self-discovery (not to mention the spectre of a long jail sentence and attempts on his life while in prison) convinced him to admit to his involvement in the murder of five people — Michel Marion, Giuseppe Montegano, Nicolas Morello, Michel Pozza, and Mario Héroux. In the process he implicated his accomplices and co-conspirators, including Frank Cotroni.

Police now had enough evidence to lay murder charges against Frank Cotroni for the death of Montegano. On October 10, 1986, Montreal police arrested Cotroni, his son Franky Junior, as well as Simard's two accomplices in the murder, Danny Arena and Francesco Raso. Simard was the first to be prosecuted

for his confessed role in the other murders and was convicted of one charge of second-degree murder and four charges of manslaughter. Many wagered he would not last that long; when he pleaded guilty to murdering Montegano, it became public that he had turned police informant and would testify against Frank Cotroni.

Réal Simard is shown in the back of a police car in Toronto, October 16, 1986, after being found guilty of second-degree murder.

Despite a contract being placed on his head, Simard did not back away from his commitment to give evidence against his former boss, whose trial was slated to begin in January 1988. But the courtroom confrontation between Simard and Cotroni would not take place. Before the trial was scheduled to begin, Frank Cotroni and the three other men cut a deal with the Crown and pleaded guilty to manslaughter charges in the death of Giuseppe Montegano. At his sentencing trial, the Crown prosecutor told the court that Cotroni ordered the slaying based on his suspicions that Montegano was talking to police. The fifty-six-year-old Cotroni was sentenced to eight years, his son received three years, while Arena and Raso got seven and five years, respectively. It was the first time Frank Cotroni had ever been convicted in Canada.

In March 1988, Simard testified at Richard Clément's trial for his role in the murder of Mario Héroux. Based on Simard's evidence, the thirty-five-year-old Clément, who had returned from Lebanon in 1987, was convicted and sentenced to life. Despite his admitted involvement in the murder of five men, Simard was released in 1994 and given a new identity. While out on parole, he put his strong organizing skills to good use when he became the campaign manager for a Bloc Québécois candidate in the 1994 federal election. When police informed the Bloc candidate of his manager's true identity, Simard was forced to leave his high-profile job. For the next ten years, Simard lived under an alias while trying to avoid police. While on parole, he committed welfare fraud to the tune of $13,000 and, when the offence was discovered, his parole was revoked and a warrant was issued for his arrest. Police captured Simard in 1999, but he was able to escape and disappeared for the next five years. When police caught up with him again in 2004, he was married and working as a security guard at College Jean de Brebeuf, a prestigious private school in Montreal. Simard was put back in prison and his application for parole in 2005 and again in 2006 were both turned down.

THE COLOMBIA OF QUAALUDES

By the mid-1970s, the hearings of the Quebec Crime Commission as well as constant police surveillance of the province's mobsters drove many to a locale popular among Quebec snowbirds: Florida. In 1983, the Florida Governor's Council on Organized Crime estimated that at least three hundred people associated with Canadian criminal organizations had operated in Florida since the mid-1970s. This led authorities to conclude that the Canadian crime groups constituted a "considerable presence in the State, operating in much the same manner as domestic groups, finding their customers and victims among both Floridians and the nearly one million Canadians who visit Florida each year." Further, according to the report, police in Florida "believe that the state has become a haven for Canadian fugitives, who pass easily into the United States because there are no passport requirements.

Once in the U.S., they become permanent residents generally through purchase of property, or by marriage to a U.S. citizen."

The criminal activities carried out by the Quebec gangsters in Florida included drug trafficking, loasharking, bookmaking, and the smuggling of stolen automobiles and firearms. "The trade in stolen cars to and from Canada is substantial, involving many Canadian gang members," a 1986 report from the President's Commission on Organized Crime stated. "The trade in handguns smuggled to Canada is also lucrative, since the weapons are easily available in Florida, but are heavily regulated in Canada. Canadian gangs buy pistols in Florida under false identification and sell these untraceable weapons in Canada for up to five times their American retail cost. According to Canadian police, the guns are then used in robberies and murders."

Speaking with the media in 1983, one official with the Governor's Council on Organized Crime said that the Canadian mobsters frequently commit crimes against other Canadians living in Florida because many of the victims are living there illegally and do not report the crimes for fear of deportation. The spokesperson added that the victims were—

> ... extremely fearful of the Canadian gangster. The Montreal media is full of reprisal killings and torturings in gangland style. Canadians do not testify against the mob. In the same vein, the Canadian gangster does not testify against another Canadian gangster. If the typical "stand up" U.S. gangster is tight-lipped, the typical Canadian "stand up" gangster has no mouth. The discipline and determination of the Canadian gangster far exceeds that of the U.S. gangster. In all my career I have only found one other type of individual who is more secretive and that is a Swiss banker.

Canadian criminals were blending in with the larger French-Canadian population in areas like Hollywood, Florida, where the concentration of Quebecers was so great it was known as "Little Quebec." The gangster snowbirds were also busy investing in restaurants, hotels, and real estate in Florida and were not reluctant to use strong arm-tactics to further their business and residential investments in the Sunshine State. They intimidated real estate agents as well as homeowners selling properties to obtain a favourable price. Police also feared that a war for control of the Miami area and other parts of Southern Florida was on the verge of breaking out between Canadian criminals and New York's Gambino, Lucchese, and Genovese mafia families, which were also establishing a presence in Southern Florida. Police intelligence information indicated that the Gambino Family had sent one hundred "muscle men" to the greater Miami area to counter the influx of Canadian mobsters. A violent conflict was already being fought over control of pizza businesses in Southern Florida; between 1982 and 1983, there were at least eleven bombings of eight pizza parlours. Two members of the Gambino Family, who had been trying to open a pizza restaurant in what apparently was Canadian-claimed territory, were found dead in the trunk of their car in Dade County. During the same period, a special police task force in the Miami area arrested five of Canada's ten most wanted criminals, most of whom were members or associates of the Montreal mafia or the Dubois brothers' gang.

Among the Quebecers arrested in Florida longtime Cotroni associate William Obront, who had relocated there in the early 1980s after fleeing Canada. Willie already had invested in a disco in Miami Beach in the 1970s. He also operated a fruit and vegetable business and had plans to develop a shopping centre. Among Obie's co-investors in his Florida companies were Montreal mafia member Joe Di Maulo, who also departed Quebec for sunnier climes when the provincial crime commission began to take an interest in his local activities.

Notwithstanding their semi-legitimate property and business investments, the greatest source of income for the Quebec criminals in Florida was drug trafficking. Beginning in the early 1980s, Obront became involved in a network that mass-produced methaqualone (a sedative commonly known as Quaalude) as well as a fake version (using the less potent and cheaper diazepam). Since the late 1970s, clandestine labs in Greater Montreal were manufacturing millions of tiny diazepam pills stamped with the trademark "Lemmon 714." The pills were then shipped south in trucks carrying loads of peat moss and lumber where they were taken to a warehouse in Miami and then distributed across the United States as the popular Quaalude. Police accused Obront of taking part in a $50 million-a-year drug ring that sent millions of phony Quaaludes into the United States and brought back kilos of cocaine into Canada.

Police caught up with the Canadians in the summer of 1983 when Obront was arrested for drug trafficking. In what was being called the "French-Canadian Connection," U.S. law enforcement agents rounded up more than forty people who were being indicted. In July 1984, Obront was dealt a twenty-year sentence and fined $50,000 following his conviction on twelve drug-related charges. A follow-up investigation concluded in March 1987 with the arrest of forty-nine other people thought to be involved in the ongoing drug ring that police said accounted for 70 percent of counterfeit Quaalude sales in the United States. The most recent indictments targeted twenty Canadians, twenty-seven Americans, and two Colombians. Among the Canadians charged were William Obront and the man police claimed was the mastermind behind the manufacturing of the counterfeit Quaaludes, Roger Dufour, a forty-seven-year-old Montreal pharmacist and businessman with no previous criminal convictions. A Drug Enforcement Administration official said that 13.5 million pills were produced between 1981 and 1986 at four clandestine labs in Montreal. Upon announcing the arrests, a DEA official called Canada "the Colombia of Quaaludes." Willie Obront would not be released from jail until March 7, 2002, when he was seventy-eight years old.

"ONE WORD CAN MEAN SO MUCH"

While Frank Cotroni and Willie Obront were aspiring to expand their criminal operations to Ontario and Florida, respectively, the Rizzuto Family was solidifying its hold over the mafia in Montreal. By the early 1980s, the Calabrian leadership had been completely purged from the Bonanno's Canadian crew while its made members and associates had little choice but to pledge their allegiance to the Rizzutos.

Nicolò Rizzuto, the Sicilian-born maverick who rebelled against and eventually spearheaded the overthrow of the Calabrian Cotroni-Violi regime, was now living in semi-retirement in Caracas. Despite his frequent visits to Montreal, the reins of power had been passed to his capable son Vito. Over the next few years, Vito Rizzuto would become one of the most powerful and respected criminals in Canada. He had become a made man in the Bonanno Family sometime during the 1970s or early 1980s and was the acknowledged head of the family's Montreal crew (even though technically he was only a soldier in the family). As the leader of the Montreal mafia, Vito evolved into what some mob watchers called the "epitome of the modern global gangster." He had outposts and cells strategically placed throughout Canada and abroad and was forging a global organized criminal conglomerate that would surpass the reach, wealth, and power of any of the five New York families.

While the Montreal crew may have only had twenty or so made members, Rizzuto could count on hundreds of associates around Canada and the world. He maintained order among the once-warring mafia factions in Montreal while establishing ties to other established criminal groups, including the American Cosa Nostra, the Sicilian Mafia, the Calabrian 'Ndrangheta, the Hells Angels, the West End Gang, Colombian cocaine dealers, and the Chinese Big Circle Boys. In conjunction with these many partners, but most importantly through his affiliation with the Caruana-Cuntrera mafia subsidiary, he presided over one of the world's largest drug trafficking networks. The Montreal mafia was also accumulating a fortune through a maze of large-scale gambling and book-making operations. Beginning in the 1980s, Rizzuto expanded his gaming interests to include video lottery terminals, which were fast becoming the most lucrative form of gambling in Quebec. Profits generated from these illegal activities were banked, invested, and laundered throughout the world. Rizzuto paid homage to his bosses in the Bonanno Family, and was sending millions of dollars in tribute to New York annually, while slowly planning for the day that he would run his own autonomous family, free from the confining shackles of the Cosa Nostra. Indeed, as Lee Lamothe and Adrian Humphrey's write in their book *The Sixth Family* (a title that alludes to the independence and power of the Montreal mafia under the Rizzutos by equating it with the five New York families), "Few fully

recognized the growing influence of the Sixth Family" and "fewer still understood that what was once a small, outpost of subservient gangsters had grown into an independent and powerful entity that could hold its own in any underworld on any continent."

Vito Rizutto circa 1980s

The wealth, power, and prestige of the Montreal mafia as a global criminal network largely came from financing, smuggling, and trafficking in drugs; in fact, Rizzuto's criminal organization was one of the few in the world that dealt in large quantities of hash, heroin, and cocaine. The 1992 annual report of the Criminal Intelligence Service Canada observed that the "sophisticated structure of this crime group enables members to oversee the entire drug importation operation from source country to street level trafficking ensuring maximum profit." While this may have been true, when Rizzuto became involved in a drug deal, he was either the financier or played the role of intermediary, bringing together a supplier with a buyer. Regardless, he only became involved in deals that involved hundreds of kilos and rarely brought in a load unless he already had a buyer.

Under Rizzuto, many drug shipments were bypassing the Montreal port and instead were routed through Nova Scotia or Newfoundland where there was less enforcement at the ports, not to mention hundreds of miles of unguarded coastline perfect for the surreptitious unloading of illegal cargo. In 1985,

13 metric tons of hashish was seized by the RCMP from a fishing boat that docked at Lockeport on Nova Scotia's South Shore. In 1986, police confiscated a 14-ton truckload of hashish on Cape Breton Island, and another 16 tons from a ship at the Halifax port. The captain of the ship told police that he had to pay off senior militia officers with the Christian Phalangists in Lebanon to get the shipment out of the country. Like the West End Gang, the Montreal mafia had direct ties with hashish exporters in Lebanon that date to at least the early 1970s. According to a 1989 *Montreal Gazette* article, members of the Montreal mafia established a mutually beneficial trading partnership with Lebanese Christian Phalangist militias, which bartered hash for weapons and cash. In 1980, the FBI confirmed that a large shipment of weapons including M16s and ammunition had been stolen from a Boston armoury, smuggled to Montreal, and then sent to Lebanon in exchange for hashish. Police also established a link between Frank Cotroni and senior figures in Lebanon's government and military. Wiretaps on Frank Cotroni's phone in the mid-1970s revealed that he was making calls directly to the home of Suleiman Franjieh, who at the time was president of Lebanon. Cotroni also allegedly made several trips during the 1970s to Lebanon to organize hash shipments with senior Lebanese officials.

In early December 1987, a two-month investigation by the RCMP resulted in the seizure of 13 metric tons of Lebanese hash off the Newfoundland coast and the arrest of six Montreal men. The investigation began in October when RCMP officers seized 500 kilos of hash from a trawler at the port of Blanc Sablon, Quebec, on the north coast of the Gulf of St. Lawrence, near Labrador. The seizure led the RCMP to suspect that large hash shipments were being loaded aboard small craft in the area from mother ships anchored in international waters off the coast of Newfoundland. Following tips from fishermen about unusual ship traffic around Trinity Bay, the RCMP made a series of other seizures from boats and trucks in Newfoundland in late November. Among those charged in connection with the seizures were Vito Rizzuto and thirty-four-year-old Raynald Desjardins, the man police alleged to be in charge of the importations. Desjardins was not merely a drug importer; he has been described

as "the most influential non-Italian in the Montreal mafia since William Obront and Armand Courville." He was the brother-in-law of long-time mob member Joe Di Maulo and, in 1973, he and Di Maulo accompanied Paolo Violi to New York City to participate in the election of Phil Rastelli as the new boss of the Bonanno Family.

On November 18, 1988, while out on $150,000 bail from his 1987 arrest, Rizzuto was again arrested for conspiring to smuggle 32 metric tons of Lebanese hash into the country, which police believe was scheduled to land in Sept-Îles, Quebec. Police charged him solely on the word of Normand Dupuis, the owner and captain of the boat where the drugs were found. Rizzuto was acquitted of all charges in December 1989, after Dupuis was caught on tape making an offer to Jean Salois, Rizzuto's lawyer. He was trying to persuade Salois to provide him with a "lifetime pension" if he would agree to disappear before Rizzuto's trial. Salois had already been contacted by Dupuis and had a tape recorder running when the offer was made in person in his office. Salois took the tapes to police, who in turn handed them over to prosecutors. Their star witness no longer had any credibility and the decision was made to drop the charges against Rizzuto. It was Dupuis who would go to jail on a thirty-two-month sentence for obstructing justice (on top of his sentence for the drug charges).

In December 1990, Rizzuto would receive his second acquittal in less than twelve months. Along with Desjardins and two other accused men, he was absolved of the earlier drug charges laid against him when a Newfoundland Supreme Court ruled that police evidence had been obtained illegally. The court ruled that secret RCMP recordings made of meetings of Rizzuto's legal team while dining at a St. John's hotel restaurant jeopardized his chances of a fair trial (the offending RCMP officers swore in an affidavit they were conducting surveillance as part of an entirely separate investigation). Usually a man who refrains from talking to the media, Rizzuto did tell a reporter when leaving the courtroom, "One word can mean so much — especially when that word is acquittal."

Desjardins and Rizzuto would continue their drug dealing relationship and, along with Quebec Hells Angels leader Maurice Boucher, they were allegedly behind a botched 750-kilo shipment of cocaine that was to be smuggled into the Port of Halifax in 1993. At the time, police believed the coke had been dumped into the ocean by smugglers who panicked when their boat began to malfunction. The drugs were never retrieved, but police were confident they had enough evidence to lay charges. When RCMP officers were tailing Desjardins in the summer of 1993, they watched as he regularly held meetings with Boucher and other senior Angels. Desjardin was eventually convicted for his part in the conspiracy and received fifteen years, while Rizzuto and Boucher were left untouched due to a lack of evidence.

Vito's father did not seem to share his son's luck in escaping the clutches of police and prosecution. On February 12, 1988, Venezuelan national police arrested Nick Rizzuto at his home in Caracas on drug trafficking charges after they found around 800 grams of cocaine hidden in a special belt (most likely a sample for an upcoming purchase). Rizzuto was arrested along with four other men, all of whom had ties to the Montreal mafia. He was acquitted at his first trial, but prosecutors successfully appealed the decision and obtained a conviction for one count of cocaine possession. As a result, Nick Rizzuto was sentenced to eight years in prison. After almost five years in a Venezuelan jail, he was paroled and flew to Montreal on May 23, 1993, where he was greeted at the airport by his son Vito and more than two dozen friends and relatives. Not long after his release, speculation was rampant that government palms in Venezuela were greased to secure Nick's early parole. Domenic Tozzi, an associate of the Rizzuto Family, told an undercover RCMP officer he personally took $800,000 to Venezuela in 1993 to purchase Nick's release.

Born in the early 1940s, Domenico Tozzi specialized in money laundering for the Montreal mafia and, for years, worked with long-time mafioso Vincenzo (Jimmy) Di Maulo. Along with Giuseppe (Joseph) Lagana, a lawyer whose principal client was Vito Rizzuto, Tozzi was caught up in an RCMP sting operation in which the Mounties set up a phony currency exchange business in the early 1990s in downtown Montreal to nab money launderers and to infiltrate the drug operations that generated the illicit cash. In their allegations against Tozzi, the RCMP said he

began frequenting the undercover Centre International Monétaire de Montréal in late 1991 to exchange cash. In less than three years, from December 2, 1991 to July 28, 1994, Tozzi brought more than $27 million into the fake currency exchange business. Police alleged the money was exclusively derived from the drug trafficking activities connected to the Montreal mafia.

The sting operation was shut down on August 30, 1994, and fifty-seven people were arrested on hundreds of counts of money laundering and drug trafficking offences. Along with Tozzi, other Rizzuto associates were arrested included Joseph Lagana, who, along with a couple of junior lawyers in his law firm, had delivered millions of dollars in Canadian cash to undercover officers. (One observer estimated that Lagana and his associates laundered a staggering $91 million.) Other services availed by the lawyers were purchases of monetary instruments and arranging for overseas wire transfers. Lagana, who was described in court as the right-hand man of Vito Rizzuto and an intermediary with Colombian drug traffickers, confessed to laundering $47.4 million in drug proceeds and participating in a conspiracy to import 558 kilos of cocaine to Canada. He pleaded guilty in June 1995 and was sentenced to thirteen years in prison. Tozzi was charged with money laundering and conspiracy to traffic in drugs and in March 1996, he admitted to his role in laundering over $27 million and plotting three cocaine shipments to Canada. He was sentenced to ten years in prison and fined $150,000. Both Tozzi and Lagana were paroled after serving a fraction of their sentences.

Jimmy Di Maulo was also caught in the police proceeds-of-crime net and was charged with forty-six counts of money laundering and drug trafficking. In 1996, he admitted to laundering more than $10.5 million from 1990 to 1994 through the undercover operation and was also convicted for his role in importing 2,500 kilos of cocaine from Colombia into the country. For these offences, he was sentenced to twelve years. Two of Di Maulo's associates were also imprisoned after they were caught offering a $100,000 bribe to a Mountie to secure his efforts to convince the prosecutor to reduce the prison sentence he was pursuing for Di Maulo.

Another long-time Montreal mafioso charged as part of the money laundering sting operation was

Sabatino (Sammy) Nicolucci. Born in the late 1940s, Nicolucci had convictions for drug possession and counterfeiting that date back to the early 1970s. He was close enough to Vito Rizzuto that he travelled with him to Caracas in 1984. A year later, he was sentenced to fourteen years in prison for narcotics offences after police seized around 13 kilos of cocaine in Vancouver. Nicolucci was paroled in 1991, and threw himself back into the cocaine trafficking and money laundering business. Police quickly caught up with Nicolucci, charging him with 437 counts of drug trafficking and money laundering, which stemmed in part from his role in helping to ship more than 500 kilos of cocaine to the Hells Angels in Great Britain. Before he could be arrested, Nicolucci was kidnapped at gunpoint while lounging at a Montreal strip club. He was first transported to the Laurentians, just north of Montreal, then flown to Miami and finally taken to Colombia, where he was held captive by members of a cocaine cartel over repayment of a $1.7-million drug debt. Although there were suspicions that Nicolucci had been killed by his captors, he was picked up by Colombian police in February 1995. It is still unclear whether he escaped, had his ransom paid, or cut a deal with the hostage-takers. After another eighteen months in a Colombian prison, he was extradited to Canada in May 1996. In 1997, Nicolucci was found guilty on more than 150 criminal counts, including conspiracy to import drugs into Canada and laundering $31 million in drug money. He was sentenced to nineteen years in prison, which could only be served after the remainder of his fourteen-year drug conviction from 1985 was finished.

As in the past, Vito Rizzuto, Canada's own "Teflon Don," escaped any charges stemming from the undercover operation, despite his name appearing on a search warrant executed at Lagana's Montreal law firm. "We know that he is part of the conspiracy but because of legal principles we cannot file this evidence against Mr. Rizzuto," a Crown prosecutor told the media.

"WHAT'S ORGANIZED CRIME?"

What's organized crime? Listen, I'm 62 and I'm tired and I have to crawl out of bed every morning.
—John Papalia in a 1989 media interview

Whatever power or dominance Italian crime groups enjoyed in Ontario ended in the 1980s with the deaths of Stefano Magaddino, Paul Volpe, Michele Racco, Giacomo Luppino, and the jailings of the Commisso brothers, Rocco Zito, the Luppino brothers, and the Musitanos. Ontario's fractured criminal underworld became even more fractured as a diverse range of organized criminals, including the Chinese triads, outlaw motorcycle gangs, Russian criminal groups, the Colombian "cocaine cowboys," as well as mafiosi imported from Quebec and Italy stormed into the province.

When Joseph Todaro became the boss of Buffalo's Magaddino Family in 1984, John Papalia was anointed as his main representative for Southern Ontario, which included Toronto, Hamilton, and the Niagara Peninsula. Papalia returned to his Hamilton, base after having been released from jail in 1981 following a six-year term for defrauding and extorting stockbroker Stanley Bader. For the remainder of his life he appeared intent on filling the power vacuum, although, as in the past, he would never be able to completely impose his authority nor was the Magaddino Family under Todaro able to reign supreme in Ontario like it once did under the Grand Old Man.

John Papalia in the 1980s

Papalia's immediate plans were to establish a monopoly of gambling houses and loansharking activities in his territories. He already either controlled or was receiving a cut from the underground Italian gambling houses in Toronto and Niagara Falls and was also attempting to exercise influence in Toronto's

Jewish and Greek gambling clubs by exacting a protection fee. In addition, he was muscling his way into the loan-shark businessby advancing money to street lenders in return for a percentage of their profits. In October 1985, Louis Iannuzzelli, a Niagara Falls bookmaker and convicted loan shark disappeared. One Niagara Regional Police officer suggested to reporters that Iannuzzelli committed suicide because he was depressed. Other theories revolved around the possibility that Iannuzzelli, who had once been part of Magaddino's bookmaking operations in Ontario, got into financial difficulties with Papalia or was intruding on his territory. "I'm sure he was depressed," a Toronto police intelligence officer was quoted as saying in a 1986 *Globe and Mail* article on Papalia. "You'd be depressed, too, if you thought Johnny Pops was mad at you for some reason. He didn't commit suicide. He was killed. And with him gone, there's no competition for John in Niagara Falls." The same article described how a Toronto loan shark was assaulted by "a renegade biker" in November 1986 and was told to pay the more than $100,000 he owed Papalia.

Papalia's efforts to control the gambling halls, bookmarkers, and loan sharks in Southern Ontario were largely delegated to two of his key lieutenants: Carmen Barillaro, who was responsible for Niagara Falls, and Enio Mora, who had jurisdiction over Toronto. Barillaro was a made member of the Magaddino Family and one of a dozen men who reported directly to Papalia. By the late 1980s, Barillaro was considered by police as one of the ten most powerful mafia members in Ontario (his boss was considered number one at the time) and may even have risen to become Papalia's number-two man by the 1990s. Barillaro also had his own circle of criminal associates in the Niagara Region that helped him carry out Papalia's orders while executing other mostly loansharking, bookmaking, and drug trafficking activities for Barillo. He was a ruggedly handsome man, with a passing resemblance to Warren Beatty. Neighbours characterized the father of two girls as quite sociable; he regularly greeted them on the street and liked to barbeque in his backyard. Every Sunday he went to church and had dinner with his mother. Born in Italy on July 24, 1944, he moved to Canada before the age of ten. His first conviction came in 1978 when he received two years in prison

for conspiracy to traffic in heroin. While out on parole in 1980 he was arrested and then handed a three-year sentence after selling three ounces of heroin to an undercover police officer. When he emerged from jail he began working for Papalia in their mutual quest to dominate underground gambling and loansharking operations in the Niagara Region.

Carmen Barillaro

Weighing in at around 260 pounds, Enio Mora was a hulk of a man who lost the lower half of one leg in 1979 from a shotgun blast during a robbery attempt at a Toronto gambling hall under his protection. The prime suspect in the robbery was a small time criminal named Anthony Carnevale, who was never charged, but who was killed by a shotgun blast in the basement of his parents' home in January 1980 (not long after Mora was fitted for an artificial leg). Born in 1949 in Sora, Italy, Mora immigrated to Canada in 1968. Before working for Papalia, he was linked to Siderno Group member Rocco Zito and later Paul Volpe. Of those who subscribe to the theory that Papalia was the trigger man behind Volpe's murder in 1983, some believe it was Mora who lured Volpe to the construction yard

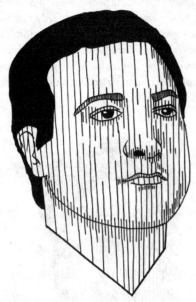

Enio Mora

where he met his demise. Like Barillaro, Mora was one of Papalia's most reliable enforcers. When one man supposedly took too long to pay a debt to Papalia, Mora allegedly doused him with gasoline and drove him to his boss, who just happened to be playing with his cigarette lighter at the time.

In 1985, Mora and Barillaro were among ten people arrested in what police were calling a protection racket that preyed upon Greek gambling clubs on Toronto's Danforth Avenue. The arrests were part of "Project Outhouse," a joint forces operation targeting Papalia's efforts to take over independent gambling and bookmaking operations in Southern Ontario. Also charged with extortion was thirty-five-year-old Peter Scarcella, Paul Volpe's former aid and godfather to Mora's child. In laying the charges, police noted that a shot was fired late at night through a window of one of the clubs while the owner of another club had his ear slashed with a knife. No charges were laid against Papalia and when asked about the arrests of his associates, he told a *Globe and Mail* reporter, "Yeah, I know the people they charged, they're friends of mine. But that doesn't mean I was involved. I wasn't, because I wouldn't have anything to do with Greeks. I don't like them, I don't like their restaurants, I don't

like their food." Police eventually dropped the charges against Barillaro and Mora.

In 1989, Barillaro was sentenced to three years for counselling to commit murder against Roy Caja, an ex-member of the Outlaws Motorcycle Gang. Caja was in Barillaro's debt but escaped any harm after the hit woman hired to kill him became a police informant. Barillaro only served half of that sentence and once back on the outside he was quickly arrested on drug charges stemming from a police investigation in which cocaine and marijuana with a wholesale value of US$2.2 million was seized. In June 1993, he and three other men were charged with extortion, uttering threats and assault after number of people from Niagara Falls complained that large sums of money were being demanded from them.

When Barillaro was hauled before the court as part of the pre-trial hearings for his attempted hit on Caja, RCMP corporal Reginald King, a noted mob expert for Ontario, testified that Papalia was a top crime figure in Ontario. "We're looking at approximately 275 organized crime subjects that we monitor into about 15 different groups in the province of Ontario, and we have Mr. Barillaro as the head of one of these groups based in Niagara Falls under the sphere of John Papalia." By 1992, the Canadian Association of Chiefs of Police was reporting that fourteen "traditional organized crime groups" (mafia and 'Ndrangheta groups) were active in Ontario. "Members of these organizations are established in Toronto, Windsor, Hamilton, Ottawa and the Niagara Region," according to the report. "All of these groups associate with their counterparts in Quebec, the United States and Italy. Connections have been confirmed between the American LCN in Detroit, Michigan and organized crime groups in Ontario."

In addition to the Cosa Nostra's Canadian contingent headed by Papalia, the Calabrian 'Ndrangheta continued to thrive in Ontario despite the death of former leader Michele Rocco and the imprisonment of his heirs, Rocco Zito and the Commisso brothers. The Criminal Intelligence Service Canada reported in 1985 that in Ontario the 'Ndrangheta continued to operate "a number of loosely structured 'cells,' which are branches of crime families based in Calabria, Italy. These cells exist in the London, Hamilton, Ottawa and Toronto area."

A 1990 report by the Canadian Association of Chiefs of Police noted that members of the 'Ndrangheta cells in Toronto were behind a large-scale counterfeiting ring that was distributing American $100 counterfeit bills in the Toronto area. "Many members" of the 'Ndrangheta in the Toronto area were also "heavily involved in drug trafficking between Toronto, New York and Italy," according to the report. Indeed, the Calabrian Mafia in Canada was a central player in an international heroin trafficking conspiracy that linked 'Ndrina groups on the eastern shores of Calabria, which supplied the heroin, and those in New York State, which were the recipients of most of the heroin. The group also supplied cocaine that was traded for the heroin and destined for European markets.

Despite the successful barter system, cash was still used to purchase cocaine in North America, as evidenced by the February 12, 1989, arrival of Vincenzo Restagno at Toronto's Pearson International Airport on a flight from Rome with 370 million Italian lire (about CDN$370,000) inside a shoebox. Although suspicious, Canadian Customs agents let him go because carrying large amounts of cash into Canada was not a crime. Police later found out that Restagno was working for a notorious 'Ndrangheta chieftain in Calabria and engaged in smuggling heroin through Canada into New York. From there, the heroin was exchanged for cocaine which would then be mailed to relatives in Italy mixed in with baby clothes. A few days after arriving in Toronto, Restagno flew to New York and, once off the plane, drove immediately to a Manhattan branch of the Bank of America where he withdrew $60,000 in U.S. currency that had been wired the day before by the owner of a travel agency in Toronto's Little Italy. While in New York, Restagno phoned his father and uncle in Toronto, who arranged to have another $90,000 wired to them via the same travel agency. The money was then used to purchase five kilos of cocaine, which was mailed to the grandmother of an accomplice back in Italy. On February 27, Restagno and seven others were arrested by the FBI following a joint American-Canadian-Italian investigation into international drug trafficking by 'Ndrangheta clans.

In 1985, Constable Giovanni Persichetti, an undercover RCMP officer, was initiated into one 'Ndrangheta cell in London, Ontario. Three separate ceremonies, held in a high-rise apartment in the city, were captured on police videotape. The targets of the undercover operation were brothers Giovanni (John) and Saverio (Sam) Zangari, and it was Giovanni who presided over the ceremony and initiated the undercover officer in a tightly drawn circle made up of six existing members of his secret society. He told the new recruit that he would be entering "The Honoured Society of Calabria" and "the Family" at the rank of *picciotto* (soldier). The ceremony became public in March 1988 when a Crown prosecutor used it as evidence in the trial of the Zangari brothers in a bid to strengthen the allegation of a criminal conspiracy. Both brothers were charged with one count of conspiring to traffic in cocaine, which resulted from the RCMP undercover operation in which Persichetti told the brothers he had a reliable source for 1.2 kilos of almost pure cocaine if the Zangari brothers could produce a seller. Shortly after videotapes of the swearing-in ceremony were shown, the trial ended abruptly when Giovanni and Saverio changed their pleas to guilty. After firing their lawyers and switching their pleas back to not guilty the brothers were tried once more, but again they decided to plead guilty to lesser charges and received minimal sentences as a result.

A few years later, two other mafia-wannabe brothers were having their own problems. In April 1995, twenty-eight-year-old Domenic Violi and his twenty-four-year-old brother Giuseppe were among eight people arrested in what the Hamilton-Wentworth deputy police chief called the city's "most significant drug bust involving organized crime" in more than a quarter century. Domenic and Giuseppe were the sons of deceased Montreal mobster Paolo Violi and his widow, Grazia, herself the daughter of Giacomo Luppino, the long-time leader of the Hamilton wing of the Magaddino Family. She had moved back to her hometown following the 1978 death of her husband and raised her two boys in Hamilton, where police believe they were being groomed for leadership positions within the local Magaddino crew. The eight men were accused of conspiring to smuggle cocaine from Colombia to Ontario via the U.S. The police operation culminated with the seizure of more than 100 kilos of cocaine in Joplin, Missouri, and four kilos in Toronto.

Along with four others, Giuseppe pleaded guilty to conspiracy to import a narcotic, although charges were withdrawn against his brother Domenic.

The Musitano brothers of Hamilton were also reeling after Anthony was sentenced to fifteen years in prison in 1983 for the string of bombings he orchestrated as part of his wave of extortion bids against local Italian businesses. While in prison, Anthony, his brother Domenic and their nephew Giuseppe Avignone plotted the death of Domenic Racco, the out-of-control son of deceased Siderno Group leader Michele Racco. In 1985, Anthony Musitano pleaded guilty to conspiring to murder Domenic Racco and was sentenced to twelve years. His brother Domenic was sentenced to just six years after pleading guilty to being an accessory and was released on parole after serving only two years. In 1995, Domenic's fifty-seven-year-old heart finally gave out under all that excess weight and he was pronounced dead of a heart attack at McMaster University Medical Centre.

Before his death, Domenic and his wife, Carmelina, raised five children in a modest semi-detached house in Hamilton's old Italian district (and a ten-minute walk from John Papalia's Railway Street headquarters). His eldest son, Pasquale (Pat) Musitano, carried on the criminal tradition of his family with the support of his younger brother, Angelo, and their cousin Giuseppe Avignone, who also spent time in prison for his part in the Racco murder plot. Born in 1968, Pasquale inherited his father's girth as well as his criminal tendencies. At the age of sixteen he quit school to take over the family's businesses. He later became president of P & L Recycling, a tire dump his father purchased in 1983. In 1992, the Musitanos were found guilty of failing to heed an environmental order to clean up the site. The province took control of the dump and the Musitanos were ordered to pay $1.8 million for the cleanup costs (which Pasquale dodged by pleading bankruptcy). He also ran a popular restaurant in Hamilton and was said to have been an affable and welcoming host.

In the summer of 1996, Pasquale and his brother-in-law John Trigiani were acquitted of conspiracy to commit arson for the purpose of insurance fraud, after someone tried to burn down the Collins Hotel located in a Hamilton suburb. On the morning of March 5, 1992, a hotel resident called the fire department to complain about smelling gasoline. When firefighters entered the historic premises, they discovered toasters rigged to timers in rooms soaked with gasoline. The resulting investigation, called "Project Toast," was an effort to determine why Musitano-owned properties kept going up in flames.

That same summer, the Hamilton-Wentworth Regional Police began investigating the illegal gaming activities of the Musitano family. Using information from an informant, the preliminary inquiry blossomed into a joint forces operation dubbed "Project Windfall." Evidence collected by police indicated that the Musitano group was making $14 million in annual profits from bookmaking, underground lotteries, and the illegal distribution of video lottery terminals. Between February 10 and April 7, 1997, police surveillance caught Vincenzo (Vince) Campanella receiving approximately 1,528 bets worth around $583,799 on sporting events, primarily professional basketball and hockey games. It was determined that Campanella was a bookie working for Pasquale Musitano and he was arrested and charged with gaming offences. In December 1997, the Windfall investigation resulted in criminal charges against another two dozen people in relation to the distribution of illegal gaming machines, most of which were operated out of two bars connected to the Musitanos. Pasquale was charged with illegal bookmaking. In a surprise move, however, the charges were withdrawn when Campanella and seven other accused took the rap and pleaded guilty. Musitano's cousin Giuseppe Avignone was not so lucky; he pleaded guilty to keeping illegal gambling machines and was fined $3,500.

THE ENFORCER LOOKED OLD

When John Papalia was released from jail in the early 1980s, his biographer, Adrian Humphreys, described him as having aged terribly. "His hair, which had started thinning and greying when he left for prison was now almost white, and a huge swath on the top of his head was essentially bald. He needed glasses to see clearly, his cheeks were jowly; his brow furrowed with thick wrinkles when he frowned. The Enforcer looked old." The prognosis for the future of Johnny Pops was equally downbeat. After decades as a gangster, and emerging from prison into a changed criminal underworld with far more players, there was no shortage of competition or people who would like him out of the picture. But Papalia hung on, and even prospered, for the next fifteen years. But time finally ran out on The Enforcer one spring day in 1997.

In the early afternoon on May 30, 1997, Papalia was conducting what had become an almost daily routine to avoid bugs planted in his offices: he was walking across the parking lot of his Galaxy Vending company on Railway Street, just across from the home where he grew up, talking business with a younger man. Without warning, the man, who witnesses described as about five-foot-nine around thirty-five years old and wearing a Nike baseball cap, turned, drew a gun, and fired a shot into the head of John Papalia. After the man jumped into a pickup truck and sped away, Papalia was rushed to a nearby hospital. About an hour after he was carted through the doors of the emergency room, he died.

After Pops was gunned down, Carman Barillaro began acting like he was Papalia's heir apparent and was even talking about becoming Buffalo's new representative in Southern Ontario. But Barillaro's hubris was short-lived. On August 12, 1997, he was killed at his Hamilton home. When paramedics arrived, it was clear they stood little chance of resuscitating him. He would have been fifty-three years old the next day.

For more than a year, the two murders remained unsolved, although there was no shortage of hypotheses. Some believed that the slayings were ordered by Buffalo because Papalia was becoming too independent and allowing other mobsters (such as Frank Cotroni) into Ontario. Another theory was that the Montreal mafia was embarking on a bid to wrest control of Ontario away from the once-powerful Magaddino Family. Still others pointed out that the nature of both murders did not reflect the hallmarks of mob hits in Canada, which are often done in relative seclusion — not in parking lots or homes in broad daylight. They are also carried out with some form of symbolism; Paul Volpe's bullet-riddled body was found in the trunk of his wife's car at Pearson International Airport while Paolo Violi was murdered in the bar he once owned. Police also contrasted Papalia's death with the September 11, 1996, murder of his lieutenant, Enio Mora, who was shot four times in the head at close range and whose body was stuffed in the trunk of his Cadillac with his hands bound and his prosthetic leg lying near his head. Before the end of the year, Giacinto Arcuri, a native of Sicily who was a good friend of Mora's, co-owned some real estate with him, and had joined him for coffee just hours before the murder, was arrested and charged with first-degree murder. Police found little to link the murder of Mora to that of Papalia and Barillaro and, six years after his arrest, the seventy-two-year-old Arcuri was acquitted by a jury.

A few months before Papalia and Barillaro died, police had formed "Project Expiate," a task force that was to investigate the 1987 murder of Ronald MacNeil and the 1985 murder of Salvatore (Sam) Alaimo. Sensing that the same killer may have also been responsible for all four murders, the task force was mandated to investigate the Papalia and Barillaro slayings as well. Their trail eventually led to Ken Murdock, a former bouncer-turned-enforcer-turned-hit-man who had a reputation for petty crimes, violence, and a cocaine addiction. In their investigation of Papalia's murder, police compiled a physical description that closely matched that of Murdock. Even the man who hired Murdock later told him that police and Papalia's former gang members knew it was he who carried out the hit and that both were closing in on him.

Ken Murdock

Several months after the Papalia and Barillaro murders, Murdock was sitting in jail on charges of extortion and assault. Suspecting that he was the trigger man, police played on his suspicions that a contract had been placed on his head by Papalia's mob associates. Fearing for his life, he confessed to police in October 1998. Through his lawyer, he then cut a deal and, in return for a lenient sentence, he agreed to provide the names of and testify against the men who hired him to kill Barillaro and Papalia.

Murdock pleaded guilty to three counts of second-degree murder for the deaths of Papalia and Barillaro as well as the drive-by shooting of Salvatore Alaimo, a fifty-three-year-old janitor at Stelco Inc. who died instantly when a bullet struck him in the head as he worked in the garage of his Hamilton home. Five shots were fired in his general direction from a small yellow car that neighbours said had been cruising the area for several days. But police made little progress on the case. Murdock, who was just twenty-two at the time of this, his first murder, told police the hit on Alaimo was ordered by the late Dominic Musitano. He said that he was approached by two men with an offer to kill Alaimo for $10,000 (although he stated he only received $3,000 of the promised amount). Murdock confessed to police that he was told in the vaguest of terms that Alaimo must die because of "money and family." Two theories have been proposed as to why Musitano wanted Alaimo killed: he owed a debt to Musitano (and the shots were supposed to have been just a warning), or he simply had angered Musitano, who and felt obliged to respond to the slight in a traditional mafia manner. Regardless, for the three murders, Murdock received a life sentence with no eligibility for parole for thirteen years.

On November 24, 1998, Murdock was charged, tried, convicted, and sentenced in perhaps the most expedient murder trial in Ontario history. "I killed Papalia for $2,000 and forty grams of cocaine, then I killed Barillaro," he told the judge. A few hours before Murdock's rapid-fire trial, police acted on the information he provided and simultaneously visited the homes of Pasquale Musitano and his brother Angelo. Pat was charged with first-degree murder in Papalia's death while Angelo was charged with first-degree murder in both Papalia's and Barillaro's slayings.

As part of Barillaro's sworn statements to police (before he himself was murdered) he said that Papalia was marked for death by the brothers because Pasquale owed Johnny money. Conversely, police have speculated that Pasquale ordered the hit so he could take over Papalia's gambling and other criminal activities in Hamilton and the Niagara Region. The Musitanos had already expanded their bookmaking and gambling operations to Guelph, London, and Toronto, and police intelligence even suggests that Papalia had turned over some of his gambling and protection rackets to the Musitanos (which either may have infuriated Buffalo mob bosses enough to have Papalia killed or perhaps because they pressured Papalia to relinquish control because he was getting too old). Either way, a mob hit on Papalia would first have to be cleared by Buffalo. Police intelligence collected during Project Windfall uncovered at least one meeting between the Musitanos and made members from the Magaddino Family, which supports this particular theory.

Pat Musitano (left) and his brother Angelo are shown leaving provincial court in Hamilton in September 1998.

Lee Coppola, a former reporter from western New York who covered the Magaddino Family for more than two decades, told the media in 1998 that a Buffalo-sanctioned hit "is a very unlikely scenario. I don't think there is enough organization, structure, power or authority in the Buffalo mob to have any input or sanction into a murder in Canada." Coppola, who was the dean of the journalism school at St. Bonaventure University in New York State when he made these comments, was adamant that "for all intents and purposes, the Buffalo mob — as it once was when Magaddino actually ruled that part of Toronto and the Papalias and Violis were under him — is all diminished and has been diminishing over the last couple of decades to a point now where there is no leadership, there is no structure, and there certainly is not power." Coppola believed that if the Musitanos were responsible for the killings of Papalia and Barillaro, they were probably acting on their own.

Another plausible theory is that Vito Rizzuto ordered Papalia dead to pave the way for a full-scale invasion of Southern Ontario. The Montreal mafia, under Rizzuto, was already carrying out gambling operations in Eastern Ontario and had aligned themselves with the Musitanos, who were expanding across the more populous southern and western parts of the province. On October 23, 1997, Pasquale Musitano and his cousin Giuseppe Avigone met with Vito Rizzuto in Toronto, lending credence to this theory.

The murder of Barillaro was advantageous to the Musitano brothers for two reasons. First, it would further clear the way for the brothers to take over Papalia's rackets, given Barillaro's reasonable quest to ascend to Papalia's throne. Second, they believed that Barillaro suspected them of killing his boss and it was only a matter of time before he sought revenge. In fact, two days after Papalia was killed, police surveillance cameras picked up Pat Musitano and Barillaro in a heated discussion outside of Musitano's eatery. Barillaro accused Musitano of ordering the hit on Papalia and even had information that Murdock was the trigger man. Musitano denied any involvement in the killing, but Barillaro apparently would not be dissuaded.

The Musitano brothers were originally charged with first-degree murder, but in the middle of their preliminary hearing in February 2000, they both entered guilty pleas to the lesser charge of conspiracy to commit murder of Barillaro. The Crown withdrew both murder counts involving Papalia. Pat Musitano's decision in February 2000 to plead guilty to conspiring to murder Barillaro was particularly surprising given that he was only charged with the murder of Papalia; he was not charged with the murder of Barillaro. Musitano's defence lawyer told the media that his client was securing a plea bargain for his younger brother, who was facing two counts of murder in the slayings of both Barillaro and Papalia. The plea agreement stipulated that the

Crown would withdraw both murder counts relating to Papalia if the Musitanos would take responsibility for the death of Barillaro alone. The motive behind Pat Musitano's plea bargain was also to distance himself and Angelo from the murder of the legendary mobster. On February 5, 2000, the two brothers were convicted of conspiracy to murder Carmen Barillaro and each was sentenced to ten years in jail.

OMERTA

When Frank Cotroni's eldest son, Francesco, was released from jail in the early 1990s for his part in murdering Giuseppe Montegano, he inherited his father's drug network. He even travelled to Columbia in February 1995 to meet with Gilberto Rodriguez Orejuela, the head of the Cali Cartel, to discuss shipments of cocaine to Canada. Francesco was also seen meeting with other major drug traffickers at the Villa Sorrento hotel in Mexico, which was co-owned by his father at the time. But this was an especially perilous time for anyone aspiring to become a big-time coke dealer in Quebec; the province was engulfed in a brutal war over who would dominate the cocaine market, pitting the Hells Angels against the Rock Machine. On August 3, 1993, Francesco's car, which was parked in front of Expotronique, a video lottery machine company he ran in the Saint-Leonard neighbourhood of Montreal, exploded. A little more than a week later, another explosion went off in front of the building. Nobody was harmed, but the damage caused by the two bombings was estimated at $400,000. Police had been monitoring Expotronique since the mid-1980s when it was linked to the distribution of illegal video lottery terminals and was raided by police in May 1988 as part of an investigation into illegal gambling in Montreal. Most interpreted the bombings as a warning to Cotroni to get out of the cocaine business, and police arrests in relation to the explosions appeared to justify this speculation. On October 20, 1993, two men believed to be associates of the Quebec Hells Angels, Bruno Boutin and Christain Caron, were charged with the bombings. The two pleaded guilty, without revealing who was behind the order to bomb Cotroni's business, but according to some media accounts, Boutin and Caron were hired by Cotroni so he could collect on the insurance.

On September 28, 1995, Frank Senior was released from jail and once on the outside he became involved in a cocaine importing partnership with Daniel The Arab Serero, a reputed associate of the West End Gang. Police claimed the network negotiated directly with suppliers in Cali, Colombia, and Lima, Peru, and were importing hundreds, if not thousands, of kilos of cocaine into Canada. Following the seizure of 170 kilos of cocaine in 1996, Frank, his son Francesco, and twenty-two others were nabbed by police and charged with various drug offences. (When Francesco was arrested at his home, police found a manual on bomb making.) In April 1997, just three days before their trial was to begin, Frank Cotroni and his son pleaded guilty to conspiring to import cocaine into Canada and received seven and eight years, respectively. Serero pleaded guilty the previous year to conspiracy to import 3,000 kilos of hashish into Canada and was sentenced to eleven years in prison.

Frank Cotroni is led away in handcuffs after his arrest in April 17, 1996, in Montreal.

While behind bars, Frank Cotroni received horrible news. On August 23, 1998, Paolo, the second of his five sons, was ambushed by two men as he was getting out of his car at his suburban Montreal home. He was shot six times, including two shots to the head. A couple of days after the attack, the family made the decision to remove the forty-two-year-old from life support. According to police, Paolo ran his own lucrative drug network in Montreal that sold drugs out of nightclubs and bars. Police believe he was a victim of Quebec's cocaine war, although they did not rule out the possibility that he was murdered by the Sicilian wing of the Montreal mafia.

In 2001, Frank Cotroni was paroled after serving four years in prison. He was seventy years old and had now spent close to thirty years of his life in a Canadian or America prison. His parole came with tight conditions, which included restrictions on where he could travel and with whom he could associate. Cotroni was arrested on June 3, 2002 for allegedly violating the conditions of his parole because he was fraternizing with known criminals. He was given a conditional release in August 2002 and two years later, on August 17, 2004, he died of brain cancer at his Montreal home.

At best, Frank Cotroni and his sons were a major irritant to the Sicilian wing of the Montreal mafia and a daily reminder of its past reviled Calabrian leadership. Frank's never-ending jailings were anathema to Vito Rizzuto, who prided himself on his ability to avoid jail time and demanded that his men maintain a low profile. And while Cotroni had a strong drug network in place, Vito Rizzuto needed little help in building up his own international drug empire.

The main engine of Rizzuto's drug dealing vehicle were the Caruana-Cuntrera families, who were so intertwined with the Rizzutos that Italian authorities began referring to them collectively as the "Agrigento Mafia," a title referring to the province in Sicily where all three families originated. The patriarchs of the two clans, Pasquale Cuntrera and bothers Leonardo and Liborio Caruana, were all born in Siculiana, a village in Agrigento. Joined by blood and intermarriages, the two families formed a criminal clique that ruled their village. Between 1950 and 1965, five Cuntrera brothers — Pasquale, Gaspare, Liborio, Paolo and Agostino — immigrated to Canada and were followed in the late 1960s by the three Caruana brothers: Gerlando, Alfonso, and Pasquale. The Caruana and Cuntrera families were instrumental in helping Nick Rizzuto build up the finances and power he needed to overthrow the Calabrian wing of the Montreal mafia, which included using family members to murder Paolo Violi. While Nick and the Cuntrera family were establishing a strategic base in Caracas, Vito Rizzuto and the Caruana brothers remained in Montreal to help coordinate the importation of heroin and cocaine. By the mid-1970s, the Caruana-Cuntrera group was running a global drug operation that dealt in tens of millions of dollars of heroin, cocaine, and hashish annually.

As mafia-linked drug traffickers they were innovators of sorts. In the early 1980s, they began buying heroin produced in Asia's Golden Triangle from suppliers in Thailand. Pasquale and Alfonso Caruana relocated to England in 1982 and three years later, two shipments of heroin hidden in furniture originating in Thailand was seized in London and Montreal. Thirty-six kilograms were seized in London on May 30, 1985, while another 22 kilos were discovered when members of the RCMP drug squad swooped down on a warehouse in Montreal's west end in June. Among those arrested in Montreal was Gerlando Caruana, who was later convicted of drug trafficking and received an eighteen-year sentence (although he was paroled in less than half that time).

The drug bust prompted a larger investigation into the Caruana and Cuntrera families by police in Canada, the United States, and Italy. The RCMP estimated that between 1978 and 1985, the Agrigento Mafia had imported into Montreal more than 700 kilos of heroin and, between 1984 and 1987, 70 tons of hashish. During roughly the same period, it was conservatively estimated that Alfonso Caruana and his associates had moved $33 million through personal and corporate bank accounts in Canada. Thanks in part to a corrupt branch manager, Alfonso Caruana supervised the laundering of more than $15 million in drug money through the City and District Savings Bank in Montreal. So much cash was being delivered to the branch that it was stuffed into tote bags, loaded onto pickup trucks, and then backed up to its front door. Between late April and early November 1981 alone, $10 million, mostly in small American bills, was brought into the bank branch. The amount of U.S. cash being delivered was so plentiful it supplied all the other branches of the bank in the Montreal area

with U.S. currency, with enough left over to be sold to competitors. By the end of that year, suspicious senior management at the bank refused to service Caruana anymore and ordered all his accounts closed. Cash was also being laundered through foreign banks; on November 27, 1978, Alfonso and his close colleague Giuseppe Cuffaro arrived in Zurich, Switzerland, on a Swiss Air flight from Montreal, and were fined for failing to declare $600,000 in American money concealed in false-bottomed suitcases. Italian police began calling the Caruana-Cuntrera group "the Rothchilds of the Mafia" due to their global financial prowess.

Beginning in 1985, members of the Caruana and Cuntrera families were under intense police scrutiny due to recent drug busts. The amount of cash flowing through their bank accounts also attracted the attention of Revenue Canada and, in 1986, the federal agency seized approximately $876,000 from a personal account belonging to Alfonso Caruana. In 1992, Gaspare, Pasquale, and Paolo Cuntrera were extradited from Venezuela to Italy and, in 1998, they were convicted on a number of offences, amongst them drug trafficking. Alfonso Caruana was also charged and received, *in absentia*, a sentence of twenty-two years and a fine of 180 million lira.

Alfonso avoided extradition to Italy and in 1995 he resurfaced in Montreal to declare personal bankruptcy, a move that was made to escape an assessment of $29.8 million levied against him two years earlier by Revenue Canada for unpaid taxes and penalties. As the decade drew to a close, police gathered more evidence surrounding the organization's international drug trafficking activities. As part of "Project Omerta," an RCMP-led, joint force, multinational investigation that was one of the largest and costliest in Canadian history, police obtained sworn testimony from Oreste Pagano, a member of the Camorra based in Brescia, Italy, and a middleman between Alfonso Caruana and Colombian drug suppliers. Pagano revealed that he had supplied Caruana with cocaine from South America between 1991 and 1998. This included two back-to-back cocaine shipments of enormous proportions: 4,526 kilos into Canada and 8,200 kilos into Italy. Pagano estimated that these shipments netted the organization CDN$36 million and US$36 million, respectively.

Law enforcement in the U.S. and Canada were also closing in. On May 16, 1998, while transporting 200 kilograms of cocaine to Canada, John Curtis Hill and Richard Todd Court were arrested and charged by police in Texas. The Caruana-Cuntrera organization, and Alfonso Caruana in particular, was identified as the primary facilitator of this drug shipment. Two months later, Project Omerta culminated with a series of pre-dawn raids throughout Greater Toronto that targeted the leaders and members of the Caruana-Cuntrera drug trafficking group. Among the eight people arrested was Alfonso Caruana, whose principal residence was now in the Toronto suburb of Woodbridge. His brothers Gerlando and Pasquale were also arrested and charged. At the time of the takedown, police described the Caruana-Cuntrera group as one of the world's largest and most successful drug trafficking networks with outposts or connections in Miami, New York, Mexico City, Toronto, Montreal, Houston, Italy, England, France, Germany, Spain, The Netherlands, Venezuela, Aruba, Thailand, and India.

When search warrants were executed at the Woodbridge home of Alfonso Caruana, police found $40,000 in cash and jewellery worth $304,229 hidden in a secret compartment. In a building considered to be the Toronto headquarters of the Caruana–Cuntrera group, a suitcase containing $200,000, in twenty-dollar denominations was found hidden in the ceiling of the office of Giuseppe Cuntrera Dimora (son of Liborio Cuntrera). The cash was later confirmed by Oreste Pagano to be partial payment for a drug shipment. Found in the office of Giuseppe Cuntrera (son of Paolo Cuntrera) were two safety deposit box keys. A search of the safety deposit boxes uncovered $390,047 in Canadian currency, $11,170 in American currency, as well as jewellery and coins with an appraised value of approximately $314,592. A concurrent investigation in Venezuela resulted in a number of arrests of individuals associated with the Caruana-Cuntrera organization. Bank accounts containing $14 million in Venezuela and 400,000 hectares of land in Bolivia were seized by authorities in both countries.

In the Greater Toronto Area alone, eighteen companies associated with the Caruana and Cuntrera families were identified by police. These businesses included import-export companies, fitness clubs, nightclubs, restaurants, supermarkets, auto leasing

Alfonso Caruana upon his arrest in 1998

and sales companies, a tanning parlour, a car-cleaning company, a pool hall, a decorating company, a real estate firm, a travel agency, a meat-packing company, a record distribution company, and hotel management businesses. Numerous numbered and holding companies — with no stated lines of business — were also identified. One of these companies reported annual revenues of under $10,000, yet police identified cash deposits and withdrawals from its corporate bank account that ran into millions of dollars annually.

Illegal revenues were also invested into real estate. Police identified at least eleven homes in the Greater Toronto Area that belonged to members of the Caruana and Cuntrera families. Of the eleven homes, two were registered in the names of active members of the criminal organization, two were registered in the names of numbered companies belonging to members, and seven were registered in the names of wives or daughters of members or associates of the criminal group. Of these seven properties, three had private mortgage financing by group members or their associates.

On February 25, 2000, key members of the Caruana-Cuntrera group pleaded guilty in court and received lengthy jail terms. Alfonso Caruana was sentenced to two concurrent eighteen-year prison terms for masterminding the importation of Colombian cocaine into Canada. He also faced extradition to Italy to serve the twenty-two-year sentence he received *in absentia* for drug trafficking and other offences. His brothers Gerlando and Pasquale were handed eighteen and ten years, respectively. Oreste Pagano pled guilty on December 9, 1999 to conspiracy to import and traffic in a controlled substance. He was sentenced to time served and then was immediately extradited to Italy as a co-operating witness. Before he left Canada, he described to police how Vito Rizzuto received a cut from Alfonso Caruana's cocaine trafficking activities and even detailed how he was ordered to kill a lawyer in Venezuela whom Rizzuto had suspected of stealing $500,000 that was meant to secure the release of Nick Rizzuto from prison. Pagano said the hit was never carried out.

PROTECTING THE ORGANIZATION FROM BETRAYAL AND INFILTRATION

Once again Vito Rizzuto, escaped the charges that befell his close colleagues. Despite the arrest and successful prosecution of many of his minions, Rizzuto had not been convicted of any criminal infraction since his arson offence in 1972 (he was fined several hundreds of thousands of dollars by Revenue Canada for failing to pay taxes on $1.5 million in revenue between 1986 and 1988 and, in 2001, he reached an out-of-court settlement in part to avoid the exposure of his criminal ties that would have resulted from a public trial).

By the turn of the millennium, Vito Rizzuto was all powerful, and as he entered his fifth decade, he very much looked the part of the mafia don; he had aged well and his well-trimmed, slicked-back greying hair complemented his elegant attire. For years, he lived in a 4,500-square-foot home on Montreal's Antoine-Berthelet Avenue (otherwise known as "Mafia Road" because of the other homeowners, including his father, who lived two doors down, and Paolo Renda, Vito's brother-in-law and the man convicted of conspiracy to commit arson alongside him in 1972). Vito was also known as an avid collector of luxury and classic cars, and at one time owned a Porsche, a Lincoln, two Jaguars, and three Corvettes.

The 2001 annual report of the Criminal Intelligence Service Canada asserted that the Rizzuto Family "remains one of the most influential and powerful criminal organizations in the Montreal area, exerting extensive influence over other criminal organizations operating in Montreal." His power was so unchallenged in Quebec's criminal underworld that he was credited with playing a major role in "persuading" the leaders of the Hells Angels and the Rock Machine to negotiate a truce to their war. The 2001 CISC report also noted that the Montreal mafia's "influence may be spreading beyond its Québec base." Vito was making regular trips to Ontario, to check up on his business investments. To some, his frequent visits were also a signal that he was intent on expanding his criminal enterprises into the province, especially following the death of John Papalia. One indication of this interprovincial growth was revealed in April 2001 when a $200-million gambling operation in Montreal, Ottawa, Hamilton, and Toronto was disrupted by the arrest of fifty-four people in Quebec and Ontario. The ten-month investigation zeroed in on a high-tech bookmaking operation linked to Rizzuto, which used storefronts, the Internet, cell phones, Palm Pilots, and BlackBerrys to take bets on sporting events from across North America. Police also discovered a parallel loansharking operation and heard from one bettor who was given a loan to pay off his $75,000 gambling debt, but then had to deal with interest that totalled around $60,000.

In its 2002 annual report, the Criminal Intelligence Service Canada made another not-so-veiled reference to the Rizzuto Family, "A Montréal-based Sicilian crime family continues to expand its influence throughout the Canadian Italian-based criminal community and maintains connections with other organized crime groups to facilitate joint criminal endeavors." As the CISC infers, one of the reasons that Rizzuto had become so successful was that he was building partnerships with other like-minded criminal organizations. In their book, *The Sixth Family*, Lamothe and Humphreys identified some other reasons why the Montreal mafia under Vito Rizzuto was able to achieve success during the 1980s and 1990s, a time when mafia groups throughout Canada and the U.S. were imploding:

> The Sixth Family blends the traditions of
> the Sicilian Mafia with a modern corporate

structure, building a rugged durable, ever-expanding corporate Mafia. It maintains the secretiveness of the Mafiosi tradition but keeps its inner circle more tightly controlled than in the American Mafia. The Sixth Family has shed the old militaristic organizational structure of the Five Families — which has soldiers answering to captains who answer to a boss. It has been replaced with a structure that is even more ancient — the family. It is not merely a Mafia initiation ceremony that binds its core, but rather, almost without exception, marriage vows and blood ties. It is far more effective at engendering loyalty and trust; for protecting the organization from betrayal and infiltration.

As the power of the Montreal mafia grew, Vito Rizzuto became less and less concerned about his ties to New York's Bonanno Family. Signals that Rizzuto was pulling away from New York's orbit were not lost on the leadership of the Bonanno Family, who responded in the early 1990s by sending senior members to Montreal to reignite a closer relationship. Dispatching a delegation to Montreal was an obvious illustration of how important the Montreal crew was to New York. The irony is that Montreal was not only the most profitable subsidiary of the Bonanno Family, contributing millions in illegal revenues to its coffers, but it was now larger than the New York "headquarters" in terms of its international reach, its partnerships with other criminal groups, and the number of members and associates. An even greater irony is that while Vito Rizzuto was slowly extricating himself and his organization from the confining bonds of the Bonanno Family, it would be the New York mafia that would ultimately betray and bring him down.

Despite the respect Rizzuto was accorded in the criminal underworld, his stature made him a target. In the summer of 2001, police announced that they foiled a plot to kill Rizzuto along with a key lieutenant, Francesco Arcadi, and another associate named Frank Martorana. Two men, Christian Deschínes and Denis-Rolland Girouard, were arrested on July 13 by the Sûreté du Québec and later charged with conspiracy to murder, conspiracy to kidnap, and weapons offences. Police linked Deschínes to several drug schemes in-

volving the Rizzuto organization, including a 1992 case where 4,000 kilos of cocaine were flown into Canada direct from Colombia. The investigation into Rizzuto's possible assassination had been under way since April 2001, when Quebec provincial police were tipped off about a potential holdup. While following that lead, they discovered a hit was being planned and a tactical team moved in when two men, driving separate cars, were blocks from the Consenza Social Club, a small café housed in a strip mall in the St. Léonard neighbourhood of Montreal that served as an unofficial meeting place for Rizzuto and his men. Police suspected an attempt on Rizzuto's life was looming, but when the two suspects were apprehended neither was carrying a weapon. When police searched the home of one of the men, however, they turned up an AK-47 rifle, a .357-calibre Magnum revolver, two 9-mm pistols, two bulletproof vests, and ammunition. The plot to assassinate Rizzuto was not a conspiracy for control of the underworld, but apparently the brainchild of Salvatore Gervais, a reputed member of the Montreal mafia who was angry with Rizzuto for allowing the Hells Angels to murder his son, who was allegedly dealing drugs to their archrivals the Rock Machine. Seeking revenge, the grieving father reportedly hired Deschínes. Gervais would later be shot dead as he sat behind the wheel of his car.

The constant attention paid to Rizzuto by police was catching up with him. On May 30, 2002, he was pulled over and charged with drinking and driving after Montreal police caught him weaving across the road. Rizzuto refused to take a breathalyzer and was arrested. Two months later he pleaded not guilty to the charges. In September of that year, the RCMP named Vito Rizzuto as part of a conspiracy to import cocaine into Canada, although he was not arrested. Three counts alleging drug trafficking were laid against José Guede, a criminal lawyer working in the Montreal law firm of Loris Cavaliere, which was representing Rizzuto on the drunk-driving charge.

Guede was charged with brokering a deal with Colombian suppliers to import hundreds of kilos of cocaine ultimately destined for the Hells Angels in Quebec and associates of the Montreal mafia breaking into Ontario's profitable cocaine market. Guede's arrest was the result of an RCMP investigation that seized a cocaine-laden shipping container in Halifax and another illicit shipment from a small plane in Toronto. Police made sure that Rizzuto's name figured prominently in the documents that accompanied the formal charges laid against Guede, who voluntarily turned himself in to the RCMP. Guede had apparently been approached by men linked to Rizzuto to work out a deal with Colombian suppliers. The use of a lawyer to negotiate a drug deal was a tactic that was increasingly being used by Rizzuto because it meant that strict solicitor-client privilege could be invoked if police ever attempted to intercept any communications that may involve lawyers working for the family.

Guede was acquitted of his charges when a judge ruled that an RCMP officer lied to protect the credibility of an informant who was the main witness against the lawyer. Guede was set free and once again Rizzuto slipped through the fingers of police. In 2004, however, police and prosecutors in America accomplished something that eluded Canadian police for years: they laid serious criminal charges against the Montreal mafia don that would eventually stick.

On January 20, fifty-seven-year-old Vito Rizzuto was picked up by Canadian police in response to an American warrant on three murders that dated back to 1981. Rizzuto was one of thirty men arrested, most of whom were members of the now-reeling Bonanno Family, including the acting boss, Anthony (Tony Green) Urso, underboss, Joseph (Joe Saunders) Cammarano, seven captains or former captains and at least thirteen soldiers. A U.S. Attorney in New York called the arrests "the broadest and deepest penetration ever of a New York City-based organized crime family." Rizzuto was accused of being the lead gunman in the May 1981 murders of three high-ranking members of the Bonanno Family: Philip (Philip Lucky) Giaccone, Alphonse (Sonny Red) Indelicato, and Dominick (Big Trin) Trinchera. Federal officials in the U.S. quickly began extradition proceedings against the man they described as "the most influential Bonanno family member in Canada, the only family with a significant presence in Canada."

American authorities argued that the killings were the result of a power struggle within the Bonanno Family, which, during the late 1970s and early 1980s was divided into two factions: those who supported Philip (Rusty) Rastelli as the new boss and those who supported Alphonse Indelicato (the man who once ordered Frank Cotroni to be killed because he thought he was co-operating with U.S. authorities). Joseph (Big Joey) Massino, the portly, strategically minded senior captain in the family, supported Rastelli. The bloc that opposed Rastelli included such other powerful captains as Philip Giaccone and Dominick Trinchera. The murder of the three men was orchestrated by Massino, along with another Bonanno captain, Gerlando Sciascia, to remove any obstacles to Rastelli's power. Sciascia was the Bonanno Family's official captain of its Montreal crew and spent so much time in Quebec he was called "George from Canada."

The doomed men were lured to a modest two-storey social club in Brooklyn on the pretence of a meeting of Bonanno captains. When they arrived, they were caught in an ambush. Indelicato's body, wrapped in a bedsheet, was found about two weeks later by some children playing in a vacant lot in Queens. The bodies of the other two men were exhumed from the same lot in October 2004, after Massino provided police with information on their whereabouts. Amazingly, the murder of the three Bonanno captains remained unsolved for more than twenty years, in part due to the silence of all those involved in the killings, those who witnessed the murders, or those who were ordered to dispose of the dead bodies.

The FBI had long suspected Rizzuto's involvement in the murders, in part because of a surveillance photo that captured him along with Joe Massino, Gerlando Sciascia, and a heroin-dealing Sicilian named Giovanni Ligamarri (who was later found hanging in the basement of his home), leaving a Bronx motel the day after the murders occurred. But police had little to link Rizzuto to the murders, although eventually that missing link would be supplied by Salvatore (Good Looking Sal) Vitale and Frank Lino, two senior members of the Bonanno Family, who were charged with other killings and who decided to co-operate with the FBI.

In July 2004, Vitale became a key state witness against Joseph Massino, Good Looking Sal's boss, brother-in-law and sponsor for induction into the Bonanno Family in the early 1970s. Vitale had been picked up by police on January 9, 2003 for the murder

FBI photograph taken May 19, 1981, the day after the murder of the Bonanno captains. From left to right: Gerlando Sciascia, Vito Rizzuto, Giovanni Ligamarri, and Joe Massino

of a *New York Post* employee and within weeks of his arrest, he agreed to become a witness for the prosecution. Massino was arrested shortly thereafter. Vitale implicated Massino in the murders of seven members of the Bonanno Family and also fingered Rizzuto in the 1981 slayings of Giaccone, Trinchera, and Indelicato. Affidavits released by the U.S. Attorney's Office in New York to support Rizzuto's extradition request, stated that the government had "co-operating witnesses" who would testify that Rizzuto was one of the gunmen and that Gerlando Sciascia conspired with Massino and Rizzuto to set up the murders.

Vitale testified in Massino's 2004 murder and racketeering trial that his former boss wanted members from the Montreal crew to take the lead in the 1981 murders. The Canadians were brought in "because of a security issue," Vitale would tell an American judge. "It would never leak out. And after the murders, they would go back to Montreal." Among the imported hit men was Rizzuto, another suspected member of the Montreal mob named Emanuele Ragusa, and a silver-haired man simply referred to as the "old timer" (whose identity was never revealed but who possibly was an associate of Nick Rizzuto's).

According to Vitale, all the shooters hid in a closet in the social club. When the three intended victims arrived, Sciascia signalled his fellow conspirators, who burst out of the closet firing. On Massino's orders, Rizzuto and Ragusa were the lead gunmen, while Vitale and the "old timer" guarded the exits.

The shooters wore ski masks to conceal their identity from other Bonanno captains who would be present at the social club, but who were not to be harmed. Also on Massino's orders Rizzuto reportedly yelled, "Don't anybody move, this is a holdup" when bursting out of the closet so the intended victims would line up against the wall and be killed in an orderly, execution-style manner.

Following the murders, Massino's power in the Bonanno Family grew and he even took over as boss in 1991 after Rastelli died. Rizzuto's role in the murders earned him the respect of Massino and Gerlando Sciascia continued to be the official captain of the Canadian crew while also serving as an important link between the Montreal heroin suppliers and their New York mafia customers. Years later, Sciascia fell out of favour with Massino because he increasingly sided with the Montreal crew against the wishes of its New York masters (the tipping point appeared to be when Sciascia supported Rizzuto's refusal to send men from Canada to kill the *New York Post* employee, which forced Massino to delegate the job to Salvatore Vitale). Massino ordered "George from Canada" dead and, in 1999, Sciascia's body was found in New York with multiple gunshot wounds.

After Sciascia's murder, Vitale travelled to Montreal on orders of Massino to try and placate Rizzuto, who was angered over the Sciascia hit. Rizzuto was offered the formal position of captain of the Montreal crew, but in a stunning display of defiance, he turned the offer down. Despite future entreaties by Massino, Rizzuto was now in the process of completely severing ties between the Montreal mafia and the Bonanno Family. By the end of the 1990s, he was no longer sending tribute money to New York. This was more than symbolic, according to Lee Lamothe and Adrian Humphreys. While the Bonanno Family was in steep decline during the 1980s and 1990s, due to deadly internecine battles and successful federal prosecutions, the Montreal mafia under Rizzuto was growing in strength, wealth, and international reach. Rizzuto's relationship with the Bonanno Family was now "irrelevant to the modern business structure that Vito had been building. It was a bit like a waning reliance on the postal system with the advent of the Internet. The Sixth Family had not only eclipsed the wealth and strength of the Bonanno Family in New York, they now seemed to have extricated themselves from the family hierarchy and were truly setting themselves apart from any of the Five Families in New York." But as Rizzuto was abandoning a relationship that had lasted for more than fifty years, his former bosses in New York were now dragging him down with them.

Based on the evidence provided by Vitale, Joe Massino was charged with Sciascia's murder and on July 30, 2004, the sixty-one-year-old was found guilty of ordering seven murders, which included the deaths of four of his own captains. In June 2005, Massino confessed to the murder of Gerlando Sciascia, and, more surprisingly, became the first boss of a New York mafia family ever to become a state witness, a precedent that was spurred by prosecutors' growing calls for Massino to face the death penalty. His defection would prove to be another crippling blow to Rizzuto and his attempts to avoid extradition to the U.S. where he would stand trial for the 1981 murders.

While Rizzuto was fighting extradition, police in Italy issued arrest warrants for him and eighty-year-old Giuseppe Zappia. The warrants claimed the two were part of a mafia-backed consortium that was trying to win a billion-dollar contract to build a bridge between Sicily and mainland Italy. In February 2005, Italian authorities charged Vito Rizzuto and four others with laundering the proceeds of crime through a company that Zappia set up to act as a front for Rizzuto's bid to build the bridge. Zappia, who was arrested at his home in Rome, was already known in Canada as a controversial contractor for the 1976 Olympics in Montreal. In 1988, he was cleared of fraud charges that resulted from his work on Olympic facilities after two key witnesses died before testifying at his trial.

Italian authorities would have to wait until they could get their hands on Rizzuto. On August 17, 2006, after more than two years of legal wrangling, including a trip to the Supreme Court of Canada, the godfather of the Montreal mafia and grandfather of five was extradited to the United States to face charges in connection with the 1981 gangland killings.

While Rizzuto awaited his legal proceedings in New York, police in Canada dealt another blow to his organization. In the early-morning hours of November 23, 2006, coordinated raids were carried

Joe (Big Joey) Massino

out, resulting in the arrest of ninety people with alleged connections to the Montreal mafia. Among them were Vito's eighty-two-year-old father, Nick, his sixty-five-year-old brother-in-law Paolo Renda, fifty-three-year-old Francesco Arcadi, (who police believe became interim head of the Montreal mafia after Vito's arrest in 2004), and Rocco Sollecito, another senior member of the family. The four men were described as the leaders of several criminal operations and key targets of "Project Colisée," an investigation that entailed allegations of more than thirteen major cocaine importations worth millions of dollars. The Montreal mafia was also accused of infiltrating Montreal's Pierre Elliott Trudeau International Airport to import the cocaine and police issued warrants for two agents with Canada Border Services and about ten employees of airline and food service companies based at the airport. Approximately one thousand criminal conspiracy charges related to illegal drugs, online gambling, corruption and extortion would be laid.

Project Colisée was a three-year investigation in which police bugged and videotaped the inside of the favourite meeting place for members of the Montreal mafia: the Consenza Social Club. Police surveillance captured couriers transporting thousands of dollars in tightly packed wads of cash in and out of the club. A description of the tribute system of the

Nicolò Rizzuto sits in a police car in Montreal following his arrest on November 22, 2006.

Montreal mafia, and of recipients of the cash tributes, was captured by police surveillance on May 23, 2005, when Rocco Sollecito cryptically told another man, "When they do something — and it doesn't matter when they do it — they always bring something here so that it can be divided up among us five: me, Vito, Nicolò, Paolo." (The fifth man was Francesco Arcadi.) All five men were observed by police cameras at one time or another counting the money in the club and then dividing it amongst themselves. Nick Rizzuto came to the club several times a week to pick up his tribute (and that owing to his son after his arrest). He would place the cash in his socks, pockets, wallet or any combination of the three, depending on the size of the wad. Appropriately enough, a day following the raids, the Canada Revenue Agency announced it had executed two dozen search warrants as part of a parallel investigation that sought to collect taxes on undeclared revenues. Among its targets was Nick

Rizzuto, who the agency claimed owed $1.5 million in unpaid taxes, interest, and penalties.

While the targets of Project Colisée were fighting these charges and trying to stay out of jail, the fate of their boss was announced in a New York courtroom. On May 4, 2007, Vito Rizzuto, looking thin and tired, pleaded guilty to a racketeering charge. As part of a plea agreement, Vito was handed a ten-year sentence (half of what he would have faced if he had gone to trial) to be followed by a three-year supervised release. With the time he had already served in Quebec and U.S. jails factored in, the sixty-one-year-old Rizzuto could have been out of prison in less than six years. The plea bargain required that Rizzuto confess to his role in the murders. "I was one of the guys who participated in this. My job was to say that it was a holdup so [the captains] would stand still," Rizzuto told the judge. "The other guys came in and started shooting."

Vito Rizzuto conferring with one of his lawyers, Jean Salois, after a court appearance in Montreal on February 6, 2004, regarding his extradition

In November 2008, Nick Rizzuto was sentenced to three years probation on proceeds-of-crime charges. A plea bargain with the Crown allowed him to avoid the more serious drug trafficking charges laid against him. Two other conspirators did not get off so lightly. Francesco Del Balso and Francesco Arcadi each received the equivalent of a fifteen-year prison term.

SOCIETIES GET THE CRIME THEY DESERVE

In sentencing Vito Rizzuto, the judge told him: "Today marks the final chapter in the sad story of the execution of three people 26 years ago in pursuit of power and money. It has been the subject of books, multiple prosecutions and at least one motion picture. Despite such efforts to glamourize these incidents, as the history of these events unfolded in this courthouse it is apparent to the court that such a sordid and cynical act deserves only our scorn and condemnation."

The above condemnation could very well be part of an epitaph for Italian organized crime in North America. Whether called the mafia, La Cosa Nostra, or 'Ndrangheta, Italian crime groups were once the most powerful force in the criminal underworld in Canada and the United States. Their roots could be found in small villages in Sicily or Calabria and in tenement neighbourhoods in New York or Toronto. The evolution of the mafia from local bands of extortionists to an international drug trafficking cartel set the mould for all other organized crime genres to follow. The success and resilience of the mafia was a product of an organizational structure that borrowed equally from governmental, paramilitary, business, and family constitutions, an unwavering subservience of its members to the organization and its leaders, a highly opportunistic nose for profitable opportunities, and the strategic use of violence and intimidation. But like any great dynasty, the mafia fell from power in North

America, fuelled by insatiable greed, a Machiavellian lust for power, intra-family and inter-family wars, defections, stepped-up enforcement, as well as competition from other organized crime genres. By the turn of the millennium, the five New York families were merely a shadow of their former selves. The one "family" that appears to have risen above the ashes was the Rizzuto clan. But Vito Rizzuto is just another Macbeth-like character whose own unrequited quest for power, combined with a slavish obedience to tradition, caused him to wade through blood, leading to his own fall.

A couple of years before Rizzuto was arrested in Canada on an American warrant for murder, the man who began the family that would both sponsor and ultimately betray him died. On May 10, 2002, Joseph Bonanno was found dead at the age of ninety-seven. In addition to being one of the seminal figures in the American Cosa Nostra, Bonanno can rightly be seen as a godfather figure to organized crime in Canada. For it was he, along with such other historical American criminals as Al Capone, Lucky Luciano, Carmine Galante, and Stefano Magaddino that would turn Canada into a branch plant of American organized crime for much of the 20th century.

The die was now cast, as criminal organizations from around the world — Chinese triads, American outlaw motorcycle gangs, Colombian cocaine cartels, and Nigerian fraud artists among others — invaded Canada. But to characterize organized crime in Canada as exclusively the product of some foreign invasion of criminal cultures ignores the many indigenous conditions that made this country ripe for organized criminality.

One of the many constants in the history of organized crime in Canada has been smuggling, from whale bones in the 18th century, to tea and opium in the 19th century, to liquor and cigarettes in the early 20th century, not to mention a deluge of drugs and a cornucopia of contraband in the postwar era. Perhaps no other country in the world has as many conditions in place that are conducive to a vibrant smuggling trade: Canada has thousands of miles of poorly enforced coastline; thousands of miles of unguarded border with the United States of America, the largest supplier and consumer of drugs and contraband in the world, and, most uniquely, a large concentration of people living within a short distance of that border (thereby providing a convenient market for the contraband as well as a sympathetic and skilled labour pool from which to draw smugglers and distributors).

There have been few substantial changes in organized smuggling over the centuries. The underground activity is largely precipitated and sustained by government policies, such as the enactment of prohibitive taxes on tea and cigarettes, or the criminalization of liquor, opium, and other drugs. The commodities of choice for the professional smuggler — liquor, cigarettes, drugs, and people — as well as the routes taken into and out of the country have also changed little over the years. Regardless of the commodity or the period, the earliest stages of any particular smuggling maelstrom are characterized by pure competition, with a large number of individuals and small groups operating relatively autonomously. Eventually, however, oligopolies are formed as small operations consolidate under the more successful criminal entrepreneurs or well-established criminal groups enter the arena to take advantage of its existing capacities, networks, and economies of scale, to exploit its proclivities for corruption and violence.

The historic smuggling trade also accentuates the realization that organized crime is a reflection of the broader economic, political, and social forces of Canada. The massive cross-border traffic in legal and illegal goods simply reflects (and takes advantage of) the massive trading relationship between Canada and the United States. The fact that organized crime in Canada was long a branch plant of American organized crime is just another expression of the umbilical economic relationship between the two countries. Guided by the laws of supply and demand, organized drug trafficking and contraband markets represent the darker side of the free market economic system. The multi-ethnic character of organized crime is a reflection of the multicultural nature of Canadian society. The liberal immigration policies of Canada must also be seen as a factor in fuelling organized crime in this country. This is aggravated by what some view as historically rooted institutionalized racism in the country whereby certain "ethnic" immigrant groups — the Irish, Jews, Chinese, Italians, Hispanics, Jamaicans — have been shut out of legitimate economic opportunities en masse and therefore have had to turn to organized crime. In short, like any historical analysis, the commentary resulting from an examination of the history of organized crime in Canada can be used to help shed light on the character of the country and its people.

When examining organized crime in an historical context, one can also be excused from evoking the tired, yet telling, French axiom *"Plus ça change, plus c'est la même chose"* (the more things change, the more they stay the same). While the scope, sophistication, and number of players may have changed over the years, organized crime has not changed much since pirates were robbing merchant ships or smugglers began filling the demand for low-priced tea in the British colonies. In his 1991 book chronicling the history of crime in Canada, D. Owen Carrigan wrote:

> Gangs of organized criminals throughout our history have exhibited many common characteristics. They are commanded by strong, usually ruthless leaders who have organizational skills and personal qualities that instill loyalty and fear in their followers. Most gangs maintain discipline through some informal or defined code of conduct. Family ties, national origins, friendships, common interests, status, fear, and severe punishment are some of the factors that bring and keep the gangs together. They are a microcosm of the criminal world, drawn from all strata of society and from all backgrounds.

Another constant in the history of organized crime is the realization that its eradication — or even containment — through the criminal justice system remains a highly elusive and, some would argue, an unattainable goal. (The most effective measures implemented to counter organized crime have been the reversal of public policy decisions that helped spur underground industries in the first place, such as the repeal of liquor prohibition laws or the lowering of federal taxes on cigarettes.) While numerous criminal groups and illegal markets have been disrupted and gangland bosses and their underlings put behind bars, organized crime will be with us for some time to come. In its 2007 annual report, the Criminal Intelligence Service of Canada estimated there were 950 known organized crime groups in the country, an increase of nearly 20 percent over the previous year. The vast majority of these groups (80 percent, according to the CISC) are involved in the illegal drug market. In British Columbia alone, the estimated number of organized crime gangs more than doubled — from fifty-two in 2003 to 108 in 2005. In a public speech, the assistant commissioner in charge of the RCMP in the province said that this increase was largely fuelled by marijuana production. He added that limited law enforcement resources mean that "only 30 percent of known organized crime groups can be targeted every year."

Within either an historical or current context, organized crime must be viewed as an ephemeral and flexible system that easily and opportunistically adapts to changes and external circumstances (including changes in public preferences, technological advances, government policies, and law enforcement). The resilience of organized crime stems from the fact that, like crime in general, it is very much rooted in the institutions and cultures of the societies it inhabits, making it an enduring historical fixture on the Canadian landscape. As Robert Leslie Bellem wrote in *Preview of Murder*, his 1949 pulp fiction classic, "That was fourteen years ago, but the fourteen years faded and vanished like a lap dissolve shot so that time was telescoped and the past merged into the present, the present became the past."

GLOSSARY

Ace deuce suit — three-piece suit

Ace-deuce — three

Alky-cooking — illegal distilling

Ankle (verb) — to move away slowly

Ballyhoo — a boisterous sensationalism designed to attract a crowd

Banfang — jail

Banfanged — jailed

Bangfei — kidnapper

Baoli — violence

Barbeque stool — electric chair

Barleybroth — beer

Barred hotel — prison

Beat out and stand — the departure of a ship

Beng — money

Bent — corrupt

Berries — dollars

Betwixt — between

Big House — prison

Big sleep — death

Bindle — drugs

Bindle-dealing deucers — drug dealers

Binnacle — a case or box on the deck of a ship, generally mounted in front of the helmsman, in which navigational instruments are placed

Blobber — police informant

Blowing off the groundsails — to have sex

Boater — man's hat fashionable during the 1920s

Boiler — automobile

Bones — dice

Bootleg — contraband liquor

Bootlegger — one who is involved in the production and/or sale of contraband liquor

Booze foundry — illegal liquor distilling operation

Boozehister — one who is involved in the production and/or sale of contraband liquor

Bowsy — drunk; to get drunk

Brewhister — bootlegger

Bris — a religious ceremony within Judaism to welcome infant Jewish boys into a covenant between God and the Children of Israel through ritual circumcision performed by a mohel

Brogans — tough guys; enforcers

Bronfen shmuglens — whiskey smugglers

Bubkis — nothing, but less than nothing if possible

Bull — enforcement officer

Bunko artist — fraudster

Button — police officer

Calaboose — prison

Canary — informant

Cannon's mouth — to engage in piracy or privateering

Captain-Hackum — a fighting, blustering bully

Cat-o'-nine-tails — whip

Changfu — prostitute

Chazzer — a pig (one who eats like a pig)

Chiing — beat (attack)

Chutzpeh — brazenness, gall

Clams — dollars

Clapperdogeon — thieve, rogue, pirate

Clean sneak — to escape without leaving any clues

Clip joint — illegal gambling hall

Clipster — deceitful professional gambler

Cloyers — thieves, robbers, rogues

Cloying — stealing, thieving, robbing

Conk — head

Copped — arrested

Copper — police officer

Copper factory — police station

Corsair — pirate

Court jester — lawyer

Cow thumper — cowboy, ranch hand

Cowpoke — cowboy, ranch hand

Cowpuncher — cowboy, ranch hand

Craps — dice game popular among gamblers

Crimson blossoms — blood

Croak — to die

Cropper — low-level member of a criminal group

Crown glove-puppet — government lawyer (criminal prosecutor)

Crown Lips — government lawyer (criminal prosecutor)

Crown's court jester — government lawyer (criminal prosecutor)

Cull — an honest man

Cutlash — cutlass, sword

Daibued — arrested

Dao — knife

Daoed — to be knifed

Dance the hempen jig — to be executed by hanging

Davy Jones' Locker — to die at sea

Deek — police detective

Dell — thief, rogue, pirate

Detroit Iron — automobile

Dick — investigator (public dick — police officer; private dick — private investigator)

Dime-a-pops — police

Dirk — a long knife

Dousing — murder

Dragged-out — tired

Drill — to punch or to be shot by a gun

Droog — gang member

Dry-gulch — to attack someone by surprise and beat them

Dutch — debt

Eagle eyes — police

Easing powder — opium, morphine, heroin

E-flat Dillinger — gangster

Elbows — police

Elephant ears — police

Fachadick — extremely confused

Fahklumpt — confused, mixed up

Fandu — narcotic drug

Fanguan — restaurant

Finest — police

Finger — to identify someone

Flannel mouth — derogatory term for easterners

Flophouse — cheap hotel

Fob — to cheat, deceive

Foolish powder — powdered opium

Freebooters — pirates

Fresh bull — an incorruptible, energetic policeman (carrying the suggestion of someone new to the job)

Galley — a small, oared fighting ship (frigate)

Gamogue — a silly trick

Gantser k'nacker! — big shot!

Gaunef — a deceiver or thief; derived from the Hebrew word *ganav* "thief"

Gee — drug courier

Gelt — money

Giggle water — intoxicating liquor

Gin jogger — bootlegger

Glazier — thief, rogue, pirate

Glom — to see

Glove-puppet — state lawyer

G-note — thousand dollars/thousand-dollar bill
Gongda — attack
Gondaed — attacked
Gow — opium
Gownick — Jewish drug trafficker
Grease — bribe
Grog — liquor; spiked rum
Groggeries — underground drinking establishment
Gull and Gut — to rob (to clean out)
Gum — opium
Gumption — nerve, courage, daring
Gun moll — female gangster
Gunpoke — gun-wearing cowboy or outlaw
Guallaver — head
G'vir — rich man

Hailouying — heroin
Hammer and saws — law enforcement officials (police, state attorneys, judges)
Harness bulls — uniform police officers
Hawk — to sell something
Heat — the police; police investigation
Heine — buttocks
Hell-fer-leather — to move quickly
Hep cat — cool guy
High-falutin — mildly derogatory reference to pretentiousness
Hincty — stuck up; pretentious; fancy
Hinky — suspicious, almost to the point of certainty
Hogsheads — barrels
Hooch — liquor; intoxicating beverage
Hoods — gang members, criminals
Hood-wink'd — blindfolded
Hoosegow — prison
Hop — opium
Hop sticks — opium pipes
Hong — school
Hop — opium
Hot lead — bullets
Huang — blood
Huanging — bleeding
Humdinger — excellent, influential
Hurdy-gurdy houses — brothels
Huzzahs — cheers
Hype — heroin

Ice — diamond jewellery
Igloo — home
Ile Royale — Cape Breton Island (Nova Scotia)
Illicit linctus — illegal opium
Iron pills — bullets

Jalopy — automobile
Jazz water — liquor
Jettison — to be thrown from a ship overboard
Jian — letter
Jiangyu — territory
Jigger — bootleg liquor
Jingfang — police
Jinjin — muscle (enforcer)
Jitney — taxi
John Law — police officer
Jolly Irene — the original fat women in P.T. Barnum's circus
Jolly Roger — pirate flag
Joy dust — powdered opium
Jue — stab
Jug — jail
Juniper juice — liquor; intoxicating beverage

K'nackers — a know-it-all who thinks he can do everything better than anyone else
Kaddishel — baby son; endearing term for a boy or man
Kekeyin — cocaine
Kezhan — nightclub
Kick-off — to die
Kishef macher — magic-worker
Klip– to gab incessantly
K'nish — baked dumpling filled with potato, meat, liver, or barley
Knot — crew or gang of villans
Kop — head
Kvell — to beam with pride and pleasure
Kvetch — to complain in a very aggravating way

Lewdies — people
Linctus — drugs (opium)
Lip — lawyer
Liquid damnation — liquor; intoxicating beverage
Lougui — theft
Longuied — robbed

Louqian — extort

Loogans — criminal gang members especially strong-arm enforcers

Lorry — truck

Macher — big shot, person with access to authorities, man with contacts

Magoo — bullshit

Malchick — boy

Mashers — pimps, white slavers (those who procure women for prostitution purposes)

Mashugga — crazy

Matzoh — cracker-like flatbread made of plain white flour and water

Mazuma — money

Mekler — go-between

Meng — people

Metal squirting — the firing of a gun or guns

Mob gee — low-level soldier in a criminal organization

Motor can — car

Moyel — a person (usually a rabbi) who performs circumcisions

Mudsill — lowlife

Nazzis — breasts

Nick — to steal

Nifter — dead person

Nifter — deceased

Nippy — quick

Nishtikeit — nothing, or possibly less than nothing

Nosh — to eat

Numbers racket — illegal lottery or bookmaking operation

Oddy knocky — lonesome

Oil of angels — graft money

Opnarers — trickster, shady operator

Pao — gun

Paddington frisk — to be executed by hanging

Pieceways — a long way away or a long time away

Pinch — to arrest

Pineapple — bomb

Pisher — young annoying punk, a little squirt, a nobody

Plotz — walk in a lumbering way

Plug — to shoot someone

Plugged — to get shot

Plunder — to steal

Pontious Pilot — judge

Poteen — traditional Irish grain spirit

Pour-out man — someone who deals in contraband liquor

Powder monkeys — young boys aboard a ship-of-war tasked within transporting gun power from the magazine to the canons

Press-gang — to recruit seamen onto a sailing vessel by force

Press-ganged — to be forced to work on a pirate ship

Pulchrum scelus — an honourable crime

Puller — someone who smuggles liquor

Qiang — to kill, murder

Qianging — killing

Qingnan — youth

Racket — an illegal activity, generally ongoing, and profit oriented involving theft, fraud, extortion

Radosty — joy

Rapped — criminally charged

Rattle — to move, to transport

Rattle trap — automobile

Red-light — to eject from a car or train

Rod — gun

Rosoe — gun

Rot — mouth

Roundhands — pirates; a ship's crew

Roustabouts — those up to no good, criminals, loiterers waiting for action or trouble

Rye sap — liquor

Savey — to know something

Sawbuck — ten dollars

Schlimazel — a born loser

Schlump — sloppy or dowdy person

Schmada — garments, clothing (reference to the garment industry)

Schmaltz — rendered pig, chicken, or goose fat used for frying or as a spread on bread

Schnapps — liquor

Schnorrer — a Jewish person who has some pretensions to respectability

Scofflaw — an unsavoury character

Scram — to leave

Scratch — money

Screw — prison guard or police officer

Scuffer — low-level member of a criminal gang

Shabbat — Jewish Sabbath

Shab'd-off — to leave or flee in a hurry

Shagetz — vermin

Sharries — buttocks

Shav — cold spinach soup, sorrel grass soup, sour-leaves soup

Sheji — shoot

Shejied — bullet

Shine mover — one who transports contraband liquor (liquor smuggler)

Shine peddler — one who sells contraband liquor

Shlemiel — idiot, moron, loser

Shlumperdik — unkempt, sloppy

Shmeckle — penis (public shmeckle = public dick = police officer)

Shmeer — the business; the whole works

Shmendrik — an inept person; incompetent, nincompoop

Shmugle — smuggle

Shopt — imprisoned or put in irons

Shtarkers — strong-arm men

Shtetl — typically a small town with a large Jewish population in pre-Holocaust Central and Eastern Europe

Shtik naches — great joy

Shtocker — strong-arm man

Shtrudel — pastry

Shtup — to carry, transport

Shutfims — partners; associates

Shvegerin — sister-in-law

Shvindel — fraud, deception, swindle

Shylock — loan shark

Shyster — lawyer

Slap leather — to draw a gun from its holster

Sloop — a type of ship

Slug — bullet

Smeck — opium, heroin

Smouch — to steal, rob

Soft shoe — police officer

Soykher — salesman

Spikotz — police informant

Spying — watching

Squirl/Squirrel/ squirrel's dew — intoxicating liquor

Squirt metal — to fire a gun

State hotel — prison

Steer joint — illegal gambling hall

Stiff — dead body

Stogie — cigar

Straw boater — men's straw hat fashionable during the 1920s

Stump — to steal

Sukky — quickly

Swaddler — thief, rogue, pirate

Swag — to steal, capture, plunder

Swallow the anchor — the surrender of a pirate ship to enforcement

Swig-man — thief, rogue, pirate

Talmud — a book containing the treasury of Jewish law interpreting the Torah into livable law

Tatteh — father

Three fingers — a measured shot of booze

Tsuris — big troubles

Tuchis — buttocks

Under glass — in jail

Undub — to open or unlock forcibly

Unglommed — to be unseen, unspotted

Unshuck — remove, extract

Verklempt — choked with emotion

Vipes — sexy person

Vittles — food

Vops — crimes

Waishen — testicles

Wear iron — to carry a gun

Whip-jack — thieve, rogue, pirate

White cross — opium

Wiper — hired killer

Wuwu — drunk, stoned

Yarmelkeh — traditional Jewish skull cap

Yan — eye

Yiddisher kop — Jewish head

Yiquin — gang
Yufan — to convict
Yutz — idiot, loser

Zhanshi — fighting
Zhan — war
Zhou — wine
Zuixng — crime
Zuzhang — leader

PHOTOS AND ILLUSTRATIONS

123   Reprinted with permission from the Archives of Ontario, File No. RG 22-392-0-6308, Container 167, File Title: "Defendant: Italiano, Guiseppe; Charged with Sending threatening letters (2 counts); Robbery (3 counts); Conspiracy (2 counts), Welland County."

124   Reprinted with permission from the Archives of Ontario, File No. RG 22-392-0-6308, Container 167, File Title: "Defendant: Italiano, Guiseppe; Charged with Sending threatening letters (2 counts); Robbery (3 counts); Conspiracy (2 counts)."

133   Illustration by Ben Frisch.

148   Reprinted with permission from Library and Archives Canada, C-072064.

165   Reprinted with permission from Library and Archives Canada and the Royal Canadian Mounted Police, RG 18, Vol. 3309, File 1925-HQ-189-4-C-1.

169   Illustration by Ben Frisch.

170   Illustration by Ben Frisch.

176   Courtesy of Antonio Nicaso, author of *Rocco Perri: The Story of Canada's Most Notorious Bootlegger*. Wiley, 2004.

183   City of Vancouver Archives, CVA 480-215.

192   Walter Calder photo, City of Vancouver Archives, MSS 54, Port N56 (183-D-2).

202   Illustration by Ben Frisch.

208   Photo by Moore, W.J., City of Vancouver Archives, MSS 54, Bu N288 (183-D-1).

209   Illustration by Ben Frisch.

215   Courtesy of the Glenbow Archives, NA-1136-1.

213   Courtesy of the Glenbow Archives, NA-3282-2.

229   Illustration by Ben Frisch.

231   Illustration by Ben Frisch.

232   Illustration by Ben Frisch.

241   Reprinted with permission from the Library and Archives Canada and Southam Inc./*Montreal Gazette*, PA 144557.

242   Reprinted with permission from Library and Archives Canada and Southam Inc./*Montreal Gazette*, PA 144555.

243   (*l.*) Illustration by Ben Frisch; (*r.*) Reprinted with permission from Library and Archives Canada and Southam Inc./*Montreal Gazette*, PA 144554.

245   Illustration by Ben Frisch.

246   Illustration by Ben Frisch.

249   Reprinted with permission from Library and Archives Canada and the Royal Canadian Mounted Police, PA 144551.

251   Illustration by Ben Frisch.

254   Illustration by Ben Frisch.

260   Illustration by Ben Frisch.

262   Illustration by Ben Frisch.

266   Illustration by Ben Frisch.

271   Illustration by Ben Frisch.

274   The Canadian Press.

275   La Presse/The Canadian Press.

278   Courtesy of Stephen Schneider.

279   The Canadian Press.

281   The Canadian Press.

287   Illustration by Ben Frisch.

291   Courtesy of Adrian Humphreys.

295   Illustration by Ben Frisch.

296   Illustration by Ben Frisch.

300   Illustration by Ben Frisch.

303   Illustration by Ben Frisch.

311   Illustration by Ben Frisch.

317   Illustration by Ben Frisch.

325   *Toronto Star*/The Canadian Press.

327   Illustration by Ben Frisch.

330   Illustration by Ben Frisch.

334   Illustration by Ben Frisch.

335   Illustration by Ben Frisch.

347   Illustration by Ben Frisch.

348   Illustration by Ben Frisch.

349   Illustration by Ben Frisch.

355   The Canadian Press(Tannis Toohey).

359   The Canadian Press(Tobin Grimshaw).

361   The Canadian Press(Tobin Grimshaw).

368   The Canadian Press.

385   *Gazette* (Royal Canadian Mounted Police). "Outlaw motorcycle gangs." Vol. 42, No. 10, 1980.

392   Illustration by Ben Frisch.

395   Illustration by Ben Frisch.

396   *Montreal Gazette*.

401   *Gazette* (Royal Canadian Mounted Police) "Outlaw motorcycle gangs: Provincial profiles." Vol. 56, No. 3 & 4, 1994.

408   John Mahoney, The Gazette (Montreal).

409   Illustration by Ben Frisch.

412   Montreal Star/The Gazette (Montreal).

419   The Canadian Press(Jacques Boissinot).

421   *Kingston Whig Standard*/The Canadian Press(Jennifer Pritchet).

423 The Canadian Press.

426 John Mahoney, *The Gazette*(Montreal).

427 *Winnipeg Free Press*/The Canadian Press.

428 St. Catharines Standard/The Canadian Press(Denis Cahill).

430 *Chatham Daily News*/The Canadian Press(Dan Janisse).

435 *Toronto Star*/Colin McConnell.

438 Illustration by Adam Hilborn.

439 Illustration by Adam Hilborn.

440 Illustration by Adam Hilborn.

441 Illustration by Adam Hilborn.

449 Image F-07470 courtesy of Royal British Columbia Museum, British Columbia Archives.

458 Illustration by Ben Frisch.

460 Illustration by Ben Frisch.

464 From the collection of James Dubro, originally published in *Dragons of Crime: Asian Mobs in Canada*, and with the permission of Ben Eng.

478 Illustration by Ben Frisch.

479 Mark Van Manen/*Vancouver Sun.*

487 The Canadian Press(Nick Procaylo).

490 Nick Didlick/*Vancouver Sun.*

499 The Canadian Press/El Tiempo.

501 The Canadian Press(Fernando Liano).

502 Illustration by Ben Frisch.

515 Illustration by Ben Frisch.

530 *Globe and Mail*/The Canadian Press(Tim McKenna).

533 Courtesy of Adrian Humphreys.

536 *Toronto Star*/Don Dutton.

537 Illustration by Ben Frisch.

538 Illustration by Ben Frisch.

541 Courtesy of the *Hamilton Spectator.*

542 Courtesy of the *Hamilton Spectator.*

544 *Journal de Montréal*/The Canadian Press.

546 *The Hamilton Spectator*/The Canadian Press(John Rennison).

551 Illustration by Ben Frisch.

552 *La Presse*/The Canadian Press(Ivanoh Demers).

553 The Canadian Press(Ryan Remiorz)

INDEX

Stephen Schneider is Associate Professor in the Department of Sociology and Criminology at Saint Mary's University in Halifax. As one of Canada's foremost researchers and educators in the field of organized crime, he has conducted a number of classified studies on organized crime for the federal government. He has analyzed police case files, affidavits, wiretap transcripts, and classified documents. He has taught numerous courses on organized crime and has published several scholarly articles on this subject. Along with Margaret Beare, he is the co-author of the 2007 book *Money Laundering in Canada: Chasing Dangerous and Dirty Dollars*.